President and Publisher
IRA SHAPIRO

Executive Vice President
ANN MIDDLEBROOK

Senior Vice President
WENDL KORNFELD

Controller
BRENDA MASSY

Director of Marketing
and Sales
KAREN HADAM

Director of Production
and Manufacturing
ZULEMA RODRIGUEZ

Director of Digital Communications
ADOLFO VARGAS

Design Director
DAN DYKSEN

ADVERTISING SALES

Sales Coordinator
RANDY PUDDU

Sales Representatives
JOHN BERGSTROM
JO ANN MILLER
JOE SAFFERSON

MARKETING

Marketing Administration Manager
LISA WILKER

Marketing Coordinator
MICHAEL MCGRUDER

CREATIVE

Graphic Designer
DAVID DEASY

Freelance Designers
STEPHANIE LAPORTE
YONG OH

PRODUCTION

Senior Production Manager
CHUCK ROSENOW

Production Coordinators
PAUL CHIN
LILLIAN LOPEZ

Traffic Coordinator
MILTON SUAREZ

**DIGITAL COMMUNICATIONS
AND DISTRIBUTION**

Digital Communications Coordinator
ANNE SMITH

Book Distribution Coordinator
JAMES KRAVITZ

ADMINISTRATION

Office Manager
JANET HIGGINS

Accounts Manager
LESLEY-ANN PEREIRA-HALL

Accounting Assistants
ALEXANDRIA MANIATAKIS
MICHELLE ROBERTS

Special thanks to
DAMIEN ACEVEDO
THERESA AFFUSO
BRIDGETTE BARTLETT
MICHELLE BROWN
CASSANDRA COOK
LINDA CORNIEL
DAVID GROSSMAN
JOE KRAVITZ
ED MEDINA
KEVIN ROBERTS
TERRANCE SCRIVEN
JOSEPH SOLANO

Front Cover Illustration: BRAD HOLLAND
Lead Page Illustration: GARY BASEMAN

US Book Trade Distribution

American Showcase, Inc.
915 Broadway, 14th Floor
New York, NY 10010
Tel 212.673.6600 or 800.894.7469
www.showcase.com

For Sales Outside the US
Rotovision SA
Sheridan House, 112/116A,
Western Road, Hove BN3 2AA, England
Tel 44 1273 72 72 68
Fax 44 1273 72 72 69

Service Bureau
The Ace Group, Inc.

Color Separation
ASA Ltd., Inc.
through PrintPro Ltd., Hong Kong

Printing and Manufacturing
Tien Wah Press (PTE) Limited

Directory Listings Typesetting
Judi Orlick Design

Published by
American Showcase, Inc.
915 Broadway, 14th Floor
New York, NY 10010
Tel 212.673.6600 or 800.894.7469
Fax 212.673.9795
email info@amshow.com
url www.showcase.com

American Illustration Showcase 22
BOOK 2 of 2
ISBN 1-887-165-25-8
ISSN 0278-8128

© 1999 American Showcase, Inc.
All Rights Reserved

american

showcase

American Showcase Illustration

Twenty-Second Edition

C O N T E N T S

ILLUSTRATORS & DESIGNERS

ILLUSTRATORS & DESIGNERS

ILLUSTRATORS & DESIGNERS

ILLUSTRATORS & DESIGNERS

ILLUSTRATORS & DESIGNERS

showca

illustrators | designers | digital artists | interactive talent | photographers

EVERY ONE
OF OUR ARTISTS
IS ON-LINE.

se.com

Newly redesigned,

our site is the place

to locate all the

information you need.

With the highest caliber

of artists, we've

made it even easier to

find talent within.

RICHARD A GOLDBERG 15 CLIFF ST ARLINGTON MA 02476

TELEPHONE: 781-646-1041 FAX: 781-646-0956

SEE NEW WORK: WWW.THEISPOT.COM/ARTIST/RAG

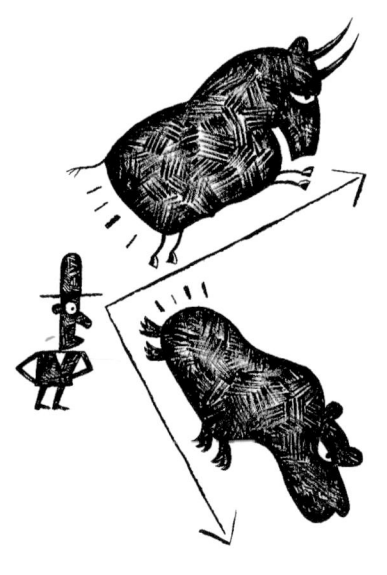

John S. Dykes 203-254-7180
E-MAIL: jsdart@freewwweb.com

Robert Saunders

Brookline MA • (617) 566-4464 • Fax 739-0040 • drnibs@world.std.com • http://world.std.com/~drnibs

Robert Saunders

Brookline MA • (617) 566-4464 • Fax 739-0040 • drnibs@world.std.com • http://world.std.com/~drnibs

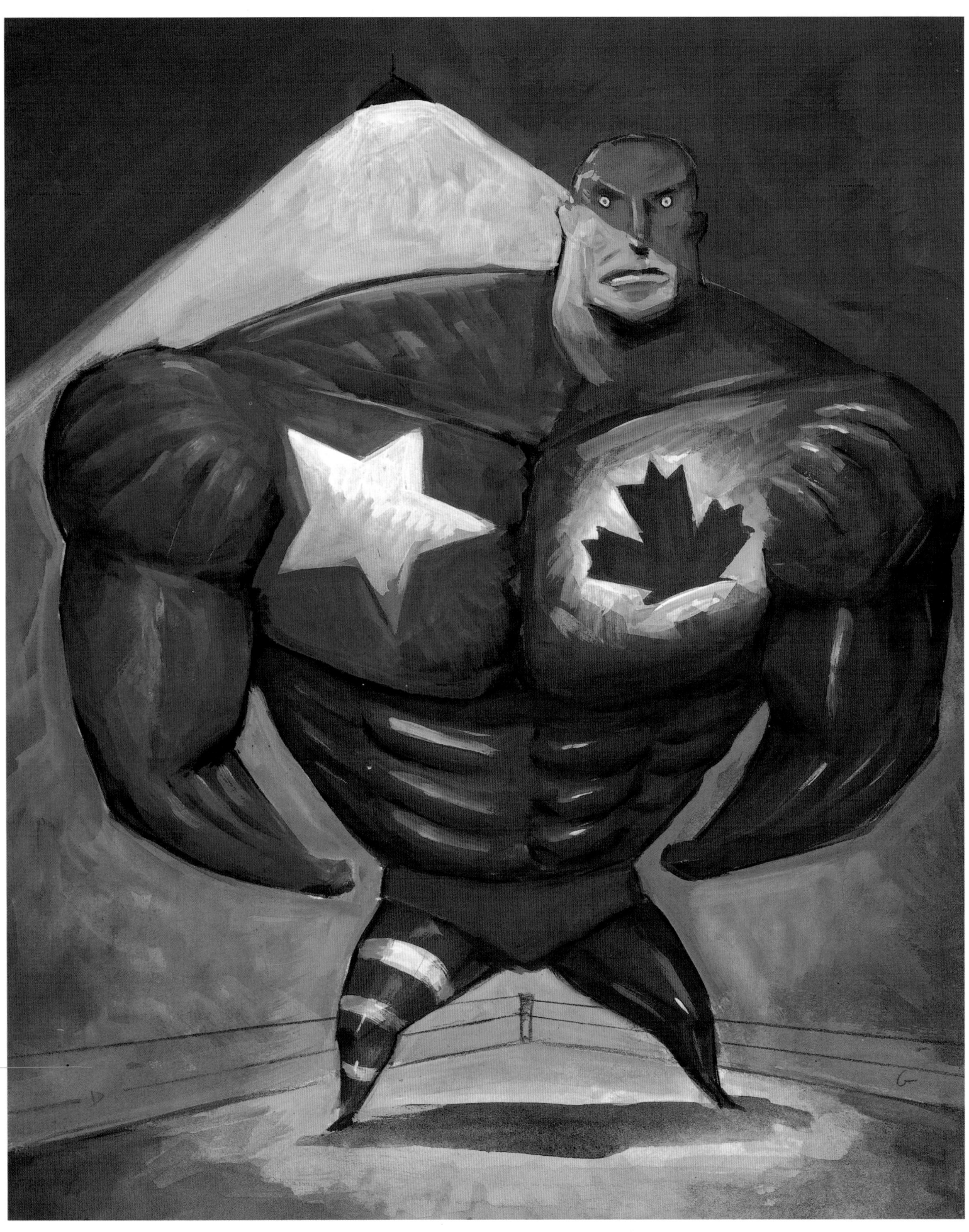

DAVID GORDON
510::547::1685

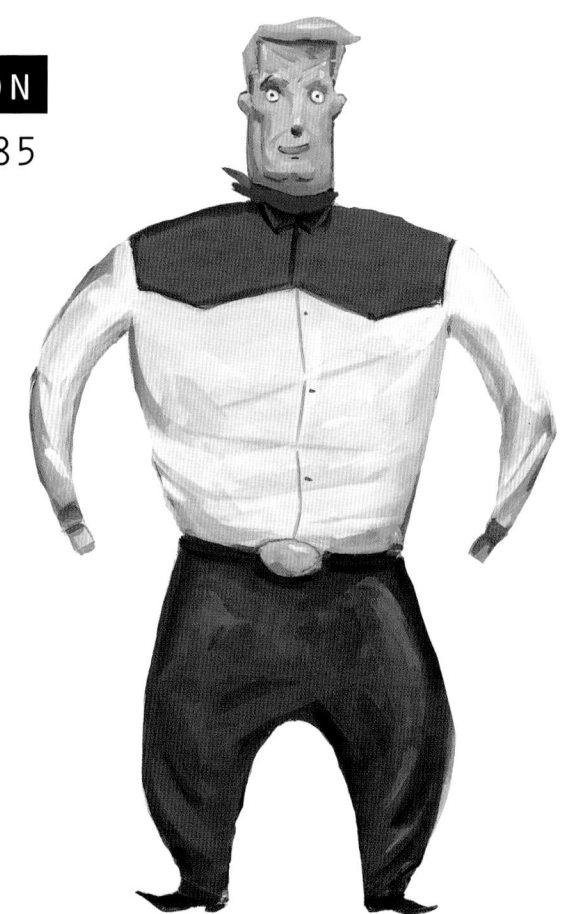

Brad Holland

96 Greene Street New York, NY 10012 Telephone: (212) 226.3675 Fax: (212) 941.5520

**CATHLEEN
TOELKE**

RHINEBECK NY
•
914·876·8776
•
ADVERTISING

CORPORATE

& EDITORIAL

PORTFOLIOS
•
STOCK IMAGES

**C A T H L E E N
T O E L K E**

RHINEBECK NY

914·876·8776

ADVERTISING

CORPORATE

& EDITORIAL

PORTFOLIOS

STOCK IMAGES

Mike Lester
706-234-7733
fax 706-234-0086
www.mikelester.com

Mike Lester
706-234-7733
fax 706-234-0086
www.mikelester.com

Min Jae Hong • 54 Points of View • Warwick, NY 10990 • Tel: 914-986-8040 • Fax: 914-987-1002 • Email: blink@warwick.net • www.blinkstudio.com

Min Jae Hong • 54 Points of View • Warwick, NY 10990 • Tel: 914-986-8040 • Fax: 914-987-1002 • Email: blink@warwick.net • www.blinkstudio.com

Gary Baseman

Represented by Jan Collier (415) 383-9026 (415) 383-9037 fax collierreps.com
East & Editorial (323) 934-5567 (323) 934-5516 fax

Gary Baseman Represented by Jan Collier (415) 383-9026 (415) 383-9037 fax collierreps.com
East & Editorial (323) 934-5567 (323) 934-5516 fax

212-228-2606

Jeff Seaver

130 W 24th Street • 4B
New York, N Y • 10011

email • jeff@seaver.com
web • www.seaver.com

phone • 212 / 741-2279
fax   •   212 / 255-3823

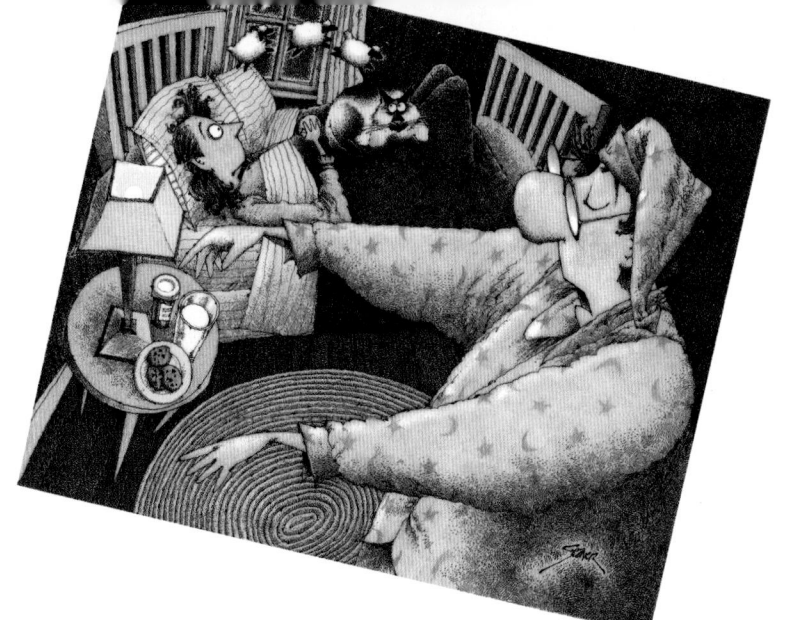

Jeff Seaver
130 W 24th Street • 4B
New York, N Y • 10011

email • jeff@seaver.com
web • www.seaver.com

phone • 212 / 741-2279
fax • 212 / 255-3823

DFS Group Ltd.

Gallery Mall

JVC Jazz Festival

N.Y. University

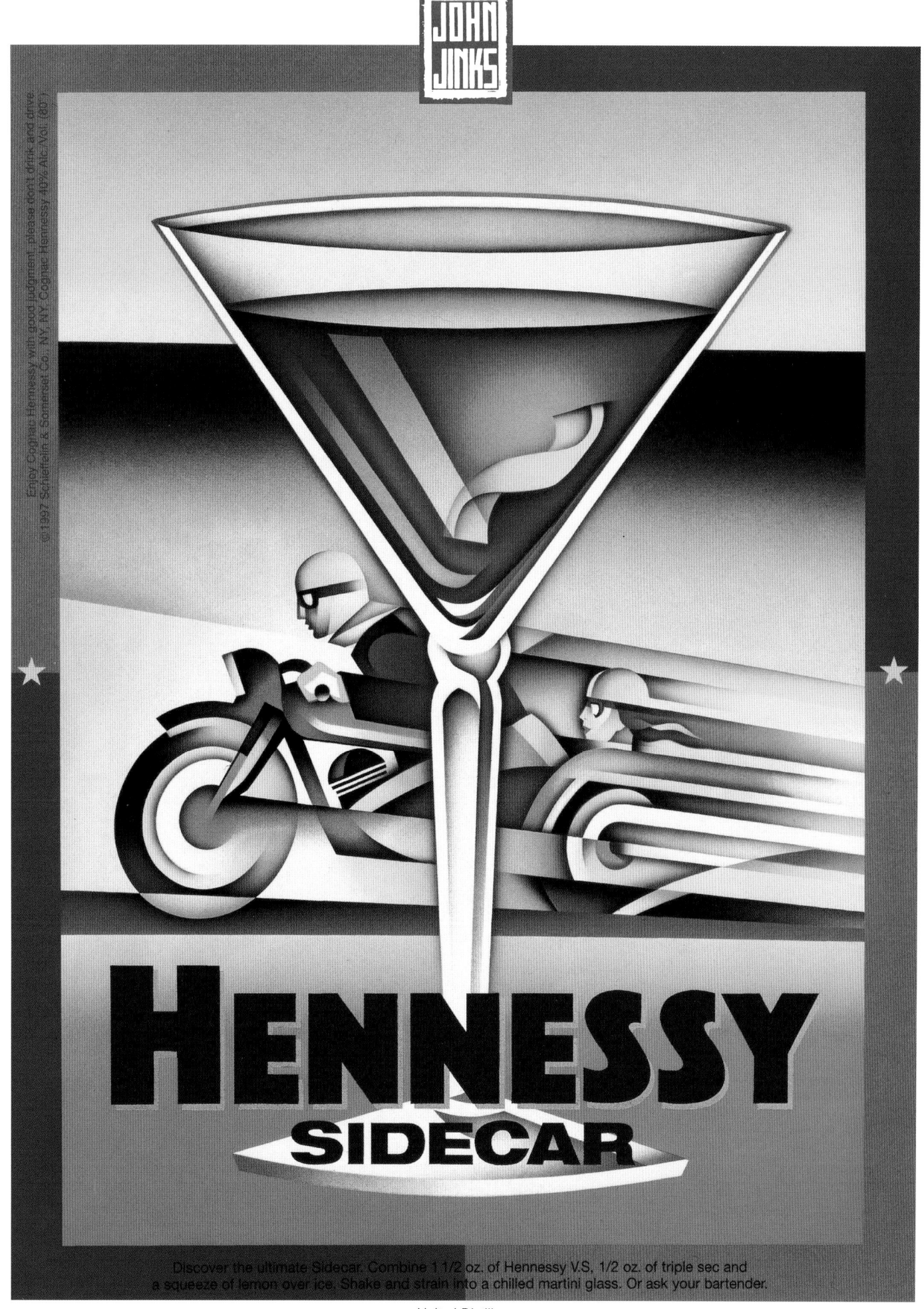

©dave miller

DAVE MILLER

☎ 773-264-1152

FAX 773-264-0916

©dave miller

943

SLOAN

SLOAN

MICHAEL SLOAN ILLUSTRATION • NYC • 212-253-2047

945

robert neubecker   212 219 8435 www.xmission.com/~rubob

ROBERT NEUBECKER

212 219 8435   www.xmission.com/~rubob

947

STEVE GRAY...

Sam Viviano Illustrator, 25 West 13th Street, New York, NY 10011
Telephone (212) 242-1471 • Fax (212) 691-4271

Travis Foster

Represented by Jan Collier (415) 383-9026 (415) 383-9037 fax collierreps.com
Editorial (615) 227-0895

Travis Foster Represented by Jan Collier (415) 383-9026 (415) 383-9037 fax collierreps.com
Editorial (615) 227-0895

955

Steve Björkman

New York
Renard Represents 212.490.2450
Fax 212.697.6828

Studio 949.261.1411 Fax 949.261.7528
WWW.stevebjorkman.com

Chicago
Vincent Kamin 312.787.8834
Fax 312.787.8172

Steve Björkman

New York
Renard Represents 212.490.2450
Fax 212.697.6828

Studio 949.261.1411 Fax 949.261.7528
WWW.stevebjorkman.com

Chicago
Vincent Kamin 312.787.8834
Fax 312.787.8172

ANNFIELD
310.450-6413
represented by
friend & johnson
new york 212.337-0055
san francisco 415.927-4500
southwest 214.559-0055
midwest 312.435-0055

EAT

ANN
310.450-6413
FIELD

represented by
friend & johnson
new york 212.337-0055
san francisco 415.927-4500
southwest 214.559-0055
midwest 312.435-0055

tom white.images • *phone* 212.866.7841 • *e-mail* tom@twimages.com • *website* http://www.twimages.com •

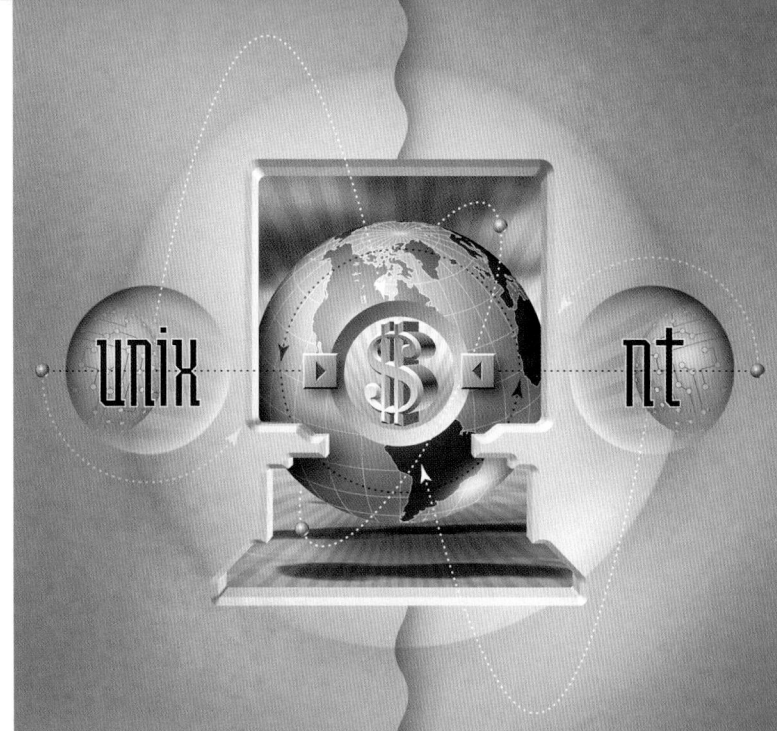

unix $ nt

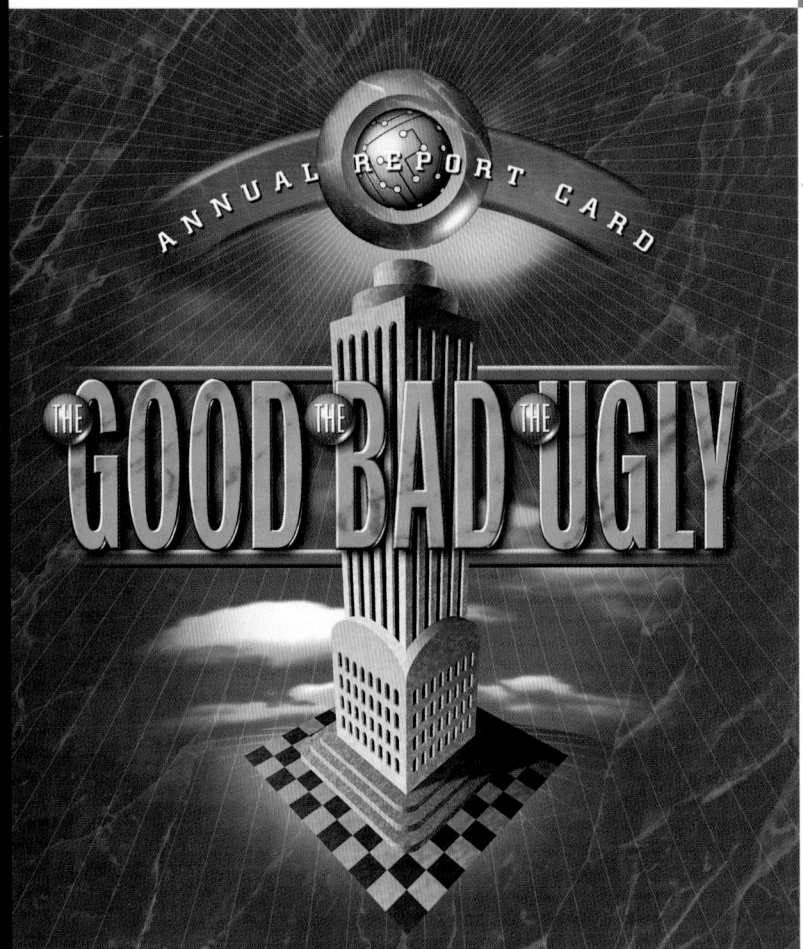

ANNUAL REPORT CARD

THE GOOD THE BAD THE UGLY

Headlines

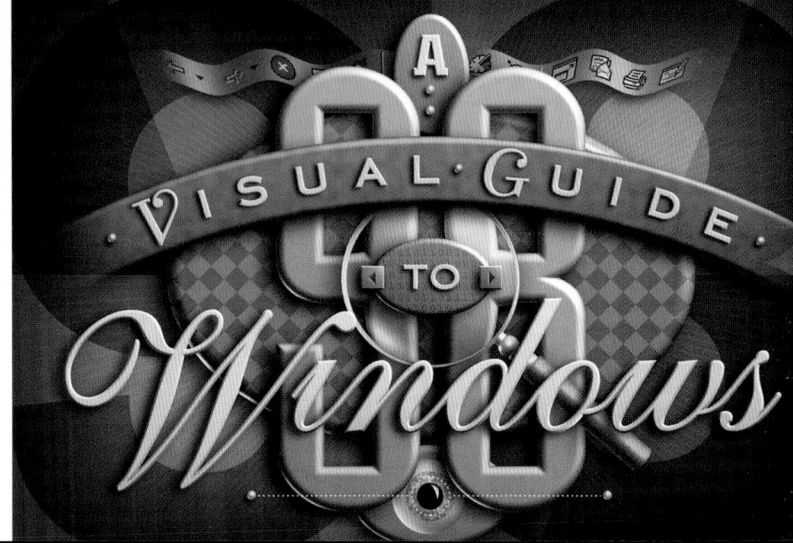

A VISUAL·GUIDE· TO Windows

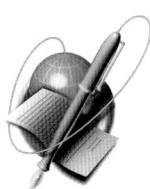
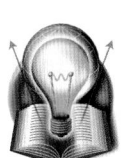
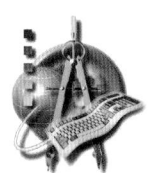
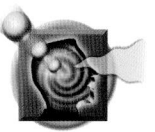

• to SEE a full range of our work, view our interactive portfolio and presentation at our website • http://www.twimages.com

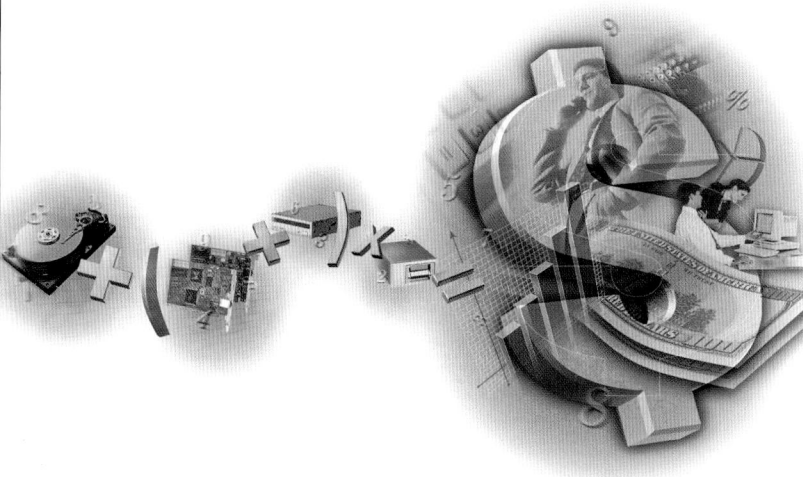

ILLUSTRATION & DESIGN FOR ALL MEDIA

tom white.images

212.866.7841

tom@twimages.com • http://www.twimages.com

CARY HENRIE

PH 801.298.2044

FAX 801.299.1919

C A R Y   H E N R I E

P H   8 0 1 . 2 9 8 . 2 0 4 4
FAX   8 0 1 . 2 9 9 . 1 9 1 9

ROBERT HUNT

ROBERT HUNT

Robert Hunt Studio (415) 459 6882 Fax 415 459 0343
Email: RobtHunt@aol.com
Represented in Los Angeles by Randy Pate (805) 529 8111
Artwork delivered as original art, Large format transparencies, or digital files

LA: 323-467-1700

NY: 212-206-9162

SEE LAURA'S STOCK AT:
HTTP://HOME.EARTHLINK.NET/~DORETSMITH/

©1999 LAURA SMITH

SUSAN ISHIGE

MICROSOFT

MICROSOFT

MICROSOFT

NEW ENGLAND JOURNAL OF MEDICINE

537 CHESTNUT STREET NEEDHAM, MASSACHUSETTS 02192 TELEPHONE 781.449.7761 FAX 781.449.9092

 # SUSAN ISHIGE

DREYFUS CORPORATION

537 CHESTNUT STREET NEEDHAM, MASSACHUSETTS 02192 TELEPHONE 781.449.7761 FAX 781.449.9092

THE SISCO KID   1561 NARVA RD., MISSISSAUGA, ON., CANADA L5H 3H4 PH/FAX (905) 278•2716

SAM SISCO

PH/FAX 905 278•2716

973

ken orvidas
telephone 425 867 3072
fax 425 867 3092

Business Competition

ken orvidas

telephone 425 867 3072
fax 425 867 3092

Conscience

Information Age

Managing Investments

Collaboration

R E P R E S E N T E D   B Y   J I M   L I L I E   4 1 5 • 4 4 1 • 4 3 8 4

E R I C   B O W M A N

Rick Griffin (1944–1991)

Cantina la Información

R E P R E S E N T E D   B Y   J I M   L I L I E   4 1 5 • 4 4 1 • 4 3 8 4

WWW.COCOTOS.COM

TOM NICK COCOTOS

212.620.7556

Bonnie Rieser

[206] 633-2334

AMERICAN LUNG ASSOCIATION BOSTON CONSULTING GROUP
FIDELITY INVESTMENTS GENRAD JAPAN AIRLINES MACWORLD
NYNEX TELEPHONE CO. SEATTLE SYMPHONY TEKTRONIX

(206) 633-2334

to see more of my portfolio,
look me up on www.showcase.com

NEIL BRENNAN

7 5 7   8 7 5 · 0 1 4 8

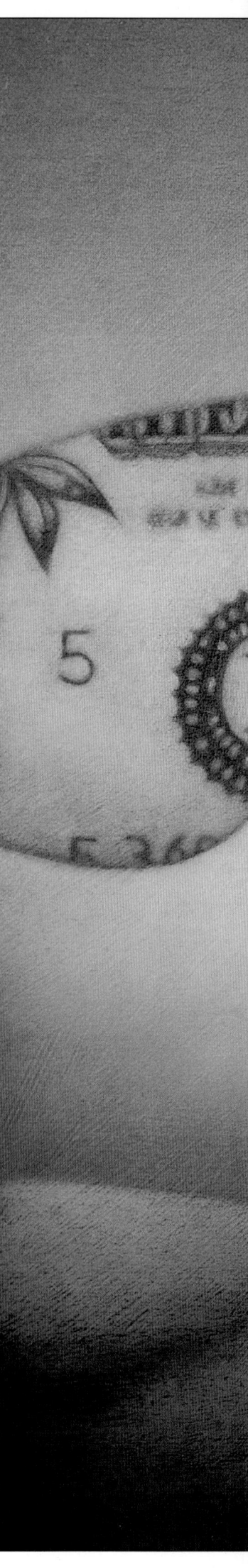

NIKOLAI PUNIN

NIKOLAI PUNIN

Kellogg's ®

Michèle Manning

Represented by Jan Collier (415) 383-9026 (415) 383-9037 fax collierreps.com

Michèle Manning Represented by Jan Collier (415) 383-9026 (415) 383-9037 fax collierreps.com

CHRIS·BUTLER
(303)494·4118·Fax:(303)530·5036

CALL FOR 3 PROMOTIONS WITH MORE THAN 160 ILLUSTRATIONS!

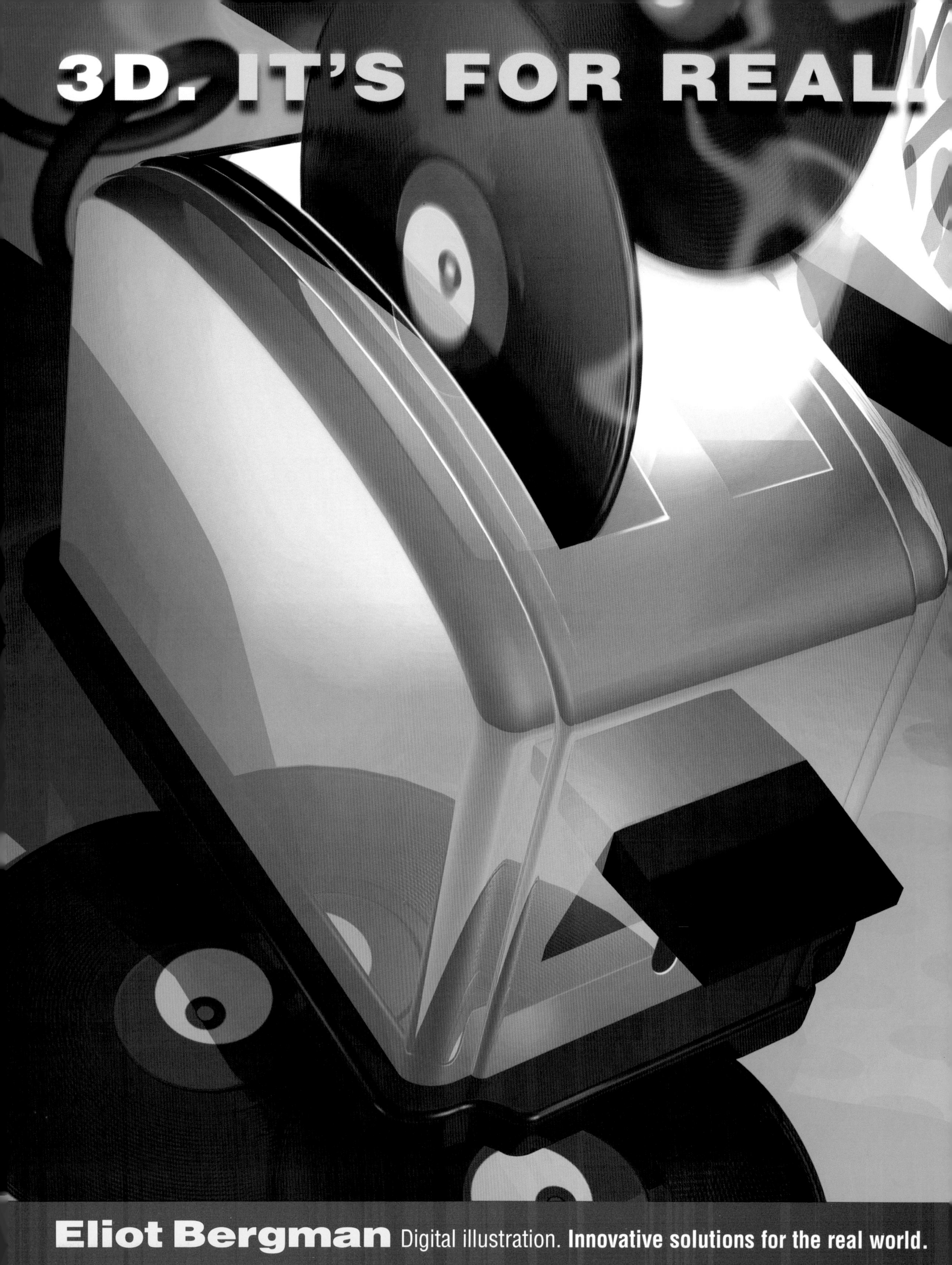

3D. IT'S FOR REAL

Eliot Bergman Digital illustration. **Innovative solutions for the real world.**

Packaging

Publishing

Apparel

Advertising

ADAM COHEN ILLUSTRATION

Golf Digest

Globalstar

Connecticut Laborers' Fund

212. 691 4074 TEL
212. 691 2109 FAX
email: admstudio@earthlink.com

ADAM COHEN

ILLUSTRATION

email: admstudio@earthlink.com

212.691 4074 TEL 212.691 2109 FAX

American Express

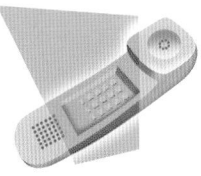

The Coca Cola Company

Dean Witter

995

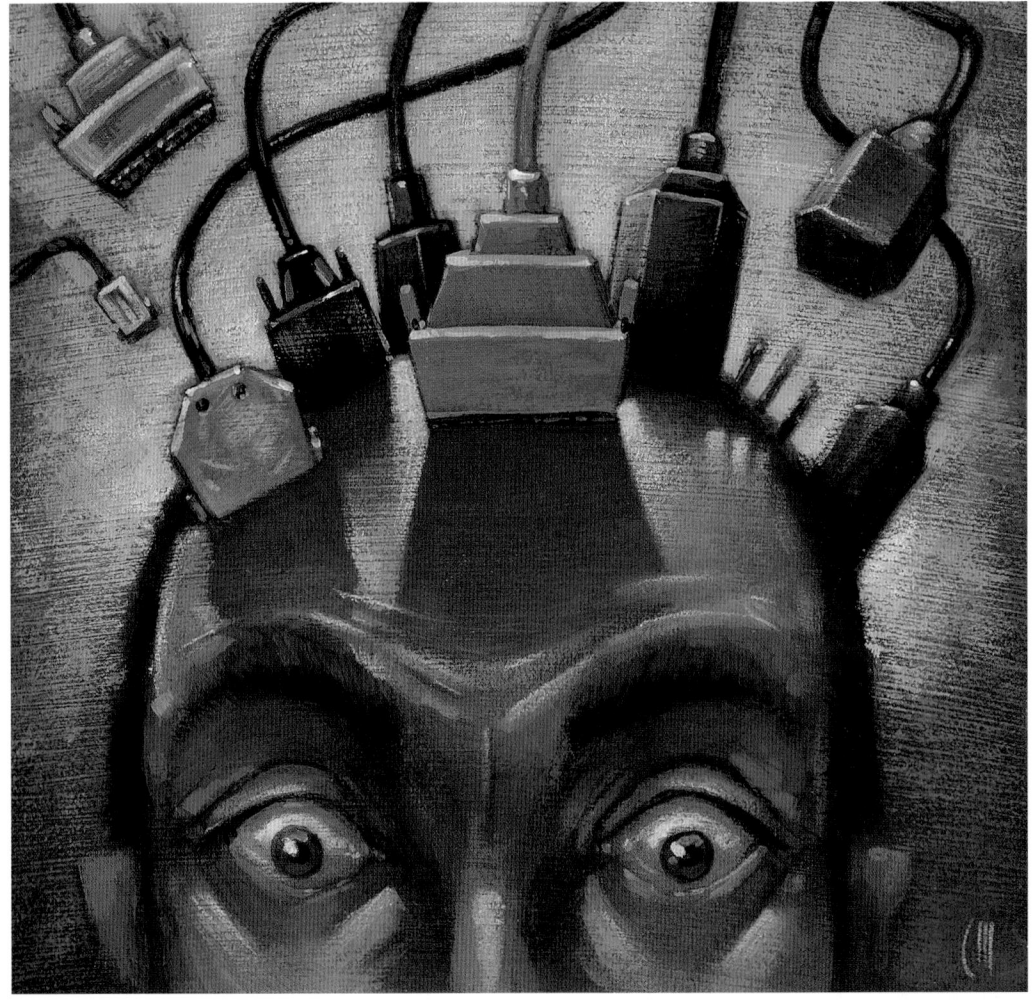

CHRIS McALLISTER ILLUSTRATION

218 · 828 · 8786

Online Portfolio and Stock Library: www.theispot.com/artist/mcallister

CHRIS McALLISTER ILLUSTRATION

218·828·8786

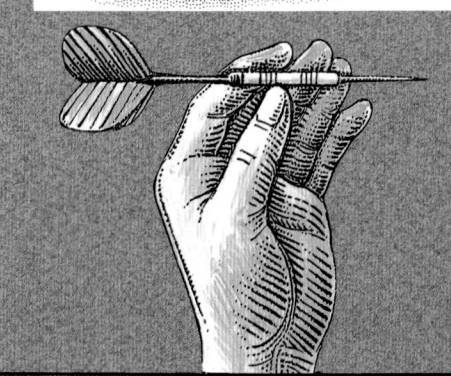

THE VICTOR BUI

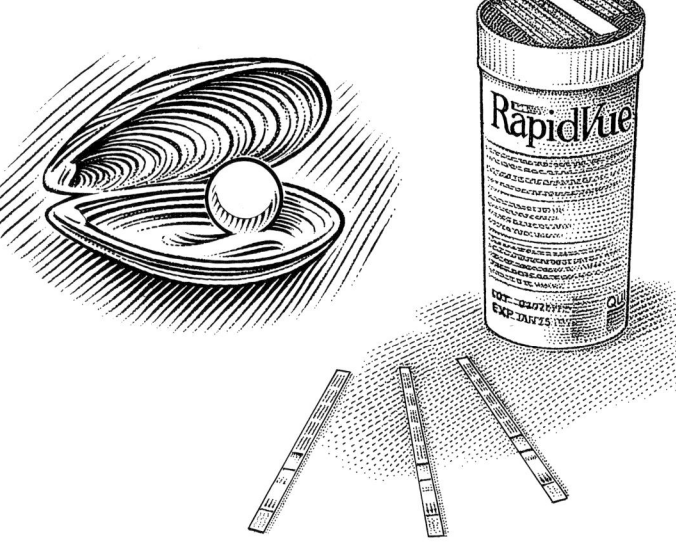

American *Eagle*

RapidVue

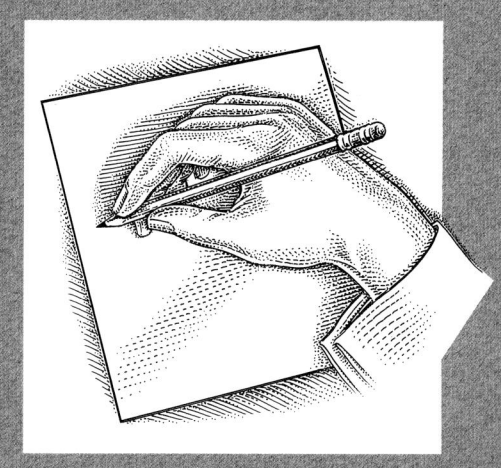

DIANE FENSTER

PHOTO
illustration

→ PORTFOLIO ONLINE AT www.sirius.com/~fenster

EDITORIAL & STUDIO   PHONE & FAX 650.355.5007   EMAIL fenster@sfsu.edu

CORPORATE & ADVERTISING REPRESENTED BY FREDA SCOTT   PHONE 415.398.9121   FAX 415.398.6136

1000

DIANE FENSTER

AIDS

"Floating Paper" © Nicholls Design Inc. 1997

CALVIN NICHOLLS

(705)878-1640 FAX 878-5675

CALVIN NICHOLLS

(705)878-1640 FAX 878-5675

Randy Lyhus • 301-986-0036 • fax 301-907-4653 • www.randylyhus.com

Phone: 303.837.1888   MARK JASIN   Lightbendr@aol.com

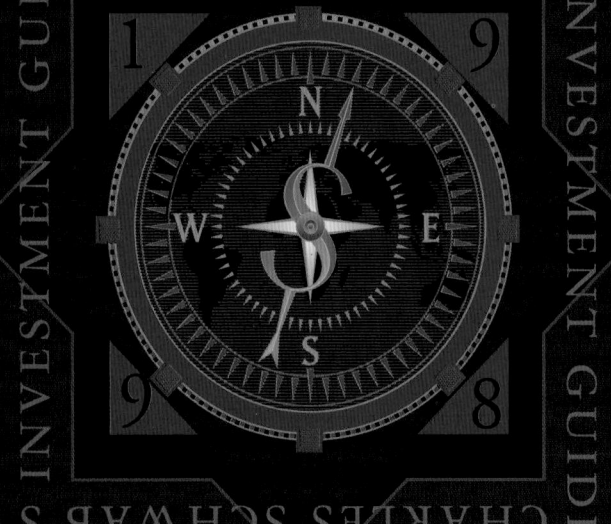

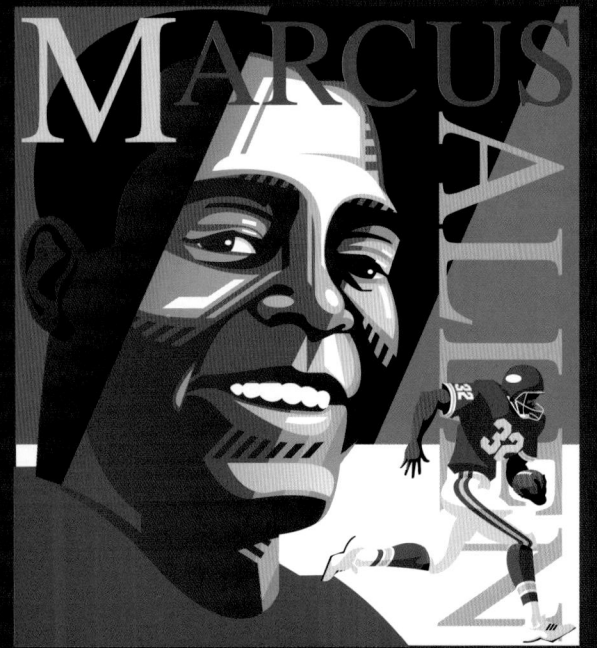

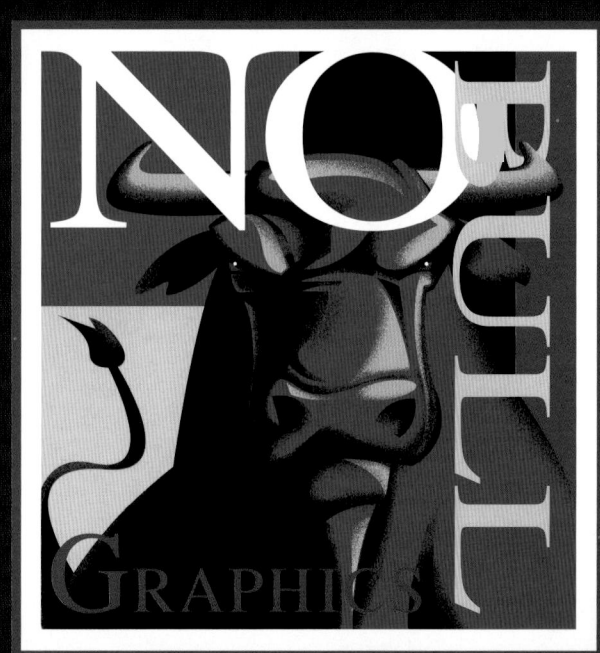

Phone: 303.837.1888   MARK JASIN   Lightbendr@aol.com

News   Events   Entertainment   Accommodations   Transportation   Marketplace   Business   History   Forum

EESTI PANK

5
VIIS KROONI

P. KERES 1916-1975

Armandina Lozano
*(949) 559-1397 • FAX 559-0338 • rep. **Jim Lilie** (415) 441-4384*

Marc Yankus

212 -242- 6334

www.niceboy.com

PANTHEON
Schocken

FALL 1998

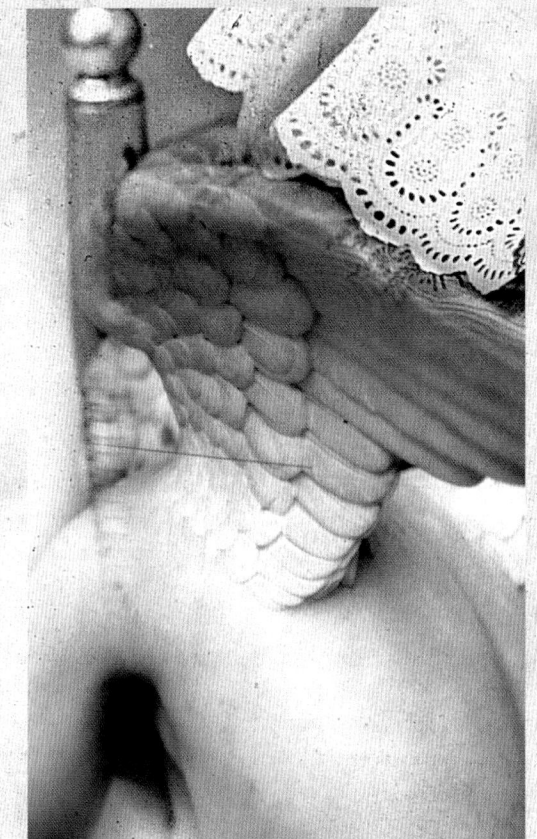

Brian Jensen

RKB STUDIOS  MINNEAPOLIS

(6 1 2)   3 3 9 - 7 0 5 5

fax [612] 339-8689   e-mail: brian@rkbstudios.com

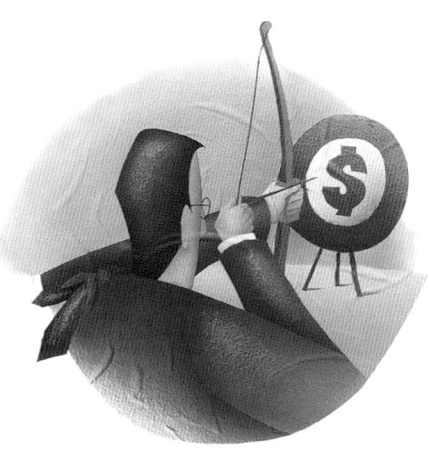

Brian Jensen

RKB STUDIOS MINNEAPOLIS

(612) 339-7055

fax [612] 339-8689   e-mail: brian@rkbstudios.com

John **Rowe Illustration**

Los Angeles *westcoast*
818.790.2645 · f 818.790.2655

New York *eastcoast*
212.986.5680 · f 212.818.1246

mendola artist

See our portfolio website
www.mendolaart.com

Moonlight. 20 x 22, oil.

Human-i-tees. 22 x 24, oil.

Julia. 20 x 24, oil.

Underwater World. 21 x 26, oil.

John **Rowe Illustration**

Los Angeles *westcoast*
818.790.2645 · *f* 818.790.2655

New York *eastcoast*
212.986.5680 · *f* 212.818.1246

mendola artist

See our portfolio website
www.mendolaart.com

Animal Kingdom. 9 x 16, oil.
© *Walt Disney Company 1998*

DALE GLASGOW & ASSOC.

INFORMATION ILLUSTRATION•INTERACTIVE MULTIMEDIA•VIDEO

Dale Glasgow & Assoc.
448 Hartwood Road
Fredericksburg,
Virginia 22406

VOICE
(540) 286-2539

FAX
(540) 286-0316

AMERICA ON-LINE
infoban@aol.com

INTERNET E-MAIL
dale@glasgowmedia.com

WEB SITE
www.glasgowmedia.com

TO VIEW MORE WORK:
- *Creative Illustration Book*, 1991-1999
- *American Showcase*, 1992-1999
- *New Media Showcase*, 1993-1995
- *Creative Sourcebook*, 1992-1998
- *Workbook*, 1995-1999
- *Diagraphics*, Vol. 2, JCA, 1995
- *Information Illustration*, 1994
- Home Page, www.glasgowmedia.com

SAMPLES
540-286-2539

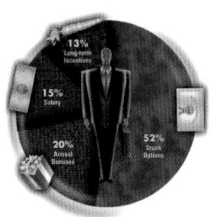

Johnson Hill Press—Executive salaries

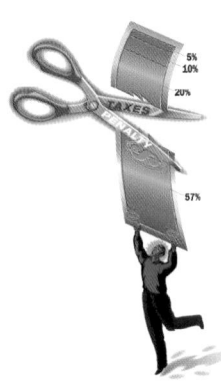

Capital Research & Management—
Taxes cutting into our dollar

US West—Weigh your strengths

ADI Technologies—Harness the power of Print Flow

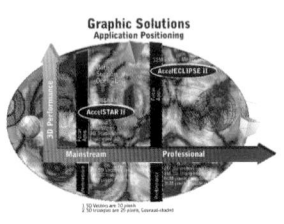

NEC— 3-D accelerator board performance

IGN—Network of gambling online

US West—Fly your business to new heights

Builder Magazine—Housing market rodeo

US West—Value your fax

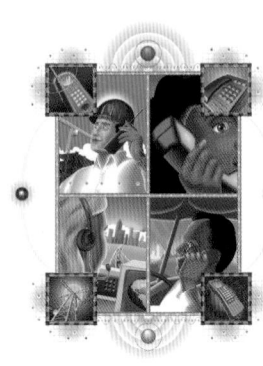

Pittencrief Communications—
Communications market

Capital R&M—Rollover your IRA

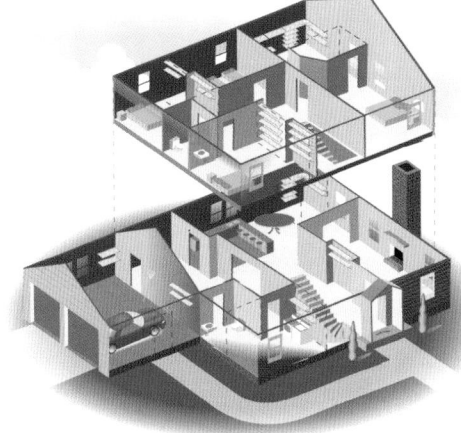
Closet Maid—Maximizing Closet Space

Elitch Gardens—Theme poster

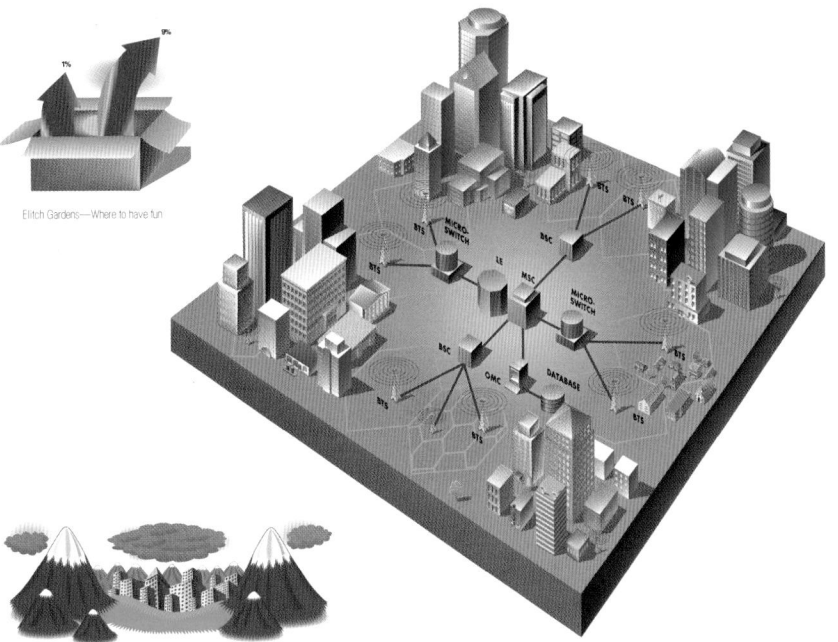
Elitch Gardens—Where to have fun

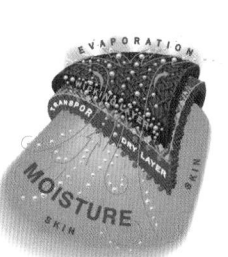
Universal Studios—How to find us

InterWave Communications—Network over a city

Houghton Mifflin—Pollution over Mexico

Titlest-FootJoy—DryFiber sock wicking moisture

BUCK LEWIS
AKA H.B.
8 0 0 . 5 2 2 . 1 3 7 7

BLACK

LISA BLACKSHEAR • 208 W. 23RD ST. #805 • NEW YORK NY 10011 • (212) 675-1083

SHEAR

LISA BLACKSHEAR • 208 W. 23RD ST. #805 • NEW YORK NY 10011 • (212) 675-1083

Digital images created in Illustrator

FAX (212) 242-3314

WEB http://www.users. interport.net/~lisab

1021

611 South Loma Vista Circle / Mesa, Arizona 85204 / 602 854 3121

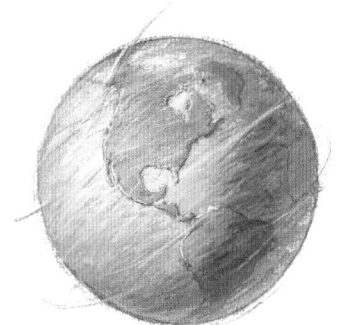

611 South Loma Vista Circle / Mesa, Arizona 85204 / 602 854 3121

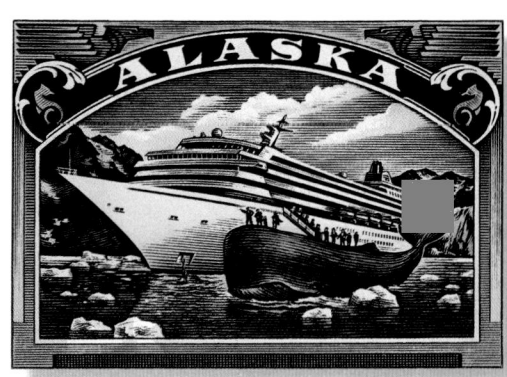

ABSOLUT PHILADELPHIA.

Confronting Your Stalker

illustration

T. F. COOK ILLUSTRATION
1907 EAGLE ST. MURFREESBORO, TN 37130
PH. (615) 895-9484 • FAX (615) 867-3870

T. F. COOK ILLUSTRATION
1907 EAGLE ST. MURFREESBORO, TN 37130
PH. (615) 895-9484 • FAX (615) 867-3870

Olizia

(KLEETS-EEAH)

914•734•4756

Clizia

(KLEETS-EEAH)

914 • 734 • 4756

1029

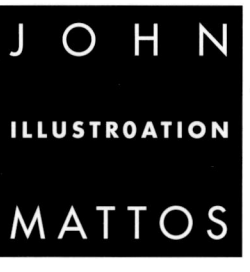

JOHN
ILLUSTROATION
MATTOS

415.397.2138

Studio E-Mail
mattos@sirius.com
Studio Fax Number
415-397-1174

Represented in the
Southern Midwest and
Southeast by

CLARE
JETT
& Associates

502-561-0737

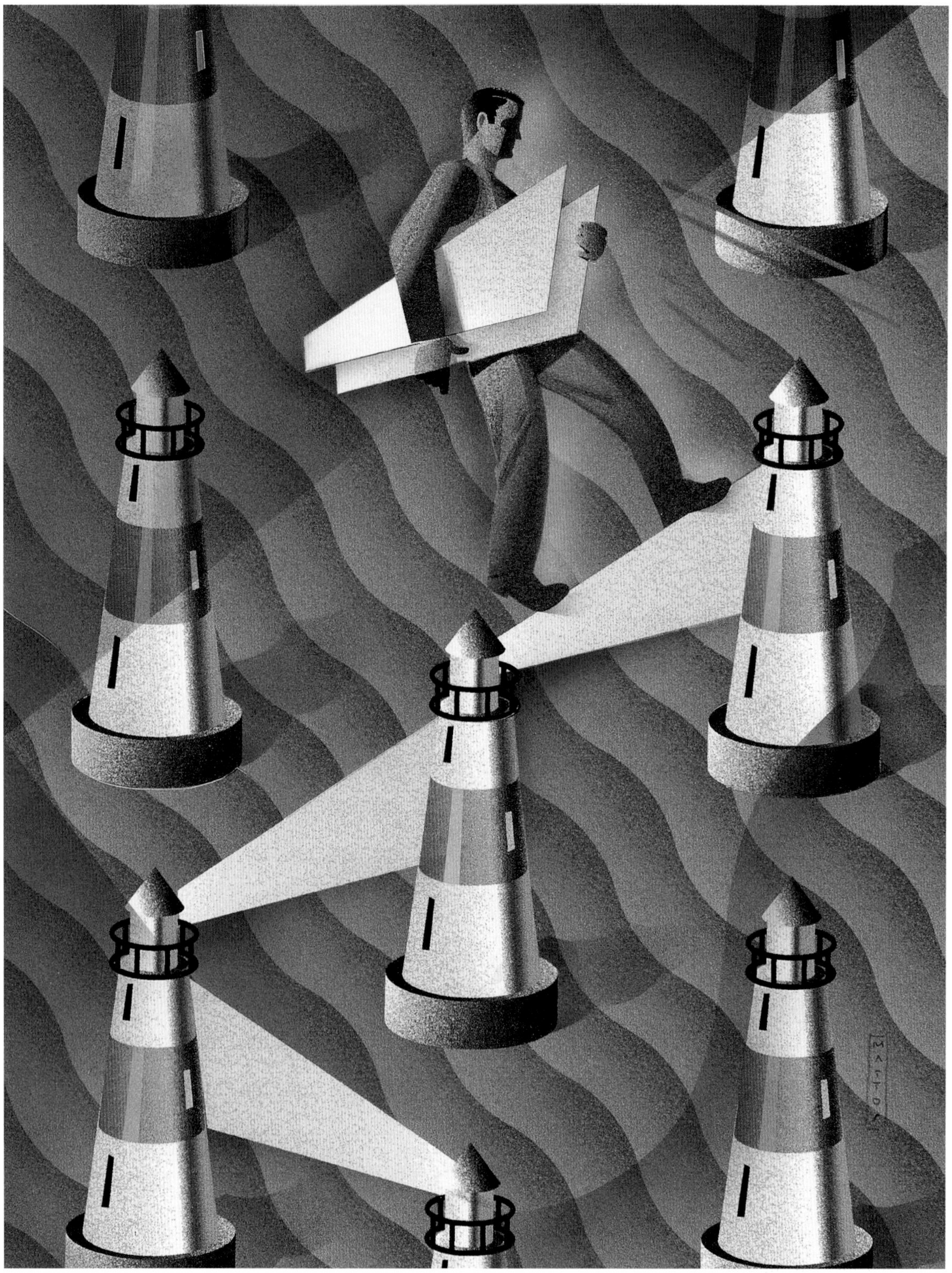

JOHN

ILLUSTROATION

MATTOS

415.397.2138

Studio E-Mail
mattos@sirius.com
Studio Fax Number
415-397-1174

Represented in the
Southern Midwest and
Southeast by

CLARE
JETT
& Associates

502-561-0737

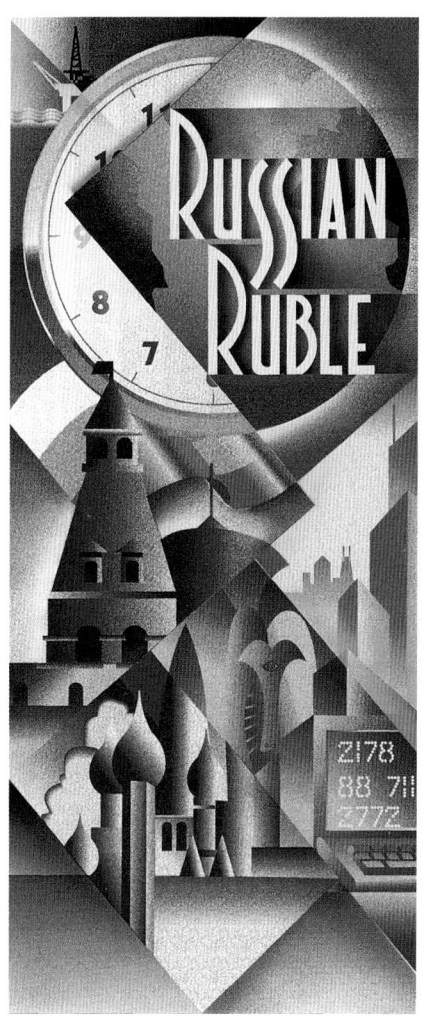

(614) 228.0900

614.228.0909 FAX

SPORK DESIGN incorporated

illustrators: Dominic LaRocca and Andrew Robinson

(614) 228.0900   614.228.0909 FAX

SPORK DESIGN incorporated

illustrators: Dominic LaRiccia and Andrew Robinson

Elizabeth, that's the wrong answer.

But that's what is written on the desk.

Dad, what does extinct mean?

Look it up, Rebecca.

SCIENCE FAIR

MOON ROCK →

Mom, I've changed my mind. I want this puppy instead of a little brother.

JARED D. LEE

(513)932-2154

FAX (513)932-9389

2942 Hamilton Road / Lebanon, Ohio 45036

JARED
LEE

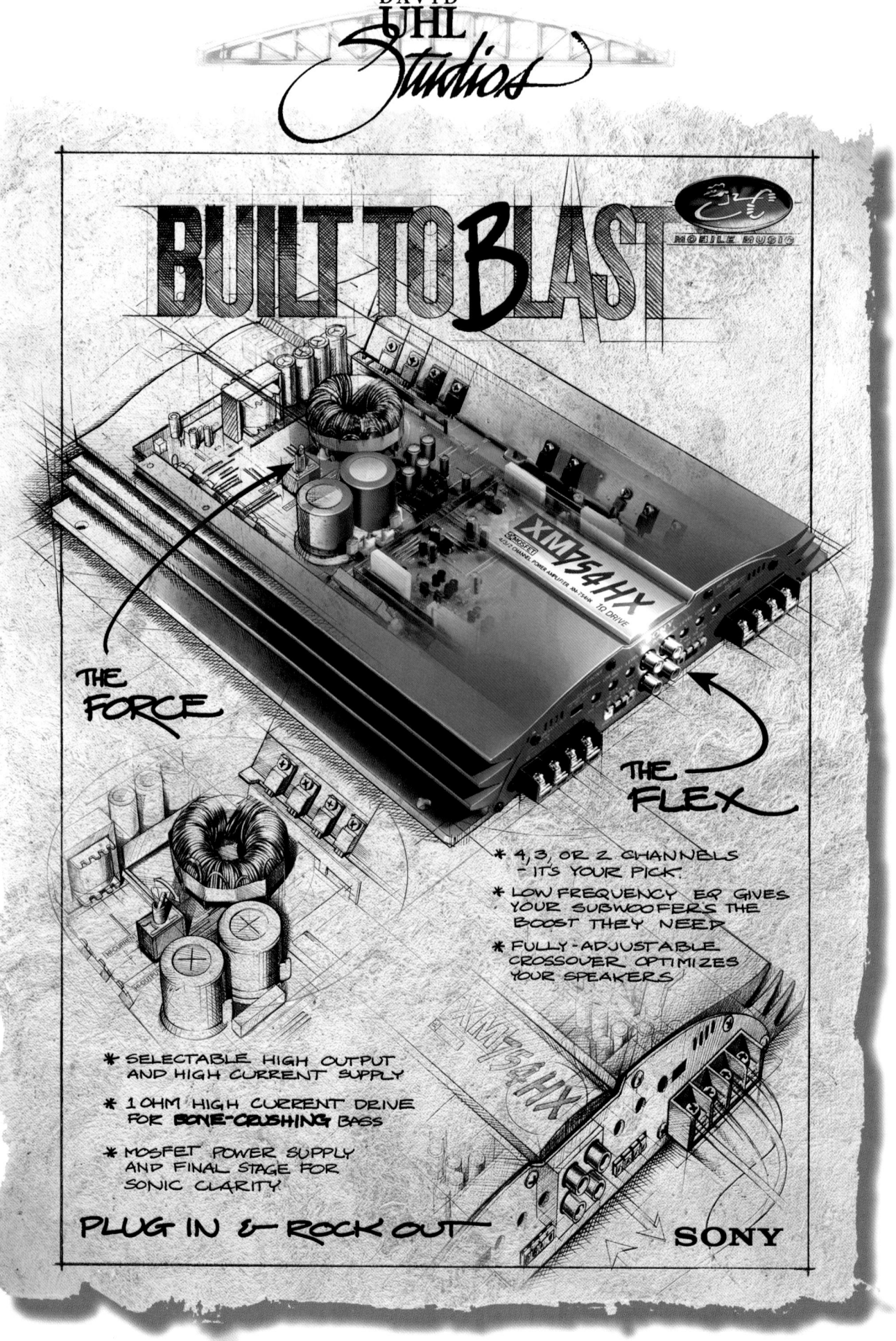

DAVID
UHL
Studios

"No Boundaries" For Hewlett Packard

Harley Davidson

1261 Delaware St. Denver, Colorado 80204 • 303.534.2054 • Fax 303.534.2056
email daviduhl@sni.net

GAD

JOEL
SPECTOR

REPRESENTED BY VICKI MORGAN ASSOCIATES · 212 475 0440

1044

TED WRIGHT

FOREST PARK

EQUESTRIAN CLASSIC

STUDIO: 314-797-4264
4237 HANSARD LANE/HILLSBORO/MISSOURI/63050
WWW.TEDWRIGHT.COM ■ EMAIL: TWRIGHTART@AOL.COM

T E D W R I G H T

O L Y M P I C
DIVING

O L Y M P I C
BASEBALL

O L Y M P I C
TRACK & FIELD

O L Y M P I C
GYMNASTICS

STUDIO: 314-797-4264
4237 HANSARD LANE/HILLSBORO/MISSOURI/63050
WWW.TEDWRIGHT.COM ▪ EMAIL: TWRIGHTART@AOL.COM

Sky MAGAZINE

DANIEL VASCONCELLOS

CALL: 781.829.8815

FAX: 781.829.8867

VIEW MORE @ www.theispot.com/artist/vasconcellos

TVSM/TOTAL TV

DANIEL VASONCELLOS.

CALL: 781.829.8815

FAX: 781.829.8867

DATAMATION

VIEW MORE @ www.theispot.com/artist/vasconcellos

Dale Stephanos

508-543-2500

Dale Stephanos

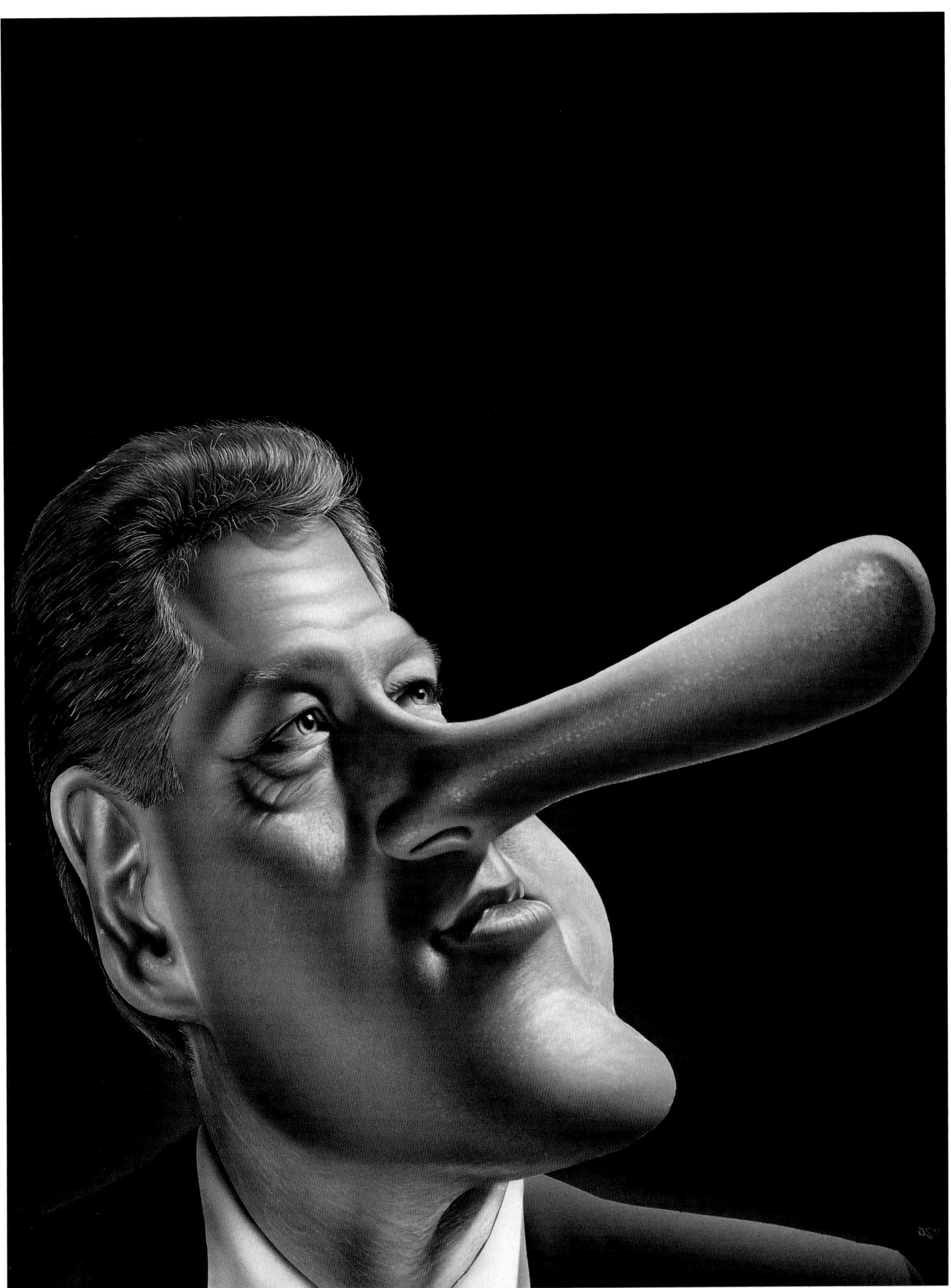

508-543-2500

For more samples see Showcase 21 & Directory of Illustration 13. Online portfolio : www.theispot.com/artist/stephanos

STEVEN NOBLE

Louis Armstrong

S&W Tri Valley Growers

"The Cable Guy:" annual report

Haggen, Inc.

Coors Logo

Travelers' Group

Sutter Home Winery

Phone (530) 477-1950   Fax (530) 477-2310

Gary Pierazzi

For more samples see earlier editions of Showcase and Workbook

SANDRA BRUCE

studio 530.477.1909
fax 530.477.2232

Mark Stutzman

100 6 Street Mtn. Lake Park MD 21550
V. 301 334-4086 F. 301 334-4186
eloqui@aol.com **Eloqui** www.eloqui.com

Eloqui is a studio devoted exclusively to illustration

Arizona Theatre Group

© 1998 Nickelodeon

© 1998 Walt Disney Attractions, McDonald's Cup Promotion

Laura Stutzman

100 G Street Mtn. Lake Park MD 21550
V. 301 334-4086 F. 301 334-4186
eloqui@aol.com Eloqui www.eloqui.com

Eloqui is a studio devoted exclusively to illustration

Review and Herald Publishing

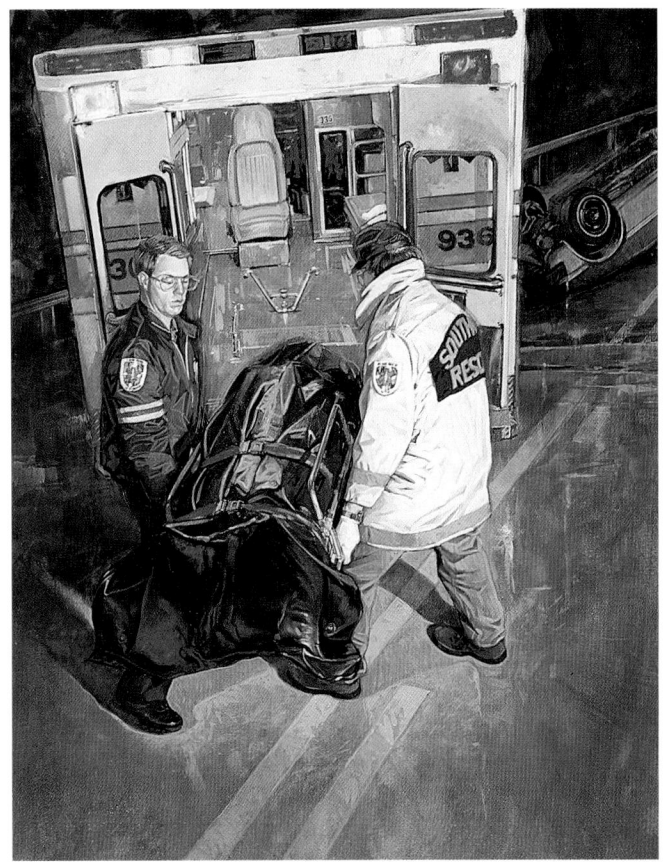

American Forces Information Services

US Mint

Association of Scrap Recycling

214.720.2272

REPRESENTED BY PHOTOCOM / FAX 214.720.2274

STUDIO 214.922.9757

FOR MORE WORK, PLEASE SEE SHOWCASE 19,20,21 AND WORKBOOK 18,19,20&21

WOMAN VS. MANAGEMENT

DON ARDAY

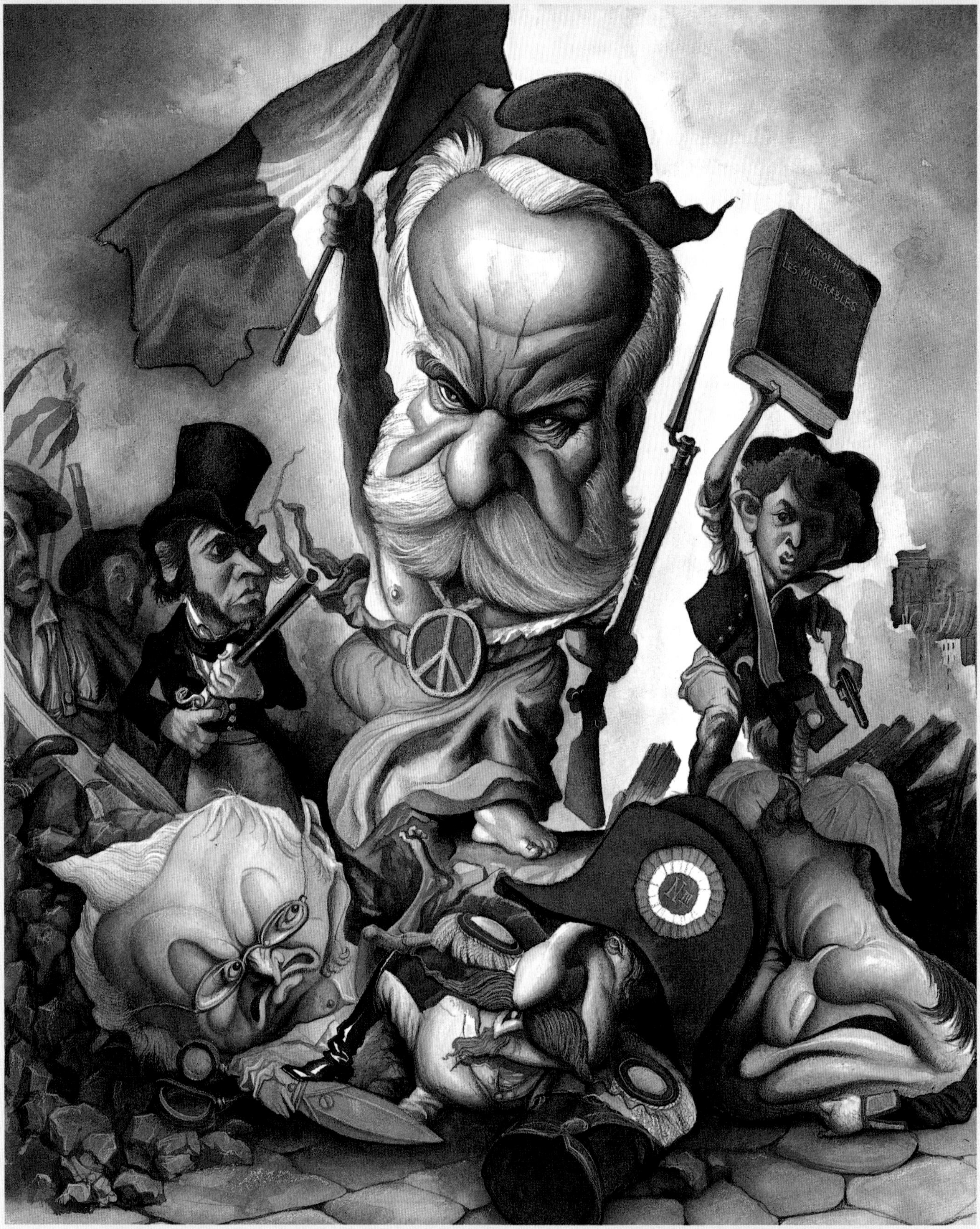

"Clockwise: Victor Hugo, King Louis-Philipe, Emperor Napoleon III, President Louis-Adolphe Thiers"

R.Genn

Represented by Barbara Markowitz
(323) 939 5927

"Robin Williams"

"Madeleine Albright"

"Manchurian Candidates"

ROMAN GENN

Represented by Barbara Markowitz (323) 939 5927

ANGRY COW
Dan Hobbs
(416) 767-6035

PETER HORJUS

For speed & convenience all illustrations are provided on disk or emailed as Illustrator EPS files. PHONE **619 299 0729** FAX **619 574 7774**

DENNIS ZIEMIENSKI

JIM LILIE   415 441·4384   FAX 415 395·9809

JOE FARNHAM
80 EDGECLIFF ROAD, WATERTOWN, MA 02472; PHONE/FAX: (617) 926-3266

jason farris one 800 887 7146

http://www.jasonfarris.com

NICHOLAS WILTON

JENNIE OPPENHEIMER

DAN YACCARINO

Japan: CWC
813-3496-0745
fax 813-3496-0747

Studio: (212) 675-5335
www.danyaccarino.com
reel available

UK: Beint & Beint
0171-793-7000
fax 0171-735-2565

CARLA BAUER ▪ 156 FIFTH AVENUE ▪ SUITE 1100 ▪ NEW YORK CITY 10010 ▪ 212.807.8305 ▪ 212.727.8094 FAX ▪ WOODCUT ILLUSTRATION

shelly meridith   55 mercer street Floor 4 nyc, ny 10013   212 941 1905
fax 212 226 3227   e mail leocat@spacelab.net

Outrunning A Market Correction

Kick the Habit

*eyecon

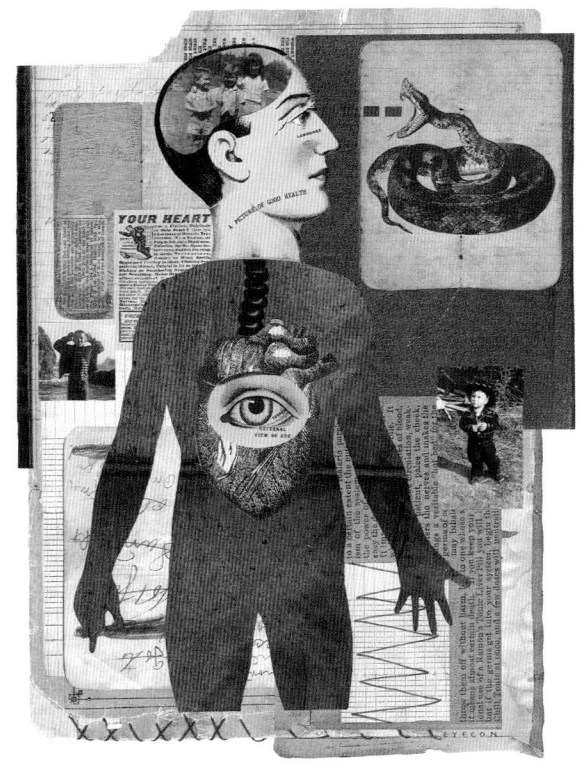

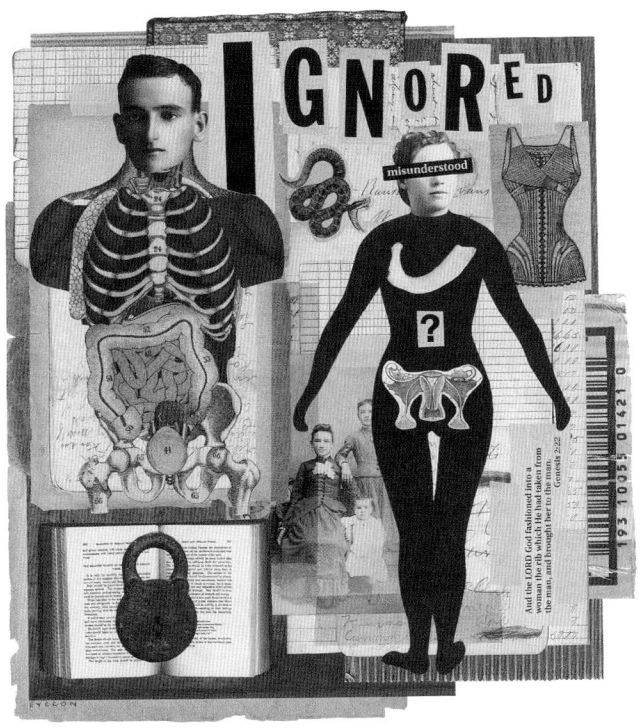

JANIS LLEWELYN

2318 MAPLETON AVE

BOULDER, COLORADO 80304

PHONE: (303)545-9380 FAX: (303)727-7670

E-MAIL: EYECONDSGN@AOL.COM

Liz Lomax

Rudy Giuliani

Marv Albert

Bill Clinton

Bob Marley, Jerry Garcia, Jimi Hendrix

914 · 666 · 7345

81 Seven Bridges Rd. Chappaqua, N.Y. 10514

RICK POWELL

PHONE 757-440-1723, FAX 757-440-0952, www.studiopowell.com

Oh, oh, what a mistake I made?!

Kurt D. Hollomon
Studio ~ 503·636·4221
» REPRESENTED IN THE NORTHWEST BY «
Donna Jorgensen / Annie Barrett
{ Phone ~ 206 634·1880 Fax ~ 206 632·2024 }

EUGENE

N°
3

Michael Miracle, Boston, MA 888·393·3779 www.michaelmiracle.com

Greg Huber

LESLIE COBER-GENTRY

203·255·9780
PHONE + FAX →

224 SHERWOOD FARM
FAIRFIELD, CT 06430

GLeeWall

http://www.mindspring.com/~gleewall/   gleewall@mindspring.com   804-673-3632

JANET CLELAND

ILLUSTRATOR

One Mono Lane • San Anselmo, CA 94960 • TEL 415.457.1049 • FAX 415.453.5851

Suling Wang

(415) 474-0259 • 2885 Bush Street #9 San Francisco, CA 94115
Suling_Wang@designlink.com • http://www.best.com/~sulingw/

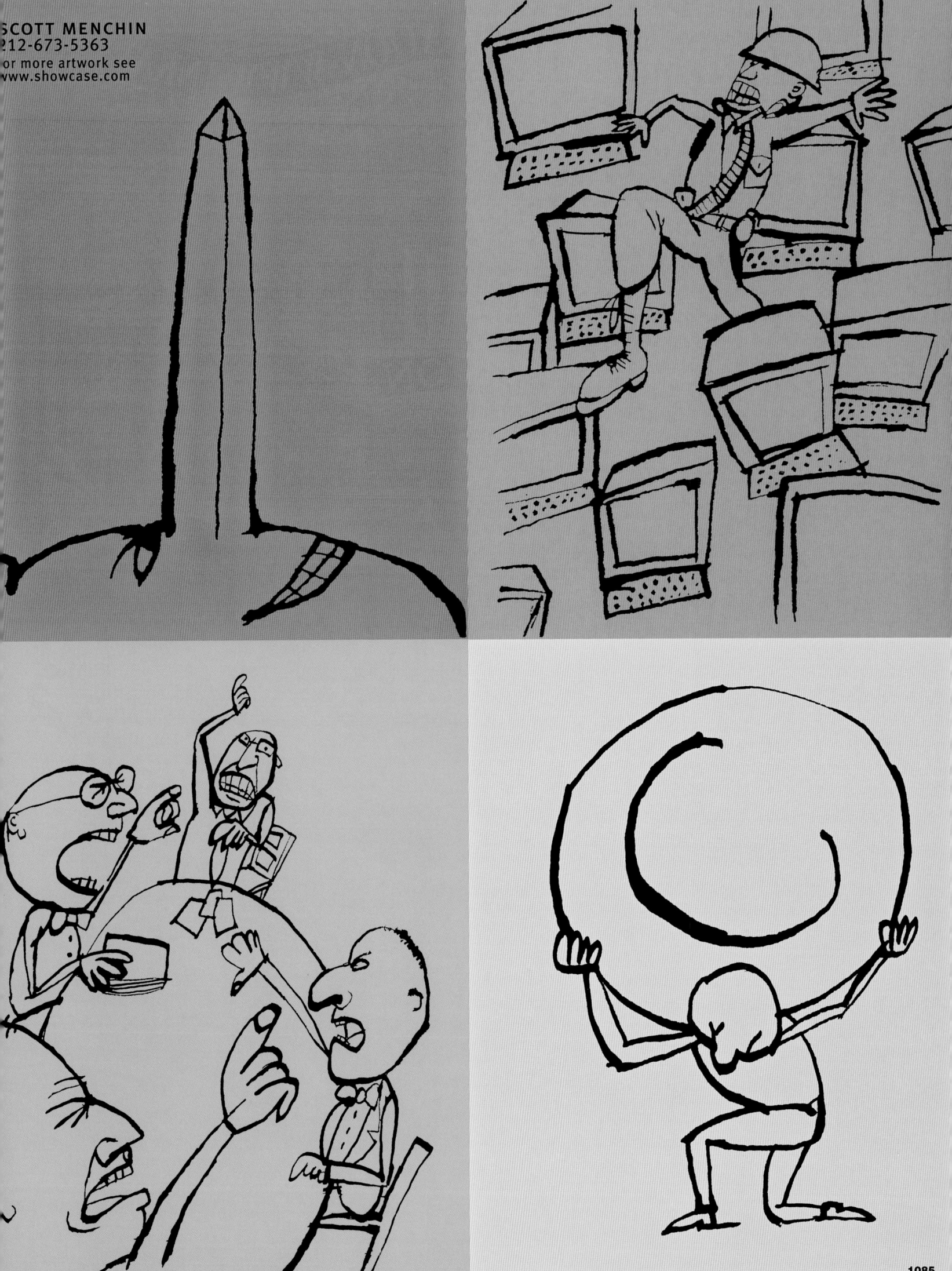

1085

BOSTON

BOBBYE COCHRAN

studio
773.404.0375

fax
773.404.0377

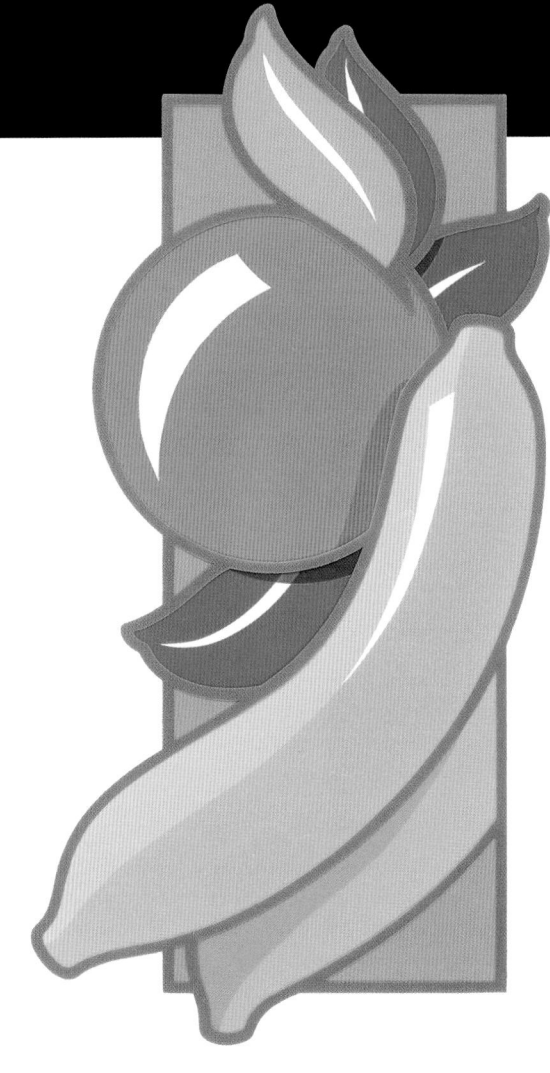

Barnett Is Florida's Bank.®

JUDE MACEREN

STUDIO TEL & FAX

(732) 752-59-31

92 KOSSUTH ST. PISCATAWAY, NJ 08854   E-MAIL: judeM.art@worldnet.att.net

tanya brokaw

310 394 8456

LEO ESPINOSA NEOCOMIC ILLUSTRATION PHONE 914 725 9103 FAX 914 725 9704 E-MAIL LEI@INCH.COM

For additional samples see: GAG 8, 9, 10, 11, 12, 13, 14 & Alternative Pick 1, 2, 3

dOUgLaS aNdELiN

415.927.1945

GREG TUCKER
ILLUSTRATION

ENVOY MAGAZINE: IS CATHOLIC GOOD ENOUGH?

COMMUNICATION ARTISTS OF NEW MEXICO

COVER, ZANDERS IKONO PAPER SAMPLER

*Recently included in: Society of Illustrators of Los Angeles (**Gold Medal in Editorial Illustration**); Graphis Design 96 & 98; CA Illustration Annual 1997 & 1998; American Illustration 16 & 17; Society of Illustrators 37 & 39; California Image 1997. Call for additional samples.*

Farida Zaman

U.S.A. 973 744-9377   Canada 416 489-3769
E-Mail   fzaman@cybernex.net

1093

KYLE DREIER

TONAL VALUES ILLUSTRATION | TEL 214.943.2569 | FAX 214.942.6771 | TOLL FREE 800.484.8592 code 2787 | E.MAIL tonalvalues@mindspring.com

Work should be fun! | | | INTERNET www.dreier.com

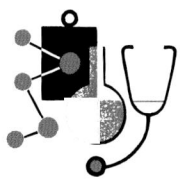

TIMOTHY COOK

PHONE 301.949.5002

FAX 301.949.5003

WEB www.timothycook.com

AIGA

MACY'S

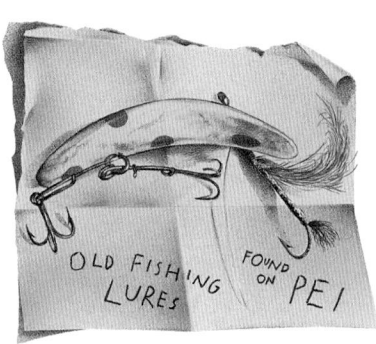

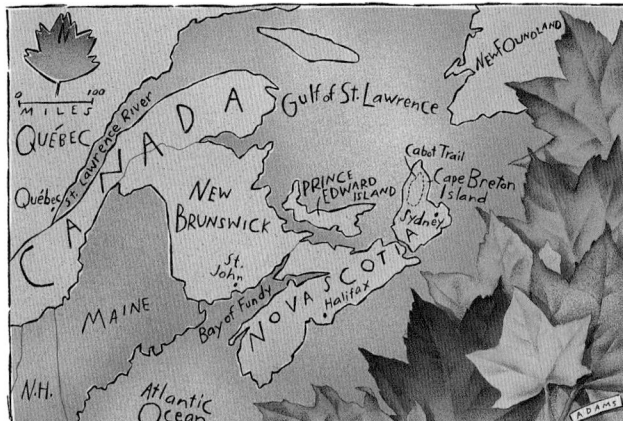

THE ATLANTIC MONTHLY (3)

MACMILLAN

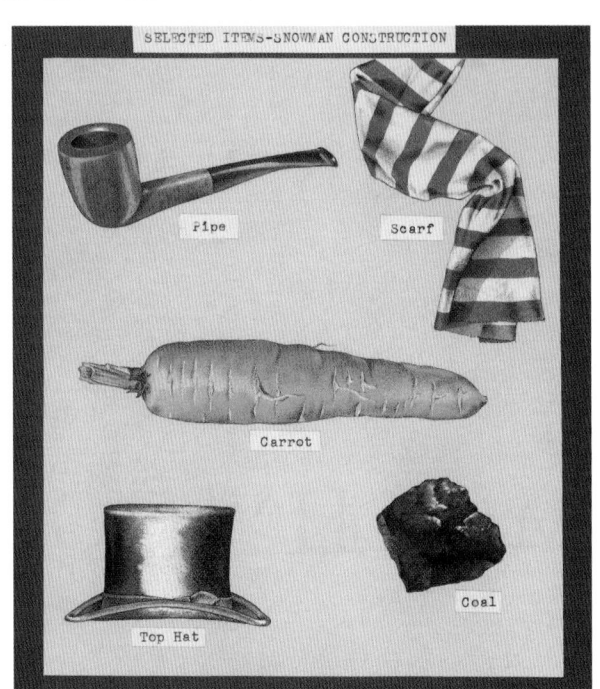

GREETING CARD

LISA ADAMS

✳

40 Harrison Street | Nº·29f | NYC | 10013 | tel: 212.385.8189 | fax: 212.385.9630

VA*L*ENTI

lisa valenti

☎ *914 738 1995*

FX *914 738 5273*

MARK RYDEN   Tel 626-355-1750   •   Fax 626-355-1138

Amy Vangsgard

RUNNING 'ROUND THE CLOCK

TURNING THE WORLD AROUND

RACING TOWARD THE MILLENNIUM

Tel: (323) 461-3094   **Fax:** (323) 461-5024   **Email:** AmyNatChaz@aol.com

Portfolio: www.theispot.com/artist/vangsgard   **Stock:** www.sisstock.com

1099

David Aldrich • 416/960-6005

MEDICAL ILLUSTRATION

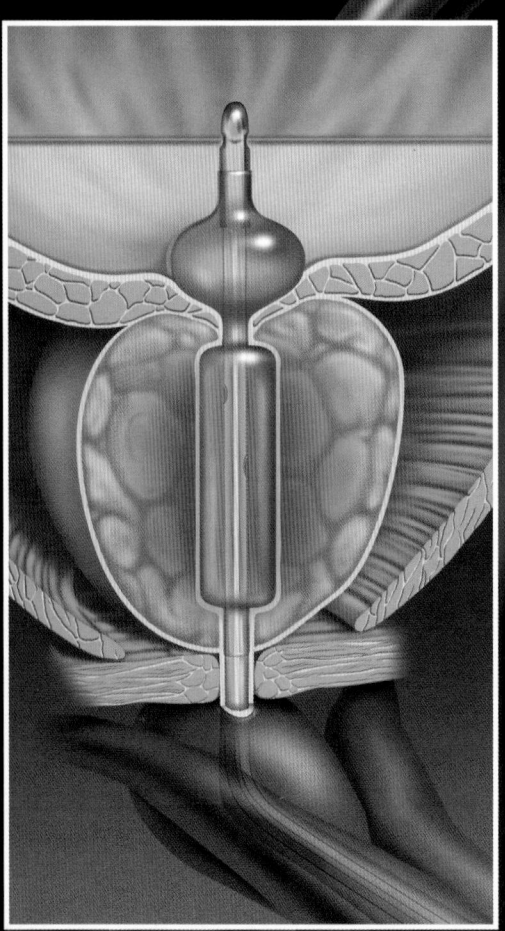
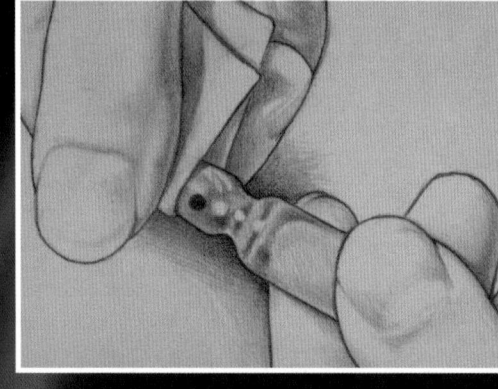

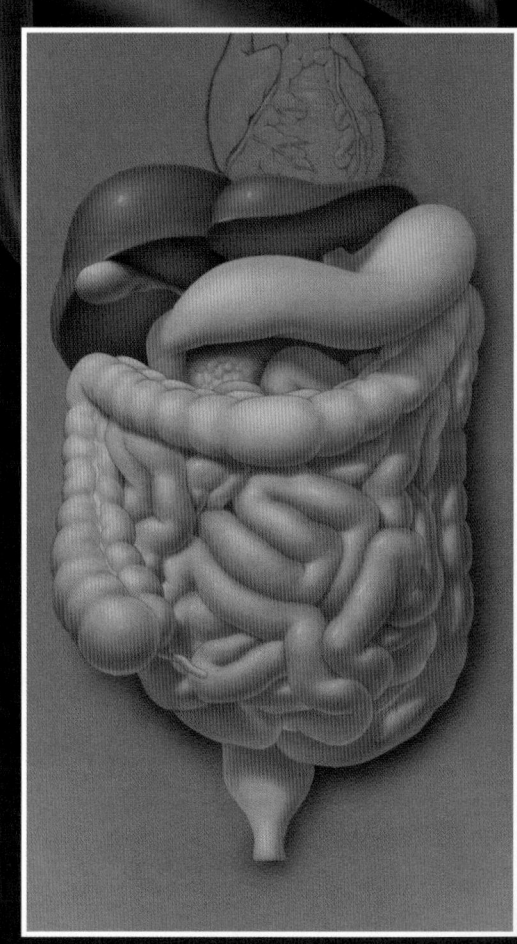

CHARLIE HILL
DIGITAL ILLUSTRATION

DAVID WILEY REPRESENTS
415.442.1822
FAX.442.1823

DAVID
W
WILEY

KELLY ALDER ILLUSTRATION

7 NORTH MONROE ST. 2ND FLOOR • RICHMOND, VIRGINIA 23220
TELEPHONE & FAX: 804•643•5761

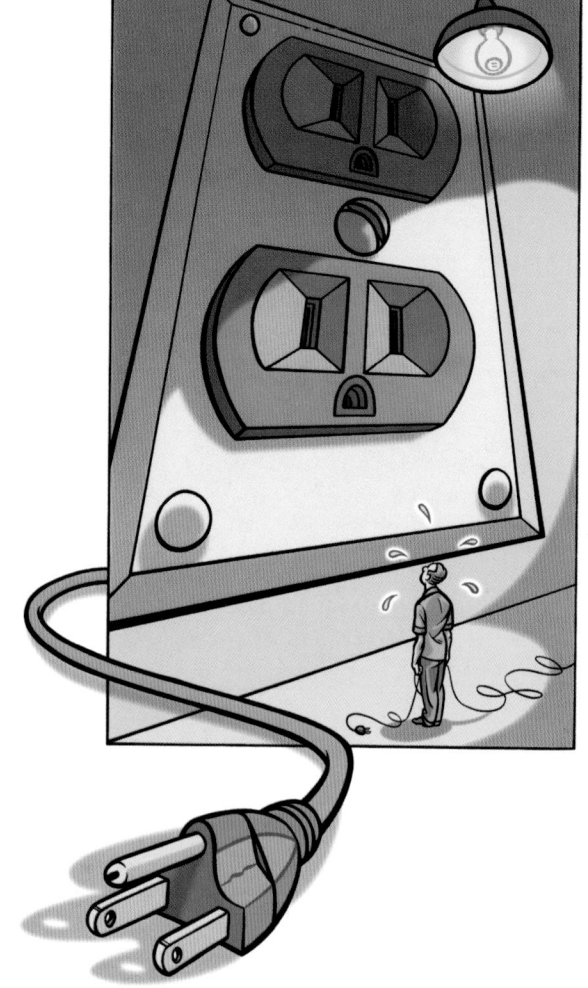

For additional work, see Communication Arts Illustration
Annual 1997 and Directory of Illustration #s 12, 13, and 14.
Call for free electronic portfolio.

Ellen Thompson

732 422-0233

KONG LU

illustration

LEHMEN ◎ DABNEY

representatives

....

Tel 206.325.8595

Fax 206.325.8594

Melissa Sweet

PH. [207]772-4850
FAX [207]874-7649

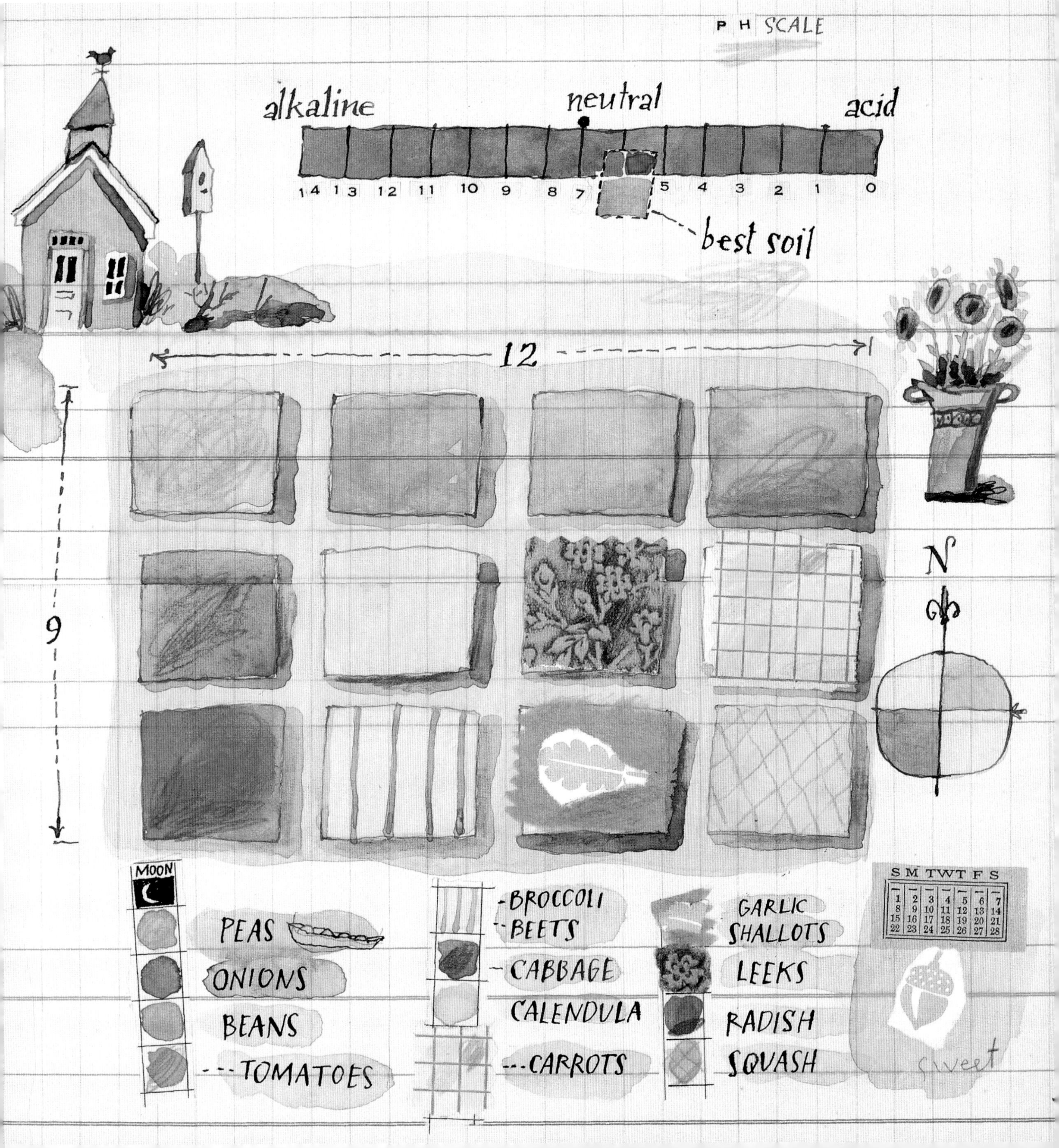

PH SCALE

alkaline   neutral   acid

| 14 | 13 | 12 | 11 | 10 | 9 | 8 | 7 | 6 | 5 | 4 | 3 | 2 | 1 | 0 |

best soil

12

9

N

MOON

PEAS

ONIONS

BEANS

TOMATOES

BROCCOLI
BEETS

CABBAGE

CALENDULA

CARROTS

GARLIC
SHALLOTS

LEEKS

RADISH

SQUASH

S	M	T	W	T	F	S
1	2	3	4	5	6	7
8	9	10	11	12	13	14
15	16	17	18	19	20	21
22	23	24	25	26	27	28

Sweet

Jeff West

INFORMATION DESIGN AND ILLUSTRATION

Concept Models, Anatomies, Processes, Structures, Relationships,
Data, and Products through Diagrams, Charts, Graphs, Maps,
Exploded view, See-thru, Cutaway, Axiometric, & 3D visuals.

☎ **831.688.6075**   fax 831.688.6072

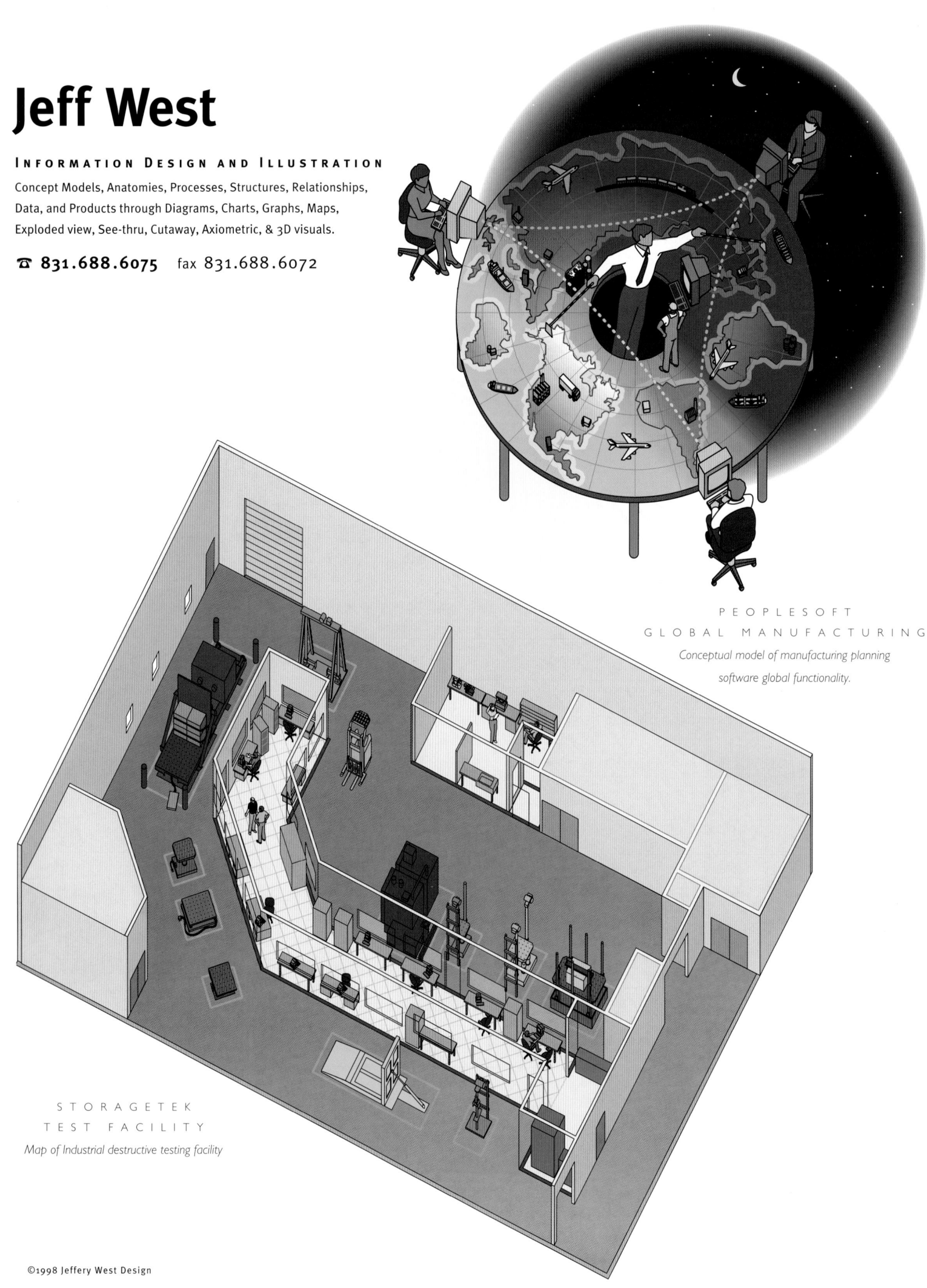

PEOPLESOFT
GLOBAL MANUFACTURING

*Conceptual model of manufacturing planning
software global functionality.*

STORAGETEK
TEST FACILITY

Map of Industrial destructive testing facility

Tim Jessell

SUZANNE CRAIG REPRESENTS
INCORPORATED

CENTRAL TIME   TEL & FAX 918 749 9424   EAST 405 377 3619   CHICAGO 918 749 9424

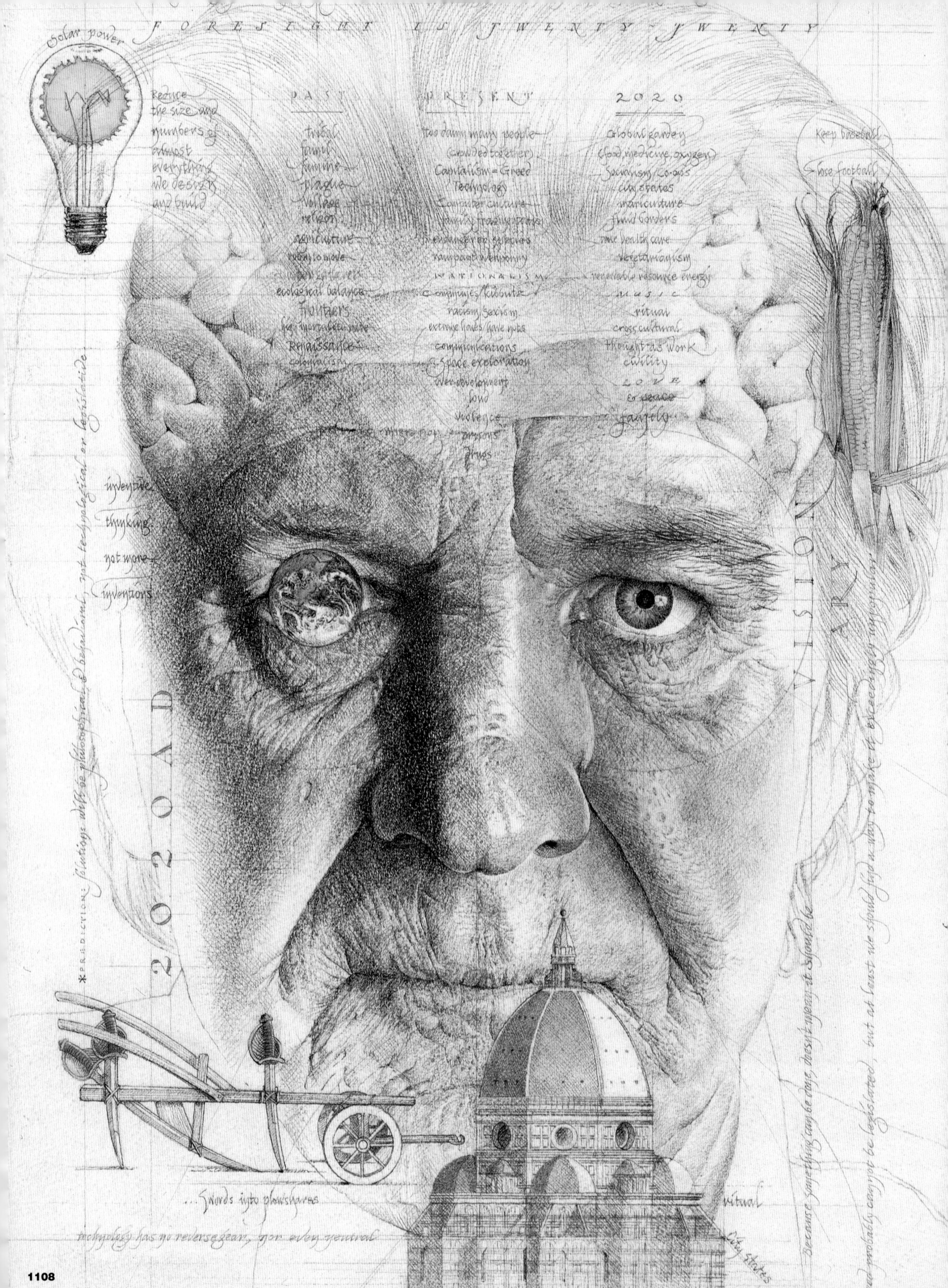

FORESIGHT IS TWENTY-TWENTY

Solar power

Reduce
the size and
numbers of
almost
everything
we desire
and build

PAST   PRESENT   2020

tribal   too damn many people   Global garden
family   (crowded together)   (food, medicine, oxygen)
famine   Capitalism = Greed   Socialism, co-ops
plague   Technology   city states
voltage   Computer culture   mariculture
religion   fluid borders
agriculture   nine health care
need to move   rampant weaponry   vegetarianism
                   NATIONALISM   renewable resource energy
ecological balance communes/kibbutz   music
hunters   racism, sexism   ritual
                   extreme loans/have nots cross cultural
Renaissance   communications   thought as work
colonialism   space exploration   civility
                   war development   2028
                   food   ex peace
                   violence   largely

inventive
thinking,
not more
inventions

...Swords into plowshares

technology has no reverse gear, nor even neutral

tel 416-516-2835 — **lorraine tuson** — fax 416-516-0955

FAITH, LOVE & DEVOTION / WATERCOLOR

MARY T. MONGE
I L L U S T R A T I O N
Studio: 949-831-2762

Represented By Hall & Associates
Marni Hall and Lisa Ellison 323-962-2500

GET YOUR KICKS ON ROUTE 66

ASSOCIATION OF SCHOOL BUSINESS OFFICIALS

LOS ANGELES TIMES MAGAZINE / WATERCOLOR

BUZ studio

tel/fax 877.614.8111

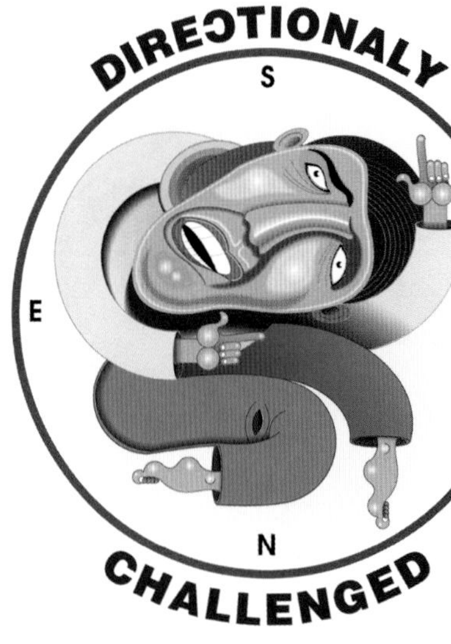

Marcia Staimer
I L L U S T R A T I O N

studio (703) 960-4196 • fax (703) 960-5392 • e·mail marsta@aol.com

The Directory of Illustration #15 • The Creative Sourcebook Vol. 9,10,11 • www.theispot.com

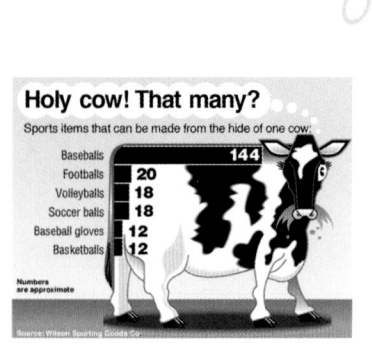

Holy cow! That many?
Sports items that can be made from the hide of one cow:

Baseballs		144
Footballs	20	
Volleyballs	18	
Soccer balls	18	
Baseball gloves	12	
Basketballs	12	

Numbers are approximate

Source: Wilson Sporting Goods Co.

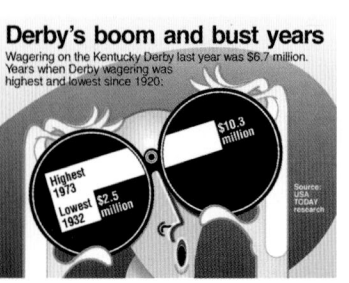

Derby's boom and bust years
Wagering on the Kentucky Derby last year was $6.7 million. Years when Derby wagering was highest and lowest since 1920:

$10.3 million

Highest 1973

$2.5 million

Lowest 1932

Source: USA TODAY research

All-time top Grammy winners
John Williams' winning of a 16th Grammy for his Schindler's List music week ties Paul Simon and Leonard Bernstein[1] for sixth place on the all-time winners list. The top 5:

1– Deceased

Sir Georg Solti	30
Quincy Jones	26
Vladimir Horowitz[1]	25
Henry Mancini[1]	20
Stevie Wonder	17

Source: National Academy of Recording Arts and Sciences

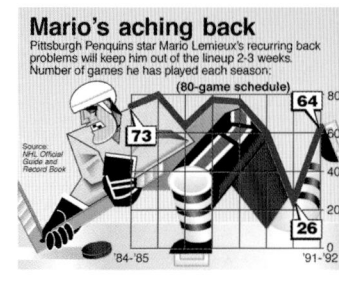

Mario's aching back
Pittsburgh Penguins star Mario Lemieux's recurring back problems will keep him out of the lineup 2-3 weeks. Number of games he has played each season:

(80-game schedule)

73

64

26

'84-'85   '91-'92

Source: NHL Official Guide and Record Book

ORGANICALLY GROWN
Tender Harvest
MINESTRONE DINNER
CERTIFIED ORGANIC
Gerber®
NET WT. 4 OZ. (113g)

AndreaBrooks
212.633.1477

On the west coast call:
Corey Graham
415.956.4750

To view more work:
www.coreygrahamreps.com

Raspberry Jam

Apricot and Pecan Scones

Hot Coffee & CREAM

Little Otto's
MAGIC STORE
Loads of fun for almost anyone!

jim spiece

logos
lettering
illustration
type design

[219-436-9549]

Wacky Cactus
R A N C H

SPRING BOUQUET

Mr. Fancy
HATS GALORE

ANCIENT chinese DRAGONS

WUG & DIZ

TERRY
KOVALCIK

WARD SCHUMAKER

TELEPHONE 415.398.1060

DICK BOBNICK

9801 DUPONT AVE. SO. · SUITE 165 · BLOOMINGTON, MN 55431 · (612) 881-1008

Websites: www.theispot.com/artist/bobnick and www.showcase.com

RALPH KELLIHER

11 SEQUOIA ROAD

FAIRFAX, CA 94930

PH: 415. 457-4535

RKI@SIRIUS.COM

FX: 415. 459-4586

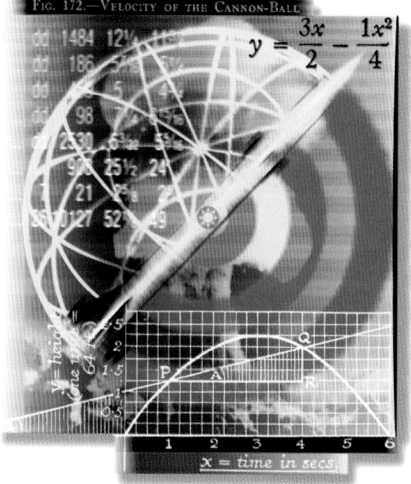

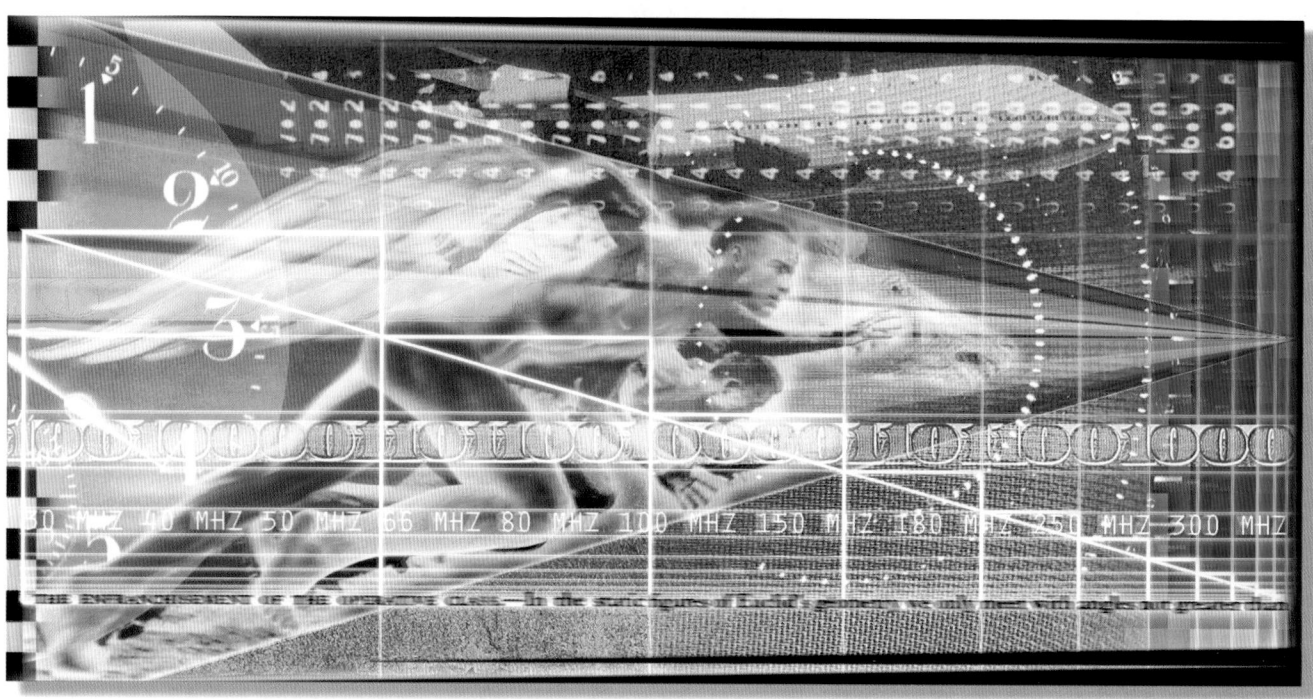

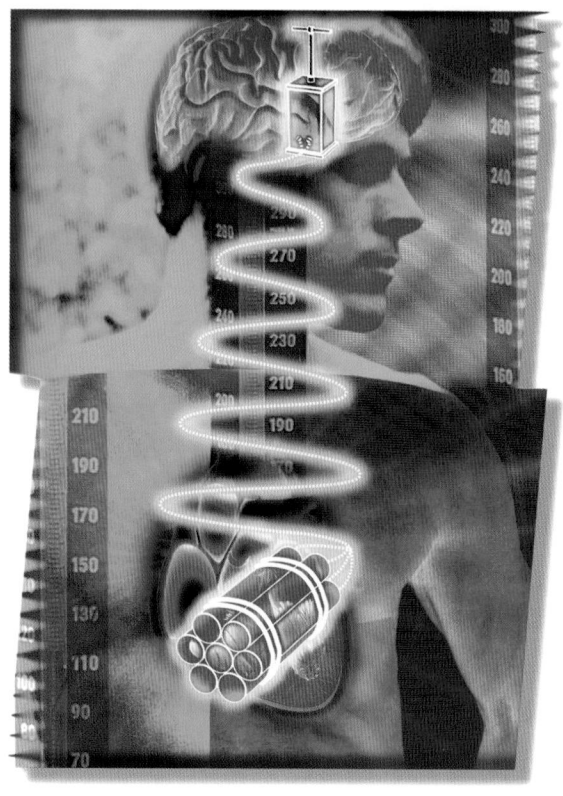

Red Rose Tea Package

Departures Magazine: AD Anna Ratman

CINDY SASS

ILLUSTRATION
15 Torne Road
Sloatsburg, NY 10974
914.753.5119
fax 914.753.5411

110 Lovato Lane / Sante Fe / New Mexico / 505-989-8483

Stardust

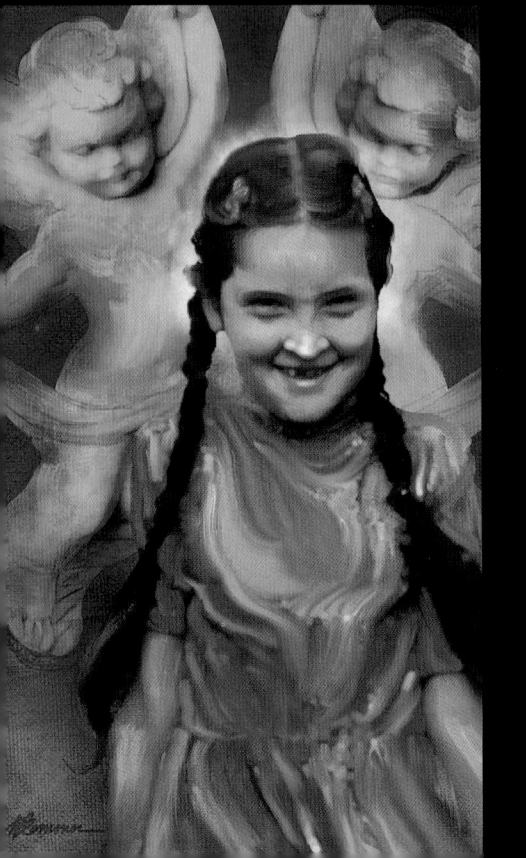

MARK BREMMER 303·932·8759

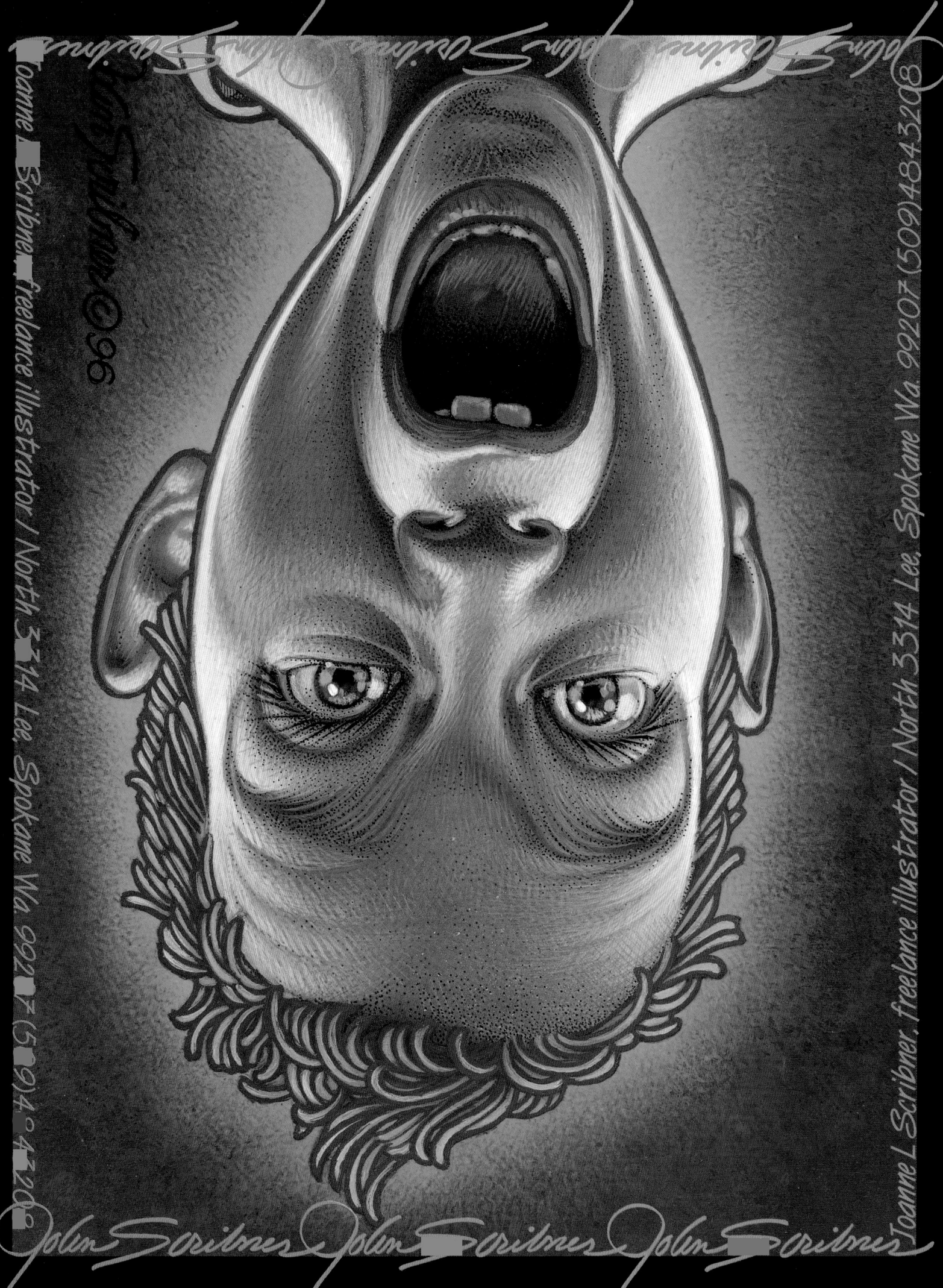

stephanie langley illustration **650.857.9539** **fax.857.0445** *619 maybell avenue palo alto, ca 94306*

George Krauter
Digital Illustration and Animation
(415)753-5305 • fax:(415)665-7054 • email: kronos1@aol.com

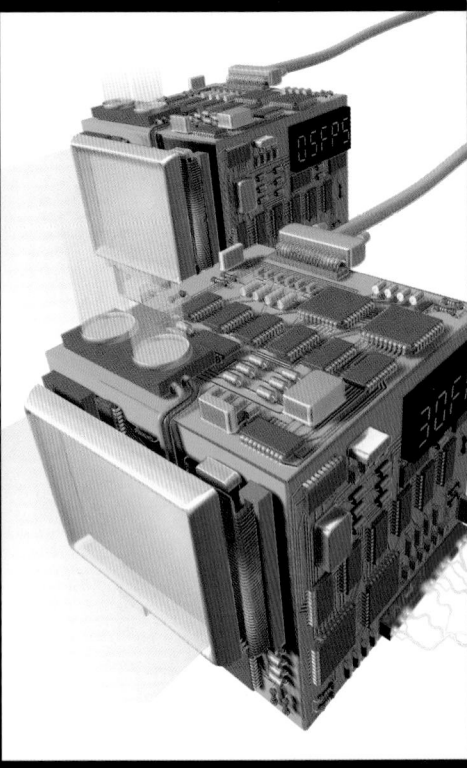

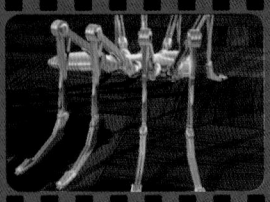
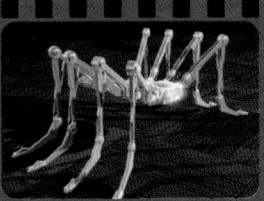
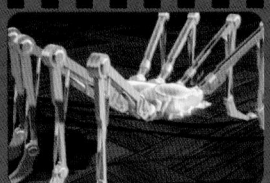
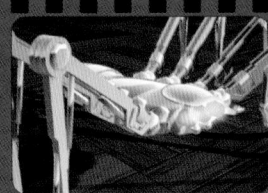
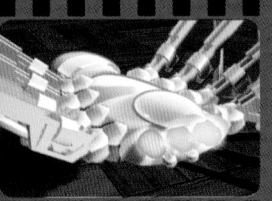
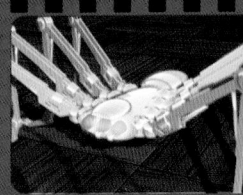

clients include : I B M BankersTrust AT&T Forbes Playboy US News L A Times Newsweek HarperCollins Simon & Schuster

NED SHAW STUDIO
Digital Illustration

The Future is Portable.

CHARLES STUBBS

638 CORDELIA DRIVE, SUITE 1 · SANTA ROSA, CA · PHONE/FAX 707.544.8358

1131

Robert Jew

Phone & Fax: 760·731·6416

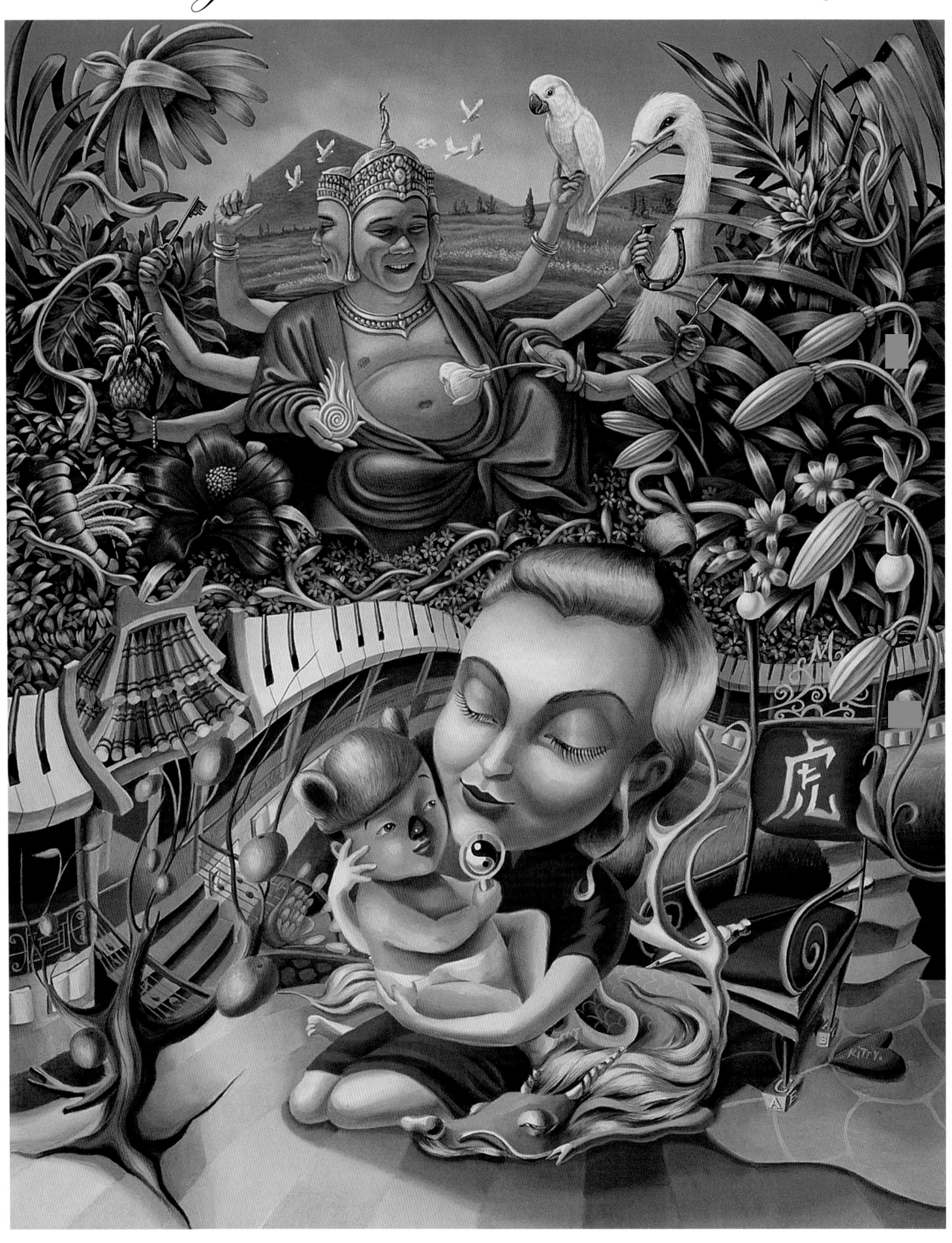

Phone & Fax: 760·731·6416

Kitty Meek

CHARLIE PARKER

Client:
Fasone
Garrett
Boehm

Client: The Chicago Tribune

Neil Shapiro
773·975·9657
fax 773·975·9659
NShap981@aol·com

"TIME waits for NO ONE, and it won't WA for ME

Client:
The
Raleigh
News &
Observer

Client: The Nation

Also See
the 40th
Society of
Illustrators
Annual

212-222-8351

See more work @ showcase.com

JEFF JONES

STUDIO 602.331.4599
FAX 602.331.4799

1135

Jon C. Lund

330-655-0784

Also see Showcase 18-21, Showcase.com, and Workbook 16, 18, & 20.

Paul Schulenburg

508 255.9554

SCOTT GWILLIAMS

TEL (416) 929-8432

FAX (416) 926-8875

Hal Brooks

(212) 531-0255

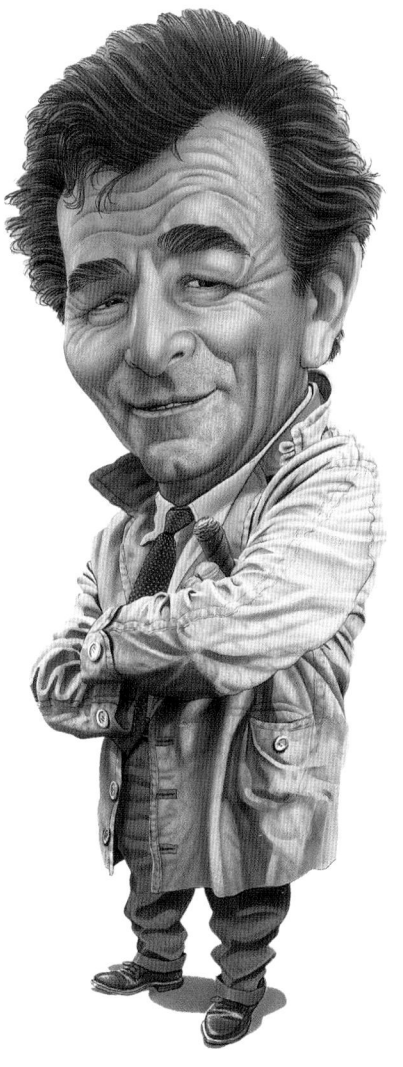

WEST COAST REP - TERRI METZLER (415) 431-8474

Stephen Schudlich

(STEE-FIN SHOOD-LICK)

Professional Artwork Provided In An Expedient And Courteous Manner.

The Science of Illustration

C. M. CHAPMAN

PHONE 1.888.422.0320 PIN 6870

 CMCHAPMAN@CMGRAFIK.COM

WWW.CMGRAFIK.COM

JIM CARSON
(617) 661.3321 phone and fax

There's an easier way to round up patients.

JOHN BURGOYNE

310-376-1448
BOB SCHUCHMAN
3-D Computer Character Modeling & Animation
Film
Video
Print

MERRY CHRISTMAS

©Warner Bros.

Animation reel available upon request

ROB BLACKARD

ILLUSTRATION

212.366.5831

Maral Sassouni Illustration

1416 QUEENS ROAD, WEST HOLLYWOOD, CALIFORNIA 90069 • TEL/FAX (213) 650-5865 • E-MAIL : marals@starnet.fr

ST.JACQUES
ILLUSTRATION DESIGN

60 Speedwell Avenue, Morristown, NJ 07960
1-800-70-TWINS   www.stjacques.com

Clients include: ADP, AlliedSignal, Becton Dickinson, Bill Communications, Bristol–Myers Squibb, Coldwell Banker, Dolce International, Dun & Bradstreet, FCB Healthcare, Lucent Technologies, Merck, Nomura Capital, NJ Transit, Reader's Digest, Saatchi & Saatchi

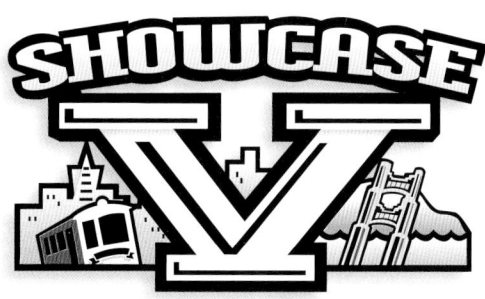

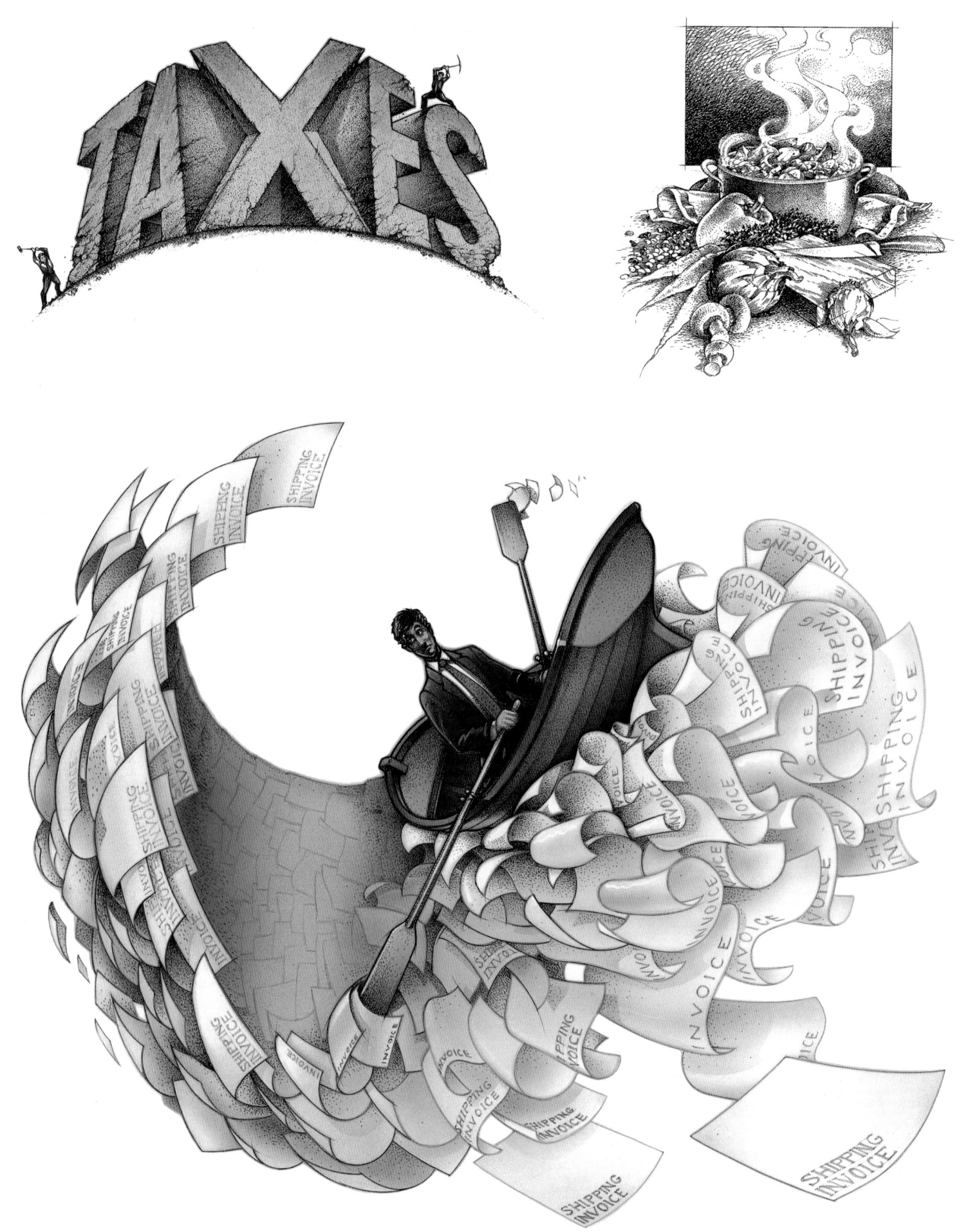

DAVID SCANLAN · 310.545.0773 · FAX 310.545.7364

135 S. LaBrea Ave. #1

Christian Clayton

Phone: (213) 936-8448

email: oldways@ix.netcom.com

Los Angeles, CA 90036

Fax: (213) 933-2519

VADIM VAHRAMEEV

415 751 5471 fax (415) 751 1766

sports

wildlife

advertising

business

lifestyle

PIXEL
pushers
d e s i g n

po box 802635 dallas texas 75380-2635

CONCEpt
ILLUStRATioN
& dESigN

97² 814.0690

1153

ROB COLVIN

801.451.6858

CD cover (Kerosene Dream)

Book cover (Beyond Words Publishing)

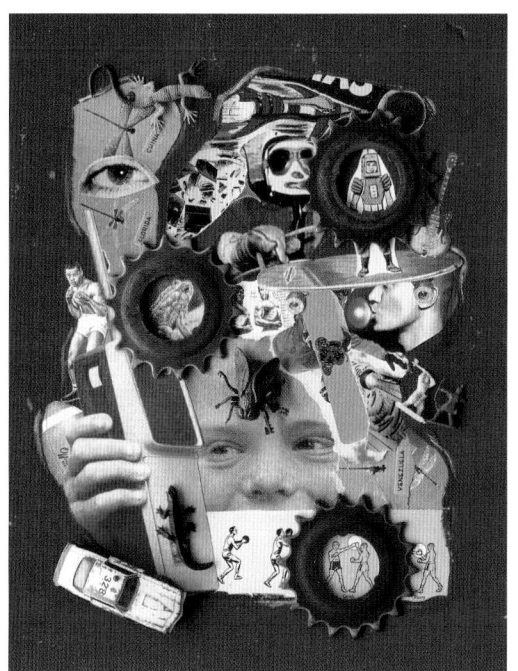

Beyond Words Publishing

CD cover (Autonomous Records)

(http://www.quarterdeck.com)

(http://www.industry.net)

(http://www.pointcom.com)

(http://www.ypn.com)

(http://www.scip.org)

(http://www.altavista.digital.com)

(http://www.quarterdeck.com)

RIEGEL ILLUSTRATION

MARGARET RIEGEL ✳ 800 WEST END AVENUE, APT 8D NEW YORK NY 10025 ✳ 212.866.8466 T 212.662.2881 F

FOR ADDITIONAL SAMPLES SEE DIRECTORY OF ILLUSTRATION 11 & 13, AMERICAN SHOWCASE 21, NEW MEDIA SHOWCASE 2, WWW.SHOWCASE.COM OR CALL FOR A PORTFOLIO

U.S. Gypsum

Pinkerton Inc.

Bob Commander
4 3 5   6 4 9   4 3 5 6
West — Ann Koeffler 323 957-2327
East — Lori Nowicki 212 243-5888
w w w . L o r i n o w i c k i . c o m

Pinkerton Inc.

Duke Communications

MARIA RENDON

tel. 909.889.8979
fax. 909.888.9932

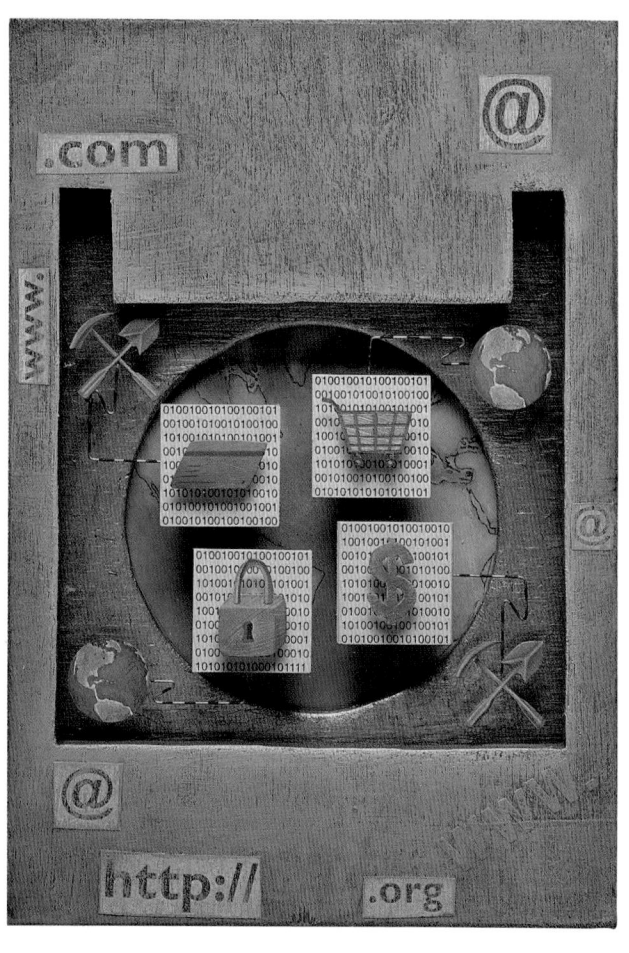

6997 perris hill road san bernardino, california 92404

JIM LAMBRENOS 609.768.0580

macsketch@aol.com

KEVIN
RECHIN
Phone: 703·560·1209
Fax:703·698·1257

WILL WORK FOR LOAVES AND FISHES

deb hoeffner

973-838-5490   538 Cherry Tree Lane, Kinnelon, NJ 07405

soft realism

www.swan-net.com/deb

ROBERT CRAWFORD

STUDIO- 123 Minortown Rd., Woodbury, CT   06798   203-266-0059
CHICAGO- Represented by Dan Sell   T-312-578-8844   F-312-578-8847

BARBARA REID

(416) 461-9793

124 Hoyt Street in Boerum Hill, Brooklyn, New York ll217-2215
718.237.0145 FAX: 718.237.2430 Hand-stitched and machine-
appliqued artwork: quilts, samplers, soft sculpture, props, and
mixed media. Call for my portfolio. Also, if you're on a budget,
there are many images available for second usage.

MARGARET CUSACK

Clients include: Time Magazine, Avon, Forbes Magazine, Texaco,
Village Voice, Wamsutta, Seagram's, Reader's Digest, Macmillan,
The New York Times, Book of the Month Club, and Yankee Magazi
Also: American Showcase #21, p. 1251; #20, p. 1098; #19,
p. 1292; and #18, p. 1121. Member: Graphic Artists Guild

TIME MAGAZINE

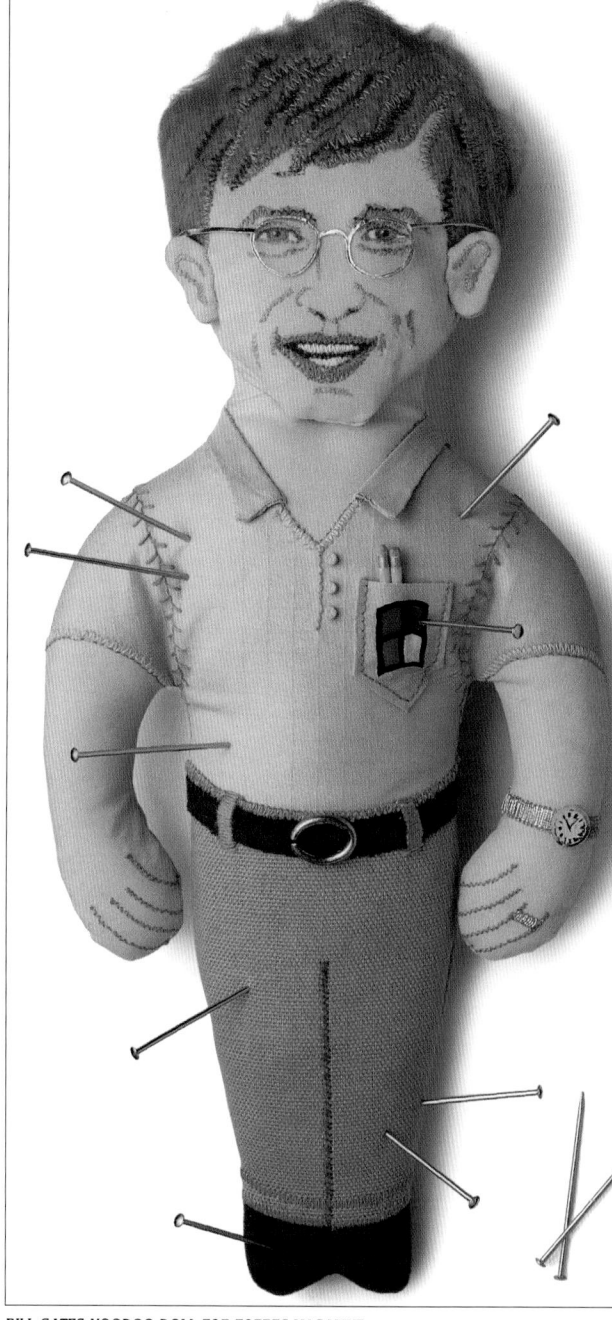

BILL GATES VOODOO DOLL FOR FORBES MAGAZINE

THE VILLAGE VOICE

DAIMARU DEPARTMENT STORE

WOMAN'S DAY MAGAZINE

KATHY PETRAUSKAS
312 642 • 4950 • FAX 312 642 • 6391

HARRY PULVER JR.

PHONE 612·377·1797 FAX!

COCA COLA,CO, GENERAL MILLS, PIZZA HUT, 3M
SONY MUSIC / EPIC, WENDY'S, SCHOLASTIC INC.,
LEVIS 501 JEANS, DAVE MATTHEWS BAND
DIGITAL DELIVERY!

Roxana Villa

818.906.3355 / roxanavilla.com

JOANN DALEY

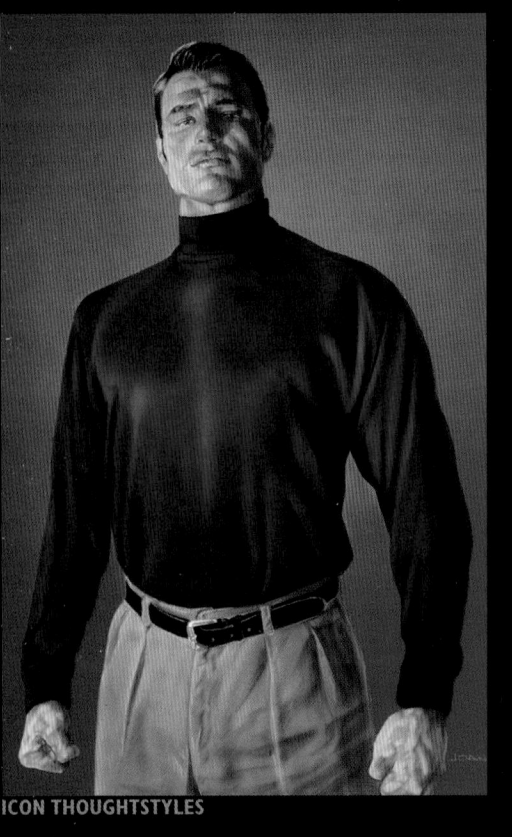

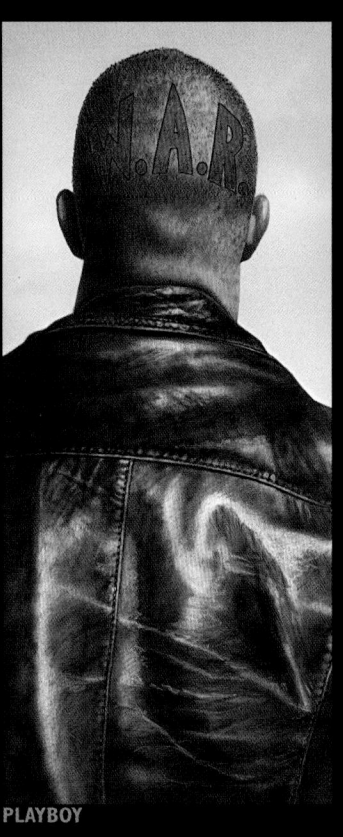

ICON THOUGHTSTYLES

PLAYBOY

HARLEQUIN

STUDIO 805.985.16

FAX   805.985.10

IN THE MIDWEST
CONNIE KORALIK
312. 944.5680

IN THE SOUTHWEST
KIM BOEGE
602. 265.4389

ROADSTORIES

COMPS

ADT magazine

Qualcomm

Alaris Medical

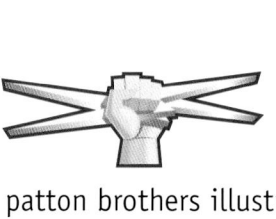

patton brothers illustration
619.463.4562
619.463.4763 fax
patton@pattonbros.com
www.pattonbros.com

1171

Northeastern University

Coopers and Lybrand

Occidental

US News and World Report

Microsoft

Additional Work: Showcase 19, 20, 21; Workbook 19, 20; Directory of Illustration 12, 13, 14, 15.

ROBERT M. PASTRANA
818 • 548 • 6083

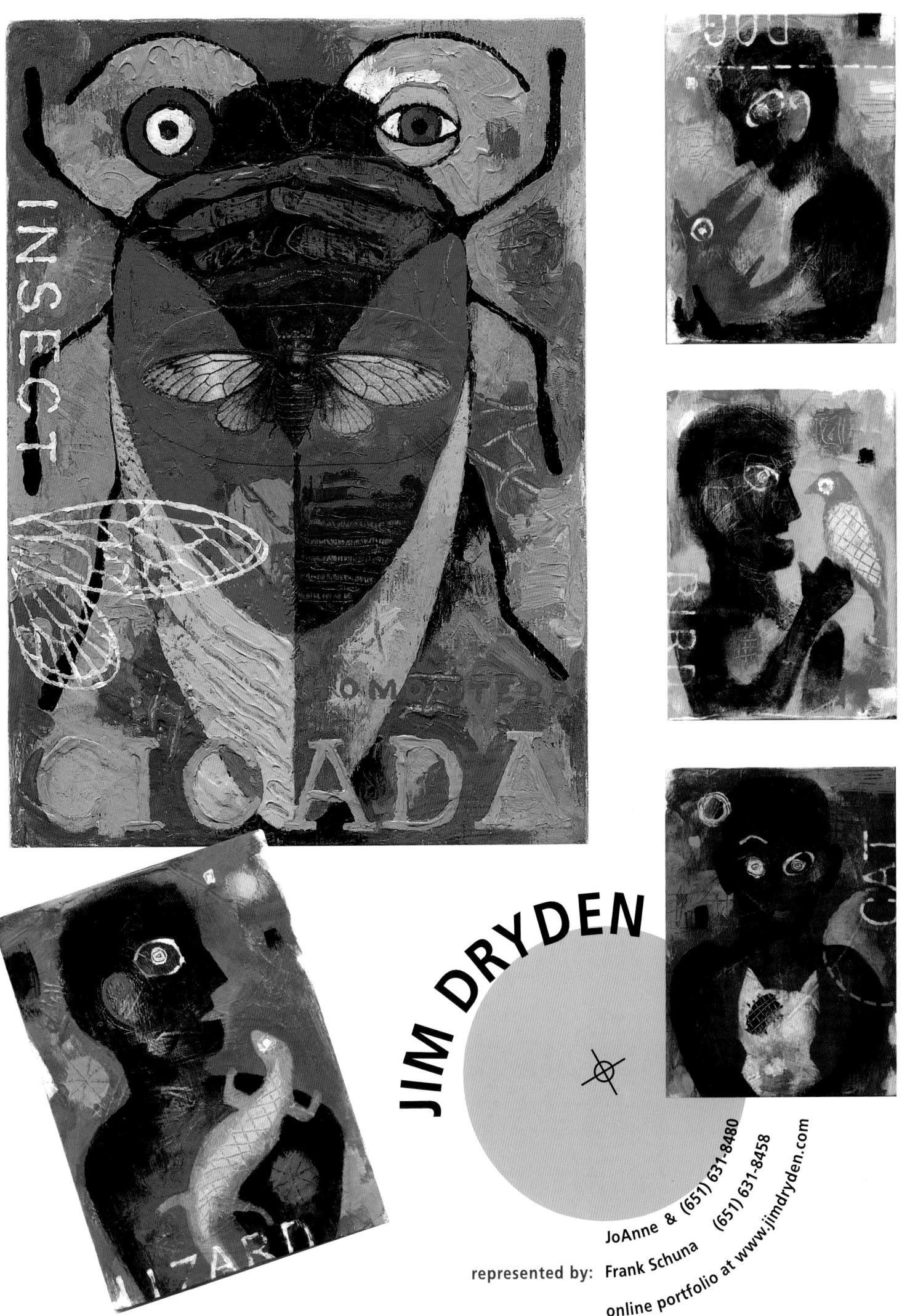

INSECT

CICADA

JIM DRYDEN

represented by: JoAnne & Frank Schuna
(651) 631-8480
(651) 631-8458

online portfolio at www.jimdryden.com

MICHAEL J DEAS

5 0 4 · 5 2 4 · 3 9 5 7

GARRY NICHOLS

TEL 317.861.6550 ▪ FAX 317.861.6552
3094 WEST 200 SOUTH ▪ GREENFIELD, IN 46140

© 1999 OSUNA

EURIWARE / PARIS / AUTRE, PLANÈTES

MACWORLD

NET-IT

SUNEXPERT

MACWORLD

W W W . H A N K O S U N A . C O M

4 1 5 . 8 2 1 . 5 8 9 3

D I G I T A L I L L U S T R A T I O N

AMERICAN SHOWCASE VOL 21 PG.1116

SHOWCASE STOCK BOOK 1998 PG.90-91

INFOWORLD

As consumer loyalty grows more evasive, and markets become fragmented,

NAME ADVERTISING

TAKES CENTER STAGE

Fig.2. Client

Fig.3. Designers

Fig.1. Consumer

Fig.4. Copywriters
Illustrators
Photographers

Illustration
INGUNA IRBE

voice 773.271< 6508
paper 6493

For the Sun, Moon, and Planets.

Put n = the equatorial horizontal parallax;
Δ = the distance of the object from the earth;
ζ and ζ' = the geocentric and apparent zenith distances respectively;
A and A' = the geocentric and apparent azimuths respectively;
ϕ and ϕ' = the geographical and geocentric latitudes respectively;
ρ = the earth's radius corresponding to ϕ;
a and a' = the geocentric and apparent right ascensions of the object respectively;
δ and δ' = the geocentric and apparent declinations of the object;
h = the hour angle of the object (reckoned + when west of meridian).

COMPATIBLE

Digital Studio of
IGORS IRBE

Digital Illustration
Visual Expression
Conceptual Design
Computer Manipulation

P 773.271.6508   F 773.271.6493

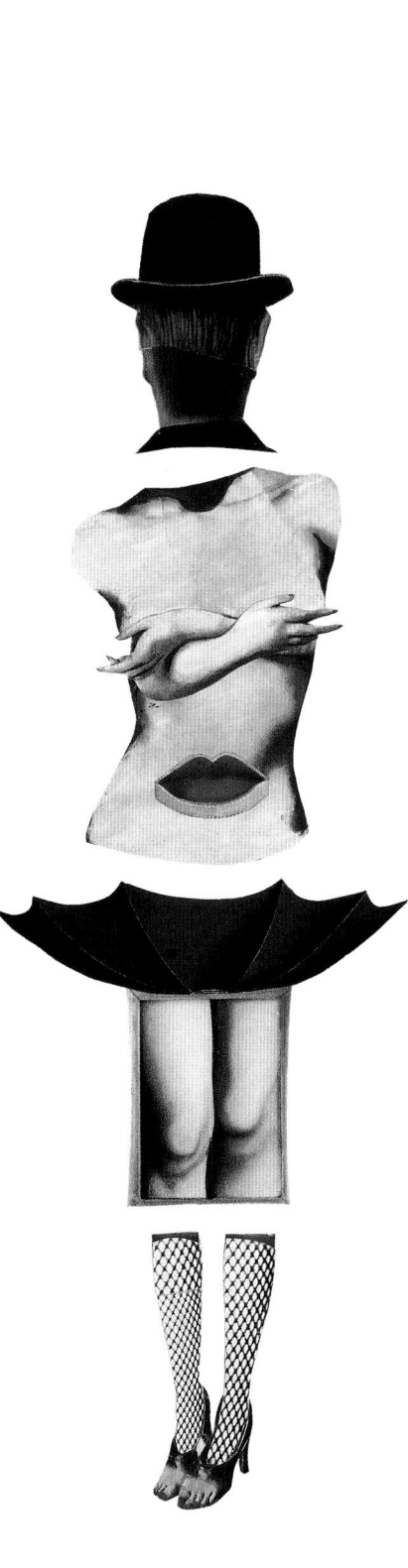

Kari Kroll

626.795.9292 fax:626.449.5513

ROBERT CRAIG

VOICE: (716) 882-0102 / FACSIMILE: (716) 884-1047

INTERNET: WWW.INKWELLSTUDIOS.COM

HULL+HONEYCUTT

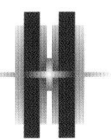

tel **916 929 477**
fax **916 929 173**
e-mail shull@hhmarketinganddesign.cc

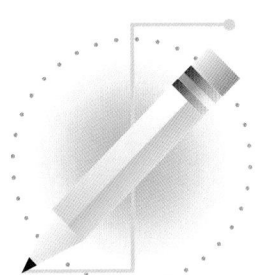

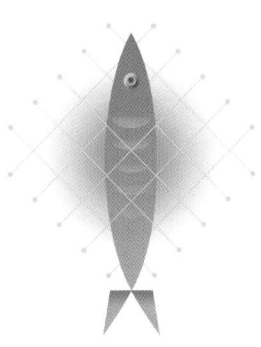

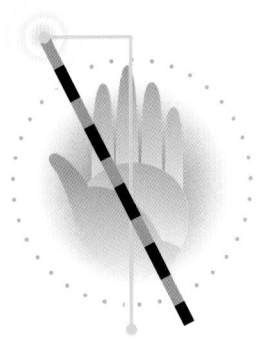

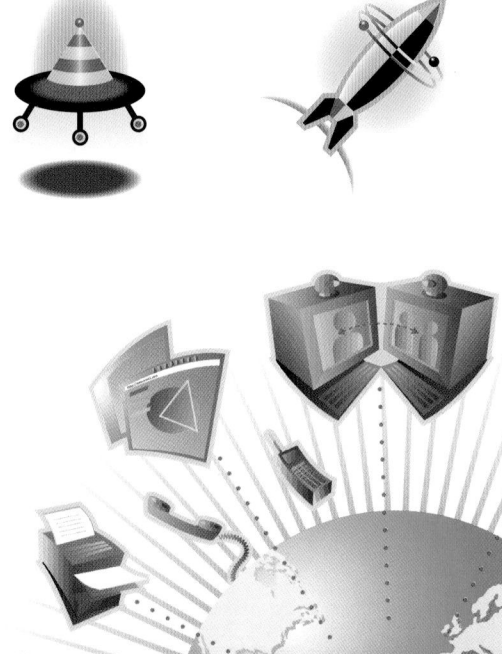

DIGITAL ILLUSTRATION+DESIGN

ERICKA MELTZER O'ROURKE
I L L U S T R A T I O N

732 | 438 8402
online portfolio: WWW.ELMDESIGN.COM
ERICKA@ELMDESIGN.COM
ALSO IN AMERICAN SHOWCASE # 21

MARINES

NAVY

AIR FORCE

Client: The Integer Group, Denver, CO.

COAST GUARD

ARMY

DOMINO'S FRANCHISEE ASSOCIATION

DESIGN
iLLUSTRATION
PHOTOMANIPULATION

303-617-1386

EAGLEYE
CREATIVE

Steven Schader • 19745 E. Bellewood Dr. • Aurora, Colorado 800
Look for more of my work in the 96/97 and 97/98 Rocky Mountain Creative
Sourcebooks and American Showcase Illustration Volume 21.

TONI KURRASCH (415) 464-0744

represented on the east coast by

MENDOLA, LTD. (212) 986-5680

Toni Kurrasch

MONOPOLY HEIRLOOM EDITION

ANATOLY CHERNISHOV 201-327-2377

FAX 201-236-9469

STUART *Bradford*

Represented by **MASLOV WEINBERG** *415.641.1285*
Editorial: 415.485.6903

GaryGray

DIABETES BROCHURE "ORALS TO INSULIN" / WATERCOLOR

DIABETES BROCHURE "ORALS TO INSULIN" / WATERCOLOR

ONE OF A SERIES FOR BOOK OF ESSAYS ON HARLEM / WATERCOLOR

10 HIGHLAND DRIVE   PENFIELD NY   716 586 1357

DIGITAL ART®

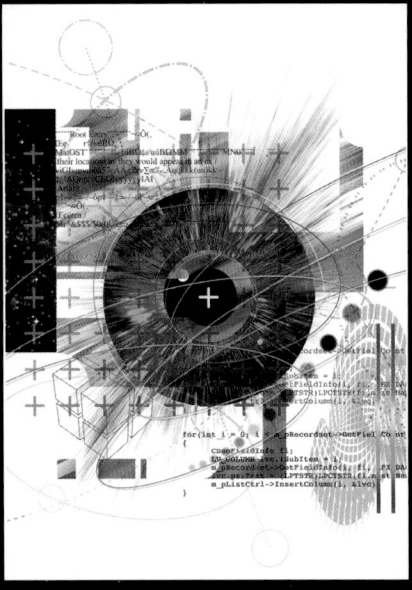

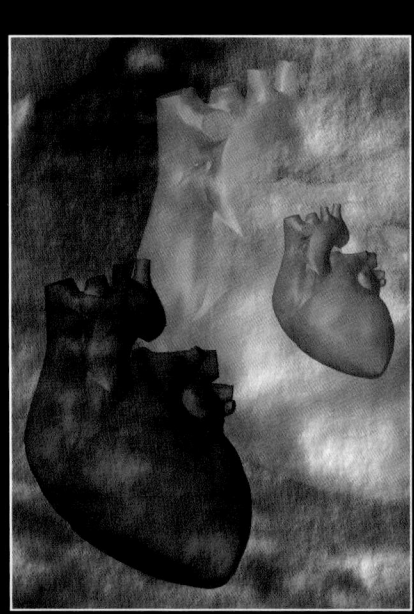
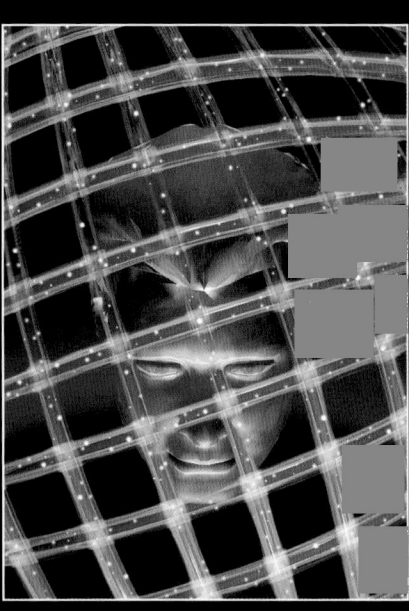

3166 EAST PALMDALE BLVD. SUITE 120 PALMDALE, CA 93550
805.265.8092 FAX 265.8095
STOCK AND ASSIGNMENT

KEN DUBROWSKI

781-837-3457

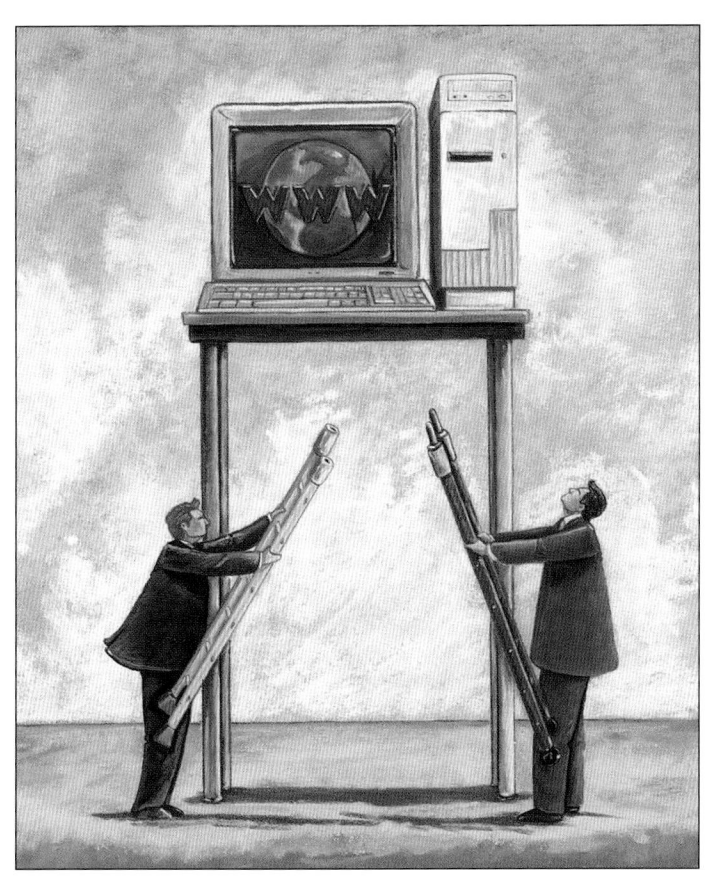

KEN TOYAMA

DIGITAL ILLUSTRATION

WILEY GROUP

TELEPHONE 415. 442. 1822   FACSIMILE 415. 442. 1823

©1

GARY MOSES

206. 323. 1441   WWMOSES@HALCYON.COM

WWW.HALCYON.COM/WWMOSES/PORTFOLIO

Terese Nielsen

Phone 626.451.0454

Fax 626.451.0544

6049 Kauffman Ave

Temple City, CA 91780

world weary   watercolor

untitled   oil, gold leaf

sparks of life   oil

dissolution of perception   oil

felipe echevarria

970   224 - 5534

OgDeMLi
FeLdMAn &
DESIGN
ILLUSTRATION

OGDEMLI/FELDMAN DESIGN & ILLUSTRATI

818•760•1759 FAX: 818•760•158

http://www.ogdemlifeldman.co

E-MAIL: daniel@ogdemlifeldman.co

SEE WORKBOOK #19 p41, #20 p75, &

Kristina Weiss   Illustrator

Phone-Fax 925.426.8964

GEORGE PETERS DESIGN
& ILLUSTRATION

209 TURNERS
CROSSROAD SOUTH

MINNEAPOLIS, MN 55416

TEL: (612) 546-4808

FAX: (612) 595-8063

E-MAIL:
ZEEINKSTER@AOL.COM

Caffeine-induced visuals brewed fresh daily!

Potato
LOVERS

Comfort
FOOD

Mmmm, Meatloaf...

The maximum dosage of digital humor allowed by law!

THE LONELY COWBOY BLUES

Ma dawg died and left me all aloooone...

The finance companeeee dropped by today, and repOoossessed my home...

DAVID W. DOUGLASS

6251 RIDGEBURY BOULEVARD ■ MAYFIELD VILLAGE, OHIO 44124 ■ (440) 442-3283 ■ dougzeug@earthlink.net

Zurich Insurance

Squirrel Hill Eyetique

Gallo Winery

Pittsburgh Magazine

WH Smith Stores

Eat'n Park Restaurants

Juliana **Morris**

CREATED ON
THE MACINTOSH

TO VIEW MORE, SEE
SHOWCASE 18, 19 & 20
PORTFOLIO AVAILABLE
ON REQUEST

RAY VELLA   AOL: rayvella

Jeff Lorber

state of grace

Business Week Magazine, Federal Express,
Chase Bank, Black & Decker, The New York Times,
Conde' Nast Publications, The World Health Organization,
Chrysler, IBM, Ernst & Young, CMP Publishing, AT&T,
Time Warner, Ziff-Davis, McMillan Publishing,
and a lot of other really big companies !!!

ILLUSTRATOR

20 NORTH BROADWAY
WHITE PLAINS, N.Y. 10601

Phone/Fax/Modem
914·997·1424

SMART ART

Public Relations Society of America, Brochure Cover

M.E. COHEN

PH (212) 627-8033 ■ FX (212) 627-1167

smartartme@aol.com ■ www.theispot.com/artist/mecohen

MARK WATTS STUDIOS

215 ◆ 343 ◆ 8490

HI-TECH 3D COMPUTER ILLUSTRATION-ANIMATION-CONCEPT-TYPE-DESIGN-AIRBRUSH ILLUSTRATIO
PACKAGE DESIGN & ILLUSTRATION, BROCHURES, POSTERS, NATIONAL ADDS, MULTIMEDIA & INTERACTIVE CD ROMS PRODUCED WITH HIGH E
ANIMATION FOR GAMES, PRESENTATIONS, SALES, EDUCATION, ADVERTISING. 20 YEARS OF EXCELLENCE IN ADVERTISING. CLIENTS - WALT DISN
WARNER BROS.- PARAMOUNT PICTURES - BUDWEISER - LEVER BROTHERS - SONY - KRAFT FOODS - M&M MARS - TYCO TOYS - MATTEL - KENNER - HASBRO - LE
PORTFOLIO & CD ROM AVAILABLE ON REQUEST   WEB SITE http://members.aol.com/wattsart   EMAIL WATTSART@AOL.COM   FAX 21_ 43-8

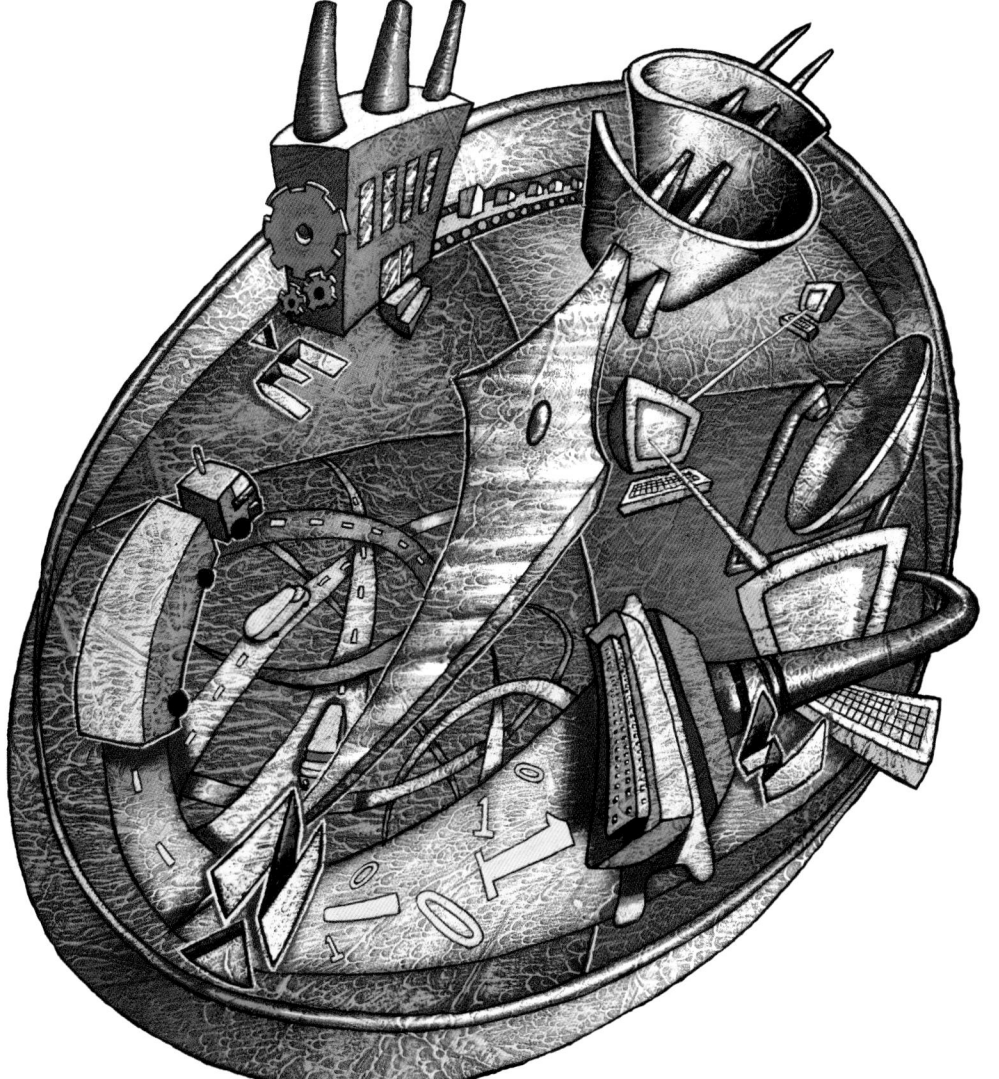

692A MOULTON AVENUE ▪ LOS ANGELES CA 90031-3237

tel
323
223
4242

fax
323
223
1344

"Quality Healthcare"

"Profits Pie Chart"

This show ain't big enough for th' both of us

Joltin' Joe

MICHELE AMATRULA

PHONE:212·255·7413 FAX:212·989·4374

259 WEST 10TH STREET·SUITE 4J·NEW YORK, NEW YORK·10014

DIKAYL

Jeff ZIMMERMAN

810-731-4674 — 4010 Montgomery, Shelby Township, MI 48316

CLIFFORD FAUST
212·581·9461

Charlie A. Zabarte

408.985.4841

3479 Agate Dr. #1. Santa Clara CA 95051
z-net@ix.netcom.com

Fresh Items Always in Supply

at the Megan Montague Cash Studio we always have the following and more

digital files

mittens

communications

fetching palettes

busy hammers

pets

monkeys

nice cocoa

Stan

surprises

universal themes

shears

identical twins

mad money

new ideas

funny hats

hydrants

your best friend

entertainments

bells + whistles

scarves

elbow grease

adventures

call me

fun + games

squeezeboxes

sudden inspirations

IT'S OUR PLEASURE TO SERVE YOU

Megan Montague Cash
will put you on her mailing list,
just phone/fax: (718) 388-3473

85 N Third Street, Brooklyn, NY 11211
website: //members.aol.com/megancash/home.html

clients:
The Brooklyn Children's Museum
The Museum of Modern Art
Disney Enterprises, Inc.
Nickelodeon
Parents Magazine
Family Fun Magazine
Family Life Magazine
eeBoo Corporation
Barnes & Noble
Harcourt Brace & Co.
Simon & Schuster
Stewart, Tabori & Chang
Galison Books
Silicon Graphics
Elektra Entertainment, Inc.
Big Apple Circus
New York Kids, WNYC
The City of New York

ANDREW FAULKNER

415-332-3521

www.afstudio.com

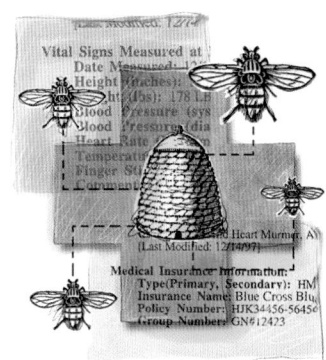

Clients Include:

American Airlines • Adobe Systems Inc. Apple Computer • Chronicle Books • Harper Collins • Los Angeles Times • Macworld Oracle • Southwest Airlines • Worth

MATHEW MCFARREN

Travel by Train/Oil

Key West Fantasy Fest/Oil

Data Factory/Oil

1553 PLATTE STREET/SUITE 302   DENVER, COLORADO 80202   (303) 458-7445   FAX (303) 458-7161   EMAIL: macart@ecentral.com

GREGORY MARTIN

760 753 4073
FAX 436 6931

MARC GABBANA

2453 OLIVE CT. WINDSOR ONTARIO CANADA N8T 3N4 PHONE / FAX (519) 948-2418

Sandy Haight

Call: 206-343-0656   Fax: 206-343-5697

Mercedes McDonald

 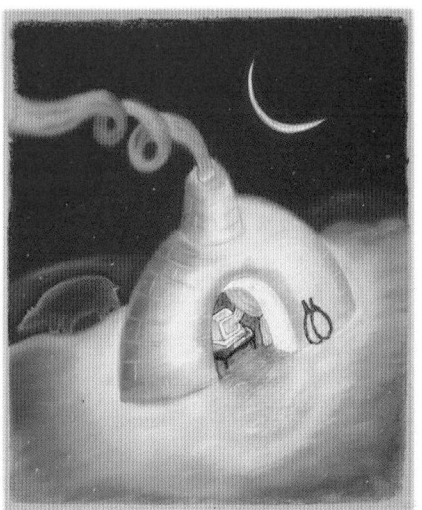

Friend & Johnson
Southwest 214 559 0055 • East 212 337 0055 • Midwest 312 435 0055 • West 415 927 4500

Carrie Perlow
Southern California 310 540 5958

Studio
818 505 8085 or mermc@aol.com

GLENN HARRINGTON

610 294 8104

Rebecca Lyon

Studio/Fax (415) 751-7343, San Francisco, CA

fōn 7o3.683.1544 **Becky Heavner** fax 7o3.683.o872

Hawaiian Islands

Visit my website at www.beckyheavner.com

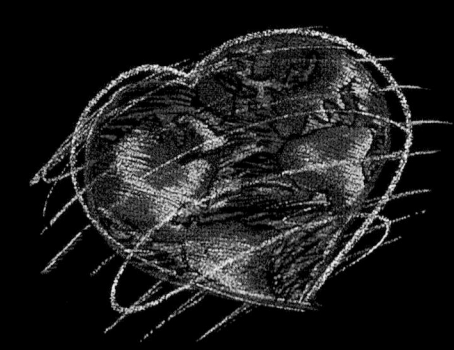

debi lee mandel

www.catsprite.com

530.389.8312

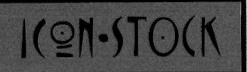

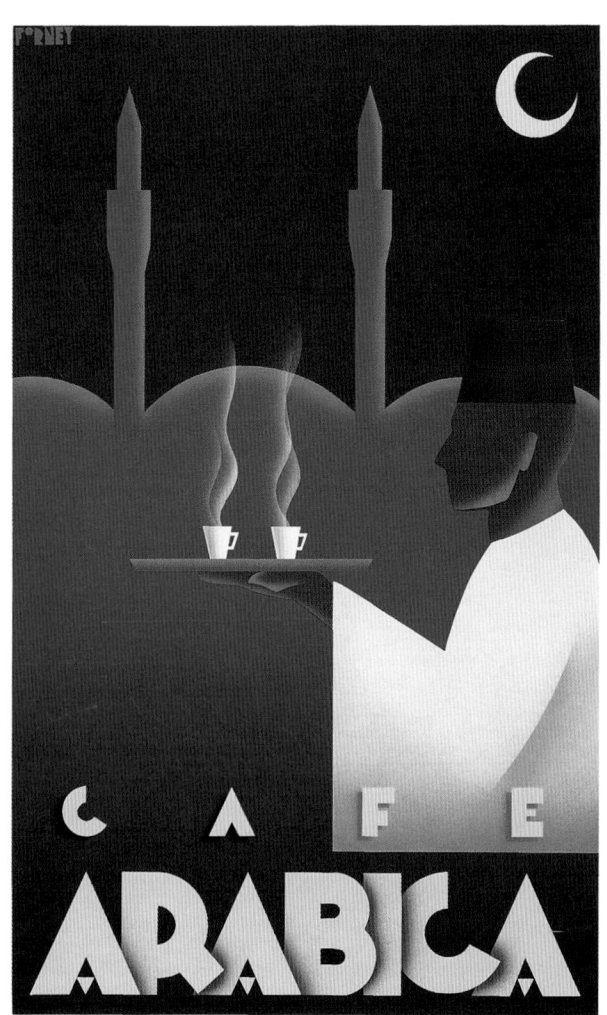

Tel: 510.653.4523 · Fax: 510.653.6506

A² Studio
Leon Zernitsky
(416) 638-9271 Phone/FAX

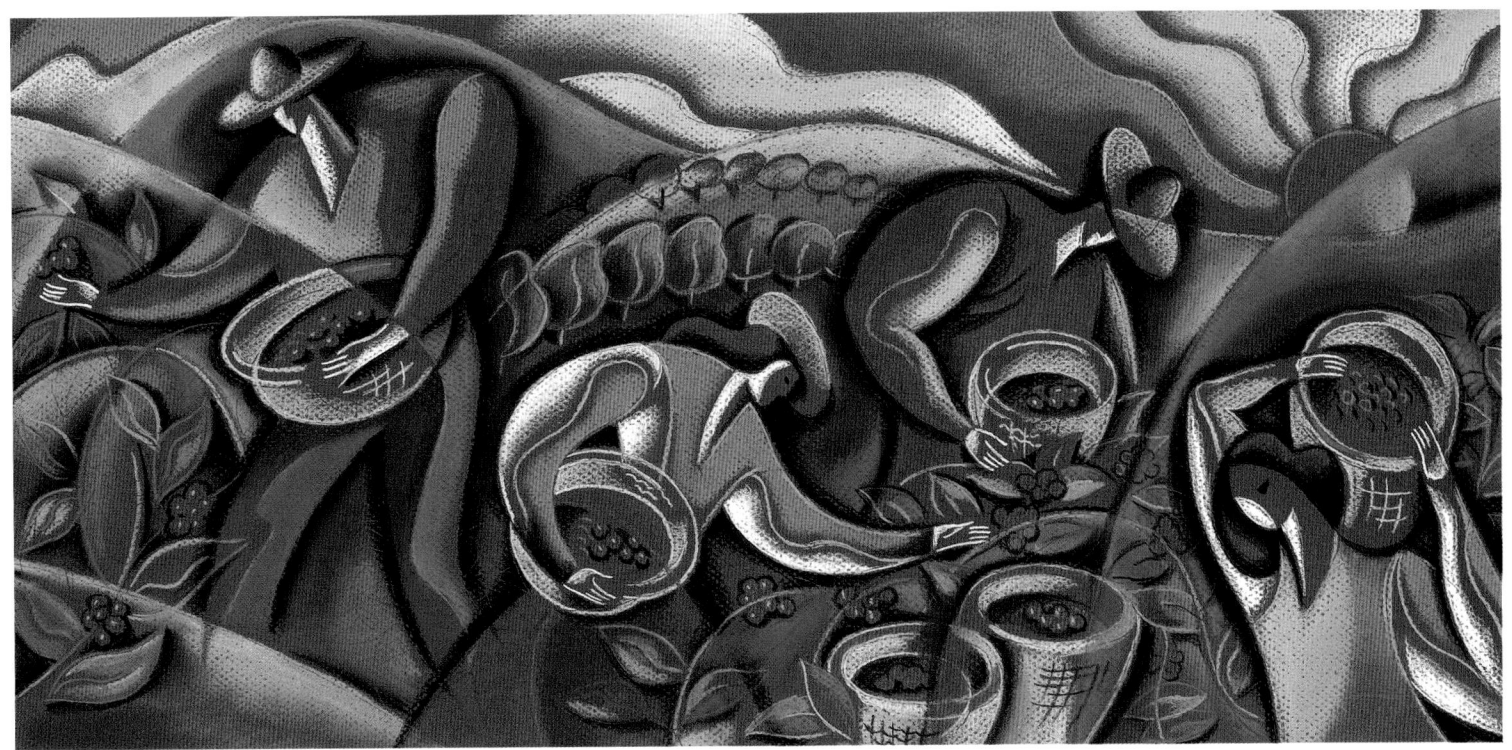

Winky Adam
370 Central Park West
New York, New York 10025
(212) 423-0746
FAX: Available

Clients include: Land's End, Little
Simon/Simon & Schuster, Scholastic,
Mudpuppy Press, Lenox Hill Hospital,
Dover Publications, Macmillan/McGraw-
Hill, The American Museum of Natural
History, The New York Botanical
Garden, The Bronx Zoo, Unicef and
others.

To view more work, please see American
Showcase Volumes 18, 19, 20 and 21
and Graphis T-Shirt 1 and Graphis
Letterhead 3. Member of The Society of
Illustrators.

Kenneth Robert Ampel
014 Black Oak Drive
Medford, Oregon 97504
(541) 779-3859 phone/fax
mail: kampel@jeffnet.org
www.showcase.com

Elizabeth Anderson
EA Illustration & Design
15544 SE 175th Court
Renton, Washington 98058
(425) 204-9400
(425) 204-9333 FAX

(206) 608-5057 Pager
email: eaillustration@hotmail.com

Graphic Artist
Digital Illustration
Web Design
Conceptual Prototyping

The Money Trail

Earthbile

Saving Trees after a Storm

Search results: 2,981 matches

Taxis of the Future...

Fian Arroyo
(305) 866-6370
FAX: (305) 866-1192
email: fianarroyo@aol.com
http://www.fian.com

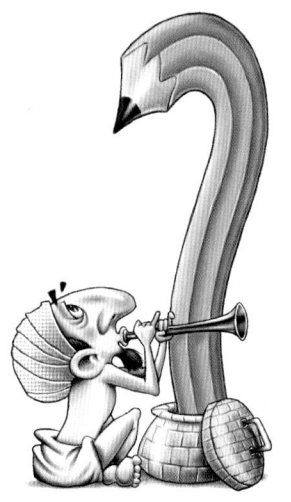

showcase.com

illustrators | designers | digital artists | interactive talent | photographers

The Art Machine Inc.
2224 North 38th Avenue
Hollywood, Florida 33021
www.gate.net/~artmach

Techniques include:
• Line Drawing
• Exploded View
• Cutaway
• Phantom
• Interactive

Ask for our new interactive and 2-D
animation portfolio.

INTERACTIVE
Illustration

PRESENTATIONS
ADVERTISING
TRAINING
TECH SUPPORT
COMMUNICATION

V/R

CUTAWAY

LAYERED

EXPLODED

CONCEPT
DESIGN
SCALE
MATERIALS
PARTS
ASSEMBLY

APPLICATIONS

MULTIMEDIA
TRANSPORTATION
ARCHITECTURE
PROCEDURES
EDUCATION
PATENTS
LITIGATION
TECHNOLOGY
MECHANICAL

PHONE (954)-967-0409

ARTIST KEVIN ELLSWORTH

Zita Asbaghi
104-40 Queens Boulevard, #12X
Forest Hills, New York 11375
(718) 275-1995

ita Asbaghi
04-40 Queens Boulevard, #12X
orest Hills, New York 11375
18) 275-1995

Kurt Aspland
305 North Harbor, #215
Fullerton, California 92832
(714) 738-5587
FAX: (714) 738-0974
email: kaspland@asplandesign.com
www.asplandesign.com

Illustrations, design and animation for
packaging, printing, advertising and
electronic media.

All illustrations are created in either
Photoshop or Illustrator applications.

View additional work and
sample animations at
www.asplandesign.com
or email Kurt at
kaspland@asplandesign.com

Michael Aveto
10 Bennett Avenue, #2E
New York, New York 10033
(212) 923-7485 Phone/FAX
email: trubka@aol.com

Represented by
Cliff Knecht
309 Walnut Road
Pittsburg, Pennsylvania 15202
(412) 761-5666
FAX: (412) 761-4072

Additional Work In:
American Showcase #21 p. 1221
Directory of Illustration #15

Lew Azzinaro
11630 Old Brookville Court
Reston, Virginia 20194
(703) 834-6419
FAX: (703) 478-9750
www.theispot.com/artist/azzinaro

To view additional samples, see
American Showcase Vol. 18,
Workbook Vol.18, Directory of
Illustration Vol. 14, and Creative
Illustration Book 1993-94. . .

Promotional Brochures and portfolio
available upon request, or view my
website at address listed.

Johnna Bandle
7726 Noland Road
Lenexa, Kansas 66216
(913) 962-9595 Phone/FAX
email: bandle@qni.com
www.jbandle.com

Call for representation in your area.

Also see Showcase 8 - 21
(8 -12 used the maiden name,
Hogenkamp).

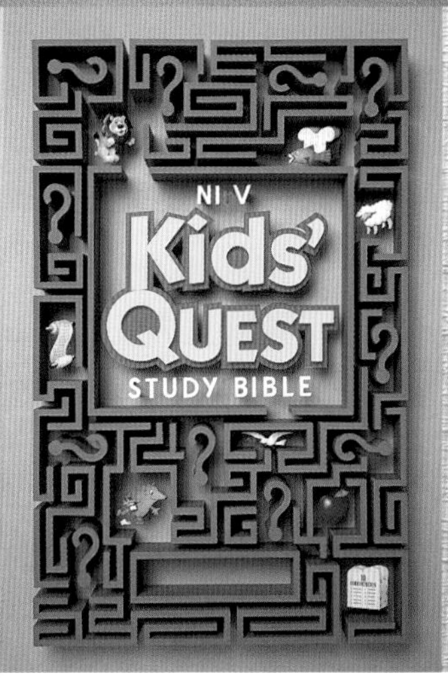

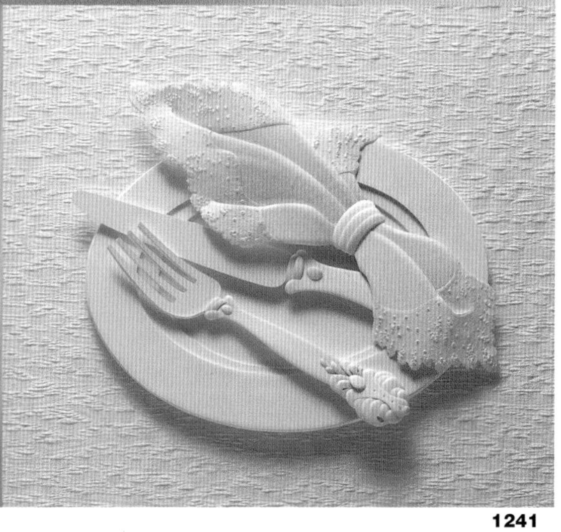

Sergio Baradat
210 West 70th Street, #1606
New York, New York 10023
(212) 721-2588
(212) 724-4013
email: baradat@aol.com
www.walrus.com/~sergiob

Suzette Barbier
124 Winchester Street
Newton, Massachusetts 02161
(617) 527-8388
FAX: (617) 244-0266
email: HolyFish@aol.com

Additional Work In:
The Creative Illustration Book 4 and
5, Directory of Illustration 12, and
American Showcase 20.

Portfolio and samples available upon
request.

Member:
Graphic Artists Guild.

Nancy Barnet

Studio phone: 916.685.4147   Email: NBarnetArt@aol.com

Batelman Illustration
Kenneth & Jill Batelman
407 Buckhorn Drive
Belvidere, New Jersey 07823
(908) 475-8124
FAX: (908)475-8924
email: batelman@epix.net

Clients: McGraw Hill, Macmillan,
Prentice Hall, Conde Nast Publications,
Simon & Schuster, Young & Rubicam,
Newsweek, Businessweek, Readers
Digest, Risk Management, Popular
Science, Mayo Clinic, Coca-Cola,
Clinique, Revlon, Lucent Technologies

Specializing in:
Digital illustration for advertising, editorial,
packaging, text books, infographics,
annual reports, charts & maps
Awards include:
How's Online Design, Step-by-Step,
Digitalink, TheVisual Club

Additional work samples:
New Media Showcase 3, 5, 6, 7
Directory of Illustration 13, 14, 15, 16
California Image '98
Book Production Buyer's Guide '97, '98
www.theispot.com

Harry Bates
Inkgraved Illustration
(914) 679-4695
FAX: (914) 679-4292

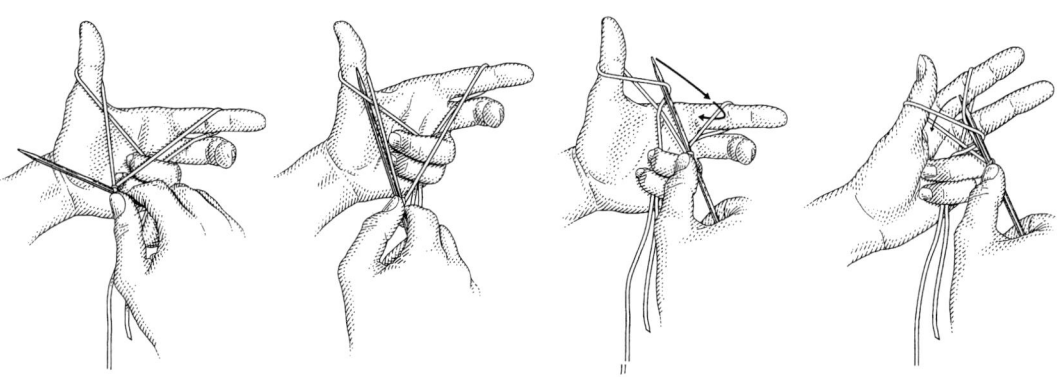
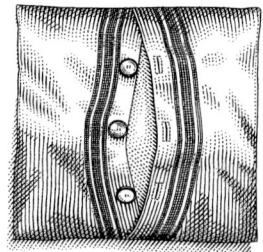

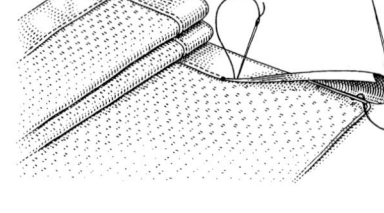
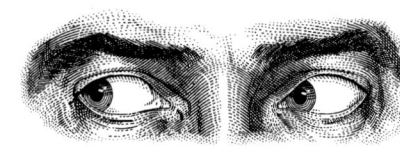

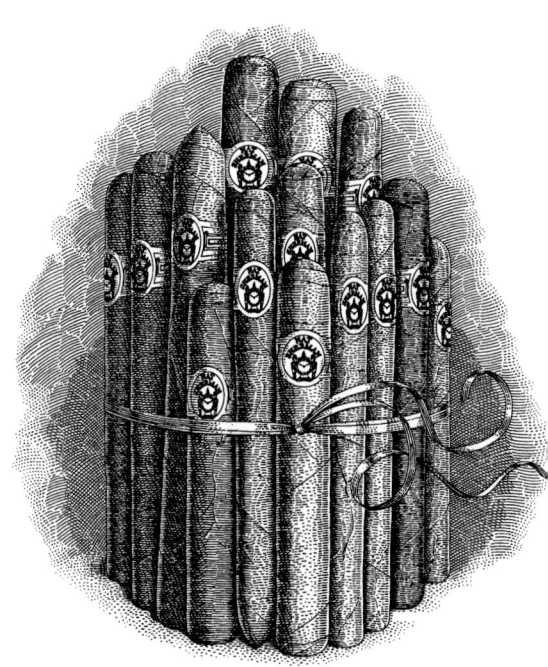

HARRY BATES

INKGRAVED ILLUSTRATION

914-679-4695   Fax:914-679-4292

Eric Berendt
1989-A Santa Rita Road, Suite 307
Pleasanton, California 94566
(925) 462-6809
FAX: (925) 462-6807
email: eric@berendtstudio.com
www.berendtstudio.com

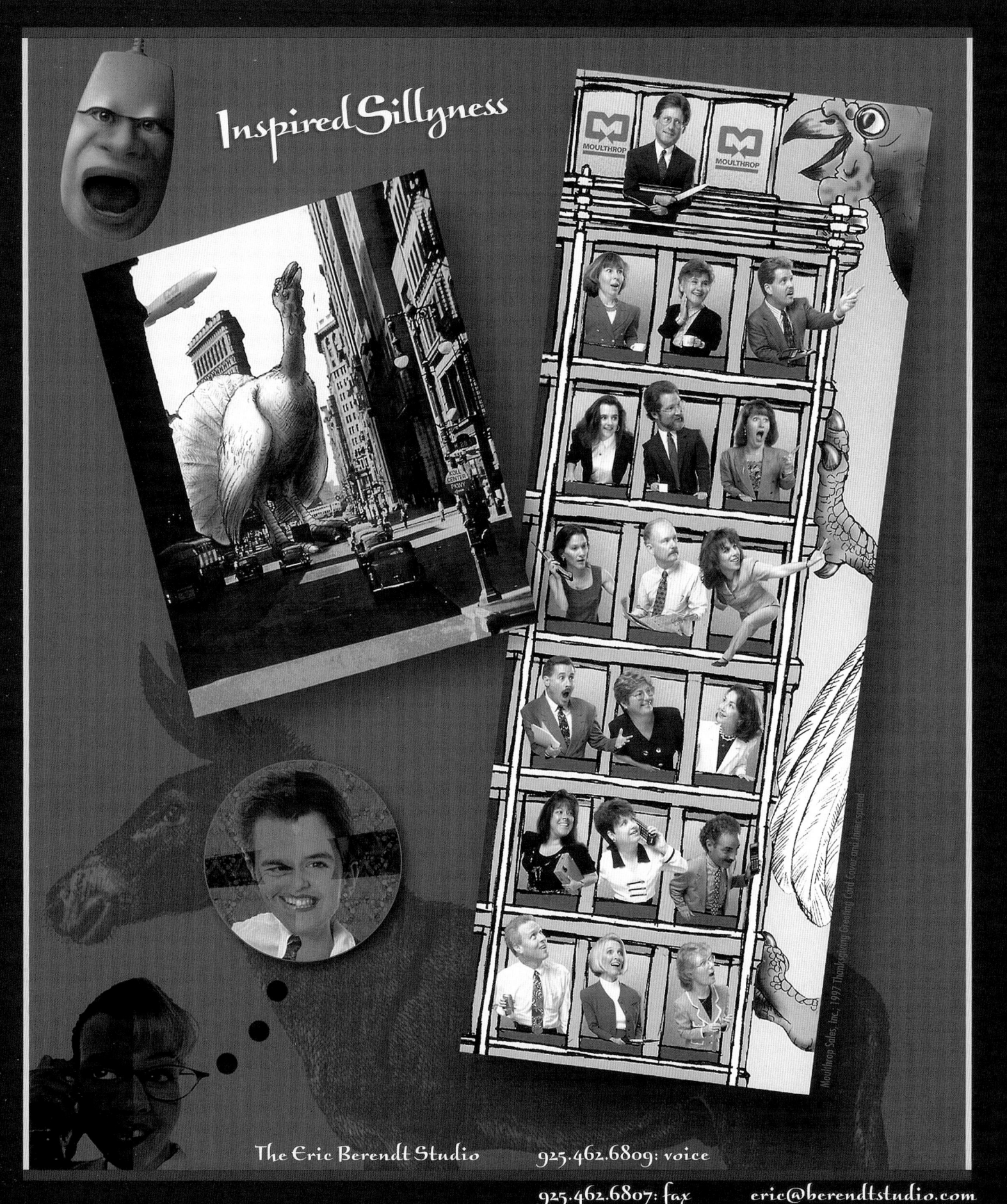

John Berg
110 Cottage Street
Buffalo, New York 14201
(716) 884-8003
FAX: (716) 885-4281

For additional samples see
Showcase 14-20, or call.

John Berg
110 Cottage Street
Buffalo, New York 14201
(716) 884-8003
FAX: (716) 885-4281

For additional samples see
Showcase 14-20, or call.

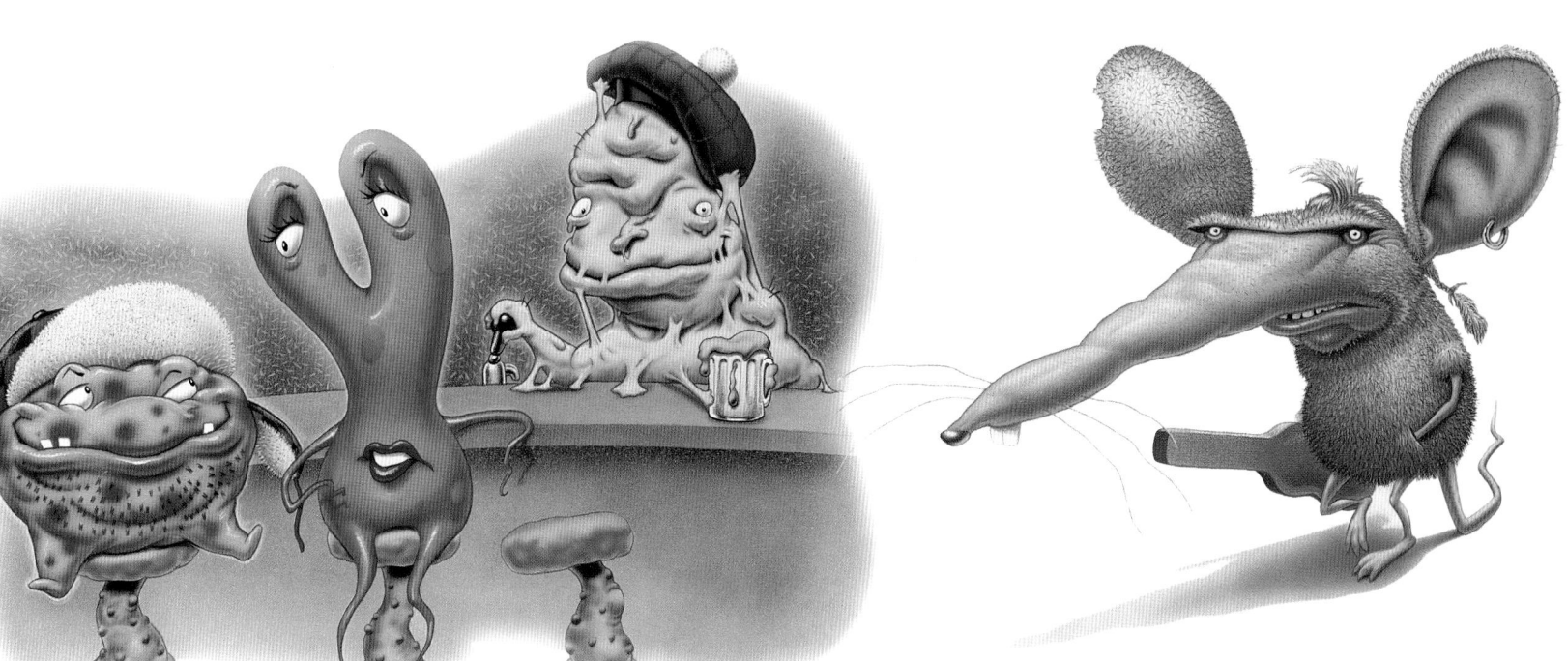

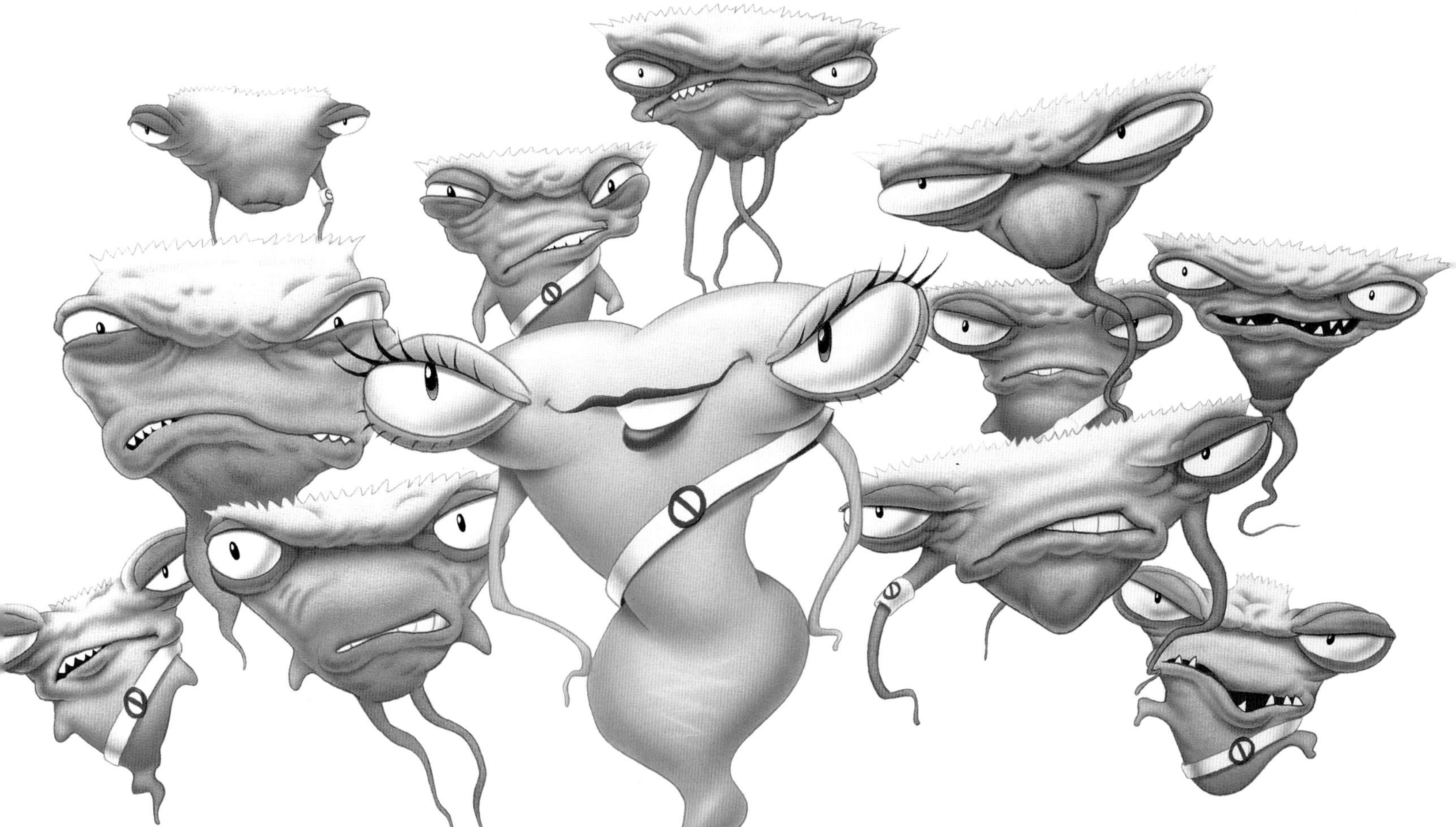

Guy Billout
225 Lafayette Street, Suite 1008
New York, New York 10012-4015
(212) 431-6350
FAX: (212) 941-0787
http://www.theispot.com/artist/billout

Illustration for Time Magazine (U.K.),
for a story about Italy having to clean
up her act, in order to meet the
Maastricht's standards.

John Bleck
3636 North Bosworth
Chicago, Illinois 60613
(773) 975-8232
FAX: (773) 975-8233
email: jbleck@suba.com

All images are produced digitally.

Clients include: MacWorld, PCWorld, Microsoft, Adobe Systems Inc., Silicon Graphics, U.S. News & World Report, Motorola, The Wall Street Journal, Lockheed/Martin, Information Week, American Express, Putnam Investments, Business Week, Money Magazine, BYTE Magazine, Chicago Tribune, IBM, Dell Computers, Prevasive Software

Martha Anne Booth
P.O. Box 208
990 Acacia Street
Montara, California 94037
(650) 728-8332 Phone/FAX

West Coast: **Ann Koeffler**
(323) 957-2327 / FAX: (323) 957-1910
email: annartrep@aol.com

East Coast: **Lori Nowicki & Associates**
(212) 243-5888 / FAX: (212) 243-5955
www.lorinowicki.com

Midwest: **Suzanne Craig Represents**
(918) 749-9424 TEL & FAX

Matt Brownson
Golden, Colorado 80403
(303) 582-0787
FAX: (303) 582-0787
email: brownson@ecentral.com

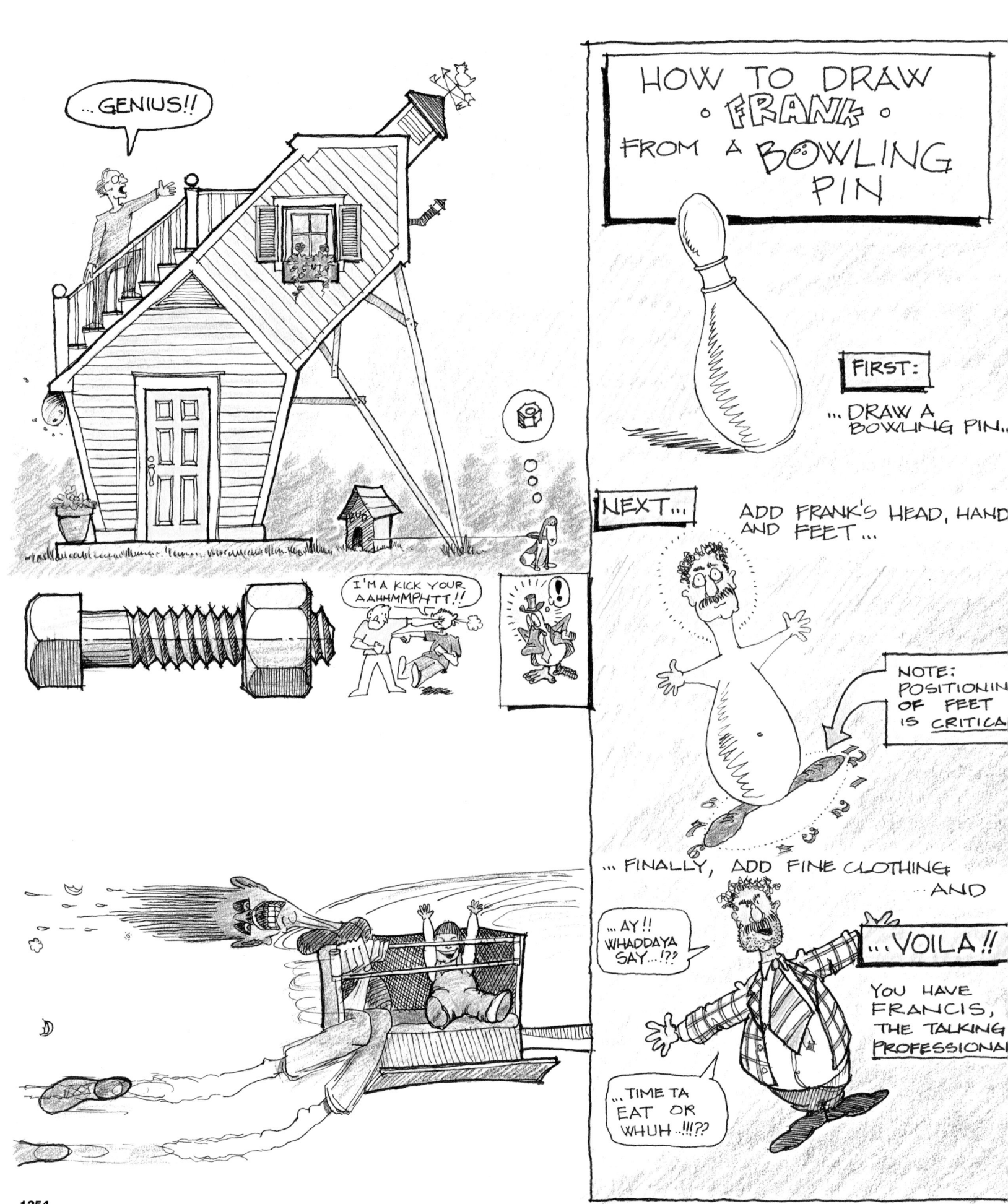

Bob Burnett
237 Lowell Street
Wakefield, Massachusetts 01880
(781) 245-3474
email: boburnett@earthlink.net

Denise Hilton Campbell
(619) 485-6771 Phone/FAX
email: Rcamp1193@aol.com

Salzman International
(415) 285-8267 San Francisco
(212) 997-0115 New York

D E N I S E   H I L T O N   C A M P B E L L

SALZMAN
international

Richard Salzman and Brian McMahon Artist's Representatives

San Francisco 415.285.8267   Fax 415.285.8268
Chicago 312.782.2244   New York 212.997.0115

Penny Carter
(212) 473-7965
(803) 324-1024

Joe Cepeda
3340 Ivar Avenue
Rosemead, California 91770
(626) 288-8205 Phone/FAX
email: cepeda@earthlink.net

Clients include:
Health Net, Unocal, Hilton Hotels, Inc.
Magazine, Hispanic Magazine, Harper-
Collins, Simon & Schuster, Putnam,

Cahners Pub. Co., Individual Investor
Group, Buzz Magazine, Coyote
Design Group, Scholastic Inc., Latina
Magazine, L.A. Lawyer.

Additional Samples:
American Showcase 20, 21, Society
of Illustrator Annuals.

Member Grapic Artists Guild

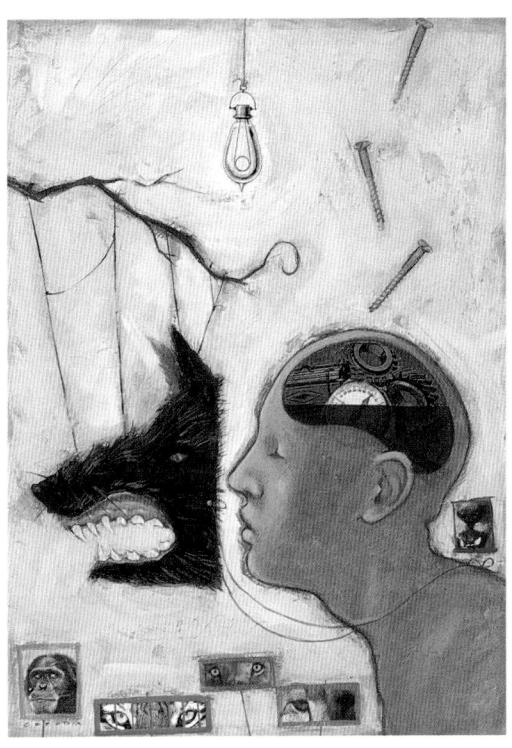

Gloria Chenoweth
8026 31st Avenue N.W.
Seattle, Washington 98117
(206) 789-7633
FAX: (206) 784-4571
email: g.chenoweth@aol.com

Christopher
(916) 421-2983

Additional images on:
www.showcase.com

Giovannina Colalillo
(416) 604-0057 phone/fax

For more samples see:
www.showcase.com, Showcase CD
Volume 20, American Showcase 19,
20 & 21, Creative Illustration Book
1994 & 1995, Creative Source 11, 14, 15,
16, 17, 18 & 19

JANE PARKER BREADS

AMERITECH

AMERITECH

CANADIAN LAWYER

ILLUSTRATION

Terry Colon
554 Lombard
San Francisco, California 94133
(415) 835-2422

Clients:
The Atlantic Monthly, Family Circle,
Fast Company, Fortean Times,
InfoWorld, LAN Times, the Oxford
American, PC World, Suck.com

John Corbitt
150 West Brambleton Avenue
Norfolk, Virginia 23510
(757) 446-2729
FAX: (757) 623-5283
email: jcorbitt@infi.net

Brian Corey
(888) 287-9880

In loving memory of Chris Farley

showcase.com

illustrators | designers | digital artists | interactive talent | photographers

ohn Courtney
79 11th Avenue, #5-D
Paterson, New Jersey 07514
(973) 345-7652 home
(201) 599-7340 office

Dave Cutler
7 West Street
Warwick, New York 10990
(914) 987-1705
FAX: (914) 987-1706
email: spots@warwick.net

Clients include: Microsoft, Dupont, ADP, EDS, AT&T, Sprint, MCI, Mercedes-Benz, GE, NetCom, Ernst & Young, Mitsubishi, HBO, Energizer, Ceridian, MCA, Time, Businessweek, Forbes, Glamour, Wall Street Journal, NY Times, McDonalds, Newsweek, Metlife, Standard & Poor, Hewlett Packard, AGFA

See more in:
Society of Illustrators Annuals, Workbook
American Showcase 14-21
Internet: www.theispot.com

Stock available at:
www.sisstock.com
www.theispot.com
www.spotsonthespot.com

Dave Cutler

7 West Street
Warwick, New York 10990
(914) 987-1705
FAX: (914) 987-1706
email: spots@warwick.net

Clients include: Microsoft, Dupont,
ADP, EDS, AT&T, Sprint, MCI,
Mercedes-Benz, GE, NetCom, Ernst &
Young, Mitsubishi, HBO, Energizer,
Ceridian, MCA, Time, Businessweek,
Forbes, Glamour, Wall Street Journal,
NY Times, McDonalds, Newsweek,

Metlife, Standard & Poor, Hewlett
Packard, AGFA

See more in:
Society of Illustrators Annuals, Workbook
American Showcase 14-21
Internet: www.theispot.com

Stock available at:
www.sisstock.com
www.theispot.com
www.spotsonthespot.com

showcase.com

Bob Dahm
166 Arnold Avenue
Cranston, Rhode Island 02905
(401) 781-5092

•Editorial
•Advertising
•Electronic

See my web page for recent samples
and contact information.

Daniels & Daniels
14-S Madrid Avenue
Newbury Park, California 91320
(805) 498-1923
FAX: (805) 499-8344
email: ariaart@aol.com

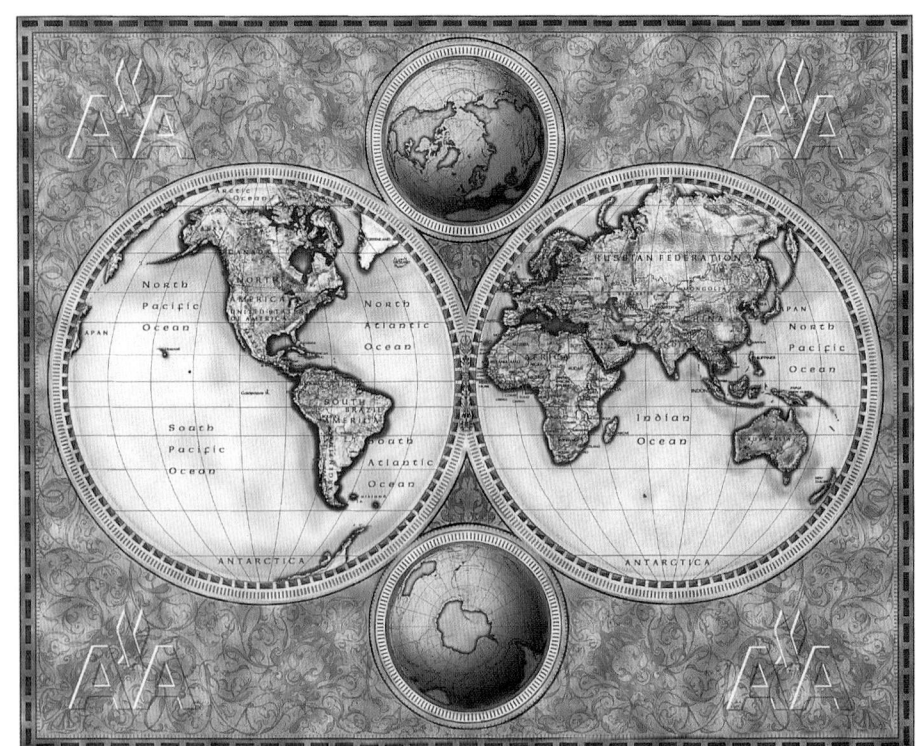

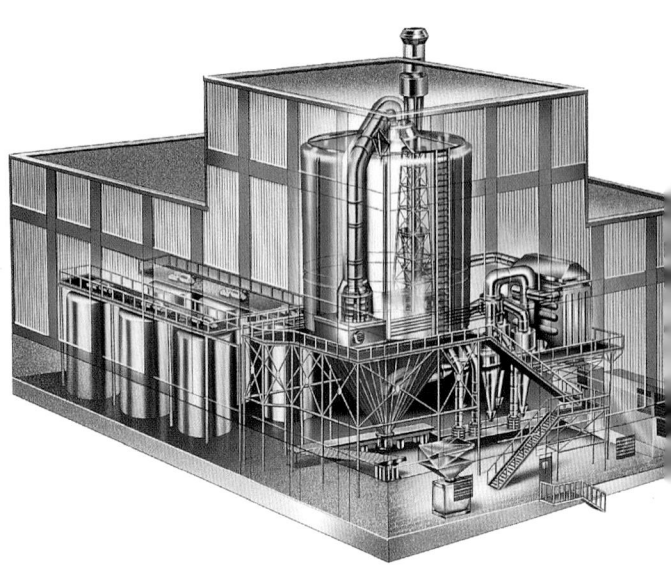

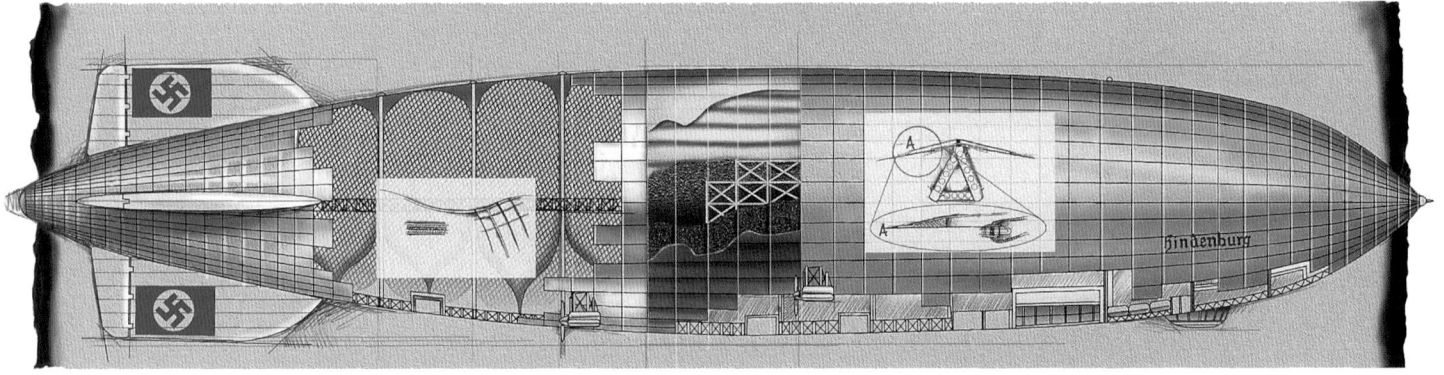

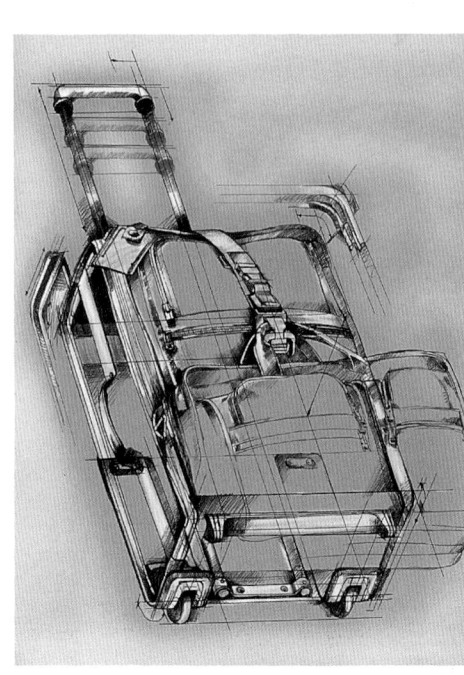

Daniels & Daniels
4-S Madrid Avenue
Newbury Park, California 91320
(805) 498-1923
FAX: (805) 499-8344
e-mail: ariaart@aol.com

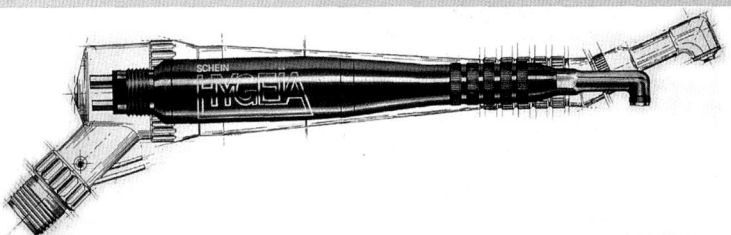

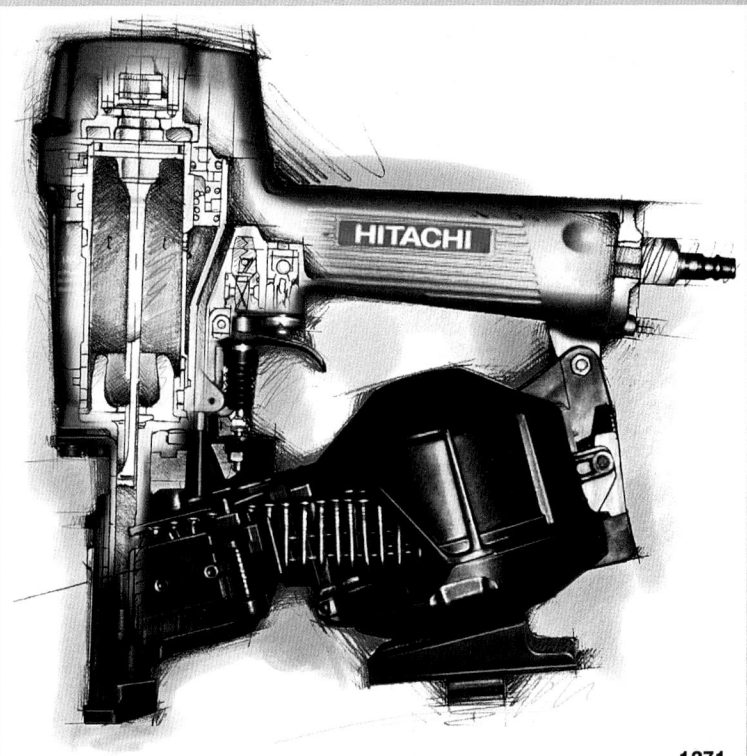

Bruce Day
6080 Arney Lane
Boise, Idaho 83703
(208) 853-8336

Dan DeCarlo
570 First Avenue
Suite 6C
New York, New York 10028
(212) 879-8660

More work in:
American Showcase Volume 21
(p.1261)
American Showcase Volume 20
(p.1365)

Astrid Dininno
457 John Joy Road
Woodstock, New York 12498
(914) 679-7929
FAX: (914) 679-8357

For additional samples:
Directory of Illustration Volumes 14, 15
Stock Illustration Source Volumes 5, 6
www.sisstock.com

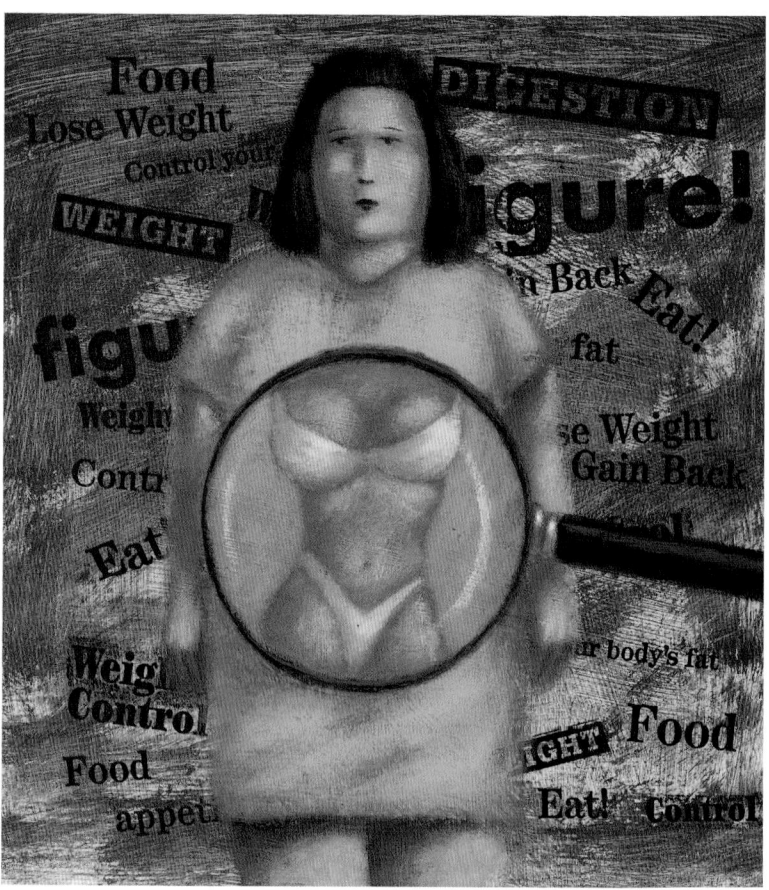

Mike Dowling
1729 South Wayland Avenue
Sioux Falls, South Dakota 57105
(605) 332-5150
(605) 336-1745
FAX: (605) 336-9577

Additional work may be seen in
American Showcase 20 and 21.

Clients include:
Cahner's Publishing
JP Kids, Hubbard Feeds, Inc.
Prince Manufacturing
Y-Tex Corporation
Grand Laboratories

Mike
DOWLING
ILLUSTRATION

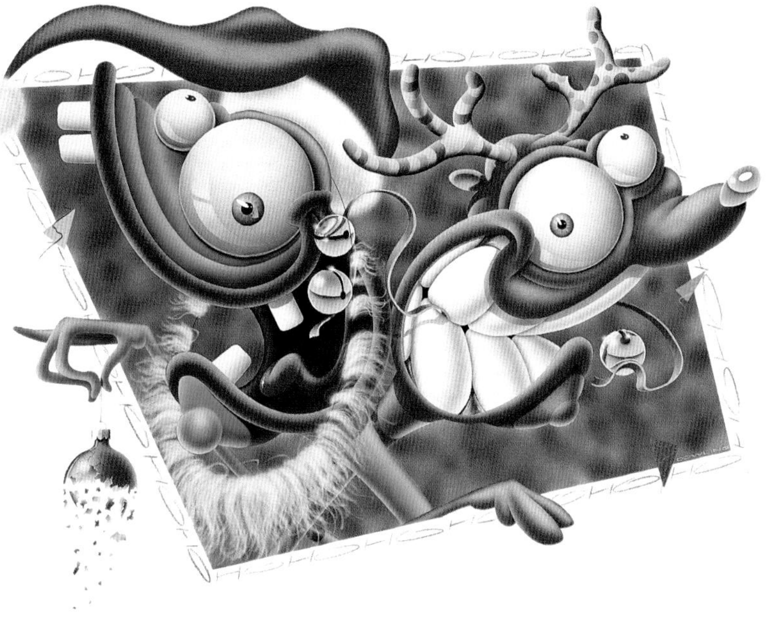

showcase.com

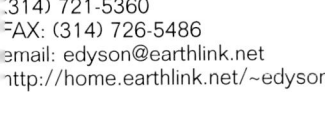

Ed Dyson
74 Greendale Drive
St. Louis, Missouri 63121-4702
(314) 721-5360
FAX: (314) 726-5486
email: edyson@earthlink.net
http://home.earthlink.net/~edyson/

From the home of Bowling Hall of Fame, St. Louis, Missouri, comes an experienced digital artist who brings plenty of problem-solving, concept generating energy to every project.

Call now and play "Bowling for Art" today. Previous winners include Ralston Purina, Southwestern Bell, Pet Inc., Monsanto, and Anheuser-Busch.

Richard Elmer
504 East 11th Street
New York, New York 10009
(212) 598-4024
FAX: (212) 473-1655
email: R2elmer@worldnet.att.net

Stock Options:
Showcase Stock Premier Illustration
Volume 1
The i spot: www.theispot.com

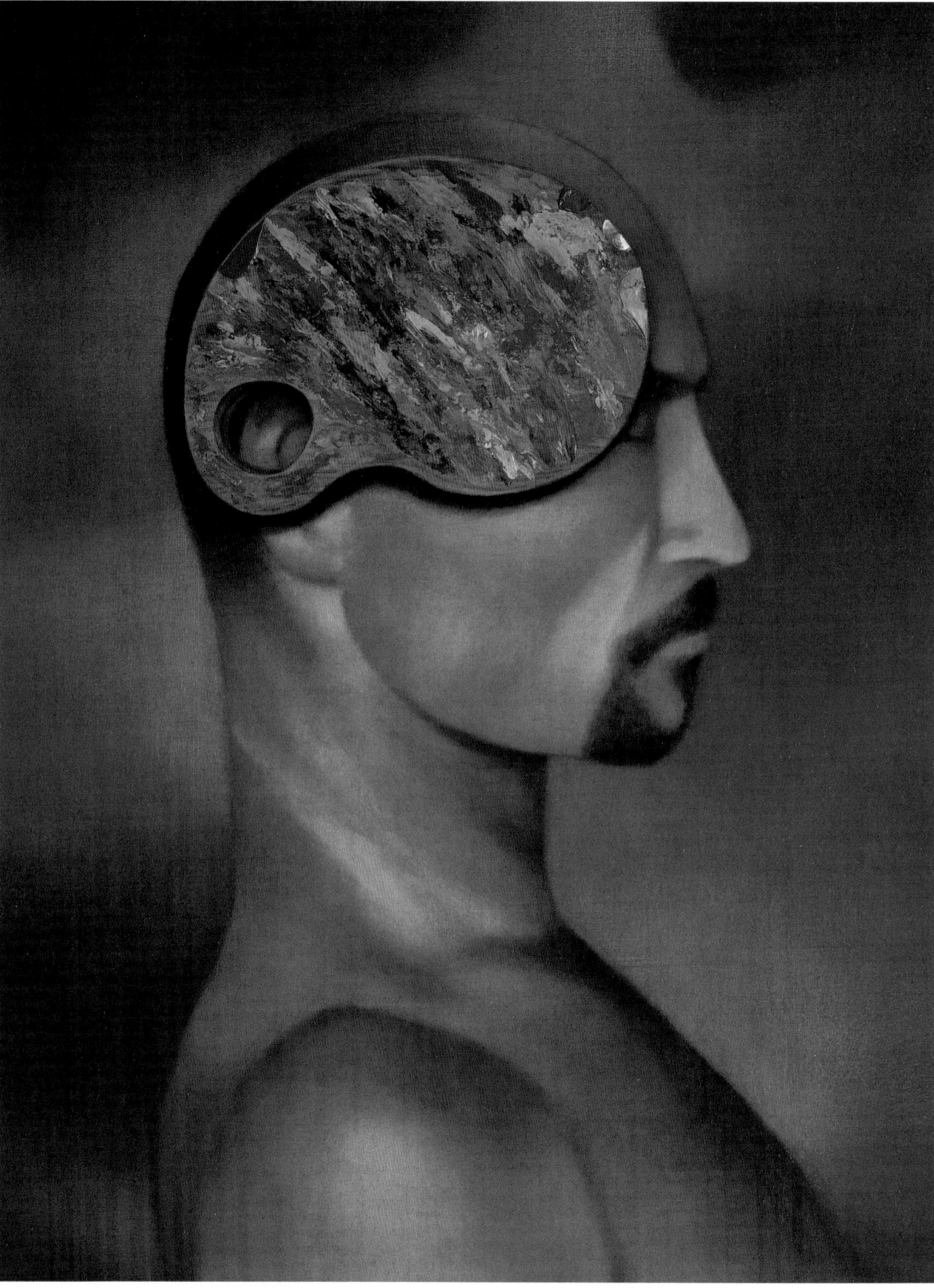

Richard Elmer
504 East 11th Street
New York, New York 10009
(212) 598-4024
FAX: (212) 473-1655
email: R2elmer@worldnet.att.net

Stock Options:
Showcase Stock Premier Illustration,
Volume 1
The i spot: www.theispot.com

Patty West Elstrott
9604 Robin Lane
New Orleans, Louisana 70123
(504) 738-0833

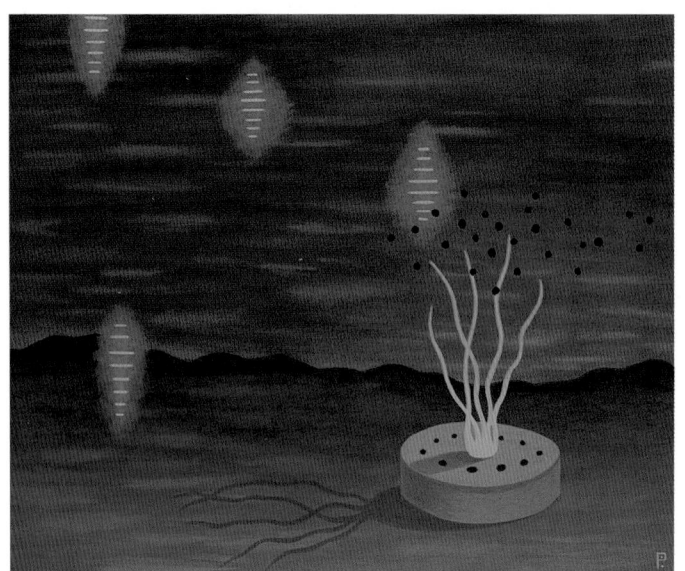

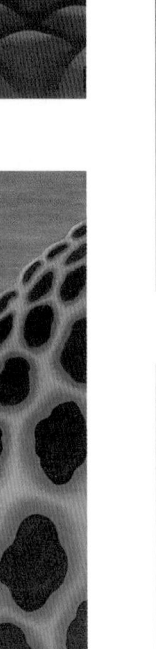

PATTY WEST
ELSTROTT
504 738 0833

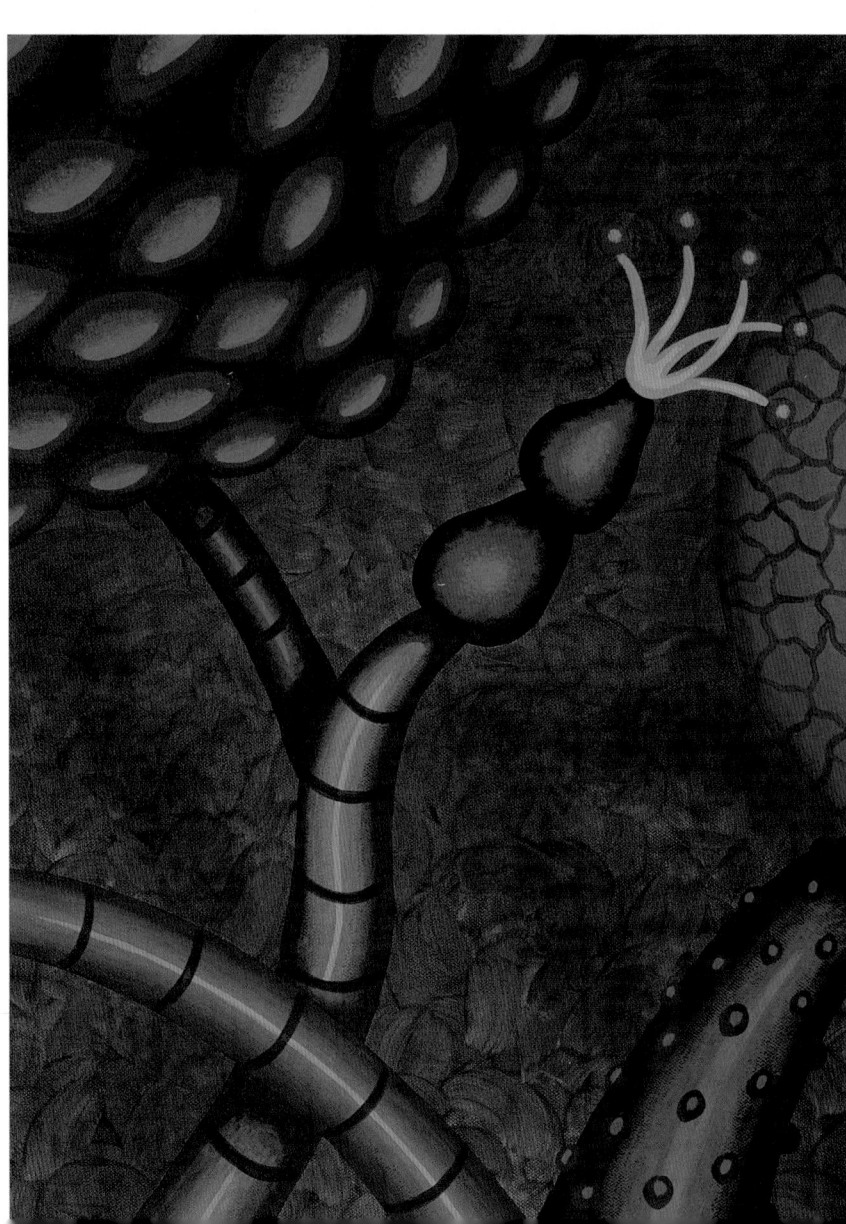

Sarah Jane English
23 Hepworth Drive
Toronto, Ontario
Canada M9R 3W1
(416) 410-5777
Call for fax

Clients have Included: Ford,
Kellogg's, IBM, Parke-Davis,
World Wildlife Foundation,
CCW Wines, Chudleigh's Fruit Juices,
Financial Post, Imax Corporation,
Macmillan Publishing,
Harlequin-Worldwide Mystery,
Harcourt Brace & Company,
Addison-Wesley Longman,
Silver Burdette Ginn, Kids Can Press
© Sarah Jane English, 1998

To view additional work see
American Showcase 19 & 20,
The Creative Illustration Book 1995

Richard Ewing
Richard Ewing Drawings
3966 Gaviota Avenue
Long Beach, California 90807
(888) 403-1004
FAX: (562) 989-9539

For more work -
See showcase 18, 19 & 21
Or look me up @ www.showcase.com

**I Can Make Anyone
Do Anything You
Want Them To Do!**

Natalie Fabian
1 Minetta Street, #5B
New York, New York 10012
(212) 505-0155
email: fabian@ultinet.net
www.nataliefabian.com

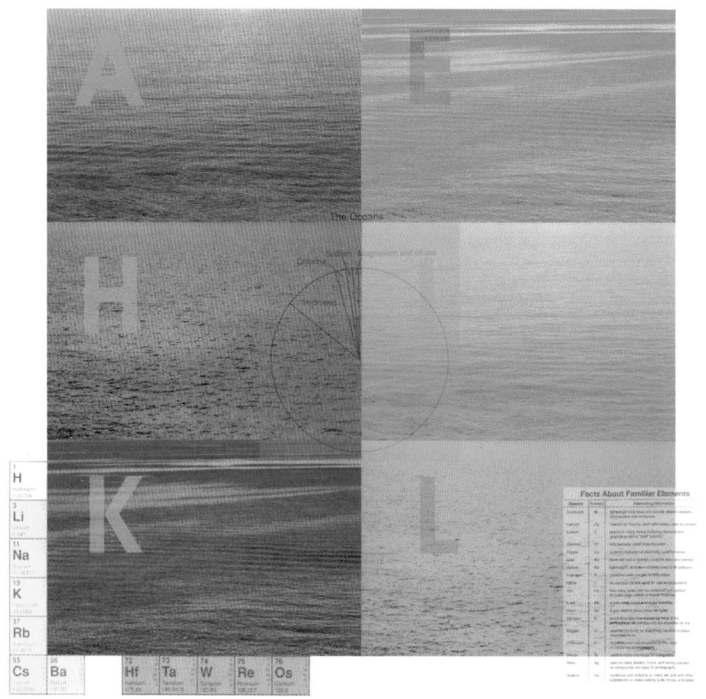

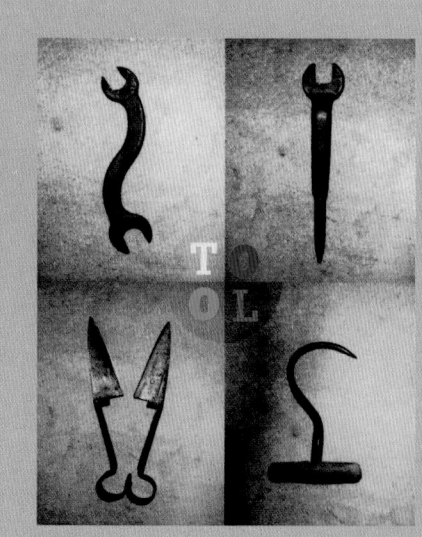

ZOE DANAE FALLIERS
DIGITAL ILLUSTRATION AND PHOTOGRAPHY

505 989 5061   505 989 5091 FAX   zdmf@ix.netcom.com EMAIL

369 MONTEZUMA AVENUE SUITE 387 SANTA FE, NEW MEXICO 87501

David FeBland
570 West End Avenue, #11-B
New York, New York 10025
(212) 580-9299
FAX: (212) 580-3030

An Immigrants Tale / Oil on Canvas

Red Time / Oil on Linen

Vivienne Flesher
(415) 921-2440

Illustration for children's book,
An Mei's Strange
and Wondrous Adventure,
by Stephan Molnar-Fenton

Nicholas Forder
"Delphi" Albert Road
Hedge End, Southampton
England, United Kingdom
S030 ODH
+44 1489 798 435 phone/fax

I specialize in modern ultra realistic illustrations using traditional tools for that unique image. All briefs fully researched for maximum attention to detail. Tight briefs adhered to, or, if preferred creative input no problem. Full colour or black and white visuals supplied as required.

Clients include:
Publishers: Random House, Hodder Headline, Dorling & Kindersley, Future, Matt, Practical Beaulieu NMM, B.T., Moody Yachts and Princess Boats.

Karen Forkish
(888) 686-8863
kforkish@aol.com

from *The Power of Flowers* card deck and book, published by US Games Systems, Inc.

John Francis
1610 Wynkoop Suite 600
Denver, Colorado 80202
(303) 595-3805
FAX: (303) 595-3808
www.jfrancis.com

JOHN
FRANCIS
ILLUSTRATION

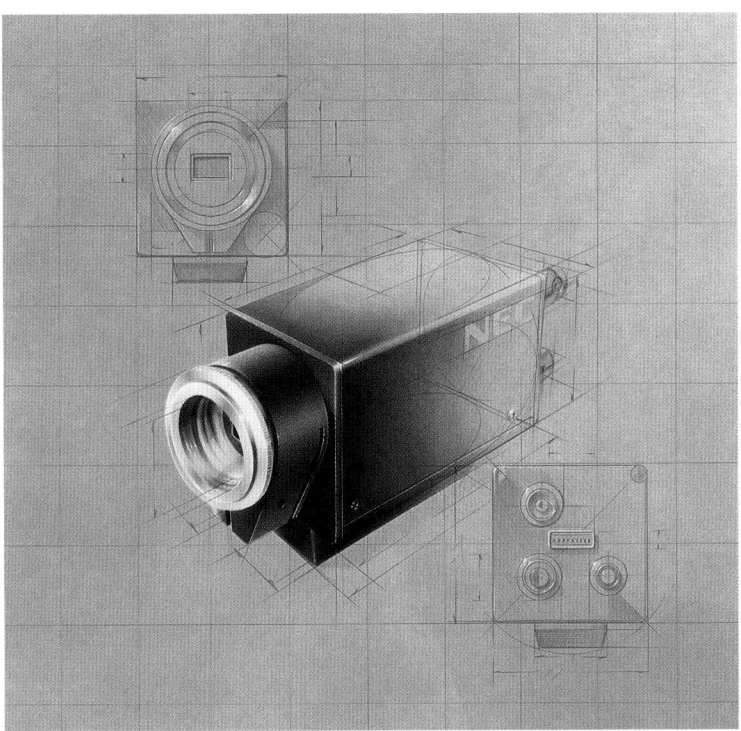

Judy Francis
(212) 866-7204
(212) 734-6113
FAX: (212) 734-3263

Member Society of Illustrators
Member Graphic Artists Guild
Member Fashion Art Source

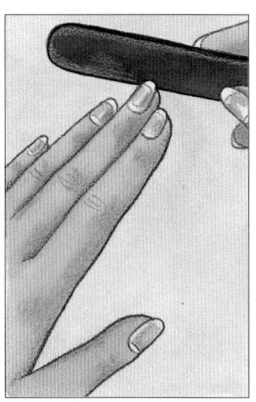
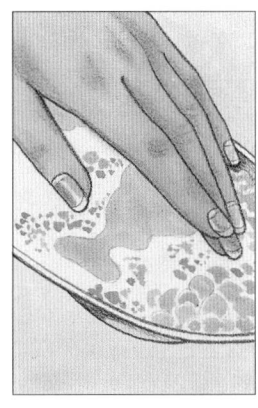
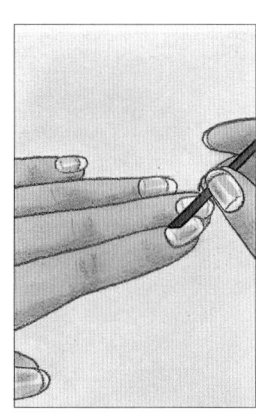

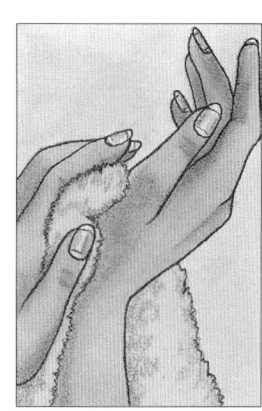
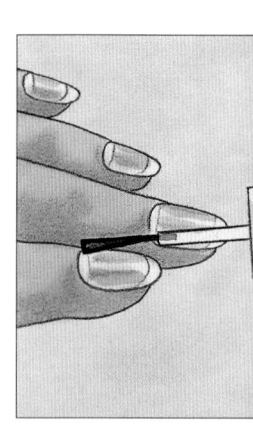

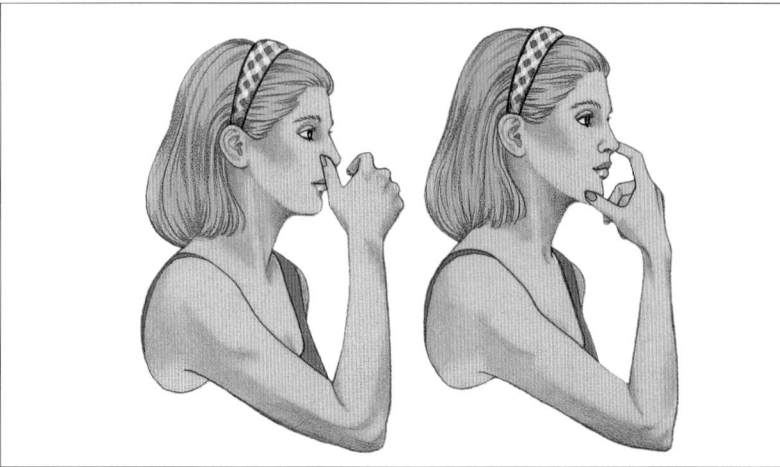

James Frisino
(800) 578-4433

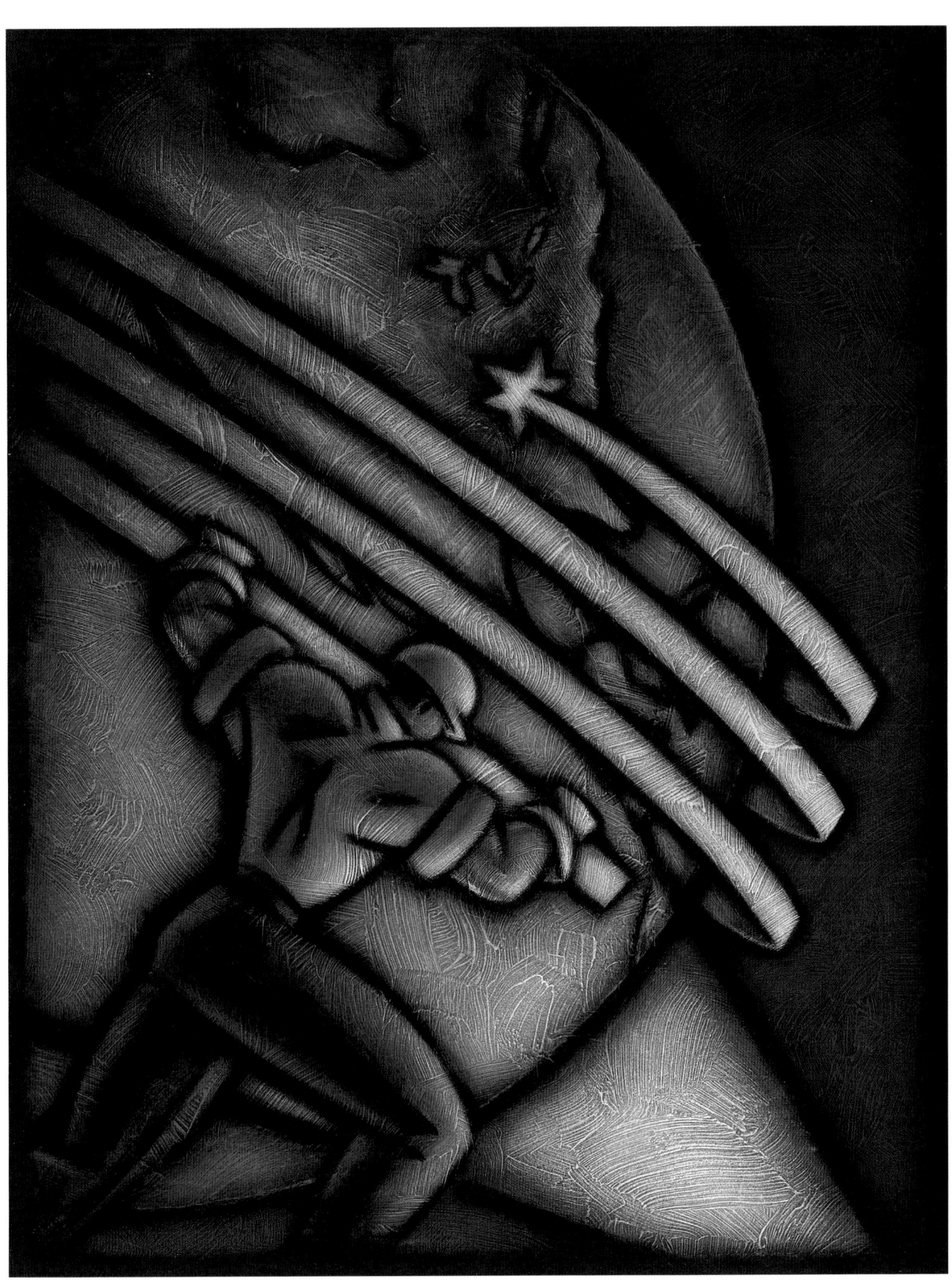

STEEL TECHNOLOGIES AR

showcase.com

illustrators | designers | digital artists | interactive talent | photographers

Kristen Funkhouser
(310) 452-4240

Salzman International
(415) 285-8267
FAX: (415) 285-8268

K R I S T E N   F U N K H O U S E R

SALZMAN
international

Richard Salzman and Brian McMahon Artist's Representatives

San Francisco 415.285.8267   Fax 415.285.8268
Chicago 312.782.2244   New York 212.997.0115

Michael Garland
79 Manor Road
Patterson, New York 12563
(914) 878-4347
FAX: (914) 878-4349
email: Garlandmp@aol.com
www.bestweb.net/~artmtn/

Michael Garland
79 Manor Road
Patterson, New York 12563
(914) 878-4347
FAX: (914) 878-4349
email: Garlandmp@aol.com
www.bestweb.net/~artmtn/

MARSHALL ISLANDS

32

David Garner
Illustrator at Large (and small)
311 West 97th Street, #7E
New York, New York 10025
(212) 663-9548
FAX: (212) 666-9359

Additional work can be found in:
American Showcase 11, 13, 15, 18 or
Directory of Illustration 10, 12, 13, 14

Warren Gebert
New York
(914) 354-2536
FAX: (914) 362-8635

WARREN GEBERT

Mordicai Gerstein
186 Crescent Street
Northampton, Massachusetts 01060
(413) 268-7549
email: risumo@javavanet.com

Illustration of all kinds, as well as
direction, design and storyboard for
animated films.

Below:
The Wild Boy, Farrar, Strauss & Giroux.

Other clients include: HarperCollins,
Hyperion Books, Simon & Schuster,
Harcourt Brace

OPTIMA SERVICES, POSTER

UNITED HEALTH CARE, BROCHURE

UNITED HEALTH CARE, COVER

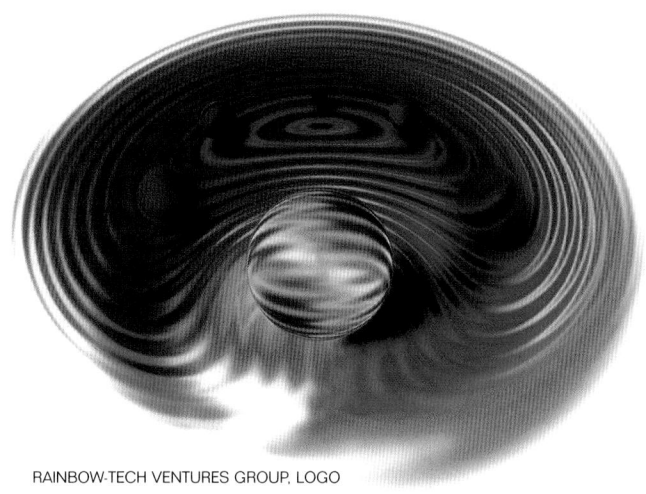

RAINBOW-TECH VENTURES GROUP, LOGO

FRANCESCO GIANNETTI · 1.888.339.3172

showcase.com

illustrators | designers | digital artists | interactive talent | photographers

Nancy Gibson-Nash
88 Welch Street
Peaks Island, Maine 04108
(207) 766-5761
FAX: (207) 766-4472

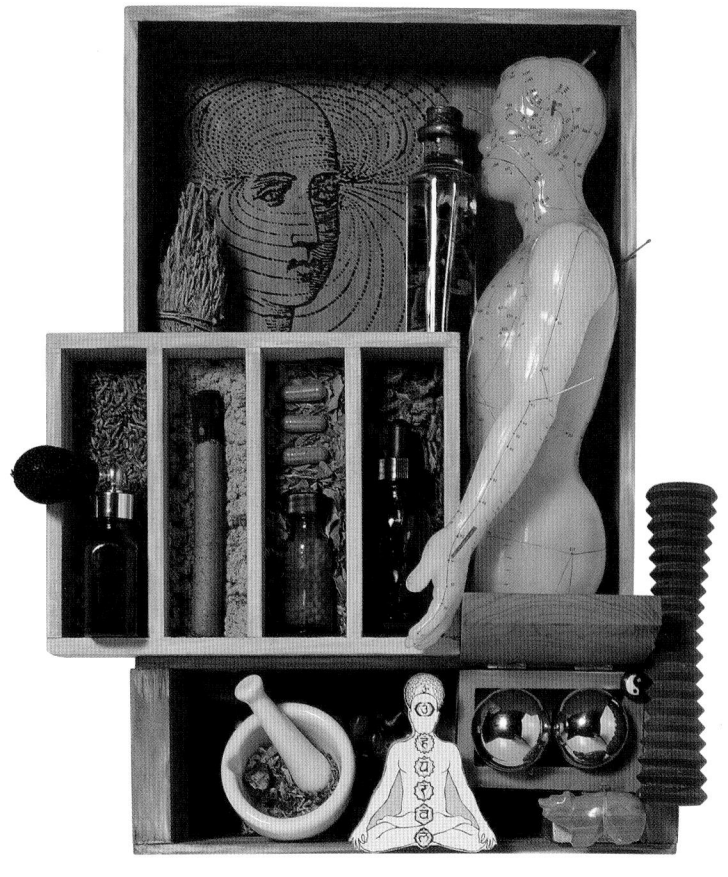

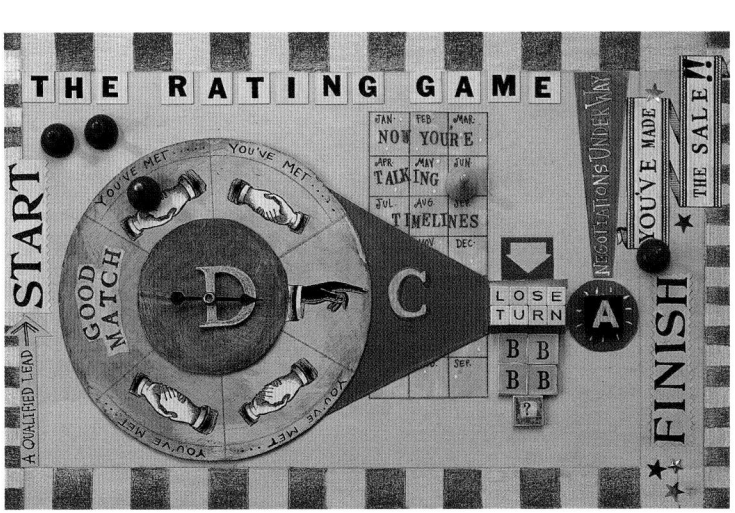

Carter Goodrich
18 Imperial Place, #6-E
Providence, Rhode Island 02903
(401) 272-6094

Carter Goodrich
18 Imperial Place, #6-E
Providence, Rhode Island 02903
(401) 272-6094

Danny Gordon
5500 NW 111th Street
Oklahoma City, Oklahoma 73162
(405) 728-1350
(405) 728-9813 FAX

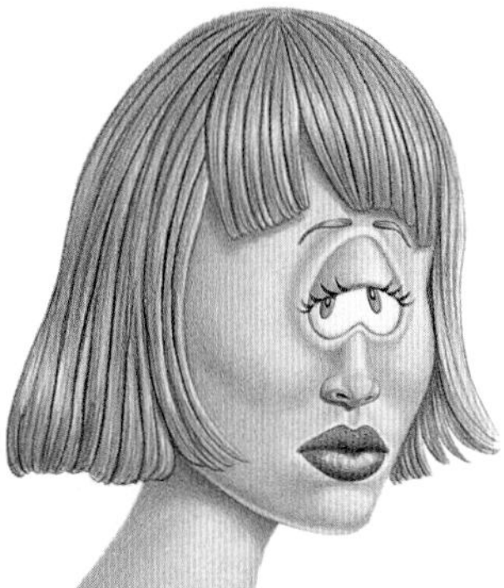

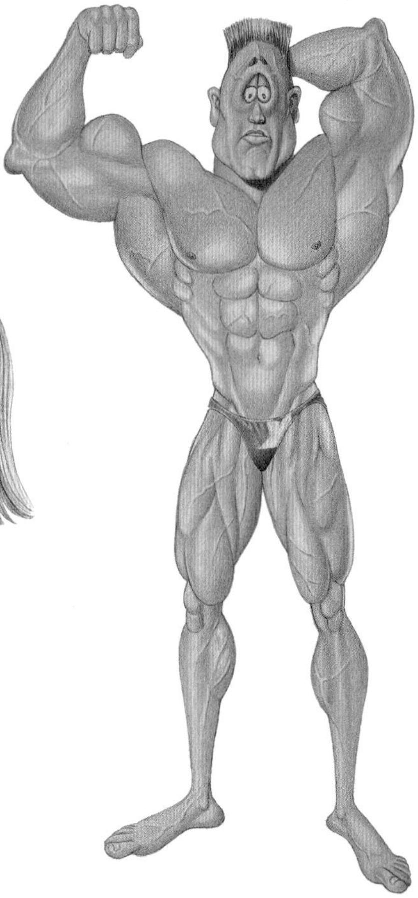

Rob Gregoretti
1-07 56th Street
Woodside, New York 11377
(718) 779-7913
FAX: (718) 779-7913
http://www.showcase.com

Clients include:
CBS Records, RCA/BMG Records,
Lifetime Television, Kirchoff/Wohlberg,
Inc., Macmillan/McGraw Hill,
Guideposts, Billboard Magazine

Exhibitions and Awards include:
The National Arts Club Gallery with
the Pastel Society of America, The
American Artists Professional League
Inc., and the Salmagundi Club of New
York, where he received the Alice B.
McReynolds Award for his portrait of
B.B. King

Portfolio Available upon request.
Additional work appears in American
Showcase Volumes 14, 15, 16, 18,
and 19
© Rob Gregoretti 1999

Rhoda Grossman
216 Fourth Street
Sausalito, California 94965
(415) 331-0328
FAX: (415) 332-1960
rhoda@digitalpainting.com
www.digitalpainting.com

Computer Illustration for print or
electronic media

See additional images:
www.showcase.com
Workbook, Volume 18, p.957
Workbook, Volume 19, p.707
California Image '95, p.184

Member Graphic Artists Guild
Member San Francisco Society of
Illustrators

Caricature

digital painting

Domestic Violence—Making a Difference

Dirk Hagner
(714) 493-5596

Salzman International
(415) 285-8267
(212) 997-0115

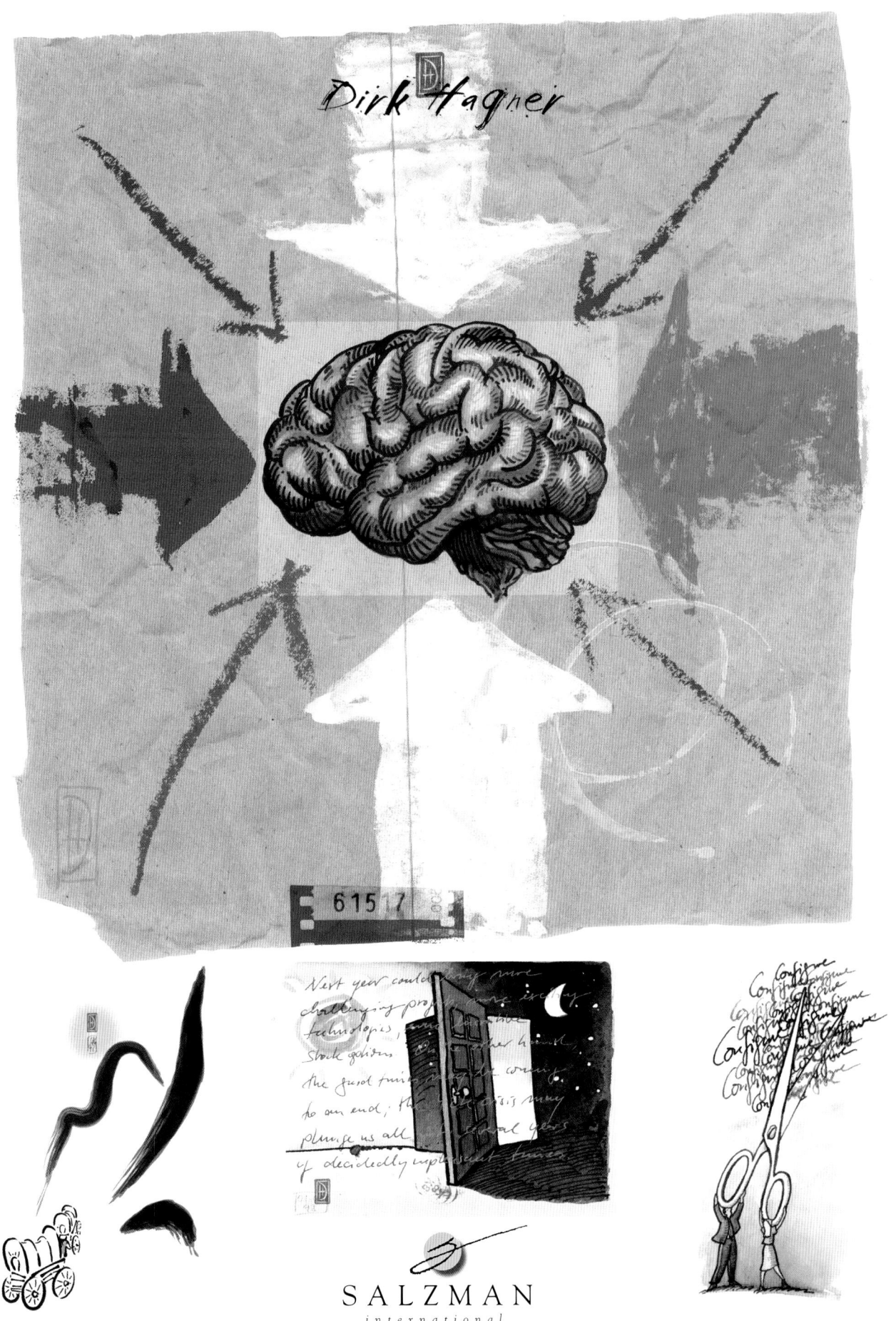

S A L Z M A N
international
Richard Salzman and Brian McMahon Artists' Representatives

San Francisco 415.285.8267   Fax 415.285.8268   Chicago 312.782.2244   New York 212.997.0115

showcase.com

illustrators | designers | digital artists | interactive talent | photographers

Joan Hall
155 Bank Street
Studio H954
New York, New York 10014
(212) 243-6059
FAX: (212) 924-8560

2 and 3 Dimensional Collage Illustration

Instructor of 'Collage Now'
The School of Visual Arts, New York
Additional work: SIS Volume 6
American Showcase 14-21

Clients include: Atlantic Records, The
Bank of NY, Citibank, Cunard Lines,
Doubleday, Estee Lauder, Gourmet,
GTE Spacenet, HBO, IBM, L'Express,
NYNEX, POZ Remy Martin, Sony,
Time/Life, Tokyo Bay Lalaport

JOAN HALL

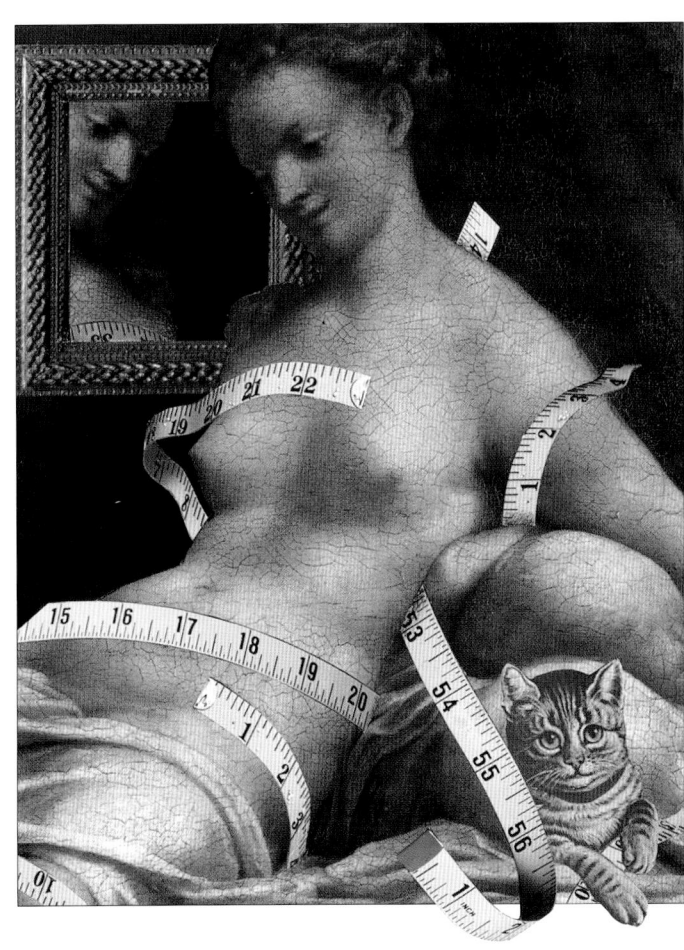

Meredith Hamilton
Brooklyn, New York
(800) 963-7896

VISA International training video

Eastern & Orient Express Burma guide

Sandalwood

Temple Etiquette

Thanaka

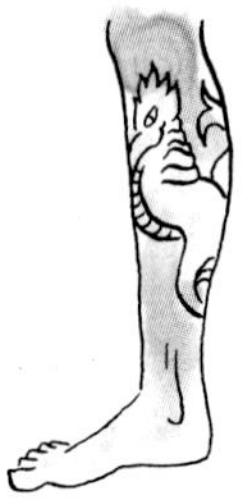

Naga

Earthquakes

Music

Food

The hunter + the Monk

White Elephant

Templest trees

Minorities

Temple Slave

Tattooing

Ox cart

Temple vs. Stupa

Meredith Hamilton
Brooklyn, New York
(800) 963-7896

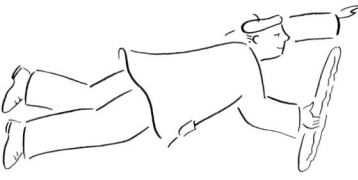

Singapore Airlines European destinations TV ad

Supermarket sweepstake

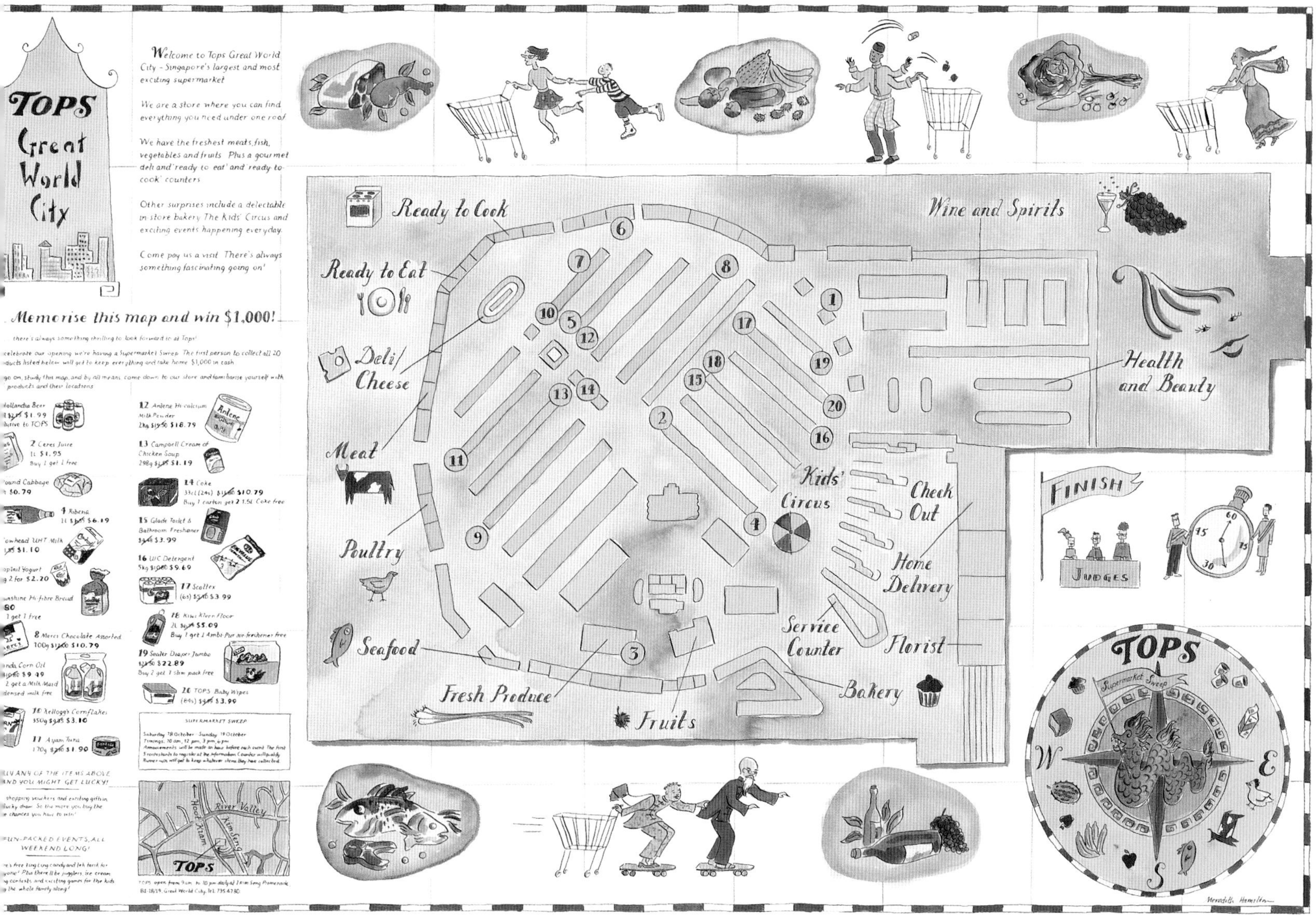

Debra Hardesty
(916) 446-1824

DEBRA HARDESTY

1017 VALLEJO WAY   SACRAMENTO, CA 95818   TEL 916.446.1824   FAX 916.446.5661

Nancy Harrison
4671 Durham Road
Gardenville, Pennsylvania 18926
(215) 766-9829
(610) 390-4540
Fax in studio.

Obadinah Heavner
10310 Mary Avenue NW
Seattle, Washington 98177-5329
(206) 789-8899 studio
FAX: (206) 782-1572
email: obadinah@nwlink.com

Harcourt Brace
Quaker Oats
Microsoft
American Airlines Publishing
Cricket Magazine Group
Group Health

Houghton Mifflin
Monsanto
Plastics Technology
The Wright Group

Obadinah
H e a v n e r

Jennifer Hewitson
1145 Wotan Drive
Encinitas, California 92024
(760) 944-6154
FAX: (760) 943-0322

Portfolio on the web at
www.showcase.com
Also see Showcase 14-21 and SIS #5
and 6
© Jennifer Hewitson 1998

Clients include:
AT&T, Disney, Frito Lay, Los Angeles
Times, The Wall Street Journal

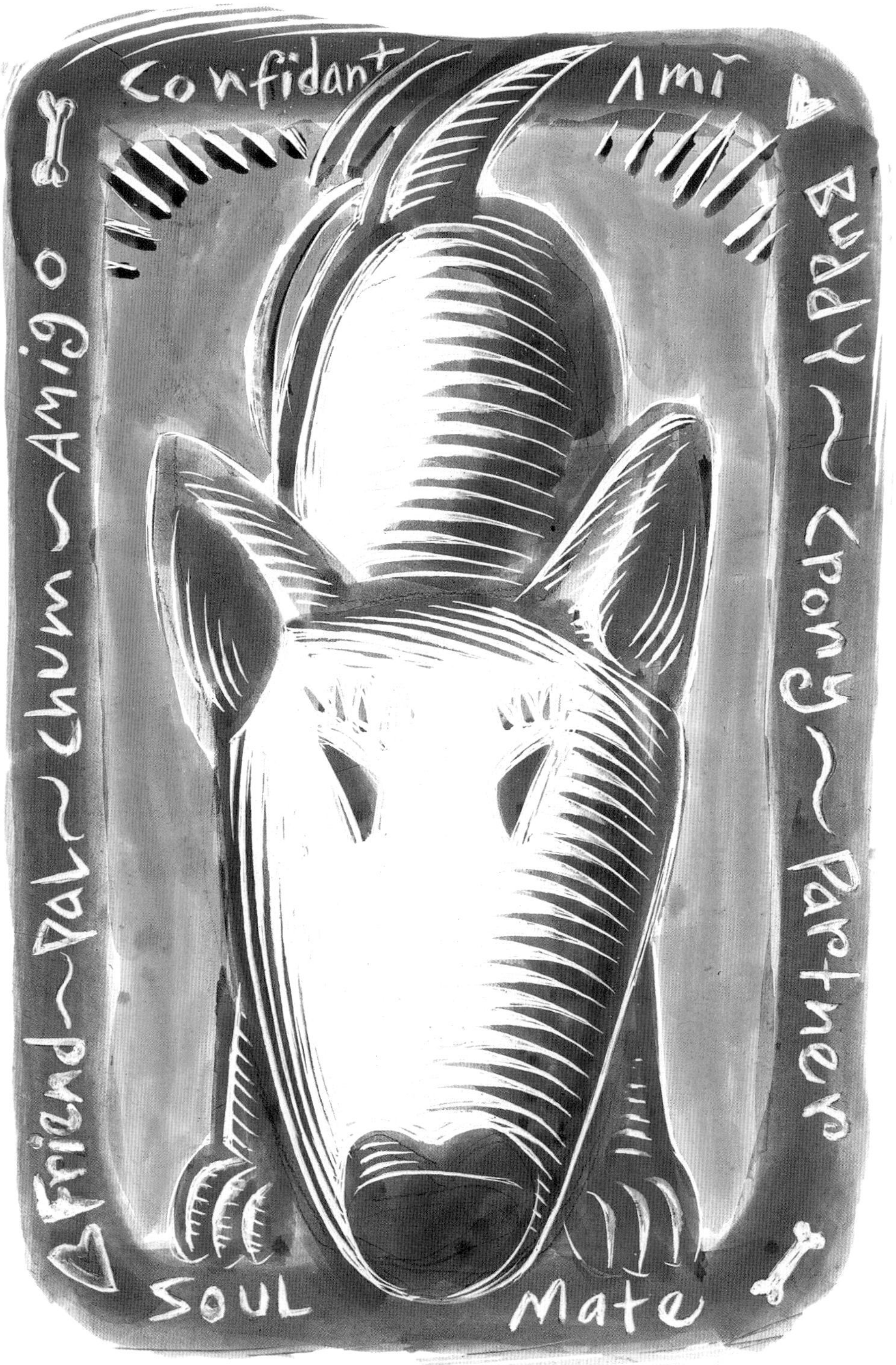

Laurie A. Hicklin
8028 Dusenberg Court
Sacramento, California 95828
(916) 689-6725 Phone/FAX

LAURIE A HICKLIN

illustrator

9 1 6 . 6 8 9 . 6 7 2 5

HieroGraphiX Productions
636 Broadway, #1210
New York, New York 10012
(212) 529-2771
FAX: (212) 473-0509
email: true@hieroprod.com
www.hieroprod.com

Illustration • animation
character & logo design
for print & electronic media

1996 Atlanta Games, Beat Down (hip hop mag), CDNOW, Chopping Block, ConsumerInfo, Disney, GTE Online, i-traffic, L.A. Times, Manhattan Files, Men's Club Magazine (Japan), MGM's "Pink Panther" CD-rom Series,

Micrsoft's "Magic School Bus" CD-rom Series, Bill Moyers' PBS Online Series, New York Magazine, New York Times, St. Martin Press, Time Warner, Travel Holiday, Village Voice & YOU!

Diane Hillier
170 Corte Madera Road
Portola Valley, California 94028
(650) 851-9715
FAX: (650) 851-9715

Scratchboard Illustration

ITALIAN FOOD PRODUCTS

Eileen Hine
1078 West Lake Avenue
Guilford, Connecticut 06437
(203) 453-8798
FAX: (203) 458-2567

J. Michael Hite
11166 West Arbor Drive
Littleton, Colorado 80127
(303) 979-9527
FAX: (303) 904-9025
email: mhdesigns@earthlink.net

David Ho
www.davidho.com

3586 Dickenson Common, Fremont, CA 94538 **tel.** 510.656.2468 **fax.** 510.656.2224 **email.** ho@davidho.com

Doug Hoch
140 Highland Avenue
Arlington, Massachusetts 02174
(781) 483-3763

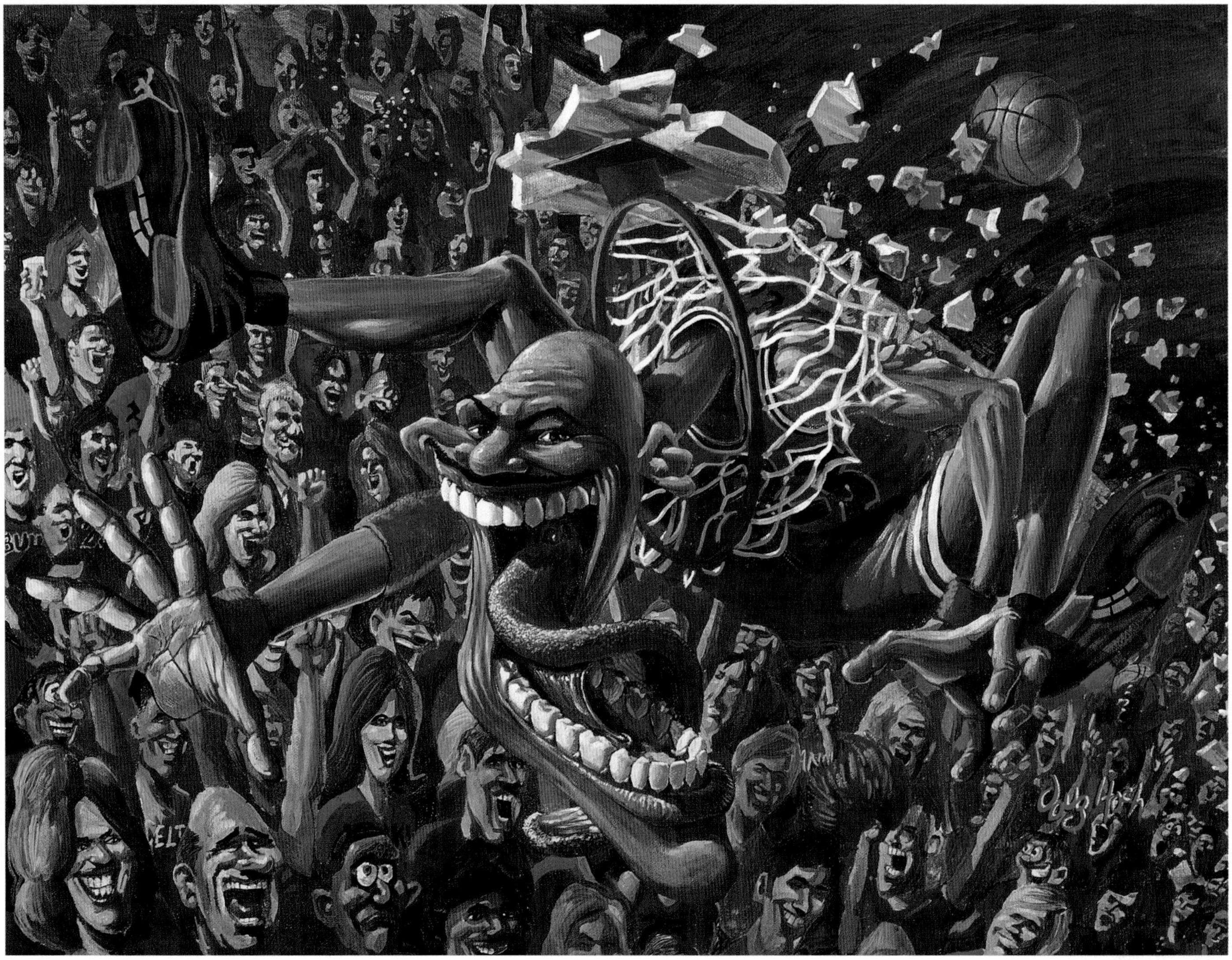

Ilumination Studio
Alex Bostic
L.C. Thompson
9629 Dove Hollow Lane
Glen Allen, Virgina 23060
(804) 755-7455
FAX: (804) 755-6792

L.C. Thompson *3 Dimensional paper illustration*

Alex Bostic *Mixed media illustration*

Phone 804.755.7455   Fax 804.755.6792

Partial Client List:
*Time-Life Books, Budweiser, The Martin Agency, U.S. Navy,
Virginia Power, AT&T, Hallmark Cards, Sunrise Publications,
NYNEX, Denny's, John Deere, NASA, and Mutual of Omaha.*

Cliff Iwai

WHEN BAD THINGS HAPPEN TO GOOD PEOPLE / DIGITAL

BOY ARE MY ARMS TIRED / DIGITAL

SHEILA OF THE CATS / DIGITAL

1604 Tyler St.   Berkeley, CA 94703   Ph. 510-540-6125   Fax: 510-540-7580   e-mail ciwai@AOL.com

Nancy Januzzi
306 East 91st Street
New York, New York 10128
(212) 774-7790

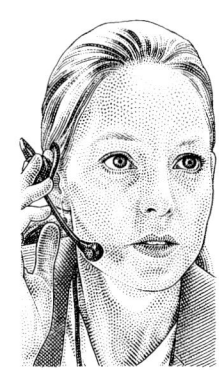

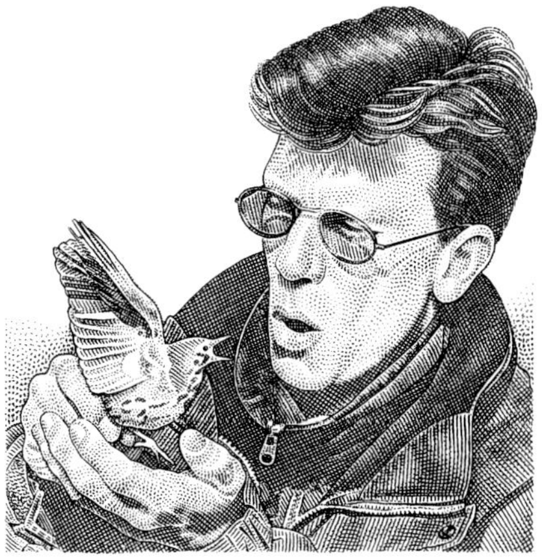

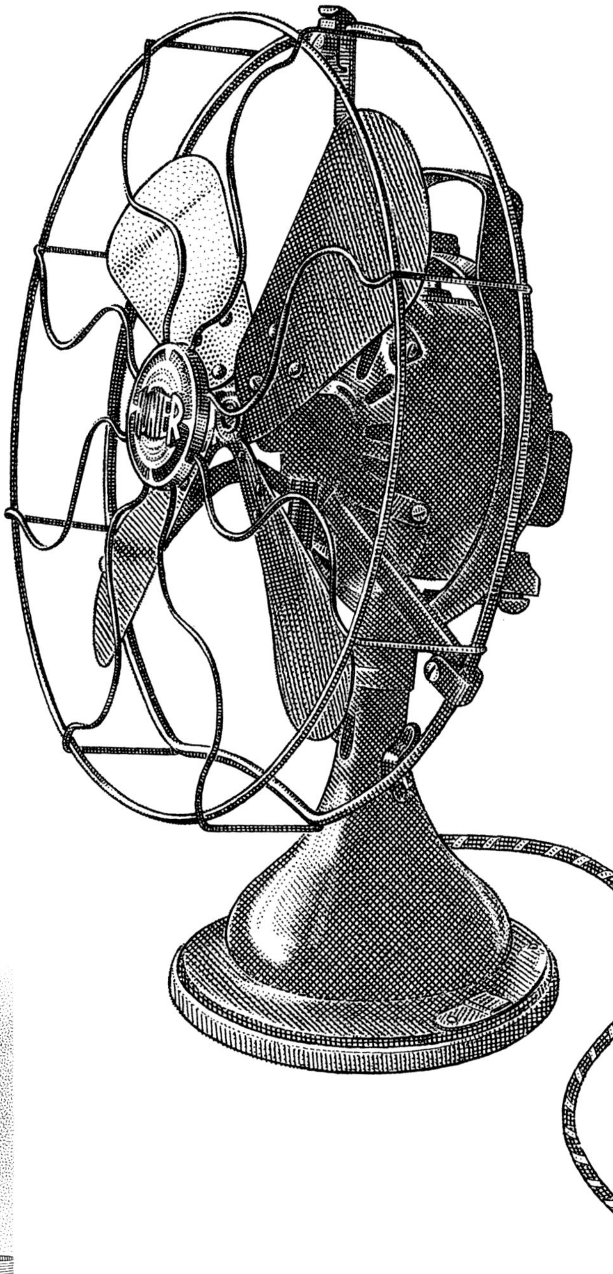

1325

Mark Jaquette
P.O. Box 21932
Eugene, Oregon 97402
(888) 318-7876
(541) 461-1382 Phone/FAX
email: bamm@pond.net

Clients include: Pulse!; REact; Guitar Player; The Rocket; The Stranger; The Nation; CCM; Boot; Alternatives Journal; Sappo; The Bear Essential; The Progressive; Spitball; Breakaway.

Member: A.I.G.A.

Beth Griffis Johnson
2 Brimmer Street, #3A
Beacon Hill
Boston, Massachusetts 02108
(617) 742-6134

Clients include:
Woman's Day Magazine, Home Magazine,
The Millbrook Press, Bon Appetit,
Highlights for Children, Colorbök,
Marcel Schurman, Colors By Design

Beth Griffis Johnson
illustrations

Dan Jones
3101 Bancroft St.
San Diego, CA 92104
(619) 281-3413
email: asiaj@aol.com

Salzman International
(212) 997-0115
(415) 285-8267

·DAN JONES·

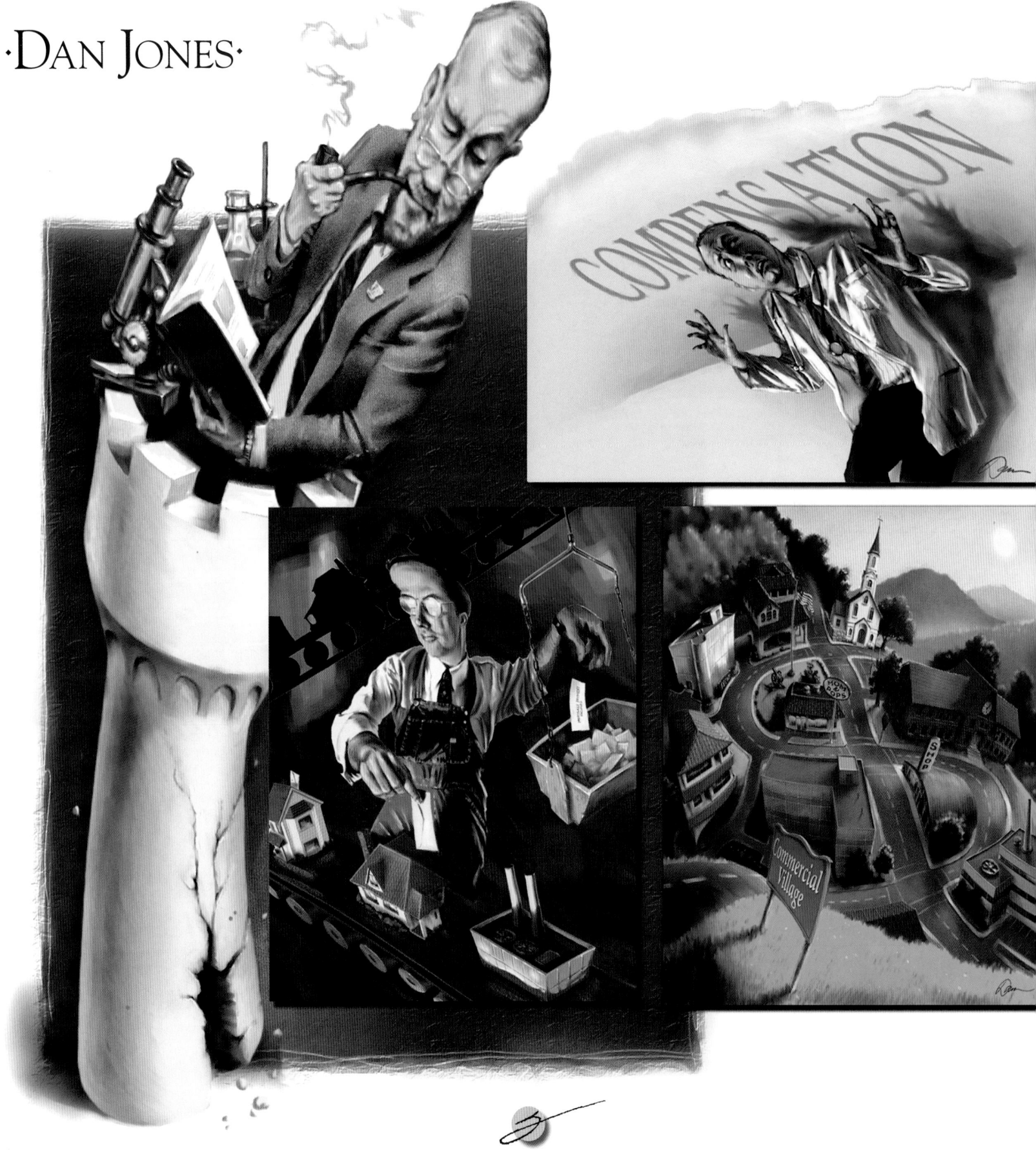

SALZMAN
international
San Francisco 415.285.8267   Fax 415.285.8268
Chicago 312.782.2244   New York 212.997.0115

Stanford Kay
Paragraphics
(914) 358-0798
FAX: (914) 358-3284

For more samples of illustrations
and/or infographics see
Showcase #19, #20, #21
or see the portfolio on the web at
www.spyral.net/para

Ruth Sofair Ketler
101 Bluff Terrance
Silver Spring, Maryland 20902
(301) 593-6059
(301) 593-1236
email: ruth.ketler@tcs.wap.org

Kathleen Kimball
(206) 522-2710
FAX: (206) 528-4808

Clients:
Simon & Schuster, Sage Publications,
U.V. Limited Partnership

Simon & Schuster

U.V. Ltd. Partnership

U.V. Ltd. Partnership

Lisa Krieshok
15 Old Creek Road
Petaluma, California 94952
(707) 769-8124 Phone/FAX
email: krieshok@slip.net

Julie B. Lawrence
174 Summit Avenue #306
Summit, New Jersey 07901
(908) 273-1934

Illustration/Caricatures/Cartoons

JULIE LAWRENCE

174 Summit Ave #306
Summit, NJ 07901
908-273-1934

Illustration • Caricatures • Cartoons

Bill Lee
792 Columbus Avenue, # 1 - 0
New York, New York 10025
(212) 866-5664 Phone/FAX

Rebecca J. Leer
440 West End Avenue, 12E
New York, New York 10024
(212) 595-5865
FAX: (212) 595-5940

Clients include:
Alfred A. Knopf
Bell Atlantic
Direct Results Group
Duty Free Stores
Heublein Beverages

Kimberly-Clark
Miller Freeman, Inc.
Orchard Books
Putnam & Grosset
Saatchi & Saatchi
Viking Penguin

Additional work in:
American Showcase 14-21
CA Illustration 35
Illustrators 36
SILA Illustration West 33, 35, 36

SOMETHING TO SMILE ABOUT

MANTRA SQUASH

Lance Lekander
(907) 243-8889
FAX: (907) 245-1773

ENT / DATA DEBATERS

THE McCLATCHY COMPANY / DIGITAL

LANTIMES / STOPPING THE E-MAIL FLOOD

showcase.com

illustrators | designers | digital artists | interactive talent | photographers

Todd Leonardo
9110 Almond Road
Castro Valley, California 94546
(510) 728-1076
Fax in studio.

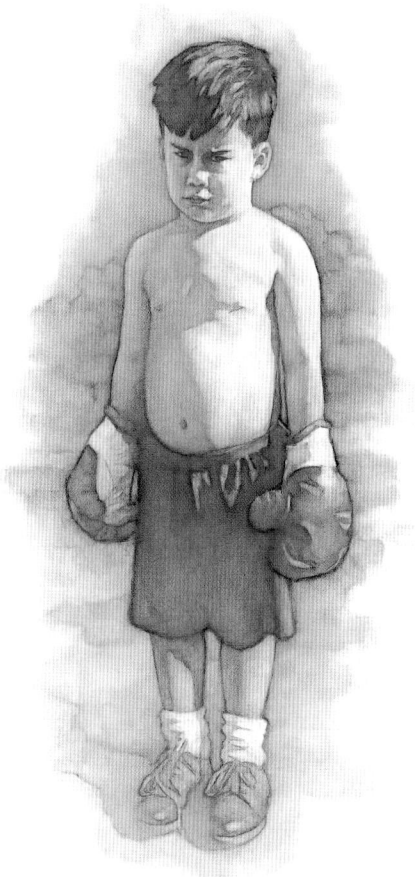

Andy Levine
23-30 24th Street
Astoria, New York 11105
(718) 956-8539

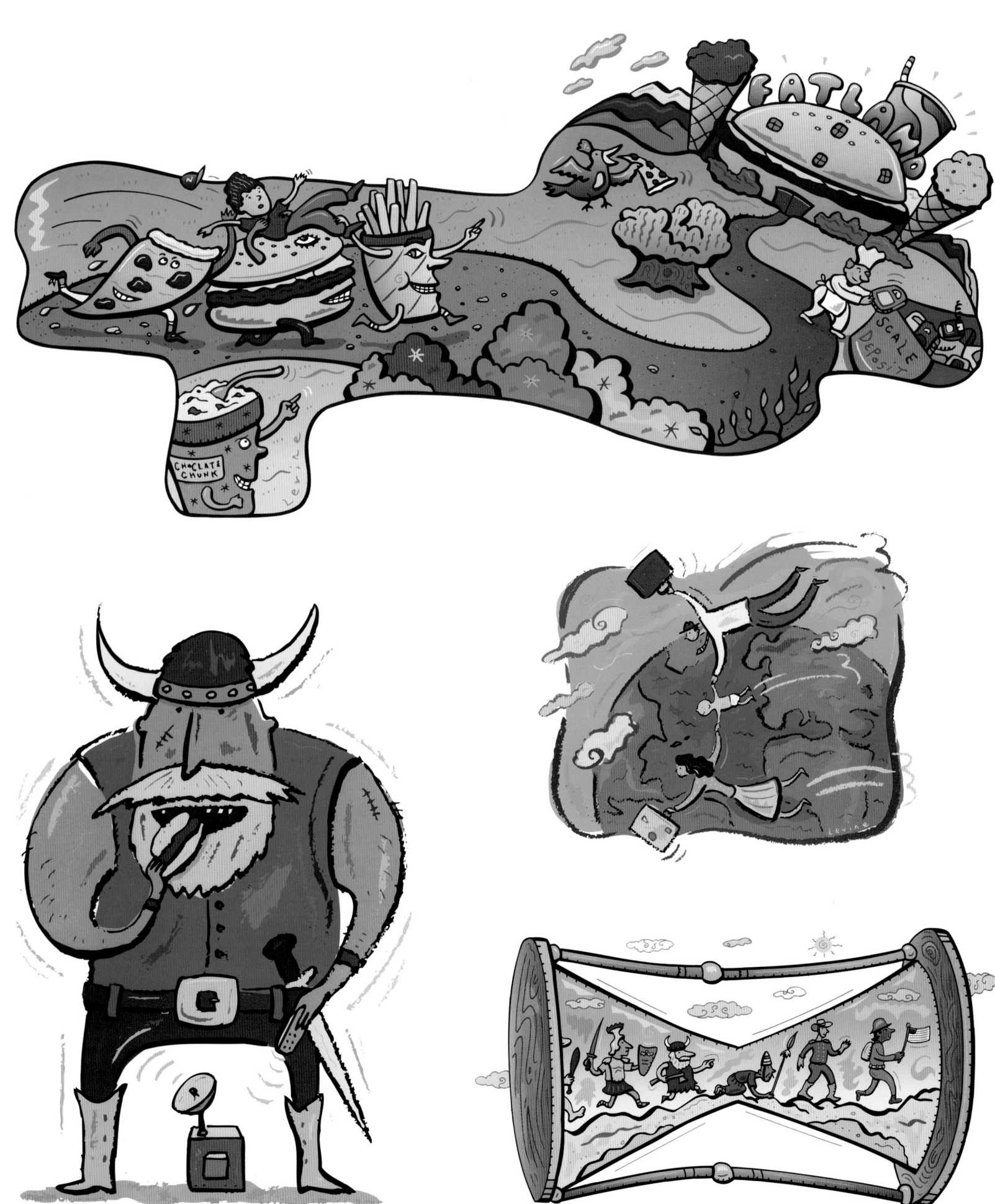

Andy Levine
3-30 24th Street
Astoria, New York 11105
(718) 956-8539

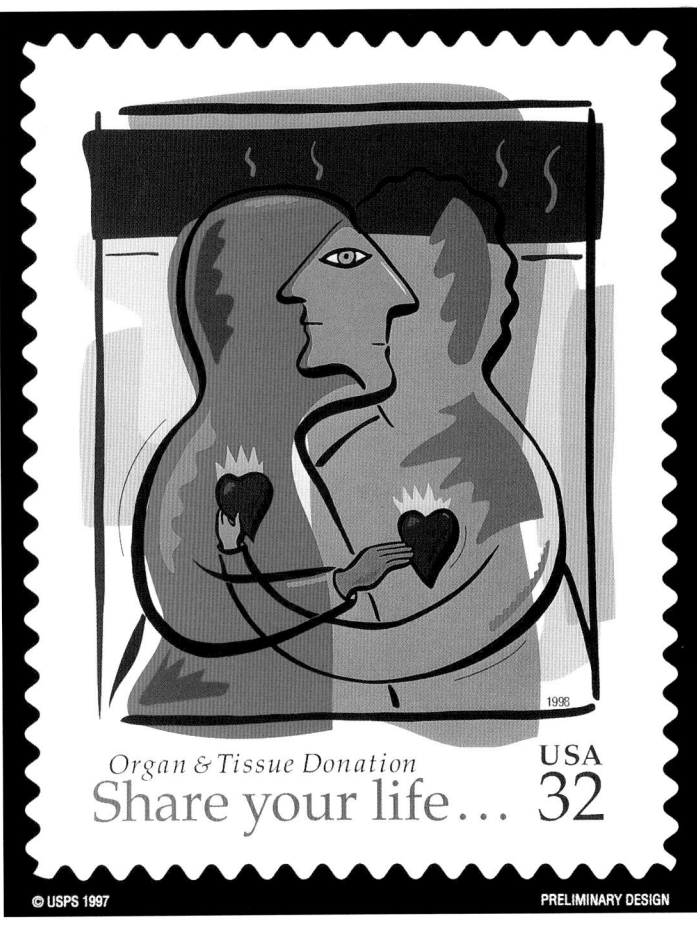

Organ & Tissue Donation
Share your life...

USA
32

© USPS 1997   PRELIMINARY DESIGN

Cardinal®

Aimee Levy
527 San Vincente Boulevard, #301
Santa Monica, California 90402
(310) 319-3788

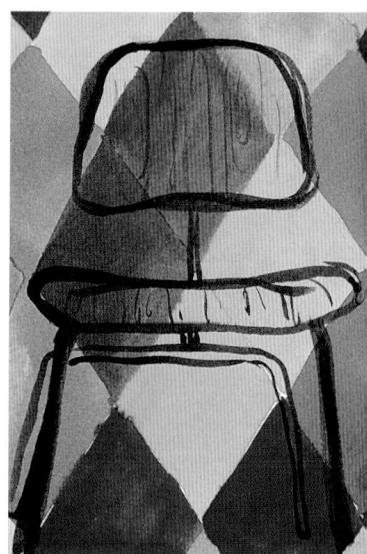

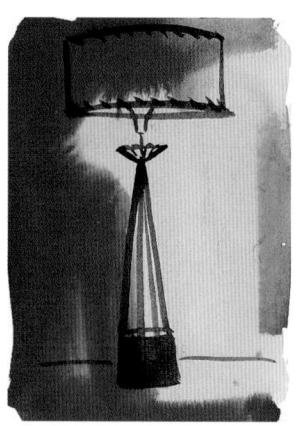

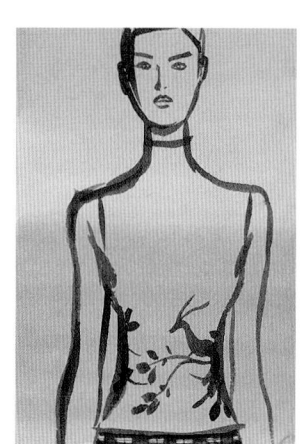

Fred Lynch
One Eaton Court
Winchester, Massachusetts 01890
(781) 729-3813 Phone/FAX

John Lytle
Post Office Box 5155
Sonora, California 95370
(209) 928-4849
FAX: (209) 928-4575

Delivery: 17301 Fitch Ranch Road
Sonora, California 95370

Additional illustrations:
American Showcase Volumes 5-21

Katherine Mahoney
60 Hurd Road
Belmont, Massachusetts 02478
(617) 868-7877 Voice
(617) 497-4262 FAX

Clients represented on this page:
MCI, BusinessWeek,
Harvard Business Review

Comping is usage
Ask first.

M. Maurer
304 Corbin Drive
Newport News, Virginia 23606
(757) 595-5921
email: mmi@widomaker.com

showcase.com

illustrators | designers | digital artists | interactive talent | photographers

Glenn Mitsui
Studio M D
1512 Alaskan Way
Seattle, Washington 98101
(206) 682-6221
FAX: (206) 682-6283
email: glenn@studiomd.com

Clients include:
Microsoft, NEC, IBM, Sun Microsystems,
Apple Computer, Sony, Bell Canada,
Sybase, Newsweek, Time, Atlantic
Monthly, MacWorld Magazine,
Entertainment Weekly, MacWorld
Tokyo and Forbes.

Glenn's work is also on display at the
Seattle Pacific Science Center and the
National Museum of Science and
Technology of Canada.

www.studiomd.com

Glenn Mitsui
Studio M D
1512 Alaskan Way
Seattle, Washington 98101
(206) 682-6221
FAX: (206) 682-6283
email: glenn@studiomd.com

Clients include:
Microsoft, NEC, IBM, Sun Microsystems,
Apple Computer, Sony, Bell Canada,
Sybase, Newsweek, Time, Atlantic
Monthly, MacWorld Magazine,
Entertainment Weekly, MacWorld
Tokyo and Forbes.

Glenn's work is also on display at the
Seattle Pacific Science Center and the
National Museum of Science and
Technology of Canada.

www.studiomd.com

Glenn Mitsui
Studio M D
512 Alaskan Way
Seattle, Washington 98101
(206) 682-6221
FAX: (206) 682-6283
email: glenn@studiomd.com

Clients include:
Microsoft, NEC, IBM, Sun Microsystems,
Apple Computer, Sony, Bell Canada,
Sybase, Newsweek, Time, Atlantic
Monthly, MacWorld Magazine,
Entertainment Weekly, MacWorld
Tokyo and Forbes.

Glenn's work is also on display at the
Seattle Pacific Science Center and the
National Museum of Science and
Technology of Canada.

www.studiomd.com

1-800-466-4060   Fax: (650) 355-8051   www.J2morrow.com

JT
Morrow

showcase.com

Keiko Motoyama
1607 East Glenhaven Drive
Phoenix, Arizona 85048
(602) 460-2743 Phone/FAX
email: mokkun@aol.com

For Children's Book, Call
Christina A. Tugeau
Artist Agent
(203) 438-7307

For additional work see:
American Showcase 21
Picturebook 98, 99
(under Christina Tugeau Artist Agent)

Eric Mueller
eM2 Illustration
4625 Drew Avenue South
Minneapolis, Minnesota 55410
(612) 926-0594
FAX: (612) 926-0703
email: emhome@usinternet.com

www.eM2pix.com

Clients include:
3M Corporation
American Express
Timberland
Windows Magazine
InfoWorld Magazine

Oracle Magazine
Byte Magazine
InformationWeek Magazine
Goverment Executive Magazine
Selling Power Magazine

ERIC MUELLER
[612] 926.0594

SELLING POWER MAGAZINE

Eric Mueller
eM2 Illustration
4625 Drew Avenue South
Minneapolis, Minnesota 55410
(612) 926-0594
FAX: (612) 926-0703
email: emhome@usinternet.com

www.eM2pix.com

INFOWORLD MAGAZINE

ORACLE MAGAZINE

ERIC MUELLER
[612] 926.0594

INFOWORLD MAGAZINE

BYTE MAGAZINE

Donald Mulligan
418 Central Park West, Suite 81
New York, New York 10025
(212) 666-6079 Studio/FAX

Illustration and Design Studio.
Portfolio or Faxfolio on request.
See Showcase 12-21 for other samples.

Clients include:
T.V. Guide, Chocolatier, Diversion,
Wall Street Journal, Chase, Federal
Express, Mount Sinai, Greek &
Spanish Tourist Associations.

DONALD MULLIGAN
GRAPHIC ARTS
ILLUSTRATION & DESIGN

MOSAIC

GREECE / Life Today

ITALY / Chocolatier

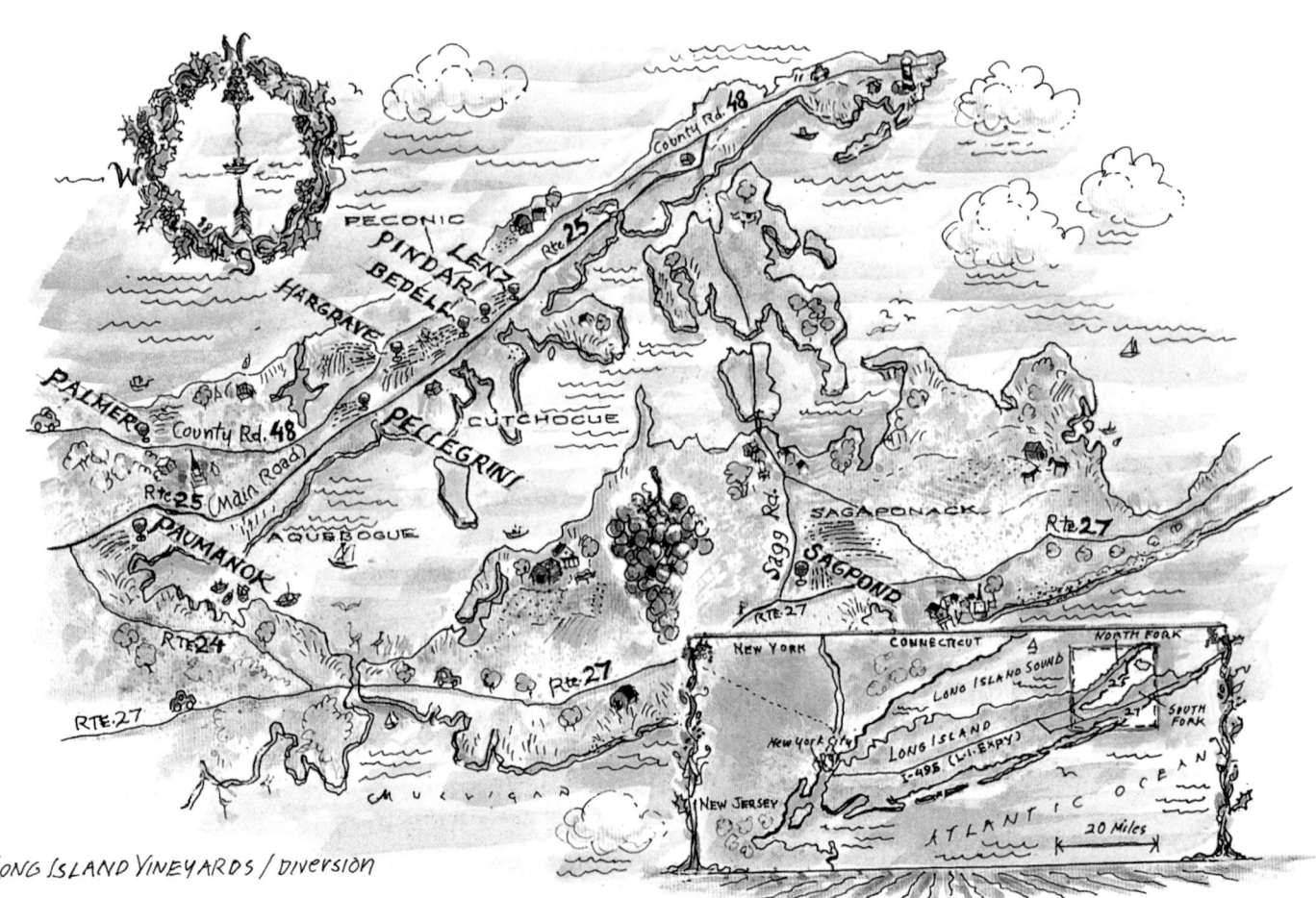

LONG ISLAND VINEYARDS / DIVERSION

1358

Scott Nelson & Son
22 Rayburn Drive
Millbury, Massachusetts 01527
(508) 865-5045 Phone/FAX
email: NelsonandSon@Juno.com

Please see American Showcase #21
for additional samples.

Britannia - Image Arts - (over easy)
DaySpring
Paramount
Gibson
Current
American Greetings

Cartoonist / Illustrator
508-865-5045
Scott Nelson & Son
22 rayburn dr.
millbury, ma 01527

Kathleen Newman
12325 90th Avenue
Palos Park, Illinois 60464
(708) 361-0679
FAX (708) 361-5063

Signature member of Midwest
Watercolor Society; Midwest Pastel
Society; 1997 American Watercolor
Society Show, NYC; 1997 National
Watercolor Society Show, LA; Graphic
Artists Guild; SCBWI; Published in
"Best of Portraits," Northlight Books.

Samples of watercolor work shown in
Workbook 20

Larry Norton
918 North Craig Avenue
Altadena, California 91001
(626) 797-9837
(626) 791-1170 FAX

William O'Connor
28 Central Street
Huntington, New York 11743
(516) 271-9827 Phone/FAX
(516) 673-8350 alt.
email: wocillo@aol.com

Clients include:
Doubleday Books
Harper Prism Books
WhiteWolf Publishing
Wizards of the Coast
TSR Inc.
AEG INC. etal.

Awards and Memberships:
1996 Philcon: Best Fantasy
1996 Lunacon: Judges Choice
1995 Origins: Best of Year, Best Color
Graphic Artists Guild
Association of Science Fiction and
Fantasy Artists

" . . . William O'Connor's illustrations add a depth of imagination to the project that elevates the work from basic storytelling to work of art . . ."
—The Tome, November 1997

Patty O'Leary
30 Darlene Drive
Southborough, Massachusetts 01772
(508) 480-0720 Phone/FAX

Lori Osiecki
123 West 2nd Street
Mesa, Arizona 85201
(602) 962-5233 Phone/FAX

John Ottinger
(909) 279-7758

ILLUSTRATION

Pierre-Paul Pariseau
(514) 849-2964
FAX: (514) 843-4808

For additional artwork:
www.showcase.com
American Showcase #20, #21

Karen Patkau
(416) 260-1915
FAX: (416) 260-1916

Traditional & Digital Collage

see also:
Black Book Illustration 7, 8
Creative Source 9, 10, 12, 15, 16, 17, 18

Karen Patkau | traditional and digital collage

phone 416.260.1915 · fax 416.260.1916

Daniel Pelavin
80 Varick Street, #3B
New York, New York 10013
(212) 941-7418
FAX: (212) 431-7138
email: daniel@pelavin.com
www.pelavin.com

Lettering, typographic design,
logotypes and icons

Daniel Pelavin
30 Varick Street, #3B
New York, New York 10013
(212) 941-7418
FAX: (212) 431-7138
email: daniel@pelavin.com
www.pelavin.com

Illustration

Daniel Pelavin

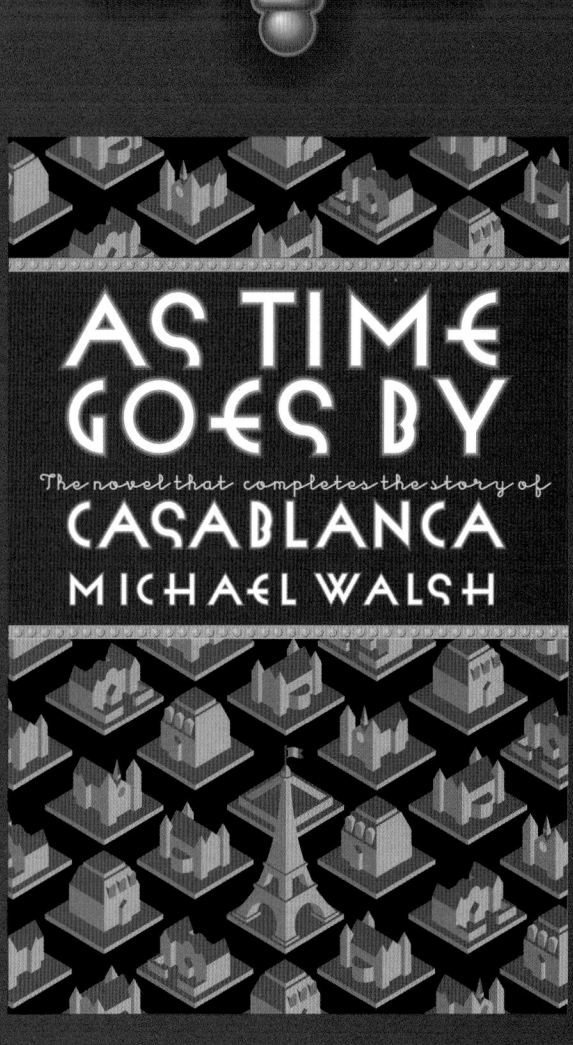

Leticia Plate
192 Fifth Avenue, #2
Brooklyn, New York 11217
(212) 807-9728

Clients:
The New York Times, The Boston
Globe, Mademoiselle, Brooklyn
Bridge, Time, Diversion, Showtime,
Ms. Magazine, Crown Publishers,
New Woman, McCann Erickson

Additional places to see more work:
Workbook 18, 19, 20, 21
Stock Illustration Source
www.theispot.com

Randy Pollak
(718) 396-0027
ranbin@aol.com
www.randomacts.com

Clients include:
IBM, The Sci-Fi Channel, The Village
Voice, Pontiac, America Online, Tri-Star,
The Unlimited Magazine, Warner
Brothers, Polygram, Newsday

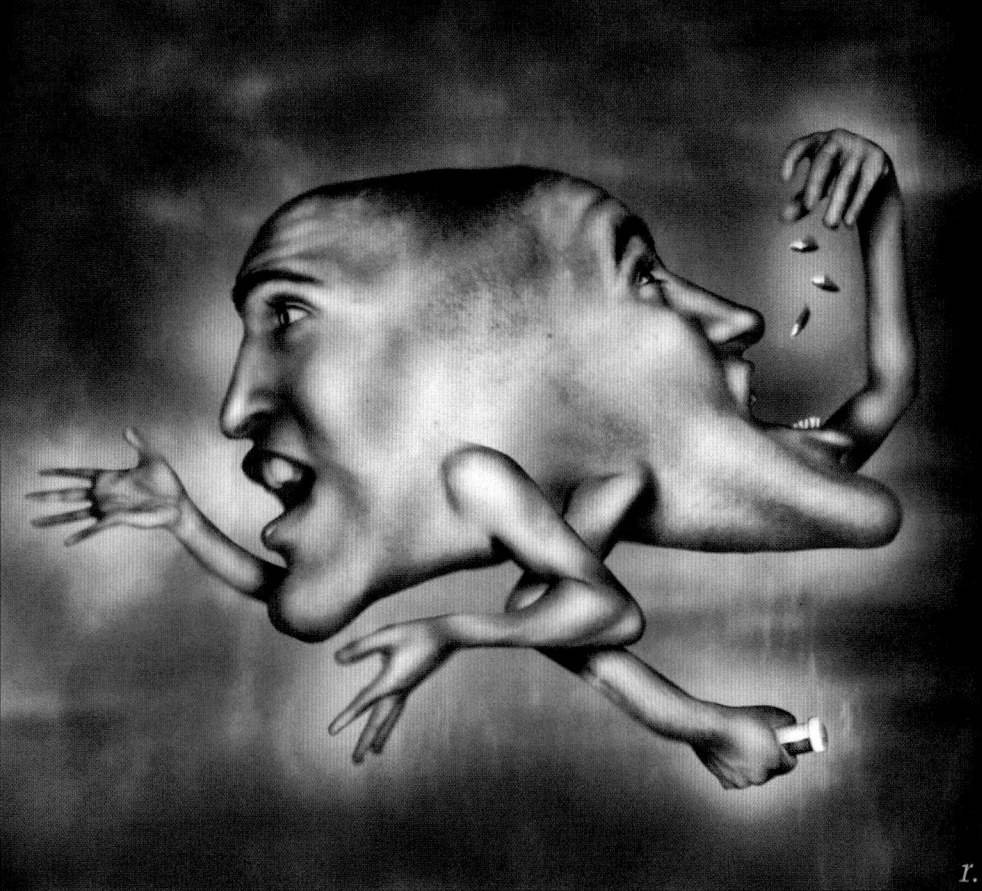

Polly Powell
2319 J Street
Sacramento, California 95816
(916) 444-1646
FAX: (916) 441-5714

Clients Include:
PepsiCo; Hal Riney & Partners
(Saturn); Walt Disney Co.; Intel;
Nickelodeon; Foote; Cone &
Belding/NY (US Postal Service);
Scholastic Books; Harcourt Brace &
Co.; MCA/Universal; Warner Records;

Klasky-Csupo, Inc.; Las Vegas Hilton;
CalPERS; Los Angeles Times
Magazine; Simon & Schuster; Better
Homes & Gardens, etc.
Also: Read my kids' book "Just
Dessert" (it won't take long) and look
for "Monster Math" coming soon!

Greg Ragland
(800) 346-1227
(435) 645-9232
FAX: (435) 645-9309
email: greg@gregragland.com
www.gregragland.com

phone
800.346.1227
browse
www.gregragland.com
for stock & portfolio

Christin Ranger
500 Aurora Avenue North, #406c
Seattle, Washington 98109
(206) 818-0879
FAX: (206) 326-5270
email: christinranger@hotmail.com

Clients include:
Sage Publishing
Lincoln Park Zoo
Union Pacific
Member: AIGA

CHRISTIN RANGER

Carole Raschella
8607 Bothwell Road
Northridge, California 91324
(818) 349-6742
FAX: (818)349-5842
email: CRaschella@aol.com

1375

Wendy Rasmussen
P.O. Box 131
950 Durham Road
Durham, Pennsylvania 18039
(610) 346-8117 Phone/FAX

Brian Raszka
(415) 673-4479
email: braszka@worldnet.att.net
www.theispot.com/artist/raszka

Clients include: Adobe Magazine, Bloomberg Magazine, Chicago Tribune, Discover Magazine, Inc. Magazine, Kiplinger's Personal Finance, Los Angeles Times, Musician, Microsoft Magazine, Novell, Sony Music, The Washington Post and many more!

Awards:
The Illustration West 35, The San Francisco Society of Illustrators, The Society of Publication Designers

For more work see:
www.showcase.com,
The Directory of Illustration 15,
The Alternative Pick '97-'99

Member: Graphic Artists Guild

BLOOMBERG MAGAZINE

Shane Reiswig
(206) 523-9579

shane @speakeasy.org
http.www.speakeasy.org/~shane

Clients include; America West Airlines, Fly Rod and Reel Magazine, Sea Kayaker Magazine, Sail Mahazine, Crazy Shirts/Mainland Co., Times Mirror Group, High Range Graphics, Cune Publishing, Review and Herald Publishing, Presbyterians Today, Ragged Mountain Press, McGraw Hill International Marine and Simon & Schuster.Member of Society of Chidrens Book Writers and Illustrators and The Graphic Artists Guild.

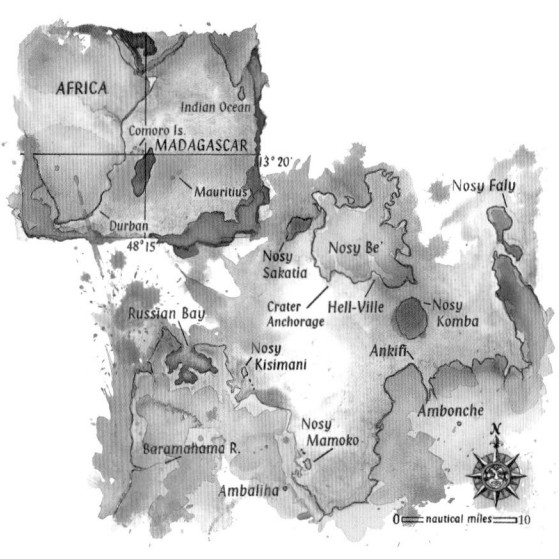

Dorothy Remington
632 Commercial Street
San Francisco, California 94111
(415) 397-4668
FAX: (415) 392-8354
email: akarem@aol.com

Tom Richmond
3421 East Burnsville Parkway
Burnsville, Minnesota 55337
(612) 882-9133 Phone/FAX
email: tom@richmondillus.com
www.richmondillus.com

Specializing in caricature, cartoons
and humorous illustration in many
mediums including airbrush,
watercolor, pen and ink and digital.

Winner 1998 "Caricaturist of the
Year" from National Caricaturist
Network. Clients include the
Minnesota Twins, MSP Publications,
Rolaids, S.F. Giants, Palladium
Interactive, Detour Magazine and others.

Ic Roberts

057 Bennett Avenue
Long Beach, California 90804
562) 433-3599
FAX: (562) 433-4599
email: droberts@ix.netcom.com
www.monsterzero.com

Clients include:
Burger King, E! Entertainment
Network, Kellogg's, School Marketing
Partners, ShowBiz Pizza Time, Giant
Apparel, Gotcha Sportswear

Bob Robinson
3704 Roxbury Lane
Plano, Texas 75025
(972) 208-9215 Phone/FAX

Bob Robinson Digital Illustration
(972) 208-9215

smael Roldan
90 Greenwich Street, #5E
New York, New York 10014
212) 691-5841 Phone/FAX

Time, Sports Illustrated, The
Washington Post, The Wall Street
Journal, Adweek, Individual Investor,
Golf Digest, Cowles Business Media,
The American Spectator, The New
York Post, The American Enterprise,

Computer World, Forbes, Artista
Records, Warner Music International,
The Baltimore Sun, The Washington
Times, U.S. News and World Report,
Harper-Collins

Member Graphic Artists Guild.
More of my work may be seen in the
Directory of Illustration #12, #14, and
American Showcase #19, #20, #21

Bill Ross
602 Davidson Road
Nashville, Tennessee 37205
(615) 352-3729
FAX: (615) 356-1122

Joseph Ruf
36 Franklin Avenue
Deer Park, New York 11729
(516) 586-5633

Animal and Nature Illustrations
Prehistoric or Current

Michael Sabanosh
433 West 34th Street, #18B
New York, New York 10001
(212) 947-8161

THE
ALLURE
OF
HOLLYWOOD

Michael Sabanosh
433 West 34th Street, #18B
New York, New York 10001
(212) 947-8161

MICHAEL
SABANOSH

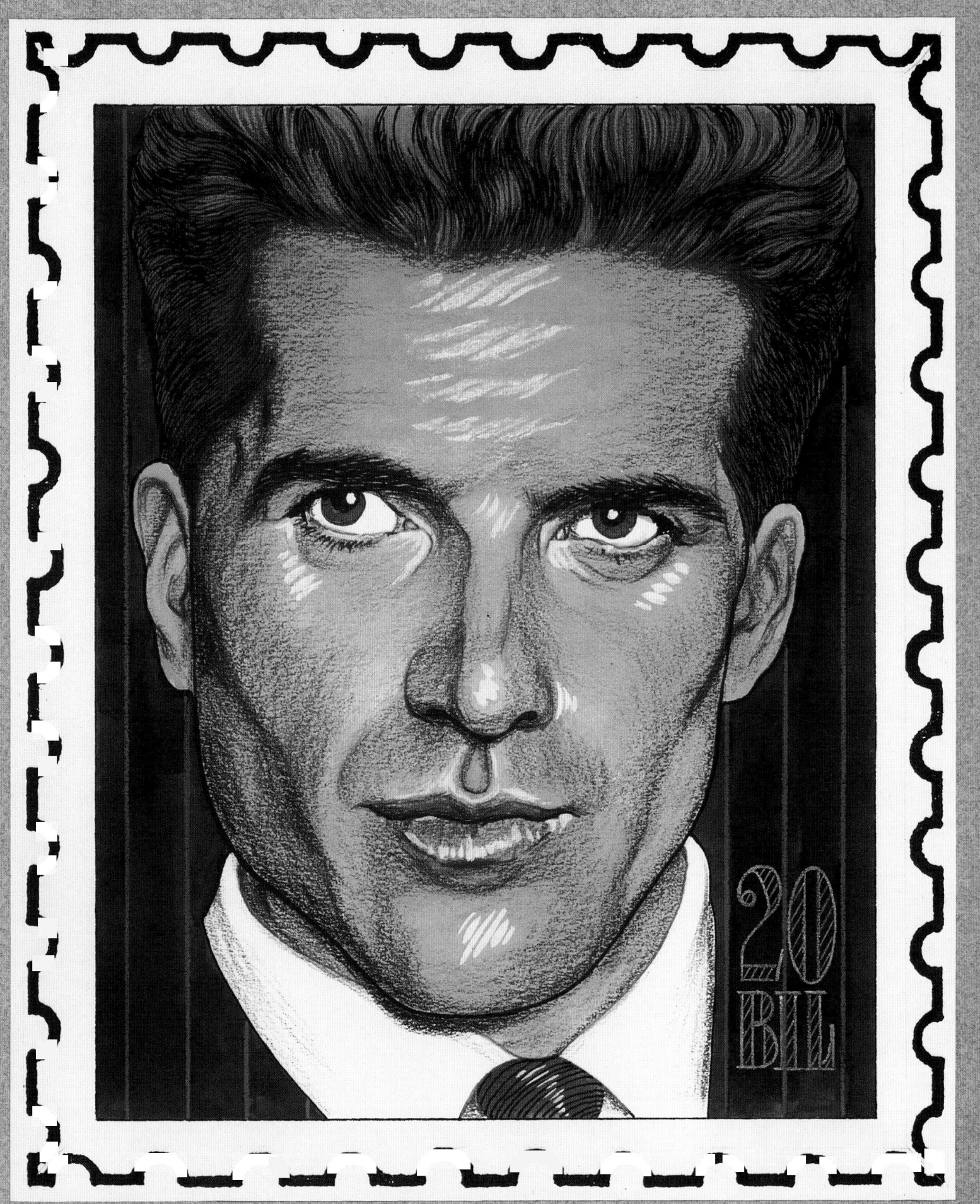

Chelsea Sammel
482 South Street
Hollister, California 95023
(831) 636-7443 Phone/FAX

Chelsea Sammel

831 - 636 - 7443

Steve Sanford
41 Union Square West
Suite 615
New York, New York 10003
(212) 243-6119
FAX: (212) 924-3074

Bob Scott
4108 Forest Hill Avenue
Richmond, Virginia 23225
(804) 232-1627
FAX: (804) 233-7737
email: bscott5@aol.com

Additional work can be seen in
American Showcase Volumes 10-21
Directory of Illustration #13
And on the world wide web at:
http://members.aol.com/bscott5
now featuring digital samples and the
Small Gems stock art file.

HTTP://MEMBERS.AOL.COM/BSCOTT5

Joseph Sellars
2423 West 22nd Street
Minneapolis, Minnesota 55405
(612) 377-8766
FAX: (612) 377-5243

Bruce Sharp
15808 SE 47th Street
Bellevue, Washington 98006
(425) 373-4752

Clients:
The Atlantic Monthly, Disney, Geo
Magazine, Henry Holt & Co., The
Miami Herald, Microsoft, Omni
Magazine, Outside Magazine,
Random House, The Seattle Times,
Sierra On-Line, Simon & Schuster,

The Travelers Insurance, The
Washington Post Magazine, The
Washington Post

Sharp Designs
Paul Sharp
Alice Sharp
(800) 999-4417
(520) 282-7696
FAX: (520) 204-6442
email: sharp@kachina.net

Clients include:
Addison Wesley, Western Publishing,
Publications Intl. Ltd., Creative
Expressions, Children's Press, Curtis
Publishing, Good Times Publishing/
Entertainment, Rose Art

Additional illustrations can be seen in
Directory of Illustration 13, 14, and 15
and on the world wide web at:
www.di14.com and
www.di15.com and
www.showcase.com

SHARP DESIGNS™
DESIGNS THAT POP!

Products that POP!

Packaging that POPS!

Jeff Shelly
2330 San Marco Drive
Los Angeles, California 90068
(800) 314-3244
(323) 460-4604
FAX: (323) 464-6630
email: jlshelly@aol.com

For additional work, see
American Showcase Vol.'s 18, 19,
20, & 21
Blackbook Illustration 96, 97, 98, & 99
www.theispot.com/artist/shelly
www.showcase.com

Client List:
McDonalds, Sun-Rype, Microsoft,
Columbia House, AT&T, Gibson
Greetings, The Walt Disney Co., Time
Warner, The Virginia State Lottery,
Merck, Scholastic, America On Line,

North Shore Bank, Children's
Television Workshop, Sports Illustrated
For Kids, Publishers Weekly, Family PC
Dog Fancy

Dan Sipple
(714) 848-7216
FAX: (714) 848-2416

Clients include:
NobleWorks, Prudent Publishing, Recycled Paper Greetings, Road & Track and more!

Member Graphic Artists Guild

Additional work can be seen in California Image 98 and at my web site:
http://members.aol.com/dansipple

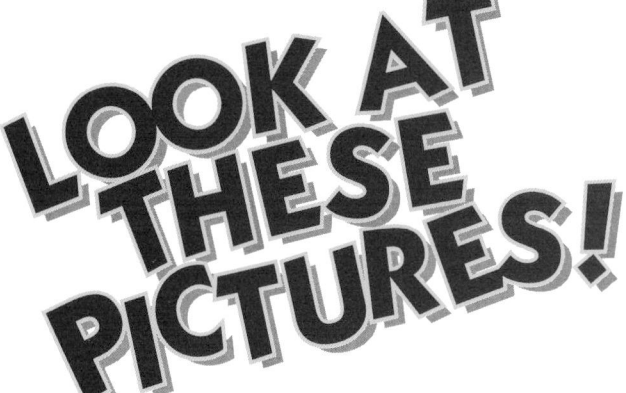

Steve Skelton
3205 5th Street
Boulder, Colorado 80304
(303) 546-0117
FAX: (303) 546-0112

Elwood H. Smith
2 Locust Grove Road
Rhinebeck, New York 12572

Represented by:
Maggie Pickard
(914) 876-2358
FAX: (914) 876-5931
email: elwood@pojonews.infi.net

web sites:
www.elwoodsmith.com
www.theispot.com/artist/esmith
www.showcase.com

Jackie Snider
(705) 924-1487

JACKIE SNIDER
(705) 924-1487

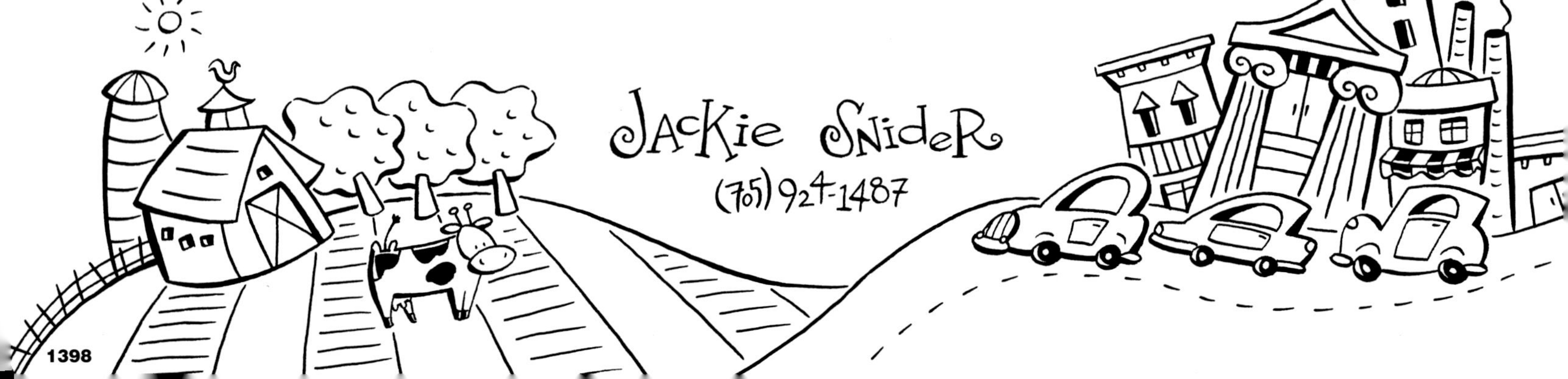

Stephen J. Sotnick
20 W. Santa Fe Avenue
Placentia, California 92870
(714) 447-9050 Home
(714) 993-9099 Work
FAX: (714) 993-9098

John P. Ringo, The Final Hours

Nellie Cashman/Frontier Angel

Moonlight Press Studio
Chris Spollen
362 Cromwell Avenue
Ocean Breeze, New York 10305-2304
(718) 979-9695
FAX: (718) 979-8919
email: CJSpollen@aol.com

Website: http: www.inch.com/~cspollen/
Illustration & Design
Over 1200 Quality Stock Cuts
Contained in our three Catalogs
All Catalogs are available free
Sample Kit on Request

Studio by the Ocean
Reduce, Reuse, Recycle

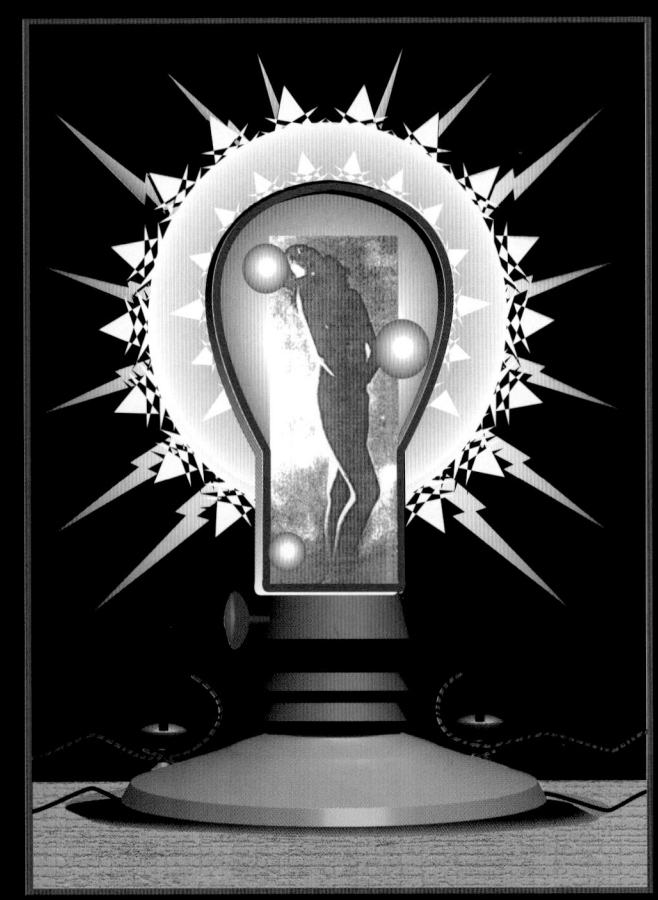

Moonlight Press Studio
Chris Spollen
362 Cromwell Avenue
Ocean Breeze, New York 10305-2304
(718) 979-9695
FAX: (718) 979-8919
email: CJSpollen@aol.com

Website: http: www.inch.com/~cspollen/
Illustration & Design
Over 1200 Quality Stock Cuts
Contained in our three Catalogs
All Catalogs are available free
Sample Kit on Request

Studio by the Ocean
Reduce, Reuse, Recycle

Entrepreneur Mag

Internet Connect

Business Trends

Yankee Magazine

AT&T

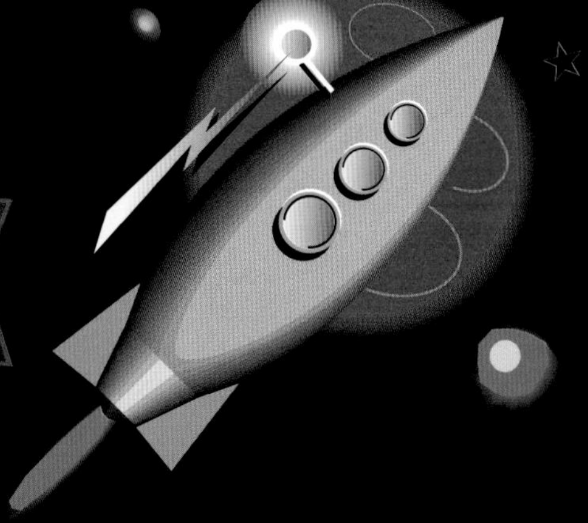

Datamation Magazine

Gee Bee

Anheuser Busch

Software Productivity Group

showcase.com

illustrators | designers | digital artists | interactive talent | photographers

Sally Springer
1510 North Thumb Point Drive
Fort Pierce, Florida 34949
(561) 467-0095

Barbara Spurll
(416) 594-6594
FAX: (416) 601-1010

Royal Trust *MoneyGuide*

In-Flight Magazine

Wildlife Conservation Magazine

Barbara Spurll
(416) 594-6594
FAX: (416) 601-1010

For more samples see:
Creative Illustration (Black Book) '95,
'96, '97
American Showcase 19, 20 & 21 and
American Showcase CD Vol. 20

Christie Brown & Co.

Paul Stoddard
524 Main Street
Stoneham, Massachusetts 02180
(781) 438-0266 Studio/FAX
email: PStodd8434@aol.com

Clients include:
Better Homes & Gardens
Business Travel News
Guidepost for Teens
Inc. Magazine
Organic Gardening
PC Magazine

Software Magazine
Windows NT Magazine
Your Health & Fitness

For additional work see:
American Showcase #20
Member of The Graphic Artists Guild

Walter Stuart
(619) 455-5573
FAX: (619) 455-5519

Salzman International
(212) 997-0115 New York
(415) 285-8267 San Francisco
FAX: (415) 285-8268

Clients:
Jurassic Park, Dakin, Microsoft,
Parker Brothers, Smithsonian

Magazines: National Geographic
World, Omni, Discover, Disney

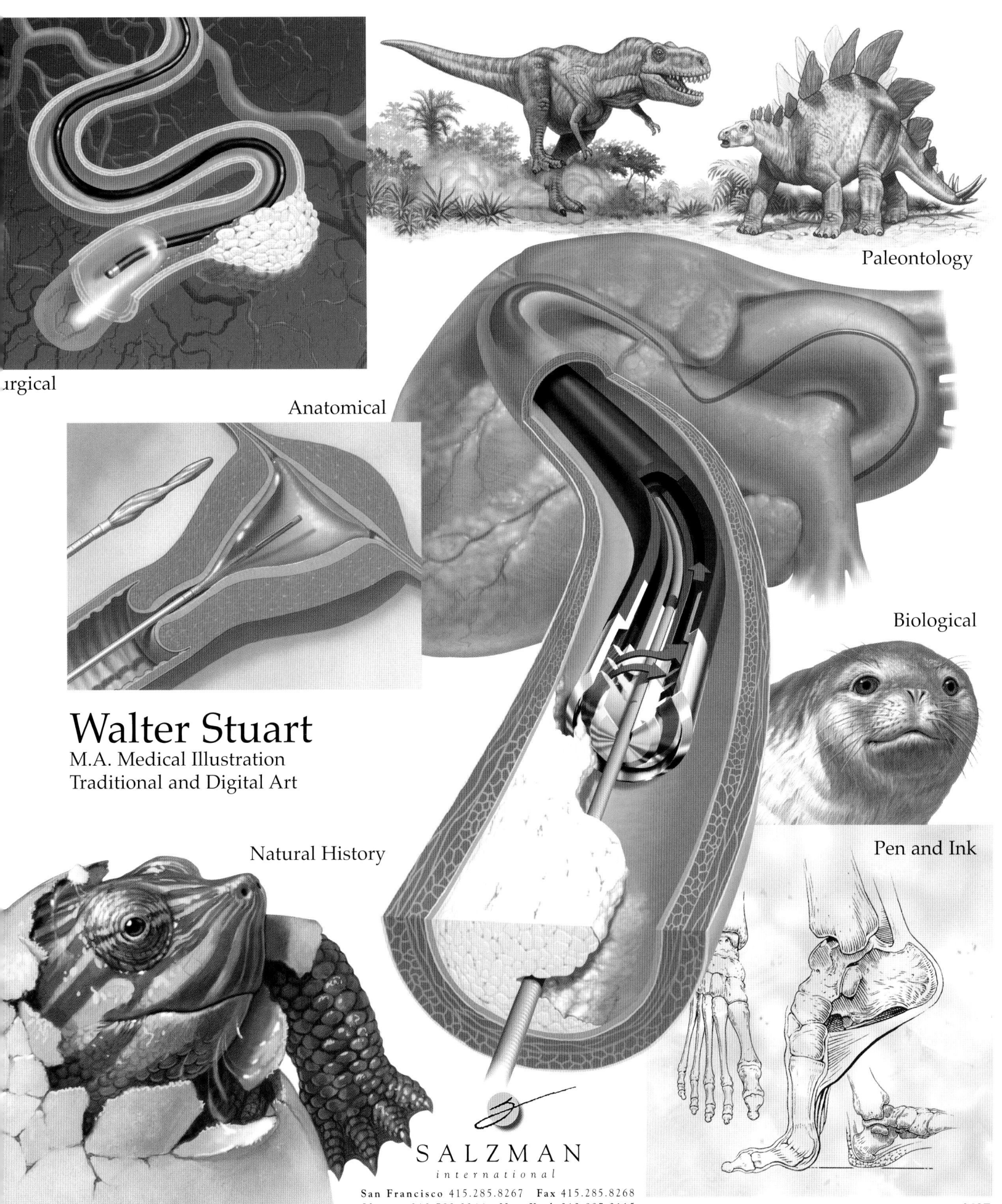

Surgical

Paleontology

Anatomical

Biological

Walter Stuart
M.A. Medical Illustration
Traditional and Digital Art

Natural History

Pen and Ink

SALZMAN
international
San Francisco 415.285.8267   Fax 415.285.8268
Chicago 312.782.2244   New York 212.997.0115

Linda Sturm
1763 Dogwood Drive
Yorktown Heights, New York 10598
(914) 245-7981
FAX: (914) 245-0297
lswm@aol.com

Computer generated illustration
Clients include publishing, ad agencies
and graphic design firms: advertising
and editorial clients.

For additional work, refer to the
Directory of Illustration - Volumes #14
and #15

John Sundwall
Eye Catcher Ink
509 Fulton Street
Waverly, New York 14892
(607) 565-3375

Scott Swales
419 Main Street
Phoenix, New York 13135
(315) 695-4519

Laura Tarrish
2450 SW Sherwood Drive
Portland, Oregon 97201
(503) 224-8686

Collage Illustration
See also Showcase 13, 17, 18, 19,
20, 21

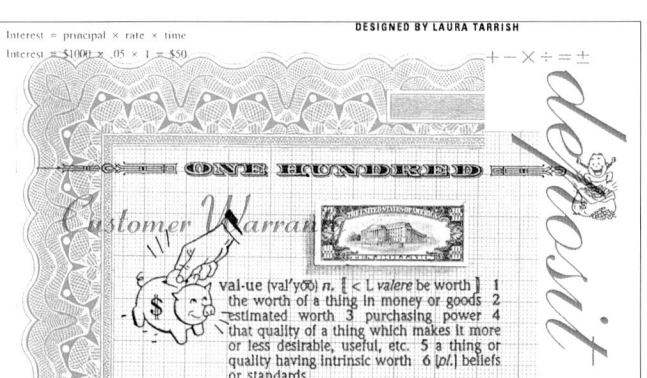

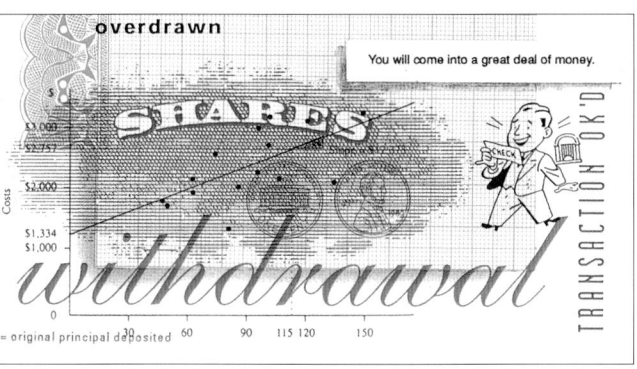

CHECKBOOK COVER / FRONT & BACK

Emily Thompson
433 West 43rd Street, #3E
New York, New York 10036
(212) 245-2543 Phone/FAX

American Health, American Cheerleader, Aspire Magazine, Assets International, Bridal Guide, Christian Parenting, Fit Magazine, Girls Life, Hallmark, National Gardening, NJ Bride, Newsday, New York Times, Oscar Mayer, Oxford Health Plans, Roadsmart, Scholastic, Selling Power, Sesame Street Parents

Look for other examples of my work in Showcase 19 and 21, RSVP 18 thru 23 and Book Production Buyers Guide 1998. Call for a free pack of samples.

Debbie Tilley
(760) 432-6282
FAX: (760) 738-8019

Salzman International
(212) 997- 0115
(415) 285-8267
FAX: (415) 285-8268

GREAT MOTHERS IN HISTORY

MOTHER EARTH

QUEEN MOTHER

MOTHER THERESA

WHISTLER'S MOTHER

MOTHER NATURE

MOTHER OF INVENTION

SALZMAN
international
San Francisco 415.285.8267 Fax 415.285.8268 Chicago 312.782.2244 New York 212.997.0115

1413

Mike Tofanelli
2424 Hurley Way, #24
Sacramento, California 95825
(916) 927-4809 Phone/FAX

For additional work see:
Black Book Illustration '96, '97
American Showcase 20, 21

Top: Way Out West. Sacramento
Public Library Kids' Reading Club.

Bottom L to R: One Norse Town,
Hot-Tempered Farmers. Book covers
for Kinetic City Super Crew series,
McGraw-Hill, client.

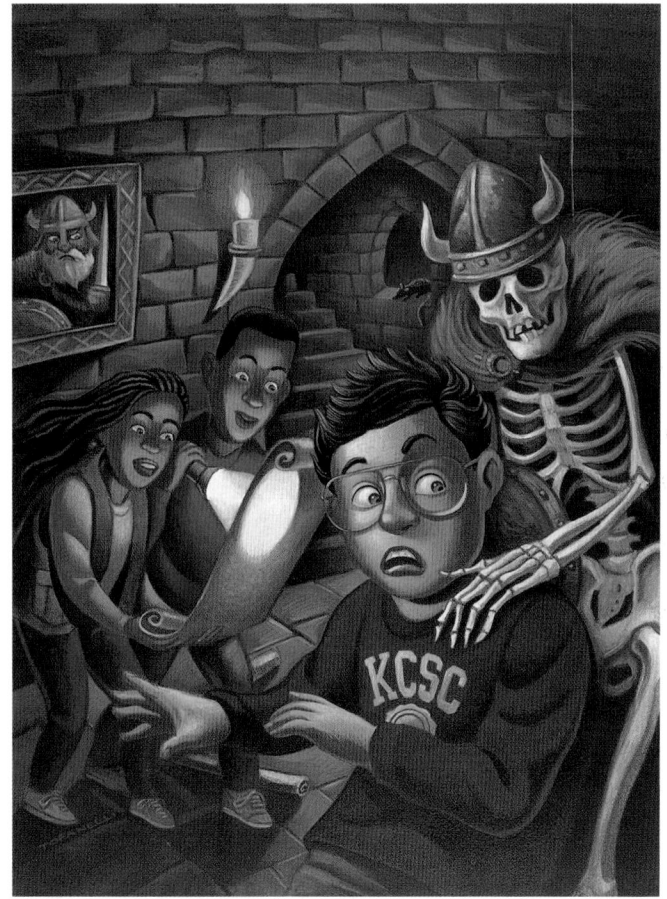

Ket Tom-Conway
607 Maple Street
Aptos, California 95003
(831) 684-2378 Phone/FAX

Clients:
The Boston Globe, Changing Times
Magazine, The Cousteau Society,
Cross & Associates, Disney Adventures,
Harrowsmith Magazine, Outside
Magazine, Physician's Weekly, Post
Graduate Medicine, Simpson Papers,
Seymour Duncan Guitars and Pickups,
Scholastic Magazine, Security Pacific
Bank, Toy & Hobbie World, Wadsworth
Publishing.
Children's Book:
The Young Explorer's Guide to
Undersea Life

Gary Townswick
(402) 593-7115

Gary Townswick Design
(402) 593 - 7115

John Trinh
9221 East Longden Avenue
Temple City, California 91780
(626) 287-5989
(877) 268-1298

John Trinh
877-268-1298

Norman Schwarzkopf (Acrylics)

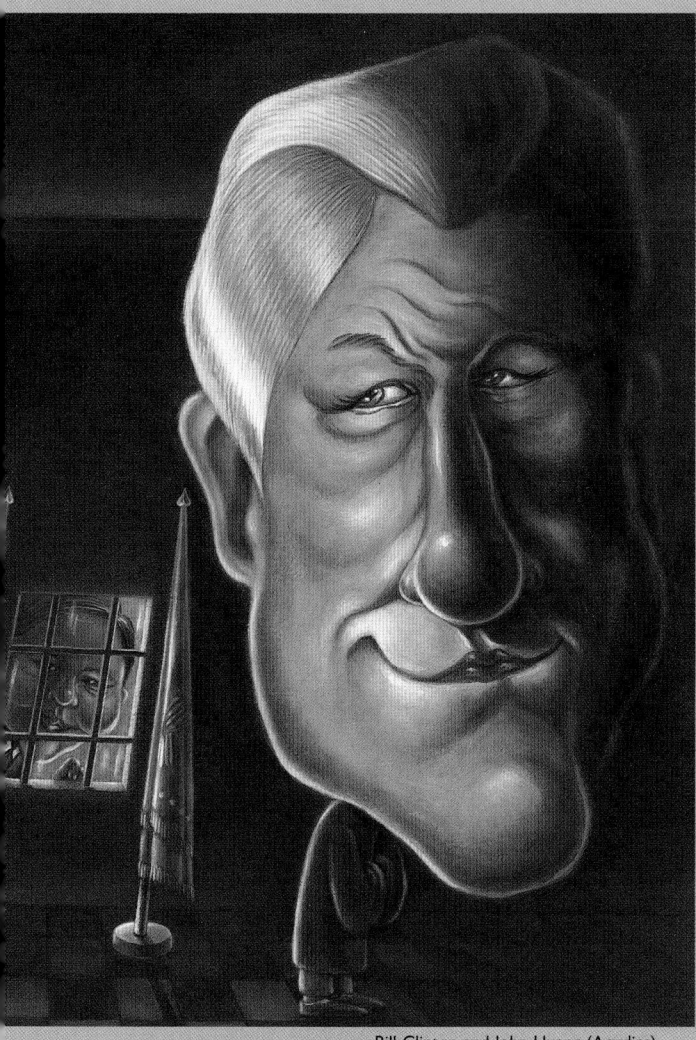

Bill Clinton and John Huang (Acrylics)

Pat Buchanan (Gouache)

Santiago Uceda
(714) 754-0651
FAX: (714) 545-7816

David Veal
(303) 756-2527
email: dvealart@aol.com
www.showcase.com

Advertising, Corporate, Editorial,
Publishing, Storyboard

THE GREAT BALLOON RACE / MIXED MEDIA

BUILDING A DATABASE (GETTING TO KNOW YOU)

ACK AND THE BEANSTALK: THE CORPORATE WORLD / MIXED MEDIA

BATHING THE DOG / MIXED MEDIA

Alexander Verbitsky
507 West 111 Street, Apt. 4
New York, New York 10025
(212) 749-9707
email: averbitsky@aol.com

Clients include:
Bantam Doubleday Dell, ABC Inc.,
McGraw-Hill Companies, Latina
Magazine, General Foods, Cahners
Business Information, Revlon, Sharp,
Sony, Pfizer, Reed Elsevier Inc.,
American College of Cardiology,

Chilton Publishing, University of
California, Carter/Cosgrove & Co.,
Plenum Publishing, Peregrine Theatre
Company, Merchandising Workshop
Inc., Sterling Winthrop, Worldvision
Home Video Inc.

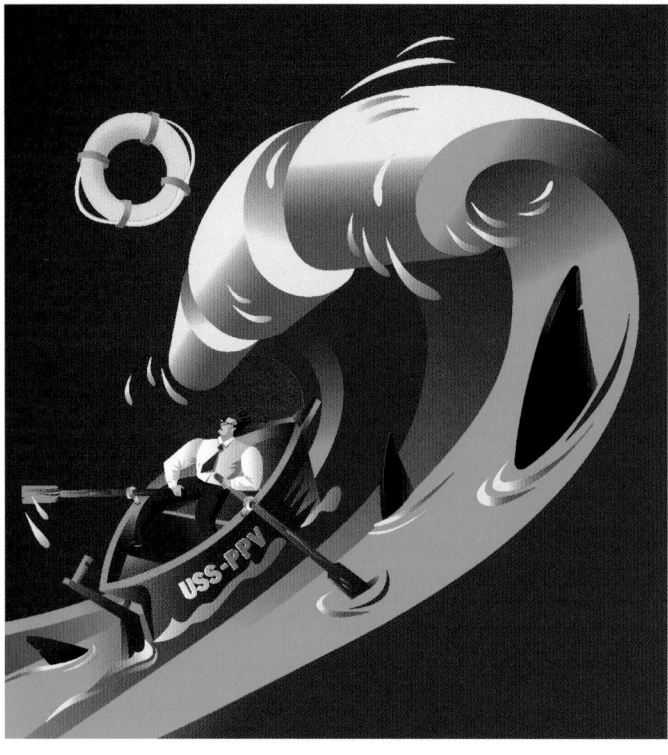

COMPUTER
ILLUSTRATIONS

Mark E. Verna
66 Martinot Avenue
Rochester, New York 14609
(716) 288-5762 Phone/FAX

Tina Vey
11 East 7th Street, #5W
New York, New York 10003
(212) 460-9697 Phone/FAX

Visionary Studios
417 West Patti Page Boulevard
Claremore, Oklahoma 74017
(918) 343-9865 Phone/FAX

Scott Youtsey

Warner Brothers
WGN -TV
Chicago White Sox
Igloo
American Demographics Magazine
Marketing Tools Magazine
Kellogg's

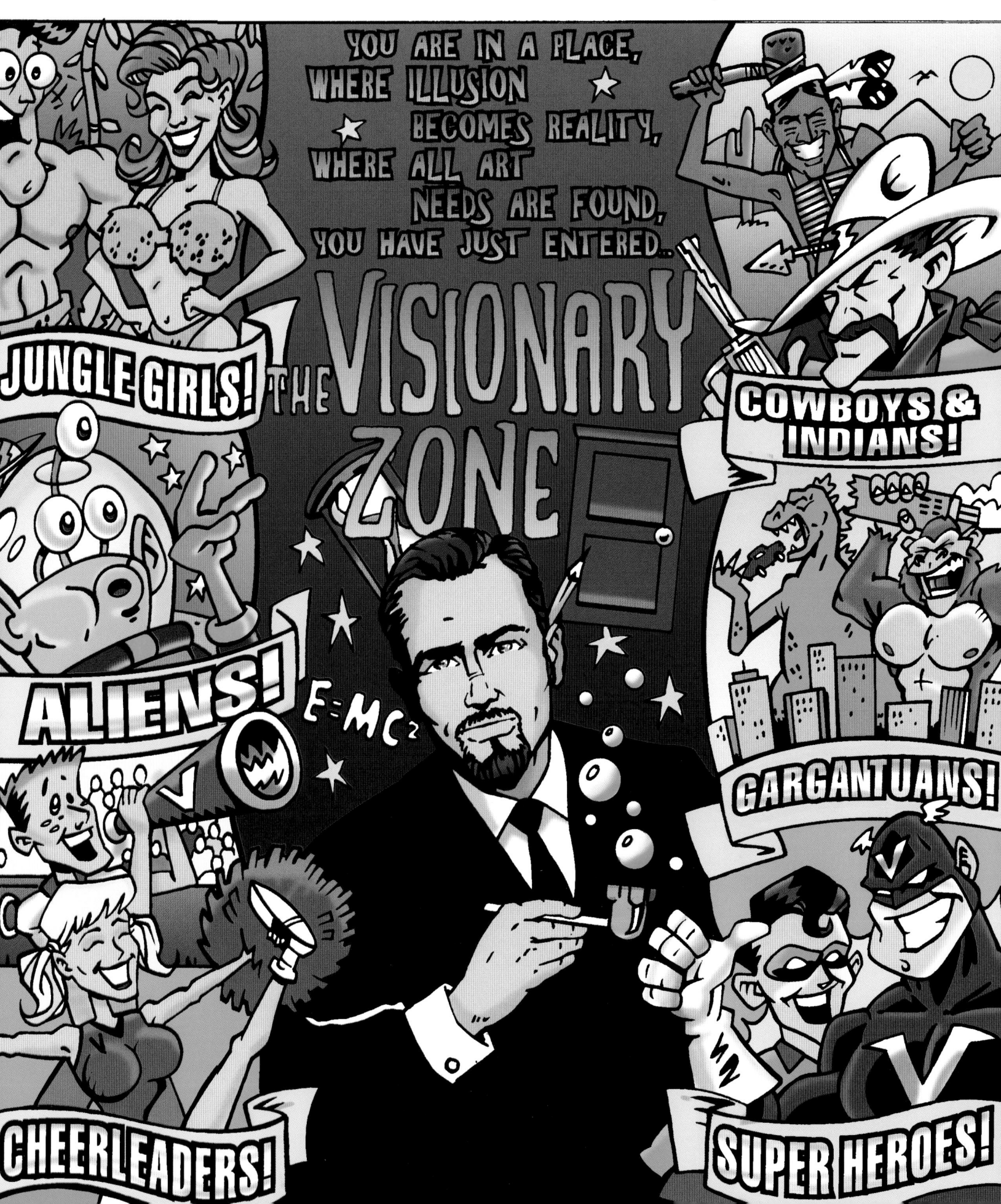

Paul Vismara
(888) VISMARA
(888) (847-6272)

Carol Wagner
2015 North Beachwood Drive
Los Angeles, California 90068
(323) 461-6446
FAX (323) 463-4515
email: YudduhsLA@aol.com

Who's Winning?

Zooooooom!

Debra Wainwright
95 Carriage House Lane
Wrentham, Massachusetts 02093
(508) 384-2759 Phone/FAX
email: DebraWai@aol.com

Paul S. Weiner
Illustrator
4 Cypress Street, #2
Brookline, Massachusetts 02445
(617) 738-0446 Phone/FAX

pweiner@world.std.com
world.std.com/~pweiner/

Patrick J. Welsh
(609) 232-3130
FAX: (609) 232-6050
email: welshdesign@p3.net
Online Samples:
www.p3.net/~welshdesign

Whim Whams Illustration Studio
3314 Oberon Street
Kensington, Maryland 20895
(301) 933-4912
FAX: (301) 933-4923
www.whimwhams.com

Bryan Wiggins
26 High View Road
Cape Elizabeth, Maine 04107
(207) 799-2918
FAX: (207) 767-7131
website: home.maine.rr.com/wiggins

Mac portfolio slideshow emailed upon request.

WIGGINS ILLUSTRATION
STRONG ART BUILT TO LAST

DeLorme Mapping

MacWorld

MacWorld

Gopher Hill
Communications

Atlantic Rancher
Clothing

The Healing Wheel

BRADLEY WILLIAMS

862 HOLROYD DRIVE, OGDEN, UTAH 84403 • **(801) 479 8055**

Kasia M. Wilusz
Moon Ranch
249 Southeast Road
New Hartford, Connecticut 06057
(860) 693-4062

Clients include:
Fancy Publications, Chemical
Engineering, The Fitness Centre For
Women and other around town odd
ball jobs.
Whimsy is our specialty, all deadlines
met with jubilation.

ILLUSTRATIONS
THAT FLY

TASTES GREAT!

POLITICALLY CORRECT?

WILL WORK FOR PEANUTS & BANANAS

Elizabeth Wolf
3303 North Mountain Lane
Boise, Idaho 83702
(208) 387-0031
FAX: (208) 387-0119
email: LizWolf13@aol.com

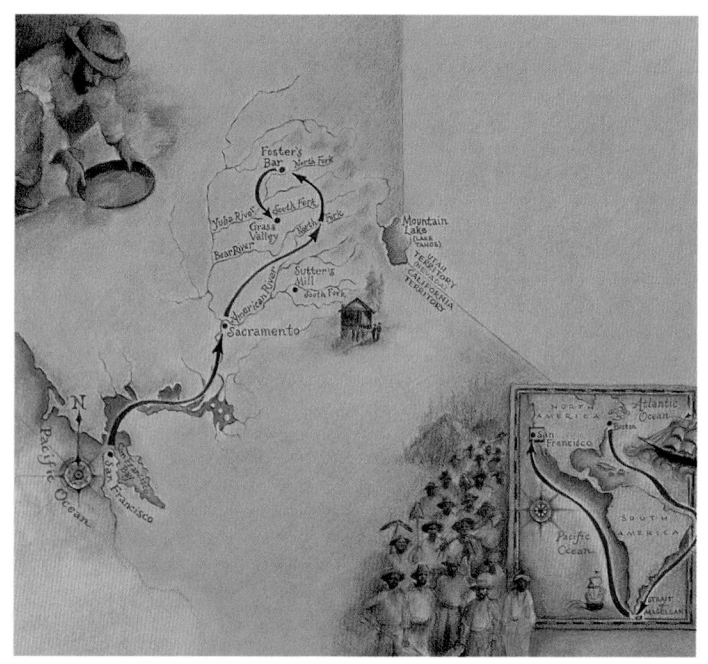

Karen Woo
60 Lawton Street
Brookline, Massachusetts 02445
(617) 277-8598 Phone/FAX
karenwoo@thecia.net

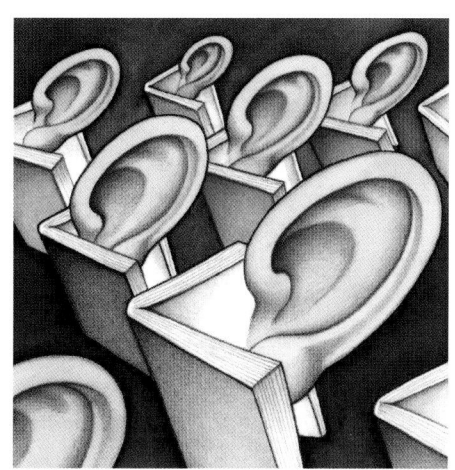

Aqua Images
Jon Q. Wright
P.O. Box 290055
Minneapolis, Minnesota 55429
(888) 658-5211
email: aquaimages@aol.com

Specializing in aquatic illustrations of freshwater and saltwater species.

A variety of color, b/w, and computer illustration styles are available.

Promotional brochure and/or portfolio available upon request.

AQUA
IMAGES

NORTH AMERICAN
T R O U T

Bill Yermal
62 Carey Road
Succasunna, New Jersey 07876
(973) 927-8909
(973) 927-6744

In addition to digital illustration for print
I also deal in content for multimedia
(web, CD-Rom) as well as animation.

BILL YERMAL

PN 973·927·8909

FX 973·927·6744

62 CAREY RD.

SUCCASUNNA NJ 07876

Ron Young
7 Gifford Lane
Medusa, New York 12120
(518) 239-6551
FAX: (518) 239-4935

Clients include:
American Publishing
CBS Publications
Golf Magazine
Jack & Jill Magazine
McGraw Hill Publications

Parents Magazine
Prevention Magazine
Putnam Publishing
Scholastic Books
Simon & Schuster
The Bronx Zoo

Stefanie Young
2427 Bay Street
San Francisco. California 94123
(415) 776-1218 Phone/FAX

On Badu Time / Pastel

The Untouchable / Mixed Media

showcase.com

illustrators | designers | digital artists | interactive talent | photographers

DESIGN & LETTERING

BRANDED APPAREL

BRANDED APPAREL

BRANDED APPAREL

TAYLOR GUITARS / POINT OF PURCHASE

FUSION

AGASSI ENTERPRISES

MULTI-DISCIPLINARY ART CENTER

EAR THERMOMETER

NIKE / DEION SANDERS CROSS-TRAINING SHOE

NIKE

CD-ROM PUBLISHER

SPECIALTY FISHING LURES

BOYDS COFFEE

HARCOURT BRACE & CO.

SPECIALTY BRANDS, INC.

SPARROW RECORDS / PACKAGING

BOYDS COFFEE / PACKAGING

AGASSI ENTERPRISES / POINT-OF-PURCHASE

QUALCOMM / PACKAGING

1443

GRAPHICS

Voice/Fax: (425) 488-2573

email: arendt@eskimo.com

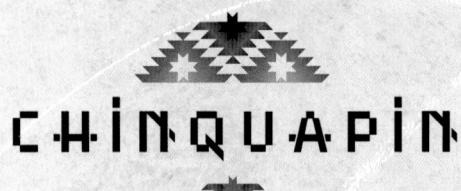

CHINQUAPIN

CORNERSTONE

Bachanalia

NANCY STENTZ
LETTERFORMS

Represented
by Jorgensen / Barrett /
fax 206.632.2024
206.634.1880
in Seattle

Encore Media Group

SEATTLE CHOCOLATES

Souriga-Nacional,

the finest of grapes

for Porto

DOTY

Creative solutions
that work.

LA CELLULAR WEBSITE

VICTORIA'S SECRET WEBSITE - JAPAN

TECHNICOLOR
THE GREATEST NAME IN COLOR

Kodak
Image Magic

---

*tsuchiya*sloneker
COMMUNICATIONS

Vision inspired, Strategy driven, Problem solvers.
Advertising design from concept to completion for print and web.

www.tscom.com   [415] 986 5365
e-mail: mail@tscom.com

VERTISING   PROMOTION   EDITORIAL   PACKAGING   IDENTITY   TV   FILM

PEOPLE MAGAZINE

VERS / CORNERSTONE DESIGN ASSOCIATES, INC.

Flirting with spring

BLOOMINGDALE'S

PROCTER & GAMBLE / GREY

Vibrant Reds

L'OREAL COSMETICS

follow the sun

AMERICAN HOMESTYLE MAGAZINE

PEPSI COLA / THOMPSON & COMPANY

B.Dalton
BOOKSELLER

B. DALTON BOOKS / MICHAEL PETERS DESIGN, INC.

UPS / BRIERLEY & PARTNERS

BATMAN™

DC COMICS

AT&T / BRONNER, SLOSBERG, HUMPHREY

OZARKA / CORNERSTONE DESIGN ASSOCIATES, INC.

THE *Three* SOPRANOS

ATLANTIC RECORDS

ANTHONY BLOCH
212-927-6856
FAX 928-4792
Work done by hand or on the mac.

REDBOOK MAGAZINE

1447

LAURA KAY DESIGN

Phone 800 497-1752
http://opendoor.com/laurakaydesign/
email: laurakaydesign@opendoor.com

Logos, Trademarks, Icons
Corporate Identity Packages
37 international & national design awards

MAIL ORDER 500

PSYCHO-CIRCUS

Scandal

ABM

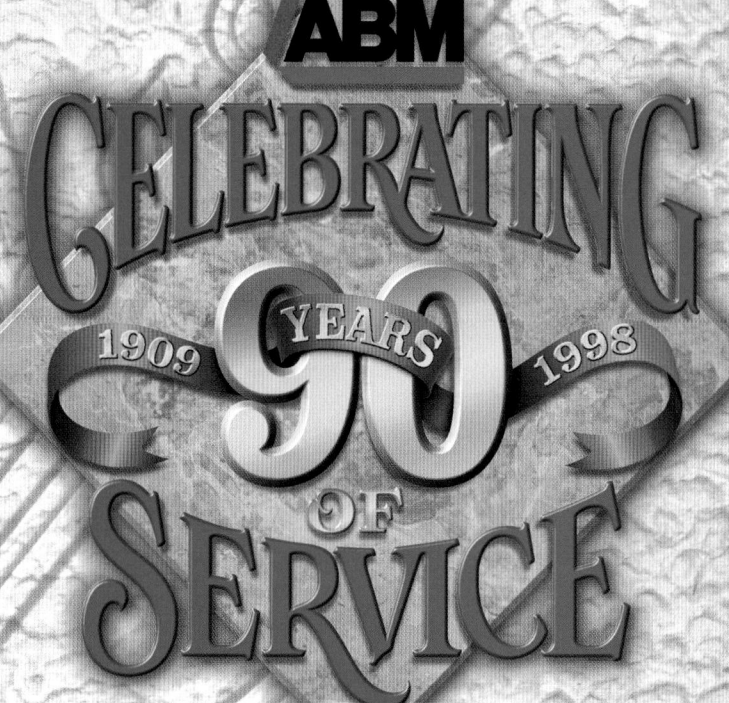

CELEBRATING 90 YEARS OF SERVICE

1909 1998

CHAIN OF COMMAND

GRAND SLAM

USL

DEAL

Start the New Year Right

TYPOGRAPHIC DESIGN

Lebbad

BY MAC OR BY HAND

JAMES A. LEBBAD

212•645•5260   609•737•3458

Holly Dickens Design, Inc.   312.280.0777   Fax 312.280.1725   e-mail HolDickens@aol.com

Pizzazz!

ANDERSON FLOORING

I would become fluent in French.

FIDELITY INVESTMENTS

GUINNESS

Better than Milk?

BRISTOL MEYERS

PLANTERS
Relax. Go Nuts.

NABISCO

WILD THINGS

A JOHN McNAUGHTON FILM

PACE. THE REAL DEAL.

CAMPBELL SOUP COMPANY

KRAFT FOODS

Imagine yourself in a Mercury

MERCURY

DENIM BLUES

DENIM BLUES RETAIL

BEST BUY
Now that's a great idea!

BEST BUY

intel inside

INTEL

Digital Output Available

Sample No. 507

The Quick Brown Fox jumps over the lazy dog The Quick Brown Fox

Sample No. 512

The Quick Brown

Sample No. 513

The Quick Brown

Sample No. 508

The Quick Brown Fox jumps over the lazy dog. The Q

Sample No. 514

The Quick Bro

Sample No. 509

The Quick Brown Fox jumped over the lazy dog. The

Sample No. 515

The Quick

Sample No. 510

The Quick Brown Fox JUMPS Over

Sample No. 511

THE QUICK BROWN FOX

CHARACTERS IN FONT
*

ABCDEFGHIJK
LMNOPQRST
UVWXYZ&
abcdefghijklm
nopqrstuvwxyz
',;:-!?()""
$1234567890

Represented by **JOANIE BERNSTEIN • ART REP** Tel: (941) 403-4393 Fax: (941) 403-0066

Michael Doret

LOGOS / LETTERING / GRAPHIC & TYPOGRAPHIC DESIGN

TEL: 323-467-1900 / FAX: 323-467-4555 / NY: 212-929-1688
EMAIL: DORETSMITH@EARTHLINK.NET

Disney's River Country Water Park

© THE WALT DISNEY CO.

Your Personal Internet

All★Star Weekend

Madison Square Garden

New York

NBA

Bankspeek Brand

Line of Credit

Speech

Local Flavors

See More At

HTTP://HOME.EARTHLINK.NET/~DORETSMITH/

1453

showcase.com

COMPS

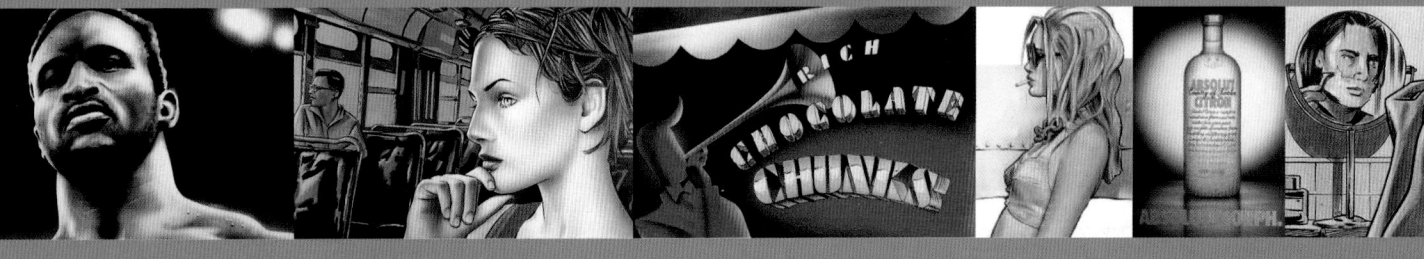

Denis Luzuriaga

Alexandra Gabanyi

Laszlo Schreiber

212·283·3401
Contact Diane Boston or Emile Svitzer

WAY ART ▶

Storyboards·Animatics
Comps·Illustration
w w w . w a y a r t . c o m

Aristídes Ruiz

Michael D'Antuono

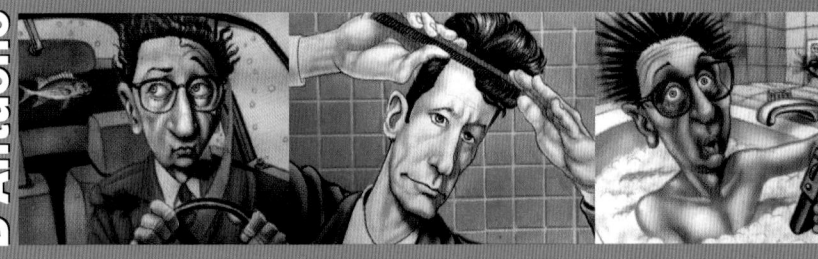

Rich Ransley

Bruce Rauffenbart

Suzanne Simmons

Denis Luzuriaga

Alexandra Gabanyi

Laszlo Schreiber

Scott Mcbee

Brian Stymest

Lucian Mihaesteanu

Harry Borgman

Weston Emmart

Obedient Illustrator. Comes when you call him.

1459

COMPING IS USAGE. **ASK FIRST.**

DIGITAL

SCHLOWSKY
COMPUTER
ILLUSTRATION

73 OLD ROAD
WESTON, MA 02193
781.899.5110 FAX: 781.647.1608
e-mail: bob@schlowsky.com

Lois Schlowsky - Illustration • Bob Schlowsky - Digital Photography

Education

Advocacy

COMPUTER
SCHLOWSKY
ILLUSTRATION

73 OLD ROAD
WESTON . MA . 02193
781.899.5110 . FAX: 781.647.1608
e-mail: bob@schlowsky.com

Lois Schlowsky - Illustration • Bob Schlowsky - Digital Photography

Creative Photo-Illustration.

Superior Image Modification.

Sam Haltom

970.871.0151 voice

970.871.0150 fax

sam@digitalnation.com e-mail

www.anothercolor.com URL

Clients include:
IBM, Bell Atlantic, NASA,
Time Life Books/Video,
Lockheed Martin,
American College of Radiology,
Steamboat Ski & Resort

another color

Shenandoah Dreamer

dedicated.
dependable.

ServInt
ServInt
A whole new way of doing business

radiation

quality
continuous
improvement

Sprint

SKI TOWN USA
WORLD CUP
at Steamboat.

STEINER

I | S | NORDIC COMBINED
W O R L D   C U P

acr

History
of acr

click
to login/register

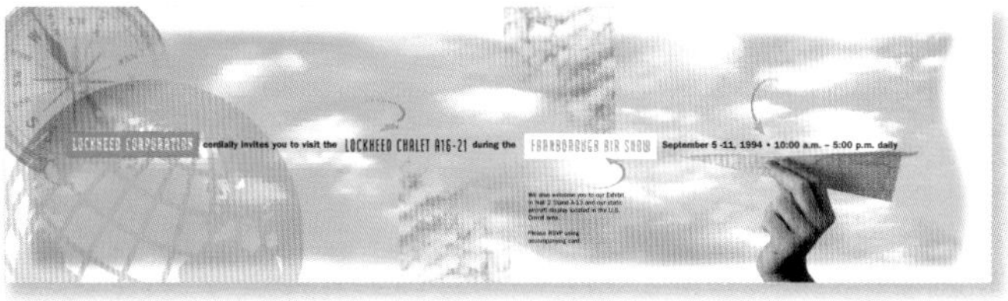

photos: Cynthia Hunter

LOCKHEED CORPORATION cordially invites you to visit the LOCKHEED CHALET A16-21 during the FARNBOROUGH AIR SHOW September 5-11, 1994 • 10:00 a.m. – 5:00 p.m. daily

photo: Johan Malkoski

Creative Photo-Illustration.

Superior Image Modification.

Sam Haltom

970.871.0151 voice

970.871.0150 fax

sam@digitalnation.com e-mail

www.anothercolor.com URL

Clients include:
IBM, Bell Atlantic, NASA,
Time Life Books/Video,
Lockheed Martin,
American College of Radiology,
Steamboat Ski & Resort

Elle studio
photo illustration
214 526 6712

Elle *studio*

photo illustration   214 526 6712

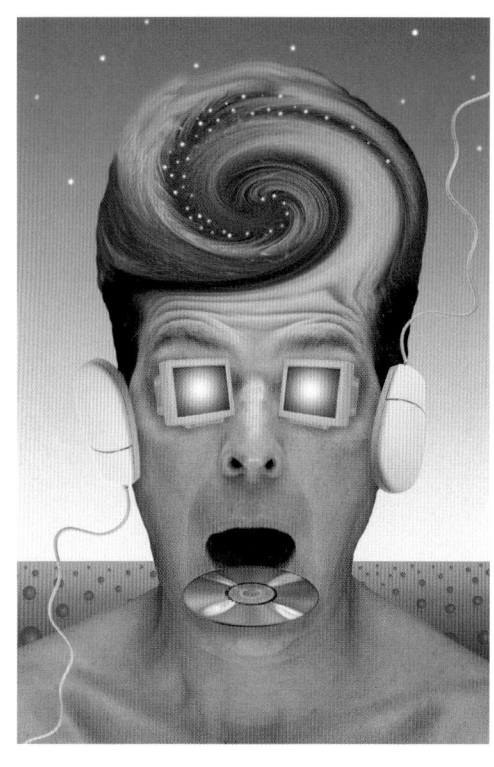

LEE STOKES
illustrative retouching

(612) 339–5770 email: lstokes@intxxnet.com web site: retoucher.com

imagen
a digital design firm

phone 214.871.2747   fax 214.871.2748   web http://www.imageninc.com

Digital Illustration & Photo Retouching

Music CD Cover Retouching:
Daryl Hall & John Oates

©PUSH Records

Lighter Illustration:
Anheuser-Busch

Annual Report Retouching:
TRC

Puzzle/Packaging Illustration:
BePuzzled

Poster Illustration:
IBM

2000

Brochure Illustration:
Paradigm Communications

Web Page & Brochure Illustration:
General Electric

Clients Include:
Anheuser-Busch, BePuzzled,
Dell Magazines, General Electric, Hall & Oates,
IBM, Paradigm Communications, Reebok,
Sears, Spalding, Stanley, Timex, TRC.

Giana GraphX

www.gianagraphx.com

Alan Giana   860-658-2938
17 Colonial Drive, Simsbury, CT 06089

MARK SCHROEDER
ILLUSTRATION & RETOUCHING

PHONE : 415 - 421 - 3691 • FAX 415 - 421 - 1135

414 Jackson St. Suite 207, San Francisco, CA 94111

Member: San Francisco Society of Illustrators

CLIENTS INCLUDE:

Fujitsu, Bio Rad, Kingsford Charcoal, Del Monte, Clorox, Ortho, Chevron, Blue Star Lines, Amtrak, Peterbuilt, Hewlett Packard, Galoob Toys, Seagate, Skidmore, Owings, & Merrill, Applied Materials, National Semiconductor, IBM, Gloria Ferrer, Paul Masson

E-MAIL: 104147.1313@compuserve.com

ADDITIONAL WORK: california **image,** 95, 96, 97, 98

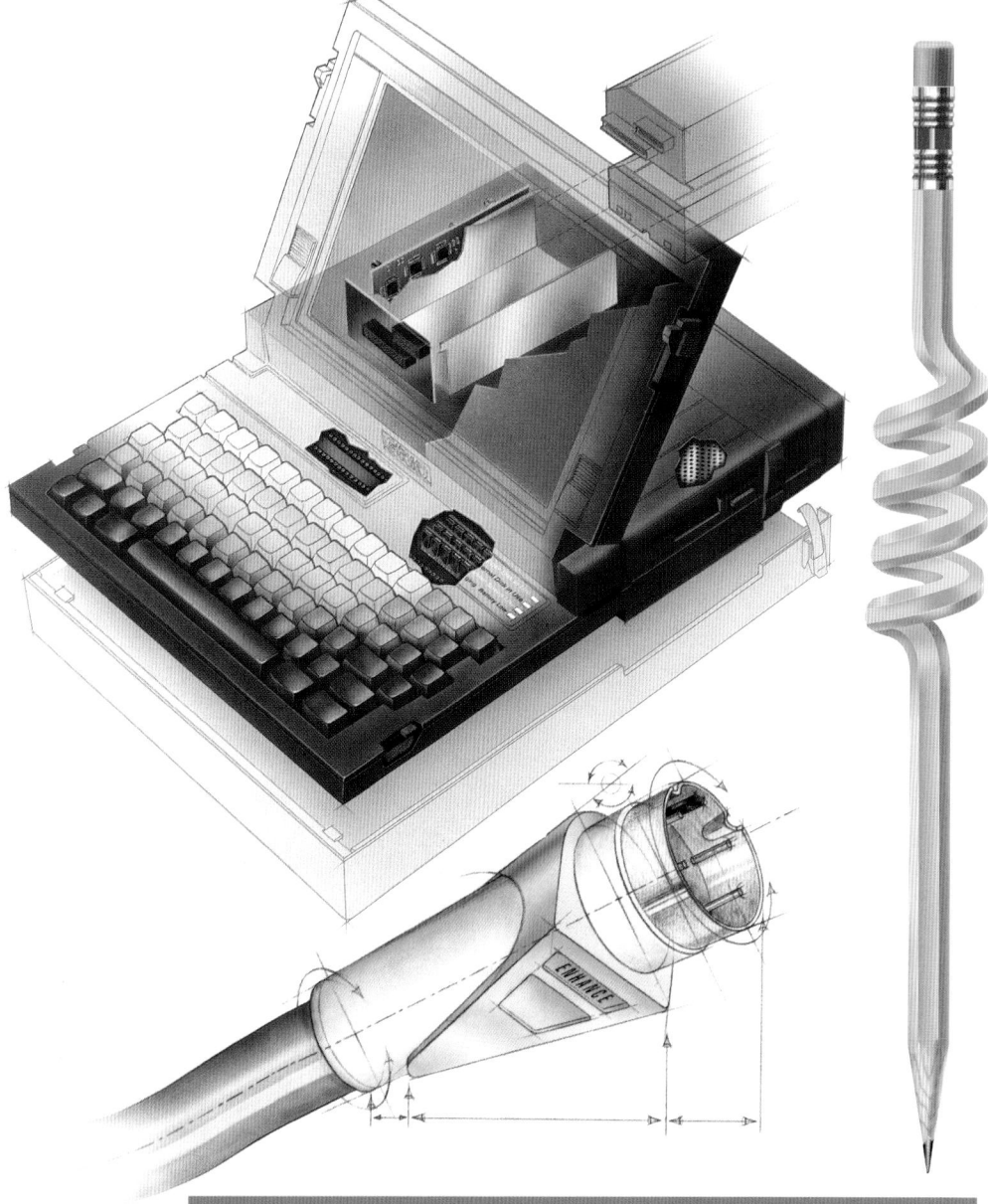

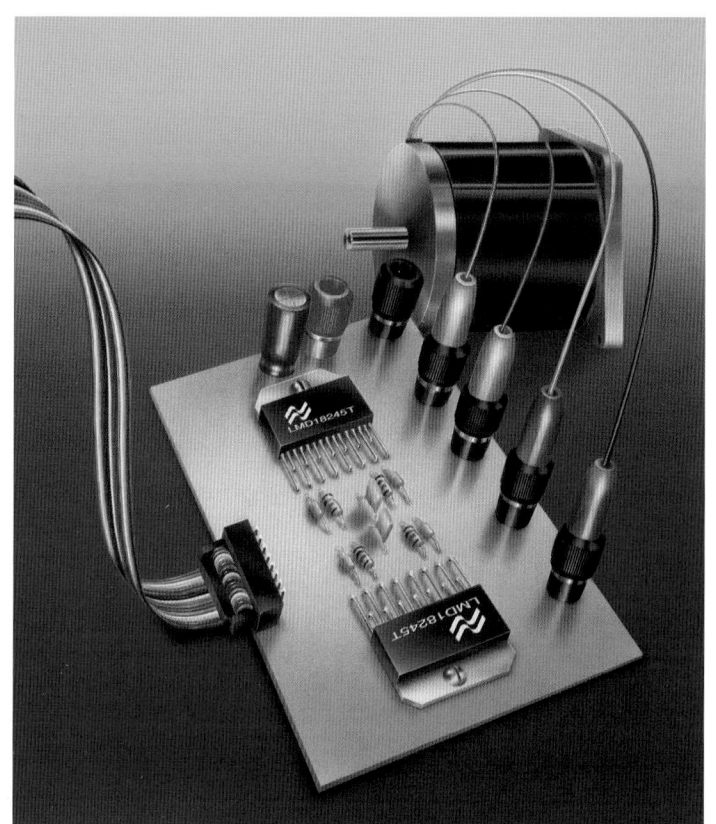

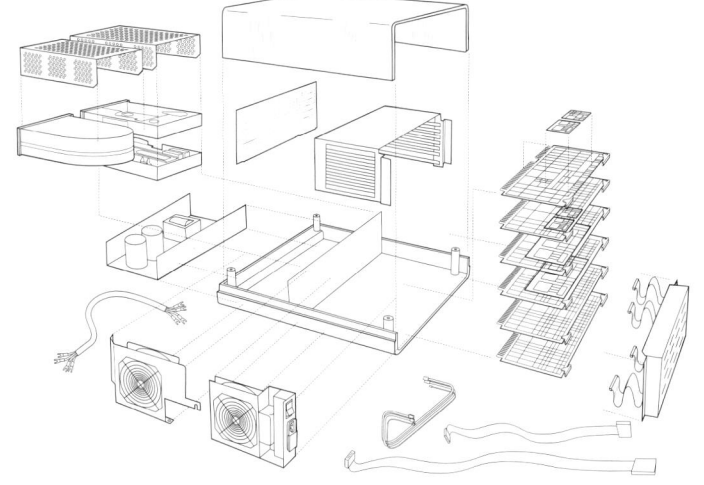

Doug Struthers

ANIMATION AND ILLUSTRATION

CD
Demo Reel

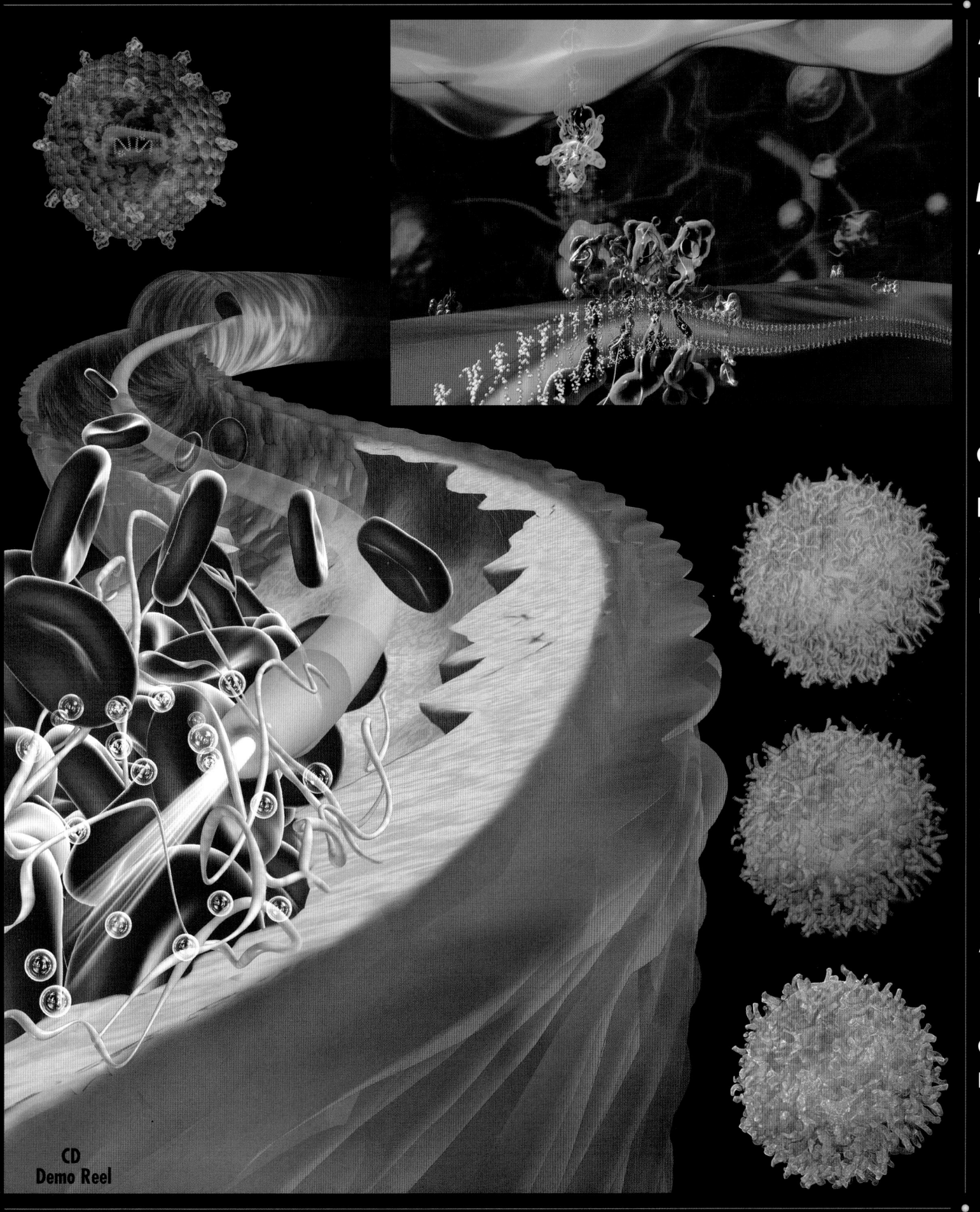

Doug Struthers

Levy creative Management, LLC 300 eaST 46TH STreeT Suite 4G New York, New York 10017
Tel:212-687-6463 Fax:212-661-4839   In CA: 415-626-6510   maIl:Sari@LevyCreative.COm

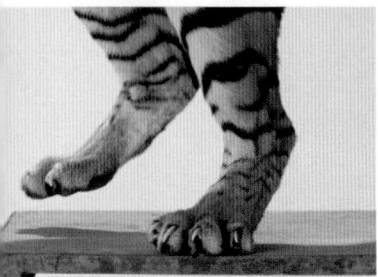

Jacques Devaud *io* IMAGE Randy Nelsen

Randy Nelsen *io* IMAGE Jacques Devaud

THE HEISMAN MEMORIAL TROPHY

COORS LIGHT
COLLEGE FOOTBALL
HEISMAN

NAME THE HEISMAN TROPHY WINNER!

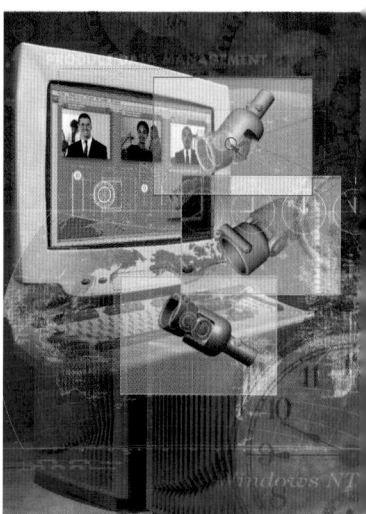

Forbes 400

Baron's Marketing

Little Brown & Company Publishers

American Health for Women

RIEGEL ILLUSTRATION

MARGARET RIEGEL ✳ 160 EAST 3RD STREET APT 4G, NEW YORK NY 10009 ✳ 212.254.8240 T 212.475.7804 F

FOR ADDITIONAL SAMPLES SEE DIRECTORY OF ILLUSTRATION 11 & 13, AMERICAN SHOWCASE 21, WWW.SHOWCASE.COM OR CALL FOR A PORTFOLIO

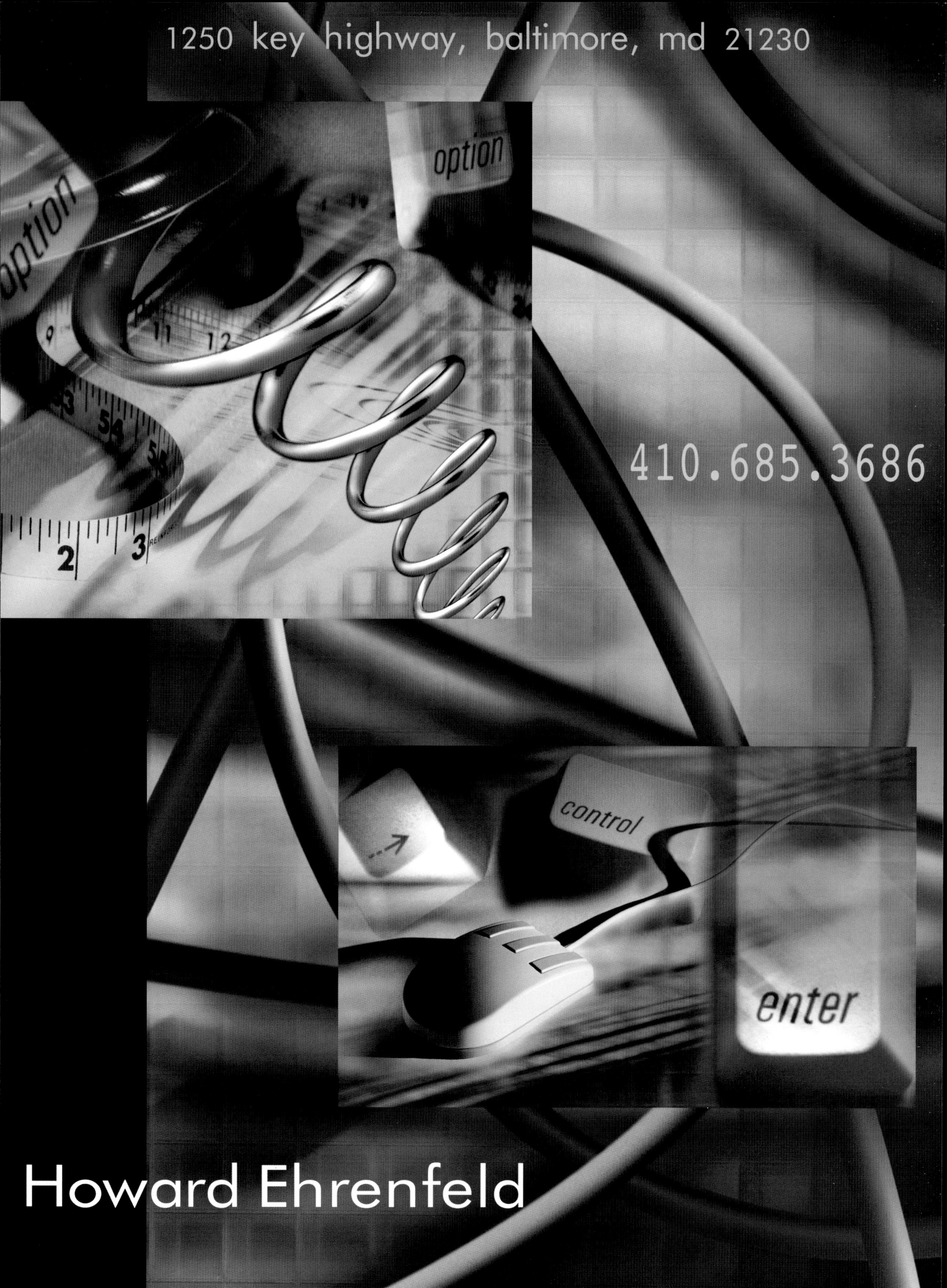

1250 key highway, baltimore, md 21230

410.685.3686

Howard Ehrenfeld

Tony Klassen
219.926.2045

David Peters Design

digital illustration

c o l l a g e

orchestrated chaos

tel 310-390-3528

fax 310-397-5383

(201) 868-9585 • FAX (201) 868-9584 • EMAIL: ANDYLACKOW@AOL.COM

Andy
LACKOW

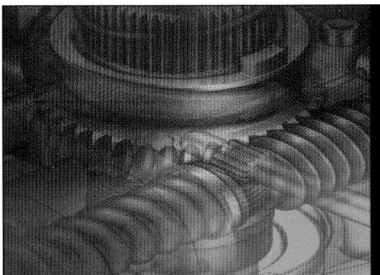

Michael Llewellyn

Technical Illustration

Phone: 713-462-5331 Fax: 713-462-8950

www.MikeLLLL.com

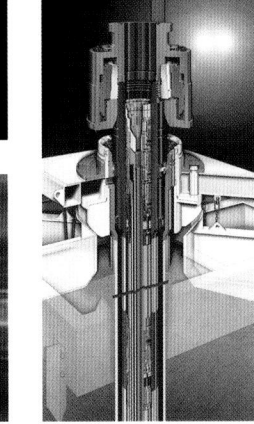

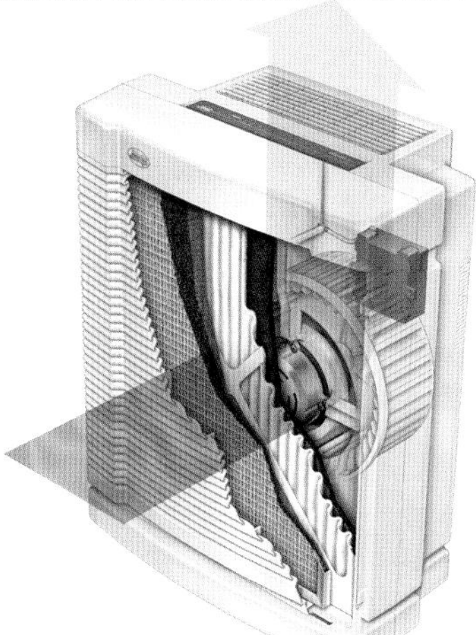

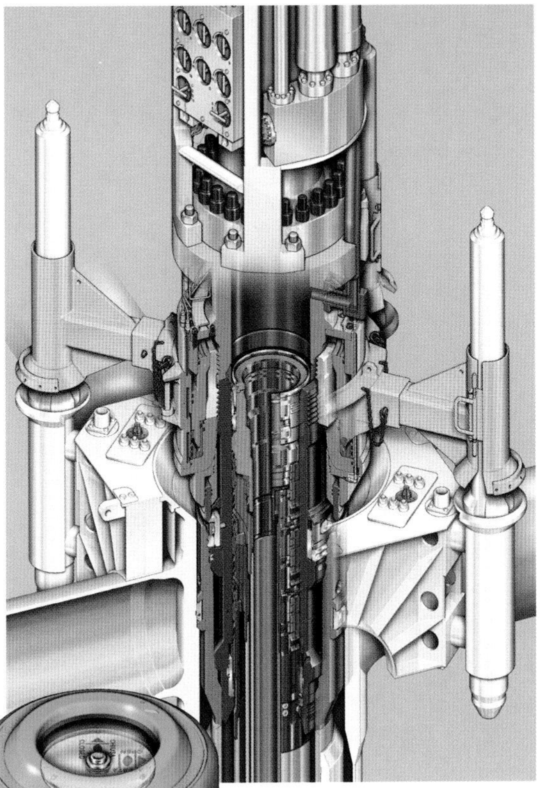

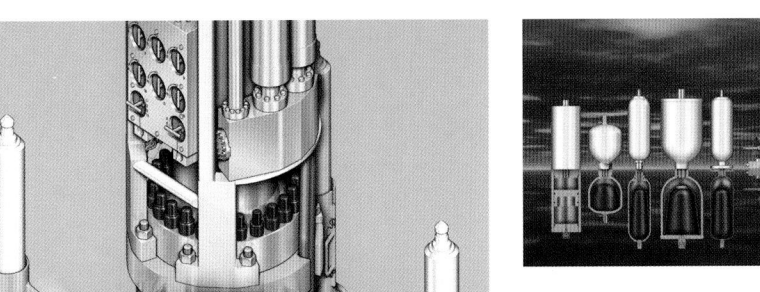

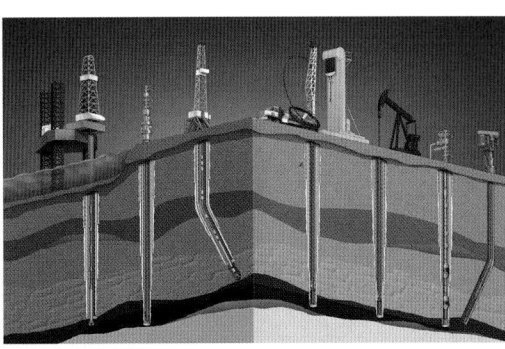

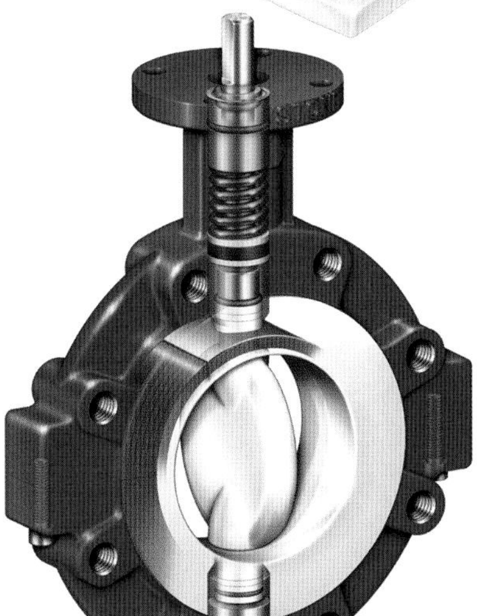

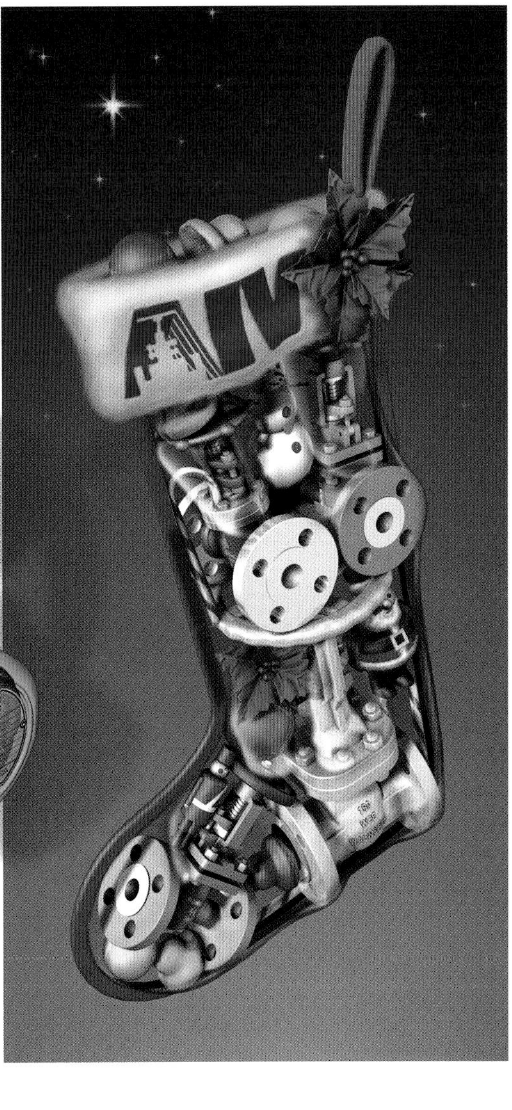

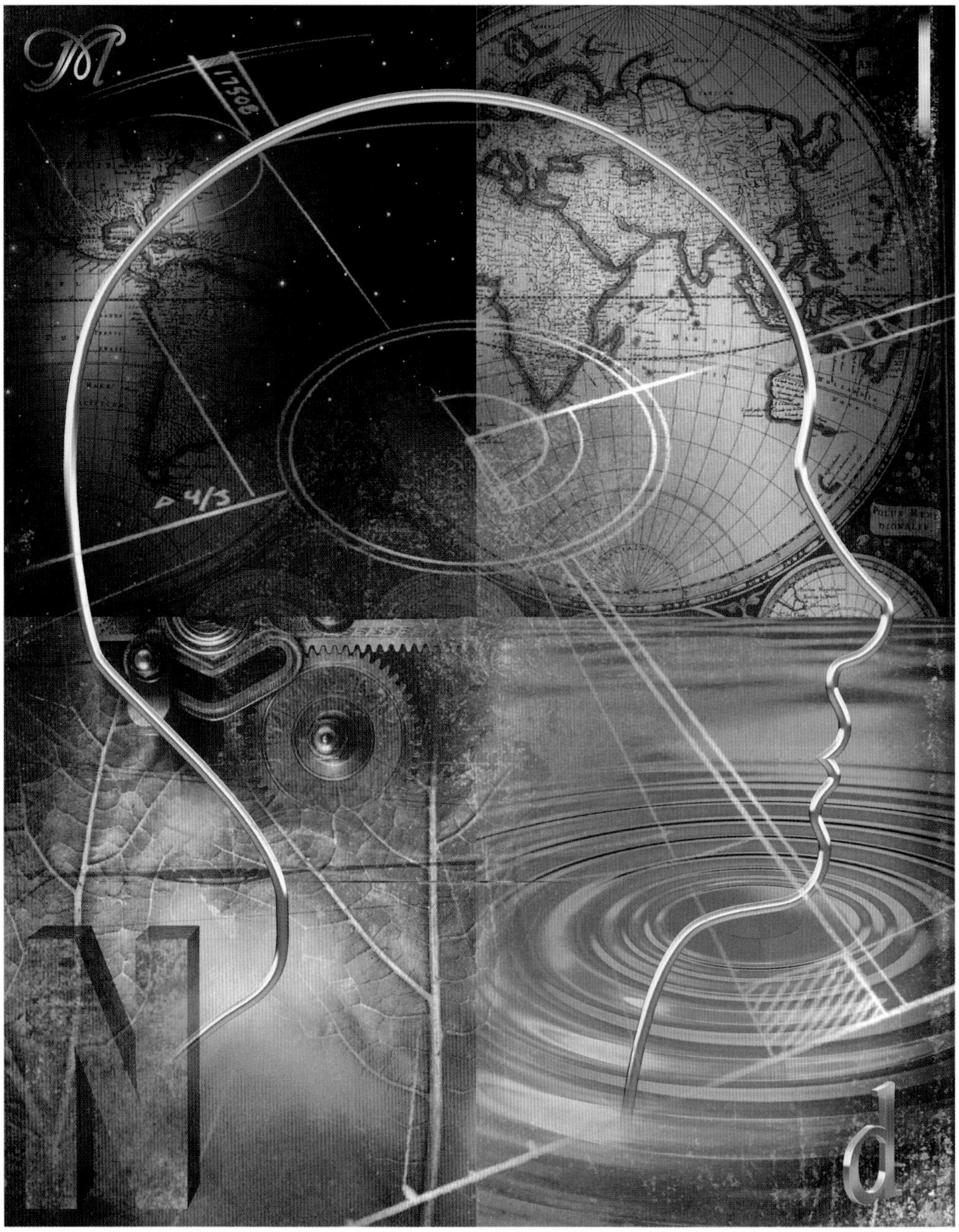

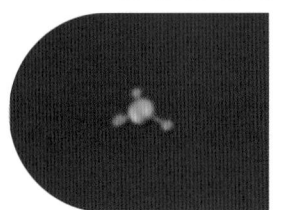
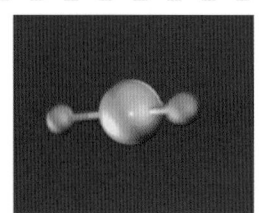
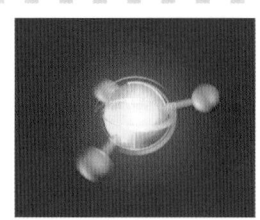
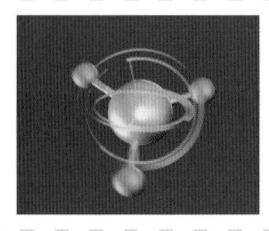
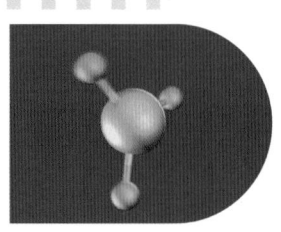

henk DAWSON

425·882·3303

henk DAWSON

425·882·3303

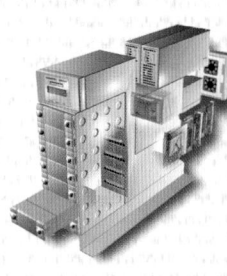

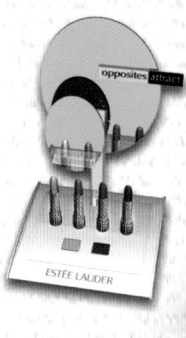

Mind of the Machine is a digital
Studio Producing 2D and 3D
graphics for print, video and
interactivity. We have been
designing digitally for over 12
years and have unmatched
expertise in the field. Our
immersion in the technical
aspects of the craft is complete;
but we still focus on the idea
behind the mechanics to produce
truly memorable pieces.

Mind of the Machine

David Teich, Mind of the Machine   41 Tamara Drive, Roosevelt, NJ 08555   609-448-5036 phone • 609-443-3228 fax

mindmachine@mindspring.com   http://www.mindofthemachine.com

JAE SHIM

Digital Conceptual Illustrations

8 1 8 - 7 5 2 - 1 5 2 4

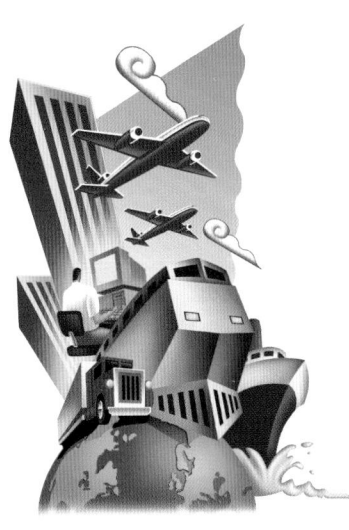

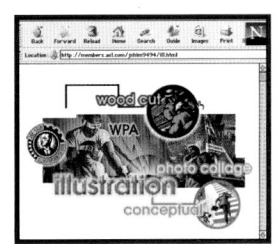

VISIT WEBSITE FOR MORE SAMPLES

http://members.aol.com/jshim9494

tom white.images

presents

the 4 BASIC NEEDS of
AN ART PROFESSIONAL

JEFF BARNES · DIGITAL ILLUSTRATION

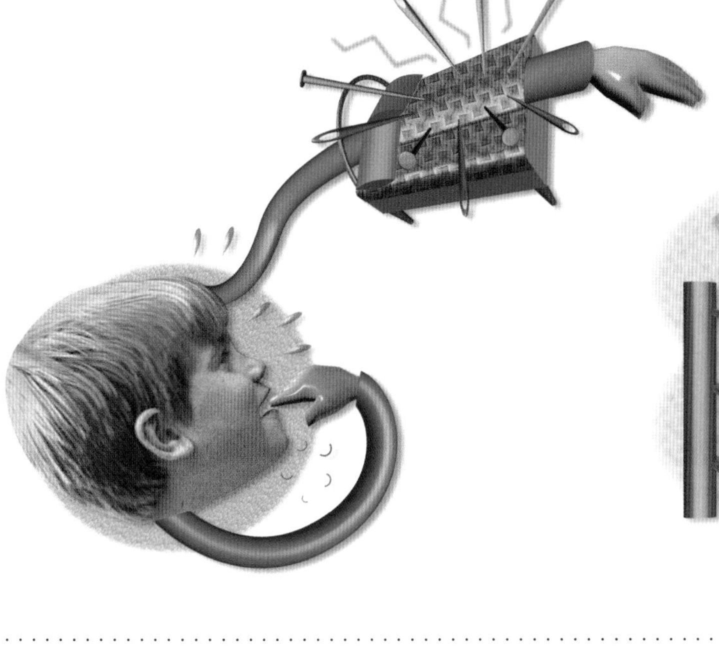

918-496-9598   jbpix@worldnet.att.net

Eric Yang | digital illustrations

phone: 626.284.4727

fax: 626.282.5536

email: etyang@pacbell.net

DOGLIGHT STUDIOS: VOICE 213-222-1928   E-MAIL doglight@aol.com
FAX 213-222-8151   Homepage www.doglight.com

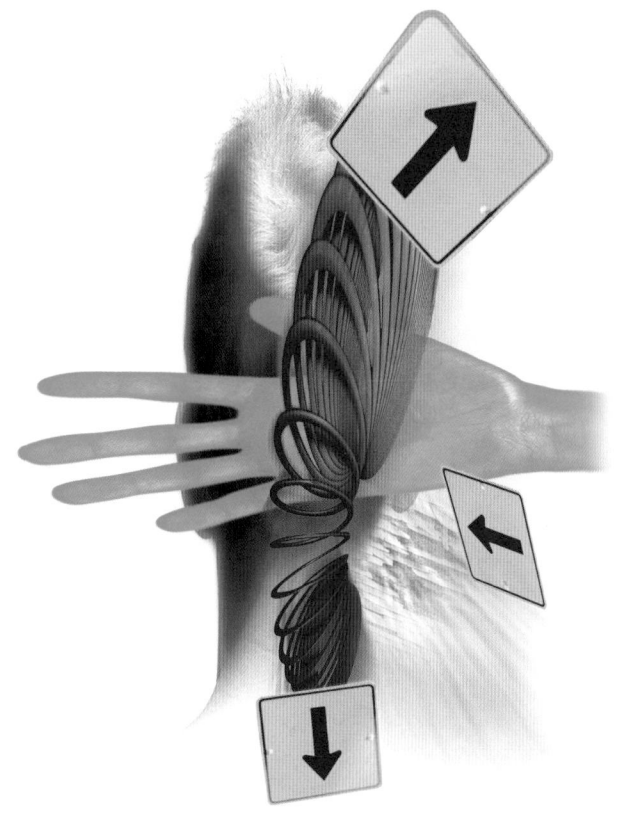

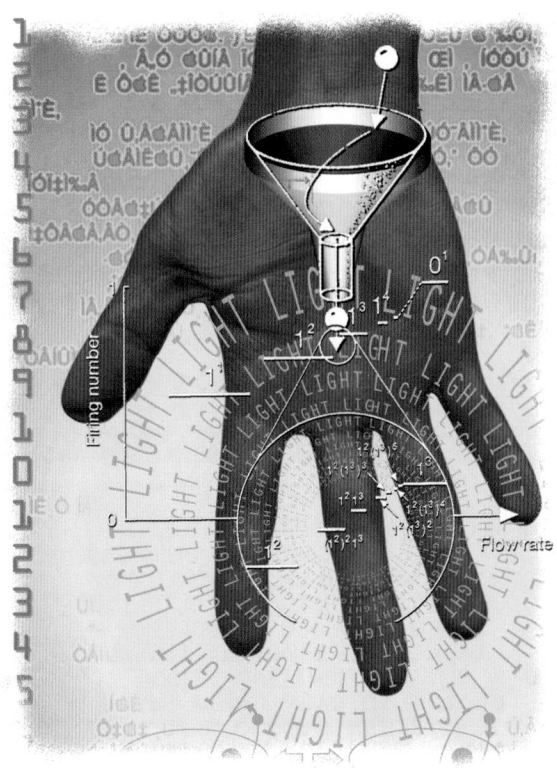

Digital Illustration	Digital Studio of	Conceptual Design
Visual Expression	**IGORS IRBE**	Computer Manipulation
P 773.271.6508		F 773.271.6493

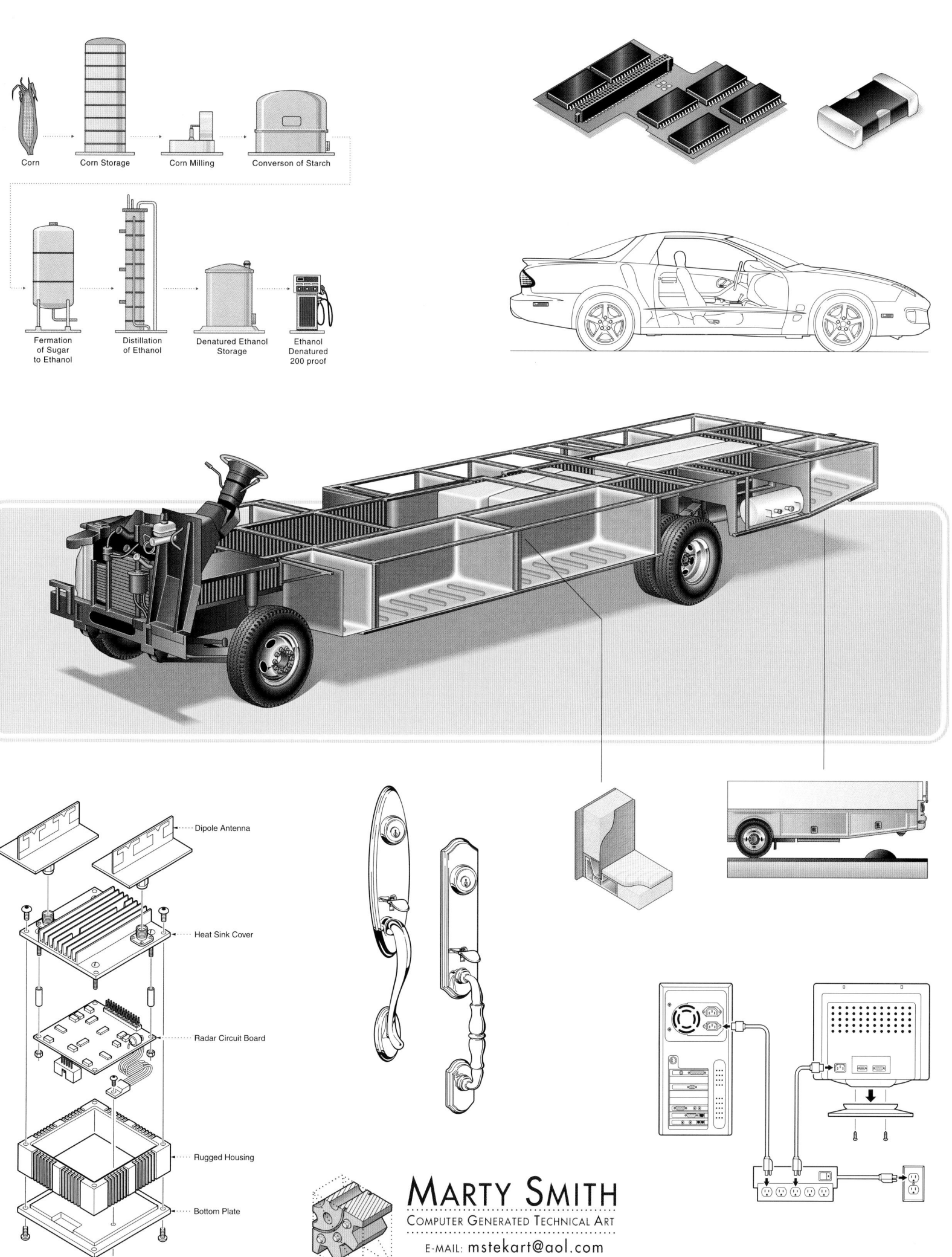

Corn

Corn Storage

Corn Milling

Converson of Starch

Fermation of Sugar to Ethanol

Distillation of Ethanol

Denatured Ethanol Storage

Ethanol Denatured 200 proof

Dipole Antenna

Heat Sink Cover

Radar Circuit Board

Rugged Housing

Bottom Plate

MARTY SMITH
COMPUTER GENERATED TECHNICAL ART
E-MAIL: mstekart@aol.com
PHONE: (714) 962.0461

SAN FRANCISCO: Barb Hauser (415) 647.5660   NEW ENGLAND: Chip Caton (860) 523.4562
ADDITIONAL WORK: Workbook 15,17,18,19,20, New Media Showcase 4,5,6,7

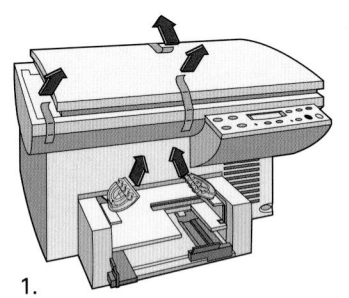

1.

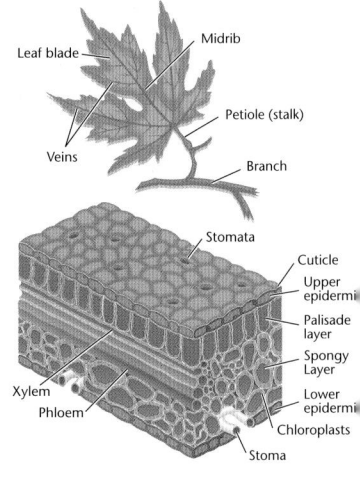

Leaf blade
Midrib
Veins
Petiole (stalk)
Branch
Stomata
Cuticle
Upper epidermi
Palisade layer
Spongy Layer
Lower epidermi
Xylem
Phloem
Chloroplasts
Stoma

2.

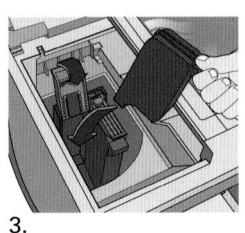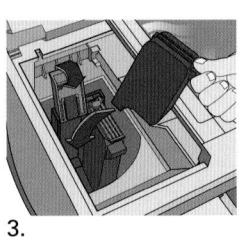

3.

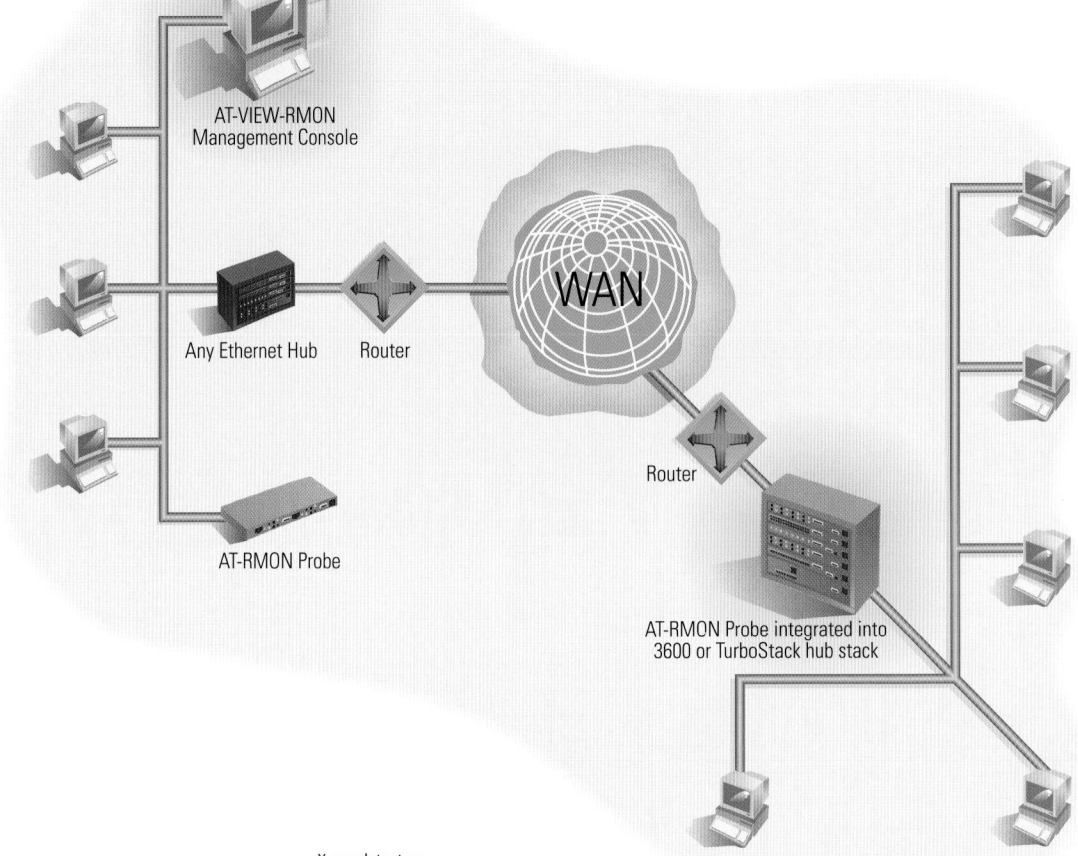

AT-VIEW-RMON
Management Console

Any Ethernet Hub   Router

WAN

Router

AT-RMON Probe

AT-RMON Probe integrated into
3600 or TurboStack hub stack

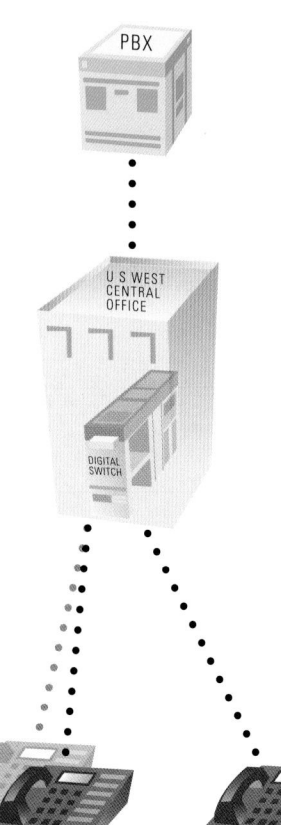

PBX

U S WEST
CENTRAL
OFFICE

DIGITAL
SWITCH

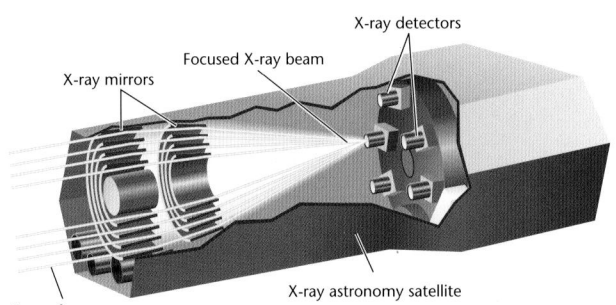

X-ray detectors
Focused X-ray beam
X-ray mirrors
X-ray astronomy satellite
X-rays from space

COLIN HAYES
DIGITAL ILLUSTRATION
Studio: (425) 338-5452 / chayes267@aol.com

D O N N A N N I E
DONNA JORGENSEN/ANNIE BARRETT
ARTISTS REPRESENTATIVES
206   634-1880
FAX 206 632-2024

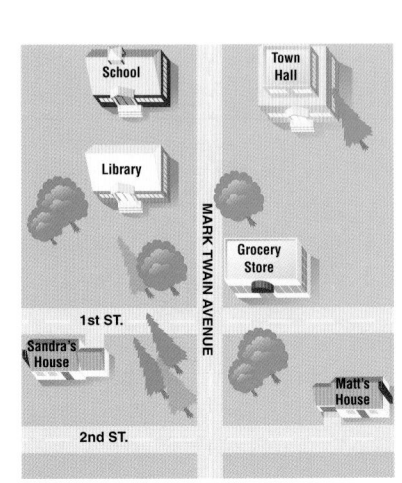

School
Town Hall
Library
MARK TWAIN AVENUE
Grocery Store
1st ST.
Sandra's House
Matt's House
2nd ST.

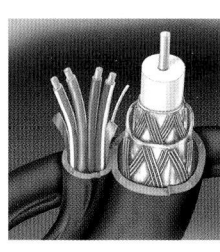

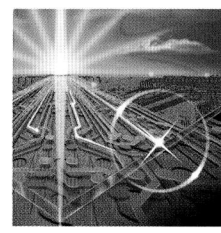

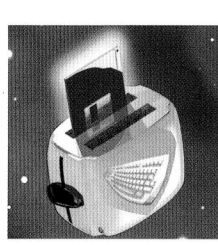

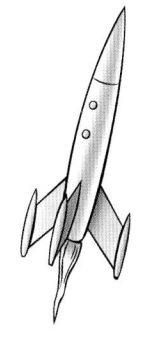

Jim McDonald

Digital Rendering / 3-D Web Art and Animation
Studio: 602-494-0747
Mail: airpwr@earthlink.net
http://home.earthlink.net/~airpwr/

Represented by:
Atelier Kimberley Boege
602-265-4389

DARYL STEVENS

digital artist

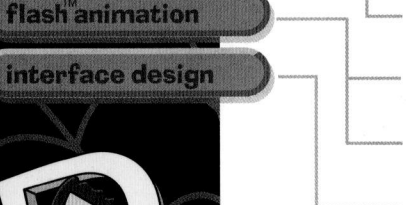

- freehand™ artwork
- flash™ animation
- interface design

- eps files for print
- gif & jpeg files for web
- vector animation
- gif animation
- icon and banner art
- button & navigation

◄ Information Week Magazine

Consumer Reports ▲

Children's Television Workshop ▲

Yahoo! Internet Life Magazine ▲

see portfolio website:
www.studio202.com ▼

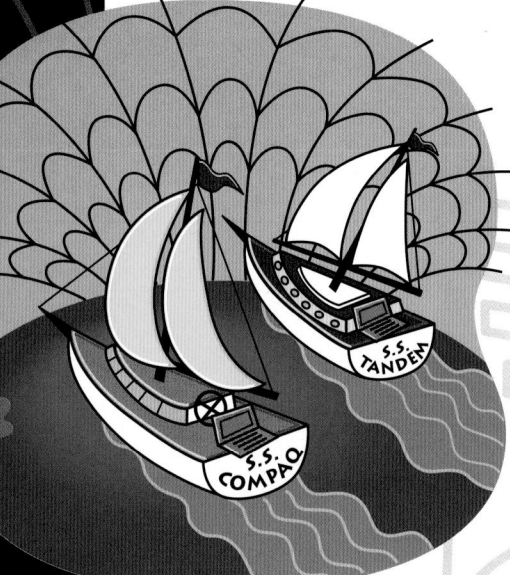

 BASEBALL
 GOLF
FOOTBALL

 PHOTO GALLERY
 SI STORE
 SI FORUM

Icons for Sports Illustrated Compuserve website ▲

Go To: http://www.studio202.com

d.stevens
@studio202.com

BOOK · WORK · ARTIST · CONTACT · HOME

macromedia®
PEOPLE'S CHOICE
97 AWARDS
FINALIST

▲ Nominated for Macromedia's People's Choice Awards 1997

212-741-1610
phone

CONTACT

DARYL STEVENS

illustration | animation

for print | for web

212-741-1610 — phone

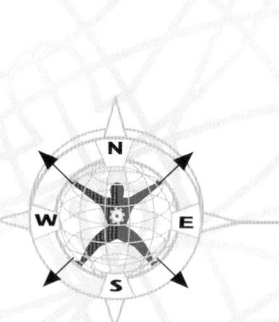

◀ Mortgage Technology
Magazine

Specializing in **2d** vector illustration
and animation for print and internet.
Art files delivered via e-mail or disk.

STUDIO202.COM

editorial illustration

interactive design

▲ Major League Baseball for Kids Magazine

recent clients ▼

Children's Television Workshop

Consumer Reports

Computer Life Magazine

Information Week Magazine

Major League Baseball

National Hockey League

Sports Illustrated

New York Life Insurance Co.

Parent Life Magazine

US Banker Magazine

Yahoo! Internet Life Magazine

dstevens@studio202.com — e-mail

212-620-4145
fax

INDEX

INDEX

INDEX

INDEX

INDEX

PHONE LISTINGS
& ADDRESSES

DIRECTORY

REPRESENTATIVES

A

Adams, Mary Jane:
3006B W Division St, Arlington, TX 76012 817-265-2821
AIR Studio:
203 E Seventh St, Cincinnati, OH 45202 513-721-1193
Illustrator: P D Cooper, Walt Curlee, Jim Effler, Kathleen Estes, Jim Fitzpatrick, Lawrence Goodridge, Jennifer Knaack, Tim Langenderfer, Matt Manley, Craig McKay, David Miller, Amy Price, Jim Schrier, Tim Stout, Jim Wainscott, Sean Wallace, Jack Whitney, Kurt Alan Williams
AKA Reps:
153 Waverly Pl 5th Fl, New York, NY 10014 212-620-4777
Albrecht & Associates, Anne:
405 North Wabash Avenue, Chicago, IL 60611 312-595-0300
Illustrator: Ted Burn, T.S. Carson, Fred Ingram, Randee Ladden, Barton Stabler, Jim Steck, Keith Witmer
Photographer: Jim Fiscus, Kevin Sanchez, Kevin Smith
• **Alexander/Pollard, Inc: pg 641**
848 Greenwood Ave NE, Atlanta, GA 30306 404-875-1363
Illustrator: Diane Borowski, Lindy Burnett, Sally Wern Comport, Cheryl Cooper, Chris Ellithorpe, Thomas Gonzalez, Alan Hashimoto, Kathy Lengyel, Don Morris, Brian Otto, Al Pisano, Nip Rogers, James Soukup, Karen Strelecki, Kate Thomssen, Mark Weakley, Stephen Wells
Photographer: David Guggenheim
Aline Assocs, France:
1367 N Las Palmas Ave, Hollywood, CA 90028 213-469-3400
Electronic Imaging: Stewart Daniels, Craig Mellins
Illustrator: Thomas Blackshear, Elisa Cohen, Scott Fike, Lendon Flanagan, Thomas Hennessy, Jacqui Morgan, Jacquie Morgan, Robert Revels, Ezra Tucker, Bruce Wolse
Lettering: Peter Greco
Music: Mark Mothersbaugh
Photographer: Grove Pashley, Jill Sabella
Alternative Vision/Michele Mei:
17 SE Third Ave #502, Portland, OR 97214 ....
Photographer: Dan Bronson, Rich Iwasaki, Bryan Peterson
Altman, Elizabeth:
3300 N Lake Shore Dr, Chicago, IL 60657 773-935-9007
• **American Artists Rep Inc: pg 788,789**
353 W 53rd St #1W, New York, NY 10019 ....**212-682-2462**
e-mail: info@americanartists.com / url: www.americanartists.com / fax: 212-582-0090
Illustrator: Keith Batcheller, Steve Celmer, John Churchman, Gary Ciccarelli, Andrew Condon, Bob Depew, Jacques Fabre, Russell Farrell, Bill Garland, Garth Glazier, Scott Grimando, Doug Henry, John Holm, John & Phillip Hom, Michael Jaroszko, Maurice Lewis, Jerry Lofaro, Alan Male, Shawn McKelvey, Jean-Claude Michel, Dave Miller, Shawn Murphy, Tony Randazzo, Bot Roda, Joe Scrofani, Jim Starr, Rod Vass, Rhonda Voo, Stan Watts, Jonathan Wright, Eddie Young
Anderson, Laurel:
28 Rich St #201, Larkspur, CA 94904 415-332-0437
Film: Axis Media Boutique
Photographer: John Cleare
Anderson, Stephanie:
38 Greene St 5th Fl, New York, NY 10013 212-925-2999
Photographer: Howard Berman, Steve Bronstein, Bret Wills
Ann Represents, Jill:
1770 Broadway #301, San Francisco, CA 94109 415-626-7440
Photographer: Biondo Productions, Charles Bush, Butler Photography, Dale Higgins Photography, Richard C Jung
Anton, Jerry:
119 W 23rd St #203, New York, NY 10011 212-633-9880
Illustrator: Norman Green, Oliver Williams
Photographer: Inc, Aaron Rezny, Chris Vincent
Arena:
144 Royal College St, London, England, UK NW1 OTA..................71-267-9661
Aresu-Goldring Studio:
160 Varick St 8th Fl, New York, NY 10013 212-604-0606
Photographer: Paul Aresu
Arnold Inc, Peter:
1181 Broadway 4th Fl, New York, NY 10001 212-481-1190
Photographer: Fred Bavendam, Martha Cooper, Manfred Kage, Jeffrey L Rotman, Galen Rowell, Kevin Schafer, David Scharf, Erika Stone, Norbert Wu, Bruno Zehnder
Art & Commerce:
755 Washington St, New York, NY 10014 212-206-0737
Cartoonist: David James, Glenn O'Brien
Illustrator: Raul Martinez, A R Media, Alex Gonzalez, Mats Gusatfson, Ronnie Cooke Newhouse
Photographer: William Abranowicz, Anette Aurell, Richard Burbridge, Clint Clemens, Lynn Davis, William Eggleston, Fabrizio Ferri, Jan Groover, John Huba, Inez Van Lamsweerde/Matadin, William Klein, Annie Leibovitz, Glen Luchford, Mary Ellen Mark, Wayne Maser, Craig McDean, Steven Meisel, Frank W Ockenfels, Perry Ogden, Sebastio Salgado, Luis Sanchez, Steven Sebring, Laurie Simmons, Bill Steele, Max Vadukel, Max Vadukul, Ellen Von Unwerth, William Wegman
Art Agency, The:
2405 NW Thurman St, Portland, OR 97210 503-203-8300
Illustrator: Robin Ator, Peter Beach, Diana Rice Bonin, Dale Champlin, Nancy Coffelt, Dennis Cunningham, Debra Spina Dixon, Bill Firewood, Stephen F Hayes, Laure Heinz, Craig Holmes, Sheila Lucas, Joanne Radmilovich, Ben Killen Rosenberg, Gary Whitley, Matt Wuerker, Jane Zwinger
Photographer: Dennis Cunningham, Jim Lommasson, Brad Ness, Brandy Pace
Art Bunch, Inc, The:
180 N Michigan Ave #1720, Chicago, IL 60601 312-368-8777
Illustrator: Phil Babb, Randy Chaffee, Jay Fisher, Rich Lo, Tak Murakami, Jerry Salinas
Art Department:
48 Greene St 4th Fl, New York, NY 10013 212-925-4222
Art Rep Services:
123 N Third St, Minneapolis, MN 55401 612-672-9940
Photographer: Tony Kubat, Studio Central
Art Services Int'l:
One Timber Ln, Westport, CT 06880 203-227-5687

Art Source, The:
PO Box 2193, Grapevine, TX 76099 817-481-2212
Illustrator: Elliot Park, Rick Whipple
Art Source/Diane Barkley:
PO Box 257, Pleasantville, NY 10570 914-747-2220
Illustrator: James Barkley, Larry Bennetti, Paul Birling, Vince Caputo, Liz Conrad, Rick Faist, Betsy Feeney, Robert J Lee, Robert Marinelli, Richard Rockwell
Art Staff, Inc:
1000 John R Rd #201, Troy, MI 48083 248-583-6070
Illustrator: Paul Chen, Pam Colecchia, Larry Cory, Heiner Hertling, Ben Jaroslaw, Rainer Laubach, Dick Meissner, Linda Nagle, Gary Richardson, Jeff Ridky, Ken Taylor, Alan Wilson
• **Artbank International: pg 578**
8 Woodcroft Avenue, London, England NW7 2AG **44-181-906-2288**
e-mail: info@artbank.ltd.uk / url: www.artbank.ltd.uk / fax: 44-181-906-2289
• **Artco: pg 657-671**
227 Godfrey Rd, Weston, CT 06883 ....**203-222-8777**
e-mail: artcoct@snet.net / fax: 203-454-9940
Illustrator: George Angelini, Gary Carlson, Ray Downing, Joe St Pierre, John Stephens, Jason Sutton, Larry Taugher, Alex Tiani,
Artisan:
4300 Campus Dr #110, Newport Beach, CA 92660 714-260-1720
Artisan Professional Freelance Reps, Inc:
10 E 40th St #2901, New York, NY 10016 212-448-0200
Artist Representatives of Texas:
11601 Katie Frwy #105, Houston, TX 77079 ....
Illustrator: Alice Campbell Boyd, Jason Daniels, Victor Higginbotham, CJ Latta, Ashley Mims, Christine Mosley, Robert L. Pharr
Artists Assocs:
4416 La Jolla Dr, Bradenton, FL 34210 941-756-8445
Shrub Oak, NY 212-755-1365
Illustrator: Norman Adams, Michael C Dudash, Mark English, Bob Heindel, Steve Karchin, Dick Krepel, Fred Otnes
Artists Int'l:
320 Bee Brook Rd, Washington, CT 06777 860-868-1011
Illustrator: Peter Barrett, David Chestnut, Eric D'Zenis, Gino, Michael Hampshire, Jerry Harston, Barbara Lanza, John Lunch, Jane Maday, Paul Miller, Kathy Mitchell, John Nez, Gail Roth, Jim Spence, Anne Thornburgh, Richard Walz
Artlab:
609 9th Ave #4S, New York, NY 10036 212-754-0700
Artline:
439 S Tryon St, Charlotte, NC 28202..704-376-7609
Illustrator: Steve Barbaria, Indigo Studios, Eric Joyner, David Wink
Multimedia: Electro Entertainment Group
Photographer: Alex Bee, Jim Fiscus, Steve Murray
Stock: Picturesque
Arts Counsel, Inc:
853 Broadway #606, New York, NY 10003 212-777-6777
Illustrator: Greg Christie, Lisa Cohen, James Dignan, Matt Downs, Glen Hanson, Doreen Kibler, Pamela Kogen, Mark Korsak, Barbara McGregor, David McGrievey, Jackie Pardo, Sara Singh, Sally Sturman, Annalisa Vivarelli, Liselotte Watkins, Jenny Williams
ARTS Resource:
545 Sutter St #305, San Francisco, CA 94102..............................415-775-0709
Illustrator: Arthur Bell, John Wotipka
• **Artworks Illustration: pg 522-541**
89 Fifth Ave #901, New York, NY 10003 ....**212-627-1554**
fax: 212-627-1719
Illustrator: Paul Bachem, Kim Barnes, Dan Brown, Deborah Chabrian, Ellis Chapell, Adrian Chesterman, Christopher R. Clarke, Peter Fiore, Stephen Gardner, Mike Harper, Rick Lovell, Dennis Lyall, Tony Meers, Molly O'Gorman, Peter Siu, Brad Teare, Victoria Vebell
• **Artworks, The: pg 707-715**
455 W 23rd St #8D, New York, NY 10011......................................**212-366-1893**
url: www.andtheart.com / fax: 212-604-9643
Illustrator: Sophie Allport, Christian Birmingham, Giles Burton Chapple, Greg Clarke, Izhar Cohen, Matthew Cook, Penny Dann, Andrew Davidson, Jeffrey Decoster, Gurbuz D Eksioglu, Graham Evernden, Jody Hewgill, John Lawrence, Peter Malone, Mark Fox of Blackdog Studio, Desdemona McCannon, Sarah McMenemy, John Montgomery, Anton Morris, Joe Morse, Graham Percy, Clare Pettinati, Hanoch Piven, Jenny Powell, Isadore Seltzer, Meilo So, Mark Ulriksen, Rupert Van Wyk, Marco Ventura, Mary Woodin, Christopher Wormell
Photographer: Ron Sanford
Ascher & Assocs, Catherine:
3210 Overlook Cir, Goshen, KY 40026..502-288-9561
Asciutto Art Reps:
1712 E Butler Cir, Chandler, AZ 85225..602-899-0600
Illustrator: Anthony Accardo, Alex Bloch, Deborah Borgo, Olivia Cole, Mark Corcoran, Jack Crompton, Susanne DeMarco, Len Epstein, Kersti Frigell, Meryl Henderson, Alan Leiner, Loretta Lustig, Charles Peale, Jan Pyk, Gary Undercuffer
Ash, Michael:
1180 6th Ave PH, New York, NY 10036 212-655-6500
Atelier Kimberly Boege:
PO Box 7544, Phoenix, AZ 85011 602-265-4389
Illustrator: Robert Case, Joann Daley, Roberta Hancock, Tracy Hill, Paul Janovsky, Jim McDonald Design, Jim McDonald, John Nelson, Adair Payne, Howard Post, Kevin Short, Dale C Verzaal, Charles Wilkin
Photographer: Jacques Barbey, Kevin Cruff Photo, Rick Gayle
Atols & Hoffman:
440 N Wabash #3101, Chicago, IL 60611 312-222-0504
Photographer: Gary Cipinko, Tony D'Orio, Beth Galton, Mark Laita, Richard Hamilton Smith
Austrian, Susan:
12605 Hilloway Rd, Minnetonka, MN 55305.................................
Photographer: Mike Jensen, Richard Hamilton Smith, Nick Vedros
Ayerst Artists' Agent, Deborah:
2546 Sutter St, San Francisco, CA 94115 415-567-3570
Music: Charley Brown & Co
Photographer: John Casado, Davies & Starr, Andre Lansal, Scott Morgan, Robert Olding, Stephanie Rausser

B

Bacall Reps, Robert:
350 Seventh Ave 20th Fl #2004, New York, NY 10001 212-695-1729
Illustrator: Matt Baier
Photographer: Colin Cooke, Jeff Dunas, David Hautzig, Bruce James, Britt Lundquist,
Patrick McNamara, Peter Morello, Ross Whitaker
Bacher, Nancy:
2654 Rodeo Dr NE, Blaine, MN 55449.....................................612-786-1200
Illustrator: Bryan Anderson, Mary Bergherr, Jan-Willem Boer, Derek Brigham, John
Dearstyne, Bret Meredith, Doug Talalla, Pepper Tharp, Adam Turner
Badd, Linda:
568 Broadway #601, New York, NY 10012 212-431-3377
Photographer: Tom Clayton
Bahm, Bob:
25488 Bryden Rd, Beachwood, OH 44122...............................440-542-0145
Graphic Designer: Roger Huyssen
Illustrator: David McCall Johnston, Gordon Kibbee, Joan Landis, Don Ivan Punchatz,
John M Thompson
• **Baker, Kolea: pg 672-683**
2814 NW 72nd St, Seattle, WA 98117.....................................**206-784-1136**
e-mail: kolea@kolea.com / url: www.kolea.com / fax: 206-784-1171
Illustrator: George Abe, Don Baker, Christopher Baldwin, Jeff Brice, Margaret Chodos Irvine,
Brant Day, Hilber Nelson, Jere Smith, Riccardo Stampatori
Bancroft & Friends, Carol:
121 Dodgingtown Rd Box 266, Bethel, CT 06801 203-748-4823
Illustrator: Gary Bialke, Cliff Faust, Linda Graves, Catherine Huerte, Karen Loccisano,
Steve Marchesi, Yoshi Miyake, Frank Ordaz, Don Weller, Linda Weller
Baranski Art Reps, Sue:
3200 N Lake Shore Dr #2310, Chicago, IL 60657 773-477-3188
Illustrator: Storyboard Studio
Photographer: Wayne Cable, Greg Heck
Barany, Leslie:
121 W 27th St #202, New York, NY 10001 212-627-8488
Barba, Maria:
33 Greene #3E, New York, NY 10013 212-941-7580
Photographer: Danny Clinch
Barboza Assocs, Ken:
853 Broadway #1603, New York, NY 10003 212-505-8635
Hair: Daryle Bennett, Johnny Gentry, Oscar James, Marque, Rudy Townsell
Hair & Make-up: Allyson Carey, Zianni Coates, Troy Jensen
Illustrator: Gil Ashby, Leonard Jenkins, Dennis S McArthur, Willie Tobert
Make-up: Annastazia, Daniel Green, La Lette LittleJohn, Tony Marshall, Tracey Penning-
ton, Reggie Wells, Tobe West
Photographer: Anthony Barboza, Adger Cowens, Joe Grant, Jerry Jack, Peter Morehand,
Marcus Tullis, Mel Wright
Stock: Black Images
Stylist: Alexx Brown, Debbie Medieros
Wardrobe: Lois Barrett, Debra Ginyard, Johnetta Hamilton Vasquz, Derek Lee, Rick Ramsey
Barnard, Pat:
Universal House/Queens Parade Pl, Bath, England, UK BA1 2NN 122-542-7521
Barracca & Assocs, Sal:
381 Park Ave S #1120, New York, NY 10016 212-889-2400
Illustrator: Alan Ayers, Franklin Ayers, Donato Giancola, Rich Grote, Tim Jacobus, Richard
Lauter, Roger Loveless, Kevin Murphy, Keith Paul, Eric Peterson, Christopher Pugliese,
Greg Roman, Brad Schmehl, Tom Sciacca, Larry Selman, Matt Stawicki, John Zielinski
• **Bartels & Assocs, Ceci: pg 1180**
3286 Ivanhoe, St Louis, MO 63139...**314-781-7377**
e-mail: ceciba@stlnet.com / fax: 314-781-8017
Illustrator: Bartels & Co, Marta Blanford, Bill Bruning, Lindy Burnett, Kevin Conran,
Robert Craig, Jim Dandy, Chris Dellorco, Sheryl Dickert, Jonathan Evans, Mary Flock-
Lempa, Mike Gardner, Leland Klanderman, Mary Flock Lempa, Larry McEntire, Rollin
McGrail, John Nelson, Jon Nelson, Kevin Newman, Deborah Palen, Charlie Podrebarac,
Guy Porfirio, Guy Porfiro, Jean Probert, Kyle Raetz, Deborah Rediger, Francisco
Rodriguez-Maruca, Jonathan & Georgina Rosenbaum, Chris Sharp, Stephen Thompson,
Wayne Watford, Stan Watts, Russ Widstrand, Ted Wright
Photographer: Chris Amaral, Jacques Barbey, Brian Kuhlmann & Associates, Ryan Roessler
Bartholomew, Gillian:
One Captain Dr #D358, Emeryville, CA 94608 510-653-3996
Illustrator: Patrick Réault
Barton Reps, Sue:
101 Calumet Ave, San Anselmo, CA 94960 415-457-3695
Photographer: Mark Gamba, Michael Golden, Peter Langone, Philip-Jon, Racine Photo Arts
Bastille & Assocs, Marie:
Paris, France 145-26-7009
Bates & Assocs, Pat:
300 W 12th St #3-I, New York, NY 10014 212-807-8420
Hair & Make-up: Paul Fields
Photographer: Francesca Galliani, Ted Hartshorn, Stewart Heir, Carolyn Knops
Stylist: Kris Jensen, David Yarritu
Baugher Associates, Liz:
300 N State St #4511, Chicago, IL 60610 312-832-9888
Illustrator: Shock Digital Art, Paul Somers
Photographer: Marc Hauser, Dave Jordano, Mark Lind Photography, Mark Luinenberg,
Bob Peterson, Chris Sanders, Thomas Smugala, Peter Zander
Beate Works:
2400 Shenandoah St, Los Angeles, CA 90034 310-558-1100
Graphic Designer: Maura McCarthy
Photographer: Larry Bartholomew, Grey Crawford, Jeff Novack, Rudy Schwab, Rick Stauss
Beck, Susanne:
2721 Cherokee Rd, Birmingham, AL 35216 205-871-6632
Photographer: Charles Beck
Beckett, Rosie:
55 Rochester Pl, London, England, UK NW1 PJU 71-482-3400
Beilin, Frank:
405 E 56th St, New York, NY 10022 212-751-3074
Photographer: Giovanni Stefano Ghidini, Victor Skrebneski
• **Beint & Beint: pg 1069** London, UK.................................**0171-793-7000**
fax: 0171-735-2565
Illustrator: Dan Yaccarino

Bender & Assocs, Lawrence:
846 Portola Rd #C, Portola Valley, CA 94028 415-851-0594
Bender, Brenda:
4170 S Arbor Cir, Marietta, GA 30066.....................................770-924-4793
Graphic Designer: Thomas Cleveland
Illustrator: Shawn Brasfield, Thomas Cleveland, Stephen Gallegos, Hellman Assoc,
Richard Edward Hicks, Paul Lackner, Marc Rochon, Geo Sipp, Skidmore Inc, Kyle Stone,
Jim Turgeon, Keith Witmer
Photographer: Jim Arbogast, Knight/Bilham, Jon Mazey, Ron Modra, Chuck St John, Jim
Wenger, Debrah Wihitlau
Benjamin Photographers/NY:
149 5th Ave #803, New York, NY 10010 212-253-8688
Photographer: Skip Caplan, Rafael Fuchs, Dennis Gottlieb, Zan Productions
Benton Nyce:
15 W 26th St #1001, New York, NY 10010 212-686-8444
Beranbaum, Sheryl:
RI 401-737-8591
Illustrator: David Barber, Doug Bowles, Michael Brenan, Richard Cook, James Edwards,
John Kastner, Manuel King, Mary King, Albert Molnai, Stephen Moscowitz, Matthew Pip-
pin, Sergio Roffo, Roy Scott, Susan Seed, Gary Symington, Erin Terry
Berendsen & Assocs, Inc:
2233 Kemper Ln, Cincinnati, OH 45206 513-861-1400
Illustrator: David Chestnut, Jake Ellison, Bill Fox, Rocky Fuller, George Hardebeck, Mar-
cia Hartsock, Daniel Krovatin, Mahammad Mansoor, Tom Marcotte, Thomas O Miller,
Garry Nichols, Frank Ordaz, Duff Orlemann, Jack Pennington, Dave Reed, Garry Richard-
son, Brent Riley, Ursula Roma, Robert Schuster, Fariba Shiadaz, Kevin Torline, Dave
Warren, Wendy Wassink Ackison, Misty Wheatley-Maxwell, Lee Woolery
Photographer: Jim Callaway, Doug Lempkee, Dan Patterson
Berliant, Ardath:
723 West Wrightwood, Chicago, IL 60614 773-525-0011
• **Bernstein & Andriulli: pg 1291**
60 E 42nd St #822, New York, NY 10165 ....**212-682-1490**
e-mail: Artinfo@ba-reps.com / fax: 212-286-1890
Illustrator: Tony Antonios, Pat Bailey, Johnathon Barkat, Jacques Brady, Don
Brautigam, Neil Brennan, Gregory Bridges, Rick Brown, Leonello Calvetti, Barbara
Camp, Karen Chandler, Cloe Cheese, The CIA, Haydee Corner, Haydn Cornner, Cre-
ative Capers Ent. Inc., Grant Delin, Grace DeVito, Anatoly Dverin, Julia Eggeringhaus,
Pauline Ellison, Ronald Finger, Dean Fleming, Ron Fleming, James Frisino, Victor
Gadino, Fred Gambino, Joe Genova, Lynda Gray, Brian Grimwood, John Harwood,
Bryan Haynes, David Holmes, Peter Horridge, Catherine Huerta, Daniel Kirk, Thea
Kliros, Peter Kramer, Mary Ann Lasher, John Lawrence, Vicki Lowe, Lee MacLeod,
Jacqueline Mair, Charles Masters, Darlene Olivia McElroy, McEwan, David McMacken,
Paul Micich, Frances Middendorf, Chris Moore, Pete Mueller, Fabian Negrin, Craig Nel-
son, Jeff Nishinaka, Neil Packer, Leah Palmer Preiss, Larry Paulsen, Greg Petan, Laura
Phillips, Michael Plank, Peggi Roberts, Paul S Robinson, Jeremy Sancha, Goro Sasaki,
Robert Shadbolt, Michael Sheehy, Erwin Sherman, Simon Spilsbury, Peter Stallard,
Tommy Stubbs, Thomas Thewes Jr, Jean-Paul Tibbles, Russell Walker, Pam Wall,
Matt Warford, Brent Watkinson, Catherine Wessel, David Wilgus, Leslie Wu, Farida
Zamas
Photographer: Melanie Acevedo, David Bartolomi, Dean Freeman, Brett Froomer, Philip
Habib, Stuart Hall, Gregory Heisler, Thibault Jeanson, Jock McDonald, Hans Neleman,
Pete Seward, Daniella Stallinger, Paul Wakefield
• **Bernstein, Joanie: pg 1452**
756 S 8th Ave, Naples, FL 34102 ....**941-403-4393**
fax: 941-403-0066
Illustrator: Todd Apjones, Allen Brewer, Tom Garrett, Eric Hanson, Jack A Molloy,
Dan Picasso, Joe Sorren, Elvis Swift
Lettering: Todd Apjones
Bertola Benz, Amy:
144 Barley Neck Rd, Orleans, MA 02653 508-255-1773
Photographer: Angela Coppola, Henderson/Cartledge
Bertotti Reps, Thomas:
456 Vallejo St, San Francisco, CA 94133 415-391-2573
Biernat, Anna: Troy, MI 248-545-2363
Bina Reps:
632 Broadway, New York, NY 10012 212-533-1734
Birenbaum, Molly:
7 Williamsburg Dr, Cheshire, CT 06410 203-272-9253
Illustrator: Bernstein & Andriulli Intl, P Beach Illustration, Paul Selwyn
Photographer: Sean Kernan, Frank Moscati, Joanne Schmaltz, Bill Thompson
Black Star:
116 E 27th St, New York, NY 10016..212-679-3288
Photographer: John W Alexanders
Black, Inc:
2512 E Thomas Rd #2, Phoenix, AZ 85016...............................602-381-1332
Illustrator: Laura Bailey, Coni Bourin, Greta Buchart, Giovanina Colliilio, Bob Diercksmeier,
John Huxtable, Alan Neider, Peggi Roberts, Wilma Shell, Angela Simon, Tad Smith
Photographer: Enric Aromi, Jim Carroll, Dan Coogan, Golf Stock, Bill Mckellar, Tim Pan-
ell, Bruce Peterson, Richard Petrillo, Lana Tucker
Black, Pamela:
149 Fifth Ave 8th Fl, New York, NY 10010 212-979-2636
Photographer: William Heuberger, James Levin, Mariano Pastor, Frank Veronsky
Black, White & Color, Inc:
2232 E 14 Mile Rd, Warren, MI 48092 810-795-4620
Blackburn, Christopher:
Westech Industrial Park #28, Tyngsboro, MA 01879 508-649-7788
Photographer: Peter Kaskons
• **Boege, Kim: pg 1170**
Phoenix, AZ **602-265-4389**
Illustrator: Joann Daley
Boghosian, Marty:
201 E 21st St, New York, NY 10010 212-353-1313
Photographer: David Katzenstein, David Massey
Boho Studio, The:
254 Elizabeth St #5A, New York, NY 10012 212-334-8302
Photographer: Cesar Vera
Bold Montage:
8955 Wenderland Park Ave, Los Angeles, CA 90046 213-851-0621
Photographer: Christy Bush, Alison Dyer, Dennis Keeley, Mark Liddell, Rick Steil, Art
Strieber, Matthew Welch, Jim Wright

Bonavita, Rocco:
32 Downing St #4D, New York, NY 10014 212-633-1310
Bookmakers Ltd:
PO Box 1086, Taos, NM 87571 505-776-5435
Illustrator: Susan Banta, Andrea Barrett, Lloyd Birmingham, Carol Byer, Barbara Cousins, Deirdre Griffin, George Guzzi, Lydia Halverson, Ronda Henrichsen, David Hohn, Keith Lo Bue, Kathleen McCord, Mark Mohr, Karen Pellaton, Marsha Serafin, Dick Smolinski, Angela Werneke
Booth & Assocs, Greg:
1322 Roundtable, Dallas, TX 75247 214-688-1855
Booth Inc, Tom:
425 W 23rd St #17A, New York, NY 10011 212-243-2750
Photographer: Hiro, Matthew Hranek, Steve Lewis
Bos & Co:
London, England, UK 81-847-7274
Boshard, Lisa:
CA 303-413-0830
• **Boston, Diane: pg 1456,1457**
39 Hamilton Terr, New York, NY 10031 ....**212-283-3401**
url: www.wayart.com
Illustrator: Harry Borgman, Michael D'Antuono, Weston Emmart, Alexandra Gabanyi, Denis Luzuriaga, Scott McBee, Lucian Mihaesteanu, Rich Ransley, Bruce Rauffenbart, Aristides Ruiz, Laszlo Schreiber, Suzanne Simmons, Brian Stymest
Botaish Group, Janet:
1633 Electric Avenue, Venice, CA 90291 310-314-1571
Photographer: Patrik Andersson, Eika Aoshima, Michael Faye, Fergus Greer, Kevin Kerslake, Stephanie Pfriender, Diego Uchitel, Firooz Zahedi
Brackman, Henrietta:
415 E 52nd St, New York, NY 10022 212-753-6483
Braun, Betsy:
109 Somerstown Rd, Ossining, NY 10562 914-762-5335
Photographer: Whitney Lane
Braun, Kathy:
2925 Griffith St, San Francisco, CA 94124 415-467-9676
Graphic Designer: Koji Takei
Illustrator: Pat Allen, Vivian Wu Browning, Michael Bull, Eldon Doty, John Huxtable, Scott Matthews, Sudi McCollum, Jacqueline Osborn, Stephen Osborn, Dan Raabe, Heidi Schmidt
Photographer: Laurence Bartone
Breitmayer, Becky:
1306 Summit Ave, Cleveland, OH 44107 216-226-1455
Photographer: Anthony Gray, Geoffrey Pankhurst, Trepal Photography
Brenneman, Cindy:
1856 Elba Cir, Costa Mesa, CA 92626 714-641-9700
Brenner, Harriet:
3131 SW Martin Downs Blvd, Palm City, FL 34990 561-286-9781
Photographer: Dick Krueger
• **Brewster, John D: pg 790,791**
597 Riverside Ave, Westport, CT 06880 ....**203-226-4724**
url: brewstercreative.com / fax: 203-454-9904
Brindle, Inc, Carolyn:
203 E 89th St #3D, New York, NY 10128 212-534-4177
Brody, Sam, The Mavins, Inc:
77 Winfield St #4, E Norwalk, CT 06855 203-854-0805
Bronstein Berman Wills:
38 Greene St, New York, NY 10013 212-925-2999
url: www.bbwstudio.com / fax: 212-925-3799
Photographer: Howard Berman, Steve Bronstein, Bret Wills
Brooke & Co:
4323 Bluffview Blvd, Dallas, TX 75209 214-352-9192
Illustrator: Karen Blessen, Lee Lee Brazeal, Paul Fleming, Bryan Haynes, Michael Haynes, Gary Head, Mike Reed, Carol Zuber-Mallison
Photographer: Jay Dickman, Jeffrey Heger, David Lyles, Richard Seagraves, Greg Watermann
Brooks & Assocs, Doug:
Chicago, IL 773-792-2662
Photographer: Deborah Van Kirk
Brown & Assocs, Deborah:
80 Fourth Ave 7th Fl, New York, NY 10003 212-674-2002
Photographer: Jeff Corwin, Mark Godfrey, Michael Melford, Nancy Moran, Ron Wu
Brown & Assocs, Shelley: pg 560-577
155 Lippincott St, Toronto, ON M5S 2P3 ....**416-505-9522**
....**888-277-7200**
e-mail: shelly@sbaillustrates.com / url: www.sbaillustrates.com
Illustrator: Harvey Chan, Helen D'Souza, Joe Fleming, Kevin Ghiglione, Laurie Lafrance, Glenn Ryan, Tracy Walker, Tim Zeltner
Brown & Assocs, Shin:
60 E 42nd St #1060, New York, NY 10165 212-953-0088
Photographer: Dennis Blachut, Lee Crum, Giles Hancock, Kelvin Hudson, Serge Korniloff, Stephen Wilkes
Brown, Dianne:
402 N Windsor Blvd, Los Angeles, CA 90004 213-462-5598
Brown, Regina:
307 S Trooper Rd, Norristown, PA 19403 610-539-1130
Electronic Imaging: Scott MacNeil
Illustrator: Jean Bryer van Dornick, Gary Carlson, Lucas Deaver, Max Garcia, Jeff Holewski, Seth Jaben, Linda S Nye, Terry Watkinson, Michael Weaver, Ed Wexler
Lettering: Luis Sola
Photographer: Angelo Caggiano, Bruce Cramer
• **Bruck & Moss: pg 806-815**
100 Bleecker St, New York, NY 10012 ....**212-982-6533**
fax: 212-358-1586
333 E 49th St, New York, NY 10017 ....**212-980-8061**
url: www.theispot.com/rep/bruckandmoss / fax: 212-832-8778
Illustrator: Dave Black, Tom Curry, Lydia Hess, Barbara Hranilovich, DB Johnson, Katie Keller, Elizabeth Lada, Susan LeVan, Adam Niklewicz, Rebecca Rüegger

• **Bruck, Nancy: pg 806-815**
100 Bleecker St, New York, NY 10012 ....**212-982-6533**
url: www.theispot.com/rep/bruckandmoss / fax: 212-358-1586
See Bruck & Moss for client list
Bruml, Kathy:
161 Valley View, Ridgewood, NJ 07450 212-874-5659
Photographer: Monica Buck, Charles Maraia, David & Carin Riley, Luca Travotta
Buck & Kane:
481 8th Ave #1530, New York, NY 10001 212-631-0009
Illustrator: Shawn Banner, Jay Belmore, Ken Call, Michel Canetti, Dee Densmore D'Amico, Philip Huber, Mark Kaufman, Robert Melendez, Wally Neibart, Robert Passantino, Joanie Popeo, Dave Redl, Eva Sakmar, Gerry Schurr, Kevin Spaulding, Glenn Tunstull, Marcia G Verman, Ron Victor
Buck, Sid & Kane, Barney:
481 8th Ave #1530, New York, NY 10036 212-221-8090
Illustrator: Shawn Banner, Jay Belmore, Ken Call, Michel Canetti, Mario Henri Chakkour, Dee Densmore D'amico, Natalie Fabian, Nate Giorgio, Mark Kaufman, Bertrand Le Pautremat, Robert Melendez, Robert Passantino, Dave Redl, Gerry Schurr, Kevin Serwacki, Robin Skoglund, Kevin Spaulding, Eva Sullivan, Roman Szolkowski, Glenn Tunstull
Burg Fine Art Editions, Randall:
4224 Glencoe Ave, Marina Del Rey, CA 90292
Illustrator: Christina De Musée
Burg, Kathleen:
228 S First St, Milwaukee, WI 53204 414-273-5555
Illustrator: Neal Aspinall
Burke/Triolo Productions:
307 N Michigan Ave #1006, Chicago, IL 60601 312-704-0500
Photographer: Jeff Burke, Tim Hawley, Bruce James, Lew Robertson
Stylist: Lorraine Triolo
Burlingham, Tricia:
10355 Ashton Ave, Los Angeles, CA 90024 310-275-3495
Photographer: Sam Jones, Carin Krasner, Shawn Michienzi, Bill Miles, Peggy Sirota, Jonelle Weaver, Chris Wimpey
Burnett, Yolanda:
6478 Chestnut Hill Rd, Flowery Branch, GA 30542 770-967-0039
Illustrator: Clem Bedwell, Vince Chiaramonte, Barbara Emmons, Thomas L Fluharty, Paul Johnson, Tim Jonke, Nobee Kanayama, Nancy Kurtz, Don Margolis, Jeff Meyer, Jeff O'Connor, James Shepherd, Keith Skeen, Jay Smith, Luis Sola, Tim Spransy, Keith Ward, Jim Wilson, Matt Zumbo
Photographer: Joe Beauchamp, Mike Granberry
Bush, Nan:
135 Watts St 5th Fl, New York, NY 10013 212-226-0814
Photographer: Barry Lategan, Bruce Weber
Bussler, Tom:
451 West Wrightwood Ave, Chicago, IL 60614 773-342-3709
Illustrator: Phoenix Studio Inc

C

Cadenbach Assocs, Marilyn:
115 Upland Rd, Cambridge, MA 02140 617-868-2004
Photographer: William Huber, John Huet, Raymond Meeks, Martijn Oort, Jack Richmond
Caltis, Kate:
439 S Tryon St, Charlotte, NC 28202 704-376-7609
Campbell, Marianne:
Pier 9 Embarcadaro #102, San Francisco, CA 94111 415-433-0353
Photographer: Jim Erickson, Michael Lamotte
Caputo, Elise:
240 E 27th St, New York, NY 10016 212-725-0503
Film: David Wagreich
Photographer: Didier Dorot, Dennis Mosner, John Rizzo
PF: Jeffrey Apoian
Carelas, Joan:
313 W Martin St, Raleigh, NC 27601 919-833-6659
Carter, Katherine T:
24 Fifth Ave #703, New York, NY 10011 212-533-9530
P.O. Box 2449, St Leo, FL 33574 352-523-1948
Cary & Co:
666 Bantry Ln, Stone Mountain, GA 30083 404-296-9666
Illustrator: Robert August, Johnna Bandle, Howard & Margie Fullmer, Mike Hodges, Kevin Hulsey, David Marks, Shawn McKelvey Studio, Shawn McKelvey, Charlie Mitchell, Greg Olsen
Photographer: Axiom Inc/Chuck Carlton, Peter Fownes
Casala Ltd:
8383 Wilshire Blvd #954, Beverly Hills, CA 90211 213-465-7577
Hair & Make-up: Jacquline Neely, Sheri Short
Casey & Assocs, Marge:
150 W 28th St #1803, New York, NY 10001 212-929-3757
Illustrator: Mark Hall
Photographer: Augustus Butera, Wayne Calabrese, Jeffrey Clifford, Chris DeGray, Brian Fraunfelter, Yoshiomi Goto, Ryazard Horowitz, Joel Larson, David Mendelsohn, Judd Pilossof, Christopher Schrameck, Michael Scott, Joyce Tenneson
Casey, Inc, Judy:
114 E 13th St, New York, NY 10003 212-228-7500
Hair: Shay Ashval, Azuma, Antonio Diaz, Michele Garziano, Maria Schiavetti
Hair & Make-up: Cyril Lanoir, Donald Mikula, Rob Van Dorssen
Music: Keiko Morisaki, Shally Zucker
Make-up: Hiromi Ando, Ariella, Gianpaolo Ceciliato, Maria De Schneider, Lorraine Leckie
Photographer: Michael Arnaud, Franceska Cotti, Alan Cresto, Greg Delves, Torkil Gudnason, George Holz, Maria Robledo
Stock: Irene Bilo, Conrad Blane, Mimi Fisher, Sarah Gore, Carlos Mota
Stylist: Bradley Garlock, Christine Mottau, Robertino Trovati
Catipillar Graphics:
232 Paliament St, Toronto, ON M5A 3A4 416-368-4999
• **Caton, Chip: pg 656, 984,985,1495**
15 Warrenton Ave, Hartford, CT 06105 ....**860-523-4562**
Illustrator: Anatoly, Angie Applebee, Diana Minisci Appleton, Doug Besser, Mark Busacca, Gary Davis, Phillip Dvorak, Jeff Faria, Andy Giarnella, Joe Klim, Terry Lennox, Roger Leyonmark, Jon Lezinsky, Michelle Lougee, Michael McCurdy, Nikolai Punin, Aina Roman, Linda Schiwall, Marty Smith, Jim Smola, Janet Street, David Tow, Jon Valk, Bryan Wiggins, Randall Zwingler
Photographer: Melanie Eve Barocas, David Mendelsohn, Peter Weidlein

Cedeno, Lucy:
44 Arroyo Viejo Rd, Santa Fe, NM 87505 505-473-2745
Photographer: David Michael Kennedy
Charles, Bill:
126 Madison Ave ste 2F, New York, NY 10016 212-213-6810
Photographer: Max Cardelli, Alesia Exum, Larry Fink, Spencer Jones Photography,
Spencer Jones, Jennifer Lee, Svend Lindbbaek, Joseph Pluchino, Amanda Pratt, Joseph
Rodriquez, Steven Stickler
Chicago Artist Reps:
PO Box 11902, Chicago, IL 60611 312-409-6211
• **Chislovsky Design, Inc, Carol: pg 817-819**
853 Broadway #1201, New York, NY 10003.............................**212-677-9100**
e-mail: chislovsky@aol.com / fax: 212-353-0954
Illustrator: Gil Adams, Randal Birkey, Jerry Blank, Daniels & Daniels, Scott Ernster, Susan
Foster, Chris Gall, Jeff George, Ignacio Gomez, Jack Graham, John Hart, John J Hart,
Mark Herman, Nobee Kanayama, Murray Kimber, Jim Kopp, Gary Krejca, Joe Lapinski,
John Margeson, Jeff Marinelli, Larry Moore, Joe Ovies, Julie Pace, Chuck Schmidt, RM
Schneider Illustration, Sandra Shap, Neil Shigley, Carla Siboldi, Randy South
Christell & Assocs, Jim:
660 N Deerborn St #208, Chicago, IL 60610 312-337-6005
Film: Carbo Films, Electric Ave
Music: Elias Assoc
Photographer: Norm Clasen
Cichocki, Lisa:
140 W 22nd St 8th Fl, New York, NY 10011 212-255-0710
Photographer: Bill Milne
Clare Reps, Pam:
9812 Glynshire Way, Potomac, MD 20854.................................301-424-9298
Cohn, Carol:
137 W 25th St, New York, NY 10001 212-924-4450
Photographer: Frederic Brenner, Ric Cohn, Ric Photography Cohn, Jill Enfield, Bret
Lopez, Cheryl Maeder, Pierre Reinhard, Johnathon Torgovnik
Colavecchio, Bob:
555 Oradell Ave, Oradell, NJ 07649 201-261-9247
Cole, Randy:
24 W 30th St 5th Fl, New York, NY 10001 212-679-5933
Photographer: Lori Adamski-Peek, Andrew Brusso, Barbara Cole, Cameron Davidson,
Jill Greenberg, Laurie Rubin
Coleman, Woody:
490 Rockside Rd, Cleveland, OH 44131 216-661-4222
Electronic Imaging: Royce Fitzgerald, Michael Koester, Bill Morse
Illustrator: Tom Antonishak, Eric Apel, Alexander Bostic, Bruce Bowles, Mark Brown, Eric
Bryant, Mark Busacca, Paul Butvila, Mike Corcoran, Denise Cuttitta, Alano Daniels, Bear
Daniels, JC Duffy, John Dzedzy, Larry Elmore, Sid Evans, Robert Fraser, Gary Glover,
Jenny Graham, Andrew Grivas, Abe Gurvin, R Hartzler, Bella Hollingworth, Bruce Holwer-
da, Thomas Hudson, Herb James, Thomas Jester, Buena Johnson, Reginald Jones, Eric
Joyner, David Kelley, Toni Kurrasch, John Letostak, Roger Leyonmark, Charles Manus, Al
Margolis, Camille McBride, Bob Novak, Fred Padberg, Joani Pakula, Vincent Perez, Sally
Pogwizd, Peter Quidley, Bob Radigan, Rick Reeves, Jesse Reisch, Gerry Saent-Johns,
Tim Scoggins, Natalie Sehn, James Seward, Steven Seward, Marla Shega, Tom Shep-
hard, William Silvers, Victor Stabin, Don Stewart, Alan Studt, James Swanson, Robert
Tanenbaum, David Taylor, Greg Thorkelson, Ezra Tucker, Victor Valla, Barry Waldman,
Lawrence Walker, Tim Webb, Mark Weber, David Wenzel, Eric Williams, Chuck Wim-
mer, Greg Wray, Roger Xavier, Randall Zwingler
• **Collier, Jan: pg 252,253,376.377,934,935,952,953,986,987**
1205 W California Ave, Mill Valley, CA 94941 ....**213-934-5567**
fax: 213-934-5516
PO Box 470818, San Francisco, CA 94147 ....**415-383-9026**
e-mail: jan@collierreps.com / url: www.collierreps.com / fax: 415-383-9037
Illustrator: Barbara Banthien, Gary Baseman, Rich Borge, Gerald Bustamante, Kathleen
Dunne, Rae Ecklund, Travis Foster, Douglas Fraser, Craig Frazier, Michele Manning,
Raphael Montoliu, Robert Gantt Steele, Alain Stivell
• **Collington, Danielle: pg 792,793**
200 W 15th St #16A, New York, NY 10011 ....**212-243-4209**
Command, Betsy:
15621 N Hillcrest, Minneapolis, MN 55406 612-291-1954
• **Comport, Allan: pg 641-645**
208 Providence Rd, Annapois, MD 21401 ....**410-349-8669**
e-mail: acomport@aol.com
Illustrator: Lori Bilter, Sally Wern Comport, Vicki Gullickson, Stan Makowski, Chuck Rancorn
Comstock:
49 Bathurst St #401, Toronto, ON M5V 2P2 416-504-9177
Condon, Jennifur:
1035 W Lake St, Chicago, IL 60607 ....
Photographer: e-Light Studios, Walter Gray, Heidi Wells
Coningsby, Andrew:
30 Tottenham St, London, England, UK W1 9PN...........................1716-361064
Conlon, Jean:
461 Broome St, New York, NY 10013...212-966-9897
Illustrator: Elizabeth Brady
Photographer: Kenro Izu, Minh & Wass, Sergio Purtell
Connolly, Elyse:
23 W 16th St, New York, NY 10011 212-255-0886
Photographer: Thomas Heinser, Rudy Molacek, Fred Ohringer, Peggy Sirota, Charles
Tracy, Paul Westlake
• **Conrad Represents: pg 473-501**
2149 Lyon St #5, San Francisco, CA 94115 ....**415-921-7140**
e-mail: art@conradreps.com / url: www.conradreps.com / fax: 415-921-3939
Illustrator: Paul Anderson, Jerry Blank, David Chen, David Austin Clar, James Endicott,
Michael Gibbs, Dante Jarecka, Andrew Judd, Jerzy Kolacz, Rafael Lopez, Eric Peterson,
Max Seabaugh, Dave Stevenson, Paul Vismara
Cook, Warren:
PO Box 2159, Laguna Hills, CA 92653 714-770-4619
Photographer: Kathleen Norris Cook
Corbis:
920 Broadway 5th Fl, New York, NY 10018 212-777-6200
Photographer: David Allen, John Bellisimo, Richard Bowditch, Renee Cox, Mitch Gerber,
Joe Giron, Lynn Goldsmith, Alan Levenson, Matt Mendolsohn, Barry Morgenstein, Tim
Mosenfelder, Will Van Overbeek, Pacha, John Roca

Cornelia Photo Reps, Inc:
380 Madison Ave 7th Fl, New York, NY 10017 212-697-0069
Photographer: Christopher Baker, Michael Mundy, Richard Pierce, Aldo Rossi
Cornell & Co:
737 Milwood Ave, Venice, CA 90291...310-301-8059
Film: Crossroads Films, Nomad Editorial, Taylormade Editorial, X-1 Films, X-Ray Films
Illustrator: Joe Saputo
Photographer: Charles Hopkins
Cornell, McCarthy:
2D Cross Hwy, Westport, CT 06880..203-454-4210
Corporate Art Planning:
27 Union Square West ste 407, New York, NY 10003 212-242-8995
Electronic Imaging: Suzanne Brookens, Caroline Corey, Charles Friedman, Nebraska Gif-
ford Shestak, Charles Messina, Eric Monteiro, Richard Rockwell
Cowan, Pat:
68 E Division Rd, Valparaiso, IN 46383 219-462-0199
Photographer: Ralph Cowan
• **Craig Reps, Suzanne: pg 1107**
4015 E 53rd St, Tulsa, OK 74135...**918-749-9424**
Illustrator: Gil Adams, Martha Anne Booth, Cameron Clement, Paul Corrigan, Michael
Hogue, Tim Jessell, Gary Locke, Keith Locke, Genevieve Meek, David Merrell, Aletha Reppel
Photographer: Robin Kachantones
Creative Advantage, Inc:
620 Union St, Schenectady, NY 12305 518-370-0312
Illustrator: Jack Graber
Creative Connection, Inc:
PO Box 253 Stillwater Rd, Gibson Island, MD 21056 410-360-5981
Creative Freelancers:
99 Park Ave #210A, New York, NY 10016 800-398-9544
Illustrator: Gil Ashby, Cary Austin, Marcel Bordei, Stephen Bornstein, Lloyd Briming-
ham, Henry Buerckholz, Wende Caporale, Carolyn Carpenter, Chris Celusniak, Roger
Chandler, James Cooper MD, Jim DeLapine, John Edens, Clifford Faust, Anne Feiza,
John Gampert, Rick Geary, Gary Hanna, Traci Harmon, Phil Howe, Chet Jezierski,
Sandy Kossin, Salem Krieger, Rob Lawson, Frank McShane, AJ Miller, Greg Newbold,
Jan North, Jim Owens, Elena Poladin, Meryl Rosner, Reg Sandland, Glen Schofield,
Scott Snow, Steve Sullivan, David Tamura Design/Illustration, David Tamura, Winson
Trang, Lou Vaccaro, David Wink, Yemi
Photographer: Greg Newbold
• **Creative Illustrators Agency: pg 784-787**
231 E 76th St #5D, New York, NY 10021 ....**212-535-0438**
fax: 212-535-1624
Creative Management Partners:
1180 6th Ave PH, New York, NY 10036 212-655-6500
Photographer: Shu Akashi, Kaz Arahama, Lillian Bassman, Anita Calfro, Clang, Jim
Erickson, Fergus Grier, Simon Harsent, David Leach, Dennis Manarchy, Doug Menuez,
Chris Nicholls, Jeff Riedel, Duncan Sim, Karina Taira, Alastair Thain, Olaf Veltman
Creative Network:
100 Wyndham Cir W, New Brighton, MN 55112 612-631-2353
Illustrator: Tim Blouch, Terry Boles, Dave Danz, Virginia Kylberg, Keith Lango,
C Spencer Morris, Chris Nye, Linda O'Leary, Bryon Vollman
Creative Network East:
1089 Brook Rd #100, Milton, MA 02186 800-309-1102
Illustrator: Brad Gaber, Heather Holbrook
Photographer: Ken Childress, Rocky Kneten, Hal Lott, Beryl Striewski
Creative Network South:
4316 Cynthia St, Bellaire, TX 77401 281-870-1102
Illustrator: Brad Gaber
IP: Steven Belchér
Photographer: Ken Childress, Rocky Kneten, Hal Lott, Beryl Striewski
Creative Options, Inc:
50 Washington St, S Norwalk, CT 06854 203-854-9393
Creative Photographers, Inc:
444 Park Ave S #502, New York, NY 10016 212-683-1455
Photographer: Colin Bell, Polly Borland, Gwendolyn Cates, Richard Croft, Melanie Dunea,
Guido Hanari, Ralph Mecke, Nigel Parry, TC Reiner, Andrew Southam, Wayne Stambler,
Art Streiber, Veronique Vial
Creative Resources:
12056 Summit Cir, Beverly Hills, CA 90210................................310-276-5282
Illustrator: Roger Chandler, John Chui, Dorothy Gulick, Shane John, Toni Kurrasch, Rob
Lawson, Darlene Olivia McElroy, Carlos Sanchez, Terri Starrett, ET Steadman, Dave
Stevenson, Anne Teisher, Bret Wagner, Marijke P Wagner
Photographer: Eliot Crowley, Jack Eadon, Claudia Kunin, Colin McRae, David Miller,
Norm Stevens, Elise Weinger
Creative Source, Inc:
360 N Michigan Ave #805, Chicago, IL 60601 312-201-1020
Cullom, Ellen:
55 E 9th St, New York, NY 10003 212-777-1749
Photographer: Robert Grant
Custack, David:
Raleigh, NC 919-833-5522
• **CWC: pg 1069**
Tokyo, Japan **813-3496-0745**
fax: 813-3496-0747
Illustrator: Dan Yaccarino

D

Dakota, Irene:
2121 Lucerne Ave, Miami Beach, FL 33140 305-674-9975
Photographer: Michael Dakota
Darnell, Jim, The Art Source:
2820 Rainforest Ct, Southlake, TX 76092 817-481-2212
Das Grup:
311 Ave H #D, Redondo Beach, CA 90277.................................310-540-5958
Illustrator: Loudvik Akopyan, Mona Daly, Brian Fujimori, Ray Goudey, John Hull, Jui
Ishida, Rachael McCampbell, Mercedes McDonald, Robert Rodriguez, Brad Weinman,
Michael Wepplo
Photographer: Richard Rendon
Day, Ursula:
24 Fifth Ave #531, New York, NY 10011 212-505-3322
Photographer: Gerhard Yurkovic

• De Moreta, Linda: pg 822-825
1839 Ninth St, Alameda, CA 94501 ....**510-769-1421**
e-mail: ldmreps@earthlink.net / fax: 510-521-1674
Illustrator: Shannon K Abbey, Johnston Clark, John Firesheets, Diane Hays, James Henry, Verne Lindner, Peter McDonnell, Diane Naugle, Colin Poole, Charles Pyle, Richard Sheppard
Lettering: Barbara Callow, Verne Lindner
Photographer: Joe Baraban, James Chiang, John Lund, Ron Miller

Deddens & Deddens:
Los Angeles, CA 310-203-9714
Photographer: Robb Scharetg

• Dedell, Inc, Jacqueline: pg 282-312
58 W 15th St, New York, NY 10011 ....**212-741-2539**
url: www.showcase.com / fax: 212-741-4660
Illustrator: Scott Baldwin, Amy Binder, Cathie Bleck, Edward Briant, Philip Brooker, Alicia Buelow, Brian Cairns, Ron Chan, Ivan Chermayeff, Christopher Corr, Nancy Davis, David Frampton, Linda Frichtel, Bryan Leister, Frank Miller, Paula Munck, Paul Oxborough, Ed Parker, Kimberly Bulken Root, Fletcher Sibthorp, Gordon Studer, Richard Tuschman, Alexandria Weems, Mick Wiggins, Heidi Younger

Deegan, Marian:
2508 Belleview Pl #41, Milwaukee, WI 53211 414-964-8088

Demont, Thiery:
7266 Franklin Ave #421, Los Angeles, CA 90046 213-876-3742
Photographer: William Claxton, Melvin Sokolsky

Des Vergers, Diana:
6153 Lower York Rd, New Hope, PA 18938 215-794-3793
Photographer: Paccione

Design Marketing Group, Inc:
375 Interstate Blvd, Sarasota, FL 34240 941-377-6709
Illustrator: Phil Jones

Di Parisi, Peter:
250 W 99th St #3A, New York, NY 10025 212-663-8330

Diane Boston Group, Way Art:
39 Hamilton Terrace, New York, NY 10031 212-283-3401

Dice, Ron:
1700 North North Park, Chicago, IL 60614 312-266-6313
Electronic Imaging: John De Salvo
Illustrator: Paul Miller
Photographer: Bruce DeBoer, Kurt Gerber, David Lyles, Ken Redding, Kathy Sanders

Dictenberg, Robin:
348 W 11th St #2B, New York, NY 10014 212-620-0995
Photographer: Sandi Fellman, Graham Ford, John Huet, Mark Laita, Philip Porcella, Graham Westmoreland

Dimension Creative Artwork:
9801 DuPont Ave S #168, Minneapolis, MN 55431 612-884-4045
Electronic Imaging: Jennifer Vee
Film: Wobat Interactive, Frank Ordaz, Marshall Woksa
Illustrator: Keith Grove, Chad Peterson, Chad A. Peterson, Dennis Rogers, Kathy Rogers, Dan Salmela
Photographer: John Lehn & Assocs

DLM Artist Reps:
570 Seventh Ave #1803, New York, NY 10018 212-840-8100
Photographer: Dana Buckley, Chas Bush, Corinne Colen, Mervyn Franklin, Julie Gang, Jim Huibregtse, Les Jorgensen, Michael Lippino, David Maisel, John Manno, James Porto, Pete Stone, Denis Waugh, David Weiss, Peter Zander

Dodge + Assocs, Sharon:
3033 13th Ave W, Seattle, WA 98119 206-284-4701
Illustrator: Bart Bemus, Bill Brown, Robert BrŸnz, Nancy Davis, Jonathan Evans, John Fortune, Chris Gall, Allen Garns, Jud Guitteau, Pablo Haz, G Brian Karas, Mike Kowalski, Julia LaPine, Stephanie Morgan Rogers, Mark Schofield, Kevin Short, Beata Szpura, Keith Witmer
Photographer: Robin Bartholick, Patricia Ridenour

Dolby Reps, Karen:
333 N Michigan #1100, Chicago, IL 60601 312-855-9336
Illustrator: Matt Ambre, Kevin Bapp, Mark Busacca, Mona Daly, Diane Kay Davis, Patrick Faricy, Fran Gregory, Dave Joly, Kelly Kennedy, Jennifer Knaack, Charlie Mitchell, Paul Ristau, Dan Wiemer
Photographer: Allan Birnbach, Paul Rung

Dorman, Paul:
430 E 57th St, New York, NY 10022 212-826-6737

Dotzler Creative Arts:
4202 S 90th St, Omaha, NE 68127 402-592-1901
Illustrator: JC Illus

Douraghy, Jamie:
1950 S Sawtelle Blvd #320, Los Angeles, CA 90025 310-312-2062

Drost, Cindy:
1829-2 Grove, Glenview, IL 60025 847-729-0957
Graphic Designer: Steve Reynolds
Illustrator: Paul E Niemeyer
Photographer: Scott Simms

Dubois, Dennis Reps, Francoise:
305 Newbury Ln, Newbury Park, CA 91320 805-376-9738
Photographer: Michael Baciu, Andrew Bernstein, Ron Derhacopian, Michel Dubois, Stephen Lee, Eric Sander

Dunn & Assocs, Roark:
121 Reade Street #7E, New York, NY 10013 212-566-4900

E

Edberg, Grace:
835 Moraga Dr #2, Los Angeles, CA 90049 310-471-2288
Hair & Make-up: Dian Bethune-Coble, Jeffrey Fetzer, Renne Parenteau, Gloria Pasqua, Jeanne Rios, Mickey Song
Photographer: Amedeo, Cynthia Brown, Gary Cloud, Todd Gray, Enida Vanderwyck, Robert Zuckerman
Stylist: Traci Marmon

Edders, Scott:
PO Box 4018, Naperville, IL 60567 630-961-0237

Edge:
5757 Wilshire Blvd PH-20, Los Angeles, CA 90036 213-954-9422
596 Broadway 11th Fl, New York, NY 10012 212-343-2260
Make-up: Susan Houser
Photographer: Dan Borris, Gentl & Hyers, Michael Lavine, Norman Jean Roy, Nitin Vadukul
Stylist: Wendy Schecter

Edsey & Sons, Steve:
401 N Wabash, Chicago, IL 60611 312-527-0351
Graphic Designer: Roberts Barnes, Kelly Hume
Illustrator: Keith Batcheller, Michael Carroll, Mike Dammer, Lary Day, Tom Durfee, Dennis Dzielak, Michael Edsey, Dennis Franzen, Bryan Friel, Gene Givan, George Hamblin, Seitu Hayden, Mitchell Heinze, Tim Huhn, Victor Kennedy, Doug Knutson, Gary Krejca, Rick Lieder, David Loew, Dan Lotts, Rick Lundeen, Rob Magiera, Ron Mahoney, Betty Maxey, Tom McKee, Jay Moore, Manuel Morales, Terry Olson, Matt Paoletti, Mike Philips, Harlan Scheffler, Mike Sobey, Richard Stergulz, Don Stinson, Bobbi Tull, Jim Wisniewski, John Zielinski
Photographer: Robert Barnes, Steve Liss

• Eiss, Kelly: pg 821
401 Second Ave #800, Minneapolis, MN 55401 ....**612-338-9138**
....**612-747-0001**
e-mail: kjeiss@pioneerplanet.infi.net / fax: 612-338-9148

Elder, Heather:
1027 Church St, San Francisco, CA 94114 415-391-1181
Photographer: Hunter Freeman, Stephen Wilkes

Embler, Jennifer:
10 Fairway Dr #212, Deerfield Beach, FL 33441 954-760-4195
Cartoonist: Walter Curlee
Illustrator: Bob Cline, Sid Daniels, Kevin Ellsworth, Sid Evans, David FeBland, Alan Heider, Reggie Holladay, Dick Mahoney, Colin Poole, Bob Radigan, Jim Stillwell, Monte Varah, Brian Wiggins, Bryan Wiggins
Multimedia: Gary Colby, Brian Fein

Ennis, Inc:
451 D St, Boston, MA 02210 617-261-3970
Hair & Make-up: Lynne Avallone, Jane Choi, Christine Clemente, Christine Dooley, Anne Jones, Cynthia Murphy, Heidi Wells
Stock: Joji Goto, Lisa Greenfield
Stylist: Manuella Amzallag, Mary Arch, Myrosha Dziuk, Margie Eis, Eileen Eisele, Stella Goodall, Carmine Micciulla, Joseph Serpa, Lisa Smith, Sybylla Smith, Tui Stark, Kelly Upson, Irene Vass, Raquel Vidal, Nan Whitney, Assaff Ziv
Z: Sara Egan, Deborah Freedman, Lauren Kramer, Joan Morency, Susan Strauss

Envoy Creative Consultants, Inc:
1523 King St, Alexandria, VA 22314 703-706-5729
Illustrator: Daiji Asami, Debra Schaeffer
Photographer: Michelle Frankfurter, Aaron Goodman, Mark Lee, Craig Paternostro, Jim Vecchione, Mark Wieland

Epstein, Rhoni:
11977 Kiowa Ave #307, Los Angeles, CA 90049 310-207-5937
Photographer: Charles Bush, Marcelo Coelho, Vic Huber, John Kelley, Bret Lopez, Cheryl Maeder, Jim McHugh, Anthony Nex, Meredith Parmelee, Rocki Pederson

Ericson, William:
1024 Mission St, S Pasadena, CA 91030 213-461-4969

Erwin, Robin:
54 Applecross Cir, Chalfont, PA 18914 215-997-2311
Stock: Signal Stock

Eskimo, Joel:
175 5th Ave, New York, NY 10010 212-807-8338

Esto Photo:
222 Valley Pl, Mamaroneck, NY 10543 914-698-4060
Photographer: Peter Aaron, Jeff Goldberg, Tim Griffith, Peter Mauss, Jock Pottle

Evans, Dilys:
Box 430, Norfolk, CT 06058 860-542-5433

F

Famous Frames:
5855 Green Valley Cir #308, Culver City, CA 90230 310-642-2721
Illustrator: Jennifer Baker, Kathy Bieck, Paul Binkley, Mark Bloom, George Booker, Vonnie Brenno, Jason Brubaker, Mia Carpenter, Gary Ciccati, Rick Clubb, Philippe Collot, Wil Cormier, Kurt Cyr, Gus DeGuzman, Paul Didier, Jerry Dolan, Cash Donovan, Patty Dryden, Rod Dryden, Gabriella Farkas, Kevin Farrell, Sean Farrell, Trevor Goring, Collin Grant, Ramon Gregorio, Reggie Hendrix, Shannon Hogan, Tim Holtrop, Jack Hsu, Tak Ioka, Merle Keller, Andy Lee, Michael Lee, Walter Lee, Hector Lopez, Meridee Mandio, Chad McGown, Hogie Mcmurtrie, Alex McOwan, Marc Messenger, Mark Millicent, Luis Molina, Alex Morris, Duff Moses, Brian Murray, Jeanne Norman, Scott Ownbey, Neal Parrow, Ivan Pavlovits, Bill Perry, Steve Pica, Mick Reinman, Ruben Sarkissian, Michael Swift, Dave Threadgold, Bob Towner, Jerry Viviit, Mark Wagner, Steve Werblun, Shari Wickstrom, Lee Wilson, Jill Winterbottom, Steve Worthington, Nob Yamashita, Mark Yates, Debbie Young, Barbara Ziering

• Faure, Laurence: pg 641,1088
Europe **33-1-46-06-2936**
Illustrator: Jude Maceren

Ferderbar Studios:
2356 S 102nd St, Milwaukee, WI 53227 414-545-7770

• Fiat Rabin & Assocs: pg 654
918 Sheridan Rd, Glencoe, IL 60022 ....**847-835-3999**
fax: 847-835-9156
Illustrator: Jon Conrad
Photographer: Carrie Branovan, Daniel Mulka, Victor John Penner, Laurie Rubin, Sandro, Todd Winters

Fishback Illus, Inc, Lee:
350 W 21st St, New York, NY 10011 212-929-2951
Illustrator: Peter Attard, Andrew Bacha, Nancy Cheadle, Mac Conner, Bruce Eagle, Trini Eiche, Samson Pollen, Mike Russell, Barbara Siegel, Joseph Taffo, Bryna Waldman, Kevin Wasden, George Wilson

Fisher Reps, Bunny:
730 N Franklin #605, Chicago, IL 60610 312-280-1961
Illustrator: James Caulfield, Roberta Polfus, Jennifer Riggler
Photographer: Tony Glaser

• Flanders, Shelly: pg 827-831
1424 Las Positas Place, Santa Barbara, CA 93105 ....**805-682-6775**
fax: 805-687-1350

Fleming, Laird Tyler:
12240 Montana Ave #107, Los Angeles, CA 90049 310-556-0541

Folio:
PO Box 1251, New York, NY 10023 212-774-4271
Graphic Designer: Steve Jones
Illustrator: Bayo Akinsiku, Richard Allen, Mark Arundale, David Atkinson, Paul Bateman, Katherine Baxter, Claudio Berni, Malcolm Bird, Michael Bishop, Kay Boyce, John Bradley, Syd Brak, Jane Brewster, Judy Byford, Paul Campion, Reg Cartwright, Chris Coady, Jonathan Cooper, Don Cordery, Eddie Corkery, Sydney Couldridge, David Cutter,

John Davis, Nina Davis, Mike Delany, Simon Dewey, Jovan Djoedevic, Christophe Drochon, Jacques Fabre, David Farren, Steve Fricker, Manuel Geerinck, Tim Gill, Jo Goodberry, Charlotte Grann, Alex Green, Roger Harris, Robert Heesom, Paul Hogarth, Andrew Ingamells, Kevin Jones, Tim Jonke, Sophie Joyce, David Juniper, JC Knaff, David Lawrence, Andy Lawson, Larry Learmonth, Stewart Lees, Gary Long, Alyson MacNeill, Martin Macrae, Chandraa Manga, Helen Manning, David McAllister, John McIlvancy, Stuart McKay, Ed McLachlan, Tony Meeuwissen, Jonathan Milne, Bekah O'Neill, Roger O'Reilly, Micheal Ogden, Viv Oxley, Nick Pace, Andrew Pepworth, Alan Preston, Graham Redfern, John Reilly, Larry Richmond, David Riley, David Russell, Jonathan Satchell, Nick Schon, Anne Sharp, Mike Sharp, Tony Spaul, Tamara Sternberg, Leo Stevenson, Gay Sturrock, Tim Taylor, Mike Terry, Ken Thompson, Nancy Tolford, Michael Toohig, George Underwood, Chris Vine, Diz Wallis, Andy Ward, Povl Webb, Laurence Whiteley, Sue Williams, Ray Winder, Stephan Wohlgemuth, Andela Wood, Murray Zanoni

Folio London:
10 Gate St Lincoln Inn Fields, London, England, UK WC2 A 71-242-9562
Richard Jordan, See NYC listing for clients

Ford, Denise:
5114 Milam, Dallas, TX 75206 214-821-6788

Fortuni:
2508 E Belleview Pl #41, Milwaukee, WI 53211 414-964-8088

• **Foster Artists Rep, Pat: pg 794,795**
32 W 40th Street, New York, NY 10018 ....**212-575-6877**
e-mail: pfosterrep@aol.com / fax: 212-953-0728
Illustrator: Alessandro Biffignandi, Keith Birdsong, Dru Blair, Louis Henderson, Marcos Monteiro, Ken Otsuka, Lionel Talaro, Neil Watson, Hua Zhu

Foster Reps, Teenuh:
1051 S Big Bend Blvd #210, St Louis, MO 63117 314-647-7377
Illustrator: Sandy Appleoff, Paul Blakey, Matt Foster, Mark Frueh, Tuko Fujisaki, Ian Greathead, Jim Hancock, Bryan Haynes, Michael P Haynes, Daphne Hewett, Kelly Hume, Mark Langeneckert, Jeff May, Mark Oakley, Brian Otto, Harlan Scheffler, Jim Steck, Frank Steiner, Terry Tidwell, Beth Tipton, Arden von Haeger
Photographer: Scott Ferguson, Robert Grimm, Mark Katzman, James Olvera, Greg Rannells

Fountainhead:
527 Marquette Ave #640, Minneapolis, MN 55402 612-288-9925

Fox Art, Inc, Marsha:
3033 Fernwood Ave, Los Angeles, CA 90039............................213-662-0020
Illustrator: Bruce Eagle, Raphaelle Goethals, Raphaelle Goethals, Abe Gurvin, Sue Rother, Joe Spencer
Lettering: Michael Manoogian
Photographer: Jay Ahrend, Sue Bennett, David Guilburt, Tim Hale, Blake Little, Philip Salaverry

Fox Creek Photographix:
129 S Washington #300, Green Bay, WI 54301 ....
Photographer: John M Touscany

Francisco, Carol:
419 Cynwyd Rd, Bala Cynwyd, PA 19004............................610-667-2378
Illustrator: Renée Daily

Freelance Advancers:
420 Lexington Ave #2007, New York, NY 10170 212-661-0900

Freeman, Lisa:
740 E 52nd St #8, Indianapolis, IN 46205............................317-920-0068
Illustrator: Julie Bauker, Brian Behnke, Calef Brown, Harry Campbell, Dan Carney, Barbara Friedman, Liz Grace, Todd Graveline, Terry Julien, Sara Love, Tracey Mitchell, Susan Moore, Paul Moschell, Carol O'Malia, Einat Peled, Chris Pyle, Elizabeth Uyehara, Jerry Velasco, Matt Wawiorka

Friedman Creative Showcase, Eric:
16 Oak Pkwy, Sparta, NJ 07871 212-689-2343

• **Friend & Johnson: pg 958,959,1221**
53 W Jackson Blvd #1454, Chicago, IL 60604 ....**312-435-0055**
137 W 14th St #204, New York, NY 10011............................**212-337-0055**
325 Wilson Way, Larkspur, CA 94939............................**415-927-4500**
4606 Cedar Spring #1527, Dallas, TX 75219............................**214-559-0055**
Illustrator: Dave Cutler, Ann Field, Barbara Lambase, Mercedes McDonald, R Kenton Nelson, Giselle Potter, James Noel Smith, Kelly Stribling-Sutherland
Photographer: Hans Gissinger, Michael Johnson, Geof Kern, Scogin Mayo, Bill Phelps, Chuck Shotwell, Jim Sims

G

Garafola Reps, Lorraine:
206 Linda Ln, Edison, NJ 08820............................908-756-9254
Illustrator: Ralph Garafola, Bob Hardin, Don Martinetti, Peter Neumann, Robert Nicol

Garden Studio:
23 Ganton St, London, England, UK WIV 1LA 71-287-9191
Illustrator: Mike Atkinson, Graham Austin, Philip Bannister, Rowan Barnes-Murphy, Colin Brown, Caroline Church, Sue Climpson, Linda Dacey, Nick Diggory, Antonia Enthoven, Micheal Fisher, Keith Fowles, Sian Frances, John Havargal, Paul Hess, Simon Jones, Rod & Kira Josey, Doreen McGuiness, Mark Oliver, Gill Platt, Andrew Riley, Rosanne Sanders, John Spencer, STIK, Petula Stone, Simon Williams

Gardner, Jean:
444 N Larchmont Blvd #207, Los Angeles, CA 90004 213-464-2492
Photographer: Herman Agopian, John Reed Forsman, Brian Leatart, Rick Rusing, Jeremy Samuelson, Mark Scott, Steve Smith, Bryan Trebelcock

• **Gatlin Reps, Rita: pg 770-775**
83 Walnut Ave, Corte Madera, CA 94925............................**415-924-7881**
toll-free............................**800-924-7881**
url: www.ritareps.com / fax: 415-924-7891
Graphic Designer: John Pirman
Illustrator: Andrew Boerger, Russ Charpentier, Anne Crosse, Ellen Del Valle, Chris Dellorco, John J Hart, Thomas Hennessy, Elizabeth Hinshaw, Jack Lutzow, John Pirman, Tana Powell, Delro Rosco, Mary Ross, Paul Rossi
Photographer: Jackson Vereen

Gatta Design & Co:
286 Spring St #301, New York, NY 10013............................212-229-0073

Gaynin, Gail, Vicki Morgan Assocs: pg 161-191
url: www.vickimorganassociates.com / fax: 212-353-8538
194 Third Ave, New York, NY 10003............................**212-475-0440**
Illustrator: Nanette Biers, Karen Blessen, Dave Calver, Tom Christopher, Paul Colon, Nicholas Gaetano, Beppe Giacobbe, Sandra Kaplan, William Low, Joyce Patti, Elizabeth Rosen, Robert Sauber, Joanie Schwarz, Joel Spector, Dahl Taylor, Lauren Uram, Kris Wiltse, Bruce Wolfe, Wendy Wray

Gelman, Candace:
400 E Randolph #2108, Chicago, IL 60601 312-540-0086
Photographer: Joe Baraban, Lauren Greenfield, Susan Kinast

Gem Studio, Inc:
420 Lexington Ave #220, New York, NY 10170 212-687-3460

George, Melody:
542 S Second St, Bellaire, TX 77401 713-661-6521
Photographer: Michael Hart Photography, Bryan Kuntz Photo, Jeff Myers, Paul Schmidt

George, Nancy:
1259 Highland Rd, Santa Ynez, CA 93460............................805-688-3772
Illustrator: Dianne Bennett, Robert Cooper, Diane Kay Davis, Bruce Dean, Bob Gleason, Penelope Gottlieb, Carol Heiman-Greene, Steve Hendricks, Hank Hinton, Gary Hoover, Richard Kriegler, Gary Lund, Corey Wolfe

Giannini, Judi:
1932 McFall St, Mclean, VA 22101............................703-534-8316
Photographer: William Dempsey, Karen Holzberg, Breton Littlehales, Greg Pease, Mark Segal, Stock Agency

Gillies, Page:
251 Greenwood Ave, Bethel, CT 06801 203-797-8188

Ginsburg, Michael:
240 E 27th St #24E, New York, NY 10016 212-679-8881
Photographer: Butch Belair, Karen Capusilli, Chris Cheetam, Darryl Estrine, Matt Gunther, Chris Sanders, Mark Weiss

Glenn, Chris W:
340 Diversey St, Chicago, IL 60657............................312-670-7737
Illustrator: Tom Bachtell, Alex Boies, David FeBland, Chuck Gonzales, Michael Haynes, Carlos Marrero, Beck Nead, Will Northerner
Photographer: Jack Perna, Victor Skrebneski, Dave Slivinski

• **Glick & Assocs, Ivy: pg 832-835**
PO Box 30485, Walnut Creek, CA 94598 ....**925-944-0304**
New York, NY **212-869-0214**
San Francisco, CA **415-543-6056**
Illustrator: Catherine-Rose Crowther, Jerry Dadds, Derek Grinnell, Matthew Holmes, Terence Lawlor, Map Makers, Tony Morse, John Roman
Lettering: Jane Dill

Godfrey, Ally:
2030 Main St #501, Dallas, TX 75201 214-827-2559
Photographer: Neal Farris, Carolyn McGovern, Jeff Stephens, Lynn Sugarman, Jim Vecchione, Jake Wallis

Godfrey, Dennis:
201 W 21st St #10G, New York, NY 10001 212-807-0840
Illustrator: Jeffrey Adams, John Blackford, David Parker, Wendy Popp, David Stimson, Michael Wepplo
Photographer: John Blackford

• **Goldman Agency, David: pg 764-768**
41 Union Sq W #918, New York, NY 10003............................**212-807-6627**
url: www.idt.net/~dgagency / fax: 212-463-8175
Illustrator: Nishan Akguilan, Nishan Akgulian, Michelle Barnes, Norm Bendell, Keith Bendis, Steve Dininno, Rosemary Fox, Mazemaster David Anson Russo, Kazushige Nitta, Mitch Rigie, Gary Taxali, Kurt Vargo, Mark Wiener, James Yang

Goodale, Rick:
8 Woodcroft Ave, London, England, UK NW7 2AG............................1819-062288

• **Goodman, Christine (Munro Goodman Reps): pg 627-641**
5 E 17th St 6th Fl, New York, NY 10003 ....**212-691-2667**
url: www.spar.org / fax: 212-633-1844
4 E Ohio Studio B, Chicago, IL 60611............................**312-321-1336**
fax: 312-321-1350
Illustrator: Shelly A Bartek, Tom Bookwalter, Mark Chickinelli, Sally Wern Comport, Phillip Dunlap, Pat Dypold, Dennis Dzielak, Malcolm Farley, Tom Foty, Ben Garvie, Clint Hansen, Greg Hargreaves, Dan Hatala, Quang Ho, John Holm, Iskra Johnsin, Mike Kasun, Douglas Klauba, Holly Kowitt, Tatjana Krizmanic, Paul Lackner, Jack A Molloy, Randy Nelson, Bryan Peterson, Tim Robinson, David Schweitzer, Steve Shock, Richard Hamilton Smith, Ryle Smith, Michael Steirnagle, David Uhl, Peter Wells, Corey Wilkinson
Photographer: Chris Coxwell, Peter Freed, Richard Hamilton Smith

Goodman, Inc, Tom:
626 Loves Lane, Wynnewood, PA 19096 610-649-1514
Electronic Imaging: Bob Lambiase
Photographer: Kevin Black, Tom Crane, Ed Eckstein

Goodson, Anna:
CP 325 Succ Westmount, Montreal, QU H3Z 2T5 514-983-9020

Goodwin, Phyllis:
10 E 81st St #5, New York, NY 10028............................212-570-6021
Photographer: Carl Furuta

• **Gordon Assocs Ltd, Barbara: pg 836-842**
165 E 32nd St, New York, NY 10016............................**212-686-3514**
fax: 212-532-4302
Illustrator: Susan Avishai, Ron Barry, Robin Brickman, Wendy Christensen, Valerie Constantino, Jim Dietz, Gary Glover, Glenn Harrington, Robert Hunt, Nenad Jakesevic, Bill James, Jackie Jasper, George Ladas, Sonja Lamut, Tim Lundgren, Jim Smola, Jim Smolla, John Suh

• **Gordon, Tami: pg 641,1088**
PO Box 4112, Montebello, CA 90640 ....**213-887-8958**
Illustrator: Pearl Beach, Sally Wern Comport, Jude Maceren
Photographer: Susan Lakin

Grafton Reps, Lisa:
26121 Malaga Ln, Mission Viejo, CA 92692............................714-582-2081

• **Graham Represents, Corey: pg 646-656,1115**
Pier 33 North, San Francisco, CA 94111 ....**415-956-4750**
e-mail: crg@slip.net / url: www.coreygrahamreps.com / fax: 415-391-6104
Illustrator: Frank Ansley, Jon Conrad, Manuel Geerinck, Matt Manley, Joel Nakamura, David Tillinghast, Robin Zingone

Graham Reps, Mary:
450 34th Ave, San Francisco, CA 94121............................415-668-2900
Photographer: Daniel Furon, Leslie Hirsch, Marc Simon

Gray, Hamilton:
3519 W 6th St, Los Angeles, CA 90020............................213-380-3933
Photographer: Jay Blakesburg, Gwendolen Cates, Chris Cuffaro, Vern Evans, Michael Grecco, Maggie Hamilton, Stan Klimek, Michael Kremer, Cynthia Levine, Dudley Reed, TC Reiner, Jake Wallis, Theo Westenberger

Green, Anita:
257 W 17th St #4C, New York, NY 10011 212-807-7545
Photographer: Ernie Friedlander, Bruce Plotkin, Shaffer/Smith Photo
• **Grien, Anita: pg 843**
155 E 38th St, New York, NY 10016.........................**212-697-6170**
e-mail: agrien@aol.com / url: www.anitagrien.com / fax: 212-697-6177
Illustrator: Dolores Bego, Fanny Mellet Berry, Julie Johnson, Hal Just, Mona Mark, Jerry McDaniel, Don Morrison, Alan Neider, Alan Reingold, Alex Zwarenstein
Grims, Peter:
115 Arch St, Philadelphia, PA 19106 215-925-4233
Photographer: Michael Furman Photography/ERGO Digital Imaging
Groeschel, Erika:
15 E 32nd St 11th Fl, New York, NY 10016............212-685-3291
Cartoonist: Karen Leon, Bob McMahon, Bert Tanner
Illustrator: Denise Derosiers, Bil Donovan, Liz Jorg Studio, Joy Monte, Frank Sofo, Mike Wanke
Photographer: Tony Mandarino
Gross Assocs, Lee:
119 W 57th Street ste 1215, New York, NY 10019 212-582-0440
Group West, Inc:
5455 Wilshire #1212, Los Angeles, CA 90036............
Illustrator: Ren Wicks
• **Guenzi Agents, Inc, Carol: pg 736-745,1474,1475**
865 Delaware St, Denver, CO 80204 ....**303-820-2599**
toll free............**800-417-5120**
url: www.artagent.com / fax: 303-820-2598
Illustrator: Gus Alavezos, Shelly Bartek, Marc Brown, Dan Bulleit, Dan Bullett, John Ceballos, Peter Cunis, Patrick Daughtery, Jacques Devaud, Dave Ember, Christer Eriksson, Brian Evans, Mike Fisher, Greg Hargreaves, Kelly Hume, Steve Hunter, io image, Jeff Jones, Dean Kennedy, Tatjana Krizmanic, Todd Lockwood, Joe McDermott, Heidi Merscher, Randy Nelsen, Sue Rother, Ryle Smith, Don Sullivan, Marina Tito, Tom Ward, Bryan Wiggins, Tim Yearington
Guided Imagery Productions:
2995 Woodside Rd #400, Woodside, CA 94062 ....

H
• **Hackett Artist Representation, Pat: pg 844-847**
1809 7th Ave #1710, Seattle, WA 98101............**206-447-1600**
url: www.pathackett.com / fax: 206-447-0739
Illustrator: Bryan Ballinger, Ken Barnes, Janice Kooch Campbell, Jonathan Combs, Steve Coppin, Eldon Doty, Larry Duke, Edwin Fotheringham, Martin French, John Fretz, John L Fretz, David Harto, Celeste Henriquez, Chris Hopkins, Daniel McGowan, Bill Meyer, Leo Monahan, Bruce Morser, Dennis Ochsner, Chuck Pyle, Elizabeth Read, Laurie Rosenwald, Yutaka Sasaki, Kathlyn Shadle, Chuck Solway, Bobbi Tull, Kris Wiltse, Mark Zingarelli
Lettering: Lilly Lee, Ted Witus
Photographer: Bill Cannon, Diane Padys, Marco Prozzo
Hackney, Lee:
339 Home Ave #2C, Oak Park, IL 60302............708-383-9178
Hahn [H2 & Co], Holly:
837 W Grand Ave 4th Fl, Chicago, IL 60622............312 633-0500
Illustrator: Nan Brooks, Lina Chesak, Doug Githens, Tim Peterson, Tim D Peterson, Steve Snodgrass, Sara Swan, Kirsten Ulve
Photographer: Jeff Sciortino, Kipling Swehla, Greg Whitaker
Haims, Joshua:
900 S Wabash #404, Chicago, IL 60605............773-528-3151
Music: John Tharnstrom Music
Photographer: Chris Cassidy, Lee Page
• **Hall & Assocs: pg 1110**
606 N Larchmont Blvd #4C, Los Angeles, CA 90004............**213-962-2500**
Illustrator: Dave Arkle, Kevin Conran, Jim Doody, Fred Hilliard, Mary T. Monge Illustration, Raphael Montoliu
Photographer: Myron Beck, Derek Gardner, Marshall Harrington, Douglas Kirkland, Markku Lahdesmaki, Aaron Rapoport, Deborah Roundtree, Craig Saruwatari, Gil Smith, James Wood
Hall Reps, Rich:
20434 S Santa Fe Ave, Long Beach, CA 90810............310-637-1112
Photographer: John Early, David Le Bon
Hall, Marni:
606 N Larchmont Blvd #4C, Los Angeles, CA 90004............213-962-2500
Halley Resources:
37 W 20th St #603, New York, NY 10011............212-206-0901
Hair: Algene, Terry Foster
Hair & Make-up: Joseph Boggess, David Maderich, Ricardo Marin, Gregory Paul, Martin Pretorius, Michael Reimer, Rick Teal
Music: Michel Galen, Amy Sacco
Make-up: Karlo
Stock: Irene Albright, Caroline Morrison, Norine Smith
Stylist: Stephen Ang, Angie Arnett, Jean Doyen de Montaillou, Scott Gordon, Sharon Ryan
Halley, Russell:
37 West 20th St #603, New York, NY 10011............212-206-0901
Hamilton, Gray:
3519 W 6th St, Los Angeles, CA 90020............213-380-3933
• **Hankins & Tegenborg Ltd, Artists Reps: pg 416-445**
60 E 42nd St, New York, NY 10165-1940............**212-867-8092**
e-mail: DHLT@aol.com / url: www.HT-LTD.com / fax: 212-949-1977
Film: David Gaadt
Illustrator: Matt Archambault, Jeff Barson, Bob Berran, Paul Blumstein, Joe Burleson, Dan Burr, Donald Case, Chris Cocozza, David Cook, John B Crane, Pino Daeni, Carla Daguanno, Vittorio Dangelico, Donna Diamond, Bill Dodge, Danilo Ducak, Danilo Dulak, John Dzedzy, Bryant Eastman, Jon Paul Ferrara, Crista Forest, Hal Frenck, Antonio J Gabrielle, David Gandt, Mark Garro, Kerri Gibbs, William Giese, Sergio Giovine, Jim Griffin, Phil Hefferman, Phil Heffernan, Edwin Herder, Michael Herring, Tony Hertz, Philip Howe, Aleta Jenks, Rick Johnson, Jean-Kves Kervevan, Uldis Klavins, Rick Lieder, Bob Maguire, Kei Masuda, Neal McPheeters, Linda Messier, Cliff Miller, Rudy Muller, Keith Newton, Ernie Norcia, Kevin Odhner, Gary Penca, Walter Rane, Sergio Roffo, Ken Rosenberg, Mitzura Salgian, Harry Schaare, Bill Schmidt, Robert Schuster, Miro Sinovcic, Donald Sipley, Diane Sivavec, Ted Sizemore, John W Sledd, Cliff Spohn, Victor Stabin, Robert Swanson, Jean Targete, Jean Taroete, Peter Van Ryzin, Richard Waldrep, Jeff Walker, Conrad Weiss, Judy York, Paul Youll, John Youssi
Hanson/Artist Agent, Jim:
777 N Michigan Ave #706, Chicago, IL 60611............312-337-7770
Illustrator: Michael Dinges, Garrian Manning, Rob Porazinski, Craig Smallish
Photographer: Michael Dinges, Leonard Gertz, Glen Gyssler, Maria Krajcirovic

Hardy, Allen:
Pier 59 Chelsea Piers 2nd Fl, New York, NY 10011............212-787-5566
Photographer: Marco Glaviano, Jeff Licata, Steve Simko
• **Harlib Assocs, Joel: pg 380,381**
10 E Ontario #4708, Chicago, IL 60611............**312-573-1370**
Illustrator: Richard Anderson, Nick Backes, Michael Backus, Julie Bell, Rick Brown, Gerry Chapleski, Russell Cobane, Mike Dean, Lawrence Duke, Alex Ebel, Chuck Eckert, Abe Gurvin, Karel Havlicek, Joe & Kathy Heiner, Tim Langenderfer, Kent Leech & Associates, Fred Pepera, Buc Rogers, Delro Rosco, RV2, David Sawyer, Tim Stout, Robert Tyrrell, Boris Vallejo, Ron Villani, Kim Whitesides, Bruce Wolfe
Photographer: Marty Evans, Robert Farber, Bret Lopez, David Maisel, Jean Moss, Steve Nozicka, Lee Page
Harold Lee Miller:
53 W Jackson Blvd #1454, Chicago, IL 60604............312-435-0055
Illustrator: Dave Cutler, Ann Field, Barbara Lambase, Mercedes McDonald, R Kenton Nelson, Giselle Potter, James Noel Smith, Stribling-Sutherland
Photographer: Hans Gissinger, Michael Johnson, Geof Kern, Scogin Mayo, Bill Phelps, Chuck Shotwell, Jim Sims
Harris & Assocs, Gretchen:
5230 13th Ave S, Minneapolis, MN 55417............612-822-0650
Illustrator: Ted Gadecki, John Kleber, Jane Mjolsness, Jody Winger, Mary Worcester
Hart, Vikki:
780 Bryant St, San Francisco, CA 94107............415-495-4278
Illustrator: Kevin Hulsey, Aleta Jenks, Jonathan Wright
Photographer: GK Hart
• **Hauser, Barb, Another Girl Rep: pg 849-851,1495**
525 Brannan St #406, San Francisco, CA 94107............**415-647-5660**
url: www.girlrep.com
Electronic Imaging: Suzanne Staud
Illustrator: Nick Backes, Tracy Britt, Lawrence Duke, Fred Hilliard, Paul Kratter, Ed Lindlof, Ben Perini, Miro Salazar, Marty Smith, Suzanne Staud, Judy Unger
Photographer: Kevin Sanchez
Havergal, John:
23 Ganton St, London, England, UK W1V 1LA............1712-288882
Hayes, Tom:
236 W 27th St, New York, NY 10001............212 463-8550
Head Productions:
42 Delavan St, Brooklyn, NY 11231............718-624-1906
Head, Olive:
155 Riverside Dr #10C, New York, NY 10024............212-580-3323
Photographer: Nesti Mendoza, Monica Stevenson
Hedge, Joanne:
1415 Gadren St, Glendale, CA 91201............818-244-0110
Illustrator: Tony De Luz, Greg Epkes, Rick McCollum, David McMacken, David Mollering, Marjorie Muns, Ken Perkins, Laura Phillips, Stacey Previn, Ken Rosenberg, Jim Salvati, David Schweitzer, Tsuchiya Sloneker Comms, Brent Watkinson
• **Heflin & The Artworks, Sally: pg 707-715**
455 W 23rd St #8D, New York, NY 10011............**212-366-1893**
url: www.andtheart.com / fax: 212-604-9643
Illustrator: Sophie Allport, Christian Birmingham, Giles Burton Chapple, Greg Clarke, Izhar Cohen, Matthew Cook, Penny Dann, Andrew Davidson, Jeffrey Decoster, Gurbuz D Eksioglu, Graham Evernden, Jody Hewgill, John Lawrence, Peter Malone, Mark Fox of Blackdog Studio, Desdemona McCannon, Sarah McMenemy, John Montgomery, Anton Morris, Joe Morse, Graham Percy, Clare Pettinati, Hanoch Piven, Jenny Powell, Isadore Seltzer, Meilo So, Mark Ulriksen, Rupert Van Wyk, Marco Ventura, Mary Woodin, Christopher Wormell
Photographer: Ron Sanford
Held Reps, Cynthia:
6516 W 6th St, Los Angeles, CA 90048............213-655-2979
Photographer: Steve Hix, Craig McMillan, RJ Muna, Peter Rodger, Ron Strong
Hellman Assocs, Inc:
400 First Ave N #218, Minneapolis, MN 55401............612-375-9598
Illustrator: Kim Behm, Deb Bovy, Greg Hargreaves, Dan Hatala, Steve Hunter, Dean Kennedy, Doug Knutson, Paul Lackner, Pat Muchmore, Rick Nass, John Thompson, Todd Treadway
Herron, Pat:
80 Madison Ave, New York, NY 10016............212-683-9039
Photographer: Kip Meyer
Hersey, Renee:
923 Preston Ave, Los Angeles, CA 90026............213-666-3310
Graphic Designer: Beth Middleworth, Marika VanAdelsberg
Photographer: Michael Llewellyn, James R Minchin III, Lisa Powers
Heyl Assocs, Fran:
230 Park Ave #2525, New York, NY 10169............800-327-0333
Hillebrandt, Bo:
3110 1/2 Roswell Rd NW, Atlanta, GA 30305............404-846-0444
Hillman, Betsy:
P.O. Box 77644, San Francisco, CA 94107............415-381-4728
Illustrator: Istvan Banyai, Greg Couch, Cathy Deeter, Jud Guitteau, Greg Spalenka, Joe Spencer, Jeremy Thornton, Dona Turner
Photographer: Brandtner & Staedeli, John S Dykes, Gordon Edwardes, Dennis Gray, Randy Schwartz, Holly Stewart
Hintze, Lise:
26 Main St, Setauket, NY 11733............516-689-7054
Photographer: Rob Lang
• **HK Portfolio: pg 684-695**
666 Greenwich St #860, New York, NY 10014............**212-675-5719**
e-mail: HKPfolio@aol.com / url: www.hkportfolio.com / fax: 212-675-6341
Illustrator: Ron Barrett, Nan Brooks, Abby Carter, Gwen Connelly, Eldon Doty, Leonid Gore, Rob Hefferan, John Manders, Mike Reed, Remy Simard, Theresa Smith, Randy Verougstraete
Hoch & Assocs, Christopher:
101 N Wacker Dr #CM 190, Chicago, IL 60606............312-689-8077
Film: Wild Onion Studio
Hodges, Jeanette:
12401 Bellwood Rd, Los Alamitos, CA 90720............562-431-4343
Illustrator: Ken Hodges

• Holland & Co, Mary: pg 800-802
6638 N 13th St, Phoenix, AZ 85014 ....**602-263-8990**
fax: 602-277-0680
Illustrator: Shelly Bartek, Roland Dahlquist, Dave Ember, Jack Graham, Jimmy Holder, Doug Horne, Rose Johnson, Jeff Jones, Gary Krejca, Judy Miller, CB Mordan, Julie Pace, Pepper Tharp, Cathryne Trachok, Monte Varah, Tim Yearington
Photographer: Marc Feldman, Paul Loven, Judy Miller, Studio X Digital Photography

• Holmberg, Irmeli: pg 852-866
280 Madison Ave #1110, New York, NY 10016.........................**212-545-9155**
e-mail: Irmeli@aol.com / url: www.spar.org / fax: 212-545-9462
Illustrator: Gary Aagaard, Kaz Aizawa, Melanie Barnes, Alexander Barsky, Tivadar Bote, Dan Bridy, Bob Byrd, Rita Chow, Lo Cole, Sylvie Daigneault, Jim Dandy, Potter Hall, Barbara Kelley, Roger Leyonmark, Tina Limer, Kristina Louhi, Lu Matthews, Linda Montgomery, Wally Neibart, Meredith Nieves, Steven Noble, Bob Radigan, Lynne Riding, Schauman, Clare Schaumann, Linda Schiwall, Tom Sevalrud, Melissa Sweet, Lydia Taranovic, Kat Thacker, Tinam Valk, Hannele Vanha-Aho

Holt, Bill:
1509 Brandywoine Blvd, Wilmington, DE 19809 302-762-8373

Holt, Rita:
2327 Ewing Dr, Atlanta, GA 30319 404-634-6400
Film: Bruce Scharfenberg
Photographer: Leland Bobbe, Glenn Daly, Chuck Ealovega, Susan Johann, Rodney Rascona

Hopkins, John: 212-427-1451
Photographer: Jim Graham

Hopson Reps, Melissa:
1605 Stemmons Freeway #C, Dallas, TX 75207...........................214-747-3122
Illustrator: Pat Binder, Bill Jenkins, Miles Lewis, Cody Lucido, Kevin Mishak, Peggy Mozley, Colin Poole, Keith Steiger, Studio 212/

Howard, Marilyn:
99 Park Ave #210A, New York, NY 10016 212-344-7067

Hubauer GMBH, Margarethe:
Erika Strasse, Hamburg, Germany, 20251 49-40-486003
Illustrator: Tamar Haber-Schaim

Hughes, Judy:
90 South St, Boston, MA 02111..617-426-9111
Photographer: Michael Malyszko

Hull Assocs, Scott:
68 E Franklin St, Dayton, OH 45459..937-433-8383
Illustrator: Dave Albers, Tim Anderson, David Beck, David Bowers, Tracy Britt, Andy Buttram, John Ceballos, Young Sook Cho, Greg Dearth, Helen Dsouza, Andrea Eberbach, Doug Fryer, Josef Gast, Clint Hansen, Peter Harritos, Stacey Innerst, Bob James, Greg Lafever, Dave Lafleur, Jon Lezinsky, John Maggard, Larry Martin, Curtis Parker, John Patrick, Evangelia Phillippidis, Ted Pitts, Andy Powell, Mark Riedy, Geoff Smith, Geoffrey P Smith, Tammy Smith, Tracy Walker

Hunter, Nadine:
PO Box 307, Ross, CA 94957 415-456-7711
Illustrator: Rebecca Archey, Mercedes McDonald, Cathrine Thompson, Liz Wheaton

Hurewitz & Assocs, Gary:
305 Madison Ave ste 710, New York, NY 10165 212-682-2600
Photographer: Tony D'Orio, Vincent Dente, Scott Frances, Mark Havriliak, Alan Kaplan, Allan Penn, James Robinson, Garry Wade

I

Iconomics:
155 N College Ave #225, Ft Collins, CO 80524...........................970-493-0087

Image Studios:
1100 S Lynndale Dr, Appleton, WI 54914 920-738-4080
Photographer: Will Croff, Steve Eliasen, Glenn Hartjes, Jeff Lendrum, John Luke, Bill Reini, John Von Dorri, Dave Wallace, Harvey Wallner

In Flight Productions:
3114 St Mary's Ave, Omaha, NE 68105.....................................402-345-2164
Film: Michael Harting

In Focus Assocs:
251 W 92nd St #3B, New York, NY 10025 ....212 799-2100
Photographer: EJ Camp, Jeff McNamara, Bill Miles

Inman, E W:
6723 N Lightfoot, Chicago, IL 60646..773-792-9169
Illustrator: Chris Sheban, Russell Thurston
Photographer: Greg Gannells, Barbara Karant, John Payne

Intermarketing Group, The:
29 Holt Rd, Amherst, NH 03031 603-672-0499

Ivy League of Artists:
18 W 21st Street 17th Floor, New York, NY 10010 212-243-1333
Film: BK Taylor
Illustrator: Lori Anzalone, Cheryl Chalmers, Ric Del Rossi, John Dyess, John Paul Genzo, Paula Goodman, Chris Murphy, Justin Novak, Tom Powers, Tanya Rebelo, John Rice, Steve Smallwood

J

Jameson, Diane:
2 Silver Ave #205, Toronto, ON M6R 3A2..................................416-530-1500
Illustrator: Nina Berkson, Mike Constable, Katrin Dockrill, Clancy Gibson, Grant Innis, Pierre Pratt
Photographer: Peter Chou, Russell Monk

Jarrett, Don:
1920 E Warner Ave #3J & K, Santa Ana, CA 92705 714-250-3377
Photographer: Michael Jarrett

Jaz & Jaz, The Artists' Rep:
4033 Aurora Ave N, Seattle, WA 98103.....................................206-633-3445
Electronic Imaging: Tom Wilkins
Illustrator: Vaughn Aldredge, Christopher Baldwin, Jim Chow, Todd Connor, John Fretz, John L Fretz, James Frisino, Jim Frisino, Steve Hepburn, Si Huynh, Stephen Konz, Dev Madan, Larry Milam, Leslie Newman, Shawn Ogle, Julie Paschkis, Bonnie Rieser, Fred Saunders, Heather Scholl, Richard Stine, Pat Turner, Lorne Winters
Photographer: Bryan Allen, Rick Etkin, Dale Windham

Jedell, Joan:
370 E 76th St, New York, NY 10021 212-861-7861
Photographer: George Aglias, Ken Chung, Bruno Frontino, Tim Pannell

Jenni & Assocs, Jane:
472 Portland Ave, St Paul, MN 55102 612-224-6763
Illustrator: Amy Butler, David Butler, Joelle Nelson
Photographer: Julie Delton, Georgina E Frankel

• Jett & Assocs, Clare: pg 542-559
7118 Upper River Rd, Prospect, KY 40059 ....**502-228-9427**
url: www.jettreps.com / fax: 502-228 8857
Illustrator: Lou Beach, Mark Betcher, Jennifer Bolten, Dan Brawner, Annette Cable, Mark Cable, Antonio Cangemi, Cameron Eagle, Claudia Hammer, Dave Jonason, John Mattos, Jan Nickum, Mario Noche, Billy Renkl, Lori Siebert, David Wariner, Roy Wiemann

Johnson Reps, Sally:
1643 W Swallow Rd, Ft Collins, CO 80526 970-223-3027
Illustrator: Walt Curlee, Myron Grossman, Kelly Stribling Sutherland, Ken Tiessen

Johnson, Arlene:
35 Stillman #105, San Francisco, CA 94107 415-543-1131
Photographer: Dan Escobar, Philip Salaverry

Johnson, Bud & Evelyne:
201 E 28th St, New York, NY 10016 212-532-0928
Illustrator: Lynn Adams, Cathy Beylon, Peter Bollinger, Lisa Bonforte, Joanne Cannon, Frank Daniel, Larry Daste, Jill Dubin, Carolyn Ewing, Bill Finewood, George Ford, Lia Frasinetti, Simon Galkin, June Golsborough, Mel Grefinger, Marsha Halleck, Turi MacCombie, Darcy May, Cheryl Nathan, Robert Noreika, Joan O'Brien, John O'Brien, Heidi Petach, Steven Petruccio, Barbara Soloff-Levy, Barbara Steadman, Pat Stewart, Tom Tierney, Sylvia Walker

Johnston, Suzy:
39 Cranfield Rd, Toronto, ON M4B 3H6 416-285-8905
Illustrator: Mir Lada, Doug Martin
Photographer: Mir Lada, Robert Lear, Anson Liaw, Dan Lim

• Jones, Betsy: pg 796,797
2491 West 22nd Avenue, Vancouver, BC V6L 1M3 ....**604-733-4422**
url: www.repart.com / fax: 604-684-6826
Illustrator: Robin Arkell, Charles Bell, Peter Bishop, John Bolesky, Kelly Brooks, Jeff Burgess, Lorne Cames, Mark Heine, Steve Hepburn, Si Huynh, Barbara Klunder, Michael Knox, Kim LaFave, James Lorintz, Dietrich Madsen, Michael McKinnell, Gary McLaughlin, Domonic Ng, Gavin Orpen, Mark Schofield, Elizabeth Simpson, Sharon Smith, Steve Van Gelder, Brad Yeo

Jordan, Richard:
10 Gate St Lincoln Inn Fields, London, England, UK WC2 A...........71-242-9562

• Jorgensen /Barrett: pg 1078,1445
753 N 35th, Seattle, WA 98103 ....**206-634-1880**
fax: 206-632-2024
Illustrator: Fred Birchman, Liz Grace, Debbie Hanley, Colin Hayes, Fred Hilliard, Kurt D Hollomon, Mits Katayama, Richard Kehl, Stephanie Langley Illustration, David Lund, Greg MacDonald, Cheri Ryan, Jane Shasky
Lettering: Nancy Stentz
Photographer: Angie Norwood Browne, Mel Curtis Photography, Mel Curtis, Donna Day, Joyce Tenneson

Josell Communications, Robin:
185 West End Ave #22C, New York, NY 10023 212-877-5560

Josell, Jessica:
185 West End Ave #22C, New York, NY 10023 212-877-5560

Joyce, Tricia:
79 Chambers St, New York, NY 10007 212-962-0728
Animator: Steve Speer
Hair & Make-up: Boushelle Alvarez
Photographer: Todd Burris, Roger Cabello, Roger Diadul, Paul Empson, Barry Harris, Bruce Plotkin, Sophie Rolland, Paul Warchol, Tina West, Neil Winokur
Stock: Joselyn Braxton
Stylist: Sara Feldman, Sarah Gore

K

K & K Studios, Inc:
401 Second Ave S #800, Minneapolis, MN 55401 612-338-9138

Kahn Artists:
4317 Cornelia Cir, Minneapolis, MN 55435.................................612-925-1699
Illustrator: Tom Lochray, Mike McMillen, Brian Otto, Rick Peterson, Cindy Wrobel

Kahn, Harvey:
155 Millburn Ave, Milburn, NJ 07041 212-752-8490
Illustrator: Bernie Fuchs, Gerry Gersten

Kahn, Harvey:
155 Millburn Ave, Millburn, NJ 07041 212-752-8490
Illustrator: Bernie Fuchs, Gerry Gersten

Kalish, Renee:
1707 Keeney, Evanston, IL 60202...312-704-0010
Illustrator: Gary Glover, Barry Jackson, Bob Krogle, Greg Loudon, Karen Snave, Jim Sutton

Kalms Reps, Nadine:
1518 Harvard St #5, Santa Monica, CA 90404 310-829-5233
Photographer: Joe Baraban, Steve Bonini, Rick Chou, Carl Corey, Laura Crosta, Jeff Sarpa

• Kamin & Assocs, Vince: pg 956,957
260 E Chestnut #3005, Chicago, IL 60611 ....**312-787-8834**
Illustrator: Sara Anderson, Steve Bjorkman, Linda Bleck, Andrzej Dudzinski, Gail Greenfield Randall
Photographer: Steven Conway, Susan Drinker, Dick Durrance, Peter Gabriel, David Guilbert, Len Irish, Dorit Lombroso, Simon Metz, Dan Morrill, Boudewijn Smit, Andrew Terzes, Bill Tucker, Jim Veccioni

• Kasak, Harriet: pg 684-695
666 Greenwich St #860, New York, NY 10014 ....**212-675-5719**
url: www.hkportfolio.com / fax: 212-675-6341
See HK Portfolio for client list

Kastaris & Assocs, Harriet:
3301A S Jefferson Ave, St Louis, MO 63118 314-773-2600
Illustrator: Sarah Beise, Jim Carroll, Gary Ciccarelli, Eric Dinyer, Betsy Everitt, Greg Johannes, Rip Kastaris, Michael Kilfoy, Darin Murray, Christian Musselman, Rhonda Nass, Nikolai Punin, Terry Ravanelli, Tracy Rea, Carlos Sanchez, RJ Shay, Peter Stallard, Chris Szetela, Joseph Taylor, Doug Thompson, Jenay Vainisi, Amanda Warren, Linda Webb, April Goodman Willy, Keith Witner, Cindy Wrobel
Lettering: Dia Calhoun

Katz Represents, Susan:
2828 N Burling #406, Chicago, IL 60657 773-549-5379
Photographer: Robert Frerck, Harrison Jones, Panoramic Images, Susan Reich, Mark Segal
Stock: Phtographic Resources

Kaufman, Katrin:
  144 W 27th St, New York, NY 10001 212-255-1976
  Photographer: Mickey Kaufman
Kaurala & Assocs, Ed:
  903 N Main St, Royal Oak, MI 48067 248-548-4500
Kauss, Jean-Gabriel:
  161 Ave of Americas 13th Fl, New York, NY 10013 212-243-5454
  Make-up: Yasuo
  Photographer: Gilles Bensimon, Michel Comte, Jonathan Glynn-Smith, Francois Halard, Mike Reinhardt, Isabel Snyder, Antoine Verglas
  Stylist: Jocelyne Beaudoin
Keating, Peggy:
  30 Horatio St #3B, New York, NY 10014 212-691-4654
  Illustrator: Charles Dillion, Carol Vennell, Sylvia Walker
Kenney & Clifford:
  1505 Hanover St, Yorktown Heights, NY 10598.............914-962-0002
Kenney Represents, John:
  1505 Hanover St, Yorktown Heights, NY 10598.............914-962-0002
  Photographer: Bruce Charlesworth, Paul Elledge, Shawn Michienzi, Joe Paczkowski, Craig Perman, George Petrakes
Kenny, Steven T:
  3557 Slate Mills Rd, Sperryville, VA 22740 800-789-9389
  Illustrator: Steven Adler
Ketcham, Laurie:
  210 E 36th St #6C, New York, NY 10016 212-481-9592
  Photographer: MacDuff Everton, Sally Gall, Peter Gregoire, Lizzie Himmel, Pete McArthur, Dick Nystrom, Dan Peebles, Warren Salowe, Mark Viker
• **Kimche, Tania: pg 868-870**
  137 Fifth Ave 11th Fl, New York, NY 10010 ....**212-529-3556**
  fax: 212-353-0831
• **Kirchoff/Wohlberg Inc: pg 872,873**
  866 United Nations Plaza, New York, NY 10017 ....**212-644-2020**
  url:www.spar.org
• **Kirsch Represents, Melanie: pg 769**
  218 Elm Ct, Rhinelander, WI 54501 ....**715-369-2130**
  toll-free **800-456-3706**
  Illustrator: David Kimble, Judy Koenig
Klein Represents, Jane:
  1635 E 22nd St, Oakland, CA 94606 510-535-0495
  Illustrator: Jannine Cabossel, Carolyn Fisher, Tuko Fujisaki
  Photographer: Kirk Amyx, Reid Ashton, Marshall Gordon, Christian Peacock
Klimt Represents, Bill & Maurine:
  15 W 72nd St, New York, NY 10023 212-799-2231
  Illustrator: Wayne Alfano, David Blattel, Paul Henry, Katherine Manzo, Frank Morris, Ben Stahl
Knable & Assocs, Ellen:
  1233 S La Cienega Blvd, Los Angeles, CA 90035 310-855-8855
  Animator: Roger Chouinard
  Photographer: Dean Siracusa, Kirk Weddle
• **Knecht, Cliff: pg 1239**
  309 Walnut Rd, Pittsburgh, PA 15202.............................**412-761-5666**
  Illustrator: Michael Aveto, Pamela Becker, Mark Bender, Gary Colby, Jim Deigan, Milan Kecman, Melinda Levine, Lauren Ling, Ron Magnes, Lyn Martin, Robert Meganck, Mark Murphy, Lori Osiecki, Wayne Parmenter, Debbie Pinkney, Karen Pritchett, George Schill, Lee Steadman, Jim Trusilo, Phil Wilson
• **Koeffler, Ann: pg 1157,1200,1252**
  5015 Clinton St #306, Los Angeles, CA 90004 ....**323-957-2327**
  Illustrator: Ron Barry, Martha Anne Booth, Dick Cole, Bob Commander, Catherine Deeter, Jan Evans, Paul Jermann, Judy Koenig, Susan Legnami, Constance McLennan, Eugene Mitta, Juliana Morris, Kevin O'Shea, Rik Olson, Randy South, Kevin Spaulding, James Stagg, Charles Thomas, Jenny Vainisi, Teresa Woodward
• **Koralik Assocs: pg 1170**
  900 W Jackson Blvd #7W, Chicago, IL 60607 312-944-5680
  fax: 312-421-5948
  Illustrator: Randal Birkey, Tim Campell, Tony Crakovich, Ron Criswell, Joann Daley, Susan Edison, Lori Nelson Field, Arthur Friedman, Myron Grossman, Loren Kirkwood, Salem Kreiger, Karen Kuchar, Jim Lange, Rob Lawson, Chuck Ludeke, Joe McDermott, Michele Noiset, LS Pierce, Tom Price, Ilene Robinette, Brian Schrader, Bob Scott, Dennis Soderstrom, Terri Starrett, Ken Tiessen, Andy Zito
  Photographer: Bill Graham, Robert Keeling, Dan McCreehan, Scott Smudsky
Korman & Co:
  135 W 24th St PH A, New York, NY 10011 212-727-1442
  Photographer: David Bishop, Richard Bradbury, Carlo Pieroni, David Harry Stewart
• **Korn & Assoc, Pamela: pg 776-779**
  333 Lower Seese Hill Rd, Canadensis, PA 18325.........**717-595-9298**
  fax: 717-595-9392
  Illustrator: Brian Ajhar, Jeff Moores
Korn Assocs Ltd, Elaine:
  372 Fifth Ave #2E, New York, NY 10018 212-760-0057
  Photographer: Edward Celnick, John Fortunato, Frank Yarborugh
Kortz & Co, David:
  PO Box 2042, Minneapolis, MN 55402............................612-824-0218
Kramer & Assocs, Joan:
  10490 Wilshire Blvd #1701, Los Angeles, CA 90024 310-446-1866
  Photographer: Richard Apple, Bill Bachmann, Roberto Brosan, David Cornwell, Clark Dunbar, Bruce Fier, Stan Flint, Stephen Frink, Peter T Kane, John Luke, Carey Moore, Frank Moscati, Bill Nation, John Russell, Glenn Steiner Photo, Mel Weinstein, Ken Whitmore, Edward Young
Kramer & Assocs, Joan:
  New York, NY 212-567-5545
  Photographer: Richard Apple, Bill Bachmann, Roberto Brosan, David Cornwell, Clark Dunbar, Bruce Fier, Stan Flint, Stephen Frink, Peter T Kane, John Luke, Cary Moore, Frank Moscati, Bill Nation, John Russell, Glenn Steiner Photo, Mel Weinstein, Ken Whitmore, Edward Young
Kramer & Kramer, Inc:
  156 Fifth Ave #303, New York, NY 10010 212-645-8787
  Hair: Colleen Creighton, James Dodes, Moiz, Perrine Rougemont, Ronnie Stan
  Hair & Make-up: Alexis Caydam
  Illustrator: Carlotta
  Make-up: Ana Marie, Carolina Gonzalez, Helene Macaulay, Lydia Snyder, Mary Wiles
  Photographer: Jeff Manzetti, Ben Watts
  Stock: Robin Page
  Stylist: Susan Breindel, Kendall Farr, Emily Fitch, Marisa Crawford Indri

Kramer, Ina:
  928 Broadway, New York, NY 10010 212-614-0616
Kristo-Nagy, Elka:
  57 E 11th St 9th Fl, New York, NY 10003 212-475-5156
  Photographer: Albano Ballerini, Steven Cohen, Andreas Pollok
KSC Reps:
  121 West 19th St 10th Fl, New York, NY 10010 212-627-7171
  Electronic Imaging: Tim Tucker Images
  Illustrator: Bob Conge, Andre LaRoche
  Multimedia: Mark Conge
  Photographer: Christopher Clor, Walter Colley, Kurt Gardner, George Kamper, Todd Powell, Dave Radler, Derek Snape, Brian Sprouse
Kuehnel & Assocs, Peter:
  30 E Huron Plaza #2108, Chicago, IL 60611 312-642-6499
  Electronic Imaging: Mad Dog Digital, TOPIX
  Film: Neoglyphics
  Illustrator: Phoenix Studio Inc
Kurlansky, Sharon:
  192 Southville Rd, Southborough, MA 01772 508-872-4549
  Illustrator: John Gamache, Bruce Hutchison, Tim Lewis, Mary Anne Lloyd

L

La Moine:
  6059 Melrose Ave, Los Angeles, CA 90038 213-467-9730
  Photographer: Charles William Bush, Robert Fleischauer, Bob Frame, Jonny Hernandez, Melanie Nissen, Carlos Serrao
LA Rep:
  8149 Kirkwood Dr, Los Angeles, CA 90046 213-656-1720
  Hair & Make-up: Kathy Doss, Robin Frederiksz, Mario Lara, Elizabeth Sloan, Jettie Vander Tuin
  Photographer: Peter Brown, Darren Keith, Lisa Peardon, Meila Penn, Grant Sainsbury, Ken Sax
  Stylist: Leslie Gardner, Jacki Roach
Lachapelle Reps, Linda:
  420 E 54th St, New York, NY 10022...............................212-838-3170
  Hair: Dov, Gabriel Saba
  Hair & Make-up: Barbara Fazio, Koji, Mutsumi
  Photographer: Martha Camarillo, Carlo Dalla Chiesa, Richard Dunkley, Pieter Estersohn, James Galloway, Tim Geaney, Thom Jackson, Patricia de Warren, Peter Woloszynski
  Stylist: Martin Bourne, Beverly Hyde, Pamela Silver
Laird, Sarah:
  12 Charles Ln, New York, NY 10014 212-989-9666
  Hair: Lawrence DePalma, Michael Johnson
  Hair & Make-up: Pat Carroll, Ilise Heitzner Harris, Herve, Brett Jackson, Sara Johnson, Michael Reh, Regine Thorre
  Make-up: Margaret Avery, Racine Christensen, Glenna Franklin, Wei Lang, Matthew Sky
  Photographer: Stewart Ferebee, Richard Imrie, Jim Reiher
  Stylist: Lee Clower, Cheryl Galante
Lamb, Jennie:
  23 New Mount St, Manchester, England, UK M4 4DE 1619-534034
Lambert & Assocs, Laurie:
  2870 Romana, Cincinnati, OH 45209 513-841-0073
Lamont, Mary:
  New York, NY 212-242-1087
  Photographer: Jim Marchese
Langley Artist Rep, Sharon:
  111 E Wacker 26th, Chicago, IL 60601 312-540-9470
  Illustrator: Clem Bedwell, Barbara Emmons, Thomas L Fluharty, Paul Johnson, Nobee Kanayama, Jeff Meyer, Jeff O'Connor, Tim Spransy, Keith Ward, Matt Zumbo
Larkin, Mary:
  220 E 57th St #5J, New York, NY 10022 212-832-8116
  Illustrator: Ken Fallin, Loren Long
  Photographer: Lynn St John
Larkworthy Artist Rep Ltd, Kate:
  32 Downing St #4D, New York, NY 10014 212-633-1310
  Illustrator: Nick Dewar, Olaf Hajek, Michael Hill, Anja Kroencke, Zohar Lazar, Miyuki Morimoto, David Navaseurs, Geoffrey Parker, Susan Saas, Hiroshi Tanabe, Dominique Vitali
• **Lavaty, Frank & Jeff: pg 502-521**
  217 E 86th St Box 212, New York, NY 10028 ....**212-427-5632**
  url: http://www.LavatyArt.com / fax: 212-427-6372
  Illustrator: Lori Anzalone, Craig Attebery, David Biedrzycki, Gary Davis, Don Demers, Chris Duke, Tim Hildebrandt, Gervasio Gallardo, John Paul Genzo, Yuan Lee, Robert LoGrippo, Carlos Ochagavia, Peter Scanlan, Shannon Stirnweis, Ben Verkaaik
Lawrence Reps, Robert:
  25 Buckineer, Marina Del Rey, CA 90292 310-827-0457
  Illustrator: Ray Dougela, Dave Lowe
  Photographer: Geoffrey C Clifford, Mark McIntyre, Carl Schneider Photo, Charlie Schriddie
LeCouvre, Lynne:
 800-348-6911
  Illustrator: Ron Bomba, Doug Bowles, Lawrence Knighton, Paula Pertile, Gene Sparkman, Malcolm Tarlofsky, Dave Titus, Robert Zammarchi
  Photographer: James Dickens
Lee & Lou Productions, Inc:
  8522 National Blvd #108, Culver City, CA 90232 310-287-1542
  Graphic Designer: Skidmore Studio
  Photographer: Rick Casemore, Rick Graves, James Haefner Photo Inc, Chuck Kuhn, John Marian, John Oliver
Lee/Lloyd Reps:
  145 W 58th St #10M, New York, NY 10019 212-717-7654
  Photographer: Neil Beckerman, Jay Corbett, Erik Rank
Leff Assocs, Inc., Jerry:
  420 Lexington Ave #2760, New York, NY 10170 212-697-8525
  Film: Michael Plank
  Illustrator: Greg Beecham, Tom Beecham, Maryjane Begin, Ron Broda, Brian Callanan, Gwen Connelly, Denise Crawford, Wayne Ensrud, Joe Fleming, Manuel Geerinck, Charles Gehm, Alex Guben, Richard High, Fred Hilliard, Mike Hodges, Terry Hoff, Lars Justinen, Lingta Kung, Bertrand Le Pautremat, Ron Lesser, Kung Lingta, Francis Livingston, Fred Lynch, Michele Manning, David O'Keefe, Rik Olson, Pierre-Paul Pariseau, Michael Plank, Rob Roth, Sue Rother, John Sayles, Nancy Stentz, Mary Thelen, Farida Zaman
Legend, Inc:
  6922 Hollywood Blvd #620, Los Angeles, CA 90028 213-467-1533
  Photographer: Philip Dixon, Neil Kirk, Dah Len, Marco Michelitti, Isabel Snyder

- **Lehmen Dabney, Inc: pg 1104**
  1431 35th Ave S, Seattle, WA 98144 ....**206-325-8595**
  fax: 206-325-8594
  Illustrator: Cherie Bender, Ruben De Anda, Jim Deal, John Dinser, Suzanne Dunaway, Diane Fenster Illustration, Rolf Goetzinger, Obadinah Heavner, Jeremy Kidd, Kong Lu Illustration, Julie Pace, Stan Shaw, Carla Siboldi, Steve Slaske, Kirk Richard Smith, Debra Solomon, David Wink, Allen Yamashiro, Jeff Yeomans
  Photographer: Rosanne Olson

- **Leighton & Co: pg 716-726**
  7 Washington Street, Beverly, MA 01915 ....**978-921-0887**
  e-mail: leighton@leightonreps.com / url: www.leightonreps.com / fax: 978-921-0223
  Illustrator: Scott Angle, Steve Atkinson, Rob Bolster, Linda Bronson, Traci O'Very Covey, Laura DeSantis, Robert Evans Illustration, Annette Kraus, Mary Anne Lloyd, Michael Lotenero, Lisa Manning, Steve Meek, Scott Nash, Tim Nihoff, Rod Savely, Steven Stankewicz, Steven Stankiewicz, August Stein, Jennifer Thermes, Art Valero, Jane Winsor

  Leone, Mindy:
  381 Park Ave S #710, New York, NY 10016 212-696-5674
  Photographer: Bill Kouirinis

  Leonian, Phillip:
  114 E 13th St #TH1, New York, NY 10003 212-420-1860

  Lesli-Art, Inc:
  PO Box 6693, Woodland Hills, CA 91365 818-999-9228
  Illustrator: Kurt Anderson, Raymond Bayless, John Bruce, Frank Caldwell, Don Clark, Jim Daly, Thomas Darro, Walter Graham, Diane Green, Gregory Harris, Al Helner, Christa Kieffer, Roger La Manna, Tom McLaughlin, Wajih Nahleh, Rick Peterson, Richard Pionk, Jan Saether, Bob Savino, Bob Schmalzried, Brian Shapiro, Harry Somers, John Stephens, George Thompson, Edward Turner, Connie Van Dyk, James Verdugo, SZ Wang

  Levin, Dorr Assocs:
  1123 Broadway #1005, New York, NY 10010 212-627-9871
  Photographer: Mark Feaster, Fabrizio Gianni, Dominick Guillemot, Matthew Klein, Lee Page, Remi Rebillard, Stan Shaffer, Kevin Twomey, Carl Vanderschuit, Ivo Von Renner, George Whiteside

  Levy Creative Management: pg 727-735
  e-mail: sari@LeviCreative.com / fax: 212-661-4839
  300 E 46th St #4G, New York, NY 10017 ....**212-687-6463**
  Illustrator: Alan D Dingman, Shane W Evans, Roberto Parada, Doug Struthers

  Lewin, Samantha:
  242 E 19th St, New York, NY 10003 212-228-5530
  Photographer: Dennis Chalkin, Gary Goldberg, Heungman, Ralph Masullo

  Leyden Diversified:
  976 Old Huntingdon Pike, Huntingdon Valley, PA 19006 215-663-0587
  Electronic Imaging: Floyd Dean, John Dzedzy
  Film: Tom Daniels
  Illustrator: Animates/Hellman Assoc Animation, Kim Behm, Deb Bovy, John Emil Cymerman, Donna Bair Delich, Len Epstein, Bruce Evans, Alex Forbes, Greg Hargreaves, Dan Hatala, Robert Hochgertel, Joanne Hoffman, Steve Hunter, Kathleen King, Paul Lackner, John Langdon, Tony Mascio, Marcos Monteiro, Pat Muchmore, Wayne Parmenter, John Miles Simon, Craig Simpson, John Thompson, Todd Treadway, Mary Wilsbach
  Photographer: Philip Isaiah Katz, Ed Marco, Gary Mattie, Scott Nibauer

  Li Inc, Liz:
  260 Fifth Ave, New York, NY 10001 ....**212-889-7067**
  Photographer: Lorentz Gullachsen, Martin Mistretta, Roy Volkmann

- **Lilie, Jim: pg 976,977,1008,1009,1064,1108**
  729 Castro St, San Francisco, CA 94114 ....**415-441-4384**
  fax: 415-395-9809
  Illustrator: Eric Bowman, Armandina Lozano, Dennis Ziemienski, Dugald Stermer

- **Lindgren & Smith: pg 372-415,970,971**
  250 W 57th St #521, New York, NY 10107 ....**212-397-7330**
  url: www.stockillustrated.com (or) www.lindgrensmith.com
  Illustrator: Regan Dunnick, Joseph Fielder, Doug Fraser, Joe & Kathy Heiner, Jennifer Herbert, Miles Hyman, Jeff Jackson, Kim Johnson, Susan Leopold, Francis Livingston, Lori Lohstoeter, Richard Mantel, Bill Mayer, Vincent McIndoe, Jonny Mendelsson, Yan Nascimbene, Chris O'Leary, Bruno Paciulli, Mickey Paraskevas, Rick Peterson, Charles S Pyle, Tim Raglin, Steven Salerno, Marti Shohet, Valerie Sokolova, Robert Gantt Steele, JW Stewart, Mary Thelen, Bethann Thornburgh, Pol Turgeon, Stefano Vitale, Robert Wagt, Jean Wisenbaugh, Brian Zick

- **Lindgren, Pat: pg 372-415,970,971**
  250 W 57th St #521, New York, NY 10107 ....**212-397-7330**
  url: www.stockillustrated.com / See Lindgren & Smith NY for client list

  London, Valerie:
  1601 N Stanley Ave, Los Angeles, CA 90046 323-436-0123
  Photographer: Jennifer Cheung, Michael Haber, Steven Nilsson, F Scott Schafer

  Lopez, Claudia:
  PO Box 19538, Atlanta, GA 30325 404-350-8364
  Photographer: Louis Cahill

  Lorraine & Assocs:
  2311 Farrington St, Dallas, TX 75207 214-688-1540
  Illustrator: Jacques Lamy, Mary Thelen
  Photographer: David Bullock, Lee Gordon, Keith Madigan

- **Lott Reps: pg 758-763**
  60 E 42nd St #1146, New York, NY 10165 ....**212-953-7088**
  Illustrator: Sean Beavers, Tony Cove, Lori Earley, Mike Evans, Ed Kurtzman, Eric Lee, Mark Nagata, Tim O'Brien, Barbara Tyler, Craig White

  Lulu Creatives:
  4645 Colfax Ave South, Minneapolis, MN 55409 612-825-7564
  Illustrator: Doug Bowles, Alan Brunettin, Jannine Cabossel, Matt Foster, Tina Lee Hill, Fran O'Neill, Virginia Peck, Tracy Rea, Filip Yip Illus

  Luna, Tony:
  39 E Walnut St, Pasadena, CA 91103 626-584-4000
  Film: Dean Cundy, Robert Mehnert
  Photographer: Dan Wolfe

  Lund, Kent:
  306 S Washington Blvd #228, Royal Oak, MI 48067 248-548-2100
  Film: McKinsey Film Production
  Photographer: Davo, Jim Haefner, Ron Strong, Greg Zajack

  Lurie Fine Arts:
  8657 Wonderland Ave, Los Angeles, CA 90046 213-654-8983
  Illustrator: Daniel Brice, Agop Gemdjian, Greg Gronowski, Alfonce Pagano, David Serrano, Rene Vasquez
  Photographer: Steve Olson, Ben Sedererowsky

- **Lux & Assocs, Inc, Frank: pg 1218**
  401 N Wabash #532, Chicago, IL 60611 ....**312-222-1361**
  Illustrator: Dan Clyne, Karla Ginzinger, Terry Jasinski, Gregory Martin, Kathy Petrauskas, Jim Price, Evan Schwarze, Michael Stepanek, John Walker, David Wehrstein

  Lynch, Alan:
  11 Kings Ridge Rd, Long Valley, NJ 07853 908-813-8718
  Illustrator: Martin Andrews, Michael Armson, A. Azpiri, Colin Backhouse, Simon Bertram, John Peter Brown, Jim Burns, Nigel Chamberlain, John Clementson, Brigid Collins, Gordon Crabb, Carla Daly, Merritt Dekle, Les Edwards, Faranak, Yvonne Gilbert, Peter Goodfellow, Peter Gudynas, Elizabeth Harbour, John Harris, Matilda Harrisson, David Hitch, Philip Hood, John Howe, Diane Lumley, Milo Manara, Edward Miller, Terry Oakes, Mark Oldroyd, Liane Payne, Miguel Angelo Prado, Tony Roberts, Luis Royo, Liz & Brian Sanders, Brian Sweet, Len Thurston, Daniel Torres, Jenny Tylden-Wright, Jim Warren, Tim White, David Williams, Janet Woolley, Paul Wright

  Lynn, Dana:
  2748 Garfield Ave, Silver Spring, MD 20910 301-585-3045

  Lyon-Smith, Harry:
  #1 Vicarage Crescent, London, UK SW11 1712-288882

  Lysohir, Chris:
  77 Seventh Ave #12U, New York, NY 10011 212-741-3187
  Photographer: Jay Alan Lefkowitz

M

Madore, Lise: QU 514-767-8663

Mahar, Therese Ryan:
233 E 50th St #2F, New York, NY 10022 212-753-7033
Hair & Make-up: Dawn Jacobson
Photographer: Michael Biondo, Jonnie Buick, Mike Donnelly, William Garrett, Marc Hispand, Mark Platt, Andre Rau
Stylist: Marybeth Yates

Malakoff, Julia:
1523 King St, Alexander, VA 22314 703-706-5739

- **Maloney & Assocs, Tom: pg 817,874**
  307 N Michigan Ave #1006, Chicago, IL 60601 ....**312-704-0500**
  fax: 312-704-0501
  Illustrator: Steve Bondurant, Dennis Carmichael, Tungwai Chau, Dan Cooper, Dennas Davis, Gary Davis, Jean Delahoussaye, Scott Ernster, John Lenker, Mike Lester, Keith Meehan, Luis Molina, Mitch O'Connell, David Olmstead, Rik Olson, Oscar Senn, Marla Shega, Jim Starr, Paul Vaccarello

  Manasse, Michele:
  200 Aquetong Rd, New Hope, PA 18938 215-862-2091
  Illustrator: Maxine Boll, Eric Dever, Sheldon Greenberg, Greg King, Genevieve Leloup, Mike Reagan, Matthew Trueman, Terry Widener

  Mandel, Gary:
  928 Broadway #803, New York, NY 10010 212-614-8485
  Photographer: Michael Brunn, Rick Burda, Christian Chaize, Michael Cuno, Shay Hasson, Carol Weinberg Studio

  Manham, Allan:
  70 Rosaline Rd, London, England, UK SW6 7QT 1716-101801

  Mann, Ken:
  20 W 46th St, New York, NY 10036 212-944-2853
  Photographer: David Burnett, Brian Lanker, Bette Marshall, Allan McPhail, Gary Owens, Ulf Skogsbergh

  Marek & Assocs, Inc:
  170 Fifth Ave 7th Fl, New York, NY 10010 212-924-6760
  Hair: Ray Allington, Carmel, Rick Gradone, Alberto Guzman, Kazuya
  Hair & Make-up: Chase Aston, Christopher Lockhart, Nicholas Morley, Helena Occhipinti, Clorinda Yitale
  Make-up: Jim Breese, Mark Hayles, Susan McCarthy, Alison Raffaelo, Lynn Russell, Vanessa Scali, Shade, Susan Sterling, Olga Titova
  Photographer: Arnaldo Anaya-Lucca, Christopher Astley, Walter Chin, Jacques DeHornois, Robert Erdmann, Freddie Leiba, Frederik Lieberath, Nicholas Moore, Carlotta Moye, Manuela Pavesi, Timothy Reukauf, Myers Robertson, Scavullo, Kate Sebbak, Bert Stern, Timothy Tract, Deborah Turbeville, Ernesto Urdaneda, Emil Wilbekin
  Stylist: Basia Zamorska

- **Marie, Rita: pg 584,585,746-752**
  Los Angeles, CA **213-934-3395**
  fax: 213-936-2757
  1464 Linden Ave, Chicago, IL 60035 ....**847-432-2415**
  fax: 773-883-0375
  Illustrator: John Dismukes, Mort Drucker, Dick Durrstein, Rick Farrell, Marla Frazee, Stan Gorman, Peter Green, Robert Gunn, Robert Pryor, Relic, Renwick, Paul Rogers, Fathulla Shakirov, Danny Smythe, Blake Thornton, Jon Watson, Dave Willardson

  Marino, Marlene:
  75 E Wacker Dr #2500, Chicago, IL 60601 312-201-1776
  Music: Paul Libman, Kerry Rasikas
  Photographer: Rob Anderson

  Market Point Publishing:
  29 Barnes High St, London, England, UK SW13 81-876-8666

- **Markowitz, Barbara: pg 1060,1061**
  Los Angeles, CA **323-939-5927**
  Illustrator: Roman Genn

  Markus, Norma Jean:
  144 W 86th #15A, New York, NY 10024 212-579-2613
  Photographer: Todd Eberle, Matthew Rolston

  Marlena Agency, The:
  278 Hamilton Ave, Princeton, NJ 08540 609-252-9405
  Film: Paul Zwolak

  Martha Productions, Inc:
  11936 W Jefferson Blvd #C, Culver City, CA 90230 310-390-8663
  Illustrator: Bob Brugger, Bradley Clark, Royce Fitzgerald, Allen Garns, Byron Gin, Joe & Kathy Heiner, Nathan Kane, Steve Keller, Hiro Kimura, Catherine Leary, Mike Meaker, Bill Morrison, Mukai Studio, Jody Reed Silver, Peter Siu, Steve Vance, Eric Westbrook

  Marzena:
  229 E 79th St #8A, New York, NY 10021 212-772-2522
  Photographer: Chris Callis, Craig Cutler

  Maslov, Norman:
  608 York St, San Francisco, CA 94110 415-641-4376
  Photographer: Cristina Ceppas, Michele Clement Studios Inc, Shay Hasson, Deborah Jones, David Maisel, Mika Manninen

• **Maslov/Weinberg: pg 753-757**
608 York St, San Francisco, CA 94110 ....**415-641-1285**
fax: 415-641-5500
Illustrator: Polly Becker, Stuart Bradford, Sean Flanagan, Stefan Gutermuth, Pamela Hobbs, Jordan Isip, Tatjana Krizmanic, Mark Matcho, Adam McCauley, Jay Mercado, Bill Russell, Susan Sanford, Mark Urliksen, Cynthia von Buhler, Eric White

Mason Illus:
3810 Edmund Blvd, Minneapolis, MN 55406 612-729-1774
Illustrator: Neal Aspinall, Neil Aspinall, Kenn Backhaus, Patrick Faricy, Paul Fricke, Glenn Gustafson, Joe Heffron, Dan Lotts, Jeff Meyer, Mark Mille, Randy Rogers, Tom Rosborough, Harlan Scheffler, Dan Wiemer
Photographer: Chris Monroe

Matson Reps, Marla:
1429 N 1st Street, Phoenix, AZ 85004 602-252-5072
Illustrator: Michael Carroll, Mark Fredrickson, Chris Gall, Allen Garns, Mike Gushock, Rick Kirkman, John Kleber, Darrel Kolosta, Julia LaPine, Bob Lynch, Ann Morton, Curtis Parker, Walter Porter, Barbara Samanich, Jim Starr, Charles Thomas, Gary Yealdhall, John Zielinski
Photographer: Ellen Barnes, Scott Baxter, William McKellar, Mark Segal, John Wagner

Mattelson Assocs Ltd:
New York, NY 212-684-2974
Illustrator: Karen Kluglein, Marvin Mattelson, Phill Singer

McCallum, Melissa:
1020 Elm St, Winnetka, IL 60093 847-441-8993

McConnell McNamara & Co:
182 Broad St, Wethersfield, CT 06109 860-563-6154
Lisa Corson
Photographer: Jack McConnell
Stock: McConnell McNamara & Co

McCray, Donna:
38 E First St, New York, NY 10003 212-505-6195
Photographer: Henry Borne, Don Freeman, Michael James O'Brien

McCusker, Kathleen E:
3178 Belgrade St, Philadelphia, PA 19134 215-427-6114
Illustrator: Ken Hobson, Connie Kennedy, Keith Neely, Steve Smallwood, Thalia Stratton, Victor R Valla

McGee, Linda:
1126 Zimmer Dr, Atlanta, GA 30306 404-885-1640
Photographer: E Alan McGee

McKay, Colleen:
229 E 5th St #2, New York, NY 10003 212-598-0469
Photographer: Russell Porcas, Lilo Raymond, Marden Smith, Robert Tardio, Cesar Vera

McLean & Friends Reps:
2460 Peachtree Rd NW #1705, Atlanta, GA 30305 404-881-6627
Illustrator: Garry Colby, Martin Pate

McMahon & Co, Eileen:
PO Box 1062, Bayonne, NJ 07002 201-436-4362
Film: Clare Mackie
Illustrator: Michael Foreman, Andre Francois, Edward Gorey, Ronald Searle

McMahon, Brian:
1535 N Western Ave, Chicago, IL 60622 773-227-6778

McNaughton, Toni:
333 N Michigan #200, Chicago, IL 60601 312-855-1225

Mead & Assocs, Robert:
421 Park Ave, Rye, NY 10580 212-688-7474
Photographer: Burgess Blevins, Steve Bonini, Antonin Kratochvil, Nick Vedros, Michael Yamashita, Elizabeth Zeschin

• **Meiklejohn Illus, Paul & Chris: pg 875**
28 Shelton St, Covent Garden, London, England, UK WC2H **1712-402077**
fax: 1718-360199
Illustrator: Alan Cracknell, Matt Eastwood, Andrew Farley, Jake Rickwood, Paul Sample

• **Mendola Ltd, Artist Reps: pg 108-168,1014,1015,1185**
420 Lexington Ave, New York, NY 10170 ....**212-986-5680**
url: www.mendolaart.com / fax: 212-818-1246
Graphic Designer: Ltd New York Film & Animation Co, Bill Vann
Illustrator: Gus Alavezos, Paul Alexander, TL Ary, Gil Ashby, Rowan Barnes-Murphy, Kevin Beilfuss, Russell Benfanti, Brent Benger, Ron Berg, Barry Blackman, Mark Busacca, Chris Cahill, Jim Campbell, Inc Capstone Studios, Carl Cassler, Douglas Chezem, Steven Chorney, Gary Colby, Jonathan Combs, Michael Crampton, Michael Davis, Chris Dellorco, Denise & Fernando, Cathy Diefendorf, Jason Dowd, Jon Ellis, Bob Elsdale, Dan Fell, Phil Franke, Brad Gaber, Hector Garrido, Chuck Gillies, Mitch Greenblatt, Lisa Chauncy Guida, Dale Gustafson, Michael Halbert, Attila Hejja, Dave Henderson, Robert Hynes, James Ibusuki, Bill James, Scott Johnston, Alfons Kiefer, Joyce Kitchell, Bob Krogle, Kurt Krubs, Toni Kurrasch, Kent Leech & Associates, Ashley Lonsdale, Jeffrey Lynch, Rob MacDougall, Jeffrey Mangiat, Paul Manz, Edward Martinez, Bill Maughan, Geoffrey McCormack, Mick McGinty, Daniel McGowan, Mark McMahon, MDC Art Studio, Mike Mikos, Jonathan Milne, Roger Motzkus, Mark Mueller, Carol Newsom, Tom Newsom, Gregory Newsome, Chris Notarile, Peter Pagano, Heather Price, Mike Radencich, Lynn Reed, Frank Riccio, Linda Richards, John Rowe, Cornel Rubino, Jill Sabella, Francesco Santalucia, Joe Saputo, Gillie Schatner, David Schleinkofer, Eliza Schulte, Rick Sealock, Stanley Silver Jr, Bill Silvers, Mike Smollin, Wayne Anthony Still, Jim Talbot, Robert Tanenbaum, Joseph Taylor, Jeffrey Terreson, Thierry Thompson, Bill Vann, Wayne Vincent, Jeff Wack, Sam Ward, Amy L Wasserman, Rob Westerberg, Don Wieland, Dean Williams, Mike Wimmer, Larry Winborg, Keith Witmer, Stephan Wolgemuth, Jennie Yip, Boris Zlotsky
Photographer: Jill Sabella

Meo, Frank:
54 Morningside Dr #54, New York, NY 10025 212-965-9396
Photographer: Robert Ammirati, Guy Grundy, Bob Peterson, James Salzano

Metafolio/Michael Conn:
320 Manhattan Ave, Manhattan Beach, CA 90266 ....
Photographer: Tim Damon, Peggy Day

• **Metzler, Terri: pg 1139**
San Francisco, CA **415-431-8474**
Illustrator: Hal Brooks

Midcoast Studio:
2616 Industrial Row, Troy, MI 48084 248-280-0640
Photographer: Madison Ford, Phil Gratorex, Mark Harmer, Eric Perry, Dennis Wiand

Midwest Assocs:
2021 Barrett, Royal Oak, MI 48067 248-546-0884
Photographer: Inc, Lucky Curtis Photography

Miller, Doug:
420 Lexington Ave, New York, NY 10170 212-692-9200

Miller, Judith:
20 E 35th St, New York, NY 10016 212-447-5551
Photographer: Abrams/Lacagnina, John Dolan, Eitan, Frank Herholdt, Grant Matthews, James Merrell, Michael O.Neill, Wilhelm Scholz, Marlene Wetherell

Mills & Co, Jane:
600 N Bishop, Dallas, TX 75208 214-946-6569
Illustrator: Bob Shema
Photographer: Eric Pearle

Mizuno, Barbara:
32129 Lindeso Canyon Rd #103, West Lake Village, CA 91361 310-472-1446

Monaco Reps:
389 Bleecker St, New York, NY 10014 212-647-0336

Montagano & Assocs, David:
11 E Hubbard 7th Fl, Chicago, IL 60611 312-527-3283
Electronic Imaging: Eye Design, Joseph Taylor
Illustrator: Tom DuBois, Joel Heinz, John Hyatt, Mary Jones, Burton Morris, Bruno Paciulli, Larry Paulsen, Mike Randall, James Swanson
Photographer: Hans Rott

Montage Photographic Agency:
8955 Wonderland Park Ave, Los Angeles, CA 90068 213-851-0621
Photographer: Alison Dyer, Loren Haynes, Dennis Keeley, Bonnie Schiffman, Rick Steil, Art Streiber, Matthew Welch, Jim Wright

Moore & Assocs, Gigante:
360 N Michigan Ave #1908, Chicago, IL 60601 312-541-9595
Animator: Will Vinton Studios
Film: Compulsive, Industrial Light & Magic
Photographer: Wilson Griak Productions, Silent Partner

Morawski & Assocs:
135 Park St, Troy, MI 48083 248-589-8050
Photographer: Charles Hopkins, Scott Lane, Steve Petrovich, Larry Rice

• **Morgan Assocs, Vicki: pg 169-191**
194 Third Ave 3rd Fl, New York, NY 10003 ....**212-475-0440**
url: www.vickimorganassociates.com / fax: 212-353-8538
Illustrator: Nanette Biers, Karen Blessen, Dave Calver, Tom Christopher, Raul Colon, Nicholas Gaetano, Beppe Giacobbe, Sandra Kaplan, William Low, Joyce Patti, Elizabeth Rosen, Robert Sauber, Joanie Schwarz, Joel Spector, Dahl Taylor, Lauren Uram, Kris Wiltse, Bruce Wolfe, Wendy Wray

Morin & Assocs, Jacqueline:
51 Bulwer St #200, Toronto, ON M5T 1A1 416-506-1411

Morneau, France:
4398 Saint Laurent, Montréal, QU H2W 1Z5 514-848-9870

• **Morris, Sharon: pg 877**
580 Washington St, Ste 204, San Francisco, CA 94111 ....**415-362-8280**
e-mail: smasf@aol.com/ fax: 415-362-8310

Moses, Janice:
99 Battery Place #11m, New York, NY 10280 212-898-4898
Photographer: Brad Guice, Karen Kuehn, David Lawrence, Luciana Pampalone

Moskowitz Reps, Inc, Marion:
315 E 68 St, New York, NY 10021 212-517-4919
Illustrator: Phillip Dvorak, Diane Teske Harris, Beth McCash, Geoffrey Moss, Roger Roth

• **Moss, Eileen: pg 806-815**
333 E 49th St, New York, NY 10017 ....**212-980-8061**
url: www.theispot.com/rep/bruckandmoss / fax: 212-832-8778
See "Bruck & Moss" for client list

Motion Artists:
1400 N Hayworth Ave #36, Los Angeles, CA 90046 213-851-7737
Film: Simon Murton, Patrick Tatopoulos
Illustrator: Gabriel Abraham, Jim Bandsuh, Harold Belker, Ted Boonthanakit, Mauro Borelli, Tim Burgard, Jim Byrkit, Raymond Consing, Robert Consing, John Coven, Juan Diaz, Mariano Diaz, Guy Dyas, Giacomo Ghiazza, Christopher Glass, Darek Gogol, Ray Harvie, Peter Heer, Marc Hurtado, Patrick Janicke, Bruton Jones, Petko Kadiev, Phil Keller, Tani Kunitake, Diane Labuda, Wil Madoc Rees, Joseph Musso, Susan Nininger, Emily Owens, Scot Ritchie, Jim Salvati, Christian Scheuerer, Oliver Scholl, Joshua Sheppard, Khang Trong-Pham, Carlos Vesa, Tracey Wilson, Anthony Zierhut

Muir, Dani:
65 E 93rd St #A, New York, NY 10128 212-828-1238

Mullins Photo, Max:
PO Box 14620, Chicago, IL 60614 773-477-6548

• **Munro Goodman Reps: pg 627-641**
5 E 17th St 6th Fl, New York, NY 10003 ....**212-691-2667**
url: www.spar.org / fax: 212-633-1844
4 E Ohio Studio B, Chicago, IL 60611 ....**312-321-1336**
fax: 312-321-1350
Illustrator: Shelly A Bartek, Mark Chickinelli, Sally Wern Comport, Phillip Dunlap, Tom Foty, Ben Garvie, Greg Hargreaves, Dan Hatala, Mike Kasun, Douglas Klauba, Bryan Peterson, Tim Robinson, Michael Steirnagle, Corey Wilkinson

Muth, John:
37 W 26th St, New York, NY 10010 212-532-3479
Photographer: Pat Hill

N

Nachreiner Boie Art Factory Ltd, Tom:
925 Elm Grove Rd, Elm Grove, WI 53122 414-785-1940

Nah, Pat:
111 N Bridge Rd #8-17 Peninsula Plz, Singapore, 0617 336-8808
Photographer: Scott Lightner

Nathan, Eunice:
370 E 76th St, New York, NY 10021 212-772-1776
Photographer: Bob Brody, Kevin Galvin

Nation, Monica:
344 W 47th St #2E, New York, NY 10036 212-265-7222
Photographer: Nicholas Eveleigh, Robert Lewis, Adam Weiss

• **Neis Group, The: pg 878,879**
P.O. Box 174, 11440 Oak Dr, Shelbyville, MI 49344 ....**616-672-5756**
e-mail: neisgroup@wmis.net / url: www.neisgroup.com / fax: 616-672-5757
Illustrator: Tom Bookwalter, Lyn Boyer-Nelles, G William Cole, Michael Ingle, Ken Karsen, Rainey Kirk, Berney Knox, Matt LaBarre, Erika LeBarre, Matt LeBarre, Don McLean, Laura Meadows, Bill Ross, David Schweitzer, Joyce Stiglich, John White, Danny Wilson
Lettering: Barbara McAdams
Photographer: Fred Bender, Phil Gray
Nevill, Charlene, VIS-A-VIS:
717 Capp St, San Francisco, CA 94110 415-824-4772
Photographer: Peter Fox, Tom Rider, Rich Turner, Thomas Upton Photography
Newborn Group, The:
115 West 2nd Street, New York, NY 10011....................212-989-4600
Illustrator: Julian Allen, Roy Carruthers, Teresa Fasolino, Robert Giusti, Robert Goldstrom, Mark Hess, John H Howard, Victor Juhasz, James Marsh, Wilson McLean, David Wilcox, Christopher Zacharow
Newman & Assocs, Carole:
1119 Colorado Ave #23, Santa Monica, CA 90401 310-576-0757
Electronic Imaging: Tom Slatky
Graphic Designer: Outerspace
Illustrator: Jenny Adams, Scott Angle, Ted Burn, Christian Ellithorpe, Tim Huhn, Michael Humphries, Paul Janovsky, Luis Molina, Randy Noble, Darcie Park, Leslie Roberts, Hiroko Sanders, Robert Schultz, Larry Taugher, Eddie Young
Photographer: Karen Anderson, Val Gelineau, Mike Granberry, Ronnda Heinrich, Knight/Bilham Photography, Kaz Kurisu, William Mackenzie-Smith, Gabriela Ortuzar
Nittolo Studio, Mary:
216 E 45th St 14th Fl, New York, NY 10017 212-661-1363
• **Nowak, Wanda: pg 784-787**
231 E 76th St #5D, New York, NY 10021 ....**212-535-0438**
fax: 212-535-1624
Illustrator: Ilja Bereznickas, Ferderique Bertrand, Herve Blondon, Laurent Cilluffo, Jo Chen Gerner, Vlad Guzner, Tim Hussey, Stein Loken, Martin Matje, David Miller, Chris Sharp, Coutler Young, Yoyo
• **Nowicki & Assocs, Lori: pg 1157,1200,1252**
37 West 20th Street #902, New York, NY 10011....................**212-243-5888**
url: www.xensei.com/users/nowicki
Illustrator: Argus, Martha Anne Booth, Bob Commander, Dave Cottone, Jean Hirashima, Paul Jermann, Mellissa@ McGill, Burton Morris, Juliana Morris, Hank Osuna, Tony Persiani, Doug Ross, Mark Schroder, Bryon Thompson, Dona Turner, Joe Veno, Tim Webb
Nowicki's, Inc:
4 Oak St, Needham, MA 02492 617-423-2800
Photographer: Daniel Arsenault Photography, Harry De Zitter, Francine Zaslow
Nygreen, Ann:
250A Seaview Ave, Piedmont, CA 94610 510-652-1744

O

O'Gorman/Schramm:
642 Washington Street #1A, New York, NY 10014 212-620-0284
Photographer: Shannon Greer, Janet Maya, Ron Nicolaysen, Frank Schramm, Tom Wool
Oasis Art Studio:
952 Medina Rd, Wayzata, MN 55391....................612-860-1701
Illustrator: Bill Bruning, Dan Craig, Ronald Finger, Corbett Gauthier, Ken Goldammer, Leland Klanderman, Dave LaFlur
Photographer: Dan Craig
Ogden, Robin:
4409 Washburn Ave S, Minneapolis, MN 55410 612-925-4174
Illustrator: Dianne Bennett, Bob Brugger
Lettering: Kelly Hume
Photographer: Steve Ewert, John Reed Forsman, Jeff Johnson, Bret Lopez
Olthuis, Stan:
49 Bathurst St #400, Toronto, ON M5V 2P2....................416-703-5300
One:
270 Lafayette #401, New York, NY 10012 212-925-1111
Hair & Make-up: Helene Andersson, Hiromi Kobari
Photographer: Matthias Clamer, Joseph Cultice, Takao Ikejiri, Jasper James, Eva Mueller, Benjamin Oliver, Pauline St. Denis
Stylist: Simone Colina, George Cortina, Rod Cummings, Michaela Angela Davies, Nicole Garrett, Dana Allyson Greenberg, Todd Hartnett, John Moore, Kevin Stewart
Orbit:
2 Everett Crescent, Toronto, ON M4C 4P2 416-429-2840
Photographer: Dan Couto
Organisation, The:
69 Caledonian Rd, London, England, UK N 19BT 1712-785176
42 Delavan St, Brooklyn, NY 11231 718-624-1906
Illustrator: Grahame Baker, Zafer Baran, Emma Chichester Clark, Mark Entwisle, Michael Frith, Neil Gower, Susan Hellard, Natacha Ledwidge, Lawrence Mynott, Michael O'Shaughnessy, Ruth Rivers, Max Schindler, Linda Smith, Nadine Wickenden
Ornstein, Beverly:
435 W Broadway, New York, NY 10012 212-334-6667
Photographer: Howard Schatz
Oscard Agency, Fifi:
24 W 40th St, New York, NY 10018....................212-764-1100
Illustrator: Per Arnoldi, Joe Farris
Photographer: William Claxton, Jeanne Moutousammy-Ashe, Mark Newman, Carole Reiff, Henri Silverman, Edmond Van Hoorick

P

Page, Jackie:
219 E 69th St, New York, NY 10021 212-772-0346
Photographer: Christian Belpaire, Richard Biegun, John Curtis, Sam Haskins, Michael Horikawa, Peter Langone, David Madison, Lincoln Potter, Phil Uhl, Mary Van Der Ven, Gert Wagner, Steve Wilkings
Pais Creative Rep, Jodi:
80 Raymond Ave #101, Pasadena, CA 91103....................626-795-1340
Photographer: Mario de Lopez, Ed Honowitz, Seth Joel, Ken Merfeld, Kathlene Persoff
Palulian Reps, Joanne:
18 McKinley St, Rowayton, CT 06853....................203-866-3734
Illustrator: Philippe Beha, Greg Couch, David Goldin, Bonnie Hofkin, Gayle Kabaker, Peter Kitchell, Dick Palulian, Trip Park, Tom Saecher, Bonnie Timmons

Paolantonio, Angela:
6750 Mulholland Dr, Los Angeles, CA 90068 323-874-9880
Photographer: Abrams/Lacagnina, Ty Allison, Nicola Dill, Tracy Lamonica, Fred Studios Licht, Eric Tucker
Papitto, Aurelia:
300 Commercial St #807, Boston, MA 02109....................617-742-3108
Illustrator: Ken Condon, Joe Heffron, Bruno Paciulli, Ron Tanovitz, Shaul Tsemach
Parallel Productions Inc:
2010 1st Ave S, Minneapolis, MN 55404....................612-874-1999
Parios Studio:
21 Toledo Dr, Brick, NJ 08723 908-477-5529
• **Pate & Company, Randy: pg 964,965**
2510G Las Posas Rd #431, Camarillo, CA 93010....................**805-529-8111**
Illustrator: John Alvin, Steven Chorney, Robert Florczak, Cunio Hagio, Bryan Haynes, Chris Hopkins, Robert Hunt, Mick McGinty, Kazuhiko Sano, Rumio Santo, Hugh Syme
Pateman, Michael:
155 E 35th St, New York, NY 10016 212-685-6584
Payne Assocs:
32 W 31st St 5th Fl, New York, NY 10001 212-239-4283
Illustrator: Ronald Slabbers
Payne, Liane:
144 Royal College St, London, England, UK NW1 OTA....................1712-679661
Pema Browne Ltd:
Pine Rd HCR Box 104B, Neversink, NY 12765 914-985-2936
Illustrator: Robert Barrett, Laura Bryant, Todd Doney, Bob Dorsey, Richard Hull, Charles Jordan, Dilleen Marsh, John Sandford, Bob Schochet, Maren Scott, Terry Sirrell
Penny & Stermer Group, The:
19 Stuyvesant Oval #2D, New York, NY 10009 212-505-9342
Illustrator: Steve Ellis, Scott Gordley, Glynnis Osher, Tom Payne, Terri Starrett, Rick Stromoski, Judy Unger
• **Perlow, Carrie: pg 1221**
311 Ave H #D, Redondo Beach, CA 90277 ....**310-540-5958**
Illustrator: Barbara Cummings, Mona Daly, Ray Goudey, Greg Hally, John Hull, Jui Ishida, Nora Koerber, Rachael McCampbell, Mercedes McDonald, Robert Rodriguez, Chuck Schmidt, Michael Wepplo
Photographer: Richard Rendon
PG Reps:
211 Manson Turnpike Rd, Ware, MA 01082 413-967-9855
• **Photocom, Inc: pg 1058,1059**
3005 Maple Ave #104, Dallas, TX 75201 ....**214-720-2272**
Illustrator: Abrams/Lacagnie, Don Arday, Jon Flaming, Michael Steirnagle
Photographer: Bernstein & Andriulli, Ric Cohn, Ric Photography Cohn, Phillip Esparza, Nancy Moran, Greg Stevens, Richard Wahlstrom
Photogroup, Inc:
3500 SE 22nd Ave Bldg 41, Portland, OR 97202 503-797-7817
Photographer: Jerry Taylor
• **Pickard, Maggie: pg 1397**
2 Locust Grove Rd, Rhinebeck, NY 12572 914-876-2358
fax: 914-876-5931
Illustrator: Elwood H Smith
Pincus, Rachel:
520 Washington Blvd. #107, Marina Del Rey, CA 90292 310-827-5496
Pinkstaff, Marsha:
25 W 81st St 15th Fl, New York, NY 10024....................212-799-1500
Photographer: Akos, Beth Galton, John Goodman, Lois Greenfield, Charles Purvis, Glen Wexler
Pinnacle Creative Co:
8136 Mullen Rd, Lenexa, KS 66215 913-438-1888
Illustrator: Peter Cole, Chris Willey
Piscopo, Maria:
2973 Harbor Blvd #229, Costa Mesa, CA 92626 714-556-8133
Photographer: Stan Sholik
Pix Producers Inc., Linda:
380 Lafayette St, New York, NY 10003....................212-533-3800
Photographer: Davies & Starr, Gary Hush, Gerhard Linnekogel, Duane Michals
Pizer, Alyssa:
13121 Garden Land Rd, Los Angeles, CA 90049 310-440-3930
Photographer: Marc Addleman, Mark Addleman, Robert Deutschman, Nels Israelson, Steven Lippman, David Michalek, Amyin Nesser, Stephen Sidoloff
• **Planet Rep-Williams Group West: pg 1346**
5 Tower Dr., MillValley, CA 94941 ....**800-847-5101**
Illustrator: J F Martin
Pohlman Studios, Inc:
535 N 27th St Box 08296, Milwaukee, WI 53208....................414-342-6363
Poje, Elizabeth:
1001 S Alfred St, Los Angeles, CA 90035....................310-556-1439
Illustrator: Mark Bussaca, Frank Kozik, Michele Lally, Alain Massicotte, Miyuki Sena, Oscar Senn, David Turner, Judy Unger, Stan Watts, Dave Woodman
Photographer: Jack Anderson, Robert Butler, Tony Garcia, Craig McMillen, David Perry, Bill Robbins, Eric Schmidt, Jeff Sedlik, Trudi Unger
Polizzi, Antonia:
125 Watts St, New York, NY 10013 212-925-1571
Photographer: Andrew Garn
Pomegranate Pictures:
5 W 19th St, New York, NY 10011....................212-633-2313
Photographer: Jimmy Bruch, Robert Farber, Phil Mucci, Joe Standart
Pool, Linda:
34701 E Hammond Rd, Grain Valley, MO 64029....................816-697-3984
Illustrator: Lone Jade, Robert Newton, Mike Radencich, Karen Woodburn
Photographer: Kent DeFault, Molly Plummer, Walt Seng
Positive Images:
89 Main St, Andover, MA 01810 508-749-9901
Photographer: Patricia Bruno, Karen Bussolini, Les Campbell, Dick Canby, Candace Cochrane, Jack Foley, Dennis Frates, Harry Haralambou, Margaret Hensel, Jerry Howard, Donna Ilkenberry, Roger Leo, Scott Leonhart, Roger Luft, Kathy Mansfield, Ivan Massar, Martin Miller, Jacob Mosser, John Parker, David Pratt, Catharine Reeve, Paul Rezendes, Pam Spaulding, Albert Squillace, Lee Anne White

• **Potts & Assocs, Carolyn:** pg 803-805,1080
1872 N Clybourn #404, Chicago, IL 60614 ....**773-935-8840**
fax: 773-935-6191
Graphic Designer: Joe Plume
Illustrator: Karen Bell, John Craig, Byron Gin, Greg Huber, Julia LaPine, Rhonda Voo
Lettering: Joe Plume
Photographer: Terry Collier, Ralph Daniel, Debra Doffing, Paul Goirand, Todd Haiman, Derek Seaward, Craig Van der Lende, Douglas Walker

Potts, Vicki:
PO Box 13518, Chicago, IL 60613 773-296-2940

Powditch Assocs, Michael:
CA 805-497-0952
Illustrator: Denny Osborn
Photographer: Steve Cooper, Bo Hylen, S Peter Lopez, O'Brien & Schridde, Les Ward

Powdith Associates:
863 Hartglen Ave, Westlake Village, CA 91361 805-497-0069

Prapas, Christine:
12480 SE Wiess Rd, Boring, OR 97009 503-658-7070
Illustrator: Marla Baggetta, Brian Battles, Dan Braun, Michael Carroll, Steve Cauden, Steve Ellis, Mitch Frye, Ted Gadecki, Leslie Gorsline, Tom Hassler, Stephen Hogan, Doug Horne, Blaise Jette, Alan Just, Jeff Labbe, Darlene Olivia McElroy, Charles Varner, Madeline Vasquez, Brad Weinman, Michael Wepplo
Photographer: Damien Conrad, Mark Scott

Pred, Becky:
10012 Perry Dr, Overland Pk, MO 66212 913-438-7733
Electronic Imaging: Dave Altis
Graphic Designer: Margaret Carsello
Illustrator: Jean Holmgren, Angela Moore, Jim Paillot, Tom Patrick, Rick Richter
Photographer: Donovan Reese

• **Prentice Assocs, Inc, Vicki:** pg 881
630 Fifth Ave 20th Fl, Rockefeller Ctr, New York, NY 10111 ....**212-332-3460**
fax: 212-674-4042
Illustrator: Rocco Baviera, Robert Byrne, Tom Edgarton, Joan Farber, Nasaaki Ogai, Leo Pando, Marjorie E Pesek, Hisashi Sekine, Mary Spencer, Tom Voss Illustration, Tom Voss
Photographer: Reuben Njaa

Prentice, Nancy:
2917 N Fulton Dr NE, Atlanta, GA 30305 404-266-0088
Illustrator: Steve McAfee, Mark E Schuler, Robbie Short, Bruce Young

Proof:
18 E 16th St #308, New York, NY 10003 212-727-7445
Make-up: Mitchell Behr
Photographer: Dan Chavkin, Bob Frame, Brian Hagiwara, Lisa Limer, Alan Richardson, Mark Seliger

Publishers Graphics:
251 Greenwood Ave, Bethel, CT 06801 203-797-8188
Illustrator: Joann Adinolfi, RW Alley, Dan Andreasen, Rowan Barnes-Murphy, Huang Benrei, Paige Billin-Frye, Eric Brace, Susan Calitri, Jean Cassels, Donald Cods, Eulala Conner, Jane Conteh-Morgan, Laura Cornell, Lynne Crowath, Felipe Davalos, Kees de Kiefte, Shelley Dieterichs, Bert Dodson, Leslie Dunlap, Julie Durrell, Alan Eitzen, Nate Evans, Gioia Fiammenghi, Cynthia Fisher, Teresa Flavin, Brian Floca, Patrick Girouard, Joan Holub, Berrei Huang, Pamela G Johnson, G Brian Karas, Kathy Kelleher, Lisa McCue, Marilyn Mets, Pam Paparona, RA Parker, Cory Pillo, Dana C. Regan, SD Schindler, Joel Snyder, Jeff Spackman, Rebecca Thornburgh, Lucia Wasburn, James Watlins, Terry Weidner, Bari Weissman, Kenyo White, Jerry Williams, Vik Woodworth

Pulse Communications:
7518 W Madison St, Forest Park, IL 60130 708-366-1770
Photographer: Frank Konrath

Pushpin Group Inc, The:
18 E 16th St 7th Fl, New York, NY 10003 212-255-6456
Illustrator: Seymour Chwast

Putscher, Terry:
PO Box 461, Narberth, PA 19072 610-667-8890
Illustrator: Tracie Aretz, Bob Byrd, Dale Crawford, Marie Garafano, Tom Herbert, Neal Hughes, Bob Jones, Adam Mathews, Heidi Merscher, Bot Roda

Q R

Quicksilver, Diana:
7281 Bren Ln, Eden Prairie, MN 55346 ....
Photographer: Detrick Gesk, Buck Holzemer, Greg Martin

Rabin & Assocs, Bill:
680 N Lake Shore Dr #1020, Chicago, IL 60611 312-944-6655
Graphic Designer: Michael Schwab
Illustrator: Cunio Hagio
Photographer: Bruce Wolf

Raines Creative, Robert:
224 Cuba Hill Rd, Huntington, NY 11743 516-261-2263

Ramin, Linda:
6239 Elizabeth Ave, St Louis, MO 63139 314-781-8851
Illustrator: Robert Barnum, Phil Benson, Richard Bernal, Tom Buttner, Carol Carter, Don Curran, Brian Fine, William O'Donnell, Righard High, Richele Garcia Slecke, Roy Smith, Linda Solovic, Jim Turgeon, Jack Whitney, Mike Whitney, Terry Ziegelman, John Zielinski

• **Rapp, Inc, Gerald & Cullen:** pg 12-107,1450, Back Cover Books 1 & 2
108 E 35th St #2, New York, NY 10016 ....**212-889-3337**
url: www.theispot.com/ / fax: 212-889-3341
Graphic Designer: Bernard Maisner
Illustrator: Beth Adams, Philip Anderson, Natalie Ascencios, Garin Baker, Tim Bower, Stuart Briers, Lon Busch, Johnathon Carlson, Jonathan Carlson, Jack Davis, Robert de Michiell, Richard Downs, Henrik Drescher, The Dynamic Duo, Randall Enos, Phil Foster, Mark Fredrickson, Jacki Gelb, Thomas Hart, Peter Hoey, Peter Horvath, David Hughes, Kevin Hulsey, Celia Johnson, James Kaczman, Steve Keller, JD King, Laszlo Kubinyi, Davy Liu, P.J Loughran, Bernard Maisner, Hal Mayforth, David McLimans, Rick Meyerowitz, Bruce Morser, Alex Murawski, Marlies Najaka, Christian Northeast, James O'Brien, Jean-Francois Podevin, Marc Rosenthal, Alison Seiffer, Seth, James Steinberg, Drew Struzan, Elizabeth Traynor, Michael Witte, Noah Woods, Brad Yeo

Rappaport, Jodi:
6305 Yucca St #600, Los Angeles, CA 90028 213-464-4481
Photographer: Guzman, David Jensen, Andrew McPherson

Raskob, Rich:
1285 Sixth Ave 6th Fl, New York, NY 10019 212-459-5316

Ravenhill Reps:
1215 W 67th St, Kansas City, MI 64113 816-333-0744
Graphic Designer: Judy Rush
Illustrator: Sandy Appleoff, John Diebel, Kelli Everett, Jim Fanning, CB Mordan, Darryl Shelton, Steve Skelton, Matt Walton
Photographer: Jim Krantz

Ray, Marlys:
350 Central Park W #3C, New York, NY 10025 212-222-7680
Photographer: Bill Ray

• **Ray, Rodney:** pg 746-752
1464 Linden Ave, Chicago, IL 60035 ....**847-432-2415**
fax: 773-883-0375
Los Angeles **213-934-3395**
fax: 213-936-2757
See Rita Marie for client list

re: Sources/Melody Meisel:
34 E Sola St, Santa Barbara, CA 93101 805-730-1277

Reactor Art & Design:
51 Camden St, Toronto, ON M5V 1V2 416-703-1913
Illustrator: Jaime Bennett, Roxanna Bikadoroff, Federico Botana, Shelley Browning, Blair Drawson, Henrik Drescher, Louis Fishauf, Bob Fortier, Gail Geltner, Carolyn Gowdy, Steven Guarnaccia, Margaret Hathaway, John Hersey, Tom Hunt, Huntley/Muir, Jeff Jackson, Jerzy Kolacz, Ross MacDonald, James Marsh, Simon Ng, Frank Nissen, Tomio Nitto, Christian Northeast, Alain Pilon, Stephanie Power, Bill Russell, Fiona Smyth, Jean Tuttle, Maurice Vellekoop, Tracey Wood, Rene Zamic, Andreas Zaretzki

Red Circle Studios, Inc:
5 W 19th St 5th Fl, New York, NY 10011 212-924-4545
Photographer: Phil Mucci, Joe Standart

Reese-Gibson, Jean:
4 Puritan Rd, N Beverly, MA 01915 508-927-5006
Photographer: John Bellenis, Steve Rubicam

Reid-Chauvet ltd, Pamela:
162 Fifth Ave #1003, New York, NY 10010 212-675-1151
Hair & Make-up: Antonio Diaz, Joe Iannitti
Photographer: Russell James, Christophe Jouany, Bert Stern
Stylist: Agnes Baddoo, Mane Duplan

• **Reilly Reps, Kerry:** pg 641
1826 Asheville Pl, Charlotte, NC 28203 ....**704-372-6007**
Cartoonist: Alex Tiani
Illustrator: Robert Bergin, Ken Bowser, Tim Bruce, Alan Brunettin, Sally Wern Comport, Richard Cowdrey, Gary Crane, Ernie Eldredge, Jerry Frazee, Marsha Grossman, Michael Hagel, John Huxtable, Reid Icard, Rick Kroninger, Gary Palmer, Ben Perini, Chuck Rancorn, Greg Rudd, Skidmore Inc, Walter Stanford, David Stevenson, David Taylor, Jack Vaughan, David Wariner, David Wilgus, Robin Wilgus
Lettering: Mike McMahon
Photographer: Gerin Choiniere, Jim McGuire

Remen-Willis Design Group:
2964 Colton Rd, Pebble Beach, CA 93953 408-655-1407
Illustrator: Peg Magovern

• **Renard Reps:** pg 192-243,956,957,992,993
501 Fifth Ave, New York, NY 10017 ....**212-490-2450**
url: www.renardrepresents.com / fax: 212-697-6828
Illustrator: Steve Bjorkman, James Bozzini Illustration, Rob Brooks, Bill Cigliano, Stéphan Daigle, Carol Donner, Gary Eldridge, Dan Garrow, Audra Geras, Tim Girvin Design, Tim Girvin Design, Wendy Grossman, Jud Guitteau, William Harrison, Jonathan Herbert, Roger Hill, Matthew Holmes, Tim Lee, John MacDonald, John Martin, Matsu, Michael McGurl, Wayne McLoughlin, René Milot, Richard Newton, Jeffrey Pelo, Kevin Pope, Robert Rodriguez, Theo Rudnak, Kazuhiko Sano, Valerie Sinclair, Kim Whitesides

• **Rep Art:** pg 796-797
2491 W 2nd Ave, Vancouver, BC B6L 1M3 ....**604-684-6826**
url: www.repart.com / fax: 604-684-6826

Rep Connection, The:
PO Box 1806, Lomita, CA 90717 310-530-5470

Repertoire:
2029 Custer Pkwy, Richardson, TX 75080 972-761-0500
Illustrator: Amy Bryant, Denise Crawford, Eric Dinyer, Matt Foster, Glenn Gustafson, Jennifer Harris, Frederick Jordan, Dave Kramer, CB Mordan, Ambrose Rivera, RJ Shay, Rhonda Voo
Photographer: Morton Beebe, Robie Capps, Lisa Cargill, Carl Corey, Ben Cornford, Charlie Fremmer, Skeeter Hagler, Marc Hauser, Aaron Jones, Ed Lallo, Gary Nolton, Glenn Provenzano, Kevin Rose, Robert Sebree, John Shipes

Repertory:
847A Second Ave #150, New York, NY 10017 212-486-0177
Illustrator: Richard Arruda, Kirk Botero, Rhonda Burns, Cristos, John Hanley, Hom & Hom, Haruo Ishioka, Philip Knowles, Paul Kratter, Teresa Powers, Don Stewart, Jackie Urbanovic, Steve Walters
Photographer: Tom O'Brien, Karl Parry, Don Saban

Reps in the West:
17 Osgood Pl, San Francisco, CA 94133 415-283-2400

Resnick, Matthew J:
515 W 48th St, New York, NY 10036 212-541-7738
Photographer: Charlie Bidwell, Phillip Jean, Jay Strauss, Cristoph Wilhelm

Rhyne, Paulette:
2075 S University #246, Denver, CO 80210 303-871-9166
Cartoonist: John Dearstyne Illust, Don Dudley
Film: John Hull
Illustrator: Mark Bremmer, Thomas Buchanan, Bill Cigliano, Mona Daly, Malcolm Farley, Lisa Haughom, Laura Hesse, Ron Hicks, Jeffery Hitch, John Hull, John Huxtable, Steve Keller, Clare Kelly, Tammie Lane, Darlene Olivia McElroy, Mathew McFarren, Jill McIntyre, David Moyers, Elizabeth Read, Jeff Slemons, Keith Witmer
Lettering: Sandy Marvin

Richards, Julian:
262 Mott St, New York, NY 10012 212-219-1269
Photographer: David Barry, Chris Buck, Michael McLaughlin, Ashkan Sahihi, James Smolka

Rick Creative Services:
2310 Denison Ave, Cleveland, OH 44109 216-398-1494
Photographer: Mike Steinberg, Mike Wilkes

Ridgeway, Inc, Ronald:
530 Broadway 4th Fl, New York, NY 10012 212-966-9696

- **Riley Illus: pg 600-613**
  155 W 15th St, New York, NY 10011......................................**212-989-8770**
  fax: 212-989-7892
  Illustrator: Benoit, William Bramhall, Paul Degen, Isabelle Dervaux, Jeffrey Fisher, Rebecca Gibbon, Edward Koren, Pierre Le-Tan, Warren Linn, Kathy Osborn, Robert Andrew Parker, Philippe Petit-Roulet, Victoria Roberts, Marina Sagona, Jean Jacques Sempe, Danny Shanahan, Mark Von Ulrich, Philippe Weisbecker, Sarah Wilkins

Ring Creative Rep, Thomas:
  1015 N Central Ave, Phoenix, AZ 85004..602-447-9186
  Illustrator: Keith Biele, Karen Strelecki, Russ Wall
  Photographer: Arthur A Holeman Photo, Michael Norton

Rittenberg, Michelle:
  3632 Maplewood Ave, Los Angeles, CA 90066...........................310-391-8488
  Photographer: Sidney

- **RKB Studios: pg 1012,1013**
  420 N 5th St, Minneapolis, MN 55401......................................**612-339-7055**
  Film: Kristi Schaeppi

Roberts, Mary Beth:
  114 E 13th St #2C, New York, NY 10003 212-780-2150

Robinson, Jens:
  67 Riverside Dr #1D, New York, NY 10024..................................212-362-9256

Robinson, Madeleine:
  27 Aubrey Rd, Upper Montclair, NJ 07043...............................973-655-0386
  Photographer: Russell Kirk, Russel Kirk/Golf Links

Roche Reps, Diann:
  709 W 90th Terr, Kansas City, MO 64114 816-822-2024
  Film: CA Nobens
  Illustrator: Rich Bowman, Cynthia Fitting, Kim Janssen, Steve Lee, Gary Otteson, Marty Roper, Brad Sneed
  Photographer: Thane Brethour, Tracey Thompson

Rodi, Domenico:
  14-18 Ham Yard/Gr Windmill St, London, England, UK W1V 8DE 1717-347991

- **Rogers Studio, Lilla: pg 696-706**
  6 Parker Rd, Arlington, MA 02174...**781-641-2787**
  fax: 781-641-2244
  Illustrator: Makiko Azakami, Diane Bigda, Ann Boyajian, Susan Farrington, Donna Ingemanson, Anne Smith, Susy Pilgrim Waters

Rohani, Mushka:
  9229 215th St SW, Edmonds, WA 98020 425-771-2905
  Illustrator: Michael Sours Rohani
  Photographer: Richard DeWeese

Roland Group, Inc:
  4948 St Elmo Ave #201, Bethesda, MD 20814..........................301-718-7955
  Illustrator: Max Altekruse, Tungwai Chau, Michael Crampton, Garth Glazier, Ralph Hughes, Kurt Krebs, Paul Manz, Karen Stolper, Mark Weber
  Photographer: Michael Pohuski

Rome Studio:
  364 Manville Rd, Pleasantville, NY 10570................................914-747-1422
  Photographer: Jerry Errico

Root, Inc, Jed:
  225 Lafayette ste 406, New York, NY 10012..............................212-226-6600
  Photographer: Ruven Afanador, Philippe Cometti, Joshua Jordan, Thierry LeGones, Joag Reichardt, Michael Thompson, Jay Zukerkorn

Rosen, Donna:
  15209 Rockport Dr, Silver Spring, MD 20905............................301-384-8925
  Illustrator: Lew Azzinaro, Matthew Beak, Jim Haynes, Rob Johnson, James Kowalski, Bruce MacPherson, Steve Pica, Jo Rivers, Renata Roberts, Dale Rutter, Bruce Sharp, Erik Tunnéll

Rosenberg, Arlene:
  377 W 11th St, New York, NY 10014..212-675-7983
  Photographer: James Cohen, Frank Marchese

Rosenthal Reps:
  3850 Eddingham Ave, Calabasas, CA 91302.............................818-222-5445
  Film: Terry Anderson, Norm Bendell, Catherine Huerta, Judy Koenig, Dirk J Wunderlich
  Illustrator: Kelly Akins, Norm Bendell, Sandra Bergeron, Nan Brooks, Marjory Buckley, Gwen Connelly, Renée Daily, Richard Duerrstein, Kathleen Dunne, Teddy Edinjiklian, Steven Michael Gardner, John Paul Genzo, Jack Graber, Robert G Gunn, Bill Hall, James Henry, Lewis Johnson, Alan London, Gale Pitt, Larry Salk, Stewart Sherwood, June Sobel, Dorothy Stott, Bill Vann, Kenny Yamada, Randall Zwingler

Roth-Karpe, Michele:
  11959 Woodbridge St, Studio City, CA 91604 818-760-0491
  Illustrator: Jennifer Geiger, Greg Spalenka, Michal Venera
  Photographer: Victoria Pearson, Horst Stasny
  SJ: David McLean

Rozden, Ilya:
  223 Harrison Ave, Boston, MA 02111.......................................617-338-4695
  Illustrator: Bruce Rogovin Photography
  Photographer: Logan Seale

Rubin, Adrienne:
  416 E 78th St, New York, NY 10021...212-243-7904
  Photographer: Tom Arma

Ruderman, Linda:
  1245 Park Ave, New York, NY 10128.......................................212-369-7531
  Photographer: Albert Jade, Carl Zapp

Russo, Karen:
  New York, NY 212-749-6382
  Photographer: Dick Durrance, Charles Gold, Susan Orinker, Neil Selkirk

Rutt Assocs, Dick:
  234 Shorline Dr Yacht Cove/Lake Murray, Columbia, SC 29212 803-407-2030
  Illustrator: Kim Behm, Deb Bovy, Gary Ciccarelli, Linda Clark, Stuart Cooper, Greg Hargreaves, Dan Hatala, Lu Matthews, Randall McKissick, John Thompson, Todd Treadway, Scott Travers Wright

Ryan, Steve:
  43 W 24th St #9A, New York, NY 10010..................................212-924-4744
  Photographer: Shig Ikeda

S

Saba Press Photos:
  116 E 16th St 8th Fl, New York, NY 10003 212-477-7722
  Photographer: Marc Asnin, Adrian Bradshaw, David Butow, Peter Charlesworth, Keith Dannemiller, Najlah Feanny, Colin Finlay, Erica Freudenstein, Paul Gero, Jason Grow, Ron Haviv, Ralf-Finn Hestoft, Filip Horvat, Gary Knight, Antonin Kratochvil, Ken Kulish, Andre Lambertson, Jim Leynse, Ken Light, Robbie McClaran, Mark Peterson, Ed Quinn, Chris Rainier, Lara Jo Regan, Ricki Rosen, Jeffrey Salter, Martin Schoeller, Michael Schumann, Shepard Sherbell, Martin Simon, Greg Smith, Steve Starr, Ann States, Maggie Stebber, Robert Wallis, Peter Yates

Sacramone, Dario:
  302 W 12th St, New York, NY 10014.......................................212-929-0487
  Photographer: Marty Umans, John Wilkes

- **Salzman Int'l: pg 1255,1293,1307,1328,1407,1413**
  716 Sanchez St, San Francisco, CA 94114..............................**415-285-8267**
  e-mail: Salzman@designlink.com / fax: 415-285-8268
  Chicago, IL **312-782-2244**
  New York, NY **212-997-0115**
  Illustrator: Denise Hilton Campbell, Kristen Funkhouser, Rhoda Grossman, Marty Gunsaullus, Dirk Hagner, Denise Hilton Campbell, Denise Hilton-Campbell, Dan Jones, Scott Medlock, Nancy Gibson Nash, Everett Peck, Robert Rayevsky, Greg Shed, Walter Stuart, Debbie Tilley

Sander, Vicki:
  48 Gramercy Park S, New York, NY 10010...............................212-420-1333

- **Sanders Agency, Liz: pg 882-893**
  16 Phaedra, Laguna Niguel, CA 92677 ....**949-495-3664**
  url: www.showcase.com / fax: 949-495-0129
  Illustrator: Johnee Bee, Sherie Bender, Gina Binkley, Clemente Botelho, Clemente Botelho, Bruce Carnes, Martha Collins, Jody Eastman, Jud Guitteau, Johanna Hantel, Steve Hayes, Margaret Hewitt, Chris Lensch, Bachrun LoMele, Pete Mueller, Kevin Newman, Amy Ning, Tom Pansini, Kim Passey, Judy Pedersen, Dorothy Reinhardt, Chelsea Sammel, Mark Shaver, Cameron Wasson
  Photographer: Michael Lariche

Sands Artist Rep, Trudy:
  2410 Farrington, Dallas, TX 75207...214-905-9037
  Illustrator: John Cook, Beth McCash, Tim McClure, Michael Sours Rohani
  Photographer: Richard DeWeese

Santa-Donato Studio:
  42 W 38th St, New York, NY 10018...212-921-1550

Saunders, Michele:
  345 Ocean Dr, Miami Beach, FL 33139....................................305-673-5838

Scher, Dorothea:
  235 E 22nd St, New York, NY 10010.......................................212-689-7273
  Photographer: Frank White

Schlager, Inc, Barbara:
  225 Lafayette St #902, New York, NY 10012 212-941-1777
  Photographer: Francois Deconinck, Jean-Louis Gregoire

Schmidbauer, Michele:
  PO Box 1197, Lake Zurich, IL 60047.......................................847-438-7128
  Illustrator: Phil Kirchmeier, Terry Schmidbauer, Joe Sibilski

Schmidt, Pam:
  96 S Wheeler St, St Paul, MN 55105......................................
  Photographer: Jennifer Frost, Karen Melvin, Steve Niedorf, Vik Orenstein, Joe Viesti

Schochat, Kevin R:
  49 MacDougal Street Ste#1, New York, NY 10012 212-633-8750
  Photographer: Chuck Carlton, Mark Ferri, George Kavanagh, Sanjay Kothari, George Otero, Kevin Reardon, Bill White

Schumann, Patty:
  1009 West 6th St #207, Austin, TX 78703...............................512-481-0907
  Illustrator: Pearl Beach, Anthony Butkouich, Larry Goode, Chris Lockwood, Costa Design Lockwood, John Rutkowski, Brian White
  Photographer: Paul Bardagjy, Robb Kendrick, Ralph Smith, Jose Manuel Vidaurre, Terry Vine

- **Schuna Group, Inc, The: pg 1173**
  1503 Briar Knoll Dr, Arden Hills, MN 55112 ....**651-631-8480**
  ....**651-631-8458**
  Illustrator: Pete Bastiansen, Cindy Berglund, Neverne Covington, Teresa Cox, Theresa Cox, Jim Dryden, Tom Foty, Tony Griego, Warren Hanson, Beth Hatlen, Cathy Lundeen Huber, Kristen Miller, Anastasia Mitchell, Joe Nordstrom, Faye Passow, Ruth Pettis, Will Terry

Schwartz, Deborah:
  443 E Alameda St, Altadena, CA 91001..................................626-794-7371

- **Scott, Freda: pg 1000,1001**
  1015-B Battery St, San Francisco, CA 94111 ....**415-398-9121**
  Illustrator: Bruce Bowles, Kelly Burke, Diane Fenster, Cynthia Fitting, Matt Foster, Bethany Gully, Abe Gurvin, Terry Hoff, Michael Iofin, Scott Johnston, Francis Livingston, Alan Mazzetti, Nancy Nimoy, Jeffrey Pelo, Tim Racer, Thorina Rose, Sue Rother, Rosiland Solomon, Randy South, Debra Spina-Dixon, Carolyn Vibbert
  Lettering: Sherry Bringham
  Photographer: Ty Allison, Daniel Arsenault Photography, John Blaustein, Bruce Brown, Lon Clark, Ernie Friedlander, Rose Hodges, Edward Holub, Kevin Irby, Christopher Irion, Stephen Kennedy, Tom Landecker, RJ Muna, Stan Musilek, Susan Schelling, Robert Schlatter, Ron Starr Photography, Mark Tuschman, Michael Venera, Richard Wahlstrom, Elizabet Zeilon, Bill Zemanek

Scott-Sahler:
  2836 Blue Brick Dr., Nashville, TN 37214 800-690-6186

Seawell Photography:
  2565 Third Street Studio 303, San Francisco, CA 94107 415-550-1807
  Photographer: Tom Seawell

Secret Agent Man:
  16421 Olvine St, Ramsey, MN 55303.....................................612-753-1115
  Electronic Imaging: Electric Soup
  Graphic Designer: Stress Lab Art & Design
  Photographer: Bob McNamara, Paul Westbrook

See Pictures:
  2626 Cole Ave #400, Dallas, TX 75204..................................214-665-9490
  Photographer: Scott Metcalfe, Rocky Powell, Paul Swen, John Wong

Segerstrom, Rebecca:
  109 W 27th St 3rd Fl, New York, NY 10001.............................212-741-0688
  Photographer: Susumu Sato Photography

Seigel, Fran:
  160 West End Ave #23-S, New York, NY 10023 212-486-9644
  Illustrator: Kinuko Y Craft, John Dawson, Catherine Deeter, Lisa Falkenstern, Mark Harrison, Hokanson/Cichetti, Earl Keleny, Ron Miller, John Mullane, Myles Pinkney, Dan Sneberger

• **Sell, Inc, Dan: pg 641,1164**
333 N Michigan Ave, Chicago, IL 60601 .... **312-578-8844**
fax: 312-578-8847
Electronic Imaging: Tom Lochray
Illustrator: Johnna Bandle, Bob Boyd, Lee Lee Brazeal, Daryl Cagle, James Carlson, Rose A Cassano, Bobbye Cochran, Sally Wern Comport, Robert Crawford, Jerry Dadds, Bill Ersland, Dick Flood, Bill Gerhold, Bill Harrison, Jeff Jones, Bernie Kapuza, Gregory Manchess, Bill Mayer, Mike McMillen, Frank Morris, Gary Overacre, WB Park, Miles Parnell, Roy Pendleton, Ian Ross, RJ Shay, Bill Vann, Arden von Haeger, Richard Waldrep, Scott T Wright, John Youssi
Photographer: Don Carstens, Miles Lowry, Gregory Manchess, Denis Scott, James B Wood

Sellentin, Greg:
56 W 22nd St 12th Fl, New York, NY 10010 212-645-0508
Photographer: Stephen Hellerstein

Seltenreich, Margaret:
202 Granada Way, Los Gatos, CA 95030 408-370-1663
Photographer: Mert Carpenter

Shanahan, Nancy:
35 Stillman #101, San Francisco, CA 94107 415-243-8283
Photographer: Jay Blakesberg, Paul Franz-Moore, Heather Monahan, David Peterson

• **Shannon Assocs L.L.C: pg 313-371**
327 E 89th St #3E, New York, NY 10128 .... **212-831-5650**
fax: 212-831-6241
1306 Alabama St, Huntington Beach, CA 92648 714-969-7766
fax: 714-374-3744
Illustrator: Patrick Arrasmith, Cary Austin, Doug Beekman, Mary Jane Begin, James Bernardin, Peter Bollinger, Steve Brodner, Greg Call, Lynne Cannoy, Richard Cowdrey, Dave Devries, Mike Dietz, Mark Elliott, Tristan Elwell, Patrick Faricy, Tim Gabor, Cunio Hagio, Michael Harris, Silver Kid, Hiro Kimura, Michael Koelsch, Mike McMillen, Cliff Nielsen, David O'Keefe, Marc Phares, Carlos Torres

Sharpe & Assocs:
25 W 68th St #9A, New York, NY 10023 212-595-1125
7536 Ogelsby Ave, Los Angeles, CA 90045 310-641-8556
Illustrator: Robert Case, Peter Simpson Cook, Greg Moraes, Dan Richards, Judy Reed Silver
Photographer: Neal Brown, Ann Elliott Cutting, Hugh Kretschmer, Lise Metzger, Jamey Stillings, Everard Williams Jr

Sharpshooter Creative, Inc:
49 Bathurst St #400, Toronto, ON M5V 2P2 416-703-5300
Illustrator: Christine Bunn, Francois Chartier, Norman Eyolfson, Nancy Ruth Jackson, Jacobson/Fernandez, Olena Kassian, JC Knaff, Anita Kunz, Martin Lane, Neil MacLachlan, Stuart Mclachlan, KC Rasmussen, Balvis Rubess, Gordon Sauve, Laura Wallace, Rick Zettler
Photographer: Michel Pilon, Eden Robbins, Brian Smale, Olivier Staub, Lorelia Zanetti

Sheehan, Betsy:
19 Ruxview Ct #301, Baltimore, MD 21204 410-828-4020
Illustrator: Don Dudley, RJ Shay
Photographer: Steve Uzzell

Shekut, Linda:
PO Box 928, Mount Prospect, IL 60056 312-977-9171

Shelley Brown Associates:
155 Lippincott Street, Tornonto, ON M5S 2P3 416-505-9522
Illustrator: Philippe Bena, Harvey Chan, Helen D'Souza, Joe Fleming, Kevin Ghiglione, Laurie Lafrance, Matsu, Raphael Montoliu, Glenn Ryan, Thom Sevalrud, Remy Simard, Tinka Anjali Sloss, Alan Stivell, Tracy Walker, Tim Zeltner

Shepherd, Judith:
344 W 23rd St, New York, NY 10011 212-242-6554
Photographer: Edward Holub, Mark Thomas

Shigeta Assocs:
1546 N Orleans St, Chicago, IL 60610 312-642-8715

Shin, Judi:
60 E 42nd St #1060, New York, NY 10165 212-986-5782
Photographer: Dennis Blachut, Lee Crum, Giles Hancock, Kelvin Hudson, Serge Korniloff, Stephen Wilkes

Shomakhiya, Alexandria:
139E 33rd St #9J, New York, NY 10016 212-698-4238

Shooting Star:
1441 N McCadden Pl, Los Angeles, CA 90028 213-469-2020
1178 Broadway 4th Fl, New York, NY 10001 212-447-0666
Illustrator: Arturo, Lynn Bennett, Robin Ghelerter O'Connell, JT Steiny
Photographer: Christopher Barr, Ron Batzdorff, Beckett & Beckett, Steven Begleiter, EJ Carr, Joe Comick, Charlie Daniels, Ted Dayton, Robert Ferrone, Robin Ghelerter O'Connell, Kerry Hayes, Steve Hirsch, Christina Lessa, Dorothy Low, Elliot Marks, Darren Michaels, Anthony Pardines, Allan Penn, John Sann, JT Steiny, Dean Tokuno, Alex Vertikoff, Bernard Vidal, Laura Wagner

SI Int'l:
43 E 19th St, New York, NY 10003 212-254-4996
Illustrator: Carolyn Bracken, Cardona Studio, Mario Cortes, Ted Enik, Segundo Garcia, Mel Grant, Holly Hannon, Steve Haskamp, Jane Kurisu, John Kurtz, Mike Malkovas, Franc Mateu, Isdre Mones, Carlos Nine, Bob Ostrom, Gabriel Picart, Jesus Redondo, Francesc Rigol, Gusti Rosenefet, Martin Salvador, Sanjulian, Serrat-Sans, Ortiz Tafalla
Photographer: Karen Baumann, Carolyn Bracken, Horacio Elena, Ted Enik, Segundo Garcia, Pepe Gonzalez, Mel Grant, Steve Haefele, Holly Hannon, Steve Haskamp, Nick Jainschigg, John Kurtz, Fred Marvin, Franc Mateu, Isidre Mones, Carlos Nine, Kathy Passen, Gabriel Picart, Francesc Rigol, Ed Tadiello, Del & Dana Thompson

Siegel, Tema:
234 Fifth Ave 4th Fl, New York, NY 10001 212-696-4680

Sillen, Florence:
55 W 11th St, New York, NY 10011 212-243-9490
Illustrator: Meredith Hamilton
Photographer: Harvey Wang

Silverstein, Patti:
230 E 15th St, New York, NY 10003 212-228-7924
Photographer: Kim Golding, Amy Neunsinger, Silvia Otte

Simitch, Leslie:
270 Lafayette St #1300, New York, NY 10012 212-925-2668
Photographer: Bumper, Philip-Lorca diCorcia, Pamela Hanson

Simpson, Elizabeth:
1222 Manufacturing, Dallas, TX 75207 214-761-0001
Photographer: Michael Simpson

Skacha/Magnificent, Patrick:
85, Rue Billancourt, Boulogne, FR 29100 46045910

SKB / Keifer, Scott:
1880 Birchwood, Troy, MI 48083 248-619-0066
Photographer: Reid Ashton, Rick Rusing, Gil Smith, Brad Stanley

Skidmore, Inc:
29580 Northwestern Hwy, Southfield, MI 48034 248-353-7722
Illustrator: Bob Andrews, Wayne Appleton, John Ball, Ann Bauer, Rob Burman, Gary Cooley, Larry Dodge, Rudy Laslo, Stephen Magsig, Jerry Monley, Scott Olds

Smith, Cheryl:
920 N Citrus Ave, Hollywood, CA 90038 213-466-6030
Film: Jay Silverman Productions

Smith, Jeff:
11 6th Ave, Atlantic Highlands, NJ 07716 732-291-7889
Photographer: Jeff Smith

• **Smith, Piper: pg 372-415,970,971**
250 W 57th St #521, New York, NY 10107 .... **212-397-7330**
url: www.lindgrensmith.com (or) www.stockillustrated.com
See Lindgren & Smith NY for client list

Snyder, Deborah:
5321 W 62nd St, Edina, MN 55436 612-922-3462
Illustrator: Edwin Beylerian, Scott Buchschacher, Lynn Fellman, Jack Lindstrom, Beth McLarnan, Terri Mitchelson, Mary Quinlivan, Glenn Quist

• **Solomon, Richard: pg 244-281**
121 Madison Ave #5F, New York, NY 10016 .... **212-683-1362**
fax: 212-683-1919
Illustrator: Kent Barton, James Bennett, Richard Cline, John Collier, Paul Cox, Jack E Davis, David Johnson, Stephen Johnson, Gary Kelley, Murray Kimber, Loren Long, Gregory Manchess, Bill Nelson, CF Payne, Douglas Smith, Mark Summers, Ezra Tucker, Andrea Ventura, Raymond Verdaguer

Solomon, Wendy:
815 Ivy St, Pittsburgh, PA 15232 412-362-4766

Somlo, Carolyn:
456 N Morgan St, Chicago, IL 60622 312-226-2272
Photographer: Mark Gamba, Steve Grubman, Andrea Mandel, Sheryl Unger

Sonneville, Dane:
67 Upper Mountain Ave, Montclair, NJ 07042 973-744-4465
Illustrator: Jack Balnave, Bryn Barnard, Tim Barrall, Jim Fanning, Pierre Fortin, Rich Grote, Jeff Holewski, Art Kretzschmar, Alex Leonard, Leonard Morgan, Steve & Jacqui Osborne, Earl Parker, Jared Phillips, Kevin Somerville, Gregory Voth, Pam Voth
Photographer: Barry Blackman, John F Cooper, Joseph Sachs

Soodak, Arlene:
393 Tehama, San Francisco, CA 94107 415-284-0555
Photographer: Renee Comet, David Gaz, Martin Rogers

Spectrum Studio, Inc:
1503 Washington Ave S 3rd Fl, Minneapolis, MN 55454 612-332-2361
Illustrator: Martin Harris, Anthony Hilscher, Mark Jensen, Roger Lundquist, Jim Rownd, Larry Ruppert, Kim Sakstrup

Spelman, Steve:
526 W 26th St, New York, NY 10001 212-242-9381
Photographer: Steve Garforth, Michael Mazzeo, Dudley Reed, Dani Steele

Spencer, Torrey:
11201 Valley Spring Ln, Studio City, CA 91602 818-505-1124
Illustrator: Robert August, Cam DeLeon, Rob Magiera
Photographer: Jock McDonald, Scott Montgomery, Holly Stewart, Jana Taylor, Paul Taylor

Spiegel, Melanie:
3005 Maple Ave #104, Dallas, TX 75201 214-720-2272
Photographer: Abrams/Lacagnia

Squire, Terry:
4233 Mountainbrook Rd, Apex, NC 27502 919-772-1262
Illustrator: Linda Davick, Rodney Davidson, Jim Owens, Pamela Rossi
Photographer: Mark Schroeder, Greg Slater, Willa Stein

St John, Julia:
5730 Arlington Blvd, Arlington, VA 22204 703-845-5831
Photographer: David Hathcox

Stefanski Represents, Janice:
2022 Jones St, San Francisco, CA 94133 415-928-0457
Illustrator: Barbara Kelley, Maria Korusiewicz, Beth Whybrow Leeds, Mark Mattioli, Jeffrey Oh, Bob Roth, Katherine Salentine, Bryan Wiggins

Steichen, Shelly:
1731 Reynolds Ave, Irvine, CA 92714 714-261-5844
Photographer: Bill Cash, Vic Huber

Stemrich, J David:
1334 W Hamilton St, Allentown, PA 18102 610-776-0825

Stern, Andrea:
617 Crestmoore PL #E, Venice, CA 90291 310-574-0076

Stern, Meredith:
300 E 34th St, New York, NY 10016 212-689-9888
Illustrator: The Art Director's Studio Inc

Stevens, Norma:
20 E 74th St #10F, New York, NY 10021 212-879-6325
Photographer: Richard Avedon

Stevens, Robin:
410 N Michigan #1080, Chicago, IL 60611 312-689-3442
Illustrator: Paul Miller, Andre Miripolsky, Monica Rangne, Bill Reynolds, David Scanlan
Photographer: Agnes Donnadieu, Greg Gillis, Stephen Scott Gross, James Imbrogno, Michael Northrop, Earl Ripling, Dean Tokuno, Terry Vine

Stieglitz, Clifford:
1985 Swarthmore Ave, Lakewood, NJ 08701 732-364-2111

Still Life Studios:
1886 Thunderbird Rd, Troy, MI 48084 248-362-3111
Photographer: Emil Croes, Tony Segielski

Stocki, Tom:
925 Elm Grove Rd, Elm Grove, WI 53122 414-785-1940
Illustrator: Mark Bixby, Chuck Boie, Tom Buchs, Todd Dakins, Linda Godrey, Terry Herman, Larry Mikec, Tom Nachreiner, Bill Scott, Susan Tolonen, Stewart Zastrow

Stockland Martel:
5 Union Sq W 6th Fl, New York, NY 10003 212-727-1400
Photographer: Jorg Badura, Joel Baldwin, Richard Corman, Georg Fischer, Rolph Gobits, Anthony Gordon, Timothy Greenfield-Sanders, Hashi, Ruedi Hofmann, Walter Iooss, Nadav Kander, Tony Meneguzzo, Eric Meola, Uli Rose, Leen Thijsse, Timothy White, Bruce Wolf, Michael Zeppetello

Stone, Will:
545 Sutter St #305, San Francisco, CA 94012...........415-775-0709
Storyboards Inc:
1426 Main St, Venice, CA 90291...........................310-581-4050
Streeters USA Inc:
568 Broadway #504A, New York, NY 10012...............212-219-9566
Hair: Jonathan Connelly, Giovanni DiStefano, Pasquale Ferrante, Rick Haylor, Luigi Murenu, Ken O'Rourke, Johnnie Sapong
Make-up: Billy B, Liam Dunn, Katarina Hakansson, Leanne Hirsh, Kay Montano, Lucia Pieroni, Tracy Sondern, Rose-Marie Swift
Photographer: Miles Aldridge, Kim Andreolli, Alex Antitch, Jake Chessum, George Kokolis, Steen Sundland
Stylist: Victoria Bartlett, Cathy Dixon, Tiina Laakkonen, Havana Laffitte, Annett Monheim, Andrew Richardson, Kevin Robinson, Alexandra White
Studio 360:
3131 Western Ave #513, Seattle, WA 98121..............206-285-5662
Photographer: Dan Taylor
Sturges, Frank/Scott Hull Assoc:
142 W Winter St, Delaware, OH 43015....................740-369-9702
See Hull Assoc for client list
Sullivan & Assocs:
3805 Maple Ct, Marietta, GA 30066........................770-971-6782
Illustrator: Terry Buchanan, Joann Daley, PJ Meacham, Henry Patton, Phil Perry, Charles Scogins, Simon Sholnik, Anne Teisher
Photographer: Ken Chesler, Alan David, Sylvia Martin, Harrison Northcutt, Ron Sherman, Ed Wolkis
Sullivan Artist Rep, Maureen:
1942 SE Larch Ave, Portland, OR 97214..................503-236-7493
Photographer: David Emmite, Robbie McClaran
• **Sumpter & Assocs, Will: pg 1180**
Atlanta, GA...**770-460-8438**
Illustrator: David Boyd, Charles Chashwell, Britt Taylor Collins, Bob Cooper, Robert Craig, Dee DeLoy, Paul Dempsey, Chris Ellison, David Gaadt, Robert Gunn, Robert G Gunn, Bill Morse, David Moses, Jackie Pittman, Drew Rose, David Watts
Photographer: Jerry Burns, Flip Chalfant
• **Susan & Co Artist Rep (Susan Trimpe): pg 614-626**
5002 92nd Ave SE, Mercer Island, WA 98040...........**206-232-7873**
fax: 206-232-7908
Illustrator: Linda Holt Ayriss, George Cheney, Wendy Edelson, Chris Hinrichs, Fred Ingram, Larry Jost, Eric Larson, Greg Stadler, Carolyn Vibbert
• **Svitzer, Emile: pg 1456,1457**
39 Hamilton Terr, New York, NY 10031..................**212-283-3401**
url: www.wayart.com
Illustrator: Harry Borgman, Michael D'Antuono, Weston Emmart, Alexandra Gabanyi, Denis Luzuriaga, Scott McBee, Lucian Mihaesteanu, Rich Ransley, Bruce Rauffenbart, Aristides Ruiz, Laszlo Schreiber, Suzanne Simmons, Brian Stymest
Sweet Represents, Ron:
716 Montgomery St, San Francisco, CA 94111...........415-433-1222
Illustrator: Anatoly, Mike Blatt, Charley Brown, Dick Cole, Jonathan Combs, Robert Evans Illustration, Robert Evans, Ben Garvie, Randy Glass, Kent Leech & Associates, Rachel McCambell, Rachael McCampbell, Derek Mueller, Will Nelson, Jim Nichols, Steven Noble, Todd Nordling, Bruce Wolfe
Photographer: Curt Fischer, James B Wood
Swing, Jo Anne:
16370 Lucky Rd, Los Gatos, CA 95030...................408-354-2569
Illustrator: Jerry McLaughlin

T

T-Square Etc:
1426 Main St, Venice, CA 90291........................310-581-2200
Team Russell:
210C-AABC, Aspen, CO 81611............................970-920-1431
Teri O:
1045 Diamond Ave NE, Grand Rapids, MI 49503...........616-454-1278
Illustrator: Nell Floeter, Tim Foley, Rob Lawson, Ed Wong Ligta
Photographer: Roger Hill
Testino, Giovanni:
145 Hudson St 2nd Fl, New York, NY 10013..............212-343-9889
Photographer: Enrique Badulescu, Sean Ellis, Marc Hom, Kelly Klein, Mario Testino, Javier Vallhonrat
Those Three Reps:
2909 Cole Ave #118, Dallas, TX 75204..................214-871-1316
Illustrator: Dave Albers, Art Gecko, Phil Boatwright, Mark Chickinelli, Gary Ciccarelli, Michael Crampton, Lisa Dodson, Regan Dunnick, Mike Fisher, Keith Graves, Myron Grossman, Arthur James, Greg King, Kathleen Kinkoph, Greg McCullogh, June Michel, George Toomer, Terry Widener
Photographer: Will Crocker, Art Gecko, Craig Kuhner, Toby Threadgill, Ka Yeung
Three:
236 W 26th St #805, New York, NY 10001................212-463-7025
Graphic Designer: Frank Marchese
Illustrator: Max Tokyo
Three in a Box, Inc:
Panama City, FL.......................................904-747-8415
Chicago, IL...312-663-5506
UK/Western Europe,....................................186-543-5654
New York, NY..212-643-0896
Los Angeles, CA.......................................213-688-7428
468 Queen St E #104, Toronto, ON M5A 1T7..............416-367-2446
Illustrator: Kathryn Adams, Illian Ambrosia, Wesley Bates, Jackie Besteman, Brad Black, Francis Blake, Marty Braun, Andre Brissette, Dominic Bugatto, Eric Colquhoun, John Cresnick, Bob Daly, Mohamed Danawi, Stephanie Denis, Peter Ferguson, Bill Frampton, Maria Friske, Kim Fujiwara, Paul Gilligan, Von R Glitschka, Callie Gray, Jaime Hogan, Oleg Koulilou, Peter Lacalamita, Martin Lane, Patricia Leidl, Ross Paul Lindo, Robert Littleford, Lindsay Lozon, Tadeusz Majewski, Renee Mansfield, Daniel Mizuguchi, Steve Munday, Alex Murchison, Sandy Nichols, John Oresnik, Jeff Panek, Lisa Ringnalda, Scot Ritchie, Eden Robbins, David Rolfe, Jimminy Roux, Roy Schneider, Fred Sebastian, Keri Smith, Mark Snyder, Pete Spino, Anne Stanley, Otto Steininger, Greg Stevenson, Margot Thompson, Richard Thompson, Susan Todd, Naomi Wallis, Paul Watson, Dave Whamond, Jeremie White, Russ Willms, Rosemary Woods, Peter Yundt, Rose Zgodzinski, Marlena Zuber

• **Thurm Represents, Gail: pg 579-599**
232 Madison Ave #512, New York, NY 10016..............**212-889-8777**
fax: 212-447-1475
Illustrator: Tim Barnes, Doron Ben-Ami, Mort Drucker, Lisa Henderling, James Kirkland, Bret Meredith, Dimitrios Patelis, Lisa Rivard, Victor Vaccaro, Sally Vitsky
Tiffany Represents:
2000 Second Ave #906, Seattle, WA 98121...............206-441-7701
Illustrator: Neal Aspinall
Tila New House Production Services:
1711 Hazard, Houston, TX 77019........................713-529-7916
Film: Tim Newman, Wright/Banks Films
Tise, Katherine:
200 E 78th St #8C, New York, NY 10021.................617-558-1883
Tonal Values, Inc:
133 N Montclair Ave, Dallas, TX 75208.................214-943-2569
Illustrator: Nigel Buchanan, Anatoly Chernishov, Kyle Dreier, Karen L Greenberg, D Mark Kingsley, Susan Masterson, David Pohl, Nikolai Punin, Mark Schroder, Pauline Cilmi Speers, Supotux, Mark Tremlett, Gus Van Eck, Carol Wyatt
Toyama Represents, Kathee:
1260 El Mirador Dr, Pasadena, CA 91103................
Tricia:
163 S Center, Lowell, MI 49331........................616-897-6668
• **Trimpe, Susan: pg 614-626**
5002 92nd Ave SE, Mercer Island, WA 98040.............**206-232-7873**
fax: 206-232-7908
See Susan & Co. for client listing
Trott, David:
1237 Chicago Rd, Troy, MI 48083.......................248-583-2828
Photographer: Steve Karr, Tom Kirby, Paul Primeau
• **Tugeau, Christina A: pg 895-897,1355**
110 Rising Ridge Rd, Ridgefield, CT 06877.............**203-438-7307**
Illustrator: Winky Adam, Ann Barrow, Sarah Beise, James Bernardin, Lloyd Birmingham, Craig Brown, Jonathan Bumas, Priscilla Burris, Sally JK Davies, Larry Day, Marlene Ekman, Bill Farnsworth, Crista Forest, Nancy Pelham Foulke, Nancy Giffy, Susan Greenstein, Laurie Harden, Naomi Howland, Melissa Iwai, Karen A Jerome, John Kanaler, John Kanzler, Richard Kirk, Lauren Klementz-Harte, Jan Machalek, Erin Mauterer, Chris Miles, Keiko Motoyama, Cheryl Kirk Noll, Kathleen O'Malley, Andrew Portwood, Daniel Powers, Stacey Scheutt, Stacey Schuett, Teri Sloat, David Slonim, Sally Springer, Meryl Treatner, Jeremy Tugeau, Jason Wolff
Tuke, Joni:
325 W Huron, Chicago, IL 60610........................312-787-6826
Illustrator: Kaz Aizawa, Fian Arroyo, Gary Ciccarelli, Brian Fujimori, Jud Guitteau, Jennifer Hansen, Laura Hesse, Chris Hopkins, John Hull, Kitty Meek, Cyd Moore, Gary Penca, Terry Sirrell, Jeffrey Stock, Dick Thorn, Ezra Tucker, Pam Wall, DL Warfield, Ken Westphal
Photographer: Eric Klein, Ted Tamburo, Bill Thomson
• **Turk, Melissa: pg 798,799**
9 Babbling Brook Ln, Suffern, NY 10901................**914-368-8606**
fax: 914-368-8608
Illustrator: Barbara Bash, Ka Botzis, Nancy Didion, Drew/Brook/Cormack, Robert Frank, Dara Goldman, Pedro Julio Gonzalez, Joe LeMonnier, Kevin O'Malley, Claudia Karabaic Sargent, Mark Siegel, Wendy Smith-Griswold, BK Taylor, Bridget Starr-Taylor, Mary Teichman, Neecy Twinem, Elsa Warnick, Jane Chambless Wright
Turner Photo Rep Inc, John:
55 Bethune St #348, New York, NY 10014................212-243-6373
Photographer: Mark Andrew, Michael Myers, Troy Word
2D Illus Agency:
114 Ladbroke Grove, London, England, UK W10 5NE.......171-727-5243
Illustrator: 2D or not 2D Limited, Rachel Ashton, John Batten, Geraldine Bracey, Vanessa Cuthbert, Tiffiny Lynch, Phillip Morrison, Juliette Pearce, Brian Whitehead, Becky Williams
Ty Reps:
920 1/4 N Formosa Ave, Los Angeles, CA 90046..........213-850-7957
Photographer: Buck Holzemer, Kathryn Russell

U V

Underwood, Delight:
8025C Hollywood Blvd, Hollywood, CA 90046.............213-874-2057
Illustrator: Harland Williams
Unicorn:
120 American Rd, Morris Plains, NJ 07950..............973-292-6854
Illustrator: David Boller, Lou Harrison, Chris Hawkes, Greg Hildebrandt, Tim Hildebrandt, Joe Quesada
VA Represents:
5436 Monticello Ave, Dallas, TX 75206.................214-826-7063
Photographer: Spook Bolt, Dragon Street Studio, Dan Ham, Rusty Hill
Vallon, Arlene:
411 E 53rd St #8K, New York, NY 10022.................212-980-1522
Photographer: Susan Goldman, Theo Westenberger
Van Arnam, Lewis:
881 Seventh Ave #817, New York, NY 10019..............212-541-4787
Photographer: Paul Amato, Carl Bengtsson, Hiromasa, Joseph Montezinos, Brian Nice, Steven Silverstein, Matthew Jordan Smith
Vargo/Bockos:
211 E Ohio Suite 2404, Chicago, IL 60611..............312-661-1717
Film: Bill Chair Productions, Cognito Films, Lawdaer Films, Shaddwrock Productions
Illustrator: Norm Bendell, Kurt Graves, Barbara Samanich
Photographer: Greg Heck, David Leach, Brian Lipchik, Regina Murphy
Veloric Assocs, Phillip:
200 S Roberts Rd #F6, Bryn Mawr, PA 19010.............610-520-3470
Illustrator: Susan Avishai, Beatrice Bork, Deb Troyer Bunnell, Rick L Cooley, Jack Crane, Len Ebert, Sherry L Fissel, Marvin Friedman, Deborah Healy, John Holder, Robert R Jackson, Rebecca A Merrilees, Keith Neely, Dennis Schofield, Nina Wallace, Stephen Wells, Jennifer Wharton, Lane Yerkes
Velvet Photography Agency:
3010 Lake Glen Dr., Beverly Hills, CA 90210...........310-458-1906
Vincent Creative Group, The:
140 Bentwood Dr, Stanford, CT 06903...................203-322-2332
Photographer: Neal Aspinall, Don Hammerman, Inc, Michael Weiss Studio
• **Virnig, Janet: pg 780-783**
5236 W 56th St, Minneapolis, MN 55436.................**651-926-5585**
fax: 651-926-3347
Illustrator: Rick Allen, Kara Fellows, Mary GrandPre, Kate Brennan Hall, Cindy Lindgren, Adam Ritchie, Kate Thomssen

Visages:
7750 Sunset Blvd 2nd Fl, Los Angeles, CA 90046....................213-650-8880
Photographer: Pascal Andre, Tracy Bayne, William Claxton, Sofia Coppola, John Dunne, Roger Erickson, Kevin Foley, Kate Garner, Angelika Grundler, Paul Jasmin, Roxann Mills, James Sorensen, Richard Wright

Von Schreiber, Barbara:
380 Lafayette St #300C, New York, NY 10003 212-460-5000
Photographer: Jean Maillard Claude, Oberto Gili, Gabriella Imperatori-Penn, Carolyn Jones, McDermott & McGough, Sarah Moon, Aernout Overbeeke, Peter Rodger, Neal Slavin, Laura Wilson

W

W/C Studio Inc:
208 Providence Rd, Annapolis, MD 21401 410-349-8669
Illustrator: Lori Bilter, Vicki Gullickson, Chuck Rancorn, Tom Sciacca
Photographer: Chris Coxwell

Wagoner, Jae:
654 Pier Ave #C, Santa Monica, CA 90405 ....310-392-4877Moline Kramer
Illustrator: Rick Allen, Dennis Doheny, Stephen Durke, Eva Ashley Emmert, William Harrison, Gary Johnson, Moline Kramer, Maurice Lewis, Mark McIntosh, Brad McMahon, Jane Mjolsness, Leo Monahan, Derek Mueller, Jeff Nishinaka, Tom Nordstrom, Miles Parnell, Don Weller, Benjamin Wu

Wagonheim, Rick:
350 W 39th St, New York, NY 10018........................212-239-6767

Wallen, Marilyn:
170 E 83rd St, New York, NY 10028 212-794-2479
Photographer: Anthony Edgeworth, Larry Dale Gordon

Walters, Gwen:
50 Fuller Brook Rd, Wellesley, MA 02181 781-235-8658
Illustrator: Tom Barrett, Heidi Chang, Dee DeLoy, Alan Espinoza, Arthur Friedman, Dave Garbo, Lane Gregory, Larry Johnson, Dan Krovatin, Pat Paris, Judith Pfeiffer, Salley Shadeler, Janise Skivington, Patrick Soper, Requel Soysa, Susan Spellman, Gary Torrisi, Rosario Valderrama, Fabrisio Vandenbroeck, Joe Veno, Jane Wright

Warner & Assocs, Bob:
1425 Belleview Ave, Plainfield, NJ 07060 908-755-7236
Illustrator: Tumo Narashima, Alex Petersen, Dimitry Schidlovsky, Victor R Valla
Photographer: Markus Meyenhofer, Hank Morgan, Frederick Skvara

• Warshaw Blumenthal, Inc.: pg 1458
New York, NY **212-867-4225**
url: www.illustrations-nyc.com

Washington Artists Rep:
22727 Cielo Vista, San Antonio, TX 78255....................210-698-1409
Illustrator: Fian Arroyo, Walt Curlee, Darius Detwiler, Stephen Durke, Mark Harlien, Jay Mercado, Kevin Peake, Herb Schnabel, Jim Steck, Michelle Wilby, John Wilson

Washington, Dick:
22727 Cielo Vista, San Antonio, TX 78255....................210-698-1409

Watson & Spierman:
524 Broadway 4th Fl, New York, NY 10012 212-431-4480
Illustrator: Dan Cotton, Monica Lind, Andrew Mockett
Photographer: Jim Allen, Marc Antoni, Kan Phtography, Rob Lewine, Frank Siteman, North Sullivan, Steve Vaccariello, Louis Wallach

• Way Art: pg 1456,1457
39 Hamilton Terr, New York, NY 10031 ....**212-283-3401**
url: www.wayart.com
Illustrator: Harry Borgman, Michael D'Antuono, Weston Emmart, Alexandra Gabanyi, Denis Luzuriaga, Scott McBee, Lucian Mihaesteanu, Rich Ransley, Bruce Rauffenbart, Aristides Ruiz, Laszlo Schreiber, Suzanne Simmons, Brian Stymest

• Webber, Tricia: pg 118372-415,970,971
250 W 57th St #521, New York, NY 10107 ....**212-397-7330**
url: www.lindgrensmith.com (or) www.stockillustrated.com
See Lindgren & Smith NY for client list

Weinberg, Larry:
608 York St, San Francisco, CA 94110 415-641-1285

• Weinberg, Maslov: pg 1187
San Francisco, CA **415-641-1285**
Illustrator: Stuart Bradford

Weiss, Caryn:
6311 Romaine St #7234, Los Angeles, CA 90038....................213-461-1084
Photographer: Marina Chavez, Caroline Greyshock, Albert Sanchez, Pamela Springsteen, Randee St Nicholas, Dana Tynan, Nathaniel Welch

Weiss, Debra:
1123 1/2 N Sweetzer, Los Angeles, CA 90069....................213-656-5029
Photographer: Ron Perry, Mark Segal, Douglas Walker
Stock: Panoramic Images

Weissberg, Elyse:
225 Broadway #700, New York, NY 10007 212-227-7272
Photographer: Eddie Adams, Markow Southwest, Paul Markow, Jack Reznicki

Wells, Karen:
14027 Memorial #125, Houston, TX 77079 281-579-3220
Illustrator: Karen Bell, Robert Crawford, Bill Firestone, Kit Hevron-Mahoney, Doug Horne, Daphne McCormack, Sharron O'Neil, Randy Rogers, Jeff Sanson, Stephen Wells

Wells, Susan:
5134 Timber Trail NE, Atlanta, GA 30342....................404-255-1430
Illustrator: Mark Andresen, Shelly Bartek, Ted Burn, Chad Cameron, David Clegg, Alex Hackworth, Jon Nelson, Matt Phillips, Colin Poole, Bob Radigan, Lynne Riding, Tommy Stubbs, Jack Unruh, Tracy Walker
Lettering: Elaine Dillard

West End Studio:
1501 Main St #201, Venice, CA 90291 310-664-9200
Animator: Robert Blair
Illustrator: Joe Cibere, Jim Krogle, Ken Roberts

White, Paula:
32 Shelton St, Covent Garden, London, England, UK WC2H 1714-972555

Whitehead, Brian:
Studio 4, Dickson House, Queens Rd, Richmond, Surrey,
England, UK TW106SP....................1812-558880

• Wilie Group: pg 1101,1192
94 Natoma St #200, San Francisco, CA 94105....................**415-442-1822**
url: www.dwrepresents.com/dwr / fax: 415-442-1823
Illustrator: Janet Cleland, Steve Forney, Ben Garvie Illustration, Ben Garvie, Mike Gray, Pablo Haz, Charlie Hill, Kathy Mcnicholas, Ken Toyama, David Watts, Paul Wiley, Keith Witmer
Photographer: Underwood Photography

Will, Jeannie:
2000 W Carroll Ave, Chicago, IL 60612 847-755-1351
Illustrator: David Will
Photographer: Eliot Crowley, Barry Elz, Ronnda Heinrich, Nick Pavloff

William Gerrad Productions:
420 N Wabash, Ste 500, Chicago, IL 60611 312-467-5560

Williams Group West, The:
5 Tower Dr, Mill Valley, CA 94941....................415-388-9391

Williams Group, The:
731 Stovall Blvd NE, Atlanta, GA 30342 800-791-1189
Illustrator: Luis Fernandez, Abe Gurvin, Rick Lovell, Bill Mayer, Steve McAfee, David McKelvey, Tom Patrick, John Robinette, Jim Theodore, Carlos Torres, Dale Verzaal, Russ Wilson
Photographer: Boris Pittman

Wilson Represents, Betty:
225 Lafayette #1001, New York, NY 10012 212-334-5557
Photographer: Barron Claiborne, Wolfgang Ludes, Norman, Peter Poby, Carl Posey, Cleo Sullivan

Wilson/Wenzel:
149 Wooster St 4th Fl, New York, NY 10012....................212-614-9500
Hair: Mike Lundgren
Photographer: Frederic Averbach, Martin Brading, Sophia Cappola, Mikael Jansson, Paul Jasmin
Stylist: Kari Hirzonin

Wilson/Zumbo Illustration Group:
301 N Water St, Milwaukee, WI 53202 414-271-3388
Illustrator: Joey Beauchamp, Clem Bedwell, Vince Chiaramonte, Eddy Corkery, Barbara Emmons, Thomas L Fluharty, Jack Graham, Pamela Hamilton, Paul Johnson, Tim Jonke, Nobee Kanayama, Nancy Kurtz, John Lambert, Don Margolis, Jeff Meyer, Mark Mille, Chris Musselman, Jeff O'Connor, Mary Jo Phalen, Jim Shepherd, Keith Skeen, Jay Smith, Luis Sola, Tim Spransy, Chris Szetela, Judy Unger, Keith Ward, Peter Wells, Matt Zumbo

Winners Circle:
12659 Moorpark St #1, Studio City, CA 91604 818-766-3441

Winston West:
130 W 25th Street 12th Floor, New York, NY 10013 212-925-2999
204 S Beverly Dr #108, Los Angeles, CA 90212 310-275-2858
Photographer: Jerry Avenaim, Thierry Bearzatto, Jim Jordan, Marc Kayne, Graham Kuhn, Marcus Morianz, Amyn Nasser, Eran Offek, Adam Olszewski, Tom Rafalovich, Richard Reinsdorf, Simko

• Wolfe Ltd, Deborah: pg 446-472, 1482
731 N 24th St, Philadelphia, PA 19130....................**215-232-6666**
url: www.deborahwolfeltd.com / fax: 215-232-6585
Illustrator: Steve Armes, Stephen Bauer, Linda Cane, Paul Dempsey, Jeff Fitz-Maurice, Patrick Gnan, Steve Greenberg, Marianne Hughes, Lynn Jeffery, Joseph Page Kovach, Dean Kube, Jeff LeVan, Barbara McAdams, JT Morrow, Julian Mulock, Leif Peng, Lisa Pomerantz, Irena Roman, Jonathan & Georgina Rosenbaum, Saul Rosenbaum, Scott Ross, Nick Rotondo, Don Stewart, Chris Vanes, Richard Waldrep, Larry Winborg, Amy Wummer

Wolff & Co Inc:
215 Glyndon Meadows Rd, Glyndon, MD 21136....................410-526-9840
Photographer: Dean Alexander, Steven Biver, Peter Howard

Wolter, Bob:
440 N Wabash #1909, Chicago, IL 60611 312-670-8770
Illustrator: Sandy Ostroff, Marty Roper, Sandbox Digital Playground
Photographer: Dennis Galante, Ralph Mercer Photogrpahy, Jody Nilsen, Kathy Sanders, Joel Sheagren, John Welzenbach, Art Wise
Retoucher: Chicago Artist Reps

Woodfin Camp & Assoc:
116 E 27th St 8th Fl, New York, NY 10016 212-481-6900
Photographer: Nubar Alexanian, John Blaustein, Gary Braasch, Robert Frerck, Catherine Karnow, Yousuf Karsch, Paula Lerner, Gerd Ludwig, George Olson, Sepp Seitz, Robert Severi, Leif Skoogfors, William A Strode, Michael Yamashita

Woodworth Assocs, Maurice:
....................902-443-6255

Y Z

Yantis, Day:
5706 Sprinter Ln, Bonita, CA 91902....................619-479-2622

Yengo, Laura:
321 Ave C #6-C, New York, NY 10009....................212-420-1121
Photographer: Bill Bernstein, John Rusnak, Alphonse Telymonde

You Three:
32049 Milton Ave, Madison Hgts, MI 48071 248-588-6544
Photographer: Tom Burkhart, Don Johnston, Keith Jolly, George Pizzo, Troy Wood

Zabowski Creative Reps, Lulu Z:
4645 Colfax Ave S, Minneapolis, MN 55409....................612-825-7564
Electronic Imaging: Filip Yip
Illustrator: Doug Bowles, Alan Brunettin, Jannine Cabossel, Matt Foster, Tina Lee Hill, Steve Kennevan, Tony Novak, Fran O'Neill, Fran O'Neill, Virginia Peck, Tracy Rea, Paul Schmid

Zaccaro & Assocs, Jim:
315 E 68th St, New York, NY 10021 212-744-4000

Zaleski, Janet:
624 W Willow, Chicago, IL 60614....................312-944-9744
Photographer: Mark Battrell, Jeff Schewe

Zari Int'l:
853 Broadway #1516, New York, NY 10003....................212-388-8541
Photographer: Natasha Terik Alexanda, Regis Fialaire, Marc Hauser, Christina Hope, Brooke Hunyady, Michael Korte, Famiglia Trentto, Frank P Wartenberg

ILLUSTRATORS & DIGITAL ARTISTS

A

• **A^2 Studio: pg 1231** 605 Finch Ave W #71-6, Willowdale, ON M2R 1P1......**416-638-9271**
fax: 416-638-9271
Aagaard, Gary: 280 Madison Ave #1110, New York, NY 10016......................212-545-9155
• **Abbey, Shannon K: pg 824** 1839 Ninth St, Alameda, CA 94501................**510-769-1421**
e-mail: ldmreps@earthlink.net / fax: 510-521-1674
Abbott, JJ: 16 Buchanon Ct, West Orange, NJ 07052....................................908-223-8770
• **Abe, George: pg 676,677** 2814 NW 72nd St, Seattle, WA 98117..............**206-784-1136**
url: www.kolea.com / fax: 206-784-1171
Abe, Yoshiko: 165 Jacoby St, Maplewood, NJ 07040..201-378-9188
Abella, Sheffield B: 9631 Hawaiian Summer St, Las Vegas, NV 89123............702-270-8828
Aberg, Karen: 175 Fifth Ave #2148, New York, NY 10010..................................800-286-4895
Aboelela, Nazly: 10116 Rhapsody Dr, Baton Rouge, LA 70815..........................201-304-0960
Abraham, Daniel: 372 Fifth Ave #3, Brooklyn, NY 11215...................................718-499-4006
Abramovic, Carl: 11648 SW Military Lane, Portland, OR 97219........................503-697-3315
Abramowitz Fine Arts Inc: 884 Washington St, Canton, MA 02021..................617-575-0063
Abrams, Ed & Jodell: 1966 6th Ave, San Diego, CA 92101...............................619-700-2917
Abrams, Kathie: 299 Western Dr S, S Orange, NJ 07079....................................718-499-4408
Abramson, Elaine: PO Box 330008, Ft Worth, TX 76163.....................................817-292-1855
Abriatis, Vitas: 1413 Highland Ave, Plainfield, NJ 07060.................................908-754-1463
Accardo, Anthony: 1712 E Butler Cir, Chandler, AZ 85225.................................602-899-0600
Accornero, Franco: 420 Lexington Ave #2760, New York, NY 10170..................212-697-8525
Acevedo, Victor: 167 Ave B #3F, New York, NY 10009..212-777-6516
Ackison, Wendy Wassink: 144 High St, Fayetteville, WV 25840.........................304-574-4808
Acuna, Ed: 232 Madison Ave #402, New York, NY 10016....................................212-889-8777
Adam Filippo & Moran: 1206 Fifth Ave, Pittsburgh, PA 15219...........................412-261-3720
• **Adam, Winky: pg 1232** 370 Central Park West, New York, NY 10025.........**212-423-0746**
• **Adams, Beth: pg 12,13** 108 E 35th St #2, New York, NY 10016..................**212-987-8700**
url: www.theispot.com/artist/adams/ / fax: 212-889-3341
Adams, Cheryl: 2124 NW 139th St, Des Moines, IA 50325..................................515-223-7174
Adams, Dianne: 3453 Rt 40, Washington, PA 15301..704-583-0230
Adams, Gil: 853 Broadway #1201, New York, NY 10003......................................212-677-9100
Adams, Jeanette: PO Box 130 Turkey Shoot Rd, Acworth, NH 03601...............603-835-2439
Adams, Jeffrey: 201 W 21st St #10G, New York, NY 10001...............................212-807-0840
Adams, Jenny: 1119 Colorado Ave #23, Santa Monica, CA 90401.......................310-576-0757
Adams, Katharine Murta: 2038 Meridian Ave Unit E, S Pasadena, CA 91030......213-349-0763
Adams, Kathryn: UK/Western Europe,..186-543-5654
Los Angeles, CA...213-688-7428
Chicago, IL...312-663-5506
Panama City, FL...904-747-8415
New York, NY...212-643-0896
468 Queen St E #104, Toronto, ON M5A 1T7..416-367-2446
• **Adams, Lisa: pg 1096** 40 Harrison St #29F, New York, NY 10013................**212-385-8189**
fax: 212-385-9630
Adams, Michael W: 3002 Fifth St, Trooper, PA 19403...215-539-5679
Adams, Norman: Shrub Oak, NY...212-755-1365
Adams, Paul: 1000 John R Rd #201, Troy, MI 48083..248-583-6070
Adams, Rodney: 3626 Boy Wood Rd, Graham, NC 27253....................................910-222-9333
Adams, William: 1019 E Elgin Ave, Salt Lake City, UT 84104.............................801-484-3319
Adams, William T: 4016 Spruell Dr, Kensington, MD 20895...............................301-949-9475
Adel, Daniel: 50 W 22nd St 6th Fl, New York, NY 10024.....................................212-989-6114
Adigard, Erik: 237 San Carlos Ave, Sausalito, CA 94965....................................415-331-1023
Adkins, James: 18550 Prairie #11, Northridge, CA 91324..................................818-993-4967
Adler, Steven: 3557 Slate Mills Rd, Sperryville, VA 22740.................................800-789-9389
Aeurbach, Larry: 116 Bedford Ave #1R, Brooklyn, NY 11211..............................718-384-5826
Agrell, Lewis: 430 Hillcrest Dr, Prescott, AZ 86303..520-445-7038
Aguilar, Rob: 171 Coventry Dr, Campbell, CA 95008..408-378-6402
Ahearn, John D: 151 S Elm, St Louis, MO 63119...314-781-3389
Ahern, Kevin: 8029 Enfley Ln, Leawood, KS 66206...913-383-2877
Ahle, Dorothy: 8 Grimshaw St, Malden, MA 02148..617-321-8302
Ahlemeyer, Karla: 9011 Jackson Rd, Sacramento, CA 95826..............................916-363-3241
Ahmed, Ghulan Hassan: 1258 Walker Ave, Baltimore, MD 21239.........................410-433-0478
Aho, Paul: 1610 S Dixie Hwy, West Palm Beach, FL 33401.................................407-833-9117
Ahrens Interactive: 400 N State #200, Chicago, IL 60610...................................312-494-9999
Aiese, Bob: 60 Pineapple St, Brooklyn, NY 11201..914-693-7220
Air Hero's Studio: 30 Duke St, St Catharines, ON L2S 6Z4................................905-984-6140
Aizawa, Kaz: 280 Madison Ave #1110, New York, NY 10016...............................212-545-9155
• **Ajhar, Brian: pg 776,777**
333 Lower Seese Hill Rd,Canadensis, PA 18325..**717-595-9298**
url: www.theispot.com/artist/ajhar / fax: 717-595-9392
Akers, Kevin: 13 Har7t St, San Rafael, CA 94901...415-455-0562
• **Akguilan, Nishan: pg 767** 41 Union Sq W #918, New York, NY 10003.......**212-807-6627**
url: idt.net/~dgagency / fax: 212-463-8175
Akins Design, Charles: 2276 Virginia Pl #3, Atlanta, GA 30305.........................404-231-1312
Akins, Kelly: 3850 Eddingham Ave, Calabasas, CA 91302...................................818-222-5445
Akiyama, Megumi: 2330 Schoolside Ave, Monterey Park, CA 91754...................626-584-4137
Akopyan, Loudvik: 1306 Alabama St, Huntington Beach, CA 92648....................714-969-7766
Akopyan, Loudvik: 327 E 89th St #3E, New York, NY 10128................................212-831-5650
Alaimo, Terry: 2233 Martin St #113, Irvine, CA 92715..714-724-8899
Alavezos, Gus: 19050 Merrymen Cir, Monument, CO 80132..................................719-488-9078
Albahae, Andrea: 2368 Bringham St 1st Fl, Brooklyn, NY 11229........................718-934-7004
Albanese, Ernest: 136 Park Ave #2, Hoboken, NJ 07030.....................................201-659-9335
Alberg, Kari: 11125 Kane Trail, Northfield, MN 55057..507-645-2272
Albers, Dave: 6549 Eleventh Ave NW, Seattle, WA 98117....................................206-781-7933
Albrektson Studio, Jean: 1050 Main St #14, East Greenwich, RI 02818...............401-884-9993
Alco Computer Graphics: 1 Calvo Pl, Hawthorne, NJ 07506...............................201-423-1894
Alcorn, Bob: 434 South Main St, Heightstown, NJ 08520.....................................609-448-4448
Alde, David: 1801 Clydesdale Pl NW, Washington, DC 20009..............................202-234-1196
• **Alder Illustration, Kelly: pg 1102**
7 North Monroe St 2nd Fl, Richmond, VA 23220...**804-643-5761**
fax: 804-643-5761
Aldredge, Vaughn: 4033 Aurora Ave N, Seattle, WA 98103.................................206-633-3445
• **Aldrich, David : pg 1100** 143 Amelia St, Toronto, ON M4X 1E6..................**416-960-6005**
Aldworth, Susan: 2315 NW 70th, Seattle, WA 98117...206-783-3062
Alejandro, Cliff: 228 Jewett Ave, Jersey City, NJ 07304.....................................201-451-0441
Alexander & Turner: 232 Madison Ave #402, New York, NY 10016........................212-889-8777
• **Alexander, Paul: pg 156** 420 Lexington Ave, New York, NY 10170...............**212-986-5680**
url: www.mendolaart.com / fax: 212-818-1246
Ali, Mikal: 3926 Holmes, Kansas City, MO 64110..816-531-7052
Alivater, LJ: 3435 Army St #212, San Francisco, CA 94110...............................415-824-9417
Allaux, Jean Francois: Thompson, PA 18465...717-756-3034
• **Allen Design, Mark: pg 1226** 152 W 14th St #15, New York, NY 10011....**212-243-4508**
2209 Ocean Ave, Venice, CA 90291...**310-396-6471**
e-mail: mallendesign@earthlink.net / url: www.markallendesign.com
Allen Illus, Gina: 7755 S Kingston #2N, Chicago, IL 60649................................773-734-6418
Allen, Bryan: 103 Church St, Boonton, NJ 07005..201-402-0099
Allen, Dave: 3188 Eagle's Way Dr, Lafayette, IN 47905.....................................317-474-9704
Allen, David W: 18108 Martin Ave #2F, Homewood, IL 60430...............................708-798-3283
Allen, Gary: PO Box 35584, Houston, TX 77235...301-891-3530
Allen, Gina Minor: 7755 S Kingston #2N, Chicago, IL 60649................................773-734-6418
Allen, Harrison: 5811 Braesheather Rd, Houston, TX 77096................................713-729-3938
Allen, Jim: 1612 W 5th St, Coal Valley, IL 61240...309-799-3366
Allen, Joy: 12182 St Mark Street, Garden Grove, CA 92845................................714-894-8618
Allen, Julian: 115 West 2nd Street, New York, NY 10011....................................212-989-4600
Allen, Kelly: 2811 McKinney Ave #320 LB111, Dallas, TX 75204........................214-922-9080
Allen, Pat: 4510 Alpine Rd, Portola Valley, CA 94028..650-851-3116
Allen, Rick: 2532 Kipling Ave S, Minneapolis, MN 55416.....................................612-926-5585
Allen, Terry: 84 Campfire Rd, Chappaqua, NY 10514...914-238-1422
Allen, Victoria: 1203 Bolton St, Baltimore, MD 21217..410-383-0893
Allendorf, Richard M: 15 Bellwood Cir, Bellingham, MA 02019............................508-966-9047
Allers, Max: 618 2nd Ave SE, Minneapolis, MN 55414...612-362-8477
Allert, Kathy: 201 E 28th St, New York, NY 10016..212-532-0928
Allison, John: 7645 Jarboe, Kansas City, MO 64114...816-444-7782
Allison, Linda: PO Box 2646, San Anselmo, CA 94979...415-485-0630
• **Allport, Sophie: pg 713** 455 W 23rd St #8D, New York, NY 10011...............**212-366-1893**
url: www.andtheart.com / fax: 212-604-9643
Alma, Ray: 42-32 215th St #3, Bayside, NY 11361...718-631-0531
Aloisio, Richard: 145 E 16th St, New York, NY 10003...212-473-5635
Alpert, Olive: 9511 Shore Rd, Brooklyn, NY 11209..718-833-3092
Alphonse, Gary: 189 Delaware Ave, Toronto, ON M6H 2T2.................................416-534-8522
• **Alpiss, Linda: pg 625** 5002 92nd Ave SE, Mercer Island, WA 98040............**206-232-7873**
fax: 206-232-7908
Alsberg, Kari: 11125 Kane Trail, Northfield, MN 55057..507-645-2272
Alsberg, Peter: 33 Columbia Ave, Takoma Park, MD 20912.................................301-891-3530
• **Alt, Tim: pg 1190** 3166 E Palmdale Blvd #120, Palmdale, CA 93550.........**805-265-8092**
fax: 805-265-8095
Altamore, Vincent: 152-48 Melbourne Ave, Flushing, NY 11367..........................718-263-2264
Altera, Bina: 23 Stillings St 2nd Fl, Boston, MA 02210..617-451-6860
Alvarado, Leon: 1207 Dunlavy, Houston, TX 77019...713-834-0180
Alvarez, Lamberto: 2612 Galemeadow Dr, Ft Worth, TX 76123............................817-346-6971
Alvin, John: 18929 Granada Cir, Northridge, CA 91326.......................................818-831-8626
ALY Illustration: 14165 Garfield Dr, Spring Lake, MI 49456.................................616-847-1630
• **Amatrula, Michele: pg 1207** 259 W 10th St #4J, New York, NY 10014......**212-255-7413**
fax: 212-989-4374
Ambler, Barbara Hoopes: 2769 Nipoma St, San Diego, CA 92106.......................619-222-7535
Ambre, Matt: 743 Brompton Ave #GA, Chicago, IL 60657....................................773-935-5170
Ambrose, Darren: 1283 New York Rt 11, Castle Creek, NY 13744........................607-648-2197
Amedee Illustration: 126 Fifth Ave, New York, NY 10011.....................................212-620-0728
Ameijide, Ray: 108 E 35th St #2, New York, NY 10016..212-889-3337
Amendola, Steve: 95 Horatio St #610, New York, NY 10014................................212-989-3246
Amicosante, Vincent: 280 Madison Ave #1402, New York, NY 10016..................212-545-9155
Amit, Emmanuel: 108 E 35th St #2, New York, NY 10016....................................212-889-3337
4322 Sunset Ave, Montrose, CA 91020..818-249-1739
Amorosi, Thomas: 20 Sherman St, Brooklyn, NY 11215.......................................718-832-2873
Amos & Sons Inc, Jack: 18 E Main St, Richmond, VA 23219...............................804-780-0993
Amoss, John: 1177 Willivee Dr, Decatur, GA 30033..404-636-0275
• **Ampel, Kenneth Robert: pg 1233**
1014 Black Oak Dr, Medford, OR 97504...**541-779-3859**
e-mail: Kampel@Jeffnet.org / url: www.showcase.com / fax: 541-779-3859
Amrine, Cynthia: PO Box 547, Naples, NY 14512..716-374-5847
Amundson, Eric: 1100 W Cambridge Cir Dr #550, Kansas City, KS 66103.........913-281-4433
Anatoly: 716 Montgomery St, San Francisco, CA 94111.......................................415-433-1222
Ancas, Karen: 84 Keystone St, W Roxbury, MA 02132...617-323-8466
• **Andelin, Douglas : pg 1091** 19 Bayview Ave, Larkspur, CA 94939..............**415-927-1945**
Anderson & Assocs, Suzanne: PO Box 8307, Atlanta, GA 31106........................404-872-7272
Anderson Design, Charles: 30 N First St, Minneapolis, MN 55401......................612-339-5181
Anderson, Barry: 7 Ivory Ln, Darlington, Australia, NSW 2................................029-319-0847
Anderson, Charmaine: 14320 SW Red Haven Dr, Beaverton, OR 97008..............503-644-7501
Anderson, Darrel: 1420 Territory Trail, Colorado Springs, CO 80919....................719-535-0407
• **Anderson, Elizabeth: pg 1234** 15544 SE 175th CT, Renton, WA 98058......**425-204-9400**
e-mail: eaillustration@hotmail.com / fax: 425-204-9333
Anderson, John: 501 N Calvert St, Baltimore, MD 21278....................................410-332-6508
Anderson, Joni: 4724 Lincoln #223, Marina Del Rey, CA 90292..........................310-305-7806
Anderson, Kevin: 1267 Orkney Ln, Cardiff by the Sea, CA 92007.......................619-753-8410
Anderson, Lew: 260 George Waterman Rd, Johnston, RI 02919............................401-232-9342
Anderson, Mark: 8222 SW Hawthorne Lane, Vashon Island, WA 98070................206-567-4514
• **Anderson, Paul:**
pg 474,475 2149 Lyon St #5, San Francisco, CA 94115.......................................**415-921-7140**
email: art@conradreps.com / url: www.conradreps.com / fax: 415-921-3939
• **Anderson, Philip: pg 14,15** 108 E 35th St #2, New York, NY 10016...........**212-889-3337**
url: www.theispot.com/artist/anderson / fax: 212-889-3341
Anderson, Reed: 4320 S 700 E #1, Salt Lake City, UT 84107..............................801-265-0530
Anderson, Richard: 490 Bleeker Ave #2C, Mamaroneck, NY 10543.....................914-381-2682
Anderson, Rolf: 168 Lunado Ct, San Francisco, CA 94127.................................415-333-1626
Anderson, Sara: 3131 Western Ave #516, Seattle, WA 98121..............................206-285-1520
Anderson, Scott: 4949 Grange Rd, Santa Rosa, CA 95404.................................707-584-5196

Bac, Bong Sung: 5315-7 Stonehedge Blvd, Ft Wayne, IN 46835....................219-485-3463
Bacall, Aaron: 204 Arlene St, Staten Island, NY 10314....................718-494-0711
Bachalo, Jim: 1243 Broadview Ave #311, Toronto, ON M4K 2T3....................416-425-3121
• **Bachem, Paul: pg 523,528** 89 Fifth Ave #901, New York, NY 10003....................**212-627-1554**
fax: 212-627-1719
Bachtell, Tom: 220 South State #1930, Chicago, IL 60604....................312-939-6603
Back, Francis: 4706 rue Marquette, Montréal, QU H3Z 2T5....................514-983-9020
• **Backer, Marni: pg 873** 866 United Nations Plaza, New York, NY 10017....................**212-644-2020**
url: www.spar.org
Backes, Nick: 10 E Ontario #4708, Chicago, IL 60611....................312-573-1370
Backus, Michael: 1945 Tigertail Rd, Eugene, OR 97405....................541-687-0284
Bacon, Paul: PO Box 275, Clintondale, NY 12515....................914-883-9036
Bad Katz Graphics: 1550 Lunar Dr, Monterey Pk, CA 91754....................213-261-2871
Bader, David A: 3257 Revlon Dr, Kettering, OH 45420....................937-298-7516
Badgley, Marcus: 1016 McNear Ave, Petaluma, CA 94952....................707-778-0165
Badlands Media: 165 Larose Ave #1017, Etobicke, ON M9P 3V9....................416-245-3494
Baehr, AIA, Richard C: 217 E 86th St Box 212, New York, NY 10028....................212-427-5632
Baer, Roxanna: 850 Amsterdam Ave#13-c, New York, NY 10025....................212-865-2183
Baggs, Mike: 160 E 38th St #20G, New York, NY 10016....................800-492-2447
Baglieri, Peter & Mike: 160 E 38th St #20F, New York, NY 10016....................212-687-5227
Baier, Matt: 30 Second Plc #2, Brooklyn, NY 11231....................718-802-9483
Baileor, Brent: 466 Lexington Ave 2nd Fl, New York, NY 10017....................212-661-0257
Bailey, Craig: 24102 Cheddar Ct, Tomball, TX 77375....................713-351-6283
Bailey, John: 7709 W Lisbon Ave, Milwauke, WI 53222....................414-442-1367
Bailey, Laura: 2512 E Thomas Rd #2, Phoenix, AZ 85016....................602-381-1332
Bailey, Pat: 60 E 42nd St #822, New York, NY 10165....................212-682-1490
Bailey, RC: 281 Glendale Dr, Miami Springs, FL 33166....................305-888-6309
Bair, Glenn: 912 Blanco St, Austin, TX 78703....................512-477-7092
Baker, Charissa: 159 John St 6th Fl, New York, NY 10038....................212-825-1475
• **Baker, Don: pg 674,675** 2814 NW 72nd St, Seattle, WA 98117....................**206-784-1136**
url: www.kolea.com/ / fax: 206-784-1171
• **Baker, Garin: pg 20,21** 108 E 35th St #2, New York, NY 10016....................**212-889-3337**
url: www.theispot.com/artist/baker / fax: 212-889-3341
Baker, Grahame: 42 Delavan St, Brooklyn, NY 11231....................718-624-1906
Baker, Jennifer: 402 Market St #306, San Diego, CA 92101....................206-744-1119
Baker, Julie: 6619 Haley Ave, Cincinnati, OH 45227....................513-272-1662
Baker, Lori: RR1 Box 880, Plainfield, VT 05061....................802-426-3800
Baker, Louise M: 223 W Erie St, Chicago, IL 60610....................312-915-0570
Baker, Skip: 731 N 24th St, Philadelphia, PA 19130....................215-232-6666
Baker, Spencer: 242 Camino Descanso, Palm Springs, CA 92264....................714-724-3870
Baker, Susan Harriet: 315 West Side Dr #303, Gaithersburg, MD 20878....................301-258-0126
Bakley, Craig: 68 Madison Ave, Cherry Hill, NJ 08002....................609-428-6310
Baldwin Jr, Gunnar: RR1 Box 3271, Plymouth, NH 03264....................603-536-1836
• **Baldwin, Christopher: pg 683** 2814 NW 72nd St, Seattle, WA 98117....................**206-784-1136**
url: www.kolea.com / fax: 206-784-1171
Baldwin, James: 1467 Jordan Ave, Crofton, MD 21114....................410-721-1896
Baldwin, Scott: 58 W 15th St, New York, NY 10011....................212-741-2539
Balistreri West End Art Co: PO Box 70, Delafield, WI 53018....................414-646-8578
Ball, Harvey: 340 Main St, Worcester, MA 01608....................617-752-9154
Ball, John: 29580 Northwestern Hwy, Southfield, MI 48034....................248-353-7722
Ballard, Dan: PO Box 85187, Seattle, WA 98145....................206-634-0084
Ballinger, Bryan: 0 South Madison Street, Windield, IL 60190....................630-871-3001
Balnave, Jack: 7 B Yacenda Dr, Morris Plains, NJ 07950....................201-984-1982
Balouch, Kristen: 57 Norman Ave #4R, Brooklyn, NY 11222....................718-349-2311
Bamundo, David: 146 Chandler Ave 2nd Fl, Staten Island, NY 10314....................718-370-7726
Banashek, Jill: 578 29th Ave, San Francisco, CA 94121....................415-751-5336
• **Bandle, Johnna: pg 1241** 7726 Noland Rd, Lenexa, KS 66216....................**913-962-9595**
e-mail: bandle@qni.com / fax: 913-962-9595
Bandsuch, Matt: 497 Prentis St #4, Detroit, MI 48201....................313-831-7324
Banfield, Elliott: 341 E 10th St #2E, New York, NY 10009....................212-473-6772
Bangham, Richard: 2006 Cascade Rd, Silver Spring, MD 20902....................301-649-4919
Banner, Shawn: 53 Duncan Ave #56, Jersey City, NJ 07304....................201-333-6652
Banner, Shawn: 99 Park Ave #210A, New York, NY 10016....................800-398-9544
Bannerman, Isabella: 100 W 80th St #2F, New York, NY 10024....................212-873-5539
Bannister, Philip: 23 Ganton St, London, England, UK WIV 1LA....................71-287-9191
Banta, Susan: 17 Magazine St, Cambridge, MA 02139....................617-876-8568
Banthien, Barbara: PO Box 470818, San Francisco, CA 94147....................415-383-9026
Banyai, Istvan: P.O. Box 77644, San Francisco, CA 94107....................415-381-4728
Banyai, Istvan: 666 Greenwich St #420, New York, NY 10014....................212-627-2953
Bapp Illus, Kevin: 269 Vanderbilt St #2, Brooklyn, NY 11205....................718-398-6675
Bapp, Kevin: 333 N Michigan #1100, Chicago, IL 60601....................312-855-9336
Baquero, George: 4 Westlay Ln, New Milford, NJ 07646....................201-261-6011
• **Baradat, Sergio: pg 1242** 210 W 70th St #1606, New York, NY 10023....................**212-721-2588**
e-mail: baradat@aol.com / url: www.walrus.com/~sergiob / fax: 212-724-4013
Baran, Zafer: 42 Delavan St, Brooklyn, NY 11231....................718-624-1906
Barancik, Cathy: 18 E 78th St, New York, NY 10021....................212-472-3838
Barbante, Ben: 1245 Chula Vista Dr, Belmont, CA 94002....................415-525-3414
Barbaria, Steve: 1990 Third St #400, Sacramento, CA 95814....................916-442-3200
Barbee, Joel: 209 Avenida San Pablo, San Clemente, CA 92627....................714-498-0067
Barber, Brian: 3533 18th St Ave S, Minneapolis, MN 55407....................612-874-0835
Barber, David: 21 Taft St, Marblehead, MA 01945....................617-631-6130
Barber, Rob: 4809 Lincoln Ave, Beltville, MD 20705....................301-931-1157
Barbey, Jacques: 3034 E. Marlette, Phoenix, AZ 85016....................602-956-1536
Barbie, Michael: 463 Old Post Rd, Niceville, FL 32578....................904-897-3441
• **Barbier, Suzette: pg 1243** 124 Winchester St, Newton, MA 02161....................**617-527-8388**
e-mail: holyfish@aol.com / fax: 617-244-0266
Barbour, Karen: PO Box 1210, Pt Reyes Stn, CA 94956....................415-663-1100
Barcita, Pamela: 3582 Campion Ave, Virginia Beach, VA 23462....................804-463-7619
Barklew, Pete: 110 Alpine Way, Athens, GA 30606....................706-546-5058
Barkley, James: 25 Brook Manner, Pleasantville, NY 10570....................914-747-2220
Barlow, Jared: 22 N Prospect Ave, Baltimore, MD 21228....................410-455-9955
Barlow, Kevin: 2360 Bayless Pl, Saint Paul, MN 55114....................612-649-0257
Barnard, Bryn: 2717 Western Ave, Seattle, WA 98121....................206-232-7873
Barnard, Doug: 28805 S Lakeshore Dr, Agoura Hills, CA 91301....................818-991-9328
Barner, Bob: 65 Mt Vernon St, Boston, MA 02108....................617-523-0953
Barner, Bob: 866 United Nations Plaza, New York, NY 10017....................212-644-2020
• **Barnes, Jeff: pg 1491** 3718 E 83rd, Tulsa, OK 74137....................**918-496-9598**
e-mail: jbpix@worldnet.att.net
Barnes, Ken: 689 Southard St, Trenton, NJ 08638....................609-394-2440
• **Barnes, Kim: pg 531** 89 Fifth Ave #901, New York, NY 10003....................**212-627-1554**
fax: 212-627-1719
• **Barnes, Melanie: pg 864** 280 Madison Ave #1110, New York, NY 10016....................**212-545-9155**
e-mail: Irmeli@aol.com / url: www.spar.org/holmberg / fax: 212-545-9462
Barnes, Michelle: 41 Union Sq W #918, New York, NY 10003....................212-807-6627
Barnes, Suzanne: 22 Pleasant St, Salem, MA 01970....................508-740-9150
Barnes, Tim: 960 N Alfred Street #215, Los Angeles, CA 90069....................213-848-7033
• **Barnes, Tim: pg 580,581** 232 Madison Ave #512, New York, NY 10016....................**212-889-8777**
fax: 212-447-1475
• **Barnes-Murphy, Rowan: pg 114,115**
420 Lexington Ave, New York, NY 10170....................**212-986-5680**
url: www.mendolaart.com (and) www.rowanbarnes_murphy.com / fax: 212-818-1246
Barnes-Murphy, Rowan: 23 Ganton St, London, England, UK WIV 1LA....................71-287-9191
• **Barnet, Nancy: pg 1244** 8928 Shady Vista Ct, Elk Grove, CA 95624....................**916-685-4147**
e-mail: nbarnetart@aol.com
Barnett, David: 41 Hidcote Rd-Oadby, Leicester, England, UK LE2 5PG....................1162-717658
Barr, Elissa: PO Box 470483, Brookline Village, MA 02147....................617-731-4487
Barr, Ken: 420 Lexington Ave #2760, New York, NY 10170....................212-697-8525
Barr, Loel: 11100 Kensington Blvd, Kensington, MD 20896....................301-774-4634
Barr, Marilyn Grant: 5721 Wildberry Dr, Greensboro, NC 27409....................910-852-4287
Barrall, Tim: 372 Bleecker St #2, New York, NY 10014....................212-243-9003
Barrera, Alberto: 55 Bethune Street Ste 914C, New York, NY 10014....................212-645-2544
• **Barrett, Andrea: pg 828**
1424 La Positas Plaza, Santa Barbara, CA 93105....................**805-682-6775**
fax: 805-687-1350
Barrett, Anne S: 163 Ocean Ave #6K, Brooklyn, NY 11225....................718-940-8133
Barrett, Debby: 49 Hamilton St, Everett, MA 02149....................617-387-2031
Barrett, Jennifer: 5510 Glenwood Rd, Bethesda, MD 20817....................301-654-4603
Barrett, Kent: 674 Keefer St, Vancouver, BC V6A 1Y4....................604-254-6030
• **Barrett, Ron: pg 692** 666 Greenwich St #860, New York, NY 10014....................**212-675-5719**
url: www.hkportfolio.com / fax: 212-675-6341
Barrett, Sabina Crosby: 120 Hudson St, New York, NY 10013....................212-343-0631
Barrett, Tom: 81 Mt Vernon St #2, Boston, MA 02108....................617-523-4072
Barrette, Doris: 297 rue de Srencois Baillarge, Laval, QU H7L 5E9....................514-622-0325
Barrington, Brian: 10541 Torrington Cir #4, Westinster, CA 92683....................714-731-8538
Barron, Mary: 3910 Orchard St, Boulder, CO 80304....................303-440-0988
Barrows, Scott: 5182 Cypress Ct, Lisle, IL 60532....................630-355-4242
Barry, Rick: 1631 W 12th St, Brooklyn, NY 11223....................718-232-2484
Barry, Ron: 21005 Tamarack Cir, Southfield, MI 48075....................810-356-8946
• **Barsky, Alexander: pg 855**
280 Madison Ave #1110, New York, NY 10016....................**212-545-9155**
e-mail: Irmeli@aol.com / url: www.spar.org/holmberg / fax: 212-545-9462
• **Barson, Jeff: pg 431** 60 E 42nd St, New York, NY 10165-1940....................**212-867-8092**
e-mail: DHLT@aol.com / url: www.HT-LTD.com (and) www.ren-man.com /
fax: 212-949-1977
Barta, Les: 812 Jeffrey Ct, Incline Village, NV 89451....................702-831-0430
Bartalos, Michael: 30 Ramona Ave #2, San Francisco, CA 94103....................415-863-4569
Bartczak, Peter: PO Box 7709, Santa Cruz, CA 95061....................408-426-4247
• **Bartek, Shelly: pg 633** 5 E 17th St 6th Fl, New York, NY 10003....................**212-691-2667**
fax: 212-633-1844
4 E Ohio Studio B, Chicago, IL 60611....................**312-321-1336**
fax: 312-321-1350
Bartholomew, Beth: 486 Graham Ave #21, Brooklyn, NY 11222....................718-384-0162
Bartlett, Christopher: 2211B Woodbox Ln, Baltimore, MD 21209....................301-484-1906
Bartlett, Michael: 45 Bulkley Ave #2, Sausalito, CA 94965....................415-331-5127
Bartling, Tom: 1205 W 43rd St, Austin, TX 78756....................512-467-7471
Bartoli, Yuri: 45-21 45th St #3F, Sunnyside, NY 11104....................718-729-0361
• **Barton, Kent: pg 246,247** 121 Madison Ave #5F, New York, NY 10016....................**212-683-1362**
fax: 212-683-1919
Barton, Paul: 1136 E Stuart St #2060, Fort Collins, CO 80525....................303-482-1254
Baruffi, Andrea: 341 Hudson Terr, Piermont, NY 10968....................914-359-9542
• **Baseman, Gary: pg 934,935** PO Box 470818, San Francisco, CA 94147....................**415-383-9026**
e-mail: jan@collierreps.com / url: www.collierreps.com / fax: 415-383-9037
Los Angeles, CA....................**213-934-5567**
fax: 213-934-5516
Bash, Barbara: 9 Babbling Brook Ln, Suffern, NY 10901....................914-368-8606
Baskett, Austin H: 4700 Edison Ln, Boulder, CO 80301....................303-443-4643
Baskin, Jason: 441 Walnut St #4, San Francisco, CA 94118....................415-923-1195
Bass Illustration & Design, Sam: PO Box 646, Concord, NC 28026....................704-455-6915
Basso, Bill: 38 Ogden Ln, Englishtown, NJ 07081....................908-431-5497
• **Batcheller, Keith: pg 788** 353 W 53rd St #1W, New York, NY 10019....................**212-682-2462**
url: www.americanartists.com / fax: 212-582-0090
• **Batelman Illustration: pg 1245** 407 Buckhorn Dr, Belvidere, NJ 07823....................**908-475-8124**
e-mail: batelman@epix.net / url: www.theispot.com / fax: 908-475-8924
• **Bates, Harry: pg 1246** PO Box 461, Bearsville, NY 12409....................**914-679-4695**
fax: 914-679-4292
Bates, Betty: 1060 Malone Rd, San Jose, CA 95125....................408-266-1972
Bates, George: 230 E 7th St #4C, New York, NY 10009....................212-475-3229
Batten, John: 286 Spring St #301, New York, NY 10013....................212-229-0073
Battikha, Jihad: 15 Oakland St, Watertown, MA 02172....................617-926-4102
Battuz, Christine: 4312 rue Saint-André, Montréal, QU H2J 2Z2....................514-522-3675
Bauder, Adam: 224 Highridge Dr, Belleville, IL 62223....................618-398-6530
Bauer, Ann: 29580 Northwestern Hwy, Southfield, MI 48034....................248-353-7722
Bauer, Bruce E: 2202 Richmond Rd, Staten Island, NY 10306....................718-667-8977
• **Bauer, Carla: pg 1070** 156 Fifth Ave #1100, New York, NY 10010....................**212-807-8305**
fax: 212-727-8094
Bauer, Robert: 987 Columbia Rd, Berkley, MI 48072....................810-541-8642
• **Bauer, Stephen: pg 464** 731 N 24th St, Philadelphia, PA 19130....................**215-232-6666**
url: www.deborahwolfeltd.com / fax: 215-232-6585
Baughman III, Murray: PO Box 365, Bluffton, SC 29910....................919-918-3965
Baughman, Christi: 467 Clearfield, Garland, TX 75043....................214-270-5925

Bauman, Jill: PO Box 152, Jamaica, NY 11415.................................718-886-5616
Bautista, David R: 50 Lillian Rd, Nesconset, NY 11767....................516-981-4092
Bautista, Rodino R.: 2116 Bldg A Galveston Ave, San Jose, CA 95122 408-295-9101
Baviera, Rocco: 41 King Williams St #210, Hamilton, ON L8R 1A2.......905-385-0047
Baxter, Daniel: RR3 Box 159, Feller Newmark Rd, Red Hook, NY 12571........914-758-0766
Beach Illus, Peter: 83 Moseley Ave, Newburyport, MA 01950 978-462-4275
• Beach, Lou: pg 544   7118 Upper River Rd, Prospect, KY 40059...........**502-228-9427**
   url: www.jettreps.com / fax: 502-228-8857
Beard, Edward Jr: 39 Niantic Trl, W Greenwich, RI 02817......................401-739-1511
Beauchamp, Jaime: 99-12 62nd Rd, Rego Park, NY 11374 212-512-2230
Beauchamp, Tom: 3110 Serra Way, Sacramento, CA 95816 916-736-9329
Beauchemin, Marie-France: 4651 rue de Salaberry, Carignin, QU J3L 3P9 514-447-4956
Beaulieu, Jean Pierre: 5116-A av.Casgrain, Montréal, QU H2T 1W7 514-272-3682
Beauregard, Christiane: 4020 rue, Montréal, QU H4C 2C7 514-935-6794
Beavers, Sean: 60 E 42nd St #1146, New York, NY 10165 212-953-7088
Bechtold, Glory: 22 N Morgan #113, Chicago, IL 60607...........................312-666-9494
Beck Comm, Joan: 2525 E Franklin Ave #301, Minneapolis, MN 55406.........612-338-8642
Beck, David: 68 E Franklin St, Dayton, OH 45459 937-433-8383
Beck, Melinda: 44 Fourth Pl, Brooklyn, NY 11231................................718-624-3266
Becker, Neesa N: 241 Monroe St, Philadelphia, PA 19147 215-925-5363
Becker, Pamela: PO Box 756, Marshall, CA 94940 415-663-1788
Becker, Polly: 156 W Newton St, Boston, MA 02118..............................617-247-0469
Becker, Ron: 265 E 78th St, New York, NY 10021 212-535-8052
Beckerman, Carol: 4350 Clark Ave, Long Beach, CA 90808.....................310-420-2603
Beckerman, Richard: 326 E 13th St #18, New York, NY 10003.................212-228-3465
Beckman, Melissa: New York, NY 212-967-7771
Bedrick, Jeffrey: 490 Rockside Rd, Cleveland, OH 44131 216-661-4222
Bedwell, Clem: 968 Watkins St NW, Atlanta, GA 30318 404-881-1101
• Bee, Johnee: pg 889   16 Phaedra, Laguna Niguel, CA 92677..............**949-495-3664**
   url: www.showcase.com/ fax: 949-495-0129
Beecham, Greg: 420 Lexington Ave #2760, New York, NY 10170 212-697-8525
Beecham, Tom: 420 Lexington Ave #2738, New York, NY 10170 212-697-8525
• Beekman, Doug: pg 318,319   327 E 89th St #3E, New York, NY 10128 ....**212-831-5650**
   fax: 212-831-6241
   1306 Alabama St, Huntington Beach, CA 92648 ....**714-969-7766**
   fax: 714-374-3744
Beelen Jr, Frank: 3404 Emerson Ave S #103, Minneapolis, MN 55408..........612-560-3629
Beerworth, Roger: 1723 S Crescent Hts Blvd, Los Angeles, CA 90035 213-933-9692
• Begin, Maryjane: pg 320,321   327 E 89th St #3E, New York, NY 10128 ....**212-831-5650**
   fax: 212-831-6241
   1306 Alabama St, Huntington Beach, CA 92648 ....**714-969-7766**
   fax: 714-374-3744
Bego, Delores: 1601 Third Ave #22A, New York, NY 10128 212-289-7467
Beha, Philippe: 5193 Rue Cartier, Montreal, QU H2H 1X6 212-581-8338
Behm, Kim: 400 First Ave N #218, Minneapolis, MN 55401......................612-375-9598
Behnke, Brian: 419 19th Ave E #6, Seattle, WA 98112..........................206-323-5470
Behrle Jr, Richard: 576 Ridgewood Rd, Maplewood, NJ 07040 201-762-1693
Behum, Cliff: 26384 Aaron Ave, Euclid, OH 44132 216-261-9266
• Beilfuss, Kevin: pg 158   420 Lexington Ave, New York, NY 10170 ....**212-986-5680**
   url: www.mendolaart.com / fax: 212-818-1246
Beisel, Dan: 4713 Ribble Ct, Ellicott City, MD 21043 410-461-6377
Belcastro, Mario: 2946 Sebolt Rd, Library, PA 15129 412-835-8470
Belchér, Steven: 1089 Brook Rd #100, Milton, MA 02186 800-309-1102
   4316 Cynthia St, Bellaire, TX 77401 281-870-1102
   232 Madison Ave #402, New York, NY 10016 212-889-8777
   227 Godfrey Rd, Weston, CT 06883 203-222-8777
Belding, Pam: 235 Byrondale Ave N, Wayzata, MN 55391....................612-476-1338
Belford, Kevin: 546 Rosewood Ln, St Louis, MO 63122..........................314-822-2424
• Bell, Charles: pg 796   2491 W 22nd Ave, Vancouver, BC B6L 1M3 ....**604-684-6826**
   url: www.repart.com / fax: 604-684-6826
• Bell, Karen: pg 803   1872 N Clybourn #404, Chicago, IL 60614................**773-935-8840**
   fax: 773-935-6191
Bell, Ron: 7118 Upper River Rd, Prospect, KY 40059.............................502-228-9427
Bella, Joset: 280 Madison Ave #1110, New York, NY 10016 212-545-9155
Bellamy, Gordon: 129 W 22nd St, New York, NY 10011 212-924-1380
Bellamy, John Ashley: 2200 N Haskell Ave, Dallas, TX 75204..................214-827-2032
Bellamy, Mike: 70 Willow Ave, Hackensack, NJ 07601 201-487-2342
Bellora, James: 1830 Columbia Pike #215, Arlington, VA 22204................703-271-1251
Bellucci, Patty: 532 La Guardia Pl, New York, NY 10012 212-924-8654
Belman, Vickie: 210 E 181st St #4A, Bronx, NY 10457 718-367-2688
Belmar, Inc: 16780 Oakomat Ave, Gaithersburg, MD 20877...................301-990-2130
Belove, Janice: 46 Carolin Rd, Montclair, NJ 07043 201-744-3760
Belser, Burkey: 1818 N St NW #110, Washington, DC 20036 202-775-0333
Bemus, Bart: 353 W 53rd St #1W, New York, NY 10019 212-682-2462
• Ben-Ami, Doron: pg 582,583
   232 Madison Ave #512, New York, NY 10016...............................**212-889-8777**
   fax: 212-447-1475
Ben-Nahum, Dovrat: 36 Wellington St, London, England, UK WC 2E 1712-408925
   58 W 15th St, New York, NY 10011 212-741-2539
Benas, Jeanne: 54 Alpine Dr, Latham, NY 12110 518-783-9556
• Bendell, Norm: pg 768   41 Union Sq W #918, New York, NY 10003.........**212-807-6627**
   url: www.idt.net/~dgagency / fax: 212-463-8175
Bender, Cherie: 455 NE 10th St, Boca Raton, FL 33432 561-368-5722
Bender, Greg: 21 N Main St #209, Port Chester, NY 10573......................914-934-7778
Bender, Howard: 515 Buxton Rd, Toms Rivers, NJ 08755 908-286-1512
Bender, Jon: 4089 San Felipe Rd, San Jose, CA 95135...........................408-238-8730
Bendis, Keith: 1423 County Route 7, Ancram, NY 12502 518-329-1986
• Benfanti, Russell: pg 112,113   420 Lexington Ave, New York, NY 10170 .....**212-986-5680**
   url: www.mendolaart.com (or) www.benfanti.com / fax: 212-818-1246
Benger, Brent: 420 Lexington Ave, New York, NY 10170.........................212-986-5680
Bengivenga, Ron: 92 Mercer Ave #2, N Plainfield, NJ 07060 908-757-4325
Benjamin, Vincent: 6001 Velasco, Dallas, TX 75206..............................214-871-0080
Benkwitz, Marcus: 141 5th Ave 8th Fl S, New York, NY 10010 212-505-9000
Benn, Nathan: 913 E Capitol St SE, Washington, DC 20003......................202-546-6182
Bennallack-Hart, Michael: 70 Rosaline Rd, London, England, UK SW6 7QT 171-610-1801
Bennett & Assocs: 415 E Villanova, Ojai, CA 93023 818-902-1440

Bennett, Bruce: 432 N Canal St #12, S San Francisco, CA 94080 415-583-8236
Bennett, Carol: 11365 W 72nd Pl, Arvada, CO 80005 303-420-8604
Bennett, Charles A: 547 E Villanova Rd, Ojai, CA 93023 805-646-0494
Bennett, Dianne: 200 W 15th St, New York, NY 10011 212-243-4209
Bennett, Gary: 7118 Upper River Rd, Prospect, KY 40059.......................502-228-9427
• Bennett, James: pg 248,249
   121 Madison Ave #5F, New York, NY 10016...............................**212-683-1362**
   url: www.renardrepresents.com / fax: 212-683-1919
Bennett, Martin: 2617 North Lovegrove St, Baltimore, MD 21218...............410-338-0785
Bennett, Mike: 20 Cornwall Dr, Windsor Locks, CT 06096......................860-627-9772
Bennett, Peter: 1340 El Prado Ave #37, Torrance, CA 90501...................310-782-7801
Bennett, Tom: 84 Withers St 5th Fl, Brooklyn, NY 11211........................718-349-2477
Benney, Robert: 50 W 96th St, New York, NY 10025 212-222-6605
Benny, Mike: 2600 Lake Austin Blvd #5108, Austin, TX 78703.................512-860-3224
• Benoit: pg 600   155 W 15th St, New York, NY 10011 ....**212-989-8770**
   fax: 212-989-7892
Benshoshan, Orna: 34 Bernard St, Lexington, MA 02173 617-863-1689
Benson, Ben: 800 Montrose Ave, South Pasadena, CA 91030...................818-441-1009
Benson, John D: 9273 Bellbeck Rd, Parkville, MD 21234.........................410-665-3395
Benson, Linda: 455 W 23rd St #8D, New York, NY 10011 212-366-1893
Bensusen, Sally: 932 S Walter Reed Dr CPAS 2nd Fl, Arlington, VA 22204 703-979-3931
Bentley, James: 2145 Parkinson St, Pierrefonds, QU H8Y 2Z3 514-894-0547
Berasi, Teresa: 39 Central Ave, Nyack, NY 10960..................................718-965-2231
Berasi-Rosen, Barbara: 457 State St #2A, Brooklyn, NY 11217.................718-522-2335
• Berendt, Eric: pg 1247
   1989-A Santa Rita Rd #307, Pleasanton, CA 94566.........................**925-462-6809**
   e-mail: eric@berendtstudio.com / url: www.berendtstudio.com / fax: 925-462-6807
Berg, Jeanne: 220 Palo Alto Ave #202, Palo Alto, CA 94301 415-853-8418
• Berg, John: pg 1248,1249   110 Cottage St, Buffalo, NY 14201..............**716-884-8003**
   fax: 716-885-4281
• Berg, Ron: pg 126,127   420 Lexington Ave, New York, NY 10170............**212-986-5680**
   url: www.mendolaart.com / fax: 212-818-1246
   71 Hewitt Ave, Toronto, ON M6R 1Y4.......................................**416-537-4069**
Bergendorff, Roger: 7429 Orien Ave, La Mesa, CA 91941.........................619-461-9807
Bergenstein, LA: 20800 Center Ridge Rd #414, Rocky River, OH 44116 216-331-9841
Berger, Bob: 52 McNairn Ave, Toronto, ON M5M 2H5 416-485-8555
Berger, Scott: 24 Dartmouth Dr, Framingham, MA 01701 508-877-8228
Berger, Vernon: 5300 Turnabout Ln, Austin, TX 78731 512-452-8866
Bergeron, Joe: 2901 Hall St #2, Endwell, NY 13760...............................607-786-0754
Bergin, Kieran: 171 Beech St, Kearny, NJ 07032 212-459-5244
• Bergman, Eliot: pg 990,991   250 South End Avenue, New York, NY 10280 .....**888-COOLPIX**
   e-mail: ebergman@emedia.net / url: www.ebergman.com
Berkey, John: 217 E 86th St Box 212, New York, NY 10028......................212-427-5632
Berkson, Nina: 2 Silver Ave #205, Toronto, ON M6R 3A2 416-530-1500
Berley, Brian: 2533 N Burling St #3, Chicago, IL 60614............................773-525-2441
Berlin, Jeff: 238A Summit Dr, Corte Madera, CA 94925 415-979-8488
Berlin, Rick & Rose: 870 Lock Lane Rd, Yorktown Hgts, NY 10598...............914-962-0526
Berman, Craig: 16 Taylor St, Dover, NJ 07801 201-366-4407
Berman, Irving S: 110 Leroy St 2nd Fl, New York, NY 10014.....................212-727-2655
Berman, Simi: PO Box 58, Chesterfield, NH 03443.................................603-256-8477
Bernal Computer Graphics: 10510 Ridgeland Ave #7, Chicago, IL 60415........708-424-7312
Bernal, Richard: 6239 Elizabeth Ave, St Louis, MO 63139 314-781-8851
Bernal, Richard: 327 E 89th St #3E, New York, NY 10128........................212-831-5650
Bernard, Charles: 38 Balsam Dr, Medford, NY 11763.............................516-654-0351
• Bernardin, James: pg 370,371,895
   327 E 89th St #3E, New York, NY 10128....................................**212-831-5650**
   fax: 212-831-6241
   1306 Alabama St, Huntington Beach, CA 92648 ....**714-969-7766**
   fax: 714-374-3744
   110 Rising Ridge Rd, Ridgefield, CT 06877..................................**203-438-7307**
Bernasconi, Jay: Group 121/1 Design, Boston, MA 02210 617-295-7837
Bernatchez, Patrick: 4398 Garnier, Montreal, QU H2J 3S2 514-523-0689
Berney, Katherine: 513 Browns Point Rd, Bowdoinham, ME 04008 207-666-8218
Bernstein, Linda A: 10-11 50th Ave, Long Island City, NY 11101.................718-784-1599
Berran, Bob: 60 E 42nd St #1940, New York, NY 10165 212-867-8092
Berrett, Randy: 1450 Morning Glory Dr, Petaluma, CA 94954...................707-763-7254
   15 W 72nd St, New York, NY 10023 212-799-2231
Berry Illus & Design, Inc, Bob: 38 Deerview Ln, Poughaug, NY 12570...........914-223-7925
Berry, Fanny Mellet: 155 E 38th St, New York, NY 10016 212-697-6170
Berry, John: 905 E Main Street, Wellsville, UT 84339 435-245-0762
Berry, Rick: 93 Warren St, Arlington, MA 02174....................................617-648-6375
Berryhill, Thomas: 1317 Maple St, Vancouver, BC V6J3S1 604-733-2492
Bersani, Shennen: 14 Rockwell Ave, Brockton, MA 02402.......................508-583-1648
Berthiaume, Pierre: 8262 rue Chambord #B, Montréal, QU H2E 1X7 514-725-7282
Bertram, Bob: St Louis, MO 314-968-4105
Bertsch, Greg: 3211 SW 10th Ave #307, Portland, OR 97201 503-228-6892
Beshwaty, Steve: 10245 rue JJ Gagnier, Montréal, QU H2B 2Z9 514-385-2274
Besser, Doug: 432 N Cuyler, Oak Park, IL 60302 708-660-9720
Besteman, Jackie: 468 Queen St E #104, Toronto, ON M5A 1T7................416-367-2446
• Betcher, Mark: pg 551   7118 Upper River Rd, Prospect, KY 40059............**502-228-9427**
   url: www.jettreps.com / fax: 502-228-8857
Bettag, Susannah: 960 Howard St, San Francisco, CA 94103 415-957-1854
Bettoli, Delana: 737 Vernon Ave, Venice, CA 90291 213-396-0296
Bevill, Jennifer: 106 Prospect Park W #2, Brooklyn, NY 11215 718-369-2758
Beylon, Cathy: 201 E 28th St, New York, NY 10016...............................212-532-0928
Bianco, Gerard: 1040 82nd St, Brooklyn, NY 11228..............................718-836-8637
Bianco, Peter: 201 Manning St, Needham, MA 02131 617-444-9077
Biber, Hugh: 666 Greenwich St #860, New York, NY 10014.....................212-675-5719
Bice, Paul Jr: 317 W 64th St, Inglewood, CA 90302................................310-677-2606
Biebl, Jim: 094 Arlian Ln, Carbondale, CO 81623 303-963-3309
Bieck, Kathy: 5855 Green Valley Cir #308, Culver City, CA 90230 310-642-2721
Bied, Donald: 180 Blackstone Blvd, Tonawanda, NY 14150 716-836-4138
Biedny, David: PO Box 151498, San Rafael, CA 94915 415-721-0638
• Biedrzycki, David: pg 517   217 E 86th St Box 212, New York, NY 10028......**212-427-5632**
   fax: 212-427-6372

Biegel, Michael David: PO Box 428, Allendale, NJ 07401 201-825-0084
Bierig, Brian: 225 Ridge Rd, Marshfield, MA 02050...............................781-834-0142
• **Biers, Nanette: pg 190,191** 194 Third Ave 3rd Fl, New York, NY 10003 ...**212-475-0440**
   url: www.vickimorganassociates.com / fax: 212-353-8538
Biever, Richard: 117 N Frederick, Evansville, IN 47711 812-426-7761
Big Pixel, The: 3108 Sumatra Pl, Costa Mesa, CA 92626...........................714-979-8001
• **Bigda, Diane: pg 698,699** 6 Parker Rd, Arlington, MA 02174 ....**781-641-2787**
   url: www.theispot.com/artist/bigda / fax: 781-641-2244
Biggs, Dan: PO Box 565, Bonita, CA 91908 619-421-2107
Bikadoroff, Roxanna: 82 Pierrepont St #4A, Brooklyn, NY 11201..............212-606-3881
Bild, Linda: PO Box 473, Agoura Hills, CA 91376..................................818-706-3906
Billin-Frye, Paige: 216 Walnut St NW, Washington, DC 20012 202-291-3105
• **Billout, Guy: pg 1250** 225 Lafayette St #1008, New York, NY 10012 ....**212-431-6350**
   url: www.theispot.com/artist/billout / fax: 212-941-0787
Bills, Mitchell: 53 Hamilton Dr, Bethany, CT 06524 203-393-2183
Billups, Ted: 1435 Addison, Chicago, IL 60613.....................................773-248-2347
Bilmes, Semyon: 2650 Highway 238, Jacksonville, OR 97530..
Bilotti, Jerry: 5900 Naples Plz #3, Long Beach, CA 90803 310-930-0192
• **Bilter, Lori: pg 644** 5353 Colewood Pl, Sarasota, FL 34232 ....**941-379-3087**
   208 Providence Rd, Annapolis, MD 21401 ....**410-349-8669**
   e-mail: acomport@aol.com / url: www.theispot.com/rep/wcstudio / fax: 410-349-8632
• **Binder, Amy: pg 308** 58 W 15th St, New York, NY 10011 ....**212-741-2539**
   url: www.showcase.com / fax: 212-741-4660
Binder, Eric: 1528 A Cherry Ave, Charlottesville, VA 22903 888-374-2278
Bing Design: 457 State St #2A, Brooklyn, NY 11217................................718-522-2335
Bing, Christopher: Boston, MA 617-674-1386
Binger, Bill: 171 Autumn Ridge Trail, Roswell, GA 30076 770-645-5528
Bingham, Edith: PO Box 51846, Pacific Grove, CA 93950..........................408-643-0922
Bingham, Sid: 2550 Kemper Ave, La Crescenta, CA 91214 818-957-0163
Biomedical Illustrations: 804 Columbia St, Seattle, WA 98104 206-682-8197
Birchman, Fred: 2561 E Madison Ave, Seattle, WA 98112 206-325-8312
Birdsall Designs, Mike: 106 Linden St #201, Oakland, CA 94607................510-433-8900
Birdsall, Scott: 441 Old Newport Blvd #306, Newport Beach, CA 92663.......714-645-4536
Birdsong, Keith: 32 W 40th Street, New York, NY 10018 212-575-6877
Birdsong, Stephanie K: 2009 Canal St, Venice, CA 90291 310-822-3509
Birdy, Dan: 280 Madison Ave #1110, New York, NY 10016 212-545-9155
Birkey, Randal: 635 S Home, Oak Park, IL 60304 708-386-5150
Birling, Paul: PO Box 257, Pleasantville, NY 10570................................914-747-2220
Birmingham, Barbara: 133 Barrow St #4A, New York, NY 10014 212-691-5587
Birmingham, Christian: 455 W 23rd St #8D, New York, NY 10011 212-366-1893
Birmingham, Lloyd P: 500 Peekskill Hollow Rd, Putnam Valley, NY 10579 914-528-3207
Birnbaum, Dianne: 17301 Elsinore Cir, Huntington Beach, CA 92647 714-847-7631
Birnbaum, Meg: 331 Harvard St #14, Cambridge, MA 02139 617-491-7826
Birtola, Theresa: 6155 Dunn Ave, San Jose, CA 95123 408-629-6517
Bischel, Mark: 112 W 9th St 2nd Fl, Kansas City, MO 64105 816-421-4473
   4419 Roanoke Pkwy, Kansas City, MO 64111 818-753-4852
Bishop, David: 610 22nd St #311, San Francisco, CA 94107 415-558-9532
Bishop, Don: 17104 NW Countryridge Dr, Portland, OR 97229 503-533-4744
Bishop, Randa: 9720 Camden Hills Ave, Las Vegas, NV 89128 212-206-1122
Bishop, Randy Mack: 6640 Lakewood Blvd, Dallas, TX 75214...................214-977-8206
Bishop, Rich: 37 Clement Dr, Asheville, NC 28805..................................704-299-4898
Bissett, Annie: 156 Crescent St, Northampton, MA 01060.........................800-515-1060
Bixby, Mark: 925 Elm Grove Rd, Elm Grove, WI 53122............................414-785-1940
Bjelland Design: 2822 Newport Blvd #A, Newport Beach, CA 92663............714-673-2855
• **Björkman, Steve: pg 220,956,957**
   260 E Chestnut #3005, Chicago, IL 60611 ....**312-787-8834**
   fax: 312-787-8172
   501 Fifth Ave, New York, NY 10017.......................................**212-490-2450**
   url: www.renardrepresents.com / fax: 212-697-6828
   2402 Michelson #200, Irvine, CA 92612 ....**949-261-1411**
   url: www.stevebjorkman.com / fax: 949-261-7528
• **Black, Dave: pg 814** 333 E 49th St, New York, NY 10017 ....**212-980-8061**
   url: www.theispot.com/artist/dblack / fax: 212-832-8778
   100 Bleecker St, New York, NY 10012......................................**212-982-6533**
   fax: 212-358-1586
Black, Fran: 853 Broadway #606, New York, NY 10003 212-777-6777
• **Blackard, Rob: pg 1145** 454 W 23rd St #4R, New York, NY 10011 ....**212-366-5831**
Blackdog: 330 Sir Francis Drake Blvd#A, San Anselmo, CA 94960 415-258-9663
Blackford, John: 201 W 21st St #10G, New York, NY 10001 212-807-0840
Blackmun, Kathryn: 1328 Kellam Ave, Los Angeles, CA 90026...................500-447-2278
• **Blackshear, Lisa: pg 1020,1021**
   208 W 23rd St #805, New York, NY 10011 ....**212-675-1083**
   url: www.users.interport.net/~lisab / fax: 212-242-3314
Blackshear, Thomas: 1367 N Las Palmas Ave, Hollywood, CA 90028 213-469-3400
Blackwell, Garie: 60 E 42nd St #505, New York, NY 10165 212-682-1490
Blackwell, Patrick: PO Box 324, N Truro, MA 02652 508-487-3336
Blae, Ken: 1089 Central Ave, Plainfield, NJ 07060 212-869-3488
Blahd, William: 3717 Alton Pl NW, Washington, DC 20016 202-686-0179
Blair, David: PO Box 174 Cooper Sta, New York, NY 10276 212-228-1514
• **Blair, Dru: pg 795** 32 W 40th Street, New York, NY 10018 ....**212-575-6877**
   fax: 212-953-0728
Blais, Richard: 8777 rue Albanel, Saint-léonard, QU H1P 2X9 514-324-2774
Blake, Bob: 359 Ft Washington Ave #6G, New York, NY 10033 212-781-4855
Blake, Juliet: 109 Crane Root #109, Royal Palm Beach, FL 33411 407-478-9210
Blake, Marty: 141-10 28th St, Flushing, NY 11354.................................212-206-0066
   PO Box 266, Jamesville Terr, Jamesville, NY 13078...........................315-492-1332
Blakey, Paul: 137 Fifth Ave 11th Fl, New York, NY 10010 212-529-3556
Blalock, Ron: 5019 Swinton Dr, Fairfax, VA 22032 703-764-2071
Blanchard, Marie: 69 Whiteheather Blvd, Scarborough, ON M1V 1P7 416-292-3527
Blanchette, Dan: 428 Charleston Dr, Bollingbrook, IL 60440 630-972-0092
Blanchette, G: 108 Patchen Rd, Burlington, VT 05403.............................802-862-1583
Blandino Illustration, Carmelo: 1535 Sherbrooke W 3rd Fl,
   Montreal, QU H3G 1L7 514-934-5583
• **Blank, Jerry: pg 490,491** 2149 Lyon St #5, San Francisco, CA 94115.........**415-921-7140**
   email: art@conradreps.com / url: www.conradreps.com / fax: 415-921-3939
Blankenship, Sandy: 36431 32nd Ave, Auburn, WA 98001 253-838-7155

Blanton, Philip: Po Box 2187, Noble, OK 73068 405-971-0123
Blasutta, Mary Lynn: 156 Huguenot St, New Paltz, NY 12561...................914-256-0830
Blauers, Nancy: 50 Walnut St, Stratford, CT 06497...............................203-377-6109
Blauweiss, Stephen: 32-15 41st St, Long Island City, NY 11103.................718-204-8335
Blavatt, Kathleen: 743 Sunset Cliffs Blvd, San Diego, CA 92107 619-222-0057
Blechman, Laurel: 7853 Mammoth Ave, Panorama City, CA 91402 818-785-7904
• **Bleck, Cathie: pg 294,295** 58 W 15th St, New York, NY 10011 ....**212-741-2539**
   url: www.showcase.com / fax: 212-741-4660
• **Bleck, John: pg 1251** 3636 N Bosworth, Chicago, IL 60613.....................**773-975-8232**
   e-mail: jbleck@suba.com / fax: 773-975-8233
Bleck, Linda: 642 W Aldine #1, Chicago, IL 60657.................................773-281-0286
• **Blessen, Karen: pg 179** 194 Third Ave 3rd Fl, New York, NY 10003 ....**212-475-0440**
   url: www.vickimorganassociates.com / fax: 212-353-8538
Bliok, Leo: 25 Old Colony Ln, Great Neck, NY 11023..............................516-466-8879
Bliss, Anna Campbell: 27 University St, Salt Lake City, UT 84102 801-364-5835
Bliss, Harry F: 45 Washington St, Nyack, NY 10960...............................914-358-8690
Bliss, Phil: 22 Briggs Ave, Fairport, NY 14450......................................716-377-9771
Bliss, Rachel: 194 Third Ave 3rd Fl, New York, NY 10003 212-475-0440
Blitt, Barry: 34 Lincoln Ave, Greenwich, CT 06830 203-622-2988
Bloch, Alex: 1712 E Butler Cir, Chandler, AZ 85225 602-899-0600
• **Bloch, Anthony: pg 1447** 854 W 181 St #6D, New York, NY 10033 ....**212-927-6856**
   fax: 212-928-4792
Bloch, Joseph I: 716 Ivy St, Pittsburgh, PA 15232.................................412-359-6405
Blonder, Ellen: 91 Woodbine Dr, Mill Valley, CA 94941 415-388-9158
Bloom, Tom: 46 Caterson Terr, Hartsdale, NY 10530..............................914-761-1877
Bloomfield, A Scott: 1972 Golden Ave, Long Beach, CA 90806 310-334-7315
Blower, Gale Holiday: 420 Lexington Ave #220, New York, NY 10170 212-687-3460
Blubaugh, Susan M: 2182 Clove Rd, Staten Island, NY 10305 212-570-6731
Blum, Marianne: 113 Stone Meadow, S Salem, NY 10590 914-533-2379
Blum, Melinda: 464 Mariposa Ave, Sierre Madre, CA 91024.....................818-798-9897
Blumenthal, Warshaw: 104 E 40th St #201, New York, NY 10016 212-867-4225
Bluming, Joel: 328 E 19th St, New York, NY 10003 212-673-0558
Blumrich, Christoph: 149 Broadway, Greenlawn, NY 11740 516-757-0524
• **Blumstein, Paul: pg 421** 60 E 42nd St, New York, NY 10165-1940...........**212-867-8092**
   e-mail: DHLT@aol.com / url: www.HT-LTD.com / fax: 212-949-1977
Board, Inge: 3340 Bowman St, Philadelphia, PA 19129............................215-438-8422
Boatman, Thomas: 1843 NE 177th, Seattle, WA 98155...........................206-361-0627
Boatwright, Phil: 2342 Stillwater Dr, Mesquite, TX 75181 214-222-7571
Bober, Kathleen: 5706 16th St NW, Washington, DC 20011 202-829-7704
• **Bobnick, Dick: pg 1119**
   9801 Dupont Ave S #165, Bloomington, MN 55431 ....**612-881-1008**
   url: www.showcase.com & www.theispot.com/artist/bobnick
Bocci, Michael: 1529 First St, Simi Valley, CA 93065 805-581-4936
Bock, Christian: 276 Lansdowne Ave, Carle Pl, NY 11514........................516-997-9887
Boddy, Joe: 5375 Skyway Dr, Missoula, MT 59804.................................406-251-3587
Boddy, William: 609 N 10th St, Sacramento, CA 95814...........................916-443-5001
Bodell, Scott: 9617 Vinewood Dr, Dallas, TX 75228 214-320-8433
Bodily, Michael: 1671 Cabrosa, Mission Viejo, CA 92691.........................714-457-1228
Boehm, Roger: Pier 33 North, San Francisco, CA 94111...........................415-956-4750
Boerger, Andrew: 83 Walnut Ave, Corte Madera, CA 94925 415-924-7881
Bogan, Paulette: 55 W 11th St PH-W, New York, NY 10011 212-243-1694
Boge, Garrett: 6606 Soundview Dr, Gig Harbor, WA 98335 206-851-5158
Boger, Claire: 2000 Madison Ave, Memphis, TN 38104 901-725-0855
Boguslav, Raphael: 200 E 78th St, New York, NY 10021 212-570-9069
Bohbot, Michel: 3823 Harrison St, Oakland, CA 94611............................510-547-0667
Bohn, Rex: 14 N First Ave #1410, St Charles, IL 60174............................630-513-1269
Bohn, Richard: 595 W Wilson St, Costa Mesa, CA 92627 714-548-6669
Boie, Chuck: 925 Elm Grove Rd, Elm Grove, WI 53122............................414-785-1940
Boies, Alex: c/o Rahoru Odagawa, Japan,...0797-81-2012
   126 N 3rd St, Minneapolis, MN 55401 612-333-2418
Boileau, Lowell: 45 Colorado, Highland Park, MI 48203 313-865-3084
Boise, Kathyjean: 1233 De Haro St, San Francisco, CA 94107 415-285-3014
Boldman, Craig: PO Box 18128, Fairfield, OH 45018 513-868-2874
• **Bolesky, John: pg 797** 2491 W 22nd Ave, Vancouver, BC B6L 1M3 ....**604-684-6826**
   url: www.repart.com / fax: 604-684-6826
Bolinsky, David: 350 Center St #207, Wallingford, CT 06492 203-284-1224
Boll, Maxine: 200 Aquetong Rd, New Hope, PA 18938 215-862-2091
Boll, Thomas: 9500 Wyoming Ave South, Bloomington, MN 55438.............642-942-6119
Bolling, Bob: 2395 NE 185th St, N Miami Beach, FL 33180 305-931-0104
• **Bollinger, Peter: pg 322-325** 327 E 89th St #3E, New York, NY 10128......**212-831-5650**
   fax: 212-831-6241
   1306 Alabama St, Huntington Beach, CA 92648 ....**714-969-7766**
   fax: 714-374-3744
Bollman, Angela: 1274 Quincy St, Ashland, OR 97520 800-435-6509
Bolno, Kathy Lynn: 330 W Springfield Ave, Philadelphia, PA 19118............215-242-9165
Bolourchian, Flora: 12485 Rubens Ave, Los Angeles, CA 90066 213-827-8457
• **Bolster, Rob: pg 723** 7 Washington Street, Beverly, MA 01915 ....**978-921-0887**
   e-mail: leighton@leightonreps.com / url: www.leightonreps.com / fax: 978-921-0223
• **Bolten, Jennifer: pg 543** 7118 Upper River Rd, Prospect, KY 40059 ....**502-228-9427**
   url: www.jettreps.com / fax: 502-228-8857
Bolz, Wolf: 3518 Eden Croft Dr, Raleigh, NC 27612 919-571-0123
Bomba, Ron: 421 N 36th St, Seattle, WA 98103 206-634-0777
Bomeisl, James: 70 Madison Ave, Demarest, NJ 07627 201-784-3480
Bommarito, Mark: 66 Sentinel Pl, Aliso Viejo, CA 92656..........................714-362-5242
Bonanno, Paul: 142 W Golf Ave, S Plainfield, NJ 07080 908-756-8867
Bonauro, Tom: 601 Minnesota St #216, San Francisco, CA 94107 415-648-5233
Bond, Dennis A: 6481 Miriam Circle, E Petersburg, PA 17520 717-569-5823
Bond, Paul: 1421 N Dearborn #302, Chicago, IL 60610 312-280-5488
Bond, Tracey: 1135 University Ave #3B, New York, NY 10010 212-563-1077
Bondante, Chris: 3015 W Speedway, Tucson, AZ 85745...........................520-624-5994
Bondurant, Steve: 34 Elton St, Rochester, NY 14607..............................716-271-7020
Bonforte, Lisa: 201 E 28th St, New York, NY 10016................................212-532-0928
Bonham, Liz: 809 Shelmar, Euless, TX 76039 817-354-1399
Bonham, Patti: 10006 Cedar Creek, Houston, TX 77042 713-977-6522
Bonilla, Michael: 763 Hidden Cir, Dayton, OH 45458 937-435-5058

- **Brooks, Andrea: pg 1115** Pier 33 North, San Francisco, CA 94111..............**415-956-4750**
url: www.coreygrahamreps.com / fax: 415-391-6104
99 Bank St #3G, New York, NY 10014 ....**212-633-1477**
Brooks, Clare Vanacore: New York, NY 212-245-3632
Brooks, Dick: 11712 N Michigan Rd #100, Zionsville, IN 46077 317-873-1117
Brooks, Ed: 20 W 87th St #6A, New York, NY 10024 212-595-5980
- **Brooks, Hal: pg 1139,** San Francisco, CA **415-431-8474**
New York, NY **212-531-0255**
- **Brooks, Lou: pg 922,923,** New York, NY **212-245-3632**
url: www.loubrooks.com
- **Brooks, Nan: pg 690** 666 Greenwich St #860, New York, NY 10014..........**212-675-5719**
url: www.hkportfolio.com / fax: 212-675-6341
- **Brooks, Rob: pg 226,227** 501 Fifth Ave, New York, NY 10017...................**212-490-2450**
url: www.renardrepresents.com / fax: 212-697-6828
Brother, Kelly: 5250 Sycamore Grove Ln, Memphis, TN 38120........................901-761-4204
Brothers, Barry: 1920 E 17th St, Brooklyn, NY 11229 718-336-7540
Browarny, Walt: PO Box 461, Halifax Central, NS B3J 2P8...............................902-425-4654
Brown Illus, Rick: PO Box 341, Furlong, PA 18925...215-794-8186
Brown, Alan J: 700 W Pete Rose Wy Lobby B360, Cincinnati, ON 45203........513-723-4440
Brown, Bradford: 43 Vassar Ave, Newark, NJ 07112 201-926-9229
Brown, Calef: 12761 Caswell Ave, Los Angeles, CA 90066.................................310-397-7603
Brown, Carolyn: 27 Edward St, St Albans, VT 05478 802-527-1911
Brown, Charley: 3450 Third St #1D, San Francisco, CA 94124 415-648-9430
Brown, Charlie: 9444 Old Katy Rd #108, Houston, TX 77055..............................713-468-8161
Brown, Christina: 3999 Brae Burn Dr, Eugene, OR 97405...................................541-344-0598
Brown, Colin: 23 Ganton St, London, England, UK WIV 1LA...............................71-287-9191
- **Brown, Dan: pg 522,524** 89 FIfth Ave #901, New York, NY 10003...........**212-627-1554**
fax: 212-627-1719
Brown, John Peter: 235 E 22nd St #16R, New York, NY 10010..........................212-684-7080
Brown, Judith Gwyn: 522 E 85th St, New York, NY 10028 212-288-1599
Brown, Kathi: 666 Bantry Ln, Stone Mountain, GA 30083 404-296-9666
Brown, Kimberly S: 19 Spratt Ave, Staten Island, NY 10306 718-667-7874
- **Brown, Marc: pg 741** 865 Delaware St, Denver, CO 80204 ....**303-820-2599**
toll-free **800-417-5120**
url: www.artagent.com / fax: 303-820-2598
Brown, Matthew: 720 Jonathon Pl, Escondido, CA 92027 760-738-4643
Brown, Michael David: 108 E 35th St #2, New York, NY 10016 212-889-3337
Brown, Nancy: 1619 Broadway, New York, NY 10019...212-265-7600
Brown, Remi: Box 186, Roselle Park, NJ 07204..908-245-1218
Brown, Rick: 60 E 42nd St #822, New York, NY 10165.......................................212-682-1490
Brown, Sue Ellen: 6315 Richmond Ave #H, Dallas, TX 75214............................214-823-9545
Brown, William L: 6704 Westmoreland Ave, Takoma Park, MD 20912 301-270-2014
Browne, Rob: 75 Arbor Rd, Menlo Park, CA 94025..415-325-6832
Browning, Vivian Wu: 12640-A Springbrook Dr, San Diego, CA 92128 415-467-9676
- **Brownson, Matt: pg 1253** 419 Athena Rd, Golden, CO 80403 ....**303-582-0787**
e-mail: brownson@ecentral.com / fax: 303-582-0787
Brownwood, Bruce: 15402 Saranac Dr, Whittier, CA 90604 310-947-5770
Browski, Richard: 453 N Genesee Ave, Los Angeles, CA 90036 213-653-2454
Bru, Salvador: 5130 Bradley Blvd, Chevy Chase, MD 20815..............................301-654-4420
- **Bruce, Sandra: pg 1055** 13997 Emerald Ct, Grass Valley, CA 95945 ....**530-477-1909**
fax: 530-477-2232
Bruce, Taylor: 853 Broadway #1201, New York, NY 10003.................................212-677-9100
Bruce, Tim: 5850 Brookway Dr, Winston-Salem, NC 27105 910-767-8890
Bruemmer, Betsy: Box 1743, Edgartown, MA 02539 508-627-9264
Brugger, Bob: 1930 Robinson St, Redondo Beach, CA 90278..............................310-372-0135
Brun, Robert: 76 State St, Newburyport, MA 01950...508-462-1948
Bruner, Rick Ernest: PO Box 1469, Shepherdstown, WV 25443 304-876-0945
Brunettin, Alan: 1031 Wesley Ave, Evanston, IL 60202......................................847-492-0979
Bruning, Bill: 118 E 26th St, Minneapolis, MN 55404 612-871-4539
60 E 42nd St #822, New York, NY 10165...212-682-1490
3286 Ivanhoe, St Louis, MO 63139...314-781-7377
Brunkus, Denise: 111 Perryville Rd, Pittstown, NJ 08867..................................908-735-2671
Bruno, Peggy: 51 Grove St Cranberry Cove, Marshfield, MA 02050....................617-837-6896
Bruntz, Bev: 1704-A North Willow Woods Dr, Anaheim, CA 92807 714-693-1285
Brünz, Robert: 600 Seventh Ave #523, Seattle, WA 98104.................................800-750-5809
Bruvel, Gil: PO Box 1187, Kula, HI 96790...800-278-8357
Bryan, Diana: PO Box 391, Saugerties, NY 12477 914-246-3182
Bryan, Mike: Chicago, IL 847-222-0337
Bryant Illus, Web: 9310 Coronado Terr, Fairfax, VA 22031 703-359-1039
Bryant, Amy: Dallas, TX...214-696-4950
Bryant, David C: 25 Puritan Rd, Somerville, MA 01245 617-629-9982
Bryant, Eric: 9903 Gravois #C, St Louis, MO 63123...314-631-7200
Bryant, Rick J: 18 W 37th St #301, New York, NY 10018....................................212-594-6718
Bryant, Wallace E: 9310 Coronado Terr, Fairfax, VA 22031 703-276-6499
Bryne, Brian: 2736 W Leland, Chicago, IL 60625..312-878-5227
Bsales, David A: 166 Hadley Ave, Clifton, NJ 07011 201-473-1101
Bua: 2044 Dracena Dr, Los Angeles, CA 90027 213-661-2510
Bucci, Richard A: 20 Narragansett Ave, Narragansett, RI 02882........................401-783-6903
Buchanan, Nigel: 133 N Montclair Ave, Dallas, TX 75208 214-943-2569
Buchanan, Steve: 317 Colebrook Rd, Winsted, CT 06098...................................203-379-5668
Buchanan, Thomas: 41 S Rainbow Crest Dr, Golden, CO 80204 303-526-0413
Buchanan, Yvonne: 18 Lincoln Pl #2L, Brooklyn, NY 11217 718-783-6682
Buchart, Greta: 2512 E Thomas Rd #2, Phoenix, AZ 85016 602-381-1332
Buchberger, Brian: 610 Water St #310, Milwaukee, WI 53202 414-273-8194
Buchman, Doug : 3108 Sumatra Pl, Costa Mesa, CA 92626.................................714-979-8001
Buchs, Thomas: 925 Elm Grove Rd, Elm Grove, WI 53122..................................414-785-1940
Buckley, Marjory: 3850 Eddingham Ave, Calabasas, CA 91302............................818-222-5445
Buckley, Paul: 222 W 14th St #2D, New York, NY 10011 212-243-1696
Buckner, Derek: 133 Spring St 2nd Fl, New York, NY 10012 212-925-4340
Budd, Ken: 30 Ipswich St #107, Boston, MA 02215 617-424-0279
- **Buelow, Alicia: pg 298,299** 58 W 15th St, New York, NY 10011................**212-741-2539**
url: www.showcase.com / fax: 212-741-4660
Bueno, Luz: 548 Cragmont, Berkeley, CA 94708 510-524-2163
Buerge, Bill: 20421 Callen Dr, Topanga, CA 90290 310-455-3181
Buffington, Hank: 26 W Rt 70 #233, Marlton, NJ 08053 609-770-0868

Bugatto, Dominic: 468 Queen St E #104, Toronto, ON M5A 1T7.........................416-367-2446
Bugzester, Ruth: 302 W 56th St, New York, NY 10019...212-757-2964
Buhler, Ray Varn: Blue Mountain Rd, Wilseyville, CA 95257 209-293-4169
Buket: 65 Seventh Ave #2, Brooklyn, NY 11217 212-333-5676
Bull, Michael: 2350 Taylor St, San Francisco, CA 94133......................................415-776-7471
Bull, Mike: 2925 Griffith St, San Francisco, CA 94124 415-467-9676
Bullerin, David: 32-25 58th St, Woodside, NY 11377 718-777-2665
- **Bulleit, Dan: pg 744** 865 Delaware St, Denver, CO 80204..........................**303-820-2599**
toll-free **800-417-5120**
url: www.artagent.com / fax: 303-820-2598
Bumas, Jonathan: 99-34 67th Rd #6A, Forest Hills, NY 11375 718-459-5903
Bunk, Richard S: 1207 S Vista View Ct, Mahomet, IL 61853 217-586-6733
Bunn, Darian: 114-81 178th St, St Albans, NY 11434 718-523-6757
Bunnell, Deb Troyer: 346 Lincoln St, Carlisle, PA 17013 717-249-0937
Burch, Allan M: 404 Red Maple, Kirbyville, MS 65679..417-335-2410
Burckhardt, Marc: 112 W 41st St, Austin, TX 78751 512-458-1690
Burgard, WC: 2785 Heather Way, Ann Arbor, MI 48104 313-971-3014
Burgess, Lucy: 569 Hacienda Dr, Scotts Alley, CA 95066 408-438-3659
Burgio, Trish: 227 Godfrey Rd, Weston, CT 06883 203-222-8777
- **Burgoyne, John: pg 1143** 26 Statler Rd, Belmont, MA 02478.......................**617-489-4960**
e-mail: level9@thecia.net / url: www.theispot.com/artist/burgoyne / fax: 617-489-0629
Burke, Jack: 301 E 7th St #201, Charlotte, NC 28202..704-333-9693
Burke, Kelly: 2443 Filmore St #280, San Francisco, CA 94115.............................415-397-2860
Burke, Kevin: 4501 Lyons Rd, Miamisburg, OH 45342 513-866-4013
Burke, Philip: 1948 Juron Dr, Niagara Falls, NY 14304.......................................716-297-0345
Burleson, Joe: 60 E 42nd St #1940, New York, NY 10165 212-867-8092
Burman, Harry: 89 FIfth Ave #901, New York, NY 10003.....................................212-627-1554
Burman, Rob: 29580 Northwestern Hwy, Southfield, MI 48034............................248-353-7722
Burn, Ted: 5134 Timber Trail NE, Atlanta, GA 30342 404-255-1430
- **Burnett, Bob: pg 1254** 237 Lowell St, Wakefield, MA 01880.........................**781-245-3474**
e-mail: boburnett@earthlink.net
Burnett, Linda: 476 Loridans Dr, Atlanta, GA 30342 404-875-1363
Burnett, Lindy: 1841 Lake Cypress Dr, Safety Harbor, FL 34695.........................813-725-4438
Burns, Brad: 11287 Rolling Hills Dr, Dublin, CA 94568 510-829-7939
Burns, Bridget: 3333 Mentone Ave #17, Los Angeles, CA 90034...........................818-879-2016
Burns, Charles: 210 Brown St, Philadelphia, PA 19123 215-925-7618
Burns, Dan: 647 Allison Dr, Cleveland, OH 44143...216-382-9633
Burns, Jim: 11 Kings Ridge Rd, Long Valley, NJ 07853...908-813-8718
Burns, John: Rte 1 Box 487A, Bluemont, VA 22012 703-955-4786
Burns, Rhonda: 847A Second Ave #150, New York, NY 10017...............................212-486-0177
Burnside, John E: 4204 Los Feliz Blvd, Los Angeles, CA 90027 213-665-8913
- **Burr, Dan: pg 426** 60 E 42nd St, New York, NY 10165-1940 ....**212-867-8092**
e-mail: DHLT@aol.com / url: www.HT-LTD.com / fax: 212-949-1977
Burris, Jon: 125 Concord St, Brooklyn, NY 11201 718-625-6261
Burrows & Assoc, Bill: 3100 Elm Ave West, Baltimore, MD 21211 410-889-3288
Burton, Caroline: 330 8th St, Jersey City, NJ 07302 201-656-6502
Burton, Jeff: 334 State St #550, Los Altos, CA 94022..415-777-1095
Busacca, Mark: 2150 Hyde St #1, San Francisco, CA 94109 415-776-4247
Busch, Lee F: 1 Fitchburg St #C503, Somerville, MA 02143 617-488-3614
- **Busch, Lonnie: pg 26,27** 108 E 35th St #2, New York, NY 10016 ....**212-889-3337**
url: www.theispot.com/artist/busch / fax: 212-889-3341
Bush, George: 381 Park Ave S #1120, New York, NY 10016...................................212-889-2400
Bush, Lorraine: 570 Church Lane Rd, Reading, PA 19606.....................................215-779-8565
Buske, Gregory A: 19 Stuyvesant Oval #2D, New York, NY 10009 212-505-9342
Bustamante, Gerald: PO Box 470818, San Francisco, CA 94147 415-383-9026
Bustamente, Orlando: 1310 Worstead Dr, Fayetteville, NC 28314 910-868-9767
Butcher, Jim: 1357 E MacPhail Rd, Bel Air, MD 21014 410-879-6380
Butkovich, Anthony: 812 Branard #3, Houston, TX 77006....................................713-523-0388
Butler, Andi: 505 E Sherman, Holy, MI 48442 810-634-8824
Butler, Callie: 4307 Alder Dr, San Diego, CA 92116...619-280-2343
- **Butler, Chris: pg 988,989** 7018 Redwing Pl, Longmont, CO 80503 ....**303-494-4118**
fax: 303-530-5036
Butler, David: 29 Public Sq, Mt Vernon, OH 43050 614-397-1236
Butler, Ralph: 18521 Tarragon Way, Germantown, MD 20874 301-972-3669
Butler, Steve: 407 Indiana Ave, Lynn Haven, FL 32444..904-271-0452
Butterfield, Ned: 278 Cedar Ave, Islip, NY 11751 516-277-3151
Buttner, Tom: 2021 Pinician Dr, Fenton, MO 63026...314-861-1134
Buttram, Andy: 68 E Franklin St, Dayton, OH 45459 937-433-8383
Butts, Christopher C: 919 St Andrews Dr, Malvern, PA 19355 610-993-2395
Buxton, John: 4584 Sylvan Dr, Allison Park, PA 15101 412-486-6588
- **Buz Studio: pg 1113** **877-614-8111**
fax: 877-614-8111
- **Buzzelli, Christopher: pg 1113**
406 East 9th Street #18, New York, NY 10009...**877-614-8111**
Buzzworks Studio: 231 Mayatt Rd, Barrington, RI 02806 401-245-8438
Byer, Lou: 1449 N Pennsylvania, Indianapolis, IN 46202...317-264-0843
Bynum, Janie: 132 Edgemoor, Kalamazoo, MI 49001...888-342-0707
Byram, Stephen: 52 68th St #1, Guttenberg, NJ 07093 201-869-7493
Byrd, Bob: 280 Madison Ave #1110, New York, NY 10016..212-545-9155
Byrnes, Patrick: 3622 N Hamilton, Chicago, IL 60618 773-472-3649
Byrnside, Lora: 212 A Street, Shelbyville, KY 40065 502-633-5726

C

Cabarga, Leslie: 7660 Beverly Blvd #416, Los Angeles, CA 90036 213-549-0700
Cabib, Leila: 8601 Buckhannon Dr, Potomac, MD 20854...301-299-4158
- **Cable, Annette: pg 547** 7118 Upper River Rd, Prospect, KY 40059..............**502-228-9427**
url: www.jettreps.com / fax: 502-228-8857
Cable, Jerry: 133 Kuhl Rd, Flemington, NJ 08822 908-788-6750
- **Cable, Mark: pg 550** 7118 Upper River Rd, Prospect, KY 40059..................**502-228-9427**
url: www.jettreps.com / fax: 502-228-8857
Cabossel, Jannine: Rt 19 Box 90-8, Santa Fe, NM 87505 505-983-4099
Caceres, Francisco: 466 W26th St, New York, NY 10001..212-627-3520
Cacy, Michael: 537 SE Ash St, Portland, OR 97214..503-233-7715
Cadman, Joel: 41-15 50th Ave #3F, Sunnyside, NY 11104 718-784-1267
Cage, Gary: 34 Flamingo Rd, Levittown, NY 11756..516-735-1983

Caggiano, Tom: 83-25 Dongan Ave, Elmhurst, NY 11373.............718-651-8993
Cagle, Daryl: CA...805-967-4529
Cain, David H: 200 W 20th St #607, New York, NY 10011...............212-633-0258
Cairns, Brian: 58 W 15th St, New York, NY 10011......................212-741-2539
Caito, Mike: 7414 Foxfield Dr, Hazelwood, MO 63042..................314-839-1714
Calabrese, Vincent: 6357 Sharon Hills Rd, Charlotte, NC 28210........704-553-9677
Calabro, Carol: 475 Massachusetts Ave #B, Lexington, MA 02173.......781-863-6206
Calanché, Magué: 545 Belvedere St, San Francisco, CA 94117..........415-664-9511
Calder, Jean E: 69 Melrose Ave, Toronto, ON M5M 1Y6.................416-484-6349
Caldicott, Karen: 40 S 6th St, Brooklyn, NY 11211.....................718-486-7704
• Caldwell, Kirk: pg 869 137 Fifth Ave 11th Fl, New York, NY 10010 ....**212-529-3556**
   fax: 212-353-0831
Caldwell, Tony: PO Box 5901, Breckenridge, CO 80424................970-547-9612
Calhoun, Dia: 2712 N 10th, Tacoma, WA 98406......................206-383-9111
• Call, Greg: pg 328,329 327 E 89th St #3E, New York, NY 10128.............**212-831-5650**
   fax: 212-831-6241
   1306 Alabama St, Huntington Beach, CA 92648 ....**714-969-7766**
   fax: 714-734-3744
Callahan, Brian: 3 Hidden St, Providence, RI 02706...................401-421-2344
Callahan, Donna: 15 Connie Dr, Foxboro, MA 02035..................508-543-2705
Callahan, Kevin: 26 France St, Norwalk, CT 06851....................203-847-2046
Callanan, Maryjane: 218 Elm Court, Rhinelander, WI 54501...........715-369-2130
Callaway, Nicholas: 70 Bedford St, New York, NY 10014..............212-929-5212
Callaway, Terry: 4518 Mt Vernon, Houston, TX 77006................713-528-6827
Calle, Chris: 316 Old Sib Rd, Ridgefield, CT 06877...................203-438-5226
Calleja, Bob: 490 Elm Ave, Bogota, NJ 07603.........................201-488-3028
Callies, Timothy J: N6441 906th St, Elk Mound, WI 54739.............715-879-5899
Calomino, Rick: 4837 W Hayward Pl, Denver, CO 80212...............303-455-0930
Calsbeek, Craig: 710 Wilshire Blvd #510, Santa Monica, CA 90401 310-394-6037
• Calver, Dave: pg 186 194 Third Ave 3rd Fl, New York, NY 10003.........212-475-0440
   url: www.vickimorganassociates.com / fax: 212-353-8538
Calvert, Jeff: 9518 Whiskey Bottom Rd, Laurel, MD 20723.............301-236-4139
Calvert, Trudy L: PO Box 7272, Bloomington, IN 47407................812-876-9969
Calviello & Cohen Multimedia: 133 Cedar Rd, E Northport, NY 11731 516-368-2031
Calviello, Joe: 23-35 Bell Blvd #6J, Bayside, NY 11360...............718-423-3797
Cam's Happy Pencil Studio: 1819 Fiske Ave, Pasadena, CA 91104.......626-797-8890
Cameron, Chad: 5134 Timber Trail NE, Atlanta, GA 30342.............404-255-1430
Cameron, Laura: 812 W 19th St #2M, Chicago, IL 60608...............773-995-1955
Camp, Barbara: 60 E 42nd St #822, New York, NY 10165...............212-682-1490
Camp, Janeane: 2746 Castle Rock Rd, Diamond Bar, CA 91765.........909-598-8747
Campbell, Annie: 5650 Fitzgerald Rd, Trumansburg, NY 14886.........607-387-9086
• Campbell, Denise Hilton: pg 1255
   716 Sanchez St, San Francisco, CA 94114........................**415-285-8267**
   e-mail: Salzman@designlink.com
   17336 Montero Rd, San Diego, CA 92128 ....**619-485-6771**
   New York, NY..**212-997-0115**
   Chicago, IL..**312-782-2244**
Campbell, Harry: 17 Plainfield, Metuchen, NJ 08840..................732-548-7544
Campbell, Jenny: 731 N 24th St, Philadelphia, PA 19130..............215-232-6666
Campbell, Jim: 420 Lexington Ave, New York, NY 10170...............212-986-5680
Campbell, Laird: 162 E 23rd St #5B, New York, NY 10010..............212-505-5552
Campbell, Mark: 91 Ocean Pkwy #1D, Brooklyn, NY 11318.............718-854-5162
Cane, Eleni: 2163 Walnut St #200, Baldwin, NY 11510................516-378-3203
• Cane, Linda: pg 462 731 N 24th St, Philadelphia. PA 19130............**215-232-6666**
   url: www.deborahwolfeltd.com / fax: 215-232-6585
• Cangemi, Antonio: pg 556 7118 Upper River Rd, Prospect, KY 40059.........**502-228-9427**
   url: www.jettreps.com / fax: 502-228-8857
Canger, Joseph: 110 Howard St, Perth Amboy, NJ 08861...............908-826-6835
Caniglia, Carmine: 295 Macintosh Rd, Westchester, PA 19382..........610-436-1545
Cannizzaro, Gregory, J: 107 York Rd, Towson, MD 21204...............410-296-2402
Cannone, Gregory: 1982 Lake Wood Rd, Toms River, NJ 08753..........908-349-4332
• Cannoy, Lynne: pg 330,331 327 E 89th St #3E, New York, NY 10128.......**212-831-5650**
   fax: 212-831-6241
   1306 Alabama St, Huntington Beach, CA 92648 ....**714-969-7766**
   fax: 714-734-3744
Cantarella, Virginia Hoyt: PO Box 54, S Westerlo, NY 12163...........518-966-4419
Cantin, Charles: 809 Cartier, Quebec, QU G1R 2R8...................418-524-1931
Canty, Ray: 1512 W Marlene Ave, Peoria, IL 61614....................309-682-7941
Canty, Thomas: 178 Old Country Way, Braintree, MA 02185............617-843-7262
Cap Productions/Comp Art Plus: 311 W 34th St 8th Fl, New York, NY 10001 212-279-0800
Capaldi, Gina: 1563 Calle Ciervos, San Dimas, CA 91773..............818-967-6483
Caponigro, John Paul: Rte 1 Box 1055, Cushing, ME 04563.............207-354-8578
Caporale, Wende: 3850 Eddingham Ave, Calabasas, CA 91302..........818-222-5445
   Studio Hill Farm Rte 116, N Salem, NY 10560...................914-669-5653
Capozzoli, Jerry: 509 N Wells #3, Chicago, IL 60610..................312-661-0169
Caprario, Dean: 178 Chandler Ave, Staten Island, NY 10314...........718-720-1545
Capshaw, Stan: 41959 County Rd #652, Mattawan, MI 49071............616-668-5556
Capstone Studios, Inc: 2820 Westshire Dr, Los Angeles, CA 90068......213-464-2787
Caputo, Vince: PO Box 257, Pleasantville, NY 10570..................914-747-2220
Caradonna, Robert: 19830 25th Ave NE, Seattle, WA 98155............206-364-4073
Carambat, David: 21339 Wilson, Covington, LA 70433.................504-893-2432
Carbone, Lou: 805 Clinton St, Hoboken, NJ 07030....................201-656-6008
Carboni, Ron: RR #1 Box 94, Millerton, NY 12546....................914-373-9228
Cardarelli, Mike: 2900 El Camino # 131, Las Vegas, NV 89102..........702-257-0343
Cardella, Elaine: 24 Elizabeth St, Port Jervis, NY 12771..............914-856-8889
Carden, Vince: 2308 E Glenoaks Blvd, Glendale, CA 91206.............818-956-0807
Cardinal, Alain: 4611 rue Boyer, Montréal, QU H2J 3E5...............514-527-2262
Cardona Studio: 43 E 19th St, New York, NY 10003...................212-254-4996
Carey, Mark: 3109 Pelham St, Chesapeake, VA 23324.................804-396-5768
Carleton, Kim: 20 Yarmouth Rd, Norwood, MA 02062.................617-762-3228
Carlo:...514-620-8912
Carlson Illus, Fred: 118 Monticello, Monroeville, PA 15146.............412-856-0982
• Carlson, Gary: pg 660,661 227 Godfrey Rd, Weston, CT 06883.........**203-222-8777**
   e-mail: artco@snet.net / fax: 203-454-9940
• Carlson, Jonathan: pg 28,29 108 E 35th St, New York, NY 10016.............**212-889-3337**
   url: www.theispot.com/artist/carlson / fax: 212-889-3341

Carlson, Larry: RR2 Box 980, Rochester, VT 05767....................802-767-4355
Carlson, Lisa: 407 14th Ave SW, Rochester, MN 55902................507-252-0311
Carlson, Sue: 102 Bonita Rd, Waretown, NJ 08758...................800-707-0980
Carlson, Sue: 1412 Jarvis Dr, Manhattan, KS 66502 913-539-5535
Carlton, Ashley: 10900 Ventura Blvd, Studio City, CA 91604...........818-761-6644
Carmack, David: 78 Kilsyth Rd #5, Boston, MA 02135.................617-728-8582
Carmichael, Dennis: 19355 Pacific Coast Hwy, Malibu, CA 90265.......310-456-5910
Carnes, Bruce: 16 Phaedra, Laguna Niguel, CA 92677................714-495-3664
Carol, Joan: 345 Lewis St, Oakland, CA 94116......................510-268-3615
Caroline S: 143 Ripley, San Francisco, CA 94110....................415-558-8760
Carpenter, Anita: 14800 NW Cornell Rd #7A, Portland, OR 97229.......303-692-1068
Carpenter, Carolyn: 99 Park Ave #210A, New York, NY 10016..........800-398-9544
Carpenter, Joe & Polly: 72 Spring St #1003, New York, NY 10012.......212-431-6666
Carr, Alan K: 51 Dean St #2, Brooklyn, NY 11201....................718-596-8850
Carr, Barbara: 245 E 40th S #19D, New York, NY 10016...............212-370-1663
Carr, Noell: 30 E 14th St #A & B, New York, NY 10003...............212-675-1015
Carr, Ted: 21865 Rainbow Rd, Barrington, IL 60010..................847-381-6976
Carreiro, Ron: 6 Hillside Dr, Plymouth, MA 02360...................508-224-9290
Carrier, Alan: 1521 Bidwell Dr, Chico, CA 95926....................916-894-5911
Carroll, Justin: 3286 Ivanhoe, St Louis, MO 63139..................314-781-7377
Carroll, Mark Scott: 3301A S Jefferson Ave, St Louis, MO 63118........314-773-2600
Carroll, Michael: 538 Bellefort, Oak Park, IL 60302.................708-386-6125
Carroll, R Scott: 501-Hayes St #17, San Francisco, CA 94102...........415-553-8000
Carroll, Tim: 1337 California St #5, San Francisco, CA 94109..........415-929-7050
Carroll, William: 316 Franklin St, Quincy, MA 02169.................617-479-4229
Carruthers, K.J.:...514-553-7875
Carruthers, Roy: 115 West 2nd Street, New York, NY 10011...........212-989-4600
Carsello, Margaret: 516 N Vine, Hinsdale, IL 60521..................630-794-9120
• Carson, Jim: pg 1142 11 Foch St, Cambridge, MA 02140.............**617-661-3321**
   fax: 617-661-3321
Carson, Rene: PO Box 6638, Jersey City, NJ 07306...................201-946-0028
Carsten, Dan: 17 Lothian Rd #9, Brighton, MA 02135................617-787-6171
Carter Illus, Stephanie: 416 W Pender St #203, Vancouver, BC V6B 1T5....604-876-8477
• Carter, Abby: pg 691 666 Greenwich St #860, New York, NY 10014.........**212-675-5719**
   url: www.hkportfolio.com / fax: 212-675-6341
Carter, Alice: 828 Pine Hill Rd, Stanford, CA 94305.................415-424-9886
Carter, Anne: 5 Oakdale St #2, Boston, MA 02130...................617-522-7097
Carter, Bunny: 200 E 78th St, New York, NY 10021.................212-570-9069
Carter, Eric Akil: 120 McMechen St, Baltimore, MD 21217.............410-462-0829
Carter, Greg: 6020 Beardsley Ct, Raleigh, NC 27609.................919-676-0238
Carter, Jane: 460 W 42nd St 2nd Fl, New York, NY 10036.............212-967-6655
Carter, Kip: 213 Elderberry Cir, Athens, GA 30605..................706-542-5384
Carter, Mike: 32 Oaken Gateway, Toronto, ON M2P 2A1..............416-250-5433
• Carter, Penny: pg 1256 12 Stuyvesant Oval #4A, New York, NY 10009 ......**212-473-7965**
   fax: 803-324-1024
• Carter, Stephanie: pg 616 5002 92nd Ave SE, Mercer Island, WA 98040....**206-232-7873**
   fax: 206-232-7908
Carter, Zane: 345 S Patrick St, Alexandria, VA 22314................703-836-2900
Cartwright, Reg: PO Box 1251, New York, NY 10023..................212-774-4271
Carverletchermiller: 3940 Spring Dr #11, Reno, NV 89502..............702-828-4700
Casals, Pepe: 758 Brookridge Dr NE, Atlanta, GA 30306..............404-872-7980
Casanas, Cristina: 779 Riverside Dr #B12, New York, NY 10032.........212-362-5738
Case, Robert: 635 W Desert Broom Dr, Chandler, AZ 85248............602-855-1959
• Cash, Megan Montague: pg 1214 85 N Third Street, Brooklyn, NY 11211....**718-388-3473**
   url: //members.aol.com/megancash/home.html / fax: 718-388-3473
Cash-Walsh, Tina: 170 Camel Vista Dr, San Rafael, CA 94901...........415-457-0698
• Casilla, Robert: pg 872 866 United Nation Plaza, New York, NY 10017......**212-644-2020**
   url: www.spar.org
Casmer, Tom: 880 Cleveland Ave S, St Paul, MN 55116...............612-696-1664
Casper, Daniel S: One Devon Way, Hastings-on-Hudson, NY 10706.......914-478-7548
Cassano, Rose A: 253 Marcy Loop, Grants Pass, OR 97527.............541-476-9074
Cassidy, Nancy: 1 Beardsley Rd, New Milford, CT 06776...............860-350-3426
Cassity, Don: 207 Pine St, Bonner Springs, KS 66012.................816-761-7314
Cassler, Carl: 420 Lexington Ave, New York, NY 10170...............212-986-5680
Casson, Sophie: 597 av Desjardins, Montréal, QU H1V 2G2............514-899-7761
Castaneda, Teresa: 53 Pennsylvania St, Denver, CO 80203.............303-744-8110
Castellanos, Carlos: 131-74 80th Ln N, West Palm Beach, FL 33412......407-791-7993
Castleman, Doug: 14629 Hilltree Rd, Santa Monica, CA 90402..........310-454-6178
Castleman, Valerie: 60 Gramercy Park #9A, New York, NY 10010........212-254-5430
Catalano, Dominic: 68 W 5th St #8, Oswego, NY 13126...............315-342-8596
Catalano, Sal: 114 Boyce Pl, Ridgewood, NJ 07450..................201-447-5318
Cathcart, Marilyn: 6933 Columbia Ave, St Louis, MO 63130...........314-862-2644
Caty, Bartholomew: 198 Seventh Ave #4R, Brooklyn, NY 11215.........718-965-0790
Cavanagh, Tom: 119 NW 93rd Terr, Coral Sprngs, FL 33071............305-753-1874
Cave, Matt: 17 NE 2nd Ave, Dania, FL 33004.......................954-925-3186
Cavey, Bob: 710 Canterbury Cir, Chanhassen, MN 55317..............612-949-2902
Cayard, Bruce: 2323 Marrywood Dr, Los Angeles, CA 90046...........213-656-7194
Cayea, John: 39 Lafayette St, Cornwall, NY 12520..................914-534-8794
Ceballos, John: 1047 Broadmoor Dr, Napa, CA 94558................707-226-1026
   68 E Franklin St, Dayton, OH 45459...........................937-433-8383
Ceccarelli, Chris: 3427 Folsom Blvd, Sacramento, CA 95816...........916-455-0596
Cedergren, Carl: 225 Gramsie Rd, St Paul, MN 55126................612-481-1429
Celis, Sal: 3712 NE 150th St, Seattle, WA 98155....................206-366-0412
Cellini, Joseph: 501 Fifth Ave, New York, NY 10017.................212-490-2450
• Celmer, Steve: pg 788 353 W 53rd St #1W, New York, NY 10019.........**212-682-2462**
   url: www.amerartists.com / fax: 212-582-0090
Celsi, Lolita: 2229 NW Everett, Portland, OR 97210.................503-241-1491
Celusniak, Chris: 99 Park Ave #210A, New York, NY 10016............800-398-9544
• Cepeda, Joe: pg 1257 3340 Ivar Avenue, Rosemead, CA 91770...........**626-288-8205**
   e-mail: cepeda@earthlink.net / fax: 626-288-8205
Cerebio, Carlos: 2177 Qualicum Dr, Vancouver, BC V5P 2M3...........604-325-8861
Cericola, Anthony: 731 N 24th St, Philadelphia, PA 19130............215-232-6666
Cerulli, Frank: 281 Mercer St, Stirling, NJ 07980..................908-580-1198
• Chabrian, D: pg 523,529 89 Flfth Ave #901, New York, NY 10003..........**212-627-1554**
   fax: 212-627-1719

Chada, Ritu: 150 E 30th St #6A, New York, NY 10016 212-684-8134
Chaffee, James: 5400 Colusa Way, Sacramento, CA 95841 415-442-1822
Chakkour, Mario Henri: 4319 Gingham Ct, Alexandria, VA 22310 703-317-1184
Chall, Barry: 21573 Foothill Blvd, Hayward, CA 94541 800-959-6994
Chambers, Clayton: 432 26th St SE, Cedar Rapids, IA 52403 319-390-8881
Chambers, Gregory: 7925 W Washington Blvd, River Forest, IL 60305 708-771-3515
Chambers, Jill: 36 E 12th St, Holland, MI 49423 616-392-7274
Chambers, Lindy: RR 1 Box 7, Hockley, TX 77447 713-467-6819
Champie, Zhon: 2500 Summit St, Kansas City, MO 64108 816-435-2000
Champlin, Dale: 2405 NW Thurman St, Portland, OR 97210 503-203-8300
Chan, David: 8 Debden Rd, Markham, ON L3R 6Y6 416-513-8741
Chan, Eric: 15046 Septo St, Mission Hills, CA 91345 818-841-1600
• **Chan, Harvey: pg 561,562,563** 155 Lippincott St, Toronto, ON M5S 2P3 ....**416-505-9522**
toll-free **888-277-7200**
e-mail: shelley@sbaillustrates.com / url: www.sbaillustrates.com
Chan, Pak Sing: 10219 Caminito Pitaya, San Diego, CA 92131 619-571-3361
• **Chan, Ron: pg 302,303** 58 W 15th St, New York, NY 10011 ....**212-741-2539**
url: www.showcase.com / fax: 212-741-4660
Chandler, Fay: 444 Western Ave-Engine Hs Std, Brighton, MA 02135 617-254-0428
Chandler, Jean: 385 Oakwood Dr, Wyckoff, NJ 07481 201-891-2381
Chandler, Karen: 80 Lettington Rd, Locust Valley, NY 11560 516-671-0388
1159 Green St #1, San Francisco, CA 94109 415-776-2972
Chandler, Roger: 597 Riverside Ave, Westport, CT 06880 203-226-4724
99 Park Ave #210A, New York, NY 10016 800-398-9544
Chang Illus, Michelle: 36 3rd St #4L, Brooklyn, NY 11231 718-797-4427
Chang, Alain: 232 Madison Ave #402, New York, NY 10016 212-889-8777
Chang, Charles: 227 Godfrey Rd, Weston, CT 06883 203-222-8777
Chang, Dr Rodney: 2119 N King #206, Honolulu, HI 96819 808-845-6216
Chang, George: 67 E 11th St #403, New York, NY 10003 212-388-0633
Chang, Gloria: 3739 Cogswell Rd, El Monte, CA 91732 818-579-2007
Chapell, Ellis: 89 FIfth Ave #901, New York, NY 10003 212-627-1554
Chapin, Patrick O: 17 E 3rd St #A, Kansas City, MO 64106 816-421-7470
• **Chapman, CM: pg 1141** 2823 27th St NW 1, Washington, DC 20008 ....**888-422-0320**
e-mail: cmchapman@cmgrafik.com / url: www.cmgrafik.com / PIN 6870
Chapman, Craig: 5775 Big Tree Rd, Orchard Park, NY 14127 716-662-6002
Chapman, Lisa: 420 Lexington Ave, New York, NY 10170 212-986-5680
• **Chappell, Ellis: pg 523,540** 89 Fifth Ave #901, New York, NY 10003 ....**212-627-1554**
fax: 212-627-1714
Charamonte, Vince: 920 19th St, Rockford, IL 61104 815-398-6657
Charest, Anne Marie: 8139 rue, Montréal, QU H2P 2L2 514-388-7385
Charlier, Mark: 33 E Cedar #5C, Chicago, IL 60611 312-421-2668
Charmatz, Bill: 25 W 68th St, New York, NY 10023 212-595-3907
• **Charpentier, Russ: pg 775** 83 Walnut Ave, Corte Madera, CA 94925 ....**415-924-7881**
toll-free **800-924-7881**
url: www.ritareps.com / fax: 415-924-7891
Chartier, Francois: Montreal, QU 514-842-7795
Chase Design, Margo: 2255 Bancroft Ave, Los Angeles, CA 90039 213-668-1055
Chau, Tungwai: 666 Greenwich St #860, New York, NY 10014 212-675-5719
Chaussé, Monique: 4580 av Coloniale, Montréal, QU H2T 1W2 514-687-8907
Chausse, Norbert: 1709 Blue Spruce Dr, Sykesville, MD 21784 410-549-1506
Chauvin, Lynn: 344 Rosewood Ave SE, E Grand Rapids, MI 49506 616-458-5634
Chayka, Douglas: 2515 Emerson Rd, Weedsport, NY 13166 315-834-6902
Che, Cindi: 1400 Bowe Ave #1911, Santa Clara, CA 95051 408-248-9580
Cheer, Colin: 129 Hudson St, Somerville, MA 02144 617-864-8502
Chelkowska, Malgosia: 1477 Chomley Crescent, Ottawa, ON K1G 0V9 613-737-7198
• **Chen, David: pg 482,483** 2149 Lyon St #5, San Francisco, CA 94115 ....**415-921-7140**
e-mail: art@conradreps.com / url: www.conradreps.com / fax: 415-921-3939
Chen, Paul: 1000 John R Rd #201, Troy, MI 48083 248-583-6070
Chen, Rick: 3289 George Cir, Pasadena, CA 91107 818-578-1718
Chen, Tini: 69 Greenway Terr, Forest Hills, NY 11375 718-263-5969
Chen, Tony: 241 Bixley Heath, Lynbrook, NY 11563 516-596-9158
• **Cheney, George: pg 619** 5002 92nd Ave SE, Mercer Island, WA 98040 ....**206-232-7873**
fax: 206-232-7908
• **Cheney, Rob: pg 860** 280 Madison Ave, New York, NY 10016 ....**212-545-9155**
e-mail: irmeli@aol.com / url: www.spar.org/holmberg / fax: 212-545-9462
Cheng Chen, Jian: 171S Normandie Ave #312, Los Angeles, CA 90004 213-384-7108
Cheng, Kevin: 10 Kelvinway Dr, Scarborough, ON M1W 194 416-495-7312
• **Chenoweth, Gloria: pg 1258** 8026 31st Ave NW, Seattle, WA 98117 ....**206-789-7633**
e-mail: g.chenoweth@aol.com / fax: 206-784-4571
Cherington, Nina: 4347 Leach Ave #1, Oakland, CA 94602 510-482-2046
Chermayeff, Ivan: 58 W 15th St, New York, NY 10011 212-741-2539
Chernin, Donna: 169 Central St, Acton, MA 01720 508-266-1000
• **Chernishov, Anatoly: pg 1186** 4 Willowbank Ct, Mahwah, NJ 07430 ....**201-327-2377**
fax: 201-236-9469
Cherry, Eric: 99 Park Ave #210A, New York, NY 10016 800-398-9544
Cherry, Jim: 902 E Palm Ln, Phoenix, AZ 85006 602-340-0715
Cheshire, Benjamin: 8500 Leesburg Pike, Vienna, VA 22182 800-759-3327
Chessare, Michele: 210 Dartmouth Pl W, Peachtree City, GA 30269 770-487-8246
Chesser, Preston: 3831 Cherry Laurel Dr, Pensacola, FL 32504 904-476-4311
Chester, Harry: 20 W 20th St #404, New York, NY 10011 212-627-8888
• **Chesterman, Adrian: pg 538** 89 FIfth Ave #901, New York, NY 10003 ....**212-627-1554**
fax: 212-627-1719
Chestnut, David: 2233 Kemper Ln, Cincinnati, OH 45206 513-861-1400
468 Queen St E #104, Toronto, ON M5A 1T7 416-367-2446
Cheung, Phil: 2149 Lyon St #5, San Francisco, CA 94115 415-921-7140
Chevrier, Andrée: Montréal, QU 514-298-5393
Chewning, Randy: 666 Greenwich St #860, New York, NY 10014 212-675-5719
• **Chezem, Douglas: pg 147** 420 Lexington Ave, New York, NY 10170 ....**212-986-5680**
url: www.mendolaart.com / fax: 212-818-1246
Chiang, George: 280 Riverside Dr #10H, New York, NY 10025 212-663-7907
Chiaramonte, Vince: 4300 N Narragansett, Chicago, IL 60634 847-670-0912
• **Chicknelli, Mark: pg 637** 5 E 17th St 6th Fl, New York, NY 10003 ....**212-691-2667**
fax: 212-633-1844
4 E Ohio Studio B, Chicago, IL 60611 ....**312-321-1336**
fax: 312-321-1350
Chid Studios: 115 Rumsey Rd, Yonkers, NY 10705 914-963-6997
Chien-Li, Wu: 71-17 Sutton Pl, Flushing, NY 11365 718-969-6704
Chinchar, Alan: PO Box 891448, Houston, TX 77289 713-922-7151
Ching, Darren: 312 E 6th St #C-3, New York, NY 10003 212-254-0963
Chipurnoi, Minda: 1085 Warburton #508, Yonkers, NY 10701 914-963-8959
Chironna, Ronald: 122 Slosson Ave 2nd Fl, Staten Island, NY 10314 718-720-6142
Cho, Young Sook: 68 E Franklin St, Dayton, OH 45459 937-433-8383
• **Chodos-Irvine, Margaret: pg 679** 2814 NW 72nd St, Seattle, WA 98117 ....**206-784-1136**
url: www.kolea.com / fax: 206-784-1171
Choi, Jae: Brooklyn, NY 718-875-9078
Chollick, Phyllis: 8507 Homelawn St, Jamaica, NY 11432 718-658-0670
Chontow, Scott: PO Box 771025, Coral Springs, FL 33077 954-340-9882
• **Chorney, Steven: pg 145** 420 Lexington Ave, New York, NY 10170 ....**212-986-5680**
url: www.mendolaart.com / fax: 212-818-1246
Chouinard, Roger: 2205 Stoner Ave, Los Angeles, CA 90064 310-478-0771
Chow, Jim: 4033 Aurora Ave N, Seattle, WA 98103 206-633-3445
Chow, Rita: 280 Madison Ave #1110, New York, NY 10016 212-545-9155
Chow, Tad: 50-44 68th St, Woodside, NY 11375 718-899-9813
Chrestatos, Cathy: 261 Jackson Ave, Syosset, NY 11791 516-364-2196
Christe, Dory: 9 Ivy Ln, Glen Burnie, MD 21060 410-553-6655
Christensen, David M: 4338 Manchester Pl, Cypress, CA 90630 714-761-3488
Christensen, Kent: 325 E 77th St #3H, New York, NY 10021 212-744-3050
Christensen, Wendy: 165 E 32nd St, New York, NY 10016 212-686-3514
Christian, Russell: 871 Driggs Ave #3, Brooklyn, NY 11211 718-499-1587
Christiana, Dave: 731 N 24th St, Philadelphia, PA 19130 215-232-6666
Christiansen, Lee: 423 S Platt St, Red Lodge, MT 59068 406-446-2284
Christie, Greg: 853 Broadway #606, New York, NY 10003 212-777-6777
Christine, Tina: 390 Queen Quay W #1614, Toronto, ON M5V 3A6 416-345-1676
Christjansen, Dorte: 4450 E 4th St, Long Beach, CA 90814 310-434-6014
Christmas, Lawrence: 161-34 120th Ave, Jamaica, NY 11434 718-525-1350
• **Christopher: pg 1259** 1 Shoal Ct #75, Sacramento, CA 95831 ....**916-421-2983**
url: www.showcase.com
• **Christopher, Tom: pg 188,189**
194 Third Ave 3rd Fl, New York, NY 10003 ....**212-475-0440**
url: www.vickimorganassociates.com / fax: 212-353-8538
Chronister, Robert: 99 Park Ave #210A, New York, NY 10016 800-398-9544
Chua, Ning: 102 E Liberty St #413, Savannah, GA 31401 912-234-6049
Chui Studio: 1772 Hendrickson Ave, Merrick, NY 11566 516-223-8474
Chui, John: 610 Humboldt St, Richmond, CA 94805 510-233-2333
Chun Graphics, Milt: 4946 Kilauea Ave #4, Honolulu, HI 96816 808-735-6436
Chung, Harry: 8347 116th St #5A, Richmond Hill, NY 11418 718-805-8766
Chung, Mei K: 82 W 3rd St, New York, NY 10012 212-228-9100
Chung, Thomas: 6969 Schilling Ave, San Diego, CA 92126 619-536-2853
Church, Caroline: 23 Ganton St, London, England, UK WIV 1LA 71-287-9191
• **Churchman, John: pg 788** 353 W 53rd St #1W, New York, NY 10019 ....**212-682-2462**
url: www.amerartists.com / fax: 212-582-0090
Chwast, Eve: 18 E 16th St 7th Fl, New York, NY 10003 212-255-6456
Chwast, Jacqueline: 23-83 37th St, Astoria, NY 11105 718-626-0840
Chwast, Seymour: 18 E 16th St 7th Fl, New York, NY 10003 212-255-6456
Cianciarulo, Krys: 10 2nd St NE #214, Minneapolis, MN 55413 612-379-7117
Ciarallo, Anna Maria: 402 Lee St, Evanston, IL 60602 847-492-0450
Ciardiello, Joe: 2182 Clove Rd, Staten Island, NY 10305 718-727-4757
• **Ciccarelli, Gary: pg 788** 353 W 53rd St #1W, New York, NY 10019 ....**212-682-2462**
url: www.amerartists.com / fax: 212-582-0090
Cicchetti, John: PO Box 57, Scarsdale, NY 10538 914-279-5573
Ciemny, Ray: 54 Fitch's Bridge Rd, Groton, MA 01450 508-448-0028
• **Cigliano, Bill: pg 221** 501 Fifth Ave, New York, NY 10017 ....**212-490-2450**
url: www.renardrepresents.com / fax: 212-697-6828
Cilio, Chuck: 38 Dorethy Rd, Redding, CT 06896 203-938-3541
Cincotti, Gerald: 42 Freeport Dr, Burlington, MA 01803 617-229-4974
Ciss Illustration, Julius: 89 Lynnhaven Rd, Toronto, ON M6A 2L1 416-784-1416
CK Design: 43 E 19th St, New York, NY 10003 212-254-4996
Clapp, John: 4961 Monaco Dr, Pleasanton, CA 94566 510-462-6444
• **Clar, David Austin: pg 496,497**
2149 Lyon St #5, San Francisco, CA 94115 ....**415-921-7140**
email: art@conradreps.com / url: www.conradreps.com / fax: 415-921-3939
Clark Design, Jennifer: 349 County Route 2, Accord, NY 12404 914-687-4011
Clark Illus, Tim: 1256 25th St, Santa Monica, CA 90404 310-453-7613
Clark Studio: 709 Stannage Ave, Albany, CA 94706 510-528-6968
Clark, Bob: 300 East 34th Street, New York, NY 10018 212-629-1519
Clark, Bradley: 19 Stuyvesant Oval, New York, NY 10009 212-505-9342
Clark, Cynthia Watts: 36 Haggerty Hill Rd, Rhinebeck, NY 12572 914-876-2615
Clark, Emma Chichester: 42 Delavan St, Brooklyn, NY 11231 718-624-1906
Clark, Gary F: 823 Light Rd, Bloomsburg, PA 17815 717-387-1689
Clark, Jennifer: 4164 S 36th St, Arlington, VA 22206 703-671-7187
Clark, Johnston: 1210 Gregory Ave, Wilmette, IL 60091 847-251-2444
Clark, K Daniel: 3218 Steiner St, San Francisco, CA 94123 415-922-7761
Clark, Scott: 212 Mt Vernon Dr, Decatur, GA 30030 404-378-2937
Clark, Steve: 2151 Springs Place, Longmont, CO 80501 303-682-0074
Clark, Tim: 101 H St Suite G, Petaluma, CA 94952 707-773-1201
Clarke, Bob: 55 Brook Rd, Pittsford, NY 14534 716-248-8683
• **Clarke, Christopher: pg 523,537**
89 Fifth Ave #901, New York, NY 10003 ....**212-627-1554**
fax: 212-627-1719
• **Clarke, Greg: pg 709** 455 W 23rd St #8D, New York, NY 10011 ....**212-366-1893**
url: www.andtheart.com / fax: 212-604-9643
Clarke, Johnson: 46 Brooksdale Rd, Brighton, MA 02135 617-783-7075
Clarke, Peter W: PO Box 2253, Plainville, MA 02762 508-695-5141
• **Clayton, Christian: pg 1151**
135 S LaBrea Ave #1, Los Angeles, CA 90036 ....**213-936-8448**
e-mail: oldways@ix.netcom.com / fax: 213-933-2519
Clee, Suzanne K: 7520 Crittenden St, Philadelphia, PA 19119 215-247-8883
Clegg, Dave: 3571 Aaron Sosebee Rd, Cumming, GA 30130 770-887-6306
• **Cleland, Janet : pg 1083** 1 Mono Lane, San Anselmo, CA 94960 ....**415-457-1049**
fax: 415-453-5851
Clement, Cameron: 3422 S Fresno St, Fort Smith, AR 72903 501-646-7734

Copie: 286 Oakwood Dr, Paramus, NJ 07652 201-265-3405
Corben, Richard: 43 E 19th St, New York, NY 10003 212-254-4996
• **Corbitt, John: pg 1262** 150 Brambleton Ave, Virginia Beach, VA 23510 ....**757-446-2729**
e-mail: jcorbitt@infi.net / fax: 757-623-5283
Cordano, Marty: PO Box BW, Bisbee, AZ 85603 602-432-4634
Cordes, Kathy: 3714 Rexmere Rd, Baltimore, MD 21218 410-467-8140
• **Corey, Brian: pg 1263** 378A Benefit St #6, Providence, RI 02903 ....**888-287-9880**
Corfield, Marie: 48 Sylvan Place, Nutley, NJ 07110 201-667-8071
Corio, Paul: 263 First Ave #3, New York, NY 10003 212-228-4630
Cork, Richard: 4158 N Greenview Ave, Chicago, IL 60613 773-549-4108
Corkery, John: 1606 Dublin Dr, Silver Spring, MD 20902 301-681-1641
Cornelius, Ray-Mel: 1526 Elmwood Blvd, Dallas, TX 75224 214-946-9405
Cornelius-Karp: 26 E Maple Rd, Greenlawn, NY 11740 516-466-4093
Cornell, Laura: 118 E 93rd St #1A, New York, NY 10128 212-534-0596
Cornner, Haydn: 60 E 42nd St #822, New York, NY 10165 212-682-1490
Cornu, Alain: 757A Ave Champangneur, Outremont, QU H2V 3P9 514-948-5888
Correll, Cory: 11511 Sullnick Way, Gaithersburg, MD 20878 301-977-7254
Corrette, Nicholas Moses: 203 College St, Burlington, VT 05401 802-864-9241
Corrigan, Paul: 12901 N MacArthur #196, Oklahoma, OK 73142 405-720-0922
Corvi, Donna: 1591 Second Ave #3, New York, NY 10028 212-628-3102
Cory, Larry: 1000 John R Rd #201, Troy, MI 48083 248-583-6070
Cosentino, Cara: 2277 SW Olympic Club, Palm City, FL 34990 561-288-3155
Cosentino, Carlo: 10752 Vianney, Montreal, QU H2B 1K1 514-384-9596
• **Cosgrove, Dan: pg 793** 200 W 15th St, New York, NY 10011 ....**212-243-4209**
203 N Wabash Ave #1102, Chicago, IL 60601 ....**312-609-0050**
url: homepage.interaccess.com/~cosgrove
Costantino, Frank M: 13B Pauline St, Winthrop, MA 02152 617-846-4766
Costantino, Valerie: 2037 New Hyde Park Rd, New Hyde Park, NY 11040 516-358-9121
Costas, Laura: 5726 Fourth St NW, Washington, DC 20011 202-291-8757
Coté, Anne: 2100 rue Saint-Denis, Montréal, QU H2X 3K7 514-499-8916
Cote, Danny: 31 Googin St, Lewiston, ME 04240 207-783-3056
Cote, Genevieve: 400 Demaisonneuge, Montreal, QU H3A 1L4 514-282-9399
Coté, Martin: 1030 rue, Montréal, QU H2Z 1P3 514-875-6723
Coto, Bob: 13 Cloverhill Place, Montclair, NJ 07042 201-509-8301
• **Cottone, Carol: pg 884** 16 Phaedra, Laguna Niguel, CA 92677 ....**949-495-3664**
url: www.showcase.com/ fax: 949-495-0129
Couch, Anna Partch: 538 Redlands Ave, Newport Beach, CA 92663 714-631-3946
Couch, Greg: 43 N Midland Ave, Nyack, NY 10960 914-358-9353
P.O. Box 77644, San Francisco, CA 94107 415-381-4728
Coulas, Mick: 99 Coleman Ave, Toronto, ON M4C 1P8 416-698-3304
Coulson, David: 1107 Goodman St, Pittsburgh, PA 15218 412-243-7064
Coulter, Marty: 10129 Conway Rd, St Louis, MO 63124 314-432-2721
Counts, Clinton: 399 Sunset Rd, Skillman, NJ 08558 908-359-5936
Cournoyer, Jacques: 6924 rue de Saint-Vallier, Montréal, QU H2S 2P9 514-273-6237
278 Hamilton Ave, Princeton, NJ 08540 609-252-9405
Court, Rob: 31815 Camino Capistrano #18, San Juan Capistrano, CA 92675 949-496-1406
Courtney Studios: 43 E 19th St, New York, NY 10003 212-254-4996
• **Courtney, John: pg 1265** 779 Eleventh Ave #5D, Paterson, NJ 07514 ....**973-345-7652**
office **201-599-7340**
Cousineau, Normand: 870 av Oak, Saint-Lambert, QU J4P 1Z7 514-672-6940
Cove, Tony: 60 E 42nd St #1146, New York, NY 10165 212-953-7088
Covell, Mark: 950 Farmington Ave #27, New Britain, CT 06053 860-348-0699
Covert, Susan: 1134 Mendon Center Rd, Honeoye Falls, NY 14472 716-624-9682
Covey, Traci O'Very: 7 Washington Street, Beverly, MA 01915 978-921-0887
Covington, Neverne: PO Box 648, St Petersburg, FL 33703 813-822-1267
• **Cowdrey, Richard: pg 332,333**
327 E 89th St #3E, New York, NY 10128 ....**212-831-5650**
fax: 212-831-6241
1306 Alabama St, Huntington Beach, CA 92648 ....**714-969-7766**
fax: 714-374-3744
Cowles, David: 775 Landing Rd N, Rocherster, NY 14625 716-381-0910
Cox, Craig: 2305 Ashland St #C, Ashland, OR 97520 800-435-6509
Cox, H Ed: 1147 S Salisbury Blvd #5, Salisbury, MD 21801 410-548-9106
• **Cox, Paul: pg 254,255** 121 Madison Ave #5F, New York, NY 10016 ....**212-683-1362**
fax: 212-683-1919
Cox, Theresa: 1503 Briar Knoll Dr, Arden Hills, MN 55112 651-631-8480
Cozzolino, Paul: 211 Glengariff Rd, Massapequa, NY 11762 516-795-2432
Crackers: 192 Spandina Ave #510, Toronto, ON M5T 2C2 416-359-0024
Crackers World: 192 Spadina Ave #510, Toronto, ON M5T 2C2 416-504-4424
Cracknell, Alan: 28 Shelton St/Covent Garden, London, England, UK WC2H 71-240-2077
Craft, Diana: PO Box 831892, Richardson, TX 75083 972-235-1700
Craft, Kinuko Y: 83 Litchfield Rd, Norfolk, CT 06058 203-542-5018
Craig, Dan: 60 E 42nd St #822, New York, NY 10165 212-682-1490
Craig, David: 5940 Glen Erin #7A, Mississauga, ON L5M 5W9 905-826-9133
Craig, John: Rt 2 Box 2224 Tower Rd, Soldiers Grove, WI 54655 608-872-2371
Craig, Patricia: 16320 SE 15th Street, Bellevue, WA 98008 425-644-5676
• **Craig, Robert: pg 1180** 3286 Ivanhoe, St Louis, MO 63139 ....**314-781-7377**
e-mail: ceciba@stlnet.com / fax: 314-781-8017
Atlanta, GA **770-460-8438**
56 South Dr, Saugerties, NY 12477 ....**914-383-3638**
Craighead, Ray: 2500 Summit St, Kansas City, MO 64108 816-435-2000
Crakovich, Tony: 5706 S Narragansett, Chicago, IL 60638 773-586-9696
Cramer, DL: 10 Beechwood Dr, Wayne, NJ 07470 201-628-8793
Cramer, George: 6000 Highway TT, Marshall, WI 53559 608-655-4654
Cramp, Cliff: 9620 Downey Ave, Downey, CA 90240 562-862-6919
• **Crampton, Michael: pg 116,117**
420 Lexington Ave, New York, NY 10170 ....**212-986-5680**
url: www.mendolaart.com / fax: 212-818-1246
Crane, Arnold: 420 E 55th St #4C, New York, NY 10022 212-486-9050
Crane, Gary: 1511 W Little Creek Rd, Norfolk, VA 23505 804-423-2664
Crane, John B: PO Box 9413, Santa Fe, NM 87501 505-988-5282
Cranmer, Thomas F: 826 Bloomfield St, Hoboken, NJ 07030 201-795-9734
Crapo, Donald R: 2750 Giffert Way, Coopersburg, PA 18036 215-541-9313
Crase, Nancy: 6855 N 17th Pl, Phoenix, AZ 85016 602-241-0354
Crawford, Denise: 420 Lexington Ave #2760, New York, NY 10170 212-697-8525
Crawford, Emma: 108 E 16th St, New York, NY 10003 212-260-2244
Crawford, Kevin: 1467 Ellesmere Ave NW, N Canton, OH 44720 330-494-3443
• **Crawford, Robert: pg 1164** 333 N Michigan Ave, Chicago, IL 60601 ....**312-578-8844**
fax: 312-578-8847
123 Minortown Rd, Woodbury, CT 06798 ....**203-266-0059**
Creager, Donna: 451 Westfield Rd, Baltimore, MD 21222 410-527-8712
Creative Capers: 60 E 42nd St #822, New York, NY 10165 212-682-1490
Creative Force Inc, The: 1235-B Colorado Ln, Arlington, TX 76015 817-467-1013
Creative Images: 27 Atlantic Ave, Toronto, ON M6K 3E7 416-516-8200
Creative Schemes: 527 Wegman Rd, Rochester, NY 14624 716-247-4960
Crehan, Linda: 7 Washington Street, Beverly, MA 01915 978-921-0887
Cressy, Mike: 5900 119th Ave SE #B58, Bellevue, WA 98006 206-603-9669
Crews, Donald: 653 Carroll St, Brooklyn, NY 11215 718-636-5773
Crimzen, Liz: 5444 Hillcrest Dr, Los Angeles, CA 90043 213-296-8142
Criss, Keith W: 4617 Camden St Suite B, Oakland, CA 94619 510-534-0340
Crist, Alan: PO Box 152, Florence, MT 59833 406-273-6415
Cristos: 847A Second Ave #150, New York, NY 10017 212-486-0177
Cristos: 450 E Foothill Blvd, Glendora, CA 91741 ....
Criswell, Ron: 2929 Wildflower, Dallas, TX 75229 214-243-8058
Crittenden, Guy: 2504 Westwood Ave, Richmond, VA 23230 804-355-8992
Cro, Alex: 3814 Fulton St, San Francisco, CA 94118 415-751-7472
Crofut, Bob: 8 New St, Ridgefield, CT 06877 203-431-4304
Croll, Carolyn: 666 Greenwich St #860, New York, NY 10014 212-675-5719
Crompton, Jack: 1712 E Butler Cir, Chandler, AZ 85225 602-899-0600
Cromwell, Janelle: 11603 Talad St, Cypress, CA 90630 213-882-6011
Cronin, Brian: 682 Broadway #4A, New York, NY 10012 212-254-6312
Cronk, Drew: Box 2218, Healdsburg, CA 95448 707-431-7664
Cross, Dan: 129 S Washington St, Green Bay, WI 54301 414-435-4140
Crosse, Anne: 105 Hill St, Oakview, CA 93022 805-649-2788
Crossgrove, Catharine: 1131 Oddstad Dr, Redwood City, CA 94063 415-599-9473
Crouch, Lisa: 422 Sackville St, Toronto, ON M4X 1S9 416-925-2655
Croucher, Kit: 50 Kipling Dr #3, Mill Valley, CA 94941 415-383-7157
Crowell, Pat: PO Box 486, Palmer, MA 01069 203-268-1526
Crowley, Bill: 2501 W Colorado Ave, Colorado Springs, CO 80904 719-471-2704
Crowley, David: 711 Washington St, Gloucester, MA 01930 508-283-7866
Crowther, Catherine-Rose: 1732 Hearst Ave, Berkeley, CA 94703 510-704-8763
Crowther, Will: 2400 Suwanee Lakes Trail, Suwanee, GA 30174 770-513-0738
Crumrine, Randall: 944 Downing Main Flr, Denver, CO 80218 303-832-6151
Cruse, Howard: 88-11 34th Ave #5D, Jackson Heights, NY 11372 718-639-4951
Crutchfield, William: 2011 S Mesa St, San Pedro, CA 90731 310-548-4132
Cruz, Arthur: 871 Hawaii Ave, San Diego, CA 92154 619-575-8279
Cruz, Eric: 927 S Cabrillo Dr, Duarte, CA 91010 818-303-0489
Csatari, Joseph: 2 Snapper Ave, South River, NJ 08882 908-257-4660
Cserna, George: 6210 20th Ave, Brooklyn, NY 11204 718-259-2385
Csicsko, David Lee: 220 S State St #1930, Chicago, IL 60604 312-939-6603
Csuri, Charles: 1224 Kinnear Rd, Columbus, OH 43212 614-292-3416
Cuan, Sergio: 92 Edgemont Pl, Teaneck, NJ 07666 201-833-4337
Cuccio-Landry, Juanita: 300 N Michaud St, Carenco, LA 70520 318-896-6842
Cuddy, Robbin: 43 E 19th St, New York, NY 10003 212-254-4996
Cudlitz, Stuart: 1745 Pacific Ave, San Francisco, CA 94109 415-775-5044
Cueto, Ruben: 6501 Stone Crest Way, Whittier, CA 90601 562-945-8546
Cuevas, George: 4640 NW Seventh St, Miami, FL 33126 305-447-3849
Cuevas, Robert: 89-85 Hollis Ct Blvd, Queens Village, NY 11427 212-479-7206
Cullen, Danna: 14 Bedford St, New York, NY 10014 212-989-8706
Culliiane Design Inc: 260 Fifth Ave, New York, NY 10001 212-779-3155
Cumbie-Jones, Claudia: 112 S Michigan/Data Bank, Chicago, IL 60603 312-345-3550
Cumming, Moira: 9754 Parkford Dr, Dallas, TX 75238 214-343-8655
Cummings, Pat: 28 Tiffany Pl, Brooklyn, NY 11231 718-834-8584
Cummings, Terrence: 210 W 64th St #5B, New York, NY 10023 212-586-4193
Cummins, Karla: 13755 102nd Ave #7, Surrey, BC V3T 1N9 604-930-1583
Cunningham, Billy: 140 Seventh Ave #C, New York, NY 10011 212-929-6313
Cunningham, Danielle: 200 Post Rd #528, Warwick, RI 02888 401-461-5722
Cunningham, Dennis: 2405 NW Thurman St, Portland, OR 97210 503-203-8300
Cunningham, Nancy: 316 Regester St, Baltimore, MD 21212 410-377-9254
Cunningham, Patrick: 131 Fourth Pl, Brooklyn, NY 11231 212-625-6902
Cunningham, Robert M: 45 Cornwall Rd (Rt 45), Warren, CT 06754 203-868-2702
Curlee, Walt: 16 Curlee Lane, Phenix City, AL 36869 334-297-2733
Curran, Don: 215 Parkland, St Louis, MO 63122 314-965-8672
Curry, Georgina: 10229 N Scottsdale Rd #C, Scottsdale, AZ 85253 520-443-8786
Curry, Kevin: 210 Harvard Drive SE, Albuquerque, NM 87106 505-268-2915
• **Curry, Tom: pg 809** 333 E 49th St, New York, NY 10017 ....**212-980-8061**
url: www.theispot.com/artist/curry / fax: 212-832-8778
100 Bleecker St, New York, NY 10012 ....**212-982-6533**
fax: 212-358-1586
Curtis, Art: 2627 S Magnolia Ave, Los Angeles, CA 90007 213-747-1355
Curtis, D Michael: 2640 Del Mar Heights Rd #242, Del Mar, CA 92014 619-794-7949
Curtis, Todd: 2032 14th St #7, Santa Monica, CA 90405 310-452-0738
• **Cusack, Margaret: pg 1166**
124 Hoyt St in Boerum Hill, Brooklyn, NY 11217 ....**718-237-0145**
fax: 718-237-2430
Cusano, Steven R: 80 Talbot Ct, Media, PA 19063 610-565-8829
Cushwa, Tom: 303 Park Ave S #511, New York, NY 10010 212-228-2615
• **Custodio, Bernard: pg 1161** 20103 Baltar St, Canoga Pk, CA 91306 ....**818-998-4242**
fax: 818-701-9617
Cuthbert, Vanessa: 286 Spring St #301, New York, NY 10013 212-229-0073
• **Cutler, Dave: pg 1266,1267** 7 West St, Warwick, NY 10990 ....**914-987-1705**
e-mail: spots@warwick.net / url: www.theispot.com / fax: 914-987-1706
Cvjetan, Happy: 1320 Islington Ave #102, Etobicoke, ON M9A 5C6 416-236-0496
Cyr Studio, Lisa: 75 Fairview Ave #46, Jersey City, NJ 07304 201-946-2967
Czechowski, Alicia: 106 Emery St, Portland, ME 04102 207-874-2206
Czeczot, Andrzei: 278 Hamilton Ave, Princeton, NJ 08540 609-252-9405

D

D'Agostino, Anthony: 2501 West Zia Rd #2-203, Santa Fe, NM 87505 800-739-7789
D'Allaird, John: RD1 Box 298 Waites Hill Rd, Eagle Bridge, NY 12057 518-677-3312

D'Andrea, Bernie: 217 E 86th St Box 212, New York, NY 10028....................212-427-5632
D'Andrea, Dominick: 217 E 86th St Box 212, New York, NY 10028...................212-427-5632
• **D'Antuono, Michael: pg 1456** 39 Hamilton Terr, New York, NY 10031........**212-283-3401**
url: www.wayart.com
D'Augusta, Louisa: 235 Sackett St 3rd Fl, Brooklyn, NY 11231.......................718-624-5609
D'Elgin, Tershia: 1345 28th St, San Diego, CA 92102 619-239-6120
• **D'Souza, Helen: pg 564,565** 487 Mortimer Ave, Toronto, ON M4J 2G6.......**416-466-0630**
D'zenis, Eric: 320 Bee Brook Rd, Washington, CT 06777 860-868-1011
Da Silva, Silvio: 78 Manhattan Ave #2D, New York, NY 10025 212-665-3670
Daatselaar, Jos: 58 Harloff Rd, Mendon, NY 14506 716-624-5850
Dabagian, Marc: 306 N Wilmington #206, Raleigh, NC 27611 919-781-0551
Dabcovich, Meral: 77 Pond Ave #1106, Brookline, MA 02146 617-566-0910
Dacey, Bob: 7213 Woodchuck Hill Rd, Fayetteville, NY 13066 315-637-4614
Dacey, Linda: 23 Ganton St, London, England, UK WIV 1LA 71-287-9191
• **Dadds, Jerry: pg 834,835** New York, NY **212-869-0214**
San Francisco, CA **415-543-6056**
fax: 415-543-6075
Dahl, Susan Lee: 4 Weston St, Lexington, MA 02173..617-863-9478
Dahlquist, Roland: 1149 E Village Cir Dr S, Phoenix, AZ 85022.......................602-993-9895
• **Dahm, Bob: pg 1269** 166 Arnold Ave, Cranston, RI 02905.........................**401-781-5092**
e-mail: bob_dahm@ids.net
Daiber, Steven: 221 S Chesterfield Rd, Williamsburg, MA 01096 413-268-3114
• **Daigle, Stéphan: pg 198,199** 501 Fifth Ave, New York, NY 10017...............**212-490-2450**
url: www.renardrepresents.com / fax: 212-697-6828
• **Daigneault, Sylvie: pg 857** 280 Madison Ave, New York, NY 10016............**212-545-9155**
e-mail: irmeli@aol.com / url: www.spar.org/holmberg / fax: 212-545-9462
Daily, Don: 217 E 86th St Box 212, New York, NY 10028..................................212-427-5632
Daily, Renée: 666 Greenwich St #860, New York, NY 10014...............................212-675-5719
Dakins, Todd: 925 Elm Grove Rd, Elm Grove, WI 53122......................................414-785-1940
Dale, Robert: 3709 S San Pablo Rd #1608, Jacksonville, FL 32224...................904-223-8412
• **Daley, Joann: pg 1170** 2740 Peninsula Rd #231, Oxnard, CA 93035.........**805-985-1608**
fax: 805-985-1038
900 W Jackson Blvd #7W, Chicago, IL 60607 ....**312-944-5680**
fax: 312-421-5948
PO Box 7544, Phoenix, AZ 85011...**602-265-4389**
fax: 602-265-8405
Dallas Graphics, Inc: 806 Fig Tree Ln, Brandon, FL 33511 800-678-1608
Dallison, Ken: 1698 Truscott Dr, Mississauga, ON L5J 1Z1.............................905-823-9601
108 E 35th St #2, New York, NY 10016 212-889-3337
Dally, Lyman: 300 Mercer St #10J, New York, NY 10003...................................212-358-9869
Dalton, Clay: 939 Leeds Castle Way, Marietta, GA 30066..................................770-425-1065
Daly, Bob: Los Angeles, CA 213-688-7428
Chicago, IL 312-663-5506
New York, NY 212-643-0896
Panama City, FL 904-747-8415
UK/Western Europe, ...186-543-5654
468 Queen St E #104, Toronto, ON M5A 1T7 416-367-2446
Daly, Mona: 12640 Zurich Pl #3, Truckee, CA 96161 530-582-9338
toll-free 888-220-3909
Daly, Sean: 85 South St, New York, NY 10038..212-668-0031
Daly, Tom: 47 E Edsel Ave, Palisades Park, NJ 07650 201-943-1837
Daman Studio, Todd: 12918 NE 122nd Lane Suite K400, Kirkland, WA 98034425-814-2800
Dameron, Ned: 14 Manchester Pl #303, Silver Spring, MD 20901.......................301-585-8512
Damm, Jeff: 4760 Colombus Ave, Sherman Oaks, CA 91403................................818-905-5267
Dammer, Mike: 203 N Wabash #1302, Chicago, IL 60601 312-782-4995
Damore, Georgan: 680 N Lakeshore Dr #222, Chicago, IL 60611........................312-266-9451
Danawi, Mohamed: 468 Queen St E #104, Toronto, ON M5A 1T7.........................416-367-2446
Dandy, Jim: 36 W Palmdale Dr, Tempe, AZ 85282...602-829-8992
Dang, Thai: 16143 Livingstone, Fountain Valley, CA 92708...................................714-775-0465
Dangle, Lloyd: PO Box 460686, San Francisco, CA 94146 510-839-4236
Daniel, Doug: 949 Fry Rd, Greenwood, IN 46142..317-882-5887
Daniel, Frank: 201 E 28th St, New York, NY 10016 212-532-0928
• **Daniels & Daniels: pg 1270,1271**
14-S Madrid Ave, Newbury Park, CA 91320 ....**805-498-1923**
e-mail: ARIAART@AOL.COM / fax: 805-499-8344
Daniels, Alan & Beau: 232 Madison Ave #402, New York, NY 10016 212-889-8777
Daniels, Sid: 1100 West Ave #1105, Miami Bch, FL 33139 305-673-4329
Danisi, Joseph: 94 Pearsall Pl, Deer Pk, NY 11729...516-667-3720
Dann, Penny: 455 W 23rd St #8D, New York, NY 10011 212-366-1893
Dannenberg, Thomas: 407 Mill St, Richmond Hill, ON L4C 4C1..............................905-884-9166
Dano, Robert: 129 Presidents Ln, Quincy, MA 02169 617-773-9742
Dansereau, Gérard: 939 rue Marie-Ann Est, Montréal, QU H2J 2B2.........................514-522-5690
Dante, Penney: 535 E 72nd St, New York, NY 10021..212-628-7085
Danz, Dave: 4680 Demyhig Ln, Placerville, CA 95667 530-622-3218
Darby, Janet: 309 Walnut Rd, Pittsburgh, PA 15202 412-761-5666
Darden, Howard: 99 Park Ave #210A, New York, NY 10016.......................................800-398-9544
Darnell, Jim/The Art Source: PO Box 2193, Grapevine, TX 10570..............................817-481-2908
Darold, Dave: 216 F St #145, Davis, CA 95616 916-758-1379
Darrow, David R: 532 N Rosemary Ln, Burbank, CA 91505......................................800-594-9132
Darrow, Whitney: 950 Klish Way, Del Mar, CA 92014 619-259-5774
Daskas, Richard: 1677 Pleasant Hills Dr, Chino, CA 91709......................................909-591-2781
Daste, Larry: 201 E 28th St, New York, NY 10016 212-532-0928
Daugavietis, Ruta: 5301 N Lakewood, Chicago, IL 60640 773-334-8213
DaVault, Elaine: 1999 S Coast Hwy #5, Laguna Beach, CA 92651 714-497-5339
Davenport, Therese: 189 Bowen St, S Boston, MA 02127 617-268-7524
Davick, Linda: 4805 Hilldale Ln, Knoxville, TN 37914 615-546-1020
David, Susan: 931 Hudson St #3, Hoboken, NJ 07030 201-798-3062
Davide, Andrea: 2087 Blanche Ln, Merrick, NY 11566 516-546-5282
• **Davidson, Andrew: pg 708** 455 W 23rd St #8D, New York, NY 10011.......**212-366-1893**
url: www.andtheart.com / fax: 212-604-9643
Davidson, Dennis: 43 E 19th St, New York, NY 10003..212-254-4996
Davidson, Kevin: 2646 Dupont Dr Ste 20-425, Irvine, CA 92715...............................714-770-9255
Davidson, Rodney: 626 54th St S, Birmingham, AL 35212...205-595-0393
Davies, Dina: AZ 520-840-5655
Davies, Paul: 1208 E 98th Terr, Kansas City, MO 64131 816-941-9313
Davies, Will: 63-A Yorkville Ave, Toronto, ON M5R 1B7 416-925-8191

Davis, Allen: 43 E 19th St, New York, NY 10003 212-254-4996
Davis, Carla: 674 10th Ave #G-F, Brooklyn, NY 11215...212-924-6464
Davis, Dennas: 904 Sutton Hill Rd, Nashville, TN 37204 615-386-0444
Davis, Diane Kay: 333 N Michigan #1100, Chicago, IL 60601 312-855-9336
Davis, Eric: 357 W 37th St #4A, New York, NY 10018 212-563-7626
• **Davis, Gary: pg 508** 217 E 86th St Box 212, New York, NY 10028............**212-427-5632**
fax: 212-427-6372
Davis, Glenn: 223 Central St, Saugus, MA 01906..617-231-3092
Davis, Harry R: 189 E 3rd St #15, New York, NY 10009...212-674-5832
RR1 Box 1738, Shohola, PA 18458..717-559-7919
• **Davis, Jack: pg 30,31** 108 E 35th St #2, New York, NY 10016...................**212-889-3337**
url: www.theispot.com/artist/davis / fax: 212-889-3341
1315 Belleview Ave, Cardiff, CA 92007 ....**619-944-7232**
• **Davis, Jack E: pg 256,257** 121 Madison Ave #5F, New York, NY 10016......**212-683-1362**
fax: 212-683-1919
Davis, John: 604 Ninth St, Carlstadt, NJ 07072 201-460-7358
Davis, Lambert: 4378 Clayford St, San Diego, CA 92117..800-344-8034
Davis, Michael: 420 Lexington Ave, New York, NY 10170 212-986-5680
• **Davis, Nancy: pg 292,293** 58 W 15th St, New York, NY 10011 ....**212-741-2539**
url: www.showcase.com / fax: 212-741-4660
Davis, Nelle: 20 E 17th St 4th Fl, New York, NY 10003..212-807-7737
Davis, Nina: 91-B Lordship Park, Stoke Newington,
London, England, UK N16 5UP 1818-091872
Davis, Paul: 14 E 4th St, New York, NY 10012 212-420-8789
Davis, Robert: 72 Belcher St, San Francisco, CA 94114 415-621-0865
Davis, Roz: PO Box 777, Booth Bay Harbor, ME 04538 207-633-7037
Davis, Sally: 702 W Halladay, Seattle, WA 98119 206-283-3800
Davis, Scott: 19 W 21st Street #301, New York, NY 10010.......................................212-989-6446
Davis, Stephen: 365 NE 156th St, Miami, FL 33162 305-940-9832
Davis, Susan: 1107 Notley Dr, Silver Spring, MD 20904 301-384-9426
Davison, Bill: 179 Main St, Winooski, VT 05404 802-655-0407
Dawdy, Sean: 12 Bond St, Cambridge, ON N1S 4B3..519-623-5296
• **Dawson, Henk: pg 1484,1485** 3519 170th Pl NE, Bellevue, WA 98008.......**425-882-3303**
Dawson, John: New York, NY 212-486-9644
116 Bedford Rd #1, Toronto, ON M5R 2K2 416-926-0730
Dawson, Will: 11004 E 11th Pl, Tulsa, OK 74128 918-234-1362
Dawson, William: 9 Fieldcrest Ct, Peekskill, NY 10566 914-739-2404
Day, Adrian: 2022 Jones St, San Francisco, CA 94133 415-928-0457
• **Day, Brant: pg 681** 2814 NW 72nd St, Seattle, WA 98117............................**206-784-1136**
url: www.kolea.com / fax: 206-784-1171
• **Day, Bruce: pg 1272** 6080 Arney Ln, Boise, ID 83703 ....**208-853-8336**
Day, Douglas: 240 Ocho Rios Way, Oak Park, CA 91301 818-879-1431
Day, Larry: 110 Rising Ridge Rd, Ridgefield, CT 06877..203-438-7307
Day, Rob: 10 State St #214, Newburyport, MA 01950 508-465-1386
6095 Ralston Ave, Indianapolis, IN 46220 317-253-9000
• **Day, Sam: pg 1459** PO Box 4425, Seattle, WA 98104...................................**206-382-7413**
url: www.samday.com
• **Dayal, Antar: pg 1024,1025**
1666 Las Canoas Rd, Santa Barbara, CA 93105..**805-965-5988**
url: www.dayalstudio.com / fax: 805-965-5989
Dayton, Warren: 3850 Meyers Rd/PO Box 717, Camino, CA 95709 916-644-7044
de Alamada, Paulo: 431 Lee St #06, Oakland, CA 94610..800-767-8845
De Anda, Ruben: 890 Entrada Pl, Chula Vista, CA 91910..619-421-2845
De Blois, Daniéle: 6341 rue Chambord, Montréal, QU H2G 3B8..................................514-274-6477
De Castro, Marion: 21 W Van Buren St, Phoenix, AZ 85003 602-252-1462
De Cerchio, Joe: 7 Annapolis Dr, Marlton, NJ 08053...609-596-0598
de la Houssaye, Jeanne: 400 N Peters, New Orleans, LA 70130 504-581-2167
De La Hoz, D'Ann: 6995 NW 82nd Ave #32, Miami, FL 33166 305-592-6887
de Sïeve, Peter: 25 Park Pl, Brooklyn, NY 11217...718-398-8099
De Soi, Michael: 1021 Lancaster Ave, Bryn Mawr, PA 19010 610-520-9522
Dea, Patrick: 372 Ste-Catherine Quest bureau 419, Montreal, QU H3B 1A2 514-875-1301
Deacon, Jim: 373 Benefit St 1st Fl, Providence, RI 02903...401-331-8742
Deal, David: 1651 Monte Vista Dr, Vista, CA 92084 619-758-2655
Deal, Jim: 1431 35th Ave S, Seattle, WA 98144 206-325-8595
DeAlmada, Paulo: 3450 Andrew's Dr #313, Pleasanton, CA 94588...............................510-734-0738
DeAmicus, John: 35 South Durst Dr, Milltown, NJ 08850...908-249-4937
Dean, Bruce: 23211 Leonora Dr, Woodland Hills, CA 91367 818-716-5632
Dean, Glenn: RD #2 Box 788, Sussex, NJ 07461 212-490-2450
Dean, Michael: 2001 Sul Ross, Houston, TX 77098...713-527-0295
Deardorff, Patricia: 729 W Valerio St, Santa Barbara, CA 93101 805-682-3507
Dearstyne Illust, John: 10 La Purisima, Rancho St Margarita, CA 92688 714-589-6447
Dearth, Greg: 68 E Franklin St, Dayton, OH 45459 937-433-8383
Dearwater, Andy: 250 W 57th St #521, New York, NY 10107 212-397-7330
• **Deas, Michael J: pg 1175,** New Orleans, LA **504-524-3957**
Deaver, Georgia: 852 Folsom St, San Francisco, CA 94107 415-541-0770
Deaver, Lucas: 10 E 23rd St #300, New York, NY 10010...212-477-5610
Debevoise, Clay: 420 13th St Storefront W, New York, NY 10009..................................212-387-0553
DeBiasso, Thomas A: Media Arts/2501 Stevens Ave S,
Minneapolis, MN 55404 612-874-3638
DeBro, James: 1381 Dodson Dr, Atlanta, GA 30344..404-755-4317
• **DeCarlo, Dan: pg 1273** 1570 First Ave #6C, New York, NY 10028..................**212-879-8660**
Deck Design, Barry: 159 W 23rd St #4F, New York, NY 10011.......................................212-777-6627
Deckado, Marshall: 99 Park Ave #210A, New York, NY 10016 800-398-9544
Decker, George: 273 E 10th St #8, New York, NY 10009 212-673-3263
• **Decoster, Jeffrey: pg 711** 455 W 23rd St #8D, New York, NY 10011 ....**212-366-1893**
url: www.andtheart.com / fax: 212-604-9643
Dedini, Eldon: 950 Klish Way, Del Mar, CA 92014 619-259-5774
Deegan, Sean: 1840 Manhattan Ave, Hermosa Beach, CA 90254 310-342-5909
Deel, Guy: 60 E 42nd St #1940, New York, NY 10165 212-867-8092
Deen, Georganne: 3834 Aloha St, Los Angeles, CA 90027..213-665-2700
Deeter, Catherine: 160 West End Ave #23-S, New York, NY 10023 212-486-9644
Defiebe Jr, Matthew: 940 Salem Rd, Union, NY 07083 908-688-2536
Defino Jr, Frank: 2917 N Latoria Ln, Franklin Park, IL 60131 800-633-7887
DeFranco, Gerard R: 52 Oliver St, Rochester, NY 14607..716-271-0413

Defreitas, Peter: pg 863 280 Madison Ave #1110, New York, NY 10016......**212-545-9155**
e-mail: irmeli@aol.com / url: www.spar.org/holmberg / fax: 212-545-9462
Degen, Paul: pg 600 155 W 15th St, New York, NY 10011......**212-989-8770**
fax: 212-989-7892
DeGrandpre, Patty: 233 Hale St, Beverly, MA 01915......508-921-0410
Deigan, Jim: 309 Walnut Rd, Pittsburgh, PA 15202......412-761-5666
Dekle, Merritt: 584 Broadway #608, New York, NY 10012......212-966-7840
4318 Lafayette St, Marianna, FL 32446......904-526-3319
Del Rossi, Ken: PO Box 0706, Baldwin, NY 11520......516-378-8969
Del Rossi, Ric: 18 W 21st Street 17th Floor, New York, NY 10010......212-243-1333
Del Rossi, Richard: 8 Washington St, Hicksville, NY 11801......516-939-0256
Delago, Ken: 134 Rowayton Ave, Norwalk, CT 06853......203-661-6547
Delahoussaye, Jean: 400 N Peters, New Orleans, LA 70130......800-524-4981
DeLancey, Alison: 4610 Cloverlawn Dr, Grants Pass, OR 97527......541-471-1340
Delaney, John: 14 Castle St, Saugus, MA 01906......617-233-1409
Delano, Art: PO Box 3659, Ann Arbor, MI 48106......313-741-1370
Delano, Jonathan: 434 E 72nd St #2A, New York, NY 10021......212-639-9117
Delany, Mary Ann: 29A Borthwick Ave, Delmar, NY 12054......518-475-0515
Delapine, Jim: 99 Park Ave #210A, New York, NY 10016......800-398-9544
Delessert, Etienne: PO Box 1689, Lakeville, CT 06039......203-435-0061
Delezenne, Christine: 4354 rue Chambord, Montréal, QU H2J 2R1......514-849-2839
Delhomme, Jean Philippe: 225 Lafayette St #902, New York, NY 10012......212-941-1777
Delich, Donna: 889 Williams Pl, Hartsville, PA 18974......215-674-2506
Dell'Aquila, Mei Ying: 2820 Cozumel Cir, Santa Clara, CA 95051......408-246-8875
Dellicolli, Ronald E: 1 Argilla Rd, Methuen, MA 01844......508-437-9459
Dellorco, Chris: pg 131 420 Lexington Ave, New York, NY 10170......**212-986-5680**
url: www.mendolaart.com / fax: 212-818-1246
Delmirenburg, Barry: 301 E 38th St, New York, NY 10016......212-573-9200
Delmonte, Steve: 328 W Delavan Ave, Buffalo, NY 14213......716-883-6086
Delorme, Guy: 4481 rue Gatineau, Laval, QU H7T 1GB......514-687-0700
DeLouise, Dan: 15 Youngs Rd, Gloucester, MA 01930......508-282-1379
Deloy, Dee: 217 E 86th St Box 212, New York, NY 10028......212-427-5632
Delrossi, Kenneth E: PO Box 0706, Baldwin, NY 11520......516-378-8969
Delton, Julie: 669 Summit Ave, St Paul, MN 55105......651-227-3848
Demarco, Kim: 6 Parker Rd, Arlington, MA 02174......617-641-2787
Demarest, Robert: 87 Highview Terr, Hawthorne, NJ 07506......201-427-9639
DeMelle, Todd: 78 Glenville Ave #6, Alston, MA 02134......617-254-9384
• **Demers, Don: pg 509** 217 E 86th St Box 212, New York, NY 10028......**212-427-5632**
fax: 212-427-6372
• **deMichiell, Robert: pg 32,33** 108 E 35th St #2, New York, NY 10016......**212-889-3337**
url: www.theispot.com/artist/demichiell / fax: 212-889-3341
Demorat, Charles J: 2621 S 376th Pl, Federal Way, WA 98003......253-874-6026
• **Dempsey, Paul: pg 471** 731 N 24th St, Philadelphia, PA 19130......**215-232-6666**
url: www.deborahwolfsltd.com / fax: 215-232-6585
DeMuth, Roger: 59 Chenango St, Cazenovia, NY 13035......315-655-8599
Denham, Karl: 20568 Ventura Blvd #315, Woodland Hills, CA 91364......818-347-1676
DeNicola, Robert: 45-49 165th St, Flushing, NY 11358......718-359-5336
Denis, Stephanie: 468 Queen St E #104, Toronto, ON M5A 1T7......416-367-2446
Denise & Fernando: 420 Lexington Ave, New York, NY 10170......212-986-5680
Denise, Christopher: 329 Wickenden St, Providence, RI 02903......401-273-3145
Denn, Walter: 13332 Slope Crest Dr, Oakland, CA 94619......415-476-1152
Dennewill, Jim: 5823 Autry Ave, Lakewood, CA 90712......310-920-3895
Dennis, Drift: 9403 Marilla Dr, Lakeside, CA 92040......619-390-8375
Denny, Barbara: 8071 Ainsworth Ln, La Plama, CA 90623......714-527-8503
DePalma, Mary Newell: 45 Bradfield Ave, Boston, MA 02131......617-327-6241
• **Depew, Bob: pg 788** 353 W 53rd St #1W, New York, NY 10019......**212-682-2462**
url: www.americanartists.com / fax: 212-582-0090
Deponte, Fabio & Sara: PO Box 393/N Main St, Petersham, MA 01366......508-724-8823
Deronzier, Sylvie: 604 3 Rang Est app 2, Bic, QU G0L 1B0......418-736-8312
deRosa, Dee: 3409 Pleasant Valley Rd, Syracuse, NY 13215......315-673-2308
Derrick, Bill: 1393 N Castlewood Dr, Franktown, CO 80116......303-470-0857
• **Dervaux, Isabelle: pg 603** 155 W 15th St, New York, NY 10011......**212-989-8770**
Fax: 212-989-7892
Desaix, Deborah: 866 United Nations Plaza, New York, NY 10017......212-644-2020
• **DeSantis, Laura: pg 726** 7 Washington Street, Beverly, MA 01915......**978-921-0887**
e-mail: leighton@leightonreps.com / url: www.leightonreps.com / fax: 978-921-0223
Desbiens, Dominique: 5813 Third Ave, Montréal, QU H1Y 2X2......514-712-9263
Deschamps, Bob: 108 E 35th St #2, New York, NY 10016......212-889-3337
DeSeta, Maxine: 202 W 107th St #6E, New York, NY 10025......212-316-3563
Deshetler, Steve: 4533 Southridge Meadows Dr, St Louis, MO 63128......314-892-6880
Design Core: 327 E 89th St #3E, New York, NY 10128......212-831-5650
Design Loiminchay: 390 Broadway 3rd Fl, New York, NY 10012......212-941-7488
Design Plus: 853 Broadway #1607, New York, NY 10003......212-645-2686
Designation, Inc: 53 Spring St 5th Fl, New York, NY 10012......212-226-6024
Desimini, Lisa: 666 Greenwich St #16, New York, NY 10014......212-645-2932
DeSpain, Pamela: #10 West Side Apts, Burgaw, NC 28425......910-259-9097
Després, Geneviève: 4452 av des ƒrables, Montréal, QU H2H 2C8......514-527-8363
Desrocher, Jack: Rt 7 Box 611, Eureka Springs, AR 72632......501-253-6615
Detrich, Susan: 253 Baltic St, Brooklyn, NY 11201......718-237-9174
Detwiller, Darius: 22727 Cielo Visto, San Antonio, TX 78255......210-698-1409
Devaney, John: 421 Broadway, Cambridge, MA 02138......617-876-4046
DeVaney, Richard: 460 W 42nd St 2nd Fl, New York, NY 10036......212-967-6655
Devarieux, Wendy: 2105 Evergreen, Tallahassee, FL 32303......904-386-7683
Devarj, Silva: 116 W Illinois, Chicago, IL 60610......312-266-1358
• **Devaud, Jacques: pg 736,737,1474,1475**
865 Delaware St, Denver, CO 80204......**303-820-2599**
toll-free......**800-417-5120**
url: www.artagent.com / fax: 303-820-2598
Devenuti, Denise: PO Box 1430 Grand Central Station, New York, NY 10163......914-725-5879
Dever Designs: 1054 West St, Laurel, MD 20707......301-776-2812
Dever, Jeffrey L: 9101 Cherry Ln #102, Laurel, MD 20708......301-776-2812
DeVito, Grace: 60 E 42nd St #822, New York, NY 10165......212-682-1490
Devlin, Bill: 108 E 35th St #2, New York, NY 10016......212-889-3337
• **Devries, Dave: pg 334,335** 327 E 89th St #3E, New York, NY 10128......**212-831-5650**
fax: 212-831-6241
1306 Alabama St, Huntington Beach, CA 92648......**714-969-7766**
fax: 714-374-3744

Dewar, Ken: 217 Tenth Ave SW #1, Calgary, AB T2R 0A4......403-263-0167
Dewar, Nick: 32 Downing St #4D, New York, NY 10014......212-633-1310
Dexter, Cliff: 419 Ocean St, Ocean Bluff, MA 02065......781-834-0211
Dey, Lorraine: 45 Johnson Ln N, Jackson, NJ 08527......908-928-5510
Di Fate, Vincent: 227 Godfrey Rd, Weston, CT 06883......203-222-8777
Di Mare, Paul: 217 E 86th St Box 212, New York, NY 10028......212-427-5632
Di Nezza, John: 55 Grant #2, Longueuil, QU J4H 3H4......514-952-2922
Di Rubbio, Jennifer: 19 Prairie Ln, Levittown, NY 11756......516-579-1872
Di Vincenzo, Mark: 61 Fordham Dr, Buffalo, NY 14216......716-873-3566
Diamond, Donna: 420 Lexington Ave PH, New York, NY 10170......212-986-5680
Diana Sutherland Art Direction: 1061 Gate Lane, Pilot Hill, CA 95664......916-933-1513
Diane Varney Design Studio: 83 Walnut Ave, Corte Madera, CA 94925......415-924-7881
Diatz-Schlaifer, Dianna: 602 N Pelham St, Alexandria, VA 22304......703-751-4064
• **Diaz, David: pg 1229** 1697 Robin Place, Carlsbad, CA 92009......**760-438-0070**
toll-free......**800-474-ICON**
e-mail: ddiaz@diazicon.com / url: www.diazicon.com / fax: 760-438-0315
Diaz, Jose: 37-15 191st St #156, Flushing, NY 11358......718-886-9506
DiBlasio, Nicholas: 207 Commonwealth Ave, Boston, MA 02116......617-266-2650
DiCarlo, Chid: 115 Rumsey Rd, Yonkers, NY 10705......914-793-5220
DiCesare, Joe: 27 Sterling Pl, Brooklyn, NY 11217......718-622-4157
DiCianni, Ron: 340 Thompson Blvd, Buffalo Grove, IL 60089......847-634-1848
• **Dickens Design, Inc, Holly: pg 1451**
50 E Bellevue #402, Chicago, IL 60611......**312-280-0777**
e-mail: holdickens@aol.com / fax: 312-280-1725
Dickey, Burrell: 4975 Elmwood Dr, San Jose, CA 95130......408-866-0820
Dickinson, Chuck: 17 Hilburn Rd, Scarsdalen, NY 10583......914-472-1730
Dickson, Ellie: 185 West End Ave #3L, New York, NY 10023......212-724-3598
DiComo, Charles: 311 W 34th St 8th Fl, New York, NY 10001......212-279-0800
Didia, Doug: PO Box 396, Bloomfield Hills, MI 48303......313-460-2451
Didier, Paul: 5855 Green Valley Cir #308, Culver City, CA 90230......310-642-2721
Diefendorf, Cathy: 420 Lexington Ave, New York, NY 10170......212-986-5680
Dierckemeier, Robert: 550 E McKellirs Rd #2072, Mesa, AZ 85203......602-962-4864
Dieterichs, Shelly: 5 Plant Ave #2, St Louis, MO 63119......314-968-4515
• **Dietz, Jim: pg 837** 165 E 32nd St, New York, NY 10016......**212-686-3514**
fax: 212-532-4302
• **Dietz, Mike: pg 336,337** 327 E 89th St #3E, New York, NY 10128......**212-831-5650**
fax: 212-831-6241
1306 Alabama St, Huntington Beach, CA 92648......**714-969-7766**
fax: 714-374-3744
Diez-Luckie, Cathy: 62728 Clive, Oakland, CA 94611......510-482-5600
DiFabio, Jessica: 301 E 75th St #20B, New York, NY 10021......212-988-9623
Diffenderfer, Ed: 32 Cabernet Ct, Lafayette, CA 94549......510-254-8235
DiGennaro, Robert: 10 Godfrey Rd W, Weston, CT 06883......203-454-9658
Diggory, Nick: 23 Ganton St, London, England, UK WIV 1LA......71-287-9191
• **Digital Art : pg 1190** 3166 E Palmdale Blvd #120, Palmdale, CA 93550......**805-265-8092**
fax: 805-265-8095
Digital Image: 36524 Grand River #B2, Farmington Hills, MI 48335......810-477-5600
• **Dikayl: pg 1208** 433 1/2 E Broadway, Salt Lake City, UT 84111......**801-359-3591**
url: www.dikayl.com
Dildine, Jim: 1989 W 5th Ave #7, Columbus, OH 43212......614-486-5679
Dill, Jane: San Francisco, CA......415-543-6056
Dill, Wally: 34019 Oakland, Farmington, MI 48335......313-476-5581
Dillard, Sarah: 41 Monument Sq, Charlestown, MA 02129......617-241-0141
Dillon, Kathryn: 10848 Morning View Ct, Riverside, CA 92505......909-359-1481
Dillon, Leo & Diane: 221 Kane St, Brooklyn, NY 11231......718-624-0023
DiMarco, Paula J: 1521 Neil Ave #A6, Columbus, OH 43201......212-228-2893
DiMartino, Paul: 560 Mountain Ave, Washington Twnshp, NJ 07675......212-764-5591
Dimensional Illustrators: 362 2nd St Pike #112, Southampton, PA 18966......215-953-1415
Dimino Assoc, Frank: 72 Grecian Garden Dr, Rochester, NY 14626......716-225-3510
Dinamation Int'l: 9560 Jeronimo Rd, Irvine, CA 92618......714-753-9630
Dineen, Tom: 8025 McGee Ave, St Louis, MO 63123......314-827-2937
Dinges, Michael: 777 N Michigan Ave #706, Chicago, IL 60611......312-337-7770
Dingler & Associates, Fred: 1805 Raleigh Dr, Burnsville, MN 55337......612-890-3122
• **Dingman, Alan: pg 734,735** 300 E 46th St #4G, New York, NY 10017......**212-687-6463**
e-mail: sara@levycreative.com / fax: 212-661-4839
• **Dininno, Astrid: pg 1274** 457 John Joy Rd, Kingston, NY 12498......**914-679-7929**
url: www.sisstock.com / fax: 914-679-8357
• **Dininno, Steve: pg 765** 41 Union Sq W #918, New York, NY 10003......**212-807-6627**
url: www.idt.net/~dgagency / fax: 212-463-8175
Dinnerstein, Harvey: 933 President St, Brooklyn, NY 11215......718-783-6879
Dinnerstein, Matt: 1918 W Foster Ave, Chicago, IL 60640......773-769-2989
Dinser, John: 9308 Merrill Rd, Whitmore Lake, MI 48189......313-449-5969
Dinyer, Eric: 3301A S Jefferson Ave, St Louis, MO 63118......314-773-2600
Dionisi, Sandra: 37 Hanna Ave #13-A, Toronto, ON M6K1W9......416-588-4588
Dior, Jerry: 9 Old Hickory Ln, Edison, NJ 08820......908-561-6536
Dippietro, Hugo: 2480 Irbine Blvd #219, Tustin Ranch, CA 92782......714-832-7674
Dircks, David: 16 Dunford St, Melville, NY 11747......516-427-9377
Dirkes, Jessica: 4223 Hymount Ave, Sarasota, FL 34231......941-924-7255
DiSalvio, Jaime: 15364 Seitz Ct, Moorpark, CA 93021......805-523-2702
• **Dismukes, John Taylor: pg 129** 420 Lexington Ave, New York, NY 10170......**212-986-5680**
url: www.mendolaart.com / fax: 212-818-1246
Dispoto, Tony: 524 W 23rd St #4035, New York, NY 10011......973-472-4004
Ditko, Steve: 3333 E Camelback #200, Phoenix, AZ 85018......602-955-2707
Dittmer, Mark: 555 N Western Ave #1, Nogales, AZ 85621......520-287-0160
Dittrich, Dennis: 395 Broadway #10A, New York, NY 10013......212-343-0096
Dixon, Christine: 6734 Kenyon Dr, Alexandria, VA 22307......703-660-8427
Dixon, David: 8 Gentry Carson Dr, Gray, TN 37615......615-283-0484
Dixon, Debra Spina: 2714 SW Leah Ct, Portland, OR 97219......503-452-8050
Dixon, Don: 2519 Cedar Ave, Long Beach, CA 90806......310-595-8487
Dixon, Ted: 594 Broadway #902, New York, NY 10012......212-226-5686
Dodds, Glenn: 392 Central Park W #9M, New York, NY 10025......212-866-7327
Dodeles, Elise: 425 Huff Rd, North Brunswick, NJ 08902......908-821-5299
Dodge, Bill: 60 E 42nd St #1940, New York, NY 10165......212-867-8092
Dodge, Larry: 29580 Northwestern Hwy, Southfield, MI 48034......248-353-7722
Dodson, Bert: RR1 Box 1660, Bradford, VT 05033......802-222-9384

Eskridge, Lynn: 2351 W Northwest Hwy #1100, Dallas, TX 75220 214-638-7255
• Espinosa, Leo : pg 1090 18 Argyle Road, Scarsdale, NY 10583 ....**914-725-9103**
  e-mail: lei@inch.com / fax: 914-725-9704
Estioko, Mario: 5416 Havenhurst Cir, Rocklin, CA 95677 916-781-8442
Etheridge, John: 4246 Trellis Crescent, Mississauga, ON L5L 2M2 416-828-2879
ETIC Studios Inc: 121 South Rd, Chester, NJ 07930 908-879-6583
Etow, Carole: 18224 Herbold St, Northridge, CA 91325 818-772-7501
Ettlinger, Doris: RD2 Box 6, Hampton, NJ 08827 908-537-6322
Eubank, Mary Grace: 8615 Midway Rd, Dallas, TX 75209 214-902-8778
Eucalyptus Tree Studio: 2221 Morton St, Baltimore, MD 21218 410-243-0211
Evans Illus, Robert: 1045 Sansome St #306, San Francisco, CA 94111 415-397-5322
Evans, Bill: 7012 Iaverary Ct, W Chester, OH 45069 513-755-9489
• Evans, Brian: pg 740 865 Delaware St, Denver, CO 80204 ....**303-820-2599**
  toll-free **800-417-5120**
  url: www.artagent.com / fax: 303-820-2598
Evans, Jan: 5015 Clinton St #306, Los Angeles, CA 90004 323-957-2327
Evans, Jonathan: 3286 Ivanhoe, St Louis, MO 63139 314-781-7377
Evans, Leslie: 17 Bay St, Watertown, MA 02172 617-924-3058
Evans, Robert: 716 Montgomery St, San Francisco, CA 94111 415-433-1222
• Evans, Shane Warren: pg 732,733
  300 E 46th St #4G, New York, NY 10017 ....**212-687-6463**
  e-mail: sara@levycreative.com / fax: 212-661-4839
Evans, Sharron: 3220 Sacramento St, San Francisco, CA 94115 415-239-7024
Evans, Virginia: 10 State St #214, Newburyport, MA 01950 508-465-1386
Evcimen, Al: 305 Lexington Ave #6D, New York, NY 10016 212-889-2995
Eve Design: 60 Plaza St E #6E, Brooklyn, NY 11238 718-398-0950
Eveland, Russ: 1103 Ralph Rd, Newark, DE 19713 302-737-9102
Everitt Illustration, Betsy: 582 Santa Rosa Ave, Berkeley, CA 94707 510-527-3239
Everitt, Paul: 2120 S Ervay, Dallas, TX 75215 214-426-6806
• Evernden, Graham: pg 713 455 W 23rd St #8D, New York, NY 10011......**212-366-1893**
  url: www.andtheart.com / fax: 212-604-9643
Everndern, Graham: 70 Rosaline Rd, London, England, UK SW6 7QT........171-610-1801
Evraets, David: 3215 Cherrywood Ave, Bellingham, WA 98225................360-734-5725
Ewers, Joseph: 1820 Old Harrisburg Rd, Gettysburg, PA 17325 717-337-3785
Ewing, Carolyn: 201 E 28th St, New York, NY 10016 212-532-0928
Ewing, Julie: 1818 County Rd #526, Bayfield, CO 81122 303-884-4265
• Ewing, Richard: pg 1282 3966 Gaviota Ave, Long Beach, CA 90807.........**888-403-1004**
  url: www.showcase.com / fax: 562-989-9539
Eynon, Debbie: Atlanta, GA 404-814-0188
Eyolfson, Norman: 30 Waller Ave, Toronto, ON M6S 1B9 416-604-7620
Ezell, Heather: PO Box 710045, Dallas, TX 75371 214-428-7046

F

• Fabian, Natalie: pg 1283 1 Minetta St #5B, New York, NY 10012.............**212-505-0155**
  e-mail: fabian@ultinet.net / url: www.nataliefabian.com
• Fabre, Jacques: pg 788 353 W 53rd St #1W, New York, NY 10019.........**212-682-2462**
  url: www.amerartists.com / fax: 212-582-0090
Fabricatore, Carol: 16 Watson Ave, Ossing, NY 10562 914-762-0376
Fagg III, Charles O: 351 Seabull Ave SW, Palm Bay, FL 32908 407-984-2334
Fahey, Gilbert: 60 Ridgewood St, Manchester, CT 06040 203-647-8955
Fain, Nick: 300 Broadway #32, San Francisco, CA 94133 415-398-3434
Fairman, Dolores: 58 W 15th St, New York, NY 10011 212-741-2539
Fairweather, Sidney: 3900 King's Highway #3A, Brooklyn, NY 11234 718-253-1504
Falcott, Julia: 74 Elmhurst Rd, Newton, MA 02158 617-964-6556
Falkenstern, Lisa: 232 Madison Ave #402, New York, NY 10016 212-889-8777
Falkowski, Daniel: 38 N Landon Ave, Kingston, PA 18704.....................215-529-0259
• Falliers, Zoe Danae: pg 1284
  369 Montezuma Ave #387, Santa Fe, NM 87501 ....**505-989-5061**
  e-mail: zdmf@ix.netcom.com / fax: 505-989-5091
Fallin, Ken: 220 E 57th St #5J, New York, NY 10022 212-832-8116
Fallon, Douglas: 50 Twin Brooks Ave, Middletown, NJ 07748 201-671-6064
Fallon, Mary: 1878 Iglchart Ave, St Paul, MN 55104 612-645-1802
Falls, Mark: 3129 Raymond Dr, Doraville, GA 30340............................770-454-7777
Falquet, Joan: 763 Ninth Ave #3S, New York, NY 10019 212-247-3854
Fanelli, Carolyn: 19 Stuyvesant Oval, New York, NY 10009 212-533-9829
Faniel, Lucie: 768 ac Bloomfield, Outremont, QU H2V 3S3 514-270-3222
Fanning, Jim: 10 E 66th St, Kansas City, MO 64113 816-361-5191
Faragher-Gomez, Patsy: 1198 Santa Ynez Ave, Los Osos, CA 93402 805-528-4542
Farber, Joan: 310 E Aliso St, Ojai, CA 93023 805-640-8949
Faria, Jeff: 937 Garden St, Hoboken, NJ 07030 201-656-3063
• Faricy, Patrick: pg 342,343 327 E 89th St #3E, New York, NY 10128......**212-831-5650**
  fax: 212-831-6241
  1306 Alabama St, Huntington Beach, CA 92648 ....**714-969-7766**
  fax: 714-374-3744
Farkas, David: PO Box 23, Amherst, MA 01004 800-809-0958
Farkas, Gabriella: 841 N Kenter Ave, Los Angeles, CA 90049 310-471-0990
Farley, Andrew: 28 Shelton St/Covent Garden, London, England, UK WC2H 71-240-2077
Farley, David M: 353 W 53rd St #1W, New York, NY 10019 212-682-2462
Farley, Malcolm: 4 E Ohio Studio B, Chicago, IL 60611 312-321-1336
  5 E 17th St 6th Fl, New York, NY 10003 212-691-2667
  San Francisco, CA 415-543-6056
Farmer, Tom: 2505 Kennedy St NE, Minneapolis, MN 55413 800-659-2001
• Farnham, Joe: pg 1065 80 Edgecliff Road, Watertown, MA 02179 ....**617-926-3266**
Farrell, Anne: 131 Huddleson, Santa Fe, NM 87501 505-983-5126
Farrell, Marybeth: 320 Highwood Ave, Tenafly, NJ 07670 201-569-1299
Farrell, Richard: 326 Sackett St #2B, Brooklyn, NY 11231 718-802-1217
Farrell, Rick: Los Angeles, CA 213-934-3395
  Chicago, IL 847-222-0337
• Farrell, Russell: pg 788 353 W 53rd St #1W, New York, NY 10019 ....**212-682-2462**
  url: www.amerartists.com / fax: 212-582-0090
Farrell, Sean: 320 E 42nd St #112, New York, NY 10017 212-949-6081
• Farrington, Susan: pg 702,703 6 Parker Rd, Arlington, MA 02174 ....**781-641-2787**
  fax: 781-641-2244
• Farris, Jason: pg 1067 1332 Evelyn St #4, Rockford, IL 61103 ....**800-887-7146**
  url: www.jasonfarris.com
Farris, Joe: 950 Klish Way, Del Mar, CA 92014 619-259-5774

Fasolino, Peter: 100 President St, Brooklyn, NY 11231 718-834-6276
Fasolino, Teresa: 115 West 2nd Street, New York, NY 10011 212-989-4600
Fasolt, Natalie: 165 Ave A #9, New York, NY 10009 212-473-5909
Fast, Ingo: 25 Broadway, Brooklyn, NY 11211 718-387-9570
Fast, Judith: 33-68 21st St, Long Island City, NY 11106.......................718-721-5426
Faucher, Virginie: 4667 rue Hutchinson, Montréal, QU H2V 4A2 514-271-8105
Faulk, Claudia: 1445 Fern Pl, Vista, CA 92083 619-945-6576
• Faulkner, Andrew: pg 1215
  3020 Bridgeway #107, Sausalito, CA 94965 ....**415-332-3521**
  url: www.afstudio.com
Faulkner, BJ: 63 Hawthorne St, Lenox St, MA 01240 413-637-4951
Faulkner, David: 6209 Academy Ridge Dr, Albuquerque, NM 87111 505-296-5944
Faulkner, Matt: 27231 W Fourteen Mile Rd, Franklin, MI 48025..............810-626-2983
Faure, Renee: 600 Second St, Neptune Beach, FL 32233......................904-246-2781
• Faust, Clifford: pg 1211 322 W 57th St #42P, New York, NY 10019 ....**212-581-9461**
Faust, Leslie A: 5 Plant Ave, St Louis, MO 63119 314-918-0464
Fauver, Chris: 601 Oak Haven Dr, Falls Church, VA 22046 703-538-4291
Favereau, Beatrice: 460 rue Saint-Catherine, Montréal, QU H3B 1A7 514-393-9750
Favreau, Marie-Claude: 7779 rue Drolet, Montréal, QU H2R 2C8 514-274-9644
Faw, Andrew M: 29 W 19th St 4th Fl, New York, NY 10011 212-633-9063
Faw, Jenny: 29 W 19th St 4th Fl, New York, NY 10011 212-633-9063
Fay, Michael: 8 Thomas Rd, Lynnfield, MA 01940 617-334-2784
• FeBland, David: pg 1285
  670 West End Ave #11B, New York, NY 10025 ....**212-580-9299**
  fax: 212-580-3030
Fecci, Jo Marie: 335 W 19th St #B5, New York, NY 10011 212-727-2667
Feeney, Betsy: PO Box 257, Pleasantville, NY 10570 914-747-2220
Feigenbaum, Joseph: 1 Bridge St, Irvington, NY 10533 914-591-5911
Feigus, Jan: Box 207, Hatboro, PA 19040 215-957-9395
Feild, Ann Rebecca: 714 E 33rd St, Baltimore, MD 21218 410-235-0240
Feinberg, Susan: 433 W 21st St, New York, NY 10011 212-929-8679
Feinen, Jeff: 4702 Sawmill Rd, Clarence, NY 14031 716-759-8406
Feingold, Ken: 140 Fifth Ave, New York, NY 10011 212-645-9485
Feininger: 5 E 22nd St, New York, NY 10010 212-533-4984
• Feldman, Daniel: pg 1196
  11911 Magnolia Blvd #39, N Hollywood, CA 91607 ....**818-760-1759**
  e-mail: daniel@ogdemlifeldman.com / url: www.ogdemlifeldman.com / fax: 818-760-1582
Feldman, Joey: 800-276-5570
Feldman, Joey: 1139 Titan St, Philadelphia, PA 19147 215-551-1960
Felker, Robert: 7118 Upper River Rd, Prospect, KY 40059 502-228-9427
Fell, Dan: 4 Normandy Blvd, Toronto, ON M5L 3K2 416-699-1525
  420 Lexington Ave, New York, NY 10170 212-986-5680
Fellman, Lynn: 121 Washington Ave South #1814, Minneapolis, MN 55401..612-359-9048
• Fellows, Kara: pg 781 5236 W 56th St, Minneapolis, MN 55436 ....**612-926-5585**
  fax: 612-929-3347
Fellows, Stan Olson: 817 S Westwood Dr, Minneapolis, MN 55416..........612-374-3169
Feltenstein, Keith: 144-10 38th Ave, Flushing, NY 11354......................718-359-5140
Fenelon, Daniel: 5 Roosevelt Pl, Montclair, NJ 07042 201-746-0319
Fennimore, Linda: 808 West End Ave #801, New York, NY 10025 212-866-0279
• Fenster, Diane: pg 1000,1001
  1015-B Battery St, San Francisco, CA 94111 ....**415-398-9121**
  e-mail: fredarep@earthlink.net / fax: 415-398-6136
  287 Reichling Ave, Pacifica, CA 94044 ....**650-355-5007**
  e-mail: fenster@sfsu.edu / url: www.sirius.com/~fenster / fax: 650-355-5007
Ferguson, Heleman: 10512 Pilla Terra Ct/Warfld Fr, Laurel, MD 20723 ...301-604-4270
Ferguson, Peter: 468 Queen St E #104, Toronto, ON M5A 1T7 416-367-2446
Fernandes, Stanislaw: 874 Broadway #305, New York, NY 10003 212-533-2648
Fernandez, Jacobson: 141-10 28th St, Flushing, NY 11354 212-206-0066
Fernandez, Luis: 731 Stovall Blvd NE, Atlanta, GA 30342 800-791-1189
Ferrato, Donna: 25 Lenard St, New York, NY 10013 212-367-7004
Ferreira, Melissa: 231 Mayatt Rd, Barrington, RI 02806 401-245-8438
Ferrera, Steve: 609 Ashbury St, San Francisco, CA 94117 415-621-2434
Ferretti, James: 207 Freedom Circle, Harleysville, PA 19438 215-361-1021
Ferris, Keith: 50 Moraine Rd, Morris Plains, NJ 07950 201-539-3363
Ferrone, Nick: 12 Remsen St #3, Brooklyn, NY 11201 718-488-0140
Ferrulli, Dan: 5370 Graceland Ave, Indianapolis, IN 46208 317-257-5438
Ferster, Gary: 756 Marlin Ave #4, Foster City, CA 94404 800-953-3535
Fertig, Howard: 7-15 162nd St #6C, Beechhurst, NY 11357 718-746-6265
Fervoy, John: 3657 N Marshfield, Chicago, IL 60613 773-327-9192
Feuereisen, Fernando: 885 Tenth Ave #2G, New York, NY 10019 212-399-3269
• Fiedler, Joseph: pg 395 250 W 57th St #521, New York, NY 10107 ....**212-397-7330**
  url: www.lindgrensmith.com (and) www.stockillustrated.com
• Field, Ann: pg 958,959 53 W Jackson Blvd #1454, Chicago, IL 60604 ....**312-435-0055**
  4606 Cedar Spring #1527, Dallas, TX 75219 ....**214-559-0055**
  325 Wilson Way, Larkspur, CA 94939 ....**415-927-4500**
  137 W 14th St #204, New York, NY 10011 ....**212-337-0055**
  2910 16th St, Santa Monica, CA 90405 ....**310-450-6413**
Field, Bob: 17 Cranston St, Jamaica Plains, MA 02130 617-983-3230
Field, Jillian: 35093 Sunflower Ln, Squaw Valley, CA 93675 209-332-2832
Field, Lori Nelson: 8 Garden St, Montclair, NJ 07042 201-783-1321
Fields, Cathy: 5111 So Orcas St, Seattle, WA 98118 206-725-9192
Fields, Gary: 30 Allen Dr, Wayne, NJ 07470 201-633-8060
Fifield, Lew: 1300 W Mt Royal-Visual Comms, Baltimore, MD 21217 410-225-2239
Fijal, Ted: 121 Carriage Rd, Chicopee, MA 01020 413-532-7334
Fike, Scott: 1200 E Colorado Blvd Studio B, Pasadena, CA 91106 818-405-9219
Filippucci, Sandra: 455 W 23rd St #8D, New York, NY 10011 212-366-1893
Fillbach, Jeff: 22 Morning Breeze, Irving, CA 92612 714-854-6322
Film Art, Jennifer Long: 3780 Wilshire Blvd #710, Los Angeles, CA 90010 ...213-480-1059
Fine, Howard: 327 E 89th St #3E, New York, NY 10128 212-831-5650
Finewood, Bill: 604 Colton Ave, Newark, NY 14513 315-331-2905
Finger, John: 1241 Mountain View Blvd, Walnut Creek, CA 94596 510-945-0612
Finger, Ronald: 60 E 42nd St #822, New York, NY 10165 212-682-1490
Finkbeiner, Robert: 257 Indian Creek Rd, Martinez, GA 30907 706-721-9529
Finlay, Steve: 1059 Fairfax Circle W, Lantana, FL 33462 561-965-4728
Finley Illustration, Tracey: 801 Jone St #309, San Francisco, CA 94109 415-749-0908

Friedman, Marvin: 17 Montague Ave, W Trenton, NJ 08628 609-883-1576
Friedman, Todd G: 1032 Euclid Ave, Miami Beach, FL 33139 305-538-8518
Friel, Bryan: 4802 E 2nd St #1, Long Beach, CA 90803 562-439-0107
Friesen, Lianne: 203 Boulton Ave, Toronto, ON M4M 2J8 416-469-3727
Frisari, Frank: 7 Washington Street, Beverly, MA 01915 978-921-0887
• **Frisino, James : pg 1291** 6822 26th St NE, Seattle, WA 98115 ....**800-578-4433**
Friske, Maria: 21 Birch Crescent, Rochester, NY 14607 716-473-0889
Fritch, Diana: 28315 Driza, Mission Viejo, CA 92692 714-458-2356
Frith, Michael: 42 Delavan St, Brooklyn, NY 11231 718-624-1906
Fritz, Glenda: 212 Winslow Wy, Columbia, SC 29223 803-736-1671
Fritz-Zavacki, Ron: 4029 Linnet Ct, Sacramento, CA 95864 916-482-9031
Frizzell, Mark: PO Box 3176, Woburn, MA 01888 617-933-0805
Frohman, Jesse: 16 Bethune St, New York, NY 10014 212-989-0026
Froman, Loralie: 168 Linda St, San Francisco, CA 94110 415-647-5697
Frome, Mitchell: 144-18 72nd Rd, Flusing, NY 11367 212-496-3703
Frumkin, Peter: 400 W 43rd St #30R, New York, NY 10036 212-694-7837
Frush, Mark: 5329 N Glenwood, Chicago, IL 60640 773-561-6584
Fry, Dan: 474 Malvern Rd, Akron, OH 44303 330-864-7544
Fry, Leslie: 48 Elm St, Winooski, VT 05404 802-655-4349
Fry, W Logan: 2835 Southern Rd, Richfield, OH 44286 216-659-3104
Frye, Tony: 232 6th St SE #3, Washington, DC 20003 202-546-7842
• **Fryer, James: pg 578**
8 Woodcroft Ave, London, England NW7 2AG ....**+44-181-906-2288**
e-mail: info@artbank.ltd.uk / url: www.artbank.ltd.uk / fax: +44-181-906-2289
Frymark, Ted: 1111 Hornblend #6, San Diego, CA 92109 619-234-6633
Frymire, Bill: 6 E Third Ave, Vancouver, BC V5T 1C3 604-875-9880
Fuchs, Bernie: 155 Milburn Ave, Milburn, NJ 07041 201-467-0223
Fujimori, Brian: 2118 Carnegie Lane #4, Redondo Beach, CA 90278 310-318-9252
Fujisaki, Tuko: 1051 S Big Bend Blvd #210, St Louis, MO 63117 314-647-7377
1635 E 22nd St, Oakland, CA 94606 510-535-0495
12 Duende Rd, Santa Fe, NM 87505 800-208-2456
Fujiwara, Kim: Los Angeles, CA 213-688-7428
Chicago, IL 312-663-5506
Panama City, FL 904-747-8415
New York, NY 212-643-0896
468 Queen St E #104, Toronto, ON M5A 1T7 416-367-2446
Fuka, Ted: 19224 Schoolhouse Rd, Mokena, IL 60448 708-479-9514
Fukuda, Fujie: 101B Sea Oats Dr, Juno Beach, FL 33408 407-626-2164
Fulk, Karen C: PO Box 518, Wheatland, CA 95692 916-633-9353
Fuller, Rocky: 2233 Kemper Ln, Cincinnati, OH 45206 513-861-1400
Fuller, Steve: 29 Terry Ave, Schnectady, NY 12303 518-356-1048
Fullmer, Howard: 100 N Pacific Hwy #140, Talent, OR 97540 541-535-8380
Fullmer, Margie & Howard: 666 Bantry Ln, Stone Mountain, GA 30083 404-296-9666
• **Funkhouser, Kristen: pg 1293** 716 Sanchez St, San Francisco, CA 94114 ....**415-285-8267**
alternate **310-452-4240**
e-mail: Salzman@designlink.com / fax: 415-285-8268
Furgalack, Roberta: 10 Maize Dr, Charlestown, RI 02813 401-364-3667
Furukawa, Mel: 116 Duane St, New York, NY 10007 212-349-3225

G

• **Gaadt, David: pg 423** 60 E 42nd St, New York, NY 10165-1940 ....**212-867-8092**
e-mail: DHLT@aol.com / url: www.HT-LTD.com / fax: 212-949-1977
Gaadt, George: 888 Thorn, Sewickley, PA 15143 412-741-5161
• **Gabanyi, Alexandra: pg 1456,1457**
39 Hamilton Terr, New York, NY 10031 ....**212-283-3401**
url: www.wayart.com
• **Gabbana, Marc: pg 1219** 2453 Olive Ct, Windsor, ON N8T 3N4 ....**519-948-2418**
fax: 519-948-2418
Gabel, Ed: 917 4th Ave, Wall (Belmar), NJ 07719 908-681-8780
Gabel, Kurt: 364 Cobblestone Dr, Colorado Springs, CO 80906 719-576-3523
• **Gaber, Brad: pg 146** 420 Lexington Ave, New York, NY 10170 ....**212-986-5680**
url: www.mendolaart.com / fax: 212-818-1246
West Coast **206-860-0670**
Gabl, Max: 4330 McLaughlin Ave #207, Los Angeles, CA 90066 310-572-9978
• **Gabor, Tim: pg 344,345** 327 E 89th St #3E, New York, NY 10128 ....**212-831-5650**
fax: 212-831-6241
1306 Alabama St, Huntington Beach, CA 92648 ....**714-969-7766**
Gabriele, Antonio J: 931 Deep Lagoon Ln, Ft Myers, FL 33919 305-433-3202
Gaczek, Carol: 29 Exeter St, Morris Plains, NJ 07950 201-644-9286
• **Gad, Victor: pg 1040,1041**
57 Charles St W #1310, Toronto, ON M5S 2X1 ....**416-410-5638**
e-mail: mail@victorgad.com / url: www.victorgad.com
Gadecki, Ted: 2909 Cole Ave #118, Dallas, TX 75204 214-871-1316
Gadino, Victor: 60 E 42nd St #822, New York, NY 10165 212-682-1490
• **Gaetano, Nicholas: pg 178** 194 Third Ave 3rd Fl, New York, NY 10003 ....**212-475-0440**
url: www.vickimorganassociates.com / fax: 212-353-8538
Gafflin, Beverly: 2500 Bryn Maur Ln, Riverside, CA 92507 909-686-2851
Gage, Hal: 2008 E Northern Lights Blvd, Anchorage, AK 99508 907-272-4356
Gagnon, Nathlie: 12045 pl de la Gracieuse, Québec, QU G2A 3C3 418-845-6207
Gagos, Gretchen: 1641 High Crest Pl, Escondido, CA 92025 619-489-2248
Gahr, David: 49 Eighth Ave, Brooklyn, NY 11217 718-789-3365
Gainley, Mary Anne: 617 Union St, Duxbury, MA 02332 617-834-3411
Gal, Susan: 1265 Monterey Ave, Berkeley, CA 94707 510-528-9343
Galifianakis, Nick: 3427 Barger Dr, Falls Church, VA 22044 703-916-9350
Galindo, Felipe: 509 W 110th St #3H, New York, NY 10025 212-864-6648
• **Gall, Chris: pg 819** 853 Broadway #1201, New York, NY 10003 ....**212-677-9100**
e-mail: chislovsky@aol.com / fax: 212-353-0954
Gallagher, Dana: 541 Hudson St, New York, NY 10014 212-924-5497
Gallagher, David: 1475 E Murdock Dr, Pleasant Grove, UT 84062 801-785-7830
Gallaher, Trey: 4951 Cherry Ave #118, San Jose, CA 95118 800-369-8739
• **Gallardo, Gervasio: pg 502**
217 E 86th St Box 212, New York, NY 10028 ....**212-427-5632**
Gallimore, Gaylen: 372A Campbell Rd, Wall, NJ 07719 908-449-4245
Gallina-Jones, Martyn: 1320 York Ave #16Z, New York, NY 10021 212-459-4229
Gallipoli, Wayne: 54 Brushy Plain Rd #4D, Branford, CT 06405 203-878-8972
Gallivan, Gretta: 11 North St #3, Marcellus, NY 13108 315-673-9123
Gallo, Frank: 2 Predmore Ave, Colonia, NJ 07067 908-382-8293
Gallow, Beth: 1649A Willis Dr, Indiana, PA 15701 508-992-7375
Galloway, Nixon: 3850 Eddingham Ave, Calabasas, CA 91302 818-222-5445
Galloway, Nolan: 1242 Pamlico, Greensboro, NC 27408 910-852-6014
Galloway, Randy: 17031 N 44th Place, Phoenix, AZ 85032 602-867-4620
Gamache, John: 192 Southville Rd, Southborough, MA 01772 508-872-4549
Gamble, Kent: 353 W 53rd St #1W, New York, NY 10019 212-682-2462
Gampert, John: 99 Park Ave #210A, New York, NY 10016 800-398-9544
Ganann, Sean: 178A Palmerston Ave, Toronto, ON M6J 2J4 416-603-4418
Gandy, Curt: 4801 Jeffery St, McHenry, IL 60050 847-497-3027
Ganley, Mary-Anne: 617 Union St, Boston, MA 02332 617-834-3411
Garafalo, Frank: 5755 E River Rd, Tucson, AZ 85750 520-577-7557
Garafola, Ralph: 206 Linda Ln, Edison, NJ 08820 908-756-9254
Garbett, Paul: RR2, Puslinch, ON N0B 2J0 416-431-7034
Garbot, Dave: 11369 SW Winterlake Dr, Tigard, OR 97223 503-579-0663
Garbowski, Gene: 7997 Columbian Pike, Laurel, MD 20723 301-498-2726
Garbriel, Kathrine: 1264 W Winona, Chicago, IL 60640 312-243-6157
Garces, A J: 8427 Bourwell, San Antonio, TX 78250 210-509-9943
Garcia Illus, David V: 806 N Hart Blvd, Harvard, IL 60033 815-943-1241
Garcia, Aaron: 8958 Elizabeth Ave, South Gate, CA 90280 213-569-8853
Garcia, Ernie: 640 NE 72nd Terr, Miami, FL 33138 305-754-5412
Garcia, James J: 430 Dongan Hills Ave, Staten Island, NY 10305 718-351-3071
Garcia, Max: 307 S Trooper Rd, Norristown, PA 19403 610-539-1130
Garcia, Segundo: 43 E 19th St, New York, NY 10003 212-254-4996
Garcia, Tom: 597 Riverside Ave, Westport, CT 06880 203-226-4724
Garcia, Victor: 911 South Skinker Blvd, St Louis, MO 63105 800-393-9497
Gardner, Bonnie T: 142 W 19th St, New York, NY 10011 212-255-0863
Gardner, Diane: PO Box 63637, Seattle, WA 98188 206-441-8914
Gardner, Emma: 585 Carlton Ave 3rd Fl, Brooklyn, NY 11238 718-857-0796
Gardner, Gail: 227 Marlborough St, Boston, MA 02116 617-266-8626
Gardner, Jean: 1623 Spruce St, Philadelphia, PA 19103 215-893-9812
Gardner, Jeffrey: 141 W 28th St 9th Fl, New York, NY 10001 212-714-1731
Gardner, Mike: 37 Buckmaster Rd, Westwood, MA 02090 617-762-0906
• **Gardner, Stephen: pg 526** 89 Fifth Ave #901, New York, NY 10003 ....**212-627-1554**
fax: 212-627-1719
Gardos, Susan: 469 Queen St #102, Toronto, ON M5A 1T7 416-867-9345
• **Garland, Bill: pg 788** 353 W 53rd St #1W, New York, NY 10019 ....**212-682-2462**
url: www.amerartists.com / fax: 212-582-0090
• **Garland, Michael: pg 1294,1295** 79 Manor Rd, Patterson, NY 12563 ....**914-878-4347**
e-mail: garlandmp@aol.com / url: www.bestweb.net/nartmtn/ / fax: 914-878-4349
• **Garner, David: pg 1296** 311 W 97th St #7E, New York, NY 10025 ....**212-663-9548**
fax: 212-666-9359
Garner, Hjordis: 1834 Lincoln Park W, Chicago, IL 60614 312-664-8673
• **Garns, Allen: pg 1022,1023** 611 S Loma Vista Circle, Mesa, AZ 85204 ....**602-854-3121**
Garon, David: 409 W Maryland St, Duluth, MN 55803 218-724-3020
Garramone, Richard: 49 Ridgedale Ave #201, East Hanover, NJ 07936 201-887-7234
Garret, Inc, The: 9322 Olive Blvd, St Louis, MO 63132 314-997-2655
Garrett, Tom: 623 3rd Ave SE, Minneapolis, MN 55414 612-331-3123
Garrick, Jacqueline: 333 E 75th St, New York, NY 10021 212-628-1018
Garrido, Hector: 420 Lexington Ave, New York, NY 10170 212-986-5680
Garrison: PO Box 35584, Houston, TX 77235 713-729-7615
Garrison, Barbara: 12 E 87th St, New York, NY 10128 212-348-6382
Garrity, Bruce: 249 S Broad St, Penns Grove, NJ 08069 609-299-3966
Garrity, Dennis: 8443 Michael Dr, Boynton Beach, FL 33437 407-734-9414
• **Garrow, Dan: pg 236,237** 501 Fifth Ave, New York, NY 10017 ....**212-490-2450**
url: www.renardrepresents.com / fax: 212-697-6828
Gartel, Laurence: 19650 Black Olive Ln, Boca Raton, FL 33498 407-477-2526
Gartner, Stephanie: 28950 Fountainwood St, Agoura Hills, CA 91301 818-889-0891
• **Garvie, Ben: pg 632** 4 E Ohio Studio B, Chicago, IL 60611 ....**312-321-1336**
fax: 312-321-1350
5 E 17th St 6th Fl, New York, NY 10003 ....**212-691-2667**
url: www.spar.org / fax: 212-633-1844
Garvin, Elaine: 2045 McClintock, McClintock, AZ 85282 520-970-6768
Garvin, Vance: 2509 W Woodlyn Way, Greensboro, NC 27410 910-684-7447
Garza, Roy: 302 Berlin Ave, San Antonio, TX 78211 210-922-7282
Gasowski, Igor: 1220 Colusa Ave, Berkeley, CA 94707 510-524-3777
Gast, Josef: 527 Wellington Ave, Seattle, WA 98122 206-720-1033
Gates Design, Jeff: 2000 Hermitage Ave, Silver Spring, MD 20902 301-949-0436
Gates, Kathleen: 1901 Felix, Memphis, TN 38114 901-725-4667
Gatherum, Ken: 5803 NE 181st St, Seattle, WA 98155 206-402-8606
Gatto, Chris: PO Box 4041, Stamford, CT 06907 203-264-2400
Gaudette, Christine: 630 rue Mott, Saint-jean-sur-ric, QU J3B 4Z2 514-349-1818
Gauthier, Aline: Montréal, QU 514-277-8176
Gauthier, Corbert: 60 E 42nd St #822, New York, NY 10165 212-682-1490
Gavin, Bill: 268 Orchard St, Millis, MA 02054 508-376-5727
Gavin, Kerry: 154 E Canaan Rd, East Canaan, CT 06024 860-824-4839
Gay-Kassel, Doreen: 53 Railroad Pl, Hopewell, NJ 08525 609-497-0783
Gayler, Anne: RR 6 Box 187, Monroe, NY 10950 914-496-4425
Gaz, Stan: 58 W 15th St, New York, NY 10011 212-741-2539
Gazsi, Ed: 327 E 89th St #3E, New York, NY 10128 212-831-5650
Gazzo, Peppi: 42 Tamaques Way, Westfield, NJ 07090 201-798-6389
Geary, Rick: 99 Park Ave #210A, New York, NY 10016 800-398-9544
• **Gebert, Warren: pg 1297** 2 Hunte Ct, Suffern, NY 10901 ....**914-354-2536**
fax: 914-362-8635
Geddes, William: 215 W 78th St, New York, NY 10024 212-799-4464
• **Geerinck, Manuel: pg 656** Pier 33 North, San Francisco, CA 94111 ....**415-956-4750**
e-mail: cgr@slip.net / url: www.coreygrahamreps.com / fax: 415-391-6104
15 Warrenton Ave, Hartford, CT 06105 ....**860-523-4562**
Gehm, Charles: 420 Lexington Ave #2760, New York, NY 10170 212-697-8525
Geiser, Janie: 340 E 9th St, New York, NY 10003 212-353-5015
• **Gelb, Jacki: pg 46,47** 108 E 35th St #2, New York, NY 10016 ....**212-889-3337**
url: www.theispot.com/artist/gelb / fax: 212-889-3341
• **Gelen, Michael: pg 1181** 68 Dorchester Rd, Buffalo, NY 14222 ....**716-882-0102**
url: www.inkwellstudios.com / fax: 716-884-1047
Gelhardt, Rob: 902 Brookwood Dr, Tallahassee, FL 32308 904-877-6185
Gellman, Rachel: 192 Bleecker St, New York, NY 10012 212-473-7502

Gellman, Sim: 475 N Prince Rd, St Louis, MO 63132 314-994-3045
Gellos, Nancy: 3634 W Lawton St, Seattle, WA 98199 206-285-5838
Gencarelli, Elizabeth: 235 W 22nd St #7K, New York, NY 10011 212-353-9073
Genco, Chuck: 201 E 17th St, New York, NY 10003..212-677-4588
• **Genn, Roman: pg 1060,1061** Los Angeles, CA **323-939-5927**
1810 Hardison Place #10, So Pasadena, CA 91030 ....**626-441-5691**
fax: 626-441-5691
Genova, Joe: 60 E 42nd St #822, New York, NY 10165..212-682-1490
Gensheimer, Frank: 5 Lawrence St Bldg 15, Bloomfield, NJ 07003 201-743-4305
Gensurowsky, Yvonne: 312 N Sparks Ave, Burbank, CA 91523 818-953-9440
Gentile, John & Anthony: 244 W 54th St 9th Fl, New York, NY 10019 212-757-1966
Gentry, John Edward: 2617 Mendocino Dr, Pinole, CA 94564...................................510-758-8456
• **Genzo, John Paul: pg 513**
217 E 86th St Box 212, New York, NY 10028 ....**212-427-5632**
fax: 212-427-6372
Geogriann, Margaret: 3314 Oberon St, Kensington, MD 20895 301-496-5566
George, Jeff: 853 Broadway #1201, New York, NY 10003...212-677-9100
George, Maureen Radcliffe: 1834 Clinton ave, Alameda, CA 94501 510-523-8170
George, Robert J: 366 Sterling Pl, Brooklyn, NY 11238 718-783-8514
Georgiann, Margaret G: 3314 Oberon St, Kensington, MD 20895 301-933-4912
Gerace, Patrick: 116 Park Ave #8, Morrison, CO 80465...303-697-1732
Gérard: 1385 av Bernard Quest, Outremont, QU H2V 1W1 514-279-9913
Gerardo, Suzan: 50 Fuller Brook Rd, Wellesley, MA 02181 617-235-8658
• **Geras, Audra: pg 243** 501 Fifth Ave, New York, NY 10017 ....**212-490-2450**
url: www.renardrepresents.com / fax: 212-697-6828
Gerber Studio: 18 Oak Grove Rd, Brookfield, CT 06804 203-775-3658
Gergely, Peter: 24 Roe Park, Highland Falls, NY 10928..914-446-2367
Gerlach, Carmeron: 99 Park Ave #210A, New York, NY 10016 800-398-9544
Germain, Phillipe: 27 chemin ile de Mai, Boisbriand, QU J7G 1R7..........................514-434-2116
Germon, Roy: 275 Bleeker St #4, NY, NY 10014 212-807-9728
Gerns, Laurie: 450 E Foothill Blvd, Glendora, CA 91741 ....
Gersch, Wolfgang: 255 Stuyvesant Dr, San Anselmo, CA 94960...............................415-258-8210
• **Gerstein, Mordicai: pg 1298** 186 Crescent St, Northampton, MA 01060 ......**413-268-7549**
e-mail: risumo@javavanet.com / url: theispot.com/artist/gerstein
Gersten, Gerry: 177 Newtown Turnpike, Weston, CT 06883 203-222-1608
Gervais, Stephen: 183 Riverside Ave, Warwick, RI 02889 401-737-8526
Gerwitz, Rick: 228 E 10th St, New York, NY 10003 212-353-9838
Geter, Tyrone: 218 Elm Court, Rhinelander, WI 54501..715-369-2130
Geyer, Jackie: 107 6th St #207 Fulton Bldg, Pittsburgh, PA 15222 412-261-1111
Ghaboussi, Sina: 666 Greenwich St #860, New York, NY 10014..............................212-675-5719
Gherardi, Bob: 8209 Tamarron Dr, Plainsboro, NJ 08563 609-936-9138
Ghidini, Giovanni: 46 Carmine #3, New York, NY 10014 212-807-0119
• **Ghiglione, Kevin: pg 561,568,569**
155 Lippincott St, Toronto, ON M5S 2P3 ....**416-505-9522**
toll-free **888-277-7200**
e-mail: shelley@sbaillustrates.com / url: www.sbaillustrates.com
Ghirardo, Claudio: 146 Geoffrey St, Toronto, ON M6R 1P5 416-530-0702
• **Giacobbe, Beppe: pg 184,185**
194 Third Ave 3rd Fl, New York, NY 10003 ....**212-475-0440**
url: www.vickimorganassociates.com / fax: 212-353-8538
Giambarba, Paul: 5851 Vine Hill Rd, Sebastapol, CA 95472......................................707-829-8921
• **Giana Graphx, Alan D Giana: pg 1470**
17 Colonial Dr, Simsbury, CT 06089..**860-658-5938**
url: www.gianagraphx.com
Giangregorio, Laurie: 6847 La Pasada, Hereford, AZ 85615..520-378-3183
• **Giannetti, Francesco: pg 1299** 31 Amity Pl, Amherst, MA 01002..................**888-339-3172**
Giannini-Hurtley, Gay: 645 Sierra Dr, Dixon, CA 95620..916-678-3645
Giardina, Laura: 12 Buckingham Ct, Pomona, NY 10970 914-354-0871
Giarnella, Andy: 259 Main St, E Berlin, CT 06023 203-828-8410
• **Gibbon, Rebecca: pg 611** 155 W 15th St, New York, NY 10011.......................**212-989-8770**
fax: 212-989-7892
• **Gibbs, Michael: pg 500,501** 2149 Lyon St #5, San Francisco, CA 94115 .....**415-921-7140**
e-mail: art@conradreps.com / url: www.conradreps.com / fax: 415-921-3939
Gibson, Barbara: 3501 Toddsbury Ln, Onley, MD 20832...301-570-9480
Gibson, Clancy: 2 Silver Ave #205, Toronto, ON M6R 3A2 416-530-1500
• **Gibson-Nash, Nancy: pg 1301** 88 Welch St, Peaks Island, MA 04108 ....**207-766-5761**
fax: 207-766-4472
Giedd, Richard: 28 Emerson Rd, Watertown, MA 02172 617-924-4350
Gieseke, Thomas A: 7909 W 61st St, Merriam, KS 66202 913-677-4593
Gifford, Leslie: 320 Carrera Dr, Mill Valley, CA 94941 415-388-4104
Giglio, Richard: 2231 Broadway #17, New York, NY 10024 212-724-8118
Gignilliat, Elaine: 420 Lexington Ave, New York, NY 10170 212-986-5680
Giguere, Ralph: 141-10 28th St, Flushing, NY 11354 212-206-0066
230 Cliveden Ave, Glenside, PA 19038 215-885-8434
Gil, Ramon: 328 E 14th St, New York, NY 10003 800-874-7442
Gilbert, Adam: 1524 E 8th St, Tucson, AZ 85719...520-884-8078
Gilbert, Douglas R: 24 Carpenter St, Amesbury, MA 01913..978-388-0029
Gilbert, Yvonne: 666 Greenwich St #860, New York, NY 10014...............................212-675-5719
Giles, Dorothy: 1751 E Whittier Blvd, La Habra, CA 90631 310-694-1424
Gilfoy, Bruce: 568 Washington St, Wellesley, MA 02181 617-235-8977
Gill, Tim: PO Box 1251, New York, NY 10023 212-774-4271
Gillies, Chuck: 420 Lexington Ave, New York, NY 10170..212-986-5680
Gilligan, Sheila: 185 Highland Ave, Somerville, MA 02143 617-628-5144
Gillot, Carol: 30-80 33rd St #3L, Long Island City, NY 11102 718-204-8791
Gilman, Mary: Star Rte 13-A, Wendell Depot, MA 01380 508-544-7425
Gilmore, Paulette: 2860 Running Pump Ln, Herndon, VA 22071.................................703-713-0949
Gimbrone, Joanne: 24 DeWitt St, Buffalo, NY 14213 716-881-2850
Gin, Byron: 1872 N Clybourn #404, Chicago, IL 60614 773-935-8840
Gingko Design: 130 Perry St, San Francisco, CA 94107...415-777-1866
Gino: 320 Bee Brook Rd, Washington, CT 06777 860-868-1011
Ginsburg, Max: 40 W 77th Street #14B, New York, NY 10024.....................................212-787-0628
Ginzinger, Karla: 20 W Hubbard #3E, Chicago, IL 60610...312-222-1361
Giordano, Edward: PO Box 226, Clifton, NJ 07011 201-772-1401
Giorgio, Nate: 481 8th Ave #1530, New York, NY 10036 212-221-8090
• **Giovannina Illustrations: pg 1260** 19 East Dr, Toronto, ON M6N 2N8..........**416-604-0057**
Giovanopoulos, Paul: 119 Prince St, New York, NY 10013 212-677-5919
Girden, JM: 2125 Cerrada Nopal E, Tucson, AZ 85718 520-628-2740
Girvin Design, Tim: 501 Fifth Ave, New York, NY 10017 212-490-2450
Gisko, Max: 2629 Wakefield Dr, Belmont, CA 94002 415-595-1893
Gissinger, Hans: 55 Warren St, New York, NY 10007..212-964-5549
Gist, Linda E: 224 Madison Ave, Fort Washington, PA 19034 215-643-3757
Giusti, Robert: 115 West 2nd Street, New York, NY 10011...212-989-4600
Glad, Deanna: PO Box 1962, San Pedro, CA 90733 310-831-6274
Gladstone, Dale: 32 Havermeyer St #2A, Brooklyn, NY 11211.....................................718-782-2250
Glasbergen, Randy J: PO Box 611, Sherburne, NY 13460...607-674-9492
• **Glasgow & Assocs, Dale: pg 1016,1017**
448 Hartwood Rd, Fredericksburg, VA 22406 ....**540-286-2539**
e-mail: dale@glasgowmedia.com & infoban@aol.com / url: www.glasgowmedia.com /
fax: 540-286-0316
Glass, Damian: 102 Cooks Bay Dr, Keswick, ON L4P 1M3 905-476-7985
Glass, Randy: 716 Montgomery St, San Francisco, CA 94111 415-433-1222
108 E 35th St #2, New York, NY 10016 212-889-3337
Glassman, Judy: 120A E 23rd St, New York, NY 10010..212-512-7800
Glazer & Kalayjian, Inc: 301 E 45th St #18F, New York, NY 10017..............................212-687-3099
Glazer, Art: 2 James Rd, Mt Kisco, NY 10549 914-666-4554
Glazer, Ted: 28 West View Rd, Spring Valley, NY 10977 914-354-1524
• **Glazier, Garth: pg 788** 353 W 53rd St #1W, New York, NY 10019..................**212-682-2462**
e-mail: info@amerartists.com / url: www.amerartists.com / fax: 212-582-0090
Gleeson, Tony: 2525 Hyperion Ave #4, Los Angeles, CA 90027...................................213-668-2704
Glenn, Mary Jane: 2 Thorne Ln, Oakdale, NY 11769 516-589-8065
Glessner, Marc: 24 Evergreen Rd, Somerset, NJ 08873 908-249-5038
Glick, Alisha: 200 Varick St #606, New York, NY 10014 212-229-1200
Glick, Judith: 301 E 79th St, New York, NY 10021 212-734-5268
Glick, Tracy: PO Box 96, New York, NY 10276...212-675-1976
Glidden, Althea: 2 Butler Rd, Reiserstown, MD 21136 301-523-5903
Glover, Ann: 1308 Factory Pl Box 25, Los Angeles, CA 90013 213-623-6203
• **Glover, Gary: pg 842** 165 E 32nd St, New York, NY 10016 ....**212-686-3514**
fax: 212-532-4302
Gmucs, Rebecca: 295 St Johns Pl #4B, Brooklyn, NY 11238...718-638-0903
• **Gnan, Patrick: pg 457** 731 N 24th St, Philadelphia, PA 19130.....................**215-232-6666**
url: www.deborahwolfeltd.com / fax: 215-232-6585
Godbout, Luc: 9098 rue Saint-ƒtienne, Saint-benoit De, QU JON 1KO............................514-258-2989
Godfrey, Linda: 925 Elm Grove Rd, Elm Grove, WI 53122 414-785-1940
Goehring, Steven: 25456 Bull Run, Alpine, OR 97456 541-424-5443
Goethals, Raphaelle: 3033 Fernwood Ave, Los Angeles, CA 90039..............................213-662-0020
Goettemoeller, Cheryl: 4319 Wilkinson Ave, Studio City, CA 91604 818-766-4929
Gok, Diana: 1522 Innes Ave, San Francisco, CA 94124...415-826-2846
Golan, Doron: 111 Mercer St, New York, NY 10012...212-925-0250
Gold, Eva: 87 Barrow St #6E, New York, NY 10014 212-337-0977
Gold, Sandi: 18 High St, Westerly, RI 02891 401-348-9571
Goldammer, Ken: 217 E 86th St Box 212, New York, NY 10028 212-427-5632
116 W Illinois St #5W, Chicago, IL 60610...312-836-0143
Goldberg, Amy: PO Box 1669, Tahoe City, CA 96145 916-581-3401
Goldberg, Ken: 1006 W Edgeware Rd, Los Angeles, CA 90026 213-740-9080
• **Goldberg, Richard A: pg 916,917** 15 Cliff St, Arlington, MA 02476 ....**781-646-1041**
url: www.theispot.com/artist/rag / fax: 781-646-0956
Golden, Gary: 300 N Schiller, Little Rock, AR 72205 501-376-4500
Golden, Harriet: 217 E 85th St #11, New York, NY 10028 212-249-4194
Golden, Helen: 460 El Capitan Pl, Palo Alto, CA 94306...415-494-3461
Golden, Jan: 2305 Ashland St #C, Ashland, OR 97520 800-435-6509
Golden, Kenneth Sean: 696 10th Ave, New York, NY 10019 212-246-3875
Golden, Peg: 822 Grand Terrace Ave, Baldwin, NY 11510...516-868-1858
Goldenberg, Lisa: 30 E 9th St #4L, New York, NY 10003 212-460-5680
Goldin, David: 111 Fourth Ave #7E, New York, NY 10003...212-529-5195
Goldinger, Andras: 215 C St SE #310, Washington, DC 20003 202-543-9029
Goldman, Bart: 360 W 36th St #8NW, New York, NY 10018...212-239-0047
Goldman, Dara: 15 May St, Boston, MA 02130...617-524-5152
• **Goldman, David: pg 764-768**
41 Union Sq W #918, New York, NY 10003...**212-807-6627**
Goldman, Marvin: RD 3 Gypsy Trail Rd, Carmel, NY 10512 914-225-8611
Goldrick, Lisa: 121 Mudtown Rd, Sussex, NJ 07461 201-702-1328
Goldsmith, Diane: 6 Monterey Terr, Orinda, CA 94563 510-253-9451
Goldstein, Edith: 1516 Wilmar Rd, Cleveland Hghts, OH 44121 216-381-7811
Goldstein, Elise: 182 E 95th St #2K, New York, NY 10128...212-534-3594
Goldstein, Howard: 7031 Aldea Ave, Van Nuys, CA 91406..818-987-2837
Goldstein, Jacqueline: 78-52 75th St, Glendale, NY 11385 718-366-4885
Goldstrom, Robert: 115 West 2nd Street, New York, NY 10011...................................212-989-4600
Golici, Ana: 225 Guy Lombardo Ave, Freeport, NY 11520..516-623-3392
Golueke, Richard: 350 Townsend St, San Francisco, CA 94107 415-546-9302
Gomez, Ignacio: 853 Broadway #1201, New York, NY 10003......................................212-677-9100
812 Kenneth Rd, Glendale, CA 91202 818-243-2838
Gomez, Loretta: 111 Fifth Ave 8th Fl, New York, NY 10003 212-420-8100
Gonnella, Rick: 229 W Illinois, Chicago, IL 60610 312-645-4500
Gonzales, Chuck: 611 Broadway #631, New York, NY 10012..212-477-1041
Gonzales, Danilo: 324 N Marengo Ave, Alhambra, CA 91801.......................................818-441-2787
Gonzalez, Dan: 286 Clinton Ave, Brooklyn, NY 11205...718-857-7530
Gonzalez, Danilo: 301 N Water St, Milwaukee, WI 53202 414-271-3388
Gonzalez, Pedro Julio: 9 Babbling Brook Ln, Suffern, NY 10901 914-368-8606
Gonzalez, Ray: 2346 Greendale Ct, Toms River, NJ 08755...201-567-6208
Gonzalez, Samuel: 3501 Gran Prix Dr, Sebring, FL 33872 908-895-0085
Gonzalez, Thomas: 1841 Lake Cypress Dr, Safety Harbor, FL 34695 813-725-4438
Gooch, Eas: 1121 Broadway Ave E #2, Seattle, WA 98102..206-726-8799
Good, Zane: 102 Temple, Woonsocket, RI 02895...401-765-7394
Goodall, Liz: 78 Bedford St #4A, New York, NY 10014 212-645-9480
Goode, Larry: 1205 W 43rd St, Austin, TX 78756 512-467-7471
Goode, Paul: 165 W 83rd St #41, New York, NY 1024 212-874-0713
Goode, Roger: PO Box 1022, Hillsboro, NH 03244 603-464-4234
Goodell Illus, Brad: 605 Arizona SE, Albuquerque, NM 87108 505-255-7889
Goodell, Jim: 42 Richards St, Worcester, MA 01603 508-756-0673
Goodfellow, Peter: 42 Delavan St, Brooklyn, NY 11231 718-624-1906

Goodfellow, Stephen: 146 Farrand Park, Detroit, MI 48203 313-883-4827
Goodin, Robert: 6541 El Roble, Long Beach, CA 92373 310-596-4311
Goodman, Aaron: 2125 N Charles St, Baltimore, MD 21218 410-547-0667
Goodman, Johanna: 222 E 51st St #4D, New York, NY 10022 212-759-8215
Goodman, Paula: 18 W 21st Street 17th Floor, New York, NY 10010 212-243-1333
Goodman, Steven P: 31 Elsom Pkwy, S Burlington, VT 05403 802-862-0077
Goodman-Willy, April: 3301A S Jefferson Ave, St Louis, MO 63118 314-773-2600
• **Goodrich, Carter: pg 1302,1303**
18 Imperial Palace #6E, Providence, RI 02903 ....**401-272-6094**
Goodwin, Theodore E: 13522 Ocean Gate Ave, Hawthorne, CA 90250 310-644-8410
Goozee, Dan: 22534 Malden St, West Hills, CA 91304 818-887-5624
Gordley, Scott: 19 Stuyvesant Oval, New York, NY 10009 212-505-9342
• **Gordon, Barbara: pg 836-842** 165 E 32nd St, New York, NY 10016 ....**212-686-3514**
Gordon, Brenda M: 1306 Riggs ST NW, Washington, DC 20009 202-462-6428
• **Gordon, Danny: pg 1304**
5500 NW 111th St, Oklahoma City, OK 73162 ....**405-728-1350**
fax: 405-728-9813
• **Gordon, David: pg 924,925** 337 A-B 41st St, Oakland, CA 94609 ....**510-547-1685**
Gordon, Donna: 29 Booth Ave #201, Toronto, ON M4M 2M3 416-463-8869
Gordon, Emily: 2022 Jones St, San Francisco, CA 94133 415-928-0457
Gordon, Hugh: 133-02 231st St, Springfield Gardens, NY 11413 718-978-2131
Gordon-Lucas, Bonnie: 2233 Kemper Ln, Cincinnati, OH 45206 513-861-1400
Gore, Elissa: 583 W 215th St #A3, New York, NY 10034 212-567-2161
• **Gore, Leonid: pg 687** 666 Greenwich St #860, New York, NY 10014 ....**212-675-5719**
url: www.hkportfolio.com / fax: 212-675-6341
Gorey, Edward: PO Box 1062, Bayonne, NJ 07002 201-436-4362
Goring, Trevor: 5855 Green Valley Cir #308, Culver City, CA 90230 310-558-4193
Gorman, Gabriel: 2911 Medical Arts St, Austin, TX 78705 512-473-2776
Gorman, Martha: 3057 Pharr Ct North NW #E6, Atlanta, GA 30305 404-261-5632
• **Gorman, Stan: pg 751** 1464 Linden Ave, Chicago, IL 60035 ....**847-432-2415**
fax: 773-883-0375
Los Angeles **213-934-3395**
Fax: 213-936-2757
Gorski, Peter: 124 Pleasant Ave, Peak's Island, ME 04108 207-766-5593
Gorton, Julia: 207 Baldwin St, Glen Ridge, NJ 07028 201-748-6997
Gorton/Kirk Studio: 207 Baldwin St, Glen Ridge, NJ 07028 201-748-6997
Gosfield, Josh: 200 Varick St #508, New York, NY 10012 212-645-8826
Goss, James: 1606 N Sierra Bonita Ave, Los Angeles, CA 90046 213-876-2205
Goss, Stephen: 1673 Kalkaua Ave, Honolulu, HI 96816 808-949-1394
Goss, Tronnie: 1635 W Decatur St, Decatur, IL 62522 217-423-4739
Gothard, David: 104 Creek Rd, Bangor, PA 18013 610-588-4937
Goto, Scott: 1655A Paula Dr #A, Honolulu, HI 96816 808-941-5394
Gottesman, Jonathan: 343 E 30th St #7F, New York, NY 10016 212-889-8917
Gottfried, Max: 82-60 116th St #CC3, Kew Gardens, NY 11418 718-441-9868
Gottlieb, Dale: 1617 Douglas Ave, Bellingham, WA 98225 206-647-2598
Goudey, Ray: 4017 Crescent Rd, Carlsbad, CA 92008 760-729-8173
Goudreau, Roc: E Main St Box 322, Ware, MA 01082 413-967-9855
Gould, Peter: PO Box1216, Belmont, CA 94002 415-547-8643
Gowdy, Carolyn: 51 Camden St, Toronto, ON M5V 1V2 416-703-1913
Gower, Neil: 42 Delavan St, Brooklyn, NY 11231 718-624-1906
Gowling, John: 3461 Tilden St, Philadelphia, PA 19129 215-844-1121
Gowman, Dave: Vancouver, BC 888-592-0968
Goyer, Mireille H: 7600 W Manchester Ave #1313,
Playa Del Ray, CA 90293 310-827-8791
Graber, Jack: 620 Union St, Schenectady, NY 12305 518-370-0312
Grace, Alexa: 530 W 236th St #3G, Riverdale, NY 10463 212-254-4424
Grace, Davies: Brooklyn, NY 718-857-6538
Grace, Laurie: 630 Ninth Ave #409, New York, NY 10036 212-956-4308
Grace, Liz: 62 State St, Guilford, CT 06437 203-458-3094
Graef, Renee: 2730 S Shore Dr, Milwaukee, WI 53207 414-481-8977
Grafica, Gergei: 24 Roe Park, Highland Falls, NY 10928 914-446-2367
Grafix-n-Toons Studios: 107 Rosewood Dr, Wappingers Falls, NY 12590 914-896-2021
Graham, Debbie: 2401 W Seldon Ln, Phoenix, AZ 85021 602-997-7777
Graham, Heather: 4 Normandy Blvd, Toronto, ON M4L 3K2 416-867-9345
Graham, Jack: 853 Broadway #1201, New York, NY 10003 212-677-9100
6151 W Shannon St, Chandler, AZ 85226 602-940-3210
Graham, Thomas: 446 80th St, Brooklyn, NY 11209 718-680-2975
Grahame, Donald: 211 Francisco St, San Francisco, CA 94133 415-626-7116
Grahn, Geoffrey: 4054 Madison Ave, Culver City, CA 90232 310-838-7824
Grajek, Tim: 213 Webber Ave, North Tarrytown, NY 10591 914-482-4036
Gramm, Mark: 2655 Shield Dr, Winston Salem, NC 27107 909-247-6220
Gran, Eliza: 6 Parker Rd, Arlington, MA 02174 617-641-2787
Gran, Julia: 3240 Henry Hudson Pkwy #6H, Riverdale, NY 10463 718-601-8820
Granberg, Al: 18 Mathew St, Milford, CT 06460 203-877-2181
• **GrandPre, Mary: pg 783** 2182 Berkeley St, St Paul, MN 55105 ....**612-699-0424**
url: www.illconceived.com / fax: 612-699-9213
5236 W 56th St, Minneapolis, MN 55436 ....**612-926-5585**
fax: 612-926-3347
Grandstaff, Chris: 345 Church St NE, Vienna, VA 22180 703-242-1245
Graning, Ken: 2602 Williamsburg Cir, Auburn Hills, MI 48326 810-299-0677
Granner, Courtney: 328 N 5th St, Patterson, CA 95363 209-892-2973
Grant Barr, Marilyn: 5721 Wildberry Dr, Greensboro, NC 27409 919-852-4287
Grant, Collin: 5855 Green Valley Cir #308, Culver City, CA 90230 310-642-2721
Grant, Mel: 43 E 19th St, New York, NY 10003 212-254-4996
Grant, Stan: 1680 Las Lunas St, Pasadena, CA 91106 818-794-8555
Graphic Designers, Inc: 700 N Central Ave #450, Glendale, CA 91203 818-247-5433
Graphic Effects: 10305 Hawthorne, Inglewood, CA 90304 310-677-7196
Graphica: 4501 Lyons Rd, Miamisburg, OH 45342 513-866-4013
Graphics Illustrated: 5720-E North Blvd, Raleigh, NC 27604 919-878-7883
Grashow, James: 14 Diamond Hill Rd, W Redding, CT 06896 203-938-9195
Graunke, David: 1500 Center Cir, Downers Grove, IL 60515 630-932-6370
Graveline, Todd: 740 E 52nd St #8, Indianapolis, IN 46205 317-920-0068
Graves, David: 84 Main St, Gloucester, MA 01930 508-283-2335
Graves, David Bruce: 270 Jay St #11-I, Brooklyn, NY 11201 718-855-0833
Gravity Workshop: 459 W 49th St, New York, NY 10019 212-262-9823

Gray Jr, James W: 8343 Brockham Dr, Alexandria, VA 22309 703-351-8753
Gray, Doug: 60 E 42nd St #1940, New York, NY 10165 212-867-8092
• **Gray, Gary: pg 1188** 10 Highland Dr, Penfield, NY 14526 ....**716-586-1357**
Gray, Lynda: 60 E 42nd St #822, New York, NY 10165 212-682-1490
Gray, Mike: 94 Natoma St #200, San Francisco, CA 94105 415-442-1822
Gray, Ramon: 10 Highland Dr, Penfield, NY 14526 716-586-1357
• **Gray, Steve: pg 948,949**
119 W Torrance Blvd #5, Redondo Beach, CA 90277 ....**310-318-3844**
fax: 310-318-3296
Gray, Susan: 42 W 12th St #5, New York, NY 10011 212-675-2243
Grayson, Rick: 5 Nash St, Westborough, MA 01581 508-898-3943
Graziano Krafft & Zale: 111 E Wacker Dr #2600, Chicago, IL 60601 312-368-4355
Greaney, Michael: 4078 Lillian Dr, Concord, CA 94521 510-825-8111
Greathead, Ian: 1591 Sandpoint Dr, Atlanta, GA 30075 404-640-6517
Greco, Peter: 5156 Baltimore St, Los Angeles, CA 90042 213-257-8046
Green Design, Howie: 250 Boylston St 7th Fl, Boston, MA 02116 617-421-4400
Green, Barry: 15205 High Grove Rd, Alpharetta, GA 30201 770-410-1231
Green, Beth: 60 Riverside Dr, New York, NY 10124 212-580-1928
Green, Nathan: 4695 Old Pipestone Rd, Eau Claire, MI 49111 616-461-6347
Green, Norman: 119 W 23rd St #203, New York, NY 10011 212-633-9880
3053 Joaquin Miller Rd, Oakland, CA 94602 510-531-3531
Green, Patricia: 1470 W Raschner Ave #2, Chicago, IL 60640 773-275-5895
Green, Peter: 4219 W Burbank Blvd, Burbank, CA 91505 818-953-2210
Green, Randy: 6 Pine St, Freyburg, ME 04037 207-935-4200
Greenberg, Karen L: 133 N Montclair Ave, Dallas, TX 75208 214-943-2569
Greenberg, Sheldon: 200 Aquetong Rd, New Hope, PA 18938 215-862-2091
1722 Virginia St, Berkeley, CA 94703 415-221-4970
• **Greenberg, Steve: pg 458** 731 N 24th St, Philadelphia, PA 19130 ....**215-232-6666**
url: www.deborahwolfeltd.com / fax: 215-232-6585
• **Greenblatt, Mitch: pg 128** 420 Lexington Ave, New York, NY 10170 ....**212-986-5680**
url: www.mendolaart.com / fax: 212-818-1246
Greenblatt, Rodney A: 61 Crosby St, New York, NY 10012 212-219-0342
Greene, Joel & Anne: 70 Rocky Pond Rd, Boylston, MA 01505 508-869-6440
Greene, Pauline: 70 Village Park Way, Santa Monica, CA 90405 310-450-4200
Greenhow, Ralph: 3305 W Harrison St, Chicago, IL 60624 312-444-1168
Greenlaw, DR: 14314 Burbank Blvd, Sherman Oaks, CA 91401 818-988-8599
Greenstein, Susan: 229-A Windsor Pl, Brooklyn, NY 11215 718-788-6447
Gregerson, Jonathan: 201 & 1/2 E Virginia #2, McKinney, TX 75069 214-562-5926
• **Gregoretti, Rob: pg 1305** 41-07 56th St, Woodside, NY 11377 ....**718-779-7913**
url: www.showcase.com / fax: 718-779-7913
Gregory, Fran: 1432 S Elmwood Ave, Berwyn, IL 60402 708-484-7201
Gregory, Helen: PO Box 711, Sedro-Woolley, WA 98284 360-855-1416
Gregory, Lane: 50 Fuller Brook Rd, Wellesley, MA 02181 781-235-8658
Greif, Gene: 58 W 15th St, New York, NY 10011 212-741-2539
Greigg, Linda: 1010 Notley Rd, Silver Spring, MD 20904 301-384-6340
Greisen, Robert: 19615 Hamlin St, Reseda, CA 91335 818-881-3088
Grejniec, Michael: 866 United Nations Plaza, New York, NY 10017 212-644-2020
Grell, Susi: 3375 Ponytrail Dr #1003, Mississauga, ON L4X 1V8 905-624-0141
Gresslin, Marion: 1804 Knob Hill, Plano, TX 75023 214-985-9991
Grethen, Donna Marie: 2847 Guilderland Ave, Schenectady, NY 12306 518-355-8023
Griesbach/Martucci: 58 W 15th St, New York, NY 10011 212-741-2539
Grieve, Judy Mayer: 66 Raleigh Crescent, Unionville, ON L3R 4W5 905-944-1938
Griffel, Barbara: 23-45 Bell Blvd, Bayside, NY 11360 718-631-1753
Griffin, Craig P: 341 E Catawba Ave, Akron, OH 44301 216-773-9419
• **Griffin, Jim: pg 440** 60 E 42nd St, New York, NY 10165-1940 ....**212-867-8092**
e-mail: DHLT@aol.com / url: www.HT-LTD.com / fax: 212-949-1977
Griffith, Linda: 13972 Hilo Ln, Santa Ana, CA 92705 714-832-8536
Griffo, Joseph: 54 North Ave, New Rochelle, NY 10805 914-633-5734
Grigg, Amy J: 327 E 89th St #3E, New York, NY 10128 212-831-5650
Grillo, Glenn: 23337 Califa St, Woodland Hills, CA 91367 310-285-8509
• **Grimando, Scott: pg 788** 353 W 53rd St #1W, New York, NY 10019 ....**212-682-2462**
e-mail: info@amerartists.com / url: www.amerartists.com / fax: 212-582-0090
Grimes, Don: 5635 Ridgedale, Dallas, TX 75206 214-821-9590
Grimes, Melissa: 901 Cumberland Rd, Austin, TX 78704 512-445-2398
Grimes, Rebecca A: 936 Stone Rd, Westminster, MD 21158 410-857-1675
Grimwood, Brian: 60 E 42nd St #822, New York, NY 10165 212-682-1490
Griner, Larry: 1 North St #2W, Hastings-on-Hudson, NY 10706 914-478-5074
• **Grinnell, Derek: pg 834,835** San Francisco, CA **415-543-6056**
fax: 415-543-6075
New York, NY **212-869-0214**
Grinnell, Derek: 621 42nd Ave #A, San Francisco, CA 94121 415-221-2820
Griswold, Theophilus Britt: 823 Holly Dr E, Annapolis, MD 21401 410-757-8379
Groff Illustration, David W: 420 N Liberty St, Delaware, OH 43015 614-363-2131
Grogan-Brochu, Shannon: 1024 N Central Avenue #B9, Kent, WA 98032 253-520-1682
Groham, Chad: 188 Heritage Rd, Tonawanda, NY 14150 716-694-4763
Grohe, Eric: 4111 77th Pl NW, Marysville, WA 98271 206-546-3010
Groppetti, Gene: 25555 Hesperian Blvd, Hayward, CA 94545 510-786-6838
Gross, Alex: 1727 La Senda Pl, S Pasadena, CA 91030 626-799-4014
Gross, Susan: 532 Cabrillo St, San Francisco, CA 94118 415-751-5879
Grossman Illus, Larry: 5309 Coldwater Canyon Ave #C,
Sherman Oaks, CA 91401 818-907-8626
• **Grossman, Rhoda: pg 1306** 216 4th St, Sausalito, CA 94965 ....**415-331-0328**
e-mail: rhoda@digitalpainting.com / url: www.digitalpainting.com / fax: 415-332-1960
Grossman, Robert: 19 Crosby St, New York, NY 10013 212-925-1965
• **Grossman, Wendy: pg 216,217** 501 Fifth Ave, New York, NY 10017 ....**212-490-2450**
url: www.renardrepresents.com / fax: 212-697-6828
Grote, Rich: 9001 Trolley Ln, Norristown, PA 19403 609-586-5896
Grothman, Lisa: 137 Fifth Ave 11th Fl, New York, NY 10010 212-529-3556
Grotsky: 21-16 28th St, Long Island City, NY 11105 718-204-6184
Grounard, Mark: 1150 Fairview Ave, Wyomissing, PA 19610 215-372-7482
Grove, David: 382 Union St, San Francisco, CA 94133 415-433-2100
Grove, Keith: 4520 Strawberry Lane, Golden Valley, MN 55416 612-374-1951
Grubb, Lisa: PO Box 388, Sparkill, NY 10976 914-921-4526
Gruel, George: 759 Charles St, Moorpark, CA 93021 805-529-2727
Grunewald, Jeff: 2120 W Waveland Ave, Chicago, IL 60618 773-281-5284

Grura, Catherine: 200 E 71st St #3F, New York, NY 10021 212-535-9255
Guancione, Karen: 262 DeWitt Ave, Belleville, NJ 07109 201-450-9490
Guarino, Lisa: 91 Poundhill St, Quincy, MA 02169 781-847-4824
Guarnaccia, Steven: 31 Fairfield St, Montclair, NJ 07042 201-746-9785
Guben, Alex: 302 Carlton Terr, Teaneck, NJ 07666 201-836-1294
Gubenko, Alex: 1 Calvo Pl, Hawthorne, NJ 07506 201-871-1076
Gude, Karl: 15 Possom Lane, Norwalk, CT 08854 212-445-4000
Gudynas, Peter: 11 Kings Ridge Rd, Long Valley, NJ 07853 908-813-8718
Guell, Fernando: 43 E 19th St, New York, NY 10003 212-254-4996
Guevara, Susan: 843 Homer Ave, Palo Alto, CA 94301 916-426-0235
Guida, Lisa Chauncy: 420 Lexington Ave, New York, NY 10170 212-986-5680
Guidice, Rick: 9 Park Ave, Los Gatos, CA 95050 408-354-7787
Guilded Imagery Prdctns: 2995 Woodside Rd #400, Woodside, CA 94062 415-324-0323
Guip, Amy: 91 E 4th St #6, New York, NY 10003 212-674-8166
• Guitteau, Jud: pg 224,225   501 Fifth Ave, New York, NY 10017 ....**212-490-2450**
  url: www.renardrepresents.com / fax: 212-697-6828
Gulick, Dorothy: 6822 N Lotus Ave, San Gabriel, CA 91775 818-287-5104
• Gullickson, Vicki: pg 642   1035 A Cherokee St, Denver, CO 80204 ....**303-592-9811**
  fax: 303-620-9120
• Gullickson, Vicki: pg 642   208 Providence Rd, Annapolis, MD 21401 ....**410-349-8669**
  e-mail: acomport@aol.com
Gullo, Tom: 391 Clinton St, Brooklyn, NY 11231 718-625-2708
Gully, Bethany: 109 Kinston st, Boston, MA 02111 617-350-3089
Guluk, Steve: 123 8th St #D, Seal Beach, CA 90740.......................310-596-9777
Gumble, Gary: 10926 NE 17th St, Bellevue, WA 98004 425-688-1961
Gundlach, Elisabeth: 17 Ferndale St, Albany, NY 12208 518-482-4375
Gunion, Jeff: 8100 Harvard Dr, Ben Lemond, CA 95005 408-336-3300
• Gunn, Robert G: pg 752   1464 Linden Ave, Chicago, IL 60035 ....**847-432-2415**
  fax: 773-883-0375
  Los Angeles   **213-934-3395**
  Fax: 213-936-2757
Gunning, Kevin: 37 Denison Rd, Middletown, CT 06457 203-347-0688
Gunsaullus, Marty: 716 Sanchez St, San Francisco, CA 94114 415-285-8267
Gunthardt, Walt: 140 Broadview Ave, Toronto, ON M4M 2G2 416-465-1086
Gurak, Ellen: 1713 Newport Pl, New Orleans, LA 70065 504-466-3950
Gurbo, Walter: 118-12 Newport Ave, Bell Harbor, NY 11694 718-634-0072
Gurche, John: 1304 Olive St, Denver, CO 80220 303-333-7181
Gurcules, Paul C: 2121 Hamstead Ct, Suwanee, GA 30174 770-339-4036
Gurney, James: PO Box 693, Rhinebeck, NY 12572 914-876-7746
Guske, Carolyn: 12449 Kagel Canyon, San Fernando, CA 91342 818-890-4122
Gusman, Annie: 15 King St, Putnam, CT 06260 860-928-1042
Gussin, Jane E: 243 E 18th St #22, New York, NY 10003 212-777-3592
Gustafson, Dale: 420 Lexington Ave, New York, NY 10170 212-986-5680
Gustafson, Glenn: 203 N Wabash Ave #1102, Chicago, IL 60601 312-609-0081
Gutermuth, Stefan: 426 Union St, San Francisco, CA 94033 415-391-1506
Gutierrez, Rudy: 330 Haven Ave #4N, New York, NY 10033 212-568-2848
Guttman, Peter: 214 Riverside Dr #305, New York, NY 10025 212-595-4274
Guy, Edmond: 309 Race Track Rd, Hohokus, NJ 07423 201-251-7660
Guy, Robert: 80 E Hartsdale Ave, Hartsdale, NY 10530 914-682-3723
Guyer, Terry: 1139 San Carlos Ave #301, San Carlos, CA 94070 650-596-0363
Guzzi, George: 11 Randlett Pk, W Newton, MA 02165 617-244-2932
• Gwilliams, Scott: pg 1138   213 Glen Rd, Toronto, ON M4W 2X2 ....**416-929-8432**
  fax: 416-926-8875
Gyson, Mitch: 4603 Simms Ave, Baltimore, MD 21206......................410-485-0207
Gyurcsak, Joe: 133 Eaton Ave, Mercerville, NJ 08619......................609-586-7007

H

Haas, Bill: 415 South Main St, Hutchinson, MN 55350.....................320-587-5016
Haas, Irene: 133 E 80th St #10A, New York, NY 10021 212-628-2444
Haasis, Michael: 941 N Croft Ave, Los Angeles, CA 90069 213-654-5412
Haber-Schaim, Tamar: 1870 Beacon St Bldg #6-B1, Brookline, MA 02146 617-738-8883
  Erika Strasse, Hamburg, Germany, 20251.................................49-40-486003
Hackett, Michael: 20789 Millard, Taylor, MI 48180.........................313-358-2660
Hackworth, Alex: 5134 Timber Trail NE, Atlanta, GA 30342 404-255-1430
Hada, Gail: 23290 Clearpool, Harbor City, CA 90710 310-539-5114
Haddad, Darrin: 628-30 Broadway, New York, NY 10012 212-645-1241
Haddon, Julie: One South Rd, Harrison, NY 10528 914-381-8400
Haedrich, Todd: 10 Byron Dr, Basking Ridge, NJ 07920 908-204-0624
Haffar, Richard: 63 S 800 East, Salt Lake City, UT 84102.................801-328-8309
Hafner, Marylin: 33 Richdale Ave #105, Cambridge, MA 02140 617-625-6944
Hagel, Mike: 15910 Jones Circle, Omaha, NE 68118 402-691-8682
Hagen, David: 14637 Stone Range Dr, Centreville, VA 22020 703-830-4208
Hager, Sherrie: 4338 Taylorsville Hwy, Statesville, NC 28677.............704-838-1894
Haggerty, Tim: 222 E Calle Laureles, Santa Barbara, CA 93105 805-687-4848
Haggland, Martin: 2345 Broadway #638, New York, NY 10024...........212-787-0500
• Hagio, Cunio: pg 346,347   327 E 89th St #3E, New York, NY 10128 ....**212-831-5650**
  fax: 212-831-6241
  1306 Alabama St, Huntington Beach, CA 92648 ....**714-969-7766**
  fax: 714-374-3744
• Hagner, Dirk: pg 1307
  27931 Paseo Nicole, San Juan Capistrano, CA 92675 ....**949-493-5596**
  San Francisco, CA **415-285-8267**
  New York, NY **212-997-0115**
Hahn, Eileen: 8 Hillwood Rd, East Brunswick, NJ 08816....................908-390-4188
Hahn, Marika: 679 Oak Tree Rd PO Box 670, Palisades, NY 10964.....914-365-3317
• Haight, Sandy: pg 1220   911 Western Ave #525, Seattle, WA 98104..........**206-343-0656**
  fax: 206-343-5697
Haiman, Kurt: 384 Blanch Ave, Closter, NJ 07624 201-767-1383
Haimowitz, Steve: 67-40 Yellowstone Blvd #5D, Forest Hills, NY 11375 718-520-1461
Hajek, Olaf: 32 Downing St #4D, New York, NY 10014 212-633-1310
• Halbert, Michael: pg 139, 1086   2419 Big Bend Rd, St Louis, MO 63143....**314-645-6480**
  url: www.inkart.com
  420 Lexington Ave, New York, NY 10170.................................**212-986-5680**
  url: www.mendolaart.com / fax: 212-818-1246
Hale, Bruce: 1201 NW Blakely Ct, Seattle, WA 98177......................206-440-9036
Haleen, Brentano: PO Box 148, Tesuque, NM 87574......................505-986-1799
Haley, David: 1400 S Highway Dr, Fenton, MO 63099 314-827-2840

Halfacre, Elizabeth: 9530A 45th NE, Seattle, WA 98115 206-529-1669
Hall, Bill: 1235-B Colorado Ln, Arlington, TX 76015 817-467-1013
Hall, David: 2785 Westshire Dr, Los Angeles, CA 90068 213-464-2495
Hall, Eric: 2146 Spring St, Philadelphia, PA 19103 215-564-0712
Hall, Jeffrie: 174 W Hollyglen Ln, San Dimas, CA 91773.................909-599-3802
• Hall, Joan: pg 1309   155 Bank St, Studio H954, New York, NY 10014 ....**212-243-6059**
  fax: 212-924-8560
Hall, Kate Brennan: 301 DeArment Pkwy, Pittsburgh, PA 15241 412-833-9648
• Hall, Melisandi Potter: pg 856
  280 Madison Ave #1110, New York, NY 10016.........................**212-545-9155**
  e-mail: irmeli@aol.com / url: www.spar.org/holmberg / fax: 212-545-9462
Hall, Scott: 4129 Ginger Creek Dr, Meridian, ID 83642 208-376-5352
Hall, Stephen: 584 Broadway #608, New York, NY 10012 212-966-7840
Hall, Susan: 7500 NW First Ct #110, Plantation, FL 33317 305-923-5111
Hallgren, Gary: 98 Laurelton Dr, Mastic Beach, NY 11951...............516-399-5531
Hallman, Tom: 2553 Mill House Rd, Macungie, PA 18062................610-395-5656
Hally, Greg: 248 Edison St, Salt Lake City, UT 84111.....................801-355-5510
Halm, Daniel: NJ 908-382-7338
Halo Design: 15 Chestnut St #1, N Tarrytown, NY 10591................914-332-5112
Halstead, Virginia: 4336 Gayle Dr, Tarzana, CA 91356...................818-705-4353
• Halton, Sam/AnotherColor Inc.: pg 1464,1465
  PO Box 775909, Steamboat Springs, CO 80477.......................**970-871-0151**
  e-mail: sam@digitalnation.com / url: www.anothercolor.com / fax: 970-871-0150
Halverson, Lydia: PO Box 1086, Taos, NM 87571.........................505-776-5435
Hamagami Carroll & Assocs: 1316 Third St #305, Santa Monica, CA 90401 310-458-7600
Hamagami, John: 1316 3rd St Promenade, Santa Monica, CA 90401.....310-458-7600
Hamann, Brad: 330 Westminster Rd, Brooklyn, NY 11218................718-287-6086
Hamann, Peter: 36 Saint Paul Street, Rochester, NY 14604 716-232-5140
Hamblin, George: 944 Beach St, LaGrange Pk, IL 60625.................708-352-1780
Hamblin, Randy: 731 N 24th St, Philadelphia, PA 19130 215-232-6666
Hamilton, Bruce & Susan: Rt 1 Box 5C, Glorieta, NM 87535 505-757-6603
Hamilton, Carolyn: 7380 South Eastern #124-216, Las Vegas, NV 89123 702-798-6000
Hamilton, Ken: 16 Helen Ave, West Orange, NJ 07052 973-736-6532
Hamilton, Laurie: 600 N McClurg Ct #2412-A, Chicago, IL 60611 312-944-3970
Hamilton, Marcus: 12225 Ranburne Rd, Charlotte, NC 28212..........704-545-3121
• Hamilton, Meredith: pg 1310,1311
  222 Hicks Street, Brooklyn, NY 11201.....................................**800-963-7896**
Hamilton, Pamela: 353 W 53rd St #1W, New York, NY 10019 212-682-2462
Hamlin, Janet: 164 9th Street, Brooklyn, NY 11215 718-768-3647
• Hammer, Claudia: pg 549   7118 Upper River Rd, Prospect, KY 40059........**502-228-9427**
  url: www.jettreps.com / fax: 502-228-8857
Hammes, Alan: 200 W 93rd St #6D, New York, NY 10025 212-691-6387
Hammond, Cris: 410 Johnson St, Sausalito, CA 94965 415-332-7556
Hammond, Franklin: 68 E Franklin St, Dayton, OH 45459................937-433-8383
Hammond, Ted: 370 Rathburn Rd #55, Mississauga, ON L4Z 1H7 905-803-9698
Hampshire, Michael: 320 Bee Brook Rd, Washington, CT 06777 860-868-1011
Hampton, Gerry: 4792 Tiara Dr #204, Huntington Harbor, CA 92649...714-840-8239
Hamrick, Chuck: 420 Lexington Ave PH-4/5, New York, NY 10170 212-986-5680
• Han, Oki: pg 873   866 United Nations Plaza, New York, NY 10017............**212-644-2020**
  url: www.spar.org
Hancock, Roberta: 1506 W Lynwood St, Phoenix, AZ 85007 602-252-6368
Haney, William: 674 S Branch River Rd, Somerville, NJ 08876 908-369-8792
Hanley, John: 4803 Wyoming Way, Crystal Lake, IL 60012..............815-459-1123
Hanley, John: 847A Second Ave #150, New York, NY 10017 212-486-0177
Hanley, Katherine: 1831 E 61st St, Indianapolis, IN 46220...............317-251-7989
Hanna, B Scott: 1306 Alabama St, Huntington Beach, CA 92648 714-969-7766
  327 E 89th St #3E, New York, NY 10128 212-831-5650
Hanna, Kim: 1766 Sand Hill Rd #101, Palo Alto, CA 94304...............703-532-2370
Hanna, Renie: 314 Locust St, W Hempstead, NY 11552 516-292-3166
Hanna, Tony: 500 State St, Glendale, CA 91203 818-551-0747
Hannah, Halstead: 1250 Addison St Stu 211B, Berkeley, CA 94705 510-644-2241
Hannan, Michel: 20 Tower Rd, Plymouth, MA 02360 508-747-0089
Hannon, Holly: 43 E 19th St, New York, NY 10003 212-254-4996
Hansen, Ann: PO Box 1121, Nevada City, CA 95959 916-265-9634
Hansen, Biruta Akerbergs: RD1 Box 39G Sun Hill, Liverpool, PA 17045....717-444-3682
Hansen, Clint: 223 Broadway, Audubon, IA 50025 712-563-3335
Hansen, Doug: 415 E Olive Ave, Fresno, CA 93728 209-497-8060
Hansen, Greg: 24427 Deepsprings Dr, Diamond Bar, CA 91765 909-860-9974
Hansen, Jennifer: 2490 Presidio Dr, San Diego, CA 92103 619-294-9788
Hansen, Kenneth J: 1140 Washington St #3, Boston, MA 02118 617-451-5447
Hanson, Eric: 4444 Upton Ave So, Minneapolis, MN 55410 612-927-9054
• Hantel, Johanna: pg 882   16 Phaedra, Laguna Niguel, CA 92677 ....**949-495-3664**
  url: www.showcase.com / fax: 949-495-0129
Harbour, Elizabeth: 11 Kings Ridge Rd, Long Valley, NJ 07853 908-813-8718
Harden, Laurie: 121 Banta Ln, Boonton Township, NJ 07005 201-335-4578
Harden, Richard: 360 Park Rd, Pleasant Valley, CT 06063................203-379-6665
• Hardesty, Debra: pg 1312   1017 Vallejo Way, Sacramento, CA 95818 ....**916-446-1824**
  fax: 916-446-5661
Hardiman, Miles: 13215 E Bethany Pl, Aurora, CO 80014 303-750-2754
Hardin, Bob: 206 Linda Ln, Edison, NJ 08820 908-756-9254
Harding, Scott: 390 Turner Ave, Glen Ellyn, IL 60137 630-545-0806
Hardman, Sean: 1591 Marilyn Dr, Syracuse, UT 84075..................801-825-9383
Hardy, Elizabeth: 4108 28th St, Mt Ranier, MD 20712....................301-927-0504
Hardy-Faraci, Cheryl: 59 Pitman, Wakefield, MA 01880..................617-245-5315
Harfield, Mark: 115 West 2nd Street, New York, NY 10011 212-989-4600
• Hargreaves, Greg: pg 628   414 Cornwall Ave, Waterloo, IA 50702 ....**319-236-6534**
  4 E Ohio Studio B, Chicago, IL 60611......................................**312-321-1336**
  url: www.spar.org / fax: 312-321-1350
  5 E 17th St 6th Fl, New York, NY 10003 ....**212-691-2667**
  fax: 212-633-1844
Harlan, Steve: 325 Chesapeake Ave, Prince Frederick, MD 20678 410-535-4399
Harman, Richard: 5126 S Elizabeth Ave, Springfield, MO 65810.........417-889-9312
Harmon, John: 11 Neptune Ave, Seal Beach, CA 90740.................310-598-3839
Harmon, Traci: 3000 Chestnut Ave #6, Baltimore, MD 21211...........410-889-9521
Harmon, Tracy: 99 Park Ave #210A, New York, NY 10016..............800-398-9544

ILLUSTRATORS

Katzowitz, Joel: 2570 Chimney Springs Dr, Marietta, GA 30331......................770-641-9718
Kaufman, Donna: 3044 Orange Ave, La Crescenta, CA 91214........................818-248-7022
Kaufman, Judith H: 1326 La Playa St, San Francisco, CA 94122 415-564-7291
Kaufman, Luana: 2635 St Paul St, Baltimore, MD 21218..................................410-366-4674
Kaufman, Mark: 5123 Reeder St, Elmhurst, NY 11373 718-672-3257
Kaufman, Shirona: 20 Chestnut St #9, Rye, NY 10580......................................914-967-4338
Kauftheil, Henry: 220 W 19th St #1200, New York, NY 10011.............................212-633-0222
• **Kay Design, Laura: pg 1448** 105 Nutley St, Ashland, OR 97520.................**800-497-1752**
e-mail: laurakaydesign@opendoor.com / url: http://opendoor.com/laurakaydesign
Kay, Michael: 4232 N Francisco Ave, Chicago, IL 60618....................................773-463-8565
• **Kay, Stanford: pg 1329** Nyack, NY **914-358-0798**
e-mail: paragraphics@spyral.net / url: www.spyral.net/paragraphics / fax: 914-358-3284
Kazi, Pat: 2813 Rocks Rd, Jarrettsville, MD 21084 410-838-9584
Kearin, Alan: 69 Engert Ave #2L, Brooklyn, NY 11222 718-388-6037
Kearney, Rob: 332 East 18th St, New York, NY 10003 212-388-0107
Keating, Andrew: 3808 Lakeshore Ave, Oakland, CA 94610 510-465-5192
Keating, Cameron: 548 N Wilson Ave, Pasadena, CA 91106...............................626-683-1159
Keats, Deborah: PO Box 6027, Schenectady, NY 12301 518-725-2664
Kecman, Milan: 2730 Somia Dr, Cleveland, OH 44134..216-741-8755
Kedar Designs, Ruth: 433 College St, Palo Alto, CA 94306................................415-326-3706
Keeling, Gregg Bernard: 5955 Harbor Dr, Oakland, CA 94611............................510-653-8518
Keenan, Rob: 100 Van Dam St 2nd Fl, New York, NY 10013...............................212-255-7700
Keene, Donald: 4606 Cedar Spring #1527, Dallas, TX 75219..............................214-559-0055
519 Main St 2nd Fl, New Rochelle, NY 10801 914-636-2128
Keeter, Susan: 666 Greenwich St #860, New York, NY 10014..............................212-675-5719
Keeton, Sharon: 30 Tenney Dr, Rogue River, OR 97537 541-582-2165
Kehl, Richard: 8622 17th NE, Seattle, WA 98115...206-634-1162
Keim, Barbara: 161 Llewellyn Dr, Westfield, MA 01084 413-572-0688
Keith, Gary: 1419 Parrott Dr, San Mateo, CA 94402 415-358-9307
Kelemen, Stephen: 161 Henry St, Brooklyn, NY 11201 718-855-7005
Kelen: 1922 W Newport, Chicago, IL 60657 773-975-9696
Keleny, Earl: New York, NY 212-486-9644
Keller, Kate: 33 Schermerhorn St #3, Brooklyn, NY 11201.................................718-522-2334
Keller, Katie: 100 Bleecker St, New York, NY 10012...212-982-6533
• **Keller, Laurie: pg 865** 280 Madison Ave #1110, New York, NY 10016.......**212-545-9155**
e-mail: irmeli@aol.com / url: www.spar.org/holmberg / fax: 212-545-9462
Keller, Linda: 240 E 76th St #5U, New York, NY 10021 212-288-4606
Keller, Merle: 5855 Green Valley Cir #308, Culver City, CA 90230 310-642-2721
• **Keller, Steve: pg 62,63** 108 E 35th St #2, New York, NY 10016.................**212-889-3337**
url: www.theispot.com/artist/keller / fax: 212-889-3341
Keller, Thomas K: 1095 Market St #41, San Francisco, CA 94103 415-558-8000
• **Kelley, Barbara: pg 854** 280 Madison Ave #1110, New York, NY 10016 ....**212-545-9155**
e-mail: irmeli@aol.com / url: www.spar.org/holmberg / fax: 212-545-9462
• **Kelley, Gary: pg 262,263** 121 Madison Ave #5F, New York, NY 10016 ......**212-683-1362**
fax: 212-683-1919
Kelley, Steve: 3501 Windom Rd, Brentwood, MD 20722......................................301-699-1766
• **Kelliher, Ralph: pg 1120** 11 Sequoia Rd, Fairfax, CA 94930 ....**415-457-4535**
e-mail: rki@sirius.com / fax: 415-459-4586
Kelly, Christopher: 200 E 37th St 4th Fl, New York, NY 10016...........................212-689-1139
Kelly, Don: 69 Ocean St, New Bedford, MA 02740 508-993-5688
Kelly, Eileen: 813 Lincoln Ave, Falls Church, VA 22046 703-241-2727
Kelly/Etienne Delessert, Gary: 301 1/2 Main St, Cedar Falls, IA 50613.................319-277-2330
• **Kelly, Kevin: pg 1153** P.O. Box 802635, Dallas, TX 75380............................**972-814-0690**
Kemp, Dan: 9543 Dublin Rd, Walkersville, MD 21793...301-845-6107
Kendall, Dawn: 3 Harvard Dr, Brookfield, CT 06804 203-740-2535
Kendall, Gideon: 408 Seventh St #4, Brooklyn, NY 11215...................................718-788-8993
Kendell, Craig: 623 West End Ave #3B, New York, NY 10024...............................212-769-0922
Kendrick, Dennis: 99 Bank St #3G, New York, NY 10014 212-594-5563
Kennedy, Anne: 666 Greenwich St #860, New York, NY 10014 212-675-5719
• **Kennedy, Dean: pg 741** 865 Delaware St, Denver, CO 80204............................**303-820-2598**
toll-free **800-417-5120**
url: www.artagent.com / fax: 303-820-2598
Kennedy, Kelly: 1025 Idaho Ave, Santa Monica, CA 90403 310-394-2239
Kennedy, T: IN 812-853-2911
Kennedy, Victor: 514 Meadowfield Ct, Lawrenceville, GA 30243 770-339-0345
Kennefick, Ed: 176 W Coolidge #C, Phoenix, AZ 85013.......................................602-277-2975
Kennevan, Steve: 2401 Thorndyke Ave, Seattle, WA 98199.................................206-285-7758
Kenny, Aggie: 51 King St, Dobbs Ferry, NY 10522 914-693-5836
Kenny, Mike: 43 E 19th St, New York, NY 10003..212-254-4996
Kenny, Steven: 3557 Slate Mills Rd, Sperryville, VA 22740 540-547-3971
Kent, Nicholas: 138 W Olive, Long Beach, NY 11561 516-431-4258
Kent, William: 12424 Wilshire Blvd #1400, Los Angeles, CA 90025 310-207-6507
Kenyon, Kathleen: 59 Tinker St, Woodstock, NY 12498 914-679-2589
Kenyon, Liz: 4225 N 36th St #6, Phoenix, AZ 85018..602-954-8824
Keppler, Margaret: 350 W 57 St #4F, New York, NY 10019 212-315-5266
Kern, Donna: 13 Amundsen St, Norwalk, CT 06855...203-854-5486
Kern, Michael: 2320 La Paz, Oceanside, CA 92054 760-752-3336
Kernan, Patrick: 26 NE 76th Ave, Portland, OR 97213 503-251-1839
Kerr, Bruce: 2530 Crawford #208, Evanston, IL 60201 847-328-0855
Kerr, Tom: 125 Bamm Hollow Rd, Middletown, NJ 07748 908-922-6000
Kerris, Paul A: 900 W Main St #3, Laurel, MD 20707 301-604-8566
Kest, Kristin: 666 Greenwich St #860, New York, NY 10014 212-675-5719
Keswick Hamilton, Kimberlee: 3519 W 6th St, Los Angeles, CA 90020...............213-380-3933
Ketchum, Charles Ray: 420 Lexington Ave #220, New York, NY 10170 212-687-3460
• **Ketler, Ruth Sofair: pg 1330** 101 Bluff Terr, Silver Spring, MD 20902 ....**301-593-6059**
e-mail: ruth.ketler@tcs.wap.org / fax: 301-593-1236
Kettler, Al: 3301 Mt Vernon Ave, Alexandria, VA 22305 703-548-8040
Keyes, Steven: 165 Christopher Street #1B, New York, NY 10014 212-255-3169
Keys, Watt: 612 E Tremont Ave, Charlotte, NC 28203 704-332-6576
Kianersi, Nadir: 309 E Harrison #206, Seattle, WA 98102...................................206-329-3461
Kibiuk, Lydia V: 8 F Cross Keys Rd, Baltimore, MD 21210..................................410-433-1107
Kidd, Jeremy: 615 Victoria Ave, Venice, CA 90291 310-827-6862
Kidd, Tom: 59 Cross Brook Rd, New Milford, CT 06776 203-355-1781
Kiefer, Alfons: 420 Lexington Ave, New York, NY 10170 212-986-5680
Kiel, Ronaldo: 661 Metroplitan Ave #3L, Brooklyn, NY 11211...............................718-782-4963
Kielty, Tracey: PO Box 696, Beverly Hills, CA 90212 213-667-0709
Kiesel, Lorian: 300 Essex St #7, Salem, MA 01970..978-744-6231
Kilfoy Design: 3301A S Jefferson Ave, St Louis, MO 63118 314-773-2600
Kilgore, Susi: 2804 W Averill Ave, Tampa, FL 33611 813-837-9759
Kilgore, Tony: PO Box 882, Bloomington, IN 47401...812-331-7920
Killian, Carlos: 261 Seaman Ave #C4 3rd Fl, New York, NY 10034....................212-567-1500
Killian, Ted: 7605 Rochester Way, Santa Barbara, CA 93117 805-685-4827
Kilmer, David: 449 Stanford Ct, Irvine, CA 92715...800-450-4451
Kilmer, Melinda: 35 Wooster St #4F, New York, NY 10013.................................212-226-6581
Kilroy, John: 28 Fairmount Way, Nantasket, MA 02045 617-925-0582
Kim, Joung Un: 866 United Nations Plaza, New York, NY 10017 212-644-2020
Kim-Jin-Hwa, Saerom: 118 Horace Harding Blvd, Great Neck, NY 11020 212-880-3577
Kimak, James: 20 Broadway, Piermont, NY 10968..914-359-1158
Kimball, Anton: 820 SE Sandy Blvd, Portland, OR 97214.....................................503-234-4777
• **Kimball, Kathleen: pg 1331** 6207 29th Ave NE, Seattle, WA 98115 ....**206-522-2710**
fax: 206-524-4808
• **Kimber, Murray: pg 264,265**
121 Madison Ave #5F, New York, NY 10016..**212-683-1362**
fax: 212-683-1919
• **Kimble, David: pg 769** 218 Elm Ct, Rhinelander, WI 54501 ....**715-369-2130**
The Palace 220 N Highland, Marfa, TX 79843..**915-729-4802**
• **Kimura, Hiro: pg 350,351** 327 E 89th St #3E, New York, NY 10128 ....**212-831-5650**
fax: 212-831-6241
1306 Alabama St, Huntington Beach, CA 92648 ....**714-969-7766**
fax: 714-374-3744
Kincade, John Orin: 27 Clove Brook Rd, Valhalla, NY 10595 914-773-0504
Kincaid, Samuel J: 242 E 38th St #1A, New York, NY 10016 212-697-2263
King, Allison: New York, NY 718-768-8921
King, Carol: 3001 W Schumacher Dr, Tucson, AZ 85741 520-622-0915
King, Fiona: PO Box 232722, Encinitas, CA 92023 760-942-1121
King, Greg: 200 Aquetong Rd, New Hope, PA 18938..215-862-2091
• **King, JD: pg 64,65** 108 E 35th St #2, New York, NY 10016..........................**212-889-3337**
url: www.theispot.com/artist/jdking / fax: 212-889-3341
King, Manuel: 118 Congress St, Orange, MA 01364...508-544-7124
King, Stephen: 2211 10th Ave E #1, Seattle, WA 98102.......................................206-328-0779
King-Judge, Cynthia: PO Box 4644, Montebello, CA 90640 213-721-3826
Kingham, David: 42 Blue Spruce Cir, Weston, CT 06883.....................................203-226-3106
Kingsbery, Guy: 305 High St, Milford, CT 06460 203-878-8939
Kingsley, D: 525 W 22nd Street #3-E, New York City, NY 10011 212-645-7379
• **Kinkopf, Kathleen: pg 138** 420 Lexington Ave, New York, NY 10107...........**212-986-5680**
url: www.mendolaart.com / fax: 212-818-1246
Kinst, Lew: 10051 Pasadena Ave #J, Cupertino, CA 95014 408-255-9100
Kinstrey, Jim: 1036 Broadway, W Longbranch, NJ 07764....................................908-229-0312
Kirby, Jill: 1559 S 16th St, Milwaukee, WI 53204...414-672-1272
Kirk Noll, Cheryl: 19 Hooker St, Providence, RI 02908..401-861-5869
Kirk, Betsy: 216 Blenheim Rd, Baltimore, MD 21212 410-377-7530
Kirk, Bev: 5815 Sovereign Dr, Cincinnati, OH 45241 513-530-5353
Kirk, Daniel: 60 E 42nd St #822, New York, NY 10165 212-682-1490
Kirk, Rainey: 11440 Oak Dr, Shelbyville, MI 49344...616-672-5756
Kirk, Richard: 155 Center St, Bellingham, MA 02019 508-883-2838
Kirkland, Cynthia: 10637 Chesapeake Dr, Dallas, TX 75217.................................214-286-6255
• **Kirkland, James: pg 588,589**
232 Madison Ave #512, New York, NY 10016..**212-889-8777**
fax: 212-447-1475
Kirkman, Rick: 2432 W Peoria Ave #1191, Phoenix, AZ 85029.............................602-997-6004
Kirov, Lydia: 4008 N Hermitage Ave, Chicago, IL 60613.....................................773-929-5535
Kitazawa, Sharon: 4451 Rockland Place #1, La Canada, CA 91011......................818-957-6258
• **Kitchell, Joyce: pg 118,119** 420 Lexington Ave, New York, NY 10170 ....**212-986-5680**
url: www.mendolaart.com / fax: 212-818-1246
Kitchell, Peter: 203-866-3734
Kitchen, Bert: 50 Derby Road, London, England, UK E18 2PS..........................1815-051433
Kitchens, Christie: 133 Spring St 2nd Fl, New York, NY 10012 212-925-4340
Kitses, John: Longmeadow Rd, Lincoln, MA 01773...617-259-0804
Kitzerow, Scott: 3505 N Pine Grove, Chicago, IL 60657......................................773-935-9234
Kiwak, Barbara: 165 E 32nd St, New York, NY 10016...212-686-3514
Kiwior, Carla: 404 Jackson St, Dickson City, PA 18159.......................................717-383-2090
KiwiStudios: 404 Jackson St, Dickson City, PA 18519 717-383-2090
Kizer, Fran: 5256, Tempe, AZ 85283 602-839-5187
Klanderman, Leland: 118 E 26th Street #302, Minneapolis, MN 55404..........612-871-4539
Klare, Tom: PO Box 370561, San Diego, CA 92137 619-565-6167
• **Klassen, Tony: pg 1478** 1492 N Furnleigh Ln, Chesterton, IN 46304 ....**219-926-2045**
• **Klauba, Douglas: pg 638** 4 E Ohio Studio B, Chicago, IL 60611....................**312-321-1336**
fax: 312-321-1350
5 E 17th St 6th Fl, New York, NY 10003 ....**212-691-2667**
url: www.spar.org / fax: 212-633-1844
• **Klavins, Uldis: pg 427** 60 E 42nd St, New York, NY 10165-1940...................**212-867-8092**
e-mail: DHLT@aol.com / url: www.HT-LTD.com / fax: 212-949-1977
Kleber, John: 2301 N 10th St, Phoenix, AZ 85006...602-253-4129
Klein, Chris: 2 The Donway E #207, Toronto, ON M3C 1X7 416-391-3774
Klein, David G: 408 Seventh St, Brooklyn, NY 11215...718-788-1818
Klein, Hannah: 207 Eighth Ave #4R, New York, NY 10011..................................212-345-5050
Klein, Hedy: 111-56 76th Dr #B3, Forest Hills, NY 11375 718-793-0246
Klein, Kathryn: 51 Melcher St, Boston, MA 02210...617-350-7970
Klein, Michael: 22 Edgewood Rd, Madison, NJ 07940 973-765-0623
Klein, Renee: 164 Daniel Low Terr, Staten Island, NY 10301 718-727-0723
Kleinsteuber, Robert: 4808 Bel Pre Rd, Rockville, MD 20853.............................301-871-1816
Kleman, Gary B: 809 S Florissant Rd, St Louis, MO 63135.................................314-521-5065
Kletsky, Olga: 63-89 Saunders St #5G, Rego Park, NY 11374............................718-897-1771
Klim, Joseph: PO Box 463, Avon, CT 06001 203-676-9933
Kline, Michael: 1106 S Dodge, Witchita, KS 67213...316-264-4112
Klineman, Peggy: 310 W 47th St #4B, New York, NY 10036................................212-757-3460
Klingensmith, Milt: 10385 Soft Castle, Fenwick, MI 48834 517-637-4183
Klopp, Karyl: 5209 8th Ave-Constitution Qtrs, Charlestown, MA 02129...............617-242-7463
Kloverstrom, Candis: 1568 Ward Circle, Franktown, CO 80116...........................303-688-0649
Klucowicz, Karen: 7270 Shallford Rd, Mississauga, ON L4T 2P7........................416-673-5132

- **Lee, Tim: pg 208,209** 501 Fifth Ave, New York, NY 10017 ....**212-490-2450**
  url: www.renardrepresents.com / fax: 212-697-6828
- Lee, Victoria: D8 Holiday Estates, Jessup, MD 20794 301-596-3532
- Lee, Wangdon: 7655 Woodbine Dr, Laurel, MD 20707 301-725-0948
- Lee, Warren: 88 Meadow Valley Rd, Corte Madera, CA 94925 415-924-0261
- **Lee, Yuan: pg 514,515** 217 E 86th St Box 212, New York, NY 10028........**212-427-5632**
  fax: 212-427-6372
- Leech, Dorothy: 1024 Ave of Americas 4th Fl, New York, NY 10018 212-354-6641
- Leeds, Beth Whybrow: 2022 Jones St, San Francisco, CA 94133 415-928-0457
- Leedy, Jeff: 141-10 28th St, Flushing, NY 11354..................212-206-0066
  190 Pelican Ln, Novato, CA 94945..................415-331-1354
- **Leer, Rebecca J: pg 1336** 440 West End Ave #12E, New York, NY 10024....**212-595-5865**
  fax: 212-595-5940
- Leete, William W: 202 Silver Lake Ave, Wakefield, RI 02879 401-783-8055
- Lefkowitz, Mark: 132 Oak Hill Dr, Sharon, MA 02067 617-784-5293
- Legaspi, Randy: 1311 E Harvard, Glendale, CA 91205..................818-244-4786
- Legnami, Susan: 389 Clementina St, San Francisco, CA 94103..................415-777-9569
- Lehew, Ron: 17 Chestnut St, Salem, NJ 08079..................609-935-1422
- Lehman, Connie: PO Box 281, Elizabeth, CO 80107 303-646-4638
- **Lehner & Whyte Digital Design/Illustration: pg 1480**
  8-10 S Fullerton Ave, Montclair, NJ 07042..................**973-746-1335**
  e-mail: lehwhy@intac.com / url: www.lehnerwhyte.com / fax: 973-746-0178
- Leicht, Christina: 12342 Hunter's Chase Dr #1313, Austin, TX 78729..................512-219-0156
- Leidl, Patricia: 468 Queen St E #104, Toronto, ON M5A 1T7 416-367-2446
- Leifheit, Diane: Hunt Bldg Rt 86, Gabriels, NY 12939..................518-327-3473
- Leigh, Tom: RR1 Box 224A Swain's Cove Rd, Little Deer Isle, ME 04650........207-348-9382
- Leiner, Alan: 353 W 53rd St #1W, New York, NY 10019..................212-682-2462
- **Leister, Bryan: pg 296,297** 58 W 15th St, New York, NY 10011 ....**212-741-2539**
  url: www.showcase.com / fax: 212-741-4660
- **Lekander, Lance: pg 1337** 4340 Woronzof Dr, Anchorage, AK 99517 ....**907-243-8889**
  fax: 907-245-1773
- Lelup, Carol: 200 Aquetong Rd, New Hope, PA 18938..................215-862-2091
- Lemant, Albert: 666 Greenwich St #860, New York, NY 10014..................212-675-5719
- Lemay, Katy: 1427 av Valois, Montréal, QU H1W 3L8 514-521-4155
- Lemelman, Martin: 1286 Country Club Rd, Allentown, PA 18106..................215-395-4536
- Lemieux, Andrée: 1 av du Boisé, Napierville, QU J0J 1L0 514-245-7059
- Lemieux, Margo: 22 Highland Ave, Mansfield, MA 02048..................508-339-7487
- Lemke, Brian: 3421 Tripp Ct #1, San Diego, CA 92121..................619-793-1033
- Lemley, David: 1904 3rd Ave #920, Seattle, WA 98101..................206-682-9480
- **Lemonnier, Joe: pg 799** 9 Babbling Brook Ln, Suffern, NY 10901..........**914-368-8606**
  fax: 914-368-8608
- LeMoult, Dolph: 597 Riverside Ave, Westport, CT 06880 203-226-4724
- Lenar, Loci B: 17 Central Ave, Mine Hill, NJ 07801..................201-989-0934
- Lendway, Andy: 203 Taft Ave, Wilmington, DE 19805 302-777-5955
- Lengyel, Kathy: 2306 Jones Dr, Dunedin, FL 34698..................813-734-1382
- **Lensch, Chris: pg 885** 16 Phaedra, Laguna Niguel, CA 9267 ....**949-495-3664**
  url: www.showcase.com / fax: 949-495-0129
- Leon, Anthony: 1350 Winstead Ct, St Louis, MO 63304..................314-664-3975
- Leon, Karen: 154-01 Barclay Ave, Flushing, NY 11355..................718-461-2050
- Leon, Thomas: 314 N Mission Dr, San Gabriel, CA 91775..................818-458-7699
- Leonard, Richard: 212 W 17th St #2B, New York, NY 10011 212-243-6613
- Leonard-Gibson, Barbara: 3501 Toddsbury Ln, Olney, MD 20832 301-570-9480
- Leonard-Stock, Lois: 3 Stratton Pl, Portland, ME 04101..................207-761-0038
- Leonardo, Curtis: 4308 Omega Ave, Castro Valley, CA 94546..................510-886-1669
- **Leonardo, Todd: pg 1339** 19110 Almond Road, Castro Valley, CA 94546....**510-728-1076**
- Leopold: 877 Carlaw Ave, Toronto, ON M4K 3L4 416-778-1879
- **Leopold, Susan: pg 388,389** 250 W 57th St #521, New York, NY 10107 ....**212-397-7330**
  url: www.lindgrensmith.com (and) www.stockillustrated.com
- Lepine, Philip W: 31 Brighton Rd, Tonawanda, NY 14150..................716-875-5490
- Leroux, Maryse: 8663 Rue Joseph-Quintal, Montreal, QC H2M 2M9 514-389-8249
- Lesh, David: 18 McKinley St, Rowayton, CT 06853 203-866-3734
- Lesh, David: 5693 N Meridian St, Indianapolis, IN 46208 317-253-3141
- Lesnick, H Robert: 1001 City Ave #EE821, Wynnewood, PA 19096 610-642-8948
- Lessard, Marie: 4641 rue Hutchinson, Montréal, QU H2V 4A2 514-272-5696
- Lesser, Ron: 420 Lexington Ave #2760, New York, NY 10170 212-697-8525
- Lester, Michelle: 15 W 17th St 9th Fl, New York, NY 10011 212-989-1411
- **Lester, Mike: pg 930,931** 17 E Third Ave #2, Rome, GA 30161 ....**706-234-7733**
  url: www.mikelester.com / fax: 706-234-0086
- Letostak, John: 7801 Fernhill Ave, Parma, OH 44129..................216-885-1753
- Letter Perfect: PO Box 785, Gig Harbor, WA 98335..................206-956-9422
- Letzig, Michael: 235 W 22nd St #6T, New York, NY 10011..................212-243-3166
- **LeVan, Jeff: pg 470** 731 N 24th St, Philadelphia, PA 19130 ....**215-232-6666**
  url: www.deborahwolfeltd.com / fax: 215-232-6585
- **LeVan, Susan: pg 813** 333 E 49th St, New York, NY 10017..................**212-980-8061**
  fax: 212-832-8778
  100 Bleecker St, New York, NY 10012 ....**212-982-6533**
  url: www.theispot.com/artist/levan / fax: 212-358-1586
- LeVan/Barbee Studio: 30 Ipswich St #211, Boston, MA 02215 617-536-6828
- Levee, Gayle: 51 Century St, Medford, MA 02155..................617-396-9656
- Levenson, Wendy: 19 Flintlock Dr, Warren Town, NJ 07059..................908-647-0900
- Leveque, Lyne: 34 av des Saules, Saint Basile le gr, QU J3N 1G8..................514-461-2935
- Levin, Arnie: 23 Glenlawn Ave, Sea Cliff, NY 11579..................516-676-1228
- Levin, Bill: 4903 N Winthrop Ave, Indianapolis, IN 46205..................317-335-6023
- Levin, Mara: 23 Water St, Holliston, MA 01746..................508-429-0762
- **Levine, Andy: pg 1340,1341** 23-30 24th St, Long Island City, NY 11105....**718-956-8539**
- Levine, Bette: 639 S Highland, Los Angeles, CA 90036..................213-935-9199
- Levine, Faye: 4609 Shoreline Dr #210, Spring Park, MN 55384..................612-471-8441
- Levine, Lucinda: 2604 Connecticut Ave NW, Washington, DC 20008 202-667-5365
- Levine, Ned: 301 Frankel Blvd, Merrick, NY 11566 516-378-8122
- Levine, Polar: 86 Thomas St, New York, NY 10013 212-732-2449
- Levine, Ron: 1619 Williams St #202, Montreal, QU H3J 1R1 212-727-1967
- Levinson, David: 86 Parson Rd #2, Clifton, NJ 07012 201-614-1627
- Levinson, W Jason: 11625 Sun Circle Way, Columbia, MD 21044 301-854-0406
- Levison, Bob: 1959 E Jefferson Ave, Detroit, MI 48207 313-567-8900
- Levstek, Ljuba: 4 Normandy Blvd, Toronto, ON M4L 3K2 416-867-9345

- **Levy, Aimee: pg 1342**
  527 San Vicente Blvd #301, Santa Monica, CA 90402 ....**310-319-3788**
- Levy, Pamela R: 7 Trapelo St, Brighton, MA 02135 617-254-5779
- Levy, Robert S: 1023 Fairway Rd, Franklin Square, NY 11010..................516-872-3713
- Lew, Kent: 452 Washington Mtn Rd, Washington, MA 01223..................413-623-0212
- Lewczak, Scott: 10970 Boutilier Ln, Manassas, VA 22111 703-335-7070
- Lewin, Laurie: 206 Sir Geoffrey Ct, Blakeslee, PA 18610..................717-643-1519
- Lewin, Ted: 152 Willoughby Ave, Brooklyn, NY 11205..................718-622-3882
- LeWinter, Renee: 41 Sewall St, Somerville, MA 02145..................617-628-5695
- **Lewis, Buck (Howard B): pg 1018,1019**
  16 Canonchet Rd, Hope Valley, RI 02832 ....**800-522-1377**
- **Lewis, Maurice: pg 788** 353 W 53rd St #1W, New York, NY 10019..........**212-682-2462**
  e-mail: info@amerartists.com / url: www.amerartists.com / fax: 212-582-0090
- Lewis, Polly Krumbhaar: 125 McClenaghan Mill Rd, Wynnewood, PA 19096......215-649-1989
- Lewis, Ray: 4675 Murat Ct, San Diego, CA 92117..................619-270-9680
- Lewis, Stacey: 225 S 18th St #1017, Philadelphia, PA 19103..................215-545-5614
- Lewis, Tim: 192 Southville Rd, Southborough, MA 01772..................508-872-4549
- Leyonmark, Roger: 280 Madison Ave #1110, New York, NY 10016..................212-545-9155
- Leyshon, Judy: 5606 Sonoma Rd, Bethesda, MD 20817 301-530-5070
- Li, Tommy: 232 Austin Dr, Markham, ON L3R 6N6 905-475-7747
- Liao Inc, Sharmen: 314 N Mission Dr, San Gabriel, CA 91775..................818-458-7699
- Liaw, Anson: 39 Cranfield Rd, Toronto, ON M4B 3H6 416-285-8905
- Liberman, Joni Levy: 99 Taylor St, Needham, MA 02194 617-986-4657
- Libetti, Thomas: 49 Briggs Ave, Yonkers, NY 10701..................914-376-7611
- Licht, Lisa: 4915 Tyrone #207, Sherman Oaks, CA 91423 818-995-5724
- Lichtenfels, Lisa: 146 Bay St, Springfield, MA 01109..................413-781-1359
- Lichty, Patrick: 8211 E Wadora NW, N Canton, OH 44720..................330-494-5593
- Lieberman, Ron: 109 W 28th St, New York, NY 10001..................212-947-0653
- Liebman, Ruth: 1565 Chestnut St #31, San Francisco, CA 94123 415-437-3888
- Lieder, Rick: 60 E 42nd St #1940, New York, NY 10165..................212-867-8092
- Liepke, Skip: 30 W 72nd St #2B, New York, NY 14304 212-724-5593
- Lies, Brian: 31 North St, Norfolk, MA 02056..................508-528-8293
- Life, Kay: 419 Southwick Rd B7, Westfield, MA 01085..................413-562-6418
- Ligasan, Darryl: 422 E 77th St #5W, New York, NY 10021 212-737-4393
- Lightburn, Ron: 232 Madison Ave #402, New York, NY 10016 212-889-8777
- Lilie, Jim: 110 Sutter St #706, San Francisco, CA 94104 415-441-4384
- Lillard, Jill M: 32 Westgate, Luguna Niguel, CA 92677..................714-661-2270
- Lim, Deborah: 505 N Lake Shore Dr #5606, Chicago, IL 60611..................312-527-3271
- **Limer, Tina: pg 852** 280 Madison Ave #1110, New York, NY 10016 ....**212-545-9155**
  e-mail: irmeli@aol.com / url: www.spar.org/holmberg / fax: 212-545-9462
- Limnidis, Larry: 75 Heaslip Terr, Scarborough, ON M1T 1W8..................416-292-6144
- Lincoln, Jay: 265 Elmwood Ave, East Aurora, NY 14052..................716-884-8010
- Lind, Monica: 524 Broadway 4th Fl, New York, NY 10012 212-431-4480
- Lindberg, Dean: 4023 14th Ave.South, Minneapolis, MN 55407..................612-823-1977
- Lindberg, Jeffrey: 449 50th St, Brooklyn, NY 11220..................718-492-1114
- Lindbloom, Bruce: 7370 Walnut Ct, Eden Prairie, MN 55346 612-937-9627
- Linden, Judy: 39 E Walnut St, Pasadena, CA 91103 818-584-4034
- **Lindgren, Cindy: pg 782** 5236 W 56th St, Minneapolis, MN 55436 ....**612-926-5585**
  fax: 612-926-3347
- Lindgren, Malin: 100 Bleecker St, New York, NY 10012..................212-982-6533
- Lindlof, Ed: 603 Carolyn Ave, Austin, TX 78705 512-472-0195
- Lindner, Verne: 1413 Sanborn Ave, Los Angeles, CA 90027..................213-667-2758
- Lindquist, Mark: 1762 First Ave, New York, NY 10028 212-534-3899
- Lindroth, David: 85 Broadway, W Milford, NJ 07480..................201-697-1965
- Lindstrom, Jack: 6300 Shingle Creek Pkwy, Minneapolis, MN 55430..................612-561-6543
- Lindt, Peggy: 1627 Calle Canon, Santa Barbara, CA 93101..................805-569-1002
- Lingta, Kung: 420 Lexington Ave #2760, New York, NY 10170..................212-697-8525
- Linker, James Alan: 324 S Spring St, Bellefonte, PA 16823..................814-353-0774
- **Linn, Warren: pg 609** 155 W 15th St, New York, NY 10011 ....**212-989-8770**
  fax: 212-989-7892
- Linnett, Charles: 99 High St, Canton, MA 02021 617-828-4972
- Lins, Rico: 18 E 16th St 7th Fl, New York, NY 10003..................212-255-6456
- Lionel Tepper Design, Inc: 449 E 14th St, New York, NY 10009..................212-505-0029
- Lipczenko, S Dimitri: 3901 Tunlaw Rd NW #402, Washington, DC 20007 202-338-1318
- Lipman, Michael: 310 Rydal Ave, Mill Valley, CA 94941 415-383-1927
  1474 W Hubbard, Chicago, IL 60622..................312-666-8381
- Lipner, Robin: 220 W 21st St #2E, New York, NY 10011 212-929-5807
- Lipowec, Alex: 304 Mulberry St #GLB, New York, NY 10012..................212-925-7663
- Lipper, Gabriel: 2305 Ashland St #C, Ashland, OR 97520..................800-435-6509
- Lippman, Peter: 410 Riverside Dr #134, New York, NY 10025..................212-865-1823
- Lipstein, Morissa: 1712 E Butler Cir, Chandler, AZ 85225..................602-899-0600
- Lisi, Victoria Poyser: 166 Sawyer Hill Rd, New Milford, CT 06776..................203-350-9404
- Lisker, Emily: 139 Rathburn St, Woonsocket, RI 02895 401-762-2503
- Liss, Julius: 446 Lawrence Ave W, Toronto, ON M5M 1C2..................416-784-1416
- Litchfield, Linda: 468 Deering Ave, Portland, ME 04103..................207-774-4750
- Little Apple Art: 409 Sixth Ave, Brooklyn, NY 11215..................718-499-7045
- Little, Chad: 4206 N Central Ave, Phoenix, AZ 85012..................602-265-9030
- Little, Ed: 232 Madison Ave #402, New York, NY 10016..................212-889-8777
- Littmann, Rosemary: 299 Rutland Ave, Teaneck, NJ 07666..................201-833-2417
- **Liu, Davy: pg 68,69** 108 E 35th St #2, New York, NY 10016 ....**212-889-3337**
  url: www.theispot.com/artist/liu / fax: 212-889-3341
- **Livingston, Francis: pg 400,401**
  250 W 57th St #521, New York, NY 10107 ....**212-397-7330**
  url: www.lindgrensmith.com (and) www.stockillustrated.com
- Livingston, Lourdes: 240 Scott, San Francisco, CA 94117..................415-252-7449
- Livingston, Randy: 4132 Faithway Dr, Murfreeboro, TN 37129..................615-896-9390
- Lizarraga, Sergio: 2759 N Hampton St, Orange, CA 92667..................714-778-5692
- **Llewellyn, Michael: pg 1483** 5820 Langfield Rd, Houston, TX 77092..........**713-462-5331**
  url: www.MikeLLLL.com / fax: 713-462-8950
- **Llewelyn, Janis: pg 1073** 2318 Mapleton Ave, Boulder, CO 80304 ....**303-545-9380**
  e-mail: eyecondsgn@aol.com / fax: 303-727-7670
- Lloyd, Gregory: 5534 Red River Dr, San Diego, CA 92120 619-582-3487
- Lloyd, Mary Anne: 192 Southville Rd, Southborough, MA 01772..................508-872-4549
- Loccisano, Karen: 121 Dodgingtown Rd Box 266, Bethel, CT 06801 203-748-4823

Lochray, Tom: 5645 10th Ave S, Minneapolis, MN 55417 612-823-7630
Locke, Gary: 2702 S.Farm Rd#227, Rogersville, MO 65742 417-823-8650
Locke, Keith: 4015 E 53rd St, Tulsa, OK 74135...918-749-9424
Lockett, Carolyn L: 265 First Ave #3, Salt Lake City, UT 84103.....................801-483-2469
Lockwood, Chris: 1210 W Clay #19, Houston, TX 77019 713-524-1860
Lockwood, Todd: 60 E 42nd St #822, New York, NY 10165...........................212-682-1490
Lockyear, Doug: 158 W 29th Street 11th Floor, New York, NY 10001 212-268-9400
Lodderhose, Bill: 6716 Sutherland, St Louis, MO 63109 314-647-7738
Lodrick, Karen: 839 Leavenworth St #409, San Francisco, CA 94109 415-885-0228
Loecke, James E: 1400 Coconino Rd #216, Ames, IA 50014............................515-296-2190
Loehle, Don: 9075 Gullatt Rd, Palmetto, GA 30268.....................................770-306-1335
Loehle, Richard: 2608 River Oak Dr, Decatur, GA 30033 404-633-5639
Loew, David: 227 Godfrey Rd, Weston, CT 06883 203-222-8777
    232 Madison Ave #402, New York, NY 10016...212-889-8777
• Lofaro, Jerry: pg 788   353 W 53rd St #1W, New York, NY 10019..............**212-682-2462**
    e-mail: info@amerartists.com / url: www.amerartists.com / fax: 212-582-0090
Lofficier, Jean-Marc: PO Box 17270, Encino, CA 91416 818-343-7942
Loftus, David: 31 Prothero Rd, Fulham, London, UK SW6 7LY 171-381-9145
    58 W 15th St, New York, NY 10011..212-741-2539
Logan, Ron: PO Box 306, Brentwood, NY 11717 516-273-4693
• LoGrippo, Bob: pg 516   217 E 86th St Box 212, New York, NY 10028 ....**212-427-5632**
    fax: 212-427-6372
• Lohstoeter, Lori: pg 406   250 W 57th St #521, New York, NY 10107 ....**212-397-7330**
    url: www.lindgrensmith.com (and) www.stockillustrated.com
• Loken, Stein: pg 786   231 E 76th St #5D, New York, NY 10021.................**212-535-0438**
    fax: 212-535-1624
• Lomax, Liz: pg 1074   81 Seven Bridges Road, Chappaqua, NY 10514..........**914-666-7345**
Lombardo, William: 491 Broadway 12th Fl, New York, NY 10012 212-226-3471
• LoMele, Bachrun: pg 891   16 Phaedra, Laguna Niguel, CA 92677 ....**949-495-3664**
    url: www.showcase.com / fax: 949-495-0129
Lomprey, Steve: 5474 Boyd Ave, Oakland, CA 94618 510-597-1157
London, Sherry: 1523 Pleasant Dr, Cherry Hill, NJ 08003 609-795-1710
Long, Bill: 1580 Courtship Dr, Lancaster, OH 43130 614-653-7058
Long, Bruce: 5539 Jefferson Blvd, Frederick, MD 21702 301-371-5264
Long, Ethan: 907 Allenview Dr, Mechanicsburg, PA 17055.............................717-691-9278
Long, Jennifer: 3780 Wilshire Blvd #710, Los Angeles, CA 90010..................213-480-1059
Long, Jim: 4415 Briarwood Court N, Annandale, VA 22003............................703-354-8052
Long, John: 666 West End Ave #16E, New York, NY 10025 212-724-0428
Long, Laurel: 23714 Aster Trail, Calabasas, CA 91302..................................818-222-8507
Long, Lennie: 100 Jenkins St, Providence, RI 02906.....................................401-274-6314
• Long, Loren: pg 266,267   121 Madison Ave, New York NY 10016...............**212-683-1362**
    fax: 212-683-1919
Long, Paulette: PO Box 519, Tatamy, PA 18085 201-224-8106
Long, Suzanne: 1076 Jackson St, Benicia, CA 94510 707-745-6123
Lonsdale, Ashley: 420 Lexington Ave, New York, NY 10170 212-986-5680
Lopez Assocs, Stewart: 550 W Kentucky St, Louisville, KY 40203 502-583-5502
Lopez, Emmanuel: 192 Spadina Ave #510, Toronto, ON M5T 2C2 416-504-4424
• Lopez, Rafael: pg 476,477
    2149 Lyon St #5, San Francisco, CA 94115...**415-921-7140**
    email: art@conradreps.com / url: www.conradreps.com / fax: 415-921-3939
Lord, David: 2100 Cord St, Indianapolis, IN 46224 317-634-1244
Lord, Rosalind: 175 W 12th St #16N, New York, NY 10011 212-807-7959
Lord, Tim: 2814 NW 72nd St, Seattle, WA 98117 206-784-1136
Lorenz, Albert: 49 Pine Ave, Floral Park, NY 11001 516-354-5530
Lorenz, Lee: 108 E 35th St #2, New York, NY 10016 212-889-3337
Lorick, Blake: Manitou Rd RR2 Box 414, Garrison, NY 10524 914-424-3549
• Lorincz, James: pg 797   2491 W 22nd Ave, Vancouver, BC B6L 1M3 ....**604-684-6826**
    url: www.repart.com / fax: 604-684-6826
Loschiavo, Doree: 2714 S Marvine St, Philadelphia, PA 19148 215-336-1724
Lose, Hal: 533 W Hortter St Toad Hall, Philadelphia, PA 19119 215-849-7635
Loudon, Greg: 1804 Pine rd, Homewood, IL 60430 708-799-4339
Lougee, Michelle: 2 Lothian Rd #3, Brighton, MA 02135 617-254-7252
• Loughran, PJ: pg 70,71   108 E 35th St, New York, NY 10016 ....**212-889-3337**
    url: www.theispot.com/artist/loughran / fax: 212-889-3341
Lounsberry, Charles: 863 Park Pl, Ocean City, NJ 08226 609-399-3105
Lourdes, Candace: 99 Coleman Ave #208, Toronto, ON M4C1P8 416-698-3304
Lovato, Rich: 4864 Valley Hi Dr, Sacramento, CA 95823 916-429-2655
Love, Judith DuFour: 68 Agassiz Ave, Belmont, MA 02178 617-484-8023
Love, Nan: PO Box 5004, Santa Rosa, CA 95402..707-527-5683
Love, Sarah: 770 E 73rd St, Indianapolis, IN 46240.....................................317-255-1197
Loveless, Jim: 4137 San Francisco Ave, St Louis, MO 63115...........................314-533-7914
Loveless, Roger: 1199 S Main St #200, Centerville, UT 84014 801-292-0943
• Lovell, Rick: pg 539   89 FIfth Ave #901, New York, NY 10003 ....**212-627-1554**
    fax: 212-627-1719
Lovitt, Anita: 308 E 78th St, New York, NY 10021 212-628-8171
• Low, William: pg 187   194 Third Ave 3rd Fl, New York, NY 10003 ....**212-475-0440**
    url: www.vickimorganassociates.com / fax: 212-353-8538
Lowden, Alisa: 4120 Fulton Street #1, San Francisco, CA 94121 ....
Lowell, Beth: 190 Millburn Ave, Millburn, NJ 07041 201-376-6838
Lowery, Denise C: 35 Flatt Rd #102, Rochester, NY 14623 716-292-5435
Lowry Graphics, David: PO Box 121861, Nashville, TN 37212 615-298-5841
Lowry, Rose: 41 Cutter Rd, Temple, NH 03084...603-532-8433
• Lozano, Armandina: pg 1008,1009
    110 Sutter St #706, San Francisco, CA 94104 ....**415-441-4384**
    2 Buckthorn St, Irvine, CA 92604 ....**949-559-1397**
    fax: 949-559-0330
Lozano, Henry Jr: 3205 Belle River Dr, Hacienda, CA 91745 818-330-2095
Lozner, Ruth: 133 Spring St 2nd Fl, New York, NY 10012 212-925-4340
LSI Graphic Evidence: 16255 Ventura Blvd #450, Encino, CA 91436 310-568-1831
• Lu Illustration, Kong: pg 1104   1431 35th Ave S, Seattle, WA 98144.........**206-325-8595**
    fax: 206-325-8594
Lubert, Randall: 17767 Mitchell, Irvine, CA 92714 714-660-9396
Lubey, Dick: 726 Harvard, Rochester, NY 14610..716-442-6075
Lubinsky, D Adolph: 7301 Argentina, Buena Park, CA 90620.........................714-523-8189
Lubsen, Laurie J Perkins: 13215 Stablebrook Way, Herndon, VA 22071 703-904-0731

• Lucas, Cedric: pg 872   866 United Nations PLaza, New York, NY 10017......**212-644-2020**
    url: www.spar.org
Lucas, Christopher M: 4000 Westbrook Dr, Brooklyn, OH 44144 216-749-7742
Lucas, Sheila: 2405 NW Thurman St, Portland, OR 97210...............................503-203-8300
Luce, Ben: 4 E Ohio Studio B, Chicago, IL 60611 312-321-1336
    5 E 17th St 6th Fl, New York, NY 10003 212-691-2667
Luce, Craig: PO Box 4003, Charlottesville, VA 22903 804-823-2745
Lucero, Andre: 333 E 49th St, New York, NY 10017.....................................212-980-8061
Lucero, Anita: 15 Deer Ln #12, Clchester, VT 05446....................................802-878-9205
Lucero, Rebecca: Box 3603, Citrus Hgts, CA 95672 916-723-5155
Lucier, Brian: 45 Constitution Dr, Leominster, MA 01453 978-534-9900
Luckett, Julie L: 810 Bellevue Rd #280, Nashville, TN 37221.........................615-646-9581
Luckom, Lawrence: 117 Prescott St, North Andover, MA 01845......................508-557-5530
Luckwitz, Matthew: 3500 Osceola St, Denver, CO 80212 303-839-8442
Luczak, Laurie B: 223 E 35th St #2WR, New York, NY 10016........................212-251-9694
Ludtke, Sharon & Jim: 1008C 9th St, Santa Monica, CA 90403 310-656-1173
Lugo, Lisette: 100 Produce Ave #F, San Francisco, CA 94080.........................415-588-3375
Lui, David: Regency Prk 3 Wah King Hill Rd, Hong Kong, ...212-925-0491
Luikart, Erika: 1550 9th Avenue #7, San Francisco, CA 94122 415-242-1770
Lukens, Jan: 2354 Chaucer Ln, Winston-Salem, NC 27107 910-788-5451
Lukova, Luba: 315 W 14th St, New York, NY 10014 212-645-1485
Lulevitch, Tom: 15222 Victoria Ave, White Rock, BC V4B 1G6, ...604-535-1909
Lum, Bernice: 205 Howland Ave, Toronto, ON M5R 3B7, ...416-923-4961
Lumley, Diane: 11 Kings Ridge Rd, Long Valley, NJ 07853...........................908-813-8718
• Lund, Jon C: pg 1136   709 Wellesley Ave, Akron, OH 44303 ....**330-655-0784**
    url: www.showcase.com
Lundgren, Alvalyn: 274 Mariposa Dr, Newbury Park, CA 91320 805-480-9600
Lundgren, Tim: 165 E 32nd St, New York, NY 10016 212-686-3514
• Lundman, Julia: pg 1225   853 W Washington #1B, Oak Park, IL 60302......**708-386-2608**
    url: www.showcase.com / fax: 708-386-2608
Lundquist, Roger: 217 E 86th St Box 212, New York, NY 10028 212-427-5632
Lung, YW: 3300 Don Mills Rd #2404, Willowdale, ON M2J 4X7 416-497-4359
Lunsford, Annie: 515 N Hudson St, Arlington, VA 22201 703-527-7696
Lussier, Robert: 18 Pleasant Cir, Methuen, MA 01844 508-670-6734
Lustig, Loretta: 330 Clinton Ave, Brooklyn, NY 11205 718-789-2496
Lutts, Heidi: 12 Rand Rd, Salem, MA 01970 508-741-1878
Lutz, Dan: 456 Lincoln Blvd, Santa Monica, CA 90402 310-393-9747
Lutzow, Jack A: 906-A Noe St, San Francisco, CA 94114 415-641-5800
• Luzuriaga, Denis: pg 1456,1457   39 Hamilton Terr, New York, NY 10031 .....**212-283-3401**
    url: www.wayart.com
• Lyall, Dennis: pg 522,532   89 Fifth Ave #901, New York, NY 10003 ....**212-627-1554**
    fax: 212-627-1719
• Lyhus, Randy: pg 1004,1005
    4853 Cordell Ave #10, Bethesda, MD 20814 ....**301-986-0036**
    url: www.randylyhus.com / fax: 301-907-4653
Lynaugh, Matt: 110 Academy Dr, Austin, TX 78704 512-416-7772
Lynch, Bob: 2639 N Charles St, Baltimore, MD 21218 410-366-6535
• Lynch, Fred: pg 1343   One Eaton Ct, Winchester, MA 01890 ....**781-729-3813**
    fax: 781-729-3813
Lynch, Jeffrey: 420 Lexington Ave, New York, NY 10170...............................212-986-5680
Lynch, Tiffiny: 286 Spring St #301, New York, NY 10013 212-229-0073
Lynn, Jeffery: 1554 Stagecoach Rd, Stowe, VT 05672 802-253-4767
Lynn, Jenny: 18 S Letitia St, Philadelphia, PA 19106....................................215-925-8967
Lynn, Kathy: 330 W Springfield Ave, Philadelphia, PA 19118 215-242-9165
Lynn, Nicholas: 305 E 86th St, New York, NY 10028 212-503-3969
Lyons, Claudia: 37490 Toronto Ave, Burney, CA 96013 530-335-3225
Lyons, Jonathan Lee: 2302 W Indianhead Dr, Tallahassee, FL 32301 850-942-9442
Lyons, Linda: 787 Schaefer Ave, Oradell, NJ 07649....................................201-262-5020
• Lyons, Rebecca: pg 1224   414 Lake St #6, San Francisco, CA 94118 ....**415-751-7343**
    fax: 415-751-7343
Lyons, Sam: 731 Stovall Blvd NE, Atlanta, GA 30342 800-791-1189
Lyons, Steven: 136 Scenic Rd, Fairfax, CA 94930.......................................415-459-7560
Lyte, Mason: 610 Anacapa St, Santa Barbara, CA 93101 805-683-4884
• Lytle, John: pg 1344   PO Box 5155, Sonora, CA 95370 ....**209-928-4849**
    fax: 209-928-4575
Lyubner, Boris: 9015 Flint Way, Park City, UT 84098...................................435-649-2129

M

Ma, Tom: 8 Wells Hill Ave, Toronto, ON M5R 3A6 416-535-9178
Mably, Greg: 52 Sagueny Ave, Toronto, ON M5N 2Y7 416-410-8744
Mac, Kenny: 888 Worcester, Wellesley, MA 02181 617-235-6800
MacAdam, Dean: 133 N Montclair Ave, Dallas, TX 75208 214-943-2569
Macanga, Steve: 20 Morgantine Rd, Roseland, NJ 07068...............................201-403-8967
MacArthur, Dave: 147 E Bradford Ave #B, Cedar Grove, NJ 07009.................201-857-1046
MacCombie, Turi: 201 E 28th St, New York, NY 10016 212-532-0928
MacDonald, Greg: 753 N 35th, Seattle, WA 98103 206-634-1880
• MacDonald, John: pg 196,197   501 Fifth Ave, New York, NY 10017 ....**212-490-2450**
    url: www.renardrepresents.com / fax: 212-697-6828
MacDonald, Ross: 56 Castle Meadow Rd, Newton, CT 06470 203-270-6438
MacDougall, Rob: 420 Lexington Ave, New York, NY 10170 212-986-5680
MacDouglas Home Press: 861 SW Webster, Topeka, KS 66606......................913-234-0336
• Maceren, Jude: pg 1088   PO Box 4112, Montebello, CA 90640..................**213-887-8958**
    92 Kossuth St, Piscataway, NJ 08854 ....**732-752-5931**
    e-mail: judem.art@worldnet.att.net / fax: 732-752-5931
    Europe **011331-46-06-29-36**
MacFarland, Jean: 2300 W Alameda #A6, Santa Fe, NM 87501 505-471-2867
Mach, Steven: 87 E Elm St, Chicago, IL 60611 312-280-0071
Machalek, Jan: 3355/108 Queen Mary Rd, Montreal, QU H3V1A5 514-341-1592
Machat, Mike: 4426 Deseret Dr, Woodland Hills, CA 91364..........................818-702-9433
MacIntosh, Guy: 714 Enright Ave, Cincinnati, OH 45205..............................513-244-7160
MacKenzie, Vic: 1913A Ruhland Ave, Redondo Beach, CA 90278...................310-374-7911
Mackey, Melissa: 5 Tower Dr, Mill Valley, CA 94941....................................800-847-5101
Mackie, Clare: PO Box 1062, Bayonne, NJ 07002 201-436-4362
Maclachian, Neil: 45 Earswick Dr, Toronto, ON M1E 1C7 416-269-8141
MacLeod, Ainslie: 25 East Pier, Kappas Marina, Sausalito, CA 94965 415-331-2588

ILLUSTRATORS

Martinetti, Don: 206 Linda Ln, Edison, NJ 08820 908-756-9254
Martinez, Edward: 420 Lexington Ave, New York, NY 10170 212-986-5680
Martinez, Isabel G: Studio M - 3200 Main Street, Dallas, TX 75226 214-653-1529
Martinez, John: 165 Hudson St, New York, NY 10013 212-941-0482
Martinez, Sergio: 43 E 19th St, New York, NY 10003 212-254-4996
Martinot, Claude: 1133 Broadway #1614, New York, NY 10010 212-229-2249
Martins, Marcos: Rua Nascimento Silva 107 #201, Rio de Janeiro, BR 22421 .021-521-0534
Martis, Michael W: 612 SE Spring, Des Moines, IA 50315 515-285-8122
Maruca, Francisco Rodriguez: 3286 Ivanhoe, St Louis, MO 63139 314-781-7377
Maruszewska, Beata: 5207 W Henderson, Chicago, IL 60641 773-202-8375
Marvin, Fred: 43 E 19th St, New York, NY 10003 212-254-4996
Marx, Jeff: 17844 Margate St, Encino, CA 91316 818-344-3572
Maryanski, Ken: 314 Chelsea St, Everett, MA 02149 617-381-1806
Marzullo, Michael: 2827 E Northern Pkwy, Baltimore, MD 21214 410-426-7713
Maschler, Lorraine: 2646 Dupont Dr Ste 20-425, Irvine, CA 92715 714-770-9255
Masciovecchio, Marie: 16 W 16th St #8JN, New York, NY 10011 212-698-4246
Masi, Kevin: 309 N Justine, Chicago, IL 60607 312-421-7858
Masla, Robert: 165 E 32nd St, New York, NY 10016 212-686-3514
Maslen, Barbara: New York, NY 212-645-5325
Mason Studio, John: PO Box 3973, Carmel, CA 93921 408-625-3868
Mason, Angie: PO Box 8232, Saddle Brook, NJ 07663 201-253-1244
Mason, Susan: 200 Henry Bldg 30, 6th Floor, Stamford, CT 06902 203-357-1248
Masse, DD: 81 Seward Ln, Aston, PA 19014 215-494-7525
Masse, Josée: 4030 rue, Montréal, QU H4C 2C7 514-937-2363
Massé, Pierre: 72 av Laurier Ouest, Montréal, QU H2T 2N4 514-277-7395
Masseau, Jean Carlson: RR 1 Box 303 Silver St, Hinesburg, VT 05461 802-482-2407
Massicotte, Alain: 1121 Rue Ste-Catherine Ouest 4, Montreal, QU H3B 1J5 514-843-4169
Masuda, Coco: PO Box 470818, San Francisco, CA 94147 415-383-9026
• **Matcho, Mark: pg 756,757** 608 York St, San Francisco, CA 94110 ....**415-641-1285**
fax: 415-641-5500
Mateu, Franc: 43 E 19th St, New York, NY 10003 212-254-4996
Matheis, Shelley: 534 East Passaic Ave, Bloomfield, NJ 07003 201-338-9506
Mathias, John: 520 2nd St #3F, Brooklyn, NY 11215 718-788-2133
Mathias, Steve: 115 E 19th St #1B, New York, NY 10035 212-426-6036
Matsick, Anni: 1000 Bayberry Dr, State College, PA 16801 814-234-4752
• **Matsu: pg 192-195** 501 Fifth Ave, New York, NY 10017 ....**212-490-2450**
url: www.renardrepresents.com / fax: 212-697-6828
Matt, Baier: 30 Second Pl #2, Brooklyn, NY 11231 718-802-9483
Mattelson, Marvin: 37 Cary Rd, Great Neck, NY 11021 516-487-1323
Matthews, Alex: 443 Lexington Ave, El Cerrito, CA 94530 212-984-3149
Matthews, Bonnie: 848 W 35th St, Baltimore, MD 21211 410-243-3514
Matthews, Lu: 280 Madison Ave #1110, New York, NY 10016 212-545-9155
Matthews, Pete: PO Box 18128, Fairfield, OH 45018 513-868-2874
Matthews, Scott: 2925 Griffith St, San Francisco, CA 94124 415-467-9676
Matthews, Scott: 7530 Ethel Ave, St Louis, MO 63117 314-647-9899
Matthieson, Brad: 310 Delaware St #210, Kansas City, MO 64105 816-221-1047
Mattingly, David B: 1112 Bloomfield St, Hoboken, NJ 07030 201-659-7404
Mattingly, Matthew: 55 S Mount Holyoke Dr, Amherst, MA 01002 413-259-1394
Mattioli, Angela: 455 N Deheny Drive #103, Beverley Hills, CA 90210 310-385-1901
Mattiucci, Jim: 247 N Goodman St, Rochester, NY 14607 716-271-2280
• **Mattos, John: pg 545,1030,1031**
7118 Upper River Rd, Prospect, KY 40059 ....**502-228-9427**
url: www.jettreps.com / fax: 502-228-8857
studio **415-397-2138**
e-mail: mattos@sirius.com / fax: 415-397-1174
Mattson, Tom: 1814 Cleveland, Santa Barbara, CA 93103 805-569-5751
• **Maughan, Bill: pg 160** 420 Lexington Ave, New York, NY 10170 ....**212-986-5680**
url: www.mendolaart.com / fax: 212-818-1246
Maun, Patrick: 255 E Kellogg Blvd #509, St Paul, MN 55101 612-227-2780
• **Maurer, Marsha: pg 1347** 304 Corbin Dr, Newport News, VA 23606 ....**757-595-5921**
e-mail: mmi@widomaker.com
Mauro, Paulo: 431 Lee St #6, Oakland, CA 94610 510-893-3328
Mauro, Ray: 228 Second St, Clifton, NJ 07011 201-546-8750
Mauterer, Erin: 51 Ascot Dr, Ocean City, NJ 07712 800-258-9287
Max, Adam: 21-16 28th St, Long Island City, NY 11105 718-204-6184
Max, Deborah Dudley: 157 Newbrook Ln, Bay Shore, NY 11706 516-968-5918
Max, Louise: 102 Quail Dr, Doylestown, PA 18901 215-345-8547
Maxedon, Terry: 718 Broadway, New York, NY 10003 212-677-3509
Maxson, Greg: 116 W Florida Ave, Urbana, IL 61801 217-359-6835
Maxwell, Sylvie: 171 Marine Parade #4, Santa Cruz, CA 95062 408-426-6452
May, Anthony: 382 Day St, San Francisco, CA 94131 415-648-2690
May, Danny: 3535 Newton St, Denver, CO 80211 303-433-4880
May, Darcy: 201 E 28th St, New York, NY 10016 212-532-0928
May, Jeff: 7368 Ahern Ave, St Louis, MO 63130 314-727-1476
May, Jody: 5413 Willowmere Way, Baltimore, MD 21212 410-435-8864
Mayberry, Douglas: 1315 Oakhill Ave, Gulfport, MS 39507 601-688-1884
Maydak, Michael: 2149 Lyon St #5, San Francisco, CA 94115 415-921-7140
Mayeda, Kaz: 243 Bickwell #A, Santa Monica, CA 90405 310-452-0054
• **Mayer, Bill: pg 378,970,971** 250 W 57th St #521, New York, NY 10107 ....**212-397-7330**
url: www.lindgrensmith.com (and) www.stockillustrated.com
240 Forkner Dr, Decatur, GA 30030 ....**404-378-0686**
fax: 404-373-1759
Mayes, Kevin: 3002 Timberlane Circle, Wichita, KS 67216 316-522-6742
• **Mayforth, Hal: pg 74,75** 108 E 35th St #2, New York, NY 10016 ....**212-889-3337**
url: www.theispot.com/artist/mayforth / fax: 212-889-3341
Mayo, Frank: 25000 Creekside Dr, Farmington Hills, MI 48336 810-661-8498
Mayo, Martin & Robert: 9 Stanford Ave, Colonia, NJ 07067 908-382-4730
Mayse, Steve: 7515 Allman, Lenexa, KS 66217 913-599-5440
Maziacyzk, Claire: 834 River Rd, Schodack Landing, NY 12156 518-732-2779
Mazoujian, Charles: 20 Brook Rd, Tenafly, NJ 07670 201-569-8057
Mazut, Mark: PO Box M1573, Hoboken, NJ 07030 201-656-0657
Mazzella, Mary Jo: 98 Youngblood Rd, Montgomery, NY 12549 914-361-1765
Mazzeo, George: 740 Broadway 4th Fl, New York, NY 10019 212-698-4263
Mazzetti, Alan: 420 Lexington Ave #2760, New York, NY 10170 212-697-8525
Mazzetti, Alan: 834 Moultrie St, San Francisco, CA 94110 415-647-7677
Mazzini, John: 68 Grey Ln, Levittown, NY 11756 516-579-6518
• **McAdams, Barbara: pg 454** 731 N 24th St, Philadelphia, PA 19103 ....**215-232-6666**
url: www.deborahwolfeltd.com / fax: 215-232-6585
McAfee, Steve: PO Box 54272, Atlanta, GA 30308 404-873-8227
McAll, Kenneth: 90 Ash, Park Forest, IL 60466 708-747-6401
McAllen, Bob: 3268 Military Ave, Los Angeles, CA 90034 310-477-8374
• **McAllister, Chris: pg 996,997**
3080 Highland Scenic Dr S, Baxter, MN 56425 ....**218-828-8786**
url: www.theispot.com/artist/mcallister
McArthur, Dennis: 170-44 130th Ave #8D, Jamaica, NY 11434 718-987-3946
• **McBee, Scott: pg 1457** 39 Hamilton Terr, New York, NY 10031 ....**212-283-3401**
url: www.wayart.com
McBride, David: 6319 Jackie Ave, Woodland Hills, CA 91367 818-884-8149
McBrine, Mike: 61 Bickford Rd, Braintree, MA 02184 617-843-2285
McCain, Kevin: 1424 La Positas Plaza, Santa Barbara, CA 93105 805-682-6775
McCampbell, Rachael: 311 Ave H #D, Redondo Beach, CA 90277 310-540-5958
McCampbell, Rachael: 716 Montgomery St, San Francisco, CA 94111 415-433-1222
McCampbell, Rachael: 2815 Grayson Ave, Venice, CA 90291 310-306-0469
McCandlish, Mark: 2205 Hilltop Dr #158, Redding, CA 96002 916-547-5424
McCann, Stephanie: 2417 Foothill Ln, Santa Barbara, CA 93105 805-966-1877
McCarthy, Emmett: 123 Elizabeth St, New York, NY 10013 212-431-4134
McCarthy, Errol: 3918 Pacific Avenue, Long Beach, CA 90807 310-424-9014
• **McCauley, Adam: pg 754,755** 608 York St, San Francisco, CA 94110 ....**415-641-1285**
alternate **510-832-0860**
url: www.adammccauley.com / fax: 415-641-5500
McCauley, Adam: 2400 Eighth Ave, Oakland, CA 94606 510-832-0860
McClary, Andrew L: 3708 Richelieu Rd, Indianapolis, IN 46226 317-897-2745
McClintock, Wendell: 60 E 42nd St #1146, New York, NY 10165 212-953-7088
McCloskey, Bill: 1215 18th St, Sacramento, CA 95816 916-448-6543
McCloskey, Kevin: 140 E Main, Kutztown, PA 19530 215-683-6546
McClure, Linda: 11111 Pickford Way, Culver City, CA 90230 310-397-5167
McClure, Nancee: 2755 B Road, Grand Junction, CO 81503 970-242-4744
McClure, Nancy Wirsig: 421 SW 6th Ave #1050, Portland, OR 97204 503-768-4866
McCollum, Rick: 232 Madison Ave #402, New York, NY 10016 212-889-8777
McCollum, Sudi: 2925 Griffith St, San Francisco, CA 94124 415-467-9676
McConnell, Gerald: 10 E 23rd St, New York, NY 10010 212-505-0950
McConnell, Mike: 6 Seven Springs Ct, Phoenix, MD 21131 410-527-0055
McCord, Kathleen: PO Box 1086, Taos, NM 87571 505-776-5435
McCormack, Daphne: 14027 Memorial #125, Houston, TX 77079 281-579-3220
McCormack, Donna: 46-26 247 St, Douglaston, NY 11362 718-229-7939
• **McCormack, Geoffrey: pg 151** 420 Lexington Ave, New York, NY 10170 ....**212-986-5680**
url: www.mendolaart.com / fax: 212-818-1246
McCormick, Peter: 13726 Aleppo Dr, Sun City West, AZ 85375 520-584-8403
McCracken, Kathi: 96 Mulberry Ln, Atherton, CA 94027 818-548-7107
McCullough, Greg: 3000 Carlisle #203, Dallas, TX 75204 214-969-6911
McCurdy, Michael: 66 Lake Buel Rd, Great Barrington, MA 01230 413-528-2749
McDaniel, Jerry: 155 E 38th St, New York, NY 10016 212-697-6170
McDermond, Patricia: 9 Gracie Square #1RW, New York, NY 10028 212-737-1982
• **McDermott, Joe: pg 745** 865 Delaware St, Denver, CO 80204 ....**303-820-2599**
toll-free **800-417-5120**
url: www.artagent.com / fax: 303-820-2598
McDermott, Michael: 12 South Main St Box 343, Stewartstown, PA 17363 717-993-2746
McDermott, Teri: 38W563 Koshare Trail, Elgin, IL 60123 847-888-2206
McDevitt, Mark: 7010 Oak Leaf Dr, Fairburn, GA 30213 770-964-8720
• **McDonald Design, Jim: pg 1497** 5703 E Evans Dr, Scottsdale, AZ 85254 ....**602-464-0747**
e-mail: airpwr@earthlink.net / url: www.http//home.earthlink.net/~airpwr
PO Box 7544, Phoenix, AZ 85011 ....**602-265-4389**
• **McDonald, Mercedes: pg 1221** 325 Wilson Way, Larkspur, CA 94939 ....**415-927-4500**
53 W Jackson Blvd #1454, Chicago, IL 60604 ....**312-435-0055**
4606 Cedar Spring #1527, Dallas, TX 75219 ....**214-559-0055**
137 W 14th St #204, New York, NY 10011 ....**212-337-0055**
4349 Cahuenga Blvd #105, Toluca Lake, CA 91602 ....**818-505-8085**
e-mail: mermc@aol.com
Redondo Beach, CA **310-540-5958**
McDonnell, Patrick: 3420 Westmore, Montreal, QU H4B 1Z8 514-483-5489
• **McDonnell, Peter: pg 825** 1839 Ninth St, Alameda, CA 94501 ....**510-769-1421**
e-mail: ldmreps@earthlink.net / fax: 510-521-1674
McDonnell, Susan: 1347 Topeka St, Pasadena, CA 91104 818-797-3926
McDougall, David: 5403 104th Pl SW, Mukilteo, WA 98275 206-787-9766
McDougall, Scott: 712 N 62nd St, Seattle, WA 98103 206-783-1403
McElhaney, Gary: 8104 Peaceful Hill Ln, Austin, TX 78748 512-282-5743
McEntire, Larry: 1931 Lexington Street, Houston, TX 77098 713-520-1298
McFarland, Tom F: 7300 Belleview, Kansas City, MO 64114 816-363-5699
• **McFarren, Mathew: pg 1216** 1553 Platte St #302, Denver, CO 80202 ....**303-458-7445**
e-mail: macart@ecentral.com / fax: 303-458-7161
McGinley, Ed: PO Box 40459, Providence, RI 02940 401-272-4535
McGinness, Jim: 3822 Janice Rd, Fairfax, VA 22030 703-691-0758
• **McGinty, Mick: pg 136** 420 Lexington Ave, New York, NY 10170 ....**212-986-5680**
url: www.mendolaart.com / fax: 212-818-1246
McGovern, Michael: 455 W 23rd St #8D, New York, NY 10011 212-366-1893
McGovern, Preston: 157 E 3rd St, New York, NY 10009 212-982-8595
McGowan, Daniel: 420 Lexington Ave, New York, NY 10170 212-986-5680
McGrail, Rollin: 12492 Westhampton Cir, W Palm Beach, FL 33414 407-795-9525
McGrath & Assocs, Judy: 809 Forrest Ave, Evanston, IL 60202 847-866-8568
McGraw, Kim: 1888 Century Park E #1104, Los Angeles, CA 90067 310-556-0500
McGraw, Laurie: RR #2, Shelbourne, ON L0N 1S6 519-925-5134
McGuiness, Doreen: 23 Ganton St, London, England, UK WIV 1LA 71-287-9191
McGuire, Bill: 111 E Wacker Dr #2600, Chicago, IL 60601 312-368-4355
McGuire, Jim: 1311 Central Ave, Charlotte, NC 28205 704-333-1052
• **McGurl, Michael: pg 204,205** 501 Fifth Ave, New York, NY 10017 ....**212-490-2450**
url: www.renardrepresents.com / fax: 212-697-6828
• **McIndoe, Vincent: pg 384,385**
250 W 57th St #521, New York, NY 10107 ....**212-397-7330**
url: www.lindgrensmith.com (and) www.stockillustrated.com
McIntosh, Guy: 714 Enright Ave, Cincinnati, OH 45205 513-244-7160
McIntosh, Jon C: 17 Devon Rd, Chestnut Hill, MA 02167 617-277-9530

McIntyre Illus, Mark J: 1566 Sugarwood Dr, Winter Park, FL 32792................407-294-9408
McKean, Katie: 1516 Deerhaven Dr, Crystal Lake, IL 60014..........................914-278-7966
McKee, Darren: 162 Classen, Dallas, TX 75218 214-343-8766
McKee, Dianne: 1832 Perkiomenville Rd, Perkiomenville, PA 18074 215-234-0377
McKee, Ron: 32362 Lake Pleasant Dr, Westlake Village, CA 91361 818-889-6692
Mckee-Anderson Group: 919 Springer Dr, Lombard, IL 60148..........................630-953-8706
McKeever, Michael: 3475 Soutwood Ct, Davie, FL 33328 305-476-6884
McKelvey, David: 731 Stovall Blvd NE, Atlanta, GA 30342 800-791-1189
• **McKelvey, Shawn: pg 788** 353 W 53rd St #1W, New York, NY 10019......**212-682-2462**
e-mail: info@amerartists.com / url: www.amerartists.com / fax: 212-582-0090
McKenzie, Crystal: 30 E 20th St #502, New York, NY 10003 212-598-4567
McKenzie, Dave: 112P Lofton Dr, Fayetteville, NC 28311..............................910-822-1536
McKenzie, Gail: 216 Bedford Rd, Greenwich, CT 06831 203-622-0161
McKeon, Patrick: 101 S Jennings #5304, Ft Worth, TX 76104.........................817-336-1118
McKie, Roy: 164 Old Clinton Rd, Flemington, NJ 08822 908-788-7996
McKiernan, James: 3088 Walnut Ave, Long Beach, CA 90807.........................310-426-1888
McKinley, John: 247 Meadowlark Ln, Aptos, CA 95003 408-662-0880
McKinnell, Michael: 2491 W 22nd Ave, Vancouver, BC B6L 1M3 604-684-6826
McKissick, Randall: PO Box 21811, Columbia, SC 29221 803-739-9080
McKissick, Stewart: 250 Piedmont Rd, Columbus, OH 43214..........................614-262-3262
McKowen, Scott: 278 Hamilton Ave, Princeton, NJ 08540 609-252-9405
McLain, W Clay: 9211 E Lake Highlands Rd, Dallas, TX 75218 214-324-0168
McLaren, Chelsey: 125 W 79th St #3F, New York, NY 10024..........................212-496-1505
McLaughlin, Cynthia: 4628 Conwell Dr, Annandale, VA 22008 703-256-4924
McLaughlin, Jerry: 16370 Lucky Rd, Los Gatos, CA 95030 408-354-2569
McLean, Don: 11440 Oak Dr, Shelbyville, MI 49344 616-672-5756
McLean, Wilson: 115 West 2nd Street, New York, NY 10011 212-989-4600
McLellan, Anne C: 285 Bennett St, Wrentham, MA 02093 508-384-7355
McLennan, Constance: 3908 Baltic Cir, Rocklin, CA 95677 916-624-1957
• **McLimans, David: pg 76,77** 108 E 35th St #2, New York, NY 10016.........**212-889-3337**
url: www.theispot.com/artist/mclimans / fax: 212-889-3341
McLoughlin, Jackie: 48 Atkinson St, Bellows Falls, VT 05101 802-457-2708
• **McLoughlin, Wayne: pg 228** 501 Fifth Ave, New York, NY 10017...............**212-490-2450**
url: www.renardrepresents.com / fax: 212-697-6828
McMacken, David: 19481 Franquelin Pl, Sonoma, CA 95476 707-996-5239
60 E 42nd St #822, New York, NY 10165..212-682-1490
McMahon, Bob: 240 S 3rd Unit 0, Burbank, CA 91502 818-955-8802
McMahon, Brad: 654 Pier Ave #C, Santa Monica, CA 90405 310-392-4877
McMahon, Kelly: 2051 1/2 255 St, Lomita, CA 90717 310-534-1013
McMahon, Mark: 321 S Ridge Rd, Lake Forest, IL 60045...............................847-295-2604
McMahon, Mike: 1826 Asheville Pl, Charlotte, NC 28203 704-372-6007
McMahon, Robert: 7260 Apperson St #212, Tujunga, CA 91042 818-352-9990
McManus, Eugenia: PO Box 39, Mayhew, MS 39753.....................................601-328-5534
McManus, Jim: 85 Park St #5, Portland, ME 04101 207-775-1372
McManus, Robert: 3333 W Wethersfield Rd, Phoenix, AZ 85029 602-993-8659
McManus, Tom: 30 Washington Park, Maplewood, NJ 07040 201-378-3875
• **McMenemy, Sarah: pg 715** 455 W 23rd St #8D, New York, NY 10011 ......**212-366-1893**
url: www.andtheart.com / fax: 212-604-9643
• **McMillan, Ken: pg 870** 137 Fifth Ave 11th Fl, New York, NY 10010 ....**212-529-3556**
fax: 212-353-0831
• **McMillen, Mike: pg 356,357** 327 E 89th St #3E, New York, NY 10128......**212-831-5650**
fax: 212-831-6241
1306 Alabama St, Huntington Beach, CA 92648 ....**714-969-7766**
fax: 714-374-3744
McMullan, James: 207 E 32nd St, New York, NY 10016..................................212-689-5527
McMullin, Dale: 11021 Balckwolf Ln, Parker, CO 80138.................................303-805-7637
McMullin, Russ: 765 N 400 E #1, Provo, UT 84606..801-375-8420
McNally, Andrew: 19 Oak Grove Rd, Caldwell, NJ 07006 201-228-6701
McNally, Jim: 3009 N Ashland, Chicago, IL 60657 773-404-5570
McNally, Kathleen: 21 North St, Saco, ME 04072 207-282-2713
McNeel, Richard: 140 Hepburn Rd #14H, Clifton, NJ 07012 201-779-0802
McNeely, Tom: 63-A Yorkville Ave, Toronto, ON M5R1B7..............................416-925-1929
McNeill, Jim: 3 Peru St, Edison, NJ 08820 732-548-9168
McNeill, Shannon: 13307 Valleyheart Dr N, Sherman Oaks, CA 91423............818-990-4627
McNicholas, Michael: 11740 S Brookside Dr, Palos Park, IL 60464 708-361-2850
McNichols, Kathy: 1736 Stockton #4, San Francisco, CA 94133 415-956-4646
McNulty, Catherine: 419 Main St, Concord, MA 01742 508-287-5492
McNulty, Johanne: 2936 rue Girouard Ouest, Saint-hyacinthe, QU J2S 3B1 514-771-1240
McOwan, Alex: 5855 Green Valley Cir #308, Culver City, CA 90230................310-642-2721
McParlane, Michael: 468 Queen St E #104, Toronto, ON M5A 1T7 416-367-2446
McPhee, Brian: 82 Frizzell Ave, Toronto, ON M4J 1E3 416-778-9146
McPheeters, Neal: 60 E 42nd St #1940, New York, NY 10165.........................212-867-8092
• **McPherson, Ron: pg 1213**
1000 Manhattan Ave #E, Manhattan Beach, CA 90266 ....**310-372-7777**
e-mail: rmcphers@ix.netcom.com / url: www.fatd.com and iSDN: 310-796-8564 /
fax: 310-318-2247
McShane, Frank: 555 North Ln, Conshohocken, PA 19428...............................215-830-0878
McSherry, Stewart: 265 San Antonio Ave, Palo Alto, CA 94306.......................415-856-6167
McVicker, Charles: PO Box 183, Rocky Hill, NJ 08553 609-924-2660
McWilliams, Stephanie: 704 Eighth Ave #2C, Brooklyn, NY 11215..................718-499-5622
Meachum, Jack: 3579 F Clubhouse Cir, Decatur, GA 30032............................404-296-8797
Mead, Kimble P: 232 Madison Ave #402, New York, NY 10016 212-889-8777
Meadows, Laura: 865 Delaware St, Denver, CO 80204 303-820-2598
Mechtly, Robert: 5536 Meadowgreen Ct, St Charles, MO 63304 314-539-6215
Medan, Dev: 2814 NW Golden Dr, Seattle, WA 98117 206-789-2601
Medbery, Sherrell: 18 Philadelphia Ave, Takoma Park, MD 20912 301-270-0314
Medeiros, John: 273 Peckham St, Fall River, MA 02724 508-676-8752
Medical Image Corp: 207 E 32nd St, New York, NY 10016 212-481-9737
Medici, Ray: 16 Hawthorn St, Rosslindale, MA 02131 617-323-0842
Medivisuals: 9211 Foresthill Ave #103, Richmond, VA 23235 800-899-2153
Medlock, Scott: 716 Sanchez St, San Francisco, CA 94114 415-285-8267
Medoff, Jack: 14 Hillside Rd S, Weston, CT 06883 203-454-3199
Meehan, Keith: 277 Alexander St #400, Rochester, NY 14607........................716-325-1530
Meek, Genevieve: 6207 Orchid Lane, Dallas, TX 75230 214-363-0680
• **Meek, Steve: pg 724** 7 Washington Street, Beverly, MA 01915 ....**978-921-0887**
e-mail: leighton@leightonreps.com / url: www.leightonreps.com / fax: 978-921-0223

Meeker, Carlene: 7 Forest St, Wakefield, MA 01880......................................617-846-5117
• **Meers, Tony: pg 536** 89 Fifth Ave #901, New York, NY 10003 ....**212-627-1554**
fax: 212-627-1719
Meganck, Robert: One North 5th St #500, Richmond, VA 23219 804-644-9200
Meier, Eric Paul: PO Box 40186, Providence, RI 02940 401-274-0271
Meier, Lori: 7336 Santa Monica Blvd #626, Hollywood, CA 90046..................310-772-8250
Meisel, Paul: 2 Pheasant Ridge Rd, Newtown, CT 06470 203-270-6692
Meisler, Meryl: 553 8th St, Brooklyn, NY 11215 718-768-3991
Meisner, Arnold: PO Box 40, Peaks Island, ME 04108 207-766-2422
Meissner, Dick: 1000 John R Rd #201, Troy, MI 48083..................................248-583-6070
Melanson, Luc: 8173 rue, Montréal, QU H2P 2L2 514-384-1336
Melendez, Robert: 481 8th Ave #1530, New York, NY 10036..........................212-221-8090
• **Mell, Sue: pg 1210** 285 Texas St, San Francisco, CA 94107..........................**415-431-6865**
Mellett, James: 500 S Meadowcroft Ave, Pittsburgh, PA 15228 412-563-4131
• **Mellon, Kristen: pg 1205** 692A Moulton Ave, Los Angeles, CA 90031..........**323-223-4242**
fax: 323-223-1344
• **Melmon, Deborah: pg 877**
580 Washington St #204, San Francisco, CA 94111 ....**415-362-8280**
fax: 415-362-8310
Melnick, Anil: 101-06 67th Dr #6F, Forest Hills, NY 11375 718-275-1008
Meloche, Lyne: Montréal, QU 514-460-3391
Melodia, Barbara: 1141 Bernal Ave, Burlingame, CA 94010 415-343-7331
Meltzer, Ericka: 223 Northumberland Way, Monmouth Junction, NJ 08852 732-438-8402
Melvin, William Jr: 211 Woodpecker Ln, Mt Holly, NJ 08060 609-267-3394
Menard, Kerri-Lynne: 60 Quincy #B, Long Beach, CA 90803 310-987-2963
• **Menchin, Scott: pg 1085** 104 Fifth Ave 19th Floor, New York, NY 10012....**212-673-5363**
url: www.showcase.com
• **Mendelsson, Jonny: pg 374** 250 W 57th St #521, New York, NY 10107 ....**212-397-7330**
url: www.lindgrensmith.com (and) www.stockillustrated.com
Mendheim, Michael: 2916 W Estes, Chicago, IL 60645 773-274-0077
Menk, France: 16 Cedar Ridge Rd, New Paltz, NY 12561...............................914-255-3755
Mercado, Jay: 608 York St, San Francisco, CA 94110....................................415-641-1285
Mercado, Vernon: 374-A Second Ave, San Francisco, CA 94118 415-386-5469
Merchan, Richard: 921 Flying Fish St, Foster City, CA 94404 707-778-9393
• **Meredith, Bret: pg 590,591**
232 Madison Ave #512, New York, NY 10016..**212-889-8777**
fax: 212-447-1475
Meredith, Jane: 333 E Ontario #4010B-B, Chicago, IL 60611..........................312-944-0731
Merewether, Patrick: 3047 Newton St, Denver, CO 80211 303-477-1220
• **Meridith, Shelly: pg 1071** 55 Mercer St 4th Fl, New York, NY 10013 ....**212-941-1905**
e-mail: leocat@spacelab.net / fax: 212-226-3227
Merkin, Richard: 500 West End Ave #12D, New York, NY 10024....................212-724-9285
Merola, Caroline: 10925 av de l'Esplanade, Montréal, QU H3L 2Y5 514-337-3009
Merrell, Patrick: 143 Ridgeway St, Mt Vernon, NY 10552...............................212-620-7777
Merrill, Dave: 11686 Stockbridge Ln, Reston, VA 22094 703-481-1776
Merrill, Lizanne: 333 Rector Pl #5N, New York, NY 10280 212-945-6115
Merritt, Norman: 621 Paseo De Los Reyes, Redondo Beach, CA 90277 310-378-4689
• **Merscher, Heidi: pg 742** 865 Delaware St, Denver, CO 80204 ....**303-820-2599**
toll-free **800-417-5120**
url: www.artagent.com / fax: 303--820-2598
Meshon, Aaron: 269 E 10th St #3, New York, NY 10009 212-253-1350
Messer, Holly: 1114 S Waterville Rd, Oconomowoc, WI 53066.......................414-646-5095
Messex, Mike: Los Angeles, CA 213-666-8822
Messi & Schmidt: 2149 Lyon St #5, San Francisco, CA 94115........................415-921-7140
Messier, Linda: 60 E 42nd St #1940, New York, NY 10165 212-867-8092
Metcalf, Eugene: 1006 E Rosewood Ave, Orange, CA 92666.........................714-538-6401
Metcalf, Paul: Webber Rd Box 35C, Brookfield, MA 01506 508-867-7754
Metz, Andrea: 1147 NW 57, Seattle, WA 206-781-8660
Meunier, Yvan: 754 rue Saint Paul Ouest, Montréal, QU H3C 1M4 514-392-0388
Meyer, Clay: 1020 N Jefferson #E, Jackson, MS 39202 601-969-5720
Meyer, G: 70 Whittingham Pl, W Orange, NJ 07052 201-736-7087
Meyer, Gary: 21725 Ybarra Rd, Woodland Hills, CA 91364 818-992-6974
Meyer, Jeff: 1427-A N Hawley Rd, Milwaukee, WI 53208 414-476-6161
Meyer, Ken: 3467 Bevis St, San Diego, CA 92111 619-571-0681
Meyer, Wendy: 5636 Souchak Dr, W Palm Beach, FL 33413 407-686-4847
• **Meyerowitz, Rick: pg 78,79** 108 E 35th St #2, New York, NY 10016 ....**212-889-3337**
url: www.theispot.com/artist/meyerowitz / fax: 212-889-3341
Meyers, Adam: 1123 Garden St, Hoboken, NJ 07030 201-222-7551
Meyers, Caroline: 66 Pearl St #606, New York, NY 10004..............................212-809-7394
Meyers, Kristine Everett: 5262 Butterwood Cir, Orangevale, CA 95662...........916-989-2420
Meyers, Pat: 139 Alala Rd, Kailua, HI 96734..808-263-0258
Meza, John: 3417 Faircrest Dr, Anaheim, CA 92804......................................714-827-8841
Mezzapelle, Bruno: 110 Sutter St #706, San Francisco, CA 94104 415-441-4384
Miceli, James: 155 Canterbury Rd, Rochester, NY 14607...............................716-271-8190
Michael Davis Group: 420 Lexington Ave, New York, NY 10170.....................212-986-5680
Michaels, Bob: 267 Fifth Ave #402, New York, NY 10016..............................212-532-0916
Michaels, Serge: 123 N Madison Ave, Monrovia, CA 91016...........................626-357-1416
Michal, Marie: 150 E 73rd St #4D, New York, NY 10021 212-288-0479
Michalak, David: 30 Mypold St, Walpole St, MA 02081 617-542-4946
Michalarias, Connie: 10432 S Kostrex, Oaklawn, IL 60453.............................312-259-4863
Michalski Jr, Joseph E: 401 N Carolina Ave, Pasadena, MD 21122 410-437-5330
Michaud, Line: 6301 rue de Saint-Vallier, Montréal, QU H2S 2P6 514-273-5619
• **Michel, Jean-Claude: pg 788** 353 W 53rd St #1W, New York, NY 10019.....**212-682-2462**
e-mail: info@amerartists.com / url: www.amerartists.com / fax: 212-582-0090
Michele, Amatrula: 259 W Tenth St #4J, New York, NY 10014 212-255-7413
Micho, Pierre: 4554 rue La Fontaine, Montréal, QU H1V 1P5 514-899-9582
Micich, Paul: 60 E 42nd St #822, New York, NY 10165 212-682-1490
Midda, Sara: 81 Greene St, New York, NY 10012..212-925-3053
Middendorf, Frances: 337 E 22nd St #2, New York, NY 10010........................212-473-3586
Middendorf, Nikki: 200 E 28th St, New York, NY 10016.................................212-863-2848
Middlebrook, Ann: 915 Broadway 14th Fl, New York, NY 10010 212-673-6600
Middleworth, Beth: 923 Preston Ave, Los Angeles, CA 90026........................213-666-3310
• **Mihaesteanu, Lucian: pg 1457** 39 Hamilton Terr, New York, NY 10031 ......**212-283-3401**
url: www.wayart.com
Mikec, Larry: 925 Elm Grove Rd, Elm Grove, WI 53122 414-785-1940

Mikolaycak, Charles: 64 E 91st St #2, New York, NY 10128..........................212-427-9628
Mikos, Mike: 420 Lexington Ave, New York, NY 10170..................................212-986-5680
Mikros, Nikita: 58-31 44th Ave, Woodside, NY 11377....................................718-458-6456
Milam, Larry: 4033 Aurora Ave N, Seattle, WA 98103 206-633-3445
Milbourn, Patrick D: 89 FIfth Ave #901, New York, NY 10003 212-627-1554
Milec, Larry: 925 Elm Grove Rd, Elm Grove, WI 53122..................................414-785-1940
Miles, Chris: 385 Douglas, Brooklyn, NY 11217 718-622-6407
Miles, Karen: 368 Broadway #209, New York, NY 10013...............................212-571-3678
Milgrim, David: 1164 Baywood Dr #18, Petaluma, CA 94954.........................707-782-9387
Miliano, Ed: Cullellen/Lowr Glenageary Rd/Dunlaoghaire, Dublin, Ireland, __ 31-280-1513
Millar, Brian: 40 Perkins t, Somerset, MA 02725...508-676-0466
Mille, Mark: 133 W Pittsburgh Ave #502, Milwaukee, WI 53204 414-278-8400
Miller, Charlie: 11 Hartack Ct, Baltimore, MD 21236 410-668-4131
Miller, Cindy: PO Box 7917, Ann Arbor, MI 48107 313-663-2144
Miller, Cliff: 60 E 42nd St #1940, New York, NY 10165 212-867-8092
• **Miller, Dave: pg 942,943** 11318 Forrestville Ave, Chicago, IL 60628 ....**773-264-1152**
fax: 773-264-0916
• **Miller, David: pg 785** 231 E 76th St #5D, New York, NY 10021 ....**212-535-0438**
fax: 212-535-1624
353 W 53rd St #1W, New York, NY 10019..**212-682-2462**
e-mail: info@amerartists.com / url: www.americanartists.com / fax: 212-582-0090
Miller, Doug: 420 Lexington Ave #3020, New York, NY 10170 212-692-9200
Miller, Edward: 231 Willow Ave #1L, Hoboken, NJ 07030...............................201-420-6457
• **Miller, Frank: pg 306,307** 58 W 15th St, New York, NY 10011 ....**212-741-2539**
url: www.showcase.com / fax: 212-741-4660
Miller, Gregory: 7317 Loch Aleme Ave, Pico Rivera, CA 90660 310-948-2915
Miller, Jack Paul: 1331 N Lincoln St, Burbank, CA 91506..............................818-841-4668
Miller, Jane: 1260 Day Valley, Aptos, CA 95003 408-684-1593
• **Miller, Judy: pg 800** 6638 N 13th St, Phoenix, AZ 85014..........................**602-263-8990**
fax: 602-277-0680
Miller, Kathleen: 2149 E Norma Ave, W Covina, CA 91791 818-966-4978
Miller, Lyle: 124 Cedar Valley Ln-Cedar Hill, Dallas, TX 75104.......................214-291-1577
Miller, Mark: 3200 N 29th Ave, Hollywood, FL 33020....................................800-328-4349
Miller, Max: 58 W 15th St, New York, NY 10011 212-741-2539
Miller, Melissa: 317 High St, Milford, CT 06460...203-389-6988
Miller, Paul: 320 Bee Brook Rd, Washington, CT 06777 860-868-1011
Miller, Roger E: 3520 W 21st St, Minneapolis, MN 55416 612-925-0781
Miller, Sandro: 2540 W Huron, Chicago, IL 60612 312-486-0300
Miller, Steve: 2586 Majella Rd, Vista, CA 92084 619-758-0804
Miller, Thomas O: 2233 Kemper Ln, Cincinnati, OH 45206 513-861-1400
Miller, Tom: 407 Mission Ave #1, San Rafael, CA 94901 415-457-6678
Miller, Vance: 0-13 Fair Lawn Pkwy, Fair Lawn, NJ 07410.............................201-703-8291
Miller, Warren: 950 Klish Way, Del Mar, CA 92014 619-259-5774
Miller-Mann, Sheila: 5 Arrow Path, S Natick, MA 01760 508-650-0998
Milligan, Dan: 33 Yonge St 12th Fl, Toronto, ON M53 1X6 416-363-3772
Mills, Elise: 4 Bloomer Rd, North Salem, NY 10021......................................914-669-5948
Millsap, Darrel: 5996 Bounty St, San Diego, CA 92120..................................619-286-8668
Milne, Jonathan: 420 Lexington Ave, New York, NY 10170.............................212-986-5680
• **Milot, René: pg 206,207** 501 Fifth Ave, New York, NY 10017.......................**212-490-2450**
url: www.renardrepresents.com / fax: 212-697-6828
Mineo, Andrea: 12 Lincoln Blvd, Emerson, NJ 07630......................................201-265-3886
Minnick, Jay: 13367 Shirley, Omaha, NE 68144..402-334-5238
Minnix, Gary: 201 S Cuyler, Oak Park, IL 60302 708-386-4484
Minor, Wendell: 15 Old North Rd, Washington, CT 06793..............................203-868-9101
Minot, Karen: 26 Deuce Ct, Fairfax, CA 94930 415-457-7559
Mintz, Margery: 307 N Michigan Ave #1006, Chicago, IL 60601......................312-704-0500
Mirabella, Tony: 1127 Shannon St, Upland, CA 91784 909-949-2238
• **Miracle, Michael: pg 1079** 1 Wall Street, Boston, MA 02476......................**888-393-3779**
url: www.michaelmiracle.com
Miralles, Jose-Maria: 43 E 19th St, New York, NY 10003...............................212-254-4996
• **Mires Design: pg 1442,1443**
2345 Kettner Blvd, San Francisco, CA 92101 ....**619-234-6631**
url: www.miresdesign.com / fax: 619-234-1807
Mirkin, Ekaterina S: 2026A Parker St, Berkley, CA 94704 510-644-3969
Mironchuk, Greg: 409 Central Ave, Saugus, MA 01906 617-941-8030
Miserendino, Peter: 33 Stonegate Dr, Southbury, CT 06488...........................203-264-0908
Miskell, Jack: 47 Walker St #2B, New York, NY 10013 212-226-0462
Mison, Vesna: 901 56th St, Brooklyn, NY 11219 718-854-7847
Mistretta, Andrea: 135 E Prospect St, Waldwick, NJ 07463.............................201-652-7531
Mistretta, Tony: 223 W Erie St #5EC, Chicago, IL 60610................................312-751-4005
Mitch, Anthony: 960 Maddux Dr, Palo Alto, CA 94303...................................415-494-3240
Mitchell Design, Dean: 10219 Caminito Pitaya, San Diego, CA 92131 619-566-1032
Mitchell, Bono: 2118 N Oakland St, Arlington, VA 22207..............................703-276-0612
Mitchell, Briar Lee: 11552 Hartsook St, N Hollywood, CA 91601 818-752-6809
Mitchell, Celia: 22-29 19th St, Long Island City, NY 11105............................718-626-4095
Mitchell, Charlie: 1034 Pepperwood Trail, Norcross, GA 30093 770-381-9929
Mitchell, Jeanne: 19361 St Mary's Dr, Santa Ana, CA 92705..........................714-731-2976
Mitchell, JoBeth: 4611 Talisman St, Torrance, CA 90503...............................310-370-1728
Mitchell, Kurt: 3004 W 66th St, Chicago, IL 60629.......................................773-476-4429
Mitchell, Lori: 10219 Camito Pitaya, San Diego, CA 92131 619-566-1033
Mitchell, Mark: 7 W 34th St, New York, NY 10001..212-576-5916
Mitchell, Sean: 2701 Newkirk Ave #3B, Brooklyn, NY 11226..........................718-462-2782
Mitchell, Sharon Augusta: 2735 Elmwood Ave, Berkeley, CA 94705................510-548-6101
Mitchell, Tim: 7718 Kingman St, Panama Beach City, FL 32408 904-230-9030
• **Mitsui, Glenn: pg 1349-1351** 1512 Alaskan Way, Seattle, WA 98101.........**206-682-6221**
e-mail: glenn@studiomd.com / url: www.studiomd.com / fax: 206-682-6283
Mitta, Eugene: 5015 Clinton St #306, Los Angeles, CA 90004 323-957-2327
Miyake, Yoshi: 121 Dodgingtown Rd Box 266, Bethel, CT 06801 203-748-4823
Mize, Charles: 633 Battery St #200, San Francisco, CA 94111 415-421-1548
Mizuguchi, Daniel: 468 Queen St E #104, Toronto, ON M5A 1T7 416-367-2446
MJE Design Studios: 212-3432089
Mjolsness, Jane: 101 Kitty Hawk Bay Dr, Kill Devil Hills, NC 27948..................919-480-0165
Mladinich, Charles: 7 Maspeth Dr, Melville, NY 11747 516-271-8525
MLH Communications Group: 51 Madison Ave #1201, New York, NY 10010 212-576-5916
Mock, Paul: 27 Old Meeting House Green, Norton, MA 02766 508-285-8309
Mockensturm, Steve: 2660 Letchworth, Toledo, OH 43606 419-474-0484
Mocri, Joe: 241 New York Ave, Massapequa Pk, NY 11762............................516-797-0941
Modaff, Linda: 8210 Creighton St, Los Angeles, CA 90045 310-641-6916
Modell, Frank: 950 Klish Way, Del Mar, CA 92014...619-259-5774
Moede, Jade: 96 S Main St, Lodi, NJ 07644 201-778-4090
Moffet, Maureen: 121 Lyall Ave, Toronto, ON M4E 1W6.................................416-691-3242
Mohr, Mark: 5106 Reinhardt Pkwy, Roeland Park, KS 66205...........................913-631-0943
Moire Studio: 3152 Elliot Ave S, Minneapolis, MN 55407...............................612-827-6407
Mojhr, Michael: 781 Mojave Trail, Maitland, FL 32751 407-644-9615
Moldenhauer, Egon: 2228 N Moisertown Rd, Sagertown, PA 16433...............814-763-4197
Moldoff, Kirk: 1116 Elm St, Peekskill, NY 10566 914-736-7823
Molina, Luis: 5855 Green Valley Cir #308, Culver City, CA 90230...................310-642-2721
Moline, Robin: 2149 Lyon St #5, San Francisco, CA 94115............................415-921-7140
Mollica, Pat: 319 E 50th St, New York, NY 10022 212-355-4020
Molloy, Jack A: 817 S Westwood Dr, Minneapolis, MN 55416........................612-374-3169
Molnar, Albert: 1875 Hialeah Dr, Orleans, ON K4A 3S7 613-841-7901
Moncrieff, Judi: 4543 SW Water Ave, Portland, OR 97201 503-294-9947
Mondok, Wayne: 27 Renault Crescent, Weston, ON M9P 1J2 416-249-2676
Mones, Isdre: 43 E 19th St, New York, NY 10003 212-254-4996
Mones-Mateu: 43 E 19th St, New York, NY 10003...212-254-4996
Monet, André: 460 rue Saint-Catherine, Montréal, QU HB3 1A7 514-393-0844
• **Monge Illustration, Mary T: pg 1110**
78 Allenwood Ln, Laguna Hills, CA 92656 ....**949-831-2762**
606 N Larchmont Blvd #4C, Los Angeles, CA 90004 ....**213-962-2500**
Mongeau, Marc: 278 Hamilton Ave, Princeton, NJ 08540 609-252-9405
Monley, Jerry: 29580 Northwestern Hwy, Southfield, MI 48034.......................248-353-7722
Monlux, Mark: 7622 S Yakima Ave, Tacoma, WA 98408.................................206-471-0820
Monroy, Bert: 11 Latham Ln, Berkeley, CA 94708 510-524-9412
Montagne: 1405 rue Bishop bur, Montréal, QU H3G 2E5 514-288-7414
Montague, Desmond: 4185 Wheelwright Cres, Mississauga, ON L5L 2X4.........416-820-4921
Montana, Leslie: 56 Highland Ave #3FL, Montclair, NJ 07042 201-744-3407
Monte, Joy: 103 Walnut St, Walden, NY 12586 914-778-5303
Monté, Robert: 1600 rue Notre Dame, Montréal, QU H3J 1M1 514-937-7279
Montecalvo, Janet: 10 Cavotorta Dr, Framingham, MA 01701.........................508-875-4209
Monteiro, Marcus: 32 W 40th Street, New York, NY 10018..............................212-575-6877
Monteiro, Mary: 32 Lyng St, N Dartmouth, MA 02747 508-999-2880
Monteleone, Patrick: Ashmill Rd Box 213, Mechanicsville, PA 18934 215-794-8919
Montero, Carmen: PO Box 02-5635, Miami, FL 33102 506-253-1800
Montgomery, Jay: 6900 Roswell Rd #E-2, Atlanta, GA 30328........................770-399-9330
Montgomery, Linda: 280 Madison Ave #1110, New York, NY 10016................212-545-9155
Monti, Jean Restivo: 232 Madison Ave #402, New York, NY 10016 212-889-8777
Montiel, David: 453 Fourth St #2L, Brooklyn, NY 11215 718-788-6118
Montoliu, Raphael: PO Box 470818, San Francisco, CA 94147........................415-383-9026
Montoya, Andy: 1800 Lear #5, Dallas, TX 75215 214-421-3993
Montoya, Ricardo: 5416 Agnes Pl, Riverside, CA 92504.................................714-533-0507
Montpetit, Loius: Mollo 6111 av du, Montréal, QU H3S 2V8 514-278-9558
Mooers, R Craig: 1075 Seco St, Pasadena, CA 91103....................................818-449-0975
Moojedi, Kamran: 900 W Sierra Madre #122, Azusa, CA 91702 818-969-5508
Mooney, Gerry: 2 Main St #3N, Dobbs Ferry, NY 10522 914-693-8076
• **Moonlight Press Studio: pg 1400,1401**
362 Cromwell Ave, Ocean Breeze, NY 10305 ....**718-979-9695**
e-mail: cjspollen@aol.com / url: www.inch.com/~espollen / fax: 718-979-8919
Moore, Chris: 60 E 42nd St #822, New York, NY 10165................................212-682-1490
Moore, Cyd: 280 Madison Ave #1110, New York, NY 10016............................212-545-9155
Moore, Jack: 131 Cedar Lake West, Denville, NJ 07834................................201-627-6931
Moore, Jay: 11946 Black Tail Mtn, Littleton, CO 80127 303-972-0559
Moore, Jo: 1314 Kearney St NE, Washington, DC 20017 202-526-2356
• **Moore, Larry: pg 818** 853 Broadway #1201, New York, NY 10003 ....**212-677-9100**
e-mail: chislovsky@aol.com / fax: 212-353-0954
Moore, Marlene: 300 E 34th St #10D, New York, NY 10016 212-481-0124
Moore, Monte: 5360 N Franklin St, Denver, CO 80216 303-294-0146
Moore, Sam: 920 Eighth Ave, Brooklyn, NY 11215...718-768-1337
Moore, Scott: 1203 Harris St, Eden, NC 27288 910-627-1559
Moore, Stephen: 1077 Country Creek Dr, Lebanon, OH 45036.......................513-932-4295
Moore, Tim: 23 Summer Rd #3, Brookline, MA 02146 617-731-7783
• **Moores, Jeff: pg 778,779** 333 Lower Seese Hill Rd,Canadensis, PA 18325....**717-595-9298**
url: www.theispot.com/artist/moores / fax: 717-595-9392
Mora, Francisco: 45 N Allen Ave, Pasadena, CA 91106..................................818-449-0356
Moraes, Greg Studio: 4760 Columbus Ave, Sherman Oaks, CA 91403 818-905-5267
Morales, Manuel: 55 Cleveland Terr, E Orange, NJ 07017 201-676-8187
Morales, Rosemary: 5775 Foothill Dr, Los Angeles, CA 90068 213-467-4674
Moran, Doug: 8897 Jeannette Ave, Sebastopol, CA 95472 707-829-3410
Moran, John: 711 W 17th St #J-2, Costa Mesa, CA 92627...........................714-722-0992
Moran, Michael: 39 Elmwood Rd, Florham Park, NJ 07932.............................201-966-6229
Moran, Robert: 759 N Park Ave, W Redding, CT 06896 203-452-1116
Morawa, Amy Lynne: 375 South End Ave #4K, New York, NY 10280 212-938-5732
Mordan, CB: 4908 Sycamore Dr, Roeland Park, KS 66205.............................913-677-4976
Morecraft, Ron: 97 Morris Ave, Denville, NJ 07834..201-625-5752
Morena, Alain: 325 Idaho Ave #11, Santa Monica, CA 90403 310-319-9506
Morenko, Michael: 255 W 10th St #5FS, New York, NY 10014........................212-627-5920
Moreschi, Alfred: 750 Zorn Ave #31, Louisville, KY 40206............................502-894-0937
Moreua, Alain: 325 Idaho Ave #11, Santa Monica, CA 90403 310-319-9506
Morgan, Craig: 966 Highland View NE, Atlanta, GA 30306..............................404-874-0743
Morgan, Jacqui: 1367 N Las Palmas Ave, Hollywood, CA 90028 213-469-3400
176 E 77th St #11C, New York, NY 10021 212-772-0627
Morgan, Leonard: 730 Victoria Ct, Bolingbrook, IL 60440..............................630-739-7705
Morgenstern, Michael: 429 E 73rd St, New York, NY 10021...........................212-861-7391
Morin, Josée: 4030 rue, Montréal, QU H4C 2C7 514-865-7258
Moritsugu, Alison: 570 9th Street, Brooklyn, NY 11215.................................718-383-1714
Morozko, Bruce: 111 First St, Jersey City, NJ 07203.....................................201-792-5974
Morpheus Technologies: 58 Fore St, Portland, ME 04101 207-772-3900
Morra, Janet: 19 Stanley Ave, Crotonville, NY 10562 914-762-7250
• **Morris, Anton: pg 715** 455 W 23rd St #8D, New York, NY 10011 ....**212-366-1893**
url: www.andtheart.com / fax: 212-604-9643
Morris, Barbara: 51 E Hunter Ave, Maywood, NJ 07607.................................201-368-8663

Palulian, Dick: 18 McKinley St, Rowayton, CT 06853 203-866-3734
Paluso, Christopher: 3217 Sweetwater Springs #89,
Rancho San Diego, CA 92078 619-670-4907
Pankey, Elizabeth: 1859 NW 202nd St, Seattle, WA 98110 206-542-1937
Pann, David: 5129 Westwood Blvd, Culver City, CA 90230 310-559-5068
• **Pansini, Tom: pg 892** 16 Phaedra, Laguna Niguel, CA 92677 ....**949-495-3664**
url: www.showcase.com/ fax: 949-495-0129
Panter, Gary: 118 Prospect Park W #5, Brooklyn, NY 11215 718-782-5420
Panton, Doug: 341 Wellesley St E, Toronto, ON M4X 1H2 416-920-5612
Pantuso, Mike: 350 E 89th St, New York, NY 10128 212-534-3511
Papadakis, George: 110 Bradley Dr, Yorktown, VA 23696 757-898-4872
Paperny, Vladimir: 1375 Kelton Ave #309, Los Angeles, CA 90024 310-444-7883
Pappas, Billy: 34 Sunnyview Dr, Phoenix, MD 21131 410-666-0922
Pappas, Christopher: 847A Second Ave #150, New York, NY 10017 212-486-0177
Paquette, Darisse A: 202 Waverly St, Arlington, MA 02174 617-643-1154
• **Parada, Roberto: pg 730,731** 300 E 46th St #4G, New York, NY 10017 ....**212-687-6463**
e-mail: sara@levycreative.com / fax: 212-661-4839
• **Paragraphics: pg 1329** Nyack, NY **914-358-0798**
e-mail: paragraphics@spyral.net / url: www.spyral.net/paragraphics / fax: 914-358-3284
• **Paraskevas, Michael: pg 379** 250 W 57th St #521, New York, NY 10107....**212-397-7330**
url: www.lindgrensmith.com (and) www.stockillustrated.com
Pardini, Patricia: 88 Lexington Ave #1F, New York, NY 10016 212-683-2010
Pardo, Jackie: 853 Broadway #606, New York, NY 10003 212-777-6777
Pardue, Jack: 2307 Sherwood Hall Ln, Alexandria, VA 22306....................................703-765-2622
• **Pariseau, Pierre-Paul: pg 1366**
3997 St Dominique 2, Montreal, QU H2W 2A4....................................**514-849-2964**
url: www.showcase.com / fax: 514-843-4808
Parisi, Richard: 194 Third Ave 3rd Fl, New York, NY 10003 212-475-0440
Parisi, Rita: 7000 20th St Lot 939, Vero Beach, FL 32966 561-567-4285
Park, Charlie: 25930 Rolling Hills Rd #420, Torrance, CA 90505....................................310-325-4177
Park, Chang: 100 Bleecker St, New York, NY 10012....................................212-982-6533
Park, Darcie: 2461 Roswell Ave, Long Beach, CA 90815....................................310-985-0506
Park, Elliot: PO Box 2193, Grapevine, TX 76099....................................817-481-2212
Park, Jun: 15 Cassidy Pl, North york, ON M3B 2S3 416-441-9422
Park, Yoonsung: 66 Forest Ave, Paramus, NJ 07652....................................201-587-7488
Parke, Steven: 1442 E Baltimore St, Baltimore, MD 21231 410-675-9087
Parker, Curtis: 1946 E Palomino Dr, Tempe, AZ 85284....................................520-820-6015
68 E Franklin St, Dayton, OH 45459....................................937-433-8383
Parker, Earl: 5 New Brooklyn Rd, Cedar Brook, NJ 08018 609-567-2925
• **Parker, Ed: pg 301** 58 W 15th St, New York, NY 10011 ....**212-741-2539**
url: www.showcase.com / fax: 212-741-4660
Parker, Geoffrey: 285 Fishcreek Rd, Saugerties, NY 12477 914-246-2166
• **Parker, Robert Andrew: pg 600** 155 W 15th St, New York, NY 10011 ....**212-989-8770**
fax: 212-789-7892
22 River Rd, W Cornwall, CT 06796....................................**203-672-0152**
Parker, Suzy: 1000 Wilson Blvd, Arlington, VA 22209....................................703-276-3458
Parkinson, Jim: 6170 Broadway Terr, Oakland, CA 94618....................................510-547-3100
Parks, Kevin: 1156 Ventura Ave, Oak View, CA 93022....................................805-649-4059
Parks, Melanie Marder: 5 Broadview Ln, Red Hook, NY 12571 914-758-0656
Parks, Phil: 806 Woodcrest, Royal Oaks, MI 48067....................................810-545-6477
Parmenter, Wayne: 10439 Parmento Rd NE, Erie, PA 16428....................................814-725-8566
Parnell, John: 167 Spring St #3W, New York, NY 10012....................................212-226-7682
Parnell, Miles: 654 Pier Ave #C, Santa Monica, CA 90405....................................310-392-4877
597 Riverside Ave, Westport, CT 06880....................................203-226-4724
Parr, Cathryn: 6864 Bonita Terr, Hollywood, CA 90068 213-874-7040
Parrucho, Anna Sheila: 84-20 51st Ave #5D, Elmhurst, NY 11373....................................718-651-8359
Parsekian, John: 5 Lawrence St Bldg 15, Bloomfield, NJ 07003....................................201-748-9717
Parson, Stephen: 2330 Bedford St #2, Durham, NC 27707 919-490-0608
Parsons Design, Glenn: 8522 National Blvd #108, Culver City, CA 90232.......310-559-6571
Parsons, Clif: 1185 Lyons Rd Bldg E, Centerville, OH 45459....................................513-434-0888
Parsons, Guy: 371 Coral Sands Terr NE, Calgary, AB T3J 3K3 403-280-8698
Parsons, John: 420 Lexington Ave #2760, New York, NY 10170....................................212-697-8525
Parsons, Marjorie: 114 E 13th St #2C, New York, NY 10003....................................212-496-3702
Partington, Michael: 301 Kessler Blvd W Dr, Indianapolis, IN 46220....................................317-577-9444
Parton, Steve: 400 W 43rd St #37S, New York, NY 10036....................................212-766-2285
Paschkis, Julie: 4033 Aurora Ave N, Seattle, WA 98103 206-633-3445
Pasqua, Lou: 309 Walnut Rd, Pittsburgh, PA 15202....................................412-761-5666
Passalacqua, David: 325 Versa Pl, Sayville, NY 11782....................................516-589-1663
Passarelli, Chuck: 353 W 53rd St #1W, New York, NY 10019 212-682-2462
Passey, Kim: 115 Hurlbut #17, Pasadena, CA 91105 818-441-4384
Passow, Faye: 1503 Briar Knoll Dr, Arden Hills, MN 55112 651-631-8480
Pasternak, Robert: 114 W 27th St #55, New York, NY 10001 212-675-0002
Paston, Herbert: 28 S Silver Ln, Sunderland, MA 01375....................................413-665-3366
Pastoreck, Robert Jr: 33 Lawndale St, Springfield, MA 01108....................................413-734-8816
• **Pastrana, Robert: pg 1172** 473A Riverdale Dr, Glendale, CA 91204....................................**818-548-6083**
Pastucha, Ron: 336 McNeans Ave, Winnipeg, MB R2C 2J7....................................204-222-3178
121 1/2 N Glassell #14, Orange, CA 92666....................................714-744-1505
Pate, Martin: 2460 Peachtree Rd NW, Atlanta, GA 30305....................................404-881-6627
• **Patelis, Dimitrios: pg 592,593**
232 Madison Ave #512, New York, NY 10016....................................**212-889-8777**
fax: 212-447-1475
Paternoster, Nance: 546 Wisconsin St, San Francisco, CA 94107....................................415-641-1922
• **Patkau, Karen: pg 1367**
401 Queens Quay West Suite 609, Toronto, ON M5V 2Y2 ....**416-260-1915**
fax: 416-260-1916
Patrick, Cyndy Jane: 5 Dresden St #1, Jamaica Plains, MA 02130....................................617-522-4433
Patrick, John: 68 E Franklin St, Dayton, OH 45459 937-433-8383
Patrick, Pamela: 100 Bleecker St, New York, NY 10012....................................212-982-6533
Patrick, Tom: 731 Stovall Blvd NE, Atlanta, GA 30342 800-791-1189
Patterson, James: 4312 Mt Olney Ln, Olney, MD 20832 301-774-8329
Patterson, Tom: 2233 Kemper Ln, Cincinnati, OH 45206 513-281-8095
Patterson/Thomas: 54 Monument Cir #800, Indianapolis, IN 46204 317-638-1002
• **Patti, Joyce: pg 174,175** 194 Third Ave 3rd Fl, New York, NY 10003 ....**212-475-0440**
url: www.vickimorganassociates.com / fax: 212-353-8538
• **Patton Brothers Illustration: pg 1171**
3768 Miles Ct, Spring Valley, CA 91977 ....**619-463-4562**
e-mail: patton@pattonbros.com / url: www.pattonbros.com / fax: 619-463-4763

Patton, Ed: 807A Baylor St, Austin, TX 78703....................................512-478-3338
Paul Illust, Peter: 15561 Blaine Ave, Bellflower, CA 90706 310-876-3880
Paul, David: 264 Feronia Way, Rutherford, NJ 07070....................................201-933-7157
Paul, Dayan: 779 Mabie St, New Milford, NJ 07646....................................201-501-0500
Paul, Edie: 859 Hollywood #136, Burbank, CA 91505 818-505-1874
• **Paul, Jon: pg 418** 60 E 42nd St, New York NY 10165-1940 ....**212-867-8092**
e-mail: DHLT@aol.com / url: www.HT-LTD.com / fax: 212-949-1977
Paul, Keith: 165 E 32nd St, New York, NY 10016....................................212-686-3514
Pauling, Galen T: PO Box 3150, Southfield, MI 48037....................................313-533-7674
Paulos, Martha: 5941 MacCall St, Oakland, CA 94609 510-601-1813
Paulsen, Larry: 60 E 42nd St #822, New York, NY 10165....................................212-682-1490
Pauly, Thomas Allen: 4224 N Hermitage Ave, Chicago, IL 60613....................................773-477-0440
Pavey, Jerry: 232 Madison Ave #402, New York, NY 10016 212-889-8777
Pavlov, Elana: 377 W 11th #1F, New York, NY 10014....................................212-243-0939
Pavlovich, Paul: 562 43rd Ave NE, St Petersburg, FL 33703 813-824-5620
Pavlovits, Ivan: 110 N Barrington, Los Angeles, CA 90049 310-471-0990
Pavlovsky, Dawn: 5419 S Nordica, Chicago, IL 60638....................................773-586-0631
Pawelka, Rick: 5720 E North Blvd, Raleigh, NC 27604....................................919-878-7883
Payne, Adair: 5921 East Inca St, Mesa, AZ 85205 602-641-7345
• **Payne, CF: pg 272,273** 121 Madison Ave #5F, New York, NY 10016.........**212-683-1362**
fax: 212-683-1919
Payne, Lawrence: 13265 SW Aragon St, Beaverton, OR 97005....................................541-644-7158
Payne, Tom: 19 Stuyvesant Oval #2D, New York, NY 10009....................................212-505-9342
Peacock, Matthew: 403 Acorn St, Lansdale, PA 19446 215-412-8210
Peake, Kevin: 133 N Montclair Ave, Dallas, TX 75208 214-943-2569
Peal, Michael: 4703 Mesa Oaks Circle, Austin, TX 78735....................................512-892-1798
Peale, Charles: 108 2nd St SW #36, Charlottesville, VA 22902....................................804-293-3394
Pearce, Juliette: 286 Spring St #301, New York, NY 10013....................................212-229-0073
Pearl, Todd: 1318 1/2 Amherst Ave, Los Angeles, CA 90025....................................310-473-4935
Pearson, Jim: 218 Elm Court, Rhinelander, WI 54501 715-369-2130
Pechanec, Vladimir: 34-43 Crescent St #4C, Long Island City, NY 11106........718-729-3973
Peck, Virginia: 34 Erie Ave, Newton, MA 02161 617-558-7014
Peck, Byron: 1857 Lamont St NW, Washington, DC 20010....................................202-331-1966
Peck, Everett: 716 Sanchez St, San Francisco, CA 94114....................................415-285-8267
Peck, Marshall: 10 Larch Ln, Londonderry, NH 03053 603-432-2108
Peck, Scott: 2701 Thorndale, Plano, TX 75074 214-422-7438
Peck, Suzanne: 420 Lexington Ave, New York, NY 10170 212-986-5680
Pedersen, Dennis: 1220 Avis Dr, San Jose, CA 95127 408-293-6503
Pederson, Judy: 16 McEwen St., Warwick, NY 10990....................................914-987-1090
Peebles, Peter: 455 W 23rd St #8D, New York, NY 10011 212-366-1893
Peele, Lynwood: 344 W 88th St, New York, NY 10024....................................212-799-3305
Peery, Joe: 962 Alloway Pl, Atlanta, GA 30316 404-627-6952
Peji, Bennett: 1110-B Torrey Pines Rd, La Jolla, CA 92037....................................619-456-8071
Pelaez, Joan: 43 E 19th St, New York, NY 10003 212-254-4996
• **Pelavin, Daniel: pg 1368,1369** 80 Varick St #3B, New York, NY 10013.....**212-941-7418**
e-mail: daniel@pelavin.com / url: www.pelavin.com / fax: 212-431-7138
Pelham-Foulke, Nancy Alliger: 2828 Superior St, Bellingham, WA 98226 360-671-0234
Pelicano, Chris: 1400 S Highway Dr, Fenton, MO 63099 314-827-2840
Pelikan, Judy: 200 E 78th St, New York, NY 10021 212-570-9069
Pell, Alan: 4728 King Rd, Loomis, CA 95650....................................916-632-7877
Pellaton, Karen: PO Box 1086, Taos, NM 87571....................................505-776-5435
• **Pelo, Jeffrey: pg 200,201** 501 Fifth Ave, New York, NY 10017....................................**212-490-2450**
url: www.renardrepresents.com / fax: 212-697-6828
Pelo, Lisa: PO Box 5295, Larkspur, CA 94977 415-464-0703
Péloquin, Carole: 3561 rue Cartier, Montréal, QU H2K 4G1 514-526-9437
Pembroke, Richard: 353 W 53rd St #1W, New York, NY 10019 212-682-2462
Penalva, Jordi: 43 E 19th St, New York, NY 10003 212-254-4996
Penberthy, Mark: 47 Greene St, New York, NY 10013....................................212-219-2664
Penca, Gary: 8335 NW 20th St, Coral Springs, FL 33071 305-752-4699
Pendleton, Nancy: 10415 N 38th St, Phoenix, AZ 85028....................................602-257-0097
Pendleton, Roy: 4725 San Pedro, Alberquerque, NM 87019....................................505-888-0601
Pendola, Joanne: 414 E 11th St #2E, New York, NY 10009 212-353-1834
Penelope: 420 Lexington Ave #2738, New York, NY 10170....................................212-679-8525
• **Peng, Leif: pg 450** 731 N 24th St, Philadelphia, PA 19130....................................**215-232-6666**
url: www.deborahwolfeltd.com / fax: 215-232-6585
Pennington, Jack: 597 Riverside Ave, Westport, CT 06880....................................203-226-4724
Pennington, Jack: 2233 Kemper Ln, Cincinnati, OH 45206 513-861-1400
Pentard, Alton: 2911 Dumaine, New Orleans, LA 70119....................................504-486-0633
Pentelovitch, Robert Alan: 340 W 55th St #2D, New York, NY 10019 ....212 397-9209
Pentleton, Carol: 685 Chestnut Hill Rd, Chepachet, RI 02814....................................401-568-0275
Pepellashi, Petra: 20500 Civic Center Dr #2800, Southfield, MI 48076 313-356-2470
Pepera, Fred: 1344 State Park Rd., Ortonville, MI 48462 248-627-6493
Pepler, Susan Elizabeth: 1206 av Seymour, Montréal, QU H3H 2A5 514-862-0420
Pepper, Bob: 157 Clinton St, Brooklyn, NY 11201 718-875-3236
Peralta, Bella: PO Box 1093, Weaverville, CA 96093 916-623-4872
Percivalle, Rosanne: 450 W 31st St Gr Fl, New York, NY 10001 212-295-7763
Peregoy, Chris: 1201 W Ostend St, Baltimore, MD 21230....................................410-539-8460
Pereira, Eduino J: 10837F Amherst Ave, Wheaton, MD 20902 301-649-4307
Perez, German: 69 W 106th St #5A, New York, NY 10025....................................212-932-8639
Perez, Luis F: 16 Scenic Ridge Dr, Brewster, NY 10509 914-279-7679
Perez, Vincent: 1279 Weber St, Alameda, CA 94501 510-521-2262
Pergament Graphics: 38 E 30th St, New York, NY 10016....................................212-213-8310
Peringer, Stephen: 2717 Western Ave, Seattle, WA 98121 206-232-7873
Perini, Ben: PO Box 421443, San Francisco, CA 94142....................................415-647-5660
Perini, Ben: 1607 Lancelot Ln, Winston Salem, NC 27103....................................910-724-2260
Perkins, Gary Reid: 117 Leola, Hot Springs, AR 71913 501-767-1683
Perkins, Ken: 1415 Gadren St, Glendale, CA 91201....................................818-244-0110
Perle, Quimetta: 265 12th St, Brooklyn, NY 11215 718-965-1858
Perlman, David: 59 Stoneham Dr, Rochester, NY 14625....................................716-381-3543
Perlow, Paul: 123 E 54th St #6E, New York, NY 10022....................................212-758-4358
Perna, Jess: 52-41 Douglaston Pkwy, Douglaston, NY 11362 718-224-5652
Perrin, Bryan: 1364 Mercer St, Jersey City, NJ 07302....................................201-432-1634
Perrin-Falquet, Joan: 763 Ninth Ave #3S, New York, NY 10019....................................212-247-3854
Perrone, Donna: 53 Second Ave #4A, New York, NY 10003....................................212-254-9453

Posey, David: 815 Devon Pl, Alexandria, VA 22314 703-836-8162
Posey, Pam: 2763 College Blvd, Oceanside, CA 92056 619-724-3566
Post, Howard: 2573 E Southwood, Queen Creek, AZ 85242 602-265-4389
Post, Tom: 2160 Julie Terr, Cincinnati, OH 45215 513-769-0364
Potter, Christopher: 2393 East Ridge Rd, Rochester, NY 14622 716-467-0388
Potts, Charlene: 30-20 43rd St, Astoria, NY 11103 718-274-6813
Potts, Linda: 10-A Victoria Park Ave, Toronto, ON M4E 3R9 416-698-2512
Pound, John: 5587 Noe Ave, Eureka, CA 95503 ....707 445-3769
Powell, Andy: 212 3rd Ave, Minneapolis, MN 55401 612-349-6611
Powell, Charlie: 1228 Martin Rd, Santa Cruz, CA 95060 408-457-9470
Powell, Jenny: 455 W 23rd St #8D, New York, NY 10011 212-366-1893
• **Powell, Polly: pg 1372** 2319 J Street, Sacramento, CA 95816 ....**916-444-1646**
  fax: 916-441-5714
• **Powell, Rick: pg 1076** 104 W Arden Circle, Norfolk, VA 23505...................**757-440-1723**
  url: www.studiopowell.com / fax: 757-440-0952
• **Powell, Tana: pg 773** 83 Walnut Ave, Corte Madera, CA 94925 ....**415-924-7881**
  toll-free...**800-924-7881**
  url: www.ritareps.com / fax: 415-924-7891
Powers, Teresa: 847A Second Ave #150, New York, NY 10017 212-486-0177
Powers, Tom: 18 W 21st Street 17th Floor, New York, NY 10010 212-243-1333
Pozefsky, Carol: 6040 Boulevard E, W New York, NJ 07093.............201-662-0111
Pozwozd, Sally: 124 N Park, Westmont, IL 60559 630-969-5854
Prado, Hugo: 3323 W Berteau Ave, Chicago, IL 60618 773-583-7627
Prager, Elizabeth: 30 E 9th St #3J, New York, NY 10003 212-475-6334
Pranica, John: 2004 W Walton St, Chicago, IL 60622......................773-276-7606
Prato, Rodica: 154 W 57th St, New York, NY 10019 212-245-5854
Pratt University: Computer Graphics Ctr ARC Bldg, Brooklyn, NY 11205..........718-636-3600
Pratt, George: 320 Seventh Ave, Brooklyn, NY 11215 718-768-6008
Pratt, Pierre: 5976 rue Jeanne-Mance, Montréal, QU H2V 4K8 514-277-0721
Pratt, Russell E: 171 Ogden Ave, Jersey City, NJ 07307 201-222-2887
Pratt, Wayne: PO Box 1421, Wilmington, VT 05363 802-368-7207
Pravato, Victor: 14 Emily Ave, Weston, ON M9L 2R1 416-742-4764
Pravda, Kit Monroe: 2148 Sand Hill Rd, Menlo Park, CA 94025 415-854-1050
Premru, Greg: 348 Congress St 3rd Fl, Boston, MA 02210 617-451-7770
Prendergast, Michael: 12 Merrill St, Newburyport, MA 01950 508-465-8598
Prescott, Carl: 746 Shrader St, San Francisco, CA 94117 415-752-7808
Presley, Greg: 12532 Timber Hollow Pl, Germantown, MD 20874........301-601-4999
Preslicka, Greg: 5000 Edgewater Dr, Savage, MN 55378 612-432-2166
Presnall, Terry: 50 Fuller Brook Rd, Wellesley, MA 02181 781-235-8658
Preston, Jeff: 6182 Sydney Dr, Huntington Beach, CA 92647 714-898-7288
Preuitt, Clayton: 420 S Detroit St #4, Los Angeles, CA 90036 213-965-8285
Previn, Stacey: 1415 Gadren St, Glendale, CA 91201 818-244-0110
Pribanic, Chris: 2340 Cleveland Rd, Sandusky, OH 44870 419-624-9023
Price, Amy: 213 Antisdel Pl NE, Grand Rapids, MI 49503 616-459-7595
Price, David: 6101 Bel-Air Dr, Texarcana, TX 75503.......................903-832-5552
Price, Donald: 204 W 88th St #4W, New York, NY 10024 212-769-0403
Price, Heather: Seattle, WA 98134 206-467-9156
Price, Jeannette: 1164 E 820 N, Provo, UT 84601 801-377-3958
Price, Jim: 542 N 68th St, Seattle, WA 98103 206-782-2592
Price, Joan: 1469 Canyon Rd, Sante Fe, NM 87501 505-986-3823
Price, Stephanie: 339 Whitaker St #1, Savannah, GA 31401 912-231-0876
Priester, Gary: 353 Laurel Ave, Novato, CA 94945 415-331-4531
Prince, Kevin: 24436 Ward St, Torrance, CA 90505 310-375-9232
Principato, Salvatore: 220 Sullivan St #4H, New York, NY 10012 212-477-8161
Pritchett, Karen: 309 Walnut Rd, Pittsburgh, PA 15202 412-761-5666
Probert, Jean: 3286 Ivanhoe, St Louis, MO 63139........................314-781-7377
Prochnow, Bill: 3855 Greenwood Ave, Oakland, CA 94602 415-777-8745
Prokell, Jim: 26 Marylee Ave #300, Pittsburgh, PA 15227 412-232-3636
Prosser, Les: 3501 Windom Rd, Brentwood, MD 20722..................301-927-8867
Proulx, Art: 1316 Third St #305, Santa Monica, CA 90401 310-458-7600
Provenzano, Anthony: 6980 W Touhy Ave #201, Niles, IL 60648......847-647-6418
Prud'homme, Jon: 4611 Talisman St, Torrance, CA 90503 310-370-1728
Prud'Homme, Jules: 4853 av Melrose, Montréal, QU H3X 3P4..........514-485-2641
Pryor, Robert: Chicago, IL 847-222-0337
Przewodek, Camille: 108 E 35th St #2, New York, NY 10016 212-889-3337
  522 East D St, Petaluma, CA 94952 707-762-4125
Puckett Design, David: 16 Prairie Falcon, Aliso Viejo, CA 92656 714-837-4417
Puente, Lyle: 296 E 4th St, Brooklyn, NY 11218 718-436-4447
Pullen, Lucy: PO Box 461, Halifax Central, NS B3J 2P8 902-425-4654
• **Pulver Jr, Harry: pg 1168** 105 Meadow Ln N, Minneapolis, MN 55422 ....**612-377-1797**
  fax: 612-377-1797
Punchatz, Don Ivan: 2605 Westgate Dr, Arlington, TX 76015 817-469-8151
Pundyk, Anne: 30 Waterside Plz #31d, New York, NY 10010 212-889-6833
• **Punin, Nikolai: pg 984,985** 15 Warrenton Ave, Hartford, CT 06105 ....**860-523-4562**
  url: www.theispot.com / fax: 860-231-9313
  161 W 16th St #18E, New York, NY 10011 ....**212-227-7863**
  url: www.nikolaiillustration.com / fax: 212-577-2868
Purcell, Chris: PO Box 692000, Houston, TX 77269 713-374-4679
Purdom, Bill: 2805 Oleander Dr, Wilmington, NC 28403 910-763-1208
Putnam, Jamie: 882 S Van Ness Ave, San Francisco, CA 94110 415-641-0513
Pyk, Jan: 1712 E Butler Cir, Chandler, AZ 85225 602-899-0600
• **Pyle, Chuck: pg 387** 250 W 57th St #521, New York, NY 10107...............**212-397-7330**
  url: www.lindgrensmith.com (and) www.stockillustrated.com
Pyle, Liz: 155 W 15th St #4C, New York, NY 10011 212-989-8770
Pyner, Marcia: 455 W 23rd St #8D, New York, NY 10011 212-366-1893

Q

Quartuccio, Dom: 410 W 24th St #9M, New York, NY 10011 212-727-7329
Quattrocchi, Mark: 48 Charme Rd, Billerica, MA 01821 508-667-9048
Quillen, Mike: 954 Delaware Ave, Columbus, OH 43201 614-299-8216
Quinlan, Stephen: 3602 Silverthorn Dr, Oakville, ON LCL 5N7 905-469-0525
Quinn, Colleen: 307 N Michigan Ave #1006, Chicago, IL 60601 312-704-0500
Quinn, Ger & Barbara: 7405 Arden Rd, Cabin Road, MD 20818.........301-229-8030
Quint, Chuck: 4539 N Paulina, Chicago, IL 60640 773-271-8056
Quirion, Daniel: 10131 rue Cartier, Montréal, QU H23 2B3 514-389-8974

Quon Design Office, Mike: 53 Spring St 5th Fl, New York, NY 10012...............212-226-6024

R

Raabe, Dan: 80 Montague St, Brooklyn, NY 11201......................718-260-9666
Rabagliati, Michel: 5505 boul, Montréal, QU H2T 1S6 514-271-5606
Rabi, Lorraine: 629 Glenwood Ave, Teaneck, NJ 07666.................201-836-4283
Rabinovitch, William: PO Box 403 Canal St Sta, New York, NY 10013........212-226-2873
Rabinowich, Leonid: 19560 S Rancho Way, Dominguez Hills, CA 90220........310-884-3492
Rabinowicz, Vicky: 301 Elizabeth St #8T, New York, NY 10012 212-603-9900
Racer, Tim: 3059 Richmond Blvd, Oakland, CA 94611 510-451-0303
Radencich, Mike: 420 Lexington Ave, New York, NY 10170.............212-986-5680
Radigan, Bob: 280 Madison Ave #1110, New York, NY 10016 212-545-9155
Radmilovich, Joanne: 2405 NW Thurman St, Portland, OR 97210 503-203-8300
Rae, William: 662 Warren St, Brooklyn, NY 11217 718-398-4423
Rafei, Bob: 11730 W Sunset Blvd #309, Los Angeles, CA 90049 818-777-6889
Raff, Lyne: 9501 Rolling Oaks Trail, Austin, TX 78750..................512-219-1208
Rafferty, Jim: 1518 139th Ln NW, Andover, MN 55304 612-755-8488
Raffetto, Teresa: 241 E 14th St #2A, New York, NY 10003 212-375-9432
• **Ragland, Greg: pg 1373** **800-346-1227**
  2500 Lucky John Dr, Park City, UT 84060 ....**435-645-9232**
  e-mail: greg@gregragland.com / url: www.gregragland.com / fax: 435-645-9309
Ragland, Wynne: One Meca Way #600, Norcross, GA 30093 770-564-5606
• **Raglin, Tim: pg 410** 250 W 57th St #521, New York, NY 10107 .....**212-397-7330**
  url: www.lindgrensmith.com(and) www.stockillustrated.com
Rainey, Kirk: 478 Craighead St #105, Nashville, TN 37204 615-463-0203
Rainock, Norman: 2921 Sentry Station Rd, Mechanicsville, VA 23111........804-559-8703
Ramage, Alfred: 5 Irwin St #7, Winthrop, MA 02152.....................617-846-5955
Ramazan, Seid: 7 Washington Street, Beverly, MA 01915 978-921-0887
  toll-free..888-793-SEID
Ramey, Ken: 435 S Ridge Rd, Hesston, KS 67062 316-327-2669
Rammer, Anthony: 950 Woodlake Rd, Kohler, WI 53044 414-459-6800
Ramos, Ruben: 4300 N Narragansett, Chicago, IL 60634 847-670-0912
Ramsey, Ted: 1623 Stowe Rd, Reston, VA 22094 703-481-9424
• **Ramune: pg 1174** 210 Hillside Ave #27, Needham, MA 02194 ....**781-444-1185**
  fax: 781-444-1185
• **Rancorn, Chuck: pg 643** 208 Providence Rd, Annapolis, MD 21401...........**410-349-8669**
  e-mail: acomport@aol.com
  additional number...**813-872-9996**
  additional number...**704-372-6007**
  additional number...**813-579-4990**
Randall, Gail Greenfield: 1912 Comstock Ave, Los Angeles, CA 90025...........310-556-9770
• **Randazzo, Tony: pg 788** 353 W 53rd St #1W, New York, NY 10019.....**212-682-2462**
  e-mail: info@amerartists.com / url: www.amerartists.com / fax: 212-582-0090
Randolph, Carlos: Av Atlantica 3576/501, Rio de Janeiro, Braz, 22070 021-521-0052
Rane, Walter: 60 E 42nd St #1940, New York, NY 10165 212-867-8092
Raneri, Marci: 2035 Richmond St, Philadelphia, PA 19125 800-522-0888
• **Ranger, Christin: pg 1374**
  500 Aurora Ave N #406C, Seattle, WA 98109 ....**206-447-9447**
  alternate..**206-818-0879**
  e-mail: cranger@parker.com / fax: 206-326-5270
Rangne, Monica: 210 First Ave #11, New York, NY 10009 212-260-5121
• **Ransley, Rich: pg 1456,1457** 39 Hamilton Terr, New York, NY 10031........**212-283-3401**
  url: www.wayart.com
Ransome, James: 71 Hooker Ave, Poughkeepsie, NY 12601 914-473-8281
Rapalee, Susan: 342 Seventh Ave #4, Brooklyn, NY 11215 718-499-2301
Raphael & Bolognese: 53 Irving Pl, New York, NY 10003 212-228-5219
Raphael, Natalia: 23 Parkton Rd #3, Jamaica Plain, MA 02130 617-524-0121
Rappaport, Jill: 11454 Elbert Way, San Diego, CA 92126 619-566-6247
• **Raschella, Carole: pg 1375** 8607 Bothwell Rd, Northridge, CA 91324.......**818-349-6742**
  e-mail: CRaschella@aol.com / fax: 818-349-5842
Rasema, Scott: 1844 McIlwirth, Muskegon, MI 49442 616-728-2435
Rashid, Mai Gebara: 93 86th St, Brooklyn, NY 11209 718-833-1982
Rashid, Sarah: 10 Grenoble Dr #202, North York, ON M3C 1CS 416-429-0410
Rasmussen, Bonnie: 8828 Pendleton, St Louis, MO 63144 314-962-1842
• **Rasmussen, Wendy: pg 1376**
  PO Box 131/950 Durham Rd, Durham, PA 18039 ....**610-346-8117**
  fax: 610-346-8117
• **Raszka, Brian: pg 1377** 40 Capra Way #12, San Francisco, CA 94123 ....**415-673-4479**
  e-mail: braszka@worldnet.att.net / url: www.theispot.com/artist/raszka
Rattin, Mark: 2300 W Wabansia Ave #105, Chicago, IL 60647..........312-642-0359
Ratz de Tagyos, Paul: 30 Eastchester Rd #6A, New Rochelle, NY 10801........914-636-2313
Rauchman, Robert: 5210 SW 60th Pl, Miami, FL 33155 305-663-9432
• **Rauffenbart, Bruce: pg 1456** 39 Hamilton Terr, New York, NY 10031 ....**212-283-3401**
  url: www.wayart.com
Raulick, ML: 219 Glenwood Dr, Houston, TX 77007 713-864-9041
Ravanelli, Terry: 3301A S Jefferson Ave, St Louis, MO 63118 314-773-2600
Ravel, Ken: 226 Arlington St, Reading, PA 19611 215-378-9313
Ravenwolf, Patricia Randall: 1 Gilmore Rd, Trenton, NJ 08628 609-882-3066
Rawley, Don: 7520 Blaisdell Ave S, Richfield, MN 55423 612-866-1023
Rawson, Jon: 1368 Waterside Dr, Bolingbrook, IL 60440 630-226-9320
Rayevsky, Robert: 1120 Swedesford Rd, N Wales, PA 19454 215-661-9566
Raymond, Kathryn: 104 Findell Way, Folsom, CA 95630 916-984-2086
Raymond, Victoria: 94 Mercer St #1, Jersey City, NJ 07302............201-332-8343
Rea, Tracy: 9969 Southwind Dr., indianapolis, IN 46256 317-578-8700
Read, Elizabeth: 2075 S University #246, Denver, CO 80210 303-871-9166
Ready, Lee: 927 164th Ave SE, Bellevue, WA 98008 206-747-8783
Reagan, Mike: 303 Fern Valley Ln, Apex, NC 27502 919-387-8230
Reamer, Tim: PO Box 551, San Diego, CA 92112 619-260-0021
Rearick, Kevin: 293 Goldenwood Cir, Simi Valley, CA 93065 805-584-9259
Réault, Patrick: One Captain Dr #D358, Emeryville, CA 94608 510-653-3996
Reay, Richard: 6010 Liebig Ave #2, Bronx, NY 10471 718-884-2317
Rebelo, Tanya: 18 W 21st Street 17th Floor, New York, NY 10010 ..212-243-1333
Rebillard, Remi: New York, NY 212-627-9871
• **Rechin, Kevin: pg 1160**
  7602-I Lakeside Village Dr, Falls Church, VA 22042 ....**703-560-1209**
  fax: 703-698-1257

- **Robinson, Tim: pg 629** 5 E 17th St 6th Fl, New York, NY 10003 ....**212-691-2667**
fax: 212-633-1844
4 E Ohio Studio B, Chicago, IL 60611 ....**312-321-1336**
fax: 312-321-1350
Robles, Bill: 424 N Larchmont, Los Angeles, CA 90004 213-936-9068
Rocco, Joe: 413 Dean St, Brooklyn, NY 11217...718-783-1205
Rochon, Marc: 29580 Northwestern Hwy, Southfield, MI 48034..........................248-353-7722
Rock, Stephen: 4830 41st St SW, Seattle, WA 98116 206-935-5788
Rockwell, Barry: 344 Beaver Dam, Brookhaven, NY 11719 516-286-5808
Rockwell, Tom: 90 Loden Lane, Rochester, NY 14623 716-359-9590
- **Roda, Bot: pg 788** 353 W 53rd St #1W, New York, NY 10019 ....**212-682-2462**
e-mail: info@amerartists.com / url: www.amerartists.com / fax: 212-582-0090
Rodell, Don: 60 E 42nd St #1940, New York, NY 10165 212-867-8092
Rodericks, Mike: 129 Lounsbury Rd, Trumbull, CT 06611 203-268-1551
Rodgers, Joel: 709 Carroll St #2R, Brooklyn, NY 11215 800-439-9217
Rodin, Christine: 38 Morton St #5A, New York, NY 10014................................212-242-3260
Rodney, Gail: 500 E 83rd St, New York, NY 10028 212-249-9572
Rodorigo, Sandro: 23-17 33rd St #7, Astoria, NY 11105..................................718-274-2764
Rodriguez, Claudio: 304 Mulberry St #4B, New York, NY 10012 212-941-0573
Rodriguez, Edel: 437 63rd St, Brooklyn, NY 11220 718-492-0259
Rodriguez, Francisco: 3286 Ivanhoe, St Louis, MO 63139................................314-781-7377
Rodriguez, Gisela: 695 Talcottville Rd #17-6, Vernon, CT 06066.......................413-782-6870
Rodriguez, Lisandro: 86 Fort Washington Blvd #4F, New York, NY 10032 212-781-5175
- **Rodriguez, Robert: pg 214,215** 501 Fifth Ave, New York, NY 10017...........**212-490-2450**
url: www.renardrepresents.com / fax: 212-697-6828
Rodriguez, Syl: 11516 Sixth Ave, Seattle, WA 98117.......................................206-364-9077
Rodriguez, Teco: 48 Lakeshore Dr, Toronto, ON M8V 1Z6.................................416-253-5992
Rodriquez, Jose: 14521 Cullen St, Whittier, CA 90603 310-693-1031
Roeger, Daniel T: 21 Elm St, Methuen, MA 01844...603-898-1087
Roffo, Sergio: 222 Thomas Clapp Rd, Scituate, MA 02066 617-787-5861
- **Rofheart-Piggot, Irene: 189 Upper Station Rd. PO Box 420,**
Garrison, NY 10524 ....**914-424-8304**
Rogala, Miroslaw: 329 W 18th Street #900, Chicago, IL 60616..........................312-243-2952
Rogers, Adam: 2491 W 22nd Ave, Vancouver, BC B6L 1M3................................604-684-6826
Rogers, Buc: 1025 W. Madison, Chicago, IL 60607..312-421-4132
Rogers, Glenda: 4049 Marlton Cir, Liverpool, NY 13090...................................315-451-3220
Rogers, Kathy: 19220 Hackamore Rd., Corcoran, MN 55340 612-478-9897
- **Rogers, Lilla J: pg 696-706** 6 Parker Rd, Arlington, MA 02174 ....**617-641-2787**
fax: 617-641-2244
Rogers, Mark: 232 Topeka Ave, San Jose, CA 95126 408-298-9737
Rogers, Mike: 17711 Margate #105, Encino, CA 91316.....................................818-344-8609
Rogers, Nip: 1841 Lake Cypress Dr, Safety Harbor, FL 34695 813-725-4438
848 Greenwood Ave NE, Atlanta, GA 30306 404-875-1363
Rogers, Paul: pg 749 12 S Fair Oaks Ave #202, Pasadena, CA 91105 ....**626-564-8729**
e-mail: rvhstudio@aol.com / fax: 626-564-8729
1464 Linden Ave, Chicago, IL 60035..**847-432-2415**
fax: 773-883-0375
Los Angeles **213-934-3395**
Fax: 213-936-2757
Rogers, Randy: 1212 N Post Oak, Houston, TX 77055.......................................713-688-0637
Rogers, RS: 212 S Front St, Philipsburg, PA 16866 814-342-6572
Rogers, Stephanie Morgan: 3033 13th Ave W, Seattle, WA 98119.....................206-284-4701
Rohani, Michael Sours: 9229 215th St SW, Edmonds, WA 98020.......................425-771-2905
Rohr, Dixon: 155 W 68th St #26E, New York, NY 10023 212-580-4065
Rohrbacher, Patricia: 1374 Midland Ave #308, Bronxville, NY 10708..................914-776-1185
Roland, George S: 435 Sunset Dr, Meadville, PA 16335....................................814-333-2006
- **Roldan, Ismael: pg 1383** 690 Greenwich St #5E, New York, NY 10014 .....**212-691-5841**
fax: 212-691-5841
Roldan, Jim: 141 E Main St, E Hampstead, NH 03826 603-382-1686
Rolfe, David: 468 Queen St E #104, Toronto, ON M5A 1T7 416-367-2446
Rollins, Kent: 690 Clearview Rd, Nashville, TN 37205......................................615-665-0411
Rom, Holly Meeker: 4 Stanley Keys Ct, Rye, NY 10580 914-921-3155
Roma, Ursula: 4236 Brookside Ave, Cincinnati, OH 45223................................513-542-5722
Roman, Barbara J: 814 Kaipii St, Kailua, HI 96734 808-262-4708
- **Roman, Irena: pg 448** 731 N 24th St, Philadelphia, PA 19130...................**215-232-6666**
url: www.deborahwolfeltd.com / fax: 215-232-6585
- **Roman, John: pg 834,835** New York, NY **212-869-0214**
San Francisco, CA **415-543-6056**
fax: 415-543-6075
Romano, Al: 10 Millinocket Trl, Guilford, CT 06437 203-245-2952
Romas: 389 Cako Ave, Keene, NH 03431 603-357-7306
Romeo Empire Design, Donna: 108 E 35th St #2, New York, NY 10016 212-889-3337
Romeo, Richard: 1066 NW 96th Ave, Ft Lauderdale, FL 33322..........................954-472-0072
Romer, Dan: 176 5th Ave #4R, Brooklyn, NY 11217..718-789-8442
Romney, Jordan: 1301 Henry St, Berkley, CA 94709...510-548-5614
Romney, Michael: 201 E 77th St PH-C, New York, NY 10021 212-288-0618
Ronald, Lawrence: 17 Chapel Ln, Buffalo, NY 14224..716-892-5152
Ronning, Margy H: 4324 W 87 St, Prairie Village, KS 66207..............................913-648-1284
Roolaart, Harry: 1318 Central Ave #A 11, Charlotte, NC 28205 704-529-1021
Roper, Marty: 6115 Brookside Blvd, Kansas City, MO 64113..............................816-361-8589
Rosa, Tony: 4 Holly Ave, West Keansburg, NJ 07734..908-787-0786
Rosandich, Dan: Box 410, Chassell, MI 49916...906-482-6234
Rosario, Rudolph: 360 Atlantic Ave #151, Brooklyn, NY 11217 718-875-7465
Rosas, Willie: 60-63 Street, West New York, NJ 07093 201-854-8142
Rosborough, Tom: 325 51st St, Des Moines, IA 50312......................................515-277-1785
Rosco, Delro: 455 W 23rd St #8D, New York, NY 10011 212-366-1893
91-822B Pohakupuna Rd, Ewa Beach, HI 96706 808-689-4635
Rose, Bob: 2915 Pinon Ct, Highland, CA 92346 909-425-3639
Rose, David: 1623 N Curson Ave, Los Angeles, CA 90046.................................213-876-0038
Rose, Lee: 4250 TC Jester Blvd, Houston, TX 77018..713-686-4799
Rose, Robert: 2915 Pinon Ct, Highland, CA 92346...909-425-3639
Rosebush, Judson: 154 W 57th St #826, New York, NY 10019...........................212-398-6600
Rosefelt, Mitch: 6006 Hawser Rd, Middleton, WI 53705.....................................608-831-1892
Rosely, Susan: 13157 Riverside Dr #107, Sherman Oaks, CA 91423...................818-783-4476
Rosen, Eileen: 412 Anglesey Terr, West Chester, PA 19380...............................215-524-8455

- **Rosen, Elizabeth: pg 180,181** 194 Third Ave 3rd Fl, New York, NY 10003....**212-475-0440**
url: www.vickimorganassociates.com / fax: 212-353-8538
Rosen, Terry: 35 W 81st St, New York, NY 10024..212-580-4784
- **Rosenbaum, Jonathan & Georgina: pg 455,791,1482**
597 Riverside Ave, Westport, CT 06880...**203-226-4724**
url: www.brewstercreative.com / fax: 203-454-9904
731 N 24th St, Philadelphia, PA 19130...**215-232-6666**
url: www.deborahwolfeltd.com / fax: 215-232-6585
- **Rosenbaum, Saul: pg 463** 731 N 24th St, Philadelphia, PA 19130 ....**215-232-6666**
url: www.deborahwolfeltd.com / fax: 215-232-6585
Rosenberg, Ben: 3743 SE Stephens, Portland, OR 97214 503-230-7735
- **Rosenberg, Ken: pg 444** 60 E 42nd St, New York, NY 10165-1940 212-867-8092
e-mail: DHLT@aol.com / url: www.HT-LTD.com / fax: 212-949-1977
Roseneck, Paul: Box 1717, Schenectady, NY 12301...518-381-6570
Rosenstein, Elliot: PO Box 20765, Seattle, WA 98102 206-682-3729
- **Rosenthal, Marc: pg 90,91** 108 E 35th St, New York, NY 10016................**212-889-3337**
url: www.theispot.com/artist/rosenthal / fax: 212-889-3341
Rosenwald, Laurie: 1809 7th Ave #1710, Seattle, WA 98101 206-447-1600
Rosier, Bruce: 62 Indian Church Rd, Buffalo, NY 14210...................................716-823-4690
Rosner, Meryl: 99 Park Ave #210A, New York, NY 10016 800-398-9544
Ross Culbert & Lavery: 15 W 20th St 9th Fl, New York, NY 10011....................212-206-0044
Ross Studio, Inc: 10231 Metro Pkwy, Ft Meyers, FL 33912...............................941-275-1991
Ross, Barry: 12 Fruit St, Northampton, MA 01060..413-585-8993
- **Ross, Bill: pg 1384** 602 Davidson Rd, Nashville, TN 37205 ....**615-352-3729**
fax: 615-356-1122
Ross, Dave: 1004 Hudson Rd, Cedar Falls, IA 50613 319-266-4849
Ross, Doug: 37 West 20th Street #902, New York, NY 10011 212-243-5888
Ross, Eileen: 6736 N 11th St, Phoenix, AZ 85014 602-234-1598
Ross, Ian: 205 E 95th St #34K, New York, NY 10128 212-828-0284
Ross, Larry: 53 Fairview Ave, Madison, NJ 07940..201-377-6859
- **Ross, Mary: pg 771** 83 Walnut Ave, Corte Madera, CA 94925......................**415-924-7881**
toll-free **800-924-7881**
url: www.ritareps.com / fax: 415-924-7891
Ross, Richard: 336 Lafayette Ave, Buffalo, NY 14213.......................................716-882-5373
- **Ross, Scott: pg 466** 731 N 24th St, Philadelphia, PA 19130 ....**215-232-6666**
url: www.deborahwolfeltd.com / fax: 215-232-6585
Rossano, Anthony: 2213 NW Market St, Seattle, WA 98107 206-525-2437
Rossi, Joseph: 45 Lockwood Dr, Clifton, NJ 07013..201-278-5716
Rossi, Pamela: 908 Main St #3, Evanston, IL 60202..847-475-2533
Rossiter, Nan: 14 Pleasant St, New Milford, CT 06776.......................................203-354-3065
Rotblatt, Steven: 13908 Fiji Way #165, Marina del Rey, CA 90292....................310-821-5919
- **Roth Design & Illustration, Marci: pg 1155**
2025 NE 50th Ave, Portland, OR 97213...**503-284-2978**
Roth, Aaron Thomas: 59 Grand St #3, New York, NY 10013...............................212-219-9101
Roth, Hy: 1300 Ashland St, Evanston, IL 60201 847-491-1937
Roth, Rob: 420 Lexington Ave #2760, New York, NY 10170 212-697-8525
Roth, Roger: 7227 Brent Rd, Upper Darby, PA 19082 610-352-3235
Roth, Wayne: 712 Main St, Boonton, NJ 07005...973-316-5411
- **Rother, Sue: pg 743** 865 Delaware St, Denver, CO 80204............................**303-820-2599**
toll-free **800-417-5120**
url: www.artagent.com / fax: 303-820-2598
Rothman, Mike: 62 E Ridge St, Ridgefield, CT 06877 203-438-4954
- **Rotondo, Nick: pg 467** 731 N 24th St, Philadelphia, PA 19130....................**215-232-6666**
url: www.deborahwolfeltd.com / fax: 215-232-6585
Rotunda, Matthew: 89 FIfth Ave #901, New York, NY 10003 212-627-1554
Roundy, Laine: 42 Buttonball Dr, Sandy Hook, CT 06482..................................203-426-9531
Roush, Ragan: 745 Poplar Ave, Boulder, CO 80304..303-440-6582
Roux, Jimminy: 468 Queen St E #104, Toronto, ON M5A 1T7 416-367-2446
Rouya, Es: 30 Winthrop Dr, Woodbury, NY 11797...516-367-1359
Row, Richard: 99 Atlantic Ave #207, Toronto, ON M6K 3J8 416-533-6787
Rowe, Charles: 133 Aronimink Dr, Newark, DE 19711.......................................302-738-0641
- **Rowe, John: pg 1014,1015** 420 Lexington Ave, New York, NY 10170.........**212-986-5680**
url: www.mendolaart.com / fax: 212-818-1246
316 Mellow Lane, La Canada, CA 91011 ....**818-790-2645**
url: www.mendolaart.com / fax: 818-790-2655
Rowland, Lauren: 176 Ludlow St #1H, New York, NY 10002...............................212-254-2731
Rowley, Carter: 116 N College Ave #7, Fort Collins, CO 80524...........................970-407-7240
Rowley, Michael: 2741 Gramercy Ave, Torrance, CA 90501 310-212-3267
Rownd, Jim: 5230 13th Ave S, Minneapolis, MN 55417.....................................612-822-0650
Roxburgh, Ed: 3720 Yonge St #7, San Diego, CA 92106 619-225-1438
Roy, Lyse-Anne: 106-A rue Papineau, Bromont, QU J0E 1L0 514-534-4963
Roy, Martin: 4667 rue Hutchinson, Montréal, QU H2V 4A2 514-271-8105
Royce, Johnathan: 350 7th st #8-1, Brooklyn, NY 11215..................................212-337-0077
Royden, Elizabeth: 309 E 18th St #4D, New York, NY 10003 212-228-1426
Royo, Luis: 11 Kings Ridge Rd, Long Valley, NJ 07853 908-813-8718
Rozasy, Frank: 2228 3rd St #12, Santa Monica, CA 90405 310-399-1891
Rubalcava, Alejandro: 16 Technology #115, Irvine, CA 92718 714-727-3126
Rubess, Balvis: 260 Brunswick Ave, Toronto, ON M5S 2M7 416-927-7071
Rubin, Terry: 1404 W Mount Royal Ave, Baltimore, MD 21217 410-383-8100
- **Rubino, Cornel: pg 135** 420 Lexington Ave, New York, NY 10170 ....**212-986-5680**
url: www.mendolaart.com / fax: 212-818-1246
Rubinstein, Josef: 320 Seventh Ave #1, Brooklyn, NY 11215 718-369-1527
Rucceri, David: 505 Court St #4H, Brooklyn, NY 11231 718-852-8987
Rudd, Michael Gregory: 220 Hoydens Ln, Fairfield, CT 06430 203-261-4462
Ruddell, Gary: 405 N Wabash #2709, Chicago, IL 60611 312-222-0337
Rudinsky, Joyce: 7311 Chamberlain Ave, St Louis, MO 63130...........................314-721-1114
- **Rudnak, Theo: pg 202,203** 501 Fifth Ave, New York, NY 10017 ....**212-490-2450**
url: www.renardrepresents.com / fax: 212-697-6828
- **Rüegger, Rebecca: pg 811** 333 E 49th St, New York, NY 10017 ....**212-980-8061**
url: theispot.com/artist/ruegger / fax: 212-832-8778
100 Bleecker St, New York, NY 10012 ....**212-982-6533**
fax: 212-358-1586
- **Ruf, Joseph: pg 1385** 36 Franklin Ave, Deer Park, NY 11729 ....**516-586-5633**
Ruff, Donna: 12 Top Sail Rd, Rowayton, CT 06853 203-866-8626
Ruffing, Eric: 620 Rosencrans Ave, Manhattan Bch, CA 90266 310-546-7135
Ruffins, Reynold: 51 Hampton St, Sag Harbor, NY 11963 516-725-3480

Ruggeri, John: 245 E 19th St, New York, NY 10003....................................212-979-6029
Rugh, Doug: 37 Gosnold Rd, Woods Hole, MA 02543.................................508-548-6684
Ruhl, Greg: 40 Alexander St PH 9, Toronto, ON M4Y 1B5..........................416-928-1997
• **Ruiz, Aristides: pg 1456** 39 Hamilton Terr, New York, NY 10031...............**212-283-3401**
url: www.showcase.com
Runnion Design, Jeff: 93 River Rd, Topsfield, MA 01983...............................508-887-2418
Runt Illustrations: 72 Lippincott St, Toronto, ON M5S 2P1............................416-504-7089
Rupp Art & Design, Katherine: 8511 Cheltenham Cir, Louisville, KY 40222......502-425-9266
Rush, John: 123 Kedzie St, Evanston, IL 60202..847-869-2078
Russell, Bill: 949 Filbert St #5, San Francisco, CA 94133..............................415-474-4159
Russell, Doug: 1452 NW 185th, Seattle, WA 98177.......................................206-542-1452
Russell, Mike: 427 First St, Brooklyn, NY 11215...212-598-9707
Russo, Anthony: 51 Fogland Rd, Tiverton, RI 02878.....................................401-351-1770
Russo, David Anson: 41 Union Sq W #918, New York, NY 10003..................212-807-6627
Rusynyk, Kathy: 2309 Twp Rd 257, Jeromesville, OH 44840..........................419-368-3664
Rutten, Nicole: 866 United Nations Plaza, New York, NY 10017......................212-644-2020
Ruzich, Denise: 120 Bishop's Gate, Grand Island, NY 14072..........................716-774-2700
Ryan, Carol: 14 Adams St, Port Washington, NY 11050..................................516-944-3953
Ryan, Cheri: 753 N 35th, Seattle, WA 98103...206-634-1880
• **Ryan, Glenn: pg 561,572,573** 155 Lippincott St, Toronto, ON M5S 2P3......**416-505-9522**
toll-free...**888-277-7200**
e-mail: shelley@sbaillustrates.com / url: www.sbaillustrates.com
Ryan, Kerrick A: 6 Gardenia Dr, Maple Shade, NJ 08052...............................609-482-9759
Ryane, Nathen: San Diego, CA...619-260-2472
Rybka, Steve: 3119 W 83rd St, Chicago, IL 60614...773-737-1981
• **Ryden, Mark: pg 1098** 541 Ramona Ave, Sierra Madre, CA 91024..............**818-355-1750**
fax: 818-355-1138
Ryder, Jennifer: 99 Amesbury St, Quincy, MA 02170......................................617-479-4774
Ryus, Michael: 4 Waverly Rd, Cape Elizabeth, ME 04107................................207-767-2228

S

S & V Enterprises: 4600 Kings Crossings Dr, Kennesaw, GA 30144.................770-928-8050
S. I. International: 43 E 19th St, New York, NY 10003....................................212-254-4996
Saas, Susan: 32 Downing St #4D, New York, NY 10014...................................212-633-1310
• **Sabanosh, Michael: pg 1386,1387**
433 W 34th St #18-B, New York, NY 10001..**212-947-8161**
Sabin, Tracy: 13476 Ridley Rd, San Diego, CA 92129.....................................619-484-8712
Sachs, Jenny: 157 E 32nd St, New York, NY 10016...212-684-0565
Sachs, Jim: 28971 Banoff Dr Box 1182, Lake Arrowhead, CA 92352.............909-337-5838
Sack, Steve: 5105 W 106th St, Bloomington, MN 55437..................................612-896-4961
Sacks, Ron: 1189 Rosebank Dr, Worthington, OH 43235................................614-846-1921
Sadowski, Wiktor: 278 Hamilton Ave, Princeton, NJ 08540.............................609-252-9405
Saffold, Joe: 490B Beaulieu Ave, Savannah, GA 31406...................................912-352-2472
Safier-Kerzner, Sonia: 9413 Locust Hill Rd, Bethesda, MD 20814...................301-530-5167
Safir, Marty: 11240 Magnolia Blvd Ste 205, N Hollywood, CA 91601..............818-509-0555
Safr, Paul: 295 Queen St, Blyth, ON N0M 1H0...519-523-9114
• **Sagona, Marina: pg 612** 155 W 15th St, New York, NY 10011......................**212-989-8770**
fax: 212-989-7892
Sahli, Barbara: 115 Indian Spring Dr, Silver Spring, MD 20901.......................301-585-5122
Saint-John, Bob: PO Box1412, Portsmouth, NH 03802....................................207-363-1249
Sakahara, Dick: 28826 Cedarbluff Dr, Rancho Palos Verdes, CA 90275..........310-541-8187
Sakai, Kazuya: 1804 Roxton, Richardson, TX 75081..214-234-0502
Sakimoto, Wayne: 3505 Cadillac Ave #B1, Costa Mesa, CA 92626...................714-513-9250
Saksa, Cathy: 10 Hidden Hollow Dr, Hamilton Township, NJ 08620..................609-259-7792
• **Salazar, Miro: pg 851** 525 Brannan St #406, San Francisco, CA 94107......**415-647-5660**
url: www.girlrep.com
Salem, Kay: 13418 Splintered Oak, Houston, TX 77065..................................713-469-0996
Salentine, Katherine: 10 Summerhill, San Rafael, CA 94903............................415-499-9329
Salerno, John: 4915 Rebel Rd, San Diego, CA 92117......................................619-272-1222
• **Salerno, Steven: pg 414,415**
250 W 57th St #521, New York, NY 10107..**212-397-7330**
url: www.lindgrensmith.com (and) www.stockillustrated.com
Salfino, Samuel: 57 Lakeside Dr, Nutley, NJ 07110..201-667-5103
• **Salgian, Mitzura: pg 439** 60 E 42nd St, New York, NY 10165-1940............**212-867-8092**
e-mail: DHLT@aol.com / url: www.HT-LTD.com / fax: 212-949-1977
Salicrup, Fernando: 1685 Lexington Ave, New York, NY 10029........................212-831-4333
Salinger, Joan: 2701 Fairview Rd/Box 5005, Costa Mesa, CA 92628................714-432-5691
Salk, Larry: 19029 Sprague St, Tarzana, CA 91356...818-776-1992
Salmon, Paul: 5826 Jackson's Oak Ct, Burke, VA 22015.................................703-250-4943
Salvaggio, Bob: 30 Lawnview Dr, Braintree, MA 02184...................................508-655-6415
Salvati, Jim: 6600 Royal Ave, West Hills, CA 91307.......................................818-348-9012
Salzman, Rick: 293 Rabideau St/Box 158, Cadyville, NY 12918.......................518-293-7004
Samanich, Barbara: 211 E Ohio Suite 2404, Chicago, IL 60611.........................312-661-1717
188 E Vista Del Cerro, Tempe, AZ 85281...602-966-3070
Saminski, Melinda: 45 Cowart Ave, Manasquan, NJ 08738.............................732-223-5937
• **Sammel, Chelsea: pg 1388** 482 South St, Hollister, CA 95023....................**831-636-7443**
fax: 831-636-7443
Sample, Paul: 28 Shelton St/Covent Garden, London, England, UK WC2H.........71-240-2077
Sampson, Heather: 434 Vimy #4, Scherbrooke, QU J1J 3M9.............................819-562-9066
Sampson, Maren: 12725 Gilmore Ave, Los Angeles, CA 90066.........................310-821-9491
Sampson, Ronnie: 268 Ninth Ave, San Francisco, CA 94118............................415-979-4980
Sams, BB: PO Box A, Social Circle, GA 30279...770-464-2956
Samson, Heather: PO Box 642, Derby, VT 05829..401-822-2537
Samuels, Barbara: 299 Riverside Dr #8D, New York, NY 10025........................212-666-5533
Samuels, Mark: 25 Minetta Ln #4A, New York, NY 10014...............................212-777-8580
Sancha, Jeremy: 60 E 42nd St #822, New York, NY 10165...............................212-682-1490
Sanchez, Carlos: 2149 Lyon St #5, San Francisco, CA 94115...........................415-921-7140
3301A S Jefferson Ave, St Louis, MO 63118...314-773-2600
Sanchez, Michael: 457 Nevada St, San Francisco, CA 94110...........................415-641-1791
Sanchez, Pat: 8603 Baumgarten, Dallas, TX 75228...214-328-2942
Sanchez, Santiago: 215 40th St Dr SE #304, Cedar Rapids, IA 52403..............319-364-8308
Sanders, Bruce: 7 Washington Street, Beverly, MA 01915..............................978-921-0887
Sanders, Jane: 47-51 40th St #6D, Sunnyside, NY 11104................................718-786-3505
Sanders, Lauren: 2558 Cochran St, Simi Valley, CA 93065..............................805-522-9121
Sanders, Rosanne: 23 Ganton St, London, England, UK WIV 1LA......................71-287-9191
Sanders, Terry W: 319 E 50th St #4B, New York, NY 10022.............................212-980-1893
Sanderson, Bill: Farnleigh, Huntindon Rd Houghton, Huntindon,
Cambs, England, UK PE17...1480-461506
Sandro, Cindy: 662 Medlock Rd., Decatur, GA 30033....................................404-633-3321
Sanford, John: 5038 W Berteau, Chicago, IL 60641.......................................773-685-0656
• **Sanford, Steve: pg 1389** 41 Union Sq W #615, New York, NY 10003.........**212-243-6119**
fax: 212-924-3074
Sanford, Susan: 19 Los Amigos Court, Orinda, CA 94563..............................510-253-3131
• **Sano, Kazuhiko: pg 992,993** 105 Stadium Ave, Mill Valley, CA 94941.........**415-381-6377**
fax: 415-381-3847
501 Fifth Ave, New York, NY 10017...**212-490-2450**
url: www.renardrepresents.com / fax: 212-697-6828
Sansevero, Tony: 501 W Fayette St #270, Syracuse, NY 13204.......................315-428-8585
Sanson, Jeff: 1212 N Post Oak St, Houston, TX 77055...................................713-688-0637
• **Santalucia, Francesco: pg 124,125**
420 Lexington Ave, New York, NY 10170..**212-986-5680**
url: www.mendolaart.com / fax: 212-818-1246
Santana, Miguel: 169 E 90th St #3, New York, NY 10128...............................212-369-8405
Santiago, Rafael: 72-100 37th Ave #18, Jackson Heights, NY 11372.................718-565-6772
Santo, Vincent: 2 Skibo Ln, Mamaroneck, NY 10543.......................................914-698-4667
Santoleri, Ray: 153 Courtelyous, Somerset, NJ 08873.....................................908-297-9116
Santoliquido, Delores: 60 W Broad St #6H, Mt Vernon, NY 10552...................914-667-3199
Santore, Charles: 138 S 20th St, Philadelphia, PA 19103..............................215-563-0430
Santos, Ellen: 165 Franklin St #203, Bloomfield, NJ 07003.............................201-748-0384
Santry, Karen: 463 West St #1025, New York, NY 10014................................212-645-9595
Sapulich, Joe: 8454 W 161st Pl, Tinley Park, IL 60477....................................708-532-8766
Saputo, Joe: 4024 Jasper Rd, Springfield, OR 97478.......................................541-746-9886
Sardinha, Anthony: 16 Sparta Rd, Toronto, ON M6L 2M5................................416-249-0285
Sarecky, Melody: 3601 Connecticut Ave NW #721, Washington, DC 20008....202-347-5276
Sargent, Claudia Karabaic: 15-38 126th St, Queens, NY 11356.......................718-461-8280
Sarn: San Francisco, CA...415-543-6056
Sarrazin, Marisol: 1507 rue des Bécassines, St Margurite, QU J0T 2K0............514-228-2855
Sasaki, Goro: 60 E 42nd St #822, New York, NY 10165....................................212-682-1490
• **Sass Illustration, Cindy: pg 1122** 15 Torne Rd, Sloatsburg, NY 10974.........**914-753-5119**
fax: 914-753-5411
• **Sassouni Illustration, Maral: pg 1146**
1416 Queens Rd, West Hollywood, CA 90069...**213-650-5865**
e-mail: marals@starnet.fr / fax: 213-650-5865
• **Sauber, Robert: pg 182,183** 194 Third Ave, New York, NY 10003..............**212-475-0440**
url: www.vickimorganassociates.com / fax: 212-353-8538
Sauer & Assocs, Christian: 1800 Olive St, St Louis, MO 63103.......................314-664-4646
Sauer, April: 40-21 196th St 2nd Fl, Flushing, NY 11358................................800-411-5454
Sauer, John: 800 Washington Ave N, Minneapolis, MN 55401..........................612-349-5511
Sauer, Kristie: 615 Cheryl Ln, Phoenix, OR 97535..541-535-1810
Saulsberry, Demitrius: 621 Clinton St, Gary, IN 46406....................................219-944-7598
Saunders, Fred: 4033 Aurora Ave N, Seattle, WA 98103..................................206-633-3445
• **Saunders, Robert: pg 920,921**
45 Bartlett Crescent 3rd Fl, Brookline, MA 02146..**617-566-4464**
e-mail: drnibs@world.std.com / url: http://world.std.com/~drnibs / fax: 617-739-0040
Saurda, Tomas: 875 Third Ave 4th Fl, New York, NY 10022.............................212-303-8326
Sauriol, Brian: PO Box 396, Bloomfield Hills, MI 48303..................................313-460-2451
Sava, Judy: 813 F St, Sacramento, CA 95814..916-427-3441
Savadier, Elivia: 45 Walnut Hill Rd, Chestnut Hill, MA 02167..........................617-661-0951
Savage, David: PO Box 1422, Boca Raton, FL 33429.......................................407-394-4644
Savard, Sister Judith: 250 Riverside Dr #24A, New York, NY 10025..................212-663-6273
Savastano, Lori: 37-27 86th St #4U, Jackson Hgts, NY 11372..........................718-426-2541
Savely, Rod: 7 Washington Street, Beverly, MA 01915....................................978-921-0887
365 W Wilson St #2, Costa Mesa, CA 92627...714-722-7750
Savely, Susan: 13157 Riverside Dr #107, Sherman Oaks, CA 91423.................818-783-4476
Savidge, Robert T: 1006 Lilac Ln, Lebanon, PA 17042.....................................202-547-5186
Sawchuk, Peter: 4519 S 31st St #202, Arlington, VA 22206.............................703-379-4011
Sawka, Jan: 353 W 53rd St #1W, New York, NY 10019.....................................212-682-2462
Sawyer, Arnie: 115 W 27th St 8th Fl, New York, NY 10001..............................212-645-4455
Sawyer, David: 1885 A Calle Quedo, Santa Fe, NM 87505...............................505-474-0296
Sawyer, Peter A: 7768 Clifton Rd, Fairfax, VA 22039.......................................703-250-3117
Sawyer, Scott: 94 Natoma St #200, San Francisco, CA 94105..........................415-442-1822
Saxe, Joe: 920 McLellan Dr, San Jose, CA 95110..408-287-7273
Sayles, Elizabeth: 60 Brookside Ave, Valley Cottage, NY 10989......................914-267-4127
Sayles, John: 420 Lexington Ave #2760, New York, NY 10170..........................212-697-8525
308 Eighth St, Des Moines, IA 50309...515-243-2922
Scabaugh, Max: 302 23rd Ave, San Francisco, CA 94121..................................415-750-1373
• **Scanlan, David: pg 1150** 1600 18th St, Manhattan Beach, CA 90266...........**310-545-0773**
fax: 310-545-7364
• **Scanlan, Peter: pg 510,511**
217 E 86th St Box 212, New York, NY 10028..**212-427-5632**
fax: 212-427-6372
Scanlon, Susan: 417 E 87th St #1A, New York, NY 10128................................212-996-0591
Scantland, Chris: 6509 Old Railroad Bed Rd, Toney, AL 35773.......................205-420-3821
Scaramozzino, Michael: 50 Clifford St, Providence, RI 02903..........................401-861-8002
Scardova, Jacqueline: CA..415-721-0707
Scarisbrick, Ed: 853 Broadway #1201, New York, NY 10003............................212-677-9100
Scarola, Vito-Leonardo: 24671 Sutton Ln, Laguna Niguel, CA 92677................714-831-1270
Scarpulla, Caren: 2832 Waverly Dr-Front, Los Angeles, CA 90039...................213-913-2458
Scatliffe, Steven: 4801 San Mateo Lane NE #262, Albuquerque, NM 87109.......505-262-2077
Scerbo, Ed: 24 Depew Ave #4, Nyack, NY 10960...914-348-9250
Schaare, Harry: 60 E 42nd St #1940, New York, NY 10165................................212-867-8092
Schacht, Michael: 925 Park Ave, New York, NY 10028.....................................212-734-5318
• **Schader/Eagleye, Steve: pg 1184**
19745 E Bellewood Dr, Aurora, CO 80015..**303-617-1386**
Schafer, John: 214 1/2 First St E, Independence, IA 50644..............................319-334-3203
Schaffer, Amanda: 445 Hanson Ln, Ramona, CA 92065....................................619-788-0388
Schall, Rene: 5 Field Green Dr, Colchester, VT 05446.....................................802-878-1086
Schaller, Tom: 2112 Broadway #407, New York, NY 10023...............................212-362-5524
Schanzer, Roz: 234 Fifth Ave 4th Fl, New York, NY 10001...............................212-696-4680
Scharf, Linda: PO Box 1562, Boston, MA 02146..617-738-9294

- **Schattner, Gillie: pg 120,121** 420 Lexington Ave, New York, NY 10170 ......**212-986-5680**
  url: www.mendolaart.com / fax: 212-818-1246
- **Schauman, Clare: pg 862** 280 Madison Ave #1110, New York, NY 10016 ....**212-545-9155**
  e-mail: irmeli@aol.com / url: www.spar.org/holmberg / fax: 212-545-9462
  Scheckel, Eric: 6432 E Freeport Dr, Highlands Ranch, CO 80126.....................303-470-5658
  Scheffer Studios: 1027 Berkshire Ln, Tarpon Springs, FL 34689 813-938-8388
  Scheld, Betsy: PO Box 257, Wading River, NY 11792 212-876-5281
  Schell, Paul: 1608 E 51st St, Brooklyn, NY 11234 718-951-8976
  Schellhorn, Jill: 465 Prospect Ave, Piscataway, NJ 08854 908-424-1243
  Schermer-Gramm, Kathy: 2655 Shieldale Dr, Winston Salem, NC 27107.........909-247-6220
  Scheuer Illustration, Philip A: 126 Fifth Ave #13B, New York, NY 10011 212-620-0728
  Scheuer, Lauren: 2 Fowler Rd, Upton, MA 01568.................................508-529-9053
  Schiavo, Marian: 335 38th Rd, Douglaston, NY 11363 718-229-3660
  Schieffer, John: PO Box 7114, Prospect, CT 06712 203-758-3176
  Schields, Gretchen: 4556 19th St, San Francisco, CA 94114.....................415-558-8851
  Schier, Jeffrey: 3928 Shafter, Oakland, CA 94609 510-653-5825
  Schill, George: 309 Walnut Rd, Pittsburgh, PA 15202 412-761-5666
  Schill, Nancy: 235 Channing Ave, Malvern, PA 19355 215-644-3426
  Schilling, John: 3033 13th Ave W, Seattle, WA 98119 206-284-4701
  Schindler, Max: 42 Delavan St, Brooklyn, NY 11231 718-624-1906
  Schiwall, Linda: 280 Madison Ave #1110, New York, NY 10016...................212-545-9155
  Schleh, Joy: 49 Pine Ave, Floral Park, NY 11001 516-354-5530
  Schleinkofer, David: 420 Lexington Ave, New York, NY 10170 212-986-5680
  Schlemme, Roy: 585 Centre St, Oradell, NJ 07649 212-921-9732
- **Schlowsky, Bob & Lois: pg 1462,1463** 73 Old Rd, Weston, MA 02193.......**781-899-5110**
  e-mail: rschlowsky@aol.com / fax: 781-647-1608
  Schmelzer, John: 1002 S Wesley Ave, Oak Park, IL 60304 708-386-4005
  Schmid, Paul: 4645 Colfax Ave S, Minneapolis, MN 55409 612-825-7564
  2702 Walnut Ave SW, Seattle, WA 98116 206-938-4516
  Schmidbauer, Terry: 37-H Terrace Lane, Lake Zurick, IL 60047....................
  Schmidt, Aaron: 730 N Glasgow Dr, Dallas, TX 75214 214-828-9389
- **Schmidt, Alberto: pg 1469** 2200 N Lamar #104, Dallas, TX 75202 ....**214-871-2747**
  url: www.imageninc.com / fax: 214-871-2748
- **Schmidt, Bill: pg 425** 60 E 42nd St, New York, NY 10165-1940 ....**212-867-8092**
  e-mail: DHLT@aol.com / url: www.HT-LTD.com / fax: 212-949-1977
  Schmidt, Chuck: 311 Ave H #D, Redondo Beach, CA 90277.....................310-540-5958
  853 Broadway #1201, New York, NY 10003 212-677-9100
  Schmidt, George: 183 Steuben St, Brooklyn, NY 11205 718-857-1836
  Schmidt, Heidi: 2925 Griffith St, San Francisco, CA 94124 415-467-9676
  Schmidt, John F: 7308 Leesville Blvd, Springfield, VA 22151 703-750-0927
  Schmidt, Lori: PO Box 4101, Chatsworth, CA 91313 805-527-4902
  Schmidt, Urs: 1 Ch De Boston 1004, Lusanne, Switzerland, ...121-625-2274
  Schminke, Karin: 5803 NE 181st St, Seattle, WA 98155 206-402-8606
  Schneegass, Martinu: 241 Eldridge St #2R, New York, NY 10002 212-529-7445
  Schneider Illus, RM: 853 Broadway #1201, New York, NY 10003.................212-677-9100
  Schneider, Douglas: 9016 Danube Ln, San Diego, CA 92126.....................619-695-6796
  2717 Western Ave, Seattle, WA 98121 206-232-7873
  Schneider, Roy: 468 Queen St E #104, Toronto, ON M5A 1T7 416-367-2446
  Schneider, William: 15 Morris Ave, Athens, OH 45701...........................614-594-3205
  Schneidman, Jared: 1 Nightingale Rd, Katonah, NY 10536.......................914-232-1499
  Schoenberger, Carl: 1925 16th St NW #701, Washington, DC 20009 202-483-3117
  Schoenfliess, Rebecca Butcher: 3811 Pleasant Pl, Baltimore, MD 21211.........410-467-8307
  Schofield, Dennis: 7013 Hegerman St, Philadelphia, PA 19135 215-624-8143
  Schofield, Glen: 99 Park Ave #210A, New York, NY 10016.......................800-398-9544
  Schofield, Glen: 4 Hillside Ave, Roseland, NJ 07068 201-226-5597
  Schofield, Russ: 5313 Waneta Rd, Bethesda, MD 20816 301-320-5008
  Scholberg, Barbara: 35 Buckboard Rd, Duxbury, MA 02332 508-934-7896
  Schonbach Graphics, Friedrich: 1851 Columbia Rd NW #603,
  Washington, DC 20009 202-265-2240
  Schongut, Emanuel: 110 Sutter St #706, San Francisco, CA 94104...............415-441-4384
- **Schoolcraft, Robert: pg 1162** 125 Prospect Park W, Brooklyn, NY 11215......**718-369-1781**
  Schooley, Greg: 207 Bellwood Circle, Mars, PA 16046............................412-776-4156
  Schopper, Bernie: 2415 Windbreak Dr, Alexandria, VA 22306 703-765-4652
  Schorr, Kathy Staico: PO Box 142, Roxbury, CT 06783 203-266-4084
  Schorr, Todd: PO Box 142, Roxbury, CT 06783.................................203-266-4084
  Schott, Robert & Cathleen: 831 40th Ave N, St Petersburg, FL 33703 813-525-4944
  Schotte, Marilyn: 7205 15th Ave, Takoma Park, MD 20912 301-357-4993
  Schottland, Miriam: 2201 Massachusetts Ave NW, Washington, DC 20008 202-328-3825
  Schreck, Eric: 2969 Jackson St #503, San Francisco, CA 94115 415-673-3244
  Schreck, John: 101 Spring Hill Rd, Fairfield, CT 06430 203-259-6824
  Schreiber, Dana: 36 Center St, Collinsville, CT 06022 203-693-6688
- **Schreiber, Laszlo: pg 1456,1457** 39 Hamilton Terr, New York, NY 10031 ....**212-283-3401**
  url: www.wayart.com
  Schreier, Joshua: 466 Washington St, New York, NY 10013 212-925-0472
  Schrenk, Nick: PO Box 198, Hamilton, VA 22068...............................603-357-8757
- **Schroeder Illus & Retouching, Mark: pg 1471**
  414 Jackson St #207, San Francisco, CA 94111..............................**415-421-3691**
  e-mail: 104147.1313@compuserve.com / fax: 415-421-1135
  Schroeppel, Richard: 1 W Rand Rd, Arlington Hts, IL 60004......................630-588-8540
- **Schuchman, Bob: pg 1144** Torrance, CA **310-376-1448**
  Schudlich, Stephen: 609 Ninth Ave #4S, New York, NY 10036...................212-754-0700
- **Schudlich, Stephen: pg 1140** 930 Acoma #318, Denver, CO 80204..........**303-575-9014**
  url: www.ssid.com / fax: 303-575-9015
- **Schuett, Stacey: pg 897** 110 Rising Ridge Rd, Ridgefield, CT 06877..........**203-438-7307**
  Schuh, Chris: 414 Winter St, Holliston, MA 01746 508-429-6928
- **Schulenburg, Paul: pg 1137** 185 Main St, Orleans, MA 02653..............**508-255-9554**
  Schuler, Mark E: 5410 W 68th St, Prairie Village, KS 66208 913-384-0646
  Schultz, CG: 1140 West Street Rd, West Chester, PA 19382......................215-793-3622
  Schultz, Chuck: 2819 1st Ave #340, Seattle, WA 98121..........................206-443-8209
  Schultz, Eileen Hedy: 7 Hanover Sq 25th Fl, New York, NY 10014 212-709-1755
  Schultz, Robert: 1409 N Alta Vista Blvd #105, Los Angeles, CA 90046...........213-850-8209
  Schumacher, Kurt: 5550 W Armstrong Ave, Chicago, IL 60646...................773-774-3012
  Schumacher, Michael: 2025 NE 123rd St, Seattle, WA 98125 206-364-7150
- **Schumaker, Ward: pg 1118**
  466 Green St #203, San Francisco, CA 94133................................**415-398-1060**

  Schumer, Arlen: 95 Kings Hwy S, Westport, CT 06880 203-454-4518
  Schuster, David: 1 Wood St, Southborough, MA 01772 508-460-6831
- **Schuster, Elle: pg 1466,1467** 3719 Gilbert Ave, Dallas, TX 75219 ....**214-526-6712**
- **Schuster, Robert: pg 437** 60 E 42nd St, New York, NY 10165-1940 ....**212-867-8092**
  e-mail: DHLT@aol.com / url: www.HT-LTD.com / fax: 212-949-1977
  Schwab, Michael: 501 Fifth Ave, New York, NY 10017 212-490-2450
  Schwartz, Carol: 8311 Frontwell Cir, Gaithersburg, MD 20879 301-926-4776
  Schwartz, Joanna H: 51 Woodland St #4, Newburyport, MA 01950..............508-465-9635
  Schwartz, Judith: 231 E 5th St, New York, NY 10003 212-777-7533
  Schwartz, Lisa: 102-25 67th Dr #5M, Forest Hills, NY 11375 718-896-8943
  Schwartz, Marty: 18 Winfield Ct, East Norwalk, CT 06855 203-838-9935
  Schwartz, Sara: 130 W 67th St #22G, New York, NY 10023 212-877-4162
  Schwartze, Evan: 104 S Home Ave #1, Oak Park, IL 60302......................708-445-0154
- **Schwarz, Joanie: pg 176,177** 194 Third Ave, New York, NY 10003 ....**212-475-0440**
  url: www.vickimorganassociates.com / fax: 212-353-8538
  Schweigert, Carol: 9 Lawnwood Pl, Boston, MA 02129 617-242-3901
  Schweitzer, David: 5 E 17th St 6th Fl, New York, NY 10003 212-691-2667
  4 E Ohio Studio B, Chicago, IL 60611 312-321-1336
  Schwinger, Larry: 455 W 23rd St #8D, New York, NY 10011 212-366-1893
  Sciacca, Tom: 77-39 66th Dr, Middle Village, NY 11379 718-326-9124
  Scialla, Stefano: Centro Direzionale di Napoli/Pal. Esedra Is.F.11,
  Napoli, Italy, ...81-734-5397
  Scibilia, Dom: 8277 Broadview Rd, Broadview, OH 44147.......................216-526-2036
  Scoggins, Timothy: 1919 Huntington Ln #1, Redondo Beach, CA 90278.........310-798-3774
  Scogins, Charles: 656 Dover St, Marietta, GA 30066............................770-924-7264
  Scopinich, Robert: 28952 Selfridge Dr, Malibu, CA 90265 310-589-9109
  Scott, Bill: 405 N Wabash Ave #1712, Chicago, IL 60611.........................312-321-0848
- **Scott, Bob: pg 1390** 4108 Forest Hill Ave, Richmond, VA 23225..............**804-232-1627**
  e-mail: bscott5@aol.com / fax: 804-233-7737
  Scott, Davis: 19 W 21st St #301, New York, NY 10010 212-989-6446
  Scott, Elizabeth B: 34 Stanton Rd, Brookline, MA 02146.........................617-264-9425
  Scott, Freda: 1015-B Battery St, San Francisco, CA 94111 415-398-9121
  Scott, Jens: 208 W 23rd St #1619, New York, NY 10011 201-222-8020
  Scott, Jerry: 225 E Michigan St #300, Milwaukee, WI 53202 414-271-5210
  Scott, Kelly: 202 W Orabi Dr, Phoenix, AZ 85027...............................602-581-9114
  Scott, Margaret: 1525 31st St NW, Washington, DC 20007 202-965-0523
  Scott, Martin: 1045 Sansome St #221, San Francisco, CA 94111 415-487-2160
  Scott, Roy: 1427 Suffolk Ln, Wynnewood, PA 19096............................610-642-4154
  Scratchmann, Max: 47 Allerton Walk, Manchester, England, UK M413 1612-727271
- **Scribner, Joanne: pg 1125** N 3314 Lee, Spokane, WA 99207 ....**509-484-3208**
- **Scrofani, Joseph: pg 788** 353 W 53rd St #1W, New York, NY 10019........**212-682-2462**
  e-mail: info@amerartists.com / url: www.amerartists.com / fax: 212-582-0090
  Scroggs, Phil: 624 Linwood Ave NE #2, Atlanta, GA 30306 404-885-1762
  Scudder, Brooke: 15 El Cerrito Ave #5, San Mateo, CA 94402....................415-342-7423
  Scullin, Maureen A: 109 W Hanover Ave, Randolph, NJ 07869...................201-907-0394
- **Seabaugh, Max: pg 486,487**
  2149 Lyon St #5, San Francisco, CA 94115................................**415-921-7140**
  email: art@conradreps.com / url: www.conradreps.com / fax: 415-921-3939
  Seabrook, Alexis: 330 E 33rd St #5G, New York, NY 10016 212-679-9320
- **Sealock, Rick: pg 134** 420 Lexington Ave, New York, NY 10170 ....**212-986-5680**
  url: www.mendolaart.com / fax: 212-818-1246
  Searle, Ronald: PO Box 1062, Bayonne, NJ 07002..............................201-436-4362
- **Seaver, Jeff: pg 938,939** 130 W 24th St #4B, New York, NY 10011 ....**212-741-2279**
  e-mail: jeff@seaver.com / url: www.seaver.com / fax: 212-255-3823
  Sebastian, Fred: 468 Queen St E #104, Toronto, ON M5A 1T7 416-367-2446
  Seckler, Judy: 11024 Acama St #216, Studio City, CA 91602 818-508-8778
  Seder, Jason: 134 E 40th St 4th Fl, New York, NY 10016 212-490-9300
  See, Henry: Art Dept/Williams Hall, Burlington, VT 05405 802-656-2014
  Seed, Susan: 3 Windigo Ln, N Truro, MA 02652................................508-487-6426
  Seflin, Sara M: 455 W 23rd St #8D, New York, NY 10011 121-366-1893
  Segal, John: 165 W 91st St #5A, New York, NY 10024...........................212-662-3278
  Sehmi, Gagan: 95-14 120th St, Richmond Hill, NY 11419.........................718-849-3882
  Seibert, Dave: 488 Curtis Corner Rd, S Kingston, RI 02879 401-782-2103
  Seibert, Sinclair: 347 W 22nd St #4, New York, NY 10011 212-741-1652
- **Seiffer, Alison: pg 92,93** 108 E 35th St #2, New York, NY 10016.............**212-889-3337**
  url: www.theispot.com/artist/seiffer / fax: 212-889-3341
  Seigel, Matthew: 33 Vandewater St #302, San Francisco, CA 94133 415-433-5817
  Sekeris, Pim: 570 Milton St #10, Montreal, QU H2X 1W4 514-844-0510
  Sekine, Hisashi: 3 Crested Butte Cir, Laguna Niguel, CA 92677...................714-363-0705
  630 Fifth Ave 20th Fl, Rockefeller, New York, NY 10111 212-332-3460
  Sela, Eliot: 220 W 21st St #7E, New York, NY 10011 212-627-2450
  Selby, Andrea: 31 Walker St #3, New York, NY 10013 212-334-9367
  Seldin, Jeff: 9127 SW 96th Ave, Miami, FL 33176...............................305-273-7660
  Selewacz, Mark: 24 French St, Watertown, MA 02172..........................617-926-6331
  Selfridge, MC: 817 Desplaines St, Plainfield, IL 60544 815-436-7197
- **Sellars, Joseph: pg 1391** 2423 W 22nd St, Minneapolis, MN 55405...........**612-377-8766**
  fax: 612-377-5243
  Selman, Jan: 79 Pinecrest Bch Dr, E Falmouth, MA 02536 508-540-4586
  Seltzer Design & Illus, Meyer: 744 W Buckingham Pl, Chicago, IL 60657.........773-883-0964
  Seltzer, Isadore: 285 Riverside Dr #2B, New York, NY 10025 212-666-1561
  Selvage, Roger: 2148 Cartwright Pl, Reston, VA 22091..........................703-264-5325
  Selwyn, Paul: 68 Whiting Ln, W Hartford, CT 06119 203-523-5752
  Semler, Robert: 308 Highland Terr, Pitman, NJ 08071 609-589-6495
- **Sempé, Jean Jacques: pg 600** 155 W 15th St, New York, NY 10011 ....**212-989-8770**
  fax: 212-989-7892
  Semyon: 2650 Highway 238, Jacksonville, OR 97530............................541-899-7993
  Sena, Miyuki: 5403 Clearsite St, Torrance, CA 90505 310-316-0027
  Senn, Oscar: 1532 Riverside Ave, Jacksonville, FL 32204.........................904-358-1445
  Seong, Young-Shin: 25 W 13th St #4DN, New York, NY 10011 212-242-4592
  Serafin, Marsha: 690 Washington St #3A, New York, NY 10014 212-206-9212
  PO Box 1086, Taos, NM 87571 505-776-5435
  Sereta, Bruce: 3010 Parklane Dr, Cleveland, OH 44134.........................216-241-5355
  Serra, Mary C: 12819 McGee Dr, Whittier, CA 90602 888-696-1488
  Serrat-Sans: 43 E 19th St, New York, NY 10003 212-254-4996
  Serratt, Ron: PO Box 1510, Laytonville, CA 95454 707-984-6462

Servick, Roger: 1716 N Gardner St, Los Angeles, CA 90046 ... 213-850-5225
Sese, Maria: 7501 Holiday Terr, Bethesda, MD 20817 ... 301-405-4619
Sesto, Carl: 10 Rolfe's Ln, Newbury, MA 01951 ... 508-462-3783
• **Seth: pg 94,95** 108 E 35th St #2, New York, NY 10016 ... **212-889-3337**
url: www.theispot.com/artist/seth / fax: 212-889-3341
Settimi Creative & Co: 334 Cobblesprings Ct, Avon, IN 46168 ... 317-272-0882
Seun, Won Hwa: 1224 Kinnear Rd, Columbus, OH 43212 ... 614-292-3416
• **Sevalrud, Thom: pg 853** 280 Madison Ave, New York, NY 10016 ... **212-545-9155**
e-mail: Irmeli@aol.com / url: www.spar.org/holmberg / fax: 212-545-9462
Severtson, Jeff: 221 E 12th St #2, New York, NY 10003 ... 212-473-8086
Sexton, Brenda: 4477 Woodman Ave #102, Sherman Oaks, CA 91423 ... 818-995-8140
Sexton, Rob: 270 Business Ctr #210, Irvine, CA 92715 ... 714-474-7525
Shachat, Andrew: Box 1767, Soquel, CA 95073 ... 408-475-7544
Shadle, Kathlyn: 1809 7th Ave #1710, Seattle, WA 98101 ... 206-447-1600
Shaff, Tom: 1862 Selby Ave, St Paul, MN 55104 ... 612-645-3822
Shaffer, Allen: 955 Duvall Highway, Pasadena, MD 21122 ... 410-437-9042
Shaffer, Curtis: PO Box 66, Ringgold, PA 15770 ... 412-397-2340
Shafie, Taher: 1 Nordica Dr, Croton on Hudson, NY 10520 ... 914-271-6822
Shah, Shaheen: 9 Begonia Ct, Sayerville, NJ 08872 ... 908-238-8458
• **Shakirov, Fathulla: pg 750** 1464 Linden Ave, Chicago, IL 60035 ... **847-432-2415**
fax: 773-883-0375
Los Angeles ... **213-934-3395**
fax: 213-936-2757
Shamburger, Steve: 5315 Lamar, Mission, KS 66202 ... 913-384-6060
• **Shanahan, Danny: pg 600** 155 W 15th St, New York, NY 10011 ... **212-989-8770**
fax: 212-989-7892
Shannon, Bill: 6800 Millikin Rd, Middletown, OH 45044 ... 513-777-5418
Shannon, David: 1328 W Morningside Dr, Burbank, CA 91506 ... 818-563-6763
Shansky Works: 48 Lamson Rd, Barrington Rd, RI 02806 ... 401-247-2248
• **Shap, Sandra: pg 818** 853 Broadway #1201, New York, NY 10003 ... **212-677-9100**
e-mail: chislovsky@aol.com / fax: 212-353-0954
Shapiro, Diane E: 111 E14th St #136, New York, NY 10003 ... 212-387-9568
• **Shapiro, Neil: pg 1133** 3253 N Lakewood, Chicago, IL 60657 ... **773-975-9657**
e-mail: nshap981@aol.com / fax: 773-975-9659
Share Reeves Active Media: 1133 6th St, Santa Monica, CA 90403 ... 310-451-9695
• **Sharp Designs: pg 1393** ... **800-999-4417**
90 Arroyo Drive, Sedona, AZ 86336 ... **520-282-7696**
e-mail: sharp@kachina.net / url: www.showcase.com (and) www.di14.com (and) www.di15.com / fax: 520-204-6442
Sharp, Ann: PO Box 1251, New York, NY 10023 ... 212-774-4271
• **Sharp, Bruce: pg 1392** 15808 SE 47th St, Seattle, WA 98006 ... **425-373-4752**
• **Sharp, Chris: pg 787** 231 E 76th St #5D, New York, NY 10021 ... **212-535-0438**
fax: 212-535-1624
Shasky, Jane: PO Box 354, Hansville, WA 98340 ... 360-638-1276
Shaul, Wendy: 7556 Rio Mondego Dr, Sacramento, CA 95831 ... 916-429-0288
• **Shaver, Mark: pg 888** 16 Phaedra, Laguna Niguel, CA 92677 ... **949-495-3664**
fax: 949-495-0129
2334 Oak St, Los Angeles, CA 90405 ... **310-450-4336**
url: www.showcase.com / fax: 310-392-9978
• **Shaw Studio, Ned: pg 1130** 4950 Bethel Ln, Bloomington, IN 47408 ... **812-333-2181**
fax: 812-331-0420
Shaw, Barclay: 170 East St, Sharon, CT 06069 ... 860-364-5974
Shaw, Kurt: 206 W Prospect Ave, Pittsburgh, PA 15205 ... 412-922-5818
Shaw, Paul: 785 West End Ave #16A, New York, NY 10025 ... 212-666-3738
Shaw, Robin: 4617 Montrose Blvd #206, Houston, TX 77006 ... 713-520-5715
Shawver, Natasha: 2750 Adeline, Berkeley, CA 94703 ... 510-548-5349
Shay, RJ: 2029 Custer Pkwy, Richardson, TX 75080 ... 972-761-0500
Shea, Michael: 47 Maple St, Burlington, VT 05403 ... 802-864-5884
Sheaffer, Tim: New York, NY ... 212-674-8270
Sheban, Chris: 6723 N Lightfoot, Chicago, IL 60646 ... 773-792-9169
Shed, Greg: 716 Sanchez St, San Francisco, CA 94114 ... 415-285-8267
Sheean, Hugh: 1935 S Bentley, Los Angeles, CA 90025 ... 310-268-1137
Sheehan, Tom: 31 Marmion Rd, Melrose, MA 02176 ... 617-734-6038
Sheehy, Michael: 60 E 42nd St #822, New York, NY 10165 ... 212-682-1490
Sheerin, Sean: 13 Edmunds Pl, Wakefield, MA 01880 ... 617-245-6984
Shega, Marla: 60 E 42nd St #822, New York, NY 10165 ... 212-682-1490
Sheild, Lori: 13 Seneca St, E Northport, NY 11731 ... 516-261-2919
Shek, WE: 1315 Ebener St #4, Redwood City, CA 94061 ... 415-363-0687
Shelley Brown Associates: 155 Lippincott Street, Toronto, ON M5S 2P3 ... 416-505-9522
• **Shelly, Jeff: pg 1394** 2330 San Marco Dr, Los Angeles, CA 90068 ... **323-460-4604**
toll-free ... **800-314-3244**
e-mail: jlshelly@aol.com / url: www.showcase.com (and) www.theispot.com/artist/shelly / fax: 323-464-6630
Shelly, Ron: 6880 SW 80th St, Miami, FL 33143 ... 305-667-0154
Shelton, Daniel: 4333 St Catherine West, Montreal, QU H3Z1P9 ... 514-630-7810
Shelton, Dean: 7632 Crow Cut Rd SW, Fairview, TN 37062 ... 615-799-0409
Shelton, Will: 362 Quintard St, Chula Vista, CA 91911 ... 619-476-6629
Shepard, Steven T: 3661 Carambola Circle N, Pompano Beach, FL 33066 ... 800-603-AXIS
Shephard, James R: 108 W.Wells St #2-D, Milwaukee, WI 53203 ... 414-291-9817
Shephard, Tom: 401 Bounty Way #245, Avon Lake, OH 44012 ... 216-930-2811
• **Sheppard, Richard: pg 823** 1839 Ninth St, Alameda, CA 94501 ... **510-769-1421**
e-mail: ldmreps@earthlink.net / fax: 510-521-1674
Sherbo, Dan: 4208 38th St NW, Washington, DC 20016 ... 202-244-0474
Sheridan, Brian: 145 Main St, Ossining, NY 10562 ... 914-941-1738
Sheridan, Todd: 399 East State Rd, Pleasant Grove, UT 84062 ... 801-796-9777
Sherman, Gene: PO Box 35, Williamson, NY 14589 ... 315-589-8939
Sherman, John: Dept of Art-Art Hist & Des, Notre Dame, IN 46556 ... 219-631-5000
Sherman, Linda: 9825 Canal Rd, Gaithersburg, MD 20879 ... 301-590-0604
Sherman, Oren: 227 Godfrey Rd, Weston, CT 06883 ... 203-222-8777
Sherman, Paul: 1915 Storm Dr, Falls Church, VA 22043 ... 703-790-1105
Sherman, Whitney: 83 Walnut Ave, Corte Madera, CA 94925 ... 415-924-7881
Sherrill, Robert: 3207 1/2 Foothill Blvd, Pasadena, CA 91107 ... 818-769-1468
Sherwood, Ginny: 3123 Old Kettle Rd, San Diego, CA 92111 ... 619-569-4853
Sherwood, Stewart: 625 Yonge St #303, Toronto, ON M4Y 1Z5 ... 416-925-8528
Shieldhouse, Stephanie: 1468 Edgewood Cir, Jacksonville, FL 32205 ... 904-384-9475
Shields, Bill: 14 Wilmot, San Francisco, CA 94115 ... 415-346-0376
Shields, Sandra: 62 Burton St, Bristol, RI 02809 ... 401-253-1922
Shiff, Andrew Z: 153 Clinton St, Hopkinton, MA 01748 ... 508-435-3607
Shigley, Neil: 853 Broadway #1201, New York, NY 10003 ... 212-677-9100
Shilda, Joy Massen: 6037 11th Ave So, Minneapolis, MN 55417 ... 612-866-0358
Shilov: Montréal, QU ... 514-494-0647
Shilstone, Arthur: 42 Picketts Ridge Rd, W Redding, CT 06896 ... 203-438-2727
• **Shim, Jae: pg 1487** 5121 Klump Ave #201, N Hollywood, CA 91601 ... **818-752-1524**
url: members.aol.com/jshim9494
Shin, Young: 162-11 9th Ave #5C, Whitestone, NY 11357 ... 718-767-5668
Shinnick, Margie: 220 12th Ave, San Francisco, CA 94118 ... 415-221-4208
Shipman, Anna: 9-28 Steeplebush Rd, Essex Junctn, VT 05452 ... 802-878-5073
Shock, Steve: 441 Allen St #4, Waterloo, IA 50701 ... 319-236-0340
Shoemaker, Doug: 6100 Green Valley Dr #220, Minneapolis, MN 55438 ... 612-831-2123
Shoenke, Shad: 611 N Tenth St 6th Fl, St Louis, MO 63101 ... 314-421-3800
• **Shoffner Illustrator Inc., Terry: pg 1121**
11 Irwin St, Toronto, ON M4Y 1L1 ... **416-967-6717**
Shogren, Anne: 220 Raphael Ave #8, Ames, IA 50014 ... 515-753-6577
• **Shohet, Marti: pg 399** 250 W 57th St #521, New York, NY 10107 ... **212-397-7330**
url: www.lindgrensmith.com (and) www.stockillustrated.com
Short, Kevin: 666 Greenwich St #860, New York, NY 10014 ... 212-675-5719
3033 13th Ave W, Seattle, WA 98119 ... 206-284-4701
Short, Robbie: 2903 Bentwood Dr, Marietta, GA 30062 ... 770-565-7811
Shoshana Rama, Susan: PO Box 393, East Windsor Hill, CT 06028 ... 860-289-4248
Shtern, Adele: 11-21 47th Rd #3L, Long Island City, NY 11101 ... 718-706-6363
Shukan, Luis: 123 Hummingbird, Livingston, TX 77351 ... 409-327-2666
Shultz, David: 1118 E Platte Ave, Colorado Springs, CO 80903 ... 719-473-1641
Shumate, Michael: 198 Chelsea Rd, Kingston, ON K7M 3Y8 ... 613-384-5019
Sibai-Martinez, Suhair: 37352 Daybreak St, Palmdale, CA 93550 ... 805-274-1658
Sibayan, Noel: 362 Cromwell Ave, Staten Island, NY 10305 ... 718-595-0812
Siboldi, Carla: 7118 Upper River Rd, Prospect, KY 40059 ... 502-228-9427
10 Bloomfield Rd, Burlingame, CA 94010 ... 415-344-5069
• **Sibthorp, Fletcher: pg 310,311** 58 W 15th St, New York, NY 10011 ... **212-741-2539**
url: www.showcase.com / fax: 212-741-4660
Siebers, Tom: 10182 Whitnall Ct, Hales Corner, WI 53130 ... 414-425-6405
• **Siebert, Lori: pg 555** 7118 Upper River Rd, Prospect, KY 40059 ... **502-228-9427**
url: www.jettreps.com / fax: 502-228-8857
Siegal, Jennifer: 2006 Hyde St, San Francisco, CA 94109 ... 415-441-1443
Siegel Creative Graphics, Mark: 8 Perabo Terr, Boston, MA 02132 ... 617-923-9021
Siegel, Dink: 100 W 57th St #10G, New York, NY 10019 ... 212-246-9757
Siegel, Mark: 9 Babbling Brook Ln, Suffern, NY 10901 ... 914-368-8606
Siegel, Stuart: 106 High Plain St, Walpole, MA 02081 ... 508-668-5392
Siemer, Patrick: 1809 W Division St, Chicago, IL 60622 ... 773-862-4244
Sienkiewicz, Bill: 327 E 89th St #3E, New York, NY 10128 ... 212-831-5650
Sienkowski, Laurie: 199 Deer Run, Ada, MI 49301 ... 616-676-3040
Sigberman, Rich: 600 Second Ave, San Francisco, CA 94118 ... 415-668-8832
Signorino, Slug: 3587 N Cross Trail, LaPort, IN 46350 ... 219-879-5221
Sikorski, Tony: 237 4th Ave #413 Invstmnt Bld, Pittsburgh, PA 15222 ... 412-391-8366
Silbert, Barbara Bert: 40 W 24th St #7N, New York, NY 10010 ... 212-741-1915
Sillen, Kim: 200 E 16th St #5G, New York, NY 10003 ... 212-260-5671
Sillman, Mary: 2015 MW Flanders St, Portland, OR 97209 ... 541-344-1266
Silva, Raul: 3507 N Racine #B, Chicago, IL 60657 ... 773-549-0361
Silver Graphics: PO Box 51, Weedsport, NY 13166 ... 315-834-6738
• **Silver Kid: pg 366,367** 327 E 89th St #3E, New York, NY 10128 ... **212-831-5650**
fax: 212-831-6241
1306 Alabama St, Huntington Beach, CA 92648 ... **714-969-7766**
fax: 714-374-3744
Silver Moon Graphics: 57 S Monroe Ave, Columbus, OH 43205 ... 614-469-0847
Silver, Judy Reed: 1808 Manning Ave #103, Los Angeles, CA 90025 ... 310-474-7701
Silver, Stanley: 701 N Arden Dr, Beverley Hills, CA 90210 ... 310-285-0800
Silveria, Gordon: 284 Juanita Way, San Francisco, CA 94127 ... 415-731-8789
Silverman, Burt: 324 W 71st St, New York, NY 10023 ... 212-799-3399
Silverman, Marc: 62 W 70th St, New York, NY 10023 ... 212-595-5464
Silvers, Bill: 420 Lexington Ave, New York, NY 10170 ... 212-986-5680
Silvestri, Lorraine: 122 Plimpton St, Walpole, MA 02081 ... 508-668-0111
Silvi, Ann: 220 South 8th St #3, Philadelphia, PA 19107 ... 215-242-5876
Simanson, Greg: 2717 Western Ave, Seattle, WA 98121 ... 206-232-7873
• **Simard, Remy: pg 688** 666 Greenwich St #860, New York, NY 10014 ... **212-675-5719**
url: www.hkportfolio.com / fax: 212-675-6341
Simmons, Keith: 107 Kilbreck Dr, Cary, NC 27511 ... 919-387-0042
• **Simmons, Suzanne: pg 1456** 39 Hamilton Terr, New York, NY 10031 ... **212-283-3401**
url: www.wayart.com
Simnacher, Kevin: 951 32nd Ave SW, Cedar Rapids, IA 52406 ... 319-365-8025
Simon, Angela: 2512 E Thomas Rd #2, Phoenix, AZ 85016 ... 602-381-1332
Simon, BJ: 1766 Olive Ave, Vista, CA 92083 ... 619-726-6683
Simon, Dennis: 16312 Yeoho Rd, Sparks, MD 21152 ... 410-329-3983
Simon, Joel: 344 Mt View Lane, Colorado Springs, CO 80907 ... 719-594-0490
Simon, William: 9431 Bonhomme Woods, St Louis, MO 63132 ... 314-993-3522
Simons, Stuart: 24 Westchester Ave, Pound Ridge, NY 10576 ... 914-764-9424
Simpson, Craig: 1546 Powell St, Norristown, PA 19401 ... 215-279-0991
Simpson, Gretchen Dow: 117 Everett Ave, Providence, RI 02906 ... 401-331-4514
• **Simpson, Elizabeth: pg 796** 2491 W 22nd Ave, Vancouver, BC B6L 1M3 ... **604-684-6826**
url: www.repart.com / fax: 604-684-6826
Simpson, Suzanne: 306 E 86th Street #2B, New York, NY 10028 ... 212-620-2227
Sims, Ronald Bennett: 10609 Sandpiper Dr, Houston, TX 77096 ... 713-271-3703
• **Sinclair, Valerie: pg 210,211** 501 Fifth Ave, New York, NY 10017 ... **212-490-2450**
url: www.renardrepresents.com / fax: 212-697-6828
Singer Design, Paul: 494 14th St, Brooklyn, NY 11215 ... 718-499-8172
Singer, Phill: New York, NY ... 212-684-2974
Singleton, Bill: 809 W Wedwick St, Tucson, AZ 85706 ... 520-294-1667
Sinnen, Cherie: 2217 Canyon Dr, Los Angeles, CA 90068 ... 213-463-0868
• **Sinovcic, Miro: pg 424** 60 E 42nd St, New York, NY 10165-1940 ... **212-867-8092**
e-mail: DHLT@aol.com / url: www.HT-LTD.com / fax: 212-949-1977
Sipp, Geo: 4170 S Arbor Cir, Marietta, GA 30066 ... 770-924-4793
• **Sipple, Dan: pg 1395**
17062 Evergreen Circle, Huntington Beach, CA 92647 ... **714-848-7216**
url: http://members.aol.com/dansipple / fax: 714-848-2416

Siquis Ltd: 3600 Clipper Mill Rd #350, Baltimore, MD 21211 410-467-7300
Sir Real Labs: 16745 Maple St, S Holland, IL 60473 312-409-3160
Sirrell, Terry: 768 Red Oak Dr, Bartlett, IL 60103 630-213-9003
Sis, Peter: 252 Lafayette St #5E, New York, NY 10012 212-226-2203
• **Sisco, Sam: pg 972,973** 1561 Narva Rd, Mississauga, ON L5H 3H4 .... **905-278-2716**
fax: 905-278-2716
Sisti, Jerald: 436 Countrywood Ln, Encinitas, CA 92024 619-944-7836
• **Siu, Peter: pg 522,530** 89 Fifth Ave #901, New York, NY 10003 .... **212-627-1554**
fax: 212-627-1719
Sivavec, Diane: 60 E 42nd St #1940, New York, NY 10165 212-867-8092
Sizemore, Ted: 60 E 42nd St #1940, New York, NY 10165 212-867-8092
Sjoberg, Dick: 1343 Stratford Ct, Del Mar, CA 92014 619-458-1102
Skeen, Keith: 3228 Prairie Dr, Deerfield, WI 53531 608-423-3020
• **Skelton, Steve: pg 1396** 3205 5th St, Boulder, CO 80304 .... **303-546-0117**
fax: 303-546-0112
Skidmore, John: 1112 Morefield Rd, Philadelphia, PA 19115 215-698-9114
Skiles, Jacqueline: 236 W 27th St, New York, NY 10001 212-675-7932
Skillicorn, Mark: 1655 N Damen, Chicago, IL 60647 773-549-9548
Skillman, Angie: 1225 Jefferson St, Red Bluff, CA 96080 800-964-2788
Skinner, Cortney: 32 Churchill Ave, Arlington, MA 02174 617-648-2875
Sklar, Andy: 4574 N Finley Ave #6, Los Angeles, CA 90027 213-913-1446
Sklar, Herb: 4 Broadway #5, Valhalla, NY 10595 914-328-8880
Sklut, Meryl: 721 Pleasant Valley Way, W Orange, NJ 07052 201-669-8078
Skok, Przemyslaw: 763 Leonard St, New York, NY 11222 718-349-1625
Skolsky, Mark: 257 12th St, Brooklyn, NY 11215 718-499-1148
Skopp, Jennifer: 1625 Emmons Ave #6H, Brooklyn, NY 11235 718-646-2344
Skrzydlewski, Carolyn: 2140 Vallejo St #10, San Francisco, CA 94123 415-931-0940
Skutnik, Andy: 175 Round Lake Rd, Rhinebeck, NY 12572 914-876-5585
Skutz, Peter: 100 W 57th St #17G, New York, NY 10019 212-581-6579
Skygh, Michael: 38 Fresh River Ave, Hingham, MA 02043 617-749-3937
Skypeck, George: 15407 Overlea Ct, Accokeek, MD 20607 301-203-9136
Slabbers, Ronald: 32 W 31st St 5th Fl, New York, NY 10001 212-239-4283
Slack, Chuck: 60 E 42nd St #822, New York, NY 10165 212-682-1490
Slackman, Charles B: 320 E 57th St #16A, New York, NY 10022 212-758-8233
Slagle, Krystal: 166 St Joseph, Long Beach, CA 90803 310-433-8459
Slandorn, Peggy: RR1 Box 561A, Bloomsbury, NJ 08804 908-479-6745
Slark Design, Albert: 109 Jameson Ave #714, Toronto, ON M6K 2X2 416-536-3865
• **Slatsky, Tom: pg 432** 60 E 42nd St, New York, NY 10165-1940 .... **212-867-8092**
e-mail: DHLT@aol.com / url: www.HT-LTD.com / fax: 212-949-1977
Slattery, Jack: 14814 Heritage Wood Dr, Houston, TX 77082 713-558-2246
Sledd, John W: 60 E 42nd St #1940, New York, NY 10165 212-867-8092
Slemons, Jeff: 2555 Walnut St #LF, Denver, CO 80205 303-298-0807
Sloan, Lois: 21 Tennis Ct NW, Albuquerque, NM 87120 505-899-2262
• **Sloan, Michael: pg 944,945**
32 Gramercy Park S #13K, New York, NY 10003 .... **212-253-2047**
Sloan, Michael: PO Box 1397, Madison, TN 37116 615-865-7018
Sloan, Rick: 9432 Appalachian Dr, Sacramento, CA 95827 916-364-5844
Sloan, William: 236 W 26th St #805, New York, NY 10001 212-463-7025
Sloane, Sarah: 37 Schiller St, Pawtucket, RI 02860 401-727-3385
Slocym, Mike: NJ 908-362-9660
Slone Illustration: 833 W Main St, Louisville, KY 40202 502-585-4670
Slonim, David: 232 South St, Chesterfield, IN 46017 317-378-6511
• **Sloss, Tinka Anjali: pg 830**
1424 Las Positas Pl, Santa Barbara, CA 93105 .... **805-682-6775**
Santa Barbara, CA **805-898-9309**
e-mail: anjali@pacrain.com / url: www.rain.org/~anjali / fax: 805-687-1350
Slote, Bob: 851 N San Mateo Dr #H, San Mateo, CA 94401 415-343-2996
Slote, Elizabeth: 34 1/2 Beacon St, Boston, MA 02108 617-547-5539
Slygh, Michael: 38 Fresh River Ave, Hingham, MA 02043 781-749-3937
Small, David: 155 W 15th St #4C, New York, NY 10011 212-989-8770
Smallish, Craig: 777 N Michigan Ave #706, Chicago, IL 60611 312-337-7770
Smallwood, Bud: 1505 Lewis O'Gray Dr, Saugus, MA 01906 617-231-2075
Smallwood, Steve: 4702 Summer Creek Ln SE, Grand Rapids, MI 49508 616-249-2845
Smart, Randy: 348 Countess Dr, West Henrietta, NY 14586 716-359-7497
Smiglowski, Michal: 1 Melissa Dr, Pembroke, NH 03275 603-485-4032
Smith, Laura: 6545 Cahuenga Terr, Hollywood, CA 90068 213-467-1700
Smith Illustration, Raymond: 602 Willow Ave, Hoboken, NJ 07030 201-653-6638
• **Smith, Anne: pg 700-701, Cover Book 1**
6 Parker Rd, Arlington, MA 02174 .... **781-641-2787**
url: www.showcase.com / fax: 781-641-2244
Smith, Brett: 353 W 53rd St #1W, New York, NY 10019 212-682-2462
Smith, Christopher: 7954 Queens Rd, Glen Burnie, MD 21061 410-766-8743
Smith, CJ: 881 Church St, Woodburn, OR 97071 541-981-0095
Smith, Dan & Tracey: 353 W 53rd St #1W, New York, NY 10019 212-682-2462
Smith, Daniel: 1157 N 185 W, Orem, UT 84057 801-368-9816
Smith, Donald: PO Box 391, Athens, GA 30603 706-543-5555
• **Smith, Douglas: pg 274,275** 121 Madison Ave #5F, New York, NY 10016 ..... **212-683-1362**
fax: 212-683-1919
Smith, Eileen: 809 E 41st St, Savannah, GA 31401 912-233-3786
Smith, Ellen: 185 South Rd, Marlborough, CT 06447 203-295-0004
• **Smith, Elwood H: pg 1397** 2 Locust Grove Rd, Rhinebeck, NY 12572 .... **914-876-2358**
e-mail: elwood@pojonews.infi.net / url: www.showcase.com (and)
www.theispot.com/artist/esmith (and) www.elwoodsmith.com / fax: 914-876-5931
Smith, Fred: 760 E Naomi Ave Unit C, Arcadia, CA 91007 626-447-8333
Smith, Genine: 606 Montana Ave, Santa Monica, CA 90403 310-451-1039
Smith, Geoffrey P: 217 Greendale Dr, Dayton, OH 45429 937-294-2288
Smith, J Randall: PO Box 812, Colfax, CA 95713 916-885-2814
Smith, James Noel: 325 Wilson Way, Larkspur, CA 94939 415-927-4500
137 W 14th St #204, New York, NY 10011 212-337-0055
4606 Cedar Spring #1527, Dallas, TX 75219 214-559-0055
Smith, Jeffrey: 642 Marlton Ave #E22, Los Angeles, CA 90031 323-224-8317
• **Smith, Jere: pg 680** 2814 NW 72nd St, Seattle, WA 98117 .... **206-784-1136**
url: www.kolea.com / fax: 206-784-1171
Smith, John C: 101 Yesler #502, Seattle, WA 98104 206-447-1600
Smith, Joseph A: 169 John St 6th Fl, New York, NY 10038 212-825-1475
Smith, Keri: 468 Queen St E #104, Toronto, ON M5A 1T7 416-367-2446
Smith, Kirk: 492 Armstrong St, Columbus, OH 43215 614-464-0928
• **Smith, Laura: pg 966,967** 6545 Cahuenga Terr, Hollywood, CA 90068 .... **323-467-1700**
url: http://home.earthlink.net/~doretsmith/
New York, NY **212-206-9162**
Smith, Lee Fitzgerrell: 1815 Woodsman Ct, Placerville, CA 95677 916-626-8113
Smith, Leigh Ann: RR 1 Box 77, Coxsackie, NY 12051 518-731-6924
Smith, Linda: 42 Delavan St, Brooklyn, NY 11231 718-624-1906
Smith, Marcia: 112 Linden St, Rochester, NY 14620 716-461-9348
Smith, Mark T: 235 E 22nd St #13V, New York, NY 10010 212-679-9485
• **Smith, Marty: pg 1495** 3033 Scott Rd, Burbank, CA 91504 .... **714-962-0461**
e-mail: mstekart@aol.com
Smith, Mary Anne: 165 Perry St #4D, New York, NY 10014 212-691-3570
Smith, Pamela: 4434 Corinth Ave, Culver City, CA 90230 310-391-3637
Smith, Paul: 402 W Simmons St, Weatherford, TX 76086 915-676-8321
Smith, Randy: 577 S200 East #200, Salt Lake City, UT 84111 801-355-9541
Smith, Rick: 1236 Tranquilla Dr, Dallas, TX 75218 214-321-6264
Smith, Rick E: 1415 Oakland Blvd #202, Walnut Creek, CA 94596 510-938-8866
Smith, Roger: 239 N.W. 13th #205, Portland, OR 97209 503-226-8252
Smith, Ryle: 105 N Second St, Missaury Valley, IA 51555 712-642-2933
Smith, Samantha Carol: 3818 Greenmount Ave, Baltimore, MD 21218 301-243-6184
Smith, Sean C: 295 S Broadway #1W, Yonkers, NY 10705 914-376-0715
Smith, Tad: 2512 E Thomas Rd #2, Phoenix, AZ 85016 602-381-1332
Smith, Terry: 14333 Tyler St, Sylmar, CA 93402 818-362-3599
1713 Dryden Way, Crofton, MD 21114 301-858-0734
• **Smith, Theresa: pg 685** 666 Greenwich St #860, New York, NY 10014 ...... **212-675-5719**
url: www.hkportfolio.com / fax: 212-675-6341
Smith-Griswold, Wendy: 9 Babbling Brook Ln, Suffern, NY 10901 914-368-8606
Smock, Doug: 741 Astor St, Norristown, PA 19401 610-272-3182
• **Smola, Jim: pg 838** 165 E 32nd St, New York, NY 10016 .... **212-686-3514**
fax: 212-532-4302
Smolenski, Peter: 55 Olive St, Northampton, MA 01060 413-584-5105
Smolinski, Dick: PO Box 1086, Taos, NM 87571 505-776-5435
Smolla, Jim: 165 E 32nd St, New York, NY 10016 212-686-3514
Smollin, Mark: 232 Madison Ave #402, New York, NY 10016 212-889-8777
Smollin, Michael: 420 Lexington Ave, New York, NY 10170 212-986-5680
Smool, Carl: 1528 Valentine Pl S, Seattle, WA 98144 206-328-7920
Smyth, Amy: 10 Thrush Way, Medford, NJ 08055 609-953-5952
Smyth, Fiona: 51 Camden St, Toronto, ON M5V 1V2 416-703-1913
Smyth, Richard F: 1235 Glenview Rd, Glenview, IL 60025 847-998-8345
Smythe, Danny: Los Angeles, CA 213-934-3395
Chicago, IL 847-222-0337
Sneberger, Dan: New York, NY 212-486-9644
Sneed, Brad: 709 W 90th Terr, Kansas City, MO 64114 816-822-2024
Snelson, Kenneth: 140 Sullivan St, New York, NY 10012 212-777-0356
• **Snider, Jackie: pg 1398**
Concession 2 West #800, RR1, Warkworth, ON KOK 3K0 .... **705-924-1487**
Snodgrass, Steve: 837 W Grand Ave 4th Fl, Chicago, IL 60622 .... 312 633-0500
Snow, Scott: 99 Park Ave #210A, New York, NY 10016 800-398-9544
1537 S Main St, Salt Lake City, UT 84115 801-484-0419
Snure, Roger: Box 1294, Orleans, MA 02653 508-255-8667
Snyder, David: 4812 Burris Dr, Louisville, KY 40291 502-239-2075
Snyder, Emilie: 50 N Pine St #107, Marietta, PA 17547 717-426-2906
Snyder, Teresa & Wayne: 25727 Mountain Dr, Arlington, WA 98223 206-435-8998
• **So, Meilo: pg 715** 455 W 23rd St #8D, New York, NY 10011 .... **212-366-1893**
url: www.andtheart.com / fax: 212-604-9643
Sobel, June: 2131 Lindengrove St, Westlake Village, CA 91361 805-495-0626
Sobel, Phillip Eric: 80-15 41st Ave #128, Elmhurst, NY 11373 718-476-3841
Sobieski, Jean: 514 West End Ave #7C, New York, NY 10024 212-749-9691
Society of Illustrators/San Diego: PO Box 704, Cardiff, CA 92007 649-297-8675
Soderlind, Kirsten: 1529 Keyes Ave, Niskayuna, NY 12309 518-372-3577
Sofo, Frank: 32C Stratton Sq, E Hampton, NY 11937 516-324-6119
Soileau, Hodges: 177 Inlets Blvd, Nokomis, FL 34275 941-484-7113
• **Sokolova, Valerie: pg 383** 250 W 57th St #521, New York, NY 10107 .... **212-397-7330**
url: www.lindgrensmith.com(and) www.stockillustrated.com
Sokolowski, Ted: RD #2 Box 408, Lake Ariel, PA 18436 717-937-4527
Solie, John: PO Box 249, Seal Rock, OR 97376 541-454-8147
Sollers, James: 120 Rankin St, Rockland, ME 04841 207-622-8877
Solomon, Alana: 2123 Belmont Dr, Reidsville, NC 27320 910-342-1095
Solomon, Debra: 1 Hudson St 3rd Fl, New York, NY 10013 212-619-7900
Solotoff, Susan AM: 61 Terrace Ave, Floral Park, NY 11001 516-328-2393
Solovic, Linda: 3509 Humphrey St, St Louis, MO 63118 314-773-7897
Soltis, Linda DeVito: 58 W 15th St, New York, NY 10011 212-741-2539
Solvang-Angell, Diane: 425 Randolph Ave, Seattle, WA 98122 206-324-1199
Soma, Matthew: 12657 Elkwood St, N Hollywood, CA 91605 818-701-9845
Somers, Paul: 333 N Michigan Ave #1105, Chicago, IL 60601 312-263-6593
Somerville, Kevin: 85 High St, Jamestown, RI 02835 401-423-1263
Sommerfield, Heather: 115 W 16th St, New York, NY 10011 212-337-0881
Songero, Jay: 17858 Rose St, Lansing, IL 60438 708-849-5676
Soper, Patrick: 214 Stephens, Lafayette, LA 70506 318-233-1635
Sopin, Nan: 9 Bradley Dr, Freehold, NJ 07728 908-462-7154
Sorel, Edward: 156 Franklin St, New York, NY 10013 212-966-3949
Sorel, Madeline: 140 Jaffray St, Brooklyn, NY 11235 718-646-8404
Sorensen Illus, Marcos: 3740 25th St #305, San Francisco, CA 94110 415-282-5796
Sorensen, Robert: 22 Strathmore Ave, Milford, CT 06460 203-874-6381
Sorensen, Vibeke: 708 Barbara Ave, Solana Beach, CA 92075 619-350-4567
Soroka, Elise: 2100 Mary St #503, Pittsburgh, PA 15203 412-381-6264
Sorren, Joe: 906 W Summit #B, Flagstaff, AZ 86001 520-214-9980
• **Sotnick, Stephen J: pg 1399** 220 W Santa Fe Ave, Placentia, CA 92870 ..... **714-993-9099**
alternate **714-447-9050**
fax: 714-993-9098
Soukup, James: Route 1, Seward, NE 68434 402-643-2339
Soule, Robert Alan: 15229 Baughman Dr, Silver Spring, MD 20906 301-598-8883
Sours, Michael: 9229 215th St SW, Edmonds, WA 98020 206-771-2905
Sowash, Randy: 550 Sunset Blvd, Mansfield, OH 44907 419-756-7139
Soyka, Ed: 231 Lafayette Ave, Peekskill, NY 10566 914-737-2230

Spacek, Peter: 2 Deforest Rd, Montauk, NY 11954 516-668-9092
Spain, Valerie: 83 Franklin St, Watertown, MA 02172....................................617-923-1989
Spalenka, Greg: 21303 San Miguel St, Woodland Hills, CA 91364 888-295-5828
Spanfeller, Jim: Mustato Rd, Katonah, NY 10536 914-232-3546
Sparacio, Mark & Erin: 30 Rover Ln, Hicksville, NY 11801 516-579-6679
Sparkman, Gene: 138 Virginia Ave, Bridgeport, CT 06610 203-368-1371
Sparks, Richard: 7 Parkhill Ave, Norwalk, CT 06851 203-866-2002
Spaulding, Kevin: 38 Mountain View Ln, Vergennes, VT 05491 802-877-3291
Spear, Charles: 456 9th St #2, Hoboken, NJ 07030...201-798-6466
Spears, Brent: 102 S Roosevelt Ave, Pasadena, CA 91107 818-564-1255
• **Spearing, Craig: pg 873** 866 United Nations Plaza, New York, NY 10017 ....**212-644-2020**
url: www.spar.org
• **Spector, Joel: pg 1044,1045** 3 Maplewood Dr, New Milford, CT 06776.......**860-355-5942**
fax: 860-355-5370
Speer, Stephan: 6105 81st St, Middle Village, NY 11379...................................718-457-7641
Speer, Terry: 181 Forest St, Oberlin, OH 44074 216-774-8319
Speers, Pauline Cilmi: 133 N Montclair Ave, Dallas, TX 75208 214-943-2569
5393 Bulman Ave SE, Port Orchard, WA 98366 360-871-2800
Speidel, Sandra: 616 1/2 West St, Petaluma, CA 94952 707-765-1151
Spellman, Susan: 50 Fuller Brook Rd, Wellesley, MA 02181 781-235-8658
Spence, Jim: 2301 Collins Ave #1540, Miami Beach, FL 33139 305-673-4088
Spencer Studios, Mary: 7816 Connie Dr, Huntington Beach, CA 92648 714-848-4954
Spencer, Joe: 11201 Valley Spring Ln, Studio City, CA 91602 818-760-0216
Spencer, John: 23 Ganton St, London, England, UK WIV 1LA...........................71-287-9191
Spencer, Laurie: 140 Providence Ave, South Portland, ME 04106 207-799-4103
Spengler, Kenneth: 2668 17th St, Sacramento, CA 95818 916-441-1932
Spetseris, Steve: 2460 Peachtree Rd NW, Atlanta, GA 30305...........................404-881-6627
Speulda, William: 363 Diamond Bridge Ave, Hawthorne, NJ 07506 201-427-6661
• **Spiece, Jim: pg 1116** 6636 Quail Ridge Ln, Ft Wayne, IN 46804...............**219-436-9549**
Spilsbury, Simon: 60 E 42nd St #822, New York, NY 10165 212-682-1490
Spina-Dixon, Debra: 2714 SW Leah Ct, Portland, OR 97219 503-452-8050
Spino, Pete: 468 Queen St E #104, Toronto, ON M5A 1T7 416-367-2446
Spiral Design Studio: 915 Broadway, Albany, NY 12207 518-432-7976
Spiral Designs: 26280 Oriole Ave, Euclid, OH 44132 216-261-2987
Spirduso, Kenneth: 6800 Sugarbush Dr, Orlando, FL 32819 407-354-0827
Splanenka, Greg: 21303 San Miguel St, Woodland Hills, CA 91364 818-992-5828
Spohn, Cliff: 597 Riverside Ave, Westport, CT 06880.......................................203-226-4724
Spohn, David: 614 Ellsworth Dr, Silver Spring, MD 20910................................301-589-3461
Spohn, Sachi: 420 Lexington Ave PH, New York, NY 10170 212-986-5680
Spoke, Lena: 70 Nina St, Toronto, ON M5R 1Z6..416-535-5508
• **Spollen, Chris: pg 1400,1401**
362 Cromwell Ave, Ocean Breeze, NY 10305 ....**718-979-9695**
e-mail: cjspollen@aol.com / url: www.inch.com/~cspollen/ / fax: 718-979-8919
• **Spork Design, Inc.: pg 1034,1035**
400 Dublin Ave #140, Columbus, OH 43215...**614-228-0900**
fax: 614-228-0909
Sposato, John: 43 E 22nd St, New York, NY 10010...212-477-3909
Sposato, Tim: 377 Monarch St, Louisville, CO 80027...303-673-9092
Sprague, Dee: Rd #2 Box 2194, Middlebury, VT 05753 802-462-2453
Spransy, Tim: Lisa Lane, Dousman, WI 53118 414-965-3961
Spring, Janet: 1305 E55th Street, Chicago, IL 60615 773-643-0144
Springer, Roby: 8111 Walnut Ridge Rd, Lafayette, IN 47905.............................317-538-3433
• **Springer, Sally: pg 1403** 1510 N Thumb Point Rd, Fort Pierce, FL 34949 ......**561-467-0095**
Springett, Martin: 40 Wanless Ave, Toronto, ON M4N 1V6................................416-235-7803
Springs, John: 51 Pelham St, London, England, UK SW7 2NJ 1715-893433
• **Sprouls, Kevin: pg 998,999** 1 Schooner Ln, Sweetwater, NJ 08037 ....**609-965-4795**
e-mail: ksprouls@bellatlantic.net / fax: 609-965-4795
Sprouse, Ray: 4514 Travis St #220, Dallas, TX 75205.......................................214-526-2888
Sprout, Tobin: 68 E Franklin St, Dayton, OH 45459..937-433-8383
Spruch, Stephanie: 16340 Mayall St, North Hills, CA 91343 818-891-9705
• **Spurll, Barbara: pg 1404,1405**
366 Adelaide St E #436, Toronto, ON M5A 3X9...**416-594-6594**
fax: 416-601-1010
Spurlock, J David: 1705 Mariposa Dr, Dallas, TX 75228 214-324-3767
• **St Jacques Illustration Design: pg 1147**
60 Speedwell Ave, Morristown, NJ 07960...**800-70-TWINS**
url: www.stjacques.com
St Jivago Desanges: PO Box 24AA2, Los Angeles, CA 90024 213-931-1984
St John, Bob: 35 Village Rd 3rd Fl, Middleton, MA 01949..................................508-762-2417
• **St Pierre, Joe: pg 664,665** 227 Godfrey Rd, Weston, CT 06883 ....**203-222-8777**
e-mail: artcoct@snet.net / fax: 203-454-9940
Staada, Glenn: 490 Schooley Mt Rd, Hackettstown, NJ 07840 908-852-4949
Staake, Bob: 726 S Ballas Rd, St Louis, MO 63122...314-961-2303
• **Stabin, Victor: pg 443,1042,1043**
84-21 Midland Pkwy, Jamaica, NY 11432 ....**212-243-7688**
url: www.victorstabin.com
60 E 42nd St, New York, NY 10165-1904 ....**212-867-8092**
e-mail: DHLT@aol.com / url: www.HT-LTD.com / fax: 212-949-1977
Stabler, Barton: 419 Tremont Ave, Westfield, NJ 07090....................................908-789-7415
Stackhouse, Donna: 145 Newbury St #3, Portland, ME 04101............................207-774-4977
• **Stadler, Greg: pg 620,621** 5002 92nd Ave SE, Mercer Island, WA 98040.....**206-232-7873**
fax: 206-232-7908
Stafford, Rod: 1491 Dewey Ave, Rochester, NY 14615 716-647-6200
Stagg, James: 272 Bay Vista Circle, Sausalito, CA 94965 415-332-7856
Stahl, Nancy: 470 West End Ave #8-G, New York, NY 10024 212-362-8779
• **Staimer, Marcia: pg 1114** 6128 Stegen Dr, Alexandria, VA 22310 ....**703-960-4196**
e-mail: marsta@aol.com / url: www.theispot.com / fax: 703-960-5392
Stalking Rabbit: 115 Bridge St, Great Barrington, MA 01230 413-528-3236
Stallard, Peter: 60 E 42nd St #822, New York, NY 10165..................................212-682-1490
Stalmer, Marcia: 6128 Stegen Dr, Alexandria, VA 22310...................................703-960-4196
Stamm, Jan: 4808 Hawley Blvd, San Diego, CA 92116.......................................619-280-6205
• **Stampatori, Riccardo: pg 672,673** 2814 NW 72nd St, Seattle, WA 98117 ....**206-784-1136**
url: www.kolea.com / fax: 206-784-1171
Stamper, Taylor: PO Box 661, Ashland, OR 97520 541-535-7180
Stanford, Walter: 102 Piedmont Dr., Kannapolis, NC 20801 704-933-8787
• **Stankewicz, Steven: pg 725** 7 Washington Street, Beverly, MA 01915.........**978-921-0887**
e-mail: leighton@leightonreps.com / url: www.leightonreps.com / fax: 978-921-0223

Stanley, Anne: UK/Western Europe 186-543-565
Los Angeles, CA 213-688-742
Chicago, IL 312-663-550
Panama City, FL 904-747-841
New York, NY 212-643-089
468 Queen St E #104, Toronto, ON M5A 1T7 416-367-244
Stanley, Barbara: 851 Cabrillo Ave, Coronado, CA 92118 619-437-412
Stanley, Tom: 1741 Prospect Ave #4, Santa Barbara, CA 93103 805-687-122
Stansberry, Sharon: 10208 Stonehurst Dr, Escondido, CA 92026 619-741-500
Stansbury Ronsaville Wood Inc: 17 Pinewood St, Annapolis, MD 21401 301-261-866
Stanton, Mark: 67 Jonesboro St, McDonough, GA 30253 770-957-596
Stanton, Reggie: 500 S Park Ave #203, Winter Park, FL 32789 305-645-166
Stanziani, Diane: 7537 Ridge Ave, Philadelphia, PA 19128 215-483-531
Starace, Tom: 210 W 21st St #5RW, New York, NY 10011 212-207-705
Stargardt, Fred: 8014 Timberlane Dr, Tampa, FL 33615 813-884-472
Stark, Emma: 1209 Reynolds, Bryan, TX 77803..409-779-072
Stark, Jamie: 420 E 79th St #7B, New York, NY 10021 212-861-450
Starman, Sally: 195 Prospect Place, Brooklyn, NY 11238.....................................718-857-674
Starosta, Boris: 802 Rockland Ave, Charlottesville, VA 22902 804-979-393
• **Starr, Jim: pg 788** 353 W 53rd St #1W, New York, NY 10019.......................**212-682-246**
e-mail: info@amerartists.com / url: www.amerartists.com / fax: 212-582-0090
Starr-Taylor, Bridget: 9 Babbling Brook Ln, Suffern, NY 10901 914-368-860
Starrett, Terri: 19 Stuyvesant Oval, New York, NY 10009.......................................212-505-934
Stashenko, Kristin: 5 Suffolk Rd, Norfolk, MA 02056..508-528-412
Stasiak, Krystyna: 5421 N E River Rd #507, Chicago, IL 60656.............................773-380-403
Stasolla, Mario: 3557 Slate Mills Rd, Sperryville, VA 22740 800-789-938
Statz, Jan Foelker: 3600 Heather Ct, Middleton, WI 53562 608-836-077
• **Staud, Suzanne: pg 850** 525 Brannan St #406, San Francisco, CA 94107 .....**415-647-566**
url: www.girlrep.com / fax: 415-285-1102
Stavros Digital Art: 117 Brenda Crescent, Scarboro, ON M1K 3C8 416-410-456
Steadham, Richard: 14085 Ryon Court, Woodbridge, VA 22193 703-590-946
Steadman, Broeck: 455 W 23rd St #8D, New York, NY 10011 212-366-189
Steadman, ET: 18 Allen St, Rumson, NJ 07760 908-758-853
Steadman, Lee: 309 Walnut Rd, Pittsburgh, PA 15202 412-761-566
• **Steam Inc: pg 747** 1464 Linden Ave, Chicago, IL 60035.................................**312-222-033**
fax: 773-883-0375
Stearney, Mark: 108 E 35th St #2, New York, NY 10016 212-889-333
Steccati, Eve: 6300 Estates Dr, Oakland, CA 94611 510-339-018
Stedman Studio: 474 Greenwich St, New York, NY 10013...212-941-013
Steele, Mark: 686 Massachussetts Ave, Cambridge, MA 02139................................617-424-060
• **Steele, Robert Gantt: pg 394**
250 W 57th St #521, New York, NY 10107 ....**212-397-733**
url: www.lindgrensmith.com (and) www.stockillustrated.com
Steger, John J: 940 Tuxedo, St Louis, MO 63119 314-827-228
Stehney, Regina: 25591 Via Inez, San Juan Capistrano, CA 92675..........................714-496-165
Stehrenberger, Michiko: NY 212-979-049
Stein III, Robert: 1575 E McAndrews, Medford, OR 97504 541-857-061
• **Stein, August: pg 719** 7 Washington Street, Beverly, MA 01915......................**978-921-088**
e-mail: leighton@leightonreps.com / url: www.leightonreps.com / fax: 978-921-0223
Stein, Marion: PO Box 1333, Lake Grove, NY 11755 516-981-068
Stein, Myron: 303-871-925
Steinberg, Eran: 372 Douglass St, San Francisco, CA 94114.....................................415-647-728
• **Steinberg, James: pg 96,97** 108 E 35th St #2, New York, NY 10016 ....**212-889-333**
url: www.theispot.com/artist/steinberg / fax: 212-889-3341
Steine, Debra: 6561 Green Gables Ave, San Diego, CA 92119 619-698-585
Steiner, Frank: 60 E 42nd St #1940, New York, NY 10165 212-867-809
Steiner, Joan: Rte 9H Box 130, Claverack, NY 12513 518-851-719
Steiner, Peter: 1948 Rockingham St, McLean, VA 22101 703-237-957
Steiner, Shawn: 117 E Colorado Blvd #300, Pasadena, CA 91105................................818-577-162
Steininger, Otto: Chicago, IL 312-663-550
Panama City, FL 904-747-841
Los Angeles, CA 213-688-742
468 Queen St E #104, Toronto, ON M5A 1T7 416-367-244
636 Broadway #1218, New York, NY 10012 212-982-522
UK/Western Europe, ...186-543-565
• **Steirnagle, Michael: pg 635** 5 E 17th St 6th Fl, New York, NY 10003 ....**212-691-266**
url: www.spar.org / fax: 212-633-1844
4 E Ohio Studio B, Chicago, IL 60611...**312-321-133**
fax: 312-321-1350
• **Stentz, Nancy: pg 1445** Seattle, WA **206-634-188**
fax: 206-632-2024
Stepanek, Michael: 200 W 15th St, New York, NY 10011 212-243-420
• **Stephanos, Dale: pg 1050,1051** 11 Shaw Pl, Foxboro, MA 02035......................**508-543-250**
url: www.theispot.com/artist/stephanos
• **Stephens, John: pg 666,667** 227 Godfrey Rd, Weston, CT 06883...........................**203-222-877**
e-mail: artcoct@snet.net / fax: 203-454-9940
Stergulz, Richard: 401 N Wabash, Chicago, IL 60611 312-527-035
3850 Eddingham Ave, Calabasas, CA 91302 818-222-544
Sterman, Sally: 195 Prospect Pl, Brooklyn, NY 11238...718-857-674
• **Stermer, Dugald: pg 1108** 600 Embarcadero, San Francisco, CA 94107 ......**415-777-011**
fax: 415-777-0177
110 Sutter St #706, San Francisco, CA 94104 ....**415-441-438**
Stern, Kalika: PO Box 808, S Fallsburg, NY 12779 914-436-405
Sternberg, Debra: 2151 California St NW #404, Washington, DC 20008.........................202-483-788
Sterrett, Jane: 160 Fifth Ave #700, New York, NY 10010..212-929-256
Steuer, Sharon: 205 Valley Rd, Bethany, CT 06524 203-393-398
Steunenberg, Peg: 2541 Rolling Hills Ct, Alamo, CA 94507..510-820-102
Steven, Daniel: 16923 Edgewater Ln, Huntington Beach, CA 92649.....................................714-846-463
Stevens & Stevens: 328 Brett Rd, Rochester, NY 14609...716-288-862
Stevens, Alex: 2816 Burkshire Ave, Los Angeles, CA 90064...310-473-693
Stevens, Darrel: 420 W 7th St, Cortland, NE 68331 402-798-215
• **Stevens, Daryl: pg 1498,1499** 6 Jones St #5D, New York, NY 10014...........................**212-741-161**
e-mail: dstevens@studio202.com / url: www.studio202.com / fax: 212-620-4145
Stevens, Heidi: 20 Tenth St, Petaluma, CA 94952 707-769-125
Stevens, Roy: 1349 Lexington Ave, New York, NY 10128..212-831-349
• **Stevenson, David: pg 488,489** 2149 Lyon St #5, San Francisco, CA 94115 ...**415-921-714**
e-mail: art@conradreps.com / url: www.conradreps.com / fax: 415-921-3939

Stevenson, Leo: PO Box 1251, New York, NY 10023 212-774-4271
Stevenson, Nancy: 43 E 19th St, New York, NY 10003 212-254-4996
Stewart, Bryan: CP 325 succ Westmount, Montréal, QU H3Z 2T5 514-983-9020
• **Stewart, Don: pg 449** 731 N 24th St, Philadelphia, PA 19130 ....**215-232-6666**
  url: www.deborahwolfeltd.com / fax: 215-232-6585
Stewart, John: 11323 Ulythe St, Sun Valley, CA 91352 213-875-2012
Stewart, Jonathan: 1530 Spruce St, Philadelphia, PA 19102 215-546-3649
• **Stewart, JW: pg 408,409** 250 W 57th St #521, New York, NY 10107 ......**212-397-7330**
  url: www.lindgrensmith.com (and) www.stockillustrated.com
Stewart, Neil: 77 Mowat Ave #216, Toronto, ON M6K3E3 416-516-3535
Stewart, Perry: 2200 Skyview Dr, Cedar City, UT 84720 435-865-0014
Stieferman, Guy: 5744 Magnolia Woods Dr, Bartlett, TN 38134 901-372-2902
Stiglich, Joyce: 11440 Oak Dr, Shelbyville, MI 49344 616-672-5756
  727 Forest Glen Ct, Maitland, FL 32751 407-644-5294
STIK: 23 Ganton St, London, England, UK WIV 1LA 71-287-9191
Stiles, Pat: 117 Brooks Ave, Venice, CA 90291 310-396-2186
Stiles, Steve: 1820 Rockcrest Rd, Richmond, VA 23235 804-320-0805
• **Still, Kyle: pg 130** 420 Lexington Ave, New York, NY 10170...................**212-986-5680**
  url: www.mendolaart.com / fax: 212-818-1246
Still, Wayne Anthony: 3850 Eddingham Ave, Calabasas, CA 91302 818-222-5445
Stillman, Susan: 25 Alexander Ave, White Plains, NY 10606 914-682-3771
Stimson, David: 201 W 21st St #10G, New York, NY 10001 212-807-0840
Stimson, James: 600 34th Ave #12, San Francisco, CA 94121 415-751-7366
Stineman, Mark: 1400 S Highway Dr, Fenton, MO 63099 314-827-1417
Stinson, James: 600 34th St #12, San Francisco, CA 94121 415-751-7366
• **Stirnweis, Shannon: pg 520**
  217 E 86th St Box 212, New York, NY 10028 ....**212-427-5632**
  fax: 212-427-6372
Stivell, Alain: 1440 Engracia Ave #B, Torrance, CA 90501 310-328-4011
Stock, Jeffrey: 10 Doaks Ln, Marblehead, MA 01945 617-639-8384
Stockstill, Mark: 4501 Lyons Rd, Miamisburg, OH 45342 513-866-4013
Stoddard, David: 1426 Welch, Arkadelphia, AR 71923 501-246-6163
• **Stoddard, Paul: pg 1406** 524 Main St, Stoneham, MA 02180 ....**781-438-0266**
  e-mail: pstodd8434@aol.com / fax: 781-438-0266
Stoecker, JJ: 19009 Hakes Rd, Edelstein, IL 61526..................................309-249-6891
• **Stokes, Lee: pg 1468** 121 S Eighth St #825, Minneapolis, MN 55402........**612-339-5770**
  e-mail: lstokes@intxxnet.com / url: retoucher.com / fax: 612-338-2080
Stolper, Karen: 160 W 16th St #1M, New York, NY 10011 212-675-5150
Stone, David K: 106 Stoneybrook, Chapel Hill, NC 27516 919-929-0853
Stone, Misty: 920 Golf Course Dr, Rohnert Pk, CA 94928 707-586-0986
Stone, Petula: 23 Ganton St, London, England, UK WIV 1LA 71-287-9191
Stone, Sandra: 20426 Delight St, Canyon Country, CA 91351 805-252-4915
Storey, Lee: 6565 Green Valley Cir #306, Culver City, CA 90230.................310-670-3477
Storozuk, Walter: 99 Park Ave #210A, New York, NY 10016 800-398-9544
Story, Karl: 3104 Mercer University Dr #100, Atlanta, GA 30341 770-986-0453
Stott, Dorothy: 666 Greenwich St #860, New York, NY 10014 212-675-5719
Stouffer, Stephanie: RR 1 Box 196, Belmont, VT 05730............................802-259-2686
Stout, Tim: 135 W Dorothy Ln #205, Dayton, OH 45429 513-298-5133
Strachan, Bruce: 999 Lorimer St, Brooklyn, NY 11222 718-383-1264
Strandell Design Inc: 218 E Ontario, Chicago, IL 60611 312-943-7553
Stranovsky, John: 6206 Eastern Pkwy, Baltimore, MD 21206 410-254-9122
Stratton, Mary M: 7708 Etiwanda, Reseda, CA 91335 818-757-1921
Stratton, Robert: 225 Sterling Pl #2H, Brooklyn, NY 11238 212-353-3123
Stratton, Thalia: 680 W Sunnyoaks Ave, Campbell, CA 95008 408-395-1463
Straub, Matt: 207 Avenue B, New York, NY 10009 212-995-9359
Straub, Philip: 50 Laurel Dr, Monroe, CT 06466 203-261-4334
Strauss, Matthew: 1021 Park Ave #3R, Hoboken, NJ 07030 201-798-5127
Strauss, Pamela: 160 W Brookline St, Boston, MA 02118 617-859-8766
Strauss, Ron: 2469 University Ave W, St Paul, MN 55114 612-644-7244
Strawn, Susan: 1216 W Olive St, Ft Collins, CO 80521 970-493-0679
Straznitskas, Matt: 119 Naubac Ave, East Hartford, CT 06118....................860-569-0035
• **Strebel, Carol: pg 1126** 2930 Hackberry St, Cincinnati, OH 45206 ....**513-281-6837**
  fax: 513-281-4213
Street, Janet: 15 Warrenton Ave, Hartford, CT 06105................................860-523-4562
Streeter, Eric: 1776 Bicentenial Way #6, N Providence, RI 02911 401-233-0414
Streetworks Studio: 13908 Marble Stone Dr, Clifton, VA 22024 703-631-1650
Streff, Michael: 3735 S Berkley Cir, Cincinnati, OH 45236 513-985-0568
Strelecki, Karen: 848 Greenwood Ave NE, Atlanta, GA 30306 404-875-1363
Stribling-Sutherland, Kelly: 1208 San Gabriel Dr, Denton, TX 76205 817-382-1253
Strode, Brad: 236 Old Gradyville Rd, Glen Mills, PA 19342 215-358-5088
Stromoski, Rick: 19 Stuyvesant Oval #2D, New York, NY 10009 212-505-9342
Stroster, Maria: 200 W 15th St, New York, NY 10011 212-243-4209
Stroud, Steven: 1031 Howe Ave, Shelton, CT 06484 203-924-2460
• **Struthers, Doug: pg 728,729,1472,1473**
  300 E 46th St #4G, New York, NY 10017 ....**212-687-6463**
  e-mail: sara@levycreative.com / fax: 212-661-4839
  227 Godfrey Rd, Weston, CT 06883 ....**203-222-8777**
  e-mail: artcoct@snet.net / url: www.portfolios.com/illustrators/artco
  / fax: 203-454-9940
Struve-Dencher, Goesta: #303 750 E 7th Ave, Vancouver, BC V5T 4H5 604-872-3439
• **Struzan, Drew: pg 98,99** 108 E 35th St #2, New York, NY 10016 ....**212-889-3337**
  url: www.theispot.com/artist/struzan & www.drewstruzan.com / fax: 212-889-3341
• **Stuart, Walter: pg 1407** 716 Sanchez St, San Francisco, CA 94114 ....**415-285-8267**
  e-mail: Salzman@designlink.com
  7460 Girard St #7, La Jolla, CA 92037 ....**619-455-5573**
  fax: 619-455-5519
  NY, NY..**212-997-0115**
Stubbs, Barbara: 8447 Mica Way, Citrus Hts, CA 95610 916-722-9982
• **Stubbs, Charles: pg 1131** 638 Cordelia Dr #1, Santa Rosa, CA 95405 ....**707-544-8358**
  fax: 707-544-8358
Stubbs, Diane N: 8855 Mia Moore Ave, Las Vegas, NV 89117 702-871-2711
Stubbs, Elizabeth: 27 Wyman St, Arlington, MA 02174 617-646-0785
Stubbs, Tommy: 5134 Timber Trail NE, Atlanta, GA 30342 404-255-1430
Stuck, Marion: 1088 Diamond Ct, Mississauga, ON L5Y1J5........................416-567-1493
• **Studer, Gordon: pg 312** 58 W 15th St, New York, NY 10011 ....**212-741-2539**
  url: www.showcase.com / fax: 212-741-4660

Studio 202: 215 W 10th St #4B, New York, NY 10014 212-741-1610
Studio Liddell: 217 E 86th St Box 212, New York, NY 10028......................212-427-5632
Studio M: 3088 Walnut Ave, Long Beach, CA 90807 562-426-1888
  60 E 42nd St #505, New York, NY 10165..212-682-1490
• **Studio M D: pg 1349-1351** 1512 Alaskan Way, Seattle, WA 98101..........**206-682-6221**
  e-mail: glenn@studiomd.com / url: www.studiomd.com / fax: 206-682-6283
Studio Productions, Inc: 650 N Bronson Ave #223, Los Angeles, CA 90004 213-856-8048
• **Studio Zocolo: pg 1068** San Anselmo, CA......................................**415-488-4710**
  fax: 415-458-8605
Studt, Alan: 8575 Broadview Rd, Broadview Heights, OH 44147 216-546-1274
Stuhmer, Robert: 26 W 17th St 6th Fl, New York, NY 10011 212-366-9776
Sturdivant, Ray: 4131 N Central #670, Dallas, TX 75204............................214-520-3383
• **Sturm, Linda: pg 1408** 1763 Dogwood Dr, Yorktown Heights, NY 10598.....**914-245-7981**
  e-mail: lswm@aol.com / fax: 914-245-0297
Sturman, Sally Mara: 853 Broadway #606, New York, NY 10003 212-777-6777
Sturtz, Donald Prescott: Campbell, CA 408-370-7106
Stutesman, Deborah Howard: 14378 Country Rd, Lyons, OH 43533 419-335-3340
• **Stutzman, Mark & Laura: pg 1056,1057**
  100 G St, Mt Lake Park, MD 21550 ....**301-334-4086**
  fax: 301-334-4186
• **Stymest, Brian: pg 1457** 39 Hamilton Terr, New York, NY 10031 ....**212-283-3401**
  url: www.wayart.com
Su, Hui-Ching: 2824 Felicia Way, Vista, CA 92084...................................619-945-9166
Sucher, Laurie: 6718 N Newgard, Chicago, IL 60626 773-764-2692
Suchit, Stu: 117 Jayne Ave, Port Jefferson, NY 11777 516-928-6775
Suh, Ellen: 500 S Lake St #411, Los Angeles, CA 90057............................213-483-8683
Suh, John: 165 E 32nd St, New York, NY 10016 212-686-3514
Suhre, James: 17 Greenwich Ave #11, New York, NY 10014 212-647-9734
Sukut, Arlo D: 205 Sunset Dr #26, Sedona, AZ 86336 520-204-2143
Sullivan, Dan: 941 S Orem Blvd, Orem, UT 84058 801-235-9191
• **Sullivan, Don: pg 744** 865 Delaware St, Denver, CO 80204 ....**303-820-2599**
  toll-free...**800-417-5120**
  url: www.artagent.com / fax: 303-820-2598
Sullivan, Donna: 10101 Foothills Blvd, Roseville, CA 95678 916-786-3800
Sullivan, James: 150 Grove Ave, Woodbridge, NJ 07095............................908-750-8747
Sullivan, Melinda May: 834 Moultrie St, San Francisco, CA 94110 415-648-2376
Sullivan, Pat: 29 Elmstead, Trumbull, CT 06611 203-628-1623
Sullivan, Robert M: 232 Madison Ave #402, New York, NY 10016 212-889-8777
Sullivan, Steve: 99 Park Ave #210A, New York, NY 10016 800-398-9544
Sully, Tom: 124 Wentworth St, Charleston, SC 29401 803-723-2734
Sulski, Victoria: PO Box 7709, Santa Cruz, CA 95061..............................408-426-4247
Sume, Debbie: 1936 S Lake St, Salt Lake City, UT 84105 801-487-8270
Sumichrast, Jozef: 501 Fifth Ave, New York, NY 10017 212-490-2450
Summerlin, Stephanie: 6895 Bolling Brook Cove, Memphis, TN 38138 901-751-0044
• **Summers, Mark: pg 276,277**
  121 Madison Ave #5F, New York, NY 10016 ....**212-683-1362**
  fax: 212-683-1919
Sumption, Brian F: 712 Concord St NW, Massillon, OH 44646 216-832-8453
Sundog Ltd/Gallucci Studio: 147 W 25th St, New York, NY 10001 212-675-0097
• **Sundwall, John: pg 1409** 509 Fulton St, Binghamton, NY 14892..............**607-565-3375**
Surman, Thomas: 446 Old Newport Blvd #201, Newport Beach, CA 92663.......714-650-3884
• **Susynski, Kenneth: pg 1072** 3938 Interlake Ave N, Seattle, WA 98103.......**206-632-7292**
  url: www.showcase.com / fax: 206-547-6408
Sutherland, Emma: 22 Wakefield Rd, Brighton, England, UK N2 3FP...............1273-673980
Sutherland, Kelly Stribling: 137 W 14th St #204, New York, NY 10011 212-337-0055
Sutliff, Joe: 14600 Farming Way, Centreville, VA 20120 703-968-6852
Sutton, Andrea Boff: 121 Nantasket Ave #808, Hull, MA 02045 781-925-8556
Sutton, Eva: 158 Spring St #3, New York, NY 10012 212-343-0952
• **Sutton, Jason: pg 668,669** 227 Godfrey Rd, Westport, CT 06883 ....**203-222-8777**
  e-mail: artcoct@snet.net / url: www.thoughtfoundry.com/artco.html / fax: 203-454-9940
Sutton, Jeremy: 245 Everett Ave, Palo Alto, CA 94301 415-325-3493
Sutton, Judith: 41 W Ferry St, New Hope, PA 18938.................................215-862-9771
Sutton, Ward: 104 McDougal St #19, New York, NY 10012........................212-460-9527
Suvityasiri, Sarn: 2419 Bonar St, Berkeley, CA 94702................................510-548-8218
Suzdaltseva, Jenny: 4735 Sepulveda Blvd #358, Sherman Oaks, CA 91403 818-981-4311
Svolos, Maria: 1635 W Chase Ave, Chicago, IL 60626 773-338-4675
Swaine, Mike: 6735 N 10th Pl, Phoenix, AZ 85014...................................602-264-5400
• **Swales, Scott: pg 1410** 419 Main St, Phoenix, NY 13135 ....**315-695-4519**
Swaminathan, S: PO Box 1547, Captola, CA 95010 408-722-3301
Swan, Joan: 133 N Montclair Ave, Dallas, TX 75208 214-943-2569
Swan, Sara: 2466 Moreno Dr, Los Angeles, CA 90039 213-661-4707
Swan, Susan: 1300 Ravenwood Dr, Arlington, TX 76013 817-265-1928
Swanson, James: 15 Richmond Ave, La Grange Park, IL 60526 708-352-3081
Swanson, Robert: 60 E 42nd St #1940, New York, NY 10165 212-867-8092
Swarts, Jeff: 308 S Cedar St, Danville, OH 43014 614-599-6516
Swartzback, Michael: 214 5th St NE, Washington, DC 20002 202-547-6217
Swasey, Scott: 1234 Earlham St, Pittsburgh, PA 15205 412-922-8560
Sweeney, Jerry: 1644 Beryl Dr, Pittsburgh, PA 15227 412-391-4471
Sweeney, Robert: 3925 Dolphin Cir, Colorado Springs, CO 80918 719-594-8857
Sweeny, Glynis: 3286 Ivanhoe, St Louis, MO 63139 314-781-7377
Sweet, Brian: 145 E Palatine Rd, Palatine, IL 60067 847-359-2608
• **Sweet, Melissa: pg 1105** 29 West St, Portland, ME 04102 ....**207-772-4850**
  fax: 207-874-7649
Sweetland, James: 16 Burnham Rd, Toronto, ON M4G 1C1 416-424-2101
Sweetland, Sally: Bridge St, Market Pl PO Box 334, Waitsfield, VT 05673........802-496-5759
Sweetlight Creative Partners: 11516 Sixth Ave NW, Seattle, WA 98177...........206-364-9077
Swenarton, Gordon: Lake Trial East, Morristown, NJ 07960........................908-953-0553
Swendsen, Paul: 4630 Fulton St, San Francisco, CA 94121 415-668-1077
Sweny, Stephen: 3121 Hollywood Dr, Decatur, GA 30033..........................404-299-7535
Swift, Elvis: 817 S Westwood Dr, Minneapolis, MN 55416 612-374-3169
Swift, Gary: 8 Hague Park Ln, S Kirkby, Pontefract,
  W Yorkshire, England, UK WF9 3SS 1977-646431
Swimm, Tom: 33651 Halyard Dr, Laguna Niguel, CA 92677 714-496-6349
Sych, Paul: 1179A King St W #112, Toronto, ON M6K 3C5.........................416-539-9977
Sylvada, Peter: 2327 Oxford Ave, Cardiff By the Sea, CA 92007 760-436-6807

Syme, Alec: 5051 Drew Ave S, Minneapolis, MN 55410 612-827-4510
Syme, Hugh: 3868 S Spiceland Rd, New Castle, IN 47362 765-529-0978
Symington, Gary: 2652 Volley Ln, Meadow Vista, CA 95722 916-878-6876
Syntax: 19 Los Amigos Ct, Orinda, CA 94563 510-253-3131
Syron, Colleen: 3 W 18th St 8th Fl, New York, NY 10011 212-807-0717
Syska, Richard: 1830 W Foster, Chicago, IL 60640 773-728-2738
Sysko, Ray: 300 E 33rd St #20L, New York, NY 10016 212-598-9710
Syverson, Henry: 950 Klish Way, Del Mar, CA 92014 619-259-5774
Szabo, Gustav: 380 Riverside Dr #5H, New York, NY 10025 212-663-1106
Szotak, Matt: 19 Niles Ave, Middletown, NJ 07748 908-671-3274
Szpura, Beata: 48-02 69th St, Woodside, NY 11377 718-424-8440
Szpura, Beata: 3033 13th Ave W, Seattle, WA 98119 206-284-4701
Szumowski, Tom: 221 Bigelow St, Marlborough, MA 01752 508-480-8757

T

Taback, Simms: 98 Hickory Rd, Willow, NY 12495 914-688-2605
Tachiera, Andrea: 7416 Fairmount Ave, El Cerrito, CA 94530 510-525-3484
Taff, Jim: 3467 Beldeer Dr, St Charles, MO 63303 314-441-0366
Tagel, Peggy: 666 Greenwich St #860, New York, NY 10014 212-675-5719
Taggart, Sean: 450 Broadway, Hastings-on-Hudson, NY 10706 914-478-8221
Taglianetti Illus, Clare: 256 Iven Ave #3A, Saint Davids, PA 19087 610-429-3774
Taglianetti, Clare: 280 Madison Ave #1110, New York, NY 10016 212-545-9155
Takagi, Michael: 60920 Larsen Rd, Bend, OR 97702 541-385-3263
Takahashi, Hideko: 637 S Cloverdale Ave #10, Los Angeles, CA 90036 213-938-8587
Talany, Keith: 6701 De Soto #106, Canoga Park, CA 91303 818-715-9095
Talaro, Lionel: 716 W Chase Ave, El Cajon, CA 92020 619-441-8545
32 W 40th Street, New York, NY 10018 212-575-6877
• **Talbot, Jim: pg 140** 420 Lexington Ave, New York, NY 10170 ....**212-986-5680**
url: www.mendolaart.com / fax: 212-818-1246
Taleporos, Plato: 333 E 23rd St #2EE, New York, NY 10010 212-689-3138
Tallant, Judy: 15215 50th Place W, Edmonds, WA 98026 425-742-9355
Tamura, David: 99 Park Ave #210A, New York, NY 10016 800-398-9544
Tanabe, Hiroshi: 32 Downing St #4D, New York, NY 10014 212-633-1310
Tanaka, Lynn: 4018 W 44th St, Edina, MN 55424 612-926-8923
Tanaka, Yasuo: 1 Irving Pl #U-12-B, New York, NY 10003 212-995-7730
• **Tanenbaum, Robert: pg 154** 420 Lexington Ave, New York, NY 10170 ....**212-986-5680**
url: www.mendolaart.com / fax: 212-818-1246
Tank, Darrel: 716 Montgomery St, San Francisco, CA 94111 415-433-1222
Tankersley, Paul: 29 Bethune St, New York, NY 10014 212-924-0015
Tanner, Sharon: 1766 Mandeville Cyn Rd, Los Angeles, CA 90049 310-496-1501
Tanovitz, Ron: 300 Commercial St #807, Boston, MA 02109 617-742-3108
6300 Estates Dr, Oakland, CA 94611 510-339-0182
Tapscott, Linda: 35212 Cand Ct, Freemont, CA 94536 510-792-6362
Tarabay, Sharif: 597 Riverside Ave, Westport, CT 06880 203-226-4724
Montreal, QU H3H 1J1 514-933-0261
Taranovic, Lydia: 280 Madison Ave #1110, New York, NY 10016 212-545-9155
Tarantolla, Daniel: 3 Ernest Ct, Kings Park, NY 11754 516-544-4387
• **Targete, Jean: pg 435** 60 E 42nd St, New York, NY 10165-1940 ....**212-867-8092**
e-mail: DHLT@aol.com / url: www.HT-LTD.com / fax: 212-949-1977
Tarleton, Suzanne: 1740 Stanford St, Santa Monica, CA 90404 310-859-7563
Tarlow, Phyllis: 131 Lawrence Pl, New Rochelle, NY 10801 914-235-9473
Tarr-Memmons, Tina: 145 Newbury St, Portland, ME 04104 207-828-9454
• **Tarrish, Laura: pg 1411** 2450 SW Sherwood Dr, Portland, OR 97201 ....**503-224-8686**
Tate, Don: 2022 Nash Dr, Des Moines, IA 50314 515-288-9155
Tatnall, Runcle: 5011 Mineola Rd, College Park, MD 20740 301-220-1821
• **Taugher, Larry: pg 670,671** 227 Godfrey Rd, Westport, CT 06883 ....**203-222-8777**
e-mail: artcoct@snet.net / fax: 203-454-9940
Taulmann, Derek: Dallas, TX 214-880-0888
Tauss, Herbert: South Mountain Pass, Garrison, NY 10524 914-424-3765
Tauss, Marc: 484 W 43rd St #40H, New York, NY 10036 212-410-2827
Tave, Sara: 28 Leigh Dr, Lakewood, NJ 08701 908-367-7723
Tavonatti, Mia: 440 Bolero Way, Newport Beach, CA 92663 714-646-6596
Taxali, Gary: 9 Hanna # Y-10, Toronto, ON M6K 1W8 212-807-6627
New York, NY 212-338-1334
Taylor, BK: 18 W 21st Street 17th Floor, New York, NY 10010 212-243-1333
Taylor, Brian: 3104 Chesapeake Dr #101, Dumfries, VA 22026 703-221-6931
• **Taylor, Bridget Starr: pg 798** 9 Babbling Brook Ln, Suffern, NY 10901 ....**914-368-8606**
fax: 914-368-8608
Taylor, C Winston: 17008 Lisette St, Granada Hills, CA 91344 818-363-5761
• **Taylor, Dahl: pg 172** 194 Third Ave 3rd Fl, New York, NY 10003 ....**212-475-0440**
url: www.vickimorganassociates.com / fax: 212-353-8538
Taylor, David: 1449 N Pennsylvania St, Indianapolis, IN 46202 317-634-2728
Taylor, Doug: PO Box 169, Guilford, NY 13780 607-895-6062
Taylor, George: Pasadena, CA 818-304-0119
Taylor, Jay: 21-16 28th St, Long Island City, NY 11105 718-204-6184
• **Taylor, Joseph: pg 165** 420 Lexington Ave, New York, NY 10170 ....**212-986-5680**
url: www.mendolaart.com / fax: 212-818-1246
Taylor, Katherine Lynn: 702 Albert St, Ottawa, ON K1R 6L4 613-233-0655
Taylor, Ken: 1000 John R Rd #201, Troy, MI 48083 248-583-6070
Taylor, Leila: 2247 Emerson Ave, Salt Lake City, UT 84108 801-582-8118
Taylor, Peter: 1559 Carletta Dr, Mississauga, ON L4X 1E2 905-896-7307
Taylor, Terry: 24 Eldridge St, Port Chester, NY 10573 914-937-7730
Teach, Buzz Walker: 4848 Thor Way, Carmichael, CA 95608 916-488-4392
Teague, Tom: 617 Hillcrest Drive SW, Vienna, VA 22180 703-281-7036
• **Teare, Brad: pg 522,525** 89 FIfth Ave #901, New York, NY 10003 ....**212-627-1554**
fax: 212-627-1719
Tedesco, Bob: 8 Payne Rd, Bethel, CT 06801 203-531-8484
Tedesco, Michael: 120 Boerum Pl #1E, Brooklyn, NY 11201 718-398-1770
Tedesco, Thomas: 24 Elizabeth St, Port Jervis, NY 12771 914-856-8889
Tedford, Karla J: 125 CityCentre Drive, Cincinnati, OH 45216 513-761-8200
• **Teich, David: pg 1486** 41 Tamara Dr, Roosevelt, NJ 08555 ....**609-448-5036**
e-mail: mindmachine@mindspring.com / url: www.windofthemachine.com
fax: 609-443-3228
Teisher, Anne: 977 Via Del Monte, Palos Verdes, CA 90274 310-375-0575
Telfer, Gary: 49 Washington Ave #2, Hawthorne, NJ 07506 201-238-0415
Tellok, Mark: 3625 av Laval, Montréal, QU H2X 3E1 514-281-5794
Ten, Arnie: 37 Forbus St, Poughkeepsie, NY 12601 914-485-8419
Tenga, Kathlyn: 25-05 Ditmars Blvd, Long Island City, NY 11105 718-626-4344
Tenorio, Juan: 830 Amsterdam Ave, New York, NY 10025 212-663-2626
Tenud, Tish: 447 Amhurst Circle, Folsom, CA 95630 916-355-8511
Terezakis, Peter: 50 W 22nd St, New York, NY 10010 212-929-8978
Ternay, Bill: 119 Birch Ave, Bala Cynwyd, PA 19004 215-667-8626
Terpin, John: 13 Spann St, Buffalo, NY 14206 716-827-8023
Terreson, Jeffrey: 420 Lexington Ave, New York, NY 10170 212-986-5680
Terry, Will: 392 E 1075N, Springville, UT 84663 801-489-0879
Tesi, Nick: 18629 Topham St, Reseda, CA 91335 818-758-3940
Tetnall, Runcie: 5011 Mineola Rd, College Park, MD 20740 301-220-1821
Teves, Miles: 1428 Ontario St, Burbank, CA 91505 818-848-2028
Thacker, Kat: 280 Madison Ave #1110, New York, NY 10016 212-545-9155
Tharler, Gary: 1131 S Burnside Ave, Los Angeles, CA 90019 213-857-0981
• **Tharp, Pepper: pg 802** 6638 N 13th St, Phoenix, AZ 85014 ....**602-263-8990**
fax: 602-277-0680
Thayer, Brett A: 1255 East 1700 South #2, Salt Lake City, UT 84105 801-486-6954
• **Thelen, Mary: pg 392,393** 250 W 57th St #521, New York, NY 10107 ....**212-397-7330**
url: www.lindgrensmith.com (and) www.stockillustrated.com
Thelen, Nick: 335 1/2 N Heliotrope, Los Angeles, CA 90004 213-953-4707
Theodore, Jim: 5 W Main St, Westerville, OH 43081 614-898-5316
• **Thermes, Jennifer: pg 722** 7 Washington Street, Beverly, MA 01915 ....**978-921-0887**
e-mail: leighton@leightonreps.com / url: www.leightonreps.com / fax: 978-921-0223
Thewlis, Diana: 5755 San Juan Way, Pleasanton, CA 94566 925-484-9777
Thiel, Libby: Rte 2 Box 181C Fenwick, Bryan's Road, MD 20616 301-283-6347
Thielin, Kathleen: 4514 Travis St #220, Dallas, TX 75205 214-526-2888
Thien Do: 510 Stockton St #101, San Francisco, CA 94108 415-982-4624
Thieu, Tran: 3000 Mission College Blvd, Santa Clara, CA 95051 408-988-2220
Thisdale, Francois: 4651 rue de Salaberry, Carignan, QU J3L 3P9 514-477-4956
Thole, Cathleen: 353 W 53rd St #1W, New York, NY 10019 212-682-2462
Thomas Harper Design: 9192 Russell Ave, Garden Grove, CA 92644 714-721-4732
Thomas, Benjamin: 1210 Encino Ave, Arcadia, CA 91006 818-574-8012
Thomas, Chris: 1101 Mill Hill Rd, Southport, CT 06490 203-255-9620
Thomas, Fred W.: 2128 NW 197th, Shoreline, WA 98177 206-546-5249
Thomas, George: 42 Merrell Ave #C14, Stamford, CT 06902 203-359-9132
Thomas, Lisa Carlson: 4318 Kraft Ave, Studio City, CA 91604 818-753-8117
Thomas, Pat: 711 Carpenter, Oak Park, IL 60304 708-383-8505
Thomas, Rod: 16 Grasmere Rd, Needham, MA 20194 617-449-0480
Thomas, Scott: 400 Bel Marin Keys #202, San Francisco, CA 94949 415-382-3388
Thomas, Terrill: 4932 Charlene Circle #4, Huntington Beach, CA 92649 714-840-2798
Thomas, Troy: 1247 Portage Ln, Woodstock, IL 60098 815-338-9455
Thompson Brothers: 43 E 19th St, New York, NY 10003 212-254-4996
Thompson Hi-Tech Illus, Jim: 3717 Wilkesboro Hwy, Statesville, NC 28625 704-876-4492
Thompson, Arthur: 39 Prospect Ave, Pompton Plains, NJ 07444 201-835-3534
Thompson, Brian: 183 E Palm, Altadena, CA 91001 818-798-5901
Thompson, Bryce: 14 Forrest Park Crescent, Thornhill, ON L3T 2M6 416-419-9917
Thompson, Bryon: 6132 Bellingham Ln, Ft Wayne, IN 46835 219-486-5941
Thompson, Darren: 404 E 38th St, Anderson, IN 46013 317-683-1788
3557 Slate Mills Rd, Sperryville, VA 22740 800-789-9389
Thompson, Del & Dana: PO Box 7016 #225, Greenville, SC 29606 803-232-5444
• **Thompson, Ellen: pg 1103** 67 De Leon Cir, Franklin Park, NJ 08823 ....**732-422-0233**
• **Thompson, Emily: pg 1412** 433 W 43rd St #3E, New York, NY 10036 ....**212-245-2543**
fax: 212-245-2543
Thompson, George: 433 W 43rd St #3E, New York, NY 10036 212-245-2543
Thompson, Heather: 444 E 81st St #81, New York, NY 10028 212-535-2052
Thompson, John: 400 First Ave N #218, Minneapolis, MN 55401 612-375-9598
Thompson, John M: 206 Haddonfield Dr, Dewitt, NY 13214 315-449-1241
Thompson, Kathryn: 333 Cascade Dr, Fairfax, CA 94930 415-459-8835
• **Thompson, L C: pg 1323** 9629 Dove Hollow Ln, Glen Allen, VA 23060 ....**804-755-7455**
fax: 804-755-6792
Thompson, Margot: 468 Queen St E #104, Toronto, ON M5A 1T7 416-367-2446
Thompson, Nick: PO Box 465, Belmont, MA 02178 617-623-4366
Thompson, Richard: 9309 Judge Place, Gaithersburg, MD 20879 301-948-3732
Thompson, Stephen: 3286 Ivanhoe, St Louis, MO 63139 314-781-7377
Thompson, Terry: 212 Dorchester Ln, Alamo, CA 94507 510-210-0155
Thompson, Thierry: 420 Lexington Ave, New York, NY 10170 212-986-5680
Thomsen, Ernie: Seattle, WA 98134 206-467-9156
Thomson, Bill: 66 Fox Run Dr, Southington, CT 06489 860-621-2764
Thomssen, Kate: 2532 Kipling Ave S, Minneapolis, MN 55416 612-926-5585
Thon, Bud: 410 View Park Ct, Mill Valley, CA 94941 415-389-9220
Thoner, Dan: 3485 Copley Ave, San Diego, CA 92116 619-282-0031
Thonnessen, Sabina: 141 Wooster St #3B, New York, NY 10012 212-254-7436
Thorn, Dick: 353 W 53rd St #1W, New York, NY 10019 212-682-2462
• **Thornburgh, Bethann: pg 396**
250 W 57th St #521, New York, NY 10107 ....**212-397-7330**
url: www.lindgrensmith.com (and) www.stockillustrated.com
Thornell, Ian: 144 St Marks Ave #1B, Brooklyn, NY 11217 718-783-4740
Thornley, Blair: 1251 University Ave, San Diego, CA 92103 619-543-9658
Thornton, Blake: Los Angeles, CA 213-934-3395
126 Main St S #B7, Hailey, ID 83333 208-788-1434
1464 Linden Ave, Highland Park, IL 60035 847-222-0337
Thornton, Brek: 15433 Country Club Dr Apt A306, Mill Creek, WA 98012 206-338-2513
Thornton, Jeremy: 389 Ethel Ave, Mill Valley, CA 94941 415-388-7240
Thornton, Michael: 7844 Starward Dr, Dublin, CA 94568 510-828-5032
Thornton, Sandra: 3129 Root Ave, Carmichael, CA 95608 916-489-2877
Thorpe, Cameron: 542 Hardaman Cir, Boone, NC 28607 704-262-3979
Thorpe, Eric: 106 N Chester Ave, Pasadena, CA 91106 818-792-5708
Thorpe, Peter: 77 Lyons Plain Rd, Weston, CT 06883 203-226-4535
Threinen, Cher: 475 San Gorgonio St, San Diego, CA 92106 619-226-6050
Thrush, Denny Lee: 220 W Market St, Lima, OH 45805 419-227-4988
Thurman, Glenn: 905-278-6846
Thurston, Curt: 8625 Wood Lake Ct #308, Charlotte, NC 28210 704-554-1804
Thurston, Russell: 4909 Middaugh, Downers Grove, IL 60515 630-852-5586
• **Tiani, Alex: pg 657** 227 Godfrey Rd, Westport, CT 06883 ....**203-222-8777**
e-mail: artcoct@snet.net / fax: 203-454-9940

Tibbetts, Christopher: 1704 Bush Ave, St Paul, MN 55106 ... 612-776-5300
Tibbles, Jean Paul: 60 E 42nd St #822, New York, NY 10165 ... 212-682-1490
Tien, Chung Ming: 1 Pocahontas Dr, Middletown, RI 02840 ... 401-849-7608
Tierney, John P: 659 Churchill St, Pittsfield, MA 01201 ... 413-442-8428
Tiessen, Ken: 1643 W Swallow Rd, Ft Collins, CO 80526 ... 970-223-3027
Tilbury, Gingi: 112 Cherokee Rd #2, Nashville, TN 37205 ... 615-297-1102
Tilden, David Anders: End of Wirt Way Box 2191, Duxbury, MA 02332 ... 617-934-0345
Tillander, Michelle: 3530 Bapaume Ave, Norfolk, VA 23509 ... 804-857-7269
Tillery, Angelo: 1449 Longfellow Ave, Bronx, NY 10459 ... 718-617-2907
• **Tilley, Debbie: pg 1413** 2051 Shade Tree Ln, Escondido, CA 92029 ... **760-432-6282**
fax: 760-738-8019
San Francisco, CA ... **415-285-8267**
fax: 415-285-8268
New York, NY ... **212-997-0115**
Chicago, IL ... **312-782-2244**
• **Tillinghast, David: pg 646,647**
3238 Griffith Park Blvd, Los Angeles, CA 90027 ... **323-664-0997**
url: www.showcase.com / fax: 323-664-0999
Pier 33 North, San Francisco, CA 94111 ... **415-956-4750**
e-mail: cgr@slip.net / url: www.coreygrahamreps.com / fax: 415-391-6104
Tillofson, Katherine: 149 9th Street #410, San Francisco, CA 94103 ... 415-255-1656
Tilney, Barnes: 473 4th St #2L, Brooklyn, NY 11215 ... 718-768-8312
Timmes, Patrick: 5 Oakmere Dr, Baldwin, NY 11510 ... 516-377-8907
Timmons, Bonnie: 18 McKinley St, Rowayton, CT 06853 ... 203-866-3734
Ting, Bob: 3301 Bay Ct, Belmont, CA 94002 ... 415-592-5247
Tink a Sloss: 1424 La Positas Plaza, Santa Barbara, CA 93105 ... 805-682-6775
Tinkelman, Murray: 110 Sutter St #706, San Francisco, CA 94104 ... 415-441-4384
Tinney, Robert: PO Box 778, Washington, LA 70589 ... 318-826-3003
Tinoco, Roberto: 36738 Munyan St, Newark, CA 94560 ... 510-797-4574
Tipton, Beth: 6164 Westminster Pl, St Louis, MO 63112 ... 314-727-5657
Tiritilli, Jerry: 3939 N Hamlin Ave, Chicago, IL 60618 ... 773-267-4955
Tirolese, Ana: 268 Grosvenor St #F128, London, ON N6A 4V2 ... 519-646-6170
Tishman, Jill Rosean: PO Box 1592, Sante Fe, NM 87504 ... 505-986-9987
Tito Graphics: 2817 Highland Ave #2A, Birmingham, AL 35205 ... 205-251-2588
Titus Illus, Dave: 126 Old Mammoth Rd #209, Mammoth Lakes, CA 93546 ... 760-935-4455
toll-free ... 800-348-6911
Tivadar, Bote: 468 Queen St E #104, Toronto, ON M5A 1T7 ... 416-367-2446
Tjostelson, Sally: 7921 149th St NW, Gig Harbor, WA 98329 ... 253-857-7552
Toal, Mark: 138 Stanford Shopping Ctr, Palo Alto, CA 94303 ... 415-326-7687
Tobiassen, Kris: 132 Thompson St #37, New York, NY 10012 ... 212-388-0870
Tod-Kat Studios: 353 W 53rd St #1W, New York, NY 10019 ... 212-682-2462
Todd, Barbara: 251 Greenwood Ave, Bethel, CT 06801 ... 203-797-8188
Todd, Mark: 155 W 15th St #4C, New York, NY 10011 ... 212-989-8770
Todd, Susan: 468 Queen St E #104, Toronto, ON M5A 1T7 ... 416-367-2446
• **Toelke, Cathleen: pg 928,929** PO Box 487, Rhinebeck, NY 12572 ... **914-876-8776**
url: www.zaks.com/illustrators/toelke
• **Tofanelli, Mike: pg 1414** 2424 Hurley Way #24, Sacramento, CA 95825 ... **916-927-4809**
fax: 916-927-4809
Tokach, Michele: 735 Grant St, Hazelton, PA 18201 ... 717-455-2144
Tokyo Design Center: 703 Market St #252, San Francisco, CA 94103 ... 415-543-4886
Tokyo, Max: 236 W 26th St #805, New York, NY 10001 ... 212-463-7025
Tolonen, Susan: 925 Elm Grove Rd, Elm Grove, WI 53122 ... 414-785-1940
Tom, Jack: 135 Lazy Brook Rd, Monroe, CT 06468 ... 203-452-0889
• **Tom-Conway, Ket: pg 1415** 607 Maple St, Aptos, CA 95003 ... **408-684-2378**
fax: 408-684-2378
Tomas, Mary: 3514 Oakgrove, Dallas, TX 76204 ... 214-296-4124
Tomasso, Armando: 230 Park Ave S 5th Fl, New York, NY 10003 ... 212-614-3899
Tomasulo, Patrick: 76 Howard St, Dumont, NJ 07628 ... 201-385-4350
Tomek, Thomas: 943 N. Winchester, Chicago, IL 60622 ... 773-227-7845
Tomlin, Lara: 108 E 35th St #2, New York, NY 10016 ... 212-889-3337
Tomlinson, Richard: 319 E 24th St, New York, NY 10010 ... 212-685-0552
• **Tonal Values Illustration: pg 1094** Dallas, TX ... **214-943-2569**
toll-free ... **800-484-8592 code 2787**
e-mail: tonalvalues@mindspring.com / url: www.dreier.com / fax: 214-942-6771
Toney, Allen: 3064 Wallace Cir, Huntington, WV 25705 ... 304-523-7744
Tong, Paul: 2847 Guilderland Ave, Schenectady, NY 12306 ... 518-355-8023
Tonkin, Thomas: 353 W 53rd St #1W, New York, NY 10019 ... 212-682-2462
Toolbox: 420 Lexington Ave, New York, NY 10170 ... 212-986-5680
Toomer, George: 3923 Cole Ave, Dallas, TX 75204 ... 214-522-1171
Toos, Andrew: 193 Clatter Valley Rd, Bridgewater, CT 06752 ... 860-350-3718
Torline, Kevin: 2233 Kemper Ln, Cincinnati, OH 45206 ... 513-861-1400
Torluemke, Tom: 3319 Orchard Dr, Hammond, IN 46323 ... 312-939-3883
Torp, Cynthia: PO Box 470818, San Francisco, CA 94147 ... 415-383-9026
7118 Upper River Rd, Prospect, KY 40059 ... 502-228-9427
• **Torres, Carlos: pg 368,369** 327 E 89th St #3E, New York, NY 10128 ... **212-831-5650**
fax: 212-831-6241
1306 Alabama St, Huntington Beach, CA 92648 ... 714-969-7766
fax: 714-374-3744
Torres, Daniel: 584 Broadway #608, New York, NY 10012 ... 212-966-7840
Torres, Jordy: 43 E 19th St, New York, NY 10003 ... 212-254-4996
Torres, Leyla: 14 N Henry St, Brooklyn, NY 11222 ... 718-389-6101
Torrisi, Gary: 50 Fuller Brook Rd, Wellesley, MA 02181 ... 781-235-8658
Torroll, Cynthia Lund: 3920 S Greenlawn Terr, New Berlin, WI 53151 ... 414-221-4540
Torzecka, Marlena: 278 Hamilton Ave, Princeton, NJ 08540 ... 609-252-9405
Tosch, Jamie S: 8732 Fair Oaks Blvd #44, Carmichael, CA 95608 ... 916-944-2097
Tourtellott, Mark: 12 Martyn St, Waltham, MA 02154 ... 617-647-9615
Touzie, Miriam: 9 E 32nd St #6A, New York, NY 10016 ... 212-532-6956
Tow, David: 22 Melrose St, Glastonbury, CT 06033 ... 860-659-1147
Towle, Wendy: 15318 Mack Ave, Grosspoint Park, MI 48230 ... 313-884-3332
Towler, Martha: 34-30 78 St #1J, Jackson Heights, NY 11372 ... 718-651-1549
Towler, Matthew: 277 Lake Ave, Worcester, MA 01604 ... 508-791-2416
Towner, Bob: 5855 Green Valley Cir #308, Culver City, CA 90230 ... 310-642-2721
• **Townswick, Gary: pg 1416** 7339 S 71 Avenue, Omaha, NE 68157 ... **402-593-7115**
• **Toyama, Ken: pg 1192** 94 Natoma St #200, San Francisco, CA 94105 ... **415-442-1822**
url: www.dwrepresents.com/dwr / fax: 415-442-1823
Trachok, Cathryne: 2080 Coombsville, Napa, CA 9458 ... 707-252-0728
Tracy, Donna: 2011 Vista Cerro Gordo St, Los Angeles, CA 90039 ... 213-666-4087
Tracy, Libba: 329 W Vernon Ave, Phoenix, AZ 85003 ... 602-254-8232
Tracy, Stan: 484 W 43rd St #32K, New York, NY 10036 ... 212-967-1665
Trainor, Sandra: 33 Montvale Ave #4, Woburn, MA 01801 ... 617-933-6196
Traub, Paul: PO Box 38173, Greensboro, NC 27438 ... 910-288-0527
Traversi, Steve: 1320 E Cotati Ave #115, Rohnert Park, CA 94928 ... 707-547-4442
Travis-Keene, Gayle: 334 Swinton Way, Severne Park, MD 21146 ... 410-647-7220
Trayham Photography, Britt: 1854 San Marco Blvd, Jacksonville, FL 32204
• **Traynor, Elizabeth: pg 100,101** 108 E 35th St #2, New York, NY 10016 ... **212-889-3337**
url: www.theispot.com/artist/traynor / fax: 212-889-3341
Treadway, Todd: 400 First Ave N #218, Minneapolis, MN 55401 ... 612-375-9598
Treatner, Meryl: 239 Monroe St, Philadelphia, PA 19147 ... 215-627-2297
Trefry, Charlie: 5220 E Colonial Dr, Orlando, FL 32807 ... 407-249-7949
Tremblay, Claire: 3035 Route du Port, Saint jean baptiste, QU J3T 1R2 ... 819-293-4134
Tremblay, Sylvain: 460 rue Saint-Catherine, Montréal, QU H3B 1A7 ... 514-393-0844
Tremlett, Mark: 133 N Montclair Ave, Dallas, TX 75208 ... 214-943-2569
Trenc, Milan: 99 Perry St, New York, NY 10014 ... 212-924-6768
Trillion Inc/Anderson: 5989 Tahor Dr SE, Grand Rapids, MI 49546 ... 616-940-9944
• **Trinh, John: pg 1417** 9221 E Longden Ave, Temple City, CA 91780 ... **626-287-5989**
toll-free ... **877-268-1298**
Trinsey, Michael: 16 Autumn Ridge Dr, Glassboro, NJ 08028 ... 609-218-9199
Trofimova, Marianna: 105 Boerum Pl #1, Brooklyn, NY 11201 ... 718-625-0294
Troller, Michael Design: 301 Gates St., San Francisco, CA 94110 ... 415-206-0326
Trook, Jim: 17 White St #5C, New York, NY 10013 ... 212 219 3854
Trostli, Elisabeth: 55 Bradford St #202, Providence, RI 02909 ... 401-351-3429
Trout & Trout: 739 Bryant St #205, San Francisco, CA 94107 ... 415-896-5275
Trow Bridge, David: 918 NW Market St, Seattle, WA 98107 ... 206-706-9204
True: 702 E 5th Street #3E, New York, NY 10009 ... 212-529-2771
Truesdale Art & Design: 5482 Complex St #112, San Diego, CA 92123 ... 619-268-1026
Trull, John: 1573 York Ave, New York, NY 10028 ... 212-535-5383
Trusilo, Jim: 309 Walnut Rd, Pittsburgh, PA 15202 ... 412-761-5666
Truxaw, Dick: 6404 W 125th St, Shawnee Mission, KS 66209 ... 913-383-1555
• **Tsuchiya / Sloneker Comms: pg 1446**
423 Washington #500, San Francisco, CA 94111 ... **415-986-5365**
e-mail: mail@tscomm.com / url: www.tscomm.com
Tsugami, Kyuzo: 156 Fifth Ave #417, New York, NY 10010 ... 212-243-1333
Tsui, George & Selena: 1772 Hendrickson Ave, N Merrick, NY 11566 ... 516-223-8474
Tucci, Domenick: 26 Tremont Pl, Nutley, NJ 07110 ... 201-284-0755
Tuchman, Mark: 145 Luquer St, Brooklyn, NY 11231 ... 718-222-1281
Tucker, Ezra: 110 Sutter St #706, San Francisco, CA 94104 ... 415-441-4384
• **Tucker, Greg: pg 1092** 1915 Lakeview SW, Albuquerque, NM 87105 ... **505-873-3727**
Tuke, Scott W: 1657 N California Blvd #207, Walnut Creek, CA 94596 ... 510-930-7576
Tull, Bobbi: 6103 Beachway Dr, Falls Church, VA 22041 ... 703-998-9292
Tull, Jeff: 3301A S Jefferson Ave, St Louis, MO 63118 ... 314-773-2600
Tung, Claudia: 150-21 77th Ave, Kew Garden Hills, NY 11367 ... 718-380-1054
Tung, Yu U: 3900 Chestnut St, Philadelphia, PA 19104 ... 215-386-0387
Tunstull, Glenn: 201 Clinton Ave #14G, Brooklyn, NY 11205 ... 718-834-8529
Turchyn, Sandie: 156 N Hamel Dr, Beverly Hills, CA 90211 ... 310-275-8877
Turgeon, Jim: 19 Stuyvesant Oval, New York, NY 10009 ... 212-505-9342
• **Turgeon, Pol: pg 382** 250 W 57th St #521, New York, NY 10107 ... **212-397-7330**
url: www.lindgrensmith.com (and) www.stockillustrated.com
Turk, Malcolm: 16 Abingdon Sq #2C, New York, NY 10014 ... 212-924-3324
Turk, Stephen: 927 Westbourne Dr, Los Angeles, CA 90069 ... 310-788-0682
3525 Mockingbird Ln, Dallas, TX 75205 ... 214-521-5156
Turk, Tasha: 4446 N 36th St #28, Phoenix, AZ 85018 ... 602-954-8116
Turner, Clay: 60 E 42nd St #822, New York, NY 10165 ... 212-682-1490
Turner, Cynthia: 3 Old Miller Pl, Santa Rosa Bch, FL 32459 ... 904-231-4112
Turner, Dave: 800 Clearview Dr, Nashville, TN 37205 ... 423-297-5377
Turner, David: 919 Portola Ave #A, Torrance, CA 90501 ... 310-212-6400
Turner, Dona: 5139 Coronado Avenue, Oakland, CA 94618 ... 510-547-8832
Turner, Jeanne: 809 Fulton Ave, Falls Church, VA 22046 ... 703-237-1108
Turner, John: 201 Forest Dr, Graham, NC 27253 ... 910-227-1035
Turner, Patrick: 117-1720 Southmore Crescent, South Surrey, BC V4A 6E3 ... 604-536-9776
Turner, Ray: Pier 33 North, San Francisco, CA 94111 ... 415-956-4750
Turner, Shawn: 3220 Somerset Rd, Sacramento, CA 95864 ... 916-481-8923
Turner, Tracy: 918 Sheridan Rd, Glentole, IL 60616 ... 312-663-5300
Turrell, Bleu: 245 Tolman Circle Rd #5, Ashland, OR 97520 ... 541-482-7253
Turtel, Jason: 574 Leheigh Ln, Woodmere, NY 11598 ... 516-569-5437
Tusa, Tricia: 619 Asbury St, Houston, TX 77007 ... 713-864-8864
Tuscan, Christopher: 2144 W Concord Pl, Chicago, IL 60647 ... 773-278-3320
• **Tuschman, Richard: pg 284,285** 58 W 15th St, New York, NY 10011 ... **212-741-2539**
url: www.showcase.com / fax: 212-741-4660
• **Tuson, Lorraine: pg 1109** 217 Indian Grove, Toronto, ON M6P 2H4 ... **416-516-2835**
fax: 416-516-0955
Tuttle, Jean: 145 Palisade suite 406, Dobbs Ferry, NY 10522 ... 914-693-7681
51 Camden St, Toronto, ON M5V 1V2 ... 416-703-1913
Tuveson, Christine: 1119 Hi Point St, Los Angeles, CA 90035 ... 213-936-5851
Twede, Brian L: 435 S 300 E, Salt Lake City, UT 84111 ... 801-534-1459
Twinem, Neecy: 9 Babbling Brook Ln, Suffern, NY 10901 ... 914-368-8606
2D or not 2D Limited: 286 Spring St #301, New York, NY 10013 ... 212-229-0073
• **2H Studio: pg Back Flap Books 1 & 2**
54 Old Post Rd, Southport, CT 06490 ... **203-256-1625**
or ... **203-256-9192**
Twohy, Tom: 1980 Park Ave #23, San Jose, CA 95126 ... 408-261-8431
Tylden-Wright, Jenny: 11 Kings Ridge Rd, Long Valley, NJ 07853 ... 908-813-8718
• **Tyler, Barbara: pg 762,763** 60 E 42nd St #1146, New York, NY 10165 ... **212-953-7088**
Tyler, Darden: 10218 Wolfe Manor Ct, Glen Allen, VA 23060 ... 804-755-1241
Tyler, Wayne R: 3035 E Middleton Way, Salt Lake City, UT 84124 ... 801-272-9320
Tyminski, Lori: 1157 Langlie Way, Rodeo, CA 94572 ... 510-799-3209
Tyrrell, Susan: 124 Mica Ln, Wellesley, MA 02181 ... 617-431-8686
Tysko, Lisa: 361 Nassau, Princeton, NJ 08540 ... 609-921-3610
Tzur, Zahava: 24 E 23rd St 3rd Fl, New York, NY 10010 ... 212-420-0656

U

• **Uceda, Santiago: pg 1418** 2400 Niagara Way, Costa Mesa, CA 92626 ... **714-754-0651**
url: www.showcase.com / fax: 714-545-7816

Vogelsang, Johanna: 4583 Via San Marco, Las Vegas, NV 89103....................702-362-9785
Voita, Steve: 2202 E Flower St, Phoenix, AZ 85016.....................................602-970-1905
Vojnar, Kamil: 64-40 Palmetto, Ridgewood, NY 11385...................................718-381-7590
Vollman Design, Bryan: 2320 W 4th St, Duluth, MN 55806.............................218-722-9491
Volp, Kathleen: 91 Bristers Hill Rd, Concord, MA 01742..............................508-371-1389
Voltz, Ralph: 1101 Westchester Blvd, Charlotte, NC 28205............................704-566-8283
von Buhler, Cynthia: 16 Ashford St, Boston, MA 02134.................................617-783-2421
Von Eiff, Damon: 2 W Argyle St, Rockville, MD 20850..................................301-251-0381
von Haeger, Arden: 7100 Patten Ln, Nashville, TN 37221..............................615-646-7022
von Kap-herr, Victoria: 1344 Lake Breeze Dr, West Palm Beach, FL 33414.....407-791-3345
Von Schmidt, Eric: 859 N Hollywood Way #214, Burbank, CA 91505 818-559-1490
• **Von Ulrich, Mark: pg 610** 155 W 15th St, New York, NY 10011.................**212-989-8770**
  fax: 212-989-7892
• **Voo, Rhonda: pg 788** 353 W 53rd St #1W, New York, NY 10019 ....**212-682-2462**
  e-mail: info@amerartists.com / url: www.amerartists.com / fax: 212-582-0090
Vorhies, Roger: 109 Old Port Rd, Kennebunk, ME 04043..............................207-967-0355
Voris, Rebecca J: 7031 Serenity Cir, Anchorage, AK 99502...........................907-243-5234
Vornberger, Cal: 910 West End Ave #3D, New York, NY 10025........................212-316-0200
• **Voss, Tom: pg 881**
  630 Fifth Ave 20th Fl, Rockefeller, New York, NY 10111.............................**212-332-3460**
  fax: 212-674-4042
Voth, Gregory: 67 Eighth Ave, New York, NY 10014 212-807-9766
Vue Productions: 16661 Ventura Blvd #120, Encino, CA 91436.......................848-905-1883
Vuksanovich, Bill & Fran: 3224 N Nordica, Chicago, IL 60634........................773-283-2138

W

Wacholder, Lisa Roma: 1515 E 27th St, Brooklyn, NY 11229 718-951-7218
• **Wack, Jeff: pg 133** 420 Lexington Ave, New York, NY 10170 ....**212-986-5680**
  url: www.mendolaart.com / fax: 212-818-1246
Wagner, Brett: 1085 Hickory View Cir, Camarillo, CA 93012..........................805-987-1123
• **Wagner, Carol: pg 1425** 2015 N Beachwood Dr, Los Angeles, CA 90068.....**323-461-6446**
  or **323-463-4515**
  e-mail: yudduhsla@aol.com
Wagner, Marijke P: 1085 Hickory View Cir, Camarillo, CA 93012.....................805-987-1123
Wagner, Stephen R: Rt 1 Box 978, Washington, VA 22747.............................703-675-3046
• **Wagt, Robert: pg 386** 250 W 57th St #521, New York, NY 10107............**212-397-7330**
  url: www.lindgrensmith.com (and) www.stockillustrated.com
• **Wainwright, Debra: pg 1426**
  95 Carriage House Ln, Wrentham, MA 02093.......................................**508-384-2759**
  e-mail: DebraWai@aol.com / fax: 508-384-2759
Wald, Carol: 5280 Lakeshore Rd #805, Burlington, ON L7L 5R1.....................416-634-3819
Waldbaum, Caryn: 460 W 42nd St 2nd Fl, New York, NY 10036....................212-967-6655
Waldman, Bruce: 18 Westbrook Rd, Westfield, NJ 07090...............................908-232-2840
Waldman, Neal: 54 Rocking Chair Rd, White Plains, NY 10607.......................914-949-5257
Waldon, Deb: 5300 Vernon Ave S #B102, Edina, MN 55436...........................612-922-4953
• **Waldrep, Richard: pg 465** 731 N 24th St, Philadelphia, PA 19130 ....**215-232-6666**
  url: www.deborahwolfeltd.com / fax: 215-232-6585
• **Waldron, Sarah: pg 1111** 3690 Primrose Ave, Petaluma, CA 95407 ....**707-778-0848**
Walker & Assoc: 18 E 64th St #4B, New York, NY 10021..............................212-759-5590
Walker, Bob: 9-23 118th St, College Point, NY 11356..................................212-326-9338
Walker, Brian: 2004 Palamar Turn, Seabrook, MD 20706.............................301-794-4574
Walker, Donna: 221 E 50th St #5F, New York, NY 10022.............................212-779-7158
Walker, Jeff: 60 E 42nd St #1940, New York, NY 10165..............................212-867-8092
Walker, John S: 47 Jane St, New York, NY 10014 212-242-3435
Walker, Ken: 2901 W 72nd St, Shawnee Mission, KS 66208..........................913-432-9461
Walker, Kevin: 15 McMakin Dr, Greenville, SC 29602.................................864-298-4419
Walker, Lawrence: 1740 W 120th St #C, Los Angeles, CA 90047....................213-777-5526
Walker, Lonnie: 1031 South 4th St, Louisville, KY 40203.............................502-581-9500
Walker, Michael: 2651 Favor Rd #H-8, Marietta, GA 30060..........................770-434-1268
Walker, Norman: 141-10 28th St, Flushing, NY 11354................................212-206-0066
Walker, Richard: 3546 Rhoda Ave, Oakland, CA 94602................................510-531-3753
Walker, SA: 8 Gifford Ct, Salem, MA 01970...508-745-6175
Walker, Todd: 2890 N Orlando Ave, Tucson, AZ 85712.................................520-327-1569
Walker, Tracy: 11936 W Jefferson Blvd #C, Culver City, CA 90230..................310-390-8663
• **Walker, Tracy: pg 561,574,575** 155 Lippincott St, Toronto, ON M5S 2P3 ....**416-505-9522**
  toll-free **888-277-7200**
  e-mail: shelley@sbaillustrates.com / url: www.sbaillustrates.com
• **Wall, G Lee: pg 1082** 6509 Wessex Ln, Richmond, VA 23226..................**804-673-3632**
  e-mail: gleewall@mindspring.com / url: www.mindspring.com/~gleewall/
Wall, Pam: 455 W 23rd St #8D, New York, NY 10011..................................212-366-1893
Wallace, Andrea: 866 United Nations Plaza, New York, NY 10017 212-644-2020
Wallace, Kurt: 99 Park Ave #210A, New York, NY 10016.............................800-398-9544
Wallace, Nina: 224 Euclid Ave, Haddonfield, NJ 08033 609-354-8718
Wallace, Peter: 23 Crown St, Milton, MA 02186......................................617-696-6662
Wallengren, Jason: 8C Ambassador Dr, Manchester, CT 06040......................860-645-6298
Wallwork, Shawn: 2920 Chama St NE, Albuquerque, NM 87110.....................505-880-0715
Walsh, Pat: 6357 Shaundale Dr, Springfield, VA 22152................................703-644-1759
Walstead, Curt: 398 Via Colinas, Westlake Village, CA 91362........................818-595-2981
Walters, Steve: 450 E Foothill Blvd, Glendora, CA 91741.............................
Walthall, Jeffrey: 2031 Rockingham St, McLean, VA 22101...........................703-538-2738
Waltmire, Charles: 2234 Oak Ct, Martinez, CA 94553................................916-321-1035
Walton, Brenda: 4015 E 53rd St, Tulsa, OK 74135...................................918-749-9424
Walton, Matt: 7525 State Line Rd, Kansas City, MO 64114...........................816-421-7474
Wan-Yee, Chia: 220 E Live Oak St #32, San Gabriel, CA 91776......................818-291-2377
Wang, Michael: 70-43 Kessel St, Forest Hills, NY 11375 212-473-7564
Wang, Shih-Wei: 144 Henry St #7, Brooklyn, NY 11201..............................718-243-0272
• **Wang, Suling: pg 1084** 2885 Bush St #9, San Francisco, CA 94115 ....**415-474-0259**
  e-mail: Suling_Wang@designlink.com / url: www.best.com/~sulingw/
Warchesik, Brain: 13564 W Utah Cir, Lakewood, CO 80228...........................303-986-4950
Ward, Jeff: 920 N Water #207, Bay City, MI 48708 517-895-1029
Ward, John: 7313 Sandy Creek, Wausau, WI 54401 715-675-6074
Ward, John C: 125 Maryland Ave, Freeport, NY 11520................................516-546-2906
Ward, John T: 20 Birch St, Saranac Lake, NY 12983 518-891-4534
Ward, Keith: 1717 N Marshall PO Box 92054, Milwaukee, WI 53202.............414-277-9909
Ward, Robert A: 6 Baldwin St, Newton, MA 02158....................................617-965-0854

• **Ward, Sam: pg 122,123** 420 Lexington Ave, New York, NY 10170 ....**212-986-5680**
  url: www.mendolaart.com / fax: 212-818-1246
  (editorial): 6829 Murray Ln, Annandale, VA 22003 ....**703-256-8313**
  fax: 703-914-8865
Ward, Tim: PO Box 3624, Santa Cruz, CA 95063......................................408-462-5193
• **Ward, Tom: pg 745** 865 Delaware St, Denver, CO 80204.......................**303-820-2599**
  toll-free **800-417-5120**
  url: www.artagent.com / fax: 303-820-2598
Ware, Richard: 339 First Ave #2F, New York, NY 10003...............................212-673-9102
Warfield, D L: 320 Kinner Circle, Alpharetta, GA 30201..............................770-569-0848
• **Wariner, David: pg 553** 7118 Upper River Rd, Prospect, KY 40059 ....**502-228-9427**
  url: www.jettreps.com / fax: 502-228-8857
Warman, Brian: 4922 Duebber Dr, Cincinnati, OH 45238.............................513-922-6326
Warnell, Ted: 2511 15 A St SW, Calgary, AB T2T 4B8................................403-244-7395
Warner, Elena & Michael: 5455 8th St #13, Carpinteria, CA 93013..................805-684-5203
Warner, Linda: 28 Sherman Dr, Hilton Head Island, NC 29928.......................803-689-5044
Warner, Michele: 4606 Cedar Spring #1527, Dallas, TX 75219.......................214-559-0055
Warnick, Elsa: 636 NW 20th Ave #7, Portland, OR 97209............................503-228-2659
Warren, Jim: 11 Kings Ridge Rd, Long Valley, NJ 07853...............................908-813-8718
Warren, Kirk: 617 Silverstone Ave, Winnipeg, MB R3T 2V6..........................204-261-7404
Warren, Shari: 127 Bonita Ave, Redwood City, CA 94061.............................415-369-6604
Warren, Valerie: 14 E 4th St #1103, New York, NY 10012.............................212-505-5366
Warrender, Patrice M: 2685 Burnside Rd, Sebastopol, CA 95472....................800-892-3325
• **Warshaw Blumenthal, Inc.: pg 1458** New York, NY **212-867-4225**
  url: www.illustrations-nyc.com
Washington, Romeo: 368 Bradford, San Francisco, CA 94110 415-821-7826
Washington, Sharon: 652 Bathurst St., Toronto, ON M5S2R1.........................416-538-7036
Wass, Chip: 35 Pineapple St #3B, Brooklyn, NY 11201................................718-596-0864
• **Wasserman, Amy L: pg 167** 420 Lexington Ave, New York, NY 10170 ....**212-986-5680**
  url: www.mendolaart.com / fax: 212-818-1246
Wasserman, Randie: 15 Sulky Cir, E Hampton, NY 11937............................516-324-7186
Wassink Ackison, Wendy: 2233 Kemper Ln, Cincinnati, OH 45206..................513-861-1400
• **Wasson, Cameron: pg 890** 16 Phaedra, Laguna Niguel, CA 92677...........**949-495-3664**
  url: www.showcase.com / fax: 949-495-0129
  1118 Sir Francis Drake Blvd #201, Kentfield, CA 94904............................**415-455-8874**
Waterhouse, Charles: 67 Dartmouth St, Edison, NJ 08837............................908-738-1804
Waters Art Studio: 1820 E Garry St #207, Santa Ana, CA 92705....................714-250-4466
Waters, Julian: 23707 Woodfield Rd, Gaithersburg, MD 20882 301-253-3422
• **Waters, Susy Pilgrim: pg 705** 11 Eden Ave, West Newton, MA 02165.......**617-965-4954**
  6 Parker Rd, Arlington, MA 02174...**781-641-2787**
  fax: 781-641-2244
Watford, Wayne: 3286 Ivanhoe, St Louis, MO 63139 314-781-7377
Watkins, Leslie: 25 Grove St #3, New York, NY 10014 212-989-2616
Watkinson, Brent: 6849 Mastin, Merriam, KS 66203..................................913-677-0062
  60 E 42nd St #822, New York, NY 10165...212-682-1490
Watson, Esther: 123 Prospect Pl #1, Brooklyn, NY 11217.............................718-783-1488
Watson, Karen: 14 Blueberry Ln, Lexington, MA 02173...............................617-674-1136
Watson, Neil: 32 W 40th Street, New York, NY 10018.................................212-575-6877
Watson, Paul: Panama City, FL 904-747-8415
  UK/Western Europe...186-543-5654
  468 Queen St E #104, Toronto, ON M5A 1T7.....................................416-367-2446
  Chicago, IL..312-663-5506
  New York, NY...212-643-0896
  Los Angeles, CA...213-688-7428
Watson, Richard Jesse: 2305 Ivy St, Port Townsend, WA 98368......................206-385-7805
Watt, Denise: 253 W 72nd St #1706, New York, NY 10023............................212-595-4957
Wattenmaker, Pamela Drury: 17 S Palomar Dr, Redwood City, CA 94062...........650-368-7878
• **Watts Studios, Mark: pg 1204** 2004 Par Dr, Doylestown, PA 18901 ....**215-343-8490**
  e-mail: wattsart@aol.com / url: http://members.aol.com/wattsart / fax: 215-343-8717
Watts, David: Rt 1 Mountain Shadow #12, Boone, NC 28607..........................704-265-2030
Watts, Ian: 468 Queen St E #102, Toronto, ON M5A 1T7.............................416-867-9345
Watts, Jeff & Robert: 1906 Avocado Ranch Rd, El Cajon, CA 92019..................619-447-1419
Watts, Sharon: 201 Eastern Pkwy, Brooklyn, NY 11238..............................718-398-0451
• **Watts, Stan: pg 788** 353 W 53rd St #1W, New York, NY 10019...............**212-682-2462**
  e-mail: info@amerartists.com / url: www.amerartists.com / fax: 212-582-0090
Watts, Tina: 3604 Fairoaks Blvd #250, Sacramento, CA 95864 916-989-4975
Wax, Wendy: 322 E 55th St #2A, New York, NY 10022..............................212-371-6156
Weakley, Mark: 141-10 28th St, Flushing, NY 11354.................................212-206-0066
  22727 Cielo Vista, San Antonio, TX 78255...210-698-1409
Weast, Jonathan: 10401 Georgetown Dr, Rancho Cordova, CA 95670...............916-638-4119
Weaver, Anne: 2951 East 3215 South, Salt Lake City, UT 84109......................801-484-5374
Weaver, Carol Maria: 70 W 95th St #21C, New York, NY 10025......................212-864-2394
Weaver, Michael: 2927 W 43rd Ave, Kansas City, KS 66103..........................913-432-5078
Weaver, Mike: 1505 Vott DR, West Bend, WI 53095...................................414-335-0868
Webb, Laura: 25 Ronada Ave #1, Oakland, CA 94611................................510-597-1083
Webb, Lisa: 110 Habersham Dr, Athens, GA 30606...................................706-549-6711
Webb, Lizanne E: 1374 Midland Ave #610, Bronxville, NY 17008.....................914-237-3080
Webb, Quentin: 99 Park Ave #210A, New York, NY 10016............................800-398-9544
Webber, Rosemary: 130 Shore Rd, Old Greenwich, CT 06870.........................203-637-9197
Webber, Warren: 559 Dutch Valley Rd, Atlanta, GA 30324............................404-881-6627
Weber, Joan: 1474 Westerly Terrace, Los Angeles, CA 90026.........................213-662-9300
Weber, John: 3637 Ridgewood Dr, Hilliard, OH 43026.................................614-777-0631
Weber, Mark: 113 E 29th St, Erie, PA 16504 814-453-2050
Weber, Robert: 950 Klish Way, Del Mar, CA 92014....................................619-259-5774
Webster & Assocs, John: 1445 Fern Pl, Vista, CA 92083..............................619-945-6576
Weeb, Herman: 2372 Rosemont, Montreal, QU H2G 1V1.............................514-271-4321
Weed, Greg: PO Box 396, Bloomfield Hills, MI 48303.................................313-460-2451
Weeks, Brenda: 35 Jane St #15, Toronto, ON M6S 3Y3...............................416-766-2942
• **Weems, Alexandra: pg 300** 58 W 15th St, New York, NY 10011..............**212-741-2539**
  url: www.showcase.com
  fax: 212-741-4660
Wegner, Brad: 333 Briarwood Dr, Winter Park, FL 32789..............................407-628-9875
Wehrman, Richard: 247 N Goodman St, Rochester, NY 14607.......................716-271-2280
Wehrman, Vicki: 2550 Country Rd 39 Box 146, East Bloomfield, NY 14443....716-657-7910
Wehrstein, David: 20 W Hubbard #3E, Chicago, IL 60610............................312-222-1361
Weiland, Garison: 19 Barry Place, Falmouth, MA 02540.............................508-540-2551
Weilbrenner, Johanne: 5158 rue Chabot, Montréal, QU H2H 1Y8....................514-525-6967

- Yang, Eric: pg 1492 213 La France Ave #F, Alhambra, CA 91801 ....**626-284-4727**
  e-mail: etyang@pacbell.net / fax: 626-282-5536
- Yang, James: pg 764 41 Union Sq W #918, New York, NY 10003 ....**212-807-6627**
  url: www.idt.net/~dgagency / fax: 212-463-8175
  Yaniv, Etty: 32 Laurence Ct, Closter, NJ 07624 201-784-8136
- Yankus, Marc: pg 1010,1011 190 W 10th St #3C, New York, NY 10014....**212-242-6334**
  url: www.niceboy.com
  Yanson, John Michael: 211 8th St NE/Carriage House,
  Washington, DC 20002 202-546-0600
  Yapp, Kenneth: 2570 rue Allard #3, Montréal, QU H4E 2L4 514-765-8981
  Yarmolinsky, Miriam: 806 Kennebec Ave #2, Takoma Park, MD 20912..........301-495-6342
  Yarnell, David Andrew: PO Box 286, Occoquan, VA 22125 703-491-3797
  Yazzolino, Brad: 6451 SE Morrison Ct, Portland, OR 97215 503-238-3776
  Yeager, Alice: 3157 Rolling Rd, Edgewater, MD 21037 301-956-4252
  Yealdhall, Gary: 353 W 53rd St #1W, New York, NY 10019 212-682-2462
  Yealdhall, Gary: 281 Shakespeare Dr, Severna Park, MD 21146...............410-315-9651
  Yearington, Tim: Box 811 RR #3, Woodlawn, ON K0A 3M0 613-832-0879
  Yee, Josie: 43 E 19th St, New York, NY 10003 212-254-4996
  Yeh, Jeff: 13100 Creek View #103, Garden Grove, CA 92644 714-638-2934
  Yemi: 99 Park Ave #210A, New York, NY 10016..................................800-398-9544
  Yenne, Bill: PO Box 460313, San Francisco, CA 94146 415-285-8799
- Yeo, Brad: pg 106,107 108 E 35th St #2, New York, NY 10016...............**212-889-3337**
  url: www.theispot.com/artist/yeo / fax: 212-889-3341
  Yeomans, Jeff: 4691 Orchard Ave, San Diego, CA 92107 619-224-2654
  Yerkes, Lane: 200 S Roberts Rd #F6, Bryn Mawr, PA 19010 610-520-3470
- Yermal, Bill: pg 1437 62 Carey Rd, Succasunna, NJ 07876..................**973-927-8909**
  fax: 973-927-6744
  Yesko, John: 5234 N Wayne Ave, Chicago, IL 60640............................312-416-7979
  Yezerski, Thomas: 270 Union Ave, Rutherford, NJ 07070......................201-939-6093
  Yiannias, Vicki: 200 W 15th St, New York, NY 10011 212-243-4209
  Yip Illus, Filip: PO Box 320177, San Francisco, CA 94132 415-757-8728
- Yip, Jennie: pg 159 420 Lexington Ave, New York, NY 10170.................**212-986-5680**
  url: www.mendolaart.com / fax: 212-818-1246
- Yoe Studio, Inc.: pg 1028,1029 209 Chateau Rive, Peekskill, NY 10566....**914-734-4756**
  fax: 914-734-4820
  Yonar, Michael: Borsteler Chaussee 85-99, Hamburg, Germany, 22453............40-514-9650
  York, Jeff: 1445 N State Pkwy #1902, Chicago, IL 60610......................312-664-8849
- York, Judy: pg 441 60 E 42nd St, New York, NY 10165-1940.................**212-867-8092**
  e-mail: DHLT@aol.com / url: www.HT-LTD.com / fax: 212-949-1977
- Youll, Paul: pg 434 60 E 42nd St, New York, NY 10165-1940.................**212-867-8092**
  e-mail: DHLT@aol.com / url: www.HT-LTD.com / fax: 212-949-1977
  Young & Laramore: 310 E Vermont, Indianapolis, IN 46204 317-264-8000
  Young Assocs, Robert: 78 N Union St, Rochester, NY 14607 716-546-1973
  Young, Amy: 14165 Garfield Rd, Spring Lake, MI 49456 616-847-1630
  Young, Bob: 1003 Diamond Ave #209, S Pasadena, CA 91030 818-441-8955
  Young, Bruce: 2917 N Fulton Dr NE, Atlanta, GA 30305........................404-266-0088
  Young, Coulter: 32 Croft Ln, Peekskill, NY 10566...............................914-739-2239
- Young, Eddie: pg 788 353 W 53rd St #1W, New York, NY 10019.............**212-682-2462**
  e-mail: info@amerartists.com / url: www.amerartists.com / fax: 212-582-0090
  Young, Emily: 2173 NE Multnomah, Portland, OR 97232.......................503-281-3923
  Young, Mary O'Keefe: 62 Midchester Ave, White Plains, NY 10606 914-949-0147
  Young, Michael: 425 Fontana Pl NE, Albuquerque, NM 87108 505-255-0670
  Young, Paul: PO Box 344, Champaign, IL 61824................................217-398-1923
- Young, Ron: pg 1438 7 Gifford Lane, Medusa, NY 12120....................**518-239-6551**
  fax: 518-239-4935
- Young, Stefanie: pg 1439 2427 Bay St, San Francisco, CA 94123............**415-776-1218**
  fax: 415-776-1218
  Young, Timothy: 30 Bridgman Rd Chiswick, London, England, UK W4 5BD.........1819-950191
  Young, Wally: 7 Birch Hill Rd, Weston, CT 06883 203-227-5672
  Youngblood, Michael S: RR1 Box 265/Kings Indian Farm,
  Carbondale, IL 62901 618-457-6497
- Younger, Heidi: pg 309 58 W 15th St, New York, NY 10011 ....**212-741-2539**
  url: www.showcase.com / fax: 212-741-4660
  Yourke, Oliver: 525A Sixth Ave, Brooklyn, NY 11215 718-965-0609
  Yourman, Judith: 1900 Princeton Ave, St Paul, MN 55105......................612-699-5987
- Youssi, John: pg 420 60 E 42nd St, New York, NY 10165-1940...............**212-867-8092**
  e-mail: DHLT@aol.com / url: www.HT-LTD.com / fax: 212-949-1977
  Youtsie, Scott: 417 W Patti Page Blvd, Claremore, OK 74017...................918-343-9865
  Yuh, Jennifer: 4828 Obispo Ave, Lakewood, CA 90712 310-425-6830
  Yule, Susan Hunt: 176 Elizabeth St, New York, NY 10012......................212-226-0439
  Yundt, Peter: 468 Queen St E #104, Toronto, ON M5A 1T7 416-367-2446
  Yurkovic, Michael: 5234 N Leamington, Chicago, IL 60630....................773-282-7445
- Yves, Jean: pg 430 60 E 42nd St, New York, NY 10165-1940 ....**212-867-8092**
  e-mail: DHLT@aol.com / url: www.HT-LTD.com / fax: 212-949-1977

Z

- Zabarte, Charlie: pg 1212 3479 Agate Dr #1, Santa Clara, CA 95051 ....**408-985-4841**
  e-mail: z-net@ix.netcom.com
  Zach, Tim: 180 Varick St #1302, New York, NY 10014.........................212-807-6868
  Zacharow, Christopher: 115 West 2nd Street, New York, NY 10011 212-989-4600
  Zadnik, Pat: 9215 Woods Way Dr, Kirtland, OH 44094.........................216-256-6273
  Zador, Lisa: 64 Morton St #3C, New York, NY 10014...........................212-242-3006
  Zagorski, Stanislaw: 142 E 35th St, New York, NY 10016......................212-532-2348
  Zahara, Lesley: 18315 Sugar Bush Ct, Middletown, CA 95461 707-987-4856
  Zaharuk, Michael: 61 Alvin Ave, Toronto, ON M4T 2A8 416-538-7410
  Zahnd, Mark: PO Box 25011, Charlotte, NC 28229.............................704-875-6117
  Zakari, Chantal: 2105 N Oakley, Chicago, IL 60646.............................773-252-2432
  Zakashansky, Hannah: 1340 E 9th St #C8, Brooklyn, NY 11230...............212-726-4098
  Zakrasjsek, Molly: 12741 Cedar Rd #B, Cleveland Heights, OH 44106 216-397-7897
  Zakrzemski, Dan: 21 Elm St, East Aurora, NY 14052 716-655-2940
  Zale, David: 3529 Highway Ave, Highland, IN 46322 219-838-4254
- Zaman, Farida: pg 1093 ....**416-489-3769**
  18 Norman Rd, Montclair, NJ 07043..**973-744-9377**
  e-mail: fzaman@cybernex.net
  Zamchick, Gary: 56 Hillside Ave, Tenafly, NJ 07670............................201-568-3727
  Zammarchi, Robert: PO Box 1147, Boston, MA 02134 617-787-9513

Zappler, Nina: 120 Gertrude St, Syracuse, NY 13203..........................315-475-6833
Zappy, Michael: 6606 rue Drolet, Montréal, QU H2S 2S8 514-948-0477
Zaresky, Don: 41 Leonard Ave, Northfield Center, OH 44067 216-467-5917
Zarins, Joyce Audy: 19 Woodland St, Merrimac, MA 01860....................508-346-8994
Zaslavsky, Morris: 13763 Fiji way #EU1, Marina Del Rey, CA 90292............213-399-3666
Zastrow, Stuart: 925 Elm Grove Rd, Elm Grove, WI 53122.....................414-785-1940
Zavell, Bonnie: 115 Woodcrest St, Elyria, OH 44035 216-365-3477
Zawacki, Alison: 2813 Pepper Oaks Dr, Sacramento, CA 95827...............916-368-7157
Zebot, George: PO Box 4295, Laguna Beach, CA 92652 714-494-7311
Zeigler, Gavin: PO Box 21076, New York, NY 10023...........................212-957-8007
Zeines, Bruce: 643 Vanderbilt St, Brooklyn, NY 11218.........................718-972-7256
Zeleznik, John: 7307 Kelvin Ave #10, Canoga Park, CA 91306 818-884-4954
Zellin, Lisa: 236 E 33rd St #D, New York, NY 10016............................212-978-2291
- Zeltner, Tim: pg 561,576,577 155 Lippincott St, Toronto, ON M5S 2P3 ....**416-505-9522**
  toll-free **888-277-7200**
  e-mail: shelley@sbaillustrates.com / url: www.sbaillustrates.com
  Zelvin, Diana: 35 Clark St #E5, Brooklyn, NY 11201 718-596-4816
  Zents, Shawn: 617 Country Club Dr Unit 1424, Ventura, CA 93003 805-578-9982
- Zernitsky, Leon: pg 1231
  605 Finch Ave W #71-6, Willowdale, ON M2R 1P1 ....**416-638-9271**
  fax: 416-638-9271
  Zgodzinski, Rose: Chicago, IL 312-663-5506
  Los Angeles, CA 213-688-7428
  New York, NY 212-643-0896
  Panama City, FL 904-747-8415
  UK/Western Europe, ...186-543-5654
  468 Queen St E #104, Toronto, ON M5A 1T7 416-367-2446
- Zhu, Hua: pg 794 32 W 40th St, New York, NY 10018 ....**212-575-6877**
  e-mail: pfosterrep@aol.com / fax: 212-953-0728
- Zick, Brian: pg 397 250 W 57th St #521, New York, NY 10107 ....**212-397-7330**
  url: www.lindgrensmith.com (and) www.stockillustrated.com
  Ziegler, Gavin: PO Box 21076, New York, NY 10023..........................212-957-8007
  Zielinski, John: 6239 Elizabeth Ave, St Louis, MO 63139 314-781-8851
  Ziemann, Mark: 529 Filmore St, San Francisco, CA 94117....................415-487-9502
- Ziemienski, Dennis: pg 1064
  110 Sutter St #706, San Francisco, CA 94104...............................**415-441-4384**
  fax: 415-395-9809
  Ziering, Bob: 108 E 35th St #2, New York, NY 10016..........................212-889-3337
  Zilberts & Assocs, Ed: 12200 E Briarwood #294, Englewood, CO 80112........303-792-3466
  Zima, Al: 64 Cooke Ave, Carteret, NJ 07008...................................908-969-0636
  Zimdars, Maureen: 9825 234th St SW, Edmonds, WA 98020 206-546-5141
  Zimmerman, Amy: 19 Salem Ln, Port Washington, NY 11050.................212-598-0133
  Zimmerman, Bruce: 8030 Woodmont Ave #300, Bethesda, MD 20814 301-656-2787
- Zimmerman, Jeff: pg 1209
  4010 Montgomery, Shelby Township, MI 48316.............................**810-731-4674**
  Zimmerman, Jerry: 351 Warwick Ave, Teaneck, NJ 07666....................201-837-7702
  Zimmerman, Robert: 16 Gertrude Pl, Asheville, NC 28801 704-252-9689
- Zingarelli, Mark: pg 846 1809 7th Ave #1710, Seattle, WA 98101 ....**206-447-1600**
  url: www.pathackett.com / fax: 206-447-0739
- Zingone, Robin: pg 652,653 Pier 33 North, San Francisco, CA 94111 ....**415-956-4750**
  e-mail: cgr@slip.net / url: www.coreygrahamreps.com
  24 Old Depot Road, PO Box 598, Chester, CT 06412..........................**860-526-1755**
  url: www.theispot.com/artist/zingone
  Zinn, Ron: 117 Village Dr, Jericho, NY 11753 516-933-2767
  Ziowodzka, Joanna: 144 W 10th Street, New York, NY 10014................212-620-7981
  Zipser, Tami: 31 Doris Ave, Franklin Square, NY 11010........................516-358-4534
  Zito Studio, Andy: 135 S La Brea Ave, Los Angeles, CA 90036................213-931-1182
  Zito, Andy: 353 W 53rd St #1W, New York, NY 10019 212-682-2462
  Zizzi, Richard: 1535 W Renee Dr, Phoenix, AZ 85027 602-869-8445
- Zlotsky, Boris: pg 137 420 Lexington Ave, New York, NY 10170..............**212-986-5680**
  url: www.mendolaart.com / fax: 212-818-1246
  Zlowodzka, Joanna: 144 W 10th St #18, New York, NY 10014................212-620-7981
  Zoot, Ira: 6755 N Artesian #2E, Chicago, IL 60645.............................312-280-0048
  Zuba, Bob: 105 W Saylor Ave, Plains, PA 18705................................717-824-5665
  Zuban, Kevin: 4 Putnam Ave, Edison, NJ 08817................................908-949-8617
  Zuber-Mallison, Carol: 2340 Edwin St, Ft Worth, TX 76110...................214-906-4162
  Zudeck, Darryl: 35 W 92nd St #5G, New York, NY 10025 212-663-9454
  Zumbo, Matt: 60 E 42nd St #822, New York, NY 10165......................212-682-1490
  Zumpfe, Rosemary: 4908 Martin St, Lincoln, NE 68504.......................402-466-4881
  Zunk, Ingrid: 758 Wildomar Street, Pacific Palisades, CA 90272................310-454-2662
- Zuzalek, Michele: pg 827
  1424 La Positas Plaza, Santa Barbara, CA 93105............................**805-682-6775**
  Santa Barbara, CA **805-962-3367**
  e-mail: monetz@silcom.com / url: www.michelezstudio.com / fax: 805-962-7617
  Zwarenstein, Alex: 155 E 38th St, New York, NY 10016.......................212-697-6170
  Zwicker, Sara Mintz: 98 Stetson St, Braintree, MA 02184.....................617-848-8962
  Zwinger, Jane: 2405 NW Thurman St, Portland, OR 97210...................503-203-8300
  Zwingler, Randall: 3301A S Jefferson Ave, St Louis, MO 63118 314-773-2600
  Zwolak, Paul: 278 Hamilton Ave, Princeton, NJ 08540 609-252-9405

GRAPHIC DESIGNERS & LETTERERS

A

A & H Design: 11844 Rncho Brndo #120-72, Rancho Bernardo, CA 92128...619-486-0777
A & M Assocs: 2727 N Central Ave Box 21503, Phoenix, AZ 85036...602-263-6504
A & S Creative Works: 1677 Tullie Circle #102, Atlanta, GA 30329...404-636-6622
A Bit Better Corporation: 127 2nd St #2, Los Altos, CA 94022...415-948-4766
A Creative Group: PO Box 612006, South Lake Tahoe, CA 96152...916-544-4701
A Designing Woman: 4651 E Vernon, Phoenix, AZ 85008...602-840-1117
A La Carte Graphics: 2024 Spring Rd, Smyrna, GA 30080...770-432-7639
A Priori Art & Design: 2722 Kaaha St, Honolulu, HI 96826...808-949-2708
A Solutions Company: 304 1/2 8th St #220, Des Moines, IL 50309...515-247-0003
A Street Design: 1284 Antwerp Ln, San Jose, CA 95118...408-266-5544
A To Z communications: 100 Ross St #212, Pittsburgh, PA 15219...412-471-4160
A-Musing Creative: 114 3rd St #201, Minneapolis, MN 55401...612-341-9333
A1 Brochure & Postcard Production: 17 Cabrillo Dr, Avalon, CA 90704...310-510-3100
A2Z Creative Services: 2020 Arboles Pl, Escondido, CA 92029...619-739-0896
Aardvark Illus & Graphics: 13000 Bel Red Rd #201, Bellevue, WA 98005...206-453-6010
Aardvark/Schill Design: 2749 S Westgate Ave, Los Angeles, CA 90064...310-445-8651
Aart-Werk Graphic Design, Inc: 1920 E 3rd St #11, Tempe, AZ 85281...602-921-3060
Abacus Graphics: 4701 Morning Canyon Rd, Oceanside, CA 92056...619-724-7750
Abbate Design: 726 Bloomfield Basement, Hoboken, NJ 07030...201-222-9046
Abbey Photo: 416 E Central Blvd, Palisades Park, NJ 07650...201-947-1221
Abbott/Barrington & Co: 2217 E Turney Ave, Phoenix, AZ 85016...602-553-81301
ABC Design: 3425 Riverknoll Way, West Lynn, OR 97068...503-699-1886
Abdo, Lynda: 22727 Schoolcraft St, West Hills, CA 91307...818-710-8108
Abracadabra Animation: 64 Loughlin Ave, Cos Cob, CT 06807...203-869-3646
Abrams Creative Services: 2049 Red Coach Ln, Encinitas, CA 92024...619-942-4380
Abrams Design Group: 100 View St #203, Mountain View, CA 94041...415-964-2388
Abrams Design, Kym: 213 W Institute Pl #608, Chicago, IL 60610...312-654-1005
Abrams, Elaine: 112 Fourth Ave, New York, NY 10003...212-254-1688
ABS Graphics: 901 S Rohlwing rd, Addison, IL 60101...630-495-2400
Absolute Graphics: 343 S Dearborn #1111, Chicago, IL 60604...312-427-2120
Accent Marketing: 800 Douglas Rd #100, Coral Gables, FL 33134...305-461-1112
Accent On Design: 1840 Barnes Circle, West Linn, OR 97068...503-657-3747
Access Creative Communications: 210 Avenue I #E, Redondo Beach, CA 90277...310-543-9820
Ace Design: 480 Gate Five Rd #310, Sausalito, CA 94965...415-332-9390
Acme Design Group: 100 North State St, Newtown, PA 18940...215-579-4946
Acorn Interactive: 23 E 10th St #226, New York, NY 10003...212-673-3333
Active 8: 601 N Eutaw St # 704, Baltimore, MD 21201...410-962-0270
Active Window Productions: 264 Newbury St, Boston, MA 02116...617-421-1511
ACTV Interactive: 1270 Avenue of the Americas, New York, NY 10020...212-262-2570
Ad Agency, The: 8605 Westwood Center Dr #200, Vienna, VA 22182...703-821-2030
Ad Art Design: 1407 Cross St, Eugene, OR 97402...503-344-8476
Ad Department, The : 6409 Ellis Rd, Ft Worth, TX 76112...817-451-7980
AD Design: 2501 W Zia Rd #2-203, Santa Fe, NM 87505...505-473-5163
Ad Gallery By Capielo: 2465 Campus Dr, Irvine, CA 92715...714-261-0280
Ad Group, The: 927 Lincoln Way, Auburn, CA 95603...916-888-0484
Ad Infinitum: 1414 2nd St #102, Santa Monica, CA 90401...310-395-7531
Ad Links: CA...310-534-8600
Ad Med Assocs, Inc: 6 Kingswoods Dr, New Hope, PA 18938...215-862-2316
Ad Media: 111 E Lincoln Rd, Spokane, WA 99208...509-466-1632
Ad Store, Inc, The : 8950 St Ives Dr, Los Angeles, CA 90069...310-276-1865
Ad-hoc Interactive: 221 Caledonia St, Sausalito, CA 94965...415-332-0180
Ad/Art Studios: 1501 Euclid Ave #830, Cleveland, OH 44115...312-832-4100
Adams Design, Gaylord: 521 Fifth Ave, New York, NY 10175...212-684-4625
Adams Graphic Design, Pam: 5274 E Broadway, Long Beach, CA 90803...310-438-5422
Adams Graphic Design, Wanda: 5098 Springhill Dr NW, Albany, OR 97321...503-926-2709
Adams, Cheryl: 2124 NW 139th St, Des Moines, IA 50325...515-223-7174
Adams, David R: 2105 Commerce St #102, Dallas, TX 75201...214-741-4007
Adams, Deborah S: 440 East 57th St #GC, New York, NY 10022...212-486-1002
Adams, Nina: 3952 Western Ave, Western Springs, IL 60558...708-246-0766
Adams, Rhett Design: 3130 Crow Canyon Rd #D, San Ramon, CA 94583...510-806-0100
Adams/Moriokas Double Vision: 9348 Civic Center Dr, Beverly Hills, CA 90201...310-246-5758
Add Design: 3565 Luke Circle NW, Albuquerque, NM 87107...505-344-3696
Addante Design, Inc: 417 W 43rd St #20, New York, NY...212-957-3769
Adelson, Lore: CA...714-650-5040
Adhouse: 4539 N 22nd St #105, Phoenix, AZ 85016...602-468-9877
Adkins/Balchunas: 163 Exchange St, Pawtucket, RI 02860...401-725-1855
Adler & Schinkel, Inc: 3842 W Peoria Ave, Phoenix, AZ 85029...602-277-9366
Adler Assocs, Stan: 305 Seventh Ave 19th Fl, New York, NY 10001...212-366-4860
Adler Design Group: 9690 Deereco Rd #230, Timonium, MD 21093...410-561-5550
Adler, Shelly: 2647 S Magnolia, Los Angeles, CA 90007...213-749-7347
Adler-Schwartz Graphics: 9690 Deerceo Rd #230, Timonium, MD 21093...410-561-5550
Adlerblum Design: 1133 Broadway #1225, New York, NY 10010...212-807-8429
Admagic Creative Services: 160 W Pomona Ave, Monrovia, CA 91016...818-303-5514
Admark Pacific: 2000 Cal Young Rd, Eugene, OR 97401...503-686-2394
Adnet Communications: 1378 Hilda Ave #203, Glendale, CA 91205...818-243-7802
Adrienne Youngstein & Assocs: 127 W24th St, New York, NY 10011...212-242-7140
Ads Plus: 15112 McRae St, Norwalk, CA 90650...310-929-0984
Adsit, Chuck: 1123 Louise St, San Leandro, CA 94578...510-483-4239
ADT Design For Marketing: 933 Lyford Dr, San Dimas, CA 91773...909-592-4768
Adv Design, Scott: 9411 Headlands Rd, Mentor, OH 44060...305-743-2116
Advance Design Center: 2501 Oak Lawn Ave #200, Dallas, TX 75219...214-526-1420
Advanced Concepts Center: 13500 Reeck Rd, Southgate, MI 48195...313-246-0323
Advantage Graphics Design Works: 434 W Colorado St #201, Glendale, CA 91204...818-545-4076
Advertising & Design Assocs: PO Box 788, Claremont, CA 91711...909-621-7454
Advertising a la Carte: 11400 W Olympic Blvd #207, Los Angeles, CA 90064...310-551-9237
Advertising Design: 1201 First Ave S #326, Seattle, WA 98134...206-587-6530
Advertising Design Assocs: 1095 Market St #411, San Francisco, CA 94103...415-558-8000
Advertising Designers, Inc: 7087 Snyder Ridge Rd, Mariposa, CA 95338...209-742-6704
Adzema, Diane: 17 Bleecker St, New York, NY 10012...212-982-5657
Aerial: 58 Federal St, San Francisco, CA 94107...415-957-9761
Aerocraft Charter Art Service: 3618 W Voltaire Ave, Phoenix, AZ 85029...602-978-1570
Aeschlima Design, Inc: 307 Fifth Ave 14th Fl, New York, NY 10016...212-685-1585
After Hours: 434 Marieta St NW #404, Atlanta, GA 30313...404-523-9950
After Hours: 1201 Jefferson #100B, Phoenix, AZ 85034...602-256-2648
After Hours Design & Adv: 16933 Shinedale Dr, Canyon Country, CA 91351...805-251-0197
After Midnight: 51 Melcher St, Boston, MA 02210...617-350-7970
Aga: 2 park ave 4Th Fl, New York, NY 10016...212-726-7000
Agency, The: 402 Friday Creek Rd, Burlington, WA 98233...206-724-3054
Agency.com Ltd.: 665 Broadway 9th Fl, New York, NY 10012...212-358-8220
AGI: 424 N Larchmont Blvd, Los Angeles, CA 90004...213-462-0821
Agnew Moyer Smith: 503 Martindale St, Pittsburgh, PA 15212...412-322-6333
Agnew, Scott: 4170 17th St #204, San Francisco, CA 94114...415-864-5233
Agra: 60 Madison Ave 9th Fl, New York, NY 10010...212-545-0510
AHA Creative Solutions: 3300 NE Expressway Bldg 4 #M, Atlanta, GA 30341...770-986-9997
Ahdoot, Samantha: 817 S Westgate Ave #302, Los Angeles, CA 90049...310-826-8716
Ainsworth Design: 2341 Moulton Pkwy #200, Laguna Hills, CA 92653...714-768-8500
Air Castle Productions: 410-40 Alexander St, Toronto, ON M4Y 1B5...416-921-4337
Aizawa & Furuta Advertising: 141 Industrial St, San Francisco, CA 94124...415-695-8700
AJ Buttler & CO: 122 Huntington St, New Brunswick, NJ 08901...908-828-4244
AJ Design & Assocs: PO Box 532, Basalt, CO 81621...970-927-4924
Ajamian, Jeanine: 25 W 45th St #203, New York, NY 10036...212-302-1325
AK Productions: 461 Second St #7558, San Francisco, CA 94107...408-356-1044
AKA Design: 1605 S Ninth St, St Louis, MO 63104...314-621-6070
AKA Hound Dog Studio: 1710 Hayes St #203, Nashville, TN 37203...615-327-9577
Akagi Design: 632 Commercial St 4th Fl, San Francisco, CA 94111...415-397-4668
Akers Designers, Kevin: 13 Hart St, San Rafael, CA 94901...415-455-0562
Akiyama Design: 16608 E Prentice Ave, Aurora, CO 80015...303-680-8298
Akobian, Hutch: 620 E Angeleno Ave #G, Burbank, CA 91501...818-557-7739
Aktari Design & Comm : 781 Raycliff Pl, Concord, CA 94518...510-686-9610
Aktulun, Kenan: 111 Southwood Rd, Austin, TX 78704...512-447-6522
Alaimo Studio, Terry M: 2233 Martin St #113, Irvine, CA 92715...714-724-8899
Alameda Group, The: 1585 The Alameda #100, San Jose, CA 95126...408-287-9055
Alan Gallery: 36 Park St, Berea, OH 44017...216-243-7794
Alaskan Designs: PO Box 41572, Tucson, AZ 85717...602-323-3282
Alaxander Design: 1201 18th St #240, Denver, CO 80202...303-298-7711
Albert, Keith: 355 Lexington Ave 4th Fl, New York, NY 10021...212-687-5760
Albertson Design: 425 SE Third/PO Box 5275, Portland, OR 97208...503-232-2549
Albrektson Studio: Wilcox Bldg/42 Waybosset/5th Fl, Providence, RI 02903...401-274-4260
Album Graphics: 1950 N Ruby St, Melrose Park, IL 60160...708-344-9100
Alden Design, Inc: 2157 India St, San Diego, CA 92101...619-544-9299
Aleida Graphics: 1555 Mesa Verde Dr East #49K, Costa Mesa, CA 92626...714-444-3403
Alessi Design, Anthony: 15737 Thomas Ln, Oak Forest, IL 60452...708-535-6542
Alexander Communications: 1000 W MacArthur Blvd #49, Santa Ana, CA 92707...714-641-7522
Alexander Design Assocs: 588 Broadway #202, New York, NY 10012...212-925-7755
Alexander Design, Inc, Jann: 4100 N 23rd St, Arlington, VA 22207...703-528-1200
Alexander Graphic Design, Jeanette: 1055 Nakata Ave, Bainbridge Island, WA 98110...206-842-6368
Alexander, Martha: Box 130144, Houston, TX 77219...713-529-0472
Alfonso Architects, Inc: 1705 N 16th St, Tampa, FL 33605...813-247-3333
Aliman Design, Inc: 134 Spring St 7th Fl, New York, NY 10012...212-925-9621
Alinsangan/Doyle: 2319 6th St #1, Santa Monica, CA 90405...310-392-7705
Aljon Graphics: 1721 E Lambert Rd, La Habra, CA 90631...310-694-3144
Allen & Assocs: 712 Midland Park, Aspen, CO 81611...303-925-5630
Allen & Assocs, William: 87 Wall St 2nd Fl, Seattle, WA 98121...206-443-9933
Allen Creative: 2573 Laurel View Ct, Snellville, GA 30278...770-972-8862
Allen Graphics: 954 Arlington, Redwood City, CA 94062...415-366-4009
Allied Graphic Arts: 2 Park Ave 4th Fl, New York, NY 10036...212-726-7000
Allison & Assocs: 1151 Amherst Ave #12, Los Angeles, CA 90049...310-820-5298
Allison Design: 7645 Jarboe St, Kansas City, MO 64114...816-444-7782
Almazan Graphics: 3136 Camino Graciosa, Thousand Oaka, CA 91360...805-492-0030
Alpha Light Communcations: 77 Pearl St, New York, NY 10007...212-363-1288
Alphabetics: 630 3rd St, San Francisco, CA 94107...415-543-1959
AlphaConn Web Design: PO Box 1954, Hartford, CT...860-376-9028
Altered Image: 7 Deerpark Dr #D, Monmouth Juncti, NJ 08852...908-274-2220
Altgelt & Korge: 3308 Broadway #203, San Antonio, TX 78209...210-829-0151
Alto Design: 3300 Business Dr, Sacramento, CA 95820...916-732-2068
Alto Design Group, Inc: 1160 Terra Bella Ave, Mountain View, CA 94043...415-968-2224
Altschul, Charles: 356 Riverbank Rd, Stamford, CT 06903...203-329-7251
Alu, Jeffrey Thomas: 633 San Leon, Irvine, CA 92606...714-261-1179
Alvarez Group: 3171 Cadet Ct, Los Angeles, CA 90068...213-876-3491
Alvey Design, Trent: 307 W 200 South #5000, Salt Lake City, UT 84101...801-363-8001
AM Business Communications: 14747 Artesia Blvd 4D, La Mirada, CA 90638...714-994-6630
Amann Design & Dir, Marilyn: 7338 Hotchkiss, El Cerrito, CA 94530...510-526-9091
Amber Enterprises: 11828 Rancho Bernardo Rd #123, San Diego, CA 92128...619-755-0847
Amber W Design: 2791 W Calle de Dalias, Tucson, AZ 85745...602-743-7549
Ambrosi & Assocs: 1100 W Washington Blvd, Chicago, IL 60607...312-666-9200
America Now, Inc: 2101 S Platt River Dr, Denver, CO 80223...303-934-7575
American Enginuity: 6395 Gunpark Dr, Boulder, CO 80301...303-530-7800
American Express Publishing Co: 1120 Ave of Americas, New York, NY 10036...212-382-5600
American Graphics: 2300 Defoor Hills Rd, Atlanta, GA 30318...404-355-7220
American Greetings: 1 American Rd, Cleveland, OH 44144...216-252-7300
American Model & Design: 496 East Main St, Denville, NJ 07834...201-627-0084
American Tech Systems: 5 Suburban Park Dr, Billerica, MA 01821...508-663-6755
American Visualists: 301 Mesa Dr, Costa Mesa, CA 92627...714-631-3260
American Web Classics: 4 Lincoln St, Baldwin, NY 11510...516-377-4749
AMG Marketing Resources: 2217 E Ninth St #306, Cleveland, OH 44115...216-621-1835
Amorosi, Philip R: 1432 E Cedar St, Tempe, AZ 85281...602-968-5530
Amos B Designs: 4073 Gresham #2, San Diego, CA 92109...619-296-8235
Amos Design, Gwen: 4909 Cottage Way #1, Carmichael, CA 95608...916-486-4491
Ampersand Assocs: 1620 S Canal St #3000, Chicago, IL 60616...630-241-2282
Ampersand Graphic Design: 15425 N Greenway Hayden Loop, Scottsdale, AZ 85260...602-998-4200
Ampersand Studios: 1290 S Columbine, Denver, CO 80210...303-733-0846

Amsterdam King Assocs, Inc: 3435 Ocean Pk Blvd #112,
Santa Monica, CA 90405 310-393-7263
Amundson Group: 1810 S 22nd St, Rogers, AR 72756 501-631-8202
Amundson, Eric: 1100 W Cambridge Circl Dr #550, Kansas City, KS 66103 913-281-4433
Anagnost Design: 17320 Burbank Blvd #36, Encino, CA 91316 818-784-4642
Anagram Design Group: 48 Lance Drive, Somers, CT 06071 860-749-5095
Anastasion Studio: 563 W 200 S, Salt Lake City, UT 84101 801-355-4400
Ancona & Assocs: 123 Townsend St #215, San Francisco, CA 94107 415-495-4828
Ancona 2: 19 W 21st St #1001, New York, NY 10010 212-807-8772
Anderholm, Jeff: 101 Huntington Ave, Boston, MA 02199 617-859-1212
Andersen Design: 37 Santa Barbara Avenue, San Anselmo, CA 94960 415-721-7630
Andersen, Bill: 27 Minkel Rd, Ossining, NY 10562 914-762-4867
Anderson Art Direction, Mike: PO Box 9315, Newport Beach, CA 92658.........714-662-6546
Anderson Debartolo Pan Inc: 1515 E Missouri #115, Phoenix, AZ 85014........602-230-9660
Anderson Design Works, Hornall: 1008 Western Ave #600,
Seattle, WA 98104....................................206-467-5800
Anderson Design, David: 539 North Linden Ave, Oak Park, IL 60302..............708-848-1020
Anderson Design, Mark: 790 High St, Palo Alto, CA 94301....................415-328-8864
Anderson Design, Michael: 28202 Cabot Rd #300, Laguna Niguel, CA 92677 714-831-3501
Anderson Jones Partners: 31726 Rancho Viejo Rd #207,
San Juan Capistrano, CA 92675 714-240-6802
Anderson, Charles S: 30 N First St, Minneapolis, MN 55401....................612-339-5181
Anderson, Jeri Lyn: 750 Berkshire Ave, Pittsburgh, PA 15226....................412-531-0145
Anderson, Lance: 5937 Shasta Ave, Dunsmuir, CA 96025....................415-788-5893
Anderson, Lisa: 15750 Crestwick Dr, La Mirada, CA 90638....................310-943-7851
Anderson, Russ & Terry: 1054 W Dragoon Ave, Mesa, AZ 85210 520-969-5299
Anderson-Thomas Design, Inc: 110 29th Ave N #301, Nashville, TN 37203......615-327-9894
Anderson/Clark Design: 10999 Riverside Dr #110, N Hollywood, CA 91602.......818-760-8881
Andre & Assocs, Brian: 3 Hutton Center #700, Santa Ana, CA 92704 714-957-1314
Andrew Davis Design, Paul: 1653 Downings St, Denver, CO 80218................303-830-9139
Andrews Co, Inc, WE: 140 South Rd, Bedford, MA 01730....................617-275-0720
Andrews, Chris: 4177 Carp Rd RR 1, Carp, ON K0A 1L0....................613-828-0261
Animated Systems & Design: 1900 Embaracero Rd #110,
Palo Alto, CA 94303....................................415-424-8586
Annis, Scott: 26099 McCiver, Aspen Park, CO 80222 303-674-1151
Annivette Stuido: 802 Belvidere Ave, Plainfield, NJ 07060....................908-561-5596
Another Artist: 2601 Thrasher Ln #2, San Jose, CA 95125 408-978-7010
Another Planet: 7430 Milan Ave, St Louis, MO 63130 314-726-5013
Ansbro Design: 1261 Green Acres Ct, Santa Cruz, CA 95062 408-475-4684
Anslow & Spathas Design: 6434 SE Milwaukie Ave, Portland, OR 97202 503-231-0806
Anspach Grossman PORTUGAL: 711 Third Ave 12th Fl, New York, NY 10017 212-692-9000
Antex Electronics: 16100 S Figueroa St, Gardena, CA 90248....................310-532-3092
Anthony Co, Robert: 10 E 23rd St 2nd Fl, New York, NY 10010 212-673-3011
Anthony-Franklin: 342 W 200 South #230, Salt Lake City, UT 84101 801-532-0670
Antisdel Image Group: 2332 Fruitdale Ave, San Jose, CA 95054 408-988-1010
Antista Fairclough Design: 64 Lenox Point NE, Atlanta, GA 30324....................404-816-3201
Antler & Baldwin Design Group: 230 5th Ave #512, New York, NY 10001 212-683-0051
Antokas Graphics, Stacey: 152 W 24th St/3rd Fl, New York, NY 10011...........212-675-6006
Antonuccio Design, David: 31-72 41st St 2nd Fl, Long Island City, NY 11103 718-956-7815
Apex Design: 906 Mulberry Ave, Hagerstown, MD 21742 301-791-9312
Aplin, Uno & Chibana: 2685 Marine Way #1415, Mountain View, CA 94043 415-966-8000
• **Apjones, Todd: pg 1452** Naples, FL **941-403-4393**
fax: 941-403-0066
Apor Design: 701 Atkins Dr, Glendale, CA 91206 818-549-0822
Appelbaum Company: 220 E 23rd St #507, New York, NY 10010 212-213-1130
Apple Design Source: 58 W 40th St 6th Fl, New York, NY 10018....................212-575-6373
Apple Design, Hal: 1112 Ocean Dr #203, Manhattan Beach, CA 90266 310-318-3823
Apple Design/CA: 1309 Milton Ave, Walnut Creek, CA 94596 510-256-6625
Appleton Design: 488 Fern St, West Hartford, CT 06107 860-521-4745
Aramian, Tammy: 663 S Bernardo Ave #7B, Sunnyvale, CA 94087 415-964-3938
Arana, Lupe & Assoc: 11533 Slater Ave #H, Fountain Valley, CA 92708 714-540-6700
Aratar: 220 Downey St, San Francisco, CA 94117 415-753-5855
Arcanna Design Comm: 650 Central Ave, Peekskill, NY 10566....................914-736-1760
Arce & Kwan Inc: 10 E 2nd St #1, New York, NY 10003 212-387-9209
Arce, Alex: 10 E 2nd St, New York, NY 10003 212-387-9209
Archambault, Donna: One Scenic Drive, Portland, CT 06480....................203-342-1023
Archer Design: 353 Folsom St 2nd Fl, San Francisco, CA 94105....................415-777-5788
Archey & Cavala: 4000 Bridgeway #309, Sausalito, CA 94965....................415-331-4592
Architectural Design Alliance Inc: 1737 Chestnut St, Philadelphia, PA 19103 ...215-561-9700
Architext: 121 Interpark Blvd #208, San Antonio, TX 78216 210-490-2240
Archuleta Design, Archie: 11200 Hume NE, Albuquerque, NM 87112 505-291-0285
Arena & Assocs: 61 Camino Alto #101, Mill Valley, CA 94941 415-383-9632
• **Arendt, Uwe: pg 1444** 15908 82nd Pl NE, Bothell, WA 98011 ....**425-488-2573**
e-mail: arendt@eskimo.com
Arias Design Group: 502 Waverley, Palo Alto, CA 94301 415-321-8138
Arias, Jamie: CA 310-535-5969
Arizona Graphics Network: 1054 W Dragoon Ave, Mesa, AZ 85210................602-969-5299
Arkkit-Forms: 692-A Moulton Ave, Los Angeles, CA 90031 213-227-0191
Arlt Graphics, Bob: 8392 Westlawn Ave, Los Angeles, CA 90045 310-568-0087
Armstrong Assocs: 1330 N Dutton Ave #201, Santa Rosa, CA 95401 707-527-8511
Armstrong Design Consultants: Box 12967, Raleigh, NC 27605 919-233-5786
Arneal, Clark Graphics: 1001 John St, Manhattan Beach, CA 90266 310-376-6666
Arnell Group: 130 Prince St, New York, NY 10011 212-219-8400
Arnold Assocs, Peter: 1 Hollis St #211, Wellesley, MA 02181 617-239-1030
Arnold Design: 105 Fifth Ave S #450, Minneapolis, MN 55401 612-339-2440
Arnott Group Design, Inc, The: 33 Davies Ave, Toronto, ON M4M 2A9 416-778-8990
Aron & Co, Michael: 156 Fifth Ave #500, New York, NY 10010 212-627-4054
Arris Studios: 1109 N Second St #C, Phoenix, AZ 85004....................602-254-0038
Arrowood Design: 318 S Birchwood Dr, Louisville, KY 40206....................502-897-2203
Art Assocs: 290 Gentry Way #5, Reno, NV 89502 702-828-3500
Art At Work: 4500 N 12th St, Phoenix, AZ 85014 602-274-9833
Art By Christian, Inc: 6343 Waterway Dr, Falls Church, VA 22044 703-642-5429
Art City: 6284 Brookhill Dr, Houston, TX 77087 713-644-1018
Art Corps, The: 4150 Duquesne Ave #2, Culver City, CA 90232 310-202-6462
Art Department: 2 W 46th St, New York, NY 10036 212-391-1826
Art Department Inc, The: 1 W Market St #205, York, PA 17401 717-845-4344
Art Department, The: 14714 Midship Woods Ct, Chesterfield, VA 23832 804-739-1198
Art Department, The: 2039 Willow Wood Ln, Encinitas, CA 92024....................619-944-7606
Art Department, The: 1779 Independence Blvd, Sarasota, FL 34234 813-355-7266
Art Depot Creative Agency, The: 710 13th St #210, San Diego, CA 92101 619-696-6545
Art Direction: 1100 W Lincoln Ave, Anaheim, CA 92805 714-778-6767
Art Direction: 3774 Westside Ave, Los Angeles, CA 90018 213-296-4858
Art Direction Services: 3319 El Dorado Blvd, Missouri City, TX 77749 713-977-0654
Art Directions: 201A Tubac Rd, Tubac, AZ 85646 520-398-9938
Art Directions, Inc: 28558 Lowell Court S, Southfield, MI 48076....................810-569-8566
Art Directors Club of Metropolitan Washington: 1620 Greenbrier Ct,
Reston, VA 20190....................................703-742-8055
Art Directors Service: 222 Waukegan Rd, Glenview, IL 60025....................847-657-1600
Art Etc: 2600 7th Street Rd, Louisville, KY 40208 502-637-6066
Art Factory: 925 Elm Grove Rd, Elm Grove, WI 53122 414-785-1940
Art Forms, Inc: 5150 Prospect Ave, Cleveland, OH 44103....................216-361-3855
Art Group, The: 3100 Smoketree Ct #1004, Raleigh, NC 27604 919-876-6765
Art Hotel: 607 Huntley Dr, West Hollywood, CA 90069....................310-854-6154
Art O Matic: 33951 Calle La Primavera, Dana Point, CA 92629 714-240-1856
Art Only, Inc: 2830 S Bannock St, Englewood, CO 80110 303-762-0422
Art Patrol Graphics Design: 25 W 89th St #4B, New York, NY 10024 212-787-3390
Art Rageous Design Services, Inc: 5904 Funston St, Hollywood, FL 33023.......305-961-7997
Art Service: 1135 Spring St NW, Atlanta, GA 30309 404-892-2105
Art Spikol: 751 S Fifth St, Philadelphia, PA 19147 215-627-4545
Art Studio, The: 110 30th Ave N #3, Nashville, TN 37203 615-329-3511
Art Works: 11418 SE 90th Ave #117, Portland, OR 97266 503-659-2103
Art Worx: 155 Teaneck Rd, Teaneck, NJ 07666 201-836-1273
Artability: 152 Village Square, Orinda, CA 94563....................510-254-4616
Artech Graphics: 11750 E 166th St, Artesia, CA 90701 310-924-5521
Arteffects, Inc: Midtown Tower #1115, Rochester, NY 14604....................716-232-7000
Artemedia: 8414 Lone Mesa, Austin, TX 78759 512-343-1781
Artemis: 721 Emerson St, Palo Alto, CA 94301 415-325-6596
Artery, The: 12 W Biddle St, Baltimore, MD 21201....................301-752-2979
Artful Education: 2913 Fulton St, Berkely, CA 94705....................510-843-7421
Arthur Design: 4751 Del Moreno Pl, Woodland Hills, CA 91364....................818-884-8748
Arthur Eckstein & Assoc Inc: 47 Pinetree Ln, Roslyn Hts, NY 11577 516-484-0606
Artifakt: 3748 22nd St, San Francisco, CA 94114 415-647-4700
Artists Studios: 668 Euclid Ave #815, Cleveland, OH 44114....................216-241-5355
Artmania: 8961 Complex Dr, San Diego, CA 92123 619-277-0071
Artmarks: 11 Rally Ct, Fairfax, CA 94930 415-721-2900
Artmaster Studios: 547 Library St, San Fernando, CA 91340....................818-365-7188
Artmill, The: 2701 N Reserve, Missoula, MT 59802....................406-543-7983
Artographix: 436 W Colorado #114, Glendale, CA 91204 818-500-1191
Artrix Interactive Studios: 71 W 23rd St #507, New York, NY 10010..............212-633-9695
Arts & Graphics: 4010 Justine Dr, Annandale, VA 22003 703-941-2560
Arts Place: 210 N Higgins #232, Missoula, MT 59802....................406-549-3460
Artsake: 900 E First St #307, Los Angeles, CA 90012 213-617-0488
Artscape: 532 El Dorado St, Pasadena, CA 91101 818-584-3997
Artwerks: 303 Potrero St #52, Santa Cruz, CA 95060 408-427-9040
Artword: 9666R Owensmouth Ave, Chatsworth, CA 91311....................818-709-7474
Artworks: 9 MT Vernon St, Winchester, MA 01890 617-721-4858
Artworks, Inc: PO Box 11001, Norfolk, VA 23517 757-624-2424
Arunski Assocs, Joe: 10660 NW 17th Pl, Plantation, FL 33322 305-473-4114
Asbury & Assocs: 3450 E Spring St #214, Long Beach, CA 90806 310-595-6481
Ascending Graphics: 1054 W Dragoon Ave, Mesa, AZ 85210....................602-969-5299
Ashcraft Design: 11832 W Pico Blvd, Los Angeles, CA 90064 310-479-8330
Asher Studio: 1700 E 17th Ave, Denver, CO 80218....................303-321-5599
Asher, Terri: 21800 Schoenborn St #162, Canoga Park, CA 91304 818-348-4278
Ashton & Co, David: 611 Cathedral St, Baltimore, MD 21201 301-727-1151
Askey Design & Illus: PO Box 591, Skaneateles, NY 13152....................315-685-3908
Aslan Media: 4801 Woodway #280E, Houston, TX 77057....................713-960-9411
Aspect Ratio Design: 1347 Cahuenga Blvd, Hollywood, CA 90028 213-467-2121
Associated Graphics: 3630 W Pioneer Pkwy #131, Arlington, TX 76013 817-459-1409
Associates Design, Inc: 509 19th St, Galveston, TX 77750....................489-762-5552
Associates Inc, The : 5319 Lee Hwy, Arlington, VA 22207....................703-534-3940
Aster: 136 High Dr, Laguna Beach, CA 92651 714-494-6192
Asterisk Graphics: 2332 Morris Ave, Union, NJ 07083....................908-851-2083
Asylum: 848 W Eastman #206, Chicago, IL 60622....................312-482-8877
Atelier 85: PO Box 491413, Los Angeles, CA 90049 310-826-1785
Atelier, Loucks: 20 Greenway Plz #624, Houston, TX 77046....................713-877-8551
Athanasius Design: 1300 N Damen Ave, Chicago, IL 60622 773-252-7271
Atkin: 301 Gold Ave SW #204, Albuquerque, NM 87102 505-843-6696
Atkins Design, Alexander: 1928 Old Middlefield Way #C,
Mountain view, CA 94043....................................415-948-6644
Atkins, Martyn: 1655 N Cherokee #300, Hollywood, CA 90028 213-653-8625
Atkins, Sharon: 20 Birch Hill Rd, Weston, CT 06883 203-222-7040
Atlanta Wristworks: 282 Southerland Terr NE, Atlanta, GA 30307 404-373-3001
Atlas Communications: 1312 N Greenview, Chicago, IL 60622 773-772-0177
Atlas Design: 27560 Falling Star Ln, Santa Clarita, CA 91350....................805-297-0013
Atomix: 1800 N Vine #310, Hollywood, CA 90028....................310-962-4745
Atrium Creative: 643 William St, Meadville, PA 16335....................814-337-0824
Attention Design!: 11938 Dorothy St #4, Brentwood, CA 90049....................310-207-6068
Attenzione Graphics: 191 S Goodman St, Rochester, NY 14607....................716-244-8028
Attiliis & Assocs: 9710 Days Farm Dr, Vienna, VA 22182 703-759-4283
Atwood Design, Donna: 1137 W Culver, Phoenix, AZ 85007....................602-254-7168
Au Design, Poung: 8550 Katy Freeway #218, Houston, TX 77024....................713-468-8288
Auburn Ad Group, The: 927 Lincoln Way, Auburn, CA 95603 916-888-0484
Aucella & Assocs: 132 Woodcliff Dr, Westfield, MA 01085 413-568-7069
Auger Design Assocs, Jacques: 1130 Washington Ave 6th Fl,
Miami Beach, FL 33139 305-534-3200
Augusta Design Group: 520 Broadway 2nd Fl, New York, NY 10012 212-941-4753
Ault Art Direction & Design, Jim: 911 Western Ave #510, Seattle, WA 98104 206-292-1914
Auras Design: 1746 Kalorama Rd NW, Washington, DC 20009 202-745-0088
Auster, Walter: 18 E 16th St, New York, NY 10003 212-627-8448
Auston Design Group: 651 Main St, St Helena, CA 94574 707-963-4152
Authentic Design: PO Box 310, Malibu, CA 90265....................818-880-5015
Auto Graphics: PO Box 1000, San Leandro, CA 94577....................510-352-5665
Autograph Designed: 10051 Pasadena Ave #J, Cupertino, CA 95014............408-255-9100
Autographic: 530 W 37th St, San Pedro, CA 90731....................310-833-3840
Automated Graphics: 6075 E Molly Rd, Syracuse, NY 13211....................315-437-7561
Autumn Communications: 665 Fairfield Ave #2, Stanford, CT 06902 203-357-0855

AV Graphics: 757 Bethel School Rd, Coppell, TX 75019....214-393-7700
Avallon Thackwell Design: 1672 Michael Ln, Pacific Palisades, CA 90272....310-459-9991
Avanti Case/Hoyt Advertising: 568 Broadway, New York, NY 10012....212-966-6661
Avatar NuMedia: 2635 Park Blvd, Palo Alto, CA 94306....415-322-3838
Avchen & Assocs: 1645 Hennepin Ave S #308, Minneapolis, MN 55403....612-339-1206
Avenue Creative Group: 10 SE First Ave, Delray Beach, FL 33444....407-274-4663
Avery Design Consultants, Eileen: 211 W Gutierrez St #8, Santa Barbara, CA 93101....805-884-0221
Avery Illus, Tony: 16662 Jib Circle #1, Huntington Beach, CA 92649....714-840-1275
Avit Corp, The: 1355 15th St #100, Fort Lee, NJ 07024....201-886-1100
AVM Graphics: PO Box 386, Tempe, AZ 85280....602-894-9365
Avrion Group, Inc: 1717 N California Blvd #3A, Walnut Creek, CA 94596....510-933-4486
AVS, Inc: 2109 Ward Ave, La Crosse, WI 54601....415-322-3838
Award Design: PO Box 82222, Fairbanks, AK 99708....907-455-8000
Aware Media: PO Box 834, Santa Cruz, CA 95061....408-457-2425
Awjm Systems: 224 Pennsylvania Way, North Brunswick, NJ 08902....908-745-9475
Axiom Communications: 36 S Paca St #108, Baltimore, MD 21201....410-727-4222
Axiom Design: 1415 S Church St #H, Charlotte, NC 2802....704-372-1600
Axiom Design & Mktg Comms: 215 S State St #285, Salt Lake City, UT 84111....801-532-2442
Axion Design, Inc: 137 Tunstead Ave, San Anselmo, CA 94960....415-258-6800
Axis Design: 5807 N Tobias Ave, Van Nuys, CA 91411....818-781-8848
Axis Design Communications, Inc: 2966 Twin Oaks Dr, Highland Park, IL 60035....847-266-9330
Axo Design Studio: 423 Tehama St, San Francisco, CA 94103....415-543-8712
Ayers Johanek Publication Design: 4750 Rolling Hills Dr, Bozeman, MT 59715....406-585-8826
Ayzenberg Design: 39 E Walnut St, Pasadena, CA 91103....818-584-4070
Azriel Design & Art Direction, Ted: 18106 Copps Hill Pl, Gaithersburg, MD 20879....301-947-8114

B

B & A Design Group: 634C W Broadway, Glendale, CA 91204....818-547-4080
B & B Design: 300 Mass Ave Mezz, Boston, MA 02115....617-859-8300
B Amos Designs: 4073 Gresham #2, San Diego, CA 92109....619-296-8235
B Productions: 7741 Alabama Ave #13, Canoga Park, CA 91304....818-347-8738
B Zign Communications, Inc: 3209 W Highland Blvd #205, Milwaukee, WI 53208....414-937-6543
B-Lin: 4918 N Harbor Dr #206-A, San Diego, CA 92106....619-223-0080
B3 Design: 2822 Kinney Dr, Walnut Creek, CA 94595....510-947-6179
Babcock & Schmid Assocs: 2138 N Cleveland-Massillon Rd, Bath, OH 44210....216-666-8826
Bachman Design Group, Inc: 6001 Memorial Dr, Dublin, OH 43017....614-793-9993
Bachner & Co: 130 W 25th St 10th Fl, New York, NY 10001....212-243-5287
Baer Design Assocs, Kimberly: 620 Hampton Dr, Venice, CA 90291....310-399-3295
Baer, Kimberly Design Assoc: 620 Hampton Dr, Venice, CA 90291....310-399-3295
Baese, Gary: 2229 N Charles St, Baltimore, MD 21218....410-235-2226
Bagby Design: 455 City Front Plz Dr 16th Fl, Chicago, IL 60611....312-755-3100
Bagnell & Socha: 861 N Taney St, Philadelphia, PA 19130....215-978-5667
Bailey Spiker, Inc: 2250 Hickory Rd #200, Plymouth Meetin, PA 19462....610-940-9030
Bailey, Claudia: 10764 Brookview Dr, North Hollywood, CA 91602....818-763-7314
Bailey, Robert: 0121 SW Bancroft St, Portland, OR 97201....503-228-1381
Bailey-Montague & Assocs: 19 E 200 South 10th Fl, Salt Lake City, UT 84111....801-328-0573
Bailie, Gail: 3 Milwaukee Ave, Bethel, CT 06801....203-790-8487
Bain, S Milo: 3 Shaw Ln, Hartsdale, NY 10530....914-946-0144
Baker & Baker Design: 8422 Valley View Dr SE, Huntsville, AL 35802....205-883-0963
Baker Assocs: 708 E Lake St, Wayzata, MN 55391....612-473-4882
Baker Design Assocs: 1450 20th St, Santa Monica, CA 90404....310-453-6613
Baker Design Assocs, Eric: 11 E 22nd St 5th Fl, New York, NY 10010....212-598-9111
Baker, Arthur: PO Box 29, Germantown, NY 12526....518-537-4438
Baker, Richard: 4230 W Porter Ave, Fullerton, CA 92633....714-994-0459
Balasas, Cora: 651 Vanderbilt St, Brooklyn, NY 11218....718-633-7753
Balbes, Sydney L: 9740 Sepulveda #17, N Hills, CA 91343....818-891-1370
Balch & Co, A: 744 Montgomery #300, San Francisco, CA 94111....415-421-3484
Baldassini, Paul: 234 Clarendon St, Boston, MA 02116....617-236-0190
Balderman & Assocs: 30191 Avenida de las Banderas, Rancho St Margarita, CA 92688....714-589-7403
Baldino Design, Patt: 305 Madison Ave #956, New York, NY 10165....212-986-5987
Baldwin Assocs Adv & Design: 5205 Ellicott Ct, Centerville, VA 20120....703-222-9686
Baldwin Design: 47 Warren St, Salem, MA 01970....508-745-6462
Baldwin, James: 1467 Jordan Ave, Crofton, MD 21114....301-721-1896
Balin Design, Raquel: 3 Simmons Dr N, Woodstock, NY 12498....914-679-4228
Ball Graphic Design: 4637 N Blythe, Fresno, CA 93722....209-275-7136
Ballard Design Inc, Carole: 52 Lemoyne Pkwy, Oak Park, IL 60302....708-848-3611
Bally Design: 424 N Craig, Pittsburgh, PA 15213....412-621-9009
Balmer, Dave: 8821 Horn Day Cir #513, Ft Worth, TX 76120....817-656-1925
Balog Group: 742 N Las Palmas Ave, Los Angeles, CA 90038....213-464-4140
Banayat Miller Communicating Design: 1702 E Highland #409, Phoenix, AZ 85016....602-234-0307
Bancer Printing: 401 Osage, Maumee, OH 43537....419-891-1234
Bang Design: 10600 Holman Ave #12, Los Angeles, CA 90024....310-475-5137
Bang Graphics: 3777 Seventh Ave #A, San Diego, CA 92103....619-574-6609
Banks & Assocs: 507 Veteran Ave, Los Angeles, CA 90024....310-476-5289
Banks Design Assoc: 6 Bel Aire Dr, Plainville, CT 06062....203-747-0701
Banks Design, Albert: 215 Church St #218, Decatur, GA 30030....404-370-1999
Banks Design, Lynda: 15 Saddlebrook Ct, Novato, CA 94947....415-898-9988
Bant Assocs, T: PO Box 183, Wrightwood, CA 92397....619-249-5897
Bantam Books, Inc: 1540 Broadway, New York, NY 10036....212-354-6500
Baranti Group, Inc: 2650 John St #22, Markham, ON L3R 2W6....905-479-0148
Barber Design, Jane: 4343 N Clarendon St #415, Chicago, IL 60613....779-472-5172
Barclay & Assocs: 306 Laurel Ave, Wilmette, IL 60091....847-251-5821
Barfuss Creative Services: 1331 Lake Dr SE, Grand Rapids, MI 49506....616-459-8888
Barhydt-Krall, Anne: 6012 Simpson Ave, North Hollywood, CA 91606....818-762-0213
Barich & Assocs, David: 830 Lake St, San Francisco, CA 94118....415-750-8048
Barker & Lee Graphic Design: 3248 Minnesota Ave, Costa Mesa, CA 92626....714-850-1935
Barker Design: 212 High St, Palo Alto, CA 94301....415-322-7272
Barker Design, Judith: 779 Eighth Ave, San Francisco, CA 94118....415-386-3531
Barnes Design/Chicago: 680 N Lakeshore Dr #625, Chicago, IL 60611....312-337-0495
Barnes Graphics, Herb: 142 W Colorado Blvd, Pasadena, CA 91105....818-682-2420
Barnes, Kathy: 20231 Orchid St, Newport Beach, CA 92660....714-852-8886
Barnett Design: 270 Lafayette St #801, New York, NY 10012....212-431-7130
Barnett, Gregory: 4869 Topanga Canyon Blvd #8, Woodland Hills, CA 91364....818-340-2123
Barnstorm Design: 2902 W Colorado Ave #200, Colorado Springs, CO 80904....719-630-7200
Baron Graphics: 147 Concress St, Portsmouth, NH 03801....603-436-3153
Baron, Inc: 2775 Billa Creek #250, Dallas, TX 75234....214-484-7100
Barrett Design, Janice: 2154 Golden Ave, Long Beach, CA 90806....310-218-8484
Barrett Laidlaw Gervais: 9260 Sunset Dr #103, Miami, FL 33173....305-596-1379
Barrett, Lisa: 6216 Murietta Ave, Van Nuys, CA 91401....818-989-1016
Barry, Jim: 69 W 68th St, New York, NY 10023....212-873-6787
Barsuhn Design: 420 N 5th St #1186, Minneapolis, MN 55401....612-339-2146
Bart Direction: 850 Battery St, San Francisco, CA 94111....415-421-1434
Bartel Design Group: 2820 Glendale Blvd, Los Angeles, CA 90039....213-662-6869
Bartels & Cartsens: 3286 Ivanhoe, St Louis, MO 63139....314-781-7377
Bartelt Design: 4055 N Downer Ave, Milwaukee, WI 53211....414-332-4031
Barth & Co: 10 Bassett Highway, Dover, NJ 07801....201-328-7776
Barth, Henrietta: 2113 Warwick Ln, Shaumburg, IL 60193....847-582-1063
Bartholomew Assocs: 433C Fourth St, Annapolis, MD 21403....301-261-1422
Barton: 17195 Newhope #110, Fountain Valley, CA 92708....714-434-7465
Barton & Barton: 3901 Westheimer St #356, Houston, TX 77027....713-626-2246
Barton Design, Gladys: 245 Everit Ave, Hewlett, NY 11557....516-295-4472
Barton-Cotton: 10099 SE White Pelican Way, Jupiter, FL 33469....561-743-4700
Baseline Designs: 445 Bryant St, San Francisco, CA 94107....415-974-1238
Basic Technology, Inc: 7125 Saltsburg Rd, Pittsburgh, PA 15235....412-795-5300
Basika, Lee Reedy: 1542 Williams St, Denver, CO 80218....303-333-2936
Baskin Group, The: 213 Bonifinated Rd, Silver Spring, MD 20905....301-989-0515
Baskin, Hal: 6931 Arlington Rd #301, Bethesda, MD 20814....301-913-2902
Bass Yager & Assocs: 7039 Sunset Blvd, Los Angeles, CA 90028....213-466-9701
Bassett Design: 90 East 11th St, Arcata, CA 95521....707-826-2550
Bassett Graphic Design: 2811 Villa Way, Newport Beach, CA 92663....714-675-2737
Bassinger: Star Route Box 20, Woodside, CA 94062....415-529-1210
Basso Valentine & Radford: 1500 Quail St 7th Fl, Newport Beach, CA 92660....714-252-1700
Bast Design, Beth: 81 Westwood Dr, San Francisco, CA 94112....415-469-8773
Bates: 8143 Hihn Rd, Ben Lomond, CA 95005....408-336-3661
Bates Design Studio: 207 E Bay St #303, Charleston, SC 29401....803-722-6009
Batley, Glenis: 1811 N Tamarind #108, Los Angeles, CA 90028....213-467-4352
Battles, Kim C: 919 Main St #211, El Segundo, CA 90245....310-322-0637
Bauders Computer Graphics, Don: 1825A Egbert Ave, San Francisco, CA 94124....415-468-5500
Bauer Design, Carla: 156 Fifth Ave #1100, New York, NY 10010....212-807-8305
Bauer Design, Laura: 2611 Broadway, Redwood City, CA 94063....415-327-3102
Baugh, Larry: 1417 N Irving Hgts, Irving, TX 75061....214-438-5696
Bauman Design, Leslie: 310 W 106th St #8D, New York, NY 10025....212-932-9423
Bausch Design: 1261 Alden Ct, Belmont, CA 94002....415-595-1955
Baxter & Korge, Inc: 8323 Westglen St, Houston, TX 77063....713-972-1600
Bay Graphics: 2030 Fifth St, Berkeley, CA 94710....510-843-0701
Bay Network: 4401 Great American Pkwy, Santa Clara, CA 95054....408-988-2400
Bazata Design, Tara: 9947 Monroe Dr, Thornton, CO 80229....303-252-7712
BBID: 270 E Main Loft, Los Gatos, CA 95032....408-354-3811
BC Studios: 3645 Jeannine Dr, Colorado Springs, CO 80917....719-550-0505
BCA Design: 71 Saddle Rd, Walnut Creek, CA 94595....510-946-1716
BCB Group: 670 Newfield St, Middletown, CT 06457....203-347-7848
BCD Ink Ltd: 108 E 16th St, New York, NY 10003....212-420-1222
Be One Design: 655 Bryant St, San Francisco, CA 94107....415-243-0361
Beach Advertising: 225 S 15th St 23rd Fl, Philadelphia, PA 19102....215-735-4747
Beach, Lou: 900 S Tremaine Ave, Los Angeles, CA 90019....213-934-7335
Beals Advtg Agency: 5225 N Chartel #201, Oklahoma City, OK 73118....405-848-8513
Bean Design, Inc: 4629 Island Ave NE, Bainbridge Island, WA 98110....206-780-0535
Bean Graphics, Inc: 310 West Main St, Greenwood, IN 46142....317-882-7222
Bear Brook Design: 69 Helms Hill Rd, Washintonville, NY 10992....914-496-2800
Bear Canyon Creative: 6753 Academy NE #A, Albuquerque, NM 87109....505-823-9150
Bear Graphics: 105 E Main St, Mason, OH 45040....513-398-2788
Beard & Assocs, Jerrie: 1516 W Redwood St #106, San Diego, CA 92101....619-298-9152
Beauchamp Group: 1743 Wazee St #321, Denver, CO 80202....303-296-1133
Bechtel Design, Bill: 1629 Ogden St, Denver, CO 80218....303-839-1818
Bechtold Studio, Bob: 471 S Fairview St, Burbank, CA 91505....818-563-1405
Beck & Graboski Design Office: 247 16th St, Santa Monica, CA 90402....310-393-9325
Beck/Durell Creative Dept: 1335 Worthington Woods Blvd, Worthington, OH 43085....614-844-5544
Becker Design Assoc: 2715 Western Ave, Seattle, WA 98121....206-448-7990
Beckett Advertising & Design, Edward: 1051 E Altadena Dr, Altadena, CA 91001....818-791-7954
Bedlam Studio: 500 Molino St #310, Los Angeles, CA 90013....213-617-1963
Bee Design, Paula: 182 Costa Mesa St, Costa Mesa, CA 92627....714-548-0366
Beech Design, Greene: 6360 NW 5th Way #302, Ft Lauderdale, FL 33309....305-771-6500
Beeline Group: 3374 Gateway Blvd, Fremont, CA 94538....510-770-9990
Beggs Design, Inc, Stephanie Langley : 619 Maybelle Ave, Palo Alto, CA 94506....415-857-9539
Behr, Mario: 2463 Pine Tree Dr #3, Miami Bch, FL 33140....305-674-8406
Behrens Design, Doug: PO Box 1674, Honolulu, HI 96806....808-625-7522
Bel Aire Assocs: 730 Fifth Ave #2000, New York, NY 10019....212-245-5700
Bell Group, The Clark: 339 Kreag Rd, Pittsford, NY 14534....716-586-8848
Bell, Andrea: 11949 Darlington Ave #6, Los Angeles, CA 90049....310-826-3898
Bell, Jill: 521 Indiana St Suite#C, El Segundo, CA 90245....310-322-5542
Bellini Design: 325 W Huron #706, Chicago, IL 60610....312-649-1710
Bellomo, Clea: 11911 Magnolia Blvd #27, N Hollywood, CA 91607....818-509-6756
Belman, Vickie: 210 E 181st St #4A, Bronx, NY 10457....718-367-2688
Belser, Burkey: 1818 N St NW #110, Washington, DC 20036....202-775-0333
Beltran, Lauren: 2963 Cowley Way #90, San Diego, CA 92117....619-276-4303
Belyea Design: 1809 7th Ave #1007, Seattle, WA 98101....206-682-4895
Benchmark Display Inc: 1001 Woodlands Parkway, Vernon Hills, IL 60061....847-541-2828
Benchmark Group, The: 700 W Pete Rose Way, Cincinnati, OH 45203....513-621-3038
Bender & Assocs, Lawrence: 512 Hamilton Ave, Palo Alto, CA 94301....415-327-3821
Bender, Diane: 2729 S Cleveland St, Arlington, VA 22206....703-521-1006
Benes Communications, Inc: 1840 Massachusetts Ave 2nd Fl, Lexington, MA 02173....617-647-2327
Benes Communications, Sigrid: 4265 Marina City Dr #317 W, Marina del Rey, CA 90292....310-827-7765

Boss Inman Graphic Design, Bo: 1383 S Eudora St, Denver, CO 80222 303-756-0222
Boston Design, Archie: 5707 Aladdin St, Los Angeles, CA 90008 213-296-2428
Bostrom Design, Cybul: 105 E Burlington, Riverside, IL 60546 708-447-6122
Boszta Costa Adv & Design: 605 W 70th St, Kansas City, MO 64113 816-333-1165
Botero Assocs, Samuel: 420 E 54th St #34G, New York, NY 10022 212-935-5155
Bottega Design, Inc: 1708 S Crescent, Park Ridge, IL 60068 847-825-3687
Bottiglieri, Dessolina: 126 E 12th St #6C, New York, NY 10003........................212-473-4592
Boullion Graphics: 6423 Willgus Trl, Houston, TX 77066 713-444-5749
Boulton Advertising, Connie: 3242 Caminito Ameca, La Jolla, CA 92037..........619-455-5397
Bouthhillier Design Assoc, Lans: 225 Water St S #402, Plymouth, MA 02360......508-747-4973
Bowerman & Collins Adv: 213 W 16th St, New York, NY 10011 212-929-3157
Bowers, John Dallas: 219 Radnor-Chester Rd, Villianova, PA 19085 610-989-9234
Bowers, Karen: 1508 Sanborn Ave, Los Angeles, CA 90027...............................213-664-5524
Bowles, Aaron: 203 Elden St #401-D, Herndon, VA 22070...................................703-318-7889
Boyajian & Assocs Design, Carole: 365 W Alameda Ave #308,
Burbank, CA 91506 818-848-2595
Boyarski Boyarski: 6958 Edgerton Ave, Pittsburgh, PA 15208.........................412-362-2626
Boyd Design, Douglas: 6624 Melrose Ave, Los Angeles, CA 90038...................213-933-8383
Boyd, Cathy:, Brooklyn, NY 718-875-7367
Boyer Design: 1221 Manitou Rd, Santa Barbara, CA 93101 805-687-3687
Boylan Assocs: 5 Lakeview Ave, Danvers, MA 01923 508-774-6655
Braatz Studio Inc, Jerry: 4 High St, Valhalla, NY 10595...................................914-428-0533
Brabner Design: 4517 Dolly Ridge Rd, Birmingham, AL 35243........................205-967-6606
Bracchi Design: 11 W 25th St 9th Fl, New York, NY 10010 212-366-1437
Bradbury Assocs, Robert: 26 Halsey Ln, Closter, NJ 07624 201-768-6395
Bradfield Design, Inc: 215 Long Beach Blvd #427, Long Beach, CA 90802........310-432-2125
Bradford Cout & Jansen Design: 953 N Plum Grove Rd #A,
Schaumburg, IL 60173...847-619-4777
Bradford, Peter: 928 Broadway #709, New York, NY 10010...............................212-982-2090
Brady & Paul Comms: 120 E Oakland Pk Blvd #105,
Ft Lauderdale, FL 33334 954-537-9040
Brady Design Consultants, John: 3 Gateway Ctr #17, Pittsburgh, PA 15222 412-288-9300
Brady, Susan: 1812 Webster St, San Francisco, CA 94115...............................415-563-4769
Brain Storm, Inc: 3347 Halifax St, Dallas, TX 75247 214-951-7791
Brainard Industrial Design, Robert: 30 Bellair Dr, Danbury, CT 06811..............203-746-5003
Brainstorm Creative: 2015 E State Highway AA, Springfield, MO 65803...........417-833-4233
Brainworks Design Group: 2 Harris Court, Monterey, CA 93940.......................408-657-0650
Braithwaite Communications: 1710 Hayes St #207, Nashville, TN 37203......615-329-4573
Bram, Brian: 381 Congress St 2nd Fl, Boston, MA 02210 617-338-7770
Bramble Design, Bill: 327 W 11th St, New York, NY 10014 212-929-6289
Bramson & Assocs, Inc: 7400 Beverly Blvd, Los Angeles, CA 90036................213-938-3595
Brancato Creative Services: 72 Cascade Dr, Rochester, NY 14614 716-262-4450
Brand Design: PO Box 30000, Wilmington, DE 19805...302-888-1648
Brand Equity Int'l: 2330 Washington St, Newton, MA 02162............................617-969-3150
Branders Creative Cafe: 1840 E 32nd St, Tulsa, OK 74105 918-743-6854
Braswell, Lynn: 320 Riverside Dr, New York, NY 10025.......................................212-222-8761
Brauer, Bruce Erik: 131 Midland Ave, Staten Island, NY 10306 718-667-8977
Braun Creative Group: 11051 N Town Sq Rd, Mequon, WI 53092 414-241-8984
Braverman Design, Stan: 200 Rector Pl #14B, New York, NY 10280 212-945-4434
Bravo Multimedia Communications: 325 Huron #404, Chicago, IL 60610.......312-337-9058
Brazell Design: 11447 S 46th St, Phoenix, AZ 85044 602-496-6680
BRD Design: 6525 Sunset Blvd 6th Fl, Hollywood, CA 90028............................213-962-4908
Breakthru Media Group: 20001 Glebe Ln, Charles City, VA 23030 804-829-2948
Breckenridge Designs: 2025 I St NW #300, Washington, DC 20006....................202-833-5700
Bree/Taub Design: 648 Broadway #703, New York, NY 10012 212-254-8383
Breiner, Joanne: 8 Cornelius Way, Cambridge, MA 02141 617-354-8378
Breiter Concepts Design: 223 N Encinitas Ave, Monrovia, CA 91016..................818-303-6550
Brejcha, Bart: 312 May St #5F, Chicago, IL 60607 312-433-7786
Brelsford Design, J: 4949 Westown Pkwy #125, West Des Moines, IA 50266......515-282-2655
Brems Eastman Glade: 3131 Elliot Ave #280, Seattle, WA 98121 206-284-9400
Brenlin Design, J: 143 Yorba St, Tustin, CA 92680 714-505-3443
Brennan Adv, Patrick: 517 1/2 Potrero Ave, San Francisco, CA 94110..............415-864-8520
Brenner Design, Barry: 1636 N Stanley Ave, Los Angeles, CA 90046................213-851-9415
Bressler Design Assoc, Peter: 2400 Market St #4, Philadelphia, PA 19103......215-561-5100
Brett Corp: 8316 Clairemont Mesa Blvd #105, San Diego, CA 92111 619-292-4919
Breuel & Unger Assocs, Inc: 1 Bridge St West Wing, Irvington, NY 10533.........914-591-5040
Bricker Design: 9709 Lock Tender Ln, Williamsport, MD 21795........................301-223-5282
Bridge: 211 W Wacker Dr #700, Chicago, IL 60606 312-814-0200
Bridges Design: 143 Main St, Rockport, MA 01966 508-546-3149
Brier, David: 38 Park Ave, Rutherford, NJ 07070...201-896-8476
Bright & Assocs, Inc: 901 Abbot Kinney, Venice, CA 90291.............................310-450-2488
Bright Water Design: 1801 Dove St #104, Newport Beach, CA 92660............714-833-3344
Brill Graphic Design: 8803 Fairway Hill Dr, Austin, TX 78750 512-258-2327
Brilliant Media: 450 Pacific Ave 1st Fl, San Francisco, CA 94133......................415-434-5040
Brinkman Assocs: 21 Pine St, Rockaway, NJ 07866 201-625-9000
Brinkmann Design, John: 123 S Baldwin Ave, Sierra Madre, CA 91024 818-355-3363
Brinkmann, John Design Offices Inc: 123 S Baldwin Ave,
Sierra Madre, CA 91024 818-355-3363
Brittainham Adv/Mullican Design: 4012 Ingraham St, Los Angeles, CA 90005.......213-383-0232
Britton Design: 737 Broadway PO Box 1653, Sonoma, CA 95476...................707-938-8378
Brochure Art: 1316 3rd St Promenade #101, Santa Monica, CA 90401 310-458-8863
Brochure Masters Creative Dept: 1220 S Bedford St, Los Angeles, CA 90035......310-273-9613
Brock Design, Michael: 8075 W 3rd St #300, Los Angeles, CA 90048............213-932-0283
Brocke Graphic Design, Robert: 425 30th St #25, Newport Beach, CA 92663 714-673-4281
Brody & Co, BL: 7961 Hollenbeck Cir, Parma, OH 44129 216-842-4484
Brogdon, Chris: 233 E Ontario St #901, Chicago, IL 60611 312-787-0245
Brogren Kelly & Assocs: 234 Columbine St #320, Denver, CO 80206.............303-399-3851
Bromley Chapin Design, Inc: 400 Renaissance Center #2250,
Detroit, MI 48243 313-259-2661
Brook Design, Lee Ann: 202 Providence Mine Rd #107,
Nevada City, CA 95959 916-265-6817
Brook Group Ltd, The: 8475 Old Frederick Rd, Ellicott City, MD 21043 410-465-7805
Brooks & Pollard Co: 400 W Capital #2900, Little Rock, AR 72201.................501-375-5561
Brooks Advertising: 23151 Verdugo Dr #105, Laguna Hills, CA 92653............714-951-8121
Brooks Assocs, Lloyd: 700 N Alabama St, Indianapolis, IN 46204...................317-488-8927
Brooks Comm: 1712 Terrace Dr, Belmont, CA 94002 415-595-1401
Brooks Design, Larry: 5249 College View Ave, Los Angeles, CA 90041............213-467-7922
Brooks Jenkins Design: 1100 Circle 75 Pkwy #650, Atlanta, GA 30339.........770-953-8183
Brooks Stevens Assocs, Inc: 1415 W Donges Bay Rd, Mequon, WI 53092 414-241-3800
Brooks/Cole Publising Co: 511 Forest Lodge Rd, Pacific Grove, CA 93950........408-373-0728
Brookson Design: 1641 E Osborn #7, Phoenix, AZ 85016...............................602-279-1961
Broom & Broom, Inc: 360 Post St #1100, San Francisco, CA 94108 415-397-4300
Brothers Bogusky: 11950 W Dixie Hwy, Miami, FL 33161 305-891-3642
Brothers Design: 188 Clintonville Rd, Northford, CT 06472..............................203-484-2897
Brotherton, Doug: 2160 Beachwood Terr, Los Angeles, CA 90068....................213-856-0968
Brouws, Jeff: 508 De la Vina St, Santa Barbara, CA 93101 805-966-2814
Brower Design, Steven: 18 E 16th St 7th Fl, New York, NY 10003..................212-633-2356
Brown & Assocs, Bill: 4640 Admiralty Way #900, Marina del Rey, CA 90292 310-822-5861
Brown & Assocs, Janis: 19434 4th Pl, Escondido, CA 92029............................619-743-1795
Brown & Assocs, Lynn: 1300 Bristol North #235, Newport Beach, CA 92660.....714-756-8018
Brown & Craig, Inc: 407 N Charles St, Baltimore, MD 21201 301-837-2727
Brown & Marvin Burke, Don: 111 Eighth Ave #1516, New York, NY 10011......212-622-4141
Brown Design & Co: 392 Fore St, Portland, ME 04101 207-879-1714
Brown Design, Gaines: 1515 S Tryon, Charlotte, NC 28203............................704-334-1442
Brown Design, Lance: 1800 St James Pl #609, Houston, TX 77056 713-622-5720
Brown Design, Scott: 323 Chester Ave, Menlo Park, CA 94025 415-473-1123
Brown Graphic Design, Joan: PO Box 60066, Palo Alto, CA 94306 415-493-5773
Brown Graphic Design, Larry: 2800 28th St #125, Santa Monica, CA 90405.....310-452-5502
Brown Marketing & Design, Barbara: 791 Colina Vista, Ventura, CA 93003 805-658-2086
Brown, David: 1220 20th St, Birmingham, AL 35205.......................................205-939-1050
Brown, Gloria: PO Box 335, Poncha Springs, CO 81242 800-372-9465
Brown, Hugh: 4543 Avocado St, Los Angeles, CA 90027 213-661-7767
Brown, Inc, Michael David: 235 Old County Rd, Rockport, MA 04856 207-596-6202
Brown, Kirk Q: 1092 Blake Ave, Brooklyn, NY 11208 718-346-8281
Brown, Lucy Design: 432 State St, Santa Barbara, CA 93101 805-966-1060
Brown, Morris R: 1736 Garth Ave, Los Angeles, CA 90035..............................310-204-2827
Brown, Paula: 11453 Rose Ave, Los Angeles, CA 90066...................................310-397-4913
Brown, Theresa: 53 Danbury Rd, Wilton, CT 06897...203-222-7040
Browning Design, Inc: 335 Wilber Ave, Columbus, OH 43215............................614-421-7037
Brownstone Studio: 685 Third Ave 25th Fl, New York, NY 10017 212-883-1090
Brubaker Group, The: 10560 Dolcedo Way, Los Angeles, CA 90077................310-472-4766
Bruce Assocs, Taylor: 730 N Franklin #603, Chicago, IL 60610 312-943-5529
Bruneau Studio, Inc: 901 W McDowell Rd, Phoenix, AZ 85007........................602-253-0014
Bruno Design Assocs: 120 Kearney Ave, Santa Fe, NM 87501 505-982-5544
Bruno Design Assocs: 151 Kalmus Dr #A104, Costa Mesa, CA 92626 714-545-5424
Bruss Design, Inc, Ellen: POB 822/E19th Ave, Denver, CO 80218.....................303-830-8323
Bryant & Assocs: 3838 1/2 Vantage Ave, Studio City, CA 91604 818-762-1433
Bryant & Co: 2 Astor Pl, New York, NY 10003..212-254-5122
Bryant Assocs, Robert: 4874 Bannock Circle, San Jose, CA 95130...................408-370-2121
Bryant, Dane A: 7746 Villa Nova Dr N, Boca Raton, FL 33433 561-447-6744
Bryant, Inc: 740 Broadway 8th Fl, New York, NY 10003...................................212-254-5122
Buchberger, Brian: 610 N Water St #310, Milwaukee, WI 53202....................414-273-8194
Bucher & Russell: 3600 Wilshire Blvd #2035, Los Angeles, CA 90010 213-738-5300
Buckett Assocs, Bill: 10 Gibbs St #310, Rochester, NY 14604 716-546-6580
Buckhorn, Merril: 25 Homedale Rd, Hopkins, MN 55343 612-931-0324
Buckles Design, Timothy: 1800 21st St #100, Sacramento, CA 95814 916-736-1473
Buckley Designs Inc: 310 E 75th St, New York, NY 10021 212-861-0626
Budd Graphic Design: CA 310-475-6477
Buffalo Brothers Corp: 812 S Tejon St, Colorado Springs, CO 80903...............719-389-1230
Buffalo Brothers Studios West: 217 State St #303, Santa Barbara, CA 93101 805-963-0904
Bugdal Group: 7308 SW 48th St, Miami, FL 33155 305-665-6686
Buhl, Taber: 4308 Goodrich Hill Road, Locke, NY 13092..................................315-497-0288
Buivid Photo Design: 1551 E River Rd, Grafton, WI 53024................................414-377-5118
Bullseye Productions: 375 Marin Ave, Mill Valley, CA 94941 415-388-8308
Bumacod Concept & Design: 1029 W 210th St, Torrance, CA 90502 310-328-7384
Bunzel & Assocs: 10331 Almayo Ave #3, Los Angeles, CA 90064...................310-286-0969
Burbott Design, Matthew: 8740 Willis #12, Panorama City, CA 91402 818-893-4265
Burch Assocs, Dan: 2338 Frankfort, Louisville, KY 40206 502-895-4881
Burch Design Group: 660 J St #490, Sacramento, CA 95814...........................916-558-4900
Burdick Group, The: 35 S Park, San Francisco, CA 94107 415-957-1666
Bureau Design: 333 Bryant St #190, San Francisco, CA 94107.......................415-495-4197
Burg Design: 150 Shoreline Hwy #B21, Mill Valley, CA 94941.........................415-332-9318
Burgund Design, Kathleen: 18 W Custis Ave, Alexandria, VA 22301 703-683-8084
Burke Design: 2060 Avenue de los Arboles #118, Thousand Oaks, CA 91362......310-280-3488
Burke Graphic Design, Angie: 1266 Camino Palomera,
Santa Barbara, CA 93111 805-964-1945
Burke, Michael: 1131 16th St, Baywood Park, CA 93402 805-528-6754
Burkley Studios: 1526 Edison St, Dallas, TX 75207 214-746-6336
Burnett Communication, Roberta: 607 E Loyola Dr, Tempe, AZ 85282 602-966-4900
Burney Design: 409 Hillsborough, Raleigh, NC 27613.......................................919-833-4819
Burns & Assocs, Inc: 2700 Sutter St, San Francisco, CA 94115 415-567-4404
Burns Design Assocs: 9747 Business Park Ave #203, San Diego, CA 92131 619-566-9166
Burns, Rhonda: 13049 Hartsook St, Sherman Oaks, CA 91423 213-913-1929
Burstein/Max Assoc: 271 Madison Ave #903, New York, NY 10016................212-986-2080
Burton & Differding: 897 Woodruff Pl/East River, Indianapolis, IN 46201 317-636-0925
Burton Design, Brian: CA 714-786-6333
Burton, Matthew L: 440 East 57th St #GC, New York, NY 10022...................212-486-1002
Busch & Assocs: 7558 Trade St, San Diego, CA 92121 619-578-9191
Bush Graphics, Robert: PO Box 4830, Long Beach, CA 90804........................310-434-1697
Business Graphics: 7321 Beverly Blvd #6, Los Angeles, CA 90036 213-930-4899
Business Information Graphics: 200 Park Ave S #1112, New York, NY 10003 212-477-4288
Business Office, The: 8645 Twin Rivers Dr, Ventura, CA 93004 805-659-2186
Business Presentation Services: 40 Cameron Ave, Sommerville, MA 02144 617-666-1161
Bussolati Assocs: 7000 B Carroll Ave, Tacoma Park, MD 20912 301-891-1062
Butler & Butler, Inc: 1404 S Quaker Ave, Tulsa, OK 74120..............................918-592-4151
Butler Designs: 4617 Montrose Blvd #228, Houston, TX 77006 713-526-3182
Butler Group, The: 940 N Highland Ave #C, Los Angeles, CA 90038..............213-469-8128
Butterfield Design, Christy: 480 Gate Five Rd #201, Sausalito, CA 94966 415-332-8591
Butz Gaskins Art Studio: 1994 Madison Rd, Cincinnati, OH 45209....................513-321-7002
Butzko & Rosenthal Design: 214 Greenbriar Rd, Fairfield, CT 06430 203-334-7396
Buy Design : 670 Newfield St 1st Fl, Middletown, CT 06457 203-347-7848
Buz Design Group: 8952 Ellis Ave, Los Angeles, CA 90034.............................310-202-0140
Buzzo, Marge: 4620 Santa Lucia Dr, Woodland Hills, CA 91364 818-340-5640
BWEH Graphics: 630 Rose Ave, Venice, CA 90291 310-392-9636
By Design: 4606-A E State Blvd, Ft Wayne, IN 46815 219-482-2815
By Design: 271 Madison Ave, New York, NY 10016...212-661-0962

By Design Productions: 211 Cypress Point Dr, Mountain View, CA 94043 415-968-8407
Bydalek Spence Kittner: 1000 Geyer Ave, St Louis, MO 63104 314-621-8002
Byerly, Thomas & Kim: 2870 Cynthia Dr, Medina, OH 44256 330-722-4181
Byrne Design, Susan: 27 W 24th St #602, New York, NY 10010 212-807-6671
Byrne Marketing & Adv, Peter: 25002 Paseo Cipres, El Toro, CA 92630..........714-859-3262
Byrne, Chuck: 5528 Lawton Ave, Oakland, CA 94618..510-658-6996
Byrne, Keith: 375 Hudson St 8th Fl, New York, NY 10014 212-929-2700
Byte Knights: 410 W Webster, Chicago, IL 60614 773-327-9251

C

C & L Writing & Design: 3101 W Coast Hwy #312,
Newport Beach, CA 92663 714-722-4511
C & S Creative Services: PO Box 4082, Park City, UT 84060 801-649-1234
C & W/lola, Inc: 748 Hwy 206 S, Bellemeade, NJ 08502...................................908-359-1600
C Gay Petach Studio: 2500 Woodlawn Dr, Nashville, TN 37212 615-292-3691
C/O Keith Berr Productions: 1420 East 31st St, Cleveland, OH 44114 216-566-7950
CA Design Inc: 1188 Bishop St #2611, Honolulu, HI 96813...............................808-533-2888
Cabat Studio: 627 N 4th Ave, Tucson, AZ 85705 602-622-6362
Cabazon Design: 322 N W 5th Ave #312, Portland, OR 97209.........................503-220-8236
Caber Graphic Design, Jennifer: 4950 N Calle Esquina, Tucson, AZ 85718.........602-577-1063
Cable Design, Jerry: 133 Kuhl Rd, Flemington, NJ 08822.................................908-788-6750
Cadence Design Systems: 2655 Seely Ave 7A1, San Jose, CA 95134 408-944-7135
Cadmus Creative: 5301 Louis Rd, Sandston, VA 23150 804-236-4500
Caesar Studios: 2602 Pickwick Ln, Austin, TX 78746 512-329-5110
Cagle Design: 5353 Hinton Ave, Woodland Hills, CA 91367 818-340-2887
Cagney & McDowell: 751 S Clark #200, Chicago, IL 60605................................312-461-0707
Cahan & Assocs: 818 Brannan St #300, San Francisco, CA 94103 415-621-0915
Cahill Dittrich Advertising: 40 Grove St, Wellesley, MA 02181 617-235-2782
Cahn, Jeff: 6200 SOM Center Rd #D25, Cleveland, OH 44139.........................440-349-1270
Calanche Design: 545 Belvedere St, San Francisco, CA 94117 415-664-9511
Calderhead, Richard: 821 Broadway 11th Fl, New York, NY 10003...................212-673-6200
Caldwell Design, John: 901 El Centro St, S Pasadena, CA 91030 213-682-2809
Calfo Assocs: 156 Fifth Ave #500, New York, NY 10010 212-627-3800
Calico Creations Ltd: 9340 Eton Ave, Chatsworth, CA 91311 818-407-5200
California Coast Advertising: 8439 White Oak Ave #109,
Rancho Cucamonga, CA 91730 909-948-7025
California Design: 219 Broadway #254, Laguna Beach, CA 92651 714-831-2188
California Design Int'l: 123 Townsend St #465, San Francisco, CA 94107 415-243-0980
Calko & Lakich: 704 Traction Ave, Los Angeles, CA 90013 213-620-8641
Call, Timothy: 312 E 92nd St #4A, New York, NY 10128 212-426-2510
Callahan Design, Bob: 181 Thornridge Dr, Stamford, CT 06903 203-329-0425
Callahan, Tom: 7964 S Madison Ave, Burr Ridge, IL 60521 630-789-1022
Callanta & Assocs, Al: 13010 Miller Ave, Norwalk, CA 90650..........................310-921-8684
Calleia, Michael: 184 E Second St #4E, New York, NY 10009............................212-505-9073
Calligraphics By Julie Ann: 3511 E Capri Ave, Mesa, AZ 85204 602-531-5747
Calligraphy By Rachael: 5800 Lake Murray Blvd # 86, La Mesa, CA 91942 619-465-5566
Calligraphy West Studio: 3101 Federal Ave, Los Angeles, CA 90066................310-837-3604
Callison Partnership, The: 1420 5th Ave #2400, Seattle, WA 98101 206-623-4646
Callygraphics: 15848 Sanctuary Dr, Tampa, FL 33647 813-975-0823
Calo'oy & Co: 3889 Clover Ln, Dallas, TX 75220 214-902-8044
Calori & Vanden Eynden Ltd: 130 W25th St, New York, NY 10001 212-929-6302
Calvello, Tony: 515 Alvarado St, San Francisco, CA 94114 415-647-1603
Calviello & Cohen Multimedia: 133 Cedar Rd, E Northport, NY 11731 516-368-2031
Camacho, Dennis: 55 Broad St, New York, NY 10004.......................................212-378-4985
Cambridge Design Group: 87 Fawcett St #201, Cambridge, MA 02138 617-873-2908
Cambridge Prepress Service: 215 First St, Cambridge, MA 02142 617-354-1991
Camera Ready Graphics: 225 Center St, San Rafael, CA 94901.......................415-457-5699
Cameron & Co: 2233 University Ave #150, St Paul, MN 55144 612-645-4002
Cameron, Inc: 9 Appleton St, Boston, MA 02116 617-338-4408
Camozzi, Teresa: 170 Capp St, San Francisco, CA 94110.................................415-863-2733
Campbell & Assocs, Tom : 2018 Meadow Valley Ter, Los Angeles, CA 90039......213-661-9288
Campbell & Gericke: 6602 Cahuenga AVe, Hollywood, CA 90068 213-469-7799
Campbell Art Studio: 2145 Luray Ave, Cincinnati, OH 45206............................513-221-3600
Campbell Design: 209 Hillside Ave, Mill Valley, CA 94941..............................415-331-3939
Campbell Design: 94 Pike St #30, Seattle, WA 94107......................................206-622-4294
Campbell Fisher Ditko Design: 3333 E Camelback Rd #200,
Phoenix, AZ 85018 602-955-2707
Campbell Harrington & Brear: 352 W Market St, York, PA 17401 717-846-2947
Campbell, Grady: 900 N Franklin #310, Chicago, IL 60610.............................312-642-6511
Campbell, JC: 7777 Bonhomme #2000, St Louis, MO 63105...........................314-726-5858
Campion Design: 400 Montgomery PH, San Francisco, CA 94104 415-362-2723
Campisi Design Inc, Ronn: 118 Newbury St, Boston, MA 02116 617-236-1339
Campos Design, Mike: 1804 Marion Ave, Novato, CA 94945 415-892-1573
Canciani International: 461 Second St #C227, San Francisco, CA 94107 415-442-0261
Cancilla Design, Joseph: 3534 Huntertown Rd, Allison Park, PA 15101 412-443-8698
Canfield Design: 45 Newbury St, Boston, MA 02116...617-247-3869
Cannan & Co, Bill: 301 Mortimer Ave, Rutherford, NJ 10036............................201-933-9883
Cannoy Design, Lynne: 711 Penn Ave #630, Pittsburgh, PA 15222 412-391-2040
Canright & Paule: 1425 W Summerdale Ave, Chicago, IL 60640 773-275-8895
Cantere Assocs, Lee: 1553 Euclid St, Santa Monica, CA 90404 310-395-3221
Cantor Design: 875 Ave of America #10001, New York, NY 10001 212-629-0130
Cantor, Andrew: 4 W 37th St 6th Fl, New York, NY 10018.................................212-629-0130
Canzani Graphics: 50 W 29th St, New York, NY 10001 212-643-1050
Caplin Design: 35 Medford Street #203, Somerville, MA 02143 617-627-9050
Caprs Cleveland Design: 673 Boylston St, Boston, MA 02116...........................617-267-7957
Caravello Studios: 165 W 18th St 3rd Fl, New York, NY 10011 212-620-0620
Cardi Assocs: 23010 Lake Forest Dr #281, Laguna Hills, CA 92653 714-768-3024
Cardinal Comms Group: 545 W 45th St, New York, NY 10036 212-489-1717
Carew Design: 49 Sunset Way, San Rafael, CA 94901 415-331-8222
Carey & Assocs, Bob: 10 Topaz Way, San Francisco, CA 94131 415-826-3497
Cariddi, Marianne K: 100 Indian Rock Rd, Merrimack, NH 03054.......................603-424-0337
Carino Graphic Design, Mercedes: 76C Belvedere St, San Rafael, CA 94901.....415-485-9299
Carl M Information Design: 769 N Orange Grove Blvd, Pasadena, CA 91103.......818-405-0827
Carleton Design: 777 San Antonio Rd #96, Palo Alto, CA 94303.......................415-858-2508
Carling Design: 257 Water St #2A, New York, NY 10023....................................212-393-9430
Carlisle/Carre Design: 1301 Montana Ave #A, Santa Monica, CA 90403 310-394-5330
Carlo Assocs: 417 E 9th St #14, New York, NY 10009.......................................212-420-1110
Carlson: 3054 Fite Cir #108, Sacramento, CA 95827 916-447-2277
Carlson Design: 107 SW 99th Terr, Gainesville, FL 32607...................................904-332-4917
Carmel, Abraham: 7 Peter Beet Dr, Peekskill, NY 10566 914-737-1439
Carnase, Tom: 30 E 21st St, New York, NY 10010...212-777-1500
Carpenter Advertising & Design, JL: 4457 Benfield Ct, San Diego, CA 92113.......619-527-2850
Carpenter Design, Inc: 10020 National Blvd, Los Angeles, CA 90034 310-837-0732
Carpenter Graphic Design: 72 Spring St 10th Fl, New York, NY 10012 212-431-6666
Carpenter Photo/Design: 20 Granada Way, Los Gatos, CA 95030 330-374-1750
Carpenter, Charles: 2501 Foothill Blvd, La Crescenta, CA 91214.......................818-541-0360
Carpinelli Graphic Design, Janet: 934 Minnesota St, San Francisco, CA 94107......415-826-5509
Carr Design Assocs: 817 A St NE, Washington, DC 20002...................................202-546-2611
Carr Design, James: 350 Main St 1st Fl, White Plains, NY 10601 914-287-0046
Carrara, Richard: 218 Lorraine Ave, Upper Montclair, NJ 07043 201-783-2872
Carriage House Design: 216 Radnor Chester Rd, Villanova, PA 19085 610-293-1555
Carroll: 3311 Winona Ave, Burbank, CA 91504...818-846-7840
Carroll, Cathy, Graphic Dimensions: 5055 Pacifica Dr, San Diego, CA 92109 619-581-9313
Carron Design, Ross: 1335 Union St #10, San Francisco, CA 94109....................415-440-4191
Carsello, Margaret: 516 N Vine, Hinsdale, IL 60521 630-794-9120
Carson & Co: 517 Mercury Lane, Brea, CA 92821 714-990-1500
Carson Design, David: 432 F St #503, San Diego, CA 92101 619-338-8080
Carstens, Daren: 342 Grove #201, Wood Dale, IL 60191 708-238-8505
Carta Communications, Joyce: 2181 NW 99th Ave,
Pembroke Pine, FL 33024 954-433-1391
Carter Cosgrove & Co: 345 S Patrick, Alexandria, VA 22314 703-836-2900
Carter Design: 555 Sutter St #401, San Francisco, CA 94102 415-781-7325
Carter Design, David: 4112 Swiss Ave, Dallas, TX 75204 214-826-4631
Carter Design, Inc: 814 E 19th Ave, Denver, CO 80218 303-832-1537
Carter Industrial Design, Don W: 8809 E 59th St, Kansas City, MO 64133.........816-356-1874
Carter, Calvin W: 1950 Stemmons Fwy #3207, Dallas, TX 75207 214-746-4266
Carter, Julie: 2890 Westshire Dr, Los Angeles, CA 90068..................................213-962-2521
Carter, Richard N: PO Box 208, Del Mar, CA 92014 619-792-6473
Carver Letcher Miller: 3940 Spring Dr #11, Reno, NV 89502 702-828-4700
Casal, Linda: 210 E 15th St, New York, NY 10003..212-353-2060
Case: 11 Dupont Cir NW #400, Washington, DC 20036.......................................202-328-5900
Casey & Company Graphic Design: 76 N Eastner Blvd #24,
Nashua, NH 03062..603-594-0758
Casey, Jim: 33 W 17th St 7th Fl, New York, NY 10011 212-929-2886
Casey, Jim: 33 W 17th St 7th Fl, New York, NY 10011 212-929-2886
Casper Design Group: 903 University Ave, Berkeley, CA 94710.........................510-549-1300
Cassidy, Darrell: 2700 Simpson Rd #240, Richmond, BC 604-276-0838
Castells, Jaime: 100 Juergens Ave, Cincinnati, OH 45220 513-221-3377
Catalano Design: 374 Congress St, Boston, MA 02210.......................................617-338-7447
Catalog Design & Production, Inc: 1825 A Egbert, San Francisco, CA 94124 415-468-5500
Catapult Entertainment: 20823 Stevens Creek Blvd, Cupertino, CA 95014 408-366-1735
Cates, Randy A: 421 Pendleton Ln, Londonderry, NH 03053 603-437-3759
Cathey Assocs: 3322 Shorecrest Dr #100, Dallas, TX 75235 214-352-6399
Cats' Pajamas, Inc: 344 Ramsey St, St Paul, MN 55102 612-227-2240
CBI Advertising: 8160 E Butherus Dr #6, Scottsdale, AZ 85260 602-948-0440
CCBS Design: 1604 Mclendon Ave NE, Atlanta, GA 30307.................................404-371-8586
CCMR ADV: 260 Fair St, Kingston, NY 12401 914-331-4620
CCW Group: 133 Coulter Ave, Ardmore, PA 19003..610-642-3330
CD Squared: 418 Meadow St, Fairfield, CT 06430...203-334-3330
Cejka Design: PO Box 4048, Crestline, CA 92325..909-338-2245
Celli Design: 103 Casterton Ave, Akron, OH 44303..330-374-1750
Center For Advanced Whimsy: 61 Crosby St, New York, NY 10012 212-219-0342
Centermedia: 186 South St, Boston, MA 02111 617-451-9902
Central Advtg Agcy: 1 Tandy Cir #300, Fort Worth, TX 76102 817-390-3011
CentriMedia: 3964 26th St, San Francisco, CA 95131 415-282-7875
Cerulli, Andrew: 82-31 63rd Ave, Middle Village, NY 11379...............................718-803-2321
Cesaroni Design Assocs, Inc: 1865 Grove St, Glenview, IL 60025......................847-724-8840
Cetta, Al: 111 Bank St, New York, NY 10010...212-989-9696
Chadick & Kimball Design: 1025 Conn Ave NW #311,
Washington, DC 20036 202-452-8112
Chambers Co, H: 1010 N Charles St, Baltimore, MD 21201 410-727-4535
Chambers Group, The: 1631 16th St, Santa Monica, CA 90404..........................310-452-5551
Chambray Design: 770 Madison Ave, New York, NY 10021................................212-535-0307
Champ Design Assocs, John: 1049 Camino Del Mar #C, Del Mar, CA 92014 619-481-2991
Champ, Heather: 37 E Seventh St, New York, NY 10003....................................212-995-8494
Champaigne Lafayette Comm: 7 Strathmore Rd, Natick, MA 01760...................508-651-0400
Chan Design: 1334 Lincoln Blvd #150, Santa Monica, CA 90401 310-393-3735
Chan Design, Kimiko: 407 Jackson St #202, San Francisco, CA 94111...............415-399-9665
Chandler & Assocs: 744 Flume St, Chico, CA 95928...916-343-1127
Chandler, Jeff: 1010 N Windomere Ave, Dallas, TX 75208 214-946-1348
Chaney Co: 272 E Deerpath Rd #200, Lake Forest, IL 60045 847-615-2602
Chang, Ivan: 30 E 10th St, New York, NY 10003 212-777-6102
Chaparos Productions Ltd: 1112 6th St NW, Washington, DC 20001 202-289-4838
Chaparral Graphics Group: 921 E 66th St, Lubbock, TX 79404...........................806-745-9292
Chaplin Graphics: 164 Edward Dr, Swedesboro, NJ 08085..................................609-467-5992
Chapman & Partners: 14 Imperial Pl #501, Providence, RI 02903 401-454-3456
Chapman, Sandra S: 122 Ashland Pl #7E, Brooklyn, NY 11201 718-855-7396
Charles Design Group, Richard: 54 Roast Meat Hill Rd,
Killingworth, CT 06417..203-663-2754
Charles, Milton: 199 Ravine Rd, Califon, NJ 07830 908-832-7076
Charlier, Mark: 33 E Cedar #5C, Chicago, IL 60611 312-421-2668
Charysyn & Charysyn: Route 42, Westkill, NY 12492 518-989-6720
Chase Design, David O: 1400 E Genesee St, Skaneateles, NY 13152.................315-685-8941
Chase Design, Margo: 2255 Bancroft Ave, Los Angeles, CA 90039.....................213-668-1055
Chateau de Loxley: PO Box 953, Loxley, AL 36551..334-964-6972
Checkman Design, Inc: 149 Fifth Ave 12th Fl, New York, NY 10010 212-674-4464
Chen Design Inc, David: 2211 Newton Drive, Rockville, MD 20850....................301-460-6575
Chen, Henry L: 115 Old Short Hills Rd #279, West Orange, NJ 07052 973-736-2379
Chen, Shih-chien: 2839 35th St, Edmonton, AB T6L 5K2...................................403-462-8617
Cheng Design, Mary Ann: 1092 Potrero Ave, San Francisco, CA 94110..............415-647-7382
Cheren Design: 233 Harvard St #32, Brookline, MA 02146................................617-734-1194
Chermayeff & Geismar: 15 E 26th St 12th Fl, New York, NY 10010 212-532-4499
Cherry Pie Graphics: 1171 Homestead Rd #220, Santa Clara, CA 95050............408-261-8210
Chesapeake Display & Pkgng Co : 1225 Grand Central, Glendale, CA 91201 818-507-7477
Chesapeake Group, The: 655 Eden Park Dr #525, Cincinnati, OH 45202.......513-345-6300
Chesire Designs: 2492 Flair Knoll Court NE, Atlanta, GA 30345........................404-633-8330

Cheskin & Masten: 255 Shore Line #100, Redwood City, CA 94065 415-802-2100
Chesler Design Assocs: 23052 Sunfield Dr, Boca Raton, FL 33433..................561-477-1525
Chestnut Creative: 610 Lake Medlock Ct, Alpharetta, GA 30202.....................770-813-0508
Chew Assocs, HR: 1900 N Vine St #108, Los Angeles, CA 90068 213-464-0156
Chiappetta, Gary: 117 S Morgan St 3rd Fl, Chicago, IL 60607 312-738-2611
Chiaro Design: 5 Thompson Rd, Patterson, NY 12563 203-746-0100
Chicago Show: 345 Lakewood Ave, Waukegan, IL 60085...................................847-263-2210
Chikamura Design Inc, Michael: 375 Alabama St #230,
San Francisco, CA 94110...415-252-9565
Children's Television Workshop: 1 Lincoln Plaza, New York, NY 10023 212-875-6905
Chillingworth Raddind: 35 E 21st St 6th Fl, New York, NY 10010...................212-674-4700
Chilton Design Group: 1008 Camino San Acacio, Santa Fe, NM 87501............505-820-1865
Chin Assocs, ET: 226 E 54th St #308, New York, NY 10021 212-645-6800
Chinnici Assocs: 49 W 27th St 5th Fl, New York, NY 10001..........................212-685-0564
Chirping Bird Communications:
1337 W Estes Ave #27, Chicago, IL 60626 773-274-0224
Choe Design: 307 Orchard City Dr #210, Campbell, CA 95008 408-364-1080
Chong, YC: 499 Jln 22, Kuala Lumpur, Salak, ML 57100...................................03-7835681
Christensen Media: 3638 Auburn Blvd #F, Sacramento, CA 95821 916-487-4722
Chroma Design & Communications: 115 Indian Spring Dr,
Silver Spring, MD 20901..301-585-5880
Chronicle Type & Design: 1255 23rd NW, Washington, DC 20036....................202-466-1090
Chu & Co Ltd, HL: 39 W 29th St, New York, NY 10001 212-889-4818
Chu, Collins: 430 W Main St, Tustin, CA 92680 714-731-7200
Chun Graphic Design, Milton: 4946 Kilauea Ave #4, Honolulu, HI 96816........808-735-6436
Church & Main: 30 Main St, Keene, NH 03431 603-357-5898
Church Street Design: 124 Church St, Decatur, GA 30030...............................404-370-0437
Churik Design, Bennardo: 1601 Mary's Ave, Pittsburgh, PA 15215.................412-782-1351
Chute Gerdeman Group: 130 E Chestnut #102, Columbus, OH 43215...........614-469-1001
Chwast, Seymour: 18 E 16th St 7th Fl, New York, NY 10003 212-255-6456
Cia Creative Group: 6430 Sunset Blvd #1001, Hollywood, CA 90028 213-461-5959
Ciavarra Design: One Design Ctr Pl #728, Boston, MA 02210 617-439-4223
Ciesa, Inc: 201 Ann St, E Lansing, MI 48823..517-351-2453
Cimarron Bacon O'Brien: 758 N Highland Ave, Hollywood, CA 90038...............213-461-5850
Cimity Art/Special Visual Effects: 800 S Robertson Blvd,
Los Angeles, CA 90035...310-659-4504
Cinema Concepts: 2030 Powers Ferry Rd #214, Atlanta, GA 30339 770-956-7460
Ciphers: 245 El Cajon Way, Los Gatos, CA 95030 408-356-9983
Cipriani Kremer Design: 2 Copley Pl, Boston, MA 02116 617-236-1422
Circa 86: 38 W 38th St 5th Fl, New York, NY 10018 212-869-8686
CKS Interactive: 10443 Bandley Dr, Cupertino, CA 95014.................................408-366-5100
Clare Graphics, George: 815 Sea Spray Ln #214, Foster City, CA 94404 415-349-4103
Clark Art Direction & Design: 1777 E Meadow Downs Way,
Salt Lake City, UT 84121..801-944-4187
Clark Communications Group: RR1 Box 61, Sharon, MD 21401......................802-763-7765
Clark Design, Jennifer: 349 County Route 2, Accord, NY 12404......................914-687-4011
Clark Illus, Tim: 1256 25th St, Santa Monica, CA 90404 310-453-7613
Clark Studio: 709 Stannage Ave, Albany, CA 94706..510-528-6968
Clark, Linda: 28 Precita Ave, San Francisco, CA 94110..................................415-282-7955
Clarke Co, William: 60 Green St, San Francisco, CA 94111............................415-291-8595
Clarke/Thompson: 30 W 22nd St #3rd Fl, New York, NY 10010........................212-645-8990
Clarkson Creative: 1472 S 800 East, Salt Lake City, UT 84105........................801-467-9993
Clasen Design: 3700 Katiia Ave #201B, Los Alamitos, CA 90720......................310-596-2202
Clasen, Gene: 10407 Los Alamitos Blvd, Los Alamitos, CA 90720....................310-596-2202
Clavenna, Barbara: 6000 Stone Ln, Birmingham, AL 35242 205-991-8909
Clayton Design: 4808 Nevada Ave, Nashville, TN 37209.................................615-383-4687
Cleary Design: 118 A N Division St, Salisbury, MD 21801 301-546-1040
Clebenger & Co: 514 W 26th St #2W, Kansas City, MO 64108 816-471-3311
Clemans & Partners: 1248 Homestead Ave, Walnut Creek, CA 94598..............510-938-3224
Clementi Assocs Design: 46 Lincoln St, Waltham, MA 02154 617-899-1661
Clementino Design, Ann: 145 Lakewood Cir N, Manchester, CT 06040............203-649-3669
Cleveland Design, John: 2433 28th St #B, Santa Monica, CA 90405 310-450-2133
Cliff & Assocs: 715 Fremont Ave, S Pasadena, CA 91030................................818-799-5906
Clockwise Design: 594 Broadway #904, New York, NY 10012..........................212-226-5686
Cloud Assocs, Gregory: 2116 Arlington Ave #236, Los Angeles, CA 90018 213-484-9479
Clune Design, Quinby : 1035 Cherokee St #A, Denver, CO 80204...................303-620-0070
CM Jackson Assoc: 85 Oxford Dr, Moonachie, NJ 07074..................................201-807-1500
CM Media: 254 Dolores St #4, San Francisco, CA 94103 415-552-5176
CMA: 1207 Dunlavy St, Houston, TX 77019 713-834-0180
CMG: 11260 Simpson Rd, Monmouth, OR 97361 503-838-2328
CMG Inc: 1200 Kings Ave, Jacksonville, FL 32207 904-346-0010
Cnet: 150 Chestnut St, San Francisco, CA 94111 415-395-7800
CO Design Services: 224 N 5th Ave, Phoenix, AZ 85003 602-252-7296
Coak, Steve: 2870 N Haven Ln, Altadena, CA 91001..818-797-5477
Coakley Heagerty Co, The: 1155 N First Ave #201, San Jose, CA 95112.........408-275-9400
Coastline Studios: 545 Delaney Ave #1, Orlando, FL 32801 407-246-1970
Coates Advertising: 320 South West Oak #300, Portland, OR 97204 503-241-1124
Cocchiarella, Nino: 201 NW 4th St #114, Evansville, IN 47708........................812-423-2500
Coddington Beyer Design: 36 Albany St, Cazenovia, NY 13035 315-655-5500
Coe Design Assocs, Laura: 4918 N Harbor Dr #206A, San Diego, CA 92106 619-223-0909
Coffman Multimedia, Tom: 45-955 Kamehameha Hghw #305,
Kaneohe, HI 96744..808-247-8181
Coffman, Claudia: 70 E Lake St #415, Chicago, IL 60601 312-236-8545
Cognata Assocs: 950 Battery St #310, San Francisco, CA 94111 415-931-3800
Cogno Centi Design: 149 Fifth Ave 7th Fl, New York, NY 10010 212-529-0857
Cohen & Co: 3210-2 Peachtree Rd NE, Atlanta, GA 30305 404-233-7331
Cohen & Godefroy: 956 Granville Ave, Los Angeles, CA 90049........................310-447-9320
Cohen Design, Inc, Michael: 65-76 162nd St, Fresh Meadows, NY 11365.......718-380-4990
Cohen Design, Norman: 201 E 28th St #8K, New York, NY 10016....................212-679-3906
Cohen Studio, Steve: 560 W 43rd St #37J, New York, NY 10036....................212-279-0246
Cohoe/Baker Design: 256 W 93rd St, New York, NY 10023..............................212-787-0943
Coker Golley Ltd: 127 Peachtree Road #900, Atlanta, GA 30030 404-523-8805
Colangelo Assocs, Ted:
340 Pemberwick Rd (The Mill), Greenwich, CT 06830....................................203-531-3600
Colavecchio Design: 684 Main St, Winsted, CT 06098 203-379-9893
Cole & Co Visual Comm: 4981 W Catalpa Dr, Boise, ID 83703 208-345-9962
Cole Design Group: 73 River Rd, Collinsville, CT 06022...................................860-693-1980
Coleman Group West, The: 125 E Sir Francis Drake Blvd, Larkspur, CA 94939 415-925-8000
Colini Design Assocs, Jeanine: 346 N Larchmont Blvd #102,
Los Angeles, CA 90004...213-462-7316
Collins, Thomas: 54 W 21st St #604, New York, NY 10010 212-627-1656
Color Assocs-Creative Imaging: 10835 Midwest Industrial Blvd,
St Louis, MO 63132 314-423-8111
Color Forms Studio: 407 E Fort St #300/Globe Bldg, Detroit, MI 48226 313-961-7100
Colorado Film & Television Studios: 2300 15th St #100, Denver, CO 80202......303-455-8200
Colorplay Design Studio: 323 W 13th Ave, Eugene, OR 97401 541-687-8262
Colquitt & Kibler Design: 4 E Madison St, Baltimore, MD 21202......................410-837-7070
Comadres Comm & Graphics: 55 W Wacker Dr #700, Chicago, IL 60601.........312-332-2233
Comark Commulications: 1636 Abbot Kinney Blvd, Venice, CA 90291............310-396-8626
Comark Group, Inc, The: 400 Renaissance Ctr #6060, Detroit, MI 48243 313-567-5100
Combs Design, Brent: 2626 Cole Ave LB37 #210, Dallas, TX 75204...............214-880-0846
Comcorp: 542 S Dearborn 9th Fl, Chicago, IL 60605 312-939-6424
Command P: 634 W Sunset, San Antonio, TX 78216 210-821-6006
Communica: 31 North Erie St, Toledo, OH 43624..419-244-7766
Communication Arts: 129 E Pascagoula, Jackson, MS 39201 601-354-7955
Communication Arts Multimedia Inc: 2013 Wells Branch Pkwy #201,
Austin, TX 78728..512-251-0074
Communication By Design: 25 Sturges Rd, Sharon, MA 02067 617-784-6000
Communication Connection, The: 2137 Mt Vernon Rd, Atlanta, GA 30338.......770-395-7483
Communication Design: 1604 Hodges Ct, Marina, CA 93933...........................408-883-1361
Communication Design, Inc: 8950 Calif Ctr Dr #235, Sacramento, CA 95826 916-362-0400
Communication/Design: 139 Peterborough Rd, Hancock, NH 03449 603-525-4726
Communications Company: 100 W Rincon Ave #209, Campbell, CA 95008 408-379-5356
Communications Consultants Grp, Inc: 929 Harrison Ave #301,
Columbus, OH 43215..614-297-5050
Communications Design, Inc: 5875 Old Millstone Rd, Rockford, IL 61114........815-633-0577
Communications Via Design: 354 Congress St 4th Fl, Boston, MA 02210.........617-338-1223
CommuniCreations: 2130 S Bellaire, Denver, CO 80222 303-759-1155
Comp Art of Louisville: 981 S Third St #300, Louisville, KY 40203 502-589-2557
Compass Design: 510 First Ave N #202, Minneapois, MN 55403.....................612-339-1595
Computech Design Studio: 13500 Chenal Parkway #340C,
Little Rock, AR 72211 501-223-9378
Computer Graphics Group: 1450 Manhattan Beach Blvd #B,
Manhattan Beach, CA 90266 310-372-3228
Computer Images, Inc: 2469 University Ave, St Paul, MN 55114 612-644-1977
Comvision: 60 E 42nd St #1365, New York, NY 10165 212-687-2708
Conber Creations: 3326 NE 60th, Portland, OR 97213 503-288-2938
Concept & Design: 1009 N Jackson St #1406, Milwaukee, WI 53202 414-289-9448
Concept & Design Assocs: 1585 Alameda #300, San Jose, CA 95126................408-993-2272
Concept Design: 154 Brushy Hill Rd, Danbury, CT 06810 203-797-0504
Concept Design Worx: 1835 E 6th St #13, Mesa, AZ 85203 602-968-4125
Concept Packaging, Inc: 5 Horizon Rd, Ft Lee, NJ 07024 201-224-5762
Concepts Corp, The: 120 Kedron Ave, Holmes, PA 19043 610-461-1600
Concepts Design Group: 8000 West Ave #1, San Antonio, TX 78213 210-342-0270
Concepts Unlimited, Inc: 1250 Capital of Texas Hwy S/B3#350,
Austin, TX 78746..512-328-3576
Conceptual Annual Reports: 65 Bleecker St, New York, NY 10001...................212-505-1607
Concrete, Inc: 633 S Plymouth Ct #208, Chicago, IL 60605 312-427-3733
Confluence Comm: 263 Chuckanut Point Rd, Bellingham, WA 98226...............360-733-2005
Conflux Design: 2819 Ware Rd, Rockford, IL 61114 815-282-4066
Connaster & Co: 3333 Mockingbird Ln, Dallas, TX 75205.................................214-522-7373
Connecting Images: 2469 University Ave, St Paul, MN 55114...........................612-644-1977
Connelly Design: 444 N Wabash #410, Chicago, IL 60611 312-565-0760
Connick Creative Svcs, Jack: 1935 8th Ave West, Seattle, WA 98119...............206-284-1142
Conrad Graphic Design: 1133 Millcreek Ln, Columbus, OH 43220 614-442-1880
Conrad Jorgensen Studio: 1219 Folsom St, San Francisco, CA 94103 415-626-9878
Constable, Janice: 11 Woodstock Ct, San Raphael, CA 94903 415-472-5530
Consultants In Design: 32 W 40th St #7B, New York, NY 10018.......................212-921-1524
Contempo Design: 212 Railroad Ave, Milpitas, CA 95035.................................408-956-9555
Context Design Research Dvlpmt: 2601 Meade Ct, Ann Arbor, MI 48105 313-622-0072
Contours Consulting Design Group: 864 Stearns Rd, Bartlett, IL 60103..........630-837-4100
Conway Design: 118 Magazine St, Cambridge, MA 02139..................................617-864-9838
Cook & Shanosky Assoc: 401 S State St, Newtown, PA 18940...........................215-860-8800
Cook Creative Srv: 260 W Hamilton Ave, Campbell, CA 95008 408-379-4333
Cook Design, Chris: 3836 Piute Dr, Grandville, MI 49418.................................616-531-5474
Cook Design, Mickey: 1647 Kitchener Dr, Sunnyvale, CA 94087 408-738-8277
Cook Design, Robert: PO Box 639, Bellaire, TX 77402 713-227-8350
Cooke & Co, Bill: 314 main St, Great Barringto, MA 01230 413-528-3808
Cooke Design, Alice: 1 East Ave, Norwalk, CT 06851 203-847-7109
Coon Design Assocs: 3711 W 12th St, Erie, PA 16505 814-838-1528
Cooney Design: 875 3rd Ave 4th Fl, New York, NY 10022...............................212-303-7604
Coons/Beirise Design Assocs: 313 Hilton Pl, Cincinnati, OH 45219.................513-751-7459
Cooper Assocs, Scott: 35 Pinelawn #212E, Melville, NY 11747........................516-249-9700
Cooper Design Assocs: 1360 S Coast Hwy, Laguna Beach, CA 92651...............714-497-5081
Cooper Graphic Design, Sam: 101 Linden, Ft Collins, CO 80524 970-484-7440
Cooper Software, Inc: 2345 Yale St, Palo Alto, CA 94308................................415-855-0250
Copeland Hirthler Design & Comm: 40 Inwood Circle, Atlanta, GA 30309..........404-892-3472
Corcetto Enterprises: 3 Skywind Dr, Reinholds, PA 17569 610-678-0867
Corchia Woliner Assocs: 130 W 56th St, New York, NY 10019 212-977-9778
Cordaro Design Inc, Rubin: 115 N First St, Minneapolis, MN 55401 612-343-0011
Cordella Design: 55 Westland Terrace, Haverhill, MA 01830............................617-437-9198
Cordesign: 3904 Jefferson, Austin, TX 78731 512-371-1230
Corey Mcpherson Nash: 9 Galen St, Watertown, MA 02172 617-924-6050
Cornelius/Keener Creative: 3326 Mapleridge Ct, Suwanee, GA 30174 770-623-3986
Cornerstone Design Group: 444 Park Ave S #202, New York, NY 10016 212-686-6046
Cornoyer Hedrick, Inc: 2425 E Camelback Rd #400, Phoenix, AZ 85016..........602-381-4848
Corpographics,Inc: 47 West St, New York, NY 10006.......................................212-483-9065
Corporate 3 Design: 2723 S 87th Ave, Omaha, NE 68124 402-398-3333
Corporate Design Assocs: 3450 Princeton Pike, LAwrenceville, NJ 08648 609-844-9797
Corporate Design Group: 256 Fifth Ave 2nd Fl, New York, NY 10001 212-889-7696
Corporate Graphics: 51-04 39th Ave, Woodside, NY 11377.............................718-651-4689
Corporate Graphics, Inc: 1633 Broadway 27th Fl, New York, NY 10019 212-887-8181
Corporate Image, The: 43 Wensley Dr, Great Neck, NY 11021 516-773-3131
Corporate Reports: 6 Lenox Pointe NE, Atlanta, GA 30324..............................404-233-2230
Corporate Visuals, Inc: 515 El Bosque, Laguna Beach, CA 92651....................714-494-6269
Corrente, Linda: 45 E 62nd St, New York, NY 10021 212-486-3015

Corson Design, Madeleine: 25 Zoe St, San Francisco, CA 94107 415-777-2492
Cory Adv: 2083 Main St, Stratford, CT 06497 203-380-5240
Cosgrove Assocs, Inc: 225 E 31 St 1st Fl, New York, NY 10016 212-889-7202
Costello & Co: 250 Summit Ave, Greensboro, NC 27401 910-273-9028
Costello Communications: 2657 N Bosworth Ave, Chicago, OH 60614 773-327-1386
Cotler, Inc, Sheldon: 568 Broadway #803, New York, NY 10012 212-719-9590
Cottle Communications, Inc: 8 S Michigan Ave #2212, Chicago, IL 60603 312-922-7009
Cotton Communications, Jim: 38 Vestry St, New York, NY 10013...................212-431-1930
Counihan Graphics, Gerald: 200 Mercer St, New York, NY 10012 212-477-7925
Cousins & Assocs, Morison S: 599 Broadway 8th Fl, New York, NY 10012.......212-751-3390
Cover To Cover: 26 W 17th St *th Fl, New York, NY 10011...........................212-675-5550
Covey, Traci O'Very: 7 Washington Street, Beverly, MA 01915 978-921-0887
cow.: 1522 Cloverfield Blvd #E, Santa Monica, CA 90404 310-264-2430
Cowen Design, Melinda: 3841 NE 2nd Ave, Miami, FL 33137 305-573-9838
Cox & Hall: 4901 Behrens Rd, Collieville, TX 76034 817-267-2340
Cox Adv, Jim: 391 S Madison, Pasadena, CA 91101 818-584-9363
Cox, Stephen: 303 N Broadway, St Louis, MO 63102 314-241-2150
Coy Los Angeles: 4230 Lafayette, Culver City, CA 90232 310-837-0173
Coyne Beahm: 8518 Triad Dr, Colfax, NC 27235...910-996-1255
Coyne Comms: The Penthouse/10 Park Pl, Morristown, NJ 02960...................201-984-1800
CPF Marketing Communications: 22015 Marine View Dr South,
Seattle, WA 98198..206-824-0688
Cpm 95 Inc: 95 Fifth Ave 4th Fl, New York, NY 10003 212-924-3815
CPS: 267 W 70th St #1A, New York, NY 10023...212-724-6700
CPS Group/Timerlane Mclane: 125 E Carpenter Frwy #600, Irving, TX 75062 214-869-3370
Crabtree & Jimison: 1137 N Highland St, Arlington, VA 22201 703-525-7798
Crabtree & Strussion Design Inc: 1712 Graham Rd, Reynoldsburg, OH 43068 614-577-1712
Craen, Inc, John :_520 Madison, San Antonio, TX 78204................................210-224-9751
Craig Design, Susan: 3118 Amherst Ave, Columbia, SC 29205 803-252-6558
Crane, Doug: 1732 NW Quimby St, Portland, OR 97209..................................503-223-6794
Cranford & Assocs, Johnson: 1st Commercial Bldg #2200,
Little Rock, AR 72201 501-376-6251
Craven Design: 234 Fifth Ave 4th Fl, New York, NY 10001.............................212-696-4680
Craven, Linda: 1737 Connecticut Ave NW, Washington, DC 20009 202-232-4838
Crawford Mikus Design: 887 W Marietta St NW #T-101, Atlanta, GA 30318......404-875-7753
Crawshaw Design, Todd: 120 Bayview Dr, San Rafael, CA 94901 415-456-5544
Creamer Dickson Basford: 1633 Broadway, New York, NY 10019 212-887-8670
Create 12: 12 Lois Ave, E Brunswick, NJ 08816 908-238-5051
Creative Avenue: 500 S Clinton St 8th Fl, Chicago, IL 60607 312-922-4500
Creative Center: 44 Garden St, Danvers, MA 01923 508-777-3500
Creative Concepts In Design: 1638 S Bayshore Ct, Miami, FL 33133 305-899-8464
Creative Dept: 5002 92nd Ave SE, Mercer Island, WA 98040...........................206-236-4548
Creative Dept: 1708 Scott Ave, Charlotte, NC 28203 704-339-0497
Creative Dept, The: 130 S 17th St, Philadelphia, PA 19103 215-988-0390
Creative Design: 1273 Old Dixie Highway, Lake Park, FL 33403 407-848-6666
Creative Design & Marketing: 48 Free St, Portland, ME 04101 207-774-7528
Creative Design Board: Hancock/875 N Michigan #2205, Chicago, IL 60611 312-266-2200
Creative Design Center, Inc: 1091 N Granada Dr, Orange, CA 92869..............714-771-7124
Creative Directions: 1776 Peachtree St NW #618 S, Atlanta, GA 30309 404-818-6407
Creative Group, The: 3201 W Sahara Suite G, Las Vegas, NV 89102...............702-248-6334
Creative Ink Design: 26 Park Rd, Shorts Hills, NJ 07078 201-467-5396
Creative Only: 610 Emory Ave, Campbell, CA 95008.......................................408-379-0151
Creative R & D: 321 Pharr Rd #6, Atlanta, GA 30305 404-261-1724
Creative Resource Center: 3621 Bury Dr #10, Eden Prairie, MN 55346..........612-937-6000
Creative Services: 2109 St James Rd, Raleigh, NC 27607 919-781-5366
Creative Solutions: 205 Rutgers St, Maplewood, NJ 07040.............................201-378-3800
Creative Works, Inc: 304 3rd St, Jupiter, FL 33458 407-745-7050
Creatives NYC: 27 W 24th St #500, New York, NY 10010.................................212-675-9592
Creativeworks Studios, Inc: 10 E 23rd St #300, New York, NY 10010 212-477-5610
Cricket Contrast: 2301 N 16th St, Phoenix, AZ 85006 602-258-6149
Crisp, Alan: 1430 Mercy St, Mountain View, CA 94041...................................415-965-8966
Critz, Anita: 2255 Cumberland Pkwy NW Bldg 1400 #A1, Atlanta, GA 30339.....770-436-6092
Crockadre Studio: 170 S Brownell Rd Suite A, Williston, VT 05495 802-865-6233
Cronan Design: 42 Decatur St, San Francisco, CA 94103...............................415-522-5800
Cronan, Michael Patrick: 1 Zoe St, San Francisco, CA 94107 415-543-6745
Crosby, Bart: 676 St Clair St, Chicago, IL 60611 312-951-2800
Crossroads Graphics, Inc: 235 Monroe Tnpke, Monroe, CT 06468...................203-268-2255
Crouch & Fuller,Inc: 853 Camino Del Mar, Del Mar, CA 92014 619-450-9200
Crow-Quill Studios: 1026 Walker Ave, Oakland, CA 94610..............................510-832-8931
Croxton Design: 2121 N California Blvd #530, Walnut Creek, CA 94596.........510-935-7003
Crum Designs, Inc, Don : 4607 W Lovers Ln, Dallas, TX 75209 214-352-1384
Cruz Design: 123 Townsend St #450, San Francisco, CA 94107 415-495-5999
CSF Design: 3658 Perada Dr, Walnut Creek, CA 94595 510-682-9967
Csoka Benato Fleurant, Inc: 134 W 26th St, New York, NY 10001 212-242-6777
Cuccia Design, Christine: 2350 Taylor St, San Francisco, CA 94133 415-771-1072
Cuerden Advertising Design: 1730 Gaylord St, Denver, CO 80206 303-321-4163
Cuh2A: 211 Carnegie Center, Princeton, NJ 08540...609-452-1212
Cuisine Studio 400: 760 Burr Oak Dr, Westmont, IL 60559.............................630-323-3616
Cukjati Designs: 2735 Rocky Heights Dr, Colorado Springs, CO 80921 719-481-4686
Culbert Lavery Russman, Ross: 15 W 20th St 9th Fl, New York, NY 10011......212-206-0044
Cully, Mike: 345 W Erie St, Chicago, IL 60610...312-440-9208
Cummings & Good: 3 N Main St/Box 570, Chester, CT 06412 860-526-9597
Cummings Design Group: 5 Park Plaza #1120, Irvine, CA 92614 714-643-2346
Cunningham & Welsh Design Grp: 633 W Main, Madison, WI 53703 608-258-1988
Curium Design: 83 Divisadero St, San Francisco, CA 94117.............................415-255-1877
Curr Design, Jane: 745 Walnut Dr, Paso Robles, CA 93446 805-227-4240
Curran & Connors: 333 Marcus Blvd, Hauppauge, NY 11788...........................516-435-0400
Curran & Connors: 55 Madison Ave, Morristown, NJ 07960.............................201-285-5212
Curran & Connors: 140 Wood Rd #200, Braintree, MA 02184 617-963-7540
Current, Inc: 1005 E Woodman Rd, Colorado Springs, CO 80920.....................719-594-4100
Curry Design: 1501 Main St/Mezzanine, Venice, CA 90291.............................310-399-4626
Curry, Steve: 1501 Main St Mezzanine, Venice, CA 90291 310-399-4626
Curtis & Co: 928 Broadway #1104, New York, NY 10010 212-475-3680
Curtis Design: 3328 Steiner St #1, San Francisco, CA 94123 415-567-4402
Curtis Design: 698 Bedford Rd, Armonk, NY 10504 914-234-3574
Curtis, Todd: 2032 14th St #7, Santa Monica, CA 90405 310-452-0738
Custom Designers, Inc: 5866 Old Centerville Rd, Centerville, VA 22020..........703-830-8582
Cutro Assocs, Inc: 47 Jewett Ave, Tenafly, NJ 07670 201-569-5548
CW & Assocs: 11601 Wilshire Blvd #1000, Los Angeles, CA 90025..............415-546-0810
CWA, Inc: 4015 Ibis St, San Diego, CA 92103 619-299-0431
CyberLive: 409 Utica Ave #D44, Huntington Beach, CA 92648 714-536-7014

D

D & D Creative Concepts: 59 Farnell Rd, Weston, CT 06883..........................203-227-9232
D Wilkinson Advertising: 55 W Chestnut St #1703, Chicago, IL 60610 312-951-0159
D'Addario: 595 Smith St, Farmingdale, NY 11735 516-391-5440
D'Anastasio Art Studio: 458 Boonton Turnpike, Lincoln Park, NJ 07035...........201-872-4593
• **D'Antuono, Michael: pg 1456** 39 Hamilton Terr, New York, NY 10031 ....**212-283-3401**
url: www.wayart.com
D'Art Studio, Inc: PO Box 299, N Scituate, MA 02060 617-545-7313
D'Astolfo Design, Frank: 80 Warren St #32, New York, NY 10007 212-732-3052
D-Zine: 34 W 15th St 3rd Fl, New York, NY 10011 212-691-6700
Daigle Design, Inc: 5W Harrison St, Seattle, WA 98119...................................206-282-1299
Dakin & Willison, Inc: 1210 Fifth Ave, San Rafael, CA 94901 415-257-5757
Dakota Design, Inc: 2160 Swedeford Rd, Malverne, PA 19355 610-647-9898
Dale Graphics: 50 George St Apt#2, Babylon, NY 11702 516-321-1042
Dale, Inc, Colopy: 850 Ridge Ave, Pittsburgh, PA 15212................................412-332-6706
Dale, Terry: 2824 Hurst Terr NW, Washington, DC 20008...............................202-244-3866
DaLee, Dianne: 2029 Santenay Dr, Marietta, GA 30060..................................770-425-4222
Daly & Daly Graphic Design, Inc: 233 Harvard St, Brookline, MA 02146 617-738-7181
Daly Design, Joan: 622 Central Ave, Wilmette, IL 60091...............................847-256-5042
Dancer Fitzgerald & Sample: 1010 Battery St, San Francisco, CA 94120..........415-981-6250
Dangremond Design Assocs: 6064 N Kirkwood, Chicago, IL 60646 773-205-2222
Danhausen Group Design: 2183 Fairview Rd #103, Costa Mesa, CA 92627 714-574-0303
Daniel, Inc: 3301 Hamilton #106, Fort Worth, TX 76107 817-334-0039
Daniels Design: 104 E 40th St #503, New York, NY 10016...............................212-889-0071
Daniels Graphics: 131 Sweeten Creek Rd, Asheville, NC 28803 704-277-8250
Danube Design, Louy: E 12348 Halweg Rd, Merrimac, WI 53561.....................608-493-2797
Danziger, Louis: PO Box 660189, Arcadia, CA 91066.......................................818-446-7717
Darby, Kevin: 6604 Six Forks Rd #201, Raleigh, NC 27615 919-676-3261
Darden Graphics, Clare: 5422 Bellingham Ave #201B,
N Hollywood, CA 91607 818-762-5673
Darden Lentz: 164 W Mariposa, San Clemente, CA 92672 714-361-2807
Darold Designs: 216 F St #145, Davis, CA 95616 916-758-1379
Darvin Design: 715 Griffith Pl, Laguna Beach, CA 92651 714-497-4840
[data-rocket] + [industries]: 2 N Main St #B332, Beacon Falls, CT 06403 203-720-1603
Davenport Design: 3677 Voltaire St, San Diego, CA 92106..............................619-224-6004
Davenport Design Assocs, Alan: 220 Montgomery St #1035,
San Francisco, CA 94105...415-362-8333
Davidson Production Design, Peter: 836 Ashland Ave #1,
Santa Monica, CA 90405 310-581-9335
Davies & Assocs: 1440 Terrace Dr, Tulsa, OK 74104 918-744-1101
Davies Assocs: 9424 Dayton Way #217, Beverly Hills, CA 90210 310-247-9572
Davis Adv & Design, Scott: N2806 Walden Ln, Lake Geneva, WI 53147 414-248-3608
Davis Delaney Arrow, Inc: 141 E 25th St, New York, NY 10010.......................212-686-2500
Davis Design: 2401 15th St #350, Denver, CO 80202 303-455-0357
Davis Design: 1055 Hillside, Naperville, IL 60540 630-305-3982
Davis Design Adv: 2200 Powell St #650, Emeryville, CA 94608.......................510-654-1231
Davis Design, Carla: 674 10th St #G-Fl, Brooklyn, NY 11215 212-924-6464
Davis Design, Neil: 119 W 57th St #615, New York, NY 10019........................212-245-4436
Davis Design, Pat: 455 university Ave #360, Sacramento, CA 95825..............916-920-9025
Davis Group: 14730 NE Eighth St #105, Bellevue, WA 98007..........................206-641-5758
Davis Group: 4631 Brown Ave, Jacksonville, FL 32207 904-398-1704
Davison Design: 444 De Haro St #212, San Francisco, CA 94107 415-864-5775
Dawn Patrol: 3767 Overland Ave #115, Los Angeles, CA 90034 310-841-6780
Dawson & Company: 21 Dean St, Assonet, MA 02702 508-644-2940
Dawson & Company: 49 Monroe Ctr NW, Grand Rapids, MI 49503 616-458-8022
Dawson Design: 7250 Beverly Blvd #101, Los Angeles, CA 90036...................213-937-5867
Dawson Design: 33 N Erie, Toledo, OH 43624 419-255-0413
Dawson Designers Assocs: 21 Dean St, Assonet, MA 02702 617-644-2940
Dawson, Chris: 7250 Beverly Blvd #101, Los Angeles, CA 90036 213-937-5867
• **Dawson, Henk: pg 1484,1485** 1319 170th Pl NE, Bellevue, WA 98008.....**425-882-3303**
Day & Assocs, David: 2152 S 109th St, Omaha, NE 68144 402-398-1108
Day Design & Assocs, David: 1310 Pendleton St #204, Cincinnati, OH 45210.....513-621-4060
Day, Brian: 646 Fillmore St, San Francisco, CA 94117.....................................415-621-4934
• **Day, Sam: pg 1459** PO Box 4425, Seattle, WA 98104..............................**206-382-7413**
url: www.samday.com
Dayne, Jeff: 731 NE Everett, Portland, OR 97232...503-232-8777
Dazel Corp: 301 Congress Ave #1100, Austin, TX 78701 512-494-7300
DB Design: 101 S Jennings #303, Fort Worth, TX 76104 817-870-2941
DBD Intl Ltd: 406 Technology Dr W, Menomonie, WI 54751 715-235-9040
DC Communications: 10505 Everest St, Norwalk, CA 90605...........................310-450-4013
DD Graphics: 44 Queens St, Rochester, NY 14609 716-288-8315
De Cesare Design: 15 Waverly Rd, Darien, CT 06820.......................................203-655-6057
De Goede, Jan: 3826 N Marshfield Ave, Chicago, IL 60613.............................773-525-6500
De Heer Rose Design: 350 Brannan St 3rd Fl, San Francisco, CA 94107..........415-512-7710
De Marting Design: 37 Main St #3, Cold Spring, NY 10516.............................212-941-9200
De Napoli Studio, Inc: 454 W 46th St #5ES, New York, NY 10036 212-333-3357
De Olivera Creative: 1750 Lafayette St, Denver, CO 80218 303-837-8717
De Pasque Graphic Design, Diane: 511 Ave Of The Americas,
New York, NY 10011 212-229-9201
De Plano Design, Inc: 1 Madison Ave 26th Fl, New York, NY 10010................212-213-2224
De Santis Design: 116 E 27th St 8th Fl, New York, NY 10016..........................212-725-2655
De Sherbinin Design: 7 Washington St, Beverly, MA 01915 508-927-6119
De Vries Communications: 3636 Westown Pkwy #101,
W Des Moines, IA 50266..515-221-9818
De Witt/Anthony Co: 126 Main St, Northhampton, MA 01060 413-586-4304
Dean Design Assocs: 1007 Nissley Rd, Lancaster, PA 17601...........................717-898-9800
Dean, Jane: 1007 Nissley Rd, Lancaster, PA 17601 717-898-9800
Debrey Design: 6014 Blue Circle Dr, Minnetonka, MN 55343 612-935-2292
DeBrey, Robert J: 6014 Blue Circle #D, Minneapolis, MN 55343 612-935-2292
Decampi Inc, Denis: 1201 Delaware Ave, Wilmington, DE 19806 302-656-0460
Decorage: 600 Hadley Rd, S Plainfield, NJ 07080 908-755-2600
Decorator House: 13801 Senlac Dr #100, Dallas, TX 75234............................214-484-8413
Decrosta Design, George: 902 Upper State St, New Haven, CT 06511 203-776-1155
Deep Design/Div Austin Kelley: 5901 Peachtree Dunwoody #200C,
Atlanta, GA 30328 770-396-6666

Deep Production New Media Consultancy: 312 May St #5F,
Chicago, IL 60607 312-433-7786
Dees Group, Inc: 12 Norcross #210, Roswell, GA 30075 770-522-8430
deFine Design: 415 Central Pk W, New York, NY 10025 212-316-2599
Defrancis Studio: 222 Newbury St, Boston, MA 02116 617-536-0036
DeFranco, Gerard R: 52 Oliver St, Rochester, NY 14607 716-271-0413
Defrin Design Inc, Bob: 140 Riverside Dr, New York, NY 212-799-4793
Degnen Assocs: 181 Thurnman Ave, Columbus, OH 43206 614-444-3334
Dejay Design: 9435 E 51st St, Tulsa, OK 74145 918-663-2702
Dekker Babian: 39 W 14th St #204, New York, NY 10011 212-242-1359
Dekrone Design: 70 E First St #3, New York, NY 10003 212-647-9870
Dektas Eger, Inc: 30 W Third St, Cincinnati, OH 45202 513-621-7070
DeLeeuw, Jeff: 23116 77th Ave SE, Woodinville, WA 98072 206-718-2075
DeLellis, Chris-Anthony: 417 Canal St 2nd Fl, New York, NY 10013 212-431-5300
Deleon Design, Inc: 3301 Edloe #204, Houston, TX 77027 713-963-0060
Delgado Design: 1133 Broadway #1614, New York, NY 10010 212-645-0097
Dellaporta Adv & Graphic: 2020 14th St, Santa Monica, CA 90405 310-452-3832
Delor Design Group: 732 W Main St, Louisville, KY 40202 502-584-5500
Demark Keller & Gardner: 141 W 28th St 9th Fl, New York, NY 10001 212-714-1731
DeMartin Marona Cranstoun Downes: 450 Seventh Ave 39th Fl,
New York, NY 10123 212-268-5450
DeMartino Design: 584 Broadway, New York, NY 10012 212-941-9200
Dennard Creative, Inc: 5050 Quorum #300, Dallas, TX 75240 214-233-0430
Denning & Denning Design: 2077 S Gessner #100, Houston, TX 77063 713-789-2076
Denny: 3613 Rolridge Rd, Richmond, VA 23233 804-360-7623
Denton Design Assocs: 491 Arbor St, Pasadena, CA 91105 818-792-7141
Deponte Design: 95 N Main St, Petersham, MA 01366 508-724-8823
Derek Sylvester Design: 1739 Rose St, Berkley, CA 94703 510-524-2205
DeRose, Andrea Legg: 1942 Shiver Dr, Alexandria, VA 22307 703-768-3193
Desert Graphics: 303 N Indian Canyon Dr, Palm Springs, CA 92262 619-325-2333
Desgra: 1532 E 3rd St, Long Beach, CA 90802 310-437-2144
Desgrippes Gobe &Assocs: 411 Lafayette St, New York, NY 10003 212-979-8900
Design & Direction: 872 5th St, Manhattan Beach, CA 90260 310-937-3669
Design & Direction: 7338 Hotchkiss, El Cerrito, CA 94530 510-526-9010
Design & Graphics: 330 E 13th St, Tucson, AZ 85701 520-623-8802
Design & Image Comm: 1900 Wazee #200, Denver, CO 80202 303-292-3455
Design & Prod: 9434 Hunts End Dr, Sandy, UT 84092 801-943-6771
Design & Time: 1026 Anclote Dr, Tarpon Springs, FL 34689 813-938-5107
Design 101: 707 Torrance Blvd #151, Redondo Beach, CA 90277 310-792-1455
Design 2: 6200 La Calma #200, Austin, TX 78752 512-452-8866
Design 291: 1903 Kalorama Pl NW #19, Washington, DC 20009 202-234-6908
Design Alliance: 418 N Pitt St, Alexandria, VA 22314 703-549-8881
Design Alliance, Inc: 105 Stearns Ave, Cincinnati, OH 45215 513-621-9373
Design Art: 6311 Romaine St #7311, Los Angeles, CA 90038 213-467-2984
Design Arts: 2343 W Estrella Dr, Chandler, AZ 85224 602-786-9411
Design Assocs: 430 N Park #402, Indianapolis, IN 46202 317-636-8053
Design Assocs: 6117 N Winthrop Ave, Chicago, IL 60660 773-338-4196
Design Assocs, Inc: 2819 Detroit Ave, Cleveland, OH 44113 216-696-1060
Design Assocs, Martin: 1960 E Grand Ave #610, El Segundo, CA 90245 310-414-9558
Design Assocs, Riley: 380 Diablo Rd #201, Danville, CA 94526 510-552-1590
Design At Work: 17047 El Camino Real #221, Houston, TX 77058 713-280-8635
Design Axis: 12 Westerville Sq #330, Westerville, OH 43081 614-448-7995
Design Basics: 1027 Monroe Dr NE, Atlanta, GA 30306 404-876-6475
Design Board: 1380 E South Temple #110, Salt Lake City, UT 84102 801-521-7090
Design Center: 734 W 800 S, Salt Lake City, UT 84104 801-532-6122
Design Center, Inc: 15119 Minnetonka Blvd, Minnetonka, MN 55345 612-933-9766
Design Central: 14925 Se Allen Rd #106B, Bellevue, WA 98006 206-747-4115
Design Central: 8737 Colesville Rd #304, Silver Spring, MD 20910 301-588-6994
Design Co: 250 State St, North Haven, CT 06473 203-230-9566
Design Co, Inc: 26 E Exchange St #315, St Paul, MN 55101 612-221-1030
Design Communication, Janin: 1445 New York Ave #401,
Washington, DC 20005 202-639-8855
Design Comp, Inc: PO Box 23, Meriden, CT 06450 203-235-9809
Design Consultants: PO Box 40894, Chicago, IL 60640 773-907-5500
Design Core: 1306 Alabama St, Huntington Beach, CA 92648 714-969-7766
Design Corps: 501 N Alfred St, Los Angeles, CA 90048 213-651-1422
Design Corral: 723 E Woodbury Rd, Altadena, CA 91001 818-798-8275
Design Design, Inc: 1333 N Kinsbury #201, Chicago, IL 60622 312-944-0099
Design Direction: 109 N Church St, West Chester, PA 19380 610-436-5382
Design Direction Group: 747 E Union #102, Pasadena, CA 91101 818-792-4765
Design Dynamics: 1681 94th Lane NE, Minneapolis, MN 55449 612-780-4911
Design Edge: 316 N Lamar, Austin, TX 78703 512-477-5491
Design Element: 8624 Wonderland Ave, Los Angeles, CA 90046 213-656-3293
Design Farm: 14 Northridge Lane, Lafayette, CA 94549 510-284-3316
Design Five: 180 Varick St 15th Fl, New York, NY 10014 212-727-8899
Design For Business: 435 Buckland Rd, South Windsor, CT 06074 860-644-3690
Design For Industry, Inc: 341 Linwood Ave, Buffalo, NY 14209 716-883-2095
Design Force: 104 Ganttown Rd, Turnerville, NJ 08012 609-232-7927
Design Form: 8250 Electric Ave, Stanton, CA 90680 714-952-3700
Design fx Interactive, L.L.C.: 1873 Rte 70 E #103, Cherry Hill, NJ 08003 800-651-7678
Design Group: 5801 Iris Ave, Las Vegas, NV 89107 702-878-6559
Design Group: 1229 S Washington, Royal Oak, MI 48067 810-546-4390
Design Group: 3444 N Washington Blvd, Indianapolis, IN 46205 317-924-2444
Design Group of Boston: 437 Boylston St, Boston, MA 02116 617-437-1084
Design Group West: 853 Camino Del Mar, Del Mar, CA 92014 619-481-5398
Design Group, The: 4411 W Market St #100, Greensboro, NC 27407 910-856-0815
Design Group, The: 48700 Pointe Lake View, New Baltimore, MI 48047 810-725-2254
Design Group, The: 2976 Triverton Pike, Madison, WI 53711 608-274-5393
Design Horizons: 3055 Cardinal Dr #200, Vero Beach, FL 32963 407-234-8001
Design Horizons Intl: 520 W Erie #330, Chicago, IL 60610 312-664-0006
Design House: 711 E Wardlow Rd #203, Long Beach, CA 90807 310-424-0433
Design III: 333 St Charles Ave #1213, New Orleans, LA 70130 504-558-0333
Design Imports: 260 Narragansett Park Dr, East Providence, RI 02916 401-438-6300
Design Innovation: 573 Hop Meadow St/Graystone Ct, Simsburg, CT 06070 203-651-1422
Design Kitchen: 1040 W Huron 1st Fl, Chicago, IL 60622 312-455-0388
Design Kupiec: 48 W 25th St 12th Fl, New York, NY 10010 212-675-2405
Design Logic: 804 Pleasant Hill Rd, Wallingford, PA 19086 610-876-9995
Design Logix, Inc: 345 Queen St #410, Honolulu, HI 96813 808-524-5055
Design Loiminchay: 390 Broadway 3rd Fl, New York, NY 10013 212-941-7488
Design Management: 12700 Park Central #1405, Dallas, TX 75251 214-239-6280
Design Marks Corp: 1462 W Irving Park, Chicago, IL 60613 773-327-3669
Design Media: 18123 Tarzana St, Tarzana, CA 91356 818-986-5134
Design Metro: 3502 SW Jerald Ct, Portland, OR 97221 503-274-0696
Design Moves, Inc: 1073 Gage St #3, Winnetka, IL 60093 847-661-0999
Design North : 8007 Douglas Ave, Racine, WI 53402 414-762-1320
Design Office: 95 Minna St 2nd Fl, San Francisco, CA 94105 415-543-4760
Design Office Inc, The: 1 Bridge St, Irvington, NY 10533 914-591-5911
Design On Devine: 3103 Devine St, Columbia, SC 29205 803-252-8069
Design One: 437 Marshman St, Highland Park, IL 60035 847-433-4140
Design Online: 804 Desnter St, Evanston, IL 60202 847-328-2733
Design Partners, Inc: 9540 Brink Rd/Po Box 86122, Gaithersburg, MD 20886 301-840-9525
Design Partnership: 500 NW 9th Ave, Portland, OR 97209 503-223-9682
Design Partnership, The: 111 3rd Ave S #150/Mill Place,
Minneapolis, MN 55401 612-338-8889
Design Perspective: 3170 Fourth Ave #200, San Diego, CA 92103 619-296-8266
Design Plus: 853 Broadway #1607, New York, NY 10003 212-645-2686
Design Resource: 700 S Henderson Rd #308B, King of Prussia, PA 19406 215-265-8585
Design Sense Studios: 341 Van Buren St, N Babylon, NY 11703 516-587-0623
Design Services: 2308 O'Keeffe Place, Davis, CA 95616 916-758-3344
Design Services, Inc: 7777 Jefferson Hwy 2nd Fl, Baton Rouge, LA 70809 504-926-2000
Design Studio: 1128 Tahoe Dr, Belmont, CA 94002 415-508-9980
Design Studio: 907 Cunningham Rd, Salem, OH 44460 330-337-0842
Design Studio II Assocs: 1107 NW 14th Ave, Portland, OR 97209 503-223-8058
Design Studio, The: 4600 Post Oak Pl #260, Houston, TX 77727 713-965-0100
Design Systems Group: 539 Bryant St #403, San Francisco, CA 94107 415-896-0539
Design Tekneka: Box 2510, Decatur, GA 30031 404-378-7900
Design Touch: 2208 River Run Dr #56, San Diego, CA 92108 619-281-9015
Design Trends: 4 Broadway PO Box 119, Valhalla, NY 10595 914-948-0902
Design Tribe: 525 Brannan #201, San Francisco, CA 94107 415-495-3113
Design Trust: 142 Danbury Rd, Wilton, CT 06897 203-761-1412
Design Twenty-Five Twenty-Five: 6220 S Orange Blossom Trl #175,
Orlando, FL 32809 407-856-2525
Design Two Ltd: 600 N McClurg Ct #330, Chicago, IL 60611 312-642-9888
Design Vectors: 725 Greenwich St 4th Fl, San Francisco, CA 94133 415-391-0399
Design Works: 1933 Otoole Ave #A202, San Jose, CA 95131 408-922-0788
Design Works, The: 292 S La Cienega Blvd #400, Beverly Hills, CA 90211 310-360-9292
Design Workshop, Inc: 7430 SW 122nd St, Miami, FL 33156 305-378-1039
Design, Inc: 9304 St Marks Pl, Fairfax, VA 22301 703-273-5053
Designation, Inc: 53 Spring St 5th Fl, New York, NY 10012 212-226-6024
Designers Three: 25 W 43rd St, New York, NY 10036 212-221-5900
Designframe: 116 E 16th St 10th Fl, New York, NY 10003 212-924-2426
Designing Interiors Design Co: 401 E 80th St #12A, New York, NY 10021 212-517-5428
Designmark, Inc: 4640 W 71st st, Indianapolis, IN 46268 317-291-0300
Designology: 7641 E Gray Rd, Scottsdale, AZ 85260 602-443-3227
Designs For Business: 721 Wilson St, Pomona, CA 91768 909-626-4472
Designs, Inc: 762 Purdy Alley, Columbus, OH 43206 614-443-3321
Designship: 2201 Pennsylvania Ave 1st Fl, Philadelphia, PA 19130 215-563-8048
Designspace: 476 Broadway 7th Fl, New York, NY 10013 212-925-9696
Designspeak: 150 W 25th St #900, New York, NY 10001 212-675-4477
Designteal: 500 Molina St #307, Los Angeles, CA 90013 213-485-1204
Designxavier: 13 Inverness Way So, Englewood, CO 80112 303-799-6640
Deskey: 50 E River Ctr Blvd #1700, Covington, KY 41011 606-655-2300
Deskey Assocs: 145 East 32nd St, New York, NY 10016 212-447-9400
Desktop Graphic Services: 2265 Westwood Blvd #105,
Los Angeles, CA 90064 310-391-5275
Desmarais Design: 108 Ponemah Rd, Amherst, NH 03031 603-673-0053
Desola Group, Inc: 477 Madison Ave 23rd Fl, New York, NY 10022 212-832-4770
Determined Productions: 1 Maritime Plaza #500, San Francisco, CA 94111 415-433-0660
Deutsch Design: 25 Mercer St 2nd Fl, New York, NY 10013 212-966-7710
Devaney Murata Design: 17125 S Dalton Ave, Gardena, CA 90247 310-782-8736
Devault Design: 2400 Sunset Pl, Nashvile, TN 37212 615-269-0202
Dever, Jeffrey L: 9101 Cherry Ln #102, Laurel, MD 20708 301-776-2812
Devlin Multimedia, Inc: 251 King St E, Toronto, ON M5A 1K2 416-363-6316
Dezine Media: 1629 Wagon Wheel Dr, Plano, TX 75023 214-669-9230
Dezinno, Richard: 348 Neipsic Rd, Glastonbury, CT 06033 203-659-1624
Dfo Creative Consultants: 767 Third Ave, New York, NY 10017 212-980-2900
DFS Creative Services: 12 Maple Ridge Dr, Burlington, MA 01803 617-229-8858
DGF Design: 3280 Cahuenga Blvd W 3rd Fl, Los Angeles, CA 90068 213-851-2244
DH Assocs: 402 E Main St, Palmyra, NY 14522 315-597-0022
Di Bacco Design: 46 Highwood Dr, Avon, CT 06001 203-675-6488
Di Cristo & Slagle Design: 735 N Water St, Milwaukee, WI 53202 414-273-0980
Di Giovine Design: 100 North State St #A, Newton, PA 18940 215-504-2244
di Liberto, Lisa: 413 3rd St #4, Brooklyn, NY 11215 718-768-3212
Dialog Design, Inc: 260 Montague Rd, Leverette, MA 01054 413-548-8198
Diamond Art Studio Ltd: 11 E 36th St 9th Fl, New York, NY 10016 212-685-6622
• **Dickens Design, Inc, Holly: pg 1451**
50 E Bellevue #402, Chicago, IL 60611 .... **312-280-0777**
e-mail: holdickens@aol.com / fax: 312-280-1725
Dickerson Group: 274 Summer St, Boston, MA 02210 617-426-7555
Diefenbach Elkins: 50 Rockefeller Plza 15th Fl, New York, NY 10020 212-332-3500
Diehl Design, Michael: 1415 Norton, Glendale, CA 91202 818-552-4110
Dietrich, Lance: 119 N Chestnut St, Palmyra, PA 17078 717-838-9590
Digital Art Exchange: 360 Newbury St, Boston, MA 02215 800-329-6266
Digital Corp: 13620 Sunrise Dr NE, Bainbridge Is, WA 98110 206-587-0286
Digital Dirigible, Inc: 38 Vestry St, New York, NY 10013 212-431-1925
Digital Facades: 1750 14th St #E, Santa Monica, CA 90404 310-581-4100
Digital Instincts, Inc: 405 Tarrytown Rd #370, White Plains, NY 10607 914-422-5883
Digital Media: 7694 S Madison Ave, Burr Ridge, IL 60521 708-789-1100
Digital Media World: 10 Barley Mow Passage, London, UK W4 4PH 181-995-3633
Digital Pictures: 1825 S Grant St #900, San Mateo, CA 94402 415-345-5300
Digital Pulp, Inc: 220 E 23rd St #607, New York, NY 10010 212-679-0676
Digital Tribe, Inc: 16 Charity, Irvine, CA 92715 714-854-5400
Dimensional Illustrators: 362 2nd St Pike #112, Southhampton, PA 18966 215-953-1415
Dimmick, Gary: 47 Riverview Ave, Pittsburgh, PA 15214 412-321-7225
Dinardo Design: 64 Palmer Way, Carlisle, MA 01741 508-371-0111
Diniz, Carlos: 3259 Deronda Dr, Los Angeles, CA 90068 213-469-7222

Direct Drive Design: 5901C Peachtree Dunwoody Rd #5, Atlanta, GA 30328......770-393-0662
Direct Mail Design: 707 S Snoqualmie, Seattle, WA 98108......206-622-7474
Disenos Graphic Designs, Inc: 1207 Cleburne, Houston, TX 77004......713-522-5558
Distler Design, Joshua: 1221 Oak Grove Ave #105, Burlingame, CA 94010......415-343-3940
Dittman & Assocs, Tom: 493 S Robertson Blvd, Beverly Hills, CA 90211......310-273-2197
Dittmann Graphic & Adv Design: 8202 14th Ave NE, Seattle, WA 98115......206-523-4778
Dittrick & Dittrick: 23 W 89th St, New York, NY 10024......212-724-5241
Dixon & Assocs: 3359 Karen Ave, Long Beach, CA 90808......310-433-8710
Dixon & Parcels Assocs: 521 Fifth Ave 39th Fl, New York, NY 10175......212-697-2522
Dixon, Ted: 594 Broadway #902, New York, NY 10012......212-226-5686
DJV & Assocs: Rt 102, Chester, NH 03036......603-887-3585
Dm Design Lab: 4420 Bunken Circle, Las Vegas, NV 89121......702-221-2808
DM&A Graphics: 1221 Van Ness #300, Fresno, CA 93721......209-485-6420
DMCD, Inc: 450 7th Ave 39th Fl, New York, NY 10123......212-268-5450
DMRC: 201 Summer St, Holliston, MA 01746......508-429-3300
DMTG : 150 W 28th St #1001, New York, NY 10123......212-924-6774
Doctor Design: 10505 Sorrento Valley Rd, San Diego, CA 92121......619-457-4545
Doeksen, Ray: 2159 W Giddings, Chicago, IL 60625......312-689-4253
Doerr Assocs: 8 Winchester Pl, Winchester, MA 01890......617-729-9020
• **Doglight Studios: pg 1493**
600 Moulton Ave #302, Los Angeles, CA 90031......**213-222-1928**
e-mail: doglight@aol.com / url: www.doglight.com / fax: 213-222-8151
Dogpaw Creative: 460 N Crooks, Clawson, MI 48017......810-444-4634
Dolan, Michael B: 6120 NW 38th Terr, Gainsville, FL 32653......352-372-1777
Dole Assocs, Inc: 3 Essex Square, Essex, CT 06426......203-767-0773
Dole Design, Tom: 22 W 23rd St, New York, NY 10010......212-924-9100
Doliber Skeffington Design: 8324 Rednock Ln, Miami Lakes, FL 33016......305-828-8252
Dollar & Assocs, John: 450 S 41St, Boulder, CO 80303......303-494-8626
Domus Advertising: 200 S Broad st 2nd Fl, Philadelphia, PA 19102......215-772-2800
Don Juan Prods & Adv: 17448 Burma St, Encino, CA 91316......818-996-4628
Donahue Studios: 1274 Minhette Dr, Roswell, GA 30075......404-998-5562
Donaldson Makoski: 1 Waterville Rd, Farmington, CT 06032......860-677-9777
Doneger Group: 463 Seventh Ave, New York, NY 10018......212-560-3787
Donmich Design Studio: PO Box 148, Newton, NJ 07860......201-927-7723
Donovan & Green, Inc: 71 Fifth Ave 4th Fl, New York, NY 10003......212-989-4050
Donovan Design: 2076 N Elston #301, Chicago, IL 60614......773-227-0050
Dorenenburg Design: 1010 Farmington Ave, West Hartford, CT 06107......860-231-1310
• **Doret, Michael: pg 1453** 6545 Cahuenga Terr, Hollywood, CA 90068......**323-467-1900**
e-mail: doretsmith@earthlink.net / url: http://home.earthlink.net/~doretsmith
fax: 323-467-4555
New York, NY......**212-929-1688**
Doss Design, Charles: 168 Jackson St, San Jose, CA 95112......408-947-7001
Dot System, Inc: 10730 E Bethany Dr #204, Aurora, CO 80014......303 337-5952
Dottinger Design: 20 Passaic Ave, Pompton Lakes, NJ 07442......201-616-9696
Doty Design, David: 661 W Roscoe, Chicago, IL 60657......773-348-1200
Double D Assocs, Inc: 12579 W Custer Ave, Butler, WI 53007......414-783-4800
Double Space: 170 Fifth Ave 2nd Fl, New York, NY 10010......212-366-1919
Double Vision Products: 2902 Pasatiempo Pl, Sacramento, CA 95833......916-921-6986
Douglas Design, Barry: 300 E 71st St #4H, New York, NY 10021......212-734-4137
DouPonce, Kirk: 801 Coit NES, Grand Rapids, MI 49508......616-456-1118
Downey Weeks & Toomey: 519 Eighth Ave 22nd Fl, New York, NY 10018......212-564-8260
Downing, Allan: 50 Francis St, Needham, MA 02192......617-449-4784
Downtown Digital: 32 Avenue of the Americas, New York, NY 10013......212-387-4856
Doyle Logan Company, The: 7836 Santa Monica Blvd,
W Hollywood, CA 90046......213-848-8492
Doyle Lynch Design: 60 Spectacle Ln, Wilton, CT 06897......203-762-2789
Drabkin, Leonard: PO Box 567, North Haven, CT 06473......203-288-7957
Draeger, Deanne: 518 E 13th St, New York, NY 10009......212-475-1316
Drake & Boucher: 175 Fifth Ave #805, New York, NY 10010......212-982-3565
Drate, Spencer: 160 Fifth Ave #613, New York, NY 10010......212-620-4672
Draw The Line: 10955 Lowell #200, Overland Park, KS 66210......913-451-6116
Drebelbis Studio, Inc, Marsha: 8150 Brookriver Dr #606, Dallas, TX 75247......214-951-0266
Drebelbis, Marsha: 8150 Brookriver Dr #606-S, Dallas, TX 75247......214-951-0266
Drenttel, William: 1123 Broadway, New York, NY 10010......212-463-8787
Dresser Design, John: 180 Crescent Knoll E, Libertyville, IL 60048......847-362-4222
Drew Hill Graphic Design Grp, Inc: Drawer 607, Fair Haven, NY 13064......800-724-8973
Dreyfuss Assocs, Henry: 114 W 26th St 5th Fl, New York, NY 10001......212-242-6500
Driscoll, Dennis: 101 Main St, Cambridge, MA 02142......617-520-7241
Drive Communications: 133 W 19th St 5th Fl, New York, NY 10011......212 989-5103
Dryden Rubino: 2 Elmhurst Rd, Baltimore, MD 21210......410-243-2140
Duane, Thomas S: 28 W 25th St 5th Fl, New York, NY 10010......212-924-5700
Dubins Design, Milt: 353 W 22nd St, New York, NY 10011......212-691-0232
Dubrow Assocs, Oscar: 18 E 48th St, New York, NY 10017......212-688-0698
Dudervision: PO Box 10416, Oakland, CA 90272......510-893-5889
Duffy Design Group: 901 Marquette Ave S #3000, Minneapolis, MN 55402......612-339-3247
Dufour & Assocs: 532 S 8th St/PO Box 414, Sheboygan, WI 53081......414-457-9191
Duke & Assocs, Charles: 1023 St Paul St, Baltimore, MD 21202......301-539-7916
Duke Marketing Communications: 5333 N Seventh St #C-226,
Phoenix, AZ 85014......602-604-8818
Dula Design, Mike : 17880 Sky Park Circle #170, Irvine, CA 92614......714-852-1397
Dula Gerrie Designs: 18401 Von Karman #130, Irvine, CA 92715......714-863-0330
Dumont Design, Don: 285 N Mclean, Memphis, TN 38112......901-278-3188
Dunkelberger, David: 281 Barberry Rd, Southport, CT 06490......203-255-7928
Dunn & Rice Design: 16 N goodman St #100, Rochester, NY 14607......716-473-2880
Duo Graphics: 3907 Manhattan Ave, Ft Collins, CO 80526......970-463-2788
Dupre Design: 415 2nd St, Coronado, CA 92118......619-435-8369
Durrell Design, Clauida: 9 Williams Rd, Bethel, CT 06801......203-744-3511
Dutko, Deborah: 245 Roselle St, Fairfield, CT 06432......203-579-1715
Dvorak Design Ltd: 36 Lexington Dr, Croton on Hudson, NY 10520......914-271-7706
Dvorak Goodspeed & Assocs: 165 Lexington Ave, New York, NY 10016......212-475-4580
Dyad Communications: 303 N Third St, Philadelphia, PA 19106......215-925-7835
Dyer Cahn: 8360 Melrose Ave 3rd Fl, Los Angeles, CA 90063......213-937-4100
Dyer Mutchnick Group: 8360 Melrose Ave 3rd Fl, Los Angeles, CA 90069......213-655-1800
Dykstra Group, William: 01845 W Leonard, Grand Rapids, MI 49544......616-677-1208
Dyna Pac: 7926 Convoy Ct, San Diego, CA 92111......619-560-0117
DynacomInc: 875 N Michigan #2948, Chicago, IL 60611......847-263-9636
Dynamic Diagrams: 12 Bassett St, Providence, RI 02903......401-331-2014
Dynamic Graphics: 6000 N Forest Park Dr, Peoria, IL 61614......309-688-8800
Dysart, Patty: 274 Cross St, Winchester, MA 01890......617-391-3516
Dzignlight Studios: 800 Forrest St, Atlanta, GA 30318......404-355-0755
DZN The Design Group: 470 S San Vicente Blvd 1st Fl,
Los Angeles, CA 90048......213-951-7377

E

EActive: 25 Barry Ln, Simsbury, CT 06070......203-651-3345
Eagle Graphics: 1220 Broadway, New York, NY 10001......212-629-0858
Eagle River Interactive: 411 SW Second Ave, Portland, OR 97204......503 223-2262
411 SW Second Ave, Denver, CO 80216......303-320-5411
East Design, Roger: 600 Townsend St #415W, San Francisco, CA 94103......415-552-2300
East West Creative: 26 W 22nd St 11th Fl, New York, NY 10010......212-620-7950
Easterly & Company: 5615 Kirby #518, Houston, TX 77005......713-529-2949
Eaton & Assocs Design: 708 S Third St #420, Minneapolis, MN 55415......612-338-2266
Eaves Design: 4869 Elmhurst Ave, Norfolk, VA 23513......804-853-0675
Ebersol, Rob: 734 Clairemont Ave, Decatur, GA 30030......404-687-8889
Echo Communications: 7801 Norfolk Ave #207, Bethesda, MD 20814......301-652-0504
Eclipse Graphics: 2020 Del Amo Blvd, Torrance, CA 90501......310-328-2255
Eddins Madison & Spitz: 6121 Lincolnia Rd #410, Alexandria, VA 22312......703-750-0030
Edelson, Doug: 340 W Passaic St, Rochelle Park, NJ 07662......201-909-8760
Eden Matrix, The: 101 W Sixth St #210, Austin, TX 78701......512-478-9900
Edge: 20 W 22nd St 11th Fl, New York, NY 10010......212-691-7021
Edge, Dennis: 900 Broadway 5th Fl, New York, NY 10003......212-420-1110
Edgerton, Brian: 10 Old Rt 28 Box 364, Whitehouse, NJ 08888......908-534-9400
Edmonds Graphics: 624 University Ave, Palo Alto, CA 94301......415-329-9166
Edquist Design: 3123 Fairview Ave E, Seattle, WA 98102......206-328-6010
EDR Media: 23330 Commerce Park Rd, Beachwood, OH 44122......216-292-7300
Educational Media, Graphics Division: GU Med Ctr 3900 Reservoir Rd,
Washington, DC 20007......202-625-2211
Edward Beckett Design: 1051 E Altadena Dr, Altadena, CA 91001......818-791-7954
Edwards Design: 119 W 77th St, New York, NY 10024......212-362-0283
Edwards Design Inc, Sean: 28 W 25th St 5th Fl, New York, NY 10010......212-924-5700
Edwards Studio, Inc: 1907 Sedge Dr, Houston, TX 77080......713-465-7080
Eells Design, Duane: 471 E Main St, Ventura, CA 93001......805-643-4952
Effective Design Studio: 1000 Lenora St #505, Seattle, WA 98121......206-621-8989
EFM Group: 3907 E LaSalle St, Phoenix, AZ 85040......602-256-2500
Egg Design Partners: 790 Centre St, Boston, MA 02130......617-522-7558
• **Ehrenfeld, Howard: pg 1477** 1250 Key Highway, Baltimore, MD 21230......**410-685-3686**
Eiber Design Inc, Rick: 31014 SE 58th St, Preston, WA 98050......206-632-8326
Eickhoff Hannan Rue: 1919 Oakwell Farms Pkwy #240,
San Antonio, TX 78218......210-828-8003
Eicon/Div E Group: 276 Fifth Ave #1106, New York, NY 10001......212-685-3340
Eidolon Comms: 156 Fifth Ave #707, New York, NY 10010......212-633-0404
Einhorn Design: 1103 Bingham St, Pittsburgh, PA 15203......412-488-3900
Eisenberg & Assocs: 3311 Oak Lawn #300, Dallas, TX 75219......214-528-5990
Eisenman Design Assocs, James: 151 Haven Ave,
Port Washington, NY 11050......516-944-6770
Eisenman Graphic Design: 6208 Verne St, Bethesda, MD 20817......301-229-1090
EK Weymouth: 207 Old Forge Rd, Riverton, CT 06065......203-738-3666
Elaine Design: 10 Nassau St, Emerson, NJ 07630......201-261-7528
Eldridge, Paul: PO Box 806, Meredith, NH 03253......603-279-5568
Electa Design: 807 Sanford Day Rd, Knoxville, TN 37919......615-470-2581
Electric Paint: 6335 Homewood Ave, Los Angeles, CA 90028......213-462-4332
Electrokinetics: 380 Lafayette #304, New York, NY 10003......212-473-1125
Electronic Hollywood: PO Box 448, Prince St Station, NY 10012......212-777-4801
Electronic Vision: 5 Depot St, Athens, OH 45701......614-592-2433
Elements: 550 College Ave, Palo Alto, CA 94306......415-493-2018
Eleven: 273 Summer St 7th Fl, Boston, MA 02210......617-204-1100
1185 Design: 119 University Ave, Palo Alto, CA 94301......415-325-4804
Elliott Agency: 8229 Boone Blvd #802, Vienna, VA 22182......703-903-8631
Ellis Design, Jan: 25 Lindsley Ave, Nashville, TN 37210......615-254-0483
Elsey & Assocs, Victor: 314 Joyce Way, Mill Valley, CA 94941......415-383-8199
Elsey Design, Kathleen: 1612 Stockton St, San Francisco, CA 94133......415-398-6383
Ely Design Group: 75 Kings Hwy Cutoff, Fairfield, CT 06430......203-333-9300
Elyria Graphics: 561 Ternis St, Elyria, OH 44035......216-365-9384
EM Power Corp: 282 W Milbrook Rd, Raleigh, NC 27609......919-870-525
EM2 Design: 530 Means St #402, Atlanta, GA 30318......404-221-1741
Ema Design: 1228 15th St #301, Denver, CO 80202......303-825-0222
Emerson Design Studio: 55134 Cobus Ln, Elkhart, IN 46514......219-262-1997
Emerson Hayes: 344 Bonita Rd, Portola Valley, CA 94028......415-327-7772
Emerson Marketing Agency: 636 Broadway #1000, New York, NY 10012......212-387-8210
Emerson Wajdowicz Studios, Inc: 1123 Broadway, New York, NY 10010......212-807-8144
Emerson, Larry: 6515 Escondido #A1, El Paso, TX 79912......915-581-0184
• **Emmart, Weston: pg 1457** 39 Hamilton Terr, New York, NY 10031......**212-283-3401**
url: www.wayart.com
Emmerling Design, Ronald: 206 Claremont Ave, Montclair, NJ 07042......201-783-7888
Emphasis 7 Comm: 43 E Ohio #1000, Chicago, IL 60611......312-951-8887
Emphasis Seven Comm, Inc: 549 W Randolph St #700, Chicago, IL 60661......312-951-8887
Emspace: 7634 Pierce St, Omaha, NE 68124......402-398-9448
Encompass Communications: 374 Congress St #408, Boston, MA 02210......617-357-1800
Encore Studios: 17 Industial West, Clifton, NJ 07012......800-526-0497
Endres & Eng: 209 10th Ave S #343, Nashville, TN 37203......615-251-3002
Endres, Joan: 54 Points of View, Warwick, NY 10990......914-987-1001
Endres, Michael: 10018 Tenbrook Dr, Silver Spring, MD 20901......301-681-6100
Energy Energy Design: 307 Orchard City Dr #310, Campbell, CA 95008......408-379-8858
Eng & Yee Designs: 205 W 80yh St #B1E, New York, NY 10024......212-580-3040
Engelhardt Design: 1738 Irving Ave S, Minneapolis, MN 55403......612-377-3389
Engen, Scott: 9058 Greenhills Dr, Sandy, UT 84093......801-942-3125
Engle & Assocs, Ray: 4726 La Villa Marina, Marina Del Rey, CA 90292......310-822-3224
Engle & Murphy, Inc: 236 E Third St #210, Long Beach, CA 90802......310-983-7270
Engler Design Assocs, Ronald: 605 Allengrove St, Philadelphia, PA 19120......215-722-4895
Englund & Donnelly design: 150 North Wiget Lane #206,
Walnut Creek, CA 94598......510-932-8646
Engstrom, Lynda: 317 W 89th St #2W1, New York, NY 10024......212-724-3961
Enright, Phil: 131 George St, Oakville, ON L6J 3B9......905-339-0750
Enteractive, Inc: 110 W 40th St #2100, New York, NY 10018......212-221-6559
Envion International: 472 Amherst, Nashua, NH 03063......603-881-7873
Environmedia: 617 Vine St #1336, Cincinnati, OH 45202......513-333-0040
Environmental Graphics, Inc: 1101 Southeastern Ave, Indianapolis, IN 46202......317-634-1458

Envision: 308 Trinity Ct, Princeton, NJ 08540....609-951-8723
Enzed Design: 1660 Lafayette, Denver, CO 80218....303-837-8304
Epigraph: 333 Bainbridge, Philadelphia, PA 19147....215-925-4700
Epsilon Interactive: 132 S La Jolla Ave, Los Angeles, CA 90048....213-655-4476
Epstein Gutwiller & Partners: 11427 Bellflower Rd, Cleveland, OH 44106....216-421-1600
Erbe Design, Maureen: 1500 Oxley St, S Pasadena, CA 91030....818-799-9892
Erceg Graphic Design, Joe: 123 NW 2nd Ave #201, Portland, OR 97209....503-227-5915
Erickson Design: 13197 W Iliff Dr, Lakewood, CO 80228....303-989-5058
Erickson, Peter: 46 Pleasant St, Marlborough, MA 01752....508-481-2288
Ernst & Assocs, Inc: 247 Velarde St, Mountain View, CA 94041....415-965-0869
Ervin Advertising & Design: 16400 Pacific Coast Hwy #217,
Huntington Beach, CA 92649....310-592-3827
Erwin Design Inc, Bob: 9235 Katy Freeway #160, Houston, TX 77024....713-464-7553
Escott Assocs: 3307 Pico blvd, Santa Monica, CA 90405....310-828-9679
Esposito Design & Mktg, Bronz: 25 Bank St, Stamford, CT 06901....203-324-1300
Esser Design, Steve: 2025 N Third St #170, Phoenix, AZ 85004....602-257-9790
Essertier, David: 2228 Blackrock Trpk #207, Fairfield, CT 06430....203-226-8850
Essex Two, Inc: 2210 W North Ave, Chicago, IL 60647....773-489-1400
Essinger Design Assocs: 36 Glen Ave, Newton, MA 02159....617-964-8803
Essl, Mike: 636 Broadway #1210, New York, NY 10012....212-473-0204
Estes Assocs, David: 3400 Montrose #505, Houston, TX 77006....713-523-9717
Estrela Design Group: 357 Medford St#2, Somerville, MA 02145....617-625-3355
Estudio Ray: 2320 N 58th St, Scottsdale, AZ 850257....602-945-1299
Etheridge Palombo Sedewitz: 1500 Broadway, New York, NY 10036....212-944-2530
Eucalyptus Tree Studio: 2221 Morton St, Baltimore, MD 21218....410-243-0211
Evans Design Assocs: 3303 Harbor Blvd #D8, Costa Mesa, CA 92626....714-957-6266
Evans Design Assocs: 18 Norfield Rd, Weston, CT 06883....203-226-8553
Evans Design, Leslie: 81 West Commercial St, Portland, ME 04101....207-874-0102
Evans Group: 6116 North Central #1100, Dallas, TX 75206....214-691-6491
Evans, Inc, Mackas: 3555 Habersham At Northlake, Tucker, GA 30084....770-938-2777
Evenson Design Group: 4445 Overland Ave, Culver City, CA 90230....310-204-1995
Everett Design: Mtng Hs Offcs/121 Mt Vernon St, Boston, MA 02108....617-227-2354
Everett Studios: 22 Baker Ave, White Plains, NY 10601....914-997-2200
Ewing & Beland: 517 S Ivy Ave, Monrovia, CA 91016....818-930-0977
Excelsior Graphics, Inc: 350 W 31st St 3rd Fl, New York, NY 10001....212-563-6100
Executive Arts: 887 W Marietta St J-105, Atlanta, GA 30318....404-875-8225
Exhibit Group/Giltspur: 200 N Gary Ave, Rosell, IL 60172....630-307-2400
Extreme Color: 1221 Lee Rd #120, Orlando, FL 32810....407-298-6384
Eye & I Design Group: 4703 Longridge Ave, Sherman Oaks, CA 91423....818-501-5439
Eye 4: 4320 W University Ave, Gainesville, FL 32607....904-338-7519
Eye For Design: 21583 La Playa Port, Cupertino, CA 95014....408-973-0340
Eye Tv: 270 Magnolia Ave, Larkspur, CA 94939....415-945-1370
Eye-Noise: 1215 E Robinson St, Orlando, FL 32801....407-894-3550
Eymer Design, Inc: 25 Dry Dock Ave, Boston, MA 02210....617-345-5434

F

F P Design: 920 Broadway #905, New York, NY 10010....212-473-0006
F Patrick LaSalle Design: 225 Sheridan St, Rockford, IL 61103....815-963-2089
Fahrenheit Design: 169 West Newton St, Boston, MA 02118....617-536-4482
Faia Design, Don: 130 Camino Pacifico, Aptos, CA 95003....408-662-8857
Fair Riley Call: 2761 Laguna Canyon Rd #200, Laguna Beach, CA 92651....714-376-9965
Fairly Painless Adv: 44 E 8th St #500, Holland, MI 49423....616-394-5900
Falcon Advertising Art: 1138 W 9th St #200, Cleveland, OH 44113....216-621-4327
Falcone Design Group: 1267 N Laurel Ave #17, Los Angeles, CA 90046....213-650-0502
Falcone Design Group: 5 Division St Bldg A, East Greenwich, RI 02818....401-886-8710
Falk Design Group, Robert: 4425 W Pine, St Louis, MO 63108....314-531-1410
Falls Studio, Inc: 1155 Oak Dale Pl, Boulder, CO 80304....303-442-4877
Faragher Design Group: 700 East Blvd #1, Charlotte, NC 28203....704-333-7424
Farber Design Group, Melvyn: 406 Bonhill Rd, Los Angeles, CA 90049....213-829-2668
Farin Design: 1904 3rd Ave #1031, Seattle, WA 98101....206-224-9989
Farkas, Bob: 1220 S Bedford St, Los Angeles, CA 90035....310-271-4909
Farleo Design, Joseph L: 4915 Heards Forest Dr, Acworth, GA 30102....770-917-9424
Farley, AC: 20 Stearns Terr, Chicopee, MA 01013....413-594-7302
Farnet Hart Design Studio: 822 Perdido St #202, New Orleans, LA 70112....504-522-6300
Faron Melrose, Inc: 19925 Stevens Creek Blvd #135, Cupertino, CA 95014....408-773-8022
Farrell Design Communicatons: 321 Ellis St, New Britain, CT 06051....203-225-3115
Farrell Design, Colonna: 899 Adams St #H, St Helena, CA 94574....707-963-2077
FASE Productions: 4801 Wilshire Blvd #215, Los Angeles, CA 90010....213-937-9911
Fassino Design: 230 Calvary St, Waltham, MA 02154....617-647-0407
Fattal & Collins: 4640 Admiralty Way #900, Marina Del Ray, CA 90292....310-822-2777
Faville Design: 1123 Bdwy #1012, New York, NY 10010....212-989-1566
Fear Design, Jeffery: 3961 Sepulveda Blvd #201, Culver City, CA 90230....310-398-5717
Fearless Design: 149 Fifth Ave, New York, NY 10010....212-253-9520
Fearless Designs, Inc: 622 E Main St #206, Louisville, KY 40202....502-584-1333
Feigenbaum, Joseph: 1 Bridge St, Irvington, NY 10533....914-591-5911
Feldman Assocs: 505 N Lakeshore Dr, Chicago, IL 60611....312-527-1111
Felice Matare Design: 1720 N Topanga Canyon Blvd, Topanga, CA 90290....310-455-2123
Felix Design: 37 Howard Pl, Brooklyn, NY 11215....718-788-5409
Fenster Assocs, Fred: 29 Davis Rd, Port Washington, DC 11050....516-944-7108
Fenwick Design: 211 W 56th St #30A, New York, NY 10019....212-246-9722
Ferguson, Christine: 567 Queen St W 3rd Fl, Toronto, ON M5V 2B6....416-504-5045
Fernandez, Robert: 435 Hudson St, New York, NY 10014....212-462-1500
Ferranti & Schiumo: 655 Third Ave 27th Fl, New York, NY 10017....212-687-3107
Ferris Design, Peggy: 225 Dawlish Pl, Santa Barbara, CA 93108....805-969-5502
Fetz Design: 1339 S Main St, Salt Lake City, UT 84115....801-466-8817
Fevurly, Yvette: 2852 W Greenleaf, Chicago, IL 60245....773-262-1298
Fiedler & Assocs, Inc: 8012 W Berwyn Ave, Chicago, IL 60656....773-775-0192
Fiegenshue Design: 4201 Wingren Rd #103, Irving, TX 75062....214-541-0123
Figi Graphics: 3636 Gateway ctr Dr, San Diego, CA 92102....619-262-8811
Fili Studio, Louise: 71 Fifth Ave 4th Fl, New York, NY 10003....212-989-9153
Filicori Visual Comms: 4 Gramercy Park W, New York, NY 10003....212-677-0065
Filippo & Assocs, Adam: 1206 Fifth Ave, Pittsburgh, PA 15219....412-261-3720
Film & Video Service: 1550 Bryant St #200, San Francisco, CA 94103....415-626-8400
Film Art Representation: 6201 Sunset Blvd #60, Hollywood, CA 90028....213-480-1059
Filosi Jones: 560 Harrison Ave #411, Boston, MA 02118....617-542-8886
Fina, Barbara: 23 Evergreen Way, Sleepy Hollow, NY 10591....914-332-9345
Finaly, Steve: 1059 Fairfax Circle W, Lantana, FL 33462....561-965-4728
Financial Communications, Inc: 8001 Wisconsin Ave, Bethesda, MD 20814....301-657-1711
Fine Line Graphics: 237 NW Blue Pkwy #100, Lees Summit, MO 64063....816-941-2440
Fine Line Studio: 17910 Skypark Cir #104, Irvine, CA 92714....714-863-9323
Fineberg Assocs: 333 E 68th St, New York, NY 10021....212-734-1220
Finger & Smith Assocs, Inc: 1005 Sansome #240, San Francisco, CA 94111....415-788-2238
Finite Matters Ltd: 2604 Fairground Rd, Goochland, VA 23063....804-556-6631
Finlay, Steven: 1059 Fairfax Circle W, Lantana, FL 33462....561-965-4728
Fiorella Graphic Design, Inc: 248 Rushley Way, Media, PA 19063....610-358-4411
Fiorella, Franke: 1221 Nicollet Mall #230, Minneapolis, MN 55403....612-338-1700
Fiorentino & Assocs: 134 W 26th St #902, New York, NY 10001....212-243-2236
Firehouse 101: 492 Armstrong St, Columbus, OH 43215....614-464-0928
Firestone Design: 4810 Bradford Dr, Annandale, VA 22003....703-354-0247
First Experience Communication: 3011 Main St, Glastenbury, CT 06033....203-657-3815
First Impressions: 4411 W Tampa Bay Blvd, Tampa, FL 33614....813-875-0555
Firstline Creative Resources: 525 Bishop St, Atlanta, GA 30318....404-605-0797
Fischer Creative: 5050 Quorum Dr #700, Dallas, TX 75240....214-663-0520
Fischer Graphic Design Assocs: 3854 Ridgeview Rd,
Huntingdon Vall, PA 19006....215-947-9931
Fish Eng Partners, Inc: 431 S Dearborn #1001, Chicago, IL 60605....312-939-4442
Fitch Design: 10350 Olentangy River Rd Box 360, Worthington, OH 43085....614-885-3453
Fithian Design & Illustration, George: 4104 Leawood Dr, Edmond, OK 73034....405-341-6323
Fitting Kolbrener: 7 Wood St 5th Fl, Pittsburgh, PA 15222....412-434-6934
Fitzgerald & Assocs: 23 Franklin Blvd #2E, Long Beach, NY 11561....516-431-7073
Fitzpatrick Design Group: 2109 Broadway #203, New York, NY 10023....212-580-5842
Fiumara Art Direction & Photo: 1307 Harvard Rd NE, Atlanta, GA 30306....404-373-7220
5D Studio: 20651 Seaboard Rd, Malibu, CA 90265....310-317-0705
555 Design Fabrication: 1238 S Ashland Ave, Chicago, IL 60608....312-733-6777
Five Oaks Design: 3533 Hattie Rd, Nashville, NC 27856....919-459-8908
Flagler Adv, Inc: 143 Beaconsfield Rd, Brookline, MA 02146....617-566-6971
Flaherty Robinson Design: 11 First St, Barrington, RI 02806....401-245-4236
Flanders & Assocs: 368 Congress St, Boston, MA 02210....617-423-7019
Fleishman-Hillard, Inc: 200 N Broadway, St Louis, MO 63102....314-982-1700
Fleming Graphics: 510 First Ave N #6, Great Falls, MT 59401....406-761-7887
Fleming Studios: 559 Pacific Ave, San Francisco, CA 94133....415-397-4849
Fleming, Ron: 901 14th St N, Great Falls, MT 59401....406-761-7887
Fleming, Toby: 10 E 6th Ave, Conshohocken, PA 19428....610-940-2300
Fletcher Photographer, Sarah: 82 Hunters Harbor Rd, Charlestown, RI 02813....401-364-7701
Flinchum, Inc: 200 W 57th St #609, New York, NY 10019....212-582-6692
Flink Design, Hans: 224 E 50th St, New York, NY 10022....212-832-3860
Flipside Graphic Design: 5 Mandeville Ct, Monterey, CA 93940....408-649-5510
Flores Jr, Arnie: 13320 Villa Park Dr, Austin, TX 78729....512-458-3373
Florio Design, Linda: 245 W 29th St 4th Fl, New York, NY 10001....212-736-1959
Florville Design & Analysis: 226 W 21st St, New York, NY 10011....212-633-8130
Floyd Youst Art Direction: 414 Jackson St #205, San Francisco, CA 94111....415-989-8029
Flyleaf: 611 Broadway #826, New York, NY 10012....212-473-4710
Flynn Design: 1304 N Hametown Rd, Fairlawn, OH 44333....330-666-1431
Foca Company: 520 Broadway 11th Fl, New York, NY 10012....212-966-1556
Focus 2, Inc: 2105 Commerce St #102, allas, TX 75201....214-741-4007
Fokes, Quinne: 220 Del Casa, Mill Valley, CA 94941....415-383-0924
Follis Design: 520 N Fair Oaks Ave, Pasadena, CA 91103....818-792-3590
Follis Design, Dean: 520 N Fair Oaks Ave, Pasadena, CA 91103....818-792-3590
Fomandy: 4340 Stevens Creek Blvd #114, San Jose, CA 95129....408-257-3473
Fontana, Chris:, Brooklyn, NY 11201....718-338-5270
Force, Peter: 6000 N Forest Park Dr, Peoria, IL 61614....309-688-8800
Ford & Earl Assocs, Inc: 350 W Big Beaver Rd, Troy, MI 48084....810-524-3222
Fordesign Group: 87 Dayton Rd, Redding, CT 06896....203-938-0008
Forest Design: 5900 S Eastern Ave, Commerce, CA 90040....213-462-6486
Forethought Solutions: 4 Laurel St, Beverly, MA 01915....508-927-8088
Form & Function: 3394 SE Woodward ST, Portland, OR 97202....503-731-0985
Forma : 215 Glenwood Ave, Raleigh, NC 27603....919-832-1244
Forman Designs, Yale: 11 Riverside Dr, New York, NY 10023....212-799-1665
Forman, Thomas: PO Box 3174, Princeton, NJ 08543....609-275-6077
Forstel Graphic Design, Tom: 753 s Walnut St, Boise, ID 83712....208-345-6656
Forsythe Design: 142 Berkley St, Boston, MA 02116....617-437-1023
Fortune Design Firm: 1260 Pine Ave, San Jose, CA 95125....408-723-1202
Fortune, John & Lani: 414 W Lake Samish, Bellingham, WA 98226....206-936-3471
Forward Design: 848 Eastman #105, Chicago, IL 60622....312-335-0540
Forward Design, Inc: 1115 E Maine St/Box 61, Rochester, NY 14609....716-288-0250
Foster Design Group: 222 Newbury St 3rd Fl, Boston, MA 02116....617-262-5899
Foster Design, Mark: 1240 Longford Rd, West Chester, PA 19380....610-344-4940
Foster Design, Stephen: 17 51st St #5, Weehawken, NJ 07087....201-866-9040
Foster, Kim A: 1801 SW 11th St, Miami, FL 33135....305-642-1801
Foundation: 1715 E Olive Way, Seattle, WA 98102....206-860-8800
Four Corners: PO box 10426, Burbank, CA 91510....818-899-8987
4-D-Adv Web Programming: PO Box 1282, Iowa City, IA 52244....319-338-6353
4sight: 4 Columbus Cir, New York, NY 10019....212-315-3400
Fowler & Co, Tom: 9 Webbs Hill Rd, Stamford, CT 06903....203-329-1105
Fox Design: 36 Ridge Brook Dr, West Hartford, CT 06107....203-521-8227
Fox Klox: 512 Route 202, Hollis, ME 04042....207-929-8492
Frame One, Inc: 2215 Sanders Rd #360, Northbrook, IL 60062....847-564-2221
Franek Design Assocs, David: 5101 Wisconsin Ave NW #302,
Washington, DC 20016....202-363-4441
Frank & Assocs Inc, Alan: 1524 S 1100 E, Salt Lake City, UT 84105....801-486-7453
Franke & Fiorella: 1221 Nicollet Mall #230, Minneapolis, MN 55403....612-338-1700
Frankfurt Balkind: 244 E 58th St, New York, NY 10022....212-421-5888
Franklin Architects/Design: 401 N Franklin, Chicago, IL 60610....312-527-1555
Franklin Street Comms, Inc: 2515 Professional Rd, Richmond, VA 23235....804-320-2000
Franz & Company: 8403 Colesville Rd #865, Silver Spring, MD 20910....301-589-7199
Fraser & Assocs, Robert: PO Box 39035, Baltimore, MD 21212....410-433-7191
Frassinelli, Michael: 465 South St #103, Morristown, NJ 07960....800-275-5374
Frazier Design Center Inc, Craig: 600 Townsend St #412 W,
San Francisco, CA 94103....415-863-9613
Frazier, Greg: 26 Noble St Unit 3, Toronto, ON M6K2C9....416-538-3797
Frch Design Worldwide/NY: 860 Broadway 5th Fl, New York, NY 10003....212-254-1229
Frederking Design, Sarah: 433 North Harvey Ave, Oak Park, IL 60302....708-386-6886
Freelance Ink: 2924 33rd Pl NW, Washington, DC 20008....202-342-2221
Freeman Design Assocs: 2405 Bartlett St/PO 540543, Houston, TX 77098....713-523-4302
Freeman, Sean: 2105 Commerce St #102, Dallas, TX 75201....214-741-4007
French Blitzer Scott: 156 Fifth Ave, New York, NY 10010....212-807-1111

Good Idea: 811 W 15th St #2B, Newport Beach, CA 92665 ... 714-646-7913
Goode, Larry: 1205 W 43rd St, Austin, TX 78756 ... 512-467-7471
Goodman/Orlick Design, Inc: 240 E 27th St #12K, New York, NY 10016 ... 212-779-1585
Gorbatty Design, Norman: 310 Madison Ave #2101, New York, NY 10017 ... 212-599-1665
Gordon & Assoc, Sam: 226 W 4th St, New York, NY 10014 ... 212-741-9294
Gordon Design: 6305 Riverview Ln, Dallas, TX 75248 ... 972-447-9092
Gordon Design, Inc: 300 Brannon St, San Francisco, CA 94107 ... 415-957-9592
Gordon, Roger: 10799 N Gate St, Culver City, CA 90230 ... 310-559-8287
Gorelick Design, Alan: 26 Cromwell Dr, Morristown, NJ 07960 ... 210-898-1991
Gorelick, Jill: 1035 Mayfair Way, Plainfield, NJ 07060 ... 908-755-5564
Gorman Assocs, Chris: 305 Madison Ave #2214, New York, NY 10165 ... 212-983-3375
Gorman Copy & Dsgn, Allan: 215 Glenridge Ave, Montclair, NJ 07042 ... 201-509-2728
Gorman, Pat: 5 E 17th St, New York, NY 10011 ... 212-620-0506
Goss, Keller & Martinez: 853 Camino Del Mar, Del Mar, CA 92014 ... 619-792-1919
Gotlib Design: 515 Madison ave #905, New York, NY 10022 ... 212-319-5022
Goudreau Illustration: 40 E Main St/Weir River Brick, Ware, MA 01082 ... 413-967-9855
Gould & Assocs: 3970 Archdale Rd, Encino, CA 91436 ... 818-501-6965
Gould Creative, David: 1412 Pecos, Mesquite, TX 75150 ... 214-686-4851
Gournoe Inc, M: 60 E Elm, Chicago, IL 60611 ... 312-787-5157
Goutas Assocs, Evelyn: 59 W 19th St #3A2, New York, NY 10011 ... 212-627-0101
GR Graphics Audio Visual: 1850 N 15th Ave, Phoenix, AZ 85007 ... 602-252-6525
Graetzer Ackerman, Inc: 17 S Franklin Tpke, Ramsey, NJ 07446 ... 201-236-1600
Graffito, Inc: 601 N Eutaw St #704, Baltimore, MD 21201 ... 410-837-0070
Grafica: 525 E Main St, Chester, NJ 07930 ... 908-879-2169
Graficsmiths: 15 Glendale Rd, Hudson, MA 01749 ... 508-562-5494
Grafik Comm, Inc: 1199 N Fairfax St #700, Alexandria, VA 22314 ... 703-683-4686
Grafix: 12315 Oaknole Rd #400, Vonay, CA 92064 ... 619-486-9990
Grafix Design: 6562 Ridings Rd, Syracuse, NY 13206 ... 315-463-9175
Graham & Assocs, Critt: 2970 Clairmont Rd #620, Atlanta, GA 30329 ... 404-320-1737
Graham Marketing Group, Inc: 980 Lone Oak Rd #114, Eagan, MN 55121 ... 612-681-0055
Graham, Thomas: 446 80th St, Brooklyn, NY 11209 ... 718-680-2975
Gram Graphic Design, Anne: 400 Linebrook Rd, Ispswich, MA 01938 ... 508-356-1173
Granados Assocs, Inc: 1810 Byberry Rd #E3, Bensalem, PA 19020 ... 215-244-0999
Grand Design: 1746 Underwood Rd, Gambrills, MD 21054 ... 410-721-9485
Grand Design/Boston: 22-A Franklin St, Marblehead, MA 01945 ... 617-631-5072
Graney, Tom: 7735 Pomeroy St, Richmond, VA 23228 ... 804-648-2324
Granola Graphics: 37 West 20 #902, New York, NY 10011 ... 212-727-0512
Granoski, Dana: 2500 Broadway #300, Santa Monica, CA 90404 ... 310-449-5600
Graphein: 1756 Blake St, Denver, CO 80202 ... 303-298-8009
Graphic Art Resource Assocs: 257 w 10th St #5E, New York, NY 10014 ... 212-929-0017
Graphic Artists Guild: 90 John St #403, New York, NY 10038 ... 212-791-3400
Graphic Arts, Inc: 1020 Bernard St, Alexandria, VA 22314 ... 703-683-4303
Graphic Chart & Map Co: 1 North St #2W, Hastings-on-Hudson, NY 10706 ... 914-478-5074
Graphic Comms: 20 W 38th St 2nd Fl, New York, NY 10018 ... 212-764-6237
Graphic Concepts Group: 1612 Summit Ave #410, Fort Worth, TX 76102 ... 817-332-4600
Graphic Concepts Unlimited: 2109 Hamilton Rd #H, Okemos, MI 48864 ... 517-347-8900
Graphic Consortium: 205 Race St, Philadelphia, PA 19106 ... 215-923-3200
Graphic Decisions, Inc: 318 Bainbridge St, Philadelphia, PA 19147 ... 215-627-6901
Graphic Design Advertising: 10400 Loubet St, Orlando, FL 32817 ... 407-277-7461
Graphic Design Continuum: 502 Wayne Ave, Dayton, OH 45410 ... 937-223-8264
Graphic Design Maui, Inc: 173 Ho-Ohana St #103, Kahului, HI 96732 ... 808-871-8000
Graphic Designers, Inc: 700 N Central Ave #450, Glendale, CA 91203 ... 818-247-5433
Graphic Expression, The: 330 E 59th St, New York, NY 10022 ... 212-759-7788
Graphic Expressions: 695 NW 80th Terr, Margate, FL 33063 ... 305-968-3789
Graphic House, Inc: 23200 14 Mile Rd, Bloomfield, MI 48301 ... 313-647-0011
Graphic Impact: 162 Lower Main St, Sunapee, NH 03782 ... 603-763-9221
Graphic Ink: 333 Church St, Clinton, MA 01510 ... 508-365-5205
Graphic Innovations: Rt 67 Box 168-D, Cullowhee, NC 28723 ... 704-293-9178
Graphic Marketing: 1125 E Hillsdale Blvd #110, Foster City, CA 94404 ... 415-574-2525
Graphic Matters: 4235 Hillsboro Rd #205, Nashville, TN 37215 ... 615-383-3877
Graphic Shop, Inc: 1012 San Pedro, San Antonio, TX 78212 ... 210-226-1006
Graphic Solution, The: PO Box 747, W Jordan, UT 84084 ... 801-569-8761
Graphic Solutions: 304 Hudson St/4th Fl N, New York, NY 10013 ... 212-645-2700
Graphic Solutions, Inc: 1750 Kettner Blvd, San Diego, CA 92101 ... 619-239-1335
Graphic Specialties, Inc: 6800 Shingle Creek Pkwy, Minneapolis, MN 55430 ... 612-722-6601
Graphic Studio: 811 N Highland Ave, Los Angeles, CA 90038 ... 213-466-2666
Graphic Traffic: 5845 Hollis St, Emeryville, CA 94608 ... 510-428-2808
Graphic Workshop: 80 Eighth Ave 17th Fl, New York, NY 10011 ... 212-633-6333
Graphica: 1301 Carolina St #106, Greensboro, NC 27401 ... 910-230-0575
Graphica: 204 Hastings Court, Doylestown, PA 18901 ... 215-340-7750
Graphica: 4501 Lyons Rd, Miamisburg, OH 45342 ... 937-866-4013
Graphica Corp: 3184 Alpine, Troy, MI 48084 ... 313-649-5050
Graphically Speaking: 5 Richmond Hill, Laguna Niguel, CA 92677 ... 714-661-0553
Graphics & Design: 421 S Pugh St, State College, PA 16801 ... 814-238-3136
Graphics By Nostradamus: 250 W 57th St #1128A, New York, NY 10107 ... 212-581-1362
Graphics Depot: 2805 Rte 31 E, Weedsport, NY 13166 ... 315-689-6453
Graphics Et Al: 14th Fifth Ave #3C, New York, NY 10011 ... 212-475-1757
Graphics Etc: 2460 Rue Burgundy, New Orleans, LA 70117 ... 504-944-2814
Graphics Fifty-Five, Inc: 55 Avondale Ave, Clifton, NJ 07013 ... 201-472-4810
Graphics For Industry: 8 W 30th St 7th Fl, New York, NY 10001 ... 212-889-6202
Graphics III: 131 Roseland Ave, Caldwell, NJ 07006 ... 201-226-4343
Graphics Ltd: 9007 Independence Ave, Canoga Park, CA 91304 ... 818-998-6451
Graphics One Fifty: 150 Speedwell Ave, Morris Plains, NJ 07950 ... 201-267-6446
Graphics Pad: 1108 Concora Box 1155, Mansfield, TX 76063 ... 817-473-3380
Graphics Plus: 50 Merritt St, Port Chester, NY 10573 ... 914-939-0888
Graphics To Go: 133 E 36th St, New York, NY 10016 ... 212-889-9337
Graphics West: 1215 De La Vina St #G, Santa Barbara, CA 93101 ... 805-966-0885
Graphics Workshop: 312 McDonald St, Midland, MI 48640 ... 517-631-9560
Graphicstudio: 12305 NE 12th Ct, N Miami, FL 33161 ... 305-893-1015
Graphicus Corp: 2025 Maryland Ave, Baltimore, MD 21218 ... 301-727-5553
Graphien Design: 1756 Blake St, Denver, CO 80202 ... 303-298-8009
Graphikco Design Group: 2674 N 1st #206, San Jose, CA 95134 ... 498-435-1115
Graphiti Assocs: 1725 Westlake Ave N #101, Seattle, WA 98109 ... 206-285-9440
Graphix Design: 57 E Liberty St, Girard, OH 44420 ... 330-545-5611
Graphix, Inc: 651 E Paces Ferry Rd NE, Atlanta, GA 30305 ... 404-262-7832
Grasso Assocs, Lou: 425 Madison Ave 19th Fl, New York, NY 10017 ... 212-371-1820
Grau Graphics: 6 W 18th St #2D, New York, NY 10011 ... 212-807-7777
Gravdahl Design: 406 E Lake St, Ft Collins, CO 80524 ... 970-482-8807
Graves Fowler & Assocs: 14301 Layhill Rd #200, Silver Spring, MD 20906 ... 301-598-6414
Gray Studio, Cheri: 522 N Rossmore Ave #301, Los Angeles, CA 90004 ... 213-871-8967
Gray, George: 385 West End Ave, New York, NY 10024 ... 212-873-3607
Graywood Agency, Inc, The: 7 Hilltop Rd, Mendham, NJ 07945 ... 201-543-7700
Grear Designers, Malcolm: 391 Eddy St, Providence, RI 02903 ... 401-331-2891
Greatwork Electronic Ink: 2394 Mariner Sq Dr #137, Alameda, CA 94501 ... 510-721-7659
Grebe, Hank: 8209 Persimmon Hill Ln, Jacksonville, FL 32256 ... 904-348-2349
Greedboam & Company: 120 Cedar Ln, Ossining, NY 10562 ... 914-762-0954
Green Design Studio, Peter: 4219 W Burbank Blvd, Burbank, CA 91505 ... 818-953-2210
Green Graphic Design & Adv, Mel: 145 Richdale Rd, Needham, MA 02194 ... 617-449-6777
Green Tree Graphics: 88 Main St, Peapack, NJ 07977 ... 908-781-5700
Green, Douglas: 251 E 51st St, New York, NY 10022 ... 212-752-6284
Greenberg Assocs, Inc, Jon: 29355 NW Highway #300, Southfield, MI 48034 ... 313-355-0890
Greene & Co: 1227 Liberty St #301, Allentown, PA 18102 ... 610-740-0640
Greene & Co, H: 230 W Huron, Chicago, IL 60610 ... 312-642-0088
Greenebaum Design: 86 Walnut St, Natick, MA 01760 ... 617-655-8146
Greenfield Design: 1026 ave Of The Americas, New York, NY 10018 ... 212-354-0409
Greenfield, Peggy: 5 Manmar Dr #407, Plainville, MA 02762 ... 508-543-6644
Greenfield/Belser: 1818 n St NW #110, Washington, DC 20036 ... 202-775-0333
Greenhill Productions: 216 E 45th St, New York, NY 10017 ... 212-661-1363
Greenlee Hess Ind Design: 750 Beta Dr, Cleveland, OH 44143 ... 216-461-3881
Gregg & Assocs: 112 W 9th St 2nd Fl, Kansas City, MO 64105 ... 816-421-4473
Gregg, Mutsumi: 249 Alpine St #53, Pasadena, CA 91106 ... 818-449-8909
Gregorio Design: 801 Cooper Landing Rd #A410, Cherry Hill, NJ 08002 ... 609-321-1651
Gregory Design: 1045 Sansome St #445, San Francisco, CA 94111 ... 415-296-9331
Gregory Design, Albert: 21 Hanson St, Boston, MA 02118 ... 617-482-0347
Gregory Group, Inc: Box 191003, Dallas, TX 75219 ... 214-522-9360
Greiner & Assocs, John: 3111 N Ravenswood, Chicago, IL 60657 ... 773-404-0210
Grenier Design Assocs: 617 E Scranton Ave, Lake Bluff, IL 60044 ... 847-615-0505
Greteman Group: 142 N Mosley St, Wichita, KS 67202 ... 316-263-1004
Grguric, Alek: 25 Trailwood Dr #2508, Mississauga, ON L4Z 3K9 ... 416-868-9721
Grid, Steve Chang: 18 W 21st St 6th Fl, New York, NY 10010 ... 212-255-1806
Griffin Creative Co: 534 Kingfisher Dr, Sugarland, TX 77478 ... 713-242-1119
Griffin Design: 537 Armour Circle, Atlanta, GA 30324 ... 404-842-9900
Grimes Design, Don: 5635 Ridgedale, Dallas, TX 75206 ... 214-821-9590
Gritz Visual Graphics: 5595 Arapahoe Rd, Boulder, CO 80303 ... 303-449-3840
Grizzly Hill Design: 2517 Roosevelt Ave, Richmond, CA 94804 ... 510-232-3169
Groff, Jay Michael: 4650 East West Highway, Bethesda, MD 20814 ... 301-215-7221
Groot Organization: 245 Vallejo St, San Francisco, CA 94111 ... 415-788-6677
Groppi Advertising Design: 22 Spear St, Quincy, MA 02169 ... 617-773-5585
Gross Design Concepts, Mike: 2334 E Beverly Dr, Tuscon, AZ 85719 ... 520-629-0626
Gross Graphic Design, Paul: 732 Springfield Ave, Summit, NJ 07901 ... 908-522-0333
Grossman Design, Steve: 4301 Highway 7 #120, Minneapolis, MN 55416 ... 612-922-4343
Groth Design, Donna: 13 Seventh Ave E, East Northport, NY 11731 ... 516-757-1182
Group 118: 24 Fifth Ave #201, New York, NY 10011 ... 212-995-8340
Group 33 Design Assocs: 15 W 26th St 9th Fl, New York, NY 10010 ... 212-337-0333
Group Chicago: One E Delaware Pl #200, Chicago, IL 60611 ... 312-787-4504
Group Design: 401 N Third St #360, Minneapolis, MN 55401 ... 612-787-4504
Group Design Assocs: 50 Park Circle S, Farmingdale, NY 11735 ... 516-420-8796
Group Four Design: PO Box 717, Avon, CT 06001 ... 203-678-1570
Group M: 1621 Cypress St, Philadelphia, PA 19103 ... 215-546-1995
Groves Design Company: 515 28th St #109, Des Moines, IA 50312 ... 515-288-5278
Grunau, Ted: 165 Spadina Ave 3rd Fl, Toronto, ON M5T 2C3 ... 416-351-0411
Grunder Design, Robin: 27 W 20th St #404, New York, NY 10011 ... 212-727-7125
GTE Entertainment: 2035 Corte Del Nogal #200, Carlsbad, CA 92009 ... 619-431-8801
Guancione, Karen: 262 DeWitt Ave, Belleville, NJ 07109 ... 201-450-9490
Guard Design Assocs, John: 9001 Phyliss Ave, W Hollywood, CA 90069 ... 310-247-8911
Guarino Design: 1348 Cambridge St, Cambridge, MA 02139 ... 617-661-8567
Gucciardo & Shapokas: 244 Madison Ave, New York, NY 10016 ... 212-683-9378
Gudzin Design: 153 E 57th St #5E, New York, NY 10022 ... 212-758-2532
Guerard, Jim: 4223 Glencoe Ave #A223, Marina Del Rey, CA 90292 ... 213-477-8878
Guerrette, Muriel: 3 Forest Ln, Canton, CT 06019 ... 203-693-1186
Guliani, Bob: 863 Pavonia Ave, Jersey City, NJ 07306 ... 201-792-5213
Gunn Assocs: 275 Newbury St, Boston, MA 02116 ... 617-267-0618
Gunselman & Co, Michael: 1007 N Broom St, Wilmington, DE 19806 ... 302-655-7077
Gurevich, Dmitry: 381 Congress St 5th Fl, Boston, MA 02210 ... 617-357-0337
Guzman Designs, R: 21037 Superior St, Chatsworth, CA 91311 ... 818-700-9893
GVO, Inc: 2370 Watson Ct, Palo Alto, CA 94303 ... 800-727-4486
Gwen Francis Design: 334 State St #203, Los Altos, CA 94022 ... 415-949-4343

H

H Plus: 260 Fifth Ave #1201, New York, NY 10001 ... 212-689-8853
H2D Corporate Image Management: 100 E Wisconsin Ave #2370, Milwaukee, WI 53202 ... 414-226-0321
H2N Design: 1468 W 9th St #630, Cleveland, OH 44113 ... 216-623-1144
Haapaniemi Design, Inc: 1800 St James Pl #606, Houston, TX 77056 ... 713-622-3660
Hadden Design, Christopher: 44 Exchange St, Portland, ME 21045 ... 207-772-9801
Hafeman Design Group, Inc: 935 W Chestmut St #203, Chicago, IL 60622 ... 312-829-6829
Hafner Graphic Design, Christine: 68-3743 Ua Noe Pl, Waikoloa, HI 96738 ... 808-883-9573
Hake Assocs: 212 E 47th St #28E, New York, NY 10017 ... 212-751-5121
Hal Lewis Group: 1610 Chestnut St, Philadelphia, PA 19103 ... 215-563-4461
Hale Design, Bruce: 1201 NW Blakely Ct, Seattle, WA 98177 ... 206-440-9036
Haley Johnson Design: 3107 E 42nd St, Minneapolis, MN 55406 ... 612-722-8050
Hall Design Group, Carla: 261 W 85th St, New York, NY 10024 ... 212-799-4850
Hall Design, Kelly: 1021 S Wolf Rd #280, Sunnyvale, CA 94086 ... 408 720-0431
Hall, Steve: 150 Alhambra Cir #1250, Coral Gables, FL 33134 ... 305-461-9555
Halle, Doris: 355 South End Ave #4C, New York, NY 10280 ... 212-321-2671
Halleck Design Group: 470 Ramona St, Palo Alto, CA 94301 ... 415-325-0707
Halpern Adv & Design, Alan: 18 E 16th St 4TH Fl, New York, NY 10003 ... 212-633-6505
Halsey, Mike: 2525 Lebanon Rd #B2, Nashville, TN 37214 ... 615-885-6801
Halvorsen, Everett: 874 58th St, Brooklyn, NY 11220 ... 718-438-4200
Hamada Design, Gary: 1111 Fort Stockton Dr #H, San Diego, CA 92103 ... 619-294-9711
Hamer Assocs: Canal House/128 Garden St, Farmington, CT 06032 ... 203-677-1972
Hamilton Blake Design, Inc: 670 7th Ave #201, San Diego, CA 92101 ... 619-234-3930
Hamilton Displays: 9150 E 33rd St, Indianapolis, IN 46236 ... 317-898-9300
Hamilton Group, The: 6001 N Adams Rd #100, Bloomfield Hills, MI 48304 ... 810-205-2800
Hamilton/Sternglass: 54 W 21st St #705, New York, NY 10010 ... 212-727-2703

Hammond Design Assocs: 79 Amherst St, Milford, NH 03055 603-673-5253
Hammond Design, Jean: 1026 Mass Ave, Arlington, MA 02174 617-641-4386
Hampton Corp Design, David: 3311 38th Ave W, Seattle, WA 98199 206-283-1350
Hanagriff King Design: 2222 Bissonnet, Houston, TX 77005 713-522-7783
Hananero Computing Solutions, Inc: 6352 Clayton Rd #100,
St Louis, MO 63117 314-645-5522
Hancock Design/Div Hill Holliday: 200 Clarendon St, Boston, MA 02116 617-437-1600
Hancock Graphic Design, Tim: 817 Lafarge Ave, Louisville, CO 80027 303-665-7335
Hancock Rinek Design: 5019 Lido Sands Dr, Newport Beach, CA 92663 714-631-4200
Handelan Pedersen Design: 811 W Evergreen Ave, Chicago, IL 60622 312-664-1200
Handelman Graphics: 555 Madison Ave 29th Fl, New York, NY 10022 212-350-0000
Handler Group, Inc: 22 W 23rd St 3rd Fl, New York, NY 10010 212-645-3900
Handler Holden Design, Inc: 17 Ralph Ave, White Plains, NY 10606 914-997-7592
Hands Ink Adv: 2020 S Jones Blvd, Las Vegas, NV 89102 702-364-8604
Hanigan Consulting Group: 1250 Broadway 23rd Fl, New York, NY 10010 212-675-2200
Hanna Design, Jim: 4232 Lynd Ave, Arcadia, CA 91006 818-446-7558
Hannans Design, Nancy: 5221 Quarry Ln, Virginia Beach, VA 23464 804-467-3607
Hannus Design Assocs: 10 Commercial Wharf W #508, Boston, MA 02110 617-227-3725
Hans Design: 3100 Dundee Rd #909, Northbrook, IL 60062 847-272-7980
Hansen Andrus Design: 2471 S 1500 East, Salt Lake City, UT 84106 801-487-8033
Hansen Design Assocs, Ted: 1885 Third Ave, San Diego, CA 92101 619-233-0422
Hansen Design Co: 1809 Seventh Ave #1709, Seattle, WA 98101 206-467-9959
Hansengraphics, Inc: 3305 SW 9th St, Des Moines, IA 50315 515-243-0637
Hanson, Ken: 301 N Water St, Milwaukee, WI 53202 414-347-1266
Hanson/Dodge Design: 301 N Water St 5th Fl, Milwaukee, WI 53202 414-347-1266
Hara Design, Martin: 501 Fifth Ave #2010, New York, NY 10017 212-573-6377
Harbaugh Design: 1401 NE Boat St, Seattle, WA 98105 206-547-0830
Harbor Company: 855 10th St #302, Santa Monica, CA 90403 310-393-6494
Harding & Assocs Design Grp: 377 S Daniel Way, San Jose, CA 95128 408-345-4545
Hardy Design: 250 Sandcastle, Aliso Viejo, CA 92656 714-362-3810
Hardy Design, Pat: 245 Gay Rd, Groton, MA 01450 508-448-8648
Hardy Design, Paul: 448 W 37th St #6E, New York, NY 10018 212-947-5209
Harley Assocs, Don E: 1740 Livingston Ave, W St Paul, MN 55118 612-455-1631
Harmon Design, Jann: 3931 Macarthur Blvd #226,
Newport Beach, CA 92660 714-752-0913
Harne, John: 887 W Marietta St NW N105, Atlanta, GA 30318 404-325-0795
Harrington Group, The: 8 Cattano Ave, Morristown, NJ 07960 201-326-8877
Harris Design, Inc: 724 Yorklyn Rd #150, Hockessin, DE 19707 302-234-5700
Harris Magee, Inc: 6333 Reynolds Rd, Horton, MI 49246 517-563-2100
Harris, Judy: 550 Willow Creek Ct, Clarendon Hills, IL 60514 630-789-3821
Harrison Design, Inc: 665 Chestnut 3rd Fl, San Francisco, CA 94133 415-928-6111
Harrison Lettering Design, Allen: 1601 Abbot Kinney Blvd,
Venice, CA 90291 310-396-3202
Hart Communication Assocs: 29 Brewster St, North Andover, MA 01845 508-681-8844
Hart, Kay: 10818 Midwest Industrial, St. Louis, MO 63132 314-423-9300
Harte, Cheryl: 15 McKinley St #2, Norwalk, CT 06853 203-853-6986
Hartley Metzner Hunick: 3076 S CAlhoun Rd, New Berlin, WI 53151 414-784-1010
Hartley Studios: 16 Crosby St, New York, NY 10013 212-925-7269
Hartung & Assocs Ltd: 10279 Field Ln, Forestville, CA 95436 707-887-2825
Harvey & Daughters, Inc: 116 S W Old Padonida Rd,
Cockeysville, MD 21030 410-628-9220
Hasbrouck Studios: 641 Cricket Hill Trl, Lawrenceville, GA 30244 770-972-7083
Hasgrove Design Group: 2600 S Gessner #518, Houston, TX 77063 713-789-9815
Hassold Design Assocs, Eugene: 429 Via Hidalgo #54,
Greenbrae, CA 94904 415-989-7509
Hasten Design Studio: 1629 K St NW #950, Washington, DC 20006 202-293-1333
Hasto Communications: 2248 Spencerport Rd #A, Rochester, NY 14606 716-352-7095
Hatten Design, Phil: 526 S Sparks St, Burbank, CA 91506 818-559-5691
Haugaard Creative Group: 414 N Orleans, Chicago, IL 60610 312-661-0666
Haukom Assocs: 10 Lombard St, San Francisco, CA 94111 415-658-2820
Hauser Assocs, SG: 880 Hampshire Rd #A, Westlake Village, CA 91361 805-497-5810
Hauser, Sydney: 9 Fillmore Dr, Sarasota, FL 33577 813-388-3021
Hausman, Joan: 650 High St #225, Palo Alto, CA 94301 415-325-7957
Havekotte Design: 2541 Lot-A-Fun Ave, Winter Park, FL 32789 407-647-8582
Hawthorne/Wolfe, Inc: 1818 Chouteau Ave, St Louis, MO 63103 314-231-1844
Hayakawa & Assocs, Herb: 22736 Juniper Ave, Torrance, CA 90505 310-325-7755
Hayes Productions, Bruce: 959 Wisconsin St, San Francisco, CA 94107 415-282-2244
Haygeman Isobe Johnson Kracke: 2260 Rutherford Rd #110,
Carlsbad, CA 92008 619-931-1982
Hayward & Co, Blake: 1234 Sherman Ave #200, Evanston, IL 60202 847-864-9800
HC Design: 4630 Montgomery Ave #510, Bethesda, MD 20814 301-215-7111
Healy Art & Design, Anita: 3723 Birch #14, Newport Beach, CA 92660 714-252-8722
Hearn Assocs, Walter: 1099 Deerfield Dr NW, Blacksburg, VA 24060 540-951-2853
Hearn/Perrell Art Assocs: 23022 Hatteras St, Woodland Hills, CA 91367 310-394-8373
Heatly Assocs Design: 4131 Spicewood Springs #A8, Austin, TX 78759 512-343-2284
Hecht Design: 1026 Mass Ave, Arlington, MA 02174 617-643-1988
Heckler & Assocs: 2717 Western Ave, Seattle, WA 98121 206-448-4242
Hedstrom/Blessing: 5500 Wayzata Blvd #650, Minneapolis, MN 55416 612-591-6200
Hegstrom Design: 805 Quail Glen Ct, Auburn, CA 95603 916-888-7000
Heick, Patrick E: 844 East Ave, Park Ridge, IL 60068 847-825-1099
Heidelberg USA: 1000 Gutenberg Dr, Kennesaw, GA 30144 770-419-6500
Heimall Inc, Bob: 1798 Rt 565, Sussex, NJ 07461 201-702-0075
Heiney & Craig: 235 Montgomery St #956, San Francisco, CA 94104 415-781-2404
Held & Diedrich Design: 703 E 30th St #16, Indianapolis, IN 46205 317-926-6161
Helfand, Jessica: 214 Sullivan St, New York, NY 10012 212-388-1863
Helgesson Ind Design, Ulf: 4285 Canoga Ave, Woodland Hills, CA 91364 818-883-3772
Helms, Nina: 25 Forest Ln, Westbury, NY 11590 516-997-6567
Hemisphere: 915 Main St #308, Evansville, IN 47708 812-429-0878
Hemlock Design: 53 Kirkland Circle, Wellesley Hills, MA 02181 617-237-0037
Hemman Design: 311 S Chadwick St, Philadelphia, PA 19103 215-985-1780
Henderson Company, The: 222 W Huron, Chicago, IL 60610 312-951-8973
Henderson Design, Bill: 1083 Kelly Creek Circle, Oviedo, FL 32765 407-366-5336
Henderson Tyner Art Co:
315 N Spurce St #299, Winston-Salem, NC 27101 910-748-1364
Hennelly, Noel: 239 28th St #4C, New York, NY 10016 212-683-2786
Henneman Design: 365 Canal St #2050, New Orleans, LA 70130 504-529-1482
Hennes Design Inc, Catherine: 445 Highland Ave, San Mateo, CA 94401 415-348-8247
Henning Communications: 1910 Pine St #100, St Louis, MO 63103 314-436-6464

• **Henrie, Cary: pg 962,963** 1659 E Maple Hills Dr, Bountiful, UT 84010.......**801-298-2044**
e-mail: www.dhs@itsnet.com / fax: 801-299-1919
Henry Wolf Production: 167 E 73rd St, New York, NY 10021 212-472-2500
Hensler Westerkamp Giles: 432 Walnut St #1500, Cincinnati, OH 45202 513-241-0100
Herbst Lazar Rogers & Bell, Inc: 345 N Canal, Chicago, IL 60606 312-454-1116
Herman & Assocs, Sid: 36 Ticehurst Ln, Marblehead, MA 01945 617-631-0662
Herman, Ben: 701 Pennsylvania, Ft Worth, TX 76104 817-332-7679
Herman, Julie: 2727 29th St NW #522, Washington, DC 20008 202-232-3365
Hermelyn Design: 665 Third St Ste 335, San Francisco, CA 94107 415-546-9606
Hermine Design Group: 3 Lockwood Ave, Old Greenwich, CT 06870 203-698-1732
Hermsen Design Assocs: 5151 Beltline Rd #825, Dallas, TX 75240 214-233-5090
Hernandez, Raymond: 111 E 14th St #228, New York, NY 10003 212-388-7382
Herren Designs, Inc, Scott: 911 Western Ave #555, Seattle, WA 98104 ....206 343-0701
Herring Design, Jerry: 1216 Hawthorne, Houston, TX 77006 713-526-1250
Hershey Comm NY, Inc: 257 Park Ave S 8th Fl, New York, NY 10010 212-477-9100
Hess Design: 49 Eliot St, south Natick, MA 01760 508-650-4063
Hewett, Mike: 339 Palace Rd, Kingston, ON K7L 4T4 613-546-4232
Hewson Design Assocs: 270 Lafayette St #1110, New York, NY 10002 212-925-2776
Heyck, Edith: 6 Vernon St, Newburyport, MA 01950 508-462-9027
HeyerTech: 726 Marion Ave, Palo Alto, CA 94303 415-325-8522
Heywood & Sullivan, Inc: 1354 Hancock St #306, Quincy, MA 02169 617-471-1144
Hickey & Helper Graphics: 1633 Bayshore Hwy #222,
Burlingame, CA 94010 415-652-4860
Hidalgo, Manny: 29776 Teracina Ave, Laguna Niguel, CA 92677 714-495-1033
High Design, Richard: 6311 Grovewood, Houston, TX 77008 713-861-7779
High, Richard: 6311 Grovewood Ln, Houston, TX 77006 713-861-7779
Hild Nelson Design, Inc: 1400 North Ave, Bannockburn, IL 60015 847-948-7064
Hill Design: 3512 Lake, Houston, TX 77098 713-523-7363
Hill Design Group: 2120 Arch St, Philadelphia, PA 19103 215-854-0484
Hill Design, Alan: 214 Sullivan St #6D, New York, NY 10012 212-614-8893
Hill Design, Martin: 1961 Skyview Dr, Altadena, CA 91001 818-398-7561
Hill Flaherty Sabol Marketing: 1 Gateway Center, Pittsburgh, PA 15222 412-471-3700
Hill Shea & Clients: 7955 E Chaparral Rd #134, Scottsdale, AZ 85250 602-945-7289
Hill, Chris: 3512 Lake, Houston, TX 77098 713-523-7363
Hillhouse Graphic Design: 249 De Lee Dr, Kingsport, TN 37663 423-239-9384
Hillis Mackey & Co: 1550 Utica Ave S #745, Minneapolis, MN 55416 612-542-9122
Hillman Design, Thomas: 193 Middle St, Portland, ME 04101 207-773-3727
Hillmuth, James: 3613 Norton Pl, Washington, DC 20016 202-244-0465
Hiltabiddle Design: 26 Silk St, Arlington, MA 02174 617-643-6756
Hilton Co, Inc: 740 Harpeth Trace Dr, Nashville, TN 37221 615-356-8579
Hilton Graphics, Inc: 1000 N Washington, Lansing, MI 48906 517-371-1196
Hirano Design International: 875 N Michigan Ave #3443,
Chicago, IL 60611 312-335-0090
Hirata, Clarice: 795 N Rengstorff Ave #10, Mt View, CA 94043 415-964-3773
Hirsch Design: 9136 Mormon Bridge Rd, Omaha, NE 68152 402-455-0383
Hirsch O'Connor Design: 205 W Wacker Dr #622, Chicago, IL 60606 312-329-1500
Hirschhaut Designs, Bruce: 510 Otteray Dr, Highpoint, NC 27262 910-841-5666
Hirsh Co: 8051 N Central Park Ave, Skokie, IL 60076 847-267-6777
Hitchcock, Betsy: 135 Green Meadow Ln, Boulder, CO 80302 303-444-1336
Hixo & Co: 2905 San Gabriel #300, Austin, TX 78705 512-477-0050
Hixson Design: 1414 E Fifth St, Charlotte, NC 28204 704-334-8088
Hjermstad & Assocs: 666 Brighthton Rd, Pacifica, CA 94044 415-738-0405
Hlc Group: 39 W 29th St 11th Fl, New York, NY 10001 212-889-4818
Hnath, John: 271 Madison Ave #1405, New York, NY 10016 212-661-0962
Hoashi Communications: 275 madison Ave 18th Fl, New York, NY 10016 212-697-7208
Hodges Graphic Design: 530 E Main St #301, Richmond, VA 23219 804-643-1909
Hodges, Alison: 4001 Confederate Point Rd, Jacksonville, FL 32210 904-778-8568
Hodgson/Myers Adv: 610 Market St #103, Kirkland, WA 98033 206-827-2506
Hoekstra Graphics, Grant: 18 Nottingham Dr, Lincolnshire, IL 60069 847-948-7378
Hofer Graphics: 3325 Enterprise Rd, Safety Harbor, FL 34695 813-725-2426
Hoffar & Co, Barron: 11 E Hubbard 7th Fl, Chicago, IL 60611 312-922-0890
Hogan Design, Inc: 1415 Thistlewood Ln, Grapevine, TX 76051 817-481-0808
Hohler Assocs: 6 Faneuil Hall Marketplace, Boston, MA 02109 617-742-5277
Holden, Cynthia: 275 S Oakland Ave #301, Pasadena, CA 91101 818-584-6944
Holdsworth Design & Prctn, Ani: 2433 Willow Springs Ct, Apopka, FL 32712 407-884-8284
Holl, RJ: 35 Old Chicopee St, Chicopee, MA 01013 413-594-8188
Holland Design, Robert: 2914 Evergreen Way, Ellicott City, MD 21042 410-531-2481
Hollander Design, Sara: 1102 Tuckahoe Ln, Alexandria, VA 22302 703-548-0959
Hollinger Group: 9110 Theysen Dr, Houston, TX 77080 713-690-6244
Holloway, Martin: 56 Mt Horeb Rd, Plainfield, NJ 07060 908-563-0169
Hollyn Assocs, Lynn : 522 Ramona St, Palo Alto, CA 94301 415-325-9980
Hollywood Interactive: 32215 Pacific Coast Hwy, Malibu, CA 900265 310-858-0577
Hollywood Online, Inc: 1620 26th St #370, Santa Monica, CA 90404 310-586-2000
Holmes & Assocs: 4171 Seaview Ln, Los Angeles, CA 90065 213-222-0776
Holmes Design & Adv: 6832 S Mitchell Dr, Tempe, AZ 85283 602-413-2454
Holter, Catherine: 721 Broadway #606, New York, NY 10003 212-998-1605
Holter, Eric: 30 Cutler St, Warren, RI 02885 401-247-7799
Holtz Design: 539 Polk Blvd #B, Des Moines, IA 50312 515-255-4953
Holzsager Assocs, Mel: 19-19 Radburn Rd, Fairlawn, NJ 07410 201-797-3619
Hom Design, Mary: 24 Moore Lane, Northboro, MA 01532 508-393-2148
Homs, John: 813 W 31st St, Richmond, VA 23225 804-230-7951
Honanken, William: PO Box 20402 Tompkins Sq Sta, New York, NY 10009 212-627-4108
HonBlue, Inc: 501 Summer St #3B1, Honolulu, HI 96817 808-531-4611
Honda Design, Ray: 37 Fairview Terrace, Petaluna, CA 94952 707-762-6364
Hood Assocs, William: 247 Fourth St #309, Oakland, CA 94607 510-444-5939
Hope Lane Design: 121 Crandon Blvd #359, Key Biscayne, FL 33149 305-361-0481
Hopkins Baumann: 236 W 26th St #5NW, New York, NY 10001 212-727-2929
Hopp Design Office: 5245 Knox Ave S, Minneapolis, MN 55419 612-920-2540
Hopsick Design, Frank: 17222 Vashon Hwy Sw/PO Box H,
Vashon, WA 98070 206-463-5454
Horbochuk & Assocs: 4916 Willow Crest Ave, N Hollywood, CA 91601 818-508-7524
Horizon Arts Unlimithed: 3054 S 44th, Kansas City, KS 66016 913-262-4355
Horizon Communication & Design: 256 Horizon Ave, Venice, CA 90291 310-394-5439
Horizon Image Development: 1250 Addison St #212, Berkeley, CA 94702 510-843-0131
Horizons Technology: 3990 Ruffin Rd, San Diego, CA 92123 619-292-8331
Hornbacher, Sara: 1270 W Peachtree St #15 G, Atlanta, GA 30309 404-724-0412
Horosz, Carl: 10 Park Ave, Morristown, NJ 07960 201-359-3410
Horsman Design Assocs: 4665 Munroe St, La Mesa, CA 91941 619-463-2096

Horvath & Assocs Studios Ltd: 335 W 12th St, New York, NY 10014 212-741-0300
Hosick Design, Frank: PO Box H, Vashon Island, WA 98070..........................206-463-5454
Hot Spots USA: 428 N Superior #140, De Pere, WI 54115..............................414-983-9140
Hot Tech Multimedia, Inc: 46 Mercer St, New York, NY 10013 212-925-3010
Hough Assocs, Jack: 25 Seir Hill Rd, Norwalk, CT 06850...............................203-846-2666
Hough Inc, Jack: 25 Seirhill Rd, Norwalk, CT 06850.....................................203-846-2666
Houston Mowry Productions: 5601 N Macauthur 105, Irving, TX 75038..........214-550-6147
Hovaness Design: #2 Briarwood Ct, Medford, NJ 08055 609-988-7027
Howard Design Group: 20 Nassau St #115, Princeton, NJ 08542....................609-924-1106
Howard Jeldsan Assocs/Concorde: 210 N Peak Dr, Alpharetta, GA 30202........770-518-9903
Howard-Stutesman, Deborah: 14378 County Rd S, Lyons, OH 43533 419-335-3340
Howell Design: 6319 E Valley Rd, Nashville, TN 37205..................................615-356-5020
Howell Design, David: 4616 Windmere Chase Dr, Raleigh, NC 27616..............919-873-0876
Howry Design: 354 Pine St #600, San Francisco, CA 94104.........................415-433-2035
Hrivnak, James: 10822 Childs Ct, Silver Spring, MD 20901...........................301-681-9090
Hsiung & Assocs: 1063 Central Ave, Cincinnati, OH 45202 513-381-8855
Hub Graphics: 18 E 16th St 4th Fl, New York, NY 10003 212-675-8500
Huber Design: 3284 Willow Run Rd, Kutztown, PA 19530...............................610-285-2266
Hubert, Laurent: 850 Arbor Rd, Menlo Park, CA 94025...................................415-321-5182
Hubler, Olivette: 2631 Commerce, Dallas, TX 75226 214-742-2491
Huddleston Malone Design: 56 Exchange Pl, Salt Lake City, UT 84111...............801-595-6808
Huebner Design: 12 Ox Hill Rd, Newtown, CT 06470..203-270-0732
• **Huerta Design, Inc, Gerard: Back Flap Book 2**
54 Old Post Rd, Southport, CT 06490...**203-256-9192**
Huffaker Graphics: 113 Nooks Hill Rd, Cromwell, CT 06470............................203-635-3258
Hughes Communications Group: 105 Beach St, Boston, MA 02111.................617-574-9090
Hughes Design: One Bishop St, Norwalk, CT 06851..203-847-9696
Hughes Design Communications: 22 N Morgan #203, Chicago, IL 60607.......312-733-1466
Hughes Design Group: 202 Mill Wharf, Scituate, MA 02066.............................617-545-0740
Hughes, Dralene "Red": 19750 W Observatory Rd, New Berlin, WI 53146.......414-542-5547
Hulefeld Assocs: 333 E 8th St, Cincinnati, OH 45202....................................513-421-2210
Hull Design Group, Caryl: 69 Newbury St, Boston, MA 02116..........................617-536-1017
Hull, John: 353 W 53rd St #1W, New York, NY 10019.....................................212-682-2462
Human Code: 1411 W Avenue #100, Austin, TX 78701......................................512-477-5455
Human Element, The: 8120 Penn Ave S #433, Bloomington, MN 55431.........612-888-9544
Human Factors/Industrial Design: 575 Eighth Ave 15th Fl,
New York, NY 10018 212-868-2277
Humangraphic: 4015 Ibis St, San Diego, CA 92103...619-299-0431
Hume Design, Kendra: 208 SW Stark #500, Portland, OR 97204......................503-224-7618
Hunt & Fultz, J: 307 Fifth Ave 7th Fl, New York, NY 10016 212-545-7676
Hunt Creative, David: 1237 Gadsden St #101, Columbia, SC 29201 803-252-3003
Hunt Weber Clark Design: 525 Brannan St #302, San Francisco, CA 94107.......415-882-5770
Hunter Design, Rona: 133 Hillside Ave, Cresskill, NJ 07626 201-871-9434
Hunter McMain: One W Loop S #601, Houston, TX 77027 713-627-1177
Hurd & Assocs: 1250 Pine St #102, Walnut Creek, CA 94596 510-930-8580
Hurd Design, Jim: 722 Lombard St #204, San Francisco, CA 94133 415-921-4691
Hutcheson & Co: 3845 FM 1960 W #140, Houston, TX 77068 713-440-0221
Huttner: One Penn Plaza #100, New York, NY 10119 212-695-4858
• **Huyssen, Roger: Back Flap Book 1** 54 Old Post Rd, Southport, CT 06490.....**203-256-9192**
Hyde, Bill: 751 Matsonia, Foster City, CA 94404..415-345-6955
Hyperactive Interactive: 608 17th St, Santa Monica, CA 90402 310-395-8936

I

I Catcher: 1140 Terminal Twr, Cleveland, OH 44113 216-696-1686
i/o Digital Design: 841 Broadway #502, New York, NY 10003 212-533-4467
i2M: 2621 11th St, Santa Monica, CA 90405..310-396-6664
i3 Information & Imagination: 325 Riverside Ave, Westport, CT 06880.............203-227-2030
Icon: 5405 Springboro Pike, Dayton, OH 45449..937-296-0808
Icone Studio: 64 B Walod St, Atlanta, GA 30312..404-624-4006
Iconos: 118 E 26th St #201, Minneapolis, MN 55404..612-879-0504
Ida Design: 13530 Fonesca Ave, La Mirada, CA 90638......................................213-943-2660
IDC Design Group: 1989 W 5th Ave #12, Columbus, OH 43212.........................614-487-8855
Ideas: 300 Broadway #20, San Francisco, CA 94133...415-397-2777
Ideas To Images: 5256 Aero Dr #3, Santa Rosa, CA 95403................................707-542-4301
Ideaworks Presentations: 90 Bridge St, Newton, MA 02158...............................617-244-0101
Identico: 175 Canal St, Manchester, NH 03110 603-644-1408
Identity Center: 1340 Remington Rd #5, Schaumburg, IL 60173.......................847-THE-BEST
Identity Design: 1895 Park Ave, San Jose, CA 95126.......................................408-554-1022
Identity Group, The: 114 N Brand Blvd #200, Glendale, CA 91203 818-243-3630
iDEZin Digital Workgroup: 2820 West Lunt #2000, Chicago, IL 60645...........773-338-3364
IE Design: 809 Chattanooga Ave, Dalton, GA 30720...706-217-6388
Ignition: 1001 E 15th St #200, Plano, TX 75074 214-423-7070
Ignition: 2965 20th Ave, San Francisco, CA 94132..415-731-9050
Ikkanda Design Group: 2440 S Sepulveda #152/Bldg #2,
Los Angeles, CA 90064..310-477-8584
Ilium Assocs: 600 108th Ave NE #660, Bellevue, WA 98004 206-646-6525
Illuminated Media: 577 Second St #203, San Francisco, CA 94107....................415-977-0900
Illustrated Page, The: 713 Indian Way, St Charles, IL 60174 708-443-9651
Illustration Design Group: 700 Craighead St #107, Nashville, TN 37204.........615-292-6077
Imada Design Group: 814 Fairoaks #B, S Pasadena, CA 91030..........................818-799-9114
Imag'Inez: 5 Oak Flat Rd, Orinda, CA 94563..510-254-2444
Image Arts: 480 Second St 3rd Fl, San Francisco, CA 94107 415-541-0320
Image Assocs: 4909 Windy Hill Dr, Raleigh, NC 27609 919-876-6400
Image Axis: 38 W 21st St 2nd Fl, New York, NY 10010.....................................212-989-5000
Image Base Comm, Inc: 430 W Erie #600, Chicago, IL 60610...........................312-587-8700
Image Design Studio: 837 Traction Ave, Los Angeles, CA 90013 213-617-9001
Image Excellence: 3312 Shore Crest, Dallas, TX 75235......................................214-352-9958
Image Factory: 1500 San Remo Ave #249, Coral Gables (Miami), FL 33146......305-666-5559
Image Factory: 15 Olive Ln, Owings Mills, MD 21117 410-581-8600
Image Group Studio: 3923 Cole St, Dallas, TX 75204 214-745-1411
Image Machine: 274 N Goodman St Bx90, Rochester, NY 14607 716-225-3512
Image Services: 1419 Standiford Ave #3, Modesto, CA 95350 209-579-5516
Image Source: 6105 Castle Bay Dr, Las Vegas, NV 89108..................................702-647-8487
• **Imagen: pg 1459** 2200 N Lamar #104, Dallas, TX 75202 ....**214-871-2747**
url: www.imagen.com / fax: 214-871-2748
Images: 833 W Main, Louisville, KY 40202...502-584-7954
Images & Identities: 2350 Mission College Blvd #330,
Santa Clara, CA 95054 408-982-8222

Imagesmith: 335 Rte 202-206/PO Box100, Pluckemin, NJ 07978 908-658-9334
Imageworks Communications: 21020 Victory Blvd,
Woodland Hills, CA 91367..818-712-9439
Imagicians: 1126 Fairview Ave #107, Arcadia, CA 91007 818-446-9625
Imagics Design Group: PO Box 7651, Santa Cruz, CA 95061 408-426-1531
Imagigraphics: 9 Grant St, West Newton, MA 02165..617-965-7788
Imagina: 33 Midway #203, San Francisco, CA 94133 415-788-6840
Imagination Creative Svcs: 80 Justin, San Francisco, CA 94112 408-988-8696
Imagination Factory, The: 6161 28th St SE, Grand Rapids, MI 49546.............616-356-2544
Imagine Co: 4015 80th St, Kenosha, WI 53142..414-942-9355
Imago Image Productions: 1264 S Goodrich Ave,
City of Commerce, CA 90040 213-728-8852
Imergy: 48 W 38th Street, New York, NY 10018 ....212 221-8585
IMMediacy: 5753 Uplander Way, Culver City, CA 90230..................................310-642-4995
Impact Communications Group: 18627 Brookhurst St #314,
Fountain Valley, CA 92708 714-963-6760
Impact Corp Comm: 4601 Telephone Rd #117, Ventura, CA 93003 805-658-3200
Impact Media Group: 1920 Franklin St #7, San Francisco, CA 94109 415-563-9083
Impact USA: 2227 Ann Dr, St Josephs, MI 49085...616-983-4170
Impact/FCB: 101 E Erie St 10th Fl, Chicago, IL 60611......................................312-751-3500
Impress: PO Box 761, Williamsburg, MA 01096...413-268-3040
Impress, Inc: 244 Main St, Northhampton, MA 01060.......................................413-585-5752
Impressions, Inc: 200 Powerhouse Rd, Roslyn Hts, NY 11577 516-484-2233
In House Graphic Design: 0717 Waterloo-Geneva Rd, Waterloo, NY 13165......315-539-9004
Inari Information Services: 804 N College #101, Bloomington, IN 47404........812-331-2298
Indiana Design Consortium, Inc: 416 Main St Box 180, Lafayette, IN 47902....317-423-5469
Indika NYC: 13-17 Laight St/6th Fl#1, New York, NY 10013 212-226-1272
Industrial F/X: 90 Ship St, Providence, RI 02903 401-831-5796
Industrial Technological Assoc: 30675 Solon Rd, Cleveland, OH 44139...........216-349-2900
Industry: 171 South Park, San Francisco, CA 94107..415-882-9879
Info by Design: 21240 Maira Lane, Saratoga, CA 95070 408-857-2229
Info Use: 2560 Ninth St #216, Berkley, CA 94710 510-549-6520
Information Technology Design Assocs: 10800 Lyndale Ave S #110,
Bloomington, MN 55420 612-881-2046
Ing Design: 214 Homer St, Palo Alto, CA 94301..415-617-8488
Ing Design, Victor: 5810 Lincoln, Morton Grove, IL 60053................................847-965-3459
Ingalls & Assocs: 10 Arkansas St, San Francisco, CA 94107 415-626-6395
Ingenious Multimedia: 815 W Weed St, Chicago, IL 60622................................312-951-8018
Ingle Co: 11661 San Vicente Blvd #402, Los Angeles, CA 90049......................310-820-8841
Ingram Design & Assocs, Inc: 71 W 2nd St, Yuma, AZ 85364...........................520-782-3844
Inkstone Design: 210 N Higgins Ave #334, Missoula, MT 59802.......................406-542-0270
Inkwell, Inc: 5 W 30th St, New York, NY 10001 212-279-2066
Inland Group: 222A N Main St, Edwardsville, IL 62025....................................618-656-8836
Inner Price Jones: 122 N Orange Ave #K, Orlando, FL 32801 407-245-7020
Inner Thoughts: 118 E 25th St, New York, NY 10010.......................................212-674-1277
Inno Design, Inc: 577 College Ave, Palo Alto, CA 94306..................................415-493-4666
Innovation Design & Adv: 1424 Fourth St #702, Santa Monica, CA 90401 310-395-4332
Innovations: 182 Bernard St, San Francisco, CA 94109...................................415-474-6385
Innovations & Development, Inc: 115 River Rd, Edgewater, NJ 07020.............201-941-5500
Innovative Comm: 7373 N Scottsdale Rd, Scottsdale, AZ 85253 602-948-2626
Innovative Design & Graphics: 1234 Sherman Ave #214, Evanston, IL 60202......847-475-7772
Ins Advertising: 811 NW 19th St, Portland, OR 97209......................................503-221-5000
Inscape: 1933 Pontius Ave, Los Angeles, CA 90025 310-312-5705
Insight: 5335 Bar Hills Ave #310, Dayton, OH 45429.......................................513-438-2815
Insite Communications: 3617 Silverside Rd Suite E, Wilmington, MA 19810.......302-478-6345
InSite Design: 36 Leafwood Cir, San Rafael, CA 415-721-0608
Inspire Graphic House: 98 Canal St #2R, New York, NY 10002 212-233-3757
Integre Advertising By Design: N8 W22323 Johnson Dr #D,
Waukesha, WI 53186..414-544-8800
Intelplex: 12215 Dorsett Rd, Maryland Hts, MO 63043.....................................314-739-9996
Inter-Active Designs: P.O. Box 4022, Hopkins, MN 55343 612-938-1473
Interactive Data Corp: 350 S Figueroa St #501, Los Angeles, CA 90071..........213-626-3521
Interactive Design: 1501 N Walnut St, Wilmington, DE 19801..........................302-429-0143
Interactive Design, Inc: 1511 Third Ave #670, Seattle, WA 98101....................206-382-9112
Interactive Factory: 368 Congress St, Boston, MA 02210..................................617-426-0609
Interactive Illusions: 3846 Abbott Ave S, Minneapolis, MN 55410...................612-926-5924
Interactive Media Communications: 204 Second Ave, Waltham, MA 02154......617-890-7707
Interactive Media Corp: PO Box 0089, Los Altos, CA 94023 415-948-0745
Interactive Media Partners: 50 Eagle St, San Francisco, CA 94114 415-861-1672
Interactive Media Technologies: 7745 E Redfield Rd #600,
Scottsdale, AZ 85260...602-443-3093
Interbrand Schecter Group: 437 Madison Ave 10th Fl, New York, NY 10022 212-752-4400
InterCom: 3 Grogan's Pk #200, The Woodlands, TX 77380.............................713-298-1010
Intercommunicate: 135 N Beacon, Watertown, MA 02172 617-923-1188
Intergate, Inc: 32 Warren St, Columbus, OH 43215 614-421-0004
Intergrated Media: 200 Varick St #606, New York, NY 10014............................212-229-1200
Intermark Comm: 46 Corporate Pk #100, Irvine, CA 92714 714-474-3000
International Design & Adv: 5 W 19th St 6th Fl, New York, NY 10011 212-633-2388
International Imaging: 1531-J Westbrook Plaza Dr,
Winston-Salem, NC 27103 910-760-0770
Interrobang Design Studio: 526 W 26th St #803, New York, NY 10001 212-463-0195
Intersight Design, Inc: 419 Park Ave S, New York, NY 10016 212-696-0700
Intervision: 401 E 10th Ave #160, Eugene, OR 97401 503-343-7993
Interworks: 2325 Third St #422, San Francisco, CA 94107 415-865-2424
Intrepid Design & Communications: 2342 North Ridge Rd,
McKinney, TX 75070...214-562-7961
Intrepid Productions: 7 Mt Lassen Dr #A116, San Rafael, CA 94903...............415-491-4050
Intricate Decisions: PO Box 55661, Riverside, CA 92517 714-274-9829
Invisions Group Ltd: 4927 Auburn Ave, Bethesda, MD 20814..........................301-718-3450
IPG: 5611-B Foxwood Dr, Agoura Hills, CA 91301 818-865-1428
• **Irbe, Igors (Inguna): pg 1178,1494**
1466 W Gregory St #2W, Chicago, IL 60640 ....**773-271-6508**
fax: 773-271-6493
Irish Graphics, Gary: 45 Newbury St, Boston, MA 02116.................................617-247-4168
Ironwood Assocs: 49 Sabbath Day Hill, S Salem, NY 10590 914-763-9595
Isley Design, Alexander: 4 Old Mill Rd, Redding, CT 06896.............................203-544-9692
Ison Design: 12574 Barrett Ln, Santa Ana, CA 92705......................................714-997-4452
Israel, David: 6055 Barfield Rd #200, Atlanta, GA 30328 404-255-6377

It! Design: 100 W Livingston St, Orlando, FL 32801 407-857-5462
IVID Communications: 7220 Trade St #201, San Diego, CA 92121 619-537-5000
Ivy League of Design: 156 Fifth Ave #417, New York, NY 10010....................212-243-1333
IXAT Graphics/Illustration: 42 Roger Rd, Griswold, CT 06351.......................203-376-2288
Izon Design: 1415 S Church St #B, Charlotte, NC 28203..............................704-343-0000
Izquierdo Marketing Design, Inc: 213 W Institute Pl #410,
Chicago, IL 60610 312-787-9784

J

J Brooks Potters Marketing: 111 Pacifica #120, Irvine, CA 92618 714-727-7078
Jaap Assocs, Penraat: 315 Central Park W, New York, NY 10025 212-873-4541
Jaben Design, Seth: 47 E 3rd St #3, New York, NY 10003 212-673-5631
Jablonski, Andrew: 10 W 19th St 6th Fl, New York, NY 10011 212-242-1080
Jaciow Design: 396 Grinnell Court, Santa Clara, CA 95051...........................408-984-8001
Jackmauh Design: 6 Hazel Terrace, Arlington, MA 02174 617-641-4084
Jackson Design: 300 Tenth Ave S, Nashville, TN 37203................................615-255-9335
Jacobs Creative Group: 26 Bridgecourt Ln, Concord, MA 01742 508-369-8611
Jaeger & Sons Ltd: 2445 Lyttonsville Rd #605, Silver Spring, MD 20910 301-588-1655
Jaffee Design, Lee Ann: 145 E 19th St, New York, NY 10003 212-387-0100
Jager Assocs: 25 Jefferson Pl, Grand Rapids, MI 49503 616-235-7700
Jager Dipaola Kemp Design: 47 Maple St, Burlington, VT 05401 802-864-5884
Jagoda Assocs, Don: 100 Marcus Dr, Melville, NY 11747................................516-454-1800
Jaime Graphics, Inc: 1 Central Blvd, Bethpage, NY 11714 516-931-0842
Jalbert Design, Inc: 500 Commercial St #302A, Manchester, NH 03101 603-623-8086
James Design, Doris: 2118 Summertown Dr NW, Norcross, GA 30071 770-448-7355
James Design, Peter: 7495 NW 4th St, Plantation, FL 33317 305-587-2842
James Studio, Inc: 5 Freshwater Dr, Palm Harbor, FL 345684 813-938-9553
Janicz Design Group: 200 Golf View Rd, Ardmore, PA 19003 610-649-9113
Janoski Advertising Design: 2905 N High St, Columbus, OH 43202..................614-268-9484
Jansen, Alan: 3607 Hillside Rd, Evanston, IL 60201..847-673-4777
Jantzen & Assocs, Michael: 501 Center St #11, El Segundo, CA 90245...........310-322-8016
Japan Design Network: 2186 Ellwyn Dr, Atlanta, GA 30341 770-454-0393
JAWAI Interactive: 501 E Fourth St #511, Austin, TX 78701............................512-469-0502
JC Design : 100 Westford Dr, Southport, CT 06490 203-255-5388
Jefferies Association, The: 430 S Westmoreland Ave, Los Angeles, CA 90020......213-388-4002
Jelani Design & Assocs: 2202 Trede Dr, Austin, TX 78745..............................512-442-8686
Jenkins Page Design, Inc: 244 Fifth Ave 11th Fl, New York, NY 10001............212-679-9430
Jenkins, S Laird: 4350 N Fairfax Dr #810, Arlington, VA 22203......................703-528-6216
Jennings Graphics Design, Cindy: 1021-203 Nicholwood Dr,
Raleigh, NC 27605 919-828-4741
Jensen & Assocs, Grant: 3552 Beach Dr SW, Seattle, WA 98116 206-935-7300
Jensen Group, The: 67 Maple Ave, Morristown, NJ 07960...............................201-539-5070
Jerde Partnership: 913 Ocean Front Walk, Venice, CA 90291 310-399-1987
JJ & A: 405 S Flower, Burbank, CA 91502 818-849-1444
JJ White Advertising Art: 6420 Hilltop Ln, Maumee, OH 43537 419-893-1672
JMH Corp: 921 E 66th St, Indianapolis, IN 46220 317-255-3400
JNL Graphic Design: 401 W Superior St, Chicago, IL 60610 312-640-1999
Johann Design, Damore: 300 Brannan St #610, San Francisco, CA 94107......415-957-9737
Johns Design, Sally: 1040 Washington St, Raleigh, NC 27605..........................919-828-3997
Johnson Assocs, Philip: 12 Arrow St, Cambridge, MA 02138 617-492-5899
Johnson Creative Svrcs, David: 703 Market St/Cntrl Twr #1400,
San Francisco, CA 94103..415-546-7225
Johnson Creative, Doug: 45 E 19th St, New York, NY 10003 212-260-1880
Johnson Design Group, Inc: 200 Little Falls St #410,
Falls Church, VA 22046..703-533-0550
Johnson Design Group, Inc: 447 Ada Dr, Ada, MI 49301.................................616-676-5557
Johnson Design, Ciri: PO Box 18608, Tucson, AZ 85731 520-577-0818
Johnson Design, Clifford: 365 Hamilton Pk Dr, Roswell, GA 30075 770-664-6433
Johnson Design, Dean: 646 Massachusetts Ave, Indianapolis, IN 46204..........317-634-8020
Johnson Design, Inc, Stan: 21185 W Gumina Rd Box 662,
Brookfield, WI 53008 414-783-6510
Johnson Design, Paige: 290 Lowell Ave, Palo Alto, CA 94301........................415-327-0488
Johnson Design, Tadd: 3209 Ronda de Lechusas NW,
Albuquerque, NM 87120 505-831-2120
Johnson Graphic Design, Ted: 14561 SW 152nd Ct, Miami, FL 33196 305-238-5633
Johnson Pedersen Hinrichs: 141 Lexington Ave, New York, NY 10016............212-683-5450
Johnson Rodger Design: 704 Silver Spur Rd, Rolling Hills, CA 90274 213-377-8860
Johnson, Brad: 937 Grayson St, Berkley, CA 94710...510-649-8444
Johnson, Carla: 9010 Windy Crest, Dallas, TX 75243 214-522-1449
Johnson, George: 3600 Giddings Rd, Aburne Hills, MI 48326 810-475-2500
Johnson, Iskra: 911 Western Ave #405, Seattle, WA 98108 206-340-9506
Johnson, Ken: 25 Barry Ln, Simsbury, CT 06070..860-651-3345
Johnson, Len: 200 Little Falls St #410, Falls Church, VA 22046 703-533-0550
Johnston Design Office: 5912 Bernard Pl, Edina, MN 55436 612-929-7576
Joly Major Product Design Group: 4773 Sonoma Hwy #82,
Santa Rosa, CA 95409 707-641-1933
Jones & Jane Kearns, Tom: 2803 18th St NW, Washington, DC 20009 202-232-1921
Jones Adv Design Studio, Inc: 2131-2131 Wrights Way,
Pittsburgh, PA 15203...412-381-5555
Jones Design, Brent A: 328 Hayes St, San Francisco, CA 94102 415-626-8337
Jones Design, Bruce: 31 St James Ave #303, Boston, MA 02116....................617-350-6160
Jones Design, Jacqueline: Pier 9, San Francisco, CA 94111 415-982-8484
Jones Graphic Design, Nat: 1781 Hilltop Rd, Birchrunville, PA 19421 610-469-2044
Jones, Arvell: 18700 W Ten Mile Rd, Southfield, MI 48075............................248-569-8036
Jones, Donald: 10529 Sinclair, Dallas, TX 75218...214-327-0819
Jones, Jerry: 36 S Paca St #108, Baltimore, MD 21201 301-727-4222
Jones, Richmond: 2530 W Eastwood St, Chicago, IL 60625 773-588-4900
Jones, Steve: 1081 Nowita Pl, Venice, CA 90291 213-396-9111
Jonson Pedersen Hinrichs & Shakery: 620 Davis St, San Francisco, CA 94111 415-981-6612
Jordan Assocs, Inc: 3420 Surrey Ln, Falls Church, VA 22042 703-641-9466
Joseph Design, Carolyn : 15 Mallard Ln, Westport, CT 06880 ....203 255-7769
Joslin Design, Yalta: 246 Clinton Rd, Brookline, MA 02146 617-734-4829
Joss Design Group: 1 E Erie #310, Chicago, IL 60611 312-944-0644
Joss Design Group East: 50 Bentley Pl, Upper Montclair, NJ 07043.................201-783-5700
Jowaisas Design: Oxbow Rd, Cazenovia, NY 13035..315-655-3800
Juddesign: 696 State St, San Diego, CA 92101 619-234-5405
Judson Design: 3202 1/2 Argonne St, Houston, TX 77098 713-520-1096
Juett & Assocs: 2057 E Foothill Blvd, Pasadena, CA 91107.............................818-568-8244
Julian's Web Sight: UCLA Dept of Film/TV, Los Angeles, CA 310-206-8706
Jungclaus & Kreffel Studio: 145 E 14th St, Indianapolis, IN 46202..................317-636-4891
Justdesign: 160 Fifth Ave #905, New York, NY 10010 212-620-4672
Juzenas Graphics Etc, Bob: 25190 No Bottom Rd,
Olmsted TWP, OH 44138 216-235-8088

K

K Graphic Design: 555 Magnolia St, Half Moon Bay, CA 94019 415-712-1939
K2 Design Interactive Group: 55 Broad St 7th Fl, New York, NY 10004 212-968-0047
Kaars & Assocs Inc, Nick: 1001 Bishop St #300, Honolulu, HI 96813 808-522-1366
Kacsuta Parks Design: 5725 Forward Ave #300, Pittsburgh, PA 15217 412-422-1900
Kaeser & Wilson Design: 330 Seventh Ave, New York, NY 10001.....................212-563-2455
Kaestle Design: 1123 Broadway #705, New York, NY 10010............................212-691-5991
Kageyama Design, David: Seattle, WA 206-524-7870
Kahn, Donald: 39 W 29th St 12th Fl, New York, NY 10001 212-889-8898
Kaiser Cormier: 15928 Ventura Blvd, Encino, CA 91436 818-380-0145
Kaiser Design, Kathleen: 452 Plaza Estival, San Clemente, CA 92672.............714-443-3845
Kaiserdicken: 149 Cherry St, Burlington, VT 05401 802-864-4132
Kaltenbach, Inc: 1236 Weathervane Ln #100B, Akron, OH 44313 216-867-3523
Kamei-Garnas: 54 Edgehill Way, San Francisco, CA 94127...............................415-566-0868
Kaminsky Design: 347 Congress St, Boston, MA 02210 617-422-0790
Kampa Design: 2414A S Lamar St, Austin, TX 78704 512-441-6831
Kamppila: 11937 Rising Sun Way, Gold River, CA 95670 916-635-1383
Kamren Colson Design: 225 6th St, Cincinnati, OH 45202 513-784-1616
Kandt Studio, James: 1545 N Willow Ln, Wichita, KS 67208 316-681-8628
Kaneko Metzgar Assocs Visionary: 1408 Third St Prom 3rd Fl,
Santa Monica, CA 90401 310-451-1859
Kapec Design Group, Tanaka: 18 Marshall St, South Norwalk, CT 06854.........203-852-9766
Kapp & Assocs: 2729 Prospect Ave, Cleveland, OH 44115 216-621-5144
Karlen Design: 1941 Monterey St, San Luis Obispo, CA 93401 805-541-6561
Karlin Design, James: 28 Clarks Crossing, Fairport, NY 14450 716-223-5678
Karo Design: 611 Alexander St #308, Vancouver, BC V6A 1E1 604-255-6100
Karp, Rudi: 28 Dudley Ave, Landsowne, PA 19050..215-284-5949
Kashiwagi Design, Inc: PO Box 135, Shadaken, NY 12480...............................212-832-8652
Kass Communications: 529 W 42nd St 3rd Fl, New York, NY 10036..................212-868-3133
Kass Vehlins, Inc: 333 Seventh Ave, New York, NY 10001 212-465-9206
Kassner Graphics: 4847 Hopyard Rd #3-312, Pleasanton, CA 94588 510-225-0949
Katapa Art & Design: 5 W Second St, Hinsdale, IL 60521 708-986-0992
Katz Design, Joel: 1616 Walnut St #1919, Philadelphia, PA 19103 215-985-4747
Katz Marketing Comm, Alvin: 35 E 84th St, New York, NY 10028.....................212-744-1366
Kaufman & Assocs, Henry J : 2233 Wisconsin Ave NW,
Washington, DC 20007 202-333-0700
Kaufman, Richard: 2025 Wallace St, Philadelphia, PA 19130 215-232-8722
Kaufman/Kane: 2344 Laguna Circle Ave, Agoura, CA 91301.............................818-706-7606
Kauftheil, Henry: 220 W 19th St 5th Fl, New York, NY 10011..........................212-633-0222
Kaulfuss Design: 1000 N Halsted, Chicago, IL 60622 312-943-2161
Kavin Advertising Art, Sid: 1717 Glenview Rd #205, Glenview, IL 60025.......847-998-9717
Kawai, Shelly: 10 Priscilla Rd, Norwalk, CT 06850 203-866-5685
• **Kay, Laura: pg 1448** 105 Nutley St, Ashland, OR 97520 ....**800-497-1752**
e-mail: laurakaydesign@opendoor.com / url: http://opendoor.com/laurakaydesign
• **Kay, Stanford: pg 1329** 39 Central Ave, Nyack, NY 10960 ....**914-358-0798**
e-mail: paragraphics@spryal.net / url: www.spryal.net/paragraphics / fax: 914-358-3284
Kayo & Co: 21 Colchester Rd, Weston, MA 02193 617-894-8182
Kaza Assocs, Paul: 1233 Shelburne Rd #C-3, S Burlington, VT 05403 802-863-5956
Kazmar Design Group: 355 A Central Ave, Bohemia, NY 11716 516-567-7390
KDA Industrial Design: 1785 B Cortland Ct, Addison, IL 60101.........................630-495-9466
KDS Marketing: 717 Constitution Dr #102, Exton, PA 19341 610-458-7166
Kearns Design: 1110 E Central Ave, W Carrollton, OH 45449 937-859-1579
Keaton Design & Art Direction: 1694 Electric Ave, Venice, CA 90291..............310-823-5571
Keaton, Jim: 1605 Allison St NW, Washington, DC 20011 202-328-0414
Kedar Designs: 433 College Ave, Palo Alto, CA 94306 415-326-3706
Kedash Design: 1203 Philadelphia Pike, Wilmington, DE 19809.......................302-792-1484
Keetle & Company: Two Church St #2A, Burlington, VT 05401 802-863-5313
Keithley & Assocs: 39 W 14th St #R302, New York, NY 10011 212-807-8388
Keizer Design: 801 S Sixth, Las Vegas, NV 89101 702-366-1511
Kelleher Tait Design: 121 W 27th St #1003A, New York, NY 10001 212-727-8084
Keller Design: 5235 N Diversey Blvd, Milwaukee, WI 53217 414-961-2373
Kellett Group: 1200 Fifth Ave #1910, Seattle, WA 98101 206-233-9640
Kelley Organization, Hall: 929 E Duane Ave, Sunnyvale, CA 94086 408-720-0431
Kelly & Co Design, Inc: 7490 30th Ave N, St Petersburg, FL 33710 813-341-1009
Kelly Design, Diane: 3711 Lawrence Ave, Kensington, MD 20895.....................301-949-3557
Kelsh Wilson Design: 211 N 13th St, Philadelphia, PA 19107 215-751-1114
Kelter, Joseph: 4 Village Row- Logan Sq, New Hope, PA 18938.......................215-862-4860
Kelter, Joseph: 4 Village Row-Logan Sq, New Hope, PA 18938.......................215-862-4860
Kemper Design, Denise: 505 Wintergreen Dr, Wadsworth, OH 44281 216-335-5200
Kenny Design Inc, Tim: 3 Bethesda Metro Ctr #630, Bethesda, MD 20814......301-718-9100
Kent Design: 1553 Platte #303, Denver, CO 80202 303-458-5368
Keogh, Bill: 3 Park Ave 40th Fl, New York, NY 10016 212-557-9199
Keoki Design: 19 N 2nd St #202, San Jose, CA 95113 408-298-8701
Kerbs Studio, Larry: 215 Rutgers St, Maplewood, NJ 07040............................201-378-9366
Kerr Design, Pamela: 333 S 21st St, Philadelphia, PA 19103 215-731-9902
Kessler Design Group: 6931 Alington Rd #301, Bethesda, MD 20814 301-907-3233
Ketcham Design, Matt: 1008 Western Ave #400, Seattle, WA 98104 206-624-7550
Ketchum Group, Steve: 274 N Goodman St/BoxF7, Rochester, NY 14607........716-256-0110
Ketchum International: 6 PPG Place, Pittsburgh, PA 15222 412-456-3693
Khachi Design Group: 693 S Second St#10, San Jose, CA 95112......................408-298-9636
Kharibian & Assocs: 3906 Laguna Ave, Palo Alto, CA 94306 415-858-0993
Khatkate Design, Arvind: 4837 W Jerome St, Skokie, IL 60077........................847-679-4129
Kick Design : 24 E 21st St Ph, New York, NY 10010 212-358-1151
Kildahl Design: 86 Prospect St, White Plains, NY 10606 914-428-1594
Kilpatrick Design, Don: 2512 South 150 West, Bountiful, UT 84010...............801-295-8848
Kinetik Communications Graphic: 1604 17th St NW, Washington, DC 20009 202-797-0605
King Casey, Inc: 199 Elm St, New Canaan, CT 06840.......................................203-966-3581
King Graphic Design, Jan: 84 Glen Ave, Paramus, NJ 14450 201-652-4150
King Robbins, Peter: 6525 Sunset Blvd 6th Fl, Hollywood, CA 90028..............213-962-4908
Kinneary Design: 548 Fawnhill Dr, Langhorne, PA 19047...................................215-741-6030
Kirchner Graphic Design, Amy: 5019 North Capitol Ave,
Indianapolis, IN 46403...317-475-1153
Kirkwold Assocs: 2 Appletree Sq #333, Bloomington, MN 55425 612-854-6636
Kirschner Caroff Design: 900 Broadway #1003, New York, NY 10003 212-505-2211

Kisitch, Karen: 45 W 36th St 5th Fl, New York, NY 10018 212-629-6800
Kissiloff Associates: 215 E 68th St, New York, NY 10021 212-421-8448
Kizis, Karen: 45 W 36th St 12th Fl, New York, NY 10018 212-629-6800
Kjeldsen Assocs, Howard: PO Box 420508, Atlanta, GA 30342 404-266-1897
Klaetke, Fritz: 429 Columbus Ave #1, Boston, MA 02116 617-247-3658
Klaric Design: 1154 Laurel Ave, Bridgeport, CT 06604 203-366-6547
Klein: 1111 S Robertson Blvd, Los Angeles, CA 90035 213-278-5600
Klein Design Group: 180 Old Chester Rd, Chester, NJ 07930 201-765-0770
Klein, Nikolai: 109 N 9th St #3R, Brooklyn, NY 11211 718-384-3193
Klickovich Graphics: 1638 Eastern Pkwy, Louisville, KY 40204 502-459-0295
Klim Assocs, Matt: PO Box Y Avon Park N, Avon, CT 06001 203-678-1222
Klim Design : Bldg 21/Avon Park N, Avon, CT 06001 860-678-1222
Kline Graphic Design: 304 E Market St, York, PA 17403 717-845-8738
Kline Graphics Inc, Roger: 2331 University Ave SE #121,
Minneapolis, MN 55414 612-379-8181
KLN Graphic Assocs: 15 E 30th St, New York, NY 10016 212-686-8200
Klotz, Don: 296 Millstone Rd, Wilton, CT 06897 203-762-9111
Klundt & Hosmer: 216 W Pacific #201, Spokane, WA 99204 509-456-5576
Kmg Prodution: 40 E Main St/Weir River Brick, Ware, MA 01082 413-967-9855
Knabel, Lonnie S: 8506 Suburban Dr, Orlando, FL 32829 401-381-4226
Kneapler Design, John: 31 W 21st St 8th Fl, New York, NY 10010 212-463-9774
Kneeland & Assocs, Barry: 570 Admiral St, Battle Creek, MI 49015 616-964-0898
Knowledge Adventure: 1311 Grand Central Ave, Glendale, CA 91201 818-542-4200
Knowledge/Design: 147 Cross Rd, Danville, CA 94526 510-838-2803
Knowles, Kevin: 6345-1/2 82nd Ave N, Pinellas Park, FL 33781 813-547-0599
Knox & Assocs, Harry: 9914 Locust St, Glenn Dale, MD 20769 301-464-1665
Knox, David: PO Box 30307, Mesa, AZ 85275 520-295-1726
Koc Design: 32 Seventh Ave, San Francisco, CA 99118 415-399-1539
Koch/Marshall Productions: 4310 N Mozart St, Chicago, IL 60618 773-463-4010
Kocher Communications, Jerome: PO Box 15286, Santa Rosa, CA 95402 707-539-1724
Kochi, William: 54 W 22nd St 4th Fl, New York, NY 10010 212-366-0800
Koconis Design: 231 Douglas Ave, Providence, RI 02908 401-421-5652
Koda: 8 W 19th St 2nd Fl, New York, NY 10011 212-727-7081
Koehr Design: 2103 Patrician Way St, St Louis, MO 63131 314-821-0464
Koehr, Vincent A: 2103 Patrishian Way Ct, St Louis, MO 63131 314-821-0464
Koeppen Design Inc, Kathy: 2200 N Lamour #105B, Dallas, TX 75202 214-922-0260
Kohn Design: 716 Montgomery St, San Francisco, CA 94111 415-398-1646
Komarow Design, Ronni: 214 Lincoln St #108, Allston, MA 02134 617-254-9083
Kong Design, Debbie: 935 Ontario, Oak Park, IL 60302 708-386-9441
Konig Design Group: 4001 Broadway, San Antonio, TX 78209 210-824-7387
Kopang, Jeff: 1950 Stemmons #4001, Dallas, TX 75207 214-571-0000
Korshak Creative Services: 4200 Westheimer #280, Houston, TX 77027 713-961-5061
Kosaka Design: 729 Sansome #300, San Francisco, CA 94111 415-398-9348
Kosarin, Linda: 400 W 58th St #5F, New York, NY 10019 212-261-6500
Kosh Design Studios: 6671 Sunset Blvd #1574A, Los Angeles, CA 90028 213-465-9919
Kosner Design, Anthony: 660 Vly Rd, Stone Ridge, NY 12484 914-657-6852
Kotlas, Meri: 2201 Candun Dr #100, Apex, NC 27502 919-363-4454
Kottler Caldera Group: 1201 E Jefferson #A25, Phoenix, AZ 85034 602-495-1300
Kovach Design Co: 3530 N Lake Shore Dr #2B, Chicago, IL 60657 773-935-7422
Kovin Design: 236 Lehigh Dr, Richboro, PA 18954 .... 215 968-7820
Kowler Assocs: 4706 Nicollet Ave #200, Minneapolis, MN 55409 612-822-3618
Koy Design: 4000 Westheimer #208, Houston, TX 77027 713-521-2190
Kramer & Larkin: 1934 Lombard St, Philadelphia, PA 19146 215-545-2120
Kramer Design, Mya: 604 Mission 10th Fl, San Francisco, CA 94105 415-777-4433
Kratzer Graphic Design, Karen: 294 Rock Landing Rd,
Haddam Neck, CT 06424 860-267-7441
Krause Assocs: 501 Elm St #300, Dallas, TX 75202 214-741-7500
Kreger Graphics: 7109 46th St, Chevy Chase, MD 20815 301-654-6944
Kreidel Design: 11060 Artesia Blvd #C, Cerritos, CA 90703 310-860-1418
Kremers Advtg Specialtists, Inc: 3854 Crystal SW #A, Grandville, MI 49418 616-538-0340
Krent/Paffett: 711 Atlantic Ave, Boston, MA 02111 617-451-6301
Kricket Graphics: 319 E 2nd St, Fredrick, MD 21701 301-631-0373
Krogstad, Yuguchi: 3378 W 1st St, Los Angeles, CA 90004 213-383-6915
Kroha Assocs: 573 Newfield St, Middletown, CT 06457 860-346-4650
Krohn Design: 6178 W Jefferson Blvd, Los Angeles, CA 90016 310-840-5999
Krone Group: 1007 Mumma Rd, Wormleysburg, PA 17043 717-731-9020
Krukowski & Co, Jan: 74 E 79th St 3rd Fl, New York, NY 10021 212-794-3929
Ksv Communicators: 212 Battery St, Burlington, VT 05401 802-862-8261
Kubas 11 Design Assocs, George: 13000 Athens Ave, Lakewood, OH 44107 216-521-5160
Kubota & Bender: 184 Laurel Ridge, S Salem, NY 10590 914-533-6391
Kucklick Design: 116 Las Astas Dr, Los Gatos, CA 95030 408-358-4980
Kuester Group, The: 81 S 9th St #300, Minneapolis, MN 55402 612-338-6030
Kung Assocs, Hans: 491 Broadway 9th Fl, New York, NY 10012 212-226-4842
Kuntz Design, Diane: 817 Euclid St, Santa Monica, CA 90403 310-451-3601
Kunz, R: 125 Oak Grove St #211, Minneapolis, MN 55403 612-872-0163
Kunz Assocs, Willi: 2112 Broadway #500, New York, NY 10023 212-799-4300
Kurigraphics: 10770 Minette Dr, Cupertino, CA 95014 408-725-8064
Kuzich Design, John: 350 Townsend St #304, San Francisco, CA 94107 415-543-3270

L

La Haye Design, Barney: 611 Broadway, New York, NY 10012 212-505-6802
La Perle Assocs: 330 Parkview Terrace, Oakland, CA 94610 510-444-8439
Lacy Assocs Ltd, N Lee: 8446 Melrose Pl, Los Angeles, CA 90069 213-852-1414
Ladd Assocs, Inc: 517 Georges Rd, N Brunswick, NJ 08902 908-937-5777
Laidlaw Group, The: 234 Clarendon St, Boston, MA 02116 617-536-2885
Laing Communications: 16250 NE 80th St, Redmond, WA 98052 206-869-6313
Lake Design Co, Joslin: 916 S Wabash Ave #403, Chicago, IL 60605 312-360-1833
Lake, John: 124 NW Broad St #2, Southern Pines, NC 28387 ....
Lam Design Assocs: 661 N Broadway, White Plains, NY 10603 914-948-4777
Lam/Berardin: 461 Second St #109, San Francisco, CA 94107 415-546-6779
Lamar, Laura: 302 23rd Ave, San Francisco, CA 94121 415-750-1333
Lamb & Co: 650 3rd Ave S 17th Fl, Minneapolis, MN 55402 612-333-8666
Lamont Design: 7227 Oakdale Ave, Canoga Park, CA 91306 818-709-8016
Lampert, Dave: 275 E Central Pkwy #238, Altamonte Springs, FL 32701 407-695-9000
Lamson Design, Dale: 817 Main St 2nd Fl, Cincinnati, OH 45202 513-381-6121
Lanahan, John: 39 W 38th St 10th Fl, New York, NY 10018 212-840-2912
Lancaster Design: 2900 Airport Ave #A, Santa Monica, CA 90405 310-397-7792
Landes & Assocs: 20313 Mason Court, Torrance, CA 90503 310-540-0907
Landesberg Dsgn Assocs: 1100 Bingham St, Pittsburgh, PA 15203 412-381-2220
Landis Design: 653 Bryant St, San Francisco, CA 94107 415-777-2242
Landkamer Assocs: 444 Dharo St #114, San Francisco, CA 94107 415-522-2480
Landman & Co, K: 30 W 21st St 3rd Fl, New York, NY 10010 212-924-4254
Landman, Kathy: 30 W 21st St 3rd Fl, New York, NY 10010 212-924-4254
Landor Assocs: 1301 5th Ave #1600, Seattle, WA 98101 206-223-0700
Landor Assocs: 230 Park Ave S, New York, NY 10003 212-614-5050
Landor Assocs: 1001 Front, San Francisco, CA 94111 415-955-1200
Landry Creative: 251 S clarkson St, Denver, CO 80209 303-446-9329
Lane Advertising: 21 Boaks Ln, Marblehead, MA 01945 617-631-4700
Lane Design, Emily: 1397 Kersey Lane, Potomac, MD 20854 301-424-7979
Lane/Morris: 266 Delaplane Ave, Newark, DE 19711 302-731-7370
Laney, Ron: 25 Madonna Ct, Highland, IL 62249 847-654-5142
Langdon, John: 1926 Nectarine St, Philadelphia, PA 19130 215-569-8208
Lange Design Assocs, Jim: 203 N Wabash #1312, Chicago, IL 60601 312-606-9313
Langley Design, Matthew: 2500 Q St NW #122, Washington, DC 20007 202-337-7527
Langston Cherubino Group Ltd: 835 Broadway #1507, New York, NY 10010 212-533-2585
Lapham/Miller Assocs: 34 Essex St, Andover, MA 01810 508-475-8570
Largent Studios, Herron: 3300 NE Expressway #1B, Atlanta, GA 30341 770-986-0009
Larsen Design Interacitve: 7101 York Ave S, Minneapolis, MN 55435 612-835-2271
Larson Design, Sarah: 6019 N Paulina, Chicago, IL 60660 773-465-2993
Larson, Ron: 940 N Highland Ave, Los Angeles, CA 90038 213-465-8451
Lasky Studio Inc, Carol: 30 The Fenway #C, Boston, MA 02215 617-353-0500
Latto, Sophia: 723 President St, Brooklyn, NY 11215 718-789-1980
Laufer, Joseph Mark: 2201 Penn Ave #3, Philadelphia, PA 19130 215-854-8478
Laughing Dog Design: 900 N Franklin #600, Chicago, IL 60610 312-951-8399
Laughlin/Winker, Inc: 4 Clarendon St, Boston, MA 02116 617-437-1356
Lauritsen Design, Peggy: 700 S Third St #102, Minneapolis, MN 55415 612-339-5011
Lawrence Design Group, Inc: 126 Fifth Ave #803, New York, NY 10011 212-675-4838
Lazin & Katalan: 227 W 17th St 5th Fl, New York, NY 10011 212-242-7611
• **Lazuriaga, Denis: pg 1456,1457** 39 Hamilton Terr, New York, NY 10031 ... **212-283-3401**
url: www.wayart.com
Le Brun Assocs, Inc: 853 Broadway #1607, New York, NY 10003 212-477-8969
Le Mone Advertising Design: 1702 Lincoln Ave, Pasadena, CA 91103 818-791-1811
Le Shane Jaccoma Assocs, Inc: 31 Albany Post Rd Box 327,
Montrose, NY 10548 914-736-6417
Le Van Design: 208 Spangsville Rd, Oley, PA 19547 610-689-4812
Leach Design, Molly: 37 W 20th St 10th Fl, New York, NY 10011 212-627-8361
Leach, Richard: 62 W 39th St #803, New York, NY 10018 212-869-0972
Learn Technologies Interactive: 285 W Broadway #550,
New York, NY 10013 212-334-2225
Learning Co, The: 6401 Kaiser Dr, Fremont, CA 94555 510-792-2101
Leavy Design, Robin: 2116 Wilshire #250, Santa Monica, CA 90403 310-449-7791
• **Lebbad, James A: pg 1449** 24 Independence Way, Titusville, TN 08560 ..... **609-737-3458**
New York, NY **212-645-5260**
Lebowitz Gould Design: 7 W 22nd St 7th Fl, New York, NY 10010 212-645-0550
Lebowitz, Mo: 2599 Phyllis Dr, N Bellemore, NY 11710 516-826-3397
Lecat Design: 6911 N Hamilton, Chicago, IL 60645 773-465-6580
Leckner Design Assocs: 450 Seventh Ave #2302, New York, NY 10123 212-564-4250
Ledbetter, James: 10818 Ridge Spring, Dallas, TX 75218 214-341-4858
Lee & Assocs, Michael: 221 W Ohio St, Chicago, IL 60610 312-832-1300
Lee Assocs, Alan: 296 S Great Rd, Lincoln, MA 01773 617-259-0533
Lee Assocs, Inc, Tony: 130 Ward Ave, Trenton, NJ 08609 609-989-7092
Lee Communications: 11 Conant Valley Rd, Pound Ridge, NY 10576 914-533-2325
Lee Design Inc, Clarence: 2333 Kapiolani Blvd, Honolulu, HI 96826 808-941-5021
Lee Design, Steven: 135 S Park, San Francisco, CA 94107 415-546-1701
Lee, Ken H: PO Box 1226, Brookline, MA 02146 617-277-2161
Lee, Lilly: 1021 University Ave, Berkeley, CA 94710 510-849-1900
Leed Custom Design: 26 Fishkill Hook Rd, Hopewell Junctin, NY 12533 914-896-7480
Leeds Studio, Judith K: 14 Rosemont Ct, N Caldwell, NJ 07006 201-226-3552
Leef & Assocs Inc, Naomi: 12 W 27th St 18th Fl, New York, NY 1001 212-686-6300
Lees & Assocs, John : 8 Myrtle St, Boston, MA 02114 617-248-9633
• **Lehner & Whyte: pg 1480** 8-10 S Fullerton Ave, Montclair, NJ **973-746-1335**
e-mail: lehwhy@intac.com / url: www.lehnerwhyte.com / fax: 973-746-1335
Lehrer Designs, Inc, Brad: 81 Pondfield Rd Suite#6, Bronxville, NY 10708 914-793-3001
Lehrfeld, Gerald: 701 Forum Sq #507, Glenview, IL 60025 847-297-6907
Leigh & Co, Doug: 11 Tobacco Rd, Weston, CT 06883 203-226-0779
Lekasmiller Design Inc: 3210 Old Tunnel Rd #C, Lafayette, CA 94549 510-934-3971
Lemley Design, David: 1904 3rd Ave, Seattle, WA 98101 206-682-9480
Leneker Design: 919 Stratford Ave #4, Stratford, CT 06497 203-375-0830
Lenney, Ann: 3003 Van Ness St NW, Washington, DC 20008 202-363-2729
Lennon & Assocs: 734 N Highland Ave, Los Angeles, CA 90038 213-465-5104
Lenweaver Adv & Design: 239 W Fayette St/Seneca Bldg,
Syracuse, NY 13202 315-422-8729
LEO Systems, Inc: 1505 E David Rd, Dayton, OH 45429 513-298-1503
Leong Dsgn, Russell: 847 Emerson St, Palo Alto, CA 94301 415-321-2443
Leonhardt Group: 1218 Third Ave #620, Seattle, WA 98101 206-624-0551
Leotta Designers, Inc: 303 Harry St, Conshohocken, PA 19428 215-828-8820
Lerner & Co: 24 Spring Ln, Farmington, CT 06032 860-677-7744
Les Lamotte: 3002 Keating Ct, Burnsville, MN 55337 612-894-1879
Lesdesign: 24 Country Club Dr, Olympia Fields, IL 60461 708-748-0343
Lesley-Hille, Inc: 250 E 63rd St #411, New York, NY 10021 212-759-9755
Lesniewicz Assocs: 222 N Erie St, Toledo, OH 43624 419-243-7131
Lesser/Etcetera, Joan: 3565 Greenwood Ave, Los Angeles, CA 90066 310-397-4575
Lester & Butler: 475 Fifth Ave, New York, NY 10017 212-951-6100
Letter Perfect: PO Box 785, Gig Harbor, WA 98335 206-956-9422
Letterform Design: 501 N Orange Dr, Los Angeles, CA 90036 213-932-1875
Lettergraphics: 5374 State Office Dr #2, Memphis, TN 38119 901-820-0205
Levavi & Levavi: 310 W 72nd St #9D, New York, NY 10023 212-875-8160
Levin Design, Lisa: 124 Locust Ave, Mill Valley, CA 94941 415-389-9813
Levine & Assocs: 1090 Vermont Ave NW #440, Washington, DC 20005 202-842-3660
Levine & Co: 228 Main St #5, Venice, CA 90291 310-399-9336
Levine, Ron: 1619 Williams St #202, Montreal, QU H3J 1R1 212-727-1967
toll-free 800-932-8069
Levirne, Joel: 203 Mountain Ave, Hawthorne, NJ 07506 201-423-2277
Levy Design, David: 1801 Piedmont Ave #200, Atlanta, GA 30324 404-817-7049
Lewis Design: 875 Main St 5th Fl, Cambridge, MA 02139 617-661-7145
Lewis Group Inc, Hal: 1610 Chestnut St, Philadelphia, PA 19103 215-563-4461

Marcus & Assocs Inc, Aaron: 1144 65th St #F, Emeryville, CA 94608............510-601-0994
Marcus, Sarna: 4450 Montgomery Ave #602N, Bethesda, MD 20814............301-951-7044
Marcy Design Group: 50 W Broad St #1903, Columbus, OH 43215..............614-224-6226
Marietta Corp Design Group: 37 Huntington St, Cortland, NY 13045...........800-431-3023
Marion Designs: 418 New W Townsend Rd, Lunenberg, MA 01462................508-345-4428
Marion Graphics: 2900 Weslayan #150, Houston, TX 77027.......................713-623-6444
Maritz Communication Co: 1515 W 190th St #300, Gardena, CA 90248.......310-930-0955
Mark Design, Heather: 330 Hawthorne Rd, Green Oaks, IL 60048.................847-367-9644
Mark Graphics, S: 1518 N Mohawk St, Chicago, IL 60010............................312-573-1666
Market Force: 109 N Boylan Ave, Raleigh, NC 27603...................................919-828-7887
Market Street Group: 116 Market St, Lewisburg, PA 17837..........................717-524-2367
Market To Market: 3000 Gibbons Dr, Alameda, CA 94501.............................510-865-6136
Marketing Arts: Bridge St/Market Place, Waitsfield, VT 05673........................802-496-4488
Marketing Arts: 1244 Canterbury Rd #304, Shakopee, MN 55379....................612-496-2647
Marketing By Design: 2212 K St, Sacramento, CA 95816..............................916-441-3050
Marketing Consortium, The: 114 S Catalina Ave #104,
Redondo Beach, CA 90277..310-798-8244
Marketing Creative Support Services: 813 Francis St, St Joseph, MO 64501.....816-279-5869
Marketing Design Consultants: 1259 W Belden Ave, Chicago, IL 60614..........773-404-5444
Marketing Design Group: 420 Walnut Ave, San Diego, CA 92103....................619-298-1445
Marketing Out-Of-The-Box: 7200 Oak Park Ave, Niles, IL 60714......................847-869-8250
Marketing Partners: 1109 Hinman Ave, Evanston, IL 60202...........................847-492-5180
Marketing Store, The: 5362 H St, Sacramento, CA 95819..............................916-737-7310
Markofski & Assocs, Don: 106 W Lime Ave #200A, Monrovia, CA 91016........818-359-4248
Markone Visual Communiications: 1431 Oakland Blvd #205,
Walnut Creek, CA 94596...510-945-1414
Markos, Michael: 1118 Sixth St NE, Minneapolis, MN 55413........................612-379-2133
Marks Communication: 2400 N Edgemont, Los Angeles, CA 90027.................213-664-2864
Marks Designs, Terry: 91 1/2 Pine St #24, Seattle, WA 98101......................206-628-6427
Marks, David: 726 Hillpine Dr NE, Atlanta, GA 30306..................................404-872-1824
Marks, Garson: N14W24 200 Tower Pl, Waukesha, WI 53188.........................414-523-3940
Markworks Graphic Design: 1623 Cravens Ave, Torrance, CA 90501...............310-782-8121
Marla Murphy Design: 2317 Edgewater Terr, Los Angeles, CA 90039...............213-660-5254
Marquardt Art/Design: 6526 Dana St, Oakland, CA 94609.............................510-579-1381
Marquis Graphic Design Assocs: 1509 King St, Alexandria, VA 22314...............703-519-7916
Marsh & Co: 34 W Sixth St #1100, Cincinnati, OH 45202.............................513-421-1234
Marshall, Alex: 810 E Gutierrez St #C, Santa Barbara, CA 93103....................805-962-9854
Marshall Adv Design, Pat: 3325 m St NW, Washington, DC 20007...................202-342-0222
Marshall Design & Assocs: 1109 Quail St, Newport Beach, CA 92660...............714-756-0806
Marshall Design, Catherine: 522 E 83rd St # 5E, New York, NY 10028...........212-535-4910
Marshall Design, June: 3234 Beechwood Blvd, Pittsburgh, PA 15217...............412-521-2877
Martin Design Group: 33 College Hill Rd #29C, Warwick, RI 02886...................401-822-8530
Martin Design Inc, Lynn: 435 W North Ave, Chicago, IL 60610.......................312-787-3717
Martin Design, Hardy: 2458 Walnut Ridge, Dallas, TX 75229.........................214-247-5492
Martin Design, Virginia: 47 Beverley Rd, Upper Montclair, NJ 07043...............201-744-6989
Martin Graphics: 8328 Shadyside Ave, Whittier, CA 90606............................310-695-7675
Martin Scott, Bruce: 83 Sunken Meadow Rd, Ft Salonga, NY 11768................516-757-9593
Martin, Amy: 173 E 90th St #4D, New York, NY 10128...............................212-987-2395
Martin, Janet: 1112 Pearl, Boulder, CO 80302..303-442-8202
Martinez, Fernando: 1376 Bank St #202, Ottawa, ON K1H 7Y3......................613-526-1795
Martucci, John: 116 Newbury St, Boston, MA 02116.....................................617-266-6960
Marx Design: 4704-C Prospect NE, Albuquerque, NM 87110..........................505-884-6100
Mascia Design: 155 E 31st #10A, New York, NY 10016................................212-725-2630
Masi Design Consultants, Inc: 17322 115th Ave Sw,
Vashon Island, WA 98070...206-463-6627
Masoff And Scolnik Design: 39 Fields Ln, N Salem, NY 10560........................214-277-7722
Mason, Marlise: 22974 Twin Pines Rd, Bozman, MD 21612...........................410-745-6742
Mass Design, JoAnne: 625 Hyde St #5, San Francisco, CA 94109..................415-474-1794
MASSA Design: 115 Sawsome St #1250, San Francisco, CA 94104...............415-543-5700
Mateka, Jerry: 172 Madison Ave #306, New York, NY 10016.........................212-984-3149
Matheson Design, Karen: 520 SW Sixth Ave #810, Portland, OR 97204.........503-227-6837
Mathew, Mathew K: 5801 Chinquapin Pkwy, Baltimore, MD 21239.................410-433-0035
Matjasich & Assocs: 408 Bluebird Ln, Deerfield, IL 60015...........................847-541-0443
Matrix Graphic Design, Inc: 3350 Cork Oak Way, Palo Alto, CA 94303............415-852-9316
Matrix Int'l: 50 S Steele #875, Denver, CO 80209.....................................303-388-9353
Matson Navigation: 333 Market St 3rd Fl/POB 7452,
San Francisco, CA 94120...415-957-4534
Matsumoto Design: 220 W 19th St 9th Fl, New York, NY 10011....................212-807-0248
Matt Designs: 40 Devoe Rd, Chappaqua, NY 10514....................................914-238-1082
Matthews, Robert: 1101 Boise Dr, Campbell, CA 95008...............................408-378-0878
Mattingly Design, George: 820 Miramar Ave, Berkeley, CA 94707..................510-525-2098
Mauck & Assocs, Inc: 303 Locust St, Des Moines, IA 50309.........................515-243-6010
Mauk Design: 636 Fourth St, San Francisco, CA 94107...............................415-243-9277
Maurer Graphics, Glenn: 4014 Wexford Dr, Kensington, MD 20895................301-933-9527
Maurice Assocs, Paul: 138 Spring St 6th Fl, New York, NY 10012.................212-925-4224
Max Communications: 1281 Becket Dr, Atlanta, GA 30319...........................770-451-5567
Max Graphics: 1820 Poplar Ave, Redwood City, CA 94061.............................415-322-2647
May & Co: 5401 N Central Expwy #325, Dallas, TX 75205............................214-528-4770
Maya Design Group: 2100 Wharton St, Pittsburg, PA 15203.........................412-488-2900
Mayeda, Scott: 1908 Wandering Rd, Encinitas, CA 92024...........................619-284-9692
Mayer Assocs, Gene: 9 Depot St 2nd Fl, Milford, CT 06460.........................203-882-5990
Mayfield Design: 616 Ramona St #1, Palo Alto, CA 94301............................415-322-2647
• **Mcbee, Scott: pg 1457** 39 Hamilton Terr, New York, NY 10031...................**212-283-3401**
url: www.wayart.com
McBride, Tom: 509 N Robertson Blvd, Los Angeles, CA 90048........................310-247-1922
McCall Assocs, Anthony: 11 Jay St, New York, NY 10013..............................212-925-5821
McCargar Design: 3906 Silverado Trail, Calistoga, CA 94515.........................707-942-2292
McCarthy Designs: 1851 Heritage Ln #281, Sacramento, CA 95815.................916-927-7000
McCarthy, Sally: 38 Montvale Ave #225, Stoneham, MA 02180.......................781-438-8812
Mccauley Coren Design Grp: 150 Chestnut St, Providence, RI 02903..............401-831-1290
McCausland Design & Comm: 108-110 Kenwood Dr/POB 191,
Belmont, NC 28012..704-825-0665
McChesney Design: 122 Madison, San Antonio, TX 78204............................210-227-0225
McChesney Design: 8 Laurel Way, old Saybrook, CT 06475..........................860-388-2349
McClanahan Graphics, Inc: 107 W Main St #1, Heber Springs, AR 72543.........501-362-4038
McClary, Andrew: 3706 N Ocean Blvd #360, Ft Lauderdale, FL 33308...........954-783-3363
McCord Graphic Design: 2014 Cherokee Pkwy #O, Louisville, KY 40204.........502-451-0383
McCord, David: 3890 Potters Rd, Ionia, MI 48846......................................800-997-9913
McCoy & McCoy Assocs: PO Box 2001, Buena Vista, CO 81211......................719-395-4036
Mccoy Design: 331 Wethersfield Ave, Hartford, CT 06114............................203-296-6620
McCrarey Group: 3838 Carson St #218, Torrance, CA 90503.........................310-316-9363
McCulley Group, The: 434 W Cedar St #300, San Diego, CA 92101................619-236-8700
McCulley, Mike: 4041 Bosque Dr, Plano, TX 75074.....................................214-423-0703
Mccullough Design: 15 Lakeridge Dr, Marlborough, CT 06447.......................860-295-8145
McDill Assocs: 2901 San Jose Rd Box 100, Soquel, CA 95073.......................408-462-3198
McDonald Design, Daniel: 623 Carroll St, Brooklyn, NY 11215......................718-783-9757
McDonough & Co: 40 Lowell St #21, Peabody, MA 01960............................508-532-5959
McElligott, Fallow: 79 Fifth Ave 14th Fl, New York, NY 10003......................212-206-7900
McFetridge, Geoff: 2014 Las Palmas, Los Angeles, CA 90068.......................213-874-0579
McGrath Design, Michael: 1713 Chelsey Ln, Richardson, TX 75082................214-644-4358
McGuire Design, Robert L: 7943 Campbell, Kansas City, MO 64131................816-523-9164
McGurren Weber Ink: 705 King St 3rd Fl, Alexandria, VA 22314....................703-548-0003
McHorney Marketing: 4725 E Cholla, Phoenix, AZ 85258.............................602-953-9768
McKee Design, Inc: 1415 Trestle Glen Rd, Oakland, CA 94610......................510-893-6933
McKiernan Studio: 3088 Walnut Ave, Long Beach, CA 90807........................310-426-1888
McLaughlin, Kim: 921 SW Morrison #530, Portland, OR 97205......................503-225-9957
McLuckie Design Assocs: 74 Old Hart Rd, Barrington, IL 60010....................847-382-8111
McMichael Design, Scott: 247 Claremont Ave, Montclair, NJ 07042................201-746-9709
McMillan Assocs: 130 Washington St, W dundee, IL 60118..........................847-426-3500
McMillin Giacalone Thompson: 12 New Providence Rd, Watchung, NJ 07060......908-322-7707
McNall Adv & Design: 739 E Walnut St #200, Pasadena, CA 91101.................818-796-0495
Mcnally Temple, Inc: 1817 Capital Ave #A, Sacramento, CA 95814................916-447-8186
McNamee Group, Inc: 39-19 45th St, Sunnyside, NY 11104..........................718-784-4373
McNeir, Kyle A: 2902 Galt Pl, Kennesaw, GA 30144..................................770-419-9901
Mcwilliams Assocs, George: 600 Montgomery St 27th Fl,
San Francisco, CA 94111..415-983-4195
MDB Communications, Inc: 932 Hungerford Dr Bldg 24,
Rockville, MD 20850..301-762-4474
Mdg Design Group: 236 Hamilton Ave, Palo Alto, CA 94301........................415-322-5696
ME Graphics: 618 B Moulton Ave, Los Angeles, CA 90031..........................213-225-2631
Me Myself & I, Inc: 150 S 600 East #8C, Salt Lake City, UT 84102...............801-322-0665
Meadows & Fowler, R: 2200 Lakeshore Dr, Birmingham, AL 35209................205-870-5211
Medechi Design, Inc: 480 Canal St 6th Fl, New York, NY 10013...................212-941-9111
Media Affiliates: 1805 E Indian School Rd #11, Phoenix, AZ 85016..............602-279-4559
Media Architects/MM Resources: 7320 SW Hunzicker Rd #305,
Portland, OR 97223...503-639-2505
Media Concepts: 1052b North Fifth St, San Jose, CA 95112........................408-288-8010
Media Concepts: 25 N Main St, Assonet, MA 02702...................................617-437-1382
Media Direct: PO Box 302, Tenafly, NJ 07670..201-894-5548
Media Five Ltd, Inc: 345 Queen St 9th Fl, Honolulu, HI 96813.....................808-524-2040
Media Loft: 333 Washington Ave N #210, Minneapolis, MN 55401..................612-375-1086
Media Mix: 3898 Filion St, Los Angeles, CA 90065....................................213-344-3714
Media of the Minds: 701 Minnesota St #202, San Francisco, CA 94107..........415-201-1179
Media Process Group: 770 N Halstead St #507, Chicago, IL 60622................312-850-1300
Media Services Corp: 10 Aladdin Ter, San Francisco, CA 94133....................415-928-3033
Media Shop: 77 Franklin St #507, Boston, MA 02110..................................617-482-6334
Media Studio, Inc: 1115 Erie St, Oak Park, IL 60302..................................708-386-7562
Media Wave Resources: 215 W 91st St #57, New York, NY 10024..................212-787-0700
MediaDesign International: PO Box 731, Redondo Beach, CA 90277...............310-798-3668
MediaFour, Inc: 7638 Trail Run Rd, Falls Church, VA 22042........................703-573-6117
MediaSense: 383 Arkansas St, San Francisco, CA 94107............................415-285-7655
Medius IV: 52d Colin P Kelly Jr St #101, San Francisco, CA 94107...............415-905-6959
Mednick Group, The: 8522 National Blvd #101, Culver City, CA 90232..........310-842-8444
Meek Inc, Steve : 743 W Buena St, Chicago, IL 60613...............................773-477-8055
MegaMedia, Inc: 137 S Easton Rd, Glenside, PA 19038.............................215-576-7050
Meis Creative Comms: 900 Dawson Rd, Austin, TX 78704...........................512-447-5332
Melanson Assocs, Donya: 437 Main St, Charlestown, MA 02129....................617-241-7300
Melboume, Laura: 5715 Chapman Mill Dr, Rockville, MD 20852....................301-468-1052
Melia Design Group: 905 Berninia Ave, Atlanta, GA 30307..........................404-659-5584
Mellish Creative Svrcs, David: 5020 Rosario Ave, Atascadero, CA 93422.........805-462-1104
Melone Adv & Graphic Design: 615 First St, Canonsburg, PA 15317...............412-746-5165
Melone, Michael: RD 3 Box 123, Canonsburg, PA 15317.............................412-746-5165
Menasha Corparte Art Center: N83 W13280 Leon Rd,
Menomonee Falls, WI 53051...414-253-8681
Mendel, Melissa: 150 California St, Newton, MA 02158..............................617-969-6700
Mendez, Nancy: 9816 Rosensteel Ave, Silver Spring, MD 20910...................301-608-8075
Mendoza Design: 9 W Aylesbury Rd #8, Timonium, MD 21093......................410-560-6892
Menghan, Patti: 665 Third St, San Francisco, CA 94107.............................415-243-8244
Mentken, Robert: 51 E 97th St, New York, NY 10029.................................212-534-5101
Mentler & Co: 4819 Broadway, Dallas, TX 75248......................................214-233-1414
Mentus Incorporated: 8910 University Cntr Ln #750, San Diego, CA 92122.....619-455-5500
Mercer Design: 6730 El Carmen, Long Beach, CA 90815..............................310-431-5974
Mercury Creative Services: 825 Eighth Ave 26th Fl, New York, NY 10019.......212-603-7901
Mercury Int'l Corp: 19 Alice Agnew Dr Box 222, N Attleboro, MA 02761..........508-699-9000
Mercury Neon: 104 E Seventh St, New York, NY 10009...............................212-473-6366
Meridian Creative Group: 5178 Station Rd, Erie, PA 16510..........................814-898-2612
Merrifield/Centennial Plaza: 3161 Colchester Dr SE, Ada, MI 49301...............616-956-6511
Merrill Design, David: 4 N Pasture Rd, Westport, CT 06880.........................203-222-1781
Merrill, John: 123 Albany Shaker Rd, Albany, NY 12211..............................518-447-5660
Merry Men Design: 13 Water St, Holliston, MA 01746.................................508-429-0755
Merten Design Group: 3235 E Second Ave, Denver, CO 80206.......................303-322-1451
Mervil Paylor Design: 1917 Lennox Ave, Charlotte, NC 28203......................704-375-4435
Mesmerize: 701 Santa Monica Blvd #300, Santa Monica, CA 90401...............310-656-1200
Messing & Assocs: Viamonte 640 4th Fl, Buenos Aires, Argntn, ...541-322-6948
Met Design: 240 E 27th St #17N, New York, NY 10016...............................212-689-0505
Meta 4 Digital Design: 1 Evertrust Plz, Jersey City, NJ 07302.....................201-309-0005
Meta Design: 350 Pacific Ave, San Francisco, CA 94111.............................415-627-0790
Meta-4: 311 W superior #504, Chicago, IL 60610......................................312-337-4674
Metafor Imaging, Inc: 3962 Ince, Culver City, CA 90232............................310-287-3777
Metagraphics: 43-27 222 St, Bayside, NY 11361..718-428-2718
Metal Studio, Inc: 1210 W Clay #13, Houston, TX 77019............................713-523-5777
Metropolis Corp: 56 Broad St, Milford, CT 06460.......................................203-878-2600
Metropolis Dsgn & Adv: 53 River St, Milford, CT 06460..............................203-878-2600
Meyer Design Assocs: 557 Danbury Rd, Wilton, CT 06897...........................203-834-1366
Meyer, Bonnie: 259 Collignon Way #2A, River Vale, NJ 07675......................201-666-5763
Meyers Design, Ann: 24 Fifth Ave #1201, New York, NY 10011...................212-995-8340

Meyrowitz Design, Randy: 9404 Fox Hollow Dr, Potomac, MD 20854 301-299-2923
MG Advertising: 6308 South Emporia Cir, Englewood, CO 80111 303-694-0253
MG Design: 3 Forest Ln, Canton, CT 06019 860-693-1186
MGK Design: 20 Roe Ave, East Patchogue, NY 11772 516-475-8661
MH Segan & Co: 18 E 16th St, New York, NY 10003....................................212-741-0002
Michaelis Carpelis Design: 60 E 42nd St #1730, New York, NY 10165..............212-867-8190
Micolucci Design Assocs: 515 Shoemaker Rd, King Of Prussia, PA 19406........610-265-3320
MicroColor, Inc: 2345 Broadway #638, New York, NY 10024.........................212-787-0500
Micromedia Systems: 144 W 27th St #12, New York, NY 10001 212-924-5727
Middleton Design: 1200 South Church St #10, Mt Laurel, NJ 08054 609-722-1411
Middleton Design, David: 4536 N Sacramento Ave, Chicago, IL 60625............773-463-4690
Mig Design Works: 800 First Ave, Berkeley, CA 94710..................................510-849-0560
• **Mihaesteanu, Lucian: pg 1457** 39 Hamilton Terr, New York, NY 10031 ......**212-283-3401**
url: www.wayart.com
Miho Co: 1045 Fifth Ave, New York, NY 10028...212-288-2070
Mikell, Don: 9909 Highway 36 E, Lacey's Spring, AL 35754 205-880-7435
Milan Concept & Design, Inc: 26 Lawrence Dr, Groton, MA 01450 508-448-3958
Miles Fridberg Molinaroli: 4401 Connecticut Ave NW #701,
Washington, DC 20008 202-966-7700
Mill Race Studio: Durham Rd/Brick House Opp Po, Durham, PA 18039 610-346-8117
Miller & Assocs, Bob : 2021 N St #100, Sacramento, CA 95814....................916-448-3878
Miller & Schwartz: 29341 1/2 Beverly Glen Cir #419,
Los Angeles, CA 90077...818-907-1493
Miller & White Adv: 328 S 5th St, Terre Haute, IN 47807 812-232-2875
Miller Assocs: 361 Forest Ave #202, Laguna Beach, CA 92651......................714-497-2384
Miller Brooks Assocs: 11712 N Michigan Rd, Zionzville, IN 46077 317-873-8100
Miller Design, Victoria: 10650 Kinnard Ave #311, Los Angeles, CA 90024 310-473-3489
Miller Designs, Inc, Randy: 1231 E 38th St, Tulsa, OK 74105 918-744-9621
Miller Designworks: 200 Lincoln Ave #230, Phoenixville, PA 19460 610-917-0100
Miller, Edward: 231 Willow Ave #1L, Hoboken, NJ 07030...............................201-420-6457
Miller-Hobbs, Nancy: 474 Marine St, Boulder, CO 80302..............................303-444-5508
Miller/Zell Design Center: 4715 Frederick Dr SW, Atlanta, GA 30336...............404-691-7400
Mills Design: 4400 Chippewa Dr, Boulder, CO 80303 303-494-2109
Millyard Design Assocs, Ltd: 6 Claybrook Rd, Dover, MA 02030......................508-785-9843
Milwaukee Design: 735 Wyenel Dr, Elm Grove, WI 53122...............................414-797-9420
Mind of the Machine: 41 Tamara Dr, Roosevelt, NJ 08555 609-448-5036
Mind's Eye Design: 11666 Goshen Ave, Brentwood, CA 90049.........................310-444-7387
Minkus & Assocs: 100 Chetwynd Dr #200, Rosemont, PA 19010......................610-525-6769
Mint Visual Comm: 927 Rose Ave, Oakland, CA 94611....................................510-601-8188
Mirenburg, Barry L: 301 E 38th St, New York, NY 10016................................212-573-9200
• **Mires Design: pg 1442,1443**
2345 Kettner Blvd, San Francisco, CA 92101 ....**619-234-6631**
url: www.miresdesign.com / fax: 619-234-1807
Mirror Ball Studios: 707 N Lincoln St, Arlington, VA 22201 703-243-5335
Miska, John: 192 E Wallings Rd, Cleveland, OH 44147 216-526-0464
Mistretta, Tony: 223 W Erie St #5EC, Chicago, IL 60610...............................312-751-4005
Mitchell & Co: 11221 Riverview Dr, Potomac, MD 20854 301-765-0979
Mitchell & Co Grphc Dsgn, Inc: 3247 Q St NW, Washington, DC 20007 202-342-6025
Mitchell & Witchell: 1101 Stinson Blvd NE, Minneapolis, MN 55413...................612-379-1649
Mitchell Design, Dean: 10219 Caminito Pitaya, San Diego, CA 92131 ....619 566-1032
Mitchell Design, Inc: 1199 Yorkshire Dr, Cupertino, CA 95014........................408-257-8291
Mitchell Design/CA: 728 Emerson, Palo Alto, CA 94301 415-463-1938
Mitchell Studios Dsgn Cnsltnts: 1111 Fordham Ln, Woodmere, NY 11598.......516-374-5620
Mitten Design: 604 Mission St #820, San Francisco, CA 94105 415-896-5386
Mittlemam/Robinson: 3 W 18th St 2nd Fl, New York, NY 10011........................212-627-5050
Mixed Media Works: 7 Great Valley Pkwy #100, Malvern, PA 19355 610-832-5960
Mixit Productions: 465 Washington St, New York, NY 10013............................212-966-4910
Miyasaki Assocs: 291 E Pondarosa Ln, Anaheim, CA 92802 714-750-9610
Miyauchi Design, John: 923 E Third St #304, Los Angeles, CA 90013 213-621-2828
Miyawaki Creative: 1201 1st Ave S #326, Seattle, WA 98134 206-587-6530
Mize Advertising Art, Charles E: 633 Battery St #200,
San Francisco, CA 94111..415-421-1548
Mizerek Design: 318 Lexington Ave 2nd Fl, New York, NY 10016....................212-689-4885
Mizrahi, Robert: 6256 San Harco Cir, Buena Park, CA 90620..........................714-527-6182
Mizuno Design Assocs: 32129 Lindero Canyon Rd #103,
Westlake Village, CA 91361 818-865-6181
MJH Design: 1839 rustic Oak, Chesterfield, MO 63017..................................314-532-5127
Mkr Design: 250 W Broadway, New York, NY 10013.......................................212-343-8611
Mlawer, Barbara: 477 Roy St, W Hempstead, NY 11552..................................516-564-1193
MLH Communications Group: 51 Madison Ave #1201, New York, NY 10010 212-576-5916
Mlodock Hansen: 350 W Ontario #601, Chicago, IL 60610..............................312-943-1800
MM Design 2000: 20 W 20th St 4th Fl, New York, NY 10011..........................212-206-0323
Mobium: 200 World Trade Center #2000, Chicago, IL 60654 312-527-0500
Mobium Corp: 200 Varick #502, New York, NY 10014 212-727-2449
Mobius Design Assocs: 715 Broadway #320, Santa Monica, CA 90401 310-458-9458
Mock Design Assocs Inc, Mark: 1738 Wynkoop St #303, Denver, CO 80202......303-292-0801
Modern Education Services: 381 Park Ave S #713, New York, NY 10016...........212-696-5050
Modern Media Ventures: 1317 Hyde St, San Francisco, CA 49109 415-928-7564
Moderns, The: 900 Broadway #903, New York, NY 10003...............................212-387-8852
Modino, Maureen: 225 Lafayette St #511, New York, NY 10012.......................212-431-4354
Modular Graphic Services, Inc: 621 N Fourth St, Wilmington, NC 28403 910-791-1441
Modus Exhibit Dsgn: 1059 E 900 S #100, Salt Lake City, UT 84105................801-531-7775
Modus Interactive: 5101 Wisconsin Ave NW #302, Washington, DC 20016 202-537-0323
Moewe, Thomas: 4613 Philips Hwy #204, Jacksonville, FL 32207...................904-778-8568
Mok Designs, Clement: 600 Townsend St PH, San Francisco, CA 94103..........415-703-9900
Molecular Design Ltd: 5347 Lenore Ave, Livermore, CA 94550 510-373-9952
Mollica Design: 850 3rd Ave 11th Fl, New York, NY 10011...............................212-508-3446
Molten Cube Graphics and Sound: 4647 Bloomsbury Dr, Syracuse, NY 13215 315-469-3317
Mom & Pop Web Services: 6503 38th NE, Seattle, WA 206-528-5676
Monaco Viola, Inc: 351 W Hubbard #602, Chicago, IL 60610...........................312-245-7400
Monderer Design, Stewart: 10 Thacher St #112, Boston, MA 02113.................617-720-5555
Monigle & Assocs Inc, Glenn: 150 Adams, Denver, CO 80206..........................303-388-9358
Monkeyhouse Design: 5430 LBJ Freeman #1100, Dallas, TX 75240 972-776-8066
Monnens Addis Design: 2515 9th St, Berkeley, CA 94710................................510-704-7500
Monogram Group, The: 205 W Wacker #900, Chicago, IL 60606......................312-726-4300
Monroe Creative Partners: 1435 Walnut St #600, Philadelphia, PA 19102 215-563-8080
Mont Assocs, Howard: 132 E 35th St, New York, NY 10016 212-683-4360
Montague Ferry Dsgn Consltnts: 219 Lytton Ave, Pittsburgh, PA 15213 412-682-0661
Montano Inc, Daniel: 1616 17th St #369, Denver, CO 80202.........................303-628-5440
Monti Designs, Ron: 27 Ruxview Ct #102, Baltimore, MD 21204 410-823-8451
Montiero Design: 3 Winslow St, Plymouth, MA 02360....................................808-747-6236
Moody-Kleinfeld Design: 16 W 22 St 10th Fl, New York, NY 10010 212-463-0960
Moonink, Inc: 205 N Michigan Ave #1300, Chicago, IL 60601 312-565-0040
Moore & Assocs: 7 Riedesel Ave, Cambridge, MA 02138 617-497-1277
Moore & Price Design Group, Inc: 163 Everrett Ave, Palo Alto, CA 94301........415-322-9796
Moore Design, Inc, Dave: 3232 E Campbell, Phoenix, AZ 85018....................602-955-0775
Moorhead Design: 116A Research Dr, Milford, CT 06460..............................203-874-6441
Morales Adv & Design, Frank: 12770 Coit Rd #905, Dallas, TX 75251 214-233-0667
Moran Design Corp: 438 Fayette St, Hammond, IN 46240 219-931-2825
Moran, Jeffrey: 31 Mill Hill Rd, Woodstock, NY 12498..................................914-679-8065
Morava Oliver Berte: 2054 Broadway, Santa Monica, CA 90404 310-453-3523
Moravick, Don: 229 W Illinois St 5th Fl, Chicago, IL 60610.............................312-645-4500
Morey & Waddell: 8440 Woodfield Crossing Blvd #550,
Indianapolis, IN 46240...317-469-2222
Morgan & Co: 340 E Palm Ln #120, Phoenix, AZ 85004 602-256-0036
Morgan Interactive: 450 Mission St #5, San Francisco, CA 94105 415-693-9506
Morgan-Burchette Assocs: 6935 Arlington Rd, Bethesda, MD 20814 703-549-2393
Mori & Kei Designs: 30 E 20th St #202, New York, NY 10002.......................212-260-2328
Moriber & Company: 420 Lexington Ave #2034, New York, NY 10170 212-599-2277
Morla Design: 463 Bryant St, San Francisco, CA 94107 415-543-6548
Morris Design: 1030 Preakness Ave, Wayne, NJ 07470 201-956-7787
Morris Design Assocs, David: 66 York St, Jersey City, NJ 07302....................201-434-7797
Morris Design, Don: 106 E 19th St 8th Fl, New York, NY 10003.....................212-228-3364
Morris, Carroll: 6323 Mill Point Cir, Dallas, TX 75248.....................................214-931-5762
Morris/Stylism, Dean: 307 E 6th St #4B, New York, NY 10003 212-420-0673
Morrow, Michael: 5508 Dorset Shoals Rd, Douglasville, GA 30135 770-949-2745
Mortensen Design: 416 Bush St, Mountain View, CA 94041 415-988-0946
Mortier, R Shamms: Rocky Dale, Bristol, VT 05443 802-453-4293
Morvil Design, Inc: 3803 Wrightsville Ave #11, Wilmington, NC 28403.............910-791-1441
Mosaic Creative: 2702 McKinney Ave #203, Dallas, TX 75204 214-943-6913
Mosaic Design: 38 Montvale Ave #225, Stoneham, MA 02180........................617-438-8812
Moser Design Group, Inc: 153 South State St, Hampshire, IL 60140 847-683-7080
Moshier, Harry: 15 E 12th St 2nd Fl, New York, NY 10003 212-645-7554
Moskof & Assocs: 928 Broadway #807, New York, NY 10010 212-473-1707
Moss Hartman: 1501 Main St #202, Venice, CA 90291 310-314-8622
Moss, John C: 4805 Bayard Blvd, Chevy Chase, MD 20816 301-320-3912
Mossberg Design, Stuart: 11 W 73rd St, New York, NY 10023........................212-873-6130
Mosseau Beaulieu Graphic Dsgn: 8477 Farmgate Path, Cicero, NY 13009 315-698-1213
Mossman Assocs: 1600 NW 2nd Ave #14, Baton Raton, FL 33432...............407-368-5668
Mosswarner Comms, Inc: 56 Arbor St, Hartford, CT 06106............................203-233-5641
Mott & Assocs, Robert: 1133 Columbia St #201, San Diego, CA 92101 619-231-9542
Moulton Assocs: 17 Harding Ave, Falmouth, ME 04105 207-781-5243
Mountain Adv, Patrick: 59 N Santa Cruz Ave #M, Los Gatos, CA 95030 408-395-0017
Moving Graphics: 10331 Almato Ave #3, Los Angeles, CA 90064....................310-286-0969
Mozdren, Jim: 1121 E Main St #150, St Charles, IL 60174...............................630-513-555
MPC: 4 W 20th St, New York, NY 10011 212-463-8585
Mr Tees Imprinted Sportswear: 649 W Gaines St, Tallahassee, FL 32304.........904-561-8337
Mraz Design: 1721 Delaware Ave, Wilmington, DE 19806..............................302-658-9060
Mraz Design, Anderson: 103 E 1st Ave, Spokane, WA 99202 509-624-4029
Mrk&R: 1940 Fifth Ave, Pittsburgh, PA 15219...412-471-2323
Muccino Design Group: 448 S Market St, San Jose, CA 95113.......................408-993-1870
Mueller & Wister Studio: 801 E Germantown Pike #J-4,
Morristown, PA 19401 610-278-7260
Muhlhausen Design, John: 1146 Green St, Roswell, GA 30075......................770-642-1146
Muller & Co: 4739 Belleview Ave, Kansas City, MO 64112..............................816-531-1992
Muller Design: 1124 De Haro St #700, San Francisco, CA 94107 415-642-9481
Muller-Munk Assocs, Peter: 501 Martindale St, Pittsburgh, PA 15212 412-323-2992
Mulligan & Mulligan: 225 W Ohio St #280, Chicago, IL 60610 312-467-0141
Mulligan, Donald: 418 Central Park W #81, New York, NY 10025.....................212-666-6079
Multimedia Business Presentations: 4350 17th St, San Francisco, CA 94114......310-785-0512
Multimedia Connection, The: 3517 Manhattan Ave,
Manhattan Beach, CA 90266 310-785-0512
MultiMedia Makers: 1855 Carmel Valley, CA 93924 408-659-2845
Multimedia Mason: 158 Staples Ave, San Francisco, CA 94112 415-586-4718
Multimedia Strategies, Irving: 3720 Millswood Dr, Irving, TX 75062 214-650-1986
Multimedia Works Group: 27 Red Coat Rd, Westport, CT 06880 203-221-8352
Multimedia Workshop: PO Box 44-37, Somerville, MA 02144.........................617-646-1480
Mulvany, Mark: 6770 W 19th Pl #6-208, Lakewood, CO 80214.......................303-233-7610
Mumford Design: 65 1st Ave, Atlantic Highla, NJ 07716 908-872-7245
Murphy & Friends, Harry: 58 Hickory Rd, Fairfax, CA 94930..........................415-454-1672
Murphy Design, Daina: 26 Seaview Ave, Marblehead, MA 01945 617-639-1264
Murphy Epson: 130 E Chestnut St, Columbus, OH 43215 614-221-2885
Murphy Graphic Design, Rosemary: 1216 Arch St #2C,
Philadelphia, PA 19107..215-977-7093
Murray & Assocs: 1520 Brookside Dr #3, Raleigh, NC 27604 919-828-0653
Murray Design: 626 S Clark 9th Fl, Chicago, IL 60605...................................312-362-1106
Murray Lienhart Rysner & Co: 58 W Huron Ave, Chicago, IL 60610 312-943-5995
Murrell Design Group: 1280 W Peachtree St #20, Atlanta, GA 30309 404-892-5494
Musgrave & Friends: 444 Pearl #A-5, Monterey, CA 93940............................408-649-3122
Mutsumi Gregg Design: 249 Alpine St #53, Pasadena, CA 91106.....................818-449-5752
MVP : 111 3rd Ave S #230, Minneapolis, MN 55401 612-332-8939
MY Creative Service: 317 W 93rd St #3A, New York, NY 10025.......................212-316-9101
Mydlach Design: 1260 N Prospect Ave #708, Milwaukee, WI 53202..................414-276-7090
Myers & Assocs, Loren: 4553 Glencoe Ave #365, Marina Del Rey, CA 90292.....310-306-7626
Myers Assocs, Gene: 5575 Hampton, Pittsburgh, PA 15206 412-661-6314
Mystic View Design: 88 Captains Row, Chelsea, MA 02150.............................617-889-3030

N

N Vision III: 709 Fifth Ave, San Rafael, CA 94901 415-459-5077
NACA: 13 Harbison Way, Columbia, SC 29212 803-732-6222
Nadeau Copy & Design, Greg: 65 Christian Hill Rd, Amherst, NH 03031..........603-673-9366
Naganuma Design & Direction: 1100 Montgomery St,
San Francisco, CA 94133..415-433-4484
Naganuma Design, Tony K: 1100 Montgomery St, San Francisco, CA 94133.......415-433-4484
Nagel, Jan: 9340 Eton Ave, Chatsworth, CA 91311 818-727-2120
Nak, Inc: 29 E 10th St 5th Fl, New York, NY 10003.......................................212-505-9290
Nancekivell Group, The: 400 N First St #100, Minneapolis, MN 55401..........612-341-8003

Nancy, Stentz: 420 Lexington Ave #2760, New York, NY 10170 212-697-8525
Napoleon Art: 460 W 42nd St 2nd Fl, New York, NY 10036..........................212-967-6655
Napoleon Art Studio: 460 W 42nd St, New York, NY 10036..........................212-279-2000
Napoles Design Group, Inc: 89 Madrone Ave, Lark Spur, CA 94939.................415-927-8600
Napolitano & Co: 433 E 82nd St, New York, NY 10028 212-988-3686
Nassar Design: 560 Harrison Ave, Boston, MA 02118.....................................617-482-1464
Naughton & Assocs, Carol: 213 W Institute Pl #708, Chicago, IL 60610 312-951-5353
Navratil Art/Design: 717 Liberty Ave/1305 Clark Bld, Pittsburgh, PA 15222 412-471-4322
Nearing Design: 100 Park Blvd #56B, Cherry Hill, NJ 08034 609-354-2328
Needham Design: 22323 Kittridge St, Woodland Hills, CA 91303 818-348-6704
Negin Editiorial & Design Svcs: 1545 18th St NW #712,
Washington, DC 20036 202-332-8676
Nehmen & Kodner: 1507 McCausland, St Louis, MO 63117 314-644-0114
Neiger Design: 1104 Asbury Ave, Evanston, IL 60202....................................847-328-1648
Neill, Richard: 9724 Olive St, Bloomington, CA 92316.................................714-877-5824
Neitzel, John: 152 W 25th St 12th Fl, New York, NY 10001 212-989-2236
Neitzel, John: 152 W 25th St 12th Fl, New York, NY 10001 212-989-2236
Nellis, Ryan: 1101 S Tremaine Ave, Los Angeles, CA 90019............................213-934-7118
Nelson Assocs, Louis: 80 University Pl, New York, NY 10003 212-620-9191
Nelson, Irene: 5749 Landregan St, Emeryville, CA 94608..............................510-654-6050
Neoscape, Inc: 700 Massachusetts Ave, Cambridge, MA 02139.......................617-354-1085
Nesheim & Assocs: 3741 Stewart Ave #A, Los Angeles, CA 90066 310-390-6900
Nesnady & Schwartz: 10803 Magnolia Dr, Cleveland, OH 44106.......................216-791-7721
Nestor/Stermole Design: 19 West 21st St #602, New York, NY 10010...........212-229-9377
Network Connections: 668 W Oakdale, Chicago, IL 60657 312-868-1378
Network Design Studio: 276 Bowery 3rd Fl, New York, NY 10012....................212-431-4675
Neuhaus/Griffin: 1215 E Robinson St, Orlando, FL 32801 407-898-1178
Neumann & Friends, Steve: 2405 Bartlett St, Houston, TX 77098 713-629-7501
Neville Graphic Design: 892 Worchester St, Wellesley, MA 02181..................617-235-2727
New Concepts Product Design: 7960 Convoy Ct, San Diego, CA 92111 619-576-7222
New Dawn Productions: 675 Line Rd, Matawan, NJ 07747...............................908-583-0610
New Idea Design: 3702 S 16th St, Omaha, NE 68107......................................402-733-6169
New Media Designs: 1 Little John Lane, Danbury, CT 06811 203-791-8599
New Planet Studios: 18647 Pier Point Pl #1000, Gaithersburg, MD 20879.....301-948-0452
New World Media: 14568 Fancher Ave, Fair Haven, NY 13064 315-947-6016
New York Agency: 10 Gibbs St #200, Rochester, NY 14604 716-232-7060
New York Film & Animation Co, Ltd: 420 Lexington Ave,
New York, NY 10170 212-986-5680
New [Media] Directions: 808 Broadway, Nashville, TN 37203 615-742-1490
NewBold Design: 765 Allens Ave, Providence, RI 02905 401-941-1732
Newman Design, Inc, Susan: 306 Washington St, Hoboken, NJ 07030...........201-420-8205
Newman, Andrew: 54 Winding Cove Rd, Marstons Mills, MA 02648................508-420-1161
NewOrder Media: 209 10th Ave S #450, Nashville, TN 37203 615-248-4848
Newsome, Gregory: 75 St Nicholas Pl #6A, New York, NY 10032....................212-283-0871
Nexus Design & Marketing: 710 Wilshire Blvd #510,
Santa Monica, CA 90401 310-394-5143
Ngs Assocs: 112 Crockett Rd, King of Prussia, PA 19406................................610-337-2745
Nicholas Assocs: 213 W Institute Pl #704, Chicago, IL 60610 312-951-1185
Nichols Graphic Design, Inc: 80 8th Ave #900, New York, NY 10011 212-727-9818
Nichols, Mary Ann: 80 Eighth Ave #900, New York, NY 10011 212-727-9818
Nicholson Design: 364 Second St #2, Encinitas, CA 92024.............................619-942-9000
Nicholson Partnership: 353 W 53rd St 4th Fl, New York, NY 10019................212 246-4864
Nickel Design, Rich: 130 W Liberty Dr #205, Wheaton, IL 60187 630-653-2925
Nicolini Assocs: 4046 Maybelle Ave, Oakland, CA 94619...............................510-531-5569
Nicosia Creative Expresso Ltd: 16 W 56th St 3rd Fl, New York, NY 10019.......212-489-6423
Niehaus, Don: 2380 Malcolm Ave, Los Angeles, CA 90064 213-279-1559
Nielubowicz & Assocs: 1900 Glengary St, Sarasota, FL 34231 941-924-5077
Nieshoff Design: 15 Depot Square Suite #1, Lexington, MA 02173 617-864-3664
Niimi Design Assocs: 451 N Racine 2nd Fl, Chicago, IL 60622.......................312-666-8383
Nimeck, Fran: RD 4/ 358-A Riva Ave, North Brunswick, NJ 08902 908-821-8741
Niven Marketing Group: 1850 Greenleaf Ave, Elk Grove Village, IL 60007 847-640-0300
Nix Design: 426 S Dawson St, Raleigh, NC 27601...919-829-4901
Noah, Dan: 10222 Parkwood Dr, Kensington, MD 20895 301-564-1566
Noel Design, Chris: 1010 Rockville Pike #400, Rockville, MD 20852...............301-838-9001
Noi Viva Design: 34 Old Mill Rd, Chappaqua, NY 10514 914-238-3708
Nolan & Assocs: 4100 Cathedral Ave NW, Washington, DC 20016....................202-363-6553
Nolan Design: 605 Lake Ave, Spring Lake Heights, NJ 07762..........................908-449-6953
Nolan Multimedia: 22a Commercial Blvd, Novato, CA 9494............................415-883-0187
noloss.com: 182 DeGraw St #3, Brooklyn, NY 11213......................................718-797-1934
Nomadic Display: 3628 Westchase Dr, Houston, TX 77042...............................713-977-8788
Noneman & Noneman Design: 230 E 18th St, New York, NY 10003 212-473-4090
Norman Gollin Design: 9048 Wonderland Pk Ave, Los Angeles, CA 90046 213-656-2398
Norr Design, Brad: 400 N First Ave #312, Minneapolis, MN 55401 612-339-2104
Norris Reynolds & Denham: 112 N Beechwood Ave, Baltimore, MD 21228......410-788-9229
Norstar Design Star: 2720 Loker Ave W #R, Carlsbad, CA 92008 619-929-0948
North Amer Thought Combine: 270 Lafayette St #903, New York, NY 10012.....212-219-1000
North American Aerox, Inc: 14 Engineers Lane, Farmingdale, NY 11735 516-752-0088
North Charles Street Dsgn Org: 222 W Saratoga St, Baltimore, MD 21201 410-539-4040
North, Ron: 566 Dutch Valley Rd, Atlanta, GA 30324 404-892-6232
Northrop Design, Susan: 18 Imperial Pl #1D, Providence, RI 02903 401-521-2389
Northwest Interactive: 1309 NE Ravenna Blvd, Seattle, WA 98105 206-523-7879
Northwest Media Design: 326 W 12th Ave, Eugene, OR 97401 503-343-6636
Notovitz Design, Inc: 47 E 19th St 4th Fl, New York, NY 10003 212-677-9700
Nottingham Spirk Design: 11310 Juniper Rd, Cleveland, OH 44106...................216-231-7830
Nourse, Bill: 301 N Water St 6th Fl, Milwaukee, WI 53202.............................414-278-7717
Nova Marketing Communications: 165 W Central Rd, Schaumburg, IL 60195.....847-202-6682
Novation: 6612 Gunn Dr, Oakland, CA 94611..510-339-8769
Novocom: 6314 Santa Monica Blvd, Hollywood, CA 90038...............................213-461-3688
Novus Visual Communications, Inc: 18 W 27th St, New York, NY 10001.........212-689-2424
NOW Communications: 1271 California St #6, San Francisco, CA 94109........415-775-3518
Noyes Assocs Inc, Macey: 232 Danbury Rd, Wilton, CT 06897 203-762-9002
Nuance: 378 Gypsy Hill Rd, Lancaster, PA 17602 717-293-0171
Nuart: 49 Richmonville Ave, Westport, CT 06880 203-222-8181
Nuf Said: 2564 Paintbrush Ln, Lafayette, CO 80026.......................................303-665-8188
Number Seventeen: 285 W Broadway #650, New York, NY 10013....................212-966-9395
Nunez Group: 480 Mikasa Dr, Alpharetta, GA 30202 770-475-3980
Nuttall Design & Comm: 815 N First Ave #6, Phoenix, AZ 85003 602-257-4458
Nwaise & Assocs: 300 Berkley Dr #R5, Madison, TN 37115...........................615-868-8065
NZD Designworks: 1542 Woodbine Ct, Deerfield, IL 60015............................847-945-2225

O

O & J Design, Inc: 10 W 19th St 6th Fl, New York, NY 10011 212-242-1080
O'Brien Design: 301 N Poverty Rd, Southbury, CT 06488...............................203-262-1121
O'Brion Design: 10 New Meadows Rd, Winchester, MA 01890 617-729-3893
O'Mara Design Group: 4505 La Virgenes Rd #201, Calabasas, CA 91302 818-880-9220
O'Neil Communications: 1 Bridgeview Cir, Tyngsboro, MA 01879....................508-649-7538
O'Very, Covey: 682 South 700 East, Salt Lake City, UT 84102 801-363-6063
Obata & Co, Kiku: 5585 Pershing Ave #240, St Louis, MO 631112 314-361-3110
Obata Design: 1610 Menard, St Louis, MO 63104...314-241-1710
Oberg, Richard: 327 15th Ave, Moline, IL 61265 319-359-3831
Oberhand Studios: 20124 Citronia St, Chatsworth, CA 91311 818-775-1999
Ocean Graphic Design, Inc: 273 E Olive St, Long Beach, NY 11561 516-889-1667
Octane Media: 470 W Hwy 96 #260, Shore View, MN 55126 612-482-0700
Odam Design, John: 2163 Cordero Rd, Del Mar, CA 92014.............................619-259-8230
Odd World Inhabitants: 869 Monterey St, San Luis Obispo, CA 93401 805-781-6220
Odell Group: 7060 Hollywood Blvd #614, Hollywood, CA 90028 213-469-8805
Oden & Assocs: 22 N Front St, Memphis, TN 38103.......................................901-578-8055
Odyssey Communications Group: 8140 Walnut Hill Ln #200,
Dallas, TX 75231 214-369-6294
Odyssey Visual Design: 4413 Ocean Valley Ln, San Diego, CA 92130..............619-793-1900
Offenhartz Inc, Harvey: 531 Main St, New York, NY 10044 212-319-5961
Ogando, David: 270 Park Ave S #11C, New York, NY 10010 212-353-0577
Oglesby Design, Carla: 2140 Woodwind Ct, Simi Valley, CA 93063 805-579-8823
Oh Boy, A Design Company: 539 Bryant St #304, San Francisco, CA 95107......415-543-9063
Ohalla Design, Inc, Anna: 1812 Camp Ave, Rockford, IL 61103 815-968-1533
Ohkagawa Design: 4 E Holly St #219, Pasadena, CA 91103 818-577-1701
Ohman, Diann: 150 W Jefferson #100, Detroit, MI 48226...............................313-983-3600
Oka Design, Kathy: 120 Fair Oaks, San Francisco, CA 94110 415-647-5652
Okland Design Assocs: 1970 SW Temple, Salt Lake City, UT 84115.................801-484-7861
Oldachi Design, Mark: 3316 N Lincoln Ave, Chicago, IL 60657.......................773-477-6477
Olenik, Sandra: 2096 Durham Rd, Madison, CT 06443...................................203-421-4867
Olivares, Elena: 41 Union Square W #209, New York, NY 10003 212-645-7858
Oliver Design: 2054 Broadway, Santa Monica, CA 90404................................310-453-3523
Oliver Design, Douglas: 168 N Meramec #105, St Louis, MO 63105 314-725-6616
Oliver, Mark: One W Victoria St, Santa Barbara, CA 93101 805-963-0734
Olivette Hubler Design: 2631 Commerce, Dallas, TX 75226............................214-742-2491
Ollio Studio: 2710 Phillips Ave, Glenshaw, PA 15116 412-486-6516
Ollman, Raoul: 470 Potrero Ave #3, San Francisco, CA 94110........................415-552-1941
Olsen Muscara Design Group: 60 madison Ave #1010, New York, NY 10010 212-684-4580
Olson Design, Bruce: 14775 Northern Ave, Guerneville, CA 95446..................707-869-1066
Olson Design, Inc: 853 Camino Del Mar, Del Mar, CA 92014 619-450-9200
Olthaus Designs, Larry: 1149 Devil's Backbone Rd, Cincinnati, OH 45233.......513-451-2815
Olver Dunlop Assocs: 222 W Huron #2001, Chicago, IL 60610.......................312-337-2323
Omega Design Communications: 717 Lexington Ave, New York, NY 10022 212-319-4859
Omega Group, The: 1028 Route 23, Wayne, NJ 07470 201-628-1996
Omni Graphic Media: 21385 Marina Cove Circle #E12,
Miami Beach, FL 33180 305-935-1718
Omni Media, The: 2855 Boardwalk, Ann Arbor, MI 48104 313-761-8872
Omnivore: 27 Granada Ave, Long Beach, CA 90803...310-987-5244
On Graphics: 5127 Cerrillos Dr, Woodland Hills, CA 9164 818-716-9228
On Line Design: 18 Halstead Ave, Harrison, NY 10528.....................................914-835-1979
On Line Design/Visual Stratgs: 41 Pollard Pl, San Francisco, CA 94133...........415-296-9702
Ondesign: 451 D St #305, Boston, MA 02210 617-261-4820
One Flight Up Design: 150 River Rd Suite J-4, Montville, NJ 07045................201-257-9500
One World Arts: 1831 Pearl St, Boulder, CO 80302 303-444-6996
Optilife Communications: 630 S Pointe Blvd #419, Fort Myers, FL 33919.......941-433-2465
Optimum Design: 38 Clifton Place, New York, NY 11238 718-638-2137
Optimum Group: 9745 Mangham Dr, Cincinnati, OH 45215.............................513-563-2700
Option X: 601 Prince St, Alexandria, VA 22314 703-684-7004
Orak Design: 4373 25th St, San Francisco, CA 94114 415-550-7101
Orange & Blue Design Group: 80 W 40th St #72, New York, NY 10018..........212-354-9833
Orbis Productions: 837 Rosary Ln, West Chester, PA 19382 610-692-0921
Orbit Interactive Commincations: 123 N 3rd Street Ste 300,
Minneapolis, MN 55401 612-335-8260
Origin Instruments: 854 Greenview Dr, Grand Prairie, TX 75050 214-606-8740
Originators, The: 3600 S Harbor Blvd #155, Oxnard, CA 93035....................805-985-4664
Orion Communications: 2323 W Schantz Ave #217, Dayton, OH 45409........937-297-0044
Orlov, Christian: 42 W 69th St, New York, NY 10023 212-873-2381
Orr & Assocs, Michael: 75 W Market St/Hawkes Bldg, Corning, NY 14830 607-936-4607
Orr Assocs, R: 22282 Pewter Ln, El Toro, CA 92630 714-770-1277
Ortiz, Jose Luis: 66 W 77th St, New York, NY 10024......................................212-877-3081
Orton, Michael Jones: 6800 The Sunset Ridge #200, W Hills, CA 91307 818-716-7300
Osborne Design Illustration: 4801 Nevada Ave, Nashville, TN 37209..............615-385-4476
Osborne Design, Michael: 444 De Haro #207, San Francisco, CA 94107...........415-255-0125
Osborne-Tuttle: 1259 Belden, Chicago, IL 60614 773-404-5444
Oshima, Carol: 1659 E Sachs Place, Covina, CA 91724 818-966-0796
Oshsner Design, Dennis: 2812 Patten Pl W, Seattle, WA 98199 206-286-9249
Osland Design: 145 Ave Of Americas 2nd Fl, New York, NY 10013 212-627-1280
Oslund Design: 125 Lawrence St, Eugene, OR 97401 541-686-9833
Ostrander & Chu, Inc: 900 Manakea St, Honolulu, HI 96817 808-524-4700
Ott Assocs, Inc: 906 Locust St, Philadelphia, PA 19107..................................215-925-7771
Our Design: 3501 Trimble Rd, Nashville, TN 37215 615-783-0093
Our World: 7216 Washington NE, Albuquerque, NM 87109............................505-345-0945
Out Of The Blue, Inc: 1906 Wellbourne Dr NE, Atlanta, GA 30324..................404-897-5817
Output Technologies: 4251 Pennsylvania, Kansas City, MO 64111 816-435-2000
Outside Line Studio: 225 S Owasso Blvd, Roseville, MN 55113 612-483-5761
Outside The Box Interactive: 133 W 19th St #10B, New York, NY 10011.........212 463-7160
Ovation Marketing: 201 Main St, La Crosse, WI 54601 608-785-2460
Over CC Design: 599 Broadway 8th Fl, New York, NY 10012 212-925-2456
Overton, Janet: 3616 Regent Dr, Dallas, TX 75229...214-357-1272
Ovryn Design, Nina: 142 Grove Ave, Woodbridge, NJ 07095 908-602-0568
Ovryn, Ken: 2619 Windsor St #1000, Chicago, IL 60625 773-866-0866
Owen/Garritson: 603 Business Pkwy, Richardson, TX 75081 972-671-1255
Owens & Assocs Advtg, Inc: 6530 N 16th St #101, Phoenix, AZ 85016..........602-230-7557
Owens Marketing Design: 5 Hunt Field Court, Owings Mills, MD 21117 410-235-3327
Oxford & Drozoa: 12555 High Bluff Dr, San Diego, CA 92130.........................619-481-3446

Rich Assocs, Harry: 648 Oakwood Ave, W Hartford, CT 06110 203-953-2990
Richards & Graf, Inc: 101 Yesler Way #506, Seattle, WA 98104 206-343-0281
Richards & Swensen: 350 S 400 East #300, Salt Lake City, UT 84111..................801-532-4097
Richards Design Group: 4722 Old Kingston Pike, Knoxville, TN 37919 615-584-3319
Richards Group, The: 7007 Twin Hill #200, Dallas, TX 75231 214-987-4800
Richardson, Hank: 1575 Northside Dr 100Tch #210, Atlanta, GA 30318 404-636-0567
Richardson/Smith, Inc: 10350 Olentangy River Rd, Worthington, OH 43085 614-885-3453
Richland Design Assocs: 47 Studio Rd, Newton, MA 02166............................617-558-2726
Richland Design Assocs: 357 Harvard St, Cambridge, MA 02138 617-868-1384
Richman, Mel: 15 N Presidential Blvd, Bala Cynwyd, PA 19004 215-667-8900
Richmond Jones Graphics: 2530 W Eastwood Ave, Chicago, IL 60625 773-588-4900
Rickabaugh, Eric: 384 W Johnstown Rd, Gahanna, OH 43230 614-337-2229
Riddick Corp Marketing: 401 E Main St, Ricmond, VA 23219 804-780-0006
Ridgely Curry & Assocs: 87 E Green St #309, Pasadena, CA 91105................818-564-1215
Ridgeway, Inc, Ronald: 530 Broadway 4th Fl, New York, NY 10012................212-966-9696
Ridgeway, Ronald: 530 Broadway 4th Fl, New York, NY 10014........................212-966-9696
Rieb, Robert: 24 Narrow Rocks Rd, Westport, CT 06880..................................203-227-0061
Right Angle Co: 622 Emory St, San Jose, CA 95110 408-287-8541
Rigsby Design Inc, Lana: 5650 Kirby Dr #260, Houston, TX 77005 713-660-6057
Ringel Design, Leonard: 18 Wheeler Rd, Kendall Park, NJ 08824....................908-297-9084
Rio Station Graphics: 78 Manhattan Ave #2D, New York, NY 10025.................212-665-3670
Ritola Design, Roy: 431 Jackson St, San Francisco, CA 94111 415-788-7010
Ritta & Assocs: 568 Grand Ave, Englewood, NJ 07631 201-567-4400
Ritter Design, Richard: 651 Park Ave, King of Prussia, PA 19406....................610-354-9200
Ritz Design: 5024 N 83rd St, Scottsdale, AZ 85250 602-949-5348
Riverhouse Graphics, Inc: 1650 Kendale Blvd #115, E Lansing, MI 48823......517-337-2882

• **RKB Studios, Inc: pg 1012,1013**
420 N Fifth St #920, Minneapolis, MN 55401 ....**612-339-7055**
e-mail: brian@rkbstudios.com / fax: 612-339-8689

RKD: 853 Alma St, Palo Alto, CA 94301 415-324-1355
RKM, Inc: 5307 29th St NW, Washington, DC 20015 202-364-0148
RKS Design: 7407 Topanga Canyon Blvd, Canoga Park, CA 91303 818-710-9737
RL Roberson: 12307 Cross Creek, Dallas, TX 75243..214-669-9088
RL Studios: 43 Bleeker St, Newark, NJ 07102 201-624-6491
Rmda, Inc: 212 Roosevelt Way, San Francisco, CA 94111 415-255-1221
Robbins-Tesar, Inc: 43 Homestead Ave, Stamford, CT 06902 203-356-1330
Roberts & Assocs: 402 E Unaka Ave, Johnson City, TN 37601..........................423-929-7773
Roberts Design, Jillian: One Port Cortcolden Rd, Washington, NJ 07882 908-835-0694
Robertson Design: 219 Ward Cir #4, Brentwood, TN 37027 615-373-4590
Robertson Stephens & Co: 555 California St #2600,
San Francisco, CA 94104...415-781-9700
Robertz & Kobold: 35 E Wacker Dr #3900, Chicago, IL 60601..........................312-236-5522
Robie Design Assocs, James: 152 1/2 N La Brea Ave, Los Angeles, CA 90036......213-939-7370
Robinson Design, Elton: 15 Nordica Dr, Croton on Hudson, NY 10520............914-271-2718
Robinson Job: 415 Delaware, Kansas City, MO 64105 816-474-2228
Robinson Kurtin Comm: 201 E 42nd St, New York, NY 10017...........................212-983-5757
Robinson Pritchard & Boyer: 9409 Park Hunt Ct, Springfield, VA 22153 703-548-6770
Robinson, John: 2228 Papermill Rd #J, Winchester, VA 22601........................540-678-4980
Robison Advertising Design: 2020 E 16th Ave, Denver, CO 80206 303-355-2255
Rockel, Dana: 2 N Main St #B332, Beacon Falls, CT 06403 203-720-1603
Rodney Creative Services, Deborah: 1635 16th St, Santa Monica, CA 90404 310-450-9650
Rodriguez Graphics, Inc: 501 Forest Ave #1207, Palo Alto, CA 94301 415-323-3630
Rodriguez Jr, Emilio: 8270 SW 116 Terr, Miami, FL 33157 305-235-4700
Rodriguez, Syl: 11516 Sixth Ave, Seattle, WA 98177 206-364-9077
Roecker Design Group, Inc: 2401 15th St #350, Denver, CO 80202.................303-455-4800
Roerden, Doug: 588 Tremont St, Boston, MA 02118 617-262-4868
Roessner & Co, Inc: 335 Rte 202-206, Pluckemin`, NJ 07978........................908-658-9700
Rogers Design Group: 6233 W 83rd Pl, Los Angeles, CA 90045......................310-393-4014
Rogers Design, Pam: 40 Proctor St, Hopkinton, MA 01748..............................508-435-6975
Rogers Seidman Design: 20 W 20th St #703, New York, NY 10011 212-741-4687
Rogow & Bernstein Dsgn: 5971 W 3rd St, Los Angeles, CA 90036 213-936-9916
Rohrer Design, Curt: 822 Appletree Lane, Mechanicburg, PA 17055..................717-732-5127
Rojas Design: Po Box 542, Boonville, CA 95415...707-895-2663
Rokfalusi Design: 2953 Crosswycke Forest Cir, Atlanta, GA 30319 404-262-2561
Rolandesign: 21833 De La Luz Ave, Woodland Hills, CA 91364........................818-346-9752
Romanelli Advertising & Design: 2 College St Box 227, Clinton, NY 13323.......315-853-3941
Romax Studio: 32 Club Cir, Stamford, CT 06905 203-324-4260
Romeo Empire Design, Donna: 154 Spring St 3rd Fl, New York, NY 10012 212-274-0214
Romero Design Group, Javier: 24 E 23rd St 3rd Fl, New York, NY 10010..........212-420-0656
Romero Design Group, Javier: 333 W 52nd St, New York, NY 10019 888-447-6878
Ronan Design: 1608 N Milwaukee Ave #501, Chicago, IL 60647 773-252-6624
Roos Design, Roz: 220 Bodega Ave, Petaluma, CA 94952 707-763-3939
Roose Design Inc, Rich: PO Box 539, Ketchum, ID 83340................................208-622-7924
Root, Laurie: 481 Carlisle Dr, Herndon, VA 22070...703-318-7225
Ropeik & Assocs, Inc: 9518 Evergreen St, Silver Spring, MD 20901..................301-589-5159
Rosa & Wesley Design: 3348 N Kildare, Chicago, IL 60641 773-283-3982
Rose Design, Fay: 310 Centennnial Dr, Blue Bell, PA 19422.............................610-292-9595
Rose Graphics: 3 Rose Ct, Colonia, NJ 07067 908-382-0593
Rosebush Visions: 154 W 57th St #826, New York, NY 10019...........................212-398-6600
Roselius Design, Marty: 701 Dexter Ave N #212, Seattle, WA 98109...............206-282-8926
Rosenberg Design, Leslie: 2400 Lakeview Ave #2905, Chicago, IL 60614.......773-929-6277
Rosenthal Assocs, Herb: 207 E 32nd St, New York, NY 10016.........................212-685-1814
Rosenthal, Annette: 101 Huntington Ave, Boston, MA 02199...........................617-859-1212
Rosiak & Assocs: 199 Main St, Matawan, NJ 07747...908-290-1000
Ross Creative Group, Kim: 86 Seminole Way, Rochester, NY 14618 716-244-5384
Ross Design: 29160 Heathercliff Rd #200, Malibu, CA 90265............................310-589-3100
Ross Design: 4450 Erie Ave, Cincinnati, OH 45227 513-561-5542
Ross Inc, Kallir Phillips: 333 E 38th St, New York, NY 10016...........................212-856-8400
Ross Roy Communications: 100 Bloomfield Hills Pkwy,
Bloomfield Hills, MI 48304 810-433-6000
Ross-Tomey, Stephanie: 710 N Tucker Ave #512, St Louis, MO 63109...........314-241-3811
Rosser, Toby: 4 Main St, Purdys, NY 10578...914-277-1064
Rosumat Graphic Design: PO Box 23019, Riyadh, SA 11426...........................9661476-9282
Rotella Assocs: 301 S State St, Newtown, PA 18940 215-968-3696
Roth Inc, JH: 13 Inwood Ln E, Peekskill, NY 10566..914-737-6784
Roth, Judee: 712 Main St, Boonton, NJ 07005 973-316-5411
Roth, Wayne: 712 Main St 2nd Fl, Boonton, NJ 07005.....................................973-316-5411
Rotheiser, Jordan I: 3075 University St, Highland Park, IL 60035 847-433-4288
Rother, Paul: 3015 Main St, Santa Monica, CA 90405.....................................310-450-1315
Rothschild, Joyce: 305 E 46th St 15th Fl, New York, NY 10017 212-888-8680
Rothstein & Memsic: 332 N La Brea, Los Angeles, CA 90036 213-936-7209
Roulston, Gary L: 502 E 4th St #A, Bartlesville, OK 74003 918-336-1905
Roundtable Media: 111 W Goose Alley, Urbana, IL 61801 217-367-6028
Rouslton Design: 1117 SE Delaware, Bartlesville, OK 74003 918-336-0454
Rowntree 3D, Inc: 883 Boylston St, Boston, MA 02116 617-424-0610
Royter/Snow Design: 1537 S Main St, Salt Lake City, UT 84115.....................801-484-0419
Rozier Studio: 270 Lafayette St, New York, NY 10012 212-431-7070
Rozoff Dsgn: 430 Communipaw Ave, Jersey City, NJ 07304 212-620-4110
RP Communications: 2301 Kirk Ave, Baltimore, MD 21218..............................410-467-9200
RP Hibberd, Inc: 5 E 22nd St 21st Fl, New York, NY 10010............................212-358-0447
RPM Commmunications: 601 Boston Post Rd, Milford, CT 06460....................203-878-2611
Rt Productions: 3599 Indiana St #4, San Diego, CA 92103.............................619-294-3563
Rubin Design, Marc: PO Box 440, Breesport, NY 14816..................................607-739-0871
Rubin Inc, Gary : 931 E 86th St #206, Indianapolis, IN 46240........................317-251-5330
Rubinrolt Design: 1891 Main St Rear, S Windsor, CT 06074 203-289-4248
Ruby Shoes Studio: 12A Mica Ln, Wellesley, MA 02181..................................617-431-8686
Rudoy, Peter: 1619 Broadway 10th Fl, New York, NY 10019 212-265-7600
Ruemmele, Steve: 310 N Alabama St #230, Indianapolis, IN 46204 317-972-0606
Ruggles Interactive Media: 35-45 78th St #52, Jackson Heights, NY 11372....718-476-3692

• **Ruiz, Aristides: pg 1456** 39 Hamilton Terr, New York, NY 10031.................**212-283-3401**
url: www.wayart.com

Rumble & Rumble Design: 1512 W Main St, Richmond, VA 23220.................804-359-2598
Rush, Judy: 9854 Ash Dr, Overland Park, KS 66209 913-652-0125
Rushing & Assocs: 1566 Sugarwood Circle, Winter Park, FL 32792................407-679-4876
Russell Adv & Dsgn Inc, Emelene: 6312 S Fiddlers Gr Cir #415N,
Englewood, CO 80111 303-741-4488
Russell Communications Group: 6167 Bristol Pkwy #450,
Culver City, CA 90230 310-216-1414
Russell Design Assocs: 584 Broadway, New York, NY 10012..........................212-431-8770
Russo, Wondriska: 11 Talcott Notch Rd, Farmington, CT 06032 860-677-6161
Rustad & Assocs, Steven: 150 Spear St #215, San Francisco, CA 94105.........415-543-8174
Rusty Kay & Assocs, Inc: 2665 Main St #E, Santa Monica, CA 90405.............310-392-4569
Rutter, Lance: 855 W Blackhawk St, Chicago, IL 60622 312-787-6831
Ruud & Partners: 719 Yarmouth Rd #202, Palos Verdes, CA 90274 310-375-7654
RWR Designs, Inc: 5025 Arapahpo #502, Dallas, TX 75248............................214-423-7111
Ryan Co, John: 303 Excelsior Blvd #500, MInneapolis, MN 55416....................612-924-7700
Ryan Design, Thomas: 400 8th Ave S, Nashville, TN 37203............................615-254-5374
Ryan, Debbie: 1 Waterville Rd, Farmington, CT 06032 860-677-9777
RYSing Media: 154-10 Ash Ave, Flushing, NY 11355 718-358-6559
Rysner, Murrie Lienhart: 58 W Huron, Chicago, IL 60610................................312-943-5995
Rytter & Assocs, Robert: 3618 Falls Rd, Baltimore, MD 21221 410-889-8400
RZA, Inc: 3 Harriot Pl, Harrington Park, NJ 07640..201-391-8500

S

S & N Design: 121 N 8th St, Manhattan, KS 66502 913-539-3931

• **Sabanosh, Michael: pg 1386,1387**
433 W 34th St #18B, New York, NY 10001 ....**212-947-8161**

Sackett Design: 2103 Scott St, San Francisco, CA 94115 415-929-4800
Sackheim Enterprises, Morton : 1125 Daniels Dr, Los Angeles, CA 90035........310-276-5418
Sage Graphic Design & Mrktng: 545 Oriole Ln, Corona, CA 91719...................909-279-0330
Sage Interactive: 624 Northern Ave, Mill Valley, CA 94941 415-381-4622
Saggese Design: 37 Stonehenge Dr, Ocean Township, NJ 07712......................908-922-3282
Sagmeister Design: 22 W 14th St #15A, New York, NY 10011.........................212-647-1789
Said Design, Jason: 939 Greenbrier Trace, Nashville, TN 37214 615-316-9592
Saiki & Assocs: 13 Cutter Mill Rd #366, Great Neck, NY 11021 516-466-1229
Sailsman Graphics: 137 Varick St 6th Ave, New York, NY 10013.......................212-463-7245
Sakin, Sy: 443 Park Ave S 4th Fl, New York, NY 10016...................................212-889-4489
Sakowich Design: 99 Tower Rd, Lincoln, MA 01773 617-259-9601
Saks Assocs, Arnold: 350 E 81st St 4th Fl, New York, NY 10028......................212-861-4300
Saks, Arnold: 350 E 81st St 4th Fl, New York, NY 10028 212-861-4300
Saksa, Cathy: 10 Hidden Hollow Dr, Hamilton Township, NJ 08620...................609-259-7792
Salavetz, Judith: 160 Fifth Ave #613, New York, NY 10010 212-620-4672
Salesvertising: 7865 E Mississippi #705W, Denver, CO 80231.........................303-377-9211
Salisbury & Salisbury, Inc: 130 W 30th St, New York, NY 10001 212-268-5893
Salisbury Communications: 2200 Amapola Ct #202, Torrance, CA 90501 310-320-7660
Salmon, Paul: 5826 Jackson's Oak Ct, Burke, VA 22015..................................703-250-4943
Salpeter Design: 142 E 37th St, New York, NY 10016 212-779-3566
Salvato & Coe Assocs, Inc: 2015 W Fifth Ave, Columbus, OH 43212 614-488-3131
Salvin Assocs: 1335 Dodge Ave, Evanston, IL 60201 847-328-3366
Samaritan Design, Inc: 1441 N 12th St, Phoenix, AZ 85006 602-495-4254
Samata Assocs: 101 S First St, W Dundee, IL 60118.......................................847-428-8600
Samerjan/Edigraph: 45 Cantitoe St RFD 1, Katonah, NY 10536 914-232-3725
Sametz Blackstone Assocs, Inc: 40 W Newton St, Boston, MA 02118...............617-266-8577
Sams Design, Stan: 2636B S 13th St, St Louis, MO 63118...............................314-664-0797
Samson Kelly Design: 5757 Central Ave #F, Boulder, CO 80301......................303-444-4496
San Diego Art Prdctns: 2752 Imperial Ave, San Diego, CA 92102.....................619-239-6666
Sanchez: 138 S 20th St, Philadelphia, PA 19103 215-564-2223
Sanchez/Kamps Assocs: 60 W Green St, Pasadena, CA 91105.........................818-793-4017
Sanders & Co/Dsgn, Robert: 100 Loma Vista Dr, Senoma, CA 95476...............707-996-3532
Sandstrom Design: 808 SW Third Ave, Portland, OR 97204 503-248-9466
Sanft Design: 17E 7th St, Tempe, AZ 85281 602-966-4311
Sanoski Design: 166 E Superior St, Chicago, IL 60611 312-664-7795
Santora Design: 295 Madison Ave 43rd Fl, New York, NY 10017......................212-922-0344
Santos Design: 104-37 43rd Ave, Corona, NY 11368 718-458-2564
Sargent & Berman: 1337 Third St Promenade #203,
Santa Monica, CA 90401 310-576-1070
Sargent Design Company: 397 Campbell Flat Rd, Norwich, VT 05055 802-649-3230
Sasaki: 41 madison Ave 13th Fl, New York, NY 10010 212-686-5080
Sasaki Assocs, Inc: 64 Pleasant St, Watertown, MA 02172...............................617-926-3300
Satagata/Vollmer: 308 E 8th St, Cincinnati, OH 45202....................................513-651-4443
Sater Comms & Dsgn: 4204 Roland Ave, Baltimore, MD 21210........................410-889-4043
Sato/Macke Creative: 10712 Reagan St, Los Alamitos, CA 90720 310-799-9475
Saueressig Design: 222 W Custer Pk, Bismarck, ND 58501..............................701-223-3529
Savage Design Group: 4203 Montrose Blvd, Houston, TX 77006.......................713-522-1555
Savage Design, Liz: 11201 Longwood Grove, Reston, VA 20194 703-471-0166
Savion Advtg, Elias: 2424 CNG Tower, Pittsburgh, PA 15222 412-642-7700

Savlin/Petertil: 1335 Dodge Ave, Evanston, IL 60201 847-328-3366
Sawyer Studios: 115 W 27th St 8th Fl, New York, NY 10001 212-645-4455
Sawyer, Sandra: 616 Texas St #101, Ft Worth, TX 76102 817-332-1611
Sayles Design: 308 8th St, Des Moines, IA 50309 515-243-2922
Scabrini Design, Janet: 50 Washington St, S Norwalk, CT 06854 203-853-6676
Scannell Inc, Peter: 250 W 19th St #7L, New York, NY 10011 212-989-6010
Scaramozzino, Phil: 38 Montvale Ave #220, Stoneham, MA 02180 617-438-8575
Schaefer Advertising: 14950 Walters Ct, Elm Grove, WI 53122 414-789-9952
Schaefer Assocs: 635 Butterfield Rd, Oak Brook Terrace, IL 60181 630-932-8787
Schaefer Television Art, Robert: 738 N Cahuenga, Hollywood, CA 90038 213-462-7877
Schaffer Design: 474 Third Ave, Salt Lake City, UT 84103 801-364-1717
Schaffer Design, Stephanie: 175 W 87th St Fl 14A, New York, NY 10024 ....212-580 1570
Scharfman Design: 306 W 100th St #46, New York, NY 10025 212-941-6277
Schechter Group, Inc: 437 Madison Ave 10th Fl, New York, NY 10022 212-752-4400
Scheinzeit, Teri: 27 W 24th St, New York, NY 10010 212-627-5355
Schell Horn Design: 465 Prospect Ave, Piscataway, NJ 08854 908-424-1234
Schell, Paul: 1608 E 51st St, Brooklyn, NY 11234 718-951-8976
Schlaifer Nance & Co, Inc: 11 Piedmont Ctr #404, Atlanta, GA 30305 404-231-0684
Schlesinger Design: 1231 State St #204, Santa Barbara, CA 93101 805-966-2970
Schlossberg Inc, Edwin: 641 Avenue of the Americas, New York, NY 10011 212-691-0290
Schmalz Creative Svcs, Charles: 271 Santa Rosa Ave,
San Francisco, CA 94112 415-586-0866
Schmidt Assocs: 20296 Harper Ave, Harper Woods, MI 48225 313-881-8075
• **Schmidt, Alberto: pg 1469** 2200 N Lamar #104, Dallas, TX 75202 ....**214-871-2747**
url: www.imagen.com / fax: 214-871-2748
Schneider & Assocs, Howard: 87 N Raymond Ave #210,
Pasadena, CA 91103 818-795-5258
Schneider Assocs, Inc, Ken: 2 Bending Oak, Houston, TX 77024 713-464-0322
Schneider Design: 2633 N Charles St, Baltimore, MD 21218 301-467-2611
Schneider Design, Deborah: 900 N Franklin St #505, Chicago, IL 60610 312-642-3756
Schnider Design, Oscar: 568 Broadway #804, New York, NY 10012 212-431-3253
Schoeneberg Design: 337 Sherman Ave, Evanston, IL 60202 847-869-4180
Schoenfeld, Cal: 6 Colony Ct #B, Parsippany, NJ 07054 201-263-1635
Schopper, Bernie: 2415 Windbreak Dr, Alexandria, VA 22306 703-765-4652
Schorer, R Thomas: Seven Ten Silver Spur Rd #267,
Palos Verdes, CA 90274 310-377-0207
Schowalter Design: 1133 Broadway #1610, New York, NY 10010 212-727-0072
Schrecongost, Paul: 284 Liberty St, Salem, WV 26426 304-782-3499
Schreer Design, Don: 1641 E Osborn Rd #3, Phoenix, AZ 85016 602-230-1350
Schreiber & Assocs Inc, David: PO Box 1580, Media, PA 19063 610-566-7575
• **Schreiber, Laszlo: pg 1456,1457** 39 Hamilton Terr, New York, NY 10031 ....**212-283-3401**
url: www.wayart.com
Schubert Media Design: 176 King St, Redwood City, CA 94062 415-365-6878
Schulte Design: 2132 24th st, San Francisco, CA 94107 415-647-5623
Schulwolf, Frank: 524 Hardee Rd, Coral Gables, FL 33146 305-665-2129
Schum & Stober: 1750 Old Meadow Rd, McLean, VA 22102 703-448-8150
Schutz, Thomas: 9710 Ferris Ave, Morton Grove, IL 60053 847-965-7100
Schwab, Michael: 501 Fifth Ave, New York, NY 10017 212-490-2450
Schwartz Graphic Design: 2941 Fourth Ave, San Diego, CA 92103 619-291-8878
Schwartz, Bonnie & Clem: 2941 4th Ave, San Diego, CA 92103 619-291-8878
Schwarz Design: 2301 Hickory St, St Louis, MO 63104 314-773-1181
Sciorilli, Tony: 200 First Ave, Pittsburgh, PA 15222 412-261-6815
Scotko, Mike: 240 route 38 #C, Moorestown, NJ 08057 609-273-3255
Scotton Design, Dianne: 72 Tavern Cir, Middletown, CT 06457 860-344-8472
SCR Design Organization: 305 E 46th St 5th Fl, New York, NY 10017 212-421-3500
Screamin Lobster Studio: 20 W 20th St #802, New York, NY 10011 212-229-1275
Sea Studios, Inc: 810 Cannery Row, Monterey, CA 93940 408-649-5152
Seabright & Assocs, William: 3330 Old Glenview Rd #16,
Wilmette, IL 60091 847-853-8120
Seaman Design Group: 1027 N Central Ave, Glendale, CA 91202 818-240-2674
Seats Design: 1932 1st Ave #513, Seattle, WA 98101 206-441-0646
Sebastian, James: 116 E 16th St 10th Fl, New York, NY 10011 212-924-2426
Sec Design: 11024 Acama St #216, Studio City, CA 91602 818-508-8778
Segura, Carlos: 1110 N Milwaukee Ave, Chicago, IL 60622 773-862-5667
Seidenberg & Assocs: 300 S Duncan Ave #215, Clearwater, FL 34615 813-447-7635
Seidman, Gene: 20 W 20th St #703, New York, NY 10011 212-741-4687
Seiniger Advertising: 9320 Wilshire Blvd, Beverly Hills, CA 90212 310-777-6800
Seip Graphic Design: 916 Medina Ave, Coral Gables, FL 33134 305-448-6169
Selame Design Assocs: 2330 Washington St, Newton Lower Falls, MA 02162 617-969-6690
Selbert Design, Clifford: 2067 Massachusetts Ave, Cambridge, MA 02140 617-497-6605
Selective Media Adv, Inc: 960 Willis Ave, Albertson, NY 11507 516-747-0400
Selfe Design, Mark: 604 Mission St #830, San Francisco, CA 94105 415-243-8118
Selfridge, Mary: 817 Desplaines St, Plainfield, IL 60544 815-436-7197
Selig Group, The: 20 Melrose St, Boston, MA 02116 617-426-0075
Seltzer Design & Illus, Meyer: 744 W Buckingham Pl, Chicago, IL 60657 773-883-0964
Seltzer Design Office, Carl: 120 Newport Center Dr #206,
Newport Beach, CA 92660 714-720-0806
Selz Seabolt Communications: 221 N LaSalle St 35th Fl, Chicago, IL 60601 312-372-7090
Seman Design Group: 7434 Washington Ave, Pittsburgh, PA 15218 412-242-1775
Sendecke, Reed: 240 W Gilman St, Madison, WI 53703 608-256-5000
Seneca Design & Consulting: 3540 N Leavitt, Chicago, IL 60618 312-248-3531
Serio Design, Jeff:, Salt Lake City, UT 801-328-4925
Seroti Group, The: PO Box 470670, San Francisco, CA 94147 415-776-4242
Service Station Design: 167 Perry St 2B, New York, NY 10014 212-229-0988
Sessions Design, Steven: 5177 Richmond #500, Houston, TX 77056 713-850-8450
Sestito Design, Joe: 387 Danbury Rd, Wilton, CT 06897 203-762-9815
Seta Appleman Showell: 2145 Luray Ave, Cincinnati, OH 45206 513-221-3600
Setian Design: 392 Porter Rd, E Longmeadow, MA 01028 413-525-1102
Sexton Design: 2070 Business Center Dr #210, Irvine, CA 92715 714-474-7525
Sexton Graphics: 2800 Griswold, Port Huron, MI 48606 810-982-0420
Sexton, Brenda: 505 Creek Ridge Ct, Woodstock, GA 30188 770-928-0987
SFMultimedia Development Group: 2601 Mariposa St,
San Francisco, CA 94110 415-553-2300
SGB Partners: 1725 Montgomery St, San Francisco, CA 94111 415-391-9070
SGI: 1 Stamford Lndng/62 Sthfld Ave, Stamford, CT 06902 203-353-8555
Shades Of Gray: 917 S Cooper, Memphis, TN 38104 901-725-0308
Shalit Designs, Eric: 5428 49th Ave SW, Seattle, WA 98136 206-938-1449
Shapiro, Deborah: 150 Bentley Ave, Jersey City, NJ 07304 201-432-5198
Shared Knowledge Systems: 1806 W Beltline, Cdar Hill, TX 75014 214-293-9151
Shari Finger Design: 555 Milton Rd, Rye, NY 10580 914-967-0854
Sharon Holm Design: One Sweetcake Mtn Rd, New Fairfield, CT 06812 203-746-3763
Shaver Melahn Studios: 138 W 25th St 12th Fl, New York, NY 10001 212-366-9784
Shaw Design, Susan: 150 Nassu St, New York, NY 10038 212-732-6792
Shaw, Paul: 785 West End Ave #16A, New York, NY 10025 212-666-3738
Shawver Assocs: 555 Peters Ave #100, Pleasanton, CA 94566 510-484-4052
Shea Design, Eddie: 51 E Monte Vista, Phoenix, AZ 85004 602-258-9269
Shea, Michael: 47 Maple St, Burlington, VT 05403 802-864-5884
Sheaff & Co, R Dana: 23 Chatham Rd, Norwood, MA 02062 617-551-8682
Sheaff Dorman Purins: 460 Hillside Ave, Needham Heights, MA 02194 617-449-0602
Shear Partnership, The: 2 Stamford Landg/68 Southfldave,
Stamford, CT 06902 203-323-6200
Shear, Richard: 68 Southfield Ave #2-290, Stamford, CT 06902 203-323-6200
Sheibley Design: 320 N Kensington, LaGrange Park, IL 60526 708-354-2094
Sheldon Cotler & Assocs: 568 Broadway #402A, New York, NY 10012 212-941-0005
Sheldon Studios Ltd: 170 W Sixth Ave, Vancouver, BC V5Y 1K6 604-874-9363
Shelly Design, Roger: 39 Laurel Grove Ave, Kentfield, CA 94904 415-453-4379
Shelton Design: 3241 11th St, Boulder, CO 80304 303-444-5379
Shen Advertising & Design, Coryn: 550 15th St 3rd Fl,
San Francisco, CA 94103 415-864-8200
Shen Design: 707 S Snoqualmie St #3A, Seattle, WA 98108 206-623-3312
Shepard Assocs Design: 816 West Francicso, San Rafael, CA 94901 415-485-0384
Shepard Design: 900 N Franklin #504, Chicago, IL 60610 312-280-8538
Shepard Quraeshi Assocs, Inc: 501 Heath St, Chestnut Hill, MA 02167 617-232-1117
Sherard Design: 2040 W Platt St, Tampa, FL 33606 813-254-0068
Sheridan Assocs, Keith: 236 W 27th St 8th Fl, New York, NY 10001 212-645-6400
Sherman Design, Inc: 1901 E Franklin St #109, Richmond, VA 23223 804-649-9665
Shibata-Schwartz Dsgn, Michelle: 5727 Amy Dr, Oakland, CA 94618 510-601-1606
Shields Design: 415 E Olive Ave, Fresno, CA 93728 209-497-8060
Shields Design Group, Inc: 155 Mcclleland Rd, Cannonsburg, PA 15317 412-873-1499
Shiels Design, Inc: 2909 Cole Ave #105, Dallas, TX 75204 214-871-0593
Shilt Graphic Design, Jennifer: 401 S Edgewood Ave, Lomard, IL 60148 630-620-9313
Shimokoshi/Reeves Design: 4465 Wilshire Blvd #305,
Los Angeles, CA 90010 213-937-3414
Shinobu Ishizuka Design: 11835 W Olympic Blvd #825,
Los Angeles, CA 90064 310-478-4454
Shipps & Assocs, Inc: 410 Fairfax, Birmingham, MI 48009 810-644-5446
Shiramizu Graphic Design, Inc: 1442 Market St #D, Denver, CO 80202 303-623-2211
Shirley/Hutchinson: 707 N Franklin St #100, Tampa, FL 33602 813-229-6162
Shishkoff Design, Debra: 7734 SW Canyon Ln, Portland, OR 97225 503-297-9105
Shostak Studio, Mitch: 57 E 11th St 7th Fl, New York, NY 10003 212-979-7981
Shoulak Graphics, Joel: 5621 Ocean View Dr #2, Oakland, CA 94618 510-450-0298
SHR Perceptual Management: 8700 E Via de Ventura #100,
Scottsdale, AZ 85258 602-483-3700
Shreeve Design, Draper: 28 Perry St, New York, NY 10014 212-675-7534
Shriver Waterhouse Design, Inc: 1030 W Byron #1W, Chicago, IL 60613 773-871-4015
Shuler Graphic Design, Gil: 231 King St, Charleston, SC 29401 803-722-5770
Shum & Assocs: 1749 Old Meadow Rd #440, Mclean, VA 22102 703-448-8150
Shupe, Rich: 115 E 34th St #8E, New York, NY 10016 212-725-7576
Shurtz/ Capriotti: 604 Mission St 5th Fl, San Francisco, CA 94105 415-546-1677
Shuster Design Assocs, Inc: 1401 E Broward Blvd #103,
Ft Lauderdale, FL 33301 305-462-6400
Shyaco Creative Services: 5827 Falkirk Rd, Baltimor, MD 21239 410-532-7870
Sibley Peteet: 1512 W 35th St Cutoff #200, Austin, TX 78731 512-302-0734
Sibley Peteet Design : 3232 McKinney Ave #1200, Dallas, TX 75204 214-969-1050
Side Door Multimedia: 784 Columbus Ave #9D, New York, NY 10025 212-222-2322
Sidjakov, Nicolas: 1725 Montgomery St, San Francisco, CA 94111 415-931-7500
Sidney, Douglas: 10 Ritters Ln, Owings Mills, MD 21117 410-363-6555
Siebers Retoucher/Illustrator: 10182 Whitnall Ct, Hales Corners, WI 53130 414-425-6405
Siebert Design: 1600 Sycamore St, Cincinnati, OH 45210 513-241-4550
Siegel & Gale: 10 Rockefeller Plaza, New York, NY 10020 212-730-0101
Siegel Assocs: 74 Laurel Hollow Ct, Edison, NJ 08820 908-753-9722
Siegel Design, Bhote: 3231 Thayer St #LL, Evanston, IL 60201 847-424-1500
Siegel/Inocendio: 33 Vanderwater St #302, San Francisco, CA 94133 415-433-5817
Siero Design, Inc: 112 High Ridge Rd, Avon, CT 06001 860-673-2784
Sierra Web Pages: 2907 Baronet Way, Sacramento, CA 916-736-6700
Sigalos Design, Alex: 916 N Prospect Ave, Park Ridge, IL 60068 847-698-9161
Sightworks Creative Development: 414 N Shaffer St, Orange, CA 92666 714-744-8983
Sigler Group: 9059 Havasu St, Ventura, CA 93004 805-647-8356
Sigma 6: 1435 Randolph St #403, Detroit, MI 48226 313-963-2115
Signal Design: 905 W Main St #23E, Durham, NC 27701 919-688-7878
Signcom: 527 W Rich St, Columbus, OH 43215 614-228-9999
Signworks: 7710 Aurora Ave N, Seattle, WA 98103 206-525-2718
Sikorski/Slinchak: Investment Bldg #413/4th Ave, Pittsburgh, PA 15222 412-391-8366
Silanovsky, Serge: 194 Lincoln Pl, Brooklyn, NY 11217 718-789-1747
Silva Design: 236 Gardiner Rd, Quincy, MA 02169 617-472-8113
Silver Creek Design: 31815 NE 162nd St, Duvall, WA 98019 206-788-6578
Silver Shoe Graphics: 2639 N charles St, Baltimore, MD 21218 410-366-5976
Silverman Design: 45 Clearview Rd, E Brunswick, NJ 08816 908-254-3959
Silverman Design, Bob: 216 E 49th St 2nd Fl, New York, NY 10017 212-371-6472
Silverman Design, Gail: 579 Seventh St 2Fl, Brooklyn, NY 11215 718-499-2036
Silverman Group: 700 State St 3rd Fl, New Haven, CT 06511 203-562-6418
Silverstein, Ted: 245 E 54th St #28S, New York, NY 10022 212-371-0613
Silvia Design Group, Ken: PO Box 2840, Orleans, MA 02653 508-240-2600
Silvio Design, Sam: 633 S Plymouth Ct #204, Chicago, IL 60605 312-427-1735
Simanis, Vito: 4N013 Randall Rd, St Charles, IL 60175 630-584-1683
Simantel Group: 321 SW Constitution Ave, Peoria, IL 61602 309-674-7747
Simgraphics Engineering Corp: 1137 Huntington Dr #1A,
S Pasadena, CA 91030 213-255-0900
• **Simmons, Suzanne: pg 1456** 39 Hamilton Terr, New York, NY 10031 ....**212-283-3401**
url: www.wayart.com
Simon & Cirulis: 329 N Euclid, St Louis, MO 63108 314-361-8180
Simon & Co, Rick: 720 N Franklin #401, Chicago, IL 60610 312-951-7252
Simons Industrial Design, IW: 975 Amberly Pl, Columbus, OH 43220 614-451-3796
Simpkin Design, S: 23332 Mill Creek Dr #155, Laguna Hills, CA 92653 714-830-2177
Simpkins Design Group: 3042 Highland Dr, Carlsbad, CA 92008 619-434-1940
Simpson Booth Designers: 14 Arrow St, Cambridge, MA 02138 617-661-2630

Sims, Ronald Bennett: 10609 Sandpiper Dr, Houston, TX 77096 713-271-3703
Singer Design: 18 Porter Pl, New Providence, NJ 07974 908-665-8491
Singer Design: 401 E 34th St #S-11C, New York, NY 10016 212-481-3452
Singer Design, Beth: 1910 1/2 17th St NW, Washington, DC 20009 202-483-3967
Singer Design, Paul: 494 14th St, Brooklyn, NY 11215 718-449-8172
Siren Design: 10 Jay St #7, Tenafly, NJ 07670 201-871-1127
Sirrine, JE: PO Box 5456, Greenville, SC 29606 803-298-6000
Siskind Design, Stewart: 7 E 14th St #917, New York, NY 10003 212-627-0021
Siteline: 180 Varick St, New York, NY 10014 212-929-0505
Sitespecific: 132 W 21 St 12th St, New York, NY 10011 212-206-6600
Sixth Gear: 55 Broad St 11th Fl, New York, NY 10004 212-378-4985
Sji Assocs: 1133 Broadway #635, New York, NY 10010 212-727-1657
Skaar, Melinda: 225 Santa Monica Blvd #311, Santa Monica, CA 90401 310-394-8729
Skelton Design, Claude: 11 E Saratoga St, Baltimore, MD 21202 410-576-8886
Skilling, Johanna: 39 E 20th St 7th Fl, New York, NY 10003 212-254-3344
Skjei Design, Michael: 806 Mount Curve Ave S, Minneapolis, MN 55403 612-374-3528
Sklaroff Design Assocs, William: 124 Sibley Ave, Ardmore, PA 19003 610-649-6035
Skolos Wedell, Inc: 529 Main St, Charlestown, MA 02129 617-242-5179
Skrobisz, Jan: 15017 Oak Crest Ct, Montclair, VA 22026 703-680-3670
Skunta & Co, Karen: 1382 W Ninth St, Cleveland, OH 44113 216-687-0200
Skwarczek, Dave: 1000 N Milwaukee 2nd Fl, Chicago, IL 60622 773-342-7747
Skylight Graphics: 397 Hudson St, Hackensack, NJ 07601 201-440-3909
Skyline Exhibits & Graphics: 10 Sparks St, Plainville, CT 06063 860-793-2817
Slam Design: 634-A Venice Blvd, Venice, CA 90291 310-823-0071
Sleeper Graphic Design: 3460 Cowper Ct, Palo Alto, CA 94306 415-493-5628
Sloan, William: 236 W 26th St #805, New York, NY 10001 212-463-7025
Slover Design, Susan: 584 Broadway #903, New York, NY 10012 212-431-0093
Small Wonder Design, A: 8424 A Santa Monica Blvd #103,
W Hollywood, CA 90069 213-658-8353
Smarilli Exhibits & Graphics: 602 N Front St, Wormleysburg, PA 17043 717-737-8141
Smart Concepts: 4525 S Jamestown St, Tulsa, OK 74135 918-747-6006
Smart Design & Co: 137 Varick St 8th Fl, New York, NY 10013 212-807-8150
Smc Falcone: 225 Christiani St, Cranford, NJ 07016 908-272-0660
Smetts Design, Bonnie: 1798 Fifth St, Berkeley, CA 94710 510-644-1313
Smetts Design, Bonnie: 1798 Fifth St, Berkley, CA 94710 510-644-1313
Smidt, Sam: 666 High St, Palo Alto, CA 94301 415-327-0707
Smit Ghormley Lofgreen: 4251 E Thomas, Phoenix, AZ 85018 602-381-0304
Smith & Assocs, Larry: 3300 NE Expwy Bldg 4 #400, Atlanta, GA 30341 770-458-0808
Smith & Dress, Inc: 432 W Main St, Huntington, NY 11743 516-427-9333
Smith & Hall Design, Inc: 27 Walnut Blvd 2nd FL, Petersburg, VA 23805 804-861-9660
Smith Art Direction, Tyler: 127 Dorrance St, Providence, RI 02903 401-751-1220
Smith Assocs, Randall: 337 S 400 East #300, Salt Lake City, UT 84111 801-355-9541
Smith Assocs, Thom: 308 SW 1st Ave #181, Portland, OR 97204 503-243-3499
Smith Co, Glen: 119 N 4th St #411, Minneapolis, MN 55401 612-338-8235
Smith Creations, Terry: 880 C Mawde Ave, Mountain View, CA 94043 415-938-1111
Smith Creative Services, Boo : 3416 Northview Pl, Richmond, VA 23225 804-560-1757
Smith Design, Pam: 584 Broadway #304, New York, NY 10012 212-431-4361
Smith Design Assocs, Marcia: 1703 W 9th Ave, Spokane, WA 99204 509-456-6982
Smith Design Inc, Lauren: 920 Guinda St, Palo Alto, CA 94301 415-322-1886
Smith Design Inc, Paul: 400 N Broadway 5th Fl #500,
Milwaukee, WI 53202 414-271-8582
Smith Design, Christine: 120 Newport Center Dr #204,
Newport Beach, CA 92660 714-729-1099
Smith Design, Edward: 1133 Broadway #1614, New York, NY 10010 212-255-1717
Smith Design, Mark: 28 N 20th St #A, Richmond, VA 23223 804-643-2908
Smith Design, Steve: 1620 Taylor #100, Portland, OR 97205 503-233-5068
Smith Group Communications: 614 SW 11th St #405, Portland, OR 97205 503-224-1905
Smith Hinchman Grylls Assocs, Inc: 150 W Jefferson #100,
Detroit, MI 48226 313-983-3722
Smith Junger Wellman: 920 Abbot Kinney Blvd, Venice, CA 90291 310-392-8625
Smith, Agnew Moyer: 503 Martindale St, Pittsburgh, PA 15212 412-322-6333
Smith-Felver Prime: 4497 Mechanicsville Rd, Doylestown, PA 18901 215-794-8937
Smolan & Assocs, Carbone: 22 W 19th St 10th Fl, New York, NY 10011 212-807-0011
Smullen Design, Maureen: 85 N Raymond #280, Pasadena, CA 91103 818-405-0886
Snow, Aaron: 546 Chapel St, New Haven, CT 06511 203-624-6151
Snowden, George: 8608 Red Coat Ln, Potomac, MD 20854 202-362-8944
Snyder Design: 18 E 16th St 5th Fl, New York, NY 10003 212-691-4146
Sochynsky, Ilona: 200 E 36th St, New York, NY 10016 212-686-1275
Sol Design: 623 W Drummond Pl #10, Chicago, IL 60614 773-404-5882
Solazzo Design Agency: 114 Fifth Ave 18th Fl, New York, NY 10011 212-242-0300
Soleil Communications: 81 Rocky Hill Rd, Trumbull, CT 06611 203-372-5767
Solem, Robert: 3370 N 55th St, Milwaukee, WI 53216 414-445-7698
Solo Design: 2115 Vestridge Ln, Birmingham, AL 35216 205-823-2474
SoloMat: 652 Glen Brook, Stamford, CT 06906 203-325-9104
Some Interactive: 539 Bryant St #303, San Francisco, CA 94107 415-284-6464
Sonderman Design, Joe: P O Box 35146, Charlotte, NC 28204 704-376-0803
Sonneman Design Group: 20 North Ave, Larchmont, NY 10538 914-833-0128
Sons, Dana: 1320 19th St NW #600, Washington, DC 20036 202-835-0177
Soohoo Design: 425 Bush St #203, San Francisco, CA 94108 415-392-3457
Soohoo Designers, Patrick: 19191 S Vermont Ave #400,
Torrance, CA 90502 310-324-0590
Sooy & Co, Brian: 419 Hampton Dr, Elyria, OH 44035 216-366-5415
Soree, Sal: 97 Forest Hill Rd, W Orange, NJ 07052 201-325-3591
Sorel Inc, Elaine: 640 West End Ave #8-A, New York, NY 10024 212-873-4417
Sorensen Industrial Design, Hugh: 841 Westridge Way, Brea, CA 92621 714-529-8493
Sosin, Bill: 415 W Superior St, Chicago, IL 60610 312-751-0974
Soss, Johnathan Gregory: 653 Stanley Ct, Escondido, CA 92026 619-735-5890
Soto Assocs: 97 South 2nd St #200, San Jose, CA 95113 408-288-7686
Sound & Fury, Inc: 156 Mt Arlington Blvd, Landing, NJ 07850 201-398-2560
Soundlight Productions: 1915 Webster St, Birmingham, MI 48009 810-642-3502
Source & Co: 116 S Michigan 16th Fl, Chicago, IL 60603 312-236-7620
Spangler Assocs: 1110 Third Ave #800, Seattle, WA 98101 206-467-8888
Spangler Design Team, The: 4207 Excelsior Blvd, St Louis Park, MN 55416 612-927-5425
Spangler, Peter James: 7495 NW 4th St/Mark 4 Bldg, Plantation, FL 33317 305-587-2842
Sparkman & Assocs, Don: 1120 Connecticut Ave #270,
Washington, DC 20036 202-785-2414
Spartan Graphics, Inc: 200 Applewood Dr, Sparta, MI 49345 616-887-8243
Spatafore & Assocs: 50 South 600 East #100, Salt Lake City, UT 84102 801-364-8759
Spataro, Tery: 462 W 51st St, New York, NY 10019 212-245-8736
Spatial Graphics, Inc: 7131 W Lakefield Dr, Milwaukee, WI 53219 414-545-4444
Speare, Ray: 1462 Irving Pk Rd, Chicago, IL 60613 773-327-9102
Spectrum Boston: 85 Chestnut St, Boston, MA 02108 617-367-1008
Spectrum Graphics, Inc: 3561 Valley Dr, Pittsburgh, PA 15234 412-831-9933
Spectrum HoloByte: 2490 Mariner Sq Loop #100, Alameda, CA 94501 510-522-3584
Spectrum Sight & Sound: 2801 Hyperion Ave #109, Los Angeles, CA 90027 213-462-0812
Spectrum Studio: 1503 Washington Ave S 3rd Fl, Minneapolis, MN 55454 612-332-2361
Spencer Zahn & Assocs: 2015 Sansom St, Philadelphia, PA 19103 215-564-5979
Speyrgraphix Design Studio: 24858 Paseo Primario, Calabasas, CA 91302 818-222-5643
Spiekerman Assocs, Roberta: 650 Fifth St #301, San Francisco, CA 94107 415-546-9173
Spielman Design: 143 Mallard Dr, Avon, CT 06001 860-675-8016
Spilman, Stacey S: 155 Filbert St #240, Oakland, CA 94607 510-839-5835
Spirals, Inc: 197 W Spring Valley Ave, Maywood, NJ 07607 201-846-5150
Spivey Design, William: 515 Larkspur, Corona Del Mar, CA 92625 714-721-1261
Splane Design Assocs: 9242 Deering Ave, Chatsworth, CA 91311 818-366-2069
Spot Design: 775 Ave Of Americas 6th Fl, New York, NY 10001 212-645-8684
Spur Design: 3647 Falls Rd, Baltimore, MD 21211 ....410 235-7803
Square Docks: 201 W Brentwood, Glendale, WI 53217 414-351-6101
Square One Design: 970 Montroe St NW, Grand Rapids, MI 49503 616-774-9048
Squires, James: 2913 N Canton, Dallas, TX 75226 214-939-9194
Srebro Design, Rose: 140 Carlton Rd, Newton, MA 02168 617-244-2110
St Germain Graphics: 4735 Constance St, New Orleans, LA 70115 504-895-2300
St Martin Ltd: 226 W 47th St, New York, NY 10036 212-840-2188
St Vincent Milone & McConnells: 1156 Ave of Americas,
New York, NY 10036 212-921-1414
Stabins Design: 2440 S Sepulveda Blvd #152, Los Angeles, CA 90064 310-478-1708
Stahl Design: 6219 N Guilford Ave, Indianapolis, IN 46220 317-255-6900
Stahl, David: 116 E 48th St, Indianapolis, IN 46205 317-283-5000
Stalinsky Design: 10000 Memorial Dr #170, Houston, TX 77024 713-680-9723
Stalror: 341 B Blvd, Athens, GA 30601 706-548-9349
Stampscapes: 7451 Warner Ave #E124, Huntington Beach, CA 92647 714-968-5541
Stan & Lou: 720 N Post Oak Rd #605, Houston, TX 77024 713-683-8000
Stanard Inc, Michael: 1000 Main St, Evanston, IL 60202 847-869-9820
Standlee Design, Michael: 32962 Calle Miguel, San Juan Capist, CA 92675 714-240-9140
Stanley Design, Steve: 2472 Bolsover #364, Houston, TX 77005 713-522-2645
Stansbury Ronsaville Wood, Inc: 17 Pinewood St, Annapolis, MD 21401 301-261-8662
Star Design, Inc: PO Box 30, Moorestown, NJ 08057 609-235-8150
Starbright Graphics: 200 Hudson St 9th Fl Rm901, New York, NY 10013 212-966-3200
Starke Photo Imaging, Herrmann: 9017 E Mendenhall Ct,
Columbia, MD 21045 410-290-3917
Starletta Polster Design: 144 Bain Dr, La Vergne, TN 37086 615-793-4573
Starlin, Jim: 376 John Joy Rd, Woodstock, NY 12498 914-679-8065
Starr Seigle McCombs, Inc: 1001 Bishop Sq #19 Pacific Twr,
Honolulu, HI 96813 808-524-5080
Steam/Willardson: 194 Third Ave 3rd Fl, New York, NY 10003 212-475-0440
Steam/Willardson: 103 W California, Glendale, CA 91203 818-242-5688
Stecko, Dan: 627 Broadway #504, New York, NY 10012 212-539-1680
Steel Art Co, Inc: 75 Brainerd Rd, Allston, MA 02134 617-566-4079
Steel Design: 4217 E Windsong Dr, Phoenix, AZ 85044 602-759-1810
Steel Point Graphics: 8507 E Indianola Ave, Scottsdale, AZ 85251 602-947-7450
Steele Design: 641 W Lake St, Chicago, IL 60661 312-831-1200
Steinau-Fisher Studios: 2261 Victory Pkwy, Cincinnati, OH 45206 513-221-2242
Steinberg Miller Design: 167 Melroseb St, Newton, MA 02166 617-332-2505
Steiny Assocs: 828 N June St, Los Angeles, CA 90038 213-463-1024
• **Stentz, Nancy: pg 1445** Seattle, WA **206-634-1880**
fax: 206-632-2024
Stepan Design: 1849 Barnhill Dr, Mundelein, IL 60060 847-566-0488
Stephens Design, Kirby: 219 E Mt Vernon St, Somerset, KY 42501 606-679-5634
Stephenz Group: 150 Almaden Blvd, San Jose, CA 95113 408-379-4883
Sterling Group: 800 Third Ave 27th Fl, New York, NY 10013 212-371-1919
Sterling Stepping Design: 703 Kingsley, Palo Alto, CA 94301 415-462-9210
Sternbach, Ilene: 1385 York Ave #11E, New York, NY 10021 212-737-4999
Stettler Design, Wayne: 565 Glenmore Ave, Elkins Park, PA 19117 215-235-1230
Stevens Design, Martin: 1595 Avenida De Los Lirios, Encinitas, CA 92024 619-634-3056
Stewart Creative: 3290 S Cherry St, Denver, CO 80222 303-759-1445
Stewart Daniels: 24092 Marathon, Mission Viejo, CA 92691 714-586-1658
Stewart Design: 86 Milland Dr, Mill Valley, CA 94941 415-389-1239
Stewart Lopez Bonilla: 550 W Kentucky St, Louisville, KY 40203 502-583-5502
Stillon Interaction Design: 3206 Brasswood Court #3, Greenville, NC 27834 919-321-3071
Stitt, Thomas: 864 W 4th St, Winston-Salem, NC 27101 910-724-1803
Stockton Design: 2 Piney Point Ave, Croton on Hudson, NY 10520 914-271-1058
Stoltze Design: 49 Melcher St 4th Fl, Boston, MA 02210 617-350-7109
Stone & Assocs, WD: 25 W Broad St, Cookeville, TN 38501 615-526-1315
Stone Design Assocs: 2345 Washington St #201,
Newton Lower Fa, MA 02162 617-964-6882
Stone Yamashita: 355 Bryant St #408, San Francisco, CA 94107 415-536-6600
Stout Design: 320 SW Stark St #418, Portland, OR 97204 503-223-7740
Stoutt Creative Services, JC: 2817 Stratford Ln, Flower Mound, TX 75028 214-539-8455
Stoyan Adverstising & Design: 2482 Newport Blvd #8D,
Costa Mesa, CA 92627 714-631-6314
Straightline: 60 Madison Ave, New York, NY 10010 212-779-2626
Strandell Design: 218 E Ontario 3rd fl, Chicago, IL 60611 312-943-7553
Strata Studio: 2 W St George Blvd #2100, St George, UT 84770 801-628-5218
Strategies In Design: 1648 N Wolcott Rear, Chicago, IL 60622 773-276-3252
Strauss, Ross: 2367 Frankel Blvd, Merrick, NY 11566 516-546-2807
Strawbridge, Ray: 4850 Parkglen Ave, Los Angeles, CA 90043 310-559-4377
Streamline Graphics: 210 Eleventh Ave 6th Fl, New York, NY 10001 212-633-0021
Streamline Interactive: 1406 N Benton Way, Los Angeles, CA 90026 213-413-2406
Strecker, Chris: 4415 S Semoran Blvd #6, Orlando, FL 32822 407-275-7446
Stress-Lab, Inc: 212 Third Ave N #385, Minneapolis, MN 55401 612-376-7500
Stribiak & Assocs, John: 11160 Southwest Hwy, Palos Hills, IL 60465 708-430-3380
Strickland Design Group Inc, Michael: 3355 W Alabama #100,
Houston, TX 77098 713-961-1323
Stroh Inc, Don: 8015 S Zephyr Way, Littleton, CO 80123 303-973-1476
Stromberg Visual Design, Gordon H: 5423 Artesian, Chicago, IL 60625 773-275-9449
Strong Productions: 101 2nd St SE #904, Cedar Rapids, IA 52401 319-364-8859
Strong, David: 14727 NE 87th St, Redmond, WA 98052 206-883-8684

Strong, Richard: 1595 Manzanita #1, Chico, CA 95926................................916-343-3618
Stuart, Neil: RD 1 Box 64, Mahopac, NY 10541..914-618-1662
Stubenrauch & Partners: 927 Marina Dr, Napa, CA 94559 707-226-1670
Studio & Co: 9555 Trulock Ct, Orlando, FL 32817 407-671-1717
Studio 18: 2702 N 3rd St #4005, Phoenix, AZ 85012..602-280-1005
Studio 203: 323 E Matilija #110-203, Ojai, CA 93023 805-646-7877
Studio 42: 3109 Ave K, Brooklyn, NY 11210..718-377-3686
Studio 609: 609 N 10th St 2nd Fl, Sacramento, CA 95814.................................916-443-5001
Studio 7: 2440 State St NE, N Canton, OH 44721 216-877-6774
Studio A: 1736 Stockton St #5, San Francisco, CA 94133 415-956-8429
Studio A: 6274 Peachtree St, Los Angeles, CA 90040 213-721-1802
Studio A Design: 1019 Queen St, Alexandria, VA 22314....................................703-684-7729
Studio Architype: 600 Townsend St PH, San Francisco, CA 94103 415-703-9900
Studio Blue: 9 W Hubbard 2nd Fl, Chicago, IL 60610 312-222-0858
Studio Bolo: 4764 55th Ave SW, Seattle, WA 98116 206-933-1157
Studio Doctor: 6056 Bennetts Corner Rd, Memphis, NY 13112..........................315-672-8018
Studio Dog Eat Dog, Inc: 506 Theater Pl, Buffalo, NY 14202 716-856-0142
Studio Flux: 739 N Edgemont St, Los Angeles, CA 90029....................................213-660-4323
Studio G, Inc: 1007 W 6th St, Marshfield, WI 54449...715-384-0092
Studio Goodwin Sturges: 154 W Newton St, Boston, MA 02118..........................617-262-0591
Studio Grafika: 675 Drewry St NE #2, Atlanta, GA 30306 404-874-3277
Studio Group, The: 1713 Lanier Pl NW, Washington, DC 20009 202-332-3003
Studio Izbickas: 43 Winter St 8th Fl, Boston, MA 02108 617-695-0606
Studio KaMa, Inc: 3 Robin Hood Rd, Pound Ridge, NY 10576 212-355-7830
Studio Marz: 66 Crosby St Studio #4A, New York, NY 10011 212-941-7799
Studio Mongo: 5900 119th Ave SE #B58, Bellevue, WA 98006............................206-603-9669
Studio Morris: 55 Van Dam #901, New York, NY 10013 212-366-0401
Studio One: 7300 Metro Blvd #400, Edina, MN 55439.......................................612-831-6313
Studio One Graphics: 16329 Middlebelt, Livonia, MI 48154..............................313-522-7505
Studio S: 7 Cerrito Pl, Redwood City, CA 94061 415-261-9051
Studio Six Design: 6 Lynn Dr, Springfield, NJ 07081 201-379-5820
Studio Star: 2637 McGee Ave, Berkeley, CA 94703 510-848-0901
Studio Studio: 607 27th Ave, San Francisco, CA 94121 415-221-3525
Studio W: 17 Vestry St Grd Fl, New York, NY 10013...212-274-8744
Studio West, Inc: 1005 W Franklin, Minneapolis, MN 55405..............................612-871-2900
Studio Wilks: 2148 Federal Ave #A, Los Angeles, CA 90025 310-478-4442
StudioGraphics: 107 South B St #3, San Mateo, CA 94401 415-344-3855
Studiographix: 102 Decker Ct #202, Irving, TX 75062..214-541-1001
Studiosoftware: 2140 E Seventh Pl North A2S, Los Angeles, CA 90021 213-614-1126
Sturdevant Studios: 255 Third St #301, Oakland, CA 94607..............................510-834-5938
• **Stymest, Brian: pg 1457** 39 Hamilton Terr, New York, NY 10031 ....**212-283-3401**
url: www.wayart.com
Subjective Technologies: 1106 Second St, Encinitas, CA 92024 619-942-0928
Sugiyama, Kazlinn: 5924 N Washtenaw Ave, Chicago, IL 60659..........................773-271-9026
Sulewski, Connie: 2472 Bolsover #200, Houston, TX 77005...............................713-630-0454
Sullivan Perkins Design: 2811 McKinney Ave #320 LB111,
Dallas, TX 75204 214-922-9080
Sullivan Scully Design Group: 113 N San Francisco #209,
Flagstaff, AZ 86001...520-779-1020
Sullivan, Jerry : 1512 N Fremont #101, Chicago, IL 60622 312-951-5510
Sullivan, Michael: 1354 Hancock St, Quincy, MA 02169...................................617-471-1144
Summerford Design, Inc: 2706 Fairmount, Dallas, TX 75201 214-748-4638
Summers Studio: 230 E Ontario St #2306, Chicago, IL 60611 312-943-2533
Summit Comms: 15 N Michigan St, Toledo, OH 43624 419-242-6300
Summit Design: 381 Red Tail Trl, Evergreen, CO 80438....................................303-425-3478
Summit Marketing, Inc: 125 Park Ave 8th Fl, New York, NY 10017.....................212-479-2354
Sundberg & Assocs: 30 W 26th St 12th Fl, New York, NY 10010.........................212-691-5477
Sundberg Ferar: 4359 Pineview Dr, Waldlake, MI 48390 810-360-3800
Sundin Design: 25 Whittlemore Rd, Farmingham, MA 01701..............................508-877-2771
Sundog Studios: 31 Greenfield Rd, Ballstonspa, NY 12020 518-884-8144
Sunshine Graphic: 11455 Paramount Blvd #H, Downey, CA 90241 310-861-0244
Suntar Designs: PO Box 1901, Prescott, AZ 86302 520-778-2714
Super Graphics: 353 Concord Ave, Lexington, MA 02173 617-674-9821
Superior Graphic Systems: 1700 W Anaheim St, Long Beach, CA 90813 310-433-7421
Susman Prejza & Co, Inc: 3960 Ince Blvd, Culver City, CA 90232 310-836-3939
Sussman & Prejza: 8520 Warner Dr, Culver City, CA 90232 310-836-3939
Sussna, Brenda: 67 Potomac, San Francisco, CA 94117.....................................415-431-6616
Suzuki Design, Tom: 140-A W Jefferson St, Falls Church, VA 22046 703-237-0244
Svolos, Maria: 1936 W Estes, Chicago, IL 60626 773-338-4675
Swack Design Assocs, Terry: 49 Melcher St, Boston, MA 02210........................617-423-7926
Swalwell, Brian: 707 Park Meadow Rd, Columbus, OH 43081............................614-890-9558
Swan Graphics, Inc: 110 N College St #4, Ft Collins, CO 80524........................970-224-3259
Swanson & Swanson Dsgn Studio, Inc: 5801 Roberta Circle,
Tampa, FL 33604 813-238-1915
Swatek & Romanoff Design: 156 Fifth Ave #1100, New York, NY 10010 212-807-0236
Sweeny Graphic Design, Ken: 172 Park St #3, New Canaan, CT 06840 203-972-0920
Sweetlight Creative Partners: 11516 6th Ave NW, Seattle, WA 98177 206-364-9077
Swieter Design: 3227 McKinney #201, Dallas, TX 75204 214-720-6020
Swimmer Design: 15 E Palatine Rd #109, Prospect Height, IL 60070.............847-215-0900
Swoger Grafik: 12 E Scott St, Chicago, IL 60610 312-943-2491
Synstelien Design, Ben: 851 Baker St, San Francisco, CA 94115.......................415-922-5651
Synthesis: 1200 Artesia Blvd #302, Hermosa Beach, CA 90254 310-376-8093
Sypher, Alan E: 1400 NW 101 Terr, Plantation, FL 33322 305-370-2159
Syzygy Design Group, Inc: 7037 Matilija Ave, Van Nuys, CA 91405..................818-785-4989
Szabo, Michelle: PO Box 2034, Danbury, CT 06813 203-791-8599
Szeto, Gong: 841 Broadway, New York, NY 10003 212-533-4467
Szollose, Bradley: 207 W 27th St PH, New York, NY 10001 212-255-7731

T

T6R17 Design Prtnr Ship: 900 Parkway Dr, Boulder, CO 80303 303-494-8465
Taber, Russell G: 1952 Cleveland Ave, Wyoming, MI 49509.............................616-245-3830
Tackett Barbaria Design: 1990 Third St #400, Sacramento, CA 95814 916-442-3200
Taff, Barbara: 33 W 67th St PH, New York, NY 10023 212-874-1007
Takatsuki Design, Kondziolka: 5158 W Ainslie St, Chicago, IL 60630 773-777-5091
Takigawa Design, Jerry: 225 Canery Rd #G, Montery, GA 93940.......................408-372-7486
Talala Design Studio, Mshuja: PO Box 153, Palo Alto, CA 94302 415-964-2890
Tam Design, Julia: 2216 Via La Brea, Palos Verde, CA 90274 310-378-7583
Tana & Co: 9 Calaridge Court, Montclair, NJ 07042 201-655-0643
Tanaka & Co: 1 Main St SE #209/Riverplace, Minneapolis, MN 55414............612-378-3928
Tanenbaum Graphic Design, Jill: 4701 Sangamore Rd #235 S,
Bethesda, MD 20816 301-229-1135
Tangent Design Communications: 25 Sylvan Rd South #D,
Westport, CT 06880...203-221-1013
Tangram Design Group, Inc: 348 W 36th St #6N, New York, NY 10018 212-629-3778
Tani, Karl T: 1240 Wren St, San Diego, CA 92114 619-264-1701
Taras Design, Lander: 115 Mulberry, Stamford, CT 06907...............................203-968-0058
Targeted Creativity: 60 Boston Rd Box37, Groton, MA 01450 508-448-6186
Tasi & Assocs, Peter D: 21 Southgate Ave, Annapolis, MD 21401.....................410-269-1326
Tassian, George Org: 702 Gwynne Bldg, Cincinnati, OH 45202 513-721-5566
Tate Designs, Susan: 1201 Executive Dr E #101, Richardson, TX 75081 972-889-8556
Taurins Design Assocs: 280 Madison Ave #1402, New York, NY 10016.........212-679-5955
Tauss, Jack George: 484 W 43rd St #40H, New York, NY 10036 212-279-1658
Taussig & Assocs: 331 Hoffman Rd, Tully, NY 13159 315-696-8913
Tavernor Design: Po Box 284, Whitefish, MT 59937 406-862-4964
Taylor & Assocs, Carole: 112 Maywood Way, San Rafael, CA 94901 415-485-4431
Taylor & Ives: 1001 Ave of Americas 14th Fl, New York, NY 10018 212-921-9300
Taylor Corporation: 8601 Urbandale Ave, Des Moines, IA 50322......................515-276-0992
Taylor Design, Robert: 2930 Center Green Ct #200, Boulder, CO 80301 303-443-1975
Taylor Inc, Pat: 3540 S St NW, Washington, DC 20007 202-338-0962
Taylor Inc, Stan: 300 Northern Blvd, Great Neck, NY 11021.............................516-466-5707
Teague Assocs, Walter Dorwin: 14727 NE 87th St, Redmond, WA 98052 206-883-8684
Team Design: 301 N Water #620, Milwaukee, WI 53202...................................414-347-1500
Team Design: 584 Broadway #701, New York, NY 10012 212-431-8770
Team Design: 1809 Seventh Ave #500, Seattle, WA 98101...............................206-623-1044
Technology Publishing, Inc: 2100 Wharton St #310, Pittsburgh, PA 15203........412-431-8300
Tedesco, Bob: 8 Payne Rd, Bethel, CT 06801 203-778-2306
Teitelbaum & Co: 433 W Briar Pl, Chicago, IL 60657..773-871-7740
Tektonic Productions: 3034 M St NW #3A, Washington, DC 20007.................202-333-2532
Telesis: 215 W Seminary Ave, Lutherville, MD 21093 301-235-2000
Temel Co: 716 Main St, Boonton, NJ 07005..201-335-6298
Temel West: 1303 W Fort #A, Boise, ID 83702 208-345-7076
Temner Design, Howard: 95 Fifth Ave 4th Fl, New York, NY 10003..................212-633-1978
Temp Art, Inc: PO Box 030398, Ft Lauderdale, FL 33303 954-474-7770
Tempus Fugit: 437 Way, St Louis, MO 63122 314-821-2826
Tepper Studio: 183 Bennett St, Bridgeport, CT 06605......................................203-367-6172
Tepper, Lionel: 449 E 14th St, New York, NY 10009..212-505-0029
Terada Design: 1221 East Pike #200, Seattle, WA 98122 206-726-9909
Terrell Design Group: 2291 205th St #202, Torrance, CA 90501 310-782-6301
Terry, Dean: 232 Mariposa Ave, Sierra Madre, CA 91024 800-747-7097
Tessing Design: 3822 N Seeley Ave, Chicago, IL 60618 773-525-7704
Tetrad Design: 21 Southgate, Annapolis, MD 21401 410-269-1326
Teubner Kavelaras Assocs: 765 Melody Rd, Lake Forest, IL 60045...................847-735-1212
TFW Design: 1225 King St 3rd Fl, Alexandria, VA 22314 703-548-5570
TG Madison, Inc: 3340 Peachtree Rd NE #2850, Atlanta, GA 30326 404-262-2623
Tharler/Opper, Inc: 9 Bradford Rd, Natick, MA 01760 508-653-6840
Tharp and Drummond Did It: 1009 NW Hoyt St #106, Portland, OR 97209......503-222-7226
Tharp Did It: 50 University Ave #21, Los Gatos, CA 95030 408-354-6726
That's Amorra: 19 Stanley Ave, Crotonville, NY 10562 914-762-7250
Thayer Barton Assocs, Jill: 1626 19th St #11, Bakersfield, CA 93301 805-399-0653
Thayer Industrial Design, Dana: Route 1, Monroe, VA 24574 804-929-6359
Theme Entertainment Creators: 920 Hampshire Rd #A-9,
West Lake Village, CA 91361 805-381-0522
Theodore, Bradley: 776 NW 81st St, Miami, FL 33150.....................................305-693-4435
Theoharides, Inc: 303 S Broadway, Tarrytown, NY 10591 914-631-5363
Thien Schmidt: 77 E Main St, Newark, DE 19711 302-454-7233
Thill Design, Phill: 6629 University #206, Middleton, WI 53562 608-831-7447
Thin Air: 25 Seir Hill Rd, Norwalk, CT 06850..203-849-8104
Think Design: 1457 W Norwood St, Chicago, IL 60660.....................................773-761-7564
Think Design Group: 514 N Third St #201, Minneapolis, MN 55401 612-338-3226
1333 Henderson Productions: 30-78 36th St, Astoria, NY 11103 718-721-6127
30-Sixty Design: 2801 Cahuenga Blvd W, Los Angeles, CA 900068 231-850-5312
Thom & Dave Marketing Design: 28 W State St, Media, PA 19063 610-566-0566
Thomas & Assocs: 532 Colorado Ave, Santa Monica, CA 90401 310-451-8502
Thomas & Assocs Inc, Robert: 1020 Jamieson Rd, Lutherville, MD 21093 410-494-8945
Thomas Assocs, Greg: 2812 Santa Monica Blvd, Santa Monica, CA 90404 310-315-2192
Thomas Design, Keith: 3176 Pullman #109, Costa Mesa, CA 92626 714-557-1173
Thomas Marketing, Steve: 112 S Tryon St #1755, Charlotte, NC 28284..........704-332-4624
Thomas, Sean: 304 Mulberry St, New York, NY 10012 212-226-0441
Thompson Brothers: 331 W Stone Ave, Greenville, SC 29609 864-241-0810
Thompson Design Group: 524 Union St, San Francisco, CA 94133..................415-982-5827
Thompson Graphic Design, Maureen: 3041 S Giovanna Dr,
Tucson, AZ 85730 520-885-7526
Thompson, Bradbury: Jones Park, Riverside, CT 06878....................................203-637-3614
Thomson & Co: 4 Park Plaza #205, Wyomissing, PA 19610 610-376-5170
Thomson & Thomson, Inc: 500 Victory Rd, N Quincy, MA 02171 617-479-1600
Thomson Comm Design, Melanie: 100 Market Sq #10,
Newington, CT 06111 860-665-1424
Thorbeck & Lambert, Inc: 1409 Willow, Minneapolis, MN 55403.....................612-871-7979
Thorburn Design: 311 First Ave N #200, Minneapolis, MN 55401 612-339-8003
Thorpe Design & Illust, Peter: 77 Lyons Plain Rd, Weston, CT 06883 203-226-4535
Three: 444 E 82nd St #12C, New York, NY 10028...212-988-6267
Three Communication Design: 1807 W Sunnyside Ave #2C,
Chicago, IL 60640 773-878-2229
Three, Inc: 236 W 26th St #805, New York, NY 10001 212-463-7025
3DO Co, The: 600 Galveston Dr, Redwood City, CA 94063..............................415-261-3000
Thumbnail Graphics: 228 NW 32nd St, Oklahoma City, OK 73118 405-755-7587
Thumbprint Design/Adv: 120 University Pk #200, Winter Park, FL 32792.......407-672-0117
Thurber Creative Services: 6408 S 111th East Ave, Tulsa, OK 74133 918-250-6657
Tibbott, Randy: 3501 Trimble Rd, Nashville, TN 37215...................................615-783-0093
Tiberi, Mindy: 2601 Prairy Ave, Evanston, IL 60201 847-491-1545
Tiedrich Graphic Design: 37 W 20th St #910, New York, NY 10011................212 206-6730
Tieken Design & Creative Services: 2800 N Central #150, Phoenix, AZ 85004 602-230-0060
Tigertt, William D: 1435 Randolph St #403, Detroit, MI 48226 313-963-2115
Tilka Design: 921 Marquette Ave #200, Minneapolis, MN 55402 612-822-6422
Time New Media/Pathfinder: Time Life Bldng-Rockfeller Center,
New York, NY 10020 212-645-5577

Visualgraphics Design: 1211 NW Shore Blvd, Tampa, FL 33607....................813-877-3804
Visualworks: 1100 W Cermak Rd #B-423, Chicago, IL 60608 312-738-0690
Vivid Group, The: 317 Adelaide St W #302, Toronto, ON M5V 1P9 416-340-9290
Vivid Media: 6666 Odana Rd #161, Madison, WI 53719 608-276-8244
Vivid Studios: 510 Third St #200, San Francisco, CA 94107..........................415-512-7200
Vivo, Inc: 3920 North 30, Tagoma, WA 98407 206-761-8595
VNO Design: 2824 Erica Pl, Nashville, TN 37204..615-269-8924
Volan Design, LLC: 1800 38th St, Boulder, CO 80301 303-449-3838
Volpe, Louie: 53 Meadow Ln, Levittown, NY 11756..516-520-0366
Voltec Assocs: 560 N Larchmont, Los Angeles, CA 90004 213-467-2106
Volz Design, Peter: 100 S Broad St #2136, Philadelphia, PA 19110...............215-563-1416
Von Brincken, Maria: 11 Ford Rd, Sudbury, MA 01776 508-443-4540
Voss, Henry: PO Box 618036, Orlando, FL 32806..407-894-2795
Vote Graphics Inc, Ray: 1056 E Whitton Ave, Phoenix, AZ 85014 602-285-0440
Voyage Co, The: 578 Broadway #406, New York, NY 10012 212-431-5199
Vra Studios: 1413 Highland Ave, Plainfield`, NJ 07060 908-561-5305
VSA Partners: 542 S Dearborn #202, Chicago, IL 60605..................................312-427-6413

W

W & Co, Inc: 10245 Main St #8-3, Bellevue, WA 98004 206-451-3075
W Design: 411 Wahington Ave N #208, Minneapolis, MN 55401..........................612-288-0288
W Group: 3075 Charlevoix Dr SE City, Grand Rapids, MI 49546 616-940-3913
Wages Design: 887 W Marietta St/Std S111, Atlanta, GA 30318.........................404-876-0874
Wagner, Jim: 405 E 6th St #2, New York, NY 10009..212-966-6465
Wai Graphic Design, Stan: 4324 Ewing Ave, Minneapolis, MN 55410 612-925-0546
Waksman Design, Sergio: 4306 Knights Ave, Tampa, FL 33611..........................813-835-5069
Walcott-Ayers Group: 1396 Park Ave, Emeryville, CA 94608..............................510-594-1300
Waldman, Matthew: 55 Broad St #20A, New York, NY 10004 212-968-8908
Walker Design: 9708 Stirling Rd, Richland, MI 49083 616-629-4349
Walker Graphics, Inc: 111 Third Ave South, Great Falls, MT 59405....................406-727-8115
Walker Group/CNI: 320 W 13th St 5th Fl, New York, NY 10014 212-206-0444
Wallace/Church Assocs: 330 E 48th St, New York, NY 10017 212-755-2903
Wallner Harbauer Bruce & Assocs: 500 N Michigan Ave, Chicago, IL 60611.....312-787-6787
Waln Communications Group: 2900 Lively Blvd, Elk Grove, IL 6007 312-951-6363
Walsh & Assocs: 1725 Westlake North, Seattle, WA 98109...............................206-633-4420
Walter's Designs: 24 E Cota #200, Santa Barbara, CA 805-962-3677
Walzak Design: 1123 N Water St, Milwaukee, WI 53202 414-276-7800
Wang/Hunter Design: 604 Mission St 2nd Fl, San Francisco, CA 94105...........415-957-0872
Ward Design: 374 Congress St #501, Boston, MA 02210...................................617-426-3866
Warden, Bill: 438 Wellington Dr, Mesquite, TX 75149 214-634-8434
Warehouse Agency: 10 W Madison, Phoenix, AZ 85004....................................602-256-7030
Warhaftig Assocs: 361 Broadway #300, New York, NY 10013 212-941-1700
Warkulwiz Design Assocs: 2218 Race St 3rd Fl, Philadelphia, PA 19103.........215-988-1777
Warner Design Assocs, Inc: 3920 Conde St, San Diego, CA 92110...................619-297-4455
Warren Design Inc, David: 1730 Blake St #400, Denver, CO 80202 303-291-1111
Warren Group, The: 622 Hampton Dr, Venice, CA 90291 310-396-6316
• **Warshaw Blumenthal, Inc.: pg 1458** New York, NY **212-867-4225**
url: www.illustrations-nyc.com
Wasserman Design, Diane: 14 Carter Dr, Farmingham, MA 01701 508-788-3684
Waston Design, Tom: 2172 West Lake Rd, Skaneateles, NY 13152.....................315-685-6033
Watercolor Group, The: 101 1/2 E Front St, Wheaton, IL 60187 708-871-9556
Watermark Design: 621 Wythe St, Alexandria, VA 22314 703-549-0609
Waters Design Assocs, Inc: 3 W 18th St 8th Fl, New York, NY 10011 212-807-0717
Watson Design: PO Box 3176, Redondo Beach, CA 90277.................................310-376-9665
Watson Design Group: 312 E Sixth St, Tucson, AZ 85705 520-882-0688
Watson Dezin Group: 1809 Birchston Ave, Portage, MI 49002............................616-345-7222
Watson/Swope Graphic Comm: 102 1/2 E Front St #303,
Traverse City, MI 49684 616-947-7550
Wattigney, Madelyn: 307 Olivier St, New Orleans, LA 70114 504-368-5295
Watts Design, Inc: 444 N Wells St #204, Chicago, IL 60610 312-321-0191
Watts Silverstein: 1931 Second Ave #400, Seattle, WA 98101 206-443-4200
Watzman Info Design: 25 Inman Pl, Cambridge, MA 02139................................617-876-0099
Wave Communications: PO Box 5502, Santa Monica, CA 90409 310-399-2831
Wave Design Works: 560 Harrison Ave, Boston, MA 02118...............................617-482-4470
Wayne Hunt Design: 87 N Raymond Ave #215, Pasadena, CA 91103 818-793-7847
WBMG Design, Inc: 207 E 32nd St #rd Fl, New York, NY 10016 212-689-7122
Weadock, Rutka: 1627 E Baltimore St, Baltimore, MD 21231 301-563-2100
Web Design Publishing Co: PO Box 508, Opelika, AL 334-502-7957
Web Designer: 74 Hazelton Terrace, Tenafly, NJ 07670 201-568-3465
Web Page Design by Kaybee: 1540 Taylor Rd, Dothan, AL 334-702-1447
Web Site Creations: 1175 Harrison St, Santa Clara, CA 95050..........................408-261-9024
Webb, Nancy: 101 Kimberlin Heights Dr, Oakland, CA 94619 510-531-1978
Weber Design: 1439 Larimer Sq, Denver, CO 80202...303-892-9816
Weber Design: 30 E 21st St 2nd Fl, New York, NY 10010..................................212-673-6381
Weber Design, Inc: 705 Kings St 3rd Fl, Alexandria, VA 22314 703-548-0003
Webster &Assocs, John: 1445 Fern Pl, Vista, CA 92083...................................619-956-6576
Webster Design Assocs: 5060 Dodge St #2000, Omaha, NE 68132 402-551-0503
Webster Design, Inc, Bruce : 545 Sutller St #303, San Francisco, CA 94102 415-956-2252
Webster Group: 200 Four Falls Corp Cntr #411, Conshohocken, PA 19428 610-832-8010
Webster, Inc, Robert: 220 E 23rd St, New York, NY 10010..............................212-576-1070
Wechsler & Partners: 230 W 17th St 6th Fl, New York, NY 10011 212-924-3337
Wedemeyer Adv & Design: 1467 W Lambert Rd, La Habra, CA 90631 310-691-9998
Wehrman & Co, Inc: 8175 Big Bend Blvd #250, St Louis, MO 63119...................314-962-7953
Weiman Illustration, Jon: 88 Wyckoff St #3C, Brooklyn, NY 11201 718-855-8468
Weiser Design: 167 Hillrise Dr, Penfield, NY 14526...716-377-4064
Weiss Creative, Heaton: 540 Main St #1, Winchester, MA 01890.......................617-729-3564
Weiss, Jack: 1103 Mulford St, Evanston, IL 60202 ....
Weissman, Walter: 463 West St #B332, New York, NY 10014 212-989-9694
Weller Inst For Cure of Design: 1575 W Highway 32 Box 518,
Oakley, UT 84055...801-783-5378
Wells, John: 407 Jackson St, San Francisco, CA 94111 415-956-3952
Wells, Toby: 240 Poverty Hollow Rd, Redding, CT 06896..................................203-938-8483
Wendt Graphic Design, Peter: 2914 W Pratt Ave, Chicago, IL 60645................773-338-5877
Werndorf Assocs: 6315 Yucca St, Hollywood, CA 90028...................................213-467-7990
Werner Design Werks: 126 N Third St #400, Minneapolis, MN 55401 612-338-2550
Werremeyer Creative: 15 N Gore, St Louis, MO 63119......................................314-963-0505
Werther Creative, Beth: 3600 Knollwood R, Nashville, TN 37215 615-297-0333
Wertman, Chuck: 559 Pacific Ave, San Francisco, CA 94133............................415-433-4452
Wes Horlacher: PO Box 1462, Walnut, CA 91789 213-739-3805
Wesko Creative, Inc: 6430 Southpoint Dr, Dallas, TX 75248...............................214-931-5091
Wesson & Assocs: 103 W Capitol #1215, Little Rock, AR 72201 501-374-9257
West & Assocs: 1420 Springhill Rd #325, Mclean, VA 22102 703-893-0404
West Design Studio, Harlan: 1843 Woodside, Thousand Oaks, CA 91362 805-493-4049
West Design, Suzanne: 555 Bryant #282, Palo Alto, CA 94301.........................415-324-8068
West Design, Timothy: 1397 Saddleridge Dr, Orlando, FL 32835 407-299-9748
West Graphics, Anne: 195 Forest Ave, Palo Alto, CA 94301..............................415-326-8555
West Office Exhibition Design: 118 Hawthorne St, San Francisco, CA 94107 415-546-7730
West, Harlan: 1834 Woodside Dr, Thousand Oaks, CA 91362 805-493-4049
Westchester Graphic Group: 4 Jeremy Dr, New Fairfield, CT 06812 203-746-8654
Westcom Creative Group: 2295 Coburg Road #105, Eugene, OR 97401 503-484-4314
Westcott Design Group: 15 Hunt Ave, Chattanooga, TN 37411 423-510-9610
Westdal Design: 1805 A Second St, Berkeley, CA 94710...................................510-540-1116
Western Graphics: 3535 W First Ave, Eugene, OR 97402...................................451-686-2200
Weston Communications: 175 Derby St #31, Hingham, MA 02043 617-749-0944
Westport Group, The: 1071 Post Rd East, Westport, CT 06880..........................203-227-9600
Westwood Studios: 2400 North Tenata Way, Las Vegas, NV 89128 702-228-4040
Wetzel Assocs, Joseph A: 77 N Washington St, Boston, MA 02114 617-367-6300
Weymouth Design: 332 Congress St 6th Fl, Boston, MA 02110 617-542-2647
Whelan Design Office: 155 W 19th St, New York, NY 10010...............................212-727-7332
Whibley Assocs: 216 Brewster Ave, Silver Spring, MD 20901 301-587-5944
White & Assocs: 234 E Colorado Blvd, Pasadena, CA 91101 818-583-5900
White Design: 4510 E Pacific Coast Hwy #620, Long Beach, CA 90804 310-597-7772
White Design: 2001 Sul Ross, Houston, TX 77098 713-520-0478
Whitefleet Design, Inc: 440 E 56th St, New York, NY 10022 212-319-4444
Whitford, Kim: 242 Mead Rd, Decatur, GA 30030...404-371-0860
Whittington & Company: 605 W 18th St, Austin, TX 78701................................512-474-9045
Why Design: 55 Brandford St #300, Providence, RI 02903................................401-421-7622
Wickham & Assocs: 1700 K St NW #1202, Washington, DC 20006.....................202-296-4860
Wides & Holl: 866 Broadway, New York, NY 10003 212-533-6882
Widmer Assocs, Stanley: Staples Airport Ind Park RR2, Staples, MN 56479........218-894-3466
Widmeyer Design, Inc: 911 Western #305, Seattle, WA 98104..........................206-343-7170
Wiggin Design: Six Thorndal Cir, Darien, CT 06820..203-655-1920
Wijtvliet, Inc: 440 E 56th St, New York, NY 10022 212-319-4444
Wilbanks, Inc: 2256 E Mercer, Phoenix, AZ 85028..602-788-4696
Wilcher Design: 18210 Redmond Way, Redmond, WA 98052..............................206-882-2300
Wildenradt Design Assocs: 2525 Hartrey Ave, Evanston, IL 60201 847-328-2482
Wiley Design: 2150 Capitol Ave #220, Sacramento, CA 95816...........................916-447-4633
Wilke Design, Jerry: 15 Mallard Ln, Westport, CT 06880...................................203-255-7705
Wilkins & Peterson Design: 43212 Second Ave NW, Seattle, WA 98107............206-624-1695
Wilkins Design, Warren: 4927 49th Ave S, Seattle, WA 98118...........................206-725-7500
Willey & Assocs: 8021 Knue Rd #112, Indianapolis, IN 46250 317-577-3130
William & Wrenn, Inc: 4131 N Central Expwy #840, Dallas, TX 75204...............214-520-0990
Williams & Assocs: 220 Broadway #205, Lynnfield, MA 01940...........................617-599-1818
Williams & Assocs, Bryan: 118 E 25TH St 4th Fl, New York, NY 10010 212-647-1277
Williams & Assocs, Inc, Morgan: 400 First Ave N, Minneapolis, MN 55401 612-339-5000
Williams & Ziller Design: 330 Fell St, San Francisco, CA 94102 415-621-0330
Williams Design Group, Ted: 577 Howard St 4th Fl,
San Francisco, CA 94105...415-543-4404
Williams Design, J: 695 S Colorado Blvd #370, Denver, CO 80222 303-778-8329
Williams Entertainment, Inc: 10110 Mesa Rim Rd, San Diego, CA 92121........619-658-9500
Williams McBride Design: 344 E Main St, Lexington, KY 40507 606-253-9319
Williams, Christina: 5 Bixby Ln, Westford, MA 01886 508-692-5178
Williamson Design Group, The: 1621 Abbot Kinney Blvd, Venice, CA 90291 310-452-7521
Williamson, Richie: 514 W 24th St, New York, NY 10011..................................212-807-0816
Williamson, Skip: 620 Groton Dr, Burbank, CA 91504 818-955-9875
Willis Design Group, Remen: 2964 Coltin Rd, Pebble Beach, CA 93953 408-655-1407
Willoughby Design Group: 602 Westport Rd, Kansas City, MO 64111 816-561-4189
Willson Creative Group: 355 N Ashland Ave, Chicago, IL 60607.......................312-738-3555
Wilmer Fong & Assocs, Inc: 155 Filbert St #240, Oakland, CA 94607...............510-839-5835
Wilson Adv & Design: 4021 N Rosewood, Muncie, IN 47304..............................317-288-5444
Wilson Design, Peter: 23 E Colorado Blvd #203, Pasadena, CA 91105 818-795-0126
Wilson Design, Scott: 497 Washington St, Brookline, MA 02146.......................617-734-9077
Wilson Graphic Design, Bo: 4705 Brookline Dr, Bartlesville, OK 74006.............918-333-8391
Wilson Ink: 5417 Shoreline Ct, Holly Springs, NC 27540..................................919-567-8144
Wilson, Gavin: 239 Elizabeth St #3, New York, NY 10012.................................212-966-0040
Wilson, Inc: 716 Crescent Blvd, Glen Ellyn, IL 60137 630-790-1052
Wilson, Mark: 18 River Rd, W Cornwall, CT 06796..203-672-6360
Wilson, Rex Co: 330 Seventh Ave, New York, NY 10001 212-594-3646
Wilsonwork Design: 1825 T St NW #607, Washington, DC 20009 202-332-9016
Winberry Digital Design, Bob: PO Box 13023, Long Beach, CA 90803..............310-439-3841
Wind Horse Design: 128 Highland Blvd, Hayward, CA 94542 510-886-5165
Windlight Studios: 702 N First St, Minneapolis, MN 55401 612-943-1029
Windy City Communications: 350 W Hubbard #450, Chicago, IL 60610...........312-464-0390
Wine Design, John: 4818 Macarthur Blvd, washington, DC 20007 202-333-7717
Wingate Industrial Design, Barry: 4934 Bel Escou Dr, San Jose, CA 95124 408-559-4065
Winker Productions: 71 Laurel St, Marlborough, NH 03455...............................603-876-3325
Winslow Studios: 18051 Whitman Ln, Lansing, IL 60438 708-895-1048
Winter Design, Carol: 61 W 74th St #3A, New York, NY 10023 212-724-1971
Winters, Michele: 1133 Broadway #816, New York, NY 10010 212-367-8512
Winterson, Finn: 427 Warburton Ave, Hastings-on-Hudson, NY 10706 914-478-3562
Wisconsin, Jonathan: 31 N Main St, Marlborough, CT 06447 860-295-8225
Wisdom Ware, Inc: 841 Greneda Ln, Foster City, CA 94404 414-574-2683
Wise Design: 75 13th St, Atlanta, GA 30309 404-897-5200
Withers Graphic Design, Bruce : 305 E 46th St 15th Fl,
New York, NY 10017 212-935-2552
Witherspoon Design: 1844 W 5th Ave, Columbus, OH 43212...........................614-486-5428
Wittenberg Inc, Ross: 301 W 18th St 4th Fl, New York, NY 10011 212-255-7450
Witus, Ted: 1809 7th Ave #1710, Seattle, WA 98101 206-447-1600
Wohler, Luann: 6201 Leesburg Pike #403, Falls Church, VA 22044 703-536-1773
Wohlmut Media Services: 2600 Central Ave #L, Union City, CA 94587 510-487-1073
Wojnar Productions, Lee: 326 Kater St, Philadelphia, PA 19147 215-922-5266
Woldman Design: 6 Weld St, Roslindale, MA 02131 617-323-6505
Wolen, Merle: 150 E Huron St, Chicago, IL 60611...312-787-9040
Wolf, Anita: 26 Golden Ave, Arlington, MA 02174...781-646-4502
Wolf, Inc, Henry: 167 E 73rd St, New York, NY 10021 212-472-2500
Wolfe & Assocs: 5725 Fourwood Ave #300, Pittsburgh, PA 15217 412-422-2346

Wolfe Design, Leonard: 19 Ludlow Rd, Westport, CT 06880 203-454-0566
Wolff Co, Rudi: 135 Central Park W #12NC, New York, NY 10023.................212-873-5800
Wolfson Ink: 853 Broadway #1208, New York, NY 10003............................212-475-9510
Wolk Graphic Design Inc, Toby: 5 Captain Ln, Hingham, MA 02043.........617-740-4296
Woloch Design, Dennis: 1700 York Ave, New York, NY 10128....................212-427-1746
Wong & Assocs, Patricia: 2091 Business Ctr Dr #215, Irvine, CA 92715........714-476-1213
Wong & Assocs, Steve: 425 Bush St Ph Level, San Francisco, CA 94105........415-421-3303
Wong & Yeo: 146 Eleventh St, San Francisco, CA 94103..........................415-861-1128
Wong Design, Benedict: 450 Sansome St #1600, San Francisco, CA 94111....415-781-7590
Wong Design, Christina: 215 W 92nd St #6-I, New York, NY 10025............212-496-0453
Wong Mechanicals/Div Grey, Fran: 345 California St,
 San Francisco, CA 94104...415-291-4900
Wong, George: 935 W Chestnut #500, Chicago, IL 60622 312-733-2391
Wong, Rick: 379-A Clementina, San Francisco, CA 94103 415-243-0588
Woo, Calvin: 4015 Ibis St, San Diego, CA 92103 619-299-0431
Wood Design c/o Louis Dreyfuss: 405 Lexington Ave 57th Fl,
 New York, NY 10174..212-490-2626
Wood Design Office, Mark: 517 S Ivy Ave, Monrovia, CA 91016..................818-930-0955
Wood, Tom: 3925 Peachtree Rd NE, Atlanta, GA 30319.............................404-262-7424
Wood, William: 68 Windsor Pl, Glen Ridge, NJ 07028................................201-743-5543
Woods &Woods: 414 Jackson St #304, San Francisco, CA 94111 415-399-1984
Word of Mouth: 495 West End Ave, New York, NY 10024............................212-724-8302
Work: 2019 Monument Ave, Richmond, VA 23220......................................804-358-9366
Working Design: 3060 Peachtree Rd NW #320, Atlanta, GA 30305 404-261-7813
Worthington, Carl A: 3773 Wonderland Hill Ave, Boulder, CO 80302.............303-444-1699
Wovers Art Direction, Nancy: 371 Beacon St #4, Boston, MA 02116............617-236-2226
Wow Digital: 520 Broadway, New York, NY 10012......................................212-941-4600
Wozney Design, Greg: 80 Eighth Ave #1308, New York, NY 10011 212-620-7776
Wright Art Direction: Rte 7-303 Lazy O Ranch, Brazoria, TX 77422.............409-798-6574
Wright Communications: 67 Irving Pl 12th Fl, New York, NY 10003.............212-505-8200
Wright Design Assocs: 339 Boston Post Rd, Sudbury, MA 01776 508-443-9909
Wright Design Inc, Krueger: 6409 City West Pkwy #207,
 Eden Prairie, MN 55344..612-827-7570
Wright Design, Thomas: 6349 Torrington Rd, Nashville, TN 37205 615-356-2515
Wright Graphic Design, Evan: 332 Pine St PH, San Francisco, CA 94104........415-421-2520
Write Design: 2261 Market St #325, San Francisco, CA 94414..................415-431-5646
Writeline: 19 Bridle Rd, Billerica, MA 01821...617-866-3832
Wu, Brian: 149 Fifth Ave 8th Fl, New York, NY 10010..............................212-691-0352
Wunderlich Design: 5510 Biloxi Ave, N Hollywood, CA 91601.....................818-763-4848
Wurman, Richard Saul: 180 Narragansett Ave, Newport, RI 02840 401-848-2299
WW Two Design: 2150 Post Rd 3rd Fl, Fairfield, CT 06430.........................203-256-4812
WW3 Papagalos & Assocs: 5333 N Seventh St #222, Phoenix, AZ 85014 602-279-2933
Wyant Simboli Group, The: 96 East Ave, Norwalk, CT 06851......................203-838-0191

X Y

Xavier Studios, Gae: 9818 Timber Ridge Pass, Austin, TX 78733 512-263-9822
Xeno Group: 651 Brannan St #200, San Francisco, CA 94107 415-284-0400
Xilinx, Inc: 2100 Logic Dr, San Jose, CA 95124.......................................408-559-7778
XMedia: 1127C Loma Dr, Hermosa Beach, CA 90254..................................310-535-5032
Yacinski Design: 18 W Windsor Ave, Alexandria, VA 22301 703-683-3079
Yamada Design Consultants, Tom: 801 Franklin St #603,
 Oakland, CA 94607..510-839-2468
Yamaguma Assocs: 255 N Market St #120, San Jose, CA 95110 408-279-0500
Yamamoto Moss, Inc: 252 First Ave N, Minneapolis, MN 55401...................612-375-0180
Yanovick Coburn: 312 Washington Ave N #A, Minneapolis, MN 55401 612-375-0092
Yashi Okita Design: 2355 3rd St #220, San Francisco, CA 94107 415-255-6100
Ybarra Design: 2235 Laguna St #201, San Francisco, CA 94115..................415-923-1758
Yee Design, Ray: 424 N Larchmont Blvd, Los Angeles, CA 90004 213-465-2514
Yellow Ink: 1038 Washington St, Holliston, MA 01746 508-429-7904
Yeo Design: 146 11th St, San Francisco, CA 94103..................................415-861-1128
Yerkey Design Group: 340 Bryant St #201, San Francisco, CA 94107 415-882-9400
Yip Studio, Gene: 559 Pacific Ave #24, San Francisco, CA 94133 415-788-7074
Yonezawa Design: 4300 Aurora Ave N #101, Seattle, WA 98103.................206-545-8018
Yoshimura-Fisher Design: 60 E 42nd St #1003, New York, NY 10165............212-431-4776
Young & Lynch Design: 1328 Emerald St, San Diego, CA 92109 619-270-4214
Young & Roehr Adv: 28 SW 1st Ave #500, Portland, OR 97204....................503-222-0626
Young & Thomas: 7 Birch Hill Rd, Weston, CT 06883.................................203-227-5672
Young Assocs, Robert: 78 N Union St, Rochester, NY 14607 716-546-1973
Young Goldman Young, Inc: 320 E 46th St, New York, NY 10017 212-697-7820
Yurdin Industrial Design, Carl: 2 Harborview Rd,
 Port Washington, NY 11050..516-944-7811

Z

Z Design: 7000 Central Pkwy #1700, Atlanta, GA 30328 770-399-1920
Z Group: 105 Hudson St #300, New York, NY 10013 212-941-9272
Z-Group Design: 2121 First Ave #102, Seattle, WA 98121.........................206-728-2105
Zachary Group, J: 581 Bergen Blvd, Ridgefield, NJ 07657...........................201-941-8900
Zahn & Assocs, Spencer: 2015 Sansom St, Philadelphia, PA 19103 215-564-5979
Zahor & Bender: 200 E 33rd St #3E, New York, NY 10016...........................212-532-7475
Zahra Design Group: 2811 McKinney Ave #218, Dallas, TX 75204...............214-855-1255
Zaidi, Nadeen: 166 Fifth Ave 5th Fl, New York, NY 10010 212-633-1999
Zaine, Carmile: 110 E 17th St, New York, NY 10003 212-674-0375
Zaino Design: 110 E 17th St, New York, NY 10003 212-674-0375
Zamchick, Gary: 56 Hillside Ave, Tenafly, NJ 07670...................................201-568-3727
Zamparelli & Assocs: 1450 Lomita Dr, Pasadena, CA 91106 818-799-4370
Zaprauskis Assocs, Levinson: 15 W Highland Ave, Philadelphia, PA 19118 215-248-5242
Zaref, Marc: 135 W 26th St, New York, NY 10001 212-989-6631
Zarek Packaging & Design: 769 N Ascan St, Elmont, NY 11003..................516-825-3608
Zaremda Visual Comms: 60 Federal St #302, San Francisco, CA 94107........415-957-9635
Zastrow Studios: 10555 N Port Washington Rd #202, Mequon, WI 53092 414-241-8828
Zazula Inc, Hy: 2 W 46th St 2nd Fl, New York, NY 10036............................212-581-2747
Zebra Design: 5 Beatrice Cove, Fairport, NY 14450....................................716-223-0150
Zeewy Design: 19 Cobblestone Dr, Paoli, PA 19301...................................610-644-7150
Zeines, Bruce: 103 Albamarle Rd, Brooklyn, NY 11218................................718-972-7256
Zeiss Design Group, Inc: 2083 Old Middlefeild Way #204,
 Mountain View, CA 94043..415-962-1151
Zeitsoff, Elaine: 241 Central Park W, New York, NY 10024..........................212-580-1282
Zender & Assocs: 2311 Park Ave, Cincinnati, OH 45206 513-961-1790
Zeni & Assocs, Bob: 425 N Park Rd, Lagrange Park, IL 60525 708-352-4700

Zenn Graphic Design: 1639 McCollum St, Los Angeles, CA 90026 213-413-4369
Ziba Design: 334 NW 11th Ave, Portland, OR 97209 503-223-9606
Ziegler Assocs, Inc: 107 E Cary St, Richmond, VA 23219............................804-780-1132
Ziegler Design Works, Nancy: 1542 Woodbine Ct, Deerfield, IL 60015...........847-945-2225
Zierhut Industrial Design: 2014 Platinum, Garland, TX 75042.......................214-276-1722
Ziga Design: 24 Harstrom Pl, Rowayton, CT 06853 203-852-1640
Ziller & Assocs, Barbara: 330 Fell St, San Francisco, CA 94102 415-621-0330
Zimmerman Crowe Design: 90 Tehama St, San Francisco, CA 94105 415-777-5560
Zimmerman Design, Roger: 234 W 14th St #2F, New York, NY 10011 212-741-4687
Zimmerman Graphic Design, Amy: 19 Salem Ln, Port Wasington, NY 11050....516-767-7302
Zimmermann & Assocs: 317 N 11th St #1101, St Louis, MO 63101 314-241-3939
Zoe Graphics: 32 N Main St, Pennington, NJ 08534 609-730-0500
Zoom Computer Art Center: 800-A School St, Napa, CA 94559 707-226-7808
Zu Design: 150 Chestnut St, Providence, RI 02903....................................401-272-3288
Zukor Graphics: 666A State St, San Diego, CA 92101 619-235-8191
Zurkow, Marina: 636 Broadway #1204, New York, NY 10012 212-253-1226
Zuzzolo Graphics, Inc: 316 Princeton Rd, Rockville Centr, NY 11570.............516-763-1249